③ Name origin. Historical information about the origin of the county's name.

④ Area. The total area of the county is given in square miles, followed by individual figures for the land area and water area of the county (also in square miles).

⑤ Population. The total population for the county is given first. This is followed (parenthetically) by the racial/ethnic breakdown of the population figures into five categories: White; Black or African American; Hispanic or Latino; Asian; and Other.

Note: Individuals designated Hispanic or Latino might be of any race, or any combination of races; those designated as members of one specific race belong to that race only and are not Hispanic or Latino. The "Other" designation includes respondents categorized in the 2000 Census as American Indian/Alaska Native, Native Hawaiian/Other Pacific Islander, or persons who are members of more than one race. Due to these and other factors, the percentages for the five categories given in *Counties USA* do not necessarily add up to 100%.

⑥ Foreign born. Percentage of the county population born in a country other than the United States.

⑦ Median age. The median age for that county's residents.

⑧ State rank. Denotes the county's rank in its state in terms of total population size.

⑨ Pop change 1990-2000. The percentage by which the county has increased or decreased in population between the 1990 and 2000 censuses.

⑩ Income. Income figures are presented in terms of both per capita income and median household income. (*Per capita* means "per person." Per capita income for a county represents the total income of county residents divided by the number of county residents. *Household income* refers to the sum of money received in the previous calendar year by all household members aged 15 and older, including those not related to the householder, as well as persons living alone and others in nonfamily households.)

⑪ Pop below poverty level. The percentage of the population that falls below the amount of income designated as "poverty level." (Poverty thresholds incorporate a number of varying factors such as family size, age of householder, number of children under 18, etc., and are updated annually to reflect changes in the Consumer Price Index.)

⑫ Unemployment. The percentage of the county's residents who are unemployed. (Persons are classified as *unemployed* if they do not have a job, have actively looked for work in the prior four weeks, and are currently available for work. Persons are considered *employed* if they did any work at all for pay or profit during the previous survey week, including part-time or temporary work as well as regular full-time, year-round employment. Persons are also considered employed if they have a job but did not work during the survey week due to illness, vacation, etc.)

⑬ Median home value. The median dollar value of owner-occupied housing units in the county.

⑭ Median travel time to work. The median amount of time that it takes county residents who are 16 years of age or older, and who do not work at home, to get from their homes to their places of work.

Counties USA

Counties USA

A Directory of United States Counties

2nd Edition

Containing Addresses, Telephone Numbers, Fax Numbers, and Web Site Addresses for All U.S. Counties and County-Equivalent Entities, as well as Population-Related Statistics and Other Statistical Data Related to Income, Employment, and Housing. Arranged Alphabetically by State, with Similar Information and Maps Provided for Each State. Also includes Counties Index and Other Features.

615 Griswold Street • Detroit, Michigan 48226

Editorial

Darren Smith, *Managing Editor*

Proofreading: Sharlene C. Glassman
Verification: Sue Lynch
Production Assistance: Patricia H. Cook

* * * * *

Matthew P. Barbour, *Senior Vice President*
Kay Gill, *Vice President — Directories*
Kevin Hayes, *Operations Manager*
Leif Gruenberg, *Development Manager*
David P. Bianco, *Marketing Consultant*

Peter E. Ruffner, *Publisher*
Frederick G. Ruffner, Jr., *Chairman*

ISBN 0-7808-0546-1

Printed in the United States of America

Omnigraphics, Inc.
615 Griswold Street • Detroit, MI 48226
Toll-Free Phone: 800-234-1340 • Toll-Free Fax: 800-875-1340
www.omnigraphics.com • E-mail: editorial@omnigraphics.com

Contents

Counties USA

See page 7, U.S. Counties in State Order, for an expanded table of contents that includes page references for county listings in each state.

Introduction

Counties USA provides statistical, descriptive, and contact information for the 3,140 counties and county-equivalent entities in the United States. Similar information is also provided for the 50 U.S. states.

More Statistical Data in This Edition

This second edition of *Counties USA* contains several categories of statistics for each county that were not included in the previous edition:

1. Breakdown of population by race/ethnicity
2. Percentage of population who are foreign born
3. Median age of total population
4. State rank (i.e., where the county ranks within its state in terms of total population)
5. Percentage of population change from 1990-2000
6. Per capita and median household income figures
7. Percentage of total population below the poverty level
8. Unemployment rate
9. Median home value
10. Median travel time to work.

All of the statistics provided in this directory are based primarily on information available from the U.S. Bureau of the Census. Unemployment rates were taken from information provided by the U.S. Bureau of Labor Statistics. Unemployment data given for states is seasonally adjusted, so the state rates are more recent than those given for counties. Dollar figures for per capita income are based on 1999 estimates. All other statistics are based on the 2000 Census.

Counties and County-Equivalent Entities

Forty-eight of the 50 states have governmental entities that operate at a county level. (Connecticut and Rhode Island are divided into geographic regions *called* counties, but these regions don't actually have functioning governments.) The 3,140 county listings in this directory comprise the following entities:

- 3007 counties
- 64 parishes (Louisiana)
- 15 boroughs (Alaska)
- 11 census areas (Alaska)
- 42 independent cities
- 1 municipality

The parishes of Louisiana were originally formed as ecclesiastical districts of the Roman Catholic Church under Spanish rule. Today they function the same as counties, as do the boroughs of Alaska. The one municipality that functions as a county is Anchorage, which has a consolidated city-borough government. Of the 42 independent cities listed, 39 are in Virginia; the others are Baltimore, MD, St. Louis, MO, and Carson City, NV. Independent cities function with an autonomy similar to counties, but legally they are separate entities from the counties in which they are located.

Arrangement of Information

Information in *Counties USA* is organized by states, with the following types of information included for each state grouping:

1. A state map outlining the names and boundaries of the counties and statistically equivalent areas for each state. The county outlines are based on information reported to the U.S. Bureau of the Census to be legally in effect on January 1, 2000. County changes since that date are not reflected on these maps.

2. A brief listing for that state, with a number to call for general information about the state; the state's web site; and statistical data in the same

categories as the data provided for county listings.

3. Detailed listings for each of the counties/county equivalents in that state, including contact and statistical data as well as some descriptive information.

Content of Counties Listings

Information provided for each county includes:

Contact data. Name, address, and telephone number for the county seat; fax numbers and county web sites also given as available.

Description. Brief description of the general location of the county. May also include other background information, such as dates of incorporation or organization, where available.

Name origin. Historical notes on the origin of the county name.

Area. Total county area in square miles, along with separate figures for land and water areas.

Statistical data. Includes total county population and related population data as well as statistics related to income, employment, and housing.

Index to Counties and Other Special Features

All of the counties and comparable legal entities listed in *Counties USA* are interfiled alphabetically in the **Counties Index** located at the back of the book. Index citations include the telephone number for each county, together with a reference to the page on which that county's listing appears in the main body of the book. (A detailed state-by-state list of all counties in *Counties USA* follows this Introduction.)

The **Sample Entry** located inside the front cover of this publication includes additional details about the specific content of the county listings. (Explanations of statistical data for counties are also applicable to the 50 state listings.)

Five **Statistical Tables** found inside the back cover of this book contain lists of the top 25 counties in the U.S. in terms of:

Population (2000)
Population change – numeric (1990-2000)
Population change – percentage (1990-2000)
Size (in square miles)
Per capita income (1999)

Acknowledgments

The editors are grateful for the cooperation and assistance provided to us by representatives of the U.S. Bureau of the Census and the U.S. Bureau of Labor Statistics.

Comments Welcome

Comments from readers concerning this publication, including corrections and/or suggestions for additions or improvement, are welcome. Please send to:

Editor – Counties USA
Omnigraphics, Inc.
2301 W. Sample Rd., Bldg. 3 Suite 7A
Pompano Beach, FL 33073

U.S. Counties in State Order

Hawaii

Idaho

Illinois

North Carolina

North Dakota

Ohio

Oklahoma

Wisconsin

Wyoming

Counties USA

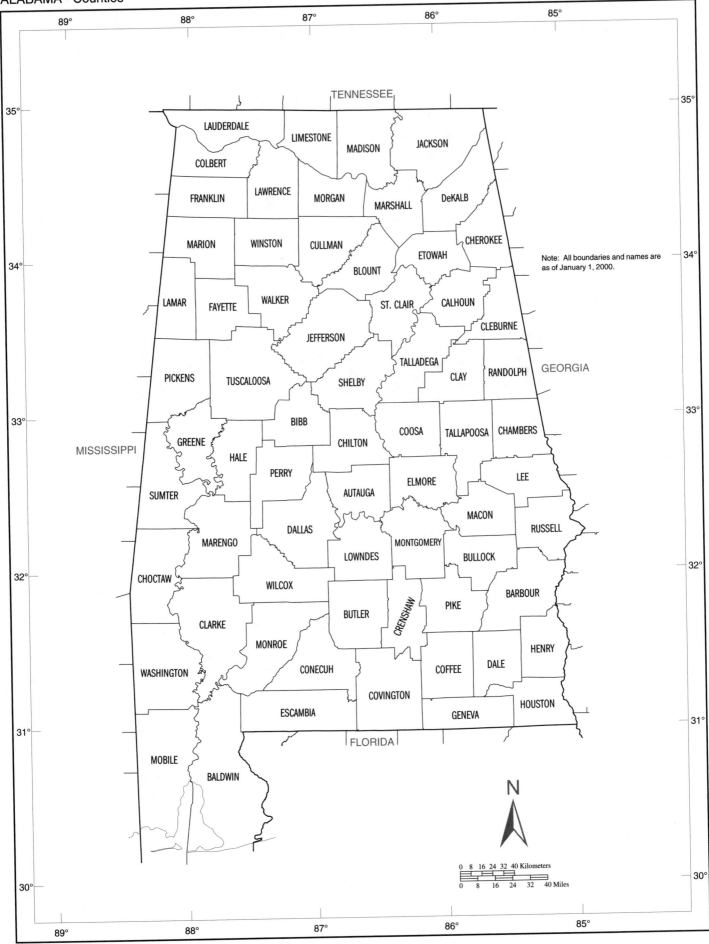

ALABAMA - Counties

Note: All boundaries and names are as of January 1, 2000.

Alabama

ALABAMA STATE INFORMATION

www.alabama.gov

Ph: 334-242-8000

Area (sq mi): 52,419.02 (land 50,744; water 1675.01).

Pop: 4,447,100 (White 70.3%; Black or African American 26%; Hispanic or Latino 1.7%; Asian 0.7%; Other 2.2%). **Foreign born:** 2%. **Median age:** 35.8. **Pop change 1990-2000:** +10.1%.

Income: per capita $18,189; median household $34,135. **Pop below poverty level:** 16.1%.

Unemployment: 5.6%. **Median home value:** $85,100. **Median travel time to work:** 24.8 minutes.

AUTAUGA COUNTY

134 N Court St Rm 106
Prattville, AL 36067

Ph: 334-361-3701
Fax: 334-361-3724

In central AL, northwest of Montgomery; organized Nov 30, 1818 (prior to statehood) from Montgomery County. **Name Origin:** For Autauga Creek, probably from Creek Indian @at1atigi 'border.'

Area (sq mi): 604.45 (land 595.97; water 8.48).

Pop: 43,671 (White 79.7%; Black or African American 17.1%; Hispanic or Latino 1.4%; Asian 0.5%; Other 1.7%). **Foreign born:** 1.2%. **Median age:** 35.1. **State rank:** 28. **Pop change 1990-2000:** +27.6%.

Income: per capita $18,518; median household $42,013. **Pop below poverty level:** 10.9%.

Unemployment: 3.7%. **Median home value:** $94,800. **Median travel time to work:** 26.5 minutes.

BALDWIN COUNTY

312 Court House Sq Suite 12
Bay Minette, AL 36507
www.co.baldwin.al.us

Ph: 251-937-9561
Fax: 251-580-2500

In southwestern AL, east of Mobile, forms part of border with Florida; organized Dec 21, 1809 from Washington County (prior to statehood). **Name Origin:** For Abraham Baldwin (1754-1807), American clergyman and U.S. senator from GA (1799-1807); founded Franklin College (now University of Georgia).

Area (sq mi): 2026.93 (land 1596.35; water 430.58).

Pop: 140,415 (White 86.1%; Black or African American 10.3%; Hispanic or Latino 1.8%; Asian 0.4%; Other 2.1%). **Foreign born:** 2.1%. **Median age:** 39. **State rank:** 7. **Pop change 1990-2000:** +42.9%.

Income: per capita $20,826; median household $40,250. **Pop below poverty level:** 10.1%.

Unemployment: 4.1%. **Median home value:** $122,500. **Median travel time to work:** 25.9 minutes.

BARBOUR COUNTY

PO Box 398
Clayton, AL 36016

Ph: 334-775-3203
Fax: 334-775-1102

On southeastern border of AL, southwest of Columbus; organized Dec 18, 1832 from Pike County and territorial land. **Name Origin:** For James Barbour (1775-1842), governor of VA (1812-14), minister to England (1828-29).

Area (sq mi): 904.52 (land 884.9; water 19.61).

Pop: 29,038 (White 50.9%; Black or African American 46.3%; Hispanic or Latino 1.6%; Asian 0.3%; Other 2.1%). **Foreign born:** 1.5%. **Median age:** 35.8. **State rank:** 39. **Pop change 1990-2000:** +14.2%.

Income: per capita $13,316; median household $25,101. **Pop below poverty level:** 26.8%.

Unemployment: 7.7%. **Median home value:** $68,600. **Median travel time to work:** 23.1 minutes.

BIBB COUNTY

35 Court Sq E
Centreville, AL 35042
www.dbtech.net/bibbco

Ph: 205-926-3103
Fax: 205-926-3132

In central AL, southeast of Tuscaloosa; organized Feb 9, 1818 (prior to statehood) from Monroe and Montgomery counties. **Name Origin:** For William Wyatt Bibb (1781-1820), U.S. senator from GA (1813-16) and first governor of AL (1817-20).

Area (sq mi): 626.16 (land 623.03; water 3.14).

Pop: 20,826 (White 76.2%; Black or African American 22.2%; Hispanic or Latino 1%; Asian 0.1%; Other 1%). **Foreign born:** 0.4%. **Median age:** 34.7. **State rank:** 50. **Pop change 1990-2000:** +25.6%.

Income: per capita $14,105; median household $31,420. **Pop below poverty level:** 20.6%.

Unemployment: 10%. **Median home value:** $74,600. **Median travel time to work:** 31.6 minutes.

BLOUNT COUNTY

220 2nd Ave E Rm 106
Oneonta, AL 35121
www.coveredbridge.org

Ph: 205-625-4160
Fax: 205-625-5961

In north-central AL, east of Gadsden; organized Feb 6, 1818 (prior to statehood) from Montgomery County. **Name Origin:** For William

Please see sample entry on inside front cover for detailed information about the statistics presented with each county listing.

Blount (1749-1800), NC delegate to Continental Congress and U.S. senator from Tennessee (1796-97).

Area (sq mi): 650.6 (land 645.59; water 5.02).

Pop: 51,024 (White 92.1%; Black or African American 1.2%; Hispanic or Latino 5.3%; Asian 0.1%; Other 3.6%). **Foreign born:** 3.1%. **Median age:** 36.4. **State rank:** 24. **Pop change 1990-2000:** +30%.

Income: per capita $16,325; median household $35,241. **Pop below poverty level:** 11.7%.

Unemployment: 2.8%. **Median home value:** $86,800. **Median travel time to work:** 34.7 minutes.

BULLOCK COUNTY
PO Box 472   **Ph:** 334-738-3883
Union Springs, AL 36089   **Fax:** 334-738-3839

In southeastern AL, southeast of Montgomery; organized Dec 5, 1866 from Barbour, Pike, Macon, and Montgomery counties. **Name Origin:** For E.C. Bullock, a local citizen.

Area (sq mi): 626.06 (land 625.01; water 1.04).

Pop: 11,714 (White 23.6%; Black or African American 73.1%; Hispanic or Latino 2.7%; Asian 0.2%; Other 1.5%). **Foreign born:** 3.1%. **Median age:** 35. **State rank:** 66. **Pop change 1990-2000:** +6.1%.

Income: per capita $10,163; median household $20,605. **Pop below poverty level:** 33.5%.

Unemployment: 11.6%. **Median home value:** $56,600. **Median travel time to work:** 26 minutes.

BUTLER COUNTY
PO Box 756   **Ph:** 334-382-3612
Greenville, AL 36037   **Fax:** 334-382-3506

In south-central AL; organized Dec 13, 1819 from Conecuh and Montgomery counties. **Name Origin:** For William Butler (?-1818), GA legislator and soldier, killed by Indians.

Area (sq mi): 777.92 (land 776.87; water 1.05).

Pop: 21,399 (White 58.1%; Black or African American 40.8%; Hispanic or Latino 0.7%; Asian 0.2%; Other 0.7%). **Foreign born:** 0.4%. **Median age:** 37.7. **State rank:** 48. **Pop change 1990-2000:** -2.3%.

Income: per capita $15,715; median household $24,791. **Pop below poverty level:** 24.6%.

Unemployment: 9.9%. **Median home value:** $57,700. **Median travel time to work:** 26.3 minutes.

CALHOUN COUNTY
1702 Noble St Suite 103   **Ph:** 256-241-2800
Anniston, AL 36201   **Fax:** 256-231-1749

In northeastern AL, southeast of Gadsden; organized as Benton County Dec 18, 1832 from Creek cession; name changed Jan 29, 1858. **Name Origin:** For John Caldwell Calhoun (1782-1850), U.S. statesman and champion of Southern causes. Originally for Thomas Hart Benton (1782-1858), U.S. senator from MO, but his views on the Missouri Compromise angered the residents.

Area (sq mi): 612.32 (land 608.46; water 3.86).

Pop: 112,249 (White 78%; Black or African American 18.5%; Hispanic or Latino 1.6%; Asian 0.6%; Other 2.1%). **Foreign born:** 1.7%. **Median age:** 37.2. **State rank:** 9. **Pop change 1990-2000:** -3.3%.

Income: per capita $17,367; median household $31,768. **Pop below poverty level:** 16.1%.

Unemployment: 5.6%. **Median home value:** $71,600. **Median travel time to work:** 23.4 minutes.

CHAMBERS COUNTY
Courthouse   **Ph:** 334-864-4348
Lafayette, AL 36862

On eastern border of AL, north of Auburn; organized Dec 18, 1832 from Creek cession. **Name Origin:** For Henry H. Chambers (1790-1826), physician and U.S. senator (1825-26).

Area (sq mi): 603.11 (land 597.17; water 5.94).

Pop: 36,583 (White 60.4%; Black or African American 38.1%; Hispanic or Latino 0.8%; Asian 0.2%; Other 0.8%). **Foreign born:** 0.8%. **Median age:** 37.7. **State rank:** 34. **Pop change 1990-2000:** -0.8%.

Income: per capita $15,147; median household $29,667. **Pop below poverty level:** 17%.

Unemployment: 6.5%. **Median home value:** $58,900. **Median travel time to work:** 22 minutes.

CHEROKEE COUNTY
102 Main St Rm 201   **Ph:** 256-927-3668
Centre, AL 35960   **Fax:** 256-927-3669

On northeastern border of AL, east of Gadsden; organized Jun 9, 1836 from Cherokee cession. **Name Origin:** For the Indian tribe of Iroquoian linguistic stock. Name may derive from Creek *tciloki* 'people of a different speech.'

Area (sq mi): 599.95 (land 553.12; water 46.83).

Pop: 23,988 (White 92.4%; Black or African American 5.5%; Hispanic or Latino 0.9%; Asian 0.1%; Other 1.4%). **Foreign born:** 1.1%. **Median age:** 40. **State rank:** 45. **Pop change 1990-2000:** +22.7%.

Income: per capita $15,543; median household $30,874. **Pop below poverty level:** 15.6%.

Unemployment: 4.4%. **Median home value:** $76,100. **Median travel time to work:** 30 minutes.

CHILTON COUNTY
PO Box 1948   **Ph:** 205-755-1551
Clanton, AL 35046   **Fax:** 205-280-7204
www.chilton.al.us/

In central AL, south of Birmingham; organized as Baker County Dec 30, 1868 from Bibb, Perry, Autauga, and Shelby counties; name changed Dec 17, 1874. **Name Origin:** For William Parish Chilton (1810-71), legislator, jurist, and member of the Confederate Congress.

Area (sq mi): 700.76 (land 693.98; water 6.78).

All statistics are based on the 2000 Census except the dollar figures given for per capita income, which are based on 1999 estimates.

Pop: 39,593 (White 85.6%; Black or African American 10.6%; Hispanic or Latino 2.9%; Asian 0.2%; Other 2.5%). **Foreign born:** 1.9%. **Median age:** 35.9. **State rank:** 31. **Pop change 1990-2000:** +22%.

Income: per capita $15,303; median household $32,588. **Pop below poverty level:** 15.7%.

Unemployment: 5.1%. **Median home value:** $81,800. **Median travel time to work:** 33.2 minutes.

CHOCTAW COUNTY

117 S Mulberry St Suite 9   **Ph:** 205-459-2417
Butler, AL 36904   **Fax:** 205-459-4248

On western border of AL; organized Dec 29, 1847 from Sumter and Washington counties. **Name Origin:** For the Indian tribe of Muskohegean linguistic stock; meaning of the name unknown.

Area (sq mi): 920.85 (land 913.51; water 7.34).

Pop: 15,922 (White 54.8%; Black or African American 44.1%; Hispanic or Latino 0.7%; Asian 0%; Other 0.7%). **Foreign born:** 0.6%. **Median age:** 37.9. **State rank:** 55. **Pop change 1990-2000:** -0.6%.

Income: per capita $14,635; median household $24,749. **Pop below poverty level:** 24.5%.

Unemployment: 9.1%. **Median home value:** $60,500. **Median travel time to work:** 37.8 minutes.

CLARKE COUNTY

PO Box 548   **Ph:** 251-275-3507
Grove Hill, AL 36451   **Fax:** 251-275-8517

In southwestern AL, northeast of Mobile; organized Dec 10, 1812 (prior to statehood) from Washington County. **Name Origin:** For John Clarke, a local Indian fighter.

Area (sq mi): 1252.51 (land 1238.38; water 14.13).

Pop: 27,867 (White 55.7%; Black or African American 43%; Hispanic or Latino 0.6%; Asian 0.2%; Other 0.9%). **Foreign born:** 0.5%. **Median age:** 35.5. **State rank:** 40. **Pop change 1990-2000:** +2.3%.

Income: per capita $14,581; median household $27,388. **Pop below poverty level:** 22.6%.

Unemployment: 11.6%. **Median home value:** $67,900. **Median travel time to work:** 26.2 minutes.

CLAY COUNTY

PO Box 187   **Ph:** 256-354-7888
Ashland, AL 36251   **Fax:** 256-354-3208

In east-central AL, south of Anniston; organized Dec 7, 1866 from Talladega and Randolph counties. **Name Origin:** For Henry Clay (1777-1852), U.S. senator from KY, known as the 'Great Pacificator' for his advocacy of compromise to avert national crises.

Area (sq mi): 606 (land 605.07; water 0.93).

Pop: 14,254 (White 81.5%; Black or African American 15.7%; Hispanic or Latino 1.8%; Asian 0.1%; Other 1.6%). **Foreign born:** 0.9%. **Median age:** 38.7. **State rank:** 58. **Pop change 1990-2000:** +7.6%.

Income: per capita $13,785; median household $27,885. **Pop below poverty level:** 17.1%.

Unemployment: 5.9%. **Median home value:** $62,200. **Median travel time to work:** 26.6 minutes.

CLEBURNE COUNTY

120 Vickery St Rm 202   **Ph:** 256-463-2651
Heflin, AL 36264   **Fax:** 256-463-2257

On eastern border of AL, east of Anniston; organized Dec 6, 1866 from Calhoun and Randolph counties. **Name Origin:** For Confederate Gen. Patrick R. Cleburne (1828-64).

Area (sq mi): 561.02 (land 560.21; water 0.81).

Pop: 14,123 (White 93.7%; Black or African American 3.7%; Hispanic or Latino 1.4%; Asian 0.1%; Other 1.4%). **Foreign born:** 0.9%. **Median age:** 37.5. **State rank:** 59. **Pop change 1990-2000:** +10.9%.

Income: per capita $14,762; median household $30,820. **Pop below poverty level:** 13.9%.

Unemployment: 5.5%. **Median home value:** $71,300. **Median travel time to work:** 30.3 minutes.

COFFEE COUNTY

230-M Court Ave   **Ph:** 334-897-2954
Elba, AL 36323

In southeastern AL, northwest of Dothan; organized Dec 29, 1841 from Dale County. **Name Origin:** For Gen. John Coffee (1772-1833), TN surveyor and officer who oversaw the removal of the Choctaws and Chickasaws to the OK Territory.

Area (sq mi): 680.48 (land 678.99; water 1.49).

Pop: 43,615 (White 75.6%; Black or African American 18.4%; Hispanic or Latino 2.7%; Asian 0.9%; Other 3.6%). **Foreign born:** 2.7%. **Median age:** 37.2. **State rank:** 29. **Pop change 1990-2000:** +8.4%.

Income: per capita $18,321; median household $33,664. **Pop below poverty level:** 14.7%.

Unemployment: 6.7%. **Median home value:** $76,600. **Median travel time to work:** 21.4 minutes.

COLBERT COUNTY

201 N Main St   **Ph:** 256-386-8500
Tuscumbia, AL 35674   **Fax:** 256-386-8510
www.colbertcounty.org

On northwestern border of AL, south of Florence; organized Feb 6, 1867 from Franklin County. **Name Origin:** For George and Levi Colbert, two Cherokee Indian brothers.

Area (sq mi): 623.61 (land 594.53; water 29.08).

Pop: 54,984 (White 80.9%; Black or African American 16.6%; Hispanic or Latino 1.1%; Asian 0.2%; Other 1.6%). **Foreign born:** 0.9%. **Median age:** 38.7. **State rank:** 22. **Pop change 1990-2000:** +6.4%.

Income: per capita $17,533; median household $31,954. **Pop below poverty level:** 14%.

Unemployment: 8.4%. **Median home value:** $72,300. **Median travel time to work:** 23.8 minutes.

Please see sample entry on inside front cover for detailed information about the statistics presented with each county listing.

CONECUH COUNTY

PO Box 107
Evergreen, AL 36401   **Ph:** 251-578-2066

In south-central AL; organized Feb 13, 1818 (prior to statehood) from Monroe County. **Name Origin:** Probably from Creek Indian *kono ika* 'polecat's head.'

Area (sq mi): 852.51 (land 850.79; water 1.71).

Pop: 14,089 (White 55.1%; Black or African American 43.6%; Hispanic or Latino 0.7%; Asian 0.1%; Other 0.9%). **Foreign born:** 0.4%. **Median age:** 38. **State rank:** 60. **Pop change 1990-2000:** +0.2%.

Income: per capita $12,964; median household $22,111. **Pop below poverty level:** 26.6%.

Unemployment: 7.9%. **Median home value:** $58,600. **Median travel time to work:** 26.2 minutes.

COOSA COUNTY

PO Box 10   **Ph:** 256-377-2420
Rockford, AL 35136   **Fax:** 256-377-2524

In east-central AL, north of Montgomery; organized Dec 18, 1832 from Creek cession. **Name Origin:** For the Coosa River, which flows through the county.

Area (sq mi): 666.36 (land 652.44; water 13.91).

Pop: 12,202 (White 63.4%; Black or African American 34.2%; Hispanic or Latino 1.3%; Asian 0%; Other 1.8%). **Foreign born:** 0.3%. **Median age:** 37.7. **State rank:** 64. **Pop change 1990-2000:** +10.3%.

Income: per capita $14,875; median household $29,873. **Pop below poverty level:** 14.9%.

Unemployment: 8%. **Median home value:** $59,500. **Median travel time to work:** 27.7 minutes.

COVINGTON COUNTY

County Courthouse   **Ph:** 334-428-2500
Andalusia, AL 36420   **Fax:** 334-428-2531

On south-central border of AL; organized Dec 7, 1821 from Henry County. **Name Origin:** For Leonard Wales Covington (1768-1813), MD-born legislator and army officer.

Area (sq mi): 1043.86 (land 1033.82; water 10.05).

Pop: 37,631 (White 85.7%; Black or African American 12.4%; Hispanic or Latino 0.8%; Asian 0.2%; Other 1.3%). **Foreign born:** 0.6%. **Median age:** 39.8. **State rank:** 33. **Pop change 1990-2000:** +3.2%.

Income: per capita $15,365; median household $26,336. **Pop below poverty level:** 18.4%.

Unemployment: 7.4%. **Median home value:** $56,700. **Median travel time to work:** 23.6 minutes.

CRENSHAW COUNTY

PO Box 227   **Ph:** 334-335-6568
Luverne, AL 36049

In south-central AL, south of Montgomery; organized Nov 24, 1866 from Covington, Butler, Coffee, Lowndes, and Pike counties. **Name Origin:** For Anderson Crenshaw (1783-1847), lawyer, statesman, and jurist.

Area (sq mi): 610.88 (land 609.58; water 1.3).

Pop: 13,665 (White 73.5%; Black or African American 24.8%; Hispanic or Latino 0.6%; Asian 0.1%; Other 1.3%). **Foreign born:** 0.3%. **Median age:** 38.8. **State rank:** 61. **Pop change 1990-2000:** +0.2%.

Income: per capita $14,565; median household $26,054. **Pop below poverty level:** 22.1%.

Unemployment: 7.6%. **Median home value:** $51,300. **Median travel time to work:** 31.8 minutes.

CULLMAN COUNTY

500 2nd Ave SW Rm 211   **Ph:** 256-739-3530
Cullman, AL 35055   **Fax:** 256-739-3525
www.co.cullman.al.us

In north-central AL, north of Birmingham; organized Jan 24, 1877 from Blount, Morgan, and Winston counties. **Name Origin:** For the city of Cullman.

Area (sq mi): 754.82 (land 738.43; water 16.39).

Pop: 77,483 (White 95.4%; Black or African American 1%; Hispanic or Latino 2.2%; Asian 0.2%; Other 2%). **Foreign born:** 1.7%. **Median age:** 37.5. **State rank:** 16. **Pop change 1990-2000:** +14.6%.

Income: per capita $16,922; median household $32,256. **Pop below poverty level:** 13%.

Unemployment: 4.2%. **Median home value:** $85,000. **Median travel time to work:** 28.2 minutes.

DALE COUNTY

202 Hwy 123 S Suite C   **Ph:** 334-774-6025
Ozark, AL 36360   **Fax:** 334-774-1841

In southeastern AL, northwest of Dothan; organized Dec 22, 1824 from Covington and Henry counties. **Name Origin:** For Samuel Dale (1772-1841), officer and scout in the Indian wars, and legislator in AL and MS.

Area (sq mi): 562.67 (land 561.07; water 1.6).

Pop: 49,129 (White 72.8%; Black or African American 20.4%; Hispanic or Latino 3.3%; Asian 1.1%; Other 4.1%). **Foreign born:** 3.1%. **Median age:** 34.3. **State rank:** 26. **Pop change 1990-2000:** -1%.

Income: per capita $16,010; median household $31,998. **Pop below poverty level:** 15.1%.

Unemployment: 5.3%. **Median home value:** $69,000. **Median travel time to work:** 20.7 minutes.

DALLAS COUNTY

PO Box 987   **Ph:** 334-874-2560
Selma, AL 36702   **Fax:** 334-874-2587

In southwest-central AL, west of Montgomery; organized Feb 9, 1818 (prior to statehood) from Montgomery County. **Name Origin:** For Alexander James Dallas (1759-1817), PA statesman, secretary of the treasury (1814-16) and acting secretary of war (1815); father of George Mifflin Dallas (1792-1864).

Area (sq mi): 993.37 (land 980.71; water 12.66).

Pop: 46,365 (White 35.4%; Black or African American 63.3%; Hispanic or Latino 0.6%; Asian 0.3%; Other 0.7%). **Foreign born:**

All statistics are based on the 2000 Census except the dollar figures given for per capita income, which are based on 1999 estimates.

32

0.7%. **Median age:** 35.3. **State rank:** 27. **Pop change 1990-2000:** -3.7%.

Income: per capita $13,638; median household $23,370. **Pop below poverty level:** 31.1%.

Unemployment: 11.7%. **Median home value:** $64,100. **Median travel time to work:** 23.6 minutes.

DEKALB COUNTY
111 Grand Ave SW Suite 200   **Ph:** 256-845-8500
Fort Payne, AL 35967   **Fax:** 256-845-8502

On northeastern border AL, north of Gadsden; organized Jan 9, 1836 form Cherokee cession. **Name Origin:** For Johann, Baron de Kalb (1721-80), German-born French soldier who fought with the Americans during the Revolutionary War.

Area (sq mi): 778.65 (land 777.91; water 0.74).

Pop: 64,452 (White 90.7%; Black or African American 1.7%; Hispanic or Latino 5.6%; Asian 0.2%; Other 5.6%). **Foreign born:** 4.1%. **Median age:** 36.3. **State rank:** 21. **Pop change 1990-2000:** +17.9%.

Income: per capita $15,818; median household $30,137. **Pop below poverty level:** 15.4%.

Unemployment: 4.6%. **Median home value:** $67,200. **Median travel time to work:** 23.9 minutes.

ELMORE COUNTY
PO Box 310   **Ph:** 334-567-1124
Wetumpka, AL 36092   **Fax:** 334-567-5957

In east-central AL, north of Montgomery; organized Feb 15, 1866 from Montgomery, Coosa, and Autauga counties, and from Tallapoosa County in 1867. **Name Origin:** For Revolutionary War veteran John Archer Elmore, an early settler (1821) and state legislator.

Area (sq mi): 657.21 (land 621.26; water 35.96).

Pop: 65,874 (White 76.5%; Black or African American 20.6%; Hispanic or Latino 1.2%; Asian 0.4%; Other 1.9%). **Foreign born:** 1.1%. **Median age:** 35.3. **State rank:** 18. **Pop change 1990-2000:** +33.9%.

Income: per capita $17,650; median household $41,243. **Pop below poverty level:** 10.2%.

Unemployment: 3.9%. **Median home value:** $98,000. **Median travel time to work:** 28.7 minutes.

ESCAMBIA COUNTY
PO Box 856   **Ph:** 251-867-0305
Brewton, AL 36427   **Fax:** 251-867-0365
www.co.escambia.al.us

On southern border of AL; organized Dec 10, 1868 from Baldwin and Conecuh counties. **Name Origin:** For Escambia River, probably a Spanish rendering of a Choctaw or Chickasaw Indian word but origin is in dispute. There may be a connection to Spanish *cambiar* 'to exchange, trade, barter.' River formerly called the *Pensacola*.

Area (sq mi): 952.95 (land 947.38; water 5.57).

Pop: 38,440 (White 63.9%; Black or African American 30.8%; Hispanic or Latino 1%; Asian 0.2%; Other 4.5%). **Foreign born:** 0.6%. **Median age:** 36.9. **State rank:** 32. **Pop change 1990-2000:** +8.2%.

Income: per capita $14,396; median household $28,319. **Pop below poverty level:** 20.9%.

Unemployment: 5.8%. **Median home value:** $66,700. **Median travel time to work:** 25.5 minutes.

ETOWAH COUNTY
800 Forrest Ave   **Ph:** 256-549-5300
Gadsden, AL 35901   **Fax:** 256-549-5400
www.etowahcounty.org

In northeastern AL, northwest of Anniston; organized as Baine County Dec 7, 1866; name changed Dec 1, 1868. **Name Origin:** Originally for David W. Baine, Confederate officer killed in the war. County abolished Dec 3, 1867 because he was a secessionist. Recreated and renamed for the Etowah Indian mound in GA. Meaning of Cherokee *itawa* is unknown but may be related to Creek *italwa* 'town, tribe.'

Area (sq mi): 548.75 (land 534.82; water 13.93).

Pop: 103,459 (White 82.1%; Black or African American 14.7%; Hispanic or Latino 1.7%; Asian 0.4%; Other 1.9%). **Foreign born:** 1.6%. **Median age:** 38.3. **State rank:** 11. **Pop change 1990-2000:** +3.6%.

Income: per capita $16,783; median household $31,170. **Pop below poverty level:** 15.7%.

Unemployment: 7.4%. **Median home value:** $71,200. **Median travel time to work:** 24.5 minutes.

FAYETTE COUNTY
103 1st Ave NW Courthouse Annex Suite 2   **Ph:** 205-932-4510
Fayette, AL 35555   **Fax:** 205-932-4370

In west-central AL, north of Tuscaloosa; organized Dec 20, 1824 from Marion and Pickens counties. **Name Origin:** For the Marquis de Layfayette (1757-1834), French statesman and soldier who fought with Americans during the Revolutionary War.

Area (sq mi): 629.34 (land 627.66; water 1.68).

Pop: 18,495 (White 86.5%; Black or African American 11.9%; Hispanic or Latino 0.8%; Asian 0.2%; Other 1%). **Foreign born:** 0.7%. **Median age:** 39. **State rank:** 51. **Pop change 1990-2000:** +3%.

Income: per capita $14,439; median household $28,539. **Pop below poverty level:** 17.3%.

Unemployment: 7.5%. **Median home value:** $64,100. **Median travel time to work:** 28.5 minutes.

FRANKLIN COUNTY
PO Box 1028   **Ph:** 256-332-1210
Russellville, AL 35653   **Fax:** 256-332-8855

On northwestern border of AL, south of Florence; organized Feb 4, 1818 (prior to statehood) from Cherokee cession. **Name Origin:** For Benjamin Franklin (1706-90), U.S. patriot, diplomat, and statesman.

Area (sq mi): 646.51 (land 635.64; water 10.86).

Please see sample entry on inside front cover for detailed information about the statistics presented with each county listing.

Pop: 31,223 (White 87.3%; Black or African American 4.2%; Hispanic or Latino 7.4%; Asian 0.1%; Other 6%). **Foreign born:** 5.6%. **Median age:** 36.7. **State rank:** 36. **Pop change 1990-2000:** +12.3%.

Income: per capita $14,814; median household $27,177. **Pop below poverty level:** 18.9%.

Unemployment: 8.4%. **Median home value:** $62,800. **Median travel time to work:** 24.4 minutes.

GENEVA COUNTY
PO Box 86   **Ph:** 334-684-5620
Geneva, AL 36340   **Fax:** 334-684-5605
www.alaweb.com/~gcounty

On southern border of AL, south of Dothan; organized Dec 26, 1868 from Coffee, Dale, and Henry counties. **Name Origin:** For Geneva, Switzerland, former home of the early settlers.

Area (sq mi): 578.9 (land 576.28; water 2.62).

Pop: 25,764 (White 86.1%; Black or African American 10.6%; Hispanic or Latino 1.8%; Asian 0.1%; Other 2.1%). **Foreign born:** 0.8%. **Median age:** 39.3. **State rank:** 41. **Pop change 1990-2000:** +9%.

Income: per capita $14,620; median household $26,448. **Pop below poverty level:** 19.6%.

Unemployment: 9.2%. **Median home value:** $55,900. **Median travel time to work:** 27.2 minutes.

GREENE COUNTY
PO Box 307   **Ph:** 205-372-3598
Eutaw, AL 35462   **Fax:** 205-372-1510

In western AL, southwest of Tuscaloosa; organized Dec 13, 1819 from Marengo and Tuscaloosa counties. **Name Origin:** For Gen. Nathanael Greene (1742-86), hero of the Revolutionary War and quartermaster general (1778-80).

Area (sq mi): 659.93 (land 645.87; water 14.07).

Pop: 9,974 (White 19%; Black or African American 80.3%; Hispanic or Latino 0.6%; Asian 0.1%; Other 0.5%). **Foreign born:** 0.7%. **Median age:** 35.9. **State rank:** 67. **Pop change 1990-2000:** -1.8%.

Income: per capita $13,686; median household $19,819. **Pop below poverty level:** 34.3%.

Unemployment: 10.7%. **Median home value:** $57,000. **Median travel time to work:** 28.8 minutes.

HALE COUNTY
PO Box 396   **Ph:** 334-624-4257
Greensboro, AL 36744   **Fax:** 334-624-1715

In west-central AL, south of Tuscaloosa; organized Jan 30, 1867 from Greene, Marengo, and Perry counties. **Name Origin:** For Stephen F. Hale (1816-78), early settler, lawyer, and Confederate army officer.

Area (sq mi): 656.47 (land 643.74; water 12.74).

Pop: 17,185 (White 39.6%; Black or African American 59%; Hispanic or Latino 0.9%; Asian 0.2%; Other 1.1%). **Foreign born:** 0.3%. **Median age:** 34.4. **State rank:** 53. **Pop change 1990-2000:** +10.9%.

Income: per capita $12,661; median household $25,807. **Pop below poverty level:** 26.9%.

Unemployment: 9.7%. **Median home value:** $66,300. **Median travel time to work:** 29 minutes.

HENRY COUNTY
101 Court Sq Suite J   **Ph:** 334-585-2753
Abbeville, AL 36310   **Fax:** 334-585-5006

On southeastern border of AL, north of Dothan; organized Dec 13, 1819 from Conecuh County. **Name Origin:** For Patrick Henry (1736-99), patriot, governor of VA (1776-79; 1784-86), and statesman, famous for declaring 'Give me liberty or give me death.'

Area (sq mi): 568.33 (land 561.8; water 6.53).

Pop: 16,310 (White 65.3%; Black or African American 32.3%; Hispanic or Latino 1.5%; Asian 0.1%; Other 1.9%). **Foreign born:** 1.1%. **Median age:** 39.3. **State rank:** 54. **Pop change 1990-2000:** +6.1%.

Income: per capita $15,681; median household $30,353. **Pop below poverty level:** 19.1%.

Unemployment: 6.5%. **Median home value:** $69,100. **Median travel time to work:** 25.5 minutes.

HOUSTON COUNTY
PO Drawer 6406   **Ph:** 334-677-4741
Dothan, AL 36302   **Fax:** 334-794-6633
www.houstoncounty.org

In southeastern corner of AL; organized Feb 9, 1903 from Dale, Geneva, and Henry counties. **Name Origin:** For George Smith Houston (1808-79), U.S. senator and governor of AL (1874-78).

Area (sq mi): 581.65 (land 580.36; water 1.29).

Pop: 88,787 (White 72.4%; Black or African American 24.6%; Hispanic or Latino 1.3%; Asian 0.6%; Other 1.7%). **Foreign born:** 1.6%. **Median age:** 36.7. **State rank:** 12. **Pop change 1990-2000:** +9.2%.

Income: per capita $18,759; median household $34,431. **Pop below poverty level:** 15%.

Unemployment: 4.2%. **Median home value:** $82,000. **Median travel time to work:** 20 minutes.

JACKSON COUNTY
Courthouse Suite 47   **Ph:** 256-574-9280
Scottsboro, AL 35768   **Fax:** 256-574-9321

On northeastern corner of AL; organized Dec 13, 1819 from Cherokee cession. **Name Origin:** For Andrew Jackson (1767-1845), seventh U.S. president.

Area (sq mi): 1126.77 (land 1078.74; water 48.02).

Pop: 53,926 (White 91.2%; Black or African American 3.7%; Hispanic or Latino 1.1%; Asian 0.2%; Other 4.2%). **Foreign born:** 0.7%. **Median age:** 37.6. **State rank:** 23. **Pop change 1990-2000:** +12.8%.

Income: per capita $16,000; median household $32,020. **Pop below poverty level:** 13.7%.

Unemployment: 8.4%. **Median home value:** $72,400. **Median travel time to work:** 27 minutes.

All statistics are based on the 2000 Census except the dollar figures given for per capita income, which are based on 1999 estimates.

JEFFERSON COUNTY

716 Richard Arrington Jr Blvd N Suite 210   **Ph:** 205-325-5555
Birmingham, AL 35203   **Fax:** 205-325-4860
www.jeffcointouch.com/

In central AL; organized Dec 13, 1819 from Blount County. **Name Origin:** For Thomas Jefferson (1743-1826), U.S. patriot and statesman; third U.S. president.

Area (sq mi): 1123.8 (land 1112.61; water 11.2).

Pop: 662,047 (White 57.4%; Black or African American 39.4%; Hispanic or Latino 1.6%; Asian 0.9%; Other 1.6%). **Foreign born:** 2.3%. **Median age:** 36. **State rank:** 1. **Pop change 1990-2000:** +1.6%.

Income: per capita $20,892; median household $36,868. **Pop below poverty level:** 14.8%.

Unemployment: 3.8%. **Median home value:** $90,700. **Median travel time to work:** 24.3 minutes.

LAMAR COUNTY

PO Box 338   **Ph:** 205-695-7333
Vernon, AL 35592   **Fax:** 205-695-8522

On western border of AL, west of Birmingham; organized as Jones County Feb 14, 1867 from Marion, Pickens, and Fayette counties; abolished the same year; recreated as Sanford County Oct 8, 1868; renamed Feb 8, 1877. **Name Origin:** For Lucius Quintus Cincinnatus Lamar (1825-93), U.S. representative from MS (1857-60; 1873-77), U.S. senator (1877-85), secretary of the interior (1885-88), and a justice of the U.S. Supreme Court (1888-93).

Area (sq mi): 605.47 (land 604.85; water 0.62).

Pop: 15,904 (White 86.1%; Black or African American 12%; Hispanic or Latino 1.3%; Asian 0.1%; Other 1.1%). **Foreign born:** 0.8%. **Median age:** 38.2. **State rank:** 56. **Pop change 1990-2000:** +1.2%.

Income: per capita $14,435; median household $28,059. **Pop below poverty level:** 16.1%.

Unemployment: 10.5%. **Median home value:** $55,200. **Median travel time to work:** 23.9 minutes.

LAUDERDALE COUNTY

PO Box 1059   **Ph:** 256-760-5750
Florence, AL 35631   **Fax:** 256-760-5703

On northwestern border of AL; organized Feb 13, 1818 (prior to statehood) from Cherokee cession. **Name Origin:** At suggestion of Gen. John Coffee (1772-1833), for Col. James Lauderdale (?-1814), who died fighting under Coffee at the Battle of Talladega.

Area (sq mi): 718.78 (land 669.46; water 49.32).

Pop: 87,966 (White 87.8%; Black or African American 9.8%; Hispanic or Latino 1%; Asian 0.4%; Other 1.5%). **Foreign born:** 1%. **Median age:** 37.6. **State rank:** 13. **Pop change 1990-2000:** +10.4%.

Income: per capita $18,626; median household $33,354. **Pop below poverty level:** 14.4%.

Unemployment: 8.1%. **Median home value:** $85,000. **Median travel time to work:** 23.7 minutes.

LAWRENCE COUNTY

PO Box 307   **Ph:** 256-974-0663
Moulton, AL 35650   **Fax:** 256-974-2403

In northwest AL, west of Decatur; organized Feb 14, 1818 (prior to statehood) from Cherokee cession. **Name Origin:** For Capt. James Lawrence (1781-1813), U.S. Navy commander in War of 1812 who said, 'Don't give up the ship!'

Area (sq mi): 718.07 (land 693.38; water 24.68).

Pop: 34,803 (White 77.3%; Black or African American 13.4%; Hispanic or Latino 1.1%; Asian 0.1%; Other 8.8%). **Foreign born:** 0.5%. **Median age:** 35.9. **State rank:** 35. **Pop change 1990-2000:** +10.4%.

Income: per capita $16,515; median household $31,549. **Pop below poverty level:** 15.3%.

Unemployment: 6.8%. **Median home value:** $75,000. **Median travel time to work:** 27 minutes.

LEE COUNTY

PO Box 666   **Ph:** 334-745-9767
Opelika, AL 36803   **Fax:** 334-742-9478

On eastern border of AL, north of Columbus; organized Dec 15, 1866 from Chambers and Macon counties. **Name Origin:** For Robert E. Lee (1807-70), American general and commander in chief of the Confederate forces during the Civil War.

Area (sq mi): 615.55 (land 608.71; water 6.84).

Pop: 115,092 (White 73.2%; Black or African American 22.7%; Hispanic or Latino 1.4%; Asian 1.6%; Other 1.6%). **Foreign born:** 2.7%. **Median age:** 27.5. **State rank:** 8. **Pop change 1990-2000:** +32.1%.

Income: per capita $17,158; median household $30,952. **Pop below poverty level:** 21.8%.

Unemployment: 3.8%. **Median home value:** $104,100. **Median travel time to work:** 20.6 minutes.

LIMESTONE COUNTY

310 W Washington St   **Ph:** 256-233-6400
Athens, AL 35611   **Fax:** 256-233-6403
www.co.limestone.al.us

On central northern border of AL, north of Decatur; organized Feb 6, 1818 (prior to statehood) from Cherokee and Chickasaw cessions. **Name Origin:** For Limestone Creek, which flows through it.

Area (sq mi): 607.08 (land 568.05; water 39.03).

Pop: 65,676 (White 82.4%; Black or African American 13.3%; Hispanic or Latino 2.6%; Asian 0.4%; Other 2.5%). **Foreign born:** 1.7%. **Median age:** 35.8. **State rank:** 19. **Pop change 1990-2000:** +21.3%.

Income: per capita $17,782; median household $37,405. **Pop below poverty level:** 12.3%.

Unemployment: 4.4%. **Median home value:** $86,400. **Median travel time to work:** 26.4 minutes.

Please see sample entry on inside front cover for detailed information about the statistics presented with each county listing.

LOWNDES COUNTY

PO Box 65
Hayneville, AL 36040

Ph: 334-548-2331
Fax: 334-548-5101

In south-central AL, southwest of Montgomery; organized Jan 20, 1830 from Butler and Dallas counties. **Name Origin:** For William Jones Lowndes (1782-1822), SC legislator and U.S. representative (1811-22).

Area (sq mi): 725.03 (land 717.94; water 7.1).

Pop: 13,473 (White 25.7%; Black or African American 73.4%; Hispanic or Latino 0.6%; Asian 0.1%; Other 0.6%). **Foreign born:** 0.3%. **Median age:** 33.9. **State rank:** 62. **Pop change 1990-2000:** +6.4%.

Income: per capita $12,457; median household $23,050. **Pop below poverty level:** 31.4%.

Unemployment: 9.4%. **Median home value:** $55,500. **Median travel time to work:** 36.3 minutes.

MACON COUNTY

101 E Northside St Courthouse
Tuskegee, AL 36083

Ph: 334-727-5120
Fax: 334-724-2621

In southwestern AL, west of Columbus; organized Dec 18, 1832 from Creek cession. **Name Origin:** For Nathaniel Macon (1757-1837), NC legislator, U.S. representative (1791-1815), U.S. senator (1815-28), and president of the NC constitutional convention (1835).

Area (sq mi): 613.24 (land 610.52; water 2.72).

Pop: 24,105 (White 13.8%; Black or African American 84.6%; Hispanic or Latino 0.7%; Asian 0.4%; Other 1%). **Foreign born:** 1.5%. **Median age:** 32. **State rank:** 44. **Pop change 1990-2000:** -3.3%.

Income: per capita $13,714; median household $21,180. **Pop below poverty level:** 32.8%.

Unemployment: 6.3%. **Median home value:** $64,200. **Median travel time to work:** 25.4 minutes.

MADISON COUNTY

100 Northside Sq
Huntsville, AL 35801
www.co.madison.al.us

Ph: 256-532-3492
Fax: 256-532-6994

On central northern border of AL; organized Dec 13, 1808 from Cherokee cession (prior to statehood). **Name Origin:** For James Madison (1751-1836), fourth U.S. president.

Area (sq mi): 812.85 (land 804.92; water 7.93).

Pop: 276,700 (White 71%; Black or African American 22.8%; Hispanic or Latino 1.9%; Asian 1.9%; Other 3.4%). **Foreign born:** 4%. **Median age:** 35.7. **State rank:** 3. **Pop change 1990-2000:** +15.8%.

Income: per capita $23,091; median household $44,704. **Pop below poverty level:** 10.5%.

Unemployment: 3.4%. **Median home value:** $103,300. **Median travel time to work:** 20.9 minutes.

MARENGO COUNTY

PO Box 480715
Linden, AL 36748

Ph: 334-295-2200
Fax: 334-295-2254

In west-central AL, south of Tuscaloosa; organized Feb 7, 1818 (prior to statehood) from Choctaw cession. **Name Origin:** Commemorates Napoleon's (1769-1821) victory over the Austrian army at Marengo, Italy (Jun 14, 1800).

Area (sq mi): 982.85 (land 977.04; water 5.8).

Pop: 22,539 (White 46.9%; Black or African American 51.7%; Hispanic or Latino 1%; Asian 0.2%; Other 0.9%). **Foreign born:** 0.7%. **Median age:** 36.4. **State rank:** 46. **Pop change 1990-2000:** -2.4%.

Income: per capita $15,308; median household $27,025. **Pop below poverty level:** 25.9%.

Unemployment: 5.3%. **Median home value:** $65,900. **Median travel time to work:** 25.5 minutes.

MARION COUNTY

PO Box 1595
Hamilton, AL 35570

Ph: 205-921-7451
Fax: 205-952-9851

On northwestern border of AL, south of Florence; organized Dec 13, 1818 (prior to statehood) from Indian lands. **Name Origin:** For Gen. Francis Marion (c. 1732-95), SC soldier and legislator, known as 'The Swamp Fox' for his tactics during the Revolutionary War.

Area (sq mi): 743.57 (land 741.41; water 2.16).

Pop: 31,214 (White 94.1%; Black or African American 3.6%; Hispanic or Latino 1.2%; Asian 0.2%; Other 1.4%). **Foreign born:** 0.5%. **Median age:** 38.9. **State rank:** 37. **Pop change 1990-2000:** +4.6%.

Income: per capita $15,321; median household $27,475. **Pop below poverty level:** 15.6%.

Unemployment: 10.5%. **Median home value:** $63,500. **Median travel time to work:** 23.6 minutes.

MARSHALL COUNTY

424 Blount Ave
Guntersville, AL 35976
www.marshallco.org/www/

Ph: 256-571-7701
Fax: 256-571-7703

In northeastern AL, south of Huntsville; organized Jan 9, 1836 from Blount County and Cherokee cession. **Name Origin:** For John Marshall (1755-1835), American jurist; fourth Chief Justice of the U.S. Supreme Court (1801-35).

Area (sq mi): 623.16 (land 567.06; water 56.1).

Pop: 82,231 (White 91.3%; Black or African American 1.5%; Hispanic or Latino 5.7%; Asian 0.2%; Other 4.8%). **Foreign born:** 4%. **Median age:** 36.9. **State rank:** 14. **Pop change 1990-2000:** +16.1%.

Income: per capita $17,089; median household $32,167. **Pop below poverty level:** 14.7%.

Unemployment: 6.2%. **Median home value:** $80,900. **Median travel time to work:** 24.2 minutes.

MOBILE COUNTY

205 Government St
Mobile, AL 36644
www.mobilecounty.org

Ph: 251-574-5077

In southwestern corner of AL on Mobile Bay; organized Aug 1, 1812 (prior to statehood) from Louisiana Purchase. **Name Origin:** For the city and the bay.

All statistics are based on the 2000 Census except the dollar figures given for per capita income, which are based on 1999 estimates.

Area (sq mi): 1644.02 (land 1233.09; water 410.93).

Pop: 399,843 (White 62.5%; Black or African American 33.4%; Hispanic or Latino 1.2%; Asian 1.4%; Other 2.1%). **Foreign born:** 2.3%. **Median age:** 34.4. **State rank:** 2. **Pop change 1990-2000:** +5.6%.

Income: per capita $17,178; median household $33,710. **Pop below poverty level:** 18.5%.

Unemployment: 6%. **Median home value:** $80,500. **Median travel time to work:** 25.2 minutes.

MONROE COUNTY
PO Box 8
Monroeville, AL 36461

Ph: 251-743-4017
Fax: 251-575-7934

In southwest-central AL; organized Jan 29, 1815 (prior to statehood) from Creek cession. **Name Origin:** For James Monroe (1758-1831), fifth U.S. president.

Area (sq mi): 1034.53 (land 1025.85; water 8.67).

Pop: 24,324 (White 57.4%; Black or African American 40.1%; Hispanic or Latino 0.8%; Asian 0.3%; Other 1.9%). **Foreign born:** 0.3%. **Median age:** 35.4. **State rank:** 43. **Pop change 1990-2000:** +1.5%.

Income: per capita $14,862; median household $29,093. **Pop below poverty level:** 21.3%.

Unemployment: 9.7%. **Median home value:** $66,900. **Median travel time to work:** 23.3 minutes.

MONTGOMERY COUNTY
PO Box 1667
Montgomery, AL 36102
www.mc-ala.org

Ph: 334-832-4950
Fax: 334-832-2533

In south-central AL; organized Dec 6, 1816 (prior to statehood) from Monroe County. **Name Origin:** For Gen. Richard Montgomery (1738-75), American Revolutionary War officer who captured Montreal, Canada.

Area (sq mi): 799.76 (land 789.76; water 9.99).

Pop: 223,510 (White 48.3%; Black or African American 48.6%; Hispanic or Latino 1.2%; Asian 1%; Other 1.6%). **Foreign born:** 2%. **Median age:** 33.5. **State rank:** 4. **Pop change 1990-2000:** +6.9%.

Income: per capita $19,358; median household $35,962. **Pop below poverty level:** 17.3%.

Unemployment: 4.1%. **Median home value:** $87,700. **Median travel time to work:** 20.2 minutes.

MORGAN COUNTY
PO Box 668
Decatur, AL 35602

Ph: 256-351-4730
Fax: 256-351-4738

In north-central AL; organized as Cotaco County Jun 8, 1818 (prior to statehood) from Indian lands; name changed Jun 14, 1821. **Name Origin:** For Gen. Daniel Morgan (1736-1802), an officer in the Revolutionary War and U.S. representative from VA (1797-99). Originally for Cotaco Creek, which runs through it.

Area (sq mi): 599.06 (land 582.21; water 16.84).

Pop: 111,064 (White 83.4%; Black or African American 11.2%; Hispanic or Latino 3.3%; Asian 0.4%; Other 3.3%). **Foreign born:** 2.7%. **Median age:** 36.6. **State rank:** 10. **Pop change 1990-2000:** +11%.

Income: per capita $19,223; median household $37,803. **Pop below poverty level:** 12.3%.

Unemployment: 5.5%. **Median home value:** $88,600. **Median travel time to work:** 23.3 minutes.

PERRY COUNTY
PO Box 505
Marion, AL 36756

Ph: 334-683-6106

In west-central AL, southeast of Tuscaloosa; organized Dec 13, 1819 from Tuscaloosa County. **Name Origin:** For Oliver Hazard Perry (1785-1819), U.S. naval officer during the War of 1812, famous for the message, 'We have met the enemy and they are ours.'

Area (sq mi): 724.08 (land 719.48; water 4.59).

Pop: 11,861 (White 30.7%; Black or African American 68.4%; Hispanic or Latino 0.9%; Asian 0%; Other 0.7%). **Foreign born:** 0.5%. **Median age:** 33.3. **State rank:** 65. **Pop change 1990-2000:** -7%.

Income: per capita $10,948; median household $20,200. **Pop below poverty level:** 35.4%.

Unemployment: 13.6%. **Median home value:** $47,600. **Median travel time to work:** 33.7 minutes.

PICKENS COUNTY
PO Box 460
Carrollton, AL 35447

Ph: 205-367-2020
Fax: 205-367-2025

On central-western border of AL, west of Tuscaloosa; organized Dec 19, 1820 from Tuscaloosa County. **Name Origin:** Probably for Gen. Andrew Pickens (1739-1817), Revolutionary War hero, and U.S. representative from SC (1793-95). Others claim Israel Pickens, GA governor (1821-25).

Area (sq mi): 890.05 (land 881.42; water 8.63).

Pop: 20,949 (White 55.7%; Black or African American 43%; Hispanic or Latino 0.7%; Asian 0.1%; Other 0.9%). **Foreign born:** 0.4%. **Median age:** 36.9. **State rank:** 49. **Pop change 1990-2000:** +1.2%.

Income: per capita $13,746; median household $26,254. **Pop below poverty level:** 24.9%.

Unemployment: 11.4%. **Median home value:** $66,000. **Median travel time to work:** 30 minutes.

PIKE COUNTY
PO Box 1147
Troy, AL 36081

Ph: 334-566-6374
Fax: 334-566-0142

In southeastern AL, southeast of Montgomery; organized Dec 17, 1821 from Henry and Montgomery counties. **Name Origin:** For Zebulon Montgomery Pike (1779-1813), U.S. army officer and discoverer of Pikes Peak in CO.

Area (sq mi): 672.1 (land 671.03; water 1.06).

Pop: 29,605 (White 60.1%; Black or African American 36.6%; Hispanic or Latino 1.2%; Asian 0.4%; Other 2.4%). **Foreign born:**

Please see sample entry on inside front cover for detailed information about the statistics presented with each county listing.

1.9%. **Median age:** 32.5. **State rank:** 38. **Pop change 1990-2000:** +7.3%.

Income: per capita $14,904; median household $25,551. **Pop below poverty level:** 23.1%.

Unemployment: 5.7%. **Median home value:** $71,400. **Median travel time to work:** 22 minutes.

RANDOLPH COUNTY
PO Box 328   **Ph:** 256-357-4551
Wedowee, AL 36278

On central-eastern border of AL; organized Dec 18, 1832 from Creek cession. **Name Origin:** For John Randolph (1773-1833), U.S. congressman from VA during the years of 1799-1827, and U.S. minister to Russia (1830-31).

Area (sq mi): 584.11 (land 581.05; water 3.06).

Pop: 22,380 (White 75.7%; Black or African American 22.2%; Hispanic or Latino 1.2%; Asian 0.2%; Other 1.1%). **Foreign born:** 1.2%. **Median age:** 37.7. **State rank:** 47. **Pop change 1990-2000:** +12.6%.

Income: per capita $14,147; median household $28,675. **Pop below poverty level:** 17%.

Unemployment: 7.8%. **Median home value:** $63,800. **Median travel time to work:** 31.2 minutes.

RUSSELL COUNTY
501 14th St   **Ph:** 334-298-0516
Phenix City, AL 36867   **Fax:** 334-297-6250

On southeastern border of AL; organized Dec 18, 1832 from Creek cession. **Name Origin:** For Col. Gilbert Christian Russell, U.S. Army officer.

Area (sq mi): 647.38 (land 641.32; water 6.06).

Pop: 49,756 (White 56.1%; Black or African American 40.8%; Hispanic or Latino 1.5%; Asian 0.4%; Other 2.2%). **Foreign born:** 2%. **Median age:** 35.4. **State rank:** 25. **Pop change 1990-2000:** +6.2%.

Income: per capita $14,015; median household $27,492. **Pop below poverty level:** 19.9%.

Unemployment: 5.7%. **Median home value:** $71,500. **Median travel time to work:** 24.6 minutes.

SAINT CLAIR COUNTY
PO Box 397   **Ph:** 205-594-2103
Ashville, AL 35953   **Fax:** 205-594-2110
www.stclairco.com

In east-central AL, east of Birmingham; organized Nov 20, 1818 (prior to statehood) from Shelby County. **Name Origin:** For Gen. Arthur Saint Clair (1736-1818), soldier, president of the Continental Congress (1787), and governor of the Northwest Territory (1787-1805).

Area (sq mi): 653.61 (land 633.75; water 19.86).

Pop: 64,742 (White 89.5%; Black or African American 8.1%; Hispanic or Latino 1.1%; Asian 0.2%; Other 1.7%). **Foreign born:** 0.6%. **Median age:** 36.4. **State rank:** 20. **Pop change 1990-2000:** +29.5%.

Income: per capita $17,960; median household $37,285. **Pop below poverty level:** 12.1%.

Unemployment: 3.7%. **Median home value:** $99,800. **Median travel time to work:** 32.3 minutes.

SHELBY COUNTY
PO Box 1810   **Ph:** 205-669-3760
Columbiana, AL 35051   **Fax:** 205-669-3786
www.shelbycountyalabama.com

In central AL, south of Birmingham; organized Feb 7, 1817 (prior to statehood) from Montgomery County. **Name Origin:** For Gen. Isaac Shelby (1750-1826), officer in the Revolutionary War, NC legislator, and governor of KY (1792-96; 1812-16).

Area (sq mi): 809.53 (land 794.69; water 14.83).

Pop: 143,293 (White 88.6%; Black or African American 7.4%; Hispanic or Latino 2%; Asian 1%; Other 1.7%). **Foreign born:** 2.4%. **Median age:** 34.9. **State rank:** 6. **Pop change 1990-2000:** +44.2%.

Income: per capita $27,176; median household $55,440. **Pop below poverty level:** 6.3%.

Unemployment: 2%. **Median home value:** $146,700. **Median travel time to work:** 28.6 minutes.

SUMTER COUNTY
PO Box 936   **Ph:** 205-652-2291
Livingston, AL 35470

On central-western border of AL, southwest of Tuscaloosa; organized Dec 18, 1832 from Choctaw cession. **Name Origin:** For Gen. Thomas Sumter (1734-1832), American Revolutionary officer nicknamed the 'Gamecock of the Revolution,' U.S. representative from GA (1789-93;1797-1801), and U.S. senator (1801-10).

Area (sq mi): 913.3 (land 904.94; water 8.37).

Pop: 14,798 (White 25.8%; Black or African American 73.2%; Hispanic or Latino 1.1%; Asian 0.1%; Other 0.8%). **Foreign born:** 0.5%. **Median age:** 32.1. **State rank:** 57. **Pop change 1990-2000:** -8.5%.

Income: per capita $11,491; median household $18,911. **Pop below poverty level:** 38.7%.

Unemployment: 10.6%. **Median home value:** $54,000. **Median travel time to work:** 28 minutes.

TALLADEGA COUNTY
PO Box 6170   **Ph:** 256-362-1357
Talladega, AL 35161   **Fax:** 256-761-2147

In east-central AL, southeast of Birmingham; organized Dec 18, 1832 from Creek cession. **Name Origin:** For the town, from Cree *talwa* 'town' and *atigi* 'border,' being the boundary between the Creeks and the Natchez.

Area (sq mi): 760.25 (land 739.53; water 20.72).

Pop: 80,321 (White 66.5%; Black or African American 31.5%; Hispanic or Latino 1%; Asian 0.2%; Other 1.2%). **Foreign born:** 0.7%. **Median age:** 36.6. **State rank:** 15. **Pop change 1990-2000:** +8.4%.

Income: per capita $15,704; median household $31,628. **Pop below poverty level:** 17.6%.

All statistics are based on the 2000 Census except the dollar figures given for per capita income, which are based on 1999 estimates.

Unemployment: 8%. **Median home value:** $72,200. **Median travel time to work:** 25.1 minutes.

TALLAPOOSA COUNTY

125 N Broadnax St Rm 131
Dadeville, AL 36853

Ph: 256-825-4268
Fax: 256-825-1009

In east-central AL, west of Auburn; organized Dec 18, 1832 from Chickasaw cession. **Name Origin:** For the Tallapoosa River, which runs through it.

Area (sq mi): 766.23 (land 717.93; water 48.3).

Pop: 41,475 (White 73.2%; Black or African American 25.4%; Hispanic or Latino 0.6%; Asian 0.2%; Other 1%). **Foreign born:** 0.4%. **Median age:** 39.3. **State rank:** 30. **Pop change 1990-2000:** +6.8%.

Income: per capita $16,909; median household $30,745. **Pop below poverty level:** 16.6%.

Unemployment: 6.7%. **Median home value:** $73,600. **Median travel time to work:** 25.1 minutes.

TUSCALOOSA COUNTY

PO Box 20113
Tuscaloosa, AL 35402
www.co.tuscaloosa.al.us

Ph: 205-349-3870
Fax: 205-758-0247

In west-central AL, west of Birmingham; organized Feb 7, 1818 (prior to statehood) from Indian lands. **Name Origin:** Indian name for the Black Warrior River, which runs through it.

Area (sq mi): 1351.23 (land 1324.37; water 26.85).

Pop: 164,875 (White 67.5%; Black or African American 29.3%; Hispanic or Latino 1.3%; Asian 0.9%; Other 1.6%). **Foreign born:** 2.1%. **Median age:** 31.9. **State rank:** 5. **Pop change 1990-2000:** +9.5%.

Income: per capita $18,998; median household $34,436. **Pop below poverty level:** 17%.

Unemployment: 3.3%. **Median home value:** $106,600. **Median travel time to work:** 21.2 minutes.

WALKER COUNTY

PO Box 1447
Jasper, AL 35502
www.walkercounty.com

Ph: 205-384-7230
Fax: 205-384-7003

In west-central AL, northwest of Birmingham; organized Dec 20, 1823 from Marion and Tuscaloosa counties. **Name Origin:** For John Williams Walker (1783-1823), U.S. senator from AL (1819-22).

Area (sq mi): 805.3 (land 794.39; water 10.91).

Pop: 70,713 (White 91.7%; Black or African American 6.2%; Hispanic or Latino 0.9%; Asian 0.2%; Other 1.5%). **Foreign born:** 0.7%. **Median age:** 38.3. **State rank:** 17. **Pop change 1990-2000:** +4.5%.

Income: per capita $15,546; median household $29,076. **Pop below poverty level:** 16.5%.

Unemployment: 7.4%. **Median home value:** $66,700. **Median travel time to work:** 33.2 minutes.

WASHINGTON COUNTY

PO Box 146
Chatom, AL 36518

Ph: 251-847-2208
Fax: 251-847-3677

On southwestern border of AL, north of Mobile; original county; organized Jun 4, 1800 (prior to statehood). **Name Origin:** For George Washington (1732-1799), American patriot and first U.S. president.

Area (sq mi): 1088.54 (land 1080.66; water 7.89).

Pop: 18,097 (White 64.5%; Black or African American 26.9%; Hispanic or Latino 0.9%; Asian 0.1%; Other 8%). **Foreign born:** 0.5%. **Median age:** 34.9. **State rank:** 52. **Pop change 1990-2000:** +8.4%.

Income: per capita $14,081; median household $30,815. **Pop below poverty level:** 18.5%.

Unemployment: 15.8%. **Median home value:** $63,000. **Median travel time to work:** 34.6 minutes.

WILCOX COUNTY

PO Box 608
Camden, AL 36726

Ph: 334-682-4126
Fax: 334-682-4025

In southwest-central AL, southwest of Montgomery; organized Dec 13, 1819 from Dallas and Monroe counties. **Name Origin:** For Lt. Joseph M. Wilcox, killed in 1814 by Creek Indians.

Area (sq mi): 907.46 (land 888.68; water 18.78).

Pop: 13,183 (White 27.4%; Black or African American 71.9%; Hispanic or Latino 0.7%; Asian 0.1%; Other 0.4%). **Foreign born:** 0.3%. **Median age:** 33.8. **State rank:** 63. **Pop change 1990-2000:** -2.8%.

Income: per capita $10,903; median household $16,646. **Pop below poverty level:** 39.9%.

Unemployment: 13.2%. **Median home value:** $52,200. **Median travel time to work:** 31.3 minutes.

WINSTON COUNTY

PO Box 309
Double Springs, AL 35553

Ph: 205-489-5533

In northwest-central AL, northwest of Birmingham; organized as Hancock County Feb 12, 1858 from Walker County; renamed Jan 22, 1858. **Name Origin:** Originally for John Hancock (1737-93), noted signer of the Declaration of Independence; then for John Anthony Winston (1812-71), Confederate army officer and governor of AL (1854-1857).

Area (sq mi): 631.86 (land 614.44; water 17.42).

Pop: 24,843 (White 96.8%; Black or African American 0.4%; Hispanic or Latino 1.5%; Asian 0.1%; Other 2.2%). **Foreign born:** 1%. **Median age:** 38. **State rank:** 42. **Pop change 1990-2000:** +12.7%.

Income: per capita $15,738; median household $28,435. **Pop below poverty level:** 17.1%.

Unemployment: 12.5%. **Median home value:** $60,800. **Median travel time to work:** 26.4 minutes.

Please see sample entry on inside front cover for detailed information about the statistics presented with each county listing.

ALASKA - Boroughs and Census Areas

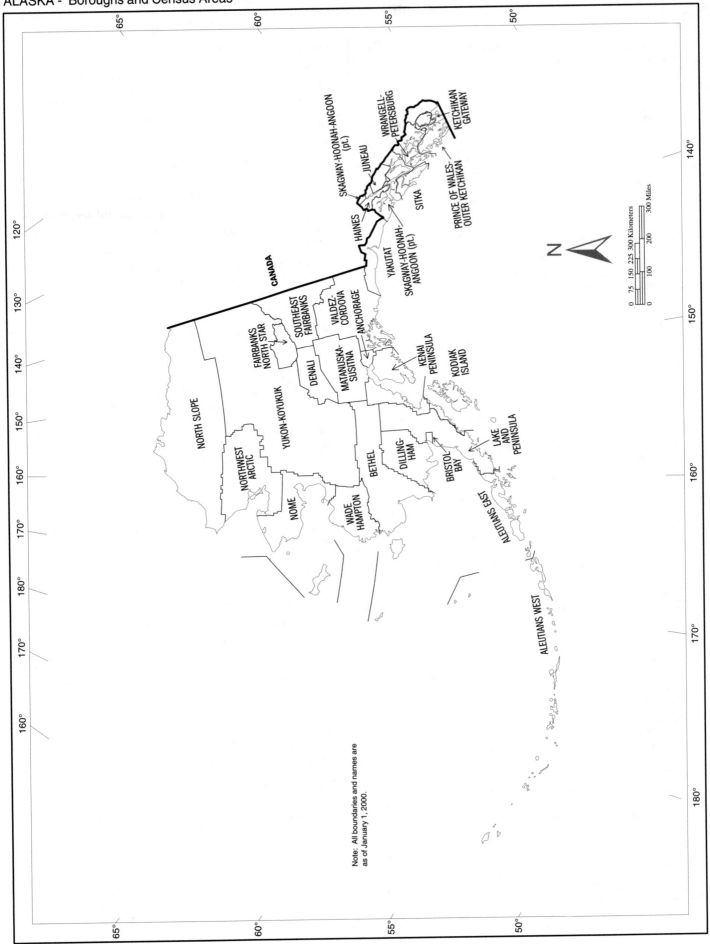

Note: All boundaries and names are as of January 1, 2000.

CANADA

WRANGELL-PETERSBURG
KETCHIKAN GATEWAY
SKAGWAY-HOONAH-ANGOON (pt.)
JUNEAU
SITKA
PRINCE OF WALES-OUTER KETCHIKAN
HAINES
YAKUTAT
SKAGWAY-HOONAH-ANGOON (pt.)
SOUTHEAST FAIRBANKS
VALDEZ-CORDOVA
ANCHORAGE
FAIRBANKS NORTH STAR
DENALI
MATANUSKA-SUSITNA
KENAI PENINSULA
KODIAK ISLAND
NORTH SLOPE
YUKON-KOYUKUK
LAKE AND PENINSULA
NORTHWEST ARCTIC
BETHEL
DILLINGHAM
BRISTOL BAY
NOME
WADE HAMPTON
ALEUTIANS EAST
ALEUTIANS WEST

N

0 75 150 225 300 Kilometers
0   100   200   300 Miles

U.S. Census Bureau, Census 2000

Alaska

ALASKA STATE INFORMATION

www.state.ak.us   **Ph:** 907-465-2111

Area (sq mi): 663,267.26 (land 571,951.26; water 91,316).

Pop: 626,932 (White 67.6%; Black or African American 3.5%; Hispanic or Latino 4.1%; Asian 4%; Other 23.1%). **Foreign born:** 5.9%. **Median age:** 32.4. **Pop change 1990-2000:** +14%.

Income: per capita $22,660; median household $51,571. **Pop below poverty level:** 9.4%.

Unemployment: 6.9%. **Median home value:** $144,200. **Median travel time to work:** 19.6 minutes.

ALEUTIANS EAST BOROUGH

PO Box 349   **Ph:** 907-383-2699
Sand Point, AK 99661   **Fax:** 907-383-3496
www.aleutianseast.org

In southwestern AK, extending south and west from the Alaska Peninsula as far west as Akutan Island; bounded on south and east by Pacific Ocean, on north by Bering Sea. Established Oct 23, 1987 from the eastern portion of the former Aleutian Islands Census Area and the southwestern portion of the Dillingham Census Area **Name Origin:** Adjective form of *Aleut*, the natives of the Aleutian Islands.

Area (sq mi): 15011.6 (land 6988.14; water 8023.46).

Pop: 2,697 (White 19.3%; Black or African American 1.7%; Hispanic or Latino 12.6%; Asian 26.5%; Other 47.9%). **Foreign born:** 18.3%. **Median age:** 37. **State rank:** 22. **Pop change 1990-2000:** +9.5%.

Income: per capita $18,421; median household $47,875. **Pop below poverty level:** 21.8%.

Unemployment: 4.3%. **Median home value:** $99,500. **Median travel time to work:** 6.3 minutes.

ALEUTIANS WEST CENSUS AREA

Southwest of Alaska Peninsula, from the Andreanof Islands in east to the Near Islands in west; bounded on north by Bering Sea and on south and east by Pacific Ocean. **Name Origin:** Adjective form of *Aleut*, the natives of the Aleutian Islands. Originally called the Aleutian Islands Census Area; name officially changed Jan 1, 1990.

Area (sq mi): 14,116.51 (land 4396.77; water 9719.74).

Pop: 5,465 (White 37.7%; Black or African American 3%; Hispanic or Latino 10.5%; Asian 24.6%; Other 32.4%). **Foreign born:** 21.5%. **Median age:** 36.1. **State rank:** 19. **Pop change 1990-2000:** -42.3%.

Income: per capita $24,037; median household $61,406. **Pop below poverty level:** 11.9%.

Unemployment: 9.2%. **Median home value:** $93,400. **Median travel time to work:** 11.3 minutes.

ANCHORAGE MUNICIPALITY

PO Box 196650   **Ph:** 907-343-4311
Anchorage, AK 995196650   **Fax:** 907-343-4313
www.ci.anchorage.ak.us

On the south-central coast of AK, at the head of Cook Inlet, 470 mi. south of Fairbanks. Founded 1914. Borough and city were consolidated as the municipality of Anchorage; includes Glen Alps and Girdwood. **Name Origin:** For Knik Anchorage, a settlement just offshore. This was named for a Tanaina village spelled *Kinik* and *Kinnick* 'fire'. Previously called *Ship Creek* and *Woodrow*.

Area (sq mi): 1961.09 (land 1697.21; water 263.88).

Pop: 260,283 (White 69.9%; Black or African American 5.8%; Hispanic or Latino 5.7%; Asian 5.5%; Other 16.4%). **Foreign born:** 8.2%. **Median age:** 32.4. **State rank:** 1. **Pop change 1990-2000:** +15%.

Income: per capita $25,287; median household $55,546. **Pop below poverty level:** 7.3%.

Unemployment: 4.3%. **Median home value:** $160,700. **Median travel time to work:** 19.5 minutes.

BETHEL CENSUS AREA

In southwestern AK with coastal area on Bering Sea. Established from the former *Kuskokwim Division*. **Name Origin:** For the city.

Area (sq mi): 45,508.46 (land 40,633.31; water 4875.15).

Pop: 16,006 (White 12.2%; Black or African American 0.4%; Hispanic or Latino 0.9%; Asian 1%; Other 86.1%). **Foreign born:** 1.4%. **Median age:** 25.3. **State rank:** 6. **Pop change 1990-2000:** +17.2%.

Income: per capita $12,603; median household $35,701. **Pop below poverty level:** 20.6%.

Unemployment: 10.6%. **Median home value:** $74,900. **Median travel time to work:** 8.6 minutes.

BRISTOL BAY BOROUGH

PO Box 189   **Ph:** 907-246-4224
Naknek, AK 99633   **Fax:** 907-246-6633
www.theborough.com

In southwestern AK at head of Kvichak Bay, an inlet of the Bering

Please see sample entry on inside front cover for detailed information about the statistics presented with each county listing.

41

Sea, west of Katmai National Park. **Name Origin:** For the bay, named in 1778 by Capt. James Cook (1728-79) for the Earl of Bristol (England). Formerly the *Bristol Bay Borough Division*.

Area (sq mi): 887.68 (land 504.92; water 382.77).

Pop: 1,258 (White 52.1%; Black or African American 0.6%; Hispanic or Latino 0.6%; Asian 0.2%; Other 46.7%). **Foreign born:** 0.6%. **Median age:** 36. **State rank:** 26. **Pop change 1990-2000:** -10.8%.

Income: per capita $22,210; median household $52,167. **Pop below poverty level:** 9.5%.

Unemployment: 10%. **Median home value:** $139,000. **Median travel time to work:** 10 minutes.

DENALI BOROUGH
PO Box 480   **Ph:** 907-683-1330
Healy, AK 99743   **Fax:** 907-683-1340
www.denaliborough.govoffice.com

In south-central AK, southwest of Fairbanks. Includes Denali National Park, where Mount McKinley, the highest point in North America, is located. Established Dec 28, 1990, primarily from the Yukon-Koyukuk Census Area and a small part of the Southeast Fairbanks Census Area. **Name Origin:** The Tanana Indian name for Mount McKinley, meaning 'the great one' or 'the high one.'

Area (sq mi): 12,774.53 (land 12,749.65; water 24.88).

Pop: 1,893 (White 84.5%; Black or African American 1.4%; Hispanic or Latino 2.5%; Asian 1.5%; Other 11.4%). **Foreign born:** 2.9%. **Median age:** 37.6. **State rank:** 24. **Pop change 1990-2000:** +7.3%.

Income: per capita $26,251; median household $53,654. **Pop below poverty level:** 7.9%.

Unemployment: 8.8%. **Median home value:** $103,400. **Median travel time to work:** 16.2 minutes.

DILLINGHAM CENSUS AREA

In southwestern AK, along Bristol Bay, northwest of Katmai National Park. Has been reduced in area as portions have been separated off to create new boroughs and census areas. **Name Origin:** For the city.

Area (sq mi): 20,928.41 (land 18,674.78; water 2253.63).

Pop: 4,922 (White 20.9%; Black or African American 0.4%; Hispanic or Latino 2.3%; Asian 0.6%; Other 77.3%). **Foreign born:** 1%. **Median age:** 28.9. **State rank:** 20. **Pop change 1990-2000:** +22.7%.

Income: per capita $16,021; median household $43,079. **Pop below poverty level:** 21.4%.

Unemployment: 9.2%. **Median home value:** $105,300. **Median travel time to work:** 10 minutes.

FAIRBANKS NORTH STAR BOROUGH
809 Pioneer Rd   **Ph:** 907-459-1000
Fairbanks, AK 99701   **Fax:** 907-459-1224
www.co.fairbanks.ak.us

In east-central AK. **Name Origin:** Formerly called the *Fairbanks Division*, for the city.

Area (sq mi): 7444.02 (land 7366.24; water 77.78).

Pop: 82,840 (White 76%; Black or African American 5.8%; Hispanic or Latino 4.2%; Asian 2.1%; Other 14.3%). **Foreign born:** 4%. **Median age:** 29.5. **State rank:** 2. **Pop change 1990-2000:** +6.6%.

Income: per capita $21,553; median household $49,076. **Pop below poverty level:** 7.8%.

Unemployment: 5.7%. **Median home value:** $132,700. **Median travel time to work:** 17.3 minutes.

HAINES BOROUGH
PO Box 1209   **Ph:** 907-766-2711
Haines, AK 99827   **Fax:** 907-766-2716
www.haines.ak.us

In AK, panhandle, northeastern (inner) portion of Alexander Archipelago, north of Juneau, bordering the province of British Columbia, Canada, to the east. **Name Origin:** For the city.

Area (sq mi): 2725.82 (land 2343.73; water 382.09).

Pop: 2,392 (White 81.9%; Black or African American 0.1%; Hispanic or Latino 1.4%; Asian 0.7%; Other 16.6%). **Foreign born:** 4.1%. **Median age:** 40.7. **State rank:** 23. **Pop change 1990-2000:** +13%.

Income: per capita $22,090; median household $40,772. **Pop below poverty level:** 10.7%.

Unemployment: 10.5%. **Median home value:** $133,100. **Median travel time to work:** 12.7 minutes.

JUNEAU CITY & BOROUGH
155 S Seward St   **Ph:** 907-586-5278
Juneau, AK 99801   **Fax:** 907-586-5385
www.juneau.org

In panhandle, southeastern AK on the Gastineau Channel, 90 mi. northeast of Sitka. State capital and largest city in the U.S. (by area). Founded 1880; designated to replace Sitka as capital in 1900, but the move to Juneau did not take place until 1906. Major industries: fishing, lumbering, tourism. Borough and city were consolidated in 1970; includes Douglas. **Name Origin:** For miner Joseph Juneau (1826-99), who discovered gold here in 1880. Formerly Harrisburg.

Area (sq mi): 3255.01 (land 2716.67; water 538.34).

Pop: 30,711 (White 73.3%; Black or African American 0.8%; Hispanic or Latino 3.4%; Asian 4.7%; Other 19.8%). **Foreign born:** 5.7%. **Median age:** 35.3. **State rank:** 5. **Pop change 1990-2000:** +14.8%.

Income: per capita $26,719; median household $62,034. **Pop below poverty level:** 6%.

Unemployment: 4.8%. **Median home value:** $195,100. **Median travel time to work:** 16.4 minutes.

KENAI PENINSULA BOROUGH
144 N Binkley St   **Ph:** 907-262-4441
Soldotna, AK 99669   **Fax:** 907-262-8615
www.borough.kenai.ak.us

In south-central AK, bounded on west by Cook Inlet, on east by the Gulf of Alaska, inlets of the Pacific. Established by combining

All statistics are based on the 2000 Census except the dollar figures given for per capita income, which are based on 1999 estimates.

the former divisions of *Kenai-Cook Inlet* and *Seward*. **Name Origin:** For a local Indian tribe; meaning of name unknown.

Area (sq mi): 24754.6 (land 16,013.26; water 8741.34).

Pop: 49,691 (White 85.1%; Black or African American 0.5%; Hispanic or Latino 2.2%; Asian 1%; Other 12.4%). **Foreign born:** 2.7%. **Median age:** 36.3. **State rank:** 4. **Pop change 1990-2000:** +21.8%.

Income: per capita $20,949; median household $46,397. **Pop below poverty level:** 10%.

Unemployment: 9.6%. **Median home value:** $118,000. **Median travel time to work:** 25.6 minutes.

KETCHIKAN GATEWAY BOROUGH

344 Front St   **Ph:** 907-228-6605
Ketchikan, AK 99901   **Fax:** 907-247-8439
www.borough.ketchikan.ak.us

In AK panhandle, southern Alexander Archipelago, east of Prince of Wales Island. **Name Origin:** For the city, which is in the southernmost portion of AK. Formerly called *Ketchican Division*.

Area (sq mi): 1753.98 (land 1233.22; water 520.75).

Pop: 14,070 (White 72.9%; Black or African American 0.5%; Hispanic or Latino 2.6%; Asian 4.3%; Other 20.9%). **Foreign born:** 5.7%. **Median age:** 36. **State rank:** 7. **Pop change 1990-2000:** +1.8%.

Income: per capita $23,994; median household $51,344. **Pop below poverty level:** 6.5%.

Unemployment: 7.7%. **Median home value:** $165,000. **Median travel time to work:** 14.8 minutes.

KODIAK ISLAND BOROUGH

710 Mill Bay Rd   **Ph:** 907-486-9311
Kodiak, AK 99615   **Fax:** 907-486-9391
www.kib.co.kodiak.ak.us

Off southern coast of AK, east of the Alaska Peninsula in the Gulf of Alaska. **Name Origin:** For the island. Formerly called *Kodiak Division*.

Area (sq mi): 12,023.67 (land 6559.85; water 5463.83).

Pop: 13,913 (White 57.5%; Black or African American 1%; Hispanic or Latino 6.1%; Asian 16%; Other 23.4%). **Foreign born:** 16.7%. **Median age:** 31.6. **State rank:** 8. **Pop change 1990-2000:** +4.5%.

Income: per capita $22,195; median household $54,636. **Pop below poverty level:** 6.6%.

Unemployment: 9%. **Median home value:** $155,100. **Median travel time to work:** 10.8 minutes.

LAKE & PENINSULA BOROUGH

PO Box 495   **Ph:** 907-246-3421
King Salmon, AK 99613   **Fax:** 907-246-6602
www.bristolbay.com/~lpboro/

In southwestern AK, including most of the upper Alaska Peninsula. Established April 24, 1989 from eastern portions of the Dillingham Census Area plus the Alaska Peninsula. **Name Origin:** For Iliamna Lake and the Alaska Peninsula.

Area (sq mi): 30,906.96 (land 23,781.96; water 7125).

Pop: 1,823 (White 18.8%; Black or African American 0.1%; Hispanic or Latino 1.2%; Asian 0.2%; Other 81%). **Foreign born:** 0.7%. **Median age:** 29.2. **State rank:** 25. **Pop change 1990-2000:** +9.3%.

Income: per capita $15,361; median household $36,442. **Pop below poverty level:** 18.9%.

Unemployment: 10.8%. **Median home value:** $87,400. **Median travel time to work:** 7.9 minutes.

MATANUSKA-SUSITNA BOROUGH

350 E Dahlia Ave   **Ph:** 907-745-4801
Palmer, AK 99645   **Fax:** 907-745-9845
www.co.mat-su.ak.us

In south-central AK, north of Anchorage. **Name Origin:** For the Metanuska River, derived from Russian for 'copper river people,' variously spelled *Matanooski, Mednofski, Miduuski*; and the Susitna River, from Tanaina Indian meaning 'sandy river'; also spelled *Sushitna, Sushit, Sutschitna, Sustchino*.

Area (sq mi): 25,259.79 (land 24,681.54; water 578.25).

Pop: 59,322 (White 86.3%; Black or African American 0.7%; Hispanic or Latino 2.5%; Asian 0.7%; Other 11.1%). **Foreign born:** 2.6%. **Median age:** 34.1. **State rank:** 3. **Pop change 1990-2000:** +49.5%.

Income: per capita $21,105; median household $51,221. **Pop below poverty level:** 11%.

Unemployment: 7.7%. **Median home value:** $125,800. **Median travel time to work:** 40.7 minutes.

NOME CENSUS AREA

In west-central AK, including much of Seward Peninsula. **Name Origin:** For the city.

Area (sq mi): 28,283.33 (land 23,000.91; water 5282.42).

Pop: 9,196 (White 19.1%; Black or African American 0.4%; Hispanic or Latino 1%; Asian 0.7%; Other 79.6%). **Foreign born:** 1.5%. **Median age:** 27.6. **State rank:** 10. **Pop change 1990-2000:** +11%.

Income: per capita $15,476; median household $41,250. **Pop below poverty level:** 17.4%.

Unemployment: 11.4%. **Median home value:** $77,100. **Median travel time to work:** 6.3 minutes.

NORTH SLOPE BOROUGH

PO Box 69   **Ph:** 907-852-2611
Barrow, AK 99723   **Fax:** 907-852-0229
www.co.north-slope.ak.us

Across northernmost AK from Pt. Hope in west to border of Yukon province, Canada in east; bounded on the north by the Arctic Ocean and Beaufort Sea. **Name Origin:** Formerly called *Barrow-North Slope Division*.

Area (sq mi): 94,762.64 (land 88,817.12; water 5945.53).

Pop: 7,385 (White 16.6%; Black or African American 0.7%; Hispanic or Latino 2.4%; Asian 5.9%; Other 76.3%). **Foreign born:**

Please see sample entry on inside front cover for detailed information about the statistics presented with each county listing.

5.8%. **Median age:** 27. **State rank:** 12. **Pop change 1990-2000:** +23.5%.

Income: per capita $20,540; median household $63,173. **Pop below poverty level:** 9.1%.

Unemployment: 8.3%. **Median home value:** $113,300. **Median travel time to work:** 7.9 minutes.

NORTHWEST ARCTIC BOROUGH

PO Box 1110   **Ph:** 907-442-2500
Kotzebue, AK 99752   **Fax:** 907-442-2930
www.northwestarcticborough.org

On northwestern coast of AK on Kotzebue Sound, north of Nome. Known as the Kobak Census Area until change to borough status on Jun 2, 1986. **Name Origin:** For its location.

Area (sq mi): 40,762 (land 35,898.34; water 4863.66).

Pop: 7,208 (White 12.2%; Black or African American 0.2%; Hispanic or Latino 0.8%; Asian 0.9%; Other 86.7%). **Foreign born:** 1.1%. **Median age:** 23.9. **State rank:** 13. **Pop change 1990-2000:** +17.9%.

Income: per capita $15,286; median household $45,976. **Pop below poverty level:** 17.4%.

Unemployment: 14.7%. **Median home value:** $89,200. **Median travel time to work:** 8.9 minutes.

PRINCE OF WALES-OUTER KETCHIKAN CENSUS AREA

In AK panhandle, southern outer portion of Alexander Archipelago, including Prince of Wales Island. Established by combining the former divisions of *Prince of Wales* and *Outer Ketchikan*. **Name Origin:** For the Prince of Wales Archipelago and nearby Ketchikan.

Area (sq mi): 12706.3 (land 7410.62; water 5295.67).

Pop: 6,146 (White 52.5%; Black or African American 0.1%; Hispanic or Latino 1.7%; Asian 0.4%; Other 46.3%). **Foreign born:** 1.8%. **Median age:** 34.7. **State rank:** 18. **Pop change 1990-2000:** -2.1%.

Income: per capita $18,395; median household $40,636. **Pop below poverty level:** 12.1%.

Unemployment: 12.3%. **Median home value:** $121,800. **Median travel time to work:** 20.9 minutes.

SITKA CITY & BOROUGH

100 Lincoln St   **Ph:** 907-747-3294
Sitka, AK 99835   **Fax:** 907-747-7403
www.cityofsitka.com

In AK panhandle, western (outer) portion of the central Alexander Archipelago, southwest of Juneau. City center on the west coast of Baranof Island, 930 mi. north of Seattle, WA. **Name Origin:** From Tlingit term for 'by the sea' or 'on Shi,' the Tlingit name for Baranof Island.

Area (sq mi): 4811.53 (land 2873.98; water 1937.55).

Pop: 8,835 (White 67.1%; Black or African American 0.3%; Hispanic or Latino 3.3%; Asian 3.8%; Other 27.4%). **Foreign born:** 5.1%. **Median age:** 35.2. **State rank:** 11. **Pop change 1990-2000:** +2.9%.

Income: per capita $23,622; median household $51,901. **Pop below poverty level:** 7.8%.

Unemployment: 4.8%. **Median home value:** $196,500. **Median travel time to work:** 13.5 minutes.

SKAGWAY-HOONAH-ANGOON CENSUS AREA

In AK panhandle, north of the Alexander Archipelago. Created from the remainder of the former Skagway-Yakutat-Angoon Census Area when the new Yakutat City and Borough was created effective September 22, 1992. **Name Origin:** For the towns that define its northern, western and eastern extent.

Area (sq mi): 11,376.73 (land 7896.48; water 3480.25).

Pop: 3,436 (White 57.5%; Black or African American 0.1%; Hispanic or Latino 2.8%; Asian 0.4%; Other 41.3%). **Foreign born:** 2%. **Median age:** 37.8. **State rank:** 21. **Pop change 1990-2000:** -6.6%.

Income: per capita $19,974; median household $40,879. **Pop below poverty level:** 12.8%.

Unemployment: 10.7%. **Median home value:** $120,900. **Median travel time to work:** 12 minutes.

SOUTHEAST FAIRBANKS CENSUS AREA

In east-central AK, southeast of Fairbanks, bordering the Yukon Territory of Canada to the east. Includes portion of former *Upper Yukon Division*. A small portion of the census area was removed to establish Denali Borough on Dec. 28, 1990. **Name Origin:** For its location.

Area (sq mi): 25,061.19 (land 24,814.86; water 246.33).

Pop: 6,174 (White 77.4%; Black or African American 2%; Hispanic or Latino 2.7%; Asian 0.7%; Other 18.3%). **Foreign born:** 9.9%. **Median age:** 33.7. **State rank:** 17. **Pop change 1990-2000:** +4.4%.

Income: per capita $16,679; median household $38,776. **Pop below poverty level:** 18.9%.

Unemployment: 10.7%. **Median home value:** $86,000. **Median travel time to work:** 15.7 minutes.

VALDEZ-CORDOVA CENSUS AREA

In southeastern AK, bounded on east by Yukon Territory of Canada and on south by the Gulf of Alaska. Established by combining the former divisions of Cordova-McCarthy and Valdez-Chitina-Whittier with part of Southeast Fairbanks Division. **Name Origin:** For the city of Valdez.

Area (sq mi): 40,199.15 (land 34319.1; water 5880.05).

Pop: 10,195 (White 74.7%; Black or African American 0.3%; Hispanic or Latino 2.8%; Asian 3.6%; Other 20.3%). **Foreign born:** 5.1%. **Median age:** 36.1. **State rank:** 9. **Pop change 1990-2000:** +2.4%.

Income: per capita $23,046; median household $48,734. **Pop below poverty level:** 9.8%.

Unemployment: 9.4%. **Median home value:** $141,300. **Median travel time to work:** 12.7 minutes.

All statistics are based on the 2000 Census except the dollar figures given for per capita income, which are based on 1999 estimates.

WADE HAMPTON CENSUS AREA

On central-western coast of AK, north of Bethel.

Area (sq mi): 19,669.24 (land 17193.5; water 2475.74).

Pop: 7,028 (White 4.7%; Black or African American 0.1%; Hispanic or Latino 0.3%; Asian 0.1%; Other 95%). **Foreign born:** 0.3%. **Median age:** 20. **State rank:** 14. **Pop change 1990-2000:** +21.4%.

Income: per capita $8,717; median household $30,184. **Pop below poverty level:** 26.2%.

Unemployment: 18.1%. **Median home value:** $38,700. **Median travel time to work:** 6.3 minutes.

WRANGELL-PETERSBURG CENSUS AREA

In AK panhandle in central-eastern Alexander Archipelago, south of Juneau. **Name Origin:** For the two chief cities.

Area (sq mi): 9021.21 (land 5834.94; water 3186.27).

Pop: 6,684 (White 72.5%; Black or African American 0.2%; Hispanic or Latino 2%; Asian 1.6%; Other 25.1%). **Foreign born:** 2.8%. **Median age:** 37.2. **State rank:** 15. **Pop change 1990-2000:** -5.1%.

Income: per capita $23,494; median household $46,434. **Pop below poverty level:** 7.9%.

Unemployment: 8.8%. **Median home value:** $156,100. **Median travel time to work:** 12.7 minutes.

YAKUTAT CITY & BOROUGH

PO Box 160
Yakutat, AK 99689

Ph: 907-784-3323
Fax: 907-784-3281

In AK panhandle, north of the Alexander Archipelago. Established Sep 22, 1992 from the former Skagway-Yakutat-Angoon Census Area (now Skagway-Hoonah-Angoon Census Area). **Name Origin:** Probably for Yakutat Bay, from the name of a Tlingit Indian village; meaning of name unknown.

Area (sq mi): 9459.28 (land 7650.46; water 1808.82).

Pop: 808 (White 50.2%; Black or African American 0.1%; Hispanic or Latino 0.7%; Asian 1.2%; Other 48.2%). **Foreign born:** 0.6%. **Median age:** 37.2. **State rank:** 27. **Pop change 1990-2000:** +14.6%.

Income: per capita $22,579; median household $46,786. **Pop below poverty level:** 13.5%.

Unemployment: 12.8%. **Median home value:** $100,700. **Median travel time to work:** 9.2 minutes.

YUKON-KOYUKUK CENSUS AREA

Spanning much of central AK to the border with Yukon Territory of Canada. Established from portions of former divisions of Kuskokwim and Upper Yukon. Some territory was removed from the census area to establish Denali Borough on Dec. 28, 1990. **Name Origin:** For the Yukon and Koyukuk rivers.

Area (sq mi): 147,842.51 (land 145,899.69; water 1942.83).

Pop: 6,551 (White 24%; Black or African American 0.1%; Hispanic or Latino 1.2%; Asian 0.4%; Other 75.2%). **Foreign born:** 1%. **Median age:** 31.1. **State rank:** 16. **Pop change 1990-2000:** -2.4%.

Income: per capita $13,720; median household $28,666. **Pop below poverty level:** 23.8%.

Unemployment: 14.4%. **Median home value:** $59,900. **Median travel time to work:** 8.9 minutes.

Please see sample entry on inside front cover for detailed information about the statistics presented with each county listing.

ARIZONA - Counties

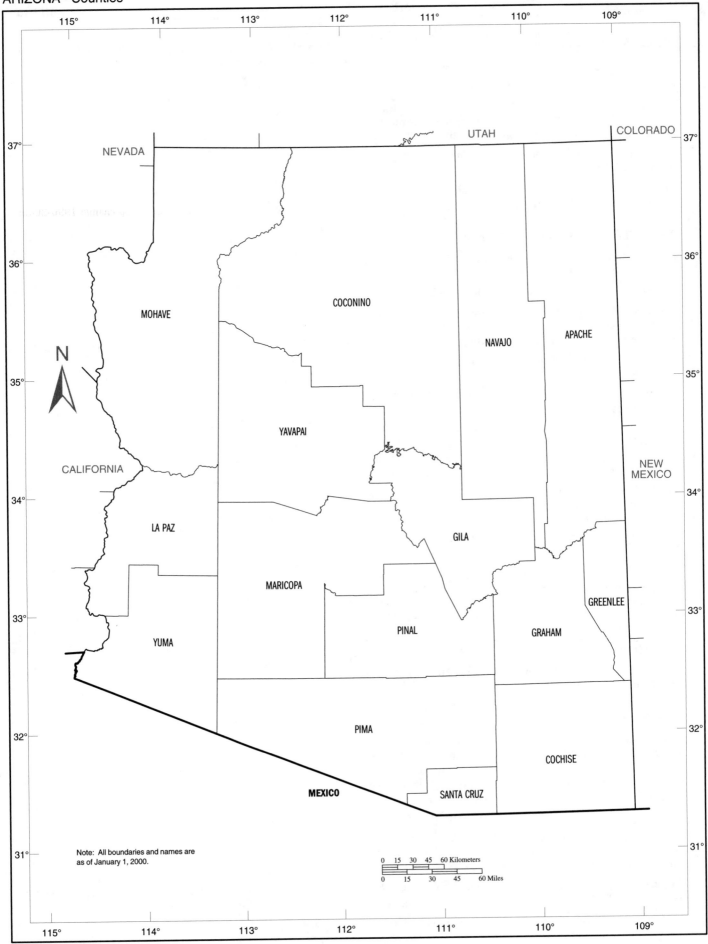

NEVADA

UTAH

COLORADO

37°

NEVADA

36°

MOHAVE

COCONINO

NAVAJO

APACHE

35°

CALIFORNIA

YAVAPAI

NEW
MEXICO

34°

LA PAZ

GILA

GREENLEE

MARICOPA

PINAL

GRAHAM

33°

YUMA

PIMA

COCHISE

32°

MEXICO

SANTA CRUZ

31°

Note: All boundaries and names are
as of January 1, 2000.

```
0   15   30   45   60 Kilometers
|___|___|___|___|___|

0   15   30   45   60 Miles
```

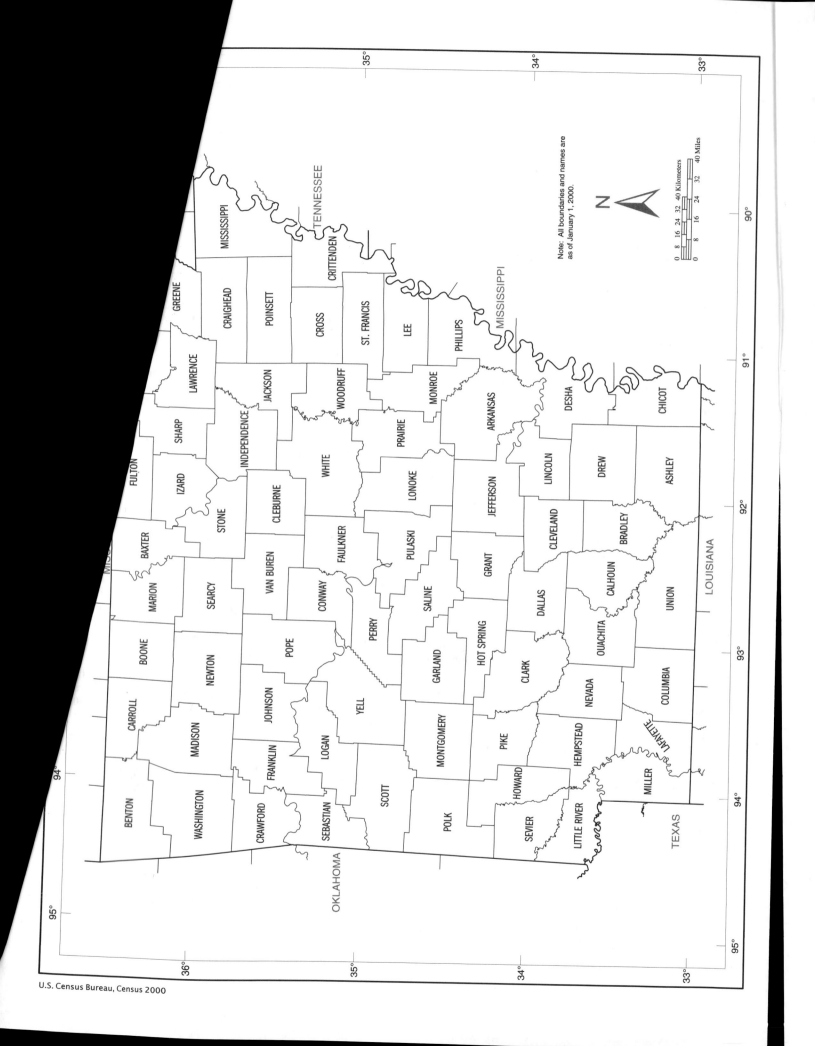

Note: All boundaries and names are as of January 1, 2000.

U.S. Census Bureau, Census 2000

Arizona

ARIZONA STATE INFORMATION

www.az.gov   **Ph:** 602-542-4900

Area (sq mi): 11,3998.3 (land 113,634.57; water 363.73).

Pop: 5,130,632 (White 63.8%; Black or African American 3.1%; Hispanic or Latino 25.3%; Asian 1.8%; Other 19.6%). **Foreign born:** 12.8%. **Median age:** 34.2. **Pop change 1990-2000:** +40%.

Income: per capita $20,275; median household $40,558. **Pop below poverty level:** 13.9%.

Unemployment: 5.6%. **Median home value:** $121,300. **Median travel time to work:** 24.9 minutes.

APACHE COUNTY

PO Box 365   **Ph:** 928-337-4364
Saint Johns, AZ 85936   **Fax:** 928-337-2771
www.co.apache.az.us

On eastern border of AZ; organized Feb 14, 1879 (prior to statehood) from Mohave County. **Name Origin:** For the Apache Indian tribe, of Athapascan linguistic stock, who inhabited the land for centuries. The name is variously said to mean 'man,' 'battles,' or 'enemy.'

Area (sq mi): 11,218.42 (land 11,204.88; water 13.54).

Pop: 69,423 (White 17.7%; Black or African American 0.2%; Hispanic or Latino 4.5%; Asian 0.1%; Other 80.2%). **Foreign born:** 0.9%. **Median age:** 27. **State rank:** 10. **Pop change 1990-2000:** +12.7%.

Income: per capita $8,986; median household $23,344. **Pop below poverty level:** 37.8%.

Unemployment: 12%. **Median home value:** $41,700. **Median travel time to work:** 28 minutes.

COCHISE COUNTY

1415 W Melody Ln   **Ph:** 520-432-9204
Bisbee, AZ 85603   **Fax:** 520-432-5016
www.co.cochise.az.us

In southeastern corner of AZ; organized Feb 1, 1881 (prior to statehood) from Pima County. **Name Origin:** For the famous Chiricahua Apache chief (c. 1812-74), who conducted raids against the U.S. after brutal treatment by U.S. Army officers and surrendered in 1871.

Area (sq mi): 6218.77 (land 6169.45; water 49.32).

Pop: 117,755 (White 60.1%; Black or African American 4.5%; Hispanic or Latino 30.7%; Asian 1.6%; Other 17.2%). **Foreign born:** 12.3%. **Median age:** 36.9. **State rank:** 7. **Pop change 1990-2000:** +20.6%.

Income: per capita $15,988; median household $32,105. **Pop below poverty level:** 17.7%.

Unemployment: 4.6%. **Median home value:** $88,200. **Median travel time to work:** 19.8 minutes.

COCONINO COUNTY

219 E Cherry Ave   **Ph:** 928-774-5011
Flagstaff, AZ 86001   **Fax:** 928-779-6785
co.coconino.az.us

In north-central AZ; organized Feb 19, 1891 (prior to statehood) from Yavapai County. **Name Origin:** Possibly from the Hopi Indian name, *Kohnina,* for the Havasupai tribe that inhabits the Grand Canyon region, which is within the county. Or derived from a Havasupai word meaning 'little water.'

Area (sq mi): 18,661.21 (land 18,617.42; water 43.79).

Pop: 116,320 (White 57.6%; Black or African American 1%; Hispanic or Latino 10.9%; Asian 0.8%; Other 35.1%). **Foreign born:** 4.3%. **Median age:** 29.6. **State rank:** 8. **Pop change 1990-2000:** +20.4%.

Income: per capita $17,139; median household $38,256. **Pop below poverty level:** 18.2%.

Unemployment: 5.4%. **Median home value:** $142,500. **Median travel time to work:** 19 minutes.

GILA COUNTY

1400 E Ash St   **Ph:** 928-425-3231
Globe, AZ 85501   **Fax:** 928-425-7802
gila.lib.az.us/gilagov/

In east-central AZ, east of Phoenix; organized Feb 8, 1881 (prior to statehood) from Maricopa and Pinal counties. **Name Origin:** For the Gila River, which forms part of the county's southern boundary. Some sources suggest the name may refer to the Gila monster.

Area (sq mi): 4795.74 (land 4767.7; water 28.03).

Pop: 51,335 (White 68.9%; Black or African American 0.4%; Hispanic or Latino 16.6%; Asian 0.4%; Other 21.4%). **Foreign born:** 3.6%. **Median age:** 42.3. **State rank:** 11. **Pop change 1990-2000:** +27.6%.

Income: per capita $16,315; median household $30,917. **Pop below poverty level:** 17.4%.

Unemployment: 5.9%. **Median home value:** $100,100. **Median travel time to work:** 20.3 minutes.

Please see sample entry on inside front cover for detailed information about the statistics presented with each county listing.

GRAHAM COUNTY

921 Thatcher Blvd
Safford, AZ 85546
www.graham.az.gov

Ph: 928-428-3250
Fax: 928-428-5951

In southeastern AZ, northeast of Tucson; organized Mar 10, 1881 (prior to statehood) from Apache and Pima counties. **Name Origin:** For its most prominent feature, Mount Graham, in the Pinaleno Mountains; elevation 10,720 ft.

Area (sq mi): 4641.14 (land 4629.32; water 11.83).

Pop: 33,489 (White 55.2%; Black or African American 1.9%; Hispanic or Latino 27%; Asian 0.6%; Other 30.3%). **Foreign born:** 2.6%. **Median age:** 30.9. **State rank:** 13. **Pop change 1990-2000:** +26.1%.

Income: per capita $12,139; median household $29,668. **Pop below poverty level:** 23%.

Unemployment: 7.3%. **Median home value:** $80,900. **Median travel time to work:** 22.6 minutes.

GREENLEE COUNTY

PO Box 908
Clifton, AZ 85533

Ph: 928-865-2072
Fax: 928-865-4417

On southeastern border of AZ; organized Mar 10, 1909 (prior to statehood) from Graham County. **Name Origin:** For Mason Greenlee (1835-1903), a Virginian who settled in the area in the 1870s.

Area (sq mi): 1848.42 (land 1847; water 1.42).

Pop: 8,547 (White 53.9%; Black or African American 0.5%; Hispanic or Latino 43.1%; Asian 0.2%; Other 25.2%). **Foreign born:** 3.4%. **Median age:** 33.6. **State rank:** 15. **Pop change 1990-2000:** +6.7%.

Income: per capita $15,814; median household $39,384. **Pop below poverty level:** 9.9%.

Unemployment: 9%. **Median home value:** $62,700. **Median travel time to work:** 20.3 minutes.

LA PAZ COUNTY

1108 Joshua Ave
Parker, AZ 853446477
www.co.la-paz.az.us

Ph: 928-669-6115
Fax: 928-669-9709

On western border of AZ, west of Phoenix; organized Jan 1, 1983 from Yuma County. **Name Origin:** For the once-prominent AZ city of La Paz, an important gold-mining center in the 1860s that eventually was abandoned. Gold had been discovered near the site on Jan 12, 1862, the date on which many Mexican and Mexican-American Catholics in early Arizona celebrated the Feast of our Lady of Peace (in Spanish, Nuestra Senora de la Paz).

Area (sq mi): 4513.36 (land 4499.95; water 13.4).

Pop: 19,715 (White 63.8%; Black or African American 0.8%; Hispanic or Latino 22.4%; Asian 0.4%; Other 24.7%). **Foreign born:** 9.7%. **Median age:** 46.8. **State rank:** 14. **Pop change 1990-2000:** +42.4%.

Income: per capita $14,916; median household $25,839. **Pop below poverty level:** 19.6%.

Unemployment: 6.3%. **Median home value:** $86,500. **Median travel time to work:** 17.2 minutes.

MARICOPA COUNTY

301 W Jefferson St 10th Fl
Phoenix, AZ 85003
www.maricopa.gov

Ph: 602-506-3415
Fax: 602-506-6402

In south-central AZ; organized Feb 14, 1871 (prior to statehood) from Yavapai and Yuma counties. **Name Origin:** From the name of an Indian tribe of Yuman linguistic stock. The name may be a variant of the spanish *mariposa*, or 'butterfly,' as the Spanish found the tribe wearing bright paints. The tribe called itself *Pipatsje*, 'people.'

Area (sq mi): 9224.27 (land 9203.14; water 21.13).

Pop: 3,072,149 (White 66.2%; Black or African American 3.7%; Hispanic or Latino 24.8%; Asian 2.2%; Other 16.7%). **Foreign born:** 14.4%. **Median age:** 33. **State rank:** 1. **Pop change 1990-2000:** +44.8%.

Income: per capita $22,251; median household $45,358. **Pop below poverty level:** 11.7%.

Unemployment: 3.9%. **Median home value:** $129,200. **Median travel time to work:** 26.1 minutes.

MOHAVE COUNTY

PO Box 7000
Kingman, AZ 86402
www.co.mohave.az.us

Ph: 928-753-0729
Fax: 928-753-5103

On western border of AZ; original county; organized Dec 21, 1864 (prior to statehood); in 1871 annexed Pah-Ute County, which had been organized in 1865. **Name Origin:** For a tribe of Yuman linguistic stock, who inhabited both the CA and AZ sides of the Colorado River. Name means 'three mountains' and refers to the Needles, the three pointed mountain peaks at the center of tribal activities. Also spelled *Mojave*.

Area (sq mi): 13,469.71 (land 13,311.64; water 158.07).

Pop: 155,032 (White 84%; Black or African American 0.5%; Hispanic or Latino 11.1%; Asian 0.8%; Other 8.6%). **Foreign born:** 5.9%. **Median age:** 42.9. **State rank:** 6. **Pop change 1990-2000:** +65.8%.

Income: per capita $16,788; median household $31,521. **Pop below poverty level:** 13.9%.

Unemployment: 4.5%. **Median home value:** $95,300. **Median travel time to work:** 20.6 minutes.

NAVAJO COUNTY

PO Box 668
Holbrook, AZ 86025
www.co.navajo.az.us

Ph: 928-524-4188
Fax: 928-524-4261

In northeastern AZ, east of Flagstaff; organized Mar 21, 1895 (prior to statehood). **Name Origin:** For the Navajo Indian tribe. Site of the Navajo National Monument.

Area (sq mi): 9959.49 (land 9953.18; water 6.31).

Pop: 97,470 (White 42.3%; Black or African American 0.9%; Hispanic or Latino 8.2%; Asian 0.3%; Other 52.7%). **Foreign born:** 1.7%. **Median age:** 30.2. **State rank:** 9. **Pop change 1990-2000:** +25.5%.

Income: per capita $11,609; median household $28,569. **Pop below poverty level:** 29.5%.

PIMA COUNTY

130 W Congress St 10th Fl
Tucson, AZ 85701
www.co.pima.az.us

Ph: 520-740-8661
Fax: 520-740-8171

On south-central border of AZ; original county; organized Dec 15, 1864 (prior to statehood). **Name Origin:** For the Pima Indian tribe, who inhabited the Gila and Salt River valleys of AZ. *Pima* was the name given the tribe by the Spanish; it means 'no' or 'I don't know,' the response the Spanish received to their questions and mistook for the tribe's name.

Area (sq mi): 9188.83 (land 9186.27; water 2.57).

Pop: 843,746 (White 61.5%; Black or African American 3%; Hispanic or Latino 29.3%; Asian 2%; Other 19.8%). **Foreign born:** 11.9%. **Median age:** 35.7. **State rank:** 2. **Pop change 1990-2000:** +26.5%.

Income: per capita $19,785; median household $36,758. **Pop below poverty level:** 14.7%.

Unemployment: 3.5%. **Median home value:** $114,600. **Median travel time to work:** 23.9 minutes.

PINAL COUNTY

PO Box 2730
Florence, AZ 85232
www.co.pinal.az.us

Ph: 520-868-6296
Fax: 520-868-6252

In south-central AZ, southeast of Phoenix; organized Feb 1, 1875 (prior to statehood) from Pima County. **Name Origin:** Probably for the Pinal tribe of the Apaches, or for an Apache chief. Name means 'deer' in Apache; in Spanish it means 'pine' or possibly 'the Apaches who live in the pines.' Pine groves and deer can be found on nearby mountains.

Area (sq mi): 5374.09 (land 5369.59; water 4.5).

Pop: 179,727 (White 58.8%; Black or African American 2.8%; Hispanic or Latino 29.9%; Asian 0.6%; Other 26.3%). **Foreign born:** 9%. **Median age:** 37.1. **State rank:** 3. **Pop change 1990-2000:** +54.4%.

Income: per capita $16,025; median household $35,856. **Pop below poverty level:** 16.9%.

Unemployment: 5.1%. **Median home value:** $93,900. **Median travel time to work:** 27.4 minutes.

SANTA CRUZ COUNTY

PO Box 1265
Nogales, AZ 85628
www.santacruzcountyaz.org

Ph: 520-761-7800
Fax: 520-761-7857

On south-central border of AZ; organized Mar 15, 1899 (prior to statehood) from Pima County. **Name Origin:** For the Santa Cruz River, which flows through the county. From the Spanish meaning 'holy cross.'

Area (sq mi): 1238.11 (land 1237.63; water 0.47).

Pop: 38,381 (White 17.8%; Black or African American 0.4%; Hispanic or Latino 80.8%; Asian 0.5%; Other 23.1%). **Foreign born:**

Unemployment: 10.5%. **Median home value:** $77,000. **Median travel time to work:** 22.9 minutes.

ARKANSAS - Counties

YAVA...

1015 ...
Prescott
www.co.y...

In central ...
21, 1860 (pr...
linguistic stoc...
explained. Mos...
'people'. Other ...
Spanish *pais* 'cou...

Area (sq mi): 8127...

Pop: 167,517 (White ...
panic or Latino 9.8%;...
5.9%. **Median age:** 44.5...
+55.5%.

Income: per capita $19,727,...
poverty level:** 11.9%.

Unemployment: 2.9%. **Media...
travel time to work:** 22.5 minu...

YUMA COUNTY

198 S Main St
Yuma, AZ 85364
www.co.yuma.az.us

In southwestern corner of AZ; original ...
1864 (prior to statehood). **Name Origin**...
tribe, who lived principally along the Colo...
given to the tribe by the Spanish, may mea...
or may come from the Spanish *umo* 'smoke.'

Area (sq mi): 5518.96 (land 5514.09; water 4.8...

Pop: 160,026 (White 44.3%; Black or African Ame...
panic or Latino 50.5%; Asian 0.9%; Other 28.5%)...
24%. **Median age:** 33.9. **State rank:** 5. **Pop change**...
+49.7%.

Income: per capita $14,802; median household $32,182...
poverty level:** 19.2%.

Unemployment: 24.4%. **Median home value:** $85,100...
travel time to work:** 18.6 minutes.

All statistics are based on the 2000 Census except the dollar figures given for per capita income, which are based on 1999 estimates.

Please see sample entry on inside front cover for detailed information about the statistics presented with each county listing.

Unemployment: 10.5%. **Median home value:** $77,000. **Median travel time to work:** 22.9 minutes.

PIMA COUNTY

130 W Congress St 10th Fl　　　　　**Ph:** 520-740-8661
Tucson, AZ 85701　　　　　　　　　**Fax:** 520-740-8171
www.co.pima.az.us

On south-central border of AZ; original county; organized Dec 15, 1864 (prior to statehood). **Name Origin:** For the Pima Indian tribe, who inhabited the Gila and Salt River valleys of AZ. *Pima* was the name given the tribe by the Spanish; it means 'no' or 'I don't know,' the response the Spanish received to their questions and mistook for the tribe's name.

Area (sq mi): 9188.83 (land 9186.27; water 2.57).

Pop: 843,746 (White 61.5%; Black or African American 3%; Hispanic or Latino 29.3%; Asian 2%; Other 19.8%). **Foreign born:** 11.9%. **Median age:** 35.7. **State rank:** 2. **Pop change 1990-2000:** +26.5%.

Income: per capita $19,785; median household $36,758. **Pop below poverty level:** 14.7%.

Unemployment: 3.5%. **Median home value:** $114,600. **Median travel time to work:** 23.9 minutes.

PINAL COUNTY

PO Box 2730　　　　　　　　　　　**Ph:** 520-868-6296
Florence, AZ 85232　　　　　　　　**Fax:** 520-868-6252
www.co.pinal.az.us

In south-central AZ, southeast of Phoenix; organized Feb 1, 1875 (prior to statehood) from Pima County. **Name Origin:** Probably for the Pinal tribe of the Apaches, or for an Apache chief. Name means 'deer' in Apache; in Spanish it means 'pine' or possibly 'the Apaches who live in the pines.' Pine groves and deer can be found on nearby mountains.

Area (sq mi): 5374.09 (land 5369.59; water 4.5).

Pop: 179,727 (White 58.8%; Black or African American 2.8%; Hispanic or Latino 29.9%; Asian 0.6%; Other 26.3%). **Foreign born:** 9%. **Median age:** 37.1. **State rank:** 3. **Pop change 1990-2000:** +54.4%.

Income: per capita $16,025; median household $35,856. **Pop below poverty level:** 16.9%.

Unemployment: 5.1%. **Median home value:** $93,900. **Median travel time to work:** 27.4 minutes.

SANTA CRUZ COUNTY

PO Box 1265　　　　　　　　　　　**Ph:** 520-761-7800
Nogales, AZ 85628　　　　　　　　**Fax:** 520-761-7857
www.santacruzcountyaz.org

On south-central border of AZ; organized Mar 15, 1899 (prior to statehood) from Pima County. **Name Origin:** For the Santa Cruz River, which flows through the county. From the Spanish meaning 'holy cross.'

Area (sq mi): 1238.11 (land 1237.63; water 0.47).

Pop: 38,381 (White 17.8%; Black or African American 0.4%; Hispanic or Latino 80.8%; Asian 0.5%; Other 23.1%). **Foreign born:**

37.7%. **Median age:** 31.8. **State rank:** 12. **Pop change 1990-2000:** +29.3%.

Income: per capita $13,278; median household $29,710. **Pop below poverty level:** 24.5%.

Unemployment: 12.8%. **Median home value:** $94,700. **Median travel time to work:** 19.7 minutes.

YAVAPAI COUNTY

1015 Fair St Rm 310　　　　　　　**Ph:** 928-771-3200
Prescott, AZ 86305　　　　　　　　**Fax:** 928-771-3257
www.co.yavapai.az.us

In central AZ, north of Phoenix; original county; organized Dec 21, 1860 (prior to statehood). **Name Origin:** For a tribe of Yuman linguistic stock who lived in western AZ. Name has been variously explained. Most probable is 'sun people,' from *enyaeva* 'sun'; *pai* 'people'. Other theories include 'hill country' from *yava* 'hill'; Spanish *pais* 'country'; and 'crooked-mouth (surly) people.'

Area (sq mi): 8127.78 (land 8123.3; water 4.48).

Pop: 167,517 (White 86.6%; Black or African American 0.4%; Hispanic or Latino 9.8%; Asian 0.5%; Other 7.2%). **Foreign born:** 5.9%. **Median age:** 44.5. **State rank:** 4. **Pop change 1990-2000:** +55.5%.

Income: per capita $19,727; median household $34,901. **Pop below poverty level:** 11.9%.

Unemployment: 2.9%. **Median home value:** $138,000. **Median travel time to work:** 22.5 minutes.

YUMA COUNTY

198 S Main St　　　　　　　　　　**Ph:** 928-329-2104
Yuma, AZ 85364　　　　　　　　　**Fax:** 928-329-2001
www.co.yuma.az.us

In southwestern corner of AZ; original county; organized Dec 21, 1864 (prior to statehood). **Name Origin:** For the Yuma Indian tribe, who lived principally along the Colorado River. The name, given to the tribe by the Spanish, may mean 'son of the captain' or may come from the Spanish *umo* 'smoke.'

Area (sq mi): 5518.96 (land 5514.09; water 4.87).

Pop: 160,026 (White 44.3%; Black or African American 2.2%; Hispanic or Latino 50.5%; Asian 0.9%; Other 28.5%). **Foreign born:** 24%. **Median age:** 33.9. **State rank:** 5. **Pop change 1990-2000:** +49.7%.

Income: per capita $14,802; median household $32,182. **Pop below poverty level:** 19.2%.

Unemployment: 24.4%. **Median home value:** $85,100. **Median travel time to work:** 18.6 minutes.

Please see sample entry on inside front cover for detailed information about the statistics presented with each county listing.

49

ARKANSAS - Counties

Note: All boundaries and names are as of January 1, 2000.

MISSOURI

TENNESSEE

MISSISSIPPI

LOUISIANA

TEXAS

OKLAHOMA

CLAY

GREENE

MISSISSIPPI

CRAIGHEAD

POINSETT

CROSS

CRITTENDEN

ST. FRANCIS

LEE

PHILLIPS

RANDOLPH

LAWRENCE

JACKSON

WOODRUFF

MONROE

ARKANSAS

DESHA

CHICOT

FULTON

SHARP

INDEPENDENCE

PRAIRIE

LINCOLN

DREW

ASHLEY

IZARD

WHITE

LONOKE

JEFFERSON

CLEVELAND

BRADLEY

STONE

CLEBURNE

BAXTER

MARION

SEARCY

VAN BUREN

CONWAY

FAULKNER

PULASKI

SALINE

GRANT

DALLAS

CALHOUN

OUACHITA

UNION

BOONE

NEWTON

POPE

PERRY

GARLAND

HOT SPRING

CLARK

NEVADA

COLUMBIA

CARROLL

MADISON

JOHNSON

YELL

MONTGOMERY

PIKE

HEMPSTEAD

LAFAYETTE

BENTON

WASHINGTON

FRANKLIN

LOGAN

SCOTT

POLK

HOWARD

SEVIER

LITTLE RIVER

MILLER

CRAWFORD

SEBASTIAN

Arkansas

ARKANSAS STATE INFORMATION

www.accessarkansas.org **Ph:** 501-682-3000

Area (sq mi): 53,178.62 (land 52,068.17; water 1110.45).

Pop: 2,673,400 (White 78.6%; Black or African American 15.7%; Hispanic or Latino 3.2%; Asian 0.8%; Other 3.6%). **Foreign born:** 2.8%. **Median age:** 36. **Pop change 1990-2000:** +13.7%.

Income: per capita $16,904; median household $32,182. **Pop below poverty level:** 15.8%.

Unemployment: 4.9%. **Median home value:** $72,800. **Median travel time to work:** 21.9 minutes.

ARKANSAS COUNTY

PO Box 719 **Ph:** 870-673-7311
Stuttgart, AR 72160

In east-central AR, east of Pine Bluff; original county; organized Dec 31, 1813 (prior to statehood). **Name Origin:** For the Arkansas Indians.

Area (sq mi): 1033.79 (land 988.49; water 45.3).

Pop: 20,749 (White 74.8%; Black or African American 23.4%; Hispanic or Latino 0.8%; Asian 0.4%; Other 1.1%). **Foreign born:** 0.4%. **Median age:** 38.7. **State rank:** 36. **Pop change 1990-2000:** -4.2%.

Income: per capita $16,401; median household $30,316. **Pop below poverty level:** 17.8%.

Unemployment: 4.9%. **Median home value:** $56,800. **Median travel time to work:** 16.5 minutes.

ASHLEY COUNTY

205 E Jefferson Ave Box 5 **Ph:** 870-853-2020
Hamburg, AR 71646 **Fax:** 870-853-2082

On southern border of AR; organized Nov 30, 1848 from Union and Drew counties. **Name Origin:** For Chester Ashley (1790-1848), U.S. senator from AR (1844-48).

Area (sq mi): 939.08 (land 921.15; water 17.93).

Pop: 24,209 (White 69%; Black or African American 27.1%; Hispanic or Latino 3.2%; Asian 0.2%; Other 2.9%). **Foreign born:** 2.2%. **Median age:** 36.2. **State rank:** 29. **Pop change 1990-2000:** -0.5%.

Income: per capita $15,702; median household $31,758. **Pop below poverty level:** 17.5%.

Unemployment: 9.1%. **Median home value:** $55,700. **Median travel time to work:** 18.5 minutes.

BAXTER COUNTY

1 E 7th St **Ph:** 870-425-3475
Mountain Home, AR 72653 **Fax:** 870-424-5105
www.baxtercounty.org

On central-northern border of AR; organized Mar 24, 1873 from Fulton County. **Name Origin:** For Elisha Baxter (1827-99), AR legislator, chief justice (1864), circuit judge (1868-72), and governor (1872-74).

Area (sq mi): 586.74 (land 554.36; water 32.38).

Pop: 38,386 (White 97.1%; Black or African American 0.1%; Hispanic or Latino 1%; Asian 0.3%; Other 1.7%). **Foreign born:** 1.6%. **Median age:** 48.1. **State rank:** 18. **Pop change 1990-2000:** +23.1%.

Income: per capita $16,859; median household $29,106. **Pop below poverty level:** 11.1%.

Unemployment: 5.7%. **Median home value:** $84,500. **Median travel time to work:** 18.4 minutes.

BENTON COUNTY

215 E Central St Suite 217 **Ph:** 479-271-1013
Bentonville, AR 72712 **Fax:** 479-271-1019
www.co.benton.ar.us

In northwest corner of AR; organized 1836 from Washington County. **Name Origin:** For Thomas Hart Benton (1782-1858), U.S. journalist and statesman; nicknamed 'Old Bullion' for championing use of gold and silver currency rather than paper money.

Area (sq mi): 880.24 (land 845.99; water 34.25).

Pop: 153,406 (White 86.8%; Black or African American 0.4%; Hispanic or Latino 8.8%; Asian 1.1%; Other 7.6%). **Foreign born:** 6.4%. **Median age:** 35.3. **State rank:** 3. **Pop change 1990-2000:** +57.3%.

Income: per capita $19,377; median household $40,281. **Pop below poverty level:** 10.1%.

Unemployment: 2.2%. **Median home value:** $94,800. **Median travel time to work:** 19.5 minutes.

BOONE COUNTY

100 N Main St Suite 201 **Ph:** 870-741-8428
Harrison, AR 72601 **Fax:** 870-741-9724

On northern border of AR; organized Apr 9, 1869 from Carroll and Marion counties. **Name Origin:** For Daniel Boone (1734?-1820), U.S. frontiersman and KY pioneer.

Area (sq mi): 601.82 (land 591.18; water 10.64).

Please see sample entry on inside front cover for detailed information about the statistics presented with each county listing.

Pop: 33,948 (White 96.9%; Black or African American 0.1%; Hispanic or Latino 1.1%; Asian 0.3%; Other 1.9%). **Foreign born:** 1%. **Median age:** 38.9. **State rank:** 21. **Pop change 1990-2000:** +20%.

Income: per capita $16,175; median household $29,988. **Pop below poverty level:** 14.8%.

Unemployment: 6%. **Median home value:** $75,300. **Median travel time to work:** 20 minutes.

BRADLEY COUNTY
101 E Cedar St   **Ph:** 870-226-3853
Warren, AR 71671   **Fax:** 870-226-8401

In south-central AR; organized Dec 18, 1840 from Union County. **Name Origin:** For William L. Bradley, a local settler.

Area (sq mi): 654.38 (land 650.63; water 3.75).

Pop: 12,600 (White 62.3%; Black or African American 28.6%; Hispanic or Latino 8.3%; Asian 0.1%; Other 8%). **Foreign born:** 4.3%. **Median age:** 38. **State rank:** 58. **Pop change 1990-2000:** +6.8%.

Income: per capita $13,895; median household $24,821. **Pop below poverty level:** 26.3%.

Unemployment: 9.1%. **Median home value:** $45,000. **Median travel time to work:** 23.2 minutes.

CALHOUN COUNTY
PO Box 1175   **Ph:** 870-798-2517
Hampton, AR 71744   **Fax:** 870-798-2428

In south-central AR; organized Dec 6, 1850 from Dallas, Ouachita, and Union counties. **Name Origin:** For John Caldwell Calhoun (1782-1850), U.S. statesman and champion of Southern causes.

Area (sq mi): 632.54 (land 628.27; water 4.27).

Pop: 5,744 (White 74%; Black or African American 23.4%; Hispanic or Latino 1.5%; Asian 0%; Other 2%). **Foreign born:** 0.9%. **Median age:** 39.2. **State rank:** 75. **Pop change 1990-2000:** -1.4%.

Income: per capita $15,555; median household $28,438. **Pop below poverty level:** 16.5%.

Unemployment: 7.2%. **Median home value:** $41,700. **Median travel time to work:** 24.8 minutes.

CARROLL COUNTY
210 W Church St   **Ph:** 870-423-2022
Berryville, AR 72616   **Fax:** 870-423-7400

On northern border of AR; organized Nov 1, 1833 (prior to statehood) from Izard County. **Name Origin:** For Charles Carroll (1737-1832), signer of the Declaration of Independence, U.S. senator from MD (1789-92), and founder of the Baltimore and Ohio railroad.

Area (sq mi): 638.81 (land 630.27; water 8.54).

Pop: 25,357 (White 87.7%; Black or African American 0.1%; Hispanic or Latino 9.7%; Asian 0.4%; Other 5.9%). **Foreign born:** 7.5%. **Median age:** 39.4. **State rank:** 28. **Pop change 1990-2000:** +35.9%.

Income: per capita $16,003; median household $27,924. **Pop below poverty level:** 15.5%.

Unemployment: 4.2%. **Median home value:** $83,900. **Median travel time to work:** 19.7 minutes.

CHICOT COUNTY
108 Main St County Courthouse   **Ph:** 870-265-8000
Lake Village, AR 71653   **Fax:** 870-265-8018

In southeastern corner of AR; organized Oct 25, 1823 (prior to statehood) from Arkansas County. **Name Origin:** For Point Chicot on the Mississippi River; *chicot* in French means 'stump,' referring to navigational difficulties there.

Area (sq mi): 690.88 (land 644.03; water 46.86).

Pop: 14,117 (White 42.4%; Black or African American 54%; Hispanic or Latino 2.9%; Asian 0.4%; Other 2.4%). **Foreign born:** 2.3%. **Median age:** 36.2. **State rank:** 55. **Pop change 1990-2000:** -10.2%.

Income: per capita $12,825; median household $22,024. **Pop below poverty level:** 28.6%.

Unemployment: 10.3%. **Median home value:** $47,300. **Median travel time to work:** 19.4 minutes.

CLARK COUNTY
401 Clay St   **Ph:** 870-246-4491
Arkadelphia, AR 71923   **Fax:** 870-246-6505

In west-central AR, south of Hot Springs; organized Dec 15, 1818 (prior to statehood) from Arkansas County. **Name Origin:** For William Clark (1770-1838), explorer, and co-leader of the Lewis and Clark Expedition.

Area (sq mi): 882.6 (land 865.43; water 17.17).

Pop: 23,546 (White 73.5%; Black or African American 22%; Hispanic or Latino 2.4%; Asian 0.6%; Other 3.1%). **Foreign born:** 2%. **Median age:** 31.8. **State rank:** 32. **Pop change 1990-2000:** +9.8%.

Income: per capita $14,533; median household $28,845. **Pop below poverty level:** 19.1%.

Unemployment: 3.7%. **Median home value:** $67,900. **Median travel time to work:** 19.4 minutes.

CLAY COUNTY
PO Box 306   **Ph:** 870-598-2813
Piggott, AR 72454   **Fax:** 870-598-2813

In northeastern corner of AR; organized Mar 24, 1873 from Randolph County. **Name Origin:** For Henry Clay (1777-1852), U.S. senator from KY, known as the 'Great Pacificator' for his advocacy of compromise to avert national crises.

Area (sq mi): 641.42 (land 639.3; water 2.12).

Pop: 17,609 (White 97.5%; Black or African American 0.2%; Hispanic or Latino 0.8%; Asian 0.1%; Other 1.7%). **Foreign born:** 0.3%. **Median age:** 40.5. **State rank:** 45. **Pop change 1990-2000:** -2.8%.

Income: per capita $14,512; median household $25,345. **Pop below poverty level:** 17.5%.

Unemployment: 8.2%. **Median home value:** $39,600. **Median travel time to work:** 21.4 minutes.

CLEBURNE COUNTY
3rd & Main Sts   **Ph:** 501-362-4620
Heber Springs, AR 72543   **Fax:** 501-362-4622

In north-central AR, north of Little Rock; organized Feb 20, 1883

All statistics are based on the 2000 Census except the dollar figures given for per capita income, which are based on 1999 estimates.

from White and Van Buren counties. **Name Origin:** For Gen. Patrick R. Cleburne (1828-64), Confederate officer.

Area (sq mi): 591.91 (land 553.05; water 38.86).

Pop: 24,046 (White 97.3%; Black or African American 0.1%; Hispanic or Latino 1.2%; Asian 0.1%; Other 1.5%). **Foreign born:** 1.1%. **Median age:** 43.7. **State rank:** 30. **Pop change 1990-2000:** +23.9%.

Income: per capita $17,250; median household $31,531. **Pop below poverty level:** 13.1%.

Unemployment: 4.7%. **Median home value:** $87,400. **Median travel time to work:** 27.1 minutes.

CLEVELAND COUNTY

PO Box 368
Rison, AR 71665

Ph: 870-325-6521
Fax: 870-325-6144

In south-central AR, south of Pine Bluff; organized Apr 17, 1873 from Dallas County. **Name Origin:** For Grover Cleveland (1837-1908), twenty-second and twenty-fourth U.S. president.

Area (sq mi): 598.8 (land 597.74; water 1.06).

Pop: 8,571 (White 84%; Black or African American 13.2%; Hispanic or Latino 1.6%; Asian 0.1%; Other 1.8%). **Foreign born:** 1.4%. **Median age:** 36.9. **State rank:** 72. **Pop change 1990-2000:** +10.2%.

Income: per capita $15,362; median household $32,405. **Pop below poverty level:** 15.2%.

Unemployment: 6.4%. **Median home value:** $48,900. **Median travel time to work:** 31.7 minutes.

COLUMBIA COUNTY

1 Court Sq Suite 1
Magnolia, AR 71753

Ph: 870-235-3774
Fax: 870-235-3773

On southern border of AR; organized Dec 17, 1852 from Lafayette County. **Name Origin:** Feminine form of Columbus, a poetic and honorific reference to Christopher Columbus (1451-1506) and America.

Area (sq mi): 766.86 (land 766.11; water 0.75).

Pop: 25,603 (White 61.6%; Black or African American 36.1%; Hispanic or Latino 1.1%; Asian 0.3%; Other 1.6%). **Foreign born:** 0.9%. **Median age:** 35.7. **State rank:** 27. **Pop change 1990-2000:** -0.3%.

Income: per capita $15,322; median household $27,640. **Pop below poverty level:** 21.1%.

Unemployment: 5.3%. **Median home value:** $55,700. **Median travel time to work:** 18.4 minutes.

CONWAY COUNTY

117 S Moose St
Morrilton, AR 72110

Ph: 501-354-9621
Fax: 501-354-9610

In central AR, northwest of Little Rock; organized Oct 20, 1825 (prior to statehood) from Pulaski County. **Name Origin:** For Henry W. Conway (1793-1827), soldier, early settler, and delegate to Congress at the time of establishment.

Area (sq mi): 566.66 (land 556.15; water 10.51).

Pop: 20,336 (White 83.5%; Black or African American 13.1%; Hispanic or Latino 1.8%; Asian 0.2%; Other 2.4%). **Foreign born:** 1.2%. **Median age:** 37.9. **State rank:** 37. **Pop change 1990-2000:** +6.2%.

Income: per capita $16,056; median household $31,209. **Pop below poverty level:** 16.1%.

Unemployment: 5.3%. **Median home value:** $59,400. **Median travel time to work:** 24.9 minutes.

CRAIGHEAD COUNTY

PO Box 1167
Jonesboro, AR 72403
www.craigheadcounty.org

Ph: 870-933-4520
Fax: 870-933-4514

In northeastern AR; organized Feb 19, 1859 from Mississippi County. **Name Origin:** For Thomas C. Craighead, state senator at the time of establishment.

Area (sq mi): 712.98 (land 710.84; water 2.14).

Pop: 82,148 (White 88.2%; Black or African American 7.8%; Hispanic or Latino 2.1%; Asian 0.6%; Other 2.3%). **Foreign born:** 2%. **Median age:** 33. **State rank:** 9. **Pop change 1990-2000:** +19.1%.

Income: per capita $17,091; median household $32,425. **Pop below poverty level:** 15.4%.

Unemployment: 4.4%. **Median home value:** $79,200. **Median travel time to work:** 18.2 minutes.

CRAWFORD COUNTY

300 Main St County Courthouse Rm 7
Van Buren, AR 72956

Ph: 479-474-1312
Fax: 479-471-3236

On western border of AR, north of Fort Smith; organized Oct 18, 1820 (prior to statehood) from Pulaski County. **Name Origin:** For William Harris Crawford (1772-1834), VA statesman.

Area (sq mi): 604.2 (land 595.39; water 8.81).

Pop: 53,247 (White 90.7%; Black or African American 0.9%; Hispanic or Latino 3.3%; Asian 1.2%; Other 5.7%). **Foreign born:** 2.4%. **Median age:** 35.1. **State rank:** 12. **Pop change 1990-2000:** +25.3%.

Income: per capita $15,015; median household $32,871. **Pop below poverty level:** 14.2%.

Unemployment: 4.1%. **Median home value:** $71,600. **Median travel time to work:** 23.7 minutes.

CRITTENDEN COUNTY

100 Court St County Courthouse
Marion, AR 72364

Ph: 870-739-4434
Fax: 870-739-3072

On eastern border of AR, east of TN; organized Oct 22, 1825 (prior to statehood) from Phillips County. **Name Origin:** For Robert Crittenden, veteran of the War of 1812 and Arkansas Territory official.

Area (sq mi): 636.69 (land 610.17; water 26.52).

Pop: 50,866 (White 50.4%; Black or African American 47.1%; Hispanic or Latino 1.4%; Asian 0.5%; Other 1.5%). **Foreign born:** 1.2%. **Median age:** 32. **State rank:** 15. **Pop change 1990-2000:** +1.9%.

Please see sample entry on inside front cover for detailed information about the statistics presented with each county listing.

Income: per capita $14,424; median household $30,109. **Pop below poverty level:** 25.3%.

Unemployment: 5.9%. **Median home value:** $70,500. **Median travel time to work:** 22.8 minutes.

CROSS COUNTY
705 E Union St Rm 8   **Ph:** 870-238-5735
Wynne, AR 72396   **Fax:** 870-238-5739

In northeastern AR, west of Memphis, TN; organized Nov 15, 1862 from Crittenden, Poinsett, and Saint Francis counties. **Name Origin:** For Edward Cross (1798-1887), jurist and U.S. representative from AR (1839-45).

Area (sq mi): 622.33 (land 615.85; water 6.49).

Pop: 19,526 (White 74.4%; Black or African American 23.7%; Hispanic or Latino 0.9%; Asian 0.3%; Other 1.1%). **Foreign born:** 1%. **Median age:** 35.9. **State rank:** 39. **Pop change 1990-2000:** +1.6%.

Income: per capita $15,726; median household $29,362. **Pop below poverty level:** 19.9%.

Unemployment: 7.5%. **Median home value:** $61,500. **Median travel time to work:** 23.4 minutes.

DALLAS COUNTY
206 W 3rd St   **Ph:** 870-352-2307
Fordyce, AR 71742   **Fax:** 870-352-7179

In south-central AR, southeast of Hot Springs; organized Jan 1, 1845 from Clark and Hot Springs counties. **Name Origin:** For George Mifflin Dallas (1792-1864), U.S. statesman and U.S. vice president (1845-49).

Area (sq mi): 668.16 (land 667.42; water 0.74).

Pop: 9,210 (White 56.4%; Black or African American 41%; Hispanic or Latino 1.9%; Asian 0.2%; Other 1.8%). **Foreign born:** 0.9%. **Median age:** 38.4. **State rank:** 69. **Pop change 1990-2000:** -4.2%.

Income: per capita $14,610; median household $26,608. **Pop below poverty level:** 18.9%.

Unemployment: 9.2%. **Median home value:** $38,700. **Median travel time to work:** 23.5 minutes.

DESHA COUNTY
PO Box 188   **Ph:** 870-877-2426
Arkansas City, AR 71630   **Fax:** 870-877-2531

On southeastern border of AR, southeast of Pine Bluff; organized Dec 12, 1838 from Arkansas County. **Name Origin:** For Capt. Benjamin Desha (?-1835), officer in the War of 1812.

Area (sq mi): 819.52 (land 764.99; water 54.53).

Pop: 15,341 (White 49.6%; Black or African American 46.3%; Hispanic or Latino 3.2%; Asian 0.3%; Other 2.9%). **Foreign born:** 2.1%. **Median age:** 35.5. **State rank:** 51. **Pop change 1990-2000:** -8.7%.

Income: per capita $13,446; median household $24,121. **Pop below poverty level:** 28.9%.

Unemployment: 11.1%. **Median home value:** $46,700. **Median travel time to work:** 18.9 minutes.

DREW COUNTY
210 S Main St   **Ph:** 870-460-6250
Monticello, AR 71655   **Fax:** 870-460-6246

In southeastern AR, southeast of Pine Bluff; organized Nov 26, 1846 from Arkansas County. **Name Origin:** For Thomas Stevenson Drew (1802-79), governor of AR (1844-49).

Area (sq mi): 835.65 (land 828.18; water 7.47).

Pop: 18,723 (White 69.7%; Black or African American 27.2%; Hispanic or Latino 1.8%; Asian 0.4%; Other 2.2%). **Foreign born:** 1.5%. **Median age:** 34. **State rank:** 40. **Pop change 1990-2000:** +7.8%.

Income: per capita $16,264; median household $28,627. **Pop below poverty level:** 18.2%.

Unemployment: 10.1%. **Median home value:** $60,100. **Median travel time to work:** 20.2 minutes.

FAULKNER COUNTY
801 Locust St   **Ph:** 501-450-4909
Conway, AR 72034   **Fax:** 501-450-4938

In central AR, north of Little Rock; organized Apr 12, 1873 from Pulaski County. **Name Origin:** Said to be for Sanford C. Faulkner, who wrote 'The Arkansas Traveler,' the state song. Other Faulkner family names occur in the area.

Area (sq mi): 664.01 (land 647.38; water 16.63).

Pop: 86,014 (White 87.4%; Black or African American 8.5%; Hispanic or Latino 1.8%; Asian 0.7%; Other 2.4%). **Foreign born:** 1.7%. **Median age:** 31. **State rank:** 6. **Pop change 1990-2000:** +43.3%.

Income: per capita $17,988; median household $38,204. **Pop below poverty level:** 12.5%.

Unemployment: 5%. **Median home value:** $92,900. **Median travel time to work:** 24.8 minutes.

FRANKLIN COUNTY
211 W Commercial St   **Ph:** 479-667-3607
Ozark, AR 72949   **Fax:** 479-667-4247

In northwestern AR, east of Fort Smith; organized Dec 19, 1837 from Crawford County. **Name Origin:** For Benjamin Franklin (1706-90), U.S. patriot, diplomat, and statesman.

Area (sq mi): 619.69 (land 609.55; water 10.13).

Pop: 17,771 (White 95.3%; Black or African American 0.6%; Hispanic or Latino 1.7%; Asian 0.3%; Other 3%). **Foreign born:** 1.3%. **Median age:** 37.6. **State rank:** 44. **Pop change 1990-2000:** +19.3%.

Income: per capita $14,616; median household $30,848. **Pop below poverty level:** 15.2%.

Unemployment: 3.4%. **Median home value:** $58,500. **Median travel time to work:** 26.6 minutes.

FULTON COUNTY
PO Box 485   **Ph:** 870-895-3310
Salem, AR 72576   **Fax:** 870-895-3383

On north-central border of AR; organized Dec 21, 1842 from Izard County. **Name Origin:** For William Savin Fulton (1795-1844), governor of the Arkansas Territory and U.S. senator (1836-44).

All statistics are based on the 2000 Census except the dollar figures given for per capita income, which are based on 1999 estimates.

Arizona

ARIZONA STATE INFORMATION

www.az.gov **Ph:** 602-542-4900

Area (sq mi): 11,3998.3 (land 113,634.57; water 363.73).

Pop: 5,130,632 (White 63.8%; Black or African American 3.1%; Hispanic or Latino 25.3%; Asian 1.8%; Other 19.6%). **Foreign born:** 12.8%. **Median age:** 34.2. **Pop change 1990-2000:** +40%.

Income: per capita $20,275; median household $40,558. **Pop below poverty level:** 13.9%.

Unemployment: 5.6%. **Median home value:** $121,300. **Median travel time to work:** 24.9 minutes.

APACHE COUNTY

PO Box 365 **Ph:** 928-337-4364
Saint Johns, AZ 85936 **Fax:** 928-337-2771
www.co.apache.az.us

On eastern border of AZ; organized Feb 14, 1879 (prior to statehood) from Mohave County. **Name Origin:** For the Apache Indian tribe, of Athapascan linguistic stock, who inhabited the land for centuries. The name is variously said to mean 'man,' 'battles,' or 'enemy.'

Area (sq mi): 11,218.42 (land 11,204.88; water 13.54).

Pop: 69,423 (White 17.7%; Black or African American 0.2%; Hispanic or Latino 4.5%; Asian 0.1%; Other 80.2%). **Foreign born:** 0.9%. **Median age:** 27. **State rank:** 10. **Pop change 1990-2000:** +12.7%.

Income: per capita $8,986; median household $23,344. **Pop below poverty level:** 37.8%.

Unemployment: 12%. **Median home value:** $41,700. **Median travel time to work:** 28 minutes.

COCHISE COUNTY

1415 W Melody Ln **Ph:** 520-432-9204
Bisbee, AZ 85603 **Fax:** 520-432-5016
www.co.cochise.az.us

In southeastern corner of AZ; organized Feb 1, 1881 (prior to statehood) from Pima County. **Name Origin:** For the famous Chiricahua Apache chief (c. 1812-74), who conducted raids against the U.S. after brutal treatment by U.S. Army officers and surrendered in 1871.

Area (sq mi): 6218.77 (land 6169.45; water 49.32).

Pop: 117,755 (White 60.1%; Black or African American 4.5%; Hispanic or Latino 30.7%; Asian 1.6%; Other 17.2%). **Foreign born:**

12.3%. **Median age:** 36.9. **State rank:** 7. **Pop change 1990-2000:** +20.6%.

Income: per capita $15,988; median household $32,105. **Pop below poverty level:** 17.7%.

Unemployment: 4.6%. **Median home value:** $88,200. **Median travel time to work:** 19.8 minutes.

COCONINO COUNTY

219 E Cherry Ave **Ph:** 928-774-5011
Flagstaff, AZ 86001 **Fax:** 928-779-6785
co.coconino.az.us

In north-central AZ; organized Feb 19, 1891 (prior to statehood) from Yavapai County. **Name Origin:** Possibly from the Hopi Indian name, *Kohnina*, for the Havasupai tribe that inhabits the Grand Canyon region, which is within the county. Or derived from a Havasupai word meaning 'little water.'

Area (sq mi): 18,661.21 (land 18,617.42; water 43.79).

Pop: 116,320 (White 57.6%; Black or African American 1%; Hispanic or Latino 10.9%; Asian 0.8%; Other 35.1%). **Foreign born:** 4.3%. **Median age:** 29.6. **State rank:** 8. **Pop change 1990-2000:** +20.4%.

Income: per capita $17,139; median household $38,256. **Pop below poverty level:** 18.2%.

Unemployment: 5.4%. **Median home value:** $142,500. **Median travel time to work:** 19 minutes.

GILA COUNTY

1400 E Ash St **Ph:** 928-425-3231
Globe, AZ 85501 **Fax:** 928-425-7802
gila.lib.az.us/gilagov/

In east-central AZ, east of Phoenix; organized Feb 8, 1881 (prior to statehood) from Maricopa and Pinal counties. **Name Origin:** For the Gila River, which forms part of the county's southern boundary. Some sources suggest the name may refer to the Gila monster.

Area (sq mi): 4795.74 (land 4767.7; water 28.03).

Pop: 51,335 (White 68.9%; Black or African American 0.4%; Hispanic or Latino 16.6%; Asian 0.4%; Other 21.4%). **Foreign born:** 3.6%. **Median age:** 42.3. **State rank:** 11. **Pop change 1990-2000:** +27.6%.

Income: per capita $16,315; median household $30,917. **Pop below poverty level:** 17.4%.

Unemployment: 5.9%. **Median home value:** $100,100. **Median travel time to work:** 20.3 minutes.

Please see sample entry on inside front cover for detailed information about the statistics presented with each county listing.

47

0.2%; Hispanic or Latino ... born: 0.4%. ...000: +16%.

9. Pop below

Median travel

01-622-3610
01-624-0665

Montgomery
832-99), AR

7.8%; Hispanic or Latino ... reign born: 1990-2000:

4. Pop below

Median travel

70-942-2631
70-942-3564

Feb 4, 1869
Grant (1822-

2.5%; Hispanic or Latino ... reign born: 1990-2000:

. Pop below

median travel

70-239-6311
70-239-3550

3 (prior to
r Gen. Na-
ar, quarter-
rmy of the

Pop: 37,331 (White 96.8%; Black or African American 0.1%; Hispanic or Latino 1.2%; Asian 0.2%; Other 2.2%). **Foreign born:** 0.5%. **Median age:** 36.2. **State rank:** 19. **Pop change 1990-2000:** +17.4%.

Income: per capita $16,403; median household $30,828. **Pop below poverty level:** 13.3%.

Unemployment: 7.8%. **Median home value:** $66,800. **Median travel time to work:** 19.2 minutes.

HEMPSTEAD COUNTY

PO Box 1420 **Ph:** 870-777-2241
Hope, AR 71802 **Fax:** 870-777-7829

In southwestern AR, northeast of Texarkana; organized Dec 15, 1818 (prior to statehood) from Arkansas County. **Name Origin:** For Edward Hempstead (1780-1817), delegate to Congress from MO.

Area (sq mi): 741.36 (land 728.77; water 12.59).

Pop: 23,587 (White 59.8%; Black or African American 30.4%; Hispanic or Latino 8.3%; Asian 0.2%; Other 6.2%). **Foreign born:** 6.4%. **Median age:** 35.2. **State rank:** 31. **Pop change 1990-2000:** +9.1%.

Income: per capita $14,103; median household $28,622. **Pop below poverty level:** 20.3%.

Unemployment: 4.9%. **Median home value:** $51,400. **Median travel time to work:** 19.2 minutes.

HOT SPRING COUNTY

210 Locust St **Ph:** 501-332-2291
Malvern, AR 72104 **Fax:** 501-332-2221

In central AR, south of Hot Springs; organized Apr 17, 1829 (prior to statehood) from Clark County. **Name Origin:** At the time of organization the famous Hot Springs were within the county boundaries.

Area (sq mi): 622.16 (land 614.93; water 7.22).

Pop: 30,353 (White 86.6%; Black or African American 10.3%; Hispanic or Latino 1.3%; Asian 0.2%; Other 2.1%). **Foreign born:** 1.2%. **Median age:** 38.4. **State rank:** 22. **Pop change 1990-2000:** +16.2%.

Income: per capita $15,216; median household $31,543. **Pop below poverty level:** 14%.

Unemployment: 6%. **Median home value:** $63,100. **Median travel time to work:** 27.9 minutes.

HOWARD COUNTY

421 N Main St Rm 10 **Ph:** 870-845-7502
Nashville, AR 71852 **Fax:** 870-845-7505

In southwestern AR, north of Texarkana; organized Apr 17, 1873 from Pike County. **Name Origin:** Said to be named for James Howard, a state senator.

Area (sq mi): 595.2 (land 587.42; water 7.78).

Pop: 14,300 (White 71.5%; Black or African American 21.9%; Hispanic or Latino 5.1%; Asian 0.5%; Other 4.1%). **Foreign born:** 3.5%. **Median age:** 36.1. **State rank:** 53. **Pop change 1990-2000:** +5.4%.

Please see sample entry on inside front cover for detailed information about the statistics presented with each county listing.

55

Arkansas   Counties USA, 2nd Edition

Income: per capita $15,586; median household $28,699. **Pop below poverty level:** 15.5%.

Unemployment: 5.5%. **Median home value:** $55,600. **Median travel time to work:** 19.2 minutes.

INDEPENDENCE COUNTY

192 E Main St   **Ph:** 870-793-8828
Batesville, AR 72501   **Fax:** 870-793-8831

In north-central AR; organized Oct 23, 1820 (prior to statehood) from Arkansas County. **Name Origin:** To honor the Declaration of Independence.

Area (sq mi): 771.57 (land 763.78; water 7.79).

Pop: 34,233 (White 94.2%; Black or African American 2%; Hispanic or Latino 1.5%; Asian 0.6%; Other 2.4%). **Foreign born:** 1.2%. **Median age:** 37.7. **State rank:** 20. **Pop change 1990-2000:** +9.7%.

Income: per capita $16,163; median household $31,920. **Pop below poverty level:** 13%.

Unemployment: 6.1%. **Median home value:** $64,300. **Median travel time to work:** 21.5 minutes.

IZARD COUNTY

PO Box 95   **Ph:** 870-368-4316
Melbourne, AR 72556   **Fax:** 870-368-4748

In north-central AR; organized Oct 27, 1825 (prior to statehood) from Independence County. **Name Origin:** For George Izard (1777-1828), general in the War of 1812 and governor of Arkansas Territory (1825-28).

Area (sq mi): 584.02 (land 580.68; water 3.34).

Pop: 13,249 (White 95.9%; Black or African American 1.4%; Hispanic or Latino 1%; Asian 0.1%; Other 2%). **Foreign born:** 0.8%. **Median age:** 42.6. **State rank:** 57. **Pop change 1990-2000:** +16.6%.

Income: per capita $14,397; median household $25,670. **Pop below poverty level:** 17.2%.

Unemployment: 6.6%. **Median home value:** $57,800. **Median travel time to work:** 26.8 minutes.

JACKSON COUNTY

208 Main St County Courthouse   **Ph:** 870-523-7420
Newport, AR 72112   **Fax:** 870-523-7404

In northeast-central AR; organized Nov 5, 1829 (prior to statehood) from Independence County. **Name Origin:** For Andrew Jackson (1767-1845), seventh U.S. president.

Area (sq mi): 641.45 (land 633.52; water 7.92).

Pop: 18,418 (White 79.9%; Black or African American 17.6%; Hispanic or Latino 1.3%; Asian 0.2%; Other 1.7%). **Foreign born:** 0.5%. **Median age:** 38.2. **State rank:** 41. **Pop change 1990-2000:** -2.8%.

Income: per capita $14,564; median household $25,081. **Pop below poverty level:** 17.4%.

Unemployment: 8.7%. **Median home value:** $45,300. **Median travel time to work:** 20.2 minutes.

JEFFERSON COUNTY

PO Box 6317   **Ph:** 870-541-5322
Pine Bluff, AR 71611   **Fax:** 870-541-5324
www.jeffersoncountyark.com

In southeast-central AR; organized Nov 2, 1829 (prior to statehood) from Arkansas and Pulaski counties. **Name Origin:** For Thomas Jefferson (1743-1826), U.S. patriot and statesman; third U.S. president.

Area (sq mi): 913.7 (land 884.82; water 28.88).

Pop: 84,278 (White 48%; Black or African American 49.6%; Hispanic or Latino 1%; Asian 0.7%; Other 1.3%). **Foreign born:** 1.1%. **Median age:** 35.1. **State rank:** 7. **Pop change 1990-2000:** -1.4%.

Income: per capita $15,417; median household $31,327. **Pop below poverty level:** 20.5%.

Unemployment: 8.2%. **Median home value:** $57,600. **Median travel time to work:** 21.6 minutes.

JOHNSON COUNTY

PO Box 57   **Ph:** 479-754-3967
Clarksville, AR 72830   **Fax:** 479-754-2286

In northwestern AR, northeast of Fort Smith; organized Nov 16, 1833 (prior to statehood) from Pope County. **Name Origin:** For Benjamin Johnson, a territorial judge.

Area (sq mi): 682.74 (land 662.17; water 20.57).

Pop: 22,781 (White 90%; Black or African American 1.4%; Hispanic or Latino 6.7%; Asian 0.3%; Other 4.6%). **Foreign born:** 4.5%. **Median age:** 36.4. **State rank:** 33. **Pop change 1990-2000:** +25%.

Income: per capita $15,097; median household $27,910. **Pop below poverty level:** 16.4%.

Unemployment: 4.3%. **Median home value:** $59,300. **Median travel time to work:** 20.5 minutes.

LAFAYETTE COUNTY

1 Courthouse Sq   **Ph:** 870-921-4858
Lewisville, AR 71845   **Fax:** 870-921-4505

On southwestern border of AR; organized Oct 15, 1827 (prior to statehood) from Hempstead County. **Name Origin:** For the Marquis de Lafayette (1757-1834), French statesman and soldier who fought with the Americans during the Revolutionary War.

Area (sq mi): 545.07 (land 526.5; water 18.57).

Pop: 8,559 (White 61.5%; Black or African American 36.5%; Hispanic or Latino 1%; Asian 0.2%; Other 1.2%). **Foreign born:** 1%. **Median age:** 39.3. **State rank:** 73. **Pop change 1990-2000:** -11.2%.

Income: per capita $14,128; median household $24,831. **Pop below poverty level:** 23.2%.

Unemployment: 5.2%. **Median home value:** $33,600. **Median travel time to work:** 26.8 minutes.

LAWRENCE COUNTY

PO Box 526   **Ph:** 870-886-1111
Walnut Ridge, AR 72476   **Fax:** 870-886-1122

In northeastern AR; organized Jan 15, 1815 (prior to statehood) from New Madrid County, MO. **Name Origin:** For Capt. James

---

MARICOPA COUNTY

301 W Jefferson St 10th Fl   **Ph:** 602-506-3415
Phoenix, AZ 85003   **Fax:** 602-506-6402
www.maricopa.gov

In south-central AZ; organized Feb 14, 1871 (prior to statehood) from Yavapai and Yuma counties. **Name Origin:** From the name of an Indian tribe of Yuman linguistic stock. The name may be a variant of the spanish *mariposa*, or 'butterfly,' as the Spanish found the tribe wearing bright paints. The tribe called itself *Pipatsje*, 'people.'

Area (sq mi): 9224.27 (land 9203.14; water 21.13).

Pop: 3,072,149 (White 66.2%; Black or African American 3.7%; Hispanic or Latino 24.8%; Asian 2.2%; Other 16.7%). **Foreign born:** 14.4%. **Median age:** 33. **State rank:** 1. **Pop change 1990-2000:** +44.8%.

Income: per capita $22,251; median household $45,358. **Pop below poverty level:** 11.7%.

Unemployment: 3.9%. **Median home value:** $129,200. **Median travel time to work:** 26.1 minutes.

MOHAVE COUNTY

PO Box 7000   **Ph:** 928-753-0729
Kingman, AZ 86402   **Fax:** 928-753-5103
www.co.mohave.az.us

On western border of AZ; original county; organized Dec 21, 1864 (prior to statehood); in 1871 annexed Pah-Ute County, which had been organized in 1865. **Name Origin:** For a tribe of Yuman linguistic stock, who inhabited both the CA and AZ sides of the Colorado River. Name means 'three mountains' and refers to the Needles, the three pointed mountain peaks at the center of tribal activities. Also spelled *Mojave*.

Area (sq mi): 13,469.71 (land 13,311.64; water 158.07).

Pop: 155,032 (White 84%; Black or African American 0.5%; Hispanic or Latino 11.1%; Asian 0.8%; Other 8.6%). **Foreign born:** 5.9%. **Median age:** 42.9. **State rank:** 6. **Pop change 1990-2000:** +65.8%.

Income: per capita $16,788; median household $31,521. **Pop below poverty level:** 13.9%.

Unemployment: 4.5%. **Median home value:** $95,300. **Median travel time to work:** 20.6 minutes.

NAVAJO COUNTY

PO Box 668   **Ph:** 928-524-4188
Holbrook, AZ 86025   **Fax:** 928-524-4261
www.co.navajo.az.us

In northeastern AZ, east of Flagstaff; organized Mar 21, 1895 (prior to statehood). **Name Origin:** For the Navajo Indian tribe. Site of the Navajo National Monument.

Area (sq mi): 9959.49 (land 9953.18; water 6.31).

Pop: 97,470 (White 42.3%; Black or African American 0.9%; Hispanic or Latino 8.2%; Asian 0.3%; Other 52.7%). **Foreign born:** 1.7%. **Median age:** 30.2. **State rank:** 9. **Pop change 1990-2000:** +25.5%.

Income: per capita $11,609; median household $28,569. **Pop below poverty level:** 29.5%.

except the dollar figures given for per capita income, which are based on 1999 estimates.

48

All statistics are based on the 2000 Census except the dollar figures given for per capita income, which are based on 1999 estimates.

56

Lawrence (1781-1813), U.S. Navy commander in War of 1812 who said 'Don't give up the ship!'

Area (sq mi): 592.34 (land 586.57; water 5.78).

Pop: 17,774 (White 97.4%; Black or African American 0.4%; Hispanic or Latino 0.7%; Asian 0.1%; Other 1.7%). **Foreign born:** 0.6%. **Median age:** 38.2. **State rank:** 43. **Pop change 1990-2000:** +1.8%.

Income: per capita $13,785; median household $27,139. **Pop below poverty level:** 18.4%.

Unemployment: 8%. **Median home value:** $45,300. **Median travel time to work:** 23.6 minutes.

LEE COUNTY

15 E Chestnut St   **Ph:** 870-295-7715
Marianna, AR 72360   **Fax:** 870-295-7766

On central-eastern border of AR; organized Apr 17, 1873 from Phillips and Monroe counties. **Name Origin:** For Robert E. Lee (1807-70), American general and commander in chief of the Confederate forces during the Civil War.

Area (sq mi): 619.47 (land 601.66; water 17.8).

Pop: 12,580 (White 40.3%; Black or African American 57.2%; Hispanic or Latino 2.2%; Asian 0.3%; Other 1.1%). **Foreign born:** 0.3%. **Median age:** 34.6. **State rank:** 59. **Pop change 1990-2000:** -3.6%.

Income: per capita $10,983; median household $20,510. **Pop below poverty level:** 29.9%.

Unemployment: 9.4%. **Median home value:** $42,800. **Median travel time to work:** 22.5 minutes.

LINCOLN COUNTY

300 S Drew St   **Ph:** 870-628-5114
Star City, AR 71667   **Fax:** 870-628-5794

In southeastern AR; organized Mar 28, 1871 from Arkansas, Bradley, Desha, Drew, and Jefferson counties. **Name Origin:** For Abraham Lincoln (1809-65), sixteenth U.S. president.

Area (sq mi): 572.17 (land 561.2; water 10.97).

Pop: 14,492 (White 64.3%; Black or African American 32.9%; Hispanic or Latino 1.8%; Asian 0.1%; Other 2.1%). **Foreign born:** 0.7%. **Median age:** 34.7. **State rank:** 52. **Pop change 1990-2000:** +5.9%.

Income: per capita $12,479; median household $29,607. **Pop below poverty level:** 19.5%.

Unemployment: 6.1%. **Median home value:** $52,200. **Median travel time to work:** 25.9 minutes.

LITTLE RIVER COUNTY

351 N 2nd St   **Ph:** 870-898-7208
Ashdown, AR 71822   **Fax:** 870-898-7207

On southwestern border; organized Mar 5, 1867 from Hempstead County. **Name Origin:** For the Little River, which forms its northern boundary.

Area (sq mi): 564.87 (land 531.73; water 33.14).

Pop: 13,628 (White 73.8%; Black or African American 21.3%; Hispanic or Latino 1.7%; Asian 0.2%; Other 4.1%). **Foreign born:** 1.7%. **Median age:** 38.2. **State rank:** 56. **Pop change 1990-2000:** -2.4%.

Income: per capita $15,899; median household $29,417. **Pop below poverty level:** 15.4%.

Unemployment: 4.4%. **Median home value:** $55,300. **Median travel time to work:** 24.5 minutes.

LOGAN COUNTY

366 N Broadway Ave   **Ph:** 479-675-2951
Booneville, AR 72927   **Fax:** 479-675-5739

In west-central AR, southeast of Fort Smith; organized as Sarber County Mar 22, 1871 from Franklin County; name changed Dec 14, 1875. **Name Origin:** For James Logan, an early settler.

Area (sq mi): 731.5 (land 709.87; water 21.63).

Pop: 22,486 (White 95.7%; Black or African American 1%; Hispanic or Latino 1.2%; Asian 0.1%; Other 2.4%). **Foreign born:** 0.9%. **Median age:** 38. **State rank:** 34. **Pop change 1990-2000:** +9.4%.

Income: per capita $14,527; median household $28,344. **Pop below poverty level:** 15.4%.

Unemployment: 5.4%. **Median home value:** $54,000. **Median travel time to work:** 24.5 minutes.

LONOKE COUNTY

PO Box 188   **Ph:** 501-676-2368
Lonoke, AR 72086   **Fax:** 501-676-3038

In central AR, east of Little Rock; organized Apr 16, 1873 from Pulaski and Jefferson counties. **Name Origin:** Variant spelling of *lone oak*, a former landmark at the county seat.

Area (sq mi): 802.43 (land 765.96; water 36.47).

Pop: 52,828 (White 90%; Black or African American 6.4%; Hispanic or Latino 1.7%; Asian 0.4%; Other 2.1%). **Foreign born:** 1.4%. **Median age:** 34.7. **State rank:** 13. **Pop change 1990-2000:** +34.5%.

Income: per capita $17,397; median household $40,314. **Pop below poverty level:** 10.5%.

Unemployment: 3.5%. **Median home value:** $85,500. **Median travel time to work:** 27.5 minutes.

MADISON COUNTY

PO Box 37   **Ph:** 479-738-2747
Huntsville, AR 72740   **Fax:** 479-738-2735

In northwestern AR, east of Fayetteville; organized Sep 30, 1836 from Washington County. **Name Origin:** For James Madison (1751-1836), fourth U.S. president.

Area (sq mi): 837.06 (land 836.81; water 0.25).

Pop: 14,243 (White 94.5%; Black or African American 0.1%; Hispanic or Latino 3.1%; Asian 0.1%; Other 3.9%). **Foreign born:** 1.8%. **Median age:** 37.7. **State rank:** 54. **Pop change 1990-2000:** +22.6%.

Income: per capita $14,736; median household $27,895. **Pop below poverty level:** 18.6%.

Please see sample entry on inside front cover for detailed information about the statistics presented with each county listing.

Unemployment: 3%. **Median home value:** $62,300. **Median travel time to work:** 32.9 minutes.

MARION COUNTY

PO Box 545
Yellville, AR 72687

Ph: 870-449-6231
Fax: 870-449-4979

On north-central border of AR; organized Nov 3, 1835 (prior to statehood) from Izard County. **Name Origin:** For Gen. Francis Marion (c. 1732-95), SC soldier and legislator, known as 'The Swamp Fox' for his tactics during the Revolutionary War.

Area (sq mi): 640.35 (land 597.7; water 42.65).

Pop: 16,140 (White 96.9%; Black or African American 0.1%; Hispanic or Latino 0.8%; Asian 0.2%; Other 2.1%). **Foreign born:** 1.1%. **Median age:** 44.1. **State rank:** 49. **Pop change 1990-2000:** +34.5%.

Income: per capita $14,588; median household $26,737. **Pop below poverty level:** 15.2%.

Unemployment: 5.6%. **Median home value:** $73,200. **Median travel time to work:** 26 minutes.

MILLER COUNTY

400 Laurel St Rm 105
Texarkana, AR 71854

Ph: 870-774-1501
Fax: 870-773-4090

On southwestern corner of AR; organized Apr 1, 1820 (prior to statehood). **Name Origin:** For Gen. James Miller (1776-1851), first territorial governor of AR (1819-25).

Area (sq mi): 637.48 (land 623.98; water 13.5).

Pop: 40,443 (White 73.2%; Black or African American 23%; Hispanic or Latino 1.6%; Asian 0.4%; Other 2.5%). **Foreign born:** 1.1%. **Median age:** 34.9. **State rank:** 17. **Pop change 1990-2000:** +5.1%.

Income: per capita $16,444; median household $30,951. **Pop below poverty level:** 19.3%.

Unemployment: 4.3%. **Median home value:** $63,700. **Median travel time to work:** 21.1 minutes.

MISSISSIPPI COUNTY

200 W Walnut St Rm 103
Blytheville, AR 72315
mcagov.missconet.com

Ph: 870-762-2411
Fax: 870-838-7784

On the northeastern border of AR, north of Memphis, TN; organized Nov 1, 1883 from Crittenden County. **Name Origin:** For the Mississippi River, which forms its eastern border.

Area (sq mi): 919.73 (land 898.25; water 21.48).

Pop: 51,979 (White 63.6%; Black or African American 32.7%; Hispanic or Latino 2.2%; Asian 0.4%; Other 2.5%). **Foreign born:** 1.2%. **Median age:** 33.1. **State rank:** 14. **Pop change 1990-2000:** -9.6%.

Income: per capita $13,978; median household $27,479. **Pop below poverty level:** 23%.

Unemployment: 13.9%. **Median home value:** $56,200. **Median travel time to work:** 19 minutes.

MONROE COUNTY

123 Madison St
Clarendon, AR 72029

Ph: 870-747-3632
Fax: 870-747-5961

In east-central AR, east of Little Rock; organized Nov 2, 1839 from Phillips and Arkansas counties. **Name Origin:** For James Monroe (1758-1831), fifth U.S. president.

Area (sq mi): 621.41 (land 606.65; water 14.76).

Pop: 10,254 (White 58.5%; Black or African American 38.8%; Hispanic or Latino 1.3%; Asian 0.1%; Other 1.7%). **Foreign born:** 0.5%. **Median age:** 38.3. **State rank:** 64. **Pop change 1990-2000:** -9.5%.

Income: per capita $13,096; median household $22,632. **Pop below poverty level:** 27.5%.

Unemployment: 7.4%. **Median home value:** $42,300. **Median travel time to work:** 21.5 minutes.

MONTGOMERY COUNTY

PO Box 717
Mount Ida, AR 71957

Ph: 870-867-3114
Fax: 870-867-4354

In west-central AR, west of Hot Springs; organized Dec 9, 1842 from Clark County. **Name Origin:** For Gen. Richard Montgomery (1736-75), American Revolutionary War officer who captured Montreal, Canada.

Area (sq mi): 800.29 (land 780.93; water 19.36).

Pop: 9,245 (White 94.5%; Black or African American 0.3%; Hispanic or Latino 2.5%; Asian 0.4%; Other 3.9%). **Foreign born:** 2%. **Median age:** 41.5. **State rank:** 68. **Pop change 1990-2000:** +17.9%.

Income: per capita $14,668; median household $28,421. **Pop below poverty level:** 17%.

Unemployment: 4.2%. **Median home value:** $54,000. **Median travel time to work:** 28.5 minutes.

NEVADA COUNTY

PO Box 621
Prescott, AR 71857

Ph: 870-887-2710
Fax: 870-887-5795

In southwestern AR, northeast of Texarkana; organized Mar 20, 1871 from Hempstead County. **Name Origin:** In reference to the state of Nevada. Possibly because the outline of the county, viewed upside down, roughly resembles that of Nevada.

Area (sq mi): 620.78 (land 619.95; water 0.83).

Pop: 9,955 (White 66.5%; Black or African American 31.2%; Hispanic or Latino 1.5%; Asian 0.1%; Other 1.9%). **Foreign born:** 1.1%. **Median age:** 37.7. **State rank:** 66. **Pop change 1990-2000:** -1.4%.

Income: per capita $14,184; median household $26,962. **Pop below poverty level:** 22.8%.

Unemployment: 4.9%. **Median home value:** $41,200. **Median travel time to work:** 23.4 minutes.

NEWTON COUNTY

PO Box 410
Jasper, AR 72641

Ph: 870-446-5125
Fax: 870-446-5775

In northwest-central AR, east of Fayetteville; organized Dec 14,

All statistics are based on the 2000 Census except the dollar figures given for per capita income, which are based on 1999 estimates.

1842 from Carroll County. **Name Origin:** For Thomas Willoughby Newton (1804-53), AR legislator and U.S. representative.

Area (sq mi): 823.18 (land 822.97; water 0.21).

Pop: 8,608 (White 96.8%; Black or African American 0.1%; Hispanic or Latino 1.1%; Asian 0.2%; Other 2.3%). **Foreign born:** 0.5%. **Median age:** 40.1. **State rank:** 71. **Pop change 1990-2000:** +12.3%.

Income: per capita $13,788; median household $24,756. **Pop below poverty level:** 20.4%.

Unemployment: 6.7%. **Median home value:** $50,100. **Median travel time to work:** 35.9 minutes.

OUACHITA COUNTY
PO Box 644   **Ph:** 870-837-2210
Camden, AR 71711

In south-central AR; organized Nov 29, 1842 from Clark County. **Name Origin:** For the Ouachita River, which runs through the county.

Area (sq mi): 739.63 (land 732.45; water 7.18).

Pop: 28,790 (White 59.4%; Black or African American 38.6%; Hispanic or Latino 0.7%; Asian 0.2%; Other 1.4%). **Foreign born:** 0.7%. **Median age:** 38.7. **State rank:** 24. **Pop change 1990-2000:** -5.8%.

Income: per capita $15,118; median household $29,341. **Pop below poverty level:** 19.5%.

Unemployment: 9.7%. **Median home value:** $50,200. **Median travel time to work:** 21.9 minutes.

PERRY COUNTY
PO Box 358   **Ph:** 501-889-5126
Perryville, AR 72126   **Fax:** 501-889-5759

In central AR, northwest of Little Rock; organized Dec 18, 1840 from Pulaski County. **Name Origin:** For Oliver Hazard Perry (1785-1819), U.S. naval officer during the War of 1812, famous for the message, 'We have met the enemy and they are ours.'

Area (sq mi): 560.47 (land 550.94; water 9.53).

Pop: 10,209 (White 95.1%; Black or African American 1.7%; Hispanic or Latino 1.2%; Asian 0.1%; Other 2.5%). **Foreign born:** 0.8%. **Median age:** 38. **State rank:** 65. **Pop change 1990-2000:** +28.1%.

Income: per capita $16,216; median household $31,083. **Pop below poverty level:** 14%.

Unemployment: 7.2%. **Median home value:** $58,700. **Median travel time to work:** 36.1 minutes.

PHILLIPS COUNTY
620 Cherry St Suite 202 County Courthouse **Ph:** 870-338-5505
Helena, AR 72342   **Fax:** 870-338-5509

On central-eastern border of AR; organized May 1, 1820 (prior to statehood) from Arkansas County. **Name Origin:** For Sylvanus Phillips (1766-1830), who explored the area along the Arkansas River in the 1790s.

Area (sq mi): 727.29 (land 692.67; water 34.62).

Pop: 26,445 (White 38.7%; Black or African American 59%; Hispanic or Latino 1.4%; Asian 0.3%; Other 1.4%). **Foreign born:** 1.1%. **Median age:** 33. **State rank:** 25. **Pop change 1990-2000:** -8.3%.

Income: per capita $12,288; median household $22,231. **Pop below poverty level:** 32.7%.

Unemployment: 10.2%. **Median home value:** $46,900. **Median travel time to work:** 20.5 minutes.

PIKE COUNTY
PO Box 219   **Ph:** 870-285-2231
Murfreesboro, AR 71958   **Fax:** 870-285-3281

In southwestern AR, southwest of Hot Springs; organized Nov 1, 1833 (prior to statehood) from Carroll and Clark counties. **Name Origin:** For Zebulon Montgomery Pike (1779-1813), U.S. army officer and discoverer of Pikes Peak in CO.

Area (sq mi): 613.88 (land 603.01; water 10.87).

Pop: 11,303 (White 91.2%; Black or African American 3.5%; Hispanic or Latino 3.6%; Asian 0.2%; Other 4.3%). **Foreign born:** 2.2%. **Median age:** 38.9. **State rank:** 62. **Pop change 1990-2000:** +12.1%.

Income: per capita $15,385; median household $27,695. **Pop below poverty level:** 16.8%.

Unemployment: 5.5%. **Median home value:** $49,600. **Median travel time to work:** 26.7 minutes.

POINSETT COUNTY
County Courthouse 401 Market St   **Ph:** 870-578-5333
Harrisburg, AR 72432

In northeastern AR, northwest of Memphis, TN; organized Feb 28, 1838 from Greene County. **Name Origin:** For Joel Roberts Poinsett (1779-1851), SC statesman and secretary of war (1837-41). He introduced the cultivation of the poinsettia flower to the U.S., having imported it from Mexico after he was a U.S. minister there (1825-29).

Area (sq mi): 763.39 (land 757.74; water 5.65).

Pop: 25,614 (White 90.5%; Black or African American 7.1%; Hispanic or Latino 1.4%; Asian 0.2%; Other 1.6%). **Foreign born:** 0.9%. **Median age:** 36.6. **State rank:** 26. **Pop change 1990-2000:** +3.9%.

Income: per capita $13,087; median household $26,558. **Pop below poverty level:** 21.2%.

Unemployment: 9.5%. **Median home value:** $49,500. **Median travel time to work:** 23.5 minutes.

POLK COUNTY
507 Church Ave   **Ph:** 479-394-8123
Mena, AR 71953   **Fax:** 479-394-8115

On western border of AR; organized Nov 30, 1844 from Montgomery County. **Name Origin:** For James Knox Polk (1795-1849), eleventh U.S. president.

Area (sq mi): 862.42 (land 859.38; water 3.04).

Please see sample entry on inside front cover for detailed information about the statistics presented with each county listing.

Pop: 20,229 (White 93.1%; Black or African American 0.2%; Hispanic or Latino 3.5%; Asian 0.2%; Other 5%). **Foreign born:** 2.7%. **Median age:** 38.6. **State rank:** 38. **Pop change 1990-2000:** +16.6%.

Income: per capita $14,063; median household $25,180. **Pop below poverty level:** 18.2%.

Unemployment: 4.4%. **Median home value:** $57,100. **Median travel time to work:** 20.4 minutes.

POPE COUNTY

102 W Main St County Courthouse Suite 6   **Ph:** 479-968-6064
Russellville, AR 72801   **Fax:** 479-967-2291

In northwest-central AR, east of Fort Smith; organized Nov 2, 1829 (prior to statehood) from Pulaski County. **Name Origin:** For John Pope (1770-1845), KY legislator and governor of Arkansas Territory (1829-35).

Area (sq mi): 830.79 (land 811.9; water 18.89).

Pop: 54,469 (White 92.8%; Black or African American 2.6%; Hispanic or Latino 2.1%; Asian 0.6%; Other 3%). **Foreign born:** 1.7%. **Median age:** 34.8. **State rank:** 11. **Pop change 1990-2000:** +18.7%.

Income: per capita $15,918; median household $32,069. **Pop below poverty level:** 15.2%.

Unemployment: 4.1%. **Median home value:** $71,100. **Median travel time to work:** 19.8 minutes.

PRAIRIE COUNTY

PO Box 1011   **Ph:** 870-256-4434
Des Arc, AR 72040

In east-central AR, east of Little Rock; organized Nov 25, 1846 from Monroe County. **Name Origin:** For its open countryside.

Area (sq mi): 675.76 (land 645.93; water 29.83).

Pop: 9,539 (White 84.5%; Black or African American 13.7%; Hispanic or Latino 0.8%; Asian 0.2%; Other 1.3%). **Foreign born:** 0.4%. **Median age:** 40.1. **State rank:** 67. **Pop change 1990-2000:** +0.2%.

Income: per capita $15,907; median household $29,990. **Pop below poverty level:** 15.5%.

Unemployment: 4.8%. **Median home value:** $55,600. **Median travel time to work:** 26.8 minutes.

PULASKI COUNTY

401 W Markham St Suite 102   **Ph:** 501-340-8431
Little Rock, AR 72201   **Fax:** 501-340-8420
www.co.pulaski.ar.us

In central AR; organized Dec 15, 1818 (prior to statehood) from Arkansas County. **Name Origin:** For Count Casimir Pulaski (1747-79), a Polish soldier who fought for America during the Revolutionary War.

Area (sq mi): 807.84 (land 770.82; water 37.02).

Pop: 361,474 (White 62.9%; Black or African American 31.9%; Hispanic or Latino 2.4%; Asian 1.2%; Other 2.9%). **Foreign born:** 3%. **Median age:** 35. **State rank:** 1. **Pop change 1990-2000:** +3.4%.

Income: per capita $21,466; median household $38,120. **Pop below poverty level:** 13.3%.

Unemployment: 4.1%. **Median home value:** $85,300. **Median travel time to work:** 20.8 minutes.

RANDOLPH COUNTY

107 W Broadway   **Ph:** 870-892-5264
Pocahontas, AR 72455

On northern border; organized Oct 29, 1835 (prior to statehood) from Lawrence County. **Name Origin:** For John Randolph (1773-1833), U.S. congressman from VA during the years 1799-1827, and U.S. minister to Russia (1830).

Area (sq mi): 656.04 (land 651.82; water 4.21).

Pop: 18,195 (White 96.5%; Black or African American 1%; Hispanic or Latino 0.8%; Asian 0.1%; Other 1.9%). **Foreign born:** 0.9%. **Median age:** 38.8. **State rank:** 42. **Pop change 1990-2000:** +9.9%.

Income: per capita $14,502; median household $27,583. **Pop below poverty level:** 15.3%.

Unemployment: 8.6%. **Median home value:** $50,600. **Median travel time to work:** 23.3 minutes.

SAINT FRANCIS COUNTY

PO Box 1653   **Ph:** 870-261-1725
Forrest City, AR 72336   **Fax:** 870-630-1210

In eastern AR, west of Memphis, TN; organized Oct 13, 1827 (prior to statehood) from Phillips County. **Name Origin:** For the Saint Francis River, which bisects the county.

Area (sq mi): 642.4 (land 633.84; water 8.56).

Pop: 29,329 (White 45.1%; Black or African American 49%; Hispanic or Latino 4.9%; Asian 0.6%; Other 2%). **Foreign born:** 0.3%. **Median age:** 33.8. **State rank:** 23. **Pop change 1990-2000:** +2.9%.

Income: per capita $12,483; median household $26,146. **Pop below poverty level:** 27.5%.

Unemployment: 8.9%. **Median home value:** $56,000. **Median travel time to work:** 22.2 minutes.

SALINE COUNTY

215 N Main St Suite 9   **Ph:** 501-303-5630
Benton, AR 72015   **Fax:** 501-303-5684
www.salinecounty.org

In central AR, west of Little Rock; organized Nov 2, 1835 (prior to statehood) from Pulaski County. **Name Origin:** For the Saline River, which has its source within the county.

Area (sq mi): 730.46 (land 723.46; water 7).

Pop: 83,529 (White 94.5%; Black or African American 2.2%; Hispanic or Latino 1.3%; Asian 0.6%; Other 1.9%). **Foreign born:** 1.3%. **Median age:** 36.8. **State rank:** 8. **Pop change 1990-2000:** +30.1%.

Income: per capita $19,214; median household $42,569. **Pop below poverty level:** 7.2%.

Unemployment: 3.3%. **Median home value:** $93,700. **Median travel time to work:** 27 minutes.

All statistics are based on the 2000 Census except the dollar figures given for per capita income, which are based on 1999 estimates.

SCOTT COUNTY

100 W 1st St Box 10   **Ph:** 479-637-2642
Waldron, AR 72958   **Fax:** 479-637-0124

On central-western border of AR; organized Nov 5, 1833 (prior to statehood) from Crawford and Pope counties. **Name Origin:** For Andrew Scott, superior court justice for the Arkansas Territory (1819-21).

Area (sq mi): 898.09 (land 893.88; water 4.21).

Pop: 10,996 (White 90.5%; Black or African American 0.2%; Hispanic or Latino 5.7%; Asian 1%; Other 5.3%). **Foreign born:** 3.5%. **Median age:** 37.3. **State rank:** 63. **Pop change 1990-2000:** +7.8%.

Income: per capita $13,609; median household $26,412. **Pop below poverty level:** 18.2%.

Unemployment: 3.5%. **Median home value:** $48,000. **Median travel time to work:** 23.6 minutes.

SEARCY COUNTY

PO Box 998   **Ph:** 870-448-3807
Marshall, AR 72650   **Fax:** 870-448-5005

In north-central AR; first established Nov 3, 1835; name changed to Marion in 1836, then in 1838 a new Searcy County was formed from Marion County. **Name Origin:** For Richard Searcy (1796-1832), lawyer, jurist, and legislator.

Area (sq mi): 668.51 (land 667.15; water 1.36).

Pop: 8,261 (White 96.8%; Black or African American 0%; Hispanic or Latino 1%; Asian 0.1%; Other 2.5%). **Foreign born:** 0.6%. **Median age:** 42.3. **State rank:** 74. **Pop change 1990-2000:** +5.4%.

Income: per capita $12,536; median household $21,397. **Pop below poverty level:** 23.8%.

Unemployment: 5%. **Median home value:** $45,600. **Median travel time to work:** 32 minutes.

SEBASTIAN COUNTY

35 S 6th St   **Ph:** 479-783-6139
Fort Smith, AR 72901   **Fax:** 479-784-1550
www.sebastiancountyonline.com

On western border of AR; organized Jan 6, 1851 from Crawford County. **Name Origin:** For William King Sebastian (1812-65), jurist and U.S. senator from AR (1846-61).

Area (sq mi): 546.04 (land 536.24; water 9.79).

Pop: 115,071 (White 80%; Black or African American 6.2%; Hispanic or Latino 6.7%; Asian 3.5%; Other 8%). **Foreign born:** 6.9%. **Median age:** 35.5. **State rank:** 4. **Pop change 1990-2000:** +15.5%.

Income: per capita $18,424; median household $33,889. **Pop below poverty level:** 13.6%.

Unemployment: 4%. **Median home value:** $73,300. **Median travel time to work:** 19.3 minutes.

SEVIER COUNTY

County Courthouse 115 N 3rd St Rm 102   **Ph:** 870-642-2852
De Queen, AR 71832   **Fax:** 870-642-3896

On southwestern border of AR; organized Oct 17, 1828 (prior to statehood) from Hempstead County. **Name Origin:** For Ambrose

Hundley Sevier (1801-48), territorial legislator (1823-27) and delegate to U.S. Congress (1828-36), later U.S. senator from AR (1836-48), and minister to Mexico (1848).

Area (sq mi): 581.35 (land 563.94; water 17.41).

Pop: 15,757 (White 72.5%; Black or African American 4.9%; Hispanic or Latino 19.7%; Asian 0.1%; Other 15.3%). **Foreign born:** 12.7%. **Median age:** 33.6. **State rank:** 50. **Pop change 1990-2000:** +15.5%.

Income: per capita $14,122; median household $30,144. **Pop below poverty level:** 19.2%.

Unemployment: 4.1%. **Median home value:** $51,700. **Median travel time to work:** 22.2 minutes.

SHARP COUNTY

PO Box 307   **Ph:** 870-994-7361
Ash Flat, AR 72513   **Fax:** 870-994-7712
www.sharpcounty.org

In northeast-central AR; organized Jul 18, 1868 from Izard County. **Name Origin:** For Ephraim Sharp, AR state legislator for the district when the county was formed.

Area (sq mi): 606.35 (land 604.35; water 1.99).

Pop: 17,119 (White 96.4%; Black or African American 0.5%; Hispanic or Latino 1%; Asian 0.1%; Other 2.3%). **Foreign born:** 0.8%. **Median age:** 44.3. **State rank:** 46. **Pop change 1990-2000:** +21.3%.

Income: per capita $14,143; median household $25,152. **Pop below poverty level:** 18.2%.

Unemployment: 6.8%. **Median home value:** $51,900. **Median travel time to work:** 26.4 minutes.

STONE COUNTY

PO Box 1427   **Ph:** 870-269-3351
Mountain View, AR 72560

In north-central AR; organized Apr 21, 1873 from Izard and Independence counties. **Name Origin:** For natural stone formations in the area.

Area (sq mi): 609.43 (land 606.59; water 2.84).

Pop: 11,499 (White 96.5%; Black or African American 0.1%; Hispanic or Latino 1.1%; Asian 0.1%; Other 2.5%). **Foreign born:** 0.8%. **Median age:** 43.1. **State rank:** 61. **Pop change 1990-2000:** +17.6%.

Income: per capita $14,134; median household $22,209. **Pop below poverty level:** 18.9%.

Unemployment: 4.9%. **Median home value:** $64,200. **Median travel time to work:** 26.5 minutes.

UNION COUNTY

101 N Washington Rm 102
County Courthouse   **Ph:** 870-864-1910
El Dorado, AR 71730   **Fax:** 870-864-1927
www.co.union.ar.us

On central-southern border of AR; organized Nov 2, 1829 (prior to statehood) from Hempstead and Clark counties. **Name Origin:** For a group of citizens who had presented petitions to the legislature in a spirit of 'Union and Unity.'

Please see sample entry on inside front cover for detailed information about the statistics presented with each county listing.

Area (sq mi): 1055.27 (land 1038.9; water 16.37).

Pop: 45,629 (White 65.6%; Black or African American 32%; Hispanic or Latino 1.1%; Asian 0.4%; Other 1.5%). **Foreign born:** 1.2%. **Median age:** 37.7. **State rank:** 16. **Pop change 1990-2000:** -2.3%.

Income: per capita $16,063; median household $29,809. **Pop below poverty level:** 18.7%.

Unemployment: 5.4%. **Median home value:** $55,400. **Median travel time to work:** 18 minutes.

VAN BUREN COUNTY
451 Main St Suite 2   **Ph:** 501-745-4140
Clinton, AR 72031   **Fax:** 501-745-7400

In north-central AR; organized Nov 11, 1833 (prior to statehood) from Independence County. **Name Origin:** For Martin Van Buren (1782-1862), eighth U.S. president.

Area (sq mi): 724.32 (land 711.51; water 12.81).

Pop: 16,192 (White 96%; Black or African American 0.3%; Hispanic or Latino 1.3%; Asian 0.2%; Other 2.7%). **Foreign born:** 1.4%. **Median age:** 44.2. **State rank:** 48. **Pop change 1990-2000:** +15.6%.

Income: per capita $16,603; median household $27,004. **Pop below poverty level:** 15.4%.

Unemployment: 6.9%. **Median home value:** $63,700. **Median travel time to work:** 32.9 minutes.

WASHINGTON COUNTY
280 N College Ave Suite 300   **Ph:** 479-444-1711
Fayetteville, AR 72701   **Fax:** 479-444-1894
www.co.washington.ar.us

On northwestern border of AR; organized Oct 17, 1828 (prior to statehood) from the eastern portion of former Lovely County. **Name Origin:** For George Washington (1732-99), American patriot and first U.S. president.

Area (sq mi): 956.01 (land 949.72; water 6.29).

Pop: 157,715 (White 84.6%; Black or African American 2.2%; Hispanic or Latino 8.2%; Asian 1.5%; Other 8.3%). **Foreign born:** 7.4%. **Median age:** 30.8. **State rank:** 2. **Pop change 1990-2000:** +39.1%.

Income: per capita $17,347; median household $34,691. **Pop below poverty level:** 14.6%.

Unemployment: 2.3%. **Median home value:** $90,100. **Median travel time to work:** 19.7 minutes.

WHITE COUNTY
300 N Spruce St   **Ph:** 501-279-6200
Searcy, AR 72143   **Fax:** 501-279-6233
www.white-county.org

In central AR, northeast of Little Rock; organized Oct 23, 1835 (prior to statehood) from Pulaski, Jackson, and Independence counties. **Name Origin:** For Hugh Lawson White (1773-1840), TN legislator and U.S. senator (1825-40); candidate for U.S. president in 1836.

Area (sq mi): 1042.36 (land 1034.03; water 8.33).

Pop: 67,165 (White 92.6%; Black or African American 3.6%; Hispanic or Latino 1.9%; Asian 0.3%; Other 2.5%). **Foreign born:** 1.5%. **Median age:** 35.1. **State rank:** 10. **Pop change 1990-2000:** +22.8%.

Income: per capita $15,890; median household $32,203. **Pop below poverty level:** 14%.

Unemployment: 5.2%. **Median home value:** $72,100. **Median travel time to work:** 23.8 minutes.

WOODRUFF COUNTY
Woodruff County Courthouse 500 N 3rd St   **Ph:** 870-347-2871
Augusta, AR 72006   **Fax:** 870-347-2608

In east-central AR, west of Memphis, TN; organized Nov 26, 1862 from White County. **Name Origin:** For William Edward Woodruff (1795-1885), publisher who established the *Arkansas Gazette*, the state's first newspaper.

Area (sq mi): 594.05 (land 586.56; water 7.49).

Pop: 8,741 (White 67.5%; Black or African American 30.8%; Hispanic or Latino 0.8%; Asian 0.1%; Other 1.3%). **Foreign born:** 0.6%. **Median age:** 38.4. **State rank:** 70. **Pop change 1990-2000:** -8.2%.

Income: per capita $13,269; median household $22,099. **Pop below poverty level:** 27%.

Unemployment: 7.9%. **Median home value:** $35,500. **Median travel time to work:** 18.4 minutes.

YELL COUNTY
PO Box 219   **Ph:** 501-495-2414
Danville, AR 72833

In west-central AR, northwest of Hot Springs; organized Dec 5, 1840 from Pope County. **Name Origin:** For Archibald Yell (1797-1847), U.S. representative from AR (1836-39) and governor (1840-44).

Area (sq mi): 948.84 (land 927.89; water 20.95).

Pop: 21,139 (White 83.5%; Black or African American 1.5%; Hispanic or Latino 12.7%; Asian 0.7%; Other 11.2%). **Foreign born:** 10.2%. **Median age:** 36.1. **State rank:** 35. **Pop change 1990-2000:** +19%.

Income: per capita $15,383; median household $28,916. **Pop below poverty level:** 15.4%.

Unemployment: 3.3%. **Median home value:** $60,600. **Median travel time to work:** 22.8 minutes.

All statistics are based on the 2000 Census except the dollar figures given for per capita income, which are based on 1999 estimates.

CALIFORNIA - Counties

OREGON

DEL NORTE
SISKIYOU
MODOC

HUMBOLDT
TRINITY
SHASTA
LASSEN

TEHAMA
PLUMAS

MENDOCINO
GLENN
BUTTE
SIERRA

NEVADA
LAKE
COLUSA
SUTTER
YUBA
PLACER

Note: All boundaries and names are as of January 1, 2000.

YOLO
EL DORADO
ALPINE

SONOMA
NAPA
SACRA-MENTO
AMADOR
CALAVERAS

SOLANO
MARIN
TUOLUMNE
MONO

SAN FRANCISCO
CONTRA COSTA
SAN JOAQUIN

NEVADA

ALAMEDA
STANISLAUS
MARIPOSA

SAN MATEO
SANTA CLARA
MERCED
MADERA

SANTA CRUZ
SAN BENITO
FRESNO
INYO

MONTEREY
TULARE

KINGS

SAN LUIS OBISPO
KERN

SAN BERNARDINO

SANTA BARBARA
VENTURA
LOS ANGELES

ORANGE
RIVERSIDE
ARIZONA

SAN DIEGO
IMPERIAL

MEXICO

N

0 15 30 45 60 Kilometers
0   15   30   45   60 Miles

California

CALIFORNIA STATE INFORMATION

www.ca.gov   **Ph:** 916-657-9900

Area (sq mi): 163,695.57 (land 155,959.34; water 7736.23).

Pop: 33,871,648 (White 46.7%; Black or African American 6.7%; Hispanic or Latino 32.4%; Asian 10.9%; Other 22.8%). **Foreign born:** 26.2%. **Median age:** 33.3. **Pop change 1990-2000:** +13.8%.

Income: per capita $22,711; median household $47,493. **Pop below poverty level:** 14.2%.

Unemployment: 6.5%. **Median home value:** $211,500. **Median travel time to work:** 27.7 minutes.

ALAMEDA COUNTY

1221 Oak St Suite 555   **Ph:** 510-272-6984
Oakland, CA 94612   **Fax:** 510-272-3784
www.co.alameda.ca.us

Along San Francisco Bay E of San Francisco; organized in Mar 25, 1853 from Contra Costa and Santa Clara counties. **Name Origin:** From Spanish 'grove of poplar trees.'

Area (sq mi): 821.15 (land 737.57; water 83.57).

Pop: 1,443,741 (White 40.9%; Black or African American 14.9%; Hispanic or Latino 19%; Asian 20.4%; Other 15.7%). **Foreign born:** 27.2%. **Median age:** 34.5. **State rank:** 7. **Pop change 1990-2000:** +12.9%.

Income: per capita $26,680; median household $55,946. **Pop below poverty level:** 11%.

Unemployment: 4.5%. **Median home value:** $303,100. **Median travel time to work:** 30.8 minutes.

ALPINE COUNTY

PO Box 158   **Ph:** 530-694-2281
Markleeville, CA 96120   **Fax:** 530-694-2491
www.alpinecountyca.com

In NE CA on Nevada border, E of Sacramento; organized Mar 16, 1864 from Calaveras, Amador, El Dorado, and Mono counties. **Name Origin:** For the mountainous terrain of the Sierra Nevada.

Area (sq mi): 743.19 (land 738.62; water 4.57).

Pop: 1,208 (White 71.8%; Black or African American 0.6%; Hispanic or Latino 7.8%; Asian 0.3%; Other 25.4%). **Foreign born:** 3.2%. **Median age:** 39.3. **State rank:** 58. **Pop change 1990-2000:** +8.5%.

Income: per capita $24,431; median household $41,875. **Pop below poverty level:** 19.5%.

Unemployment: 9%. **Median home value:** $184,200. **Median travel time to work:** 17.3 minutes.

AMADOR COUNTY

500 Argonaut Ln   **Ph:** 209-223-6470
Jackson, CA 95642   **Fax:** 209-257-0619
www.co.amador.ca.us

In NE CA, due E of Sacramento; organized May 11, 1854 from Calaveras County. **Name Origin:** For Jose Maria Amador, a construction foreman at the San Jose Mission, miner, and early landowner.

Area (sq mi): 604.69 (land 592.97; water 11.73).

Pop: 35,100 (White 82.4%; Black or African American 3.9%; Hispanic or Latino 8.9%; Asian 1%; Other 9.3%). **Foreign born:** 3.4%. **Median age:** 42.7. **State rank:** 46. **Pop change 1990-2000:** +16.8%.

Income: per capita $22,412; median household $42,280. **Pop below poverty level:** 9.2%.

Unemployment: 3.9%. **Median home value:** $153,600. **Median travel time to work:** 29.1 minutes.

BUTTE COUNTY

1 Court St   **Ph:** 530-538-7551
Oroville, CA 95965   **Fax:** 530-538-6827
www.buttecounty.net

In N central CA; original county; organized Feb 18, 1850 (prior to statehood). **Name Origin:** For the Sutter Buttes of the Sacramento Valley, or the Butte River, which flows through the county.

Area (sq mi): 1677.11 (land 1639.49; water 37.62).

Pop: 203,171 (White 80%; Black or African American 1.4%; Hispanic or Latino 10.5%; Asian 3.3%; Other 10.7%). **Foreign born:** 7.7%. **Median age:** 35.8. **State rank:** 27. **Pop change 1990-2000:** +11.6%.

Income: per capita $17,517; median household $31,924. **Pop below poverty level:** 19.8%.

Unemployment: 7%. **Median home value:** $129,800. **Median travel time to work:** 20.9 minutes.

CALAVERAS COUNTY

891 Mountain Ranch Rd   **Ph:** 209-754-6370
San Andreas, CA 95249   **Fax:** 209-754-6733
www.co.calaveras.ca.us

In NE CA, SE of Sacramento; original county; organized Feb 18, 1850 (prior to statehood). **Name Origin:** For the Calaveras River,

Please see sample entry on inside front cover for detailed information about the statistics presented with each county listing.

which flows through the county, from the Spanish 'skulls,' so named because skulls were found on the river's banks in the 1830s.

Area (sq mi): 1036.84 (land 1020.04; water 16.81).

Pop: 40,554 (White 87.5%; Black or African American 0.7%; Hispanic or Latino 6.8%; Asian 0.9%; Other 7.2%). **Foreign born:** 3%. **Median age:** 44.6. **State rank:** 45. **Pop change 1990-2000:** +26.7%.

Income: per capita $21,420; median household $41,022. **Pop below poverty level:** 11.8%.

Unemployment: 5.9%. **Median home value:** $156,900. **Median travel time to work:** 34.5 minutes.

COLUSA COUNTY
546 Jay St   **Ph:** 530-458-0500
Colusa, CA 95932   **Fax:** 530-458-0512
www.colusacountyclerk.com

In N CA, NW of Sacramento; original county; organized Feb 18, 1850 (prior to statehood). **Name Origin:** From the name of a former village of the Patwin Indians; earlier spelled *Colusi*.

Area (sq mi): 1156.22 (land 1150.68; water 5.54).

Pop: 18,804 (White 48%; Black or African American 0.5%; Hispanic or Latino 46.5%; Asian 1.2%; Other 33.9%). **Foreign born:** 27.6%. **Median age:** 31.5. **State rank:** 51. **Pop change 1990-2000:** +15.5%.

Income: per capita $14,730; median household $35,062. **Pop below poverty level:** 16.1%.

Unemployment: 17.6%. **Median home value:** $107,500. **Median travel time to work:** 22 minutes.

CONTRA COSTA COUNTY
651 Pine St 11th Fl   **Ph:** 925-335-1080
Martinez, CA 94553   **Fax:** 925-335-1098
www.co.contra-costa.ca.us

On San Pablo Bay, E of San Francisco; original county; organized Feb 18, 1850 (prior to statehood). **Name Origin:** From Spanish 'opposite coast' designating the coast opposite Marin County, north of San Francisco.

Area (sq mi): 802.15 (land 719.95; water 82.2).

Pop: 948,816 (White 57.9%; Black or African American 9.4%; Hispanic or Latino 17.7%; Asian 11%; Other 14.2%). **Foreign born:** 19%. **Median age:** 36.4. **State rank:** 9. **Pop change 1990-2000:** +18.1%.

Income: per capita $30,615; median household $63,675. **Pop below poverty level:** 7.6%.

Unemployment: 3.3%. **Median home value:** $267,800. **Median travel time to work:** 34.4 minutes.

DEL NORTE COUNTY
981 H St Suite 200   **Ph:** 707-464-7204
Crescent City, CA 95531   **Fax:** 707-464-1165
www.co.del-norte.ca.us

In NW corner of CA; organized Mar 2, 1857 from Klamath County. **Name Origin:** Spanish 'of the North,' for the county's position in the state.

Area (sq mi): 1229.75 (land 1007.81; water 221.94).

Pop: 27,507 (White 70.1%; Black or African American 4.3%; Hispanic or Latino 13.9%; Asian 2.3%; Other 14.5%). **Foreign born:** 5.7%. **Median age:** 36.4. **State rank:** 48. **Pop change 1990-2000:** +17.3%.

Income: per capita $14,573; median household $29,642. **Pop below poverty level:** 20.2%.

Unemployment: 8.7%. **Median home value:** $121,100. **Median travel time to work:** 14.8 minutes.

EL DORADO COUNTY
360 Fair Ln Bldg B   **Ph:** 530-621-5490
Placerville, CA 95667   **Fax:** 530-621-2147
co.el-dorado.ca.us

In NE CA, E of Sacramento; original county; organized Feb 18, 1850 (prior to statehood). **Name Origin:** From Spanish 'the gilded' or 'the golden,' originally applied to a legendary chief and city sought by the early Spanish explorers; here the name refers to gold discovered in the area in 1848.

Area (sq mi): 1788.1 (land 1710.85; water 77.25).

Pop: 156,299 (White 84.9%; Black or African American 0.5%; Hispanic or Latino 9.3%; Asian 2.1%; Other 7.6%). **Foreign born:** 7.2%. **Median age:** 39.4. **State rank:** 30. **Pop change 1990-2000:** +24.1%.

Income: per capita $25,560; median household $51,484. **Pop below poverty level:** 7.1%.

Unemployment: 3.8%. **Median home value:** $194,400. **Median travel time to work:** 29.7 minutes.

FRESNO COUNTY
2281 Tulare St Rm 304 Hall of Records   **Ph:** 559-488-1710
Fresno, CA 93721   **Fax:** 559-488-1830
www.co.fresno.ca.us

In central CA; organized Apr 19, 1856 from Mariposa and Merced counties. **Name Origin:** From the Spanish 'ash (tree)'; name originally applied to the river, for the ash trees that grew near it.

Area (sq mi): 6017.42 (land 5962.73; water 54.7).

Pop: 799,407 (White 39.7%; Black or African American 5.3%; Hispanic or Latino 44%; Asian 8.1%; Other 32.3%). **Foreign born:** 21.1%. **Median age:** 29.9. **State rank:** 10. **Pop change 1990-2000:** +19.8%.

Income: per capita $15,495; median household $34,725. **Pop below poverty level:** 22.9%.

Unemployment: 13.7%. **Median home value:** $104,900. **Median travel time to work:** 22.2 minutes.

GLENN COUNTY
PO Box 391   **Ph:** 530-934-6400
Willows, CA 95988   **Fax:** 530-934-6419
www.glenncountygovmt.net

In NW CA; organized Mar 11, 1891 from Colusa County. **Name Origin:** For Dr. Hugh James Glenn (1824-83), the most important wheatgrower in California during the latter half of the 1800s.

Area (sq mi): 1327.16 (land 1314.79; water 12.36).

All statistics are based on the 2000 Census except the dollar figures given for per capita income, which are based on 1999 estimates.

Pop: 26,453 (White 62.6%; Black or African American 0.6%; Hispanic or Latino 29.6%; Asian 3.4%; Other 24.3%). Foreign born: 17.8%. Median age: 33.7. State rank: 49. Pop change 1990-2000: +6.7%.

Income: per capita $14,069; median household $32,107. Pop below poverty level: 18.1%.

Unemployment: 11.2%. Median home value: $94,900. Median travel time to work: 21.1 minutes.

HUMBOLDT COUNTY

825 5th St Rm 226   Ph: 707-445-7256
Eureka, CA 95501   Fax: 707-445-7041
www.co.humboldt.ca.us

On NW coast of CA; organized Mar 12, 1853 from Trinity County, and in 1874 annexed part of Klamath County. Name Origin: For Humboldt Bay, which was named for German naturalist and traveler, [Friedrich Heinrich] Alexander von Humboldt (1769-1859).

Area (sq mi): 4052.22 (land 3572.49; water 479.74).

Pop: 126,518 (White 81.6%; Black or African American 0.9%; Hispanic or Latino 6.5%; Asian 1.7%; Other 12.7%). Foreign born: 4.5%. Median age: 36.3. State rank: 33. Pop change 1990-2000: +6.2%.

Income: per capita $17,203; median household $31,226. Pop below poverty level: 19.5%.

Unemployment: 6.1%. Median home value: $133,500. Median travel time to work: 17.8 minutes.

IMPERIAL COUNTY

940 W Main St Rm 208   Ph: 760-482-4427
El Centro, CA 92243
www.co.imperial.ca.us

In SE CA on border with Baja California; organized Aug 15, 1907 from San Diego County. Name Origin: For the Imperial Valley, itself named for the Imperial Land Company that was organized to colonize the southern Colorado Desert.

Area (sq mi): 4481.73 (land 4174.73; water 307).

Pop: 142,361 (White 20.2%; Black or African American 4%; Hispanic or Latino 72.2%; Asian 2%; Other 44.7%). Foreign born: 32.2%. Median age: 31. State rank: 31. Pop change 1990-2000: +30.2%.

Income: per capita $13,239; median household $31,870. Pop below poverty level: 22.6%.

Unemployment: 21.3%. Median home value: $100,000. Median travel time to work: 20.3 minutes.

INYO COUNTY

PO Drawer N   Ph: 760-878-0292
Independence, CA 93526   Fax: 760-878-2241
www.countyofinyo.org

On E border of CA, E of Fresno; organized Mar 22, 1866 from Tulare County. Name Origin: For the Inyo Mountains, from an Indian name said to mean 'where the great spirit dwells.'

Area (sq mi): 10,226.98 (land 10203.1; water 23.88).

Pop: 17,945 (White 74.4%; Black or African American 0.2%; Hispanic or Latino 12.6%; Asian 0.9%; Other 18.8%). Foreign born: 7.6%. Median age: 42.8. State rank: 52. Pop change 1990-2000: -1.8%.

Income: per capita $19,639; median household $35,006. Pop below poverty level: 12.6%.

Unemployment: 4.9%. Median home value: $161,300. Median travel time to work: 15.2 minutes.

KERN COUNTY

1115 Truxtun Ave 5th Fl   Ph: 661-868-3198
Bakersfield, CA 93301   Fax: 661-868-3190
www.co.kern.ca.us

In SW CA, N of Los Angeles; organized Apr 2, 1866 from Los Angeles and Tulare counties. Name Origin: For the Kern River, which was named in 1845 by explorer John C. Fremont (1813-90) for Edward M. Kern, the topographer and artist for the expedition.

Area (sq mi): 8161.42 (land 8140.96; water 20.46).

Pop: 661,645 (White 49.5%; Black or African American 6%; Hispanic or Latino 38.4%; Asian 3.4%; Other 28.9%). Foreign born: 16.9%. Median age: 30.6. State rank: 14. Pop change 1990-2000: +21.7%.

Income: per capita $15,760; median household $35,446. Pop below poverty level: 20.8%.

Unemployment: 10.5%. Median home value: $93,300. Median travel time to work: 23.2 minutes.

KINGS COUNTY

1400 W Lacey Blvd   Ph: 559-582-3211
Hanford, CA 93230
www.co.kings.ca.us

In central CA, S of Fresno; organized Mar 22, 1893 from Tulare County. Name Origin: For the Kings River, which flows through the county, itself from Spanish *Rio de los Santos Reyes* 'River of the Holy Kings,' for the Biblical figures known in English as the Three Wise Men or Magi; river discovered on Jan 6, 1806, their feast day.

Area (sq mi): 1391.49 (land 1390.99; water 0.5).

Pop: 129,461 (White 41.6%; Black or African American 8.3%; Hispanic or Latino 43.6%; Asian 3.1%; Other 35%). Foreign born: 16%. Median age: 30.2. State rank: 32. Pop change 1990-2000: +27.6%.

Income: per capita $15,848; median household $35,749. Pop below poverty level: 19.5%.

Unemployment: 13.8%. Median home value: $97,600. Median travel time to work: 20.8 minutes.

LAKE COUNTY

255 N Forbes St   Ph: 707-263-2371
Lakeport, CA 95453   Fax: 707-263-2207
www.co.lake.ca.us

In NW CA, N of San Francisco; organized May 20, 1861 from Napa County. Name Origin: For Clear Lake, the principal feature of the county.

Please see sample entry on inside front cover for detailed information about the statistics presented with each county listing.

Area (sq mi): 1329.48 (land 1257.96; water 71.52).

Pop: 58,309 (White 80.5%; Black or African American 2.1%; Hispanic or Latino 11.4%; Asian 0.8%; Other 10.8%). **Foreign born:** 6.6%. **Median age:** 42.7. **State rank:** 40. **Pop change 1990-2000:** +15.2%.

Income: per capita $16,825; median household $29,627. **Pop below poverty level:** 17.6%.

Unemployment: 7.3%. **Median home value:** $122,600. **Median travel time to work:** 29.1 minutes.

LASSEN COUNTY
220 S Lassen St Suite 5   **Ph:** 530-251-8217
Susanville, CA 96130   **Fax:** 530-257-3480
www.co.lassen.ca.us

In NE CA; organized Apr 1, 1864 from Plumas and Shasta counties. **Name Origin:** For Peter Lassen (1793-1895), a Danish-born pioneer.

Area (sq mi): 4720.37 (land 4557.27; water 163.1).

Pop: 33,828 (White 70.6%; Black or African American 8.8%; Hispanic or Latino 13.8%; Asian 0.7%; Other 9.6%). **Foreign born:** 2.3%. **Median age:** 34.6. **State rank:** 47. **Pop change 1990-2000:** +22.6%.

Income: per capita $14,749; median household $36,310. **Pop below poverty level:** 14%.

Unemployment: 6.8%. **Median home value:** $106,700. **Median travel time to work:** 19.4 minutes.

LOS ANGELES COUNTY
500 W Temple St   **Ph:** 213-974-1311
Los Angeles, CA 90012
lacounty.info

On SW coast of CA; original county; organized Feb 18, 1850 (prior to statehood). **Name Origin:** For the city.

Area (sq mi): 4752.32 (land 4060.87; water 691.45).

Pop: 9,519,338 (White 31.1%; Black or African American 9.8%; Hispanic or Latino 44.6%; Asian 11.9%; Other 29.5%). **Foreign born:** 36.2%. **Median age:** 32. **State rank:** 1. **Pop change 1990-2000:** +7.4%.

Income: per capita $20,683; median household $42,189. **Pop below poverty level:** 17.9%.

Unemployment: 5.6%. **Median home value:** $209,300. **Median travel time to work:** 29.4 minutes.

MADERA COUNTY
209 W Yosemite Ave   **Ph:** 559-675-7721
Madera, CA 93637   **Fax:** 559-675-7870
www.madera-county.com

In central CA, N of Fresno; organized Mar 11, 1893 from Fresno County. **Name Origin:** Spanish for 'lumber' because the town around which the county developed was a lumbering center.

Area (sq mi): 2153.32 (land 2135.86; water 17.46).

Pop: 123,109 (White 46.6%; Black or African American 4.1%; Hispanic or Latino 44.3%; Asian 1.3%; Other 32.4%). **Foreign born:**

20.1%. **Median age:** 32.7. **State rank:** 35. **Pop change 1990-2000:** +39.8%.

Income: per capita $14,682; median household $36,286. **Pop below poverty level:** 21.4%.

Unemployment: 12.1%. **Median home value:** $118,800. **Median travel time to work:** 26.3 minutes.

MARIN COUNTY
PO Box 4988   **Ph:** 415-499-6407
San Rafael, CA 94913
www.marin.org

Located on N coast of California, N of San Francisco; organized in 1850. **Name Origin:** Two main theories: 1) From the old Spanish name of San Rafael Bay, *Bahia de Nuestra Senora del Rosario la Marinera*, 'Bay of Our Lady of the Rosary, Mariner's Patron'; this name was given in 1775 by the surveyor Ayala. 2) For the name of a mythical Indian leader, transliterated to Marin; also applied to the islands in San Rafael Bay.

Area (sq mi): 828.2 (land 519.8; water 308.39).

Pop: 247,289 (White 78.6%; Black or African American 2.9%; Hispanic or Latino 11.1%; Asian 4.5%; Other 8.6%). **Foreign born:** 16.6%. **Median age:** 41.3. **State rank:** 24. **Pop change 1990-2000:** +7.5%.

Income: per capita $44,962; median household $71,306. **Pop below poverty level:** 6.6%.

Unemployment: 2.5%. **Median home value:** $514,600. **Median travel time to work:** 32.3 minutes.

MARIPOSA COUNTY
PO Box 28   **Ph:** 209-966-2005
Mariposa, CA 95338   **Fax:** 209-742-6860
www.mariposacounty.org

In central CA, E of San Francisco; original county; organized Feb 18, 1850 (prior to statehood). **Name Origin:** Spanish 'butterfly,' a name originally applied to an area in the county in which butterflies were numerous.

Area (sq mi): 1462.79 (land 1451.12; water 11.67).

Pop: 17,130 (White 84.9%; Black or African American 0.7%; Hispanic or Latino 7.8%; Asian 0.7%; Other 9.7%). **Foreign born:** 2.8%. **Median age:** 42.9. **State rank:** 53. **Pop change 1990-2000:** +19.8%.

Income: per capita $18,190; median household $34,626. **Pop below poverty level:** 14.8%.

Unemployment: 6.3%. **Median home value:** $141,900. **Median travel time to work:** 32.1 minutes.

MENDOCINO COUNTY
501 Low Gap Rd Rm 1020   **Ph:** 707-463-4376
Ukiah, CA 95482   **Fax:** 707-463-4257
www.co.mendocino.ca.us

On N coast of California; original county; organized Feb 18, 1850 (prior to statehood). **Name Origin:** For Cabo (Cape) Mendocino, which early records indicate was named for Antonio de Mendoza (c. 1485-1552), viceroy of New Spain in 1542, or Lorenzo Suarez

---

All statistics are based on the 2000 Census except the dollar figures given for per capita income, which are based on 1999 estimates.

de Mendoza, viceroy of New Spain (1580-83). Name merely means someone from Mendoza.

Area (sq mi): 3878.14 (land 3508.97; water 369.17).

Pop: 86,265 (White 74.9%; Black or African American 0.6%; Hispanic or Latino 16.5%; Asian 1.2%; Other 17.4%). **Foreign born:** 10.2%. **Median age:** 38.9. **State rank:** 37. **Pop change 1990-2000:** +7.4%.

Income: per capita $19,443; median household $35,996. **Pop below poverty level:** 15.9%.

Unemployment: 6.6%. **Median home value:** $170,200. **Median travel time to work:** 20.3 minutes.

MERCED COUNTY
2222 M St
Merced, CA 95340
www.co.merced.ca.us

Ph: 209-385-7637
Fax: 209-385-7375

In central CA, SE of San Francisco; organized Apr 19, 1855 from Mariposa County. **Name Origin:** Spanish 'mercy', from the original Spanish name of Lake Merced, *Nuestra Senora de la Merced* 'Our Lady of Mercy.'

Area (sq mi): 1971.87 (land 1928.69; water 43.18).

Pop: 210,554 (White 40.6%; Black or African American 3.8%; Hispanic or Latino 45.3%; Asian 6.8%; Other 33.2%). **Foreign born:** 24.8%. **Median age:** 29. **State rank:** 26. **Pop change 1990-2000:** +18%.

Income: per capita $14,257; median household $35,532. **Pop below poverty level:** 21.7%.

Unemployment: 14%. **Median home value:** $111,100. **Median travel time to work:** 26 minutes.

MODOC COUNTY
PO Box 130
Alturas, CA 96101

Ph: 530-233-6200
Fax: 530-233-2434

In NE CA; organized Feb 17, 1874 from Siskiyou County. **Name Origin:** For the Modoc Indian tribe, who had been subdued in the Modoc War of 1872-73. The name, derived from *moatokni*, means 'southerners.'

Area (sq mi): 4203.37 (land 3944.1; water 259.28).

Pop: 9,449 (White 81.1%; Black or African American 0.7%; Hispanic or Latino 11.5%; Asian 0.6%; Other 12.8%). **Foreign born:** 5.9%. **Median age:** 41.8. **State rank:** 56. **Pop change 1990-2000:** -2.4%.

Income: per capita $17,285; median household $27,522. **Pop below poverty level:** 21.5%.

Unemployment: 7%. **Median home value:** $69,100. **Median travel time to work:** 13.4 minutes.

MONO COUNTY
PO Box 237
Bridgeport, CA 93517

Ph: 760-932-5530
Fax: 760-932-5531

On W central border of CA and NV; organized Apr 24, 1861 from Calaveras and Fresno counties. **Name Origin:** For Mono Lake; the lake's name is probably a Spanish-influenced shortened form of a

Shoshonean tribal name, *monache* or *monachi* 'fly people'; their staple food was the pupae of a fly.

Area (sq mi): 3131.8 (land 3044.4; water 87.4).

Pop: 12,853 (White 76.5%; Black or African American 0.5%; Hispanic or Latino 17.7%; Asian 1.1%; Other 14.2%). **Foreign born:** 12.4%. **Median age:** 36. **State rank:** 55. **Pop change 1990-2000:** +29.1%.

Income: per capita $23,422; median household $44,992. **Pop below poverty level:** 11.5%.

Unemployment: 5.2%. **Median home value:** $236,300. **Median travel time to work:** 16.4 minutes.

MONTEREY COUNTY
PO Box 180
Salinas, CA 93902
www.co.monterey.ca.us

Ph: 831-755-5115
Fax: 831-757-5792

On central coast of CA; original county; organized Feb 18, 1850 (prior to statehood). **Name Origin:** For Monterey Bay.

Area (sq mi): 3771.07 (land 3321.95; water 449.12).

Pop: 401,762 (White 40.3%; Black or African American 3.7%; Hispanic or Latino 46.8%; Asian 6%; Other 34.2%). **Foreign born:** 29%. **Median age:** 31.7. **State rank:** 18. **Pop change 1990-2000:** +13%.

Income: per capita $20,165; median household $48,305. **Pop below poverty level:** 13.5%.

Unemployment: 9.3%. **Median home value:** $265,800. **Median travel time to work:** 23.2 minutes.

NAPA COUNTY
1195 3rd St Rm 310
Napa, CA 94559
www.co.napa.ca.us

Ph: 707-253-4421
Fax: 707-253-4176

In NW CA, N of San Francisco; original county; organized Feb 18, 1850 (prior to statehood). World-famous wine-making area. **Name Origin:** For the valley, whose name is possibly that of an Indian tribe that formerly inhabited the area.

Area (sq mi): 788.27 (land 753.73; water 34.53).

Pop: 124,279 (White 69.1%; Black or African American 1.3%; Hispanic or Latino 23.7%; Asian 3%; Other 15.6%). **Foreign born:** 18.1%. **Median age:** 38.3. **State rank:** 34. **Pop change 1990-2000:** +12.2%.

Income: per capita $26,395; median household $51,738. **Pop below poverty level:** 8.3%.

Unemployment: 3.3%. **Median home value:** $251,300. **Median travel time to work:** 24.3 minutes.

NEVADA COUNTY
201 Church St Suite 5
Nevada City, CA 95959
www.co.nevada.ca.us

Ph: 530-265-1293
Fax: 530-478-5627

On NE border of CA and NV; organized Apr 25, 1851 from Yuba County. **Name Origin:** For Nevada City, named for the Sierra Nevada range, from the Spanish words meaning 'snow-covered mountain range.'

Please see sample entry on inside front cover for detailed information about the statistics presented with each county listing.

Area (sq mi): 974.49 (land 957.61; water 16.88).

Pop: 92,033 (White 90.3%; Black or African American 0.3%; Hispanic or Latino 5.7%; Asian 0.8%; Other 5.5%). **Foreign born:** 4.4%. **Median age:** 43.1. **State rank:** 36. **Pop change 1990-2000:** +17.2%.

Income: per capita $24,007; median household $45,864. **Pop below poverty level:** 8.1%.

Unemployment: 3.7%. **Median home value:** $205,700. **Median travel time to work:** 26 minutes.

ORANGE COUNTY

12 Civic Center Plaza   **Ph:** 714-834-2500
Santa Ana, CA 92702   **Fax:** 714-834-2675
www.oc.ca.gov

On SW coast of CA, S of Los Angeles; organized Mar 11, 1889 from Los Angeles County. **Name Origin:** For local orange groves.

Area (sq mi): 947.98 (land 789.4; water 158.57).

Pop: 2,846,289 (White 51.3%; Black or African American 1.7%; Hispanic or Latino 30.8%; Asian 13.6%; Other 19.9%). **Foreign born:** 29.9%. **Median age:** 33.3. **State rank:** 2. **Pop change 1990-2000:** +18.1%.

Income: per capita $25,826; median household $58,820. **Pop below poverty level:** 10.3%.

Unemployment: 3%. **Median home value:** $270,000. **Median travel time to work:** 27.2 minutes.

PLACER COUNTY

2954 Richardson Dr   **Ph:** 530-886-5600
Auburn, CA 95603   **Fax:** 530-886-5687
www.placer.ca.gov

On NE border of CA and NV; county organized 1851 from Yuba and Sutter counties. **Name Origin:** For the many placer deposits in the county's territory.

Area (sq mi): 1502.78 (land 1404.37; water 98.41).

Pop: 248,399 (White 83.4%; Black or African American 0.8%; Hispanic or Latino 9.7%; Asian 2.9%; Other 7.7%). **Foreign born:** 7.1%. **Median age:** 38. **State rank:** 23. **Pop change 1990-2000:** +43.8%.

Income: per capita $27,963; median household $57,535. **Pop below poverty level:** 5.8%.

Unemployment: 3.6%. **Median home value:** $213,900. **Median travel time to work:** 27 minutes.

PLUMAS COUNTY

520 Main St Rm 104   **Ph:** 530-283-6305
Quincy, CA 95971   **Fax:** 530-283-6415
www.countyofplumas.com

On NE border of CA and NV; organized Mar 18, 1854, from Butte County. **Name Origin:** Spanish 'feathers,' for the Feather River, once known as *Rio de las Plumas.* Named by John A. Sutter, first settler in the Sacramento Valley, for the quantities of feathers found all around it with which the Indians decorated themselves and made blankets.

Area (sq mi): 2613.48 (land 2553.69; water 59.78).

Pop: 20,824 (White 88.7%; Black or African American 0.6%; Hispanic or Latino 5.7%; Asian 0.5%; Other 7%). **Foreign born:** 2.5%. **Median age:** 44.2. **State rank:** 50. **Pop change 1990-2000:** +5.5%.

Income: per capita $19,391; median household $36,351. **Pop below poverty level:** 13.1%.

Unemployment: 8.4%. **Median home value:** $137,900. **Median travel time to work:** 19.5 minutes.

RIVERSIDE COUNTY

4080 Lemon St 12th Fl   **Ph:** 909-955-1100
Riverside, CA 92501   **Fax:** 909-955-1105
www.co.riverside.ca.us

In S CA; organized Mar 11, 1893, from San Bernardino and San Diego counties. **Name Origin:** For the city.

Area (sq mi): 7303.13 (land 7207.37; water 95.76).

Pop: 1,545,387 (White 51%; Black or African American 6.2%; Hispanic or Latino 36.2%; Asian 3.7%; Other 24.6%). **Foreign born:** 19%. **Median age:** 33.1. **State rank:** 6. **Pop change 1990-2000:** +32%.

Income: per capita $18,689; median household $42,887. **Pop below poverty level:** 14.2%.

Unemployment: 5.2%. **Median home value:** $146,500. **Median travel time to work:** 31.2 minutes.

SACRAMENTO COUNTY

700 H St Rm 7650   **Ph:** 916-874-5833
Sacramento, CA 95814   **Fax:** 916-874-5885
www.co.sacramento.ca.us

In N central CA; original county; organized Feb 18, 1850 (prior to statehood). **Name Origin:** For the Sacramento River.

Area (sq mi): 995.48 (land 965.65; water 29.83).

Pop: 1,223,499 (White 57.8%; Black or African American 10%; Hispanic or Latino 16%; Asian 11%; Other 15%). **Foreign born:** 16.1%. **Median age:** 33.8. **State rank:** 8. **Pop change 1990-2000:** +17.5%.

Income: per capita $21,142; median household $43,816. **Pop below poverty level:** 14.1%.

Unemployment: 4.2%. **Median home value:** $144,200. **Median travel time to work:** 25.4 minutes.

SAN BENITO COUNTY

440 5th St Rm 206   **Ph:** 831-636-4029
Hollister, CA 95023   **Fax:** 831-636-2939
www.san-benito.ca.us

In W central CA, east of Monterey; organized Feb 12, 1874 from Monterey County. **Name Origin:** For San Benito, 'Saint Benedict,' the original name of San Juan Creek.

Area (sq mi): 1390.73 (land 1389.06; water 1.68).

Pop: 53,234 (White 46%; Black or African American 1.1%; Hispanic or Latino 47.9%; Asian 2.4%; Other 31.4%). **Foreign born:** 18.8%. **Median age:** 31.4. **State rank:** 43. **Pop change 1990-2000:** +45.1%.

Income: per capita $20,932; median household $57,469. **Pop below poverty level:** 10%.

All statistics are based on the 2000 Census except the dollar figures given for per capita income, which are based on 1999 estimates.

Unemployment: 8.3%. **Median home value:** $284,000. **Median travel time to work:** 33.7 minutes.

SAN BERNARDINO COUNTY

222 W Hospitality Ln
San Bernardino, CA 92415
www.co.san-bernardino.ca.us

Ph: 909-387-8306
Fax: 909-376-8940

In SE CA, east of Los Angeles; organized in 1853 from Los Angeles County. Largest county in the U.S. in land area, 20,105 sq. mi. **Name Origin:** Named for the city, Spanish 'Saint Bernard [of Siena].'

Area (sq mi): 20,105.32 (land 20052.5; water 52.82).

Pop: 1,709,434 (White 44%; Black or African American 9.1%; Hispanic or Latino 39.2%; Asian 4.7%; Other 27.3%). **Foreign born:** 18.6%. **Median age:** 30.3. **State rank:** 4. **Pop change 1990-2000:** +20.5%.

Income: per capita $16,856; median household $42,066. **Pop below poverty level:** 15.8%.

Unemployment: 4.8%. **Median home value:** $131,500. **Median travel time to work:** 31 minutes.

SAN DIEGO COUNTY

1600 Pacific Hwy
San Diego, CA 92101
www.co.san-diego.ca.us

Ph: 619-237-0502
Fax: 619-557-4155

In SW CA on border with Baja California; original county; organized Feb 18, 1850 (prior to statehood). **Name Origin:** For the bay, named for San Diego de Alcala de Henares (Saint Didacus), Spanish Franciscan saint of the 15th century.

Area (sq mi): 4525.52 (land 4199.89; water 325.62).

Pop: 2,813,833 (White 55%; Black or African American 5.7%; Hispanic or Latino 26.7%; Asian 8.9%; Other 18.9%). **Foreign born:** 21.5%. **Median age:** 33.2. **State rank:** 3. **Pop change 1990-2000:** +12.6%.

Income: per capita $22,926; median household $47,067. **Pop below poverty level:** 12.4%.

Unemployment: 3.2%. **Median home value:** $227,200. **Median travel time to work:** 25.3 minutes.

SAN FRANCISCO COUNTY

1 Dr Carleton B Goodlett Pl
San Francisco, CA 94102
www.ci.sf.ca.us

Ph: 415-554-4950

On N coast of CA; original county; organized Feb 18, 1850 (prior to statehood). **Name Origin:** For the bay, named for Saint Francis of Assisi (c. 1181-1226).

Area (sq mi): 231.92 (land 46.69; water 185.22).

Pop: 776,733 (White 43.6%; Black or African American 7.8%; Hispanic or Latino 14.1%; Asian 30.8%; Other 11.7%). **Foreign born:** 36.8%. **Median age:** 36.5. **State rank:** 11. **Pop change 1990-2000:** +7.3%.

Income: per capita $34,556; median household $55,221. **Pop below poverty level:** 11.3%.

Unemployment: 5.2%. **Median home value:** $396,400. **Median travel time to work:** 30.7 minutes.

SAN JOAQUIN COUNTY

222 E Weber St Rm 707
Stockton, CA 95202
www.co.san-joaquin.ca.us

Ph: 209-468-3211
Fax: 209-468-2875

In N central CA, E of San Francisco; original county; organized Feb 18, 1850 (prior to statehood). **Name Origin:** For the river, named for Saint Joachim, father of the Virgin Mary.

Area (sq mi): 1426.25 (land 1399.28; water 26.97).

Pop: 563,598 (White 47.4%; Black or African American 6.7%; Hispanic or Latino 30.5%; Asian 11.4%; Other 23.7%). **Foreign born:** 19.5%. **Median age:** 31.9. **State rank:** 15. **Pop change 1990-2000:** +17.3%.

Income: per capita $17,365; median household $41,282. **Pop below poverty level:** 17.7%.

Unemployment: 8.7%. **Median home value:** $142,400. **Median travel time to work:** 29.2 minutes.

SAN LUIS OBISPO COUNTY

1144 Monterey St Suite A
San Luis Obispo, CA 93408
www.slocounty.org

Ph: 805-781-5245
Fax: 805-781-1111

On central coast of CA; original county; organized Feb 18, 1850 (prior to statehood). **Name Origin:** For the mission, named for Saint Louis, Bishop of Toulouse, son of King Charles II of Naples and Sicily.

Area (sq mi): 3615.54 (land 3304.32; water 311.22).

Pop: 246,681 (White 76.1%; Black or African American 2%; Hispanic or Latino 16.3%; Asian 2.7%; Other 10.6%). **Foreign born:** 8.9%. **Median age:** 37.3. **State rank:** 25. **Pop change 1990-2000:** +13.6%.

Income: per capita $21,864; median household $42,428. **Pop below poverty level:** 12.8%.

Unemployment: 2.8%. **Median home value:** $230,000. **Median travel time to work:** 21.1 minutes.

SAN MATEO COUNTY

555 County Ctr
Redwood City, CA 94063
www.co.sanmateo.ca.us

Ph: 650-363-4712
Fax: 650-363-4843

On N central coast of CA, S of San Francisco; organized Apr 19, 1856 from San Francisco County. **Name Origin:** For the creek, named for Saint Matthew the Apostle.

Area (sq mi): 741.01 (land 449.07; water 291.95).

Pop: 707,161 (White 49.8%; Black or African American 3.5%; Hispanic or Latino 21.9%; Asian 20%; Other 16.9%). **Foreign born:** 32.3%. **Median age:** 36.8. **State rank:** 13. **Pop change 1990-2000:** +8.9%.

Income: per capita $36,045; median household $70,819. **Pop below poverty level:** 5.8%.

Unemployment: 2.8%. **Median home value:** $469,200. **Median travel time to work:** 27 minutes.

Please see sample entry on inside front cover for detailed information about the statistics presented with each county listing.

SANTA BARBARA COUNTY

PO Box 159   **Ph:** 805-568-2550
Santa Barbara, CA 93102   **Fax:** 805-568-3247
www.countyofsb.org

On S coast of CA, northwest of Los Angeles; original county; organized Feb 18, 1850 (prior to statehood). **Name Origin:** For the channel named for Saint Barbara.

Area (sq mi): 3789.08 (land 2737.01; water 1052.07).

Pop: 399,347 (White 56.9%; Black or African American 2.3%; Hispanic or Latino 34.2%; Asian 4.1%; Other 20.9%). **Foreign born:** 21.2%. **Median age:** 33.4. **State rank:** 19. **Pop change 1990-2000:** +8%.

Income: per capita $23,059; median household $46,677. **Pop below poverty level:** 14.3%.

Unemployment: 3.5%. **Median home value:** $293,000. **Median travel time to work:** 19.3 minutes.

SANTA CLARA COUNTY

70 W Hedding St   **Ph:** 408-299-2424
San Jose, CA 95110   **Fax:** 408-293-5649
claraweb.co.santa-clara.ca.us

In W central CA, north of Monterey; original county; organized Feb 18, 1850 (prior to statehood). **Name Origin:** For the river named for Saint Clare of Assisi.

Area (sq mi): 1304.01 (land 1290.69; water 13.32).

Pop: 1,682,585 (White 44.2%; Black or African American 2.8%; Hispanic or Latino 24%; Asian 25.6%; Other 17.8%). **Foreign born:** 34.1%. **Median age:** 34. **State rank:** 5. **Pop change 1990-2000:** +12.4%.

Income: per capita $32,795; median household $74,335. **Pop below poverty level:** 7.5%.

Unemployment: 4.5%. **Median home value:** $446,400. **Median travel time to work:** 26.1 minutes.

SANTA CRUZ COUNTY

701 Ocean St Rm 230   **Ph:** 831-454-2800
Santa Cruz, CA 95060
www.co.santa-cruz.ca.us

On S central coast of CA; original county; organized Feb 18, 1850 (prior to statehood). **Name Origin:** Spanish 'holy cross,' a common Spanish placename. Originally named *Branciforte* for the viceroy, but changed Apr 6, 1850.

Area (sq mi): 607.16 (land 445.24; water 161.92).

Pop: 255,602 (White 65.5%; Black or African American 1%; Hispanic or Latino 26.8%; Asian 3.4%; Other 20.5%). **Foreign born:** 18.2%. **Median age:** 35. **State rank:** 22. **Pop change 1990-2000:** +11.3%.

Income: per capita $26,396; median household $53,998. **Pop below poverty level:** 11.9%.

Unemployment: 6.1%. **Median home value:** $377,500. **Median travel time to work:** 27.8 minutes.

SHASTA COUNTY

PO Box 990880   **Ph:** 530-225-5378
Redding, CA 96099   **Fax:** 530-225-5454
www.co.shasta.ca.us

In N central CA, north of Chico; original county; organized Feb 18, 1850 (prior to statehood). **Name Origin:** For the Indian tribe of Hokan linguistic stock; the original meaning is uncertain. Also spelled *Sasty, Sastise, Chasty, Chasta.*

Area (sq mi): 3847.44 (land 3785.19; water 62.24).

Pop: 163,256 (White 86.4%; Black or African American 0.8%; Hispanic or Latino 5.5%; Asian 1.9%; Other 8.1%). **Foreign born:** 4%. **Median age:** 38.9. **State rank:** 29. **Pop change 1990-2000:** +11%.

Income: per capita $17,738; median household $34,335. **Pop below poverty level:** 15.4%.

Unemployment: 6.7%. **Median home value:** $120,800. **Median travel time to work:** 20.9 minutes.

SIERRA COUNTY

PO Drawer D   **Ph:** 530-289-3295
Downieville, CA 95936   **Fax:** 530-289-2830
www.sierracounty.ws/

On NE border of CA with NV; organized Apr 16, 1852 from Yuba County. **Name Origin:** Spanish 'mountain range,' for its location in the northern part of the Sierra Nevada.

Area (sq mi): 961.97 (land 953.38; water 8.59).

Pop: 3,555 (White 90.3%; Black or African American 0.2%; Hispanic or Latino 6%; Asian 0.2%; Other 5.4%). **Foreign born:** 3%. **Median age:** 43.7. **State rank:** 57. **Pop change 1990-2000:** +7.1%.

Income: per capita $18,815; median household $35,827. **Pop below poverty level:** 11.3%.

Unemployment: 9.7%. **Median home value:** $128,600. **Median travel time to work:** 29 minutes.

SISKIYOU COUNTY

PO Box 750   **Ph:** 530-842-8005
Yreka, CA 96097   **Fax:** 530-842-8013
www.co.siskiyou.ca.us

In N central CA on OR border; organized Mar 22, 1852 from Klamath and Shasta counties, and in 1874 annexed part of Klamath County. Site of Mt. Shasta, 14,162 ft. **Name Origin:** Possibly Chinook from Cree for 'bob-tailed horse,' or French *six cailloux* 'six boulders.'

Area (sq mi): 6347.46 (land 6286.78; water 60.68).

Pop: 44,301 (White 83.3%; Black or African American 1.3%; Hispanic or Latino 7.6%; Asian 1.2%; Other 10.4%). **Foreign born:** 5.4%. **Median age:** 43. **State rank:** 44. **Pop change 1990-2000:** +1.8%.

Income: per capita $17,570; median household $29,530. **Pop below poverty level:** 18.6%.

Unemployment: 9.4%. **Median home value:** $100,300. **Median travel time to work:** 18.2 minutes.

All statistics are based on the 2000 Census except the dollar figures given for per capita income, which are based on 1999 estimates.

SOLANO COUNTY

600 Texas St
Fairfield, CA 94533
www.co.solano.ca.us

Ph: 707-421-7485
Fax: 707-421-6311

In N central CA, NE of San Francisco; original county; organized Feb 18, 1850 (prior to statehood). **Name Origin:** For Saint Francis Solano and for Sem-yeto, a chief of the Soscol and Suisun Indians, who had accepted the Christian name of the saint at his baptism.

Area (sq mi): 906.67 (land 829.19; water 77.48).

Pop: 394,542 (White 49.2%; Black or African American 14.9%; Hispanic or Latino 17.6%; Asian 12.7%; Other 16%). **Foreign born:** 16.9%. **Median age:** 33.9. **State rank:** 20. **Pop change 1990-2000:** +15.9%.

Income: per capita $21,731; median household $54,099. **Pop below poverty level:** 8.3%.

Unemployment: 4.1%. **Median home value:** $178,300. **Median travel time to work:** 31.8 minutes.

SONOMA COUNTY

575 Administration Dr Suite 104A
Santa Rosa, CA 95403
www.sonoma-county.org

Ph: 707-565-2431
Fax: 707-565-3778

On NW coast of CA, north of San Francisco; original county; organized Feb 18, 1850 (prior to statehood). **Name Origin:** For the city, named for a Wintun Indian group that lived in the Sacramento Valley. The name means 'nose' but the reason in unknown; possibly referring to the shape of a peak. A fanciful interpretation is 'valley of the moon.'

Area (sq mi): 1768.23 (land 1575.88; water 192.35).

Pop: 458,614 (White 74.5%; Black or African American 1.4%; Hispanic or Latino 17.3%; Asian 3.1%; Other 13.9%). **Foreign born:** 14.3%. **Median age:** 37.5. **State rank:** 16. **Pop change 1990-2000:** +18.1%.

Income: per capita $25,724; median household $53,076. **Pop below poverty level:** 8.1%.

Unemployment: 2.9%. **Median home value:** $273,200. **Median travel time to work:** 26.8 minutes.

STANISLAUS COUNTY

1021 'I' St
Modesto, CA 95354
www.co.stanislaus.ca.us

Ph: 209-525-5251
Fax: 209-525-5213

In central CA, E of San Francisco; organized Apr 1, 1854, from Tuolumne County. **Name Origin:** For the Stanislaus River, the baptismal name of an Indian leader who fought bravely there. John C. Fremont (1813-90) used the anglicization of Spanish *Estanislao*.

Area (sq mi): 1514.67 (land 1493.79; water 20.88).

Pop: 446,997 (White 57.3%; Black or African American 2.6%; Hispanic or Latino 31.7%; Asian 4.2%; Other 23.8%). **Foreign born:** 18.3%. **Median age:** 31.7. **State rank:** 17. **Pop change 1990-2000:** +20.6%.

Income: per capita $16,913; median household $40,101. **Pop below poverty level:** 16%.

Unemployment: 10.2%. **Median home value:** $125,300. **Median travel time to work:** 26.8 minutes.

SUTTER COUNTY

PO Box 1555
Yuba City, CA 95992
www.co.sutter.ca.us

Ph: 530-822-7120
Fax: 530-822-7214

In N central CA, NW of Sacramento; original county; organized Feb 18, 1850 (prior to statehood). **Name Origin:** For Sutter's Creek, named for John Augustus Sutter (Johann August Suter 1803-80), on whose property gold was discovered in 1848, the beginning of the California Gold Rush.

Area (sq mi): 608.58 (land 602.54; water 6.04).

Pop: 78,930 (White 60.2%; Black or African American 1.9%; Hispanic or Latino 22.2%; Asian 11.3%; Other 19.4%). **Foreign born:** 19.3%. **Median age:** 34.1. **State rank:** 38. **Pop change 1990-2000:** +22.5%.

Income: per capita $17,428; median household $38,375. **Pop below poverty level:** 15.5%.

Unemployment: 12.3%. **Median home value:** $120,700. **Median travel time to work:** 25.4 minutes.

TEHAMA COUNTY

PO Box 250
Red Bluff, CA 96080

Ph: 530-527-3350
Fax: 530-527-1745

In N central CA, north of Chico; organized Apr 9, 1856 from Butte, Colusa, and Shasta counties. **Name Origin:** For the city, origin and meaning uncertain. It is almost certainly Indian, though an Arabian generic *tihama* 'hot lowlands' is frequently found in Arabic placenames. The Indian parallel term may also mean 'lowlands' or shallow,' as in a ford of a river.

Area (sq mi): 2962.27 (land 2950.99; water 11.28).

Pop: 56,039 (White 78.5%; Black or African American 0.6%; Hispanic or Latino 15.8%; Asian 0.8%; Other 13.9%). **Foreign born:** 7.9%. **Median age:** 37.8. **State rank:** 41. **Pop change 1990-2000:** +12.9%.

Income: per capita $15,793; median household $31,206. **Pop below poverty level:** 17.3%.

Unemployment: 6.4%. **Median home value:** $103,000. **Median travel time to work:** 22.4 minutes.

TRINITY COUNTY

PO Box 1215
Weaverville, CA 96093
www.trinitycounty.org

Ph: 530-623-1222
Fax: 530-623-8398

In NW CA, west of Redding; original county; organized Feb 18, 1850 (prior to statehood). **Name Origin:** For the Trinity River, named by Pierson B. Reading in 1845, who believed it entered Trinidad Bay. (Trinity is the English version of the Spanish Trinidad.)

Area (sq mi): 3207.54 (land 3178.61; water 28.93).

Pop: 13,022 (White 86.6%; Black or African American 0.4%; Hispanic or Latino 4%; Asian 0.5%; Other 10.2%). **Foreign born:** 1.6%. **Median age:** 44.6. **State rank:** 54. **Pop change 1990-2000:** -0.3%.

Income: per capita $16,868; median household $27,711. **Pop below poverty level:** 18.7%.

Unemployment: 10.9%. **Median home value:** $112,000. **Median travel time to work:** 24 minutes.

Please see sample entry on inside front cover for detailed information about the statistics presented with each county listing.

TULARE COUNTY
2800 W Burrel Ave
Visalia, CA 93291
www.co.tulare.ca.us

Ph: 559-733-6271
Fax: 559-733-6898

In central CA, southeast of Fresno; organized Apr 20, 1852, from Mariposa County. **Name Origin:** For Tulare Lake, Mexican-Spanish 'rush' or 'reed,' perhaps originally from Aztec *tullin* or *tollin*, 'cattail' or 'bulrush.'

Area (sq mi): 4839.09 (land 4823.97; water 15.12).

Pop: 368,021 (White 41.8%; Black or African American 1.6%; Hispanic or Latino 50.8%; Asian 3.3%; Other 37.1%). **Foreign born:** 22.6%. **Median age:** 29.2. **State rank:** 21. **Pop change 1990-2000:** +18%.

Income: per capita $14,006; median household $33,983. **Pop below poverty level:** 23.9%.

Unemployment: 15.4%. **Median home value:** $97,800. **Median travel time to work:** 21.9 minutes.

TUOLUMNE COUNTY
2 S Green St
Sonora, CA 95370
www.tcchamber.com

Ph: 209-533-5511
Fax: 209-533-5510

In E central CA, east of Stockton; original county; organized Feb 18, 1850 (prior to statehood). **Name Origin:** For the Tuolumne River, named for either the Central Miwok or Yokut Indians, of Penutian linguistic stock. Name is believed to be a corruption of Indian *talmalamne* 'cluster of stone wigwams': they lived in caves or recesses in the rocks. Variously spelled *Taulamne*, *Tahualamne*, and *Tavalames*.

Area (sq mi): 2274.34 (land 2235.41; water 38.93).

Pop: 54,501 (White 85.1%; Black or African American 2.1%; Hispanic or Latino 8.2%; Asian 0.7%; Other 7.7%). **Foreign born:** 3.2%. **Median age:** 42.9. **State rank:** 42. **Pop change 1990-2000:** +12.5%.

Income: per capita $21,015; median household $38,725. **Pop below poverty level:** 11.4%.

Unemployment: 5.5%. **Median home value:** $149,800. **Median travel time to work:** 26.8 minutes.

VENTURA COUNTY
800 S Victoria Ave
Ventura, CA 93009
www.countyofventura.org

Ph: 805-654-2267
Fax: 805-662-6343

On S coast of CA, N of Los Angeles; organized Mar 22, 1873 from Santa Barbara County. **Name Origin:** For the city, abbreviation of Spanish *San Buenaventura* 'St Bonaventure.'

Area (sq mi): 2208.2 (land 1845.3; water 362.9).

Pop: 753,197 (White 56.8%; Black or African American 1.9%; Hispanic or Latino 33.4%; Asian 5.3%; Other 22.7%). **Foreign born:** 20.7%. **Median age:** 34.2. **State rank:** 12. **Pop change 1990-2000:** +12.6%.

Income: per capita $24,600; median household $59,666. **Pop below poverty level:** 9.2%.

Unemployment: 4.5%. **Median home value:** $248,700. **Median travel time to work:** 25.4 minutes.

YOLO COUNTY
625 Court St Suite 202
Woodland, CA 95695
www.yolocounty.org

Ph: 530-666-8150
Fax: 530-666-8147

In N central CA, NE of San Francisco; original county; organized Feb 18, 1850 (prior to statehood). **Name Origin:** For a subtribe of Patwin Indians, of Wintun linguistic stock; meaning of name unclear. Possibly a corruption of *Yoloy* 'place abounding with rushes,' or *Yodoi* a Patwin village, or for a chief named *Yodo*. There was also a captain of a ranch who was named Yolo.

Area (sq mi): 1022.89 (land 1013.27; water 9.62).

Pop: 168,660 (White 58.1%; Black or African American 2%; Hispanic or Latino 25.9%; Asian 9.9%; Other 20.5%). **Foreign born:** 20.3%. **Median age:** 29.5. **State rank:** 28. **Pop change 1990-2000:** +19.5%.

Income: per capita $19,365; median household $40,769. **Pop below poverty level:** 18.4%.

Unemployment: 4.2%. **Median home value:** $169,800. **Median travel time to work:** 21.2 minutes.

YUBA COUNTY
215 5th St
Marysville, CA 95901
www.co.yuba.ca.us

Ph: 530-749-7575
Fax: 530-749-7312

In N central CA, N of Sacramento; original county; organized Feb 18, 1850 (prior to statehood). **Name Origin:** For the Yuba River, the name of which came from a Maidu Indian village and tribal name. Also spelled *Yubu*, *Yupu*, *Jubu*.

Area (sq mi): 643.73 (land 630.69; water 13.04).

Pop: 60,219 (White 65.3%; Black or African American 3.2%; Hispanic or Latino 17.4%; Asian 7.5%; Other 18.6%). **Foreign born:** 13.2%. **Median age:** 31.4. **State rank:** 39. **Pop change 1990-2000:** +3.4%.

Income: per capita $14,124; median household $30,460. **Pop below poverty level:** 20.8%.

Unemployment: 11.7%. **Median home value:** $89,700. **Median travel time to work:** 26.2 minutes.

All statistics are based on the 2000 Census except the dollar figures given for per capita income, which are based on 1999 estimates.

COLORADO - Counties

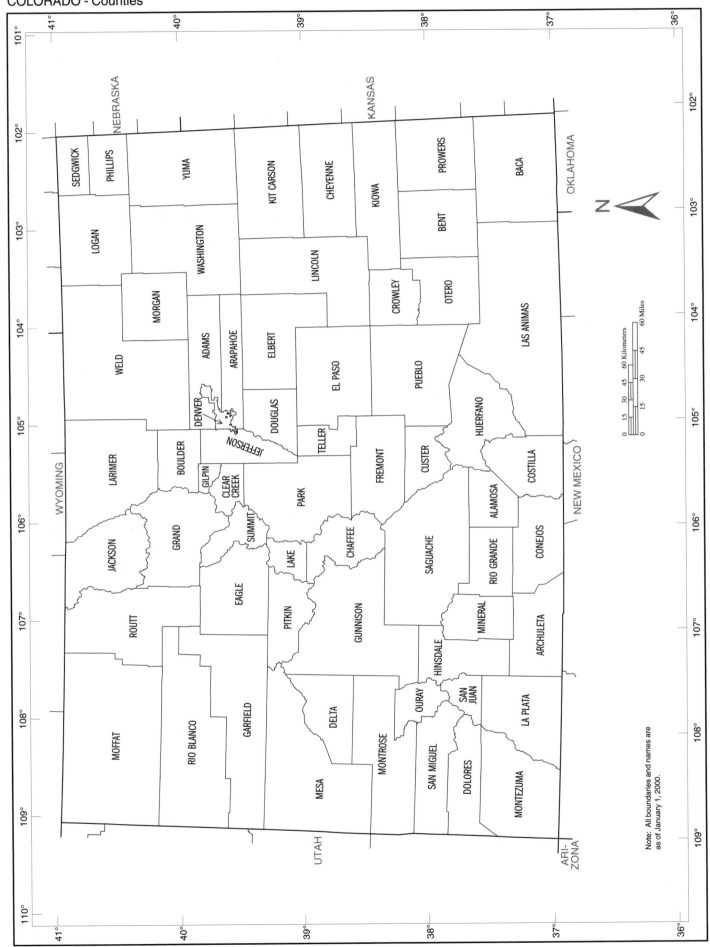

U.S. Census Bureau, Census 2000

Colorado

COLORADO STATE INFORMATION

www.colorado.gov   **Ph:** 303-866-5000

Area (sq mi): 104,093.57 (land 103,717.53; water 376.04).

Pop: 4,301,261 (White 74.5%; Black or African American 3.8%; Hispanic or Latino 17.1%; Asian 2.2%; Other 11.1%). **Foreign born:** 8.6%. **Median age:** 34.3. **Pop change 1990-2000:** +30.6%.

Income: per capita $24,049; median household $47,203. **Pop below poverty level:** 9.3%.

Unemployment: 5.4%. **Median home value:** $166,600. **Median travel time to work:** 24.3 minutes.

ADAMS COUNTY

450 S 4th Ave   **Ph:** 303-659-2120
Brighton, CO 80601   **Fax:** 303-654-6011
www.co.adams.co.us

In east-central CO, east of Denver; organized Apr 15, 1901 from Arapahoe County; annexed part of Denver County in 1909. A portion of the county was used to create Broomfield County on November 15, 2001. **Name Origin:** For Alva Adams (1850-1922), statesman and governor (1887-89; 1897-99; 1905).

Area (sq mi): 1197.71 (land 1191.93; water 5.78).

Pop: 363,857 (White 63.3%; Black or African American 3%; Hispanic or Latino 28.2%; Asian 3.2%; Other 16.5%). **Foreign born:** 12.5%. **Median age:** 31.4. **State rank:** 5. **Pop change 1990-2000:** +37.3%.

Income: per capita $19,944; median household $47,323. **Pop below poverty level:** 8.9%.

Unemployment: 3.8%. **Median home value:** $149,800. **Median travel time to work:** 27.6 minutes.

ALAMOSA COUNTY

PO Box 630   **Ph:** 719-589-5887
Alamosa, CO 81101   **Fax:** 719-589-6118

In south-central CO, southwest of Pueblo; organized Mar 8, 1913 from Costilla County. **Name Origin:** Spanish 'cottonwood trees.'

Area (sq mi): 723.53 (land 722.74; water 0.78).

Pop: 14,966 (White 54%; Black or African American 1%; Hispanic or Latino 41.4%; Asian 0.8%; Other 27%). **Foreign born:** 4.7%. **Median age:** 30.6. **State rank:** 28. **Pop change 1990-2000:** +9.9%.

Income: per capita $15,037; median household $29,447. **Pop below poverty level:** 21.3%.

Unemployment: 5.6%. **Median home value:** $87,900. **Median travel time to work:** 13.5 minutes.

ARAPAHOE COUNTY

5334 S Prince St   **Ph:** 303-795-4200
Littleton, CO 80166   **Fax:** 303-794-4625
www.co.arapahoe.co.us

In east-central CO, south of Denver; original county, organized Nov 1, 1861 (prior to statehood). **Name Origin:** For a tribe of Algonquian linguistic stock. Name is probably Pawnee *tirapihu* 'trader.' Also suggested, but not documented, 'blue-sky men' and 'cloud men.'

Area (sq mi): 805.43 (land 803.14; water 2.29).

Pop: 487,967 (White 73.9%; Black or African American 7.7%; Hispanic or Latino 11.8%; Asian 3.9%; Other 8.5%). **Foreign born:** 11%. **Median age:** 34.5. **State rank:** 4. **Pop change 1990-2000:** +24.6%.

Income: per capita $28,147; median household $53,570. **Pop below poverty level:** 5.8%.

Unemployment: 3.2%. **Median home value:** $171,700. **Median travel time to work:** 26.1 minutes.

ARCHULETA COUNTY

PO Box 2589   **Ph:** 970-264-5633
Pagosa Springs, CO 81147   **Fax:** 970-264-6423
www.archuletacounty.org

On southern border, east of Durango; organized Apr 14, 1885 from Conejos County. **Name Origin:** For Antonio D. Archuleta, a CO legislator.

Area (sq mi): 1355.48 (land 1350.22; water 5.26).

Pop: 9,898 (White 80.1%; Black or African American 0.4%; Hispanic or Latino 16.8%; Asian 0.3%; Other 11%). **Foreign born:** 2.9%. **Median age:** 40.8. **State rank:** 36. **Pop change 1990-2000:** +85.2%.

Income: per capita $21,683; median household $37,901. **Pop below poverty level:** 11.7%.

Unemployment: 4.3%. **Median home value:** $167,400. **Median travel time to work:** 19.2 minutes.

BACA COUNTY

741 Main St   **Ph:** 719-523-4372
Springfield, CO 81073   **Fax:** 719-523-4881

On southeastern border of CO; organized Apr 16 1889 from Las

Please see sample entry on inside front cover for detailed information about the statistics presented with each county listing.

77

Animas County. **Name Origin:** For an early pioneer family from Trinidad, CO.

Area (sq mi): 2557.09 (land 2555.72; water 1.37).

Pop: 4,517 (White 90.4%; Black or African American 0%; Hispanic or Latino 7%; Asian 0.2%; Other 6.1%). **Foreign born:** 2.5%. **Median age:** 42.9. **State rank:** 51. **Pop change 1990-2000:** -0.9%.

Income: per capita $15,068; median household $28,099. **Pop below poverty level:** 16.9%.

Unemployment: 2.9%. **Median home value:** $47,300. **Median travel time to work:** 15.2 minutes.

BENT COUNTY

PO Box 350   **Ph:** 719-456-1600
Las Animas, CO 81054   **Fax:** 719-456-0375

In southeastern CO, southwest of Pueblo; organized Feb 11, 1870, from Greenwood County (prior to statehood), which was organized in 1874 and abolished in 1878 by being divided between Bent and Elbert counties. **Name Origin:** For Bent's Fort on the north bank of the Arkansas River and for the Bent brothers who built it, or for one of the brothers, William Bent (1809-69), early settler, fur trader, and Indian agent.

Area (sq mi): 1541.12 (land 1513.9; water 27.22).

Pop: 5,998 (White 63.3%; Black or African American 3.7%; Hispanic or Latino 30.2%; Asian 0.6%; Other 16.3%). **Foreign born:** 4.4%. **Median age:** 37.3. **State rank:** 45. **Pop change 1990-2000:** +18.8%.

Income: per capita $13,567; median household $28,125. **Pop below poverty level:** 19.5%.

Unemployment: 4.5%. **Median home value:** $57,200. **Median travel time to work:** 18.6 minutes.

BOULDER COUNTY

PO Box 471   **Ph:** 303-441-3131
Boulder, CO 80306   **Fax:** 303-441-4863
www.co.boulder.co.us

In north-central CO, northwest of Denver; original county, organized Nov 1, 1861 (prior to statehood). A portion of the county was used to create Broomfield County on November 15, 2001. **Name Origin:** For Boulder City and Boulder Creek, themselves named for the huge rock formations in the area.

Area (sq mi): 751.37 (land 742.46; water 8.91).

Pop: 291,288 (White 83.6%; Black or African American 0.9%; Hispanic or Latino 10.5%; Asian 3.1%; Other 7.6%). **Foreign born:** 9.4%. **Median age:** 33.4. **State rank:** 6. **Pop change 1990-2000:** +29.3%.

Income: per capita $28,976; median household $55,861. **Pop below poverty level:** 9.5%.

Unemployment: 3.5%. **Median home value:** $241,900. **Median travel time to work:** 22.4 minutes.

BROOMFIELD CITY & COUNTY

1 DesCombes Dr   **Ph:** 303-469-3301
Broomfield, CO 80020   **Fax:** 303-469-8554
www.ci.broomfield.co.us

Broomfield was the only city in CO to lie in portions of four counties

(Jefferson, Adams, Weld, and Boulder), which caused problems for local residents in accessing services. Consequently, on Nov 3, 1998, the City and County of Broomfield was created by constitutional amendment. After a three-year period in which to organize, it became CO's 64th county on Nov 15, 2001. The US Bureau of the Census recognized the new county in Feb of 2002, and its census status will become official after the 2010 Census.

Area (sq mi): 33.6 (land 32.6; water 1).

CHAFFEE COUNTY

PO Box 699   **Ph:** 719-539-4004
Salida, CO 81201   **Fax:** 719-539-8588
www.chaffee-county.com

In central CO; organized as Lake County Nov 1, 1861 (prior to statehood); name changed Feb 10, 1879. **Name Origin:** For Jerome Bounty Chaffee (1825-86), CO territorial legislator and U.S. senator (1876-79); one of the founders of Denver.

Area (sq mi): 1015.01 (land 1013.45; water 1.55).

Pop: 16,242 (White 87.3%; Black or African American 1.6%; Hispanic or Latino 8.6%; Asian 0.4%; Other 7%). **Foreign born:** 2%. **Median age:** 41.8. **State rank:** 26. **Pop change 1990-2000:** +28.1%.

Income: per capita $19,430; median household $34,368. **Pop below poverty level:** 11.7%.

Unemployment: 2.8%. **Median home value:** $152,800. **Median travel time to work:** 14.8 minutes.

CHEYENNE COUNTY

PO Box 567   **Ph:** 719-767-5685
Cheyenne Wells, CO 80810   **Fax:** 719-767-5540

On central-eastern border of CO, east of Colorado Springs; organized Mar 25, 1889 from Bent and Elbert counties. **Name Origin:** For the Dakota Indian tribe of Algonquian linguistic stock; name means 'red talkers.'

Area (sq mi): 1781.37 (land 1781.35; water 0.02).

Pop: 2,231 (White 90.5%; Black or African American 0.5%; Hispanic or Latino 8.1%; Asian 0.1%; Other 6.5%). **Foreign born:** 4.1%. **Median age:** 37.9. **State rank:** 57. **Pop change 1990-2000:** -6.9%.

Income: per capita $17,850; median household $37,054. **Pop below poverty level:** 11.1%.

Unemployment: 2.3%. **Median home value:** $62,400. **Median travel time to work:** 13.5 minutes.

CLEAR CREEK COUNTY

PO Box 2000   **Ph:** 303-679-2312
Georgetown, CO 80444   **Fax:** 303-679-2440
www.co.clear-creek.co.us

In north-central CO, west of Denver; original county, organized Nov 1, 1861 (prior to statehood). **Name Origin:** For the name of a stream in the county, which was originally called Vasquez Fork, but present name adopted by 1860.

Area (sq mi): 396.46 (land 395.45; water 1.01).

Pop: 9,322 (White 94%; Black or African American 0.3%; Hispanic

All statistics are based on the 2000 Census except the dollar figures given for per capita income, which are based on 1999 estimates.

or Latino 3.9%; Asian 0.4%; Other 2.9%). **Foreign born:** 1.9%. **Median age:** 40.2. **State rank:** 38. **Pop change 1990-2000:** +22.4%.

Income: per capita $28,160; median household $50,997. **Pop below poverty level:** 5.4%.

Unemployment: 3.8%. **Median home value:** $200,400. **Median travel time to work:** 32.6 minutes.

CONEJOS COUNTY

PO Box 157   **Ph:** 719-376-5772
Conejos, CO 81129   **Fax:** 719-376-5661

On central southern border, east of Durango; original county, organized as Guadalupe County Nov 1, 1861 (prior to statehood); name changed Nov 7, 1861. **Name Origin:** For the river (which runs through the county) and town called Conejos, from the Spanish meaning 'rabbits,' for the local abundance of the animals.

Area (sq mi): 1290.87 (land 1287.22; water 3.65).

Pop: 8,400 (White 39.3%; Black or African American 0.2%; Hispanic or Latino 58.9%; Asian 0.2%; Other 26.9%). **Foreign born:** 3%. **Median age:** 34.2. **State rank:** 39. **Pop change 1990-2000:** +12.7%.

Income: per capita $12,050; median household $24,744. **Pop below poverty level:** 23%.

Unemployment: 7.9%. **Median home value:** $57,000. **Median travel time to work:** 22.4 minutes.

COSTILLA COUNTY

PO Box 301   **Ph:** 719-672-3681
San Luis, CO 81152

On central southern border of CO, southwest of Pueblo; original county, organized Nov 1, 1861 (prior to statehood). **Name Origin:** Probably for Costilla Creek, which runs through the county; Spanish 'rib' or 'furring timber'; or possibly for a local family of this name.

Area (sq mi): 1230.44 (land 1227.1; water 3.34).

Pop: 3,663 (White 28.2%; Black or African American 0.8%; Hispanic or Latino 67.6%; Asian 1%; Other 37.3%). **Foreign born:** 6.9%. **Median age:** 42.1. **State rank:** 54. **Pop change 1990-2000:** +14.8%.

Income: per capita $10,748; median household $19,531. **Pop below poverty level:** 26.8%.

Unemployment: 9.4%. **Median home value:** $61,200. **Median travel time to work:** 23.3 minutes.

CROWLEY COUNTY

603 Main St Suite 2   **Ph:** 719-267-4643
Ordway, CO 81063   **Fax:** 719-267-3114

In southeastern CO, east of Pueblo; organized May 29, 1911 from Otero County. **Name Origin:** For John H. Crowley (1849-?), state senator from Otero County when Crowley County was formed.

Area (sq mi): 800.33 (land 788.99; water 11.34).

Pop: 5,518 (White 66.5%; Black or African American 7%; Hispanic or Latino 22.5%; Asian 0.8%; Other 9.2%). **Foreign born:** 1.1%. **Median age:** 36.6. **State rank:** 48. **Pop change 1990-2000:** +39.8%.

Income: per capita $12,836; median household $26,803. **Pop below poverty level:** 18.5%.

Unemployment: 4.5%. **Median home value:** $57,200. **Median travel time to work:** 22.2 minutes.

CUSTER COUNTY

205 S 6th St   **Ph:** 719-783-2441
Westcliffe, CO 81252   **Fax:** 719-783-2885

In south-central CO, southwest of Pueblo; organized Mar 9, 1877 from Fremont County. **Name Origin:** For Gen. George Armstrong Custer (1839-76), U.S. soldier and Indian fighter.

Area (sq mi): 739.9 (land 738.89; water 1.02).

Pop: 3,503 (White 94.2%; Black or African American 0.4%; Hispanic or Latino 2.5%; Asian 0.3%; Other 3.4%). **Foreign born:** 1.7%. **Median age:** 44.9. **State rank:** 55. **Pop change 1990-2000:** +81.9%.

Income: per capita $19,817; median household $34,731. **Pop below poverty level:** 13.3%.

Unemployment: 3.5%. **Median home value:** $134,100. **Median travel time to work:** 26.4 minutes.

DELTA COUNTY

501 Palmer St Suite 211   **Ph:** 970-874-2150
Delta, CO 81416   **Fax:** 970-874-2161

In west-central CO, southeast of Grand Junction; organized Feb 11, 1883 from Gunnison County. **Name Origin:** For the city, named for its location on the delta of the Uncompahgre River.

Area (sq mi): 1148.52 (land 1142.11; water 6.42).

Pop: 27,834 (White 86%; Black or African American 0.5%; Hispanic or Latino 11.4%; Asian 0.3%; Other 6.9%). **Foreign born:** 4.2%. **Median age:** 42.3. **State rank:** 17. **Pop change 1990-2000:** +32.7%.

Income: per capita $17,152; median household $32,785. **Pop below poverty level:** 12.1%.

Unemployment: 4.1%. **Median home value:** $115,500. **Median travel time to work:** 23.5 minutes.

DENVER COUNTY

1437 Bannock St Suite 200   **Ph:** 720-865-8400
Denver, CO 80202   **Fax:** 720-865-8580
www.co.denver.co.us

In north-central CO; organized Mar 18, 1901 from Adams County. The city and county are coterminous. **Name Origin:** For Gen. James William Denver (1817-92), CA legislator, commissioner of Indian affairs, and governor of KS Territory (1857-58).

Area (sq mi): 154.94 (land 153.35; water 1.59).

Pop: 554,636 (White 51.9%; Black or African American 11.1%; Hispanic or Latino 31.7%; Asian 2.8%; Other 20.7%). **Foreign born:** 17.4%. **Median age:** 33.1. **State rank:** 1. **Pop change 1990-2000:** +18.6%.

Income: per capita $24,101; median household $39,500. **Pop below poverty level:** 14.3%.

Unemployment: 4.5%. **Median home value:** $165,800. **Median travel time to work:** 24.5 minutes.

Please see sample entry on inside front cover for detailed information about the statistics presented with each county listing.

DOLORES COUNTY

PO Box 608
Dove Creek, CO 81324

Ph: 970-677-2383
Fax: 970-677-2815

On southwestern border of CO, south of Grand Junction; organized Feb 19, 1881 from Ouray County. **Name Origin:** For the Dolores River, which runs through it; from Spanish *Rio de Nuestra Senora de los Dolores*, ' River of Our Lay of Sorrows.'

Area (sq mi): 1068.09 (land 1066.97; water 1.13).

Pop: 1,844 (White 92.8%; Black or African American 0.1%; Hispanic or Latino 3.9%; Asian 0.4%; Other 4.4%). **Foreign born:** 0.9%. **Median age:** 42.4. **State rank:** 58. **Pop change 1990-2000:** +22.6%.

Income: per capita $17,106; median household $32,196. **Pop below poverty level:** 13.1%.

Unemployment: 7.1%. **Median home value:** $76,800. **Median travel time to work:** 25.6 minutes.

DOUGLAS COUNTY

100 3rd St
Castle Rock, CO 80104
www.douglas.co.us

Ph: 303-660-7401
Fax: 303-688-1293

In central CO, between Denver and Colorado Springs; original county, organized Nov 1, 1861 (prior to statehood). **Name Origin:** For Stephen Arnold Douglas (1813-61), U.S. orator and statesman.

Area (sq mi): 842.75 (land 840.11; water 2.64).

Pop: 175,766 (White 89.7%; Black or African American 1%; Hispanic or Latino 5.1%; Asian 2.5%; Other 3.8%). **Foreign born:** 5.2%. **Median age:** 33.7. **State rank:** 9. **Pop change 1990-2000:** +191%.

Income: per capita $34,848; median household $82,929. **Pop below poverty level:** 2.1%.

Unemployment: 2.8%. **Median home value:** $236,000. **Median travel time to work:** 29.3 minutes.

EAGLE COUNTY

PO Box 850
Eagle, CO 81631
www.eagle-county.com

Ph: 970-328-8612
Fax: 970-328-8716

In west-central CO, west of Denver; organized Feb 11, 1883, from Summit County. **Name Origin:** For the Eagle River, which flows through the county; the river was named for the bird.

Area (sq mi): 1691.8 (land 1687.88; water 3.93).

Pop: 41,659 (White 74.2%; Black or African American 0.3%; Hispanic or Latino 23.2%; Asian 0.8%; Other 13.5%). **Foreign born:** 18.2%. **Median age:** 31.2. **State rank:** 15. **Pop change 1990-2000:** +90%.

Income: per capita $32,011; median household $62,682. **Pop below poverty level:** 7.8%.

Unemployment: 2.8%. **Median home value:** $369,100. **Median travel time to work:** 21.3 minutes.

EL PASO COUNTY

200 S Cascade Ave
Colorado Springs, CO 80903
www.co.el-paso.co.us

Ph: 719-520-6200

In central CO, south of Denver; original county, organized Nov 1, 1861 (prior to statehood). **Name Origin:** Spanish 'the pass' [through the mountains], referring to Ute Pass, west of Colorado Springs.

Area (sq mi): 2129.56 (land 2126.45; water 3.11).

Pop: 516,929 (White 76.2%; Black or African American 6.5%; Hispanic or Latino 11.3%; Asian 2.5%; Other 9.7%). **Foreign born:** 6.4%. **Median age:** 33. **State rank:** 3. **Pop change 1990-2000:** +30.2%.

Income: per capita $22,005; median household $46,844. **Pop below poverty level:** 8%.

Unemployment: 4.4%. **Median home value:** $147,100. **Median travel time to work:** 22.3 minutes.

ELBERT COUNTY

PO Box 579
Kiowa, CO 80117

Ph: 303-621-3132
Fax: 303-621-3166

In east-central CO, southeast of Denver; organized Feb 2, 1874, from Douglas and Greenwood counties (prior to statehood), the latter of which was organized in 1874 and abolished in 1878 by being divided between Bent and Elbert counties. **Name Origin:** For Samuel H. Elbert (1833-1907), CO territorial governor (1873-74) and chief justice of CO Supreme Court (1880-83).

Area (sq mi): 1850.89 (land 1850.78; water 0.11).

Pop: 19,872 (White 93.2%; Black or African American 0.6%; Hispanic or Latino 3.9%; Asian 0.4%; Other 3.8%). **Foreign born:** 1.9%. **Median age:** 37.2. **State rank:** 24. **Pop change 1990-2000:** +106%.

Income: per capita $24,960; median household $62,480. **Pop below poverty level:** 4%.

Unemployment: 2.8%. **Median home value:** $221,600. **Median travel time to work:** 41.1 minutes.

FREMONT COUNTY

136 Justice Ctr Rd Rm 103
Canon City, CO 81212

Ph: 719-269-0100
Fax: 719-269-0134

In central CO, southwest of Colorado Springs; original county, organized Nov 1, 1861 (prior to statehood). **Name Origin:** For John Charles Fremont (1813-90), soldier and explorer who led five expeditions to the West, U.S. senator from CA (1850-51), and governor of the AZ Territory (1878-81).

Area (sq mi): 1533.95 (land 1532.93; water 1.02).

Pop: 46,145 (White 81.1%; Black or African American 5.3%; Hispanic or Latino 10.3%; Asian 0.5%; Other 4.6%). **Foreign born:** 1.5%. **Median age:** 38.8. **State rank:** 12. **Pop change 1990-2000:** +43%.

Income: per capita $17,420; median household $34,150. **Pop below poverty level:** 11.7%.

Unemployment: 3.9%. **Median home value:** $104,900. **Median travel time to work:** 23.9 minutes.

All statistics are based on the 2000 Census except the dollar figures given for per capita income, which are based on 1999 estimates.

GARFIELD COUNTY

109 8th St Suite 200
Glenwood Springs, CO 81601

Ph: 970-945-2377
Fax: 970-947-1078

On central-western border of CO, north of Grand Junction; organized Feb 10, 1883 from Summit County. **Name Origin:** For James Abram Garfield (1831-81), twentieth U.S. president.

Area (sq mi): 2955.76 (land 2947.06; water 8.7).

Pop: 43,791 (White 81%; Black or African American 0.4%; Hispanic or Latino 16.7%; Asian 0.4%; Other 9.1%). **Foreign born:** 10.4%. **Median age:** 34.2. **State rank:** 14. **Pop change 1990-2000:** +46.1%.

Income: per capita $21,341; median household $47,016. **Pop below poverty level:** 7.5%.

Unemployment: 2.5%. **Median home value:** $200,700. **Median travel time to work:** 30.6 minutes.

GILPIN COUNTY

PO Box 429
Central City, CO 80427

Ph: 303-582-5321
Fax: 303-582-3086

In central CO, west of Denver; original county; organized Nov 1, 1861 (prior to statehood). **Name Origin:** For Col. William Gilpin (1822-94), first territorial governor of CO (1861-62).

Area (sq mi): 150.25 (land 149.87; water 0.39).

Pop: 4,757 (White 92%; Black or African American 0.5%; Hispanic or Latino 4.2%; Asian 0.7%; Other 4.4%). **Foreign born:** 3.4%. **Median age:** 38.3. **State rank:** 50. **Pop change 1990-2000:** +55%.

Income: per capita $26,148; median household $51,942. **Pop below poverty level:** 4%.

Unemployment: 3.1%. **Median home value:** $180,600. **Median travel time to work:** 34.7 minutes.

GRAND COUNTY

308 Byers Ave PO Box 120
Hot Sulphur Springs, CO 80451
www.co.grand.co.us

Ph: 970-725-3347
Fax: 970-725-0100

In north-central CO, west of Boulder; organized Feb 2, 1874 (prior to statehood) from Summit County. **Name Origin:** For Grand Lake and the Grand River; the latter was renamed the Colorado.

Area (sq mi): 1869.6 (land 1846.67; water 22.93).

Pop: 12,442 (White 93%; Black or African American 0.5%; Hispanic or Latino 4.4%; Asian 0.7%; Other 3.6%). **Foreign born:** 3.4%. **Median age:** 36.9. **State rank:** 34. **Pop change 1990-2000:** +56.2%.

Income: per capita $25,198; median household $47,759. **Pop below poverty level:** 7.3%.

Unemployment: 3.1%. **Median home value:** $205,500. **Median travel time to work:** 22.7 minutes.

GUNNISON COUNTY

221 N Wisconsin St Suite C
Gunnison, CO 81230
www.co.gunnison.co.us

Ph: 970-641-1516
Fax: 970-641-7956

In west-central CO, west of Colorado Springs; organized Mar 9, 1877, from Lake County. **Name Origin:** For John William Gunnison (1812-53), killed by Indians while surveying for a proposed railroad.

Area (sq mi): 3259.75 (land 3238.81; water 20.93).

Pop: 13,956 (White 92.3%; Black or African American 0.5%; Hispanic or Latino 5%; Asian 0.5%; Other 3.8%). **Foreign born:** 2.9%. **Median age:** 30.4. **State rank:** 32. **Pop change 1990-2000:** +35.9%.

Income: per capita $21,407; median household $36,916. **Pop below poverty level:** 15%.

Unemployment: 4.8%. **Median home value:** $189,400. **Median travel time to work:** 15.9 minutes.

HINSDALE COUNTY

PO Box 277
Lake City, CO 81235
www.hinsdalecountycolorado.us

Ph: 970-944-2225
Fax: 970-944-2630

In southwest CO, northeast of Durango; organized Feb 10, 1874, from Conejos and Summit counties (prior to statehood). **Name Origin:** For George A. Hinsdale, a former lieutenant governor of the state.

Area (sq mi): 1123.14 (land 1117.68; water 5.46).

Pop: 790 (White 96.6%; Black or African American 0%; Hispanic or Latino 1.5%; Asian 0.3%; Other 2.4%). **Foreign born:** 2%. **Median age:** 43.9. **State rank:** 62. **Pop change 1990-2000:** +69.2%.

Income: per capita $22,360; median household $37,279. **Pop below poverty level:** 7.2%.

Unemployment: 2.7%. **Median home value:** $213,300. **Median travel time to work:** 16 minutes.

HUERFANO COUNTY

401 Main St Suite 201
Walsenburg, CO 81089

Ph: 719-738-2370
Fax: 719-738-3996

In south-central CO, south of Pueblo; original county, organized Nov 1, 1861 (prior to statehood). **Name Origin:** For the Huerfano River, Spanish 'orphan,' referring to an isolated butte in the river.

Area (sq mi): 1593.24 (land 1590.87; water 2.38).

Pop: 7,862 (White 58.4%; Black or African American 2.7%; Hispanic or Latino 35.1%; Asian 0.4%; Other 15.9%). **Foreign born:** 1.6%. **Median age:** 41.7. **State rank:** 41. **Pop change 1990-2000:** +30.8%.

Income: per capita $15,242; median household $25,775. **Pop below poverty level:** 18%.

Unemployment: 5.7%. **Median home value:** $75,200. **Median travel time to work:** 24.7 minutes.

JACKSON COUNTY

PO Box 1019
Walden, CO 80480

Ph: 970-723-4660
Fax: 970-723-4706

On central northern border of CO, west of Ft. Collins; organized May 5, 1909 from Larimer County. **Name Origin:** For Andrew Jackson (1767-1845), seventh U.S. president.

Area (sq mi): 1620.95 (land 1613.21; water 7.74).

Pop: 1,577 (White 92.1%; Black or African American 0.3%; Hispanic or Latino 6.5%; Asian 0.1%; Other 3.6%). **Foreign born:** 1.9%. **Median age:** 40.5. **State rank:** 60. **Pop change 1990-2000:** -1.7%.

Please see sample entry on inside front cover for detailed information about the statistics presented with each county listing.

81

Income: per capita $17,826; median household $31,821. **Pop below poverty level:** 14%.

Unemployment: 4.6%. **Median home value:** $86,000. **Median travel time to work:** 14.4 minutes.

JEFFERSON COUNTY

100 Jefferson County Pkwy
Golden, CO 80419
www.co.jefferson.co.us

Ph: 303-271-8106
Fax: 303-271-8197

In central CO, west of Denver; original county, organized Nov 1, 1861 (prior to statehood). A portion of the county was used to create Broomfield County on November 15, 2001. **Name Origin:** From Jefferson Territory, the extra-legal government that preceded CO Territory. Named in honor of Thomas Jefferson (1743-1826), U.S. patriot and statesman; third U.S. president.

Area (sq mi): 778.06 (land 772.09; water 5.97).

Pop: 527,056 (White 84.9%; Black or African American 0.9%; Hispanic or Latino 10%; Asian 2.3%; Other 6.3%). **Foreign born:** 5.4%. **Median age:** 36.8. **State rank:** 2. **Pop change 1990-2000:** +20.2%.

Income: per capita $28,066; median household $57,339. **Pop below poverty level:** 5.2%.

Unemployment: 3%. **Median home value:** $187,900. **Median travel time to work:** 27.4 minutes.

KIOWA COUNTY

PO Box 37
Eads, CO 81036
www.kiowacountycolo.com

Ph: 719-438-5421
Fax: 719-438-5327

On southeastern border of CO, east of Pueblo; organized Apr 11, 1889, from Bent County. **Name Origin:** For the Indian tribe of Tanoan linguistic stock; name means 'principal people.'

Area (sq mi): 1785.76 (land 1770.99; water 14.76).

Pop: 1,622 (White 94.3%; Black or African American 0.5%; Hispanic or Latino 3.1%; Asian 0%; Other 3.4%). **Foreign born:** 1.4%. **Median age:** 39.7. **State rank:** 59. **Pop change 1990-2000:** -3.9%.

Income: per capita $16,382; median household $30,494. **Pop below poverty level:** 12.2%.

Unemployment: 2.5%. **Median home value:** $46,100. **Median travel time to work:** 18.3 minutes.

KIT CARSON COUNTY

PO Box 249
Burlington, CO 80807
www.kitcarsoncounty.org

Ph: 719-346-8638
Fax: 719-346-7242

On central eastern border of CO; organized Apr 11, 1889 from Elbert County. **Name Origin:** For Christopher (Kit) Carson (1809-68), frontiersman, guide, and Indian agent.

Area (sq mi): 2161.56 (land 2160.87; water 0.69).

Pop: 8,011 (White 83.4%; Black or African American 1.7%; Hispanic or Latino 13.7%; Asian 0.3%; Other 10.6%). **Foreign born:** 5.8%. **Median age:** 37.4. **State rank:** 40. **Pop change 1990-2000:** +12.2%.

Income: per capita $16,964; median household $33,152. **Pop below poverty level:** 12.1%.

Unemployment: 2%. **Median home value:** $80,400. **Median travel time to work:** 14.6 minutes.

LA PLATA COUNTY

PO Box 519
Durango, CO 81302
www.co.laplata.co.us

Ph: 970-382-6280
Fax: 970-382-6285

On southwestern border of CO; organized Feb 10, 1874, from Conejos and Lake counties (prior to statehood). **Name Origin:** For La Plata River, which runs through the county; from Spanish 'silver,' for the mines in the area.

Area (sq mi): 1699.93 (land 1692.15; water 7.78).

Pop: 43,941 (White 82.3%; Black or African American 0.3%; Hispanic or Latino 10.4%; Asian 0.4%; Other 12.1%). **Foreign born:** 2.7%. **Median age:** 35.6. **State rank:** 13. **Pop change 1990-2000:** +36.1%.

Income: per capita $21,534; median household $40,159. **Pop below poverty level:** 11.7%.

Unemployment: 3.7%. **Median home value:** $183,900. **Median travel time to work:** 20.7 minutes.

LAKE COUNTY

PO Box 917
Leadville, CO 80461

Ph: 719-486-1410
Fax: 719-486-3972

In central CO, southwest of Denver; original county, organized Nov 1, 1861 (prior to statehood); name changed from Carbonate Feb 10, 1879. **Name Origin:** For the Twin Lakes, a major feature of the county.

Area (sq mi): 383.9 (land 376.89; water 7.01).

Pop: 7,812 (White 61.6%; Black or African American 0.2%; Hispanic or Latino 36.1%; Asian 0.3%; Other 22%). **Foreign born:** 15.6%. **Median age:** 30.5. **State rank:** 42. **Pop change 1990-2000:** +30%.

Income: per capita $18,524; median household $37,691. **Pop below poverty level:** 12.9%.

Unemployment: 4.7%. **Median home value:** $115,400. **Median travel time to work:** 35.8 minutes.

LARIMER COUNTY

PO Box 1190
Fort Collins, CO 80522
www.co.larimer.co.us

Ph: 970-498-7000
Fax: 970-498-7830

On central northern border of CO; original county, organized Nov 1, 1861 (prior to statehood). **Name Origin:** For Gen. William Larimer, a founder of Denver and prominent early settler.

Area (sq mi): 2633.86 (land 2601.3; water 32.56).

Pop: 251,494 (White 87.5%; Black or African American 0.7%; Hispanic or Latino 8.3%; Asian 1.6%; Other 6.4%). **Foreign born:** 4.3%. **Median age:** 33.2. **State rank:** 7. **Pop change 1990-2000:** +35.1%.

Income: per capita $23,689; median household $48,655. **Pop below poverty level:** 9.2%.

All statistics are based on the 2000 Census except the dollar figures given for per capita income, which are based on 1999 estimates.

Unemployment: 3.5%. **Median home value:** $172,000. **Median travel time to work:** 21.4 minutes.

LAS ANIMAS COUNTY
PO Box 115
Trinidad, CO 81082   **Ph:** 719-846-3314
www.tlac.net/county   **Fax:** 719-845-2573

On southeastern border of CO, south of Pueblo; organized Feb 9, 1866 from Huerfano County (prior to statehood). **Name Origin:** From part of the original name of the Purgatoire River, which runs through the county, *El Rio de las Animas Perdidas en Purgatorio*, Spanish 'river of souls lost in Purgatory,' in memory of people killed at the river by Indians c. 1595 who died without absolution. Shortened to El Purgatorio; then to its present form by French trappers; also known by Americanized *Picketwire*.

Area (sq mi): 4775.42 (land 4772.63; water 2.79).

Pop: 15,207 (White 55.2%; Black or African American 0.4%; Hispanic or Latino 41.5%; Asian 0.4%; Other 16.5%). **Foreign born:** 2.3%. **Median age:** 40.9. **State rank:** 27. **Pop change 1990-2000:** +10.5%.

Income: per capita $16,829; median household $28,273. **Pop below poverty level:** 17.3%.

Unemployment: 4.4%. **Median home value:** $84,500. **Median travel time to work:** 20.6 minutes.

LINCOLN COUNTY
PO Box 67
Hugo, CO 80821   **Ph:** 719-743-2444
                                      Fax: 719-743-2524

In east-central CO, east of Colorado Springs; organized Apr 11, 1889 , from Bent and Elbert counties. **Name Origin:** For Abraham Lincoln (1809-65), sixteenth U.S. president.

Area (sq mi): 2586.39 (land 2586.09; water 0.3).

Pop: 6,087 (White 84.2%; Black or African American 5%; Hispanic or Latino 8.5%; Asian 0.6%; Other 8.2%). **Foreign born:** 1.8%. **Median age:** 37.8. **State rank:** 44. **Pop change 1990-2000:** +34.4%.

Income: per capita $15,510; median household $31,914. **Pop below poverty level:** 11.7%.

Unemployment: 1.6%. **Median home value:** $77,800. **Median travel time to work:** 19.2 minutes.

LOGAN COUNTY
315 Main St
Sterling, CO 80751   **Ph:** 970-522-0888
www.loganco.gov   **Fax:** 970-522-4018

On northeastern border of CO, northeast of Greeley; organized Feb 25, 1887 from Weld County. **Name Origin:** For Gen. John Alexander Logan (1826-86), officer in the Mexican-American War and Civil War; U.S. senator from IL (1871-77; 1879-86).

Area (sq mi): 1844.86 (land 1838.52; water 6.33).

Pop: 20,504 (White 84.4%; Black or African American 2%; Hispanic or Latino 11.9%; Asian 0.4%; Other 5.9%). **Foreign born:** 3.1%. **Median age:** 36.5. **State rank:** 22. **Pop change 1990-2000:** +16.7%.

Income: per capita $16,721; median household $32,724. **Pop below poverty level:** 12.2%.

Unemployment: 3.3%. **Median home value:** $87,700. **Median travel time to work:** 15.2 minutes.

MESA COUNTY
PO Box 20000
Grand Junction, CO 81502   **Ph:** 970-244-1800
www.co.mesa.co.us   **Fax:** 970-256-1588

On central western border of CO; organized Feb 14, 1883 from Gunnison County. **Name Origin:** Spanish 'table,' for the high, flat tablelands with sharply eroded sides common to the area.

Area (sq mi): 3341.11 (land 3327.75; water 13.36).

Pop: 116,255 (White 87%; Black or African American 0.5%; Hispanic or Latino 10%; Asian 0.5%; Other 6.7%). **Foreign born:** 3%. **Median age:** 38.1. **State rank:** 11. **Pop change 1990-2000:** +24.8%.

Income: per capita $18,715; median household $35,864. **Pop below poverty level:** 10.2%.

Unemployment: 4%. **Median home value:** $118,900. **Median travel time to work:** 18.4 minutes.

MINERAL COUNTY
PO Box 70
Creede, CO 81130   **Ph:** 719-658-2440
                                      Fax: 719-658-2931

In south-central CO, northeast of Durango; organized Mar 27, 1893, from Saguache and Rio Grande counties. **Name Origin:** For the rich mineral resources of the area.

Area (sq mi): 877.7 (land 875.72; water 1.99).

Pop: 831 (White 95.4%; Black or African American 0%; Hispanic or Latino 2%; Asian 0%; Other 3.1%). **Foreign born:** 0.7%. **Median age:** 45. **State rank:** 61. **Pop change 1990-2000:** +48.9%.

Income: per capita $24,475; median household $34,844. **Pop below poverty level:** 10.2%.

Unemployment: 2.4%. **Median home value:** $127,400. **Median travel time to work:** 15.9 minutes.

MOFFAT COUNTY
221 W Victory Way
Craig, CO 81625   **Ph:** 970-824-9104
www.co.moffat.co.us   **Fax:** 970-824-4975

On northwestern border of CO; organized Feb 27, 1911, from Routt County. **Name Origin:** For David Halliday Moffat (1839-1911), president of the Rio Grande Railroad (1884-91).

Area (sq mi): 4750.94 (land 4742.25; water 8.69).

Pop: 13,184 (White 88.2%; Black or African American 0.2%; Hispanic or Latino 9.5%; Asian 0.3%; Other 5.9%). **Foreign born:** 4.1%. **Median age:** 35.4. **State rank:** 33. **Pop change 1990-2000:** +16.1%.

Income: per capita $18,540; median household $41,528. **Pop below poverty level:** 8.3%.

Unemployment: 4.9%. **Median home value:** $104,600. **Median travel time to work:** 23.4 minutes.

Please see sample entry on inside front cover for detailed information about the statistics presented with each county listing.

MONTEZUMA COUNTY

109 W Main St Rm 302
Cortez, CO 81321
www.co.montezuma.co.us

Ph: 970-565-8317
Fax: 970-565-3420

On southwesternmost border of CO; organized Apr 16, 1889, from La Plata County. The corners of four states, CO, AZ, NM, and UT, meet at this point, the only place in the U.S. where this occurs. **Name Origin:** For Montezuma (1479?-1520), Aztec Indian emperor of Mexico who was conquered by Hernan Cortez (1485-1547).

Area (sq mi): 2039.97 (land 2036.63; water 3.34).

Pop: 23,830 (White 77.5%; Black or African American 0.1%; Hispanic or Latino 9.5%; Asian 0.2%; Other 18%). **Foreign born:** 2.2%. **Median age:** 38. **State rank:** 19. **Pop change 1990-2000:** +27.6%.

Income: per capita $17,003; median household $32,083. **Pop below poverty level:** 16.4%.

Unemployment: 5%. **Median home value:** $109,100. **Median travel time to work:** 21.8 minutes.

MONTROSE COUNTY

161 S Townsend
Montrose, CO 81401
www.co.montrose.co.us

Ph: 970-249-3362
Fax: 970-249-7761

On central western border of CO, south of Grand Junction; organized Feb 11, 1883 from Gunnison County. **Name Origin:** For the city, named for *The Legend of Montrose*, by Sir Walter Scott (1771-1832), for the similarity of the surrounding country; also possibly an allusion to Montrose, Scotland.

Area (sq mi): 2242.57 (land 2240.61; water 1.96).

Pop: 33,432 (White 82.4%; Black or African American 0.3%; Hispanic or Latino 14.9%; Asian 0.4%; Other 9.3%). **Foreign born:** 5.6%. **Median age:** 38.8. **State rank:** 16. **Pop change 1990-2000:** +36.9%.

Income: per capita $17,158; median household $35,234. **Pop below poverty level:** 12.6%.

Unemployment: 4.9%. **Median home value:** $121,200. **Median travel time to work:** 21.5 minutes.

MORGAN COUNTY

PO Box 1399
Fort Morgan, CO 80701

Ph: 970-542-3521
Fax: 970-542-3520

In northeastern CO, east of Boulder; organized Feb 19, 1889, from Weld County. **Name Origin:** For Fort Morgan, named for Col. Christopher Anthony Morgan (1825?-66), an army officer and inspector general of the Department of Missouri.

Area (sq mi): 1293.87 (land 1285.36; water 8.51).

Pop: 27,171 (White 67%; Black or African American 0.3%; Hispanic or Latino 31.2%; Asian 0.2%; Other 19.9%). **Foreign born:** 14.6%. **Median age:** 33.5. **State rank:** 18. **Pop change 1990-2000:** +23.8%.

Income: per capita $15,492; median household $34,568. **Pop below poverty level:** 12.4%.

Unemployment: 2.7%. **Median home value:** $95,900. **Median travel time to work:** 18.5 minutes.

OTERO COUNTY

PO Box 511
La Junta, CO 81050

Ph: 719-383-3020
Fax: 719-383-3025

In southeastern CO, southeast of Pueblo; organized Mar 25, 1889, from Bent County. **Name Origin:** For Miguel Antonio Otero (1859-1944), NM territorial governor (1896-1906).

Area (sq mi): 1269.74 (land 1262.86; water 6.89).

Pop: 20,311 (White 59.2%; Black or African American 0.8%; Hispanic or Latino 37.6%; Asian 0.7%; Other 19.6%). **Foreign born:** 4.9%. **Median age:** 37.7. **State rank:** 23. **Pop change 1990-2000:** +0.6%.

Income: per capita $15,113; median household $29,738. **Pop below poverty level:** 18.8%.

Unemployment: 5%. **Median home value:** $66,300. **Median travel time to work:** 18 minutes.

OURAY COUNTY

PO Box C
Ouray, CO 81427
www.co.ouray.co.us

Ph: 970-325-4961
Fax: 970-325-0452

In southwestern CO, north of Durango; organized as Uncompahgre County Jan 18, 1877, from San Juan County; name changed Mar 2, 1883. **Name Origin:** For the Ute Indian chief Ouray (1820-80), possibly 'the arrow.' He was chief of Uncompahgre Utes and signed a treaty with U.S. in 1863 as 'U-ray' or 'Arrow'; signed one in 1868 'U-re,' and later that year 'Ouray.'

Area (sq mi): 542.21 (land 540.47; water 1.74).

Pop: 3,742 (White 93.2%; Black or African American 0.1%; Hispanic or Latino 4.1%; Asian 0.3%; Other 3.2%). **Foreign born:** 3.2%. **Median age:** 43.4. **State rank:** 53. **Pop change 1990-2000:** +63.1%.

Income: per capita $24,335; median household $42,019. **Pop below poverty level:** 7.2%.

Unemployment: 3.2%. **Median home value:** $244,700. **Median travel time to work:** 23.6 minutes.

PARK COUNTY

PO Box 220
Fairplay, CO 80440
www.co.park.co.us

Ph: 719-836-4227
Fax: 719-836-4348

In central CO, west of Colorado Springs; original county, organized Nov 1, 1861 (prior to statehood). **Name Origin:** For the large mountain valley known as the 'South Park.'

Area (sq mi): 2210.69 (land 2200.69; water 10).

Pop: 14,523 (White 92.5%; Black or African American 0.5%; Hispanic or Latino 4.3%; Asian 0.4%; Other 3.9%). **Foreign born:** 2.2%. **Median age:** 40. **State rank:** 30. **Pop change 1990-2000:** +102.4%.

Income: per capita $25,019; median household $51,899. **Pop below poverty level:** 5.6%.

Unemployment: 3.1%. **Median home value:** $172,100. **Median travel time to work:** 44.8 minutes.

All statistics are based on the 2000 Census except the dollar figures given for per capita income, which are based on 1999 estimates.

PHILLIPS COUNTY

221 S Interocean Ave   **Ph:** 970-854-3131
Holyoke, CO 80734   **Fax:** 970-854-4745

On northeastern border of CO; organized Mar 27, 1889, from Logan County. **Name Origin:** For R. O. Phillips, an offical in the Lincoln Land Company, which organized many of the towns in eastern CO.

Area (sq mi): 687.74 (land 687.62; water 0.12).

Pop: 4,480 (White 86.3%; Black or African American 0.2%; Hispanic or Latino 11.8%; Asian 0.4%; Other 6.3%). **Foreign born:** 8.1%. **Median age:** 39.8. **State rank:** 52. **Pop change 1990-2000:** +6.9%.

Income: per capita $16,394; median household $32,177. **Pop below poverty level:** 11.6%.

Unemployment: 2.3%. **Median home value:** $79,800. **Median travel time to work:** 15.3 minutes.

PITKIN COUNTY

530 E Main St Suite 101   **Ph:** 970-920-5180
Aspen, CO 81611   **Fax:** 970-920-5196
www.pitkingov.com

In west-central CO, west of Leadville; organized Feb 23, 1881, from Gunnison County. **Name Origin:** For Frederick Walker Pitkin (1837-86), governor of CO (1879-83).

Area (sq mi): 973.23 (land 970.42; water 2.81).

Pop: 14,872 (White 90.6%; Black or African American 0.5%; Hispanic or Latino 6.5%; Asian 1.1%; Other 4%). **Foreign born:** 10.9%. **Median age:** 38.4. **State rank:** 29. **Pop change 1990-2000:** +17.5%.

Income: per capita $40,811; median household $59,375. **Pop below poverty level:** 6.2%.

Unemployment: 3.3%. **Median home value:** $750,000. **Median travel time to work:** 17.3 minutes.

PROWERS COUNTY

PO Box 1046   **Ph:** 719-336-8011
Lamar, CO 81052   **Fax:** 719-336-5306

On southeastern border of CO; organized Apr 11, 1889, from Bent County. **Name Origin:** For John Wesley Prowers (1839-84), a member of CO General Assembly who married Amanche, daughter of a Cheyenne chief, and worked with Indian agent Col. William Bent.

Area (sq mi): 1644.35 (land 1640.38; water 3.97).

Pop: 14,483 (White 65.1%; Black or African American 0.3%; Hispanic or Latino 32.9%; Asian 0.4%; Other 20.7%). **Foreign born:** 10.6%. **Median age:** 32.4. **State rank:** 31. **Pop change 1990-2000:** +8.5%.

Income: per capita $14,150; median household $29,935. **Pop below poverty level:** 19.5%.

Unemployment: 3.1%. **Median home value:** $67,900. **Median travel time to work:** 15.9 minutes.

PUEBLO COUNTY

215 W 10th St   **Ph:** 719-583-6000
Pueblo, CO 81003   **Fax:** 719-583-4894
www.co.pueblo.co.us

In south-central CO; original county, organized Nov 1, 1861, (prior to statehood). **Name Origin:** For the city, from Spanish 'town'.

Area (sq mi): 2397.73 (land 2388.69; water 9.04).

Pop: 141,472 (White 57.7%; Black or African American 1.9%; Hispanic or Latino 38%; Asian 0.7%; Other 18%). **Foreign born:** 3%. **Median age:** 36.7. **State rank:** 10. **Pop change 1990-2000:** +15%.

Income: per capita $17,163; median household $32,775. **Pop below poverty level:** 14.9%.

Unemployment: 5.1%. **Median home value:** $95,200. **Median travel time to work:** 20.7 minutes.

RIO BLANCO COUNTY

PO box 1067   **Ph:** 970-878-5068
Meeker, CO 81641   **Fax:** 970-878-3587
www.co.rio-blanco.co.us

On northwestern border of CO, north of Grand Junction; organized Mar 25, 1889, from Garfield County. **Name Origin:** Spanish name for the White River, which flows through the county; possibly referring to the white caps of the rapids; probably translated from the Ute name.

Area (sq mi): 3222.91 (land 3220.97; water 1.94).

Pop: 5,986 (White 92.6%; Black or African American 0.2%; Hispanic or Latino 4.9%; Asian 0.3%; Other 4.5%). **Foreign born:** 3.2%. **Median age:** 37.5. **State rank:** 46. **Pop change 1990-2000:** +0.2%.

Income: per capita $17,344; median household $37,711. **Pop below poverty level:** 9.6%.

Unemployment: 2.4%. **Median home value:** $94,700. **Median travel time to work:** 17.4 minutes.

RIO GRANDE COUNTY

965 6th St   **Ph:** 719-657-3334
Del Norte, CO 81132   **Fax:** 719-657-2621

In south-central CO; organized Feb 10, 1874, from Conejos County. **Name Origin:** For the Rio Grande, which flows through the county; shortened from Spanish *Rio Grande del Norte* 'Great River of the North.'

Area (sq mi): 912.14 (land 911.6; water 0.53).

Pop: 12,413 (White 56.6%; Black or African American 0.3%; Hispanic or Latino 41.7%; Asian 0.2%; Other 25.5%). **Foreign born:** 6%. **Median age:** 37.3. **State rank:** 35. **Pop change 1990-2000:** +15.3%.

Income: per capita $15,650; median household $31,836. **Pop below poverty level:** 14.5%.

Unemployment: 7.9%. **Median home value:** $82,400. **Median travel time to work:** 19.3 minutes.

Please see sample entry on inside front cover for detailed information about the statistics presented with each county listing.

ROUTT COUNTY
136 6th St
Steamboat Springs, CO 80477
www.co.routt.co.us

Ph: 970-879-0108
Fax: 970-879-3992

On central northern border of CO; organized Jan 29, 1877, from Grand County. **Name Origin:** For John Long Routt (1826-1907), last territorial governor (1876-79) and first CO state governor (1891-93).

Area (sq mi): 2368.02 (land 2361.59; water 6.43).

Pop: 19,690 (White 94.8%; Black or African American 0.1%; Hispanic or Latino 3.2%; Asian 0.4%; Other 2.6%). **Foreign born:** 4.1%. **Median age:** 35. **State rank:** 25. **Pop change 1990-2000:** +39.8%.

Income: per capita $28,792; median household $53,612. **Pop below poverty level:** 6.1%.

Unemployment: 2.2%. **Median home value:** $268,500. **Median travel time to work:** 18.5 minutes.

SAGUACHE COUNTY
501 4th St
Saguache, CO 81149

Ph: 719-655-2231
Fax: 719-655-2635

In south-central CO, west of Pueblo; organized Dec 29, 1866, from Costilla County (prior to statehood). **Name Origin:** For Saguache Creek, which flows through the county; from a Ute Indian word meaning 'blue earth,' or 'water at the blue earth.'

Area (sq mi): 3170.25 (land 3168.44; water 1.82).

Pop: 5,917 (White 51.6%; Black or African American 0.1%; Hispanic or Latino 45.3%; Asian 0.5%; Other 28.2%). **Foreign born:** 14.5%. **Median age:** 36.9. **State rank:** 47. **Pop change 1990-2000:** +28.1%.

Income: per capita $13,121; median household $25,495. **Pop below poverty level:** 22.6%.

Unemployment: 8.3%. **Median home value:** $73,900. **Median travel time to work:** 19.8 minutes.

SAN JUAN COUNTY
PO Box 466
Silverton, CO 81433

Ph: 970-387-5671
Fax: 970-387-5671

In southwestern CO, north of Durango; organized 1876, from La Plata County. **Name Origin:** Spanish Saint John (the Baptist). Name was given by early Spanish explorers to the river, the mountain range, and then the whole region.

Area (sq mi): 388.29 (land 387.42; water 0.86).

Pop: 558 (White 91.2%; Black or African American 0%; Hispanic or Latino 7.3%; Asian 0.2%; Other 2.7%). **Foreign born:** 2.5%. **Median age:** 43.7. **State rank:** 63. **Pop change 1990-2000:** -25.1%.

Income: per capita $17,584; median household $30,764. **Pop below poverty level:** 20.9%.

Unemployment: 16.2%. **Median home value:** $131,500. **Median travel time to work:** 16.1 minutes.

SAN MIGUEL COUNTY
PO Box 548
Telluride, CO 81435
www.co.san-miguel.co.us

Ph: 970-728-3954
Fax: 970-728-4808

On southwestern border of CO; organized Nov 1, 1861, from Ouray County (prior to statehood). **Name Origin:** For the river, which flows through the county; Spanish for Saint Michael (the Archangel).

Area (sq mi): 1288.49 (land 1286.5; water 1.98).

Pop: 6,594 (White 90.4%; Black or African American 0.3%; Hispanic or Latino 6.7%; Asian 0.7%; Other 5.4%). **Foreign born:** 7.3%. **Median age:** 34.2. **State rank:** 43. **Pop change 1990-2000:** +80.5%.

Income: per capita $35,329; median household $48,514. **Pop below poverty level:** 10.4%.

Unemployment: 3.8%. **Median home value:** $358,200. **Median travel time to work:** 18.8 minutes.

SEDGWICK COUNTY
PO Box 50
Julesburg, CO 80737

Ph: 970-474-3346
Fax: 970-474-0954

On northeasternmost border of CO; organized Apr 9, 1889, from Logan County. **Name Origin:** For Fort Sedgwick, named for Maj. Gen. John Sedgwick (1813-64), Indian fighter and Union officer in the Civil War.

Area (sq mi): 549.6 (land 548.24; water 1.36).

Pop: 2,747 (White 86.5%; Black or African American 0.5%; Hispanic or Latino 11.4%; Asian 0.8%; Other 8.2%). **Foreign born:** 2.7%. **Median age:** 43.2. **State rank:** 56. **Pop change 1990-2000:** +2.1%.

Income: per capita $16,125; median household $28,278. **Pop below poverty level:** 10%.

Unemployment: 3%. **Median home value:** $57,100. **Median travel time to work:** 15.7 minutes.

SUMMIT COUNTY
PO Box 1538
Breckenridge, CO 80424
www.co.summit.co.us

Ph: 970-453-2561
Fax: 970-453-3540

In central CO west of Denver; original county, organized 1861, (prior to statehood). **Name Origin:** For the mountainous terrain of the county; part of its southeastern border follows the Continental Divide.

Area (sq mi): 619.25 (land 608.16; water 11.09).

Pop: 23,548 (White 86.7%; Black or African American 0.7%; Hispanic or Latino 9.8%; Asian 0.9%; Other 6.7%). **Foreign born:** 11.6%. **Median age:** 30.8. **State rank:** 20. **Pop change 1990-2000:** +82.8%.

Income: per capita $28,676; median household $56,587. **Pop below poverty level:** 9%.

Unemployment: 2.7%. **Median home value:** $317,500. **Median travel time to work:** 16.9 minutes.

All statistics are based on the 2000 Census except the dollar figures given for per capita income, which are based on 1999 estimates.

TELLER COUNTY

PO Box 959   **Ph:** 719-689-2988
Cripple Creek, CO 80813   **Fax:** 719-689-3268
www.co.teller.co.us

In central CO, west of Colorado Springs; organized Mar 23, 1899, from El Paso and Fremont Counties. **Name Origin:** For Henry Moore Teller (1830-1914), U.S. senator from CO (1876-82; 1885-1909), and U.S. secretary of the interior (1882-85).

Area (sq mi): 558.96 (land 557.06; water 1.89).

Pop: 20,555 (White 92.9%; Black or African American 0.5%; Hispanic or Latino 3.5%; Asian 0.6%; Other 4%). **Foreign born:** 1.8%. **Median age:** 39.4. **State rank:** 21. **Pop change 1990-2000:** +64.9%.

Income: per capita $23,412; median household $50,165. **Pop below poverty level:** 5.4%.

Unemployment: 2.9%. **Median home value:** $162,000. **Median travel time to work:** 30.1 minutes.

WASHINGTON COUNTY

150 Ash Ave   **Ph:** 970-345-2701
Akron, CO 80720   **Fax:** 970-345-2702

In northeastern CO, east of Denver; organized Feb 9, 1887, from Weld County. **Name Origin:** For George Washington (1732-1799), American patriot and first U.S. president.

Area (sq mi): 2524.12 (land 2520.98; water 3.13).

Pop: 4,926 (White 92.7%; Black or African American 0%; Hispanic or Latino 6.3%; Asian 0.1%; Other 3.5%). **Foreign born:** 2.5%. **Median age:** 40.2. **State rank:** 49. **Pop change 1990-2000:** +2.4%.

Income: per capita $17,788; median household $32,431. **Pop below poverty level:** 11.4%.

Unemployment: 2.4%. **Median home value:** $70,800. **Median travel time to work:** 21 minutes.

WELD COUNTY

PO Box 758   **Ph:** 970-336-7204
Greeley, CO 80632   **Fax:** 970-352-0242
www.co.weld.co.us

On central northern border of CO, east of Fort Collins; original county, organized Nov 1, 1861, (prior to statehood). A portion of the county was used to create Broomfield County on November 15, 2001. **Name Origin:** For Lewis Ledyard Weld, first Secretary of the CO Territory.

Area (sq mi): 4021.56 (land 3992.45; water 29.11).

Pop: 180,936 (White 70%; Black or African American 0.6%; Hispanic or Latino 27%; Asian 0.8%; Other 17%). **Foreign born:** 9.3%. **Median age:** 30.9. **State rank:** 8. **Pop change 1990-2000:** +37.3%.

Income: per capita $18,957; median household $42,321. **Pop below poverty level:** 12.5%.

Unemployment: 4.1%. **Median home value:** $140,400. **Median travel time to work:** 23.7 minutes.

YUMA COUNTY

310 Ash St Suite F   **Ph:** 970-332-5809
Wray, CO 80758

On eastern border of CO, east of Denver; organized Mar 15, 1889, from Washington County. **Name Origin:** For the Yuma Indian tribe. The name, given to the tribe by the Spanish, may mean 'children of the sun' or may come from the Spanish *umo* 'smoke.'

Area (sq mi): 2369.1 (land 2365.79; water 3.3).

Pop: 9,841 (White 86.1%; Black or African American 0.1%; Hispanic or Latino 12.9%; Asian 0.1%; Other 5.6%). **Foreign born:** 7.9%. **Median age:** 37.3. **State rank:** 37. **Pop change 1990-2000:** +9.9%.

Income: per capita $16,005; median household $33,169. **Pop below poverty level:** 12.9%.

Unemployment: 2.1%. **Median home value:** $77,100. **Median travel time to work:** 15.4 minutes.

Please see sample entry on inside front cover for detailed information about the statistics presented with each county listing.

87

CONNECTICUT - Counties

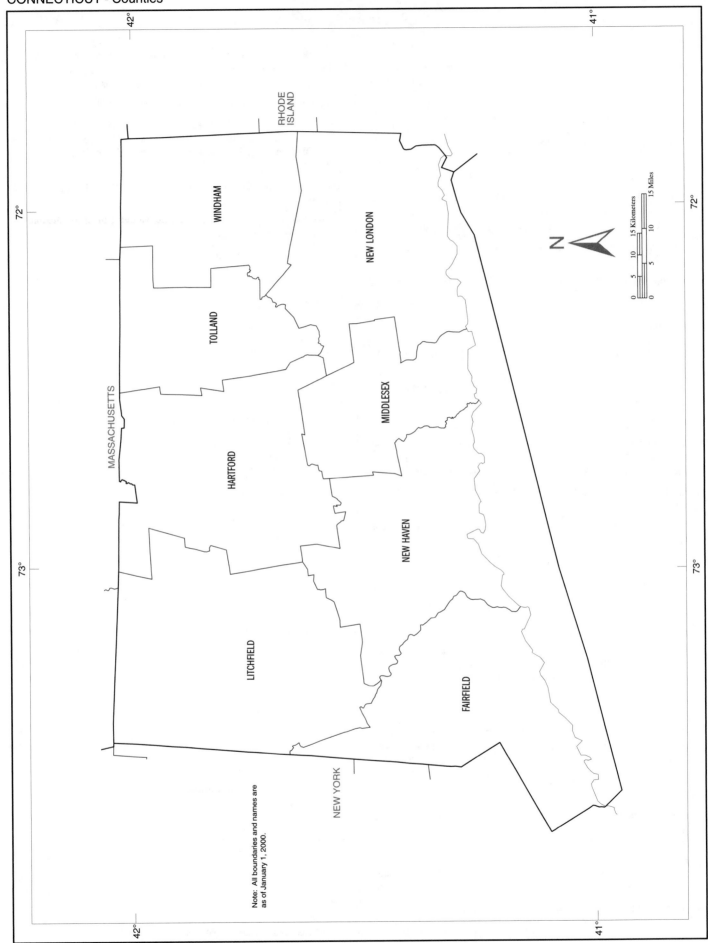

WINDHAM

NEW LONDON

TOLLAND

MASSACHUSETTS

MIDDLESEX

HARTFORD

NEW HAVEN

LITCHFIELD

FAIRFIELD

NEW YORK

RHODE ISLAND

N

15 Kilometers
15 Miles

0   5   10
0   5   10

Note: All boundaries and names are
as of January 1, 2000.

42°

72°

73°

41°

Connecticut

CONNECTICUT STATE INFORMATION

www.ct.gov   Ph: 860-622-2200

Area (sq mi): 5543.33 (land 4844.8; water 698.53).

Pop: 3,405,565 (White 77.5%; Black or African American 9.1%; Hispanic or Latino 9.4%; Asian 2.4%; Other 6.8%). **Foreign born:** 10.9%. **Median age:** 37.4. **Pop change 1990-2000:** +3.6%.

Income: per capita $28,766; median household $53,935. **Pop below poverty level:** 7.9%.

Unemployment: 4.8%. **Median home value:** $166,900. **Median travel time to work:** 24.4 minutes.

FAIRFIELD COUNTY

1061 Main St   Ph: 203-579-6527
Bridgeport, CT 06604   Fax: 203-382-8406
www.fairfieldcounty.com

In southwestern CT, bordered on the west by NY and on the south by Long Island Sound. Original county, organized May 10, 1666. **Name Origin:** Descriptive of the area.

Area (sq mi): 836.96 (land 625.8; water 211.15).

Pop: 882,567 (White 73.1%; Black or African American 10%; Hispanic or Latino 11.9%; Asian 3.3%; Other 7.4%). **Foreign born:** 16.9%. **Median age:** 37.3. **State rank:** 1. **Pop change 1990-2000:** +6.6%.

Income: per capita $38,350; median household $65,249. **Pop below poverty level:** 6.9%.

Unemployment: 3.1%. **Median home value:** $288,900. **Median travel time to work:** 28 minutes.

HARTFORD COUNTY

550 Main St   Ph: 860-543-8580
Hartford, CT 06103   Fax: 860-722-8041
www.ci.hartford.ct.us

In north-central CT. Original county, organized May 10, 1666. **Name Origin:** For Hertford or Hertfordshire, England. Spelling reflects English pronunciation.

Area (sq mi): 750.57 (land 735.44; water 15.13).

Pop: 857,183 (White 73%; Black or African American 11.7%; Hispanic or Latino 11.5%; Asian 2.4%; Other 8.9%). **Foreign born:** 11.7%. **Median age:** 37.7. **State rank:** 2. **Pop change 1990-2000:** +0.6%.

Income: per capita $26,047; median household $50,756. **Pop below poverty level:** 9.3%.

Unemployment: 3.5%. **Median home value:** $147,300. **Median travel time to work:** 21.9 minutes.

LITCHFIELD COUNTY

15 West St   Ph: 860-567-0885
Litchfield, CT 067593500   Fax: 860-567-4779
www.litchfieldcty.com

In northwestern CT, bordered on the west by NY and on the north by MA; organized Oct 14, 1751 from Hartford and Fairfield counties. **Name Origin:** For the town in England, in Hampshire County.

Area (sq mi): 944.57 (land 919.92; water 24.65).

Pop: 182,193 (White 94.5%; Black or African American 1.1%; Hispanic or Latino 2.1%; Asian 1.2%; Other 2%). **Foreign born:** 5.4%. **Median age:** 39.6. **State rank:** 5. **Pop change 1990-2000:** +4.7%.

Income: per capita $28,408; median household $56,273. **Pop below poverty level:** 4.5%.

Unemployment: 3%. **Median home value:** $156,600. **Median travel time to work:** 26.2 minutes.

MIDDLESEX COUNTY

1 Court St   Ph: 860-343-6400
Middletown, CT 06457   Fax: 860-343-6423

In south-central CT, east of New Haven, with Long Island Sound to the south and the Connecticut River to the east; organized May 2, 1785 (prior to statehood) from Hartford, New London, and New Haven counties. **Name Origin:** For a former county in southeast England.

Area (sq mi): 439.07 (land 369.26; water 69.81).

Pop: 155,071 (White 89.6%; Black or African American 4.4%; Hispanic or Latino 3%; Asian 1.6%; Other 2.8%). **Foreign born:** 6%. **Median age:** 38.6. **State rank:** 6. **Pop change 1990-2000:** +8.3%.

Income: per capita $28,251; median household $59,175. **Pop below poverty level:** 4.6%.

Unemployment: 2.7%. **Median home value:** $166,000. **Median travel time to work:** 24.5 minutes.

NEW HAVEN COUNTY

200 Orange St   Ph: 203-946-8200
New Haven, CT 06510   Fax: 203-946-7683
www.cityofnewhaven.com

In south-central CT on Long Island Sound, south of Hartford. Original county, organized May 10, 1666. **Name Origin:** For the colonial settlement at New Haven.

Please see sample entry on inside front cover for detailed information about the statistics presented with each county listing.

Area (sq mi): 862.02 (land 605.64; water 256.38).

Pop: 824,008 (White 74.8%; Black or African American 11.3%; Hispanic or Latino 10.1%; Asian 2.3%; Other 6.9%). **Foreign born:** 9%. **Median age:** 37. **State rank:** 3. **Pop change 1990-2000:** +2.5%.

Income: per capita $24,439; median household $48,834. **Pop below poverty level:** 9.5%.

Unemployment: 3.7%. **Median home value:** $151,900. **Median travel time to work:** 23.2 minutes.

NEW LONDON COUNTY
70 Huntington St   **Ph:** 860-443-5363
New London, CT 06320   **Fax:** 860-442-7703

In southeastern CT on Long Island Sound and east of the Connecticut River. Original county, organized May 10, 1666. **Name Origin:** For the city in England.

Area (sq mi): 771.66 (land 665.91; water 105.75).

Pop: 259,088 (White 84.7%; Black or African American 5.3%; Hispanic or Latino 5.1%; Asian 2%; Other 5.9%). **Foreign born:** 5.4%. **Median age:** 37. **State rank:** 4. **Pop change 1990-2000:** +1.6%.

Income: per capita $24,678; median household $50,646. **Pop below poverty level:** 6.4%.

Unemployment: 2.8%. **Median home value:** $142,200. **Median travel time to work:** 22.2 minutes.

TOLLAND COUNTY
69 Brooklyn St   **Ph:** 860-896-4920
Rockville, CT 06066

In north-central CT, east of Hartford; organized Oct 17, 1785 (prior to statehood) from Windham County. **Name Origin:** For the town in western England, in Somerset County.

Area (sq mi): 417.01 (land 410.07; water 6.94).

Pop: 136,364 (White 90.9%; Black or African American 2.7%; Hispanic or Latino 2.8%; Asian 2.3%; Other 2.7%). **Foreign born:** 5.9%. **Median age:** 35.7. **State rank:** 7. **Pop change 1990-2000:** +6%.

Income: per capita $25,474; median household $59,044. **Pop below poverty level:** 5.6%.

Unemployment: 2.3%. **Median home value:** $151,600. **Median travel time to work:** 25.4 minutes.

WINDHAM COUNTY
PO Box 191   **Ph:** 860-928-7749
Putnam, CT 06260   **Fax:** 860-928-7076

In northeastern CT, bordered on the east by RI and on the north by MA; organized May 12, 1726 from Hartford and New London counties. **Name Origin:** For Wymondham, Norfolk, England; spelling reflects pronunciation.

Area (sq mi): 521.47 (land 512.75; water 8.71).

Pop: 109,091 (White 88.6%; Black or African American 1.9%; Hispanic or Latino 7.1%; Asian 0.8%; Other 6%). **Foreign born:** 4.3%. **Median age:** 36.3. **State rank:** 8. **Pop change 1990-2000:** +6.4%.

Income: per capita $20,443; median household $45,115. **Pop below poverty level:** 8.5%.

Unemployment: 3.7%. **Median home value:** $117,200. **Median travel time to work:** 25.7 minutes.

All statistics are based on the 2000 Census except the dollar figures given for per capita income, which are based on 1999 estimates.

DELAWARE - Counties

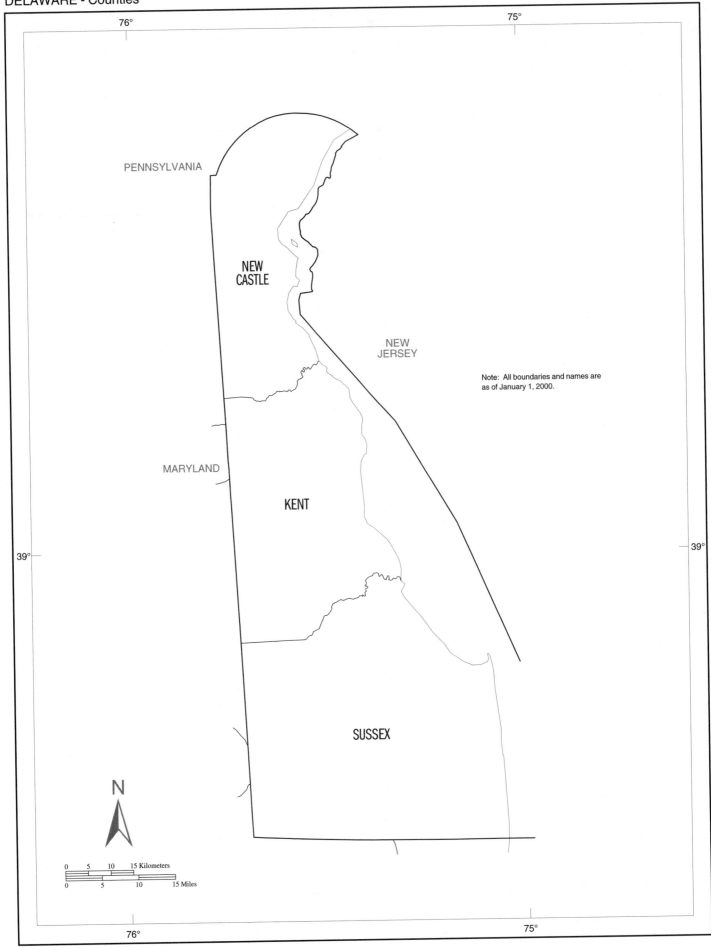

PENNSYLVANIA

NEW CASTLE

NEW JERSEY

Note: All boundaries and names are as of January 1, 2000.

MARYLAND

KENT

39°

SUSSEX

N

0   5   10   15 Kilometers

0   5   10   15 Miles

Delaware

DELAWARE STATE INFORMATION

www.delaware.gov   **Ph:** 302-739-4000

Area (sq mi): 2489.27 (land 1953.56; water 535.71).

Pop: 783,600 (White 72.5%; Black or African American 19.2%; Hispanic or Latino 4.8%; Asian 2.1%; Other 4%). **Foreign born:** 5.7%. **Median age:** 36. **Pop change 1990-2000:** +17.6%.

Income: per capita $23,305; median household $47,381. **Pop below poverty level:** 9.2%.

Unemployment: 3.4%. **Median home value:** $130,400. **Median travel time to work:** 24 minutes.

KENT COUNTY

414 Federal St   **Ph:** 302-744-2305
Dover, DE 199013615   **Fax:** 302-736-2279
www.co.kent.de.us

In central DE; organized as Saint Jones County in 1680 from Horre Kill District, which was organized in 1664; name changed in 1682. **Name Origin:** For the county in England.

Area (sq mi): 800.12 (land 589.72; water 210.4).

Pop: 126,697 (White 72.1%; Black or African American 20.7%; Hispanic or Latino 3.2%; Asian 1.7%; Other 4.1%). **Foreign born:** 4%. **Median age:** 34.4. **State rank:** 3. **Pop change 1990-2000:** +14.1%.

Income: per capita $18,662; median household $40,950. **Pop below poverty level:** 10.7%.

Unemployment: 3.7%. **Median home value:** $114,100. **Median travel time to work:** 22.7 minutes.

NEW CASTLE COUNTY

New Castle Corporate Commons
87 Reads Way   **Ph:** 302-395-5268
New Castle, DE 19720   **Fax:** 302-571-7857
www.co.new-castle.de.us

In northern DE; original county, organized 1673. **Name Origin:** Col. Richard Nicolls, in Oct. 1664, renamed the former Swedish-Dutch settlement of New Amstel to honor William Cavendish (1592-1676), Duke of Newcastle.

Area (sq mi): 493.51 (land 426.27; water 67.24).

Pop: 500,265 (White 70.7%; Black or African American 20.2%; Hispanic or Latino 5.3%; Asian 2.6%; Other 4%). **Foreign born:** 6.6%. **Median age:** 35. **State rank:** 1. **Pop change 1990-2000:** +13.2%.

Income: per capita $25,413; median household $52,419. **Pop below poverty level:** 8.4%.

Unemployment: 3.4%. **Median home value:** $136,000. **Median travel time to work:** 24.3 minutes.

SUSSEX COUNTY

PO Box 589   **Ph:** 302-855-7743
Georgetown, DE 19947   **Fax:** 302-855-7749
www.sussexcounty.net

In southern DE; organized as Deale County in 1680 from Horre Kill District, which was organized in 1664; name changed in 1682. **Name Origin:** For the county in England.

Area (sq mi): 1195.65 (land 937.58; water 258.07).

Pop: 156,638 (White 78.5%; Black or African American 14.9%; Hispanic or Latino 4.4%; Asian 0.7%; Other 4%). **Foreign born:** 4.5%. **Median age:** 41.1. **State rank:** 2. **Pop change 1990-2000:** +38.3%.

Income: per capita $20,328; median household $39,208. **Pop below poverty level:** 10.5%.

Unemployment: 3.9%. **Median home value:** $122,400. **Median travel time to work:** 24 minutes.

Please see sample entry on inside front cover for detailed information about the statistics presented with each county listing.

FLORIDA - Counties

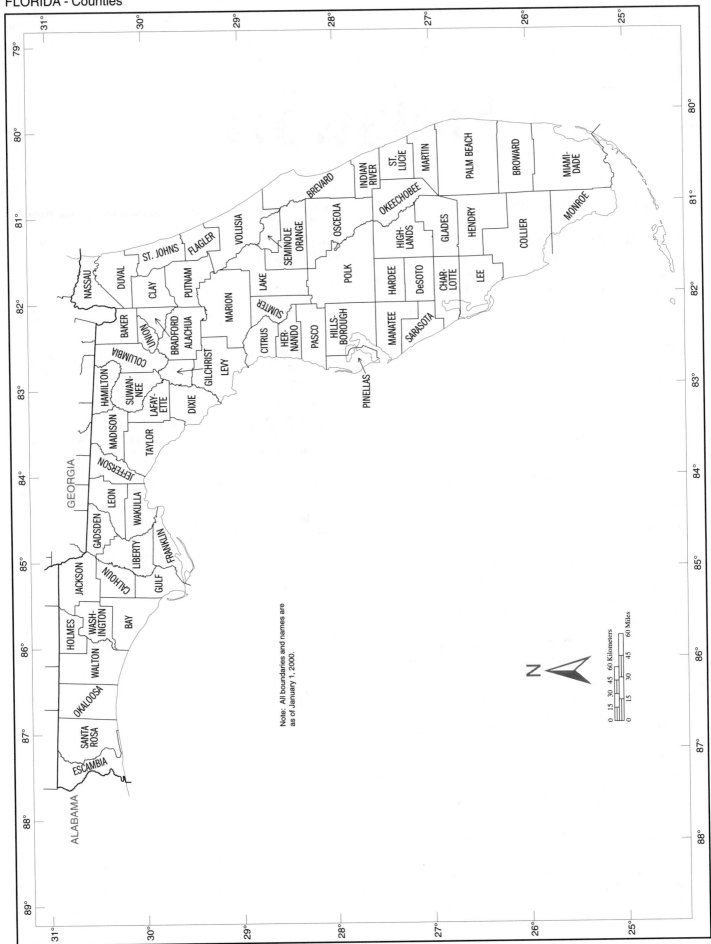

Note: All boundaries and names are as of January 1, 2000.

N

0 15 30 45 60 Kilometers
0 15 30 45 60 Miles

Florida

FLORIDA STATE INFORMATION

www.myflorida.com   **Ph:** 850-488-1234

Area (sq mi): 65,754.59 (land 53,926.82; water 11,827.77).

Pop: 15,982,378 (White 65.4%; Black or African American 14.6%; Hispanic or Latino 16.8%; Asian 1.7%; Other 5.8%). **Foreign born:** 16.7%. **Median age:** 38.7. **Pop change 1990-2000:** +23.5%.

Income: per capita $21,557; median household $38,819. **Pop below poverty level:** 12.5%.

Unemployment: 5.3%. **Median home value:** $105,500. **Median travel time to work:** 26.2 minutes.

ALACHUA COUNTY

12 SE 1st St   **Ph:** 352-374-5210
Gainesville, FL 32601   **Fax:** 352-338-7363
www.co.alachua.fl.us

In north-central FL, north of Ocala; organized Dec 29, 1824 (prior to statehood) from Duval and Saint Johns counties. **Name Origin:** For a Seminole Indian town settled by Creek Indians from Oconee, GA. Name derives from *luchuwa* 'jug,' descriptive of a chasm, probably the Devil's Millhopper, near Gainesville, FL.

Area (sq mi): 969.12 (land 874.25; water 94.88).

Pop: 217,955 (White 69.7%; Black or African American 19.3%; Hispanic or Latino 5.7%; Asian 3.5%; Other 3.6%). **Foreign born:** 7.3%. **Median age:** 29. **State rank:** 20. **Pop change 1990-2000:** +20%.

Income: per capita $18,465; median household $31,426. **Pop below poverty level:** 22.8%.

Unemployment: 2.6%. **Median home value:** $97,300. **Median travel time to work:** 21.1 minutes.

BAKER COUNTY

339 E Macclenny Ave   **Ph:** 904-259-8113
Macclenny, FL 32063   **Fax:** 904-259-4176
bakercountyfl.org

On northern border of FL, west of Jacksonville; organized Feb 8, 1861 from New River County. **Name Origin:** For James McNair Baker (1821-92), FL legislator and jurist, associate justice of the FL supreme court (1866).

Area (sq mi): 588.89 (land 585.21; water 3.67).

Pop: 22,259 (White 82.6%; Black or African American 13.9%; Hispanic or Latino 1.9%; Asian 0.4%; Other 1.6%). **Foreign born:** 1.1%. **Median age:** 34. **State rank:** 52. **Pop change 1990-2000:** +20.4%.

Income: per capita $15,164; median household $40,035. **Pop below poverty level:** 14.7%.

Unemployment: 4.5%. **Median home value:** $80,900. **Median travel time to work:** 32.7 minutes.

BAY COUNTY

300 E 4th St   **Ph:** 850-763-9061
Panama City, FL 32401   **Fax:** 850-747-5188
www.co.bay.fl.us

On northern coast of the Gulf of Mexico; organized Apr 24, 1913 from Calhoun and Washington counties; name changed from New River County in 1861. **Name Origin:** For Saint Andrews Bay, in the southeastern part of the county.

Area (sq mi): 1033.27 (land 763.68; water 269.6).

Pop: 148,217 (White 82.8%; Black or African American 10.6%; Hispanic or Latino 2.4%; Asian 1.7%; Other 3.5%). **Foreign born:** 3.6%. **Median age:** 37.4. **State rank:** 25. **Pop change 1990-2000:** +16.7%.

Income: per capita $18,700; median household $36,092. **Pop below poverty level:** 13%.

Unemployment: 6%. **Median home value:** $93,500. **Median travel time to work:** 21.6 minutes.

BRADFORD COUNTY

PO Drawer B   **Ph:** 904-964-6280
Starke, FL 32091   **Fax:** 904-964-4454
www.bradford-co-fla.org

In north-central FL between Gainesville and Jacksonville; organized as New River County Dec 21, 1858; name changed Dec 6, 1861. **Name Origin:** For Capt. Richard Bradford (1839?-61), the first Florida officer killed in the Civil War.

Area (sq mi): 300.04 (land 293.13; water 6.91).

Pop: 26,088 (White 75%; Black or African American 20.8%; Hispanic or Latino 2.4%; Asian 0.6%; Other 2.3%). **Foreign born:** 1.8%. **Median age:** 37.2. **State rank:** 50. **Pop change 1990-2000:** +15.9%.

Income: per capita $14,226; median household $33,140. **Pop below poverty level:** 14.6%.

Unemployment: 3.2%. **Median home value:** $71,700. **Median travel time to work:** 27.9 minutes.

Please see sample entry on inside front cover for detailed information about the statistics presented with each county listing.

BREVARD COUNTY
2725 Judge Fran Jamieson Way   **Ph:** 321-633-2010
Melbourne, FL 32940   **Fax:** 321-633-2115
www.brevardcounty.us

On central east coast of FL, east of Orlando; organized as Saint Lucie County Mar 14, 1844 from Mosquito County; name changed Jan 6, 1855. **Name Origin:** For Theodore Washington Brevard (1804-77), FL state comptroller (1853-61).

Area (sq mi): 1556.95 (land 1018.19; water 538.76).

Pop: 476,230 (White 83.7%; Black or African American 8.4%; Hispanic or Latino 4.6%; Asian 1.5%; Other 3.4%). **Foreign born:** 6.5%. **Median age:** 41.4. **State rank:** 9. **Pop change 1990-2000:** +19.4%.

Income: per capita $21,484; median household $40,099. **Pop below poverty level:** 9.5%.

Unemployment: 4.3%. **Median home value:** $94,400. **Median travel time to work:** 24.5 minutes.

BROWARD COUNTY
115 S Andrews Ave Rm 421   **Ph:** 954-357-7000
Fort Lauderdale, FL 33301   **Fax:** 954-357-7295
www.co.broward.fl.us

On southeastern coast of FL, north of Miami; organized Apr 30, 1915 from Dade and Palm Beach counties. **Name Origin:** For Napoleon Bonaparte Broward (1857-1910), FL governor (1905-09).

Area (sq mi): 1319.63 (land 1205.4; water 114.24).

Pop: 1,623,018 (White 58%; Black or African American 20.5%; Hispanic or Latino 16.7%; Asian 2.3%; Other 6.7%). **Foreign born:** 25.3%. **Median age:** 37.8. **State rank:** 2. **Pop change 1990-2000:** +29.3%.

Income: per capita $23,170; median household $41,691. **Pop below poverty level:** 11.5%.

Unemployment: 4.9%. **Median home value:** $128,600. **Median travel time to work:** 27.4 minutes.

CALHOUN COUNTY
20859 Central Ave E Rm 130   **Ph:** 850-674-4545
Blountstown, FL 32424   **Fax:** 850-674-5553

In the central panhandle of FL, west of Tallahassee; organized Jan 26, 1838 (prior to statehood) from Jackson County. **Name Origin:** For John Caldwell Calhoun (1782-1850), U.S. statesman and champion of Southern causes.

Area (sq mi): 574.34 (land 567.31; water 7.03).

Pop: 13,017 (White 77.6%; Black or African American 15.8%; Hispanic or Latino 3.8%; Asian 0.5%; Other 3.9%). **Foreign born:** 2.2%. **Median age:** 36.2. **State rank:** 62. **Pop change 1990-2000:** +18.2%.

Income: per capita $12,379; median household $26,575. **Pop below poverty level:** 20%.

Unemployment: 5.1%. **Median home value:** $58,500. **Median travel time to work:** 28 minutes.

CHARLOTTE COUNTY
18500 Murdoch Cir   **Ph:** 941-743-1200
Port Charlotte, FL 33948   **Fax:** 941-743-1530
www.co.charlotte.fl.us

On the Gulf coast of FL, north of Fort Myers; organized Apr 23, 1921 from DeSoto County. **Name Origin:** For Charlotte Harbor, possibly originally named for the Calusa tribe of southwestern FL, which the Spanish corrupted to Carlos or Calos. The name was later changed by English surveyors to honor Charlotte Sophia (1744-1818), wife of King George III of England.

Area (sq mi): 859.12 (land 693.6; water 165.51).

Pop: 141,627 (White 90.4%; Black or African American 4.4%; Hispanic or Latino 3.3%; Asian 0.9%; Other 2.1%). **Foreign born:** 8%. **Median age:** 54.3. **State rank:** 26. **Pop change 1990-2000:** +27.6%.

Income: per capita $21,806; median household $36,379. **Pop below poverty level:** 8.2%.

Unemployment: 3.4%. **Median home value:** $97,000. **Median travel time to work:** 23.6 minutes.

CITRUS COUNTY
110 N Apopka Ave   **Ph:** 352-341-6400
Inverness, FL 34450   **Fax:** 352-341-6491
www.clerk.citrus.fl.us

On the Gulf coast of FL, southwest of Ocala; organized Jun 2, 1887 from Hernando County. **Name Origin:** For the major agricultural crop of the region.

Area (sq mi): 773.15 (land 583.81; water 189.34).

Pop: 118,085 (White 93%; Black or African American 2.4%; Hispanic or Latino 2.7%; Asian 0.8%; Other 1.9%). **Foreign born:** 4.9%. **Median age:** 52.6. **State rank:** 31. **Pop change 1990-2000:** +26.3%.

Income: per capita $18,585; median household $31,001. **Pop below poverty level:** 11.7%.

Unemployment: 6%. **Median home value:** $84,400. **Median travel time to work:** 26.6 minutes.

CLAY COUNTY
825 N Orange Ave   **Ph:** 904-269-6302
Green Cove Springs, FL 32043
www.co.clay.fl.us

In northeastern FL, southwest of Jacksonville; organized Dec 31, 1858 from Duval County. **Name Origin:** For Henry Clay (1777-1852), U.S. senator from KY, known as the 'Great Pacificator' for his advocacy of compromise to avert national crises.

Area (sq mi): 643.69 (land 601.11; water 42.59).

Pop: 140,814 (White 84.9%; Black or African American 6.7%; Hispanic or Latino 4.3%; Asian 2%; Other 3.9%). **Foreign born:** 4.5%. **Median age:** 35.9. **State rank:** 27. **Pop change 1990-2000:** +32.9%.

Income: per capita $20,868; median household $48,854. **Pop below poverty level:** 6.8%.

Unemployment: 3.6%. **Median home value:** $108,400. **Median travel time to work:** 33.5 minutes.

All statistics are based on the 2000 Census except the dollar figures given for per capita income, which are based on 1999 estimates.

COLLIER COUNTY

3301 Tamiami Trail E
Naples, FL 34112
www.co.collier.fl.us

Ph: 239-774-8383
Fax: 239-774-4010

On the southwestern Gulf coast of FL, west of Fort Lauderdale; organized May 8, 1923 from Lee and Monroe counties. **Name Origin:** For Barron Gift Collier (1873-1939), a promoter active in the development of southern FL.

Area (sq mi): 2304.93 (land 2025.34; water 279.59).

Pop: 251,377 (White 73.8%; Black or African American 4.5%; Hispanic or Latino 19.6%; Asian 0.6%; Other 8.8%). **Foreign born:** 18.3%. **Median age:** 44.1. **State rank:** 18. **Pop change 1990-2000:** +65.3%.

Income: per capita $31,195; median household $48,289. **Pop below poverty level:** 10.3%.

Unemployment: 3.9%. **Median home value:** $168,000. **Median travel time to work:** 24 minutes.

COLUMBIA COUNTY

PO Box 2069
Lake City, FL 32056
www.columbiacountyfla.com

Ph: 386-755-4100
Fax: 386-758-1337

On northern border of FL, west of Jacksonville; organized Feb 4, 1832 (prior to statehood) from Alachua County. **Name Origin:** Feminine form of Columbus, a poetic and honorific reference to Christopher Columbus (1451-1506) and America.

Area (sq mi): 801.04 (land 797.05; water 3.99).

Pop: 56,513 (White 78%; Black or African American 17%; Hispanic or Latino 2.7%; Asian 0.7%; Other 2.5%). **Foreign born:** 2.3%. **Median age:** 37.3. **State rank:** 38. **Pop change 1990-2000:** +32.6%.

Income: per capita $14,598; median household $30,881. **Pop below poverty level:** 15%.

Unemployment: 6.4%. **Median home value:** $73,600. **Median travel time to work:** 24.1 minutes.

DESOTO COUNTY

201 E Oak St
Arcadia, FL 34266
www.co.desoto.fl.us

Ph: 863-993-4800
Fax: 863-993-4809

In southwest-central FL, east of Sarasota; organized May 19, 1887 from Manatee County. **Name Origin:** For Hernando De Soto (c. 1500-42), Spanish explorer of southern U.S.

Area (sq mi): 639.5 (land 637.27; water 2.23).

Pop: 32,209 (White 61.2%; Black or African American 12.7%; Hispanic or Latino 24.9%; Asian 0.4%; Other 13.5%). **Foreign born:** 18.7%. **Median age:** 36.5. **State rank:** 48. **Pop change 1990-2000:** +35%.

Income: per capita $14,000; median household $30,714. **Pop below poverty level:** 23.6%.

Unemployment: 6%. **Median home value:** $69,900. **Median travel time to work:** 27.9 minutes.

DIXIE COUNTY

PO Box 1206
Cross City, FL 32628
www.dixie-county.com

Ph: 352-498-1200
Fax: 352-498-1201

On the Gulf coast of FL, west of Gainesville; organized Apr 25, 1921 from Lafayette County. **Name Origin:** For the name applied to the Confederate States, from the song composed in 1859 by Daniel Decatur Emmett (1815-1904), said to be derived from a Creole pronunciation of the second name in the Mason and Dixon Line.

Area (sq mi): 863.66 (land 704.01; water 159.65).

Pop: 13,827 (White 87.7%; Black or African American 9%; Hispanic or Latino 1.8%; Asian 0.2%; Other 1.9%). **Foreign born:** 2%. **Median age:** 40.7. **State rank:** 58. **Pop change 1990-2000:** +30.6%.

Income: per capita $13,559; median household $26,082. **Pop below poverty level:** 19.1%.

Unemployment: 6.7%. **Median home value:** $61,700. **Median travel time to work:** 30.2 minutes.

DUVAL COUNTY/CITY OF JACKSONVILLE

117 W Duval St
Jacksonville, FL 32202
www.coj.net

Ph: 904-630-1178
Fax: 904-630-2906

On the northeastern coast of FL; organized Aug 12, 1822 from Saint Johns County (prior to statehood). **Name Origin:** For William Pope DuVal (1784-1854), governor of the Florida Territory (1822-34).

Area (sq mi): 918.24 (land 773.67; water 144.57).

Pop: 778,879 (White 63.5%; Black or African American 27.8%; Hispanic or Latino 4.1%; Asian 2.7%; Other 3.7%). **Foreign born:** 5.9%. **Median age:** 34.1. **State rank:** 7. **Pop change 1990-2000:** +15.7%.

Income: per capita $20,753; median household $40,703. **Pop below poverty level:** 11.9%.

Unemployment: 4.5%. **Median home value:** $89,600. **Median travel time to work:** 25.2 minutes.

ESCAMBIA COUNTY

PO Box 1591
Pensacola, FL 32597
www.co.escambia.fl.us

Ph: 850-595-4900
Fax: 850-595-4908

On northwestern border of FL, bordered on the south by the Gulf of Mexico; original county; organized Jul 21, 1822 (prior to statehood). It is one of the two first counties; the other is Saint Johns. **Name Origin:** For the river, which forms its eastern border; probably a Spanish rendering of a Choctaw or Chickasaw Indian word but origin is in dispute. River formerly called the *Pensacola*. There may be a connection to Spanish *cambiar* 'to trade.'

Area (sq mi): 875.57 (land 662.35; water 213.21).

Pop: 294,410 (White 70.9%; Black or African American 21.4%; Hispanic or Latino 2.7%; Asian 2.2%; Other 4.1%). **Foreign born:** 3.7%. **Median age:** 35.4. **State rank:** 15. **Pop change 1990-2000:** +12%.

Income: per capita $18,641; median household $35,234. **Pop below poverty level:** 15.4%.

Please see sample entry on inside front cover for detailed information about the statistics presented with each county listing.

Unemployment: 5%. **Median home value:** $85,700. **Median travel time to work:** 23 minutes.

FLAGLER COUNTY

1200 E Moody Blvd Suite 1   **Ph:** 386-437-7480
Bunnell, FL 32110   **Fax:** 386-437-7399
www.flaglercounty.org

On northeastern Atlantic coast of FL, north of Daytona Beach; organized Apr 28, 1917 from Saint Johns and Volusia counties. **Name Origin:** For Henry Morrison Flagler (1830-1913), founder of the Florida East Coast Railroad (1886) and a leader in developing Florida's east coast as a resort area.

Area (sq mi): 570.76 (land 485; water 85.77).

Pop: 49,832 (White 83.6%; Black or African American 8.8%; Hispanic or Latino 5.1%; Asian 1.2%; Other 2.8%). **Foreign born:** 9.9%. **Median age:** 50.4. **State rank:** 40. **Pop change 1990-2000:** +73.6%.

Income: per capita $21,879; median household $40,214. **Pop below poverty level:** 8.7%.

Unemployment: 4.6%. **Median home value:** $116,200. **Median travel time to work:** 25.9 minutes.

FRANKLIN COUNTY

33 Market St Suite 203   **Ph:** 850-653-8861
Apalachicola, FL 32320   **Fax:** 850-653-2261
www.franklincountyflorida.com

In eastern FL panhandle, southwest of Tallahassee and bordered on south by the Gulf of Mexico; organized Feb 8, 1832 from Jackson County (prior to statehood). **Name Origin:** For Benjamin Franklin (1706-1790), U.S. patriot, diplomat, and statesman.

Area (sq mi): 1037.48 (land 544.34; water 493.14).

Pop: 11,057 (White 79.8%; Black or African American 16.3%; Hispanic or Latino 2.4%; Asian 0.2%; Other 2.2%). **Foreign born:** 1.9%. **Median age:** 40.8. **State rank:** 64. **Pop change 1990-2000:** +23.3%.

Income: per capita $16,140; median household $26,756. **Pop below poverty level:** 17.7%.

Unemployment: 2.7%. **Median home value:** $105,300. **Median travel time to work:** 19.9 minutes.

GADSDEN COUNTY

PO Box 1649   **Ph:** 850-875-8601
Quincy, FL 32353   **Fax:** 850-875-8612

On northern border of FL panhandle, west of Tallahassee; organized Jun 24, 1823 (prior to statehood) from Jackson County. **Name Origin:** For James Gadsden (1788-1858), SC soldier and politician, negotiator of the Gadsden Purchase (1853).

Area (sq mi): 528.49 (land 516.13; water 12.35).

Pop: 45,087 (White 35.9%; Black or African American 57.1%; Hispanic or Latino 6.2%; Asian 0.3%; Other 3.9%). **Foreign born:** 4.1%. **Median age:** 35.5. **State rank:** 42. **Pop change 1990-2000:** +9.7%.

Income: per capita $14,499; median household $31,248. **Pop below poverty level:** 19.9%.

Unemployment: 4.6%. **Median home value:** $70,100. **Median travel time to work:** 29.3 minutes.

GILCHRIST COUNTY

PO Box 37   **Ph:** 352-463-3170
Trenton, FL 32693   **Fax:** 352-463-3166
www.co.gilchrist.fl.us

In north-central FL, west of Gainesville; organized Dec 4, 1925 from Alachua County. **Name Origin:** For Capt. Albert Waller Gilchrist (1858-1926), officer, FL legislator, and governor (1909-13).

Area (sq mi): 355.47 (land 348.89; water 6.58).

Pop: 14,437 (White 88.7%; Black or African American 7%; Hispanic or Latino 2.8%; Asian 0.2%; Other 2.4%). **Foreign born:** 1.7%. **Median age:** 35.4. **State rank:** 57. **Pop change 1990-2000:** +49.3%.

Income: per capita $13,985; median household $30,328. **Pop below poverty level:** 14.1%.

Unemployment: 5%. **Median home value:** $78,000. **Median travel time to work:** 33.5 minutes.

GLADES COUNTY

500 Ave J   **Ph:** 863-946-6010
Moore Haven, FL 33471   **Fax:** 863-946-0560

In south-central FL, includes part of Lake Okeechobee; organized Apr 23, 1921 from DeSoto County. **Name Origin:** A shortened form of *Everglades*: the county is at their northern extent.

Area (sq mi): 986.43 (land 773.64; water 212.79).

Pop: 10,576 (White 68.6%; Black or African American 10.5%; Hispanic or Latino 15.1%; Asian 0.3%; Other 12.1%). **Foreign born:** 7.9%. **Median age:** 40.2. **State rank:** 65. **Pop change 1990-2000:** +39.3%.

Income: per capita $15,338; median household $30,774. **Pop below poverty level:** 15.2%.

Unemployment: 9.6%. **Median home value:** $72,400. **Median travel time to work:** 29.1 minutes.

GULF COUNTY

1000 Cecil Costin Sr Blvd   **Ph:** 850-229-6113
Port Saint Joe, FL 32456   **Fax:** 850-229-6174
www.gulfcountygovernment.com

In FL panhandle, southwest of Tallahassee; organized Jun 6, 1925 from Calhoun County. **Name Origin:** For the Gulf of Mexico, which forms its southern border.

Area (sq mi): 744.59 (land 554.6; water 190).

Pop: 13,332 (White 78.7%; Black or African American 16.9%; Hispanic or Latino 2%; Asian 0.4%; Other 2.7%). **Foreign born:** 2.1%. **Median age:** 40.3. **State rank:** 60. **Pop change 1990-2000:** +15.9%.

Income: per capita $14,449; median household $30,276. **Pop below poverty level:** 16.7%.

Unemployment: 5.7%. **Median home value:** $77,200. **Median travel time to work:** 25.8 minutes.

All statistics are based on the 2000 Census except the dollar figures given for per capita income, which are based on 1999 estimates.

HAMILTON COUNTY

207 NE 1st St Rm 106   **Ph:** 386-792-1288
Jasper, FL 32052   **Fax:** 386-792-3524

On northern border of FL, between Jacksonville and Tallahassee; organized Dec 26, 1827 from Duval County (prior to statehood). **Name Origin:** For Alexander Hamilton (1757-1804), first U.S. secretary of the treasury (1789-95).

Area (sq mi): 519.31 (land 514.86; water 4.45).

Pop: 13,327 (White 55%; Black or African American 37.7%; Hispanic or Latino 6.4%; Asian 0.2%; Other 3.3%). **Foreign born:** 2.3%. **Median age:** 35.1. **State rank:** 61. **Pop change 1990-2000:** +21.9%.

Income: per capita $10,562; median household $25,638. **Pop below poverty level:** 26%.

Unemployment: 10.4%. **Median home value:** $54,600. **Median travel time to work:** 24.1 minutes.

HARDEE COUNTY

412 W Orange St Rm A-203   **Ph:** 863-773-6952
Wauchula, FL 33873   **Fax:** 863-773-0958
www.hardeecounty.net

In south-central FL, south of Winter Haven; organized Apr 23, 1921 from DeSoto County. **Name Origin:** For Cary Augustus Hardee (1876-1957), governor of FL (1921-25).

Area (sq mi): 638.33 (land 637.3; water 1.03).

Pop: 26,938 (White 54.6%; Black or African American 8.3%; Hispanic or Latino 35.7%; Asian 0.3%; Other 20.8%). **Foreign born:** 17.5%. **Median age:** 32.7. **State rank:** 49. **Pop change 1990-2000:** +38.2%.

Income: per capita $12,445; median household $30,183. **Pop below poverty level:** 24.6%.

Unemployment: 9.6%. **Median home value:** $59,600. **Median travel time to work:** 26.7 minutes.

HENDRY COUNTY

PO Box 1760   **Ph:** 863-675-5217
La Belle, FL 33975   **Fax:** 863-675-5238
www.hendryfla.net

In south-central FL, east of Fort Myers; organized May 11, 1923 from Calhoun County. **Name Origin:** For Capt. Francis Asbury Hendry (?-1917), Confederate officer, dubbed the 'Cattle King of South Florida.'

Area (sq mi): 1189.79 (land 1152.53; water 37.26).

Pop: 36,210 (White 43.9%; Black or African American 14.7%; Hispanic or Latino 39.6%; Asian 0.4%; Other 18.7%). **Foreign born:** 24%. **Median age:** 29.5. **State rank:** 44. **Pop change 1990-2000:** +40.5%.

Income: per capita $13,663; median household $33,592. **Pop below poverty level:** 24.1%.

Unemployment: 12.3%. **Median home value:** $71,500. **Median travel time to work:** 26.5 minutes.

HERNANDO COUNTY

20 N Main St Rm 460   **Ph:** 352-754-4000
Brooksville, FL 34601   **Fax:** 352-754-4477
www.co.hernando.fl.us

On central Gulf coast of FL, north of Tampa; organized Feb 24, 1843 (prior to statehood). Name changed to Benton County Mar 6, 1844, and back again Dec 24, 1850. **Name Origin:** For Hernando De Soto (c. 1500-42), Spanish explorer of southern U.S. Changed to honor Thomas Hart Benton (1782-53) who sponsored legislation to open central FL to settlement; name changed back because of his moderate position on the Missouri Compromise.

Area (sq mi): 589.08 (land 478.31; water 110.77).

Pop: 130,802 (White 89.2%; Black or African American 4.1%; Hispanic or Latino 5%; Asian 0.6%; Other 2.4%). **Foreign born:** 5.3%. **Median age:** 49.5. **State rank:** 28. **Pop change 1990-2000:** +29.4%.

Income: per capita $18,321; median household $32,572. **Pop below poverty level:** 10.3%.

Unemployment: 4.2%. **Median home value:** $87,300. **Median travel time to work:** 29.3 minutes.

HIGHLANDS COUNTY

600 S Commerce Ave   **Ph:** 863-402-6500
Sebring, FL 33871   **Fax:** 863-402-6507
www.hcbcc.net

In central FL, west of Ft. Pierce; organized Apr 23, 1921 from DeSoto County. **Name Origin:** For the hilliness of the area, in a state almost completely flat.

Area (sq mi): 1106.28 (land 1028.27; water 78.01).

Pop: 87,366 (White 76.5%; Black or African American 9.3%; Hispanic or Latino 12.1%; Asian 1%; Other 6%). **Foreign born:** 9.1%. **Median age:** 50. **State rank:** 34. **Pop change 1990-2000:** +27.7%.

Income: per capita $17,222; median household $30,160. **Pop below poverty level:** 15.2%.

Unemployment: 5.9%. **Median home value:** $72,800. **Median travel time to work:** 23 minutes.

HILLSBOROUGH COUNTY

601 E Kennedy Blvd   **Ph:** 813-276-8100
Tampa, FL 33602
www.hillsboroughcounty.org

On Tampa Bay on the central Gulf coast of FL; organized Jan 25, 1834 (prior to statehood) from Alachua and Monroe counties. **Name Origin:** For Wills Hills, Earl of Hillsborough (1718-93), Irish peer and secretary of state for the colonies (1768-72) who had received a large grant of land in FL. Named by Bernard Romans, his surveyor.

Area (sq mi): 1266.22 (land 1050.91; water 215.31).

Pop: 998,948 (White 63.3%; Black or African American 15%; Hispanic or Latino 18%; Asian 2.2%; Other 7.8%). **Foreign born:** 11.5%. **Median age:** 35.1. **State rank:** 4. **Pop change 1990-2000:** +19.8%.

Income: per capita $21,812; median household $40,663. **Pop below poverty level:** 12.5%.

Unemployment: 3.6%. **Median home value:** $97,700. **Median travel time to work:** 25.8 minutes.

Please see sample entry on inside front cover for detailed information about the statistics presented with each county listing.

HOLMES COUNTY
PO Box 397   **Ph:** 850-547-1100
Bonifay, FL 32425   **Fax:** 850-547-6630

On northern border of FL panhandle, north of Panama City; organized Jan 8, 1848 from Walton and Calhoun counties. **Name Origin:** For Holmes Creek, which forms the eastern boundary of the county. The creek was named for the valley, which was probably named for a Creek Indian chief, killed (1818) by troops under the command of Andrew Jackson (1767-1845); or possibly for Thomas J. Holmes, a settler from NC about 1830.

Area (sq mi): 488.71 (land 482.45; water 6.26).

Pop: 18,564 (White 88.9%; Black or African American 6.5%; Hispanic or Latino 1.9%; Asian 0.4%; Other 3.3%). **Foreign born:** 1.7%. **Median age:** 37.5. **State rank:** 56. **Pop change 1990-2000:** +17.7%.

Income: per capita $14,135; median household $27,923. **Pop below poverty level:** 19.1%.

Unemployment: 7%. **Median home value:** $56,200. **Median travel time to work:** 34 minutes.

INDIAN RIVER COUNTY
1840 25th St   **Ph:** 772-567-8000
Vero Beach, FL 32960   **Fax:** 772-978-1822
indian-river.fl.us

On south-central Atlantic coast of FL, north of Fort Pierce; organized May 30, 1925 from Saint Lucie County. **Name Origin:** For the Indian River, which forms its eastern border.

Area (sq mi): 616.92 (land 503.23; water 113.69).

Pop: 112,947 (White 83.4%; Black or African American 8.2%; Hispanic or Latino 6.5%; Asian 0.7%; Other 3.5%). **Foreign born:** 8.1%. **Median age:** 47. **State rank:** 33. **Pop change 1990-2000:** +25.2%.

Income: per capita $27,227; median household $39,635. **Pop below poverty level:** 9.3%.

Unemployment: 7.3%. **Median home value:** $104,000. **Median travel time to work:** 20.3 minutes.

JACKSON COUNTY
PO Box 510   **Ph:** 850-482-9552
Marianna, FL 32447   **Fax:** 850-482-7849
www.jacksoncounty-fl.com

On northern border of FL panhandle, northwest of Tallahassee; organized Aug 12, 1822 (prior to statehood) from Escambia County; in 1834 annexed Fayette County, which was organized in 1832. **Name Origin:** For Andrew Jackson (1767-1845), seventh U.S. president.

Area (sq mi): 954.58 (land 915.64; water 38.94).

Pop: 46,755 (White 68.6%; Black or African American 26.6%; Hispanic or Latino 2.9%; Asian 0.4%; Other 2.9%). **Foreign born:** 1.5%. **Median age:** 37.6. **State rank:** 41. **Pop change 1990-2000:** +13%.

Income: per capita $13,905; median household $29,744. **Pop below poverty level:** 17.2%.

Unemployment: 4.3%. **Median home value:** $66,700. **Median travel time to work:** 23.5 minutes.

JEFFERSON COUNTY
County Courthouse Rm 10   **Ph:** 850-342-0218
Monticello, FL 32344   **Fax:** 850-342-0222

On northern Gulf coast of FL, east of Tallahassee; organized Jan 20, 1827 (prior to statehood) from Leon County. **Name Origin:** For Thomas Jefferson (1743-1826), U.S. patriot and statesman; third U.S. president.

Area (sq mi): 636.65 (land 597.74; water 38.91).

Pop: 12,902 (White 58.3%; Black or African American 38.3%; Hispanic or Latino 2.2%; Asian 0.3%; Other 2.1%). **Foreign born:** 1.2%. **Median age:** 39.4. **State rank:** 63. **Pop change 1990-2000:** +14.2%.

Income: per capita $17,006; median household $32,998. **Pop below poverty level:** 17.1%.

Unemployment: 5.9%. **Median home value:** $77,000. **Median travel time to work:** 29.2 minutes.

LAFAYETTE COUNTY
PO Box 88   **Ph:** 386-294-1600
Mayo, FL 32066   **Fax:** 386-294-4231

In northern FL, northwest of Gainesville; organized Dec 23, 1856 from Madison County. **Name Origin:** For the Marquis de Lafayette (1757-1834), French statesman and soldier who fought with Americans during the Revolutionary War.

Area (sq mi): 547.92 (land 542.84; water 5.08).

Pop: 7,022 (White 75.3%; Black or African American 14.4%; Hispanic or Latino 9.1%; Asian 0.1%; Other 6.2%). **Foreign born:** 6.6%. **Median age:** 34.8. **State rank:** 66. **Pop change 1990-2000:** +25.9%.

Income: per capita $13,087; median household $30,651. **Pop below poverty level:** 17.5%.

Unemployment: 3.7%. **Median home value:** $67,100. **Median travel time to work:** 22.8 minutes.

LAKE COUNTY
PO Box 7800   **Ph:** 352-742-4102
Tavares, FL 32778   **Fax:** 352-742-4110
www.lakecountyfl.com

In central FL, west of Orlando; organized May 27, 1887 from Orange and Sumter counties. **Name Origin:** For the more than 500 lakes of 10 acres or more in the county.

Area (sq mi): 1156.4 (land 953.15; water 203.25).

Pop: 210,528 (White 84.2%; Black or African American 8.3%; Hispanic or Latino 5.6%; Asian 0.8%; Other 3.4%). **Foreign born:** 5.1%. **Median age:** 45.1. **State rank:** 21. **Pop change 1990-2000:** +38.4%.

Income: per capita $20,199; median household $36,903. **Pop below poverty level:** 9.6%.

Unemployment: 3.7%. **Median home value:** $100,600. **Median travel time to work:** 27.6 minutes.

All statistics are based on the 2000 Census except the dollar figures given for per capita income, which are based on 1999 estimates.

LEE COUNTY

PO Box 398
Fort Myers, FL 33902
www.co.lee.fl.us

Ph: 239-335-2227
Fax: 239-335-2599

On southwestern Gulf coast of FL, north of Naples; organized May 13, 1887 from Monroe County. **Name Origin:** For Robert E. Lee (1807-70), American general and commander in chief of the Confederate forces during the Civil War.

Area (sq mi): 1211.89 (land 803.63; water 408.26).

Pop: 440,888 (White 82%; Black or African American 6.6%; Hispanic or Latino 9.5%; Asian 0.8%; Other 5%). **Foreign born:** 9.2%. **Median age:** 45.2. **State rank:** 11. **Pop change 1990-2000:** +31.6%.

Income: per capita $24,542; median household $40,319. **Pop below poverty level:** 9.7%.

Unemployment: 3.2%. **Median home value:** $112,900. **Median travel time to work:** 25 minutes.

LEON COUNTY

301 S Monroe St
Tallahassee, FL 323011856
www.co.leon.fl.us

Ph: 850-487-2220
Fax: 850-488-6293

In eastern end of FL panhandle; organized Dec 9, 1824 (prior to statehood) from Gadsden County. **Name Origin:** For Juan Ponce de Leon (1460-1521), Spanish colonial governor and discoverer of Florida while in search of the 'fountain of youth.'

Area (sq mi): 701.78 (land 666.74; water 35.04).

Pop: 239,452 (White 64.1%; Black or African American 29.1%; Hispanic or Latino 3.5%; Asian 1.9%; Other 2.6%). **Foreign born:** 4.7%. **Median age:** 29.5. **State rank:** 19. **Pop change 1990-2000:** +24.4%.

Income: per capita $21,024; median household $37,517. **Pop below poverty level:** 18.2%.

Unemployment: 2.9%. **Median home value:** $110,900. **Median travel time to work:** 21.7 minutes.

LEVY COUNTY

PO Box 610
Bronson, FL 32621
www.naturecoast.org

Ph: 352-486-5100
Fax: 352-486-5166

On Gulf coast of FL, west of Ocala; organized Mar 10, 1845 from Alachua and Marion counties. **Name Origin:** For David Levy [Yulee] (1810-86), West Indian-born FL legislator, first U.S. senator from FL (1845-51; 1855-61), and member of the Confederate Congress (1861-65).

Area (sq mi): 1412.32 (land 1118.38; water 293.94).

Pop: 34,450 (White 83.2%; Black or African American 11%; Hispanic or Latino 3.9%; Asian 0.4%; Other 2.8%). **Foreign born:** 2.6%. **Median age:** 41.1. **State rank:** 47. **Pop change 1990-2000:** +32.9%.

Income: per capita $14,746; median household $26,959. **Pop below poverty level:** 18.6%.

Unemployment: 5%. **Median home value:** $75,800. **Median travel time to work:** 31.4 minutes.

LIBERTY COUNTY

PO Box 399
Bristol, FL 32321

Ph: 850-643-5404
Fax: 850-643-2866

In eastern end of FL panhandle, southwest of Tallahassee; organized Dec 15, 1855 from Franklin and Gadsden counties. **Name Origin:** For the objective of the people who founded the U.S.

Area (sq mi): 843.16 (land 835.87; water 7.29).

Pop: 7,021 (White 74.5%; Black or African American 18.4%; Hispanic or Latino 4.5%; Asian 0.1%; Other 5%). **Foreign born:** 2.1%. **Median age:** 35. **State rank:** 67. **Pop change 1990-2000:** +26.1%.

Income: per capita $17,225; median household $28,840. **Pop below poverty level:** 19.9%.

Unemployment: 3.4%. **Median home value:** $66,300. **Median travel time to work:** 33.2 minutes.

MADISON COUNTY

PO Box 237
Madison, FL 32341
www.madisonfl.org

Ph: 850-973-1500
Fax: 850-973-2059

On northern border of FL, east of Tallahassee; organized Dec 26, 1827 (prior to statehood) from Jefferson County. **Name Origin:** For James Madison (1751-1836), fourth U.S. president.

Area (sq mi): 715.8 (land 691.79; water 24).

Pop: 18,733 (White 55.4%; Black or African American 40.3%; Hispanic or Latino 3.2%; Asian 0.3%; Other 1.8%). **Foreign born:** 2%. **Median age:** 36.3. **State rank:** 55. **Pop change 1990-2000:** +13.1%.

Income: per capita $12,511; median household $26,533. **Pop below poverty level:** 23.1%.

Unemployment: 4.2%. **Median home value:** $54,800. **Median travel time to work:** 23.1 minutes.

MANATEE COUNTY

PO Box 25400
Bradenton, FL 34206
www.co.manatee.fl.us

Ph: 941-749-1800
Fax: 941-741-4083

On central Gulf coast, south of Tampa; organized Jan 9, 1855 from Hillsborough County. **Name Origin:** For the manatee, or sea cow, an endangered aquatic mammal found in the local waterways.

Area (sq mi): 892.75 (land 741.03; water 151.72).

Pop: 264,002 (White 80.6%; Black or African American 8.2%; Hispanic or Latino 9.3%; Asian 0.9%; Other 4.6%). **Foreign born:** 8.4%. **Median age:** 43.6. **State rank:** 16. **Pop change 1990-2000:** +24.7%.

Income: per capita $22,388; median household $38,673. **Pop below poverty level:** 10.1%.

Unemployment: 3.3%. **Median home value:** $119,400. **Median travel time to work:** 23.3 minutes.

MARION COUNTY

601 SE 25th Ave
Ocala, FL 34471
www.marioncountyfl.org

Ph: 352-620-3307
Fax: 352-620-3392

In north-central FL, south of Gainesville; organized Mar 14, 1844

Please see sample entry on inside front cover for detailed information about the statistics presented with each county listing.

(prior to statehood) from Alachua County. **Name Origin:** For Gen. Francis Marion (c. 1732-1795), SC soldier and legislator, known as 'The Swamp Fox' for his tactics during the Revolutionary War.

Area (sq mi): 1663.01 (land 1578.86; water 84.15).

Pop: 258,916 (White 80.4%; Black or African American 11.5%; Hispanic or Latino 6%; Asian 0.7%; Other 3.5%). **Foreign born:** 5.2%. **Median age:** 43.8. **State rank:** 17. **Pop change 1990-2000:** +32.9%.

Income: per capita $17,848; median household $31,944. **Pop below poverty level:** 13.1%.

Unemployment: 4.9%. **Median home value:** $81,300. **Median travel time to work:** 25.8 minutes.

MARTIN COUNTY
PO Box 9016   **Ph:** 772-288-5576
Stuart, FL 34995   **Fax:** 772-288-5548
www.martin.fl.us

On central Atlantic coast of FL, north of Palm Beach; organized May 30, 1925 from Palm Beach County. **Name Origin:** For John W. Martin (1884-1958), governor of FL (1925-29).

Area (sq mi): 752.79 (land 555.62; water 197.18).

Pop: 126,731 (White 85.8%; Black or African American 5.3%; Hispanic or Latino 7.5%; Asian 0.6%; Other 4.2%). **Foreign born:** 8.1%. **Median age:** 47.3. **State rank:** 29. **Pop change 1990-2000:** +25.6%.

Income: per capita $29,584; median household $43,083. **Pop below poverty level:** 8.8%.

Unemployment: 5.6%. **Median home value:** $152,400. **Median travel time to work:** 25.5 minutes.

MIAMI-DADE COUNTY
111 NW 1st St Suite 220   **Ph:** 305-375-5124
Miami, FL 33128   **Fax:** 305-375-5569
miamidade.gov

In southeastern FL, south of Fort Lauderdale; organized Feb 4, 1836 (prior to statehood) from Monroe County. Renamed as Miami-Dade County effective July 22, 1997. **Name Origin:** For Maj. Francis Langhorne Dade (1793-1835), officer killed in the Seminole War (1835-42).

Area (sq mi): 2431.26 (land 1946.06; water 485.19).

Pop: 2,253,362 (White 20.7%; Black or African American 20.3%; Hispanic or Latino 57.3%; Asian 1.4%; Other 8.6%). **Foreign born:** 50.9%. **Median age:** 35.6. **State rank:** 1. **Pop change 1990-2000:** +16.3%.

Income: per capita $18,497; median household $35,966. **Pop below poverty level:** 18%.

Unemployment: 6.9%. **Median home value:** $124,000. **Median travel time to work:** 30.1 minutes.

MONROE COUNTY
500 Whitehead St   **Ph:** 305-294-4641
Key West, FL 33040
www.co.monroe.fl.us

In southwestern FL, includes the Florida Keys; organized Jul 3,

1823 (prior to statehood) from Saint Johns County. **Name Origin:** For James Monroe (1758-1831), fifth U.S. president.

Area (sq mi): 3737.15 (land 996.91; water 2740.24).

Pop: 79,589 (White 77.2%; Black or African American 4.8%; Hispanic or Latino 15.8%; Asian 0.8%; Other 3.7%). **Foreign born:** 14.7%. **Median age:** 42.6. **State rank:** 35. **Pop change 1990-2000:** +2%.

Income: per capita $26,102; median household $42,283. **Pop below poverty level:** 10.2%.

Unemployment: 2.6%. **Median home value:** $241,200. **Median travel time to work:** 18.4 minutes.

NASSAU COUNTY
PO Box 456   **Ph:** 904-321-5700
Fernandina Beach, FL 32035   **Fax:** 904-321-5723
www.nassauclerk.org

In northeastern corner of FL, north of Jacksonville; organized Dec 29, 1824 (prior to statehood) from Duval County. **Name Origin:** For the Nassau River, which forms part of the northern border of the county, and Nassau Sound; named for the duchy in Germany associated with the House of Orange.

Area (sq mi): 725.86 (land 651.55; water 74.3).

Pop: 57,663 (White 89%; Black or African American 7.7%; Hispanic or Latino 1.5%; Asian 0.5%; Other 1.7%). **Foreign born:** 2.7%. **Median age:** 38.3. **State rank:** 37. **Pop change 1990-2000:** +31.2%.

Income: per capita $22,836; median household $46,022. **Pop below poverty level:** 9.1%.

Unemployment: 4%. **Median home value:** $126,700. **Median travel time to work:** 28.2 minutes.

OKALOOSA COUNTY
101 James Lee Blvd   **Ph:** 850-689-5000
Crestview, FL 32536   **Fax:** 850-689-5818
www.co.okaloosa.fl.us

In northwestern FL panhandle, east of Pensacola; organized Jun 13, 1915 from Santa Rosa and Walton counties. **Name Origin:** From Choctaw Indian name for the Blackwater River, which runs through the county; from *oka* 'water' and *lusa* 'black.'

Area (sq mi): 1082 (land 935.63; water 146.37).

Pop: 170,498 (White 81%; Black or African American 9.1%; Hispanic or Latino 4.3%; Asian 2.5%; Other 5%). **Foreign born:** 5.3%. **Median age:** 36.1. **State rank:** 24. **Pop change 1990-2000:** +18.6%.

Income: per capita $20,918; median household $41,474. **Pop below poverty level:** 8.8%.

Unemployment: 3.3%. **Median home value:** $101,200. **Median travel time to work:** 21.9 minutes.

OKEECHOBEE COUNTY
304 NW 2nd St   **Ph:** 863-763-6441
Okeechobee, FL 34972   **Fax:** 863-763-9529

In east-central FL, west of Fort Pierce; organized May 8, 1917 from Osceola and Palm Beach counties. **Name Origin:** For Lake Okeechobee, which forms the county's southern boundary; from Hitchiti (Muskhogan) Indian *oki* 'water' and *chobi* 'big.'

All statistics are based on the 2000 Census except the dollar figures given for per capita income, which are based on 1999 estimates.

Area (sq mi): 891.57 (land 773.94; water 117.63).

Pop: 35,910 (White 71.6%; Black or African American 7.9%; Hispanic or Latino 18.6%; Asian 0.7%; Other 12.1%). **Foreign born:** 11.5%. **Median age:** 36.7. **State rank:** 45. **Pop change 1990-2000:** +21.2%.

Income: per capita $14,553; median household $30,456. **Pop below poverty level:** 16%.

Unemployment: 7%. **Median home value:** $77,600. **Median travel time to work:** 27.7 minutes.

ORANGE COUNTY

201 S Rosalind Ave   **Ph:** 407-836-7350
Orlando, FL 32801   **Fax:** 407-836-5879
www.orangecountyfl.net

In central FL, southwest of Daytona Beach; organized as Mosquito County Dec 29, 1824 (prior to statehood) from Indian lands; name changed Jan 30, 1845. **Name Origin:** For the major crop in the region.

Area (sq mi): 1004.19 (land 907.45; water 96.74).

Pop: 896,344 (White 57.5%; Black or African American 18.2%; Hispanic or Latino 18.8%; Asian 3.4%; Other 9.8%). **Foreign born:** 14.4%. **Median age:** 33.3. **State rank:** 6. **Pop change 1990-2000:** +32.3%.

Income: per capita $20,916; median household $41,311. **Pop below poverty level:** 12.1%.

Unemployment: 4.1%. **Median home value:** $107,500. **Median travel time to work:** 26.6 minutes.

OSCEOLA COUNTY

2 Courthouse Sq   **Ph:** 407-343-3500
Kissimmee, FL 34741   **Fax:** 407-343-3699
www.osceola.org

In east-central FL, west of Melbourne; organized May 12, 1887 from Brevard and Orange counties. **Name Origin:** For Osceola (c. 1804-38), Seminole leader during the early years of the Second Seminole War (1835-42). Name is from Creek *asi-yahola* 'black drink cry,' and refers to a ceremonial drink made from leaves of the yaupon bush (Ilex vomitoria).

Area (sq mi): 1506.35 (land 1321.9; water 184.45).

Pop: 172,493 (White 59.6%; Black or African American 7.4%; Hispanic or Latino 29.4%; Asian 2.2%; Other 13.3%). **Foreign born:** 14%. **Median age:** 34.6. **State rank:** 23. **Pop change 1990-2000:** +60.1%.

Income: per capita $17,022; median household $38,214. **Pop below poverty level:** 11.5%.

Unemployment: 4.5%. **Median home value:** $99,300. **Median travel time to work:** 28.1 minutes.

PALM BEACH COUNTY

301 N Olive Ave   **Ph:** 561-355-2001
West Palm Beach, FL 33401   **Fax:** 561-355-3990
www.co.palm-beach.fl.us

On south-central Atlantic coast, north of Fort Lauderdale; organized Apr 30, 1909 from Dade County. **Name Origin:** For the coconut palms that are common in the area.

Area (sq mi): 2386.33 (land 1974.11; water 412.22).

Pop: 1,131,184 (White 70.6%; Black or African American 13.8%; Hispanic or Latino 12.4%; Asian 1.5%; Other 5.7%). **Foreign born:** 17.4%. **Median age:** 41.8. **State rank:** 3. **Pop change 1990-2000:** +31%.

Income: per capita $28,801; median household $45,062. **Pop below poverty level:** 9.9%.

Unemployment: 5.5%. **Median home value:** $135,200. **Median travel time to work:** 25.7 minutes.

PASCO COUNTY

7530 Little Rd   **Ph:** 727-847-8190
New Port Richey, FL 34654
www.pascocounty.com

On central Gulf coast of FL, north of Tampa; organized Jun 2, 1887 from Hernando County. **Name Origin:** For Samuel Pasco (1834-1917), English-born FL legislator, and U.S. senator (1887-99).

Area (sq mi): 867.95 (land 744.85; water 123.1).

Pop: 344,765 (White 89.9%; Black or African American 2.1%; Hispanic or Latino 5.7%; Asian 0.9%; Other 3.3%). **Foreign born:** 7%. **Median age:** 44.9. **State rank:** 13. **Pop change 1990-2000:** +22.6%.

Income: per capita $18,439; median household $32,969. **Pop below poverty level:** 10.7%.

Unemployment: 4.2%. **Median home value:** $79,600. **Median travel time to work:** 30 minutes.

PINELLAS COUNTY

315 Court St   **Ph:** 727-464-3485
Clearwater, FL 33756   **Fax:** 727-464-4384
www.co.pinellas.fl.us

On central Gulf coast of FL, west of Tampa, largely a peninsula, bounded on the east by Old Tampa Bay; organized May 23, 1911 from Hillsborough County. **Name Origin:** Derived from Spanish *punta pinal* 'point of pines.'

Area (sq mi): 607.67 (land 279.92; water 327.75).

Pop: 921,482 (White 82.8%; Black or African American 9%; Hispanic or Latino 4.6%; Asian 2.1%; Other 3.1%). **Foreign born:** 9.5%. **Median age:** 43. **State rank:** 5. **Pop change 1990-2000:** +8.2%.

Income: per capita $23,497; median household $37,111. **Pop below poverty level:** 10%.

Unemployment: 3.7%. **Median home value:** $96,500. **Median travel time to work:** 23.6 minutes.

POLK COUNTY

PO Box 9005 Drawer BC01   **Ph:** 863-534-6000
Bartow, FL 33831   **Fax:** 863-534-7655
www.polk-county.net

In central FL, east of Tampa; organized Feb 8, 1861 from Brevard and Hillsborough counties. **Name Origin:** For James Knox Polk (1795-1849), eleventh U.S. president.

Area (sq mi): 2009.99 (land 1874.38; water 135.6).

Please see sample entry on inside front cover for detailed information about the statistics presented with each county listing.

Pop: 483,924 (White 74.7%; Black or African American 13.5%; Hispanic or Latino 9.5%; Asian 0.9%; Other 5.9%). **Foreign born:** 6.9%. **Median age:** 38.6. **State rank:** 8. **Pop change 1990-2000:** +19.4%.

Income: per capita $18,302; median household $36,036. **Pop below poverty level:** 12.9%.

Unemployment: 6.2%. **Median home value:** $83,300. **Median travel time to work:** 25.4 minutes.

PUTNAM COUNTY
PO Box 758   **Ph:** 386-329-0361
Palatka, FL 32178   **Fax:** 386-329-0888
www.co.putnam.fl.us

In northeastern FL, east of Gainesville; organized Jan 13, 1849 from Alachua, Duval, Marion, Mosquito (now Orange), and Saint Johns counties. **Name Origin:** For Gen. Benjamin Alexander Putnam (1801-69), officer in the Seminole Indian War (1835-42), FL legislator, and surveyor-general of FL (1848-54).

Area (sq mi): 827.16 (land 721.89; water 105.27).

Pop: 70,423 (White 75.4%; Black or African American 17%; Hispanic or Latino 5.9%; Asian 0.4%; Other 4.5%). **Foreign born:** 3.4%. **Median age:** 40.5. **State rank:** 36. **Pop change 1990-2000:** +8.2%.

Income: per capita $15,603; median household $28,180. **Pop below poverty level:** 20.9%.

Unemployment: 5.9%. **Median home value:** $68,500. **Median travel time to work:** 29.3 minutes.

SAINT JOHNS COUNTY
PO Box 300   **Ph:** 904-823-2500
Saint Augustine, FL 32085   **Fax:** 904-823-2294
www.co.st-johns.fl.us

In northeastern FL, south of Jacksonville; original county; organized Aug 12, 1822 (prior to statehood). **Name Origin:** For the Saint Johns River, which forms its western border.

Area (sq mi): 821.43 (land 609.01; water 212.42).

Pop: 123,135 (White 89%; Black or African American 6.3%; Hispanic or Latino 2.6%; Asian 1%; Other 1.9%). **Foreign born:** 4.9%. **Median age:** 40.6. **State rank:** 30. **Pop change 1990-2000:** +46.9%.

Income: per capita $28,674; median household $50,099. **Pop below poverty level:** 8%.

Unemployment: 3.5%. **Median home value:** $158,400. **Median travel time to work:** 26.3 minutes.

SAINT LUCIE COUNTY
PO Box 700   **Ph:** 772-462-6900
Fort Pierce, FL 34954   **Fax:** 772-462-1283
www.stlucieco.gov

On central Atlantic coast of FL, north of Palm Beach; organized Mar 14, 1844 (prior to statehood) from Mosquito County; name changed to Brevard County on Jan 6, 1855. The present-day Saint Lucie County was organized from Brevard County May 24, 1905. **Name Origin:** For Saint Lucy (c.283-303), early Christian martyr.

Area (sq mi): 688.08 (land 572.45; water 115.63).

Pop: 192,695 (White 74.1%; Black or African American 15.4%; Hispanic or Latino 8.2%; Asian 0.9%; Other 4.5%). **Foreign born:** 10.5%. **Median age:** 42. **State rank:** 22. **Pop change 1990-2000:** +28.3%.

Income: per capita $18,790; median household $36,363. **Pop below poverty level:** 13.4%.

Unemployment: 8.3%. **Median home value:** $86,100. **Median travel time to work:** 25.9 minutes.

SANTA ROSA COUNTY
6495 Caroline St SE   **Ph:** 850-983-1974
Milton, FL 32570   **Fax:** 850-983-1986
www.co.santa-rosa.fl.us

In western end of FL panhandle, east of Pensacola; organized Feb 18, 1842 (prior to statehood) from Escambia County. **Name Origin:** For Santa Rosa Island, which lies off its southern coast; named for Santa Rosa de Viterbo (1235-52), Christian saint.

Area (sq mi): 1173.57 (land 1016.93; water 156.65).

Pop: 117,743 (White 89.1%; Black or African American 4.2%; Hispanic or Latino 2.5%; Asian 1.3%; Other 3.8%). **Foreign born:** 3%. **Median age:** 36.8. **State rank:** 32. **Pop change 1990-2000:** +44.3%.

Income: per capita $20,089; median household $41,881. **Pop below poverty level:** 9.8%.

Unemployment: 4.4%. **Median home value:** $106,000. **Median travel time to work:** 29.2 minutes.

SARASOTA COUNTY
PO Box 3079   **Ph:** 941-861-5000
Sarasota, FL 34230
www.co.sarasota.fl.us

On central Gulf coast of FL, south of Tampa; organized May 14, 1921 from Manatee County. **Name Origin:** Variously attributed to Spanish and Indian sources. One version states that the Spanish gave this name to the area, with the meaning 'place of dancing'; another explanation is that this was the site of a Seminole village named Sarasota, meaning 'point of rocks.'

Area (sq mi): 725.18 (land 571.55; water 153.63).

Pop: 325,957 (White 89.8%; Black or African American 4.2%; Hispanic or Latino 4.3%; Asian 0.8%; Other 2.3%). **Foreign born:** 9.3%. **Median age:** 50.5. **State rank:** 14. **Pop change 1990-2000:** +17.3%.

Income: per capita $28,326; median household $41,957. **Pop below poverty level:** 7.8%.

Unemployment: 2.8%. **Median home value:** $122,000. **Median travel time to work:** 21.8 minutes.

SEMINOLE COUNTY
1101 E 1st St   **Ph:** 407-665-7945
Sanford, FL 32771   **Fax:** 407-665-7939
www.co.seminole.fl.us

In east-central FL, north of Orlando; organized Apr 25, 1913 from Orange County. **Name Origin:** For the Muskhogean tribe who lived in FL until the end of the Seminole War (1835-42). Remnants of the tribe moved into the Everglades and their descendants are still

All statistics are based on the 2000 Census except the dollar figures given for per capita income, which are based on 1999 estimates.

there. The name may be from Creek @ital1ishti semoli@ital2 'wild men' or 'separate ones.'

Area (sq mi): 344.87 (land 308.2; water 36.67).

Pop: 365,196 (White 75.2%; Black or African American 9.5%; Hispanic or Latino 11.2%; Asian 2.5%; Other 5.6%). **Foreign born:** 9.1%. **Median age:** 36.2. **State rank:** 12. **Pop change 1990-2000:** +27%.

Income: per capita $24,591; median household $49,326. **Pop below poverty level:** 7.4%.

Unemployment: 3.7%. **Median home value:** $119,900. **Median travel time to work:** 27 minutes.

SUMTER COUNTY
209 N Florida St　　　　　**Ph:** 352-793-0200
Bushnell, FL 33513　　　　**Fax:** 352-793-0207
www.bocc.co.sumter.fl.us

In west-central FL, west of Orlando; organized 1853 from Marion and Orange counties. **Name Origin:** For Gen. Thomas Sumter (1734-1832), American Revolutionary officer nicknamed the 'Gamecock of the Revolution,' U.S. representative from GA (1789-93; 1797-1801), and U.S. senator (1801-10).

Area (sq mi): 580.31 (land 545.73; water 34.58).

Pop: 53,345 (White 78.4%; Black or African American 13.8%; Hispanic or Latino 6.3%; Asian 0.4%; Other 3.3%). **Foreign born:** 5.5%. **Median age:** 49.2. **State rank:** 39. **Pop change 1990-2000:** +68.9%.

Income: per capita $16,830; median household $32,073. **Pop below poverty level:** 13.7%.

Unemployment: 4.3%. **Median home value:** $100,400. **Median travel time to work:** 28.6 minutes.

SUWANNEE COUNTY
200 S Ohio Ave　　　　　**Ph:** 386-364-3498
Live Oak, FL 32064　　　　**Fax:** 386-362-0548

In northern FL, west of Jacksonville; organized Dec 21, 1858 from Columbia County. **Name Origin:** For the Suwanee River, which forms the northern and western borders of the county.

Area (sq mi): 691.9 (land 687.64; water 4.26).

Pop: 34,844 (White 81.1%; Black or African American 12.1%; Hispanic or Latino 4.9%; Asian 0.5%; Other 2.8%). **Foreign born:** 4.7%. **Median age:** 39.7. **State rank:** 46. **Pop change 1990-2000:** +30.1%.

Income: per capita $14,678; median household $29,963. **Pop below poverty level:** 18.5%.

Unemployment: 5.6%. **Median home value:** $68,500. **Median travel time to work:** 27.9 minutes.

TAYLOR COUNTY
PO Box 620　　　　　　**Ph:** 850-838-3506
Perry, FL 32348　　　　　**Fax:** 850-838-3549
taco.perryfl.com

On northern Gulf coast of FL, southeast of Tallahassee; organized Dec 23, 1856 from Madison County. **Name Origin:** For Zachary Taylor (1784-1850), twelfth U.S. president.

Area (sq mi): 1232.01 (land 1041.91; water 190.1).

Pop: 19,256 (White 76.9%; Black or African American 19%; Hispanic or Latino 1.5%; Asian 0.4%; Other 2.7%). **Foreign born:** 1.7%. **Median age:** 37.8. **State rank:** 54. **Pop change 1990-2000:** +12.5%.

Income: per capita $15,281; median household $30,032. **Pop below poverty level:** 18%.

Unemployment: 9.6%. **Median home value:** $66,000. **Median travel time to work:** 20.9 minutes.

UNION COUNTY
55 W Main St Rm 103　　　**Ph:** 386-496-3711
Lake Butler, FL 32054　　　**Fax:** 386-496-1718

In north-central FL, southwest of Jacksonville; organized May 20, 1921 from Bradford County. **Name Origin:** An expression of unity between political parties in the division of Bradford County, from which this was formed, and in the location of the county seat.

Area (sq mi): 249.71 (land 240.29; water 9.42).

Pop: 13,442 (White 71.9%; Black or African American 22.8%; Hispanic or Latino 3.5%; Asian 0.3%; Other 3.2%). **Foreign born:** 2.1%. **Median age:** 35.7. **State rank:** 59. **Pop change 1990-2000:** +31.1%.

Income: per capita $12,333; median household $34,563. **Pop below poverty level:** 14%.

Unemployment: 4%. **Median home value:** $71,700. **Median travel time to work:** 28.6 minutes.

VOLUSIA COUNTY
123 W Indiana Ave　　　　**Ph:** 386-736-5920
DeLand, FL 32720　　　　**Fax:** 386-822-5707
volusia.org

On central Atlantic coast of FL, northeast of Orlando; organized Dec 29, 1854 from Saint Lucie County. **Name Origin:** For Volusia Landing on the Saint Johns River, the latter forms the western border of the county. Origin uncertain.

Area (sq mi): 1432.44 (land 1103.25; water 329.19).

Pop: 443,343 (White 81.9%; Black or African American 9.3%; Hispanic or Latino 6.6%; Asian 1%; Other 3.5%). **Foreign born:** 6.4%. **Median age:** 42.4. **State rank:** 10. **Pop change 1990-2000:** +19.6%.

Income: per capita $19,664; median household $35,219. **Pop below poverty level:** 11.6%.

Unemployment: 4.3%. **Median home value:** $87,300. **Median travel time to work:** 25.4 minutes.

WAKULLA COUNTY
3056 Crawfordville Hwy　　　**Ph:** 850-926-0905
Crawfordville, FL 32327　　　**Fax:** 850-926-0938
www.clerk.wakulla.fl.us

On north Gulf coast of FL, south of Tallahassee; organized Mar 11, 1843 (prior to statehood) from Leon County. **Name Origin:** Possibly from Creek *wahkola* 'loon,'

Area (sq mi): 735.74 (land 606.66; water 129.08).

Pop: 22,863 (White 84.8%; Black or African American 11.5%; Hispanic or Latino 1.9%; Asian 0.2%; Other 2.1%). **Foreign born:**

Please see sample entry on inside front cover for detailed information about the statistics presented with each county listing.

105

1.5%. **Median age:** 36.8. **State rank:** 51. **Pop change 1990-2000:** +61%.

Income: per capita $17,678; median household $37,149. **Pop below poverty level:** 11.3%.

Unemployment: 3.4%. **Median home value:** $96,200. **Median travel time to work:** 35.5 minutes.

WALTON COUNTY

PO Box 1260   **Ph:** 850-892-8115
De Funiak Springs, FL 32435   **Fax:** 850-892-7551
www.co.walton.fl.us

In central part of FL panhandle, east of Pensacola; organized Dec 29, 1824 (prior to statehood) from Jackson County. **Name Origin:** For Col. George William Walton (1740-1804), secretary of the Territory of West Florida under Andrew Jackson (1821-22).

Area (sq mi): 1238.03 (land 1057.56; water 180.47).

Pop: 40,601 (White 87.3%; Black or African American 7%; Hispanic or Latino 2.2%; Asian 0.5%; Other 4.2%). **Foreign born:** 3.2%. **Median age:** 40.5. **State rank:** 43. **Pop change 1990-2000:** +46.3%.

Income: per capita $18,198; median household $32,407. **Pop below poverty level:** 14.4%.

Unemployment: 3.3%. **Median home value:** $96,400. **Median travel time to work:** 31.3 minutes.

WASHINGTON COUNTY

PO Box 647   **Ph:** 850-638-6285
Chipley, FL 32428   **Fax:** 850-638-6297
www.washingtonfl.com

In central part of FL panhandle, north of Panama City; organized Dec 9, 1825 (prior to statehood) from Jackson and Walton counties. **Name Origin:** For George Washington (1732-99), American patriot and first U.S. president.

Area (sq mi): 615.79 (land 579.93; water 35.86).

Pop: 20,973 (White 80.5%; Black or African American 13.7%; Hispanic or Latino 2.3%; Asian 0.4%; Other 4.2%). **Foreign born:** 2.5%. **Median age:** 38.8. **State rank:** 53. **Pop change 1990-2000:** +24%.

Income: per capita $14,980; median household $27,922. **Pop below poverty level:** 19.2%.

Unemployment: 5%. **Median home value:** $70,000. **Median travel time to work:** 28.9 minutes.

All statistics are based on the 2000 Census except the dollar figures given for per capita income, which are based on 1999 estimates.

GEORGIA - Counties

Note: All boundaries and names are as of January 1, 2000.

N

| 0 | 8 | 16 | 24 | 32 | 40 Kilometers |
| 0 | 8 | 16 | 24 | 32 | 40 Miles |

Georgia

GEORGIA STATE INFORMATION

www.georgia.gov   **Ph:** 404-656-2000

Area (sq mi): 59,424.77 (land 57,906.14; water 1518.63).

Pop: 8,186,453 (White 62.6%; Black or African American 28.7%; Hispanic or Latino 5.3%; Asian 2.1%; Other 4.2%). **Foreign born:** 7.1%. **Median age:** 33.4. **Pop change 1990-2000:** +26.4%.

Income: per capita $21,154; median household $42,433. **Pop below poverty level:** 13%.

Unemployment: 4.6%. **Median home value:** $111,200. **Median travel time to work:** 27.7 minutes.

APPLING COUNTY

83 S Oak St Suite A   **Ph:** 912-367-8100
Baxley, GA 31513   **Fax:** 912-367-8161

In southeast-central GA; organized 1818 (prior to statehood) from Creek cession. **Name Origin:** For Daniel Appling (1787-1818), an officer in the War of 1812.

Area (sq mi): 512.11 (land 508.51; water 3.61).

Pop: 17,419 (White 74.9%; Black or African American 19.6%; Hispanic or Latino 4.5%; Asian 0.3%; Other 3.3%). **Foreign born:** 3.4%. **Median age:** 35.4. **State rank:** 90. **Pop change 1990-2000:** +10.6%.

Income: per capita $15,044; median household $30,266. **Pop below poverty level:** 18.6%.

Unemployment: 8.9%. **Median home value:** $63,700. **Median travel time to work:** 24.1 minutes.

ATHENS-CLARKE COUNTY

PO Box 1868   **Ph:** 706-613-3031
Athens, GA 30603   **Fax:** 706-613-3033
www.athensclarkecounty.com

In north-central GA, northeast of Atlanta; organized Dec 5, 1801 from Jackson and Greene counties. **Name Origin:** For Gen. Elijah Clarke (1733-99), an officer in the American Revolution.

Area (sq mi): 121.28 (land 120.79; water 0.49).

Pop: 101,489 (White 62%; Black or African American 27.3%; Hispanic or Latino 6.3%; Asian 3.1%; Other 4.7%). **Foreign born:** 8.4%. **Median age:** 25.4. **State rank:** 14. **Pop change 1990-2000:** +15.9%.

Income: per capita $17,123; median household $28,403. **Pop below poverty level:** 28.3%.

Unemployment: 3.4%. **Median home value:** $111,300. **Median travel time to work:** 18.6 minutes.

ATKINSON COUNTY

PO Box 518   **Ph:** 912-422-3391
Pearson, GA 31642   **Fax:** 912-422-3429

In south-central GA, northeast of Valdosta; organized Aug 15, 1917 from Coffee and Clinch counties. **Name Origin:** For William Yates Atkinson (1854-99), GA governor (1894-99).

Area (sq mi): 344.1 (land 338.04; water 6.05).

Pop: 7,609 (White 62.6%; Black or African American 19.6%; Hispanic or Latino 17%; Asian 0.1%; Other 13.5%). **Foreign born:** 12.1%. **Median age:** 30.7. **State rank:** 141. **Pop change 1990-2000:** +22.5%.

Income: per capita $12,178; median household $26,470. **Pop below poverty level:** 23%.

Unemployment: 9.1%. **Median home value:** $46,700. **Median travel time to work:** 23.9 minutes.

AUGUSTA-RICHMOND COUNTY

530 Greene St   **Ph:** 706-821-2300
Augusta, GA 30911   **Fax:** 706-821-2819
www.co.richmond.ga.us

On central east coast of GA; original county; organized Feb 5, 1777 (prior to statehood) from Saint Paul Parish. **Name Origin:** For Charles Lennox, 1st Duke of Richmond (1672-1723).

Area (sq mi): 328.45 (land 324.04; water 4.41).

Pop: 199,775 (White 44.4%; Black or African American 49.8%; Hispanic or Latino 2.8%; Asian 1.5%; Other 3.2%). **Foreign born:** 3.4%. **Median age:** 32.3. **State rank:** 7. **Pop change 1990-2000:** +5.3%.

Income: per capita $17,088; median household $33,086. **Pop below poverty level:** 19.6%.

Unemployment: 5.5%. **Median home value:** $76,800. **Median travel time to work:** 22.2 minutes.

BACON COUNTY

PO Box 356   **Ph:** 912-632-5214
Alma, GA 31510   **Fax:** 912-632-2757

In southeast-central GA, northwest of Brunswick; organized Jul 27, 1914 from Appling, Pierce, and Ware counties. **Name Origin:** For Capt. Augustus Octavius Bacon (1839-1914), Confederate army officer and U.S. senator (1895-1914) from GA.

Area (sq mi): 285.92 (land 284.95; water 0.97).

Please see sample entry on inside front cover for detailed information about the statistics presented with each county listing.

109

Pop: 10,103 (White 79.9%; Black or African American 15.7%; Hispanic or Latino 3.4%; Asian 0.3%; Other 2.5%). **Foreign born:** 1.6%. **Median age:** 34.8. **State rank:** 126. **Pop change 1990-2000:** +5.6%.

Income: per capita $14,289; median household $26,910. **Pop below poverty level:** 23.7%.

Unemployment: 6.5%. **Median home value:** $56,500. **Median travel time to work:** 24.4 minutes.

BAKER COUNTY

PO Box 10   **Ph:** 229-734-3004
Newton, GA 39870   **Fax:** 229-734-7770

In southwestern GA, southwest of Albany; organized Dec 12, 1825 from Early County. **Name Origin:** For Col. John Baker (?-1792), Army officer and GA legislator.

Area (sq mi): 349.17 (land 343.22; water 5.95).

Pop: 4,074 (White 46.4%; Black or African American 50.4%; Hispanic or Latino 2.7%; Asian 0%; Other 2.1%). **Foreign born:** 1.9%. **Median age:** 35. **State rank:** 152. **Pop change 1990-2000:** +12.7%.

Income: per capita $16,969; median household $30,338. **Pop below poverty level:** 23.4%.

Unemployment: 5.1%. **Median home value:** $62,700. **Median travel time to work:** 28.3 minutes.

BALDWIN COUNTY

121 N Wilkinson St Suite 314   **Ph:** 478-445-4791
Milledgeville, GA 31061   **Fax:** 478-445-6320

In central GA, northeast of Macon; original county; organized May 11, 1803 from Creek Indian lands and Hancock, Washington, and Wilkinson counties. **Name Origin:** For Abraham Baldwin (1754-1807), member of the Continental Congress, and U.S. senator from GA (1799-1807).

Area (sq mi): 267.5 (land 258.45; water 9.05).

Pop: 44,700 (White 53.5%; Black or African American 43.4%; Hispanic or Latino 1.4%; Asian 1%; Other 1.4%). **Foreign born:** 1.9%. **Median age:** 34.2. **State rank:** 39. **Pop change 1990-2000:** +13.1%.

Income: per capita $16,271; median household $35,159. **Pop below poverty level:** 16.8%.

Unemployment: 3.7%. **Median home value:** $79,800. **Median travel time to work:** 19.9 minutes.

BANKS COUNTY

PO Box 337   **Ph:** 706-677-6240
Homer, GA 30547   **Fax:** 706-677-6294

In northeastern GA, north of Athens; organized Dec 11, 1858 from Franklin and Habersham counties. **Name Origin:** For Richard Banks (1784-1850), a noted local surgeon.

Area (sq mi): 233.87 (land 233.67; water 0.2).

Pop: 14,422 (White 91.9%; Black or African American 3.2%; Hispanic or Latino 3.4%; Asian 0.6%; Other 3.1%). **Foreign born:** 2.1%. **Median age:** 35.2. **State rank:** 105. **Pop change 1990-2000:** +39.9%.

Income: per capita $17,424; median household $38,523. **Pop below poverty level:** 12.5%.

Unemployment: 3.8%. **Median home value:** $92,400. **Median travel time to work:** 30.1 minutes.

BARROW COUNTY

233 E Broad St   **Ph:** 770-307-3111
Winder, GA 30680

In north-central GA, west of Athens; organized Jul 7, 1914 from Jackson, Walton, and Gwinnett counties. **Name Origin:** For David Crenshaw Barrow (1852-1929), professor and chancellor of the University of Georgia.

Area (sq mi): 162.84 (land 162.17; water 0.67).

Pop: 46,144 (White 83.5%; Black or African American 9.7%; Hispanic or Latino 3.2%; Asian 2.2%; Other 3.2%). **Foreign born:** 3.6%. **Median age:** 32.5. **State rank:** 37. **Pop change 1990-2000:** +55.3%.

Income: per capita $18,350; median household $45,019. **Pop below poverty level:** 8.3%.

Unemployment: 4.5%. **Median home value:** $103,400. **Median travel time to work:** 33.7 minutes.

BARTOW COUNTY

135 W Cherokee Ave Suite 251   **Ph:** 770-387-5030
Cartersville, GA 30120   **Fax:** 770-387-5023

In northwestern GA, east of Rome; organized as Cass County Dec 3, 1832 from Indian lands; name changed Dec 6, 1861. **Name Origin:** For Confederate Gen. Francis S. Bartow (?-1861), first officer of such rank to be killed in action during the Civil War.

Area (sq mi): 470.11 (land 459.43; water 10.69).

Pop: 76,019 (White 86.4%; Black or African American 8.7%; Hispanic or Latino 3.3%; Asian 0.5%; Other 3%). **Foreign born:** 2.5%. **Median age:** 33.7. **State rank:** 26. **Pop change 1990-2000:** +36%.

Income: per capita $18,989; median household $43,660. **Pop below poverty level:** 8.6%.

Unemployment: 4.5%. **Median home value:** $99,600. **Median travel time to work:** 29.6 minutes.

BEN HILL COUNTY

402A E Pine St   **Ph:** 229-426-5112
Fitzgerald, GA 31750   **Fax:** 229-426-5106
www.benhillcounty.com

In south-central GA, northeast of Albany; organized Jul 31, 1906 from Irwin and Wilcox counties. **Name Origin:** For Benjamin Harvey Hill (1823-82), GA legislator and U.S. senator.

Area (sq mi): 254.03 (land 251.79; water 2.23).

Pop: 17,484 (White 61.9%; Black or African American 32.6%; Hispanic or Latino 4.6%; Asian 0.3%; Other 3.9%). **Foreign born:** 3.4%. **Median age:** 34.8. **State rank:** 89. **Pop change 1990-2000:** +7.6%.

Income: per capita $14,093; median household $27,100. **Pop below poverty level:** 22.3%.

Unemployment: 5.4%. **Median home value:** $60,700. **Median travel time to work:** 18.3 minutes.

All statistics are based on the 2000 Census except the dollar figures given for per capita income, which are based on 1999 estimates.

BERRIEN COUNTY

PO Box 446　　　　　　　　　　　**Ph:** 229-686-5421
Nashville, GA 31639　　　　　　　**Fax:** 229-686-2785

In south-central GA, north of Valdosta; organized Feb 25, 1856 from Lowndes, Coffee, and Irwin counties. **Name Origin:** For John Macpherson Berrien (1781-1856), U.S. senator from GA (1825-29; 1841-52) and U.S. Attorney General (1829-31).

Area (sq mi): 457.78 (land 452.41; water 5.37).

Pop: 16,235 (White 84.8%; Black or African American 11.4%; Hispanic or Latino 2.4%; Asian 0.3%; Other 2.8%). **Foreign born:** 1.4%. **Median age:** 35.2. **State rank:** 94. **Pop change 1990-2000:** +14.7%.

Income: per capita $16,375; median household $30,044. **Pop below poverty level:** 17.7%.

Unemployment: 5.2%. **Median home value:** $70,700. **Median travel time to work:** 21.9 minutes.

BIBB COUNTY

601 Mulberry St　　　　　　　　　**Ph:** 478-749-6400
Macon, GA 31201　　　　　　　　**Fax:** 478-749-6329
www.co.bibb.ga.us

In central GA; organized Dec 9, 1822 from Jones, Monroe, Twiggs, and Houston counties. **Name Origin:** For William Wyatt Bibb (1781-1820), U.S. senator from GA (1813-16) and first governor of AL (1817-20).

Area (sq mi): 255.13 (land 249.96; water 5.17).

Pop: 153,887 (White 49.6%; Black or African American 47.3%; Hispanic or Latino 1.3%; Asian 1.1%; Other 1.5%). **Foreign born:** 1.9%. **Median age:** 34.7. **State rank:** 9. **Pop change 1990-2000:** +2.6%.

Income: per capita $19,058; median household $34,532. **Pop below poverty level:** 19.1%.

Unemployment: 4.3%. **Median home value:** $84,400. **Median travel time to work:** 22.2 minutes.

BLECKLEY COUNTY

306 SE 2nd St　　　　　　　　　**Ph:** 478-934-3200
Cochran, GA 31014　　　　　　　**Fax:** 478-934-0822

In central GA, southeast of Macon; organized Jul 30, 1912 from Pulaski County. **Name Origin:** For Logan Edwin Bleckley (1827-1907), Confederate soldier and chief justice of GA supreme court.

Area (sq mi): 219.14 (land 217.39; water 1.74).

Pop: 11,666 (White 72.9%; Black or African American 24.6%; Hispanic or Latino 0.9%; Asian 0.9%; Other 1.2%). **Foreign born:** 1.4%. **Median age:** 35.1. **State rank:** 114. **Pop change 1990-2000:** +11.9%.

Income: per capita $15,934; median household $33,448. **Pop below poverty level:** 15.9%.

Unemployment: 4.5%. **Median home value:** $66,500. **Median travel time to work:** 26.1 minutes.

BRANTLEY COUNTY

PO Box 398　　　　　　　　　　　**Ph:** 912-462-6285
Nahunta, GA 31553　　　　　　　**Fax:** 912-462-5538

In southeastern GA, west of Brunswick; organized Aug 4, 1920 from Charlton, Pierce, and Wayne counties. **Name Origin:** For William Gordon Brantley (1860-1934), state senator. Some claim Benjamin D. Brantley (1832-91).

Area (sq mi): 447.42 (land 444.4; water 3.02).

Pop: 14,629 (White 93.7%; Black or African American 4%; Hispanic or Latino 1%; Asian 0.1%; Other 1.5%). **Foreign born:** 0.9%. **Median age:** 34.6. **State rank:** 104. **Pop change 1990-2000:** +32.1%.

Income: per capita $13,713; median household $30,361. **Pop below poverty level:** 15.6%.

Unemployment: 5.6%. **Median home value:** $60,900. **Median travel time to work:** 34 minutes.

BROOKS COUNTY

PO Box 272　　　　　　　　　　　**Ph:** 229-263-5561
Quitman, GA 31643　　　　　　　**Fax:** 229-263-9345

On central southern border of GA, west of Valdosta; organized Dec 11, 1858 from Lowndes and Thomas counties. **Name Origin:** For a local citizen.

Area (sq mi): 497.77 (land 493.62; water 4.15).

Pop: 16,450 (White 56.6%; Black or African American 39.3%; Hispanic or Latino 3.1%; Asian 0.3%; Other 3%). **Foreign born:** 1.7%. **Median age:** 36.3. **State rank:** 93. **Pop change 1990-2000:** +6.8%.

Income: per capita $13,977; median household $26,911. **Pop below poverty level:** 23.4%.

Unemployment: 4.9%. **Median home value:** $67,900. **Median travel time to work:** 24.6 minutes.

BRYAN COUNTY

Courthouse PO Box H　　　　　　**Ph:** 912-653-4681
Pembroke, GA 31321
co.bryan.ga.totalwebgov.com

In southeastern GA, west of Savannah; organized Dec 19, 1793 from Chatham County. **Name Origin:** For Jonathan Bryan (1708-88), a founder of the Georgia Colony at Savannah, jurist, and GA legislator.

Area (sq mi): 454.49 (land 441.71; water 12.78).

Pop: 23,417 (White 81.7%; Black or African American 14.1%; Hispanic or Latino 2%; Asian 0.8%; Other 2.3%). **Foreign born:** 2.5%. **Median age:** 33.3. **State rank:** 69. **Pop change 1990-2000:** +51.7%.

Income: per capita $19,794; median household $48,345. **Pop below poverty level:** 11.7%.

Unemployment: 2.5%. **Median home value:** $115,600. **Median travel time to work:** 31.3 minutes.

BULLOCH COUNTY

PO Box 347　　　　　　　　　　　**Ph:** 912-764-6245
Statesboro, GA 30459　　　　　　**Fax:** 912-764-8634
www.bullochcounty.net

In central eastern GA, northwest of Savannah; organized Feb 8,

Please see sample entry on inside front cover for detailed information about the statistics presented with each county listing.

1796 from Bryan and Screven counties. **Name Origin:** For Archibald Bulloch (1730-77), soldier, legislator, and first governor of GA (1776-77).

Area (sq mi): 688.84 (land 682.07; water 6.77).

Pop: 55,983 (White 67.9%; Black or African American 28.8%; Hispanic or Latino 1.9%; Asian 0.8%; Other 1.7%). **Foreign born:** 3.1%. **Median age:** 26.1. **State rank:** 35. **Pop change 1990-2000:** +29.8%.

Income: per capita $16,080; median household $29,499. **Pop below poverty level:** 24.5%.

Unemployment: 3.7%. **Median home value:** $94,300. **Median travel time to work:** 22.7 minutes.

BURKE COUNTY

PO Box 89   **Ph:** 706-554-2324
Waynesboro, GA 30830   **Fax:** 706-554-0350

On central east coast of GA, south of Augusta; original county; organized Feb 5, 1777 (prior to statehood) from Saint George Parish. **Name Origin:** For Edmund Burke (1729-97), British statesman, orator, and defender of the American colonies.

Area (sq mi): 834.99 (land 830.47; water 4.52).

Pop: 22,243 (White 46.5%; Black or African American 51%; Hispanic or Latino 1.4%; Asian 0.3%; Other 1.8%). **Foreign born:** 0.8%. **Median age:** 33. **State rank:** 74. **Pop change 1990-2000:** +8.1%.

Income: per capita $13,136; median household $27,877. **Pop below poverty level:** 28.7%.

Unemployment: 7.9%. **Median home value:** $59,800. **Median travel time to work:** 29 minutes.

BUTTS COUNTY

25 3rd St Suite 4   **Ph:** 770-775-8200
Jackson, GA 30233   **Fax:** 770-775-8211

In west-central GA, northwest of Macon; organized Dec 24, 1825 from Henry and Monroe counties. **Name Origin:** For Capt. Sam Butts (1777-1814), army officer killed in the War of 1812.

Area (sq mi): 190.01 (land 186.61; water 3.4).

Pop: 19,522 (White 68.5%; Black or African American 28.8%; Hispanic or Latino 1.4%; Asian 0.3%; Other 1.6%). **Foreign born:** 0.9%. **Median age:** 35.9. **State rank:** 86. **Pop change 1990-2000:** +27.4%.

Income: per capita $17,016; median household $39,879. **Pop below poverty level:** 11.5%.

Unemployment: 5%. **Median home value:** $86,700. **Median travel time to work:** 31 minutes.

CALHOUN COUNTY

PO Box 226   **Ph:** 229-849-4835
Morgan, GA 39866   **Fax:** 229-849-2100

In southwestern GA, west of Albany; organized Feb 20, 1854 from Early and Baker counties. **Name Origin:** For John Caldwell Calhoun (1782-1850), U.S. statesman and champion of Southern causes.

Area (sq mi): 283.57 (land 280.18; water 3.39).

Pop: 6,320 (White 37.5%; Black or African American 60.6%; Hispanic or Latino 3%; Asian 0.1%; Other 1%). **Foreign born:** 1.9%. **Median age:** 35.6. **State rank:** 149. **Pop change 1990-2000:** +26.1%.

Income: per capita $11,839; median household $24,588. **Pop below poverty level:** 26.5%.

Unemployment: 6.9%. **Median home value:** $48,200. **Median travel time to work:** 26.4 minutes.

CAMDEN COUNTY

PO Box 99   **Ph:** 912-576-5649
Woodbine, GA 31569   **Fax:** 912-576-5647
www.co.camden.ga.us

On southeastern Atlantic coast; original county; organized Feb 5, 1777 (prior to statehood) from Saint Mary and Saint Thomas parishes. **Name Origin:** For Charles Pratt, 1st Earl of Camden (1714-94), English statesman who supported the American colonies before the Revolutionary War.

Area (sq mi): 782.52 (land 629.91; water 152.61).

Pop: 43,664 (White 73.2%; Black or African American 20.1%; Hispanic or Latino 3.6%; Asian 1%; Other 3.9%). **Foreign born:** 2.3%. **Median age:** 28.2. **State rank:** 41. **Pop change 1990-2000:** +44.7%.

Income: per capita $16,445; median household $41,056. **Pop below poverty level:** 10.1%.

Unemployment: 3.5%. **Median home value:** $85,300. **Median travel time to work:** 21.6 minutes.

CANDLER COUNTY

705 N Lewis St   **Ph:** 912-685-2835
Metter, GA 30439   **Fax:** 912-685-4823

In east-central GA, northwest of Savannah; organized Jul 1914 from Bulloch, Emanuel, and Tattnall counties. **Name Origin:** For Col. Allen Daniel Candler (1834-1910), GA legislator and governor (1898-1902).

Area (sq mi): 248.81 (land 246.88; water 1.94).

Pop: 9,577 (White 62.9%; Black or African American 27.1%; Hispanic or Latino 9.2%; Asian 0.3%; Other 7.2%). **Foreign born:** 6.1%. **Median age:** 35.6. **State rank:** 130. **Pop change 1990-2000:** +23.7%.

Income: per capita $12,958; median household $25,022. **Pop below poverty level:** 26.1%.

Unemployment: 4.4%. **Median home value:** $62,700. **Median travel time to work:** 24.4 minutes.

CARROLL COUNTY

PO Box 338   **Ph:** 770-830-5800
Carrollton, GA 30112   **Fax:** 770-830-5992
www.carrollcountyga.com

On central western border of GA, southwest of Atlanta; original county; established Jun 9, 1825 from Indian lands. **Name Origin:** For Charles Carroll (1737-1832), a signer of the Declaration of Independence, U.S. senator from MD (1789-92), and founder of the Baltimore and Ohio Railroad.

Area (sq mi): 503.83 (land 498.93; water 4.89).

All statistics are based on the 2000 Census except the dollar figures given for per capita income, which are based on 1999 estimates.

Pop: 87,268 (White 79.4%; Black or African American 16.3%; Hispanic or Latino 2.6%; Asian 0.6%; Other 2.5%). **Foreign born:** 2.9%. **Median age:** 32.5. **State rank:** 23. **Pop change 1990-2000:** +22.2%.

Income: per capita $17,656; median household $38,799. **Pop below poverty level:** 13.7%.

Unemployment: 5%. **Median home value:** $93,300. **Median travel time to work:** 28 minutes.

CATOOSA COUNTY
875 Lafayette St   **Ph:** 706-935-4231
Ringgold, GA 30736
www.catoosa.com

On the northern border of GA, southeast of Chattanooga, TN; organized Dec 5, 1853 from Walker and Whitfield counties. **Name Origin:** For the Cherokee Indian chief.

Area (sq mi): 162.66 (land 162.23; water 0.44).

Pop: 53,282 (White 95.7%; Black or African American 1.3%; Hispanic or Latino 1.2%; Asian 0.7%; Other 1.6%). **Foreign born:** 1.7%. **Median age:** 35.8. **State rank:** 36. **Pop change 1990-2000:** +25.5%.

Income: per capita $18,009; median household $39,998. **Pop below poverty level:** 9.4%.

Unemployment: 2.6%. **Median home value:** $90,800. **Median travel time to work:** 23.7 minutes.

CHARLTON COUNTY
100 S 3rd St   **Ph:** 912-496-2549
Folkston, GA 31537   **Fax:** 912-496-1156

In southeastern GA, southwest of Brunswick; organized Feb 11, 1854 from Camden County. **Name Origin:** For Robert Milledge Charlton (1807-54), GA legislator, jurist, and U.S. senator (1852-52).

Area (sq mi): 782.97 (land 780.77; water 2.2).

Pop: 10,282 (White 68.2%; Black or African American 29.3%; Hispanic or Latino 0.8%; Asian 0.3%; Other 1.8%). **Foreign born:** 0.9%. **Median age:** 33.4. **State rank:** 124. **Pop change 1990-2000:** +21%.

Income: per capita $12,920; median household $27,869. **Pop below poverty level:** 20.9%.

Unemployment: 3.9%. **Median home value:** $67,300. **Median travel time to work:** 33.8 minutes.

CHATHAM COUNTY
124 Bull St   **Ph:** 912-652-7869
Savannah, GA 31401   **Fax:** 912-652-7874
www.chathamcounty.org

On the southeastern Atlantic coast of GA; original county; organized Feb 5, 1777 (prior to statehood) from Saint Phillips and Christ Church parishes. **Name Origin:** For William Pitt (the Elder; 1708-78), 1st Earl of Chatham, known as 'the Great Commoner,' for his support of the American colonies before the Revolutionary War.

Area (sq mi): 632.28 (land 438.11; water 194.17).

Pop: 232,048 (White 54.2%; Black or African American 40.5%;

Hispanic or Latino 2.3%; Asian 1.7%; Other 2.5%). **Foreign born:** 4%. **Median age:** 34.4. **State rank:** 6. **Pop change 1990-2000:** +7%.

Income: per capita $21,152; median household $37,752. **Pop below poverty level:** 15.6%.

Unemployment: 3.4%. **Median home value:** $95,000. **Median travel time to work:** 22.3 minutes.

CHATTAHOOCHEE COUNTY
PO Box 299   **Ph:** 706-989-3602
Cusseta, GA 31805   **Fax:** 706-989-2005

On the central western border of GA, south of Columbus; organized Feb 13, 1854 from Muscogee and Marion counties. **Name Origin:** For the Chattahoochee River, which forms its western border. From an Indian word probably meaning 'marked rocks,' for painted stones found in the river.

Area (sq mi): 251.17 (land 248.77; water 2.4).

Pop: 14,882 (White 55%; Black or African American 29.9%; Hispanic or Latino 10.4%; Asian 1.8%; Other 10.3%). **Foreign born:** 6%. **Median age:** 23.2. **State rank:** 103. **Pop change 1990-2000:** -12.1%.

Income: per capita $14,049; median household $37,106. **Pop below poverty level:** 10.6%.

Unemployment: 6%. **Median home value:** $63,800. **Median travel time to work:** 14.3 minutes.

CHATTOOGA COUNTY
PO Box 211   **Ph:** 706-857-0701
Summerville, GA 30747   **Fax:** 706-857-0742

On the northwestern border of GA, north of Rome; organized Dec 28, 1838 from Floyd and Walker counties. **Name Origin:** For the Chattooga River, which runs diagonally through the county; a Cherokee word whose meaning is unclear.

Area (sq mi): 313.55 (land 313.33; water 0.23).

Pop: 25,470 (White 85.5%; Black or African American 11.2%; Hispanic or Latino 2.1%; Asian 0.1%; Other 1.9%). **Foreign born:** 1.9%. **Median age:** 36.5. **State rank:** 60. **Pop change 1990-2000:** +14.5%.

Income: per capita $14,508; median household $30,664. **Pop below poverty level:** 14.3%.

Unemployment: 4.4%. **Median home value:** $59,900. **Median travel time to work:** 23.9 minutes.

CHEROKEE COUNTY
90 North St Suite 310   **Ph:** 770-479-0449
Canton, GA 30114   **Fax:** 770-720-6361
www.cherokeega.com/ie.cfm

In northwest-central GA, north of Atlanta; original county; established Dec 21, 1830 from Cherokee lands. **Name Origin:** For the Indian tribe of Iroquoian linguistic stock who occupied the land at the time. Name may derive from Creek *tciloki* 'people of a different speech.'

Area (sq mi): 433.99 (land 423.68; water 10.31).

Pop: 141,903 (White 89.9%; Black or African American 2.5%; Hispanic or Latino 5.4%; Asian 0.8%; Other 4.3%). **Foreign born:**

Please see sample entry on inside front cover for detailed information about the statistics presented with each county listing.

113

5.8%. **Median age:** 34. **State rank:** 10. **Pop change 1990-2000:** +57.3%.

Income: per capita $24,871; median household $60,896. **Pop below poverty level:** 5.3%.

Unemployment: 2.3%. **Median home value:** $139,900. **Median travel time to work:** 34.4 minutes.

CLAY COUNTY

PO Box 519   **Ph:** 229-768-3238
Fort Gaines, GA 39851   **Fax:** 229-768-3672

On the southwestern border of GA, west of Albany; organized Feb 16, 1854 from Early and Randolph counties. **Name Origin:** For Henry Clay (1777-1852), U.S. senator from KY, known as the 'Great Pacificator' for his advocacy of compromise to avert national crises.

Area (sq mi): 216.99 (land 195.21; water 21.79).

Pop: 3,357 (White 38.2%; Black or African American 60.5%; Hispanic or Latino 1%; Asian 0.3%; Other 0.9%). **Foreign born:** 0.7%. **Median age:** 41.9. **State rank:** 155. **Pop change 1990-2000:** -0.2%.

Income: per capita $16,819; median household $21,448. **Pop below poverty level:** 31.3%.

Unemployment: 5.8%. **Median home value:** $53,600. **Median travel time to work:** 25.9 minutes.

CLAYTON COUNTY

112 Smith St   **Ph:** 770-477-3208
Jonesboro, GA 30236   **Fax:** 770-477-3217
www.co.clayton.ga.us

In west-central GA, south of Atlanta; organized Nov 30, 1858 from Fayette and Henry counties. **Name Origin:** For Augustin Smith Clayton (1783-1839), GA jurist and U.S. representative (1832-35).

Area (sq mi): 144.28 (land 142.62; water 1.66).

Pop: 236,517 (White 34.9%; Black or African American 51.6%; Hispanic or Latino 7.5%; Asian 4.5%; Other 6%). **Foreign born:** 10.9%. **Median age:** 30.2. **State rank:** 5. **Pop change 1990-2000:** +29.9%.

Income: per capita $18,079; median household $42,697. **Pop below poverty level:** 10.1%.

Unemployment: 4%. **Median home value:** $92,700. **Median travel time to work:** 29.8 minutes.

CLINCH COUNTY

PO Box 433   **Ph:** 912-487-5854
Homerville, GA 31634   **Fax:** 912-487-3083

On southern border, east of Valdosta; organized Feb 14, 1850 from Ware and Lowndes counties. **Name Origin:** For Brig. Gen. Duncan Lamont Clinch (1787-1849), Army officer and U.S. representative from GA (1844-45).

Area (sq mi): 824.17 (land 809.29; water 14.88).

Pop: 6,878 (White 68.5%; Black or African American 29.5%; Hispanic or Latino 0.8%; Asian 0.1%; Other 1.4%). **Foreign born:** 1.4%. **Median age:** 34.9. **State rank:** 144. **Pop change 1990-2000:** +11.7%.

Income: per capita $13,023; median household $26,755. **Pop below poverty level:** 23.4%.

Unemployment: 7%. **Median home value:** $54,600. **Median travel time to work:** 19.6 minutes.

COBB COUNTY

100 Cherokee St Suite 300   **Ph:** 770-528-3300
Marietta, GA 30090   **Fax:** 770-528-2606
www.co.cobb.ga.us

In northwest-central GA, northwest of Atlanta; organized Dec 3, 1832 from Cherokee County. **Name Origin:** For Thomas Willis Cobb (1784-1830), U.S. senator from GA (1824-28) and judge of the GA superior court (1828).

Area (sq mi): 344.51 (land 340.15; water 4.36).

Pop: 607,751 (White 68.8%; Black or African American 18.8%; Hispanic or Latino 7.7%; Asian 3.1%; Other 5.8%). **Foreign born:** 11.6%. **Median age:** 33.2. **State rank:** 3. **Pop change 1990-2000:** +35.7%.

Income: per capita $27,863; median household $58,289. **Pop below poverty level:** 6.5%.

Unemployment: 3%. **Median home value:** $147,600. **Median travel time to work:** 31.3 minutes.

COFFEE COUNTY

101 S Peterson Ave   **Ph:** 912-384-4799
Douglas, GA 31533   **Fax:** 912-384-0291

In south-central GA, northeast of Valdosta; organized Feb 9, 1854 from Clinch, Irwin, Telfair, and Ware counties. **Name Origin:** For Gen. John Coffee (1782-1836), an officer in the Indian wars, U.S. representative from GA (1833-36), and cousin to John Coffee of TN.

Area (sq mi): 602.61 (land 598.9; water 3.72).

Pop: 37,413 (White 66%; Black or African American 25.9%; Hispanic or Latino 6.8%; Asian 0.6%; Other 5.2%). **Foreign born:** 5.4%. **Median age:** 32.1. **State rank:** 48. **Pop change 1990-2000:** +26.4%.

Income: per capita $15,530; median household $30,710. **Pop below poverty level:** 19.1%.

Unemployment: 5.3%. **Median home value:** $68,800. **Median travel time to work:** 20.7 minutes.

COLQUITT COUNTY

PO Box 517   **Ph:** 229-890-1805
Moultrie, GA 31776

In south-central GA, northwest of Valdosta; organized Feb 25, 1856 from Thomas and Lowndes counties. **Name Origin:** For Walter Terry Colquitt (1799-1855), jurist, Methodist minister, and U.S. senator (1843-48).

Area (sq mi): 556.55 (land 552.27; water 4.28).

Pop: 42,053 (White 64.8%; Black or African American 23.5%; Hispanic or Latino 10.8%; Asian 0.2%; Other 8.5%). **Foreign born:** 6.5%. **Median age:** 33.7. **State rank:** 43. **Pop change 1990-2000:** +14.8%.

Income: per capita $14,457; median household $28,539. **Pop below poverty level:** 19.8%.

Unemployment: 6.7%. **Median home value:** $65,400. **Median travel time to work:** 22.5 minutes.

All statistics are based on the 2000 Census except the dollar figures given for per capita income, which are based on 1999 estimates.

COLUMBIA COUNTY

PO Box 498   **Ph:** 706-868-3379
Evans, GA 30809   **Fax:** 706-868-3348
www.co.columbia.ga.us

On central eastern coast of GA, north of Augusta; organized Dec 10, 1790 from Richmond County. **Name Origin:** Feminine form of Columbus, a poetic and honorific reference to Christopher Columbus (1451-1506) and America.

Area (sq mi): 307.78 (land 290.01; water 17.76).

Pop: 89,288 (White 81.1%; Black or African American 11.2%; Hispanic or Latino 2.6%; Asian 3.4%; Other 2.8%). **Foreign born:** 4.8%. **Median age:** 35.4. **State rank:** 21. **Pop change 1990-2000:** +35.2%.

Income: per capita $23,496; median household $55,682. **Pop below poverty level:** 5.1%.

Unemployment: 2.5%. **Median home value:** $118,000. **Median travel time to work:** 25.3 minutes.

COLUMBUS-MUSCOGEE COUNTY

PO Box 1340   **Ph:** 706-653-4013
Columbus, GA 31902   **Fax:** 706-653-4016
www.columbusga.com

On central western border of GA, southwest of Macon; organized Dec 11, 1826 from Creek lands. **Name Origin:** For the Muskogee Indians, a Shawnee tribe of Muskhogean linguistic stock.

Area (sq mi): 221 (land 216.26; water 4.74).

Pop: 186,291 (White 48.7%; Black or African American 43.7%; Hispanic or Latino 4.5%; Asian 1.5%; Other 4.3%). **Foreign born:** 4.7%. **Median age:** 32.6. **State rank:** 8. **Pop change 1990-2000:** +3.9%.

Income: per capita $18,262; median household $34,798. **Pop below poverty level:** 15.7%.

Unemployment: 4.8%. **Median home value:** $84,000. **Median travel time to work:** 19.9 minutes.

COOK COUNTY

209 N Parrish Ave   **Ph:** 229-896-2266
Adel, GA 31620   **Fax:** 229-896-7629

In south-central GA, northwest of Valdosta; organized Jul 30, 1918 from Berrien County. **Name Origin:** For Gen. Philip Cook (1817-94), Confederate officer and U.S. representative from GA (1873-83).

Area (sq mi): 233.22 (land 229.02; water 4.2).

Pop: 15,771 (White 66.7%; Black or African American 29.1%; Hispanic or Latino 3.1%; Asian 0.4%; Other 2.5%). **Foreign born:** 2.3%. **Median age:** 34.3. **State rank:** 97. **Pop change 1990-2000:** +17.2%.

Income: per capita $13,465; median household $27,582. **Pop below poverty level:** 20.7%.

Unemployment: 4.9%. **Median home value:** $60,900. **Median travel time to work:** 21.3 minutes.

COWETA COUNTY

22 E Broad St   **Ph:** 770-254-2601
Newnan, GA 30263   **Fax:** 770-254-2606
www.coweta.ga.us

In west-central GA, southwest of Atlanta; organized Jun 9, 1825 from Indian lands. **Name Origin:** For Gen. William McIntosh (1775-1825), a half-blooded Creek Indian and the head chief of the Coweta Indians of the Creek nation. The name may mean 'falls,' with reference to those on the Chattahoochee River.

Area (sq mi): 445.98 (land 442.62; water 3.36).

Pop: 89,215 (White 77.2%; Black or African American 18%; Hispanic or Latino 3.1%; Asian 0.7%; Other 2.4%). **Foreign born:** 3.7%. **Median age:** 33.6. **State rank:** 22. **Pop change 1990-2000:** +65.7%.

Income: per capita $21,949; median household $52,706. **Pop below poverty level:** 7.8%.

Unemployment: 3.3%. **Median home value:** $121,700. **Median travel time to work:** 29.7 minutes.

CRAWFORD COUNTY

PO Box 1059   **Ph:** 478-836-3782
Roberta, GA 31078   **Fax:** 478-836-5818

In west-central GA, southwest of Macon; organized Dec 9, 1822 from Houston County. **Name Origin:** For William Harris Crawford (1772-1834), VA statesman.

Area (sq mi): 326.45 (land 325.01; water 1.45).

Pop: 12,495 (White 72.3%; Black or African American 23.8%; Hispanic or Latino 2.4%; Asian 0.2%; Other 3.2%). **Foreign born:** 0.5%. **Median age:** 35.2. **State rank:** 111. **Pop change 1990-2000:** +39%.

Income: per capita $15,768; median household $37,848. **Pop below poverty level:** 15.4%.

Unemployment: 3.8%. **Median home value:** $77,800. **Median travel time to work:** 32.3 minutes.

CRISP COUNTY

210 S 7th St   **Ph:** 229-276-2672
Cordele, GA 31015   **Fax:** 229-276-2675

In south-central GA, northeast of Albany; organized Aug 17, 1905 from Dooly County. **Name Origin:** For Charles Frederick Crisp (1845-96), Confederate army officer and U.S. representative from GA (1883-96).

Area (sq mi): 281.2 (land 273.82; water 7.38).

Pop: 21,996 (White 53.5%; Black or African American 43.4%; Hispanic or Latino 1.7%; Asian 0.7%; Other 1.9%). **Foreign born:** 2.1%. **Median age:** 34.4. **State rank:** 75. **Pop change 1990-2000:** +9.9%.

Income: per capita $14,695; median household $26,547. **Pop below poverty level:** 29.3%.

Unemployment: 6.1%. **Median home value:** $74,400. **Median travel time to work:** 19 minutes.

Please see sample entry on inside front cover for detailed information about the statistics presented with each county listing.

DADE COUNTY

PO Box 417   **Ph:** 706-657-4778
Trenton, GA 30752   **Fax:** 706-657-8284

In northwestern corner of GA, south of Chattanooga, TN; organized Dec 25, 1837 from Walker County. **Name Origin:** For Maj. Francis Langhorne Dade (1793-1835), officer killed in the Seminole War (1835-42).

Area (sq mi): 174.16 (land 173.98; water 0.18).

Pop: 15,154 (White 96.9%; Black or African American 0.6%; Hispanic or Latino 0.9%; Asian 0.4%; Other 1.5%). **Foreign born:** 1.4%. **Median age:** 36.1. **State rank:** 101. **Pop change 1990-2000:** +15.3%.

Income: per capita $16,127; median household $35,259. **Pop below poverty level:** 9.7%.

Unemployment: 2.9%. **Median home value:** $79,200. **Median travel time to work:** 26.7 minutes.

DAWSON COUNTY

25 Tucker Rd Suite 102   **Ph:** 706-344-3501
Dawsonville, GA 30534   **Fax:** 706-344-3504
www.dawsoncounty.org

In north-central GA, northeast of Atlanta; organized Dec 3, 1857 from Gilmer and Lumpkin counties. **Name Origin:** For William Crosby Dawson (1798-1856), soldier, jurist, and U.S. senator from GA (1849-55).

Area (sq mi): 213.93 (land 211.04; water 2.9).

Pop: 15,999 (White 96.4%; Black or African American 0.4%; Hispanic or Latino 1.6%; Asian 0.3%; Other 2.1%). **Foreign born:** 1.4%. **Median age:** 36.2. **State rank:** 95. **Pop change 1990-2000:** +69.7%.

Income: per capita $22,520; median household $47,486. **Pop below poverty level:** 7.6%.

Unemployment: 2.6%. **Median home value:** $142,500. **Median travel time to work:** 34 minutes.

DECATUR COUNTY

PO Box 726   **Ph:** 229-248-3030
Bainbridge, GA 39818   **Fax:** 229-246-2062

On the southwestern border of GA, southwest of Albany; organized Dec 8, 1823 from Early county. **Name Origin:** For Stephen F. Decatur (1779-1820), U.S. naval officer during the War of 1812 and in actions against the Barbary pirates near Tripoli, who said '. . . may she always be in the right; but our country, right or wrong!'

Area (sq mi): 623.16 (land 596.8; water 26.36).

Pop: 28,240 (White 55.9%; Black or African American 39.9%; Hispanic or Latino 3.2%; Asian 0.3%; Other 2.5%). **Foreign born:** 2.3%. **Median age:** 34.4. **State rank:** 53. **Pop change 1990-2000:** +10.7%.

Income: per capita $15,063; median household $28,820. **Pop below poverty level:** 22.7%.

Unemployment: 6.5%. **Median home value:** $69,500. **Median travel time to work:** 22.5 minutes.

DEKALB COUNTY

556 N McDonough St   **Ph:** 404-371-2000
Decatur, GA 30030   **Fax:** 404-371-2002
www.co.dekalb.ga.us

In northwest-central GA, east of Atlanta; organized Dec 9, 1822 from Fayette, Henry, Gwinnett, and Newton counties. **Name Origin:** For Johann, Baron de Kalb (1721-80), German-born French soldier who fought with the Americans during the Revolutionary War.

Area (sq mi): 270.91 (land 268.21; water 2.7).

Pop: 665,865 (White 32.2%; Black or African American 54.2%; Hispanic or Latino 7.9%; Asian 4%; Other 5.8%). **Foreign born:** 15.2%. **Median age:** 32.3. **State rank:** 2. **Pop change 1990-2000:** +22%.

Income: per capita $23,968; median household $49,117. **Pop below poverty level:** 10.8%.

Unemployment: 4.2%. **Median home value:** $135,100. **Median travel time to work:** 31.7 minutes.

DODGE COUNTY

PO Box 818   **Ph:** 478-374-4361
Eastman, GA 31023   **Fax:** 478-374-8121

In central GA, southwest of Macon; organized Oct 26, 1870 from Montgomery, Pulaski, and Telfair counties. **Name Origin:** For William Earle Dodge (1805-83), U.S. representative from NY (1866-67) and owner of a vast estate in GA, who was active in the attempt to avoid the Civil War.

Area (sq mi): 503.17 (land 500.29; water 2.88).

Pop: 19,171 (White 68.6%; Black or African American 29.4%; Hispanic or Latino 1.3%; Asian 0.2%; Other 1.5%). **Foreign born:** 1.4%. **Median age:** 35.8. **State rank:** 87. **Pop change 1990-2000:** +8.9%.

Income: per capita $14,468; median household $27,607. **Pop below poverty level:** 17.4%.

Unemployment: 4.5%. **Median home value:** $54,200. **Median travel time to work:** 26.1 minutes.

DOOLY COUNTY

PO Box 322   **Ph:** 229-268-4228
Vienna, GA 31092   **Fax:** 229-268-4230

In west-central GA, south of Macon; original county; organized May 15, 1821 from Indian lands. **Name Origin:** For Capt. John Dooly (1740-80), American Revolutionary officer in GA, killed by British sympathizers.

Area (sq mi): 397.07 (land 392.88; water 4.19).

Pop: 11,525 (White 44.8%; Black or African American 49.5%; Hispanic or Latino 4.7%; Asian 0.4%; Other 4.1%). **Foreign born:** 1.5%. **Median age:** 35.1. **State rank:** 115. **Pop change 1990-2000:** +16.4%.

Income: per capita $13,628; median household $27,980. **Pop below poverty level:** 22.1%.

Unemployment: 6.3%. **Median home value:** $62,300. **Median travel time to work:** 22.5 minutes.

All statistics are based on the 2000 Census except the dollar figures given for per capita income, which are based on 1999 estimates.

DOUGHERTY COUNTY

PO Box 1827
Albany, GA 31702
www.dougherty.ga.us/site/

Ph: 229-431-2121
Fax: 229-438-3967

In southwestern GA, southeast of Columbus; organized Dec 15, 1853 from Baker County. **Name Origin:** For Charles Dougherty (1801-53), lawyer and western circuit judge.

Area (sq mi): 334.64 (land 329.6; water 5.04).

Pop: 96,065 (White 37.3%; Black or African American 60.1%; Hispanic or Latino 1.3%; Asian 0.6%; Other 1.4%). **Foreign born:** 1.7%. **Median age:** 32.2. **State rank:** 16. **Pop change 1990-2000:** -0.3%.

Income: per capita $16,645; median household $30,934. **Pop below poverty level:** 24.8%.

Unemployment: 6.1%. **Median home value:** $73,900. **Median travel time to work:** 18.7 minutes.

DOUGLAS COUNTY

8700 Hospital Dr
Douglasville, GA 30134
www.co.douglas.ga.us

Ph: 770-920-7264

In west-central GA, west of Atlanta; organized Oct 17, 1870 from Carroll and Campbell counties. **Name Origin:** For Stephen Arnold Douglas (1813-61), U.S. orator and statesman.

Area (sq mi): 200.26 (land 199.3; water 0.96).

Pop: 92,174 (White 75.9%; Black or African American 18.5%; Hispanic or Latino 2.9%; Asian 1.2%; Other 3%). **Foreign born:** 3.9%. **Median age:** 33.8. **State rank:** 17. **Pop change 1990-2000:** +29.6%.

Income: per capita $21,172; median household $50,108. **Pop below poverty level:** 7.8%.

Unemployment: 2.8%. **Median home value:** $102,700. **Median travel time to work:** 32.3 minutes.

EARLY COUNTY

PO Box 849
Blakely, GA 31723

Ph: 229-723-3033
Fax: 229-723-4411

On southwestern border, southwest of Albany; original county; organized Dec 15, 1818 from Creek Indian lands. **Name Origin:** For Peter Early (1773-1817), U.S. representative from GA, jurist, and governor (1813-15).

Area (sq mi): 516.27 (land 511.23; water 5.04).

Pop: 12,354 (White 49.9%; Black or African American 48.1%; Hispanic or Latino 1.2%; Asian 0.2%; Other 1.5%). **Foreign born:** 0.7%. **Median age:** 36.4. **State rank:** 112. **Pop change 1990-2000:** +4.2%.

Income: per capita $14,936; median household $25,629. **Pop below poverty level:** 25.7%.

Unemployment: 5.9%. **Median home value:** $58,600. **Median travel time to work:** 22.8 minutes.

ECHOLS COUNTY

PO Box 190
Statenville, GA 31648

Ph: 229-559-6538
Fax: 229-559-6158

On southern border of GA, east of Valdosta; organized Dec 13, 1858 from Clinch and Lowndes counties. **Name Origin:** For Gen. Robert M. Echols (1800?-47), a GA officer killed during the Mexican War.

Area (sq mi): 420.8 (land 404.13; water 16.67).

Pop: 3,754 (White 71.6%; Black or African American 6.9%; Hispanic or Latino 19.7%; Asian 0.1%; Other 15.8%). **Foreign born:** 12.6%. **Median age:** 29.7. **State rank:** 154. **Pop change 1990-2000:** +60.8%.

Income: per capita $15,727; median household $25,851. **Pop below poverty level:** 28.7%.

Unemployment: 5%. **Median home value:** $76,000. **Median travel time to work:** 25.3 minutes.

EFFINGHAM COUNTY

PO Box 307
Springfield, GA 31329
www.effinghamcounty.org

Ph: 912-754-2103
Fax: 912-754-4157

On the central eastern border of GA, north of Savannah; original county; organized Feb 5, 1777 (prior to statehood) from Saint Mathew and Saint Phillips parishes. **Name Origin:** For Thomas Howard (1746-91), Earl of Effingham, a pro-colonist English army officer.

Area (sq mi): 482.82 (land 479.41; water 3.4).

Pop: 37,535 (White 83.9%; Black or African American 13%; Hispanic or Latino 1.4%; Asian 0.5%; Other 1.8%). **Foreign born:** 1.3%. **Median age:** 33.6. **State rank:** 47. **Pop change 1990-2000:** +46.1%.

Income: per capita $18,873; median household $46,505. **Pop below poverty level:** 9.3%.

Unemployment: 2.7%. **Median home value:** $106,600. **Median travel time to work:** 31.3 minutes.

ELBERT COUNTY

PO Box 619
Elberton, GA 30635

Ph: 706-283-2005
Fax: 706-213-7286

On northeastern border of GA, northeast of Athens; organized Dec 10, 1790 from Wilkes County. **Name Origin:** For Gen. Samuel Elbert (1743-88), Revolutionary War hero and GA governor (1785-86).

Area (sq mi): 374.54 (land 368.76; water 5.78).

Pop: 20,511 (White 65.8%; Black or African American 30.9%; Hispanic or Latino 2.4%; Asian 0.2%; Other 2%). **Foreign born:** 1.9%. **Median age:** 37.2. **State rank:** 82. **Pop change 1990-2000:** +8.2%.

Income: per capita $14,535; median household $28,724. **Pop below poverty level:** 17.3%.

Unemployment: 7.2%. **Median home value:** $66,600. **Median travel time to work:** 21.2 minutes.

EMANUEL COUNTY

PO Box 787
Swainsboro, GA 30401

Ph: 478-237-3881
Fax: 478-237-2593

In east-central GA, northwest of Savannah; organized Dec 10, 1812 from Montgomery and Bulloch counties. **Name Origin:** For David Emanuel (1742-1808), GA legislator and governor (1801).

Please see sample entry on inside front cover for detailed information about the statistics presented with each county listing.

Area (sq mi): 690.33 (land 685.79; water 4.54).

Pop: 21,837 (White 62.6%; Black or African American 33.3%; Hispanic or Latino 3.4%; Asian 0.2%; Other 2.7%). **Foreign born:** 4.1%. **Median age:** 34.9. **State rank:** 77. **Pop change 1990-2000:** +6.3%.

Income: per capita $13,627; median household $24,383. **Pop below poverty level:** 27.4%.

Unemployment: 8.3%. **Median home value:** $50,800. **Median travel time to work:** 23.1 minutes.

EVANS COUNTY

3 Freeman St   **Ph:** 912-739-1141
Claxton, GA 30417   **Fax:** 912-739-0111

In east-central GA, west of Savannah; organized Aug 11, 1914 from Bulloch and Tattnall counties. **Name Origin:** For Gen. Clement Anselm Evans (1833-1911), GA officer during the Civil War, jurist, and Methodist minister.

Area (sq mi): 186.88 (land 184.92; water 1.96).

Pop: 10,495 (White 60.3%; Black or African American 33%; Hispanic or Latino 6%; Asian 0.3%; Other 5%). **Foreign born:** 4.3%. **Median age:** 34. **State rank:** 122. **Pop change 1990-2000:** +20.3%.

Income: per capita $12,758; median household $25,447. **Pop below poverty level:** 27%.

Unemployment: 3.7%. **Median home value:** $69,000. **Median travel time to work:** 21.7 minutes.

FANNIN COUNTY

171 Church St   **Ph:** 706-632-2203
Blue Ridge, GA 30513   **Fax:** 706-632-2507
www.fannincounty.org

On the central northern border of GA northeast of Rome; organized Jan 12, 1854 from Gilmer and Union counties. **Name Origin:** For James Walker Fannin (1809-36), GA soldier killed in action in the Texas War of Independence.

Area (sq mi): 391.43 (land 385.74; water 5.69).

Pop: 19,798 (White 97.5%; Black or African American 0.1%; Hispanic or Latino 0.7%; Asian 0.2%; Other 1.7%). **Foreign born:** 1.1%. **Median age:** 43.1. **State rank:** 85. **Pop change 1990-2000:** +23.8%.

Income: per capita $16,269; median household $30,612. **Pop below poverty level:** 12.4%.

Unemployment: 3.7%. **Median home value:** $86,200. **Median travel time to work:** 31.8 minutes.

FAYETTE COUNTY

140 Stonewall Ave W   **Ph:** 770-461-6041
Fayetteville, GA 30214   **Fax:** 770-460-9412
admin.co.fayette.ga.us

In west-central GA, south of Atlanta; original county; organized May 15, 1821 from Indian lands. **Name Origin:** For the Marquis de Lafayette (1757-1834), French statesman and soldier who fought with the Americans during the Revolutionary War.

Area (sq mi): 199.25 (land 197.05; water 2.2).

Pop: 91,263 (White 82%; Black or African American 11.5%; Hispanic or Latino 2.8%; Asian 2.4%; Other 2.2%). **Foreign born:** 5%. **Median age:** 38.2. **State rank:** 19. **Pop change 1990-2000:** +46.2%.

Income: per capita $29,464; median household $71,227. **Pop below poverty level:** 2.6%.

Unemployment: 1.9%. **Median home value:** $171,500. **Median travel time to work:** 30.6 minutes.

FLOYD COUNTY

PO Box 946   **Ph:** 706-291-5110
Rome, GA 30162   **Fax:** 706-291-5248
www.floydcountyga.org

On northwestern border of GA; organized Dec 3, 1832 from Cherokee County. **Name Origin:** For Gen. John Floyd (1769-1839), officer in the GA militia and U.S. representative (1827-29).

Area (sq mi): 518.46 (land 513.13; water 5.33).

Pop: 90,565 (White 79.1%; Black or African American 13.3%; Hispanic or Latino 5.5%; Asian 0.9%; Other 4.4%). **Foreign born:** 5.2%. **Median age:** 35.7. **State rank:** 20. **Pop change 1990-2000:** +11.5%.

Income: per capita $17,808; median household $35,615. **Pop below poverty level:** 14.4%.

Unemployment: 4.3%. **Median home value:** $83,500. **Median travel time to work:** 23.7 minutes.

FORSYTH COUNTY

100 Courthouse Sq Suite 010 **Ph:** 770-781-2120
Cumming, GA 30040   **Fax:** 770-886-2858
www.co.forsyth.ga.us

In north-central GA, northeast of Atlanta; organized Dec 3, 1832 from Cherokee County. **Name Origin:** For John Forsyth (1780-1841), governor of GA (1827-29) and U.S. secretary of state (1834-41).

Area (sq mi): 247.37 (land 225.8; water 21.57).

Pop: 98,407 (White 92.3%; Black or African American 0.7%; Hispanic or Latino 5.6%; Asian 0.8%; Other 3.5%). **Foreign born:** 6%. **Median age:** 34.6. **State rank:** 15. **Pop change 1990-2000:** +123.2%.

Income: per capita $29,114; median household $68,890. **Pop below poverty level:** 5.5%.

Unemployment: 2.3%. **Median home value:** $184,600. **Median travel time to work:** 33.2 minutes.

FRANKLIN COUNTY

PO Box 70   **Ph:** 706-384-2514
Carnesville, GA 30521   **Fax:** 706-384-7089
www.franklin-county.com

On northeast border of GA, northeast of Athens; original county; organized Feb 25, 1784 (prior to statehood) from Cherokee lands. **Name Origin:** For Benjamin Franklin (1706-90), U.S. patriot, diplomat, and statesman.

Area (sq mi): 266.37 (land 263.29; water 3.07).

Pop: 20,285 (White 89.1%; Black or African American 8.8%; Hispanic or Latino 0.9%; Asian 0.3%; Other 1.4%). **Foreign born:**

All statistics are based on the 2000 Census except the dollar figures given for per capita income, which are based on 1999 estimates.

118

1.2%. **Median age:** 37.6. **State rank:** 83. **Pop change 1990-2000:** +21.8%.

Income: per capita $15,767; median household $32,134. **Pop below poverty level:** 13.9%.

Unemployment: 5.1%. **Median home value:** $84,600. **Median travel time to work:** 25.7 minutes.

FULTON COUNTY

141 Pryor St SW Suite 10061   **Ph:** 404-730-8320
Atlanta, GA 30303   **Fax:** 404-730-8341
www.co.fulton.ga.us

In west-central GA; organized Dec 20, 1853 from De Kalb County; on Jan 1, 1932 annexed Campbell County (organized 1828 from Carroll, Coweta, De Kalb, Fayette, and Cherokee counties) and Milton County (organized 1857 from Cobb, Cherokee, and Forsyth counties). **Name Origin:** For Robert Fulton (1765-1815), builder of the Clermont, the first commercially successful steamboat. Some believe for Hamilton Fulton, the English engineer who surveyed a railroad through the present county.

Area (sq mi): 534.61 (land 528.66; water 5.95).

Pop: 816,006 (White 45.3%; Black or African American 44.6%; Hispanic or Latino 5.9%; Asian 3%; Other 4.3%). **Foreign born:** 9.6%. **Median age:** 32.7. **State rank:** 1. **Pop change 1990-2000:** +25.7%.

Income: per capita $30,003; median household $47,321. **Pop below poverty level:** 15.7%.

Unemployment: 4.3%. **Median home value:** $180,700. **Median travel time to work:** 29.1 minutes.

GILMER COUNTY

1 West Side Sq   **Ph:** 706-635-4361
Ellijay, GA 30540   **Fax:** 706-635-4359

In north-central GA, north of Atlanta; organized Dec 3, 1832 from Cherokee County. **Name Origin:** For George Rockingham Gilmer (1790-1859), U.S. representative from GA (1821-23; 1827-29; 1833-35) and twice governor (1829-31; 1837-39).

Area (sq mi): 431.83 (land 426.69; water 5.14).

Pop: 23,456 (White 90.8%; Black or African American 0.3%; Hispanic or Latino 7.7%; Asian 0.2%; Other 6%). **Foreign born:** 5.8%. **Median age:** 37.3. **State rank:** 68. **Pop change 1990-2000:** +75.5%.

Income: per capita $17,147; median household $35,140. **Pop below poverty level:** 12.5%.

Unemployment: 3.5%. **Median home value:** $95,700. **Median travel time to work:** 31.1 minutes.

GLASCOCK COUNTY

62 E Main St   **Ph:** 706-598-2084
Gibson, GA 30810   **Fax:** 706-598-2577

In east-central GA, southwest of Augusta; organized Dec 19, 1857 from Warren County. **Name Origin:** For Gen. Thomas Glascock (1790-1841), GA army officer during the War of 1812 and the Seminole War (1817), state legislator, and U.S. representative from GA (1835-39).

Area (sq mi): 144.45 (land 144.14; water 0.31).

Pop: 2,556 (White 90.3%; Black or African American 8.3%; Hispanic or Latino 0.5%; Asian 0%; Other 1%). **Foreign born:** 0%. **Median age:** 39.6. **State rank:** 157. **Pop change 1990-2000:** +8.4%.

Income: per capita $14,185; median household $29,743. **Pop below poverty level:** 17.2%.

Unemployment: 4.7%. **Median home value:** $48,600. **Median travel time to work:** 35.3 minutes.

GLYNN COUNTY

1803 Gloucester St Rm 114   **Ph:** 912-554-7400
Brunswick, GA 31520   **Fax:** 912-267-5691
www.glynncounty.com

On southeastern Atlantic coast of GA; original county; organized Feb 5, 1777 (prior to statehood) from Saint David and Saint Patrick parishes. **Name Origin:** For John Glynn (1722-79), a pro-colonist member of the British Parliament.

Area (sq mi): 585.17 (land 422.37; water 162.8).

Pop: 67,568 (White 68.9%; Black or African American 26.5%; Hispanic or Latino 3%; Asian 0.6%; Other 2.3%). **Foreign born:** 3.3%. **Median age:** 37.9. **State rank:** 28. **Pop change 1990-2000:** +8.1%.

Income: per capita $21,707; median household $38,765. **Pop below poverty level:** 15.1%.

Unemployment: 3.3%. **Median home value:** $114,500. **Median travel time to work:** 19.6 minutes.

GORDON COUNTY

201 N Wall St   **Ph:** 706-629-3795
Calhoun, GA 30701   **Fax:** 706-629-9516
www.gordoncounty.org

In northwestern GA, northeast of Rome; organized Feb 13, 1850 from Bartow (then called Cass) and Floyd counties. **Name Origin:** For William Washington Gordon (1796-1842), prominent GA railroad official.

Area (sq mi): 358.01 (land 355.54; water 2.48).

Pop: 44,104 (White 87.6%; Black or African American 3.5%; Hispanic or Latino 7.4%; Asian 0.5%; Other 6.4%). **Foreign born:** 6.4%. **Median age:** 34.1. **State rank:** 40. **Pop change 1990-2000:** +25.8%.

Income: per capita $17,586; median household $38,831. **Pop below poverty level:** 9.9%.

Unemployment: 6.6%. **Median home value:** $83,600. **Median travel time to work:** 23.2 minutes.

GRADY COUNTY

250 N Broad St   **Ph:** 229-377-1512
Cairo, GA 31728   **Fax:** 229-377-1039

On southern border of GA, west of Valdosta; organized Aug 17, 1905 from Decatur and Thomas counties. **Name Origin:** For Henry Woodfin Grady (1850-89), GA orator and journalist, editor, and part-owner of the *Atlanta Constitution*.

Area (sq mi): 460.34 (land 458.12; water 2.22).

Pop: 23,659 (White 63.2%; Black or African American 30.1%; Hispanic or Latino 5.2%; Asian 0.3%; Other 4.9%). **Foreign born:**

Please see sample entry on inside front cover for detailed information about the statistics presented with each county listing.

119

3.9%. **Median age:** 35.5. **State rank:** 66. **Pop change 1990-2000:** +16.7%.

Income: per capita $14,278; median household $28,656. **Pop below poverty level:** 21.3%.

Unemployment: 5.1%. **Median home value:** $74,900. **Median travel time to work:** 24.4 minutes.

GREENE COUNTY
113 N Main St 3rd Fl Suite 306   **Ph:** 706-453-7716
Greensboro, GA 30642   **Fax:** 706-453-9555

In east-central GA, southeast of Athens; organized Feb 3, 1786 (prior to statehood) from Washington, Oglethorpe, and Wilkes counties. **Name Origin:** For Gen. Nathanael Greene (1742-86), hero of the Revolutionary War, quartermaster general (1778-80), and commander of the Army of the South.

Area (sq mi): 406.24 (land 388.28; water 17.96).

Pop: 14,406 (White 51.9%; Black or African American 44.4%; Hispanic or Latino 2.9%; Asian 0.2%; Other 2.4%). **Foreign born:** 2.6%. **Median age:** 39.1. **State rank:** 106. **Pop change 1990-2000:** +22.2%.

Income: per capita $23,389; median household $33,479. **Pop below poverty level:** 22.3%.

Unemployment: 8.6%. **Median home value:** $87,100. **Median travel time to work:** 26 minutes.

GWINNETT COUNTY
Gwinnett Justice & Administration Ctr
75 Langley Dr   **Ph:** 770-822-7000
Lawrenceville, GA 30045   **Fax:** 770-822-7097
www.co.gwinnett.ga.us

In north-central GA, northeast of Atlanta; original county; organized Dec 15, 1818 from Cherokee lands. **Name Origin:** For Button Gwinnett (c. 1735-77), a signer of the Declaration of Independence and acting president of GA (1777).

Area (sq mi): 436.72 (land 432.73; water 3.99).

Pop: 588,448 (White 67%; Black or African American 13.3%; Hispanic or Latino 10.9%; Asian 7.2%; Other 6.8%). **Foreign born:** 16.9%. **Median age:** 32.5. **State rank:** 4. **Pop change 1990-2000:** +66.7%.

Income: per capita $25,006; median household $60,537. **Pop below poverty level:** 5.7%.

Unemployment: 3%. **Median home value:** $142,100. **Median travel time to work:** 32.2 minutes.

HABERSHAM COUNTY
555 Monroe St Unit 20   **Ph:** 706-754-6270
Clarkesville, GA 30523   **Fax:** 706-754-1014
www.co.habersham.ga.us

In northeastern GA; original county; organized Dec 15, 1818 from Cherokee lands. **Name Origin:** For Col. Joseph Habersham (1751-1815), member of the Continental Congress and U.S. postmaster general (1795-1801).

Area (sq mi): 279.2 (land 278.17; water 1.03).

Pop: 35,902 (White 84.9%; Black or African American 4.5%; Hispanic or Latino 7.7%; Asian 1.9%; Other 4.8%). **Foreign born:** 7.8%. **Median age:** 36.4. **State rank:** 50. **Pop change 1990-2000:** +30%.

Income: per capita $17,706; median household $36,321. **Pop below poverty level:** 12.2%.

Unemployment: 4.5%. **Median home value:** $99,700. **Median travel time to work:** 23.8 minutes.

HALL COUNTY
PO Box 1275   **Ph:** 770-531-7023
Gainesville, GA 30503   **Fax:** 770-531-7070
www.hallcounty.org

In north-central GA, northwest of Athens; original county; organized Dec 15, 1818 from Cherokee lands. **Name Origin:** For Lyman Hall (1731-90), a signer of the Declaration of Independence, and GA governor (1783-84).

Area (sq mi): 429.19 (land 393.66; water 35.53).

Pop: 139,277 (White 71%; Black or African American 7.3%; Hispanic or Latino 19.6%; Asian 1.3%; Other 10.7%). **Foreign born:** 16.2%. **Median age:** 32.2. **State rank:** 11. **Pop change 1990-2000:** +45.9%.

Income: per capita $19,690; median household $44,908. **Pop below poverty level:** 12.4%.

Unemployment: 2.9%. **Median home value:** $120,200. **Median travel time to work:** 26.1 minutes.

HANCOCK COUNTY
601 Broad St Suite 1   **Ph:** 706-444-5746
Sparta, GA 31087   **Fax:** 706-444-6221

In east-central GA, southwest of Augusta; organized Dec 17, 1793 from Greene and Washington counties. **Name Origin:** For John Hancock (1737-93), noted signer of the Declaration of Independence, governor of MA (1780-85; 1787-93), and statesman.

Area (sq mi): 478.76 (land 473.28; water 5.48).

Pop: 10,076 (White 21.2%; Black or African American 77.8%; Hispanic or Latino 0.5%; Asian 0.1%; Other 0.7%). **Foreign born:** 0.3%. **Median age:** 35.8. **State rank:** 127. **Pop change 1990-2000:** +13.1%.

Income: per capita $10,916; median household $22,003. **Pop below poverty level:** 29.4%.

Unemployment: 10.7%. **Median home value:** $53,000. **Median travel time to work:** 36.2 minutes.

HARALSON COUNTY
PO Box 489   **Ph:** 770-646-2002
Buchanan, GA 30113   **Fax:** 770-646-2035
www.haralsoncountyga.org

On the western border of GA, west of Atlanta; organized Jan 26, 1856 from Carroll and Polk counties. **Name Origin:** For Gen. Hugh Anderson Haralson (1805-54), U.S. representative from GA (1843-51).

Area (sq mi): 283.16 (land 282.11; water 1.05).

All statistics are based on the 2000 Census except the dollar figures given for per capita income, which are based on 1999 estimates.

Pop: 25,690 (White 92.6%; Black or African American 5.4%; Hispanic or Latino 0.6%; Asian 0.3%; Other 1.3%). **Foreign born:** 0.9%. **Median age:** 36.1. **State rank:** 59. **Pop change 1990-2000:** +17%.

Income: per capita $15,823; median household $31,656. **Pop below poverty level:** 15.5%.

Unemployment: 5.6%. **Median home value:** $76,500. **Median travel time to work:** 30.3 minutes.

HARRIS COUNTY
PO Box 528 **Ph:** 706-628-4944
Hamilton, GA 31811 **Fax:** 706-628-7039

On central western border of GA, north of Columbus; organized Dec 14, 1827 from Muscogee and Troup counties. **Name Origin:** For Charles Harris (1772-1827), a Savannah lawyer and city official.

Area (sq mi): 472.93 (land 463.69; water 9.24).

Pop: 23,695 (White 77.8%; Black or African American 19.5%; Hispanic or Latino 1.1%; Asian 0.5%; Other 1.6%). **Foreign born:** 1.9%. **Median age:** 38.5. **State rank:** 64. **Pop change 1990-2000:** +33.2%.

Income: per capita $21,680; median household $47,763. **Pop below poverty level:** 8.2%.

Unemployment: 3.1%. **Median home value:** $122,700. **Median travel time to work:** 29.9 minutes.

HART COUNTY
PO Box 279 **Ph:** 706-376-2024
Hartwell, GA 30643 **Fax:** 706-376-9477
www.hartwellga.com

On the northeastern border of GA, northeast of Athens; organized Dec 7, 1853 from Elbert and Franklin counties. **Name Origin:** For Nancy (Morgan) Hart (1735?-1830?), spy, sharpshooter, and heroine of the American Revolution. Called 'War Woman' by the Indians.

Area (sq mi): 256.42 (land 232.21; water 24.21).

Pop: 22,997 (White 78.6%; Black or African American 19.4%; Hispanic or Latino 0.9%; Asian 0.5%; Other 1%). **Foreign born:** 1.3%. **Median age:** 39.2. **State rank:** 70. **Pop change 1990-2000:** +16.7%.

Income: per capita $16,714; median household $32,833. **Pop below poverty level:** 14.8%.

Unemployment: 7%. **Median home value:** $89,900. **Median travel time to work:** 20.7 minutes.

HEARD COUNTY
PO Box 40 **Ph:** 706-675-3821
Franklin, GA 30217 **Fax:** 706-675-2493

On central western border of GA, southwest of Atlanta; organized Dec 22, 1830 from Carroll, Coweta, and Troup counties. **Name Origin:** For Stephen Heard (1740-1815), chief justice of the GA inferior court and governor of GA (1780-81).

Area (sq mi): 301.08 (land 296.03; water 5.06).

Pop: 11,012 (White 87%; Black or African American 10.8%; Hispanic or Latino 1.1%; Asian 0.1%; Other 1.6%). **Foreign born:**

0.7%. **Median age:** 34.1. **State rank:** 117. **Pop change 1990-2000:** +27.6%.

Income: per capita $15,132; median household $33,038. **Pop below poverty level:** 13.6%.

Unemployment: 5.5%. **Median home value:** $72,900. **Median travel time to work:** 37.5 minutes.

HENRY COUNTY
140 Henry Pkwy **Ph:** 770-954-2400
McDonough, GA 30253 **Fax:** 770-954-2418
www.co.henry.ga.us

In west-central GA, southeast of Atlanta; county organized May 15, 1821 from Indian lands. **Name Origin:** For Patrick Henry (1736-99), patriot, governor of VA (1776-79; 1784-86), and statesman, famous for declaring, 'Give me liberty or give me death.'

Area (sq mi): 324.48 (land 322.71; water 1.77).

Pop: 119,341 (White 80.1%; Black or African American 14.7%; Hispanic or Latino 2.3%; Asian 1.8%; Other 2.1%). **Foreign born:** 3.4%. **Median age:** 33.4. **State rank:** 12. **Pop change 1990-2000:** +103.2%.

Income: per capita $22,945; median household $57,309. **Pop below poverty level:** 4.9%.

Unemployment: 2.5%. **Median home value:** $122,400. **Median travel time to work:** 32.7 minutes.

HOUSTON COUNTY
200 Carl Vinson Pkwy **Ph:** 478-542-2115
Warner Robins, GA 31088 **Fax:** 478-923-5697
www.houstoncountyga.com

In central GA, south of Macon; original county; organized May 15, 1821 from Indian lands. **Name Origin:** For John Houstoun (1744-96), American Revolutionary patriot and GA governor (1778; 1784). Spelling changed by clerical error.

Area (sq mi): 379.83 (land 376.75; water 3.08).

Pop: 110,765 (White 69%; Black or African American 24.8%; Hispanic or Latino 3%; Asian 1.6%; Other 3.1%). **Foreign born:** 3.4%. **Median age:** 34. **State rank:** 13. **Pop change 1990-2000:** +24.2%.

Income: per capita $19,515; median household $43,638. **Pop below poverty level:** 10.2%.

Unemployment: 3%. **Median home value:** $88,900. **Median travel time to work:** 20.2 minutes.

IRWIN COUNTY
207 S Irwin Ave Suite 2 **Ph:** 229-468-9441
Ocilla, GA 31774 **Fax:** 229-468-9672

In south-central GA, north of Valdosta; original county; organized Dec 15, 1818 from Indian lands. **Name Origin:** For Gen. Jared Irwin (1750-1818), twice GA governor (1796-98; 1806-09).

Area (sq mi): 362.73 (land 356.81; water 5.92).

Pop: 9,931 (White 71.5%; Black or African American 25.9%; Hispanic or Latino 2%; Asian 0.3%; Other 1.8%). **Foreign born:** 1.3%. **Median age:** 34.6. **State rank:** 128. **Pop change 1990-2000:** +14.8%.

Please see sample entry on inside front cover for detailed information about the statistics presented with each county listing.

Income: per capita $14,867; median household $30,257. **Pop below poverty level:** 17.8%.

Unemployment: 6%. **Median home value:** $58,100. **Median travel time to work:** 22.5 minutes.

JACKSON COUNTY
67 Athens St
Jefferson, GA 30549

Ph: 706-367-1199
Fax: 706-367-9083

In northeastern GA, northwest of Athens; organized Feb 11, 1796 from Franklin County. **Name Origin:** For Gen. James Jackson (1757-1806), an officer in the American Revolution, GA governor (1798-1801), and U.S. senator (1793-95; 1801-06).

Area (sq mi): 343 (land 342.36; water 0.64).

Pop: 41,589 (White 87.3%; Black or African American 7.8%; Hispanic or Latino 3%; Asian 1%; Other 2.3%). **Foreign born:** 2.5%. **Median age:** 34.6. **State rank:** 44. **Pop change 1990-2000:** +38.6%.

Income: per capita $17,808; median household $40,349. **Pop below poverty level:** 12%.

Unemployment: 3.9%. **Median home value:** $102,900. **Median travel time to work:** 29.9 minutes.

JASPER COUNTY
162 N Warren St Courthouse Annex
Monticello, GA 31064

Ph: 706-468-4900
Fax: 706-468-4942

In central GA, north of Macon; organized as Randolph County Dec 10, 1807 from Baldwin County; name changed Dec 10, 1812. **Name Origin:** For Sgt. William Jasper (1750-79), Revolutionary War soldier from SC. Originally for John Randolph (1773-1833), U.S. congressman from VA, home of many early settlers; his opposition to the War of 1812 angered the populace.

Area (sq mi): 373.58 (land 370.42; water 3.16).

Pop: 11,426 (White 69.7%; Black or African American 27.3%; Hispanic or Latino 2.1%; Asian 0.2%; Other 1.6%). **Foreign born:** 2.1%. **Median age:** 36.3. **State rank:** 116. **Pop change 1990-2000:** +35.2%.

Income: per capita $19,249; median household $39,890. **Pop below poverty level:** 14.2%.

Unemployment: 4%. **Median home value:** $81,000. **Median travel time to work:** 34.2 minutes.

JEFF DAVIS COUNTY
PO Box 609
Hazlehurst, GA 31539

Ph: 912-375-6611
Fax: 912-375-0378

In southeast-central GA; organized Aug 18, 1905 from Appling and Coffee counties. **Name Origin:** For Jefferson Davis (1808-89), president of the Confederate States of America (1862-65).

Area (sq mi): 335.42 (land 333.38; water 2.04).

Pop: 12,684 (White 78.8%; Black or African American 15.1%; Hispanic or Latino 5.1%; Asian 0.4%; Other 3.2%). **Foreign born:** 3.8%. **Median age:** 35. **State rank:** 109. **Pop change 1990-2000:** +5.4%.

Income: per capita $13,780; median household $27,310. **Pop below poverty level:** 19.4%.

Unemployment: 10.1%. **Median home value:** $61,000. **Median travel time to work:** 21.7 minutes.

JEFFERSON COUNTY
PO Box 658
Louisville, GA 30434

Ph: 478-625-3332
Fax: 478-625-4007

In east-central GA, southwest of Augusta; organized Feb 20, 1796 from Burke and Warren counties. **Name Origin:** For Thomas Jefferson (1743-1826), U.S. patriot and statesman; third U.S. president.

Area (sq mi): 529.56 (land 527.65; water 1.91).

Pop: 17,266 (White 41.8%; Black or African American 56.3%; Hispanic or Latino 1.5%; Asian 0.2%; Other 1.4%). **Foreign born:** 0.5%. **Median age:** 34.9. **State rank:** 92. **Pop change 1990-2000:** -0.8%.

Income: per capita $13,491; median household $26,120. **Pop below poverty level:** 23%.

Unemployment: 9.8%. **Median home value:** $56,900. **Median travel time to work:** 29 minutes.

JENKINS COUNTY
PO Box 797
Millen, GA 30442

Ph: 478-982-2563
Fax: 478-982-4750

In east-central GA, south of Augusta; organized Aug 17, 1905 from Bulloch, Burke, Screven, and Emanuel counties. **Name Origin:** For Charles Jones Jenkins (1805-83), GA legislator, jurist, and governor (1865-67).

Area (sq mi): 352.45 (land 349.81; water 2.64).

Pop: 8,575 (White 55.6%; Black or African American 40.5%; Hispanic or Latino 3.3%; Asian 0.2%; Other 3.1%). **Foreign born:** 0.9%. **Median age:** 35.4. **State rank:** 136. **Pop change 1990-2000:** +4%.

Income: per capita $13,400; median household $24,025. **Pop below poverty level:** 28.4%.

Unemployment: 6%. **Median home value:** $49,400. **Median travel time to work:** 22.6 minutes.

JOHNSON COUNTY
PO Box 321
Wrightsville, GA 31096

Ph: 478-864-3484
Fax: 478-864-1343

In east-central GA, east of Macon; organized Dec 11, 1858 from Emanuel, Laurens, and Washington counties. **Name Origin:** For Herschel Vespasian Johnson (1812-80), middle circuit court judge, U.S. senator (1848-49), and GA governor (1853-57).

Area (sq mi): 306.52 (land 304.26; water 2.26).

Pop: 8,560 (White 62%; Black or African American 37%; Hispanic or Latino 0.9%; Asian 0.1%; Other 0.5%). **Foreign born:** 0.2%. **Median age:** 34.9. **State rank:** 137. **Pop change 1990-2000:** +2.8%.

Income: per capita $12,384; median household $23,848. **Pop below poverty level:** 22.6%.

Unemployment: 7.2%. **Median home value:** $48,000. **Median travel time to work:** 29.7 minutes.

All statistics are based on the 2000 Census except the dollar figures given for per capita income, which are based on 1999 estimates.

JONES COUNTY

PO Box 1359   **Ph:** 478-986-6405
Gray, GA 31032   **Fax:** 478-986-9682

In central GA, north of the Macon city center; organized Dec 10, 1807 from Baldwin County. **Name Origin:** For James Jones (?-1801), GA legislator and U.S. representative (1799-1801).

Area (sq mi): 395.39 (land 393.75; water 1.64).

Pop: 23,639 (White 74.7%; Black or African American 23.3%; Hispanic or Latino 0.7%; Asian 0.5%; Other 1.1%). **Foreign born:** 1%. **Median age:** 36.1. **State rank:** 67. **Pop change 1990-2000:** +14%.

Income: per capita $19,126; median household $43,301. **Pop below poverty level:** 10.2%.

Unemployment: 3.1%. **Median home value:** $91,200. **Median travel time to work:** 27.8 minutes.

LAMAR COUNTY

326 Thomaston St   **Ph:** 770-358-5146
Barnesville, GA 30204   **Fax:** 770-358-5149

In west-central GA, northwest of Macon; organized Aug 17, 1920 from Monroe and Pike counties. **Name Origin:** For Lucius Quintus Cincinnatus Lamar (1825-93), U.S. statesman and a justice of the U.S. Supreme Court (1888-93).

Area (sq mi): 185.79 (land 184.82; water 0.97).

Pop: 15,912 (White 67.1%; Black or African American 30.4%; Hispanic or Latino 1.1%; Asian 0.4%; Other 1.5%). **Foreign born:** 1%. **Median age:** 35.7. **State rank:** 96. **Pop change 1990-2000:** +22%.

Income: per capita $16,666; median household $37,087. **Pop below poverty level:** 11.2%.

Unemployment: 6%. **Median home value:** $79,900. **Median travel time to work:** 28.1 minutes.

LANIER COUNTY

100 W Main St   **Ph:** 229-482-2088
Lakeland, GA 31635   **Fax:** 229-482-8333

In south-central GA, northeast of Valdosta; organized Aug 7, 1920 from Berrien, Lowndes, and Clinch counties. **Name Origin:** For Sidney Lanier (1842-81), soldier, lawyer, musician, and important post-Civil War southern poet.

Area (sq mi): 199.83 (land 186.82; water 13.01).

Pop: 7,241 (White 70.7%; Black or African American 25.6%; Hispanic or Latino 1.7%; Asian 0.4%; Other 2.4%). **Foreign born:** 1.1%. **Median age:** 33.3. **State rank:** 142. **Pop change 1990-2000:** +30.9%.

Income: per capita $13,690; median household $29,171. **Pop below poverty level:** 18.5%.

Unemployment: 3.8%. **Median home value:** $62,200. **Median travel time to work:** 26.8 minutes.

LAURENS COUNTY

PO Box 2011   **Ph:** 478-272-4755
Dublin, GA 31040   **Fax:** 478-272-3895
www.co.laurens.ga.us

In central GA, southeast of Macon; organized Dec 10, 1807 from

Wilkinson County. **Name Origin:** For Lt. John Laurens (1753-82), officer in the American Revolution, who received the sword of Gen. Charles Cornwallis when the latter surrendered at Yorktown, VA.

Area (sq mi): 818.51 (land 812.27; water 6.24).

Pop: 44,874 (White 62.8%; Black or African American 34.5%; Hispanic or Latino 1.2%; Asian 0.8%; Other 1.2%). **Foreign born:** 1.1%. **Median age:** 35.8. **State rank:** 38. **Pop change 1990-2000:** +12.2%.

Income: per capita $16,763; median household $32,010. **Pop below poverty level:** 18.4%.

Unemployment: 4.4%. **Median home value:** $73,900. **Median travel time to work:** 23.6 minutes.

LEE COUNTY

PO Box 889   **Ph:** 229-759-6000
Leesburg, GA 31763   **Fax:** 229-759-6050
www.lee.ga.us

In southwestern GA, north of Albany; original county; established Jun 9, 1826 from Indian lands. **Name Origin:** For Richard Henry Lee (1732-94), signer of the Declaration of Independence, VA legislator, and U.S. senator (1789-92).

Area (sq mi): 362.01 (land 355.77; water 6.24).

Pop: 24,757 (White 81.6%; Black or African American 15.5%; Hispanic or Latino 1.2%; Asian 0.8%; Other 1.4%). **Foreign born:** 1.7%. **Median age:** 32.6. **State rank:** 62. **Pop change 1990-2000:** +52.4%.

Income: per capita $19,897; median household $48,600. **Pop below poverty level:** 8.2%.

Unemployment: 3.6%. **Median home value:** $102,900. **Median travel time to work:** 21.4 minutes.

LIBERTY COUNTY

PO Box 829   **Ph:** 912-876-2164
Hinesville, GA 31310   **Fax:** 912-369-0204
totalwebgov.org/LibertyCountyGA/

In southeastern GA, southwest of Savannah; original county; organized Feb 5, 1777 (prior to statehood) from Saint Andrew, Saint James, Saint Johns, and Tatnall parishes. **Name Origin:** For the fervent patriotism of the Midway community during the Revolutionary War, and to honor American independence.

Area (sq mi): 602.52 (land 519.05; water 83.47).

Pop: 61,610 (White 44.2%; Black or African American 42.8%; Hispanic or Latino 8.2%; Asian 1.8%; Other 8.7%). **Foreign born:** 5.7%. **Median age:** 25. **State rank:** 30. **Pop change 1990-2000:** +16.8%.

Income: per capita $13,855; median household $33,477. **Pop below poverty level:** 15%.

Unemployment: 4.9%. **Median home value:** $79,800. **Median travel time to work:** 21.4 minutes.

LINCOLN COUNTY

PO Box 340   **Ph:** 706-359-4444
Lincolnton, GA 30817   **Fax:** 706-359-4729

On central-eastern border of GA, north of Augusta; organized Feb

Please see sample entry on inside front cover for detailed information about the statistics presented with each county listing.

123

20, 1796 from Wilkes County. **Name Origin:** For Gen. Benjamin Lincoln (1733-1810), Revolutionary War officer, U.S. secretary of war (1781-83), and lt. gov. of MA (1788).

Area (sq mi): 257.28 (land 211.09; water 46.19).

Pop: 8,348 (White 63.7%; Black or African American 34.4%; Hispanic or Latino 1%; Asian 0.2%; Other 1.2%). **Foreign born:** 0.7%. **Median age:** 39.3. **State rank:** 138. **Pop change 1990-2000:** +12.2%.

Income: per capita $15,351; median household $31,952. **Pop below poverty level:** 15.3%.

Unemployment: 12%. **Median home value:** $82,000. **Median travel time to work:** 33.1 minutes.

LONG COUNTY
49 E McDonald St   **Ph:** 912-545-2143
Ludowici, GA 31316   **Fax:** 912-545-2150

In southeastern GA, northwest of Brunswick; organized Aug 14, 1920 from Liberty County. **Name Origin:** For Crawford Williamson Long (1815-78), prominent GA surgeon, first in history to use sulphuric ether as an anesthetic, Mar 30, 1842.

Area (sq mi): 403.49 (land 400.92; water 2.57).

Pop: 10,304 (White 64.8%; Black or African American 24.3%; Hispanic or Latino 8.4%; Asian 0.6%; Other 6.8%). **Foreign born:** 5.4%. **Median age:** 26.5. **State rank:** 123. **Pop change 1990-2000:** +66.1%.

Income: per capita $12,586; median household $30,640. **Pop below poverty level:** 19.5%.

Unemployment: 2.7%. **Median home value:** $71,100. **Median travel time to work:** 29.5 minutes.

LOWNDES COUNTY
325 W Savannah Ave   **Ph:** 229-671-2400
Valdosta, GA 31601   **Fax:** 229-245-5222
www.lowndescounty.com

On central southern border of GA; organized Dec 23, 1825 from Irwin County. **Name Origin:** For William Jones Lowndes (1782-1822), SC legislator and U.S. representative (1811-22).

Area (sq mi): 510.63 (land 504.22; water 6.41).

Pop: 92,115 (White 60.8%; Black or African American 34%; Hispanic or Latino 2.7%; Asian 1.2%; Other 2.8%). **Foreign born:** 2.7%. **Median age:** 30.2. **State rank:** 18. **Pop change 1990-2000:** +21.2%.

Income: per capita $16,683; median household $32,132. **Pop below poverty level:** 18.3%.

Unemployment: 3.7%. **Median home value:** $87,600. **Median travel time to work:** 18.7 minutes.

LUMPKIN COUNTY
99 Courthouse Hill Suite A   **Ph:** 706-864-3742
Dahlonega, GA 30533   **Fax:** 706-864-4760

In north-central GA, northeast of Atlanta; organized Dec 3, 1832 from Cherokee, Hall, and Habersham counties. **Name Origin:** For Wilson Lumpkin (1783-1870), GA governor (1831-35) and U.S. senator (1837-41).

Area (sq mi): 284.87 (land 284.47; water 0.4).

Pop: 21,016 (White 92.2%; Black or African American 1.5%; Hispanic or Latino 3.5%; Asian 0.4%; Other 4.2%). **Foreign born:** 2.9%. **Median age:** 32.5. **State rank:** 81. **Pop change 1990-2000:** +44.2%.

Income: per capita $18,062; median household $39,167. **Pop below poverty level:** 13.2%.

Unemployment: 2.3%. **Median home value:** $111,800. **Median travel time to work:** 29.6 minutes.

MACON COUNTY
PO Box 297   **Ph:** 478-472-7021
Oglethorpe, GA 31068   **Fax:** 478-472-5643

In central GA, southeast of Atlanta; organized Dec 14, 1837 from Houston and Marion counties. **Name Origin:** For Nathaniel Macon (1757-1837), NC legislator, U.S. representative (1791-1815), U.S. senator (1815-28), and president of the NC constitutional convention (1835).

Area (sq mi): 405.95 (land 403.28; water 2.67).

Pop: 14,074 (White 36.8%; Black or African American 59.5%; Hispanic or Latino 2.6%; Asian 0.6%; Other 2.5%). **Foreign born:** 1.8%. **Median age:** 35.1. **State rank:** 107. **Pop change 1990-2000:** +7.3%.

Income: per capita $11,820; median household $24,224. **Pop below poverty level:** 25.8%.

Unemployment: 7.7%. **Median home value:** $54,200. **Median travel time to work:** 24.5 minutes.

MADISON COUNTY
PO Box 147   **Ph:** 706-795-5664
Danielsville, GA 30633   **Fax:** 706-795-5668

In northeastern GA, northeast of Athens; organized Dec 5, 1811 from Clarke, Elbert, Franklin, Jackson, and Oglethorpe counties. **Name Origin:** For James Madison (1751-1836), fourth U.S. president.

Area (sq mi): 285.57 (land 283.88; water 1.69).

Pop: 25,730 (White 88.3%; Black or African American 8.5%; Hispanic or Latino 2%; Asian 0.3%; Other 2.2%). **Foreign born:** 2%. **Median age:** 35.8. **State rank:** 58. **Pop change 1990-2000:** +22.2%.

Income: per capita $16,998; median household $36,347. **Pop below poverty level:** 11.6%.

Unemployment: 3.6%. **Median home value:** $87,300. **Median travel time to work:** 26.7 minutes.

MARION COUNTY
PO Box 481   **Ph:** 229-649-2603
Buena Vista, GA 31803   **Fax:** 229-649-3702

In west-central GA, east of Columbus; organized Dec 14, 1827 from Lee and Muscogee counties. **Name Origin:** For Gen. Francis Marion (c. 1732-1795), SC soldier and legislator, known as 'The Swamp Fox' for his tactics during the Revolutionary War.

Area (sq mi): 367.49 (land 367; water 0.49).

Pop: 7,144 (White 58.5%; Black or African American 34.1%; Hispanic or Latino 5.8%; Asian 0.2%; Other 5%). **Foreign born:** 5%.

All statistics are based on the 2000 Census except the dollar figures given for per capita income, which are based on 1999 estimates.

Median age: 35.2. **State rank:** 143. **Pop change 1990-2000:** +27.8%.

Income: per capita $14,044; median household $29,145. **Pop below poverty level:** 22.4%.

Unemployment: 5.6%. **Median home value:** $70,400. **Median travel time to work:** 34.4 minutes.

McDUFFIE COUNTY
PO Box 158
Thomson, GA 30824   **Ph:** 706-595-2134
www.co.mcduffie.ga.us   **Fax:** 706-595-9150

In eastern GA, west of Augusta; organized Oct 18, 1870 from Columbia and Warren counties. **Name Origin:** For George McDuffie (1790-1851), SC governor (1834-36) and U.S. senator (1842-46).

Area (sq mi): 266.3 (land 259.77; water 6.52).

Pop: 21,231 (White 60.3%; Black or African American 37.5%; Hispanic or Latino 1.3%; Asian 0.3%; Other 1.3%). **Foreign born:** 0.6%. **Median age:** 35.2. **State rank:** 79. **Pop change 1990-2000:** +5.5%.

Income: per capita $18,005; median household $31,920. **Pop below poverty level:** 18.4%.

Unemployment: 6.9%. **Median home value:** $74,600. **Median travel time to work:** 24 minutes.

McINTOSH COUNTY
PO Box 584
Darien, GA 31305   **Ph:** 912-437-6671
                          Fax: 912-437-6416

On southeastern coast of GA, north of Brunswick; organized Dec 19, 1793 from Liberty County. **Name Origin:** Either for the McIntosh family of early settlers; or for William McIntosh (1775-1825), Creek Indian leader who fought in the Seminole War (1817-18), then became a brigadier general in the U.S. Army. He was killed as a traitor by the Creek Indians.

Area (sq mi): 574.53 (land 433.45; water 141.08).

Pop: 10,847 (White 60.9%; Black or African American 36.8%; Hispanic or Latino 0.9%; Asian 0.3%; Other 1.6%). **Foreign born:** 1%. **Median age:** 37. **State rank:** 119. **Pop change 1990-2000:** +25.6%.

Income: per capita $14,253; median household $30,102. **Pop below poverty level:** 18.7%.

Unemployment: 4.4%. **Median home value:** $81,700. **Median travel time to work:** 29.6 minutes.

MERIWETHER COUNTY
PO Box 428
Greenville, GA 30222   **Ph:** 706-672-1314
                          Fax: 706-672-1886

In west-central GA, northeast of Columbus; organized Dec 24, 1827 from Troup County. **Name Origin:** For Gen. David Meriwether (1755-1823), officer in the Revolutionary War, U.S. representative from GA (1802-07), and commissioner to the Creek Indians (1804).

Area (sq mi): 505.34 (land 503.28; water 2.06).

Pop: 22,534 (White 55.8%; Black or African American 42.2%; Hispanic or Latino 0.8%; Asian 0.2%; Other 1.4%). **Foreign born:** 0.7%. **Median age:** 36.4. **State rank:** 72. **Pop change 1990-2000:** +0.5%.

Income: per capita $15,708; median household $31,870. **Pop below poverty level:** 17.8%.

Unemployment: 6.9%. **Median home value:** $66,300. **Median travel time to work:** 31.2 minutes.

MILLER COUNTY
179 S Cuthbert St
Colquitt, GA 39837   **Ph:** 229-758-4104
                          Fax: 229-758-2229

In southwestern GA, southwest of Albany; organized Feb 26, 1856 from Baker and Early counties. **Name Origin:** For Andrew Jackson Miller (1806-56), GA legislator and superior court judge.

Area (sq mi): 283.72 (land 283.05; water 0.68).

Pop: 6,383 (White 69.8%; Black or African American 28.9%; Hispanic or Latino 0.7%; Asian 0%; Other 0.8%). **Foreign born:** 0.4%. **Median age:** 38.2. **State rank:** 147. **Pop change 1990-2000:** +1.6%.

Income: per capita $15,435; median household $27,335. **Pop below poverty level:** 21.2%.

Unemployment: 4.5%. **Median home value:** $57,600. **Median travel time to work:** 21.9 minutes.

MITCHELL COUNTY
PO Box 187
Camilla, GA 31730   **Ph:** 229-336-2000
                          Fax: 229-336-2003

In southwestern GA, south of Albany; organized Dec 21, 1857 from Baker County. **Name Origin:** For Gen. Henry Mitchell (1760-1839), Revolutionary War hero and president of the GA Senate. Some claim David Brydie Mitchell (1766-1837), GA governor.

Area (sq mi): 513.81 (land 511.96; water 1.85).

Pop: 23,932 (White 49.1%; Black or African American 47.9%; Hispanic or Latino 2.1%; Asian 0.3%; Other 2.3%). **Foreign born:** 1.6%. **Median age:** 34. **State rank:** 63. **Pop change 1990-2000:** +18%.

Income: per capita $13,042; median household $26,581. **Pop below poverty level:** 26.4%.

Unemployment: 5.2%. **Median home value:** $64,500. **Median travel time to work:** 26.5 minutes.

MONROE COUNTY
PO Box 189
Forsyth, GA 31029   **Ph:** 478-994-7000
                          Fax: 478-994-7294

In central GA, northwest of Macon; original county; organized May 15, 1821 from Indian lands. **Name Origin:** For James Monroe (1758-1831), fifth U.S. president.

Area (sq mi): 397.8 (land 395.63; water 2.17).

Pop: 21,757 (White 69.6%; Black or African American 27.9%; Hispanic or Latino 1.3%; Asian 0.3%; Other 1.2%). **Foreign born:** 1%. **Median age:** 36.4. **State rank:** 78. **Pop change 1990-2000:** +27.1%.

Income: per capita $19,580; median household $44,195. **Pop below poverty level:** 9.8%.

Unemployment: 4.7%. **Median home value:** $103,600. **Median travel time to work:** 27.6 minutes.

See explanation on inside front cover for detailed information about the statistics presented with each county listing.

MONTGOMERY COUNTY

PO Box 295
Mount Vernon, GA 30445

Ph: 912-583-2363
Fax: 912-583-2026

In east-central GA, west of Savannah; organized Dec 19, 1793 from Washington County. **Name Origin:** For Gen. Richard Montgomery (1736-75), American Revolutionary War officer who captured Montreal, Canada.

Area (sq mi): 247.32 (land 245.33; water 1.99).

Pop: 8,270 (White 68.7%; Black or African American 27.2%; Hispanic or Latino 3.3%; Asian 0.2%; Other 2.8%). **Foreign born:** 3.9%. **Median age:** 33.6. **State rank:** 139. **Pop change 1990-2000:** +15.5%.

Income: per capita $14,182; median household $30,240. **Pop below poverty level:** 19.9%.

Unemployment: 8.5%. **Median home value:** $68,300. **Median travel time to work:** 27 minutes.

MORGAN COUNTY

PO Box 168
Madison, GA 30650
www.morganga.org

Ph: 706-342-0725
Fax: 706-343-6450

In central GA, southeast of Atlanta; organized as Cotaco County Dec 10, 1807 from Baldwin County; name changed Jun 14, 1821. **Name Origin:** For Gen. Daniel Morgan (1736-1802), an officer in the Revolutionary War and U.S. representative from VA (1797-99).

Area (sq mi): 354.6 (land 349.64; water 4.96).

Pop: 15,457 (White 68.7%; Black or African American 28.5%; Hispanic or Latino 1.6%; Asian 0.3%; Other 1.4%). **Foreign born:** 1.1%. **Median age:** 36.8. **State rank:** 99. **Pop change 1990-2000:** +20%.

Income: per capita $18,823; median household $40,249. **Pop below poverty level:** 10.9%.

Unemployment: 3.2%. **Median home value:** $99,700. **Median travel time to work:** 25 minutes.

MURRAY COUNTY

PO Box 1129
Chatsworth, GA 30705

Ph: 706-695-2413
Fax: 706-695-8721

On northern border of GA, southeast of Chattanooga, TN; organized Dec 3, 1832 from Cherokee County. **Name Origin:** For Thomas W. Murray (1790-1832), GA legislator.

Area (sq mi): 346.88 (land 344.41; water 2.47).

Pop: 36,506 (White 92.8%; Black or African American 0.6%; Hispanic or Latino 5.5%; Asian 0.3%; Other 3.8%). **Foreign born:** 3.6%. **Median age:** 32.6. **State rank:** 49. **Pop change 1990-2000:** +39.6%.

Income: per capita $16,230; median household $36,996. **Pop below poverty level:** 12.7%.

Unemployment: 4.5%. **Median home value:** $85,700. **Median travel time to work:** 24.6 minutes.

NEWTON COUNTY

1113 Usher St NE
Covington, GA 30014
www.co.newton.ga.us

Ph: 770-784-2000
Fax: 770-784-2007

In central GA, southeast of Atlanta; organized Dec 24, 1821 from Henry, Walton, and Jasper counties. **Name Origin:** For Sgt. John Newton (1752-80), soldier under Gen. Francis Marion (1732?-95) in the Revolutionary War, who saved several colonial patriots from execution by surprising and capturing the British soldiers guarding them.

Area (sq mi): 279.19 (land 276.43; water 2.76).

Pop: 62,001 (White 74.2%; Black or African American 22.2%; Hispanic or Latino 1.9%; Asian 0.7%; Other 1.8%). **Foreign born:** 2.5%. **Median age:** 33.3. **State rank:** 29. **Pop change 1990-2000:** +48.3%.

Income: per capita $19,317; median household $44,875. **Pop below poverty level:** 10%.

Unemployment: 3.5%. **Median home value:** $101,300. **Median travel time to work:** 30.5 minutes.

OCONEE COUNTY

PO Box 145
Watkinsville, GA 30677
www.oconeecounty.net

Ph: 706-769-5120
Fax: 706-769-0705

In northeast-central GA, south of Athens; organized Feb 25, 1875 from Clarke County. **Name Origin:** For an Indian tribe of Muskhogean linguistic stock; meaning of name uncertain.

Area (sq mi): 186.14 (land 185.7; water 0.44).

Pop: 26,225 (White 88.1%; Black or African American 6.4%; Hispanic or Latino 3.2%; Asian 1.4%; Other 2.6%). **Foreign born:** 4.4%. **Median age:** 35.2. **State rank:** 56. **Pop change 1990-2000:** +48.9%.

Income: per capita $24,153; median household $55,211. **Pop below poverty level:** 6.5%.

Unemployment: 1.7%. **Median home value:** $151,600. **Median travel time to work:** 25 minutes.

OGLETHORPE COUNTY

PO Box 261
Lexington, GA 30648

Ph: 706-743-5270
Fax: 706-743-8371

In northeastern GA, southeast of Athens; organized Dec 19, 1793 from Wilkes County. **Name Origin:** For Gen. James Edward Oglethorpe (1696-1785), founder of GA and English humanitarian who proposed that GA be settled by former prisoners; first governor of GA under the charter granted to him.

Area (sq mi): 442.17 (land 441.11; water 1.06).

Pop: 12,635 (White 77.7%; Black or African American 19.8%; Hispanic or Latino 1.4%; Asian 0.2%; Other 1.6%). **Foreign born:** 0.8%. **Median age:** 36.8. **State rank:** 110. **Pop change 1990-2000:** +29.4%.

Income: per capita $17,089; median household $35,578. **Pop below poverty level:** 13.2%.

Unemployment: 3.7%. **Median home value:** $87,500. **Median travel time to work:** 31.6 minutes.

All statistics are based on the 2000 Census except the dollar figures given for per capita income, which are based on 1999 estimates.

PAULDING COUNTY

166 Confederate Ave   **Ph:** 770-505-1352
Dallas, GA 30132   **Fax:** 770-505-1353
www.paulding.gov

In northwestern GA, northwest of Atlanta; organized Dec 3, 1832 from Cherokee County. **Name Origin:** For John Paulding (1758-1818), one of the captors (1780) of John Andre (1750-80), British spy, during the American Revolution.

Area (sq mi): 315.06 (land 313.43; water 1.63).

Pop: 81,678 (White 89.6%; Black or African American 7%; Hispanic or Latino 1.7%; Asian 0.4%; Other 2.1%). **Foreign born:** 2.1%. **Median age:** 31.2. **State rank:** 25. **Pop change 1990-2000:** +96.3%.

Income: per capita $19,974; median household $52,161. **Pop below poverty level:** 5.5%.

Unemployment: 2.4%. **Median home value:** $106,100. **Median travel time to work:** 39.1 minutes.

PEACH COUNTY

205 W Church St   **Ph:** 478-825-2535
Fort Valley, GA 31030   **Fax:** 478-825-2678

In central GA, southeast of Macon; organized Jul 18, 1924 from Houston and Macon counties; the last county formed. **Name Origin:** For its location in one of the most fertile peach-growing areas of the state.

Area (sq mi): 151.46 (land 151.06; water 0.4).

Pop: 23,668 (White 49.2%; Black or African American 45.4%; Hispanic or Latino 4.2%; Asian 0.3%; Other 2.9%). **Foreign born:** 3.8%. **Median age:** 31.8. **State rank:** 65. **Pop change 1990-2000:** +11.7%.

Income: per capita $16,031; median household $34,453. **Pop below poverty level:** 20.2%.

Unemployment: 4.4%. **Median home value:** $78,300. **Median travel time to work:** 25.1 minutes.

PICKENS COUNTY

PO Box 130   **Ph:** 706-692-5600
Jasper, GA 30143

In north-central GA, north of Atlanta; organized Dec 5, 1853 from Cherokee and Gilmer counties. **Name Origin:** For Andrew Pickens (1739-1817), soldier and U.S. representative from SC (1793-95).

Area (sq mi): 232.78 (land 232.13; water 0.65).

Pop: 22,983 (White 95.3%; Black or African American 1.3%; Hispanic or Latino 2%; Asian 0.2%; Other 2.2%). **Foreign born:** 2%. **Median age:** 37.9. **State rank:** 71. **Pop change 1990-2000:** +59.3%.

Income: per capita $19,774; median household $41,387. **Pop below poverty level:** 9.2%.

Unemployment: 3%. **Median home value:** $113,100. **Median travel time to work:** 32.5 minutes.

PIERCE COUNTY

PO Box 679   **Ph:** 912-449-2022
Blackshear, GA 31516   **Fax:** 912-449-2024

In southeastern GA, west of Brunswick; organized Dec 18, 1857 from Appling and Ware counties. **Name Origin:** For Franklin Pierce (1804-69), fourteenth U.S. president.

Area (sq mi): 343.9 (land 343.25; water 0.65).

Pop: 15,636 (White 85.9%; Black or African American 10.9%; Hispanic or Latino 2.3%; Asian 0.2%; Other 2.1%). **Foreign born:** 2.1%. **Median age:** 36.2. **State rank:** 98. **Pop change 1990-2000:** +17.3%.

Income: per capita $14,230; median household $29,895. **Pop below poverty level:** 18.4%.

Unemployment: 4%. **Median home value:** $64,300. **Median travel time to work:** 26.2 minutes.

PIKE COUNTY

PO Box 377   **Ph:** 770-567-3406
Zebulon, GA 30295   **Fax:** 770-567-2006

In west-central GA, northwest of Macon; organized Dec 9, 1822 from Monroe County. **Name Origin:** For Gen. Zebulon Montgomery Pike (1779-1813), U.S. army officer and discoverer of Pikes Peak in CO.

Area (sq mi): 219.43 (land 218.37; water 1.06).

Pop: 13,688 (White 82.9%; Black or African American 14.8%; Hispanic or Latino 1.2%; Asian 0.4%; Other 1.2%). **Foreign born:** 1%. **Median age:** 35.7. **State rank:** 108. **Pop change 1990-2000:** +33.9%.

Income: per capita $17,661; median household $44,370. **Pop below poverty level:** 9.6%.

Unemployment: 4%. **Median home value:** $103,000. **Median travel time to work:** 30.6 minutes.

POLK COUNTY

PO Box 948   **Ph:** 770-749-2114
Cedartown, GA 30125   **Fax:** 770-749-2148

On northwestern border of GA, south of Rome; organized Dec 20, 1851 from Paulding and Floyd counties. **Name Origin:** For James Knox Polk (1795-1849), eleventh U.S. president.

Area (sq mi): 312.13 (land 311.14; water 0.99).

Pop: 38,127 (White 77.9%; Black or African American 13.3%; Hispanic or Latino 7.7%; Asian 0.3%; Other 5.7%). **Foreign born:** 6%. **Median age:** 35.1. **State rank:** 46. **Pop change 1990-2000:** +12.8%.

Income: per capita $15,617; median household $32,328. **Pop below poverty level:** 15.5%.

Unemployment: 5.1%. **Median home value:** $73,900. **Median travel time to work:** 30 minutes.

PULASKI COUNTY

PO Box 29   **Ph:** 478-783-4154
Hawkinsville, GA 31036   **Fax:** 478-783-9209

In central GA, southeast of Macon; organized Dec 13, 1808 from Laurens County. **Name Origin:** For Count Casimir Pulaski (1747-79), Polish soldier who fought for America during the Revolutionary War.

Area (sq mi): 249.89 (land 247.42; water 2.47).

Please see sample entry on inside front cover for detailed information about the statistics presented with each county listing.

Pop: 9,588 (White 61.9%; Black or African American 34.3%; Hispanic or Latino 2.8%; Asian 0.3%; Other 2.4%). **Foreign born:** 2.6%. **Median age:** 36.7. **State rank:** 129. **Pop change 1990-2000:** +18.3%.

Income: per capita $16,435; median household $31,895. **Pop below poverty level:** 16.4%.

Unemployment: 6.9%. **Median home value:** $75,400. **Median travel time to work:** 20.8 minutes.

PUTNAM COUNTY

108 S Madison Ave Suite 300   **Ph:** 706-485-5826
Eatonton, GA 31024   **Fax:** 706-485-5578

In central GA, northeast of Macon; organized Dec 10, 1807 from Baldwin County. **Name Origin:** For Gen. Israel Putnam (1718-90), Revolutionary War officer and American commander at the Battle of Bunker Hill.

Area (sq mi): 360.63 (land 344.53; water 16.1).

Pop: 18,812 (White 66.3%; Black or African American 29.9%; Hispanic or Latino 2.2%; Asian 0.7%; Other 1.9%). **Foreign born:** 2.5%. **Median age:** 39.6. **State rank:** 88. **Pop change 1990-2000:** +33.1%.

Income: per capita $20,161; median household $36,956. **Pop below poverty level:** 14.6%.

Unemployment: 3.3%. **Median home value:** $102,300. **Median travel time to work:** 26.5 minutes.

QUITMAN COUNTY

PO Box 307   **Ph:** 229-334-2578
Georgetown, GA 39854   **Fax:** 229-334-3991

On southwestern border of GA, south of Columbus; organized Dec 10, 1858 from Randolph (organized 1828) and Stewart counties. **Name Origin:** For John Anthony Quitman (1799-1858), tenth and sixteenth governor of MS (1835-36; 1850-51), and U.S. representative (1855-58).

Area (sq mi): 160.92 (land 151.54; water 9.38).

Pop: 2,598 (White 52%; Black or African American 46.9%; Hispanic or Latino 0.5%; Asian 0%; Other 0.9%). **Foreign born:** 0.7%. **Median age:** 42. **State rank:** 156. **Pop change 1990-2000:** +17.6%.

Income: per capita $14,301; median household $25,875. **Pop below poverty level:** 21.9%.

Unemployment: 6.6%. **Median home value:** $51,300. **Median travel time to work:** 27.6 minutes.

RABUN COUNTY

25 Courthouse Sq Suite 201   **Ph:** 706-782-5271
Clayton, GA 30525   **Fax:** 706-782-7588

In northeastern corner of GA; organized Dec 21, 1819 from Cherokee land. **Name Origin:** For William Rabun (1771-1819), GA legislator and governor (1817-19).

Area (sq mi): 376.99 (land 371.05; water 5.94).

Pop: 15,050 (White 93.2%; Black or African American 0.8%; Hispanic or Latino 4.5%; Asian 0.4%; Other 3.9%). **Foreign born:** 4.1%. **Median age:** 42. **State rank:** 102. **Pop change 1990-2000:** +29.2%.

Income: per capita $20,608; median household $33,899. **Pop below poverty level:** 11.1%.

Unemployment: 2.8%. **Median home value:** $112,400. **Median travel time to work:** 24.1 minutes.

RANDOLPH COUNTY

PO Box 221   **Ph:** 229-732-6440
Cuthbert, GA 31740   **Fax:** 229-732-5364

In southwestern GA, northwest of Albany; organized Dec 20, 1828 from Lee County (an earlier Randolph County was renamed Jasper County in 1812). **Name Origin:** For John Randolph (1773-1833), VA statesman and U.S. minister to Russia (1830).

Area (sq mi): 430.89 (land 429.25; water 1.64).

Pop: 7,791 (White 38.7%; Black or African American 59.5%; Hispanic or Latino 1.2%; Asian 0.2%; Other 1.3%). **Foreign born:** 0.7%. **Median age:** 36.1. **State rank:** 140. **Pop change 1990-2000:** -2.9%.

Income: per capita $11,809; median household $22,004. **Pop below poverty level:** 27.7%.

Unemployment: 9.3%. **Median home value:** $48,600. **Median travel time to work:** 23.6 minutes.

ROCKDALE COUNTY

PO Box 937   **Ph:** 770-929-4021
Conyers, GA 30012
www.rockdalecounty.org

In central GA, southeast of Atlanta; organized Oct 18, 1870 from Henry and Newton counties. **Name Origin:** For the Rockdale Church, which was named for the underlying bed of granite in this part of the state.

Area (sq mi): 132.13 (land 130.63; water 1.5).

Pop: 70,111 (White 72.7%; Black or African American 18.2%; Hispanic or Latino 6%; Asian 1.9%; Other 4.2%). **Foreign born:** 7.6%. **Median age:** 35.4. **State rank:** 27. **Pop change 1990-2000:** +29.6%.

Income: per capita $22,300; median household $53,599. **Pop below poverty level:** 8.2%.

Unemployment: 2.7%. **Median home value:** $118,000. **Median travel time to work:** 29.5 minutes.

SCHLEY COUNTY

PO Box 352   **Ph:** 229-937-2609
Ellaville, GA 31806   **Fax:** 229-937-5880

In west-central GA, southeast of Columbus; organized Dec 22, 1857 from Marion and Sumter counties. **Name Origin:** For William Schley (1786-1858), U.S. representative from GA and governor (1835-37).

Area (sq mi): 167.82 (land 167.61; water 0.21).

Pop: 3,766 (White 65.4%; Black or African American 31.3%; Hispanic or Latino 2.4%; Asian 0.1%; Other 2.9%). **Foreign born:** 1.8%. **Median age:** 34.5. **State rank:** 153. **Pop change 1990-2000:** +5%.

Income: per capita $14,981; median household $32,035. **Pop below poverty level:** 19.9%.

All statistics are based on the 2000 Census except the dollar figures given for per capita income, which are based on 1999 estimates.

Unemployment: 4.9%. **Median home value:** $57,400. **Median travel time to work:** 25.8 minutes.

SCREVEN COUNTY

PO Box 159   **Ph:** 912-564-7535
Sylvania, GA 30467   **Fax:** 912-564-2562

On central east coast of GA, north of Savannah; organized Dec 14, 1793 from Burke and Effingham counties. **Name Origin:** For Gen. James Screven (1744-78), an officer in the Revolutionary War. Originally spelled *Scriven*.

Area (sq mi): 655.59 (land 648.44; water 7.14).

Pop: 15,374 (White 53.2%; Black or African American 45.3%; Hispanic or Latino 1%; Asian 0.3%; Other 0.9%). **Foreign born:** 1.7%. **Median age:** 36.2. **State rank:** 100. **Pop change 1990-2000:** +11.1%.

Income: per capita $13,894; median household $29,312. **Pop below poverty level:** 20.1%.

Unemployment: 9.5%. **Median home value:** $64,600. **Median travel time to work:** 29.1 minutes.

SEMINOLE COUNTY

200 S Knox Ave   **Ph:** 229-524-2878
Donalsonville, GA 39845   **Fax:** 229-524-8984

In southwestern corner of GA; organized Jul 8, 1920 from Decatur and Early counties. **Name Origin:** For the Muskhogean tribe. Name is from Creek 'the separate ones.'

Area (sq mi): 256.56 (land 238.04; water 18.52).

Pop: 9,369 (White 61.2%; Black or African American 34.7%; Hispanic or Latino 3.7%; Asian 0.2%; Other 3.4%). **Foreign born:** 1.1%. **Median age:** 37.5. **State rank:** 132. **Pop change 1990-2000:** +4%.

Income: per capita $14,635; median household $27,094. **Pop below poverty level:** 23.2%.

Unemployment: 4.4%. **Median home value:** $58,600. **Median travel time to work:** 24.6 minutes.

SPALDING COUNTY

PO box 1046   **Ph:** 770-228-9900
Griffin, GA 30224
www.co.spalding.ga.us

In west-central GA, south of Atlanta; organized Dec 20, 1851 from Henry, Pike, and Fayette counties. **Name Origin:** For Thomas Spalding (1774-1851), GA legislator, U.S. representative (1805-06), and member of the GA Constitutional Convention of 1798.

Area (sq mi): 199.6 (land 197.95; water 1.65).

Pop: 58,417 (White 65.8%; Black or African American 31.1%; Hispanic or Latino 1.6%; Asian 0.7%; Other 1.8%). **Foreign born:** 2.2%. **Median age:** 34.6. **State rank:** 34. **Pop change 1990-2000:** +7.3%.

Income: per capita $16,791; median household $36,221. **Pop below poverty level:** 15.5%.

Unemployment: 4.8%. **Median home value:** $86,600. **Median travel time to work:** 27.5 minutes.

STEPHENS COUNTY

PO Box 386   **Ph:** 706-886-9491
Toccoa, GA 30577   **Fax:** 706-886-2185

On northeastern border of GA, northeast of Athens; organized Aug 18, 1905 from Franklin and Habersham counties. **Name Origin:** For Alexander Hamilton Stephens (1812-83), GA statesman and a vice president of the Confederacy (1861).

Area (sq mi): 184.23 (land 179.26; water 4.97).

Pop: 25,435 (White 85.2%; Black or African American 12%; Hispanic or Latino 1%; Asian 0.6%; Other 1.7%). **Foreign born:** 1.4%. **Median age:** 37.5. **State rank:** 61. **Pop change 1990-2000:** +9.4%.

Income: per capita $15,529; median household $29,466. **Pop below poverty level:** 15.1%.

Unemployment: 6%. **Median home value:** $80,900. **Median travel time to work:** 20.7 minutes.

STEWART COUNTY

PO Box 157   **Ph:** 229-838-6769
Lumpkin, GA 31815   **Fax:** 229-838-9856

On central-western border of GA, south of Columbus; organized Dec 23, 1830 from Randolph County. **Name Origin:** For Gen. Daniel Stewart (1759-1829), an officer in the American Revolution and the War of 1812.

Area (sq mi): 463.23 (land 458.7; water 4.53).

Pop: 5,252 (White 36.7%; Black or African American 61.5%; Hispanic or Latino 1.5%; Asian 0.2%; Other 1.1%). **Foreign born:** 1.6%. **Median age:** 38.8. **State rank:** 151. **Pop change 1990-2000:** -7.1%.

Income: per capita $16,071; median household $24,789. **Pop below poverty level:** 22.2%.

Unemployment: 7.3%. **Median home value:** $44,000. **Median travel time to work:** 28.6 minutes.

SUMTER COUNTY

PO Box 295   **Ph:** 229-928-4500
Americus, GA 31709
www.sumter-ga.com

In west-central GA, north of Albany; organized Dec 26, 1831 from Lee County. **Name Origin:** For Gen. Thomas Sumter (1734-1832), American Revolutionary officer nicknamed the 'Gamecock of the Revolution,' U.S. representative from GA (1789-93; 1797-1801), and U.S. senator (1801-10).

Area (sq mi): 492.54 (land 485.28; water 7.26).

Pop: 33,200 (White 47.2%; Black or African American 49%; Hispanic or Latino 2.7%; Asian 0.6%; Other 2.2%). **Foreign born:** 2%. **Median age:** 32.6. **State rank:** 52. **Pop change 1990-2000:** +9.8%.

Income: per capita $15,083; median household $30,904. **Pop below poverty level:** 21.4%.

Unemployment: 6.6%. **Median home value:** $66,900. **Median travel time to work:** 19.2 minutes.

Please see sample entry on inside front cover for detailed information about the statistics presented with each county listing.

TALBOT COUNTY
PO Box 325   **Ph:** 706-665-3239
Talbotton, GA 31827   **Fax:** 706-665-8637

In west-central GA, northeast of Columbus; organized Dec 14, 1827 from Muscogee County. **Name Origin:** For Matthew Talbot (1762-1827), GA legislator and ex-officio governor (1819).

Area (sq mi): 394.74 (land 393.21; water 1.52).

Pop: 6,498 (White 36.2%; Black or African American 61.6%; Hispanic or Latino 1.3%; Asian 0.3%; Other 1.3%). **Foreign born:** 0.7%. **Median age:** 39.5. **State rank:** 146. **Pop change 1990-2000:** -0.4%.

Income: per capita $14,539; median household $26,611. **Pop below poverty level:** 24.2%.

Unemployment: 6.7%. **Median home value:** $57,700. **Median travel time to work:** 32.8 minutes.

TALIAFERRO COUNTY
PO Box 182   **Ph:** 706-456-2123
Crawfordville, GA 30631   **Fax:** 706-456-2749
web.infoave.net/~taliaferro/

In east-central GA, northwest of Augusta; organized Dec 24, 1825 from Greene, Hancock, Oglethorpe, Warren, and Wilkes counties. **Name Origin:** For Capt. Benjamin Taliaferro (1750-1821), GA superior court judge, legislator, and U.S. representative (1799-1802).

Area (sq mi): 195.47 (land 195.39; water 0.08).

Pop: 2,077 (White 37.9%; Black or African American 60.3%; Hispanic or Latino 0.9%; Asian 0%; Other 1.4%). **Foreign born:** 0.5%. **Median age:** 40.2. **State rank:** 159. **Pop change 1990-2000:** +8.5%.

Income: per capita $15,498; median household $23,750. **Pop below poverty level:** 23.4%.

Unemployment: 11.9%. **Median home value:** $40,300. **Median travel time to work:** 31.2 minutes.

TATTNALL COUNTY
PO Box 25   **Ph:** 912-557-4335
Reidsville, GA 30453   **Fax:** 912-557-6088
www.tattnall.com

In east-central GA, west of Savannah; organized Dec 5, 1801 from Montgomery County. **Name Origin:** For Gen. Josiah Tattnall (1764-1803), an officer in the American Revolution, U.S. senator from GA (1796-99), and governor (1801-02).

Area (sq mi): 488.22 (land 483.69; water 4.53).

Pop: 22,305 (White 59.3%; Black or African American 31.4%; Hispanic or Latino 8.4%; Asian 0.3%; Other 7.7%). **Foreign born:** 5.8%. **Median age:** 33.9. **State rank:** 73. **Pop change 1990-2000:** +25.9%.

Income: per capita $13,439; median household $28,664. **Pop below poverty level:** 23.9%.

Unemployment: 5.2%. **Median home value:** $67,300. **Median travel time to work:** 27.5 minutes.

TAYLOR COUNTY
PO Box 278   **Ph:** 478-862-3336
Butler, GA 31006   **Fax:** 478-862-2871

In west-central GA, east of Columbus; organized Jan 15, 1852 from Macon, Marion, and Talbot counties. **Name Origin:** For Zachary Taylor (1784-1850), twelfth U.S. president.

Area (sq mi): 379.61 (land 377.44; water 2.17).

Pop: 8,815 (White 55%; Black or African American 42.6%; Hispanic or Latino 1.8%; Asian 0.2%; Other 1.8%). **Foreign born:** 1%. **Median age:** 35.7. **State rank:** 134. **Pop change 1990-2000:** +15.3%.

Income: per capita $13,432; median household $25,148. **Pop below poverty level:** 26%.

Unemployment: 5.3%. **Median home value:** $56,300. **Median travel time to work:** 28.6 minutes.

TELFAIR COUNTY
713 Telfair Ave   **Ph:** 229-868-5688
McRae, GA 31055   **Fax:** 229-868-7950

In central GA, southeast of Macon; organized Dec 10, 1807 from Wilkinson County. **Name Origin:** For Edward Telfair (1735-1807), member of the Continental Congress (1777-79; 1780-83), and GA governor (1786-87; 1790-93).

Area (sq mi): 444.08 (land 441.09; water 2.99).

Pop: 11,794 (White 59.3%; Black or African American 38.4%; Hispanic or Latino 1.8%; Asian 0.2%; Other 1.7%). **Foreign born:** 1.1%. **Median age:** 36.8. **State rank:** 113. **Pop change 1990-2000:** +7.2%.

Income: per capita $14,197; median household $26,097. **Pop below poverty level:** 21.2%.

Unemployment: 13.4%. **Median home value:** $47,600. **Median travel time to work:** 24.2 minutes.

TERRELL COUNTY
PO Box 525   **Ph:** 229-995-4476
Dawson, GA 39842   **Fax:** 229-995-4320

In southwestern GA, northwest of Albany; organized Feb 16, 1856 from Lee and Randolph counties. **Name Origin:** For Dr. William Terrell (1778-1855), GA legislator and U.S. representative (1817-21).

Area (sq mi): 337.63 (land 335.37; water 2.26).

Pop: 10,970 (White 37.4%; Black or African American 60.7%; Hispanic or Latino 1.2%; Asian 0.3%; Other 1%). **Foreign born:** 1.7%. **Median age:** 35.4. **State rank:** 118. **Pop change 1990-2000:** +3%.

Income: per capita $13,894; median household $26,969. **Pop below poverty level:** 28.6%.

Unemployment: 8.1%. **Median home value:** $59,300. **Median travel time to work:** 23 minutes.

THOMAS COUNTY
PO Box 920   **Ph:** 229-225-4100
Thomasville, GA 31799   **Fax:** 229-226-3430
www.thomascountyboc.org

On southern border of GA, west of Valdosta; organized Dec 23,

All statistics are based on the 2000 Census except the dollar figures given for per capita income, which are based on 1999 estimates.

130

1825 from Decatur and Irwin counties. **Name Origin:** For Gen. Jett Thomas (1776-1817), officer of the GA militia; supervisor of the construction of the state capitol at Milledgeville and the first university building at Athens.

Area (sq mi): 552.08 (land 548.3; water 3.78).

Pop: 42,737 (White 58.2%; Black or African American 38.9%; Hispanic or Latino 1.7%; Asian 0.4%; Other 1.8%). **Foreign born:** 1.4%. **Median age:** 36.3. **State rank:** 42. **Pop change 1990-2000:** +9.6%.

Income: per capita $16,211; median household $31,115. **Pop below poverty level:** 17.4%.

Unemployment: 4.1%. **Median home value:** $76,900. **Median travel time to work:** 19.1 minutes.

TIFT COUNTY
PO Box 354   **Ph:** 229-386-7810
Tifton, GA 31793   **Fax:** 229-386-7813
www.tiftcounty.org

In south-central GA, east of Albany; organized Aug 17, 1905 from Berrien, Irwin, and Worth counties. **Name Origin:** For Capt. Nelson Tift (1810-91), GA legislator, officer in the Confederate Navy, and U.S. representative (1868-69). Founder of the city of Albany, GA (1836).

Area (sq mi): 268.86 (land 265.05; water 3.81).

Pop: 38,407 (White 62.7%; Black or African American 28%; Hispanic or Latino 7.7%; Asian 1%; Other 5.7%). **Foreign born:** 5.5%. **Median age:** 33. **State rank:** 45. **Pop change 1990-2000:** +9.7%.

Income: per capita $16,833; median household $32,616. **Pop below poverty level:** 19.9%.

Unemployment: 4.5%. **Median home value:** $82,600. **Median travel time to work:** 17.9 minutes.

TOOMBS COUNTY
PO Box 112   **Ph:** 912-526-3311
Lyons, GA 30436   **Fax:** 912-526-1004

In east-central GA, west of Savannah; organized Aug 18, 1905 from Emanuel, Montgomery, and Tattnall counties. **Name Origin:** For Gen. Robert Toombs (1810-85), U.S. senator (1853-61), secretary of state of the Confederacy, and officer in the Confederate Army.

Area (sq mi): 368.64 (land 366.65; water 1.99).

Pop: 26,067 (White 66.1%; Black or African American 24.2%; Hispanic or Latino 8.9%; Asian 0.5%; Other 6.2%). **Foreign born:** 5.9%. **Median age:** 34.2. **State rank:** 57. **Pop change 1990-2000:** +8.3%.

Income: per capita $14,252; median household $26,811. **Pop below poverty level:** 23.9%.

Unemployment: 7.7%. **Median home value:** $66,400. **Median travel time to work:** 21.9 minutes.

TOWNS COUNTY
48 River St Suite E
Hiawassee, GA 30546   **Ph:** 706-896-2130

On northern border of GA, northwest of Athens; organized Mar 6, 1856 from Rabun and Union counties. **Name Origin:** For George

Washington Bonaparte Towns (1801-54), U.S. representative from GA (1835-36; 1837-39; 1846-47) and governor (1847-51).

Area (sq mi): 172.01 (land 166.66; water 5.35).

Pop: 9,319 (White 98.3%; Black or African American 0.1%; Hispanic or Latino 0.7%; Asian 0.3%; Other 0.8%). **Foreign born:** 2.7%. **Median age:** 48.6. **State rank:** 133. **Pop change 1990-2000:** +38%.

Income: per capita $18,221; median household $31,950. **Pop below poverty level:** 11.8%.

Unemployment: 2.7%. **Median home value:** $127,500. **Median travel time to work:** 28.5 minutes.

TREUTLEN COUNTY
PO Box 79   **Ph:** 912-529-3664
Soperton, GA 30457   **Fax:** 912-529-6062

In east-central GA; organized Aug 21, 1917 from Emanuel and Montgomery counties. **Name Origin:** For John Adam Treutlen (1726-83), first governor of GA (1777-78).

Area (sq mi): 202.19 (land 200.66; water 1.53).

Pop: 6,854 (White 65.1%; Black or African American 33.1%; Hispanic or Latino 1.2%; Asian 0.3%; Other 1%). **Foreign born:** 1.9%. **Median age:** 33.9. **State rank:** 145. **Pop change 1990-2000:** +14.3%.

Income: per capita $13,122; median household $24,644. **Pop below poverty level:** 26.3%.

Unemployment: 6.9%. **Median home value:** $56,600. **Median travel time to work:** 27.8 minutes.

TROUP COUNTY
PO Box 866   **Ph:** 706-883-1740
LaGrange, GA 30241   **Fax:** 706-883-1724
www.troupcountyga.org

On central western border of GA, north of Columbus; original county; organized Dec 11, 1826 from Indian lands. **Name Origin:** For George Michael Troup (1780-1856), U.S. senator from GA (1816-18; 1829-33) and governor (1823-27).

Area (sq mi): 445.96 (land 413.9; water 32.06).

Pop: 58,779 (White 65.1%; Black or African American 31.9%; Hispanic or Latino 1.7%; Asian 0.6%; Other 1.8%). **Foreign born:** 2%. **Median age:** 34.6. **State rank:** 33. **Pop change 1990-2000:** +5.8%.

Income: per capita $17,626; median household $35,469. **Pop below poverty level:** 14.8%.

Unemployment: 4.7%. **Median home value:** $83,700. **Median travel time to work:** 21.1 minutes.

TURNER COUNTY
PO Box 106   **Ph:** 229-567-2011
Ashburn, GA 31714   **Fax:** 229-567-0450

In south-central GA, northeast of Albany; organized 1905 from Dooly, Irwin, Wilcox, and Worth counties. **Name Origin:** For Capt. Henry Gray Turner (1839-1904), officer in the Confederate Army, U.S. representative from GA (1881-97), and associate justice of the GA supreme court (1903).

Please see sample entry on inside front cover for detailed information about the statistics presented with each county listing.

Area (sq mi): 289.85 (land 286.03; water 3.83).

Pop: 9,504 (White 55.9%; Black or African American 41%; Hispanic or Latino 2.6%; Asian 0.3%; Other 2.3%). **Foreign born:** 2.4%. **Median age:** 33.3. **State rank:** 131. **Pop change 1990-2000:** +9.2%.

Income: per capita $13,454; median household $25,676. **Pop below poverty level:** 26.7%.

Unemployment: 9%. **Median home value:** $57,600. **Median travel time to work:** 22.4 minutes.

TWIGGS COUNTY
PO Box 202   **Ph:** 478-945-3629
Jeffersonville, GA 31044   **Fax:** 478-945-3988

In central GA, east of Macon; organized Dec 14, 1809 from Wilkinson County. The geographic center of GA is within the county. **Name Origin:** For Maj. Gen. John Twiggs, an officer in the American Revolution.

Area (sq mi): 362.95 (land 360.29; water 2.66).

Pop: 10,590 (White 54.6%; Black or African American 43.7%; Hispanic or Latino 1.1%; Asian 0.1%; Other 1.3%). **Foreign born:** 0.8%. **Median age:** 35.4. **State rank:** 121. **Pop change 1990-2000:** +8%.

Income: per capita $14,259; median household $31,608. **Pop below poverty level:** 19.7%.

Unemployment: 6.3%. **Median home value:** $61,800. **Median travel time to work:** 29.3 minutes.

UNION COUNTY
114 Courthouse St Box 1   **Ph:** 706-439-6000
Blairsville, GA 30512   **Fax:** 706-439-6004
www.unioncounty.gov

On northern border of GA, northwest of Athens; organized Dec 3, 1832 from Cherokee County. **Name Origin:** By John Thomas, state legislator at the time of naming: 'Union, for none but Union men reside in it.'

Area (sq mi): 329.02 (land 322.55; water 6.47).

Pop: 17,289 (White 97.4%; Black or African American 0.6%; Hispanic or Latino 0.9%; Asian 0.2%; Other 1.2%). **Foreign born:** 1.3%. **Median age:** 44.8. **State rank:** 91. **Pop change 1990-2000:** +44.2%.

Income: per capita $18,845; median household $31,893. **Pop below poverty level:** 12.5%.

Unemployment: 2.6%. **Median home value:** $111,100. **Median travel time to work:** 27.3 minutes.

UPSON COUNTY
106 E Lee St Suite 110   **Ph:** 706-647-7012
Thomaston, GA 30286   **Fax:** 706-647-7030

In west-central GA, west of Macon; organized Dec 15, 1824 from Crawford and Pike counties. **Name Origin:** For Stephen Upson (1786-1824), attorney, jurist, and GA legislator.

Area (sq mi): 327.64 (land 325.48; water 2.15).

Pop: 27,597 (White 69.8%; Black or African American 27.9%; Hispanic or Latino 1.2%; Asian 0.4%; Other 1.1%). **Foreign born:** 2%. **Median age:** 37.4. **State rank:** 54. **Pop change 1990-2000:** +4.9%.

Income: per capita $17,053; median household $31,201. **Pop below poverty level:** 14.7%.

Unemployment: 10.5%. **Median home value:** $66,100. **Median travel time to work:** 25.1 minutes.

WALKER COUNTY
PO Box 445   **Ph:** 706-638-1437
La Fayette, GA 30728   **Fax:** 706-638-1453
www.co.walker.ga.us

On the northern border of GA, south of Chattanooga, TN; organized Dec 18, 1833 from Murray County. **Name Origin:** For Maj. Freeman Walker (1780-1827), GA legislator, U.S. senator (1819-21), and mayor of Augusta (1818-19; 1823).

Area (sq mi): 447.03 (land 446.58; water 0.45).

Pop: 61,053 (White 93.9%; Black or African American 3.8%; Hispanic or Latino 0.9%; Asian 0.3%; Other 1.5%). **Foreign born:** 1%. **Median age:** 37.1. **State rank:** 31. **Pop change 1990-2000:** +4.7%.

Income: per capita $15,867; median household $32,406. **Pop below poverty level:** 12.5%.

Unemployment: 3.9%. **Median home value:** $71,200. **Median travel time to work:** 26.5 minutes.

WALTON COUNTY
PO Box 585   **Ph:** 770-267-1301
Monroe, GA 30655   **Fax:** 770-267-1400
www.waltoncountyga.org

In central GA, east of Atlanta; original county; organized Dec 15, 1818 from Cherokee lands. **Name Origin:** For George Walton (1741-1804), a signer of the Declaration of Independence, GA governor (1779-80; 1789), and U.S. senator (1795-96).

Area (sq mi): 330.05 (land 329.18; water 0.87).

Pop: 60,687 (White 81.9%; Black or African American 14.4%; Hispanic or Latino 1.9%; Asian 0.7%; Other 1.8%). **Foreign born:** 2%. **Median age:** 33.9. **State rank:** 32. **Pop change 1990-2000:** +57.3%.

Income: per capita $19,470; median household $46,479. **Pop below poverty level:** 9.7%.

Unemployment: 3.5%. **Median home value:** $113,300. **Median travel time to work:** 33.5 minutes.

WARE COUNTY
800 Church St   **Ph:** 912-287-4300
Waycross, GA 31501   **Fax:** 912-287-4301

In southeastern GA, west of Brunswick; organized Dec 15, 1824 from Appling County. **Name Origin:** For Nicholas Ware (1769-1824), GA legislator, mayor of Augusta (1819-21), and U.S. senator (1821-24).

Area (sq mi): 906.31 (land 902.29; water 4.02).

Pop: 35,483 (White 68.9%; Black or African American 28%; Hispanic or Latino 1.9%; Asian 0.5%; Other 1.9%). **Foreign born:** 1.8%. **Median age:** 36.8. **State rank:** 51. **Pop change 1990-2000:** +0%.

Income: per capita $14,384; median household $28,360. **Pop below poverty level:** 20.5%.

All statistics are based on the 2000 Census except the dollar figures given for per capita income, which are based on 1999 estimates.

Unemployment: 5.3%. **Median home value:** $56,700. **Median travel time to work:** 20.2 minutes.

WARREN COUNTY
PO Box 46   **Ph:** 706-465-2171
Warrenton, GA 30828   **Fax:** 706-465-1300

In east-central GA, west of Augusta; organized Dec 19, 1793 from Hancock, Wilkes, Richmond, and Columbus counties. **Name Origin:** For Gen. Joseph Warren (1741-75), Revolutionary War patriot and member of the Committee of Safety who dispatched Paul Revere (1735-1818) on his famous ride.

Area (sq mi): 286.74 (land 285.52; water 1.22).

Pop: 6,336 (White 39.2%; Black or African American 59.5%; Hispanic or Latino 0.8%; Asian 0.1%; Other 1%). **Foreign born:** 0.5%. **Median age:** 37.8. **State rank:** 148. **Pop change 1990-2000:** +4.2%.

Income: per capita $14,022; median household $27,366. **Pop below poverty level:** 27%.

Unemployment: 10.2%. **Median home value:** $48,700. **Median travel time to work:** 27.9 minutes.

WASHINGTON COUNTY
PO Box 271   **Ph:** 478-552-2325
Sandersville, GA 31082   **Fax:** 478-552-7424

In east-central GA, east of Macon; organized Feb 25, 1784 (prior to statehood) from Indian lands. **Name Origin:** For George Washington (1732-99), American patriot and first U.S. president.

Area (sq mi): 684.37 (land 680.34; water 4.03).

Pop: 21,176 (White 45.4%; Black or African American 53.2%; Hispanic or Latino 0.6%; Asian 0.3%; Other 0.8%). **Foreign born:** 0.5%. **Median age:** 35.6. **State rank:** 80. **Pop change 1990-2000:** +10.8%.

Income: per capita $15,565; median household $29,910. **Pop below poverty level:** 22.9%.

Unemployment: 4.9%. **Median home value:** $66,900. **Median travel time to work:** 23.9 minutes.

WAYNE COUNTY
PO Box 270   **Ph:** 912-427-5900
Jesup, GA 31598   **Fax:** 912-427-5906
www.co.wayne.ga.us

In southeastern GA, northwest of Brunswick; original county; organized May 11, 1803 from Indian lands. **Name Origin:** For Gen. Anthony Wayne (1745-96), PA soldier and statesman; nicknamed 'Mad Anthony' for his daring during the Revolutionary War.

Area (sq mi): 648.8 (land 644.66; water 4.13).

Pop: 26,565 (White 74.7%; Black or African American 20.3%; Hispanic or Latino 3.8%; Asian 0.4%; Other 2.5%). **Foreign born:** 1.5%. **Median age:** 35.5. **State rank:** 55. **Pop change 1990-2000:** +18.8%.

Income: per capita $15,628; median household $32,766. **Pop below poverty level:** 16.7%.

Unemployment: 5.2%. **Median home value:** $71,200. **Median travel time to work:** 26.2 minutes.

WEBSTER COUNTY
PO Box 29   **Ph:** 229-828-5775
Preston, GA 31824   **Fax:** 229-828-2105

In west-central GA, southeast of Columbus; organized as Kinchafoonee County Dec 16, 1853 from Stewart County; name changed Feb 21, 1856. Originally named for the creek that runs through the county; from Creek 'nutcracker.' **Name Origin:** For Daniel Webster (1782-1852), U.S. statesman and orator from MA.

Area (sq mi): 210.26 (land 209.54; water 0.72).

Pop: 2,390 (White 49.6%; Black or African American 47%; Hispanic or Latino 2.8%; Asian 0%; Other 2.5%). **Foreign born:** 2%. **Median age:** 37.5. **State rank:** 158. **Pop change 1990-2000:** +5.6%.

Income: per capita $14,772; median household $27,992. **Pop below poverty level:** 19.3%.

Unemployment: 4.8%. **Median home value:** $49,300. **Median travel time to work:** 24.7 minutes.

WHEELER COUNTY
PO Box 181   **Ph:** 912-568-7135
Alamo, GA 30411   **Fax:** 912-568-1909

In central GA, west of Savannah; organized Aug 14, 1912 from Montgomery County. **Name Origin:** For Joseph Wheeler (1836-1906), Confederate general, author, and U.S. representative from AL (1881-82; 1883; 1885-1900).

Area (sq mi): 300.14 (land 297.72; water 2.42).

Pop: 6,179 (White 62.6%; Black or African American 33.2%; Hispanic or Latino 3.5%; Asian 0.1%; Other 2.1%). **Foreign born:** 1.9%. **Median age:** 36.1. **State rank:** 150. **Pop change 1990-2000:** +26%.

Income: per capita $13,005; median household $24,053. **Pop below poverty level:** 25.3%.

Unemployment: 10.4%. **Median home value:** $49,800. **Median travel time to work:** 29.9 minutes.

WHITE COUNTY
59 S Main St Suite A   **Ph:** 706-865-2235
Cleveland, GA 30528   **Fax:** 706-865-1324
www.whitecounty.net

In northeastern GA, northwest of Athens; organized Dec 22, 1857 from Habersham County. **Name Origin:** Believed to be for David Thomas White (1812-71), supporter of a bill to create the county. Some claim Col. John White, a hero of the American Revolution.

Area (sq mi): 242.16 (land 241.58; water 0.58).

Pop: 19,944 (White 94.3%; Black or African American 2.2%; Hispanic or Latino 1.6%; Asian 0.5%; Other 2.2%). **Foreign born:** 2%. **Median age:** 38.3. **State rank:** 84. **Pop change 1990-2000:** +53.3%.

Income: per capita $17,193; median household $36,084. **Pop below poverty level:** 10.5%.

Unemployment: 3.3%. **Median home value:** $114,000. **Median travel time to work:** 29.6 minutes.

Please see sample entry on inside front cover for detailed information about the statistics presented with each county listing.

WHITFIELD COUNTY

PO Box 248
Dalton, GA 30722
www.whitfieldcountyga.com

Ph: 706-275-7500
Fax: 706-275-7501

On northern border of GA, northeast of Rome; organized Dec 20, 1851 from Murray County. **Name Origin:** For the Rev. George Whitefield (1714-70), prominent Church of England clergyman who established Bethesda, one of the first orphanages in the U.S. Spelling changed by clerical error.

Area (sq mi): 290.65 (land 289.99; water 0.66).

Pop: 83,525 (White 72.2%; Black or African American 3.8%; Hispanic or Latino 22.1%; Asian 0.9%; Other 14.3%). **Foreign born:** 16.6%. **Median age:** 33. **State rank:** 24. **Pop change 1990-2000:** +15.3%.

Income: per capita $18,515; median household $39,377. **Pop below poverty level:** 11.5%.

Unemployment: 4.2%. **Median home value:** $91,800. **Median travel time to work:** 20.8 minutes.

WILCOX COUNTY

103 N Broad St
Abbeville, GA 31001

Ph: 229-467-2737
Fax: 229-467-2000

In central GA, northeast of Albany; organized Dec 22, 1857 from Dooly, Irwin, and Pulaski counties. **Name Origin:** Either for the Abbeville District of SC, or for the wife of David Fitzgerald, who donated the land for the county seat.

Area (sq mi): 383.3 (land 380.3; water 3).

Pop: 8,577 (White 61.8%; Black or African American 36.2%; Hispanic or Latino 1.6%; Asian 0.2%; Other 1%). **Foreign born:** 0.8%. **Median age:** 36.7. **State rank:** 135. **Pop change 1990-2000:** +22.4%.

Income: per capita $14,014; median household $27,483. **Pop below poverty level:** 21%.

Unemployment: 5.6%. **Median home value:** $51,400. **Median travel time to work:** 26 minutes.

WILKES COUNTY

23 E Court St Rm 222
Washington, GA 30673
www.washingtonwilkes.org

Ph: 706-678-2511
Fax: 706-678-3033

In eastern GA, southeast of Athens; organized Feb 5, 1777 (prior to statehood) from original territory. **Name Origin:** For John Wilkes (1725-97), member of the British House of Commons who supported the American colonies before the Revolutionary War.

Area (sq mi): 474 (land 471.37; water 2.62).

Pop: 10,687 (White 53.9%; Black or African American 43.1%; Hispanic or Latino 2%; Asian 0.2%; Other 1.6%). **Foreign born:** 1.3%. **Median age:** 39. **State rank:** 120. **Pop change 1990-2000:** +0.8%.

Income: per capita $15,020; median household $27,644. **Pop below poverty level:** 17.5%.

Unemployment: 10.2%. **Median home value:** $65,100. **Median travel time to work:** 21.6 minutes.

WILKINSON COUNTY

PO Box 161
Irwinton, GA 31042
www.accucomm.net/~wilcoboc/

Ph: 478-946-2236
Fax: 478-946-3767

In central GA, east of Macon; original county; organized May 11, 1803 from Creek cession. **Name Origin:** For James Wilkinson (1757-1825), officer under Washington, negotiated for the Louisiana Purchase, and first governor of the Louisiana Territory.

Area (sq mi): 452.01 (land 446.56; water 5.45).

Pop: 10,220 (White 57.7%; Black or African American 40.7%; Hispanic or Latino 1%; Asian 0.1%; Other 1.3%). **Foreign born:** 1.4%. **Median age:** 35.8. **State rank:** 125. **Pop change 1990-2000:** -0.1%.

Income: per capita $14,658; median household $32,723. **Pop below poverty level:** 17.9%.

Unemployment: 4.7%. **Median home value:** $61,500. **Median travel time to work:** 28.6 minutes.

WORTH COUNTY

201 N Main St Rm 30
Sylvester, GA 31791
www.worthcounty.com

Ph: 229-776-8200
Fax: 229-776-8232

In southwest-central GA, east of Albany; organized Dec 20, 1853 from Dooly and Irwin counties. **Name Origin:** For William Jenkins Worth (1794-1849), general during the Mexican War, cited by Congress for bravery.

Area (sq mi): 574.58 (land 569.73; water 4.86).

Pop: 21,967 (White 68.3%; Black or African American 29.6%; Hispanic or Latino 1.1%; Asian 0.2%; Other 1.6%). **Foreign born:** 1%. **Median age:** 35.7. **State rank:** 76. **Pop change 1990-2000:** +11.3%.

Income: per capita $15,856; median household $32,384. **Pop below poverty level:** 18.5%.

Unemployment: 6%. **Median home value:** $68,000. **Median travel time to work:** 24.8 minutes.

All statistics are based on the 2000 Census except the dollar figures given for per capita income, which are based on 1999 estimates.

HAWAII - Counties

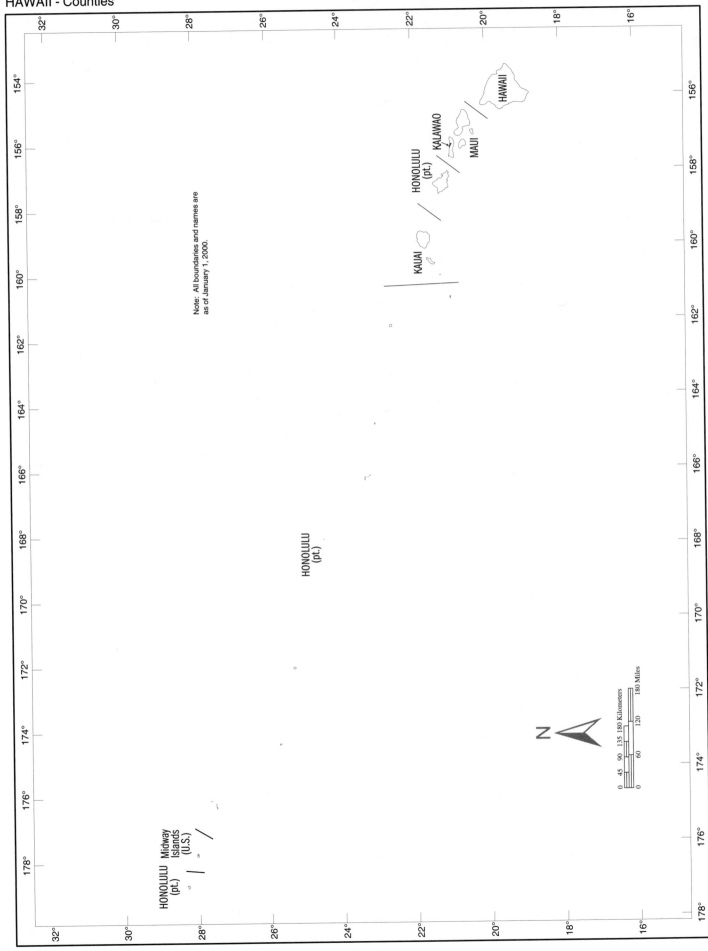

Note: All boundaries and names are as of January 1, 2000.

HONOLULU (pt.)

Midway Islands (U.S.)

KAUAI

HONOLULU (pt.)

KALAWAO

MAUI

HAWAII

N

0 45 90 135 180 Kilometers
0 60 120 180 Miles

Hawaii

HAWAII STATE INFORMATION

www.hawaii.gov   **Ph:** 808-586-2211

Area (sq mi): 10,930.98 (land 6422.62; water 4508.36).

Pop: 1,211,537 (White 22.9%; Black or African American 1.8%; Hispanic or Latino 7.2%; Asian 41.6%; Other 32.4%). **Foreign born:** 17.5%. **Median age:** 36.2. **Pop change 1990-2000:** +9.3%.

Income: per capita $21,525; median household $49,820. **Pop below poverty level:** 10.7%.

Unemployment: 3.6%. **Median home value:** $272,700. **Median travel time to work:** 26.1 minutes.

HAWAII COUNTY

25 Aupuni St Rm 209   **Ph:** 808-961-8255
Hilo, HI 96720   **Fax:** 808-961-8912
www.hawaii-county.com

Southernmost of the Islands, bordered on the north by Alenuihaha Channel; county is coextensive with the island. Established 1905 (prior to statehood). **Name Origin:** In Hawaii the name has no meaning, but in the rest of Polynesia it is the name of the underworld or of the ancestral home. Sometimes translated as 'beyond the doors of death.' Called the 'Big Island.'

Area (sq mi): 5086.7 (land 4028.02; water 1058.69).

Pop: 148,677 (White 29.7%; Black or African American 0.5%; Hispanic or Latino 9.5%; Asian 26.7%; Other 41.1%). **Foreign born:** 10.2%. **Median age:** 38.6. **State rank:** 2. **Pop change 1990-2000:** +23.6%.

Income: per capita $18,791; median household $39,805. **Pop below poverty level:** 15.7%.

Unemployment: 6.8%. **Median home value:** $153,700. **Median travel time to work:** 24.5 minutes.

HONOLULU COUNTY

530 S King St   **Ph:** 808-523-4352
Honolulu, HI 96813   **Fax:** 808-527-6888
www.co.honolulu.hi.us

Between the islands of Kauai and Molokai; bordered on west by Kauai Channel and on southeast by Kaiwi Channel. Established 1905 (prior to statehood); legally the City and County of Honolulu with one municipal government; includes the islands of Oahu and small ones northwest of Kauai. About 80% of the state's population lives in Honolulu County. **Name Origin:** From two Polynesian words, *hono* 'fair haven' and *lulu* 'calm' or 'quiet,' referring to Mamala Bay, into which Pearl Harbor opens.

Area (sq mi): 2126.85 (land 599.77; water 1527.08).

Pop: 876,156 (White 20%; Black or African American 2.4%; Hispanic or Latino 6.7%; Asian 46%; Other 30.3%). **Foreign born:** 19.2%. **Median age:** 35.7. **State rank:** 1. **Pop change 1990-2000:** +4.8%.

Income: per capita $21,998; median household $51,914. **Pop below poverty level:** 9.9%.

Unemployment: 4.1%. **Median home value:** $309,000. **Median travel time to work:** 27.3 minutes.

KALAWAO COUNTY

On the island of Molokai, southeast of the island of Oahu. Established 1905 (prior to statehood); has no county government for statistical purposes is considered as one of the judicial districts of Maui County. Site of a colony for victims of leprosy or Hansen's disease; administered by the state department of health. **Name Origin:** From the Polynesian meaning 'mountain area.'

Area (sq mi): 52.33 (land 13.21; water 39.12).

Pop: 147 (White 22.4%; Black or African American 0%; Hispanic or Latino 4.1%; Asian 17%; Other 57.1%). **Foreign born:** 20.4%. **Median age:** 58.6. **State rank:** 5. **Pop change 1990-2000:** +13.1%.

Income: per capita $13,756; median household $9,333. **Pop below poverty level:** 40.1%.

Median travel time to work: 12.9 minutes.

KAUAI COUNTY

4396 Rice St Rm 206   **Ph:** 808-241-6371
Lihue, HI 96766   **Fax:** 808-241-6349
www.kauaigov.org

Westernmost of the Islands; county includes Kauai and Niihau islands; bordered on east by Kauai Channel. Established 1905 (prior to statehood). **Name Origin:** From the Polynesian meaning 'drying place.'

Area (sq mi): 1266.37 (land 622.44; water 643.93).

Pop: 58,463 (White 27.9%; Black or African American 0.3%; Hispanic or Latino 8.2%; Asian 36%; Other 34.2%). **Foreign born:** 13%. **Median age:** 38.4. **State rank:** 4. **Pop change 1990-2000:** +14.2%.

Income: per capita $20,301; median household $45,020. **Pop below poverty level:** 10.5%.

Unemployment: 7%. **Median home value:** $216,100. **Median travel time to work:** 21.5 minutes.

Please see sample entry on inside front cover for detailed information about the statistics presented with each county listing.

MAUI COUNTY
200 S High St
Wailuku, HI 96793
www.co.maui.hi.us

Ph: 808-270-7748
Fax: 808-270-7171

Separated from Hawaii County to the southeast by Alenuihaha Channel and from Honolulu to the northwest by Kaiwi Channel. Established 1905 (prior to statehood). Includes Molokai, Lanai, Kahoolawe, and Maui islands. **Name Origin:** A Polynesian demigod.

Area (sq mi): 2398.74 (land 1159.2; water 1239.54).

Pop: 128,094 (White 31.9%; Black or African American 0.4%; Hispanic or Latino 7.8%; Asian 31%; Other 34.7%). **Foreign born:** 16.5%. **Median age:** 36.8. **State rank:** 3. **Pop change 1990-2000:** +27.6%.

Income: per capita $22,033; median household $49,489. **Pop below poverty level:** 10.5%.

Unemployment: 4.8%. **Median home value:** $249,900. **Median travel time to work:** 21.7 minutes.

All statistics are based on the 2000 Census except the dollar figures given for per capita income, which are based on 1999 estimates.

IDAHO - Counties

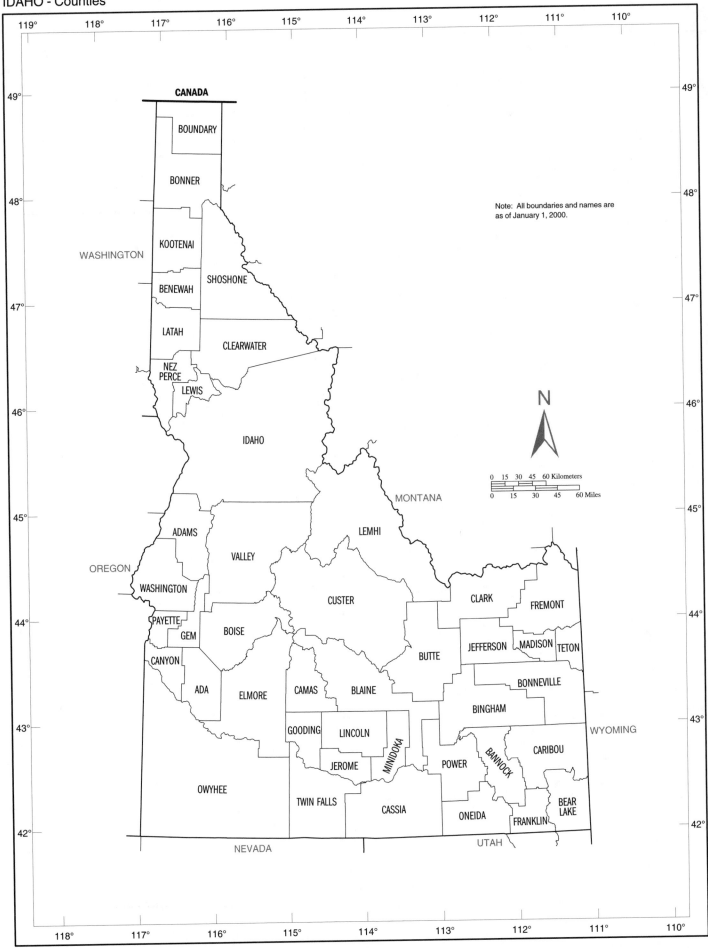

CANADA

BOUNDARY

BONNER

WASHINGTON

KOOTENAI

BENEWAH

LATAH

SHOSHONE

NEZ PERCE

LEWIS

CLEARWATER

IDAHO

Note: All boundaries and names are as of January 1, 2000.

MONTANA

N

0   15   30   45   60 Kilometers
0   15   30   45   60 Miles

OREGON

ADAMS

VALLEY

LEMHI

WASHINGTON

CUSTER

CLARK

FREMONT

PAYETTE

GEM

BOISE

BUTTE

JEFFERSON

MADISON

TETON

CANYON

BONNEVILLE

ADA

ELMORE

CAMAS

BLAINE

BINGHAM

WYOMING

GOODING

LINCOLN

MINIDOKA

POWER

BANNOCK

CARIBOU

JEROME

OWYHEE

TWIN FALLS

CASSIA

ONEIDA

FRANKLIN

BEAR LAKE

NEVADA

UTAH

Idaho

IDAHO STATE INFORMATION

www.accessidaho.org **Ph:** 208-334-2411

Area (sq mi): 83,570.08 (land 82,747.21; water 822.87).

Pop: 1,293,953 (White 88%; Black or African American 0.4%; Hispanic or Latino 7.9%; Asian 0.9%; Other 7.7%). **Foreign born:** 5%. **Median age:** 33.2. **Pop change 1990-2000:** +28.5%.

Income: per capita $17,841; median household $37,572. **Pop below poverty level:** 11.8%.

Unemployment: 5.7%. **Median home value:** $106,300. **Median travel time to work:** 20 minutes.

ADA COUNTY

200 W Front St **Ph:** 208-287-7000
Boise, ID 83702 **Fax:** 208-287-7009
www.adaweb.net

In southwestern ID; organized Dec 22, 1864 (prior to statehood) from Boise County. **Name Origin:** For Ada Riggs (1863-?), the first white child born in Boise, daughter of H. C. Riggs.

Area (sq mi): 1060.33 (land 1054.99; water 5.34).

Pop: 300,904 (White 90.6%; Black or African American 0.6%; Hispanic or Latino 4.5%; Asian 1.7%; Other 4.7%). **Foreign born:** 4.3%. **Median age:** 32.8. **State rank:** 1. **Pop change 1990-2000:** +46.2%.

Income: per capita $22,519; median household $46,140. **Pop below poverty level:** 7.7%.

Unemployment: 3.5%. **Median home value:** $124,700. **Median travel time to work:** 19.3 minutes.

ADAMS COUNTY

PO Box 48 **Ph:** 208-253-4561
Council, ID 83612 **Fax:** 208-253-4880
www.co.adams.id.us

On the central western border of ID, north of Boise; organized Mar 3, 1911 from Washington County. **Name Origin:** For John Adams (1735-1826), second U.S. president.

Area (sq mi): 1370 (land 1364.58; water 5.43).

Pop: 3,476 (White 95.5%; Black or African American 0.1%; Hispanic or Latino 1.6%; Asian 0.1%; Other 3.5%). **Foreign born:** 1.7%. **Median age:** 44.4. **State rank:** 41. **Pop change 1990-2000:** +6.8%.

Income: per capita $14,908; median household $28,423. **Pop below poverty level:** 15.1%.

Unemployment: 13.5%. **Median home value:** $88,800. **Median travel time to work:** 22.2 minutes.

BANNOCK COUNTY

PO Box 4016 **Ph:** 208-236-7210
Pocatello, ID 83205 **Fax:** 208-236-7363
www.co.bannock.id.us

In southeastern ID; organized Mar 6, 1893 from Bingham County. **Name Origin:** For the Bannack Indians whose name in Shoshonean means 'hair in backward motion,' for their habit of wearing a lock of hair tossed back over their heads. Early settlers spelled the name 'Bannock,' with an 'o' instead of an 'a'.

Area (sq mi): 1147.46 (land 1113.3; water 34.16).

Pop: 75,565 (White 89.5%; Black or African American 0.6%; Hispanic or Latino 4.7%; Asian 1%; Other 7.2%). **Foreign born:** 2.2%. **Median age:** 29.8. **State rank:** 5. **Pop change 1990-2000:** +14.4%.

Income: per capita $17,148; median household $36,683. **Pop below poverty level:** 13.9%.

Unemployment: 4.7%. **Median home value:** $90,000. **Median travel time to work:** 17.2 minutes.

BEAR LAKE COUNTY

PO Box 190 **Ph:** 208-945-2212
Paris, ID 83261 **Fax:** 208-945-2780

On the southeastern border of ID, southeast of Pocatello; organized Jan 5, 1875 from Oneida County. **Name Origin:** For Bear Lake, which lies half in ID and half in UT.

Area (sq mi): 1049.44 (land 971.38; water 78.05).

Pop: 6,411 (White 96.6%; Black or African American 0.1%; Hispanic or Latino 2.4%; Asian 0.1%; Other 2.1%). **Foreign born:** 1.1%. **Median age:** 35.8. **State rank:** 35. **Pop change 1990-2000:** +5.4%.

Income: per capita $13,592; median household $32,162. **Pop below poverty level:** 9.6%.

Unemployment: 5%. **Median home value:** $72,600. **Median travel time to work:** 21.3 minutes.

BENEWAH COUNTY

701 College Ave **Ph:** 208-245-2234
Saint Maries, ID 83861 **Fax:** 208-245-3046

On the western border of ID, southeast of Spokane, WA; organized Jan 23, 1915 from Kootenai County. **Name Origin:** For Benewah, a chief of the Coeur d'Alene Indian tribe.

Area (sq mi): 783.98 (land 776.07; water 7.91).

Please see sample entry on inside front cover for detailed information about the statistics presented with each county listing.

Pop: 9,171 (White 87.8%; Black or African American 0.1%; Hispanic or Latino 1.5%; Asian 0.2%; Other 11.1%). **Foreign born:** 0.6%. **Median age:** 39.2. **State rank:** 28. **Pop change 1990-2000:** +15.5%.

Income: per capita $15,285; median household $31,517. **Pop below poverty level:** 14.1%.

Unemployment: 10.2%. **Median home value:** $89,000. **Median travel time to work:** 19.2 minutes.

BINGHAM COUNTY

501 N Maple St Suite 205   **Ph:** 208-785-5005
Blackfoot, ID 83221   **Fax:** 208-785-4131
www.co.bingham.id.us

In southeastern ID, south of Idaho Falls; organized Jan 13, 1885 (prior to statehood) from Oneida County. **Name Origin:** By ID Territorial Governor William M. Bunn for his friend Henry Harrison Bingham (1841-1912), U.S. representative from PA (1879-1912) and a former Union officer who was awarded the Congressional Medal of Honor in 1864.

Area (sq mi): 2120.24 (land 2094.73; water 25.51).

Pop: 41,735 (White 78.6%; Black or African American 0.2%; Hispanic or Latino 13.3%; Asian 0.6%; Other 16.8%). **Foreign born:** 6.1%. **Median age:** 29.7. **State rank:** 7. **Pop change 1990-2000:** +11%.

Income: per capita $14,365; median household $36,423. **Pop below poverty level:** 12.4%.

Unemployment: 4.6%. **Median home value:** $84,400. **Median travel time to work:** 21.2 minutes.

BLAINE COUNTY

206 1st Ave S Suite 200   **Ph:** 208-788-5505
Hailey, ID 83333   **Fax:** 208-788-5501
www.co.blaine.id.us

In south-central ID, west of Pocatello; organized Mar 5, 1895 from Alturas County, which was organized in 1864 and abolished in 1895, and from Logan County, which was organized in 1889 and abolished in 1895. **Name Origin:** For James Gillespie Blaine (1830-93), U.S. representative from ME (1863-76), U.S. senator (1876-81), and U.S. secretary of state (1881; 1889-92).

Area (sq mi): 2661.02 (land 2644.78; water 16.24).

Pop: 18,991 (White 87%; Black or African American 0.1%; Hispanic or Latino 10.7%; Asian 0.7%; Other 8.4%). **Foreign born:** 10.6%. **Median age:** 37.4. **State rank:** 17. **Pop change 1990-2000:** +40.1%.

Income: per capita $31,346; median household $50,496. **Pop below poverty level:** 7.8%.

Unemployment: 2.9%. **Median home value:** $288,800. **Median travel time to work:** 18.7 minutes.

BOISE COUNTY

420 Main St   **Ph:** 208-392-4431
Idaho City, ID 83631   **Fax:** 208-392-4473
www.co.boise.id.us

In west-central ID, northeast of Boise; original county, established Feb 4, 1864. **Name Origin:** For the Boise River, which forms part of its eastern border from French *boise* 'woods.'

Area (sq mi): 1906.76 (land 1902.46; water 4.3).

Pop: 6,670 (White 93.3%; Black or African American 0.1%; Hispanic or Latino 3.4%; Asian 0.3%; Other 4.3%). **Foreign born:** 2.4%. **Median age:** 40.4. **State rank:** 34. **Pop change 1990-2000:** +90.1%.

Income: per capita $18,787; median household $38,651. **Pop below poverty level:** 12.9%.

Unemployment: 5%. **Median home value:** $126,000. **Median travel time to work:** 37.5 minutes.

BONNER COUNTY

215 S 1st Ave   **Ph:** 208-265-1432
Sandpoint, ID 83864   **Fax:** 208-265-1447
www.co.bonner.id.us

In the north of the ID panhandle, northeast of Spokane, WA; organized Feb 21, 1907 from Kootenai County. **Name Origin:** For Edwin L. Bonner, an early settler of northern ID who operated a ferry on the Kootenai River.

Area (sq mi): 1919.59 (land 1737.67; water 181.92).

Pop: 36,835 (White 95.6%; Black or African American 0.1%; Hispanic or Latino 1.6%; Asian 0.3%; Other 3%). **Foreign born:** 2%. **Median age:** 40.8. **State rank:** 9. **Pop change 1990-2000:** +38.4%.

Income: per capita $17,263; median household $32,803. **Pop below poverty level:** 15.5%.

Unemployment: 8.1%. **Median home value:** $124,500. **Median travel time to work:** 25.5 minutes.

BONNEVILLE COUNTY

605 N Capital Ave   **Ph:** 208-529-1354
Idaho Falls, ID 83402
www.co.bonneville.id.us

On the southeastern border of ID, northeast of Pocatello; organized Feb 7, 1911 from Bingham County. **Name Origin:** For Benjamin Louis Eulalie de Bonneville (1796-1878), French-born officer in the Mexican-American War and explorer of California and the Rocky Mountains region (1831-31); immortalized in the *Adventures of Captain Bonneville* (1837) by Washington Irving (1783-1859).

Area (sq mi): 1900.65 (land 1868.48; water 32.18).

Pop: 82,522 (White 90.2%; Black or African American 0.5%; Hispanic or Latino 6.9%; Asian 0.8%; Other 5.9%). **Foreign born:** 3.9%. **Median age:** 31.8. **State rank:** 4. **Pop change 1990-2000:** +14.3%.

Income: per capita $18,326; median household $41,805. **Pop below poverty level:** 10.1%.

Unemployment: 3.3%. **Median home value:** $93,500. **Median travel time to work:** 19.6 minutes.

BOUNDARY COUNTY

PO Box 419   **Ph:** 208-267-5504
Bonners Ferry, ID 83805   **Fax:** 208-267-7814
www.boundary-idaho.com

On the northern boundary of the ID panhandle; organized Jan 23, 1915 from Kootenai and Bonner counties. **Name Origin:** Because it borders Canada on the north, MT on the east, and WA on the west.

All statistics are based on the 2000 Census except the dollar figures given for per capita income, which are based on 1999 estimates.

Area (sq mi): 1278.21 (land 1268.81; water 9.4).

Pop: 9,871 (White 93.2%; Black or African American 0.2%; Hispanic or Latino 3.4%; Asian 0.6%; Other 4.1%). **Foreign born:** 2.9%. **Median age:** 38.3. **State rank:** 27. **Pop change 1990-2000:** +18.5%.

Income: per capita $14,636; median household $31,250. **Pop below poverty level:** 15.7%.

Unemployment: 9.1%. **Median home value:** $96,900. **Median travel time to work:** 21.5 minutes.

BUTTE COUNTY
PO Box 737   **Ph:** 208-527-3021
Arco, ID 83213   **Fax:** 208-527-3295

In east-central ID, west of Idaho Falls; organized Feb 6, 1917 from Bingham, Blaine, and Jefferson counties. **Name Origin:** For the landmark buttes rising from the Snake River plains.

Area (sq mi): 2233.59 (land 2232.85; water 0.74).

Pop: 2,899 (White 93.3%; Black or African American 0.3%; Hispanic or Latino 4.1%; Asian 0.2%; Other 4.9%). **Foreign born:** 3.9%. **Median age:** 38.8. **State rank:** 42. **Pop change 1990-2000:** -0.7%.

Income: per capita $14,948; median household $30,473. **Pop below poverty level:** 18.2%.

Unemployment: 3.9%. **Median home value:** $68,700. **Median travel time to work:** 22.2 minutes.

CAMAS COUNTY
PO Box 430   **Ph:** 208-764-2242
Fairfield, ID 83327   **Fax:** 208-764-2349

In south-central ID, east of Boise; organized Feb 6, 1917 from Blaine County. **Name Origin:** From the Chinook name for the camas, an edible root of the lily family.

Area (sq mi): 1079.02 (land 1074.96; water 4.06).

Pop: 991 (White 91.8%; Black or African American 1.2%; Hispanic or Latino 5.5%; Asian 0.2%; Other 3.4%). **Foreign born:** 1.8%. **Median age:** 39.7. **State rank:** 44. **Pop change 1990-2000:** +36.3%.

Income: per capita $19,550; median household $34,167. **Pop below poverty level:** 8.3%.

Unemployment: 5%. **Median home value:** $86,400. **Median travel time to work:** 29 minutes.

CANYON COUNTY
1115 Albany St   **Ph:** 208-454-7574
Caldwell, ID 83605   **Fax:** 208-454-7525
www.canyoncounty.org

On the southwestern border of ID, west of Boise; established Mar 7, 1891 from Ada County. **Name Origin:** Either for the canyon of the Boise River near Caldwell, or the Snake River canyon, which forms a county boundary.

Area (sq mi): 603.51 (land 589.72; water 13.79).

Pop: 131,441 (White 77.9%; Black or African American 0.3%; Hispanic or Latino 18.6%; Asian 0.8%; Other 15.8%). **Foreign born:** 8.6%. **Median age:** 30.5. **State rank:** 2. **Pop change 1990-2000:** +45.9%.

Income: per capita $15,155; median household $35,884. **Pop below poverty level:** 12%.

Unemployment: 5.3%. **Median home value:** $96,300. **Median travel time to work:** 22.3 minutes.

CARIBOU COUNTY
PO Box 775   **Ph:** 208-547-4324
Soda Springs, ID 83276   **Fax:** 208-547-4759

On the southeastern border of ID, east of Pocatello; organized Feb 11, 1919 from Bannock and Oneida counties. **Name Origin:** For 'Caribou (Cariboo)' Fairchild, active in mining in ID; nickname acquired in the Cariboo mine fields of British Columbia, Canada.

Area (sq mi): 1798.62 (land 1766.01; water 32.61).

Pop: 7,304 (White 94.9%; Black or African American 0.1%; Hispanic or Latino 4%; Asian 0.1%; Other 3.7%). **Foreign born:** 1.8%. **Median age:** 35. **State rank:** 33. **Pop change 1990-2000:** +4.9%.

Income: per capita $15,179; median household $37,609. **Pop below poverty level:** 9.6%.

Unemployment: 5.8%. **Median home value:** $80,400. **Median travel time to work:** 19.1 minutes.

CASSIA COUNTY
1459 Overland Ave   **Ph:** 208-878-7302
Burley, ID 83318   **Fax:** 208-878-9109
www.cassiacounty.org

On the central southern border of ID, east of Twin Falls; organized Feb 20, 1879 (prior to statehood) from Oneida County. **Name Origin:** For Cassia Creek (spelled Cassier in 1879), named either from French *cajeaux* 'raft,' for for James John Cazier, member of the Mormon Battalion and a colorful wagon train leader. Locals also believe it is for the cassia plant.

Area (sq mi): 2580.31 (land 2566.45; water 13.86).

Pop: 21,416 (White 79.3%; Black or African American 0.2%; Hispanic or Latino 18.7%; Asian 0.4%; Other 14.9%). **Foreign born:** 7.3%. **Median age:** 31.1. **State rank:** 13. **Pop change 1990-2000:** +9.6%.

Income: per capita $14,087; median household $33,322. **Pop below poverty level:** 13.6%.

Unemployment: 5.5%. **Median home value:** $83,100. **Median travel time to work:** 16.3 minutes.

CLARK COUNTY
320 W Main St   **Ph:** 208-374-5402
Dubois, ID 83423   **Fax:** 208-374-5609

On lower northern border of ID, north of Idaho Falls; organized Feb 1, 1919 from Fremont County. **Name Origin:** For Sam K. Clark, an early settler on Medicine Lodge Creek, and first state senator from the county.

Area (sq mi): 1765.21 (land 1764.63; water 0.58).

Pop: 1,022 (White 63.9%; Black or African American 0.1%; Hispanic or Latino 34.2%; Asian 0.2%; Other 25.6%). **Foreign born:** 28.2%. **Median age:** 30.7. **State rank:** 43. **Pop change 1990-2000:** +34.1%.

Please see sample entry on inside front cover for detailed information about the statistics presented with each county listing.

Income: per capita $11,141; median household $31,576. **Pop below poverty level:** 19.9%.

Unemployment: 4.4%. **Median home value:** $64,600. **Median travel time to work:** 20.5 minutes.

CLEARWATER COUNTY

PO Box 586   **Ph:** 208-476-3615
Orofino, ID 83544   **Fax:** 208-476-3127

On the eastern border of the ID panhandle, east of Lewiston; organized Feb 27, 1911 from Nez Perce County. **Name Origin:** For the Clearwater River, itself named for the translation of the Nez Perce descriptive name.

Area (sq mi): 2488.1 (land 2461.4; water 26.7).

Pop: 8,930 (White 93.8%; Black or African American 0.1%; Hispanic or Latino 1.8%; Asian 0.4%; Other 4.7%). **Foreign born:** 1.2%. **Median age:** 41.7. **State rank:** 29. **Pop change 1990-2000:** +5%.

Income: per capita $15,463; median household $32,071. **Pop below poverty level:** 13.5%.

Unemployment: 14.9%. **Median home value:** $80,500. **Median travel time to work:** 23.5 minutes.

CUSTER COUNTY

801 Main St   **Ph:** 208-879-2360
Challis, ID 83226   **Fax:** 208-879-5246
www.co.custer.id.us

In central ID; organized Jan 8, 1881 (prior to statehood) from Alturas and Lemhi counties. **Name Origin:** For the General Custer mine, named for Gen. George Armstrong Custer (1839-76), U.S. officer and Indian fighter.

Area (sq mi): 4936.79 (land 4925.45; water 11.34).

Pop: 4,342 (White 94.4%; Black or African American 0%; Hispanic or Latino 4.2%; Asian 0%; Other 2.7%). **Foreign born:** 2.3%. **Median age:** 41.2. **State rank:** 37. **Pop change 1990-2000:** +5.1%.

Income: per capita $15,783; median household $32,174. **Pop below poverty level:** 14.3%.

Unemployment: 7.6%. **Median home value:** $90,400. **Median travel time to work:** 26.1 minutes.

ELMORE COUNTY

150 S 4th East St Suite 3   **Ph:** 208-587-2129
Mountain Home, ID 83647   **Fax:** 208-587-2159
www.elmorecounty.org

In southwestern ID, east of Boise; organized Feb 7, 1889 (prior to statehood) from Alturas County. **Name Origin:** For the Ida Elmore Quartz Mine, largest producer of gold and silver during the 1860s.

Area (sq mi): 3100.51 (land 3077.57; water 22.93).

Pop: 29,130 (White 79.7%; Black or African American 3.2%; Hispanic or Latino 12%; Asian 1.7%; Other 9.8%). **Foreign born:** 7.7%. **Median age:** 29.1. **State rank:** 11. **Pop change 1990-2000:** +37.4%.

Income: per capita $16,773; median household $35,256. **Pop below poverty level:** 11.2%.

Unemployment: 6%. **Median home value:** $93,200. **Median travel time to work:** 19.3 minutes.

FRANKLIN COUNTY

39 W Oneida St   **Ph:** 208-852-1090
Preston, ID 83263   **Fax:** 208-852-1094

On the southern border of ID, southeast of Pocatello; organized Jan 30, 1913 from Oneida County. **Name Origin:** For the first settlement in ID, named for Franklin Dewey Richards (1821-99), a Mormon apostle.

Area (sq mi): 668.36 (land 665.43; water 2.92).

Pop: 11,329 (White 93.7%; Black or African American 0.1%; Hispanic or Latino 5.2%; Asian 0.1%; Other 4.6%). **Foreign born:** 3.4%. **Median age:** 27.7. **State rank:** 24. **Pop change 1990-2000:** +22.7%.

Income: per capita $13,702; median household $36,061. **Pop below poverty level:** 7.4%.

Unemployment: 3.9%. **Median home value:** $94,300. **Median travel time to work:** 23.3 minutes.

FREMONT COUNTY

151 W 1st North   **Ph:** 208-624-7332
Saint Anthony, ID 83445   **Fax:** 208-624-7335
www.co.fremont.id.us

On the lower northeastern border of ID, northeast of Idaho Falls; organized Mar 4, 1893 from Bingham County. **Name Origin:** For John Charles Fremont (1813-90), soldier and explorer who led five expeditions to the West, U.S. senator from CA (1850-51), and governor of the AZ Territory (1878-81).

Area (sq mi): 1895.59 (land 1866.76; water 28.84).

Pop: 11,819 (White 87.3%; Black or African American 0.2%; Hispanic or Latino 10.6%; Asian 0.4%; Other 8.1%). **Foreign born:** 7.3%. **Median age:** 31.9. **State rank:** 23. **Pop change 1990-2000:** +8.1%.

Income: per capita $13,965; median household $33,424. **Pop below poverty level:** 14.2%.

Unemployment: 6.5%. **Median home value:** $82,200. **Median travel time to work:** 22.4 minutes.

GEM COUNTY

415 E Main St   **Ph:** 208-365-4561
Emmett, ID 836173096   **Fax:** 208-365-6172
www.co.gem.id.us

In southwestern ID, north of Boise; organized Mar 19, 1915 from Boise and Canyon counties. **Name Origin:** For the state nickname, 'Gem State,' from the supposed Indian meaning of Idaho 'Gem of the Mountain.'

Area (sq mi): 565.75 (land 562.58; water 3.17).

Pop: 15,181 (White 90.7%; Black or African American 0.1%; Hispanic or Latino 6.9%; Asian 0.4%; Other 5.8%). **Foreign born:** 4.9%. **Median age:** 37.5. **State rank:** 20. **Pop change 1990-2000:** +28.2%.

Income: per capita $15,340; median household $34,460. **Pop below poverty level:** 13.1%.

All statistics are based on the 2000 Census except the dollar figures given for per capita income, which are based on 1999 estimates.

Unemployment: 7.9%. **Median home value:** $97,600. **Median travel time to work:** 26.9 minutes.

GOODING COUNTY

624 Main St	**Ph:** 208-934-4841
Gooding, ID 83330	**Fax:** 208-934-5085

In south-central ID, northwest of Twin Falls; organized Jan 28, 1913 from Lincoln County. **Name Origin:** For Frank Robert Gooding (1859-1928), governor of Idaho (1905-08) and U.S. senator (1921-28).

Area (sq mi): 733.84 (land 730.78; water 3.06).

Pop: 14,155 (White 80.3%; Black or African American 0.2%; Hispanic or Latino 17.1%; Asian 0.2%; Other 11.9%). **Foreign born:** 11.6%. **Median age:** 35.1. **State rank:** 21. **Pop change 1990-2000:** +21.7%.

Income: per capita $14,612; median household $31,888. **Pop below poverty level:** 13.8%.

Unemployment: 3.5%. **Median home value:** $82,500. **Median travel time to work:** 20.2 minutes.

IDAHO COUNTY

320 W Main St Rm 5	**Ph:** 208-983-2751
Grangeville, ID 83530	**Fax:** 208-983-1428
www.idahocounty.org	

At the southern base of the ID panhandle, east and south of Lewiston; original county; organized Feb 4, 1864 (prior to statehood). Originally established in 1861 as the third county of WA Territory, now in ID. **Name Origin:** For the steamer *Idaho*, launched Jun 9, 1860 on the Columbia River to serve miners in the gold rush.

Area (sq mi): 8502.48 (land 8484.88; water 17.59).

Pop: 15,511 (White 93.4%; Black or African American 0.1%; Hispanic or Latino 1.6%; Asian 0.3%; Other 5.5%). **Foreign born:** 1.2%. **Median age:** 42.3. **State rank:** 19. **Pop change 1990-2000:** +12.5%.

Income: per capita $14,411; median household $29,515. **Pop below poverty level:** 16.3%.

Unemployment: 9.5%. **Median home value:** $88,600. **Median travel time to work:** 18.4 minutes.

JEFFERSON COUNTY

134 N Clark PO Box 275	**Ph:** 208-745-7756
Rigby, ID 83442	**Fax:** 208-745-6636
www.co.jefferson.id.us	

In southeastern ID, north of Idaho Falls; organized Feb 18, 1913 from Fremont County. **Name Origin:** For Thomas Jefferson (1743-1826), U.S. patriot and statesman; third U.S. president.

Area (sq mi): 1105.55 (land 1095.08; water 10.47).

Pop: 19,155 (White 88.5%; Black or African American 0.3%; Hispanic or Latino 10%; Asian 0.2%; Other 8.7%). **Foreign born:** 5.9%. **Median age:** 28.8. **State rank:** 16. **Pop change 1990-2000:** +15.8%.

Income: per capita $13,838; median household $37,737. **Pop below poverty level:** 10.4%.

Unemployment: 3.7%. **Median home value:** $91,900. **Median travel time to work:** 25.2 minutes.

JEROME COUNTY

300 N Lincoln Ave Rm 301	**Ph:** 208-324-8811
Jerome, ID 83338	**Fax:** 208-324-2719
www.co.jerome.id.us	

In south-central ID, north of Twin Falls; organized Feb 18, 1919 from Gooding and Lincoln counties. **Name Origin:** Either for Jerome Hill, a principal figure in the Twin Falls North Side Irrigation Project (1905), or Jerome Kuhn, his son-in-law, or for Jerome Kuhn, Jr., his grandson. All were major figures in the growth of the county.

Area (sq mi): 601.87 (land 599.84; water 2.03).

Pop: 18,342 (White 80.6%; Black or African American 0.2%; Hispanic or Latino 17.2%; Asian 0.3%; Other 12.4%). **Foreign born:** 10.5%. **Median age:** 32.9. **State rank:** 18. **Pop change 1990-2000:** +21.2%.

Income: per capita $15,530; median household $34,696. **Pop below poverty level:** 13.9%.

Unemployment: 3.8%. **Median home value:** $89,800. **Median travel time to work:** 19.8 minutes.

KOOTENAI COUNTY

PO Box 9000	**Ph:** 208-769-4400
Coeur d'Alene, ID 83816	**Fax:** 208-666-1267
www.co.kootenai.id.us	

On the western border of the ID panhandle, east of Spokane, WA; original county; organized Dec 22, 1864 (prior to statehood). **Name Origin:** For the Kootenai (or Kutenai) Indian tribe, whose name means 'water people.'

Area (sq mi): 1315.69 (land 1245.12; water 70.57).

Pop: 108,685 (White 94.4%; Black or African American 0.2%; Hispanic or Latino 2.3%; Asian 0.5%; Other 3.5%). **Foreign born:** 2.4%. **Median age:** 36.1. **State rank:** 3. **Pop change 1990-2000:** +55.7%.

Income: per capita $18,430; median household $37,754. **Pop below poverty level:** 10.5%.

Unemployment: 7.6%. **Median home value:** $120,100. **Median travel time to work:** 21.7 minutes.

LATAH COUNTY

522 S Adams	**Ph:** 208-882-8580
Moscow, ID 83843	**Fax:** 208-883-7203
www.latah.id.us	

On the western border of the ID panhandle, north of Lewiston; organized May 14, 1888 (prior to statehood) from Kootenai County. **Name Origin:** For Latah Creek from a combination of two Nez Perce words, *lakah* 'place of the pines,' and *tah-ol* 'pestle.' The Indians found stones there to grind camas roots and shade in which to work.

Area (sq mi): 1076.89 (land 1076.65; water 0.24).

Pop: 34,935 (White 92.8%; Black or African American 0.6%; Hispanic or Latino 2.1%; Asian 2.1%; Other 3.4%). **Foreign born:**

Please see sample entry on inside front cover for detailed information about the statistics presented with each county listing.

4.3%. **Median age:** 27.9. **State rank:** 10. **Pop change 1990-2000:** +14.1%.

Income: per capita $16,690; median household $32,524. **Pop below poverty level:** 16.7%.

Unemployment: 3.3%. **Median home value:** $126,400. **Median travel time to work:** 17.9 minutes.

LEMHI COUNTY
206 Courthouse Dr   **Ph:** 208-756-2815
Salmon, ID 83467   **Fax:** 208-756-8424

On the central eastern border of ID; organized Mar 3, 1869 (prior to statehood) from Idaho County. **Name Origin:** For Fort Lemhi, a Mormon mission on the Salmon River, named for a character in the Book of Mormon.

Area (sq mi): 4569.5 (land 4564.16; water 5.35).

Pop: 7,806 (White 95.5%; Black or African American 0.1%; Hispanic or Latino 2.2%; Asian 0.2%; Other 3.1%). **Foreign born:** 1.5%. **Median age:** 42.7. **State rank:** 30. **Pop change 1990-2000:** +13.1%.

Income: per capita $16,037; median household $30,185. **Pop below poverty level:** 15.3%.

Unemployment: 7.6%. **Median home value:** $91,500. **Median travel time to work:** 17.5 minutes.

LEWIS COUNTY
PO Box 39   **Ph:** 208-937-2251
Nezperce, ID 83543   **Fax:** 208-937-9233

In central-western ID, southeast of Lewiston; organized Mar 3, 1911 from Nez Perce County. **Name Origin:** For Meriwether Lewis (1774-1809), co-leader of the Lewis and Clark expedition (1804-06).

Area (sq mi): 479.81 (land 479.04; water 0.77).

Pop: 3,747 (White 91.5%; Black or African American 0.3%; Hispanic or Latino 1.9%; Asian 0.4%; Other 7%). **Foreign born:** 1.1%. **Median age:** 42.5. **State rank:** 40. **Pop change 1990-2000:** +6.6%.

Income: per capita $15,942; median household $31,413. **Pop below poverty level:** 12%.

Unemployment: 7.5%. **Median home value:** $78,900. **Median travel time to work:** 21.3 minutes.

LINCOLN COUNTY
Drawer A   **Ph:** 208-886-7641
Shoshone, ID 83352   **Fax:** 208-886-2458

In south-central ID, north of Twin Falls; organized Mar 18, 1895 from Blaine County. **Name Origin:** For Abraham Lincoln (1809-65), sixteenth U.S. president.

Area (sq mi): 1205.86 (land 1205.53; water 0.33).

Pop: 4,044 (White 83.5%; Black or African American 0.5%; Hispanic or Latino 13.4%; Asian 0.4%; Other 12.5%). **Foreign born:** 10.1%. **Median age:** 34.3. **State rank:** 39. **Pop change 1990-2000:** +22.2%.

Income: per capita $14,257; median household $32,484. **Pop below poverty level:** 13.1%.

Unemployment: 3.9%. **Median home value:** $75,700. **Median travel time to work:** 30.4 minutes.

MADISON COUNTY
PO Box 389   **Ph:** 208-356-3662
Rexburg, ID 83440   **Fax:** 208-356-8396
www.co.madison.id.us

In southeastern ID, northeast of Idaho Falls; organized Feb 18, 1913 from Fremont County. **Name Origin:** For James Madison (1751-1836), fourth U.S. president.

Area (sq mi): 473.36 (land 471.52; water 1.84).

Pop: 27,467 (White 94.1%; Black or African American 0.2%; Hispanic or Latino 3.9%; Asian 0.6%; Other 3.7%). **Foreign born:** 3.5%. **Median age:** 20.7. **State rank:** 12. **Pop change 1990-2000:** +16%.

Income: per capita $10,956; median household $32,607. **Pop below poverty level:** 30.5%.

Unemployment: 2%. **Median home value:** $106,800. **Median travel time to work:** 14.7 minutes.

MINIDOKA COUNTY
PO Box 368   **Ph:** 208-436-7111
Rupert, ID 83350   **Fax:** 208-436-0737
www.minidoka.id.us

In south-central ID, west of Pocatello; organized Jan 28, 1913 from Lincoln County. **Name Origin:** For the first settlement, a railroad siding, from Shoshonean 'broad expanse,' descriptive of the Snake River plain in this area.

Area (sq mi): 762.98 (land 759.62; water 3.36).

Pop: 20,174 (White 72.1%; Black or African American 0.3%; Hispanic or Latino 25.5%; Asian 0.4%; Other 21.2%). **Foreign born:** 10.9%. **Median age:** 33.5. **State rank:** 15. **Pop change 1990-2000:** +4.2%.

Income: per capita $13,813; median household $32,021. **Pop below poverty level:** 14.8%.

Unemployment: 6.4%. **Median home value:** $74,600. **Median travel time to work:** 17.5 minutes.

NEZ PERCE COUNTY
PO Box 896   **Ph:** 208-799-3020
Lewiston, ID 83501   **Fax:** 208-799-3070
www.co.nezperce.id.us

On the western border of the ID panhandle; original county; organized Feb 4, 1864 (prior to statehood). It was previously established by WA Territory in 1861. **Name Origin:** From the French name 'pierced nose,' for an Indian tribe that called itself *Chopunnish*. The French term might be better translated as 'mashed' or 'flattened nose.'

Area (sq mi): 856.36 (land 849.08; water 7.28).

Pop: 37,410 (White 90.6%; Black or African American 0.3%; Hispanic or Latino 1.9%; Asian 0.7%; Other 7.5%). **Foreign born:** 1.9%. **Median age:** 38.1. **State rank:** 8. **Pop change 1990-2000:** +10.8%.

Income: per capita $18,544; median household $36,282. **Pop below poverty level:** 12.2%.

All statistics are based on the 2000 Census except the dollar figures given for per capita income, which are based on 1999 estimates.

Unemployment: 3.9%. **Median home value:** $105,800. **Median travel time to work:** 15.9 minutes.

ONEIDA COUNTY
10 Court St   **Ph:** 208-766-4116
Malad City, ID 83252   **Fax:** 208-766-2990
www.co.oneida.id.us

On the southern border of ID, south of Pocatello; original county; organized Jan 22, 1864 (prior to statehood). **Name Origin:** For Lake Oneida, NY, former home of early settlers, itself named for one of the Five Nations of the Iroquois. Name means 'stone people,' perhaps for their bravery.

Area (sq mi): 1201.61 (land 1200.33; water 1.28).

Pop: 4,125 (White 96.6%; Black or African American 0.1%; Hispanic or Latino 2.3%; Asian 0.1%; Other 2.3%). **Foreign born:** 2.1%. **Median age:** 36. **State rank:** 38. **Pop change 1990-2000:** +18.1%.

Income: per capita $13,829; median household $34,309. **Pop below poverty level:** 10.8%.

Unemployment: 3.6%. **Median home value:** $88,400. **Median travel time to work:** 26.4 minutes.

OWYHEE COUNTY
PO Box 128   **Ph:** 208-495-2421
Murphy, ID 83650   **Fax:** 208-495-1173
owyheecounty.net

On the southwestern border of ID, south of Boise; original county; organized Dec 31, 1863 (prior to statehood). **Name Origin:** For the Owyhee River, itself named for a corrupt spelling of Hawaii, in honor of three Hawaiians (Owyhee) who were hired to trade with the Indians; they disappeared and were presumed to have been killed.

Area (sq mi): 7696.71 (land 7677.98; water 18.72).

Pop: 10,644 (White 71.7%; Black or African American 0.2%; Hispanic or Latino 23.1%; Asian 0.5%; Other 22.5%). **Foreign born:** 11.9%. **Median age:** 32.9. **State rank:** 25. **Pop change 1990-2000:** +26.8%.

Income: per capita $13,405; median household $28,339. **Pop below poverty level:** 16.9%.

Unemployment: 4.5%. **Median home value:** $82,500. **Median travel time to work:** 25.6 minutes.

PAYETTE COUNTY
PO Drawer D   **Ph:** 208-642-6000
Payette, ID 83661   **Fax:** 208-642-6011

On western border of ID, northeast of Boise; organized Feb 28, 1917 from Canyon County. **Name Origin:** For the Payette River, which runs diagonally through the county; named for Francis Payette, Canadian fur trapper and explorer.

Area (sq mi): 410.19 (land 407.52; water 2.67).

Pop: 20,578 (White 84.7%; Black or African American 0.1%; Hispanic or Latino 11.9%; Asian 0.9%; Other 8.8%). **Foreign born:** 5.5%. **Median age:** 34.4. **State rank:** 14. **Pop change 1990-2000:** +25.2%.

Income: per capita $14,924; median household $33,046. **Pop below poverty level:** 13.2%.

Unemployment: 8.4%. **Median home value:** $87,900. **Median travel time to work:** 20 minutes.

POWER COUNTY
543 Bannock Ave   **Ph:** 208-226-7611
American Falls, ID 83211   **Fax:** 208-226-7612
www.co.power.id.us

In southeastern ID, east of Pocatello; organized Jan 30, 1913 from Bingham, Cassia, Oneida, and Blaine counties. **Name Origin:** For the American Falls Canal and Power Company.

Area (sq mi): 1442.6 (land 1405.57; water 37.03).

Pop: 7,538 (White 74.2%; Black or African American 0.1%; Hispanic or Latino 21.7%; Asian 0.3%; Other 15.8%). **Foreign born:** 10.5%. **Median age:** 31.6. **State rank:** 32. **Pop change 1990-2000:** +6.4%.

Income: per capita $14,007; median household $32,226. **Pop below poverty level:** 16.1%.

Unemployment: 7.2%. **Median home value:** $89,000. **Median travel time to work:** 17.6 minutes.

SHOSHONE COUNTY
700 Bank St   **Ph:** 208-752-3331
Wallace, ID 83873   **Fax:** 208-753-2711

On the eastern border of the ID panhandle, northeast of Lewiston. The first organized unit of government in ID, it was originally created in 1858 as part of WA Territory, effective in 1861; reorganized Feb 4, 1864 (prior to statehood). **Name Origin:** For the Shonone, one of the major Indian tribes of the northern Rocky Mountain region.

Area (sq mi): 2635.5 (land 2633.91; water 1.59).

Pop: 13,771 (White 94.7%; Black or African American 0.1%; Hispanic or Latino 1.9%; Asian 0.2%; Other 3.8%). **Foreign born:** 2%. **Median age:** 41.8. **State rank:** 22. **Pop change 1990-2000:** -1.1%.

Income: per capita $15,934; median household $28,535. **Pop below poverty level:** 16.4%.

Unemployment: 12%. **Median home value:** $70,200. **Median travel time to work:** 21.6 minutes.

TETON COUNTY
89 N Main St Suite 1   **Ph:** 208-354-2905
Driggs, ID 83422   **Fax:** 208-354-8410
www.co.teton.id.us

On the eastern border of ID, northeast of Idaho Falls; organized Jan 26, 1915 from Madison County. **Name Origin:** For the Teton Mountains.

Area (sq mi): 450.57 (land 450.36; water 0.21).

Pop: 5,999 (White 86.8%; Black or African American 0.2%; Hispanic or Latino 11.8%; Asian 0.2%; Other 8.3%). **Foreign born:** 9.9%. **Median age:** 31.3. **State rank:** 36. **Pop change 1990-2000:** +74.4%.

Income: per capita $17,778; median household $41,968. **Pop below poverty level:** 12.9%.

Please see sample entry on inside front cover for detailed information about the statistics presented with each county listing.

Unemployment: 2.5%. **Median home value:** $133,000. **Median travel time to work:** 26.9 minutes.

TWIN FALLS COUNTY
PO Box 126   **Ph:** 208-736-4004
Twin Falls, ID 83303   **Fax:** 208-736-4182

On the central southern border of ID; organized Feb 21, 1907 from Cassia County. **Name Origin:** For the falls on the Snake River.

Area (sq mi): 1928.47 (land 1925.03; water 3.44).

Pop: 64,284 (White 87.7%; Black or African American 0.2%; Hispanic or Latino 9.4%; Asian 0.8%; Other 6.6%). **Foreign born:** 6.4%. **Median age:** 34.9. **State rank:** 6. **Pop change 1990-2000:** +20%.

Income: per capita $16,678; median household $34,506. **Pop below poverty level:** 12.7%.

Unemployment: 4.1%. **Median home value:** $93,800. **Median travel time to work:** 16.7 minutes.

VALLEY COUNTY
PO Box 1350   **Ph:** 208-382-4297
Cascade, ID 83611   **Fax:** 208-382-7107

In west-central ID; organized Feb 26, 1917. **Name Origin:** For Long Valley.

Area (sq mi): 3733.66 (land 3677.82; water 55.84).

Pop: 7,651 (White 95.8%; Black or African American 0%; Hispanic or Latino 2%; Asian 0.3%; Other 3.2%). **Foreign born:** 1.4%. **Median age:** 43.5. **State rank:** 31. **Pop change 1990-2000:** +25.2%.

Income: per capita $19,246; median household $36,927. **Pop below poverty level:** 9.3%.

Unemployment: 8.3%. **Median home value:** $141,200. **Median travel time to work:** 17.2 minutes.

WASHINGTON COUNTY
PO Box 670   **Ph:** 208-414-2092
Weiser, ID 83672   **Fax:** 208-414-3925
www.ruralnetwork.net/~wcassr/

On the central western border of ID, north of Caldwell; organized Feb 20, 1879 (prior to statehood) from Boise County. **Name Origin:** For George Washington (1732-99), American patriot and first U.S. president.

Area (sq mi): 1473.54 (land 1456.32; water 17.23).

Pop: 9,977 (White 83.1%; Black or African American 0.1%; Hispanic or Latino 13.8%; Asian 1%; Other 11.4%). **Foreign born:** 7.1%. **Median age:** 39.2. **State rank:** 26. **Pop change 1990-2000:** +16.7%.

Income: per capita $15,464; median household $30,625. **Pop below poverty level:** 13.3%.

Unemployment: 8.8%. **Median home value:** $90,200. **Median travel time to work:** 19.9 minutes.

All statistics are based on the 2000 Census except the dollar figures given for per capita income, which are based on 1999 estimates.

ILLINOIS - Counties

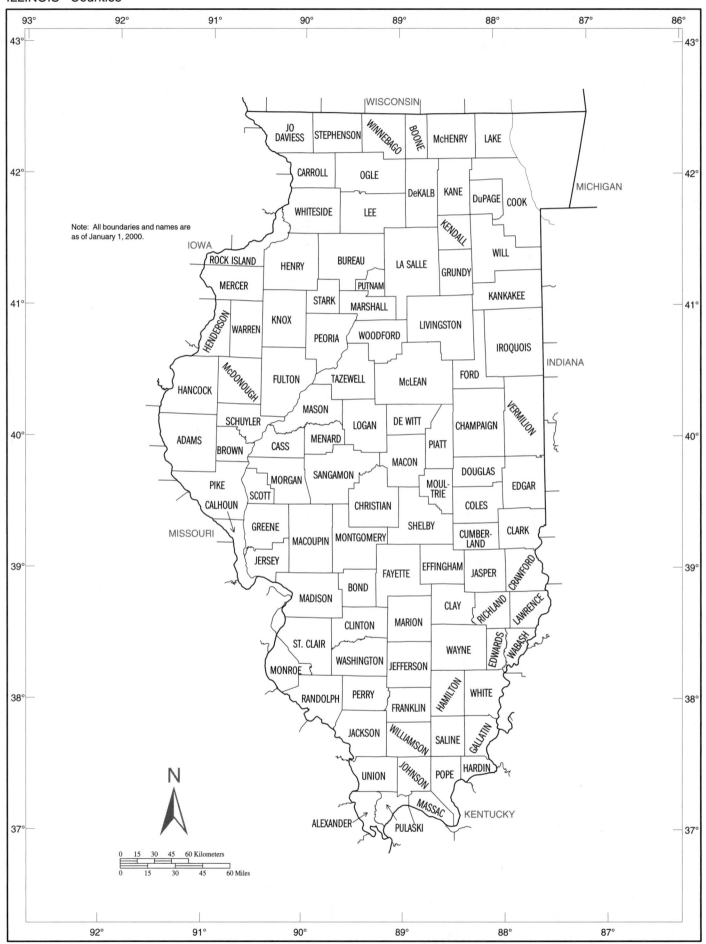

Note: All boundaries and names are as of January 1, 2000.

Illinois

ILLINOIS STATE INFORMATION

www.illinois.gov **Ph:** 217-782-2000

Area (sq mi): 57,914.38 (land 55,583.58; water 2330.79).

Pop: 12,419,293 (White 67.8%; Black or African American 15.1%; Hispanic or Latino 12.3%; Asian 3.4%; Other 7.9%). **Foreign born:** 12.3%. **Median age:** 34.7. **Pop change 1990-2000:** +8.6%.

Income: per capita $23,104; median household $46,590. **Pop below poverty level:** 10.7%.

Unemployment: 6.3%. **Median home value:** $130,800. **Median travel time to work:** 28 minutes.

ADAMS COUNTY

507 Vermont St **Ph:** 217-277-2150
Quincy, IL 62301 **Fax:** 217-277-2155
www.co.adams.il.us

On west-central border of IL west of Springfield; organized Jan 13, 1825 from Pike County. Highland County organized from Adams and Marquette counties in 1847 and eliminated in 1848. Marquette County organized in 1843 from Adams County and eliminated in 1847. **Name Origin:** For John Quincy Adams (1767-1848), sixth U.S. president.

Area (sq mi): 871.28 (land 856.63; water 14.64).

Pop: 68,277 (White 94.6%; Black or African American 3.1%; Hispanic or Latino 0.8%; Asian 0.4%; Other 1.5%). **Foreign born:** 0.8%. **Median age:** 38.3. **State rank:** 21. **Pop change 1990-2000:** +3.3%.

Income: per capita $17,894; median household $34,784. **Pop below poverty level:** 10%.

Unemployment: 4.3%. **Median home value:** $75,600. **Median travel time to work:** 16.7 minutes.

ALEXANDER COUNTY

2000 Washington Ave **Ph:** 618-734-7000
Cairo, IL 62914 **Fax:** 618-734-7002

On the southwest border southwest of Carbondale; organized Mar 4, 1819 from Johnson County. **Name Origin:** For William M. Alexander, an early settler and IL legislator (1820-24).

Area (sq mi): 252.54 (land 236.38; water 16.16).

Pop: 9,590 (White 62.2%; Black or African American 34.9%; Hispanic or Latino 1.4%; Asian 0.4%; Other 1.7%). **Foreign born:** 0.9%. **Median age:** 38. **State rank:** 89. **Pop change 1990-2000:** -9.7%.

Income: per capita $16,084; median household $26,042. **Pop below poverty level:** 26.1%.

Unemployment: 8.9%. **Median home value:** $33,400. **Median travel time to work:** 24.7 minutes.

BOND COUNTY

203 W College Ave **Ph:** 618-664-0449
Greenville, IL 62246 **Fax:** 618-664-9414

In south-central IL northeast of Belleville; organized Jan 4, 1817 (prior to statehood) from Madison County. **Name Origin:** For Shadrach Bond (1773-1832), IL legislator and first governor (1818-22).

Area (sq mi): 382.67 (land 380.2; water 2.46).

Pop: 17,633 (White 89.8%; Black or African American 7.4%; Hispanic or Latino 1.4%; Asian 0.3%; Other 1.6%). **Foreign born:** 0.8%. **Median age:** 36.8. **State rank:** 64. **Pop change 1990-2000:** +17.6%.

Income: per capita $17,947; median household $37,680. **Pop below poverty level:** 9.3%.

Unemployment: 5%. **Median home value:** $68,900. **Median travel time to work:** 24.3 minutes.

BOONE COUNTY

601 N Main St Suite 201 **Ph:** 815-547-4770
Belvidere, IL 61008 **Fax:** 815-547-3579
www.boonecountyil.org

On the north-central border of IL east of Rockford; organized Mar 4, 1837 from Winnebago County. **Name Origin:** For Daniel Boone (1734-1820), U.S. frontiersman and KY pioneer.

Area (sq mi): 281.94 (land 281.27; water 0.68).

Pop: 41,786 (White 85%; Black or African American 0.9%; Hispanic or Latino 12.5%; Asian 0.5%; Other 8.5%). **Foreign born:** 7.5%. **Median age:** 34.5. **State rank:** 32. **Pop change 1990-2000:** +35.6%.

Income: per capita $21,590; median household $52,397. **Pop below poverty level:** 7%.

Unemployment: 7.4%. **Median home value:** $123,600. **Median travel time to work:** 28.2 minutes.

BROWN COUNTY

200 W Court St Rm 4 **Ph:** 217-773-3421
Mount Sterling, IL 62353 **Fax:** 217-773-2233

In west-central IL east of Quincy; organized Feb 1, 1839 from Schuyler County. **Name Origin:** For Gen. Jacob Jennings Brown (1775-1828), an officer in the War of 1812 and commander of the U.S. Army (1821-28).

Please see sample entry on inside front cover for detailed information about the statistics presented with each county listing.

151

Area (sq mi): 307.24 (land 305.65; water 1.59).

Pop: 6,950 (White 77.2%; Black or African American 18.2%; Hispanic or Latino 3.9%; Asian 0.1%; Other 1.4%). **Foreign born:** 1.6%. **Median age:** 35.2. **State rank:** 95. **Pop change 1990-2000:** +19.1%.

Income: per capita $14,629; median household $35,445. **Pop below poverty level:** 8.5%.

Unemployment: 3%. **Median home value:** $47,400. **Median travel time to work:** 21 minutes.

BUREAU COUNTY
700 S Main St   **Ph:** 815-875-2014
Princeton, IL 61356   **Fax:** 815-879-4803

In north-central IL, east of Moline; organized Feb 28, 1837 from Putnam County. **Name Origin:** Anglicized version of Pierre de Bureo (Buero), a French trader with the Indians.

Area (sq mi): 873.3 (land 868.56; water 4.74).

Pop: 35,503 (White 93.5%; Black or African American 0.3%; Hispanic or Latino 4.9%; Asian 0.5%; Other 2.4%). **Foreign born:** 2.6%. **Median age:** 39.6. **State rank:** 42. **Pop change 1990-2000:** -0.5%.

Income: per capita $19,542; median household $40,233. **Pop below poverty level:** 7.3%.

Unemployment: 5.5%. **Median home value:** $77,800. **Median travel time to work:** 20.3 minutes.

CALHOUN COUNTY
PO Box 187   **Ph:** 618-576-2351
Hardin, IL 62047   **Fax:** 618-576-2895

On west-central border of IL southwest of Springfield; organized Jan 10, 1825 from Pike County. **Name Origin:** For John Caldwell Calhoun (1782-1850), U.S. statesman and champion of Southern causes.

Area (sq mi): 283.69 (land 253.82; water 29.87).

Pop: 5,084 (White 98.4%; Black or African American 0%; Hispanic or Latino 0.6%; Asian 0.2%; Other 1%). **Foreign born:** 1%. **Median age:** 40.5. **State rank:** 100. **Pop change 1990-2000:** -4.5%.

Income: per capita $16,785; median household $34,375. **Pop below poverty level:** 9%.

Unemployment: 5.6%. **Median home value:** $61,600. **Median travel time to work:** 40.4 minutes.

CARROLL COUNTY
PO Box 152   **Ph:** 815-244-0221
Mount Carroll, IL 61053   **Fax:** 815-244-3709

On the northwest border of IL southwest of Rockford; organized Feb 22, 1839 from Jo Daviess County. **Name Origin:** For Charles Carroll (1737-1832), a signer of the Declaration of Independence, U.S. senator from MD (1789-92), and founder of the Baltimore and Ohio Railroad.

Area (sq mi): 465.77 (land 444.21; water 21.56).

Pop: 16,674 (White 95.9%; Black or African American 0.5%; Hispanic or Latino 2%; Asian 0.4%; Other 2%). **Foreign born:** 1.9%. **Median age:** 40.8. **State rank:** 70. **Pop change 1990-2000:** -0.8%.

Income: per capita $18,688; median household $37,148. **Pop below poverty level:** 9.6%.

Unemployment: 8.4%. **Median home value:** $68,700. **Median travel time to work:** 23.1 minutes.

CASS COUNTY
100 E Springfield St   **Ph:** 217-452-7217
Virginia, IL 62691   **Fax:** 217-452-7219

In west-central IL, northwest of Springfield; organized Mar 3, 1837 from Morgan County. **Name Origin:** For Gen. Lewis Cass (1782-1866), OH legislator, military and civil governor of MI Territory (1913-31), U.S. secretary of war (1831-36), and U.S. secretary of state (1857-60).

Area (sq mi): 383.73 (land 375.9; water 7.83).

Pop: 13,695 (White 90.1%; Black or African American 0.4%; Hispanic or Latino 8.5%; Asian 0.3%; Other 4.3%). **Foreign born:** 7.8%. **Median age:** 37.2. **State rank:** 82. **Pop change 1990-2000:** +1.9%.

Income: per capita $16,532; median household $35,243. **Pop below poverty level:** 12%.

Unemployment: 4.5%. **Median home value:** $54,900. **Median travel time to work:** 22.1 minutes.

CHAMPAIGN COUNTY
1776 E Washington St   **Ph:** 217-384-3720
Urbana, IL 61802   **Fax:** 217-384-1241
www.co.champaign.il.us

In east-central IL west of Danville; organized Feb 20, 1833 from Vermilion County. **Name Origin:** For the county in OH, from French *campagne* 'field, plain.'

Area (sq mi): 997.53 (land 996.81; water 0.73).

Pop: 179,669 (White 77.4%; Black or African American 11.2%; Hispanic or Latino 2.9%; Asian 6.5%; Other 3.5%). **Foreign born:** 8%. **Median age:** 28.6. **State rank:** 12. **Pop change 1990-2000:** +3.8%.

Income: per capita $19,708; median household $37,780. **Pop below poverty level:** 16.1%.

Unemployment: 2.8%. **Median home value:** $94,700. **Median travel time to work:** 16.8 minutes.

CHRISTIAN COUNTY
PO Box 647   **Ph:** 217-824-4969
Taylorville, IL 62568   **Fax:** 217-824-5105

In central IL southwest of Decatur; organized as Dane County Feb 15, 1839 from Sangamon County; name changed Feb 1, 1840. **Name Origin:** For the county in KY, named for Col. William Christian (1743-86), army officer, Indian fighter, and legislator; brother-in-law of Patrick Henry (1736-99).

Area (sq mi): 715.71 (land 709.06; water 6.65).

Pop: 35,372 (White 95.9%; Black or African American 2.1%; Hispanic or Latino 1%; Asian 0.4%; Other 1.2%). **Foreign born:** 1.3%. **Median age:** 38.9. **State rank:** 44. **Pop change 1990-2000:** +2.8%.

Income: per capita $17,937; median household $36,561. **Pop below poverty level:** 9.5%.

All statistics are based on the 2000 Census except the dollar figures given for per capita income, which are based on 1999 estimates.

Unemployment: 5.3%. **Median home value:** $61,000. **Median travel time to work:** 24.9 minutes.

CLARK COUNTY

501 Archer Ave County Courthouse	**Ph:** 217-826-8311
Marshall, IL 62441	**Fax:** 217-826-5674
www.clarkcountyil.org	

On the east-central border of IL south of Danville; organized Mar 22, 1819 from Crawford County. **Name Origin:** For Gen. George Rogers Clark (1752-1818), officer in the Revolutionary War and frontiersman in the Northwest Territory.

Area (sq mi): 504.88 (land 501.5; water 3.38).

Pop: 17,008 (White 98.6%; Black or African American 0.2%; Hispanic or Latino 0.3%; Asian 0.1%; Other 0.9%). **Foreign born:** 0.6%. **Median age:** 39.2. **State rank:** 67. **Pop change 1990-2000:** +6.8%.

Income: per capita $17,655; median household $35,967. **Pop below poverty level:** 9.2%.

Unemployment: 5.7%. **Median home value:** $63,300. **Median travel time to work:** 22.4 minutes.

CLAY COUNTY

PO Box 160	**Ph:** 618-665-3626
Louisville, IL 62858	**Fax:** 618-665-3607

In east-central IL west of Olney; organized Dec 23, 1824 from Lawrence, Wayne, and Fayette counties. **Name Origin:** For Henry Clay (1777-1852), U.S. senator from KY, known as the 'Great Pacificator' for his advocacy of compromise to avert national crises.

Area (sq mi): 469.84 (land 469.25; water 0.59).

Pop: 14,560 (White 98.2%; Black or African American 0.1%; Hispanic or Latino 0.6%; Asian 0.5%; Other 0.8%). **Foreign born:** 0.7%. **Median age:** 39.7. **State rank:** 79. **Pop change 1990-2000:** +0.7%.

Income: per capita $15,771; median household $30,599. **Pop below poverty level:** 11.8%.

Unemployment: 7.7%. **Median home value:** $51,500. **Median travel time to work:** 19.5 minutes.

CLINTON COUNTY

PO Box 308	**Ph:** 618-594-2464
Carlyle, IL 62231	**Fax:** 618-594-0195
www.clintonco.org	

In south-central IL, east of Saint Louis, MO; organized Dec 27, 1824 from Washington, Bond, and Fayette counties. **Name Origin:** For DeWitt Clinton (1769-1828), governor of NY (1817-21; 1825-28) and supporter of the Erie Canal.

Area (sq mi): 503.48 (land 474.23; water 29.25).

Pop: 35,535 (White 93.5%; Black or African American 3.9%; Hispanic or Latino 1.6%; Asian 0.3%; Other 1.5%). **Foreign born:** 1.2%. **Median age:** 36.6. **State rank:** 41. **Pop change 1990-2000:** +4.7%.

Income: per capita $19,109; median household $44,618. **Pop below poverty level:** 6.4%.

Unemployment: 5%. **Median home value:** $83,700. **Median travel time to work:** 25.8 minutes.

COLES COUNTY

651 Jackson Ave Rm 122	**Ph:** 217-348-0501
Charleston, IL 61920	**Fax:** 217-348-7337
www.co.coles.il.us	

In east-central IL south of Urbana; organized Dec 25, 1830 from Clark and Edgar counties. **Name Origin:** For Edward Coles (1768-1868), humanitarian and IL governor (1822-26).

Area (sq mi): 510.07 (land 508.29; water 1.78).

Pop: 53,196 (White 94.6%; Black or African American 2.3%; Hispanic or Latino 1.4%; Asian 0.8%; Other 1.5%). **Foreign born:** 1.6%. **Median age:** 30.8. **State rank:** 27. **Pop change 1990-2000:** +3%.

Income: per capita $17,370; median household $32,286. **Pop below poverty level:** 17.5%.

Unemployment: 5.3%. **Median home value:** $71,500. **Median travel time to work:** 16.6 minutes.

COOK COUNTY

118 N Clark St Rm 820	**Ph:** 312-603-4660
Chicago, IL 60602	**Fax:** 312-603-4479
www.co.cook.il.us	

On the northeast border of IL bounded on east by the western shore of Lake Michigan; organized Jan 15, 1831 from Putnam County. **Name Origin:** For Daniel Pope Cook (1794-1827), first attorney general of IL and U.S. representative (1819-27).

Area (sq mi): 1635.04 (land 945.68; water 689.36).

Pop: 5,376,741 (White 47.6%; Black or African American 26.1%; Hispanic or Latino 19.9%; Asian 4.8%; Other 12.7%). **Foreign born:** 19.8%. **Median age:** 33.6. **State rank:** 1. **Pop change 1990-2000:** +5.3%.

Income: per capita $23,227; median household $45,922. **Pop below poverty level:** 13.5%.

Unemployment: 5.9%. **Median home value:** $157,700. **Median travel time to work:** 32.6 minutes.

CRAWFORD COUNTY

PO Box 616	**Ph:** 618-546-1212
Robinson, IL 62454	**Fax:** 618-546-0140
www.crawfordcountycentral.com	

On the east-central border of IL northeast of Olney; organized Dec 31, 1816 (prior to statehood) from Edwards County. **Name Origin:** For William Harris Crawford (1772-1834), U.S. senator from GA (1807-13), U.S. secretary of war (1815-16), and U.S. secretary of the treasury (1816-25).

Area (sq mi): 445.74 (land 443.53; water 2.2).

Pop: 20,452 (White 92.5%; Black or African American 4.5%; Hispanic or Latino 1.7%; Asian 0.3%; Other 1.5%). **Foreign born:** 1.3%. **Median age:** 38.6. **State rank:** 58. **Pop change 1990-2000:** +5.1%.

Income: per capita $16,869; median household $32,531. **Pop below poverty level:** 11.2%.

Please see sample entry on inside front cover for detailed information about the statistics presented with each county listing.

Unemployment: 6.5%. **Median home value:** $54,200. **Median travel time to work:** 18.1 minutes.

CUMBERLAND COUNTY

140 Courthouse Sq   **Ph:** 217-849-2631
Toledo, IL 62468   **Fax:** 217-849-2968

In east-central IL south of Urbana; organized Mar 2, 1843 from Coles County. **Name Origin:** For the Cumberland Road.

Area (sq mi): 347 (land 346.02; water 0.98).

Pop: 11,253 (White 98.5%; Black or African American 0.1%; Hispanic or Latino 0.6%; Asian 0.2%; Other 0.9%). **Foreign born:** 0.6%. **Median age:** 37.2. **State rank:** 87. **Pop change 1990-2000:** +5.5%.

Income: per capita $16,953; median household $36,149. **Pop below poverty level:** 9.5%.

Unemployment: 7%. **Median home value:** $68,700. **Median travel time to work:** 26.4 minutes.

DE WITT COUNTY

PO Box 439   **Ph:** 217-935-2119
Clinton, IL 61727   **Fax:** 217-935-4596
www.dewittcountyill.com

In central IL north of Decatur; organized Mar 1, 1839 from McLean and Macon counties. **Name Origin:** For DeWitt Clinton (1769-1828), governor of NY (1817-21; 1825-28) and supporter of the Erie Canal.

Area (sq mi): 405.15 (land 397.58; water 7.58).

Pop: 16,798 (White 97.1%; Black or African American 0.5%; Hispanic or Latino 1.3%; Asian 0.3%; Other 1.4%). **Foreign born:** 1.2%. **Median age:** 38.5. **State rank:** 69. **Pop change 1990-2000:** +1.7%.

Income: per capita $20,488; median household $41,256. **Pop below poverty level:** 8.2%.

Unemployment: 6.3%. **Median home value:** $74,300. **Median travel time to work:** 21.4 minutes.

DEKALB COUNTY

110 E Sycamore St   **Ph:** 815-895-7149
Sycamore, IL 60178   **Fax:** 815-895-7148
www.dekalbcounty.org

In north-central IL, west of Chicago; organized Mar 4, 1837 from Kane County. **Name Origin:** For Johann (1721-80), Baron de Kalb, German-born French soldier who fought with the Americans during the Revolutionary War.

Area (sq mi): 634.97 (land 634.16; water 0.81).

Pop: 88,969 (White 85.2%; Black or African American 4.6%; Hispanic or Latino 6.6%; Asian 2.3%; Other 4.6%). **Foreign born:** 5.8%. **Median age:** 28.4. **State rank:** 19. **Pop change 1990-2000:** +14.2%.

Income: per capita $19,462; median household $45,828. **Pop below poverty level:** 11.4%.

Unemployment: 4.3%. **Median home value:** $135,900. **Median travel time to work:** 23.8 minutes.

DOUGLAS COUNTY

PO Box 467   **Ph:** 217-253-2411
Tuscola, IL 61953   **Fax:** 217-253-2233

In east-central IL, east of Decatur; organized Feb 8, 1859 from Coles County. **Name Origin:** For Stephen Arnold Douglas (1813-61), U.S. orator and statesman.

Area (sq mi): 417.42 (land 416.86; water 0.56).

Pop: 19,922 (White 95.3%; Black or African American 0.3%; Hispanic or Latino 3.5%; Asian 0.3%; Other 2.2%). **Foreign born:** 2.5%. **Median age:** 37.4. **State rank:** 60. **Pop change 1990-2000:** +2.4%.

Income: per capita $18,474; median household $39,439. **Pop below poverty level:** 6.4%.

Unemployment: 3.9%. **Median home value:** $70,500. **Median travel time to work:** 19.8 minutes.

DUPAGE COUNTY

421 N County Farm Rd   **Ph:** 630-682-7035
Wheaton, IL 60187   **Fax:** 630-682-7409
www.dupageco.org

In northeast IL, west of Chicago; organized Feb 9, 1839 from Cook County. **Name Origin:** For the DuPage River, from the French name of a local Indian chief.

Area (sq mi): 336.55 (land 333.61; water 2.95).

Pop: 904,161 (White 78.7%; Black or African American 3.1%; Hispanic or Latino 9%; Asian 7.9%; Other 5%). **Foreign born:** 15.3%. **Median age:** 35.2. **State rank:** 2. **Pop change 1990-2000:** +15.7%.

Income: per capita $31,315; median household $67,887. **Pop below poverty level:** 3.6%.

Unemployment: 3.8%. **Median home value:** $195,000. **Median travel time to work:** 29 minutes.

EDGAR COUNTY

115 W Court St Rm J County Courthouse   **Ph:** 217-466-7433
Paris, IL 61944   **Fax:** 217-466-7430

On the east-central border of IL south of Danville; organized Jan 3, 1823 from Clark County. **Name Origin:** For John Edgar; pioneer merchant and politician.

Area (sq mi): 624.18 (land 623.55; water 0.63).

Pop: 19,704 (White 96.7%; Black or African American 1.8%; Hispanic or Latino 0.8%; Asian 0.2%; Other 0.9%). **Foreign born:** 0.6%. **Median age:** 39.3. **State rank:** 61. **Pop change 1990-2000:** +0.6%.

Income: per capita $17,857; median household $35,203. **Pop below poverty level:** 10.5%.

Unemployment: 4.7%. **Median home value:** $54,300. **Median travel time to work:** 19.8 minutes.

EDWARDS COUNTY

50 E Main St   **Ph:** 618-445-2115
Albion, IL 62806   **Fax:** 618-445-3505

In southeastern IL, south of Olney; organized Nov 28, 1814 (prior to statehood) from Madison and Gallatin counties. **Name Origin:**

All statistics are based on the 2000 Census except the dollar figures given for per capita income, which are based on 1999 estimates.

For Ninian Edwards (1775-1833), KY legislator and jurist, and territorial (1809-18) and civil (1826-30) governor of IL.

Area (sq mi): 222.66 (land 222.35; water 0.31).

Pop: 6,971 (White 98.5%; Black or African American 0.1%; Hispanic or Latino 0.5%; Asian 0.4%; Other 0.6%). **Foreign born:** 0.4%. **Median age:** 40.5. **State rank:** 94. **Pop change 1990-2000:** -6.3%.

Income: per capita $16,187; median household $31,816. **Pop below poverty level:** 9.8%.

Unemployment: 4.9%. **Median home value:** $46,700. **Median travel time to work:** 22.5 minutes.

EFFINGHAM COUNTY
PO Box 628 **Ph:** 217-342-6535
Effingham, IL 62401 **Fax:** 217-342-3577
www.co.effingham.il.us

In central IL southeast of Decatur; organized Feb 15, 1831 from Fayette and Crawford counties. **Name Origin:** For either Thomas Howard (1746-91), 3rd Earl of Effingham, who supported the Americans during the Revolutionary War, or Gen. Edward Effingham, who resigned from the British Army rather than fight the colonists.

Area (sq mi): 479.9 (land 478.7; water 1.2).

Pop: 34,264 (White 98.2%; Black or African American 0.2%; Hispanic or Latino 0.7%; Asian 0.3%; Other 0.9%). **Foreign born:** 1%. **Median age:** 35.7. **State rank:** 45. **Pop change 1990-2000:** +8.1%.

Income: per capita $18,301; median household $39,379. **Pop below poverty level:** 8.1%.

Unemployment: 5.1%. **Median home value:** $85,400. **Median travel time to work:** 17.4 minutes.

FAYETTE COUNTY
PO Box 401 **Ph:** 618-283-5000
Vandalia, IL 62471 **Fax:** 618-283-5004

In south-central IL, northeast of Saint Louis, MO; organized Feb 14, 1821 from Bond, Jefferson, Wayne, and Clark counties. **Name Origin:** For the Marquis de Lafayette (1757-1834), French statesman and soldier who fought with the Americans during the Revolutionary War.

Area (sq mi): 725.36 (land 716.49; water 8.87).

Pop: 21,802 (White 93.5%; Black or African American 4.9%; Hispanic or Latino 0.8%; Asian 0.2%; Other 0.9%). **Foreign born:** 0.4%. **Median age:** 37.5. **State rank:** 56. **Pop change 1990-2000:** +4.4%.

Income: per capita $15,357; median household $31,873. **Pop below poverty level:** 12.2%.

Unemployment: 7.3%. **Median home value:** $59,500. **Median travel time to work:** 22.3 minutes.

FORD COUNTY
200 W State St Rm 101 **Ph:** 217-379-2721
Paxton, IL 60957 **Fax:** 217-379-3258
www.prairienet.org/fordiroq/ford.htm

In east-central IL, east of Bloomington; organized Feb 17, 1859

from Vermilion County. **Name Origin:** For Thomas Ford (1800-1850), jurist on the IL Supreme Court (1840) and governor (1842-46).

Area (sq mi): 486.42 (land 485.9; water 0.52).

Pop: 14,241 (White 97.5%; Black or African American 0.2%; Hispanic or Latino 1.2%; Asian 0.3%; Other 1.3%). **Foreign born:** 1.1%. **Median age:** 39.4. **State rank:** 81. **Pop change 1990-2000:** -0.2%.

Income: per capita $18,860; median household $38,073. **Pop below poverty level:** 7%.

Unemployment: 4.7%. **Median home value:** $70,600. **Median travel time to work:** 21.2 minutes.

FRANKLIN COUNTY
PO Box 607 **Ph:** 618-438-3221
Benton, IL 62812 **Fax:** 618-439-4119

In south-central IL northeast of Carbondale; organized Jan 2, 1818 (prior to statehood) from White and Gallatin counties. **Name Origin:** For Benjamin Franklin (1706-90), U.S. patriot, diplomat, and statesman.

Area (sq mi): 431.4 (land 412.08; water 19.32).

Pop: 39,018 (White 98.2%; Black or African American 0.2%; Hispanic or Latino 0.6%; Asian 0.2%; Other 1%). **Foreign born:** 0.7%. **Median age:** 40.3. **State rank:** 36. **Pop change 1990-2000:** -3.2%.

Income: per capita $15,407; median household $28,411. **Pop below poverty level:** 16.2%.

Unemployment: 8.6%. **Median home value:** $45,100. **Median travel time to work:** 23 minutes.

FULTON COUNTY
100 N Main St **Ph:** 309-547-3041
Lewistown, IL 61542 **Fax:** 309-547-3326

In north-central IL, southwest of Peoria; organized Jan 18, 1823 from Pike County. **Name Origin:** For Robert Fulton (1765-1815), builder of the *Clermont*, the first commercially successful steamboat.

Area (sq mi): 882.59 (land 865.62; water 16.97).

Pop: 38,250 (White 94.3%; Black or African American 3.6%; Hispanic or Latino 1.2%; Asian 0.2%; Other 1%). **Foreign born:** 0.8%. **Median age:** 39.2. **State rank:** 37. **Pop change 1990-2000:** +0.4%.

Income: per capita $17,373; median household $33,952. **Pop below poverty level:** 9.9%.

Unemployment: 8.2%. **Median home value:** $58,100. **Median travel time to work:** 26.8 minutes.

GALLATIN COUNTY
PO Box 550 **Ph:** 618-269-3025
Shawneetown, IL 62984 **Fax:** 618-269-3343

On the southeast border of IL; organized Sep 14, 1812 (prior to statehood) from Randolph County. **Name Origin:** For Abraham Alfonse Albert Gallatin (1761-1849), Swiss-born U.S. representative from PA (1795-1801), U.S. secretary of treasury (1801-14), and U.S. minister to France (1815-23) and to Great Britain (1826-27).

Please see sample entry on inside front cover for detailed information about the statistics presented with each county listing.

155

Area (sq mi): 328.41 (land 323.73; water 4.68).

Pop: 6,445 (White 97.9%; Black or African American 0.3%; Hispanic or Latino 0.9%; Asian 0.1%; Other 1.3%). **Foreign born:** 0.4%. **Median age:** 40.7. **State rank:** 96. **Pop change 1990-2000:** -6.7%.

Income: per capita $15,575; median household $26,118. **Pop below poverty level:** 20.7%.

Unemployment: 6%. **Median home value:** $46,300. **Median travel time to work:** 27.9 minutes.

GREENE COUNTY
519 N Main St   **Ph:** 217-942-5443
Carrollton, IL 62016   **Fax:** 217-942-9323

In west-central IL northwest of Alton; organized Jan 20, 1821 from Madison County. **Name Origin:** For Gen. Nathanael Greene (1742-86), hero of the Revolutionary War, quartermaster general (1778-80), and commander of the Army of the South (1780).

Area (sq mi): 546.34 (land 543.09; water 3.25).

Pop: 14,761 (White 97.8%; Black or African American 0.7%; Hispanic or Latino 0.5%; Asian 0.1%; Other 1%). **Foreign born:** 0.3%. **Median age:** 37.9. **State rank:** 78. **Pop change 1990-2000:** -3.6%.

Income: per capita $15,246; median household $31,754. **Pop below poverty level:** 12.4%.

Unemployment: 5.5%. **Median home value:** $47,900. **Median travel time to work:** 29 minutes.

GRUNDY COUNTY
PO Box 675   **Ph:** 815-941-3222
Morris, IL 60450   **Fax:** 815-942-2222

In northeast IL, southwest of Chicago, established Feb 17, 1841 from La Salle County. **Name Origin:** For Felix Grundy (1777-1840), chief justice of KY Supreme Court, U.S. senator from TN (1829-38;1839-40), and U.S. Attorney General (1838-39).

Area (sq mi): 430.42 (land 419.9; water 10.52).

Pop: 37,535 (White 94.6%; Black or African American 0.2%; Hispanic or Latino 4.1%; Asian 0.3%; Other 2.4%). **Foreign born:** 2.7%. **Median age:** 36.3. **State rank:** 38. **Pop change 1990-2000:** +16.1%.

Income: per capita $22,591; median household $51,719. **Pop below poverty level:** 4.8%.

Unemployment: 6.5%. **Median home value:** $128,600. **Median travel time to work:** 26.4 minutes.

HAMILTON COUNTY
100 S Jackson St County Courthouse   **Ph:** 618-643-2721
McLeansboro, IL 62859

In southeastern IL northeast of Carbondale; organized Feb 8, 1821 from White County. **Name Origin:** For Alexander Hamilton (1757-1804), first U.S. secretary of the treasury (1789-95).

Area (sq mi): 435.84 (land 435.16; water 0.67).

Pop: 8,621 (White 97.8%; Black or African American 0.7%; Hispanic or Latino 0.6%; Asian 0.1%; Other 0.9%). **Foreign born:** 0.4%. **Median age:** 40.6. **State rank:** 90. **Pop change 1990-2000:** +1.4%.

Income: per capita $16,262; median household $30,496. **Pop below poverty level:** 12.9%.

Unemployment: 6.9%. **Median home value:** $47,800. **Median travel time to work:** 26.8 minutes.

HANCOCK COUNTY
PO Box 39   **Ph:** 217-357-3911
Carthage, IL 62321

On the west-central border of IL north of Quincy; organized Jan 13, 1825 from Pike County and unorganized territory. **Name Origin:** For John Hancock (1737-93), noted signer of the Declaration of Independence; governor of MA (1780-85; 1787-93), and statesman.

Area (sq mi): 814.54 (land 794.62; water 19.92).

Pop: 20,121 (White 98.3%; Black or African American 0.2%; Hispanic or Latino 0.5%; Asian 0.2%; Other 0.9%). **Foreign born:** 0.5%. **Median age:** 40.3. **State rank:** 59. **Pop change 1990-2000:** -5.9%.

Income: per capita $17,478; median household $36,654. **Pop below poverty level:** 8.3%.

Unemployment: 6.2%. **Median home value:** $58,200. **Median travel time to work:** 20.8 minutes.

HARDIN COUNTY
PO Box 187   **Ph:** 618-287-2251
Elizabethtown, IL 62931   **Fax:** 618-287-2661

On the southeastern border of IL; organized Mar 2, 1839 from Pope County. **Name Origin:** For the county in KY, former home of many settlers.

Area (sq mi): 181.53 (land 178.33; water 3.2).

Pop: 4,800 (White 94.9%; Black or African American 2.8%; Hispanic or Latino 1.1%; Asian 0.5%; Other 1.3%). **Foreign born:** 1.6%. **Median age:** 42.1. **State rank:** 101. **Pop change 1990-2000:** -7.5%.

Income: per capita $15,984; median household $27,693. **Pop below poverty level:** 18.6%.

Unemployment: 7.5%. **Median home value:** $40,800. **Median travel time to work:** 24.4 minutes.

HENDERSON COUNTY
PO Box 308   **Ph:** 309-867-2911
Oquawka, IL 61469   **Fax:** 309-867-2033

On the northwestern border of IL west of Galesburg; organized Jan 20, 1841 from Warren County. **Name Origin:** For either the county in KY, former home of many settlers, or the Henderson River, which flows through the county.

Area (sq mi): 395.12 (land 378.81; water 16.31).

Pop: 8,213 (White 97.9%; Black or African American 0.3%; Hispanic or Latino 0.9%; Asian 0.1%; Other 1.1%). **Foreign born:** 0.4%. **Median age:** 41. **State rank:** 91. **Pop change 1990-2000:** +1.4%.

Income: per capita $17,456; median household $36,405. **Pop below poverty level:** 9.5%.

Unemployment: 4.7%. **Median home value:** $57,300. **Median travel time to work:** 25.4 minutes.

All statistics are based on the 2000 Census except the dollar figures given for per capita income, which are based on 1999 estimates.

HENRY COUNTY
307 W Center St   **Ph:** 309-937-3578
Cambridge, IL 61238
www.co.henry.il.us

In northwestern IL, southeast of Davenport; organized Jan 13, 1825 from Fulton County. **Name Origin:** For Patrick Henry (1736-99), patriot, governor of VA (1776-79; 1784-86), and statesman, famous for proclaiming, 'Give me liberty or give me death.'

Area (sq mi): 825.6 (land 823.21; water 2.38).

Pop: 51,020 (White 94.9%; Black or African American 1.1%; Hispanic or Latino 2.9%; Asian 0.2%; Other 2.4%). **Foreign born:** 1.7%. **Median age:** 39.1. **State rank:** 29. **Pop change 1990-2000:** -0.3%.

Income: per capita $18,716; median household $39,854. **Pop below poverty level:** 8%.

Unemployment: 6%. **Median home value:** $77,700. **Median travel time to work:** 21.8 minutes.

IROQUOIS COUNTY
1001 E Grant St   **Ph:** 815-432-6960
Watseka, IL 60970   **Fax:** 815-432-3894
www.prairienet.org/fordiroq/iroquois.htm

On the east-central border of IL, south of Kankakee; organized Feb 26, 1833 from Vermilion County. **Name Origin:** For the Indian tribe, a French transliteration of the Algonquian name 'real adders.'

Area (sq mi): 1118.03 (land 1116.43; water 1.6).

Pop: 31,334 (White 94.4%; Black or African American 0.7%; Hispanic or Latino 3.9%; Asian 0.3%; Other 3.1%). **Foreign born:** 2.4%. **Median age:** 39.6. **State rank:** 48. **Pop change 1990-2000:** +1.8%.

Income: per capita $18,435; median household $38,071. **Pop below poverty level:** 8.7%.

Unemployment: 6.4%. **Median home value:** $77,900. **Median travel time to work:** 22.9 minutes.

JACKSON COUNTY
1001 Walnut St County Courthouse   **Ph:** 618-687-7360
Murphysboro, IL 62966   **Fax:** 618-687-7359
www.co.jackson.il.us

On the southwest border of IL southeast of Saint Louis, MO; organized Jan 10, 1816 (prior to statehood) from Randolph and Johnson counties. **Name Origin:** For Andrew Jackson (1767-1845), seventh U.S. president.

Area (sq mi): 602.53 (land 588.12; water 14.4).

Pop: 59,612 (White 79.6%; Black or African American 13%; Hispanic or Latino 2.4%; Asian 3%; Other 3.2%). **Foreign born:** 5.2%. **Median age:** 27.5. **State rank:** 24. **Pop change 1990-2000:** -2.4%.

Income: per capita $15,755; median household $24,946. **Pop below poverty level:** 25.2%.

Unemployment: 3.6%. **Median home value:** $68,200. **Median travel time to work:** 18.1 minutes.

JASPER COUNTY
204 W Washington St Suite 2   **Ph:** 618-783-3124
Newton, IL 62448   **Fax:** 618-783-4137

In east-central IL, south of Urbana; organized Feb 15, 1831 from Crawford and Clay counties. **Name Origin:** For Sgt. William Jasper (1750-79), Revolutionary War soldier from SC.

Area (sq mi): 498.02 (land 494.4; water 3.62).

Pop: 10,117 (White 98.9%; Black or African American 0.1%; Hispanic or Latino 0.5%; Asian 0.2%; Other 0.6%). **Foreign born:** 0.2%. **Median age:** 38.1. **State rank:** 88. **Pop change 1990-2000:** -4.6%.

Income: per capita $16,649; median household $34,721. **Pop below poverty level:** 9.9%.

Unemployment: 8.7%. **Median home value:** $65,000. **Median travel time to work:** 19.8 minutes.

JEFFERSON COUNTY
100 S 10th St County Courthouse   **Ph:** 618-244-8000
Mount Vernon, IL 62864   **Fax:** 618-244-8111

In south-central IL, northeast of Carbondale; organized Mar 26, 1819 from Edwards and White counties. **Name Origin:** For Thomas Jefferson (1743-1826), U.S. patriot and statesman; third U.S. president.

Area (sq mi): 583.71 (land 570.96; water 12.76).

Pop: 40,045 (White 89.2%; Black or African American 7.8%; Hispanic or Latino 1.3%; Asian 0.5%; Other 1.8%). **Foreign born:** 0.8%. **Median age:** 37.6. **State rank:** 34. **Pop change 1990-2000:** +8.2%.

Income: per capita $16,644; median household $33,555. **Pop below poverty level:** 12.3%.

Unemployment: 6.9%. **Median home value:** $63,800. **Median travel time to work:** 20.7 minutes.

JERSEY COUNTY
201 W Pearl St   **Ph:** 618-498-5571
Jerseyville, IL 62052   **Fax:** 618-498-6128

In west-central IL northwest of Alton; organized Feb 28, 1839 from Greene County. **Name Origin:** For the state of NJ.

Area (sq mi): 377.02 (land 369.16; water 7.86).

Pop: 21,668 (White 97.6%; Black or African American 0.5%; Hispanic or Latino 0.7%; Asian 0.3%; Other 1.1%). **Foreign born:** 1%. **Median age:** 37.3. **State rank:** 57. **Pop change 1990-2000:** +5.5%.

Income: per capita $19,581; median household $42,065. **Pop below poverty level:** 7.1%.

Unemployment: 5.9%. **Median home value:** $82,800. **Median travel time to work:** 28.9 minutes.

JO DAVIESS COUNTY
330 N Bench St   **Ph:** 815-777-0161
Galena, IL 61036   **Fax:** 815-777-3688

On the northwestern border of IL; organized Feb 17, 1827 from Mercer, Henry, and Putnam counties. **Name Origin:** For Col. Joseph Hamilton Daviess (1774-1811), VA soldier and jurist who unsuccessfully attempted to indict Aaron Burr (1756-1836) for treason

Please see sample entry on inside front cover for detailed information about the statistics presented with each county listing.

157

(1807). According to Jacob Piatt Dunn, 'The Colonel's name was Daveiss and he always wrote it that way'; however, the name is sometimes spelled 'Daviess' in biographical entries and in places named for him.

Area (sq mi): 618.72 (land 601.08; water 17.64).

Pop: 22,289 (White 97.5%; Black or African American 0.2%; Hispanic or Latino 1.5%; Asian 0.2%; Other 0.9%). **Foreign born:** 1.7%. **Median age:** 41.6. **State rank:** 55. **Pop change 1990-2000:** +2.1%.

Income: per capita $21,497; median household $40,411. **Pop below poverty level:** 6.7%.

Unemployment: 5.6%. **Median home value:** $89,100. **Median travel time to work:** 21 minutes.

JOHNSON COUNTY
PO Box 96   **Ph:** 618-658-3611
Vienna, IL 62995   **Fax:** 618-658-2908

In south-central IL; organized Sep 14, 1812 (prior to statehood) from Randolph County. **Name Origin:** For Col. Richard Mentor Johnson (1781-1850), officer in War of 1812, U.S. senator from KY (1819-29), and U.S. vice president (1837-41).

Area (sq mi): 348.88 (land 344.63; water 4.25).

Pop: 12,878 (White 81.9%; Black or African American 14.2%; Hispanic or Latino 2.9%; Asian 0.1%; Other 2.2%). **Foreign born:** 1.5%. **Median age:** 36.7. **State rank:** 85. **Pop change 1990-2000:** +13.5%.

Income: per capita $17,990; median household $33,326. **Pop below poverty level:** 11.3%.

Unemployment: 5.5%. **Median home value:** $64,700. **Median travel time to work:** 27.1 minutes.

KANE COUNTY
719 Batavia Ave   **Ph:** 630-232-3400
Geneva, IL 60134   **Fax:** 630-232-5866
www.co.kane.il.us

In northeastern IL, west of Chicago; organized Jan 16, 1836 from La Salle County. **Name Origin:** For Elisha Kent Kane (1796-1835), IL legislator, jurist, and U.S. senator (1825-35).

Area (sq mi): 524.08 (land 520.44; water 3.64).

Pop: 404,119 (White 67.7%; Black or African American 5.8%; Hispanic or Latino 23.7%; Asian 1.8%; Other 13.1%). **Foreign born:** 15.7%. **Median age:** 32.2. **State rank:** 5. **Pop change 1990-2000:** +27.3%.

Income: per capita $24,315; median household $59,351. **Pop below poverty level:** 6.7%.

Unemployment: 5.2%. **Median home value:** $160,400. **Median travel time to work:** 27.3 minutes.

KANKAKEE COUNTY
189 E Court St   **Ph:** 815-937-2990
Kankakee, IL 60901   **Fax:** 815-939-8831
www.co.kankakee.il.us

On the northeastern border of IL, south of Chicago; organized Feb 11, 1853 from Iroquois and Will counties. **Name Origin:** For the

Kankakee Indian tribe, possibly from Mohegan 'wolf' or 'wolfplace' but meaning is unclear.

Area (sq mi): 681.44 (land 676.75; water 4.7).

Pop: 103,833 (White 77.8%; Black or African American 15.5%; Hispanic or Latino 4.8%; Asian 0.7%; Other 4%). **Foreign born:** 3.5%. **Median age:** 35.2. **State rank:** 18. **Pop change 1990-2000:** +7.9%.

Income: per capita $19,055; median household $41,532. **Pop below poverty level:** 11.4%.

Unemployment: 5.8%. **Median home value:** $99,200. **Median travel time to work:** 23.6 minutes.

KENDALL COUNTY
111 W Fox St   **Ph:** 630-553-4104
Yorkville, IL 60560   **Fax:** 630-553-4119
www.co.kendall.il.us

In northeastern IL, southwest of Chicago; organized Feb 19, 1841 from La Salle and Kane counties. **Name Origin:** For Amos Kendall (1789-1869), U.S. postmaster general (1835-40) and publisher of the Washington *Evening Star*.

Area (sq mi): 322.67 (land 320.58; water 2.09).

Pop: 54,544 (White 89.2%; Black or African American 1.3%; Hispanic or Latino 7.5%; Asian 0.9%; Other 4.9%). **Foreign born:** 5.3%. **Median age:** 34.1. **State rank:** 26. **Pop change 1990-2000:** +38.4%.

Income: per capita $25,188; median household $64,625. **Pop below poverty level:** 3%.

Unemployment: 4%. **Median home value:** $154,900. **Median travel time to work:** 29.9 minutes.

KNOX COUNTY
200 S Cherry St   **Ph:** 309-345-3860
Galesburg, IL 61401   **Fax:** 309-345-0098
www.outfitters.com/illinois/knox/knox.html

In northwestern IL south of Moline; organized Jan 13, 1825 from Fulton County. **Name Origin:** For Gen. Henry Knox (1750-1806), Revolutionary War officer and first U.S. secretary of war (1785-95).

Area (sq mi): 719.7 (land 716.28; water 3.42).

Pop: 55,836 (White 88.4%; Black or African American 6.3%; Hispanic or Latino 3.4%; Asian 0.7%; Other 3.2%). **Foreign born:** 1.6%. **Median age:** 39.4. **State rank:** 25. **Pop change 1990-2000:** -1%.

Income: per capita $17,985; median household $35,407. **Pop below poverty level:** 11.1%.

Unemployment: 5.7%. **Median home value:** $63,500. **Median travel time to work:** 18.2 minutes.

LA SALLE COUNTY
707 E Etna Rd   **Ph:** 815-434-8205
Ottawa, IL 61350   **Fax:** 815-434-8319
www.lasallecounty.org

In north-central IL southwest of Chicago; organized Jan 15, 1831 from Putnam and Vermilion counties. **Name Origin:** For Robert

All statistics are based on the 2000 Census except the dollar figures given for per capita income, which are based on 1999 estimates.

Cavelier (1643-87), Sieur de La Salle, French adventurer and explorer who claimed the land west of the Mississippi River for France.

Area (sq mi): 1148.04 (land 1134.92; water 13.12).

Pop: 111,509 (White 91.9%; Black or African American 1.5%; Hispanic or Latino 5.2%; Asian 0.5%; Other 2.9%). **Foreign born:** 2.7%. **Median age:** 38.1. **State rank:** 17. **Pop change 1990-2000:** +4.3%.

Income: per capita $19,185; median household $40,308. **Pop below poverty level:** 9.1%.

Unemployment: 6.6%. **Median home value:** $87,000. **Median travel time to work:** 22.5 minutes.

LAKE COUNTY

18 N County St   **Ph:** 847-360-6600
Waukegan, IL 60085   **Fax:** 847-360-3608
www.co.lake.il.us

On the northeastern border of IL; organized Mar 1, 1839 from McHenry County. **Name Origin:** For Lake Michigan, which forms its eastern boundary.

Area (sq mi): 1367.95 (land 447.56; water 920.39).

Pop: 644,356 (White 73.4%; Black or African American 6.9%; Hispanic or Latino 14.4%; Asian 3.9%; Other 9%). **Foreign born:** 14.8%. **Median age:** 33.8. **State rank:** 3. **Pop change 1990-2000:** +24.8%.

Income: per capita $32,102; median household $66,973. **Pop below poverty level:** 5.7%.

Unemployment: 4.6%. **Median home value:** $198,200. **Median travel time to work:** 30.1 minutes.

LAWRENCE COUNTY

County Courthouse   **Ph:** 618-943-2346
Lawrenceville, IL 62439   **Fax:** 618-943-5205

On the east-central border of IL east of Olney; organized Jan 16, 1821 from Crawford and Edwards counties. **Name Origin:** For Capt. James Lawrence (1781-1813), U.S. naval officer in the war with Barbary pirates near Tripoli and commander of the U.S.S. *Chesapeake* in the War of 1812, who said, 'Don't give up the ship!'

Area (sq mi): 373.94 (land 371.98; water 1.96).

Pop: 15,452 (White 97.4%; Black or African American 0.8%; Hispanic or Latino 0.9%; Asian 0.1%; Other 1.1%). **Foreign born:** 0.6%. **Median age:** 40.8. **State rank:** 74. **Pop change 1990-2000:** -3.3%.

Income: per capita $17,070; median household $30,361. **Pop below poverty level:** 13.7%.

Unemployment: 6.8%. **Median home value:** $45,800. **Median travel time to work:** 20.3 minutes.

LEE COUNTY

112 E 2nd St   **Ph:** 815-288-3309
Dixon, IL 61021   **Fax:** 815-288-6492
www.leecountyillinois.com

In north-central IL south of Rockford; organized Feb 27, 1839

from Ogle County. **Name Origin:** For Richard Henry Lee (1732-1794), VA statesman, a signer of the Declaration of Independence, and U.S. senator from VA (1789-92).

Area (sq mi): 729.29 (land 725.36; water 3.92).

Pop: 36,062 (White 90.5%; Black or African American 4.9%; Hispanic or Latino 3.2%; Asian 0.6%; Other 1.8%). **Foreign born:** 1.9%. **Median age:** 37.9. **State rank:** 40. **Pop change 1990-2000:** +4.9%.

Income: per capita $18,650; median household $40,967. **Pop below poverty level:** 7.7%.

Unemployment: 5.2%. **Median home value:** $83,400. **Median travel time to work:** 21.8 minutes.

LIVINGSTON COUNTY

112 W Madison St   **Ph:** 815-844-2006
Pontiac, IL 61764   **Fax:** 815-842-1844

In east-central IL, northeast of Peoria, organized Feb 27, 1837 from La Salle and McLean counties. **Name Origin:** For Edward Livingston (1764-1836), NY legislator, LA legislator and U.S. senator (1829-31), and U.S. secretary of state (1831-33).

Area (sq mi): 1045.43 (land 1043.76; water 1.67).

Pop: 39,678 (White 91.1%; Black or African American 5.2%; Hispanic or Latino 2.7%; Asian 0.3%; Other 2.2%). **Foreign born:** 1.3%. **Median age:** 37.3. **State rank:** 35. **Pop change 1990-2000:** +1%.

Income: per capita $18,347; median household $41,342. **Pop below poverty level:** 8.8%.

Unemployment: 4.3%. **Median home value:** $79,700. **Median travel time to work:** 20.3 minutes.

LOGAN COUNTY

601 Broadway St Rm 20   **Ph:** 217-732-4148
Lincoln, IL 62656   **Fax:** 217-732-6064
www.co.logan.il.us

In central IL, northeast of Springfield; organized Feb 15, 1839 from Sangamon County. **Name Origin:** For Dr. John Logan, an immigrant from Ireland in 1823, IL legislator, and father of John Alexander Logan (1826-86), U.S. general and statesman.

Area (sq mi): 619.01 (land 618.14; water 0.87).

Pop: 31,183 (White 90.6%; Black or African American 6.6%; Hispanic or Latino 1.6%; Asian 0.5%; Other 1.2%). **Foreign born:** 1.4%. **Median age:** 37. **State rank:** 49. **Pop change 1990-2000:** +1.3%.

Income: per capita $17,953; median household $39,389. **Pop below poverty level:** 8.1%.

Unemployment: 4.1%. **Median home value:** $75,700. **Median travel time to work:** 20.3 minutes.

MACON COUNTY

141 S Main St Rm 104   **Ph:** 217-424-1305
Decatur, IL 62523   **Fax:** 217-423-0922

In central IL, east of Springfield, organized Jan 19, 1829 from Shelby County. **Name Origin:** For Nathaniel Macon (1757-1837),

Please see sample entry on inside front cover for detailed information about the statistics presented with each county listing.

159

NC legislator, U.S. representative (1791-1815), U.S. senator (1815-28), and president of the NC constitutional convention (1835).

Area (sq mi): 585.38 (land 580.52; water 4.86).

Pop: 114,706 (White 82.9%; Black or African American 14.1%; Hispanic or Latino 1%; Asian 0.6%; Other 1.9%). **Foreign born:** 1.4%. **Median age:** 38. **State rank:** 16. **Pop change 1990-2000:** -2.1%.

Income: per capita $20,067; median household $37,859. **Pop below poverty level:** 12.9%.

Unemployment: 6.3%. **Median home value:** $69,800. **Median travel time to work:** 18.2 minutes.

MACOUPIN COUNTY

PO Box 107   **Ph:** 217-854-3214
Carlinville, IL 62626   **Fax:** 217-854-8461

In west-central IL, southwest of Springfield, organized Jan 17, 1829 from Madison and Greene counties. **Name Origin:** From an Algonquian Indian word probably meaning 'white potato.'

Area (sq mi): 867.61 (land 863.57; water 4.04).

Pop: 49,019 (White 97.6%; Black or African American 0.8%; Hispanic or Latino 0.6%; Asian 0.2%; Other 0.9%). **Foreign born:** 0.5%. **Median age:** 38.9. **State rank:** 30. **Pop change 1990-2000:** +2.8%.

Income: per capita $17,298; median household $36,190. **Pop below poverty level:** 9.4%.

Unemployment: 5.9%. **Median home value:** $66,700. **Median travel time to work:** 27.1 minutes.

MADISON COUNTY

157 N Main St Suite 109   **Ph:** 618-692-6290
Edwardsville, IL 62025   **Fax:** 618-692-8903
www.co.madison.il.us

On the west-central border of IL, north of Saint Louis; organized Sep 14, 1812 (prior to statehood) from Saint Clair County. **Name Origin:** For James Madison (1751-1836), fourth U.S. president.

Area (sq mi): 740.35 (land 725.02; water 15.33).

Pop: 258,941 (White 89.3%; Black or African American 7.3%; Hispanic or Latino 1.5%; Asian 0.6%; Other 1.9%). **Foreign born:** 1.3%. **Median age:** 36.9. **State rank:** 8. **Pop change 1990-2000:** +3.9%.

Income: per capita $20,509; median household $41,541. **Pop below poverty level:** 9.8%.

Unemployment: 5.6%. **Median home value:** $77,200. **Median travel time to work:** 24.3 minutes.

MARION COUNTY

PO Box 637   **Ph:** 618-548-3400
Salem, IL 62881   **Fax:** 618-548-2226

In south-central IL west of Olney; organized Jan 24, 1823 from Fayette and Jefferson counties. **Name Origin:** For Gen. Francis Marion (c. 1732-95), SC soldier and legislator, know as 'The Swamp Fox' for his tactics during the Revolutionary War.

Area (sq mi): 575.71 (land 572.26; water 3.44).

Pop: 41,691 (White 93.4%; Black or African American 3.8%; Hispanic or Latino 0.9%; Asian 0.6%; Other 1.5%). **Foreign born:** 0.8%. **Median age:** 38.4. **State rank:** 33. **Pop change 1990-2000:** +0.3%.

Income: per capita $17,235; median household $35,227. **Pop below poverty level:** 11.3%.

Unemployment: 10.8%. **Median home value:** $53,700. **Median travel time to work:** 19.8 minutes.

MARSHALL COUNTY

PO Box 328   **Ph:** 309-246-6325
Lacon, IL 61540   **Fax:** 309-246-3667
www.co.marshall.il.us

In north-central IL north of Peoria; organized Jan 19, 1839 from Putnam County. **Name Origin:** For John Marshall (1755-1835), American jurist and fourth Chief Justice of the U.S. Supreme Court (1801-35).

Area (sq mi): 398.52 (land 386.06; water 12.45).

Pop: 13,180 (White 97.6%; Black or African American 0.3%; Hispanic or Latino 1%; Asian 0.3%; Other 1.2%). **Foreign born:** 1%. **Median age:** 40.9. **State rank:** 83. **Pop change 1990-2000:** +2.6%.

Income: per capita $19,065; median household $41,576. **Pop below poverty level:** 5.6%.

Unemployment: 4.9%. **Median home value:** $75,900. **Median travel time to work:** 25.3 minutes.

MASON COUNTY

PO Box 77   **Ph:** 309-543-6661
Havana, IL 62644   **Fax:** 309-543-2085
www.outfitters.com/~masonch/

In central IL southwest of Peoria; organized Jan 20, 1841 from Tazewell County. **Name Origin:** For the county in KY, former home of many of the settlers.

Area (sq mi): 563.37 (land 538.94; water 24.43).

Pop: 16,038 (White 98.5%; Black or African American 0.1%; Hispanic or Latino 0.5%; Asian 0.2%; Other 0.9%). **Foreign born:** 0.4%. **Median age:** 39.5. **State rank:** 73. **Pop change 1990-2000:** -1.4%.

Income: per capita $17,357; median household $35,985. **Pop below poverty level:** 9.7%.

Unemployment: 6.7%. **Median home value:** $61,200. **Median travel time to work:** 28.9 minutes.

MASSAC COUNTY

PO Box 429   **Ph:** 618-524-5213
Metropolis, IL 62960   **Fax:** 618-524-8514

On the southern border of IL; organized Feb 8, 1843 from Pope and Johnson counties. **Name Origin:** For Fort Massac, originally named Fort Ascension and then renamed to honor Massiac, a French naval minister. The 'i' was dropped to form the current spelling.

Area (sq mi): 242.12 (land 239.05; water 3.06).

Pop: 15,161 (White 92.1%; Black or African American 5.5%; Hispanic or Latino 0.8%; Asian 0.3%; Other 1.7%). **Foreign born:**

All statistics are based on the 2000 Census except the dollar figures given for per capita income, which are based on 1999 estimates.

0.4%. **Median age:** 39.6. **State rank:** 76. **Pop change 1990-2000:** +2.8%.

Income: per capita $16,334; median household $31,498. **Pop below poverty level:** 13.5%.

Unemployment: 4.9%. **Median home value:** $63,300. **Median travel time to work:** 21.1 minutes.

McDONOUGH COUNTY

1 Courthouse Sq   **Ph:** 309-833-2474
Macomb, IL 61455   **Fax:** 309-836-3368
www.outfitters.com/illinois/mcdonough/

In west-central IL southwest of Peoria; organized Jan 25, 1826 from Schuyler County. **Name Origin:** For Capt. Thomas McDonough (1783-1825), naval officer in the war against Barbary pirates near Tripoli and in the War of 1812.

Area (sq mi): 590.02 (land 589.27; water 0.75).

Pop: 32,913 (White 92%; Black or African American 3.5%; Hispanic or Latino 1.5%; Asian 2%; Other 1.6%). **Foreign born:** 2.8%. **Median age:** 29. **State rank:** 47. **Pop change 1990-2000:** -6.6%.

Income: per capita $15,890; median household $32,141. **Pop below poverty level:** 19.8%.

Unemployment: 3.1%. **Median home value:** $61,200. **Median travel time to work:** 15.6 minutes.

McHENRY COUNTY

2200 N Seminary Ave   **Ph:** 815-334-4000
Woodstock, IL 60098   **Fax:** 815-334-8727
www.co.mchenry.il.us

On the northern border of IL, northwest of Chicago; organized Jan 16, 1836 from Cook county. **Name Origin:** For Maj. William McHenry (1774-1839), officer in the War of 1812 and the Black Hawk War (1832).

Area (sq mi): 611.13 (land 603.51; water 7.62).

Pop: 260,077 (White 89.6%; Black or African American 0.6%; Hispanic or Latino 7.5%; Asian 1.5%; Other 4.1%). **Foreign born:** 7.2%. **Median age:** 34.2. **State rank:** 7. **Pop change 1990-2000:** +41.9%.

Income: per capita $26,476; median household $64,826. **Pop below poverty level:** 3.7%.

Unemployment: 4.6%. **Median home value:** $168,100. **Median travel time to work:** 32.2 minutes.

McLEAN COUNTY

104 W Front St Rm 704   **Ph:** 309-888-5190
Bloomington, IL 61701   **Fax:** 309-888-5932
www.co.mclean.il.us

In central IL, southeast of Peoria; organized Dec 25, 1830 from Tazewell County. **Name Origin:** For John McLean (1791-1830), first U.S. representative from IL (1818-19) and U.S. senator (1824-25;1829-30).

Area (sq mi): 1186.29 (land 1183.53; water 2.76).

Pop: 150,433 (White 87.9%; Black or African American 6.2%; Hispanic or Latino 2.5%; Asian 2.1%; Other 2.6%). **Foreign born:**

3.3%. **Median age:** 30.5. **State rank:** 13. **Pop change 1990-2000:** +16.5%.

Income: per capita $22,227; median household $47,021. **Pop below poverty level:** 9.7%.

Unemployment: 2.4%. **Median home value:** $114,800. **Median travel time to work:** 17 minutes.

MENARD COUNTY

PO Box 465   **Ph:** 217-632-2415
Petersburg, IL 62675   **Fax:** 217-632-4301

In central IL, north of Springfield; organized Feb 15, 1839 Sangamon County. **Name Origin:** For Lt. Col. Pierre Menard (1766-1844), jurist, first presiding officer of IL Territorial legislature (1812), and first lieutenant governor (1818-22).

Area (sq mi): 315.37 (land 314.25; water 1.13).

Pop: 12,486 (White 98%; Black or African American 0.4%; Hispanic or Latino 0.8%; Asian 0.2%; Other 0.8%). **Foreign born:** 0.7%. **Median age:** 38. **State rank:** 86. **Pop change 1990-2000:** +11.8%.

Income: per capita $21,584; median household $46,596. **Pop below poverty level:** 8.2%.

Unemployment: 4.4%. **Median home value:** $93,600. **Median travel time to work:** 27.9 minutes.

MERCER COUNTY

PO Box 66   **Ph:** 309-582-7021
Aledo, IL 61231   **Fax:** 309-582-7022

On the western border of IL, south of Davenport, IA; organized Jan 13, 1825 from Pike County. **Name Origin:** For Gen. Hugh Mercer (1721-77), Revolutionary War officer and physician.

Area (sq mi): 568.88 (land 561.02; water 7.86).

Pop: 16,957 (White 97.6%; Black or African American 0.3%; Hispanic or Latino 1.3%; Asian 0.2%; Other 1.2%). **Foreign born:** 0.6%. **Median age:** 39.5. **State rank:** 68. **Pop change 1990-2000:** -1.9%.

Income: per capita $18,645; median household $40,893. **Pop below poverty level:** 7.8%.

Unemployment: 6.5%. **Median home value:** $68,500. **Median travel time to work:** 27.8 minutes.

MONROE COUNTY

100 S Main St   **Ph:** 618-939-8681
Waterloo, IL 62298   **Fax:** 618-939-5132

On the southwest border of IL, south of Saint Louis, MO; organized Jan 6, 1816 (prior to statehood) from Randolph and Saint Clair counties. **Name Origin:** For James Monroe (1758-1831), fifth U.S. president.

Area (sq mi): 397.71 (land 388.29; water 9.42).

Pop: 27,619 (White 98.3%; Black or African American 0.1%; Hispanic or Latino 0.7%; Asian 0.3%; Other 0.9%). **Foreign born:** 0.8%. **Median age:** 37.5. **State rank:** 51. **Pop change 1990-2000:** +23.2%.

Income: per capita $22,954; median household $55,320. **Pop below poverty level:** 3.4%.

Please see sample entry on inside front cover for detailed information about the statistics presented with each county listing.

161

Unemployment: 4%. **Median home value:** $125,500. **Median travel time to work:** 29.4 minutes.

MONTGOMERY COUNTY

PO Box 595   **Ph:** 217-532-9530
Hillsboro, IL 62049   **Fax:** 217-532-9581
www.montgomeryco.com

In central IL, south of Springfield; organized Feb 12, 1821 from Bond and Madison counties. **Name Origin:** For Gen. Richard Montgomery (1736-75), American Revolutionary War officer who captured Montreal, Canada.

Area (sq mi): 709.75 (land 703.8; water 5.96).

Pop: 30,652 (White 94.4%; Black or African American 3.7%; Hispanic or Latino 1.1%; Asian 0.2%; Other 1.2%). **Foreign born:** 0.9%. **Median age:** 38.1. **State rank:** 50. **Pop change 1990-2000:** -0.2%.

Income: per capita $16,272; median household $33,123. **Pop below poverty level:** 13.4%.

Unemployment: 6.7%. **Median home value:** $54,800. **Median travel time to work:** 24.8 minutes.

MORGAN COUNTY

PO Box 1387   **Ph:** 217-243-8581
Jacksonville, IL 62651   **Fax:** 217-243-8368

In west-central IL, west of Springfield; organized Jan 31, 1823 from Sangamon County. **Name Origin:** For Gen. Daniel Morgan (1732-1802), an officer in the Revolutionary War and U.S. representative from VA (1797-99).

Area (sq mi): 572.26 (land 568.76; water 3.51).

Pop: 36,616 (White 91.7%; Black or African American 5.4%; Hispanic or Latino 1.4%; Asian 0.5%; Other 1.9%). **Foreign born:** 1.1%. **Median age:** 37.8. **State rank:** 39. **Pop change 1990-2000:** +0.6%.

Income: per capita $18,205; median household $36,933. **Pop below poverty level:** 9.7%.

Unemployment: 4.4%. **Median home value:** $75,800. **Median travel time to work:** 19.3 minutes.

MOULTRIE COUNTY

County Courthouse 10 S Main St Suite 6   **Ph:** 217-728-4389
Sullivan, IL 61951   **Fax:** 217-728-8178

In central IL southwest of Decatur; organized Feb 16, 1843 from Macon and Shelby counties. **Name Origin:** For Gen. William Moultrie (1731-1805), an officer in the Revolutionary War and governor of SC (1785-87; 1792-94).

Area (sq mi): 344.47 (land 335.6; water 8.87).

Pop: 14,287 (White 98.5%; Black or African American 0.2%; Hispanic or Latino 0.5%; Asian 0.1%; Other 0.8%). **Foreign born:** 0.6%. **Median age:** 38.7. **State rank:** 80. **Pop change 1990-2000:** +2.6%.

Income: per capita $18,562; median household $40,084. **Pop below poverty level:** 7.8%.

Unemployment: 4.5%. **Median home value:** $72,800. **Median travel time to work:** 21.4 minutes.

OGLE COUNTY

PO Box 357   **Ph:** 815-732-3201
Oregon, IL 61061   **Fax:** 815-732-6273
www.oglecounty.org

In north-central IL south of Rockford; organized Jan 16, 1836 from Jo Daviess County. **Name Origin:** For Lt. Joseph Ogle, first Methodist layman in IL and captain of the territorial militia.

Area (sq mi): 763.27 (land 758.83; water 4.43).

Pop: 51,032 (White 92.2%; Black or African American 0.4%; Hispanic or Latino 6%; Asian 0.4%; Other 3.8%). **Foreign born:** 4.3%. **Median age:** 37.2. **State rank:** 28. **Pop change 1990-2000:** +11%.

Income: per capita $20,515; median household $45,448. **Pop below poverty level:** 7.1%.

Unemployment: 5.4%. **Median home value:** $102,700. **Median travel time to work:** 22.8 minutes.

PEORIA COUNTY

324 Main St Rm 101   **Ph:** 309-672-6059
Peoria, IL 61602   **Fax:** 309-672-6063
www.co.peoria.il.us

In central IL, east of Galesburg; organized Jan 13, 1825 from Fulton County., **Name Origin:** For the Peoria tribe of the Illinois nation; anglicized from French *peourea*, a transliteration of an Illinois word. Meaning of name is in dispute; possibly 'carriers' or 'ones who are carrying packs.'

Area (sq mi): 630.89 (land 619.52; water 11.36).

Pop: 183,433 (White 78.5%; Black or African American 16.1%; Hispanic or Latino 2.1%; Asian 1.7%; Other 2.8%). **Foreign born:** 3.2%. **Median age:** 36. **State rank:** 11. **Pop change 1990-2000:** +0.3%.

Income: per capita $21,219; median household $39,978. **Pop below poverty level:** 13.7%.

Unemployment: 5.1%. **Median home value:** $85,800. **Median travel time to work:** 18.6 minutes.

PERRY COUNTY

PO Box 438   **Ph:** 618-357-5116
Pinckneyville, IL 62274

In south-central IL north of Carbondale; organized Jan 29, 1827 from Randolph and Jackson counties. **Name Origin:** For Oliver Hazard Perry (1785-1819), U.S. naval officer during the War of 1812, famous for the message, 'We have met the enemy and they are ours.'

Area (sq mi): 446.81 (land 440.96; water 5.85).

Pop: 23,094 (White 89%; Black or African American 8%; Hispanic or Latino 1.8%; Asian 0.3%; Other 2.1%). **Foreign born:** 1%. **Median age:** 37.6. **State rank:** 53. **Pop change 1990-2000:** +7.9%.

Income: per capita $15,935; median household $33,281. **Pop below poverty level:** 13.2%.

Unemployment: 8.8%. **Median home value:** $55,000. **Median travel time to work:** 23.4 minutes.

All statistics are based on the 2000 Census except the dollar figures given for per capita income, which are based on 1999 estimates.

PIATT COUNTY

PO Box 558
Monticello, IL 61856
www.piattcounty.org

Ph: 217-762-9487
Fax: 217-762-7563

In central IL, west of Urbana, organized Jan 27, 1841 from De Wiltt and Macon counties. **Name Origin:** For either James A. Piatt, Sr. (1789-1838), an early settler, or Benjamin Piatt, attorney general of IL Territory (1810-13).

Area (sq mi): 440.33 (land 440.02; water 0.31).

Pop: 16,365 (White 98.3%; Black or African American 0.2%; Hispanic or Latino 0.6%; Asian 0.1%; Other 0.8%). **Foreign born:** 0.6%. **Median age:** 39.6. **State rank:** 71. **Pop change 1990-2000:** +5.3%.

Income: per capita $21,075; median household $45,752. **Pop below poverty level:** 5%.

Unemployment: 3.8%. **Median home value:** $82,600. **Median travel time to work:** 23.6 minutes.

PIKE COUNTY

100 E Washington St Courthouse
Pittsfield, IL 62363
www.pikeil.org

Ph: 217-285-6812
Fax: 217-285-5820

On the west-central border of IL, south of Quincy; organized Jan 31, 1821 from Madison, Bond, and Clark counties. **Name Origin:** For Zebulon Montgomery Pike (1779-1813), U.S. army officer and discoverer of Pikes Peak in CO.

Area (sq mi): 848.87 (land 830.3; water 18.57).

Pop: 17,384 (White 97%; Black or African American 1.5%; Hispanic or Latino 0.5%; Asian 0.2%; Other 0.9%). **Foreign born:** 1.1%. **Median age:** 39.8. **State rank:** 65. **Pop change 1990-2000:** -1.1%.

Income: per capita $15,946; median household $31,127. **Pop below poverty level:** 12.4%.

Unemployment: 5.7%. **Median home value:** $54,000. **Median travel time to work:** 24.5 minutes.

POPE COUNTY

PO Box 216
Golconda, IL 62938

Ph: 618-683-4466
Fax: 618-683-4466

On the southeastern border of IL; organized Jan 10, 1816 (prior to statehood) from Johnson and Gallatin counties. **Name Origin:** For Nathaniel Pope (1784-1850), first territorial secretary of IL Territory (1809-16) and U.S. district judge for IL (1819-50).

Area (sq mi): 374.64 (land 370.86; water 3.77).

Pop: 4,413 (White 93%; Black or African American 3.8%; Hispanic or Latino 0.9%; Asian 0.3%; Other 2.7%). **Foreign born:** 0.7%. **Median age:** 41.1. **State rank:** 102. **Pop change 1990-2000:** +0.9%.

Income: per capita $16,440; median household $30,048. **Pop below poverty level:** 18.2%.

Unemployment: 8.6%. **Median home value:** $50,600. **Median travel time to work:** 30.4 minutes.

PULASKI COUNTY

PO Box 118
Mound City, IL 62963

Ph: 618-748-9360
Fax: 618-748-9305

On the southern border of IL; organized Mar 3, 1843 from Johnson County. **Name Origin:** For Count Casimir Pulaski (1747-79), Polish soldier who fought for America during the Revolutionary War.

Area (sq mi): 203.33 (land 200.79; water 2.55).

Pop: 7,348 (White 65.9%; Black or African American 31%; Hispanic or Latino 1.5%; Asian 0.9%; Other 1.5%). **Foreign born:** 0.7%. **Median age:** 37.7. **State rank:** 92. **Pop change 1990-2000:** -2.3%.

Income: per capita $13,325; median household $25,361. **Pop below poverty level:** 24.7%.

Unemployment: 9.4%. **Median home value:** $33,300. **Median travel time to work:** 25.8 minutes.

PUTNAM COUNTY

PO Box 236
Hennepin, IL 61327

Ph: 815-925-7129
Fax: 815-925-7549

In north-central IL, northeast of Peoria; organized Jan 13, 1825 from Fulton County. **Name Origin:** For Gen. Israel Putnam (1718-90), Revolutionary War officer and American commander at Battle of Bunker Hill.

Area (sq mi): 172.24 (land 159.8; water 12.45).

Pop: 6,086 (White 95.6%; Black or African American 0.6%; Hispanic or Latino 2.8%; Asian 0.3%; Other 1.4%). **Foreign born:** 1.8%. **Median age:** 39.6. **State rank:** 98. **Pop change 1990-2000:** +6.2%.

Income: per capita $19,792; median household $45,492. **Pop below poverty level:** 5.5%.

Unemployment: 6.2%. **Median home value:** $89,100. **Median travel time to work:** 23.8 minutes.

RANDOLPH COUNTY

1 Taylor St
Chester, IL 62233

Ph: 618-826-2510
Fax: 618-826-3750

On the southwestern border of IL; organized Oct 5, 1795 (prior to statehood) from Saint Clair County. **Name Origin:** For Edmund Jennings Randolph (1753-1813), governor of VA (1786-88), first U.S. Attorney General (1789), and U.S. secretary of state (1794-95).

Area (sq mi): 597.26 (land 578.42; water 18.84).

Pop: 33,893 (White 88.1%; Black or African American 9.3%; Hispanic or Latino 1.5%; Asian 0.2%; Other 1.8%). **Foreign born:** 0.8%. **Median age:** 37.6. **State rank:** 46. **Pop change 1990-2000:** -2%.

Income: per capita $17,696; median household $37,013. **Pop below poverty level:** 10%.

Unemployment: 5.7%. **Median home value:** $65,700. **Median travel time to work:** 22.9 minutes.

RICHLAND COUNTY

103 W Main St
Olney, IL 62450

Ph: 618-392-3111
Fax: 618-393-4005

In southeastern IL; organized Feb 24, 1841 from Clay and Lawrence counties. **Name Origin:** For the county in OH.

Please see sample entry on inside front cover for detailed information about the statistics presented with each county listing.

Area (sq mi): 362.01 (land 360.14; water 1.87).

Pop: 16,149 (White 97.7%; Black or African American 0.3%; Hispanic or Latino 0.8%; Asian 0.6%; Other 0.9%). **Foreign born:** 0.6%. **Median age:** 39.1. **State rank:** 72. **Pop change 1990-2000:** -2.4%.

Income: per capita $16,847; median household $31,185. **Pop below poverty level:** 12.9%.

Unemployment: 6.8%. **Median home value:** $62,500. **Median travel time to work:** 16.1 minutes.

ROCK ISLAND COUNTY

1504 3rd Ave   **Ph:** 309-786-4451
Rock Island, IL 61201   **Fax:** 309-786-7381
www.co.rock-island.il.us

On the northwestern border of IL; organized Feb 9, 1831 from Jo Daviess County. **Name Origin:** For an island in the Mississippi River near the mouth of the Rock River.

Area (sq mi): 451.16 (land 426.75; water 24.4).

Pop: 149,374 (White 81.5%; Black or African American 7.5%; Hispanic or Latino 8.6%; Asian 1%; Other 6%). **Foreign born:** 4.6%. **Median age:** 37.8. **State rank:** 14. **Pop change 1990-2000:** +0.4%.

Income: per capita $20,164; median household $38,608. **Pop below poverty level:** 10.7%.

Unemployment: 5.4%. **Median home value:** $78,900. **Median travel time to work:** 18.7 minutes.

SAINT CLAIR COUNTY

10 Public Sq   **Ph:** 618-277-6600
Belleville, IL 62220   **Fax:** 618-277-2868
co.st-clair.il.us

On the west-central border of IL, east of Saint Louis, MO; organized Apr 27, 1790 (prior to statehood) from Northwest Territory. **Name Origin:** For Gen. Arthur Saint Clair (1736?-1818), an officer in the French and Indian War and the Revolutionary War, president of the Continental Congress (1787), and governor of the Northwest Territory (1788-1802).

Area (sq mi): 673.95 (land 663.81; water 10.15).

Pop: 256,082 (White 66.8%; Black or African American 28.8%; Hispanic or Latino 2.2%; Asian 0.9%; Other 2.4%). **Foreign born:** 2.1%. **Median age:** 35.3. **State rank:** 9. **Pop change 1990-2000:** -2.6%.

Income: per capita $18,932; median household $39,148. **Pop below poverty level:** 14.5%.

Unemployment: 6.2%. **Median home value:** $77,700. **Median travel time to work:** 24.7 minutes.

SALINE COUNTY

10 E Poplar St   **Ph:** 618-253-8197
Harrisburg, IL 62946   **Fax:** 618-252-3073

In southeastern IL, east of Carbondale; organized Feb 25, 1847 from Gallatin County. **Name Origin:** For the Saline River, which traverses the county.

Area (sq mi): 386.98 (land 383.31; water 3.67).

Pop: 26,733 (White 93.6%; Black or African American 4.1%; Hispanic or Latino 1%; Asian 0.2%; Other 1.6%). **Foreign born:** 0.7%. **Median age:** 39.9. **State rank:** 52. **Pop change 1990-2000:** +0.7%.

Income: per capita $15,590; median household $28,768. **Pop below poverty level:** 14.2%.

Unemployment: 7.1%. **Median home value:** $48,300. **Median travel time to work:** 21.8 minutes.

SANGAMON COUNTY

200 S 9th St   **Ph:** 217-753-6706
Springfield, IL 62701   **Fax:** 217-753-6672
www.co.sangamon.il.us

In central IL, east of Decatur; organized Jan 30, 1821 from Bond and Madison counties. **Name Origin:** For the Sangamon River, which flows through the county; from Ojibway, possibly 'the outlet' or 'the land of plenty to eat.'

Area (sq mi): 877.01 (land 868.18; water 8.82).

Pop: 188,951 (White 86.8%; Black or African American 9.7%; Hispanic or Latino 1.1%; Asian 1.1%; Other 1.8%). **Foreign born:** 1.9%. **Median age:** 37.3. **State rank:** 10. **Pop change 1990-2000:** +5.9%.

Income: per capita $23,173; median household $42,957. **Pop below poverty level:** 9.3%.

Unemployment: 3.9%. **Median home value:** $91,200. **Median travel time to work:** 19 minutes.

SCHUYLER COUNTY

PO Box 200   **Ph:** 217-322-4734
Rushville, IL 62681   **Fax:** 217-322-6164

In west-central IL, northeast of Quincy; organized Jan 13, 1825 from Pike and Fulton counties. **Name Origin:** For Gen. Philip John Schuyler (1733-1804), an officer in the Revolutionary War, member of the Continental Congress (1775-77; 1778-81), and U.S. senator from NY (1789-91; 1797-98).

Area (sq mi): 441.39 (land 437.31; water 4.07).

Pop: 7,189 (White 98.6%; Black or African American 0.2%; Hispanic or Latino 0.5%; Asian 0.1%; Other 0.9%). **Foreign born:** 0.4%. **Median age:** 40.9. **State rank:** 93. **Pop change 1990-2000:** -4.1%.

Income: per capita $17,158; median household $35,233. **Pop below poverty level:** 10.1%.

Unemployment: 4.4%. **Median home value:** $54,000. **Median travel time to work:** 21.8 minutes.

SCOTT COUNTY

County Courthouse 35 E Market St   **Ph:** 217-742-3178
Winchester, IL 62694

In west-central IL, southwest of Springfield; organized Feb 16, 1839 from Morgan County. **Name Origin:** For the county in KY.

Area (sq mi): 252.77 (land 250.92; water 1.85).

Pop: 5,537 (White 99.3%; Black or African American 0%; Hispanic or Latino 0.2%; Asian 0.1%; Other 0.3%). **Foreign born:** 0.5%. **Median age:** 38.8. **State rank:** 99. **Pop change 1990-2000:** -1.9%.

All statistics are based on the 2000 Census except the dollar figures given for per capita income, which are based on 1999 estimates.

Income: per capita $16,998; median household $36,566. **Pop below poverty level:** 9.7%.

Unemployment: 5.4%. **Median home value:** $57,800. **Median travel time to work:** 24.7 minutes.

SHELBY COUNTY
PO Box 230   **Ph:** 217-774-4421
Shelbyville, IL 62565   **Fax:** 217-774-5291

In central IL, south of Decatur; organized Jan 23, 1827 from Fayette County. **Name Origin:** For Gen. Isaac Shelby (1750-1826), officer in the Revolutionary War, NC legislator, and governor of KY (1792-96; 1812-16).

Area (sq mi): 768.05 (land 758.51; water 9.54).

Pop: 22,893 (White 98.6%; Black or African American 0.2%; Hispanic or Latino 0.5%; Asian 0.2%; Other 0.6%). **Foreign born:** 0.4%. **Median age:** 39.3. **State rank:** 54. **Pop change 1990-2000:** +2.8%.

Income: per capita $17,313; median household $37,313. **Pop below poverty level:** 9.1%.

Unemployment: 6.1%. **Median home value:** $66,600. **Median travel time to work:** 26.6 minutes.

STARK COUNTY
PO Box 97   **Ph:** 309-286-5911
Toulon, IL 61483   **Fax:** 309-286-4039
www.outfitters.com/illinois/stark/

In central IL, north of Peoria; organized Mar 2, 1839 from Knox and Putnam counties. **Name Origin:** For Gen. John Stark (1728-1822), officer in the French and Indian War and the Revolutionary War.

Area (sq mi): 288.21 (land 287.94; water 0.28).

Pop: 6,332 (White 98.1%; Black or African American 0.1%; Hispanic or Latino 0.9%; Asian 0.2%; Other 1.1%). **Foreign born:** 0.4%. **Median age:** 39.9. **State rank:** 97. **Pop change 1990-2000:** -3.1%.

Income: per capita $16,767; median household $35,826. **Pop below poverty level:** 8.6%.

Unemployment: 8%. **Median home value:** $61,800. **Median travel time to work:** 25.3 minutes.

STEPHENSON COUNTY
15 N Galena Ave Suite 1   **Ph:** 815-235-8289
Freeport, IL 61032   **Fax:** 815-235-8378
www.co.stephenson.il.us

Located on northern border of IL; organized on Mar 4, 1837 from Winnebago and Jo Daviess counties. **Name Origin:** For Benjamin Stephenson (?-1821), adjutant general of IL Territory (1813), IL legislator, and prominent banker.

Area (sq mi): 564.72 (land 564.18; water 0.54).

Pop: 48,979 (White 88.6%; Black or African American 7.7%; Hispanic or Latino 1.5%; Asian 0.7%; Other 2.3%). **Foreign born:** 1.9%. **Median age:** 38.5. **State rank:** 31. **Pop change 1990-2000:** +1.9%.

Income: per capita $19,794; median household $40,366. **Pop below poverty level:** 9%.

Unemployment: 7.1%. **Median home value:** $81,400. **Median travel time to work:** 19.9 minutes.

TAZEWELL COUNTY
11 S 4th St   **Ph:** 309-477-2264
Pekin, IL 61554   **Fax:** 309-477-2244

In central IL, south of Peoria; organized Jan 31, 1827 from Fayette County. **Name Origin:** For Littleton Waller Tazewell (1774-1860), VA legislator, U.S. senator (1824-32), and governor (1834-36).

Area (sq mi): 657.89 (land 648.86; water 9.03).

Pop: 128,485 (White 96.7%; Black or African American 0.9%; Hispanic or Latino 1%; Asian 0.5%; Other 1.3%). **Foreign born:** 1.1%. **Median age:** 38.1. **State rank:** 15. **Pop change 1990-2000:** +3.9%.

Income: per capita $21,511; median household $45,250. **Pop below poverty level:** 6.3%.

Unemployment: 4.5%. **Median home value:** $89,200. **Median travel time to work:** 20.6 minutes.

UNION COUNTY
309 W Market St Rm 100   **Ph:** 618-833-5711
Jonesboro, IL 62952   **Fax:** 618-833-8712

On the southwest border of IL, south of Carbondale; organized Jan 2, 1818 (prior to statehood) from Johnson County. **Name Origin:** For the temporary union of the Baptists and Dunkards.

Area (sq mi): 422.13 (land 416.16; water 5.97).

Pop: 18,293 (White 95.2%; Black or African American 0.8%; Hispanic or Latino 2.6%; Asian 0.3%; Other 2.6%). **Foreign born:** 1.9%. **Median age:** 40.3. **State rank:** 63. **Pop change 1990-2000:** +3.8%.

Income: per capita $16,450; median household $30,994. **Pop below poverty level:** 16.5%.

Unemployment: 5.6%. **Median home value:** $59,900. **Median travel time to work:** 22.9 minutes.

VERMILION COUNTY
6 N Vermilion Courthouse Annex   **Ph:** 217-431-2615
Danville, IL 61832   **Fax:** 217-431-2806
www.co.vermilion.il.us

On the east-central border of IL, east of Urbana; organized Jan 18, 1826 from Edgar County. **Name Origin:** For the Vermilion River, which runs through the county and is colored by the red soil.

Area (sq mi): 902.14 (land 899.08; water 3.06).

Pop: 83,919 (White 84.7%; Black or African American 10.6%; Hispanic or Latino 3%; Asian 0.6%; Other 2.9%). **Foreign born:** 1.7%. **Median age:** 38. **State rank:** 20. **Pop change 1990-2000:** -4.9%.

Income: per capita $16,787; median household $34,071. **Pop below poverty level:** 13.3%.

Unemployment: 7.4%. **Median home value:** $56,000. **Median travel time to work:** 20.4 minutes.

Please see sample entry on inside front cover for detailed information about the statistics presented with each county listing.

WABASH COUNTY

PO Box 277   **Ph:** 618-262-4561
Mount Carmel, IL 62863

On the southeastern border of IL, southeast of Olney; organized Dec 27, 1824 from Edwards County. **Name Origin:** For the Wabash River, from Miami Indian *wahba* 'white' and *shik-ki* 'color-bright', usually translated as 'white water.'

Area (sq mi): 227.76 (land 223.47; water 4.29).

Pop: 12,937 (White 97.4%; Black or African American 0.4%; Hispanic or Latino 0.7%; Asian 0.4%; Other 1.3%). **Foreign born:** 0.7%. **Median age:** 39. **State rank:** 84. **Pop change 1990-2000:** -1.3%.

Income: per capita $16,747; median household $34,473. **Pop below poverty level:** 14.1%.

Unemployment: 8.5%. **Median home value:** $56,200. **Median travel time to work:** 22.4 minutes.

WARREN COUNTY

100 W Broadway   **Ph:** 309-734-8592
Monmouth, IL 61462   **Fax:** 309-734-7406
www.outfitters.com/illinois/warren/

In northwest IL, west of Galesburg; organized Jan 13, 1825 from Pike County. **Name Origin:** For Gen. Joseph Warren (1741-75), Revolutionary War patriot and member of the Committee of Safety who dispatched Paul Revere (1735-1818) on his famous ride.

Area (sq mi): 543.17 (land 542.52; water 0.65).

Pop: 18,735 (White 94.3%; Black or African American 1.6%; Hispanic or Latino 2.7%; Asian 0.3%; Other 2.5%). **Foreign born:** 1.4%. **Median age:** 37.8. **State rank:** 62. **Pop change 1990-2000:** -2.3%.

Income: per capita $16,946; median household $36,224. **Pop below poverty level:** 9.2%.

Unemployment: 4.4%. **Median home value:** $57,600. **Median travel time to work:** 18.9 minutes.

WASHINGTON COUNTY

101 E Saint Louis St County Courthouse   **Ph:** 618-327-8314
Nashville, IL 62263   **Fax:** 618-327-3582

In south-central IL, southeast of Belleville; organized Jan 2, 1818 (prior to statehood) from Saint Clair County. **Name Origin:** For George Washington (1732-99), American patriot and first U.S. president.

Area (sq mi): 564.12 (land 562.61; water 1.51).

Pop: 15,148 (White 98%; Black or African American 0.3%; Hispanic or Latino 0.7%; Asian 0.2%; Other 0.8%). **Foreign born:** 0.6%. **Median age:** 38.8. **State rank:** 77. **Pop change 1990-2000:** +1.2%.

Income: per capita $19,108; median household $40,932. **Pop below poverty level:** 6%.

Unemployment: 4.2%. **Median home value:** $74,300. **Median travel time to work:** 23.9 minutes.

WAYNE COUNTY

PO Box 187   **Ph:** 618-842-5182
Fairfield, IL 62837   **Fax:** 618-842-2556

In southeastern IL, southwest of Olney; organized Mar 26, 1819 from Edwards County. **Name Origin:** For Gen. Anthony Wayne (1745-96), PA soldier and statesman, nicknamed 'Mad Anthony' for his daring during the Revolutionary War.

Area (sq mi): 715.56 (land 713.9; water 1.66).

Pop: 17,151 (White 98.3%; Black or African American 0.2%; Hispanic or Latino 0.6%; Asian 0.3%; Other 0.8%). **Foreign born:** 0.9%. **Median age:** 39.9. **State rank:** 66. **Pop change 1990-2000:** -0.5%.

Income: per capita $15,793; median household $30,481. **Pop below poverty level:** 12.4%.

Unemployment: 6.7%. **Median home value:** $48,600. **Median travel time to work:** 21 minutes.

WHITE COUNTY

PO Box 339   **Ph:** 618-382-7211
Carmi, IL 62821

On the southeastern border of IL; organized Dec 9, 1815 (prior to statehood) from Gallatin County. **Name Origin:** For Leonard White, a delegate to the IL Constitutional Convention (1818) and state legislator.

Area (sq mi): 501.7 (land 494.87; water 6.83).

Pop: 15,371 (White 97.8%; Black or African American 0.3%; Hispanic or Latino 0.7%; Asian 0.2%; Other 1.4%). **Foreign born:** 0.3%. **Median age:** 42. **State rank:** 75. **Pop change 1990-2000:** -7%.

Income: per capita $16,412; median household $29,601. **Pop below poverty level:** 12.5%.

Unemployment: 5.3%. **Median home value:** $43,100. **Median travel time to work:** 25.2 minutes.

WHITESIDE COUNTY

200 E Knox St   **Ph:** 815-772-5100
Morrison, IL 61270   **Fax:** 815-772-7673
www.whiteside.org

On the northwestern border of IL, northeast of Moline; organized Jan 16, 1836 from Jo Daviess and Henry counties. **Name Origin:** For Gen. Samuel Whiteside, officer in the War of 1812 and the Black Hawk War; IL legislator.

Area (sq mi): 697.01 (land 684.77; water 12.24).

Pop: 60,653 (White 88.9%; Black or African American 1%; Hispanic or Latino 8.8%; Asian 0.4%; Other 5.8%). **Foreign born:** 2.8%. **Median age:** 38.5. **State rank:** 23. **Pop change 1990-2000:** +0.8%.

Income: per capita $19,296; median household $40,354. **Pop below poverty level:** 8.5%.

Unemployment: 7%. **Median home value:** $75,700. **Median travel time to work:** 18.5 minutes.

All statistics are based on the 2000 Census except the dollar figures given for per capita income, which are based on 1999 estimates.

WILL COUNTY

302 N Chicago St **Ph:** 815-740-4615
Joliet, IL 60432 **Fax:** 815-740-4699
www.willcountyillinois.com

On the northeastern border of IL, south of Chicago; organized Jan 12, 1836 from Cook and Iroquois counties. **Name Origin:** For Dr. Conrad Will (1779-1835), physician and IL legislator.

Area (sq mi): 849.39 (land 836.94; water 12.45).

Pop: 502,266 (White 77.4%; Black or African American 10.5%; Hispanic or Latino 8.7%; Asian 2.2%; Other 5.4%). **Foreign born:** 7.1%. **Median age:** 33.3. **State rank:** 4. **Pop change 1990-2000:** +40.6%.

Income: per capita $24,613; median household $62,238. **Pop below poverty level:** 4.9%.

Unemployment: 5.2%. **Median home value:** $154,300. **Median travel time to work:** 32 minutes.

WILLIAMSON COUNTY

200 W Jefferson St **Ph:** 618-997-1301
Marion, IL 62959 **Fax:** 618-993-2071

In south-central IL, east of Carbondale; organized Feb 28, 1839 from Franklin County. **Name Origin:** For Williamson County, TN, former home of many early settlers.

Area (sq mi): 444.38 (land 423.41; water 20.96).

Pop: 61,296 (White 94.6%; Black or African American 2.5%; Hispanic or Latino 1.2%; Asian 0.5%; Other 1.7%). **Foreign born:** 1.1%. **Median age:** 38.8. **State rank:** 22. **Pop change 1990-2000:** +6.2%.

Income: per capita $17,779; median household $31,991. **Pop below poverty level:** 14.6%.

Unemployment: 5.7%. **Median home value:** $63,300. **Median travel time to work:** 21.6 minutes.

WINNEBAGO COUNTY

404 Elm St **Ph:** 815-987-3050
Rockford, IL 61101 **Fax:** 815-969-0259
www.co.winnebago.il.us

On the northern border of IL; organized Jan 16, 1836 from Jo Daviess County. **Name Origin:** For the Indian tribe of Siouan linguistic stock; their name is thought to mean 'fish eaters.'

Area (sq mi): 519.27 (land 513.74; water 5.54).

Pop: 278,418 (White 79.3%; Black or African American 10.5%; Hispanic or Latino 6.9%; Asian 1.7%; Other 5.3%). **Foreign born:** 6.1%. **Median age:** 35.9. **State rank:** 6. **Pop change 1990-2000:** +10.1%.

Income: per capita $21,194; median household $43,886. **Pop below poverty level:** 9.6%.

Unemployment: 6.6%. **Median home value:** $91,900. **Median travel time to work:** 20.8 minutes.

WOODFORD COUNTY

115 N Main St Rm 202 **Ph:** 309-467-2822
Eureka, IL 61530 **Fax:** 309-467-4728

In central IL; organized Feb 27, 1841 from Tazewell and McLean counties. **Name Origin:** For Woodford County, KY, former home of many early settlers.

Area (sq mi): 542.74 (land 527.95; water 14.79).

Pop: 35,469 (White 98%; Black or African American 0.3%; Hispanic or Latino 0.7%; Asian 0.3%; Other 0.9%). **Foreign born:** 1%. **Median age:** 37.8. **State rank:** 43. **Pop change 1990-2000:** +8.6%.

Income: per capita $21,956; median household $51,394. **Pop below poverty level:** 4.3%.

Unemployment: 3%. **Median home value:** $102,900. **Median travel time to work:** 22.2 minutes.

Please see sample entry on inside front cover for detailed information about the statistics presented with each county listing.

167

INDIANA - Counties

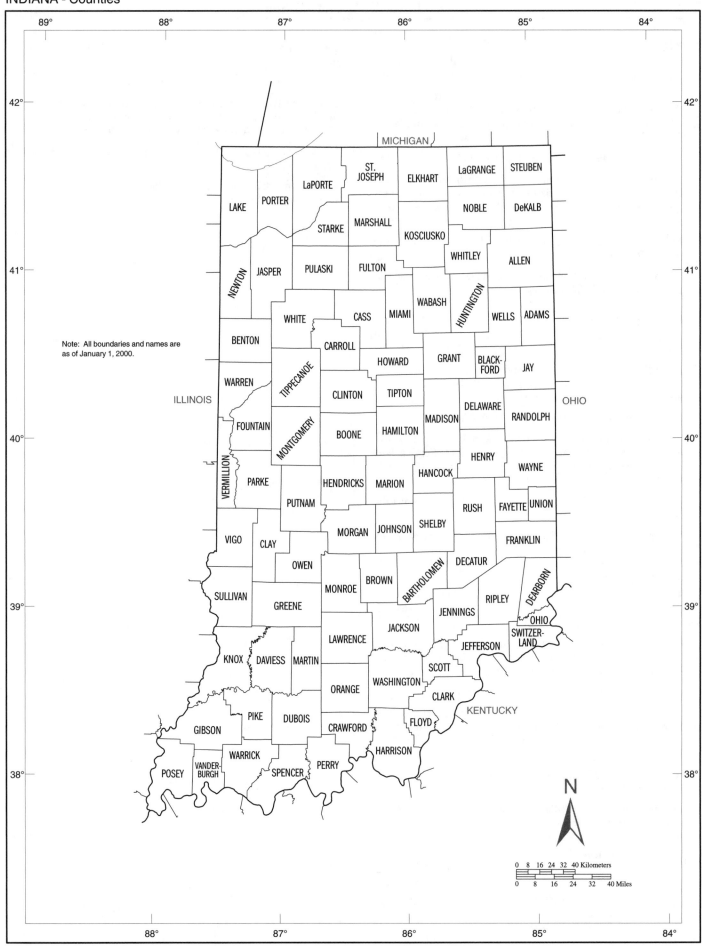

Note: All boundaries and names are as of January 1, 2000.

ILLINOIS

MICHIGAN

OHIO

KENTUCKY

N

0 8 16 24 32 40 Kilometers

0 8 16 24 32 40 Miles

Indiana

INDIANA STATE INFORMATION

www.in.gov   **Ph:** 317-232-1000

Area (sq mi): 36,417.73 (land 35866.9; water 550.83).

Pop: 6,080,485 (White 85.8%; Black or African American 8.4%; Hispanic or Latino 3.5%; Asian 1%; Other 3.1%). **Foreign born:** 3.1%. **Median age:** 35.2. **Pop change 1990-2000:** +9.7%.

Income: per capita $20,397; median household $41,567. **Pop below poverty level:** 9.5%.

Unemployment: 4.8%. **Median home value:** $94,300. **Median travel time to work:** 22.6 minutes.

ADAMS COUNTY

PO Box 189   **Ph:** 260-724-2600
Decatur, IN 46733   **Fax:** 260-724-5313

On the east-central border of IN, south of Ft. Wayne; organized Jan 23, 1836 from Warren County. **Name Origin:** For John Quincy Adams (1767-1848), sixth U.S. president.

Area (sq mi): 339.93 (land 339.36; water 0.57).

Pop: 33,625 (White 95.8%; Black or African American 0.1%; Hispanic or Latino 3.3%; Asian 0.2%; Other 2.4%). **Foreign born:** 1.1%. **Median age:** 32.9. **State rank:** 47. **Pop change 1990-2000:** +8.1%.

Income: per capita $16,704; median household $40,625. **Pop below poverty level:** 9.1%.

Unemployment: 5.5%. **Median home value:** $85,400. **Median travel time to work:** 21.7 minutes.

ALLEN COUNTY

715 S Calhoun St County Courthouse
Rm 201   **Ph:** 260-449-7245
Fort Wayne, IN 46802   **Fax:** 260-449-7929
www.co.allen.in.us

On the northeastern border of IN, northeast of Marion; organized Apr 1, 1824 from Indian lands. **Name Origin:** For Col. John Allen (?-1813), KY lawyer and army officer.

Area (sq mi): 660.1 (land 657.25; water 2.85).

Pop: 331,849 (White 81.3%; Black or African American 11.3%; Hispanic or Latino 4.2%; Asian 1.4%; Other 4.2%). **Foreign born:** 4%. **Median age:** 34.1. **State rank:** 3. **Pop change 1990-2000:** +10.3%.

Income: per capita $21,544; median household $42,671. **Pop below poverty level:** 9.1%.

Unemployment: 4.6%. **Median home value:** $88,700. **Median travel time to work:** 20.6 minutes.

BARTHOLOMEW COUNTY

PO Box 924   **Ph:** 812-379-1600
Columbus, IN 47202   **Fax:** 812-379-1675
www.bartholomewco.com

In south-central IN, south of Indianapolis; organized 1821 from Indian lands. **Name Origin:** For Gen. Joseph Bartholomew (?-1840), officer wounded at the Battle of Tippecanoe (1811) and IN state senator (1821-24).

Area (sq mi): 409.36 (land 406.84; water 2.52).

Pop: 71,435 (White 93%; Black or African American 1.8%; Hispanic or Latino 2.2%; Asian 1.9%; Other 2.1%). **Foreign born:** 3.8%. **Median age:** 36.2. **State rank:** 21. **Pop change 1990-2000:** +12.2%.

Income: per capita $21,536; median household $44,184. **Pop below poverty level:** 7.3%.

Unemployment: 3.8%. **Median home value:** $105,300. **Median travel time to work:** 18.9 minutes.

BENTON COUNTY

706 E 5th St Suite 37   **Ph:** 765-884-0930
Fowler, IN 47944   **Fax:** 765-884-0322
www.bentoncounty.org

On the northwest border of IN, northwest of Lafayette; organized Feb 18, 1840 from Indian lands. **Name Origin:** For Thomas Hart Benton (1782-1858), U.S. journalist and statesman; nicknamed 'Old Bullion' for championing the use of gold and silver currency rather than paper money.

Area (sq mi): 406.4 (land 406.31; water 0.09).

Pop: 9,421 (White 96%; Black or African American 0.2%; Hispanic or Latino 2.6%; Asian 0.1%; Other 2.8%). **Foreign born:** 0.8%. **Median age:** 36.7. **State rank:** 88. **Pop change 1990-2000:** -0.2%.

Income: per capita $17,220; median household $39,813. **Pop below poverty level:** 5.5%.

Unemployment: 3.5%. **Median home value:** $75,000. **Median travel time to work:** 24.5 minutes.

BLACKFORD COUNTY

110 W Washington St   **Ph:** 765-348-1620
Hartford City, IN 47348   **Fax:** 765-348-7222

In east-central IN, north of Muncie; organized Feb 15, 1838 from Jay County. **Name Origin:** For Isaac Newton Blackford (1786-1859), IN legislator and justice of the IN Supreme Court (1817-52).

Please see sample entry on inside front cover for detailed information about the statistics presented with each county listing.

Area (sq mi): 165.4 (land 165.1; water 0.31).

Pop: 14,048 (White 98%; Black or African American 0.1%; Hispanic or Latino 0.6%; Asian 0.2%; Other 1.3%). **Foreign born:** 0.1%. **Median age:** 38.5. **State rank:** 83. **Pop change 1990-2000:** -0.1%.

Income: per capita $16,543; median household $34,760. **Pop below poverty level:** 8.7%.

Unemployment: 6.9%. **Median home value:** $58,900. **Median travel time to work:** 23.4 minutes.

BOONE COUNTY
Courthouse Sq Rm 212   **Ph:** 765-482-3510
Lebanon, IN 46052

In central IN, northwest of Indianpolis; organized Jan 29, 1830 from Indian lands. **Name Origin:** For Daniel Boone (1734?-1820), U.S. frontiersman and KY pioneer.

Area (sq mi): 423.28 (land 422.85; water 0.42).

Pop: 46,107 (White 97.3%; Black or African American 0.4%; Hispanic or Latino 1.2%; Asian 0.5%; Other 1.3%). **Foreign born:** 1.5%. **Median age:** 36.9. **State rank:** 30. **Pop change 1990-2000:** +20.9%.

Income: per capita $24,182; median household $49,632. **Pop below poverty level:** 5.2%.

Unemployment: 2.3%. **Median home value:** $131,100. **Median travel time to work:** 23 minutes.

BROWN COUNTY
PO Box 85   **Ph:** 812-988-5510
Nashville, IN 47448   **Fax:** 812-988-5562
www.browncounty.org

In central IN, west of Columbus; organized Feb 4, 1836 from Monroe, Jackson, and Bartholomew counties. **Name Origin:** For Gen. Jacob Jennings Brown (1775-1828), an officer in the War of 1812 and commander of the U.S. Army (1821-28).

Area (sq mi): 316.62 (land 312.26; water 4.36).

Pop: 14,957 (White 97.7%; Black or African American 0.2%; Hispanic or Latino 0.9%; Asian 0.2%; Other 1.4%). **Foreign born:** 1%. **Median age:** 40.8. **State rank:** 81. **Pop change 1990-2000:** +6.2%.

Income: per capita $20,548; median household $43,708. **Pop below poverty level:** 8.9%.

Unemployment: 3.5%. **Median home value:** $114,500. **Median travel time to work:** 34.2 minutes.

CARROLL COUNTY
101 W Main St   **Ph:** 765-564-4485
Delphi, IN 46923   **Fax:** 765-564-1835

In west-central IN, west of Kokoma; organized Jan 7, 1828 from Indian lands. **Name Origin:** For Charles Carroll (1737-1832), a signer of the Declaration of Independence, U.S. senator from MD (1789-92), and founder of the Baltimore and Ohio Railroad.

Area (sq mi): 375.05 (land 372.26; water 2.8).

Pop: 20,165 (White 96.3%; Black or African American 0.2%; Hispanic or Latino 2.9%; Asian 0.1%; Other 2.1%). **Foreign born:** 2.2%. **Median age:** 37.2. **State rank:** 73. **Pop change 1990-2000:** +7.2%.

Income: per capita $19,436; median household $42,677. **Pop below poverty level:** 6.8%.

Unemployment: 3.9%. **Median home value:** $87,200. **Median travel time to work:** 23.8 minutes.

CASS COUNTY
200 Court Pk   **Ph:** 574-753-7740
Logansport, IN 46947   **Fax:** 574-722-1556

In west-central IN, northwest of Kokomo; established Dec 18, 1828 from Indian lands. **Name Origin:** For Gen. Lewis Cass (1782-1866), OH legislator, governor of MI Territory (1813-31), U.S. secretary of war (1831-36), and U.S. secretary of state (1857-60).

Area (sq mi): 414.92 (land 412.87; water 2.06).

Pop: 40,930 (White 90.2%; Black or African American 1.3%; Hispanic or Latino 7.1%; Asian 0.5%; Other 4.4%). **Foreign born:** 4.3%. **Median age:** 36.7. **State rank:** 35. **Pop change 1990-2000:** +6.6%.

Income: per capita $18,892; median household $39,193. **Pop below poverty level:** 7.6%.

Unemployment: 5.4%. **Median home value:** $71,500. **Median travel time to work:** 20.2 minutes.

CLARK COUNTY
501 E Court Ave   **Ph:** 812-285-6200
Jeffersonville, IN 47130   **Fax:** 812-285-6363
www.co.clark.in.us

On the southeast border of IN, north of Louisville, KY; organized Feb 3, 1801 (prior to statehood) from Knox County. **Name Origin:** For Gen. George Rogers Clark (1752-1818), officer in the Revolutionary War and frontiersman in the Northwest Territory.

Area (sq mi): 376.2 (land 375.04; water 1.16).

Pop: 96,472 (White 89.3%; Black or African American 6.6%; Hispanic or Latino 1.9%; Asian 0.6%; Other 2.5%). **Foreign born:** 1.7%. **Median age:** 36.5. **State rank:** 17. **Pop change 1990-2000:** +9.9%.

Income: per capita $19,936; median household $40,111. **Pop below poverty level:** 8.1%.

Unemployment: 3.8%. **Median home value:** $89,900. **Median travel time to work:** 22.2 minutes.

CLAY COUNTY
609 E National Ave Rm 213   **Ph:** 812-448-9024
Brazil, IN 47834
www.claycountyin.org

In southwest IN, east of Terre Haute; organized Feb 12, 1825 from Indian lands. **Name Origin:** For Henry Clay (1777-1852), U.S. senator from KY, known as the 'Great Pacificator' for his advocacy of compromise to avert national crises.

Area (sq mi): 360.39 (land 357.62; water 2.78).

Pop: 26,556 (White 98%; Black or African American 0.3%; Hispanic or Latino 0.6%; Asian 0.1%; Other 1.1%). **Foreign born:** 0.6%. **Median age:** 37.1. **State rank:** 60. **Pop change 1990-2000:** +7.5%.

Income: per capita $16,364; median household $36,865. **Pop below poverty level:** 8.7%.

All statistics are based on the 2000 Census except the dollar figures given for per capita income, which are based on 1999 estimates.

Unemployment: 6.1%. **Median home value:** $72,600. **Median travel time to work:** 25.9 minutes.

CLINTON COUNTY

265 Courthouse Sq   **Ph:** 765-659-6335
Frankfort, IN 46041

In central IN, east of Lafayette; organized Jan 29, 1830 from Indian lands. **Name Origin:** For DeWitt Clinton (1769-1828), governor of NY (1817-21; 1825-28) and supporter of the Erie Canal.

Area (sq mi): 405.28 (land 405.1; water 0.18).

Pop: 33,866 (White 91.7%; Black or African American 0.3%; Hispanic or Latino 7.3%; Asian 0.2%; Other 5.1%). **Foreign born:** 4.8%. **Median age:** 35.6. **State rank:** 46. **Pop change 1990-2000:** +9.3%.

Income: per capita $17,862; median household $40,759. **Pop below poverty level:** 8.6%.

Unemployment: 3.9%. **Median home value:** $85,000. **Median travel time to work:** 19.9 minutes.

CRAWFORD COUNTY

PO Box 375   **Ph:** 812-338-2565
English, IN 47118   **Fax:** 812-338-2507

On the south-central border of IN; organized Jan 19, 1818 from Harrison County. **Name Origin:** For either Col. William Crawford (1732-82), VA officer in the Revolutionary War, Indian fighter, and surveyor; or William Harris Crawford (1772-1834), senator from GA (1807-13), U.S. secretary of war (1815-16), and U.S. secretary of the treasury (1816-25).

Area (sq mi): 308.85 (land 305.68; water 3.17).

Pop: 10,743 (White 97.9%; Black or African American 0.2%; Hispanic or Latino 0.9%; Asian 0.1%; Other 1.4%). **Foreign born:** 0.3%. **Median age:** 37.3. **State rank:** 86. **Pop change 1990-2000:** +8.4%.

Income: per capita $15,926; median household $32,646. **Pop below poverty level:** 16.8%.

Unemployment: 5.4%. **Median home value:** $64,600. **Median travel time to work:** 35.4 minutes.

DAVIESS COUNTY

PO Box 739   **Ph:** 812-254-8664
Washington, IN 47501   **Fax:** 812-254-8698

In southwestern IN, east of Vincennes; established Dec 24, 1816 from Indian lands. **Name Origin:** For Col. Joseph Hamilton Daviess (1774-1811), VA soldier and jurist who unsuccessfully attempted to indict Aaron Burr for treason (1806). According to Jacob Piatt Dunn, 'the Colonel's name was Daveiss and he always wrote it that way'; however, the name is sometimes spelled 'Daviess' in biographical entries and in places named for him.

Area (sq mi): 436.86 (land 430.66; water 6.2).

Pop: 29,820 (White 96.6%; Black or African American 0.4%; Hispanic or Latino 2.1%; Asian 0.2%; Other 1.7%). **Foreign born:** 1.9%. **Median age:** 35.5. **State rank:** 54. **Pop change 1990-2000:** +8.3%.

Income: per capita $16,015; median household $34,064. **Pop below poverty level:** 13.8%.

Unemployment: 4%. **Median home value:** $70,800. **Median travel time to work:** 23.7 minutes.

DEARBORN COUNTY

215 W High St   **Ph:** 812-537-1040
Lawrenceburg, IN 47025
www.dearborncounty.org

On the southeastern border of IN, east of Columbus; organized Mar 7, 1803 (prior to statehood). **Name Origin:** For Gen. Henry Dearborn (1751-1829), an officer in the Revolutionary War, MA legislator, U.S. secretary of war (1801-09), and Minister to Portugal (1822-24).

Area (sq mi): 307.05 (land 305.21; water 1.84).

Pop: 46,109 (White 97.7%; Black or African American 0.6%; Hispanic or Latino 0.6%; Asian 0.3%; Other 1.1%). **Foreign born:** 0.8%. **Median age:** 36.2. **State rank:** 29. **Pop change 1990-2000:** +18.7%.

Income: per capita $20,431; median household $48,899. **Pop below poverty level:** 6.6%.

Unemployment: 3.5%. **Median home value:** $120,600. **Median travel time to work:** 30.5 minutes.

DECATUR COUNTY

150 Courthouse Sq Suite 244   **Ph:** 812-663-8223
Greensburg, IN 47240   **Fax:** 812-663-8642

In southeast IN, east of Columbus; established Dec 31, 1821 from Indian lands. **Name Origin:** For Stephen Decatur (1779-1820), U.S. naval officer during the War of 1812 and in actions against the Barbary pirates near Tripoli, who said '...may she always be in the right; but our country, right or wrong!'

Area (sq mi): 373.42 (land 372.6; water 0.81).

Pop: 24,555 (White 98.1%; Black or African American 0%; Hispanic or Latino 0.5%; Asian 0.7%; Other 0.7%). **Foreign born:** 1.6%. **Median age:** 35.8. **State rank:** 64. **Pop change 1990-2000:** +3.8%.

Income: per capita $18,582; median household $40,401. **Pop below poverty level:** 9.3%.

Unemployment: 2.6%. **Median home value:** $86,400. **Median travel time to work:** 19.9 minutes.

DEKALB COUNTY

PO Box 230   **Ph:** 260-925-0912
Auburn, IN 46706   **Fax:** 260-925-5126
www.dekalbnet.org

On the northeastern border of IN, north of Ft. Wayne; established Feb 7, 1835 from Allen Country. **Name Origin:** For Johann (1721-80), Baron de Kalb, German-born French soldier who fought with the Americans during the Revolutionary War.

Area (sq mi): 363.84 (land 362.88; water 0.97).

Pop: 40,285 (White 96.8%; Black or African American 0.3%; Hispanic or Latino 1.7%; Asian 0.3%; Other 1.6%). **Foreign born:** 0.8%. **Median age:** 34.7. **State rank:** 36. **Pop change 1990-2000:** +14%.

Income: per capita $19,448; median household $44,909. **Pop below poverty level:** 5.9%.

Please see sample entry on inside front cover for detailed information about the statistics presented with each county listing.

Unemployment: 5.6%. **Median home value:** $88,000. **Median travel time to work:** 19.3 minutes.

DELAWARE COUNTY
100 W Main St   **Ph:** 765-747-7730
Muncie, IN 47305   **Fax:** 765-747-7899
www.co.delaware.in.us

In east-central IN; organized Jan 26, 1827 from Indian lands. **Name Origin:** For the Delaware Indians (also called Leni or Leni-Lenape), in turn named for Thomas West (1577-1618), Lord Delaware (or De La Warr).

Area (sq mi): 395.92 (land 393.29; water 2.63).

Pop: 118,769 (White 90.1%; Black or African American 6.7%; Hispanic or Latino 1.1%; Asian 0.7%; Other 1.9%). **Foreign born:** 1.5%. **Median age:** 33.8. **State rank:** 12. **Pop change 1990-2000:** -0.7%.

Income: per capita $19,233; median household $34,659. **Pop below poverty level:** 15.1%.

Unemployment: 4.6%. **Median home value:** $75,400. **Median travel time to work:** 19.8 minutes.

DUBOIS COUNTY
1 Courthouse Sq   **Ph:** 812-481-7035
Jasper, IN 47546   **Fax:** 812-481-7044

In south-central IN, northeast of Evansville; established Dec 20, 1817 from Orange and Perry counties. **Name Origin:** For Toussaint Dubois, a French immigrant who fought with the Americans at the Battle of Tippecanoe (1811).

Area (sq mi): 435.23 (land 430.09; water 5.14).

Pop: 39,674 (White 96.5%; Black or African American 0.1%; Hispanic or Latino 2.8%; Asian 0.2%; Other 2.1%). **Foreign born:** 2.1%. **Median age:** 36.1. **State rank:** 37. **Pop change 1990-2000:** +8.4%.

Income: per capita $20,225; median household $44,169. **Pop below poverty level:** 5.3%.

Unemployment: 2.8%. **Median home value:** $92,700. **Median travel time to work:** 17.8 minutes.

ELKHART COUNTY
315 S 2nd St   **Ph:** 574-523-2233
Elkhart, IN 46516   **Fax:** 574-523-2323
www.elkhartcountygov.org

On the north-central border of IN; organized Jan 29, 1830 from Indian lands. **Name Origin:** For the Elkhart River, named for the Elkhart Indians. Name is probably a translation of either a Potawatomi or Kickapoo term for 'elk's heart', early English spelling was Elksheart.

Area (sq mi): 467.85 (land 463.81; water 4.03).

Pop: 182,791 (White 83.4%; Black or African American 5.2%; Hispanic or Latino 8.9%; Asian 0.9%; Other 7.5%). **Foreign born:** 7.1%. **Median age:** 33. **State rank:** 5. **Pop change 1990-2000:** +17%.

Income: per capita $20,250; median household $44,478. **Pop below poverty level:** 7.8%.

Unemployment: 5.4%. **Median home value:** $98,100. **Median travel time to work:** 18.4 minutes.

FAYETTE COUNTY
PO Box 607   **Ph:** 765-825-1813
Connersville, IN 47331
www.co.fayette.in.us

In east-central IN, southwest of Richmond; established Dec 28, 1818 from Wayne County. **Name Origin:** For the Marquis de Lafayette (1757-1834), French statesman and soldier who fought with Americans during the Revolutionary War.

Area (sq mi): 215.12 (land 214.96; water 0.16).

Pop: 25,588 (White 96.8%; Black or African American 1.7%; Hispanic or Latino 0.5%; Asian 0.3%; Other 0.9%). **Foreign born:** 0.5%. **Median age:** 38. **State rank:** 62. **Pop change 1990-2000:** -1.6%.

Income: per capita $18,624; median household $38,840. **Pop below poverty level:** 7.9%.

Unemployment: 8.8%. **Median home value:** $78,500. **Median travel time to work:** 22.4 minutes.

FLOYD COUNTY
PO Box 1056   **Ph:** 812-948-5411
New Albany, IN 47151   **Fax:** 812-948-4711

On the southeast border of IN, northwest of Louisville, KY; organized Jan 2, 1819 from Harrison and Clark counties. **Name Origin:** According to most sources, for Gen. John Floyd (1783-1837), VA jurist, U.S. congressman from VA (1817-29), and governor (1830-34). Others claim Col. Davis Floyd, an associate of Aaron Burr and an important member of the IN General Assembly.

Area (sq mi): 148.31 (land 148; water 0.31).

Pop: 70,823 (White 92.7%; Black or African American 4.4%; Hispanic or Latino 1.1%; Asian 0.5%; Other 1.8%). **Foreign born:** 1.2%. **Median age:** 36.8. **State rank:** 23. **Pop change 1990-2000:** +10%.

Income: per capita $21,852; median household $44,022. **Pop below poverty level:** 8.7%.

Unemployment: 3.2%. **Median home value:** $104,300. **Median travel time to work:** 21.5 minutes.

FOUNTAIN COUNTY
PO Box 183   **Ph:** 765-793-2192
Covington, IN 47932   **Fax:** 765-793-5002
www.co.fountain.in.us

On the central western border of IN, north of Terre Haute, established Dec 20, 1825 from Montgomery County. **Name Origin:** For Maj. James Fountain (originally Fontaine) (?-1790), KY army officer killed near Ft. Wayne in the Battle of Maumee.

Area (sq mi): 397.92 (land 395.69; water 2.23).

Pop: 17,954 (White 98%; Black or African American 0.1%; Hispanic or Latino 1.1%; Asian 0.2%; Other 1%). **Foreign born:** 1%. **Median age:** 37.7. **State rank:** 77. **Pop change 1990-2000:** +0.8%.

Income: per capita $17,779; median household $38,119. **Pop below poverty level:** 8.5%.

All statistics are based on the 2000 Census except the dollar figures given for per capita income, which are based on 1999 estimates.

Unemployment: 5%. **Median home value:** $69,200. **Median travel time to work:** 25.1 minutes.

FRANKLIN COUNTY
459 Main St   **Ph:** 765-647-5111
Brookville, IN 47012   **Fax:** 765-647-3224

On southeastern border of IN, south of Richmond; established Nov 27, 1810 (prior to statehood) from Wayne and Ripley counties. **Name Origin:** For Benjamin Franklin (1706-90), patriot, diplomat, and statesman.

Area (sq mi): 391.34 (land 386; water 5.33).

Pop: 22,151 (White 98.7%; Black or African American 0%; Hispanic or Latino 0.5%; Asian 0.2%; Other 0.8%). **Foreign born:** 0.6%. **Median age:** 35.9. **State rank:** 67. **Pop change 1990-2000:** +13.1%.

Income: per capita $18,624; median household $43,530. **Pop below poverty level:** 7.1%.

Unemployment: 4.4%. **Median home value:** $100,100. **Median travel time to work:** 29.9 minutes.

FULTON COUNTY
PO Box 524   **Ph:** 574-223-2911
Rochester, IN 46975   **Fax:** 574-223-8304
www.fultoncounty-in.org

In north-central IN, west of Ft. Wayne; established Feb 7, 1835 from Indian lands. **Name Origin:** For Robert Fulton (1765-1815) builder of the *Clermont*, the first commercially successful steamboat.

Area (sq mi): 371.37 (land 368.51; water 2.87).

Pop: 20,511 (White 95.1%; Black or African American 0.8%; Hispanic or Latino 2.3%; Asian 0.4%; Other 2.7%). **Foreign born:** 2%. **Median age:** 37.9. **State rank:** 71. **Pop change 1990-2000:** +8.9%.

Income: per capita $17,950; median household $38,290. **Pop below poverty level:** 7.6%.

Unemployment: 7.5%. **Median home value:** $77,000. **Median travel time to work:** 22.7 minutes.

GIBSON COUNTY
PO Box 630   **Ph:** 812-386-8401
Princeton, IN 47670   **Fax:** 812-385-5025

On the southwest border of IN, north of Evansville; organized Mar 9, 1813 (prior to statehood) from Knox County. **Name Origin:** For Gen. John Gibson (1740-1822), an officer in the French and Indian War and the Revolutionary War, jurist, and secretary of IN Territory (1801-16).

Area (sq mi): 499.05 (land 488.78; water 10.27).

Pop: 32,500 (White 96%; Black or African American 1.9%; Hispanic or Latino 0.7%; Asian 0.5%; Other 1.1%). **Foreign born:** 0.9%. **Median age:** 38. **State rank:** 50. **Pop change 1990-2000:** +1.8%.

Income: per capita $18,169; median household $37,515. **Pop below poverty level:** 8.2%.

Unemployment: 3.8%. **Median home value:** $74,700. **Median travel time to work:** 23.7 minutes.

GRANT COUNTY
101 E 4th St   **Ph:** 765-668-8121
Marion, IN 46952   **Fax:** 765-668-6541
www.grantcounty.net/grant/grant.fwx

In central IN, northwest of Muncie; organized Feb 10, 1831 from Delaware County. **Name Origin:** For Samuel and Moses Grant, killed in 1790 in Indian battles in southern IL.

Area (sq mi): 414.83 (land 414.03; water 0.81).

Pop: 73,403 (White 88%; Black or African American 7.2%; Hispanic or Latino 2.4%; Asian 0.6%; Other 2.9%). **Foreign born:** 1.2%. **Median age:** 37.4. **State rank:** 20. **Pop change 1990-2000:** -1%.

Income: per capita $18,003; median household $36,162. **Pop below poverty level:** 11.8%.

Unemployment: 6.8%. **Median home value:** $68,500. **Median travel time to work:** 19.5 minutes.

GREENE COUNTY
PO Box 229   **Ph:** 812-384-8532
Bloomfield, IN 47424   **Fax:** 812-384-8458
www.in-map.net/counties/GREENE/

In southwest IN, southwest of Bloomington; organized Jan 5, 1821 from Knox County. **Name Origin:** For Gen. Nathanael Greene (1742-86), hero of the Revolutionary War, quartermaster general (1778-80), and commander of the army in the South (1780).

Area (sq mi): 545.91 (land 541.73; water 4.18).

Pop: 33,157 (White 98.1%; Black or African American 0.1%; Hispanic or Latino 0.8%; Asian 0.2%; Other 1.1%). **Foreign born:** 0.5%. **Median age:** 38.1. **State rank:** 49. **Pop change 1990-2000:** +9%.

Income: per capita $16,834; median household $33,998. **Pop below poverty level:** 11%.

Unemployment: 8.2%. **Median home value:** $66,800. **Median travel time to work:** 29.7 minutes.

HAMILTON COUNTY
1 Hamilton County Sq Suite 106 **Ph:** 317-776-9629
Noblesville, IN 46060   **Fax:** 317-776-9664
www.co.hamilton.in.us

In central IN, north of Indianapolis; organized Jan 8, 1823 from Hancock and Marion counties. **Name Origin:** For Alexander Hamilton (1755-1804), U.S. statesman and first secretary of the treasury (1789-95).

Area (sq mi): 402.73 (land 397.94; water 4.79).

Pop: 182,740 (White 93.4%; Black or African American 1.5%; Hispanic or Latino 1.6%; Asian 2.4%; Other 1.6%). **Foreign born:** 4%. **Median age:** 34.1. **State rank:** 6. **Pop change 1990-2000:** +67.7%.

Income: per capita $33,109; median household $71,026. **Pop below poverty level:** 2.9%.

Unemployment: 2%. **Median home value:** $166,300. **Median travel time to work:** 25.3 minutes.

Please see sample entry on inside front cover for detailed information about the statistics presented with each county listing.

HANCOCK COUNTY

9 E Main St Rm 201
Greenfield, IN 46140
www.co.hancock.in.us

Ph: 317-462-1109

In central IN, east of Indianapolis; established Jan 26, 1827 from Madison County. **Name Origin:** For John Hancock (1737-93), noted signer of the Declaration of Independence and governor of MA (1780-85;1787-93).

Area (sq mi): 306.73 (land 306.12; water 0.61).

Pop: 55,391 (White 97.8%; Black or African American 0.1%; Hispanic or Latino 0.9%; Asian 0.4%; Other 1%). **Foreign born:** 0.9%. **Median age:** 37.4. **State rank:** 25. **Pop change 1990-2000:** +21.7%.

Income: per capita $24,966; median household $56,416. **Pop below poverty level:** 3%.

Unemployment: 2.7%. **Median home value:** $129,700. **Median travel time to work:** 25.9 minutes.

HARRISON COUNTY

300 N Capitol Ave
Corydon, IN 47112

Ph: 812-738-8241
Fax: 812-738-0531

On the southern border of IN; organized Oct 11, 1808 (prior to statehood) from Northwest Territory. **Name Origin:** For William Henry Harrison (1773-1841), first territorial governor of IN (1800-11) and ninth U.S. president.

Area (sq mi): 486.88 (land 485.22; water 1.66).

Pop: 34,325 (White 97.6%; Black or African American 0.4%; Hispanic or Latino 1%; Asian 0.2%; Other 1.1%). **Foreign born:** 0.9%. **Median age:** 36.6. **State rank:** 45. **Pop change 1990-2000:** +14.8%.

Income: per capita $19,643; median household $43,423. **Pop below poverty level:** 6.4%.

Unemployment: 3.3%. **Median home value:** $95,700. **Median travel time to work:** 30.5 minutes.

HENDRICKS COUNTY

PO Box 599
Danville, IN 46122
www.co.hendricks.in.us

Ph: 317-745-9231
Fax: 317-745-9306

In central IN, west of Indianapolis; established Dec 20, 1823 from Indian lands. **Name Origin:** For William Hendricks (1782-1850), IN legislator, governor (1822-25), and U.S. senator (1825-37).

Area (sq mi): 408.88 (land 408.39; water 0.48).

Pop: 104,093 (White 96%; Black or African American 1.1%; Hispanic or Latino 1.1%; Asian 0.7%; Other 1.6%). **Foreign born:** 1.6%. **Median age:** 35.6. **State rank:** 16. **Pop change 1990-2000:** +37.5%.

Income: per capita $23,129; median household $55,208. **Pop below poverty level:** 3.6%.

Unemployment: 2.4%. **Median home value:** $133,300. **Median travel time to work:** 25.6 minutes.

HENRY COUNTY

PO Box B
New Castle, IN 47362
www.co.henry.in.us

Ph: 765-529-6401
Fax: 765-521-7046

In east-central IN, south of Muncie; established Dec 31, 1821 from Delaware County. **Name Origin:** For Patrick Henry (1736-99), patriot, governor of VA (1776-79; 1784-86), and statesman, famous for proclaiming, 'Give me liberty or give me death.'

Area (sq mi): 394.9 (land 392.93; water 1.97).

Pop: 48,508 (White 97.5%; Black or African American 0.9%; Hispanic or Latino 0.8%; Asian 0.2%; Other 1%). **Foreign born:** 0.5%. **Median age:** 38.7. **State rank:** 27. **Pop change 1990-2000:** +0.8%.

Income: per capita $19,355; median household $38,150. **Pop below poverty level:** 7.8%.

Unemployment: 5.1%. **Median home value:** $84,100. **Median travel time to work:** 23.7 minutes.

HOWARD COUNTY

PO Box 9004
Kokomo, IN 46904
co.howard.in.us

Ph: 765-456-2204
Fax: 765-456-2267

In central IN, east of Marion; organized as Richardville County Jan 15, 1844 from Indian lands; name changed 1846. **Name Origin:** For Tilghman Ashurst Howard (1797-1844), TN legislator, U.S. representative from IN (1839-40), and charge d'affaires to the Republic of TX (1844).

Area (sq mi): 293.93 (land 293.07; water 0.86).

Pop: 84,964 (White 88.7%; Black or African American 6.5%; Hispanic or Latino 2%; Asian 1%; Other 2.7%). **Foreign born:** 1.8%. **Median age:** 37.1. **State rank:** 18. **Pop change 1990-2000:** +5.1%.

Income: per capita $22,049; median household $43,487. **Pop below poverty level:** 9.5%.

Unemployment: 6.3%. **Median home value:** $89,000. **Median travel time to work:** 17.4 minutes.

HUNTINGTON COUNTY

201 N Jefferson St County Courthouse
Rm 103
Huntington, IN 46750
www.huntington.in.us

Ph: 260-358-4822
Fax: 260-358-4823

In northeastern IN, southwest of Ft. Wayne; established Feb 2, 1832 from Grant County. **Name Origin:** For Samuel Huntington (1731-96), a signer of the Declaration of Independence; president of the Continental Congress (1779-81; 1783), chief justice of CT Superior Court (1784), and governor of CT (1786-96).

Area (sq mi): 387.94 (land 382.59; water 5.35).

Pop: 38,075 (White 97.6%; Black or African American 0.2%; Hispanic or Latino 1%; Asian 0.3%; Other 1.4%). **Foreign born:** 0.8%. **Median age:** 36.2. **State rank:** 39. **Pop change 1990-2000:** +7.5%.

Income: per capita $19,480; median household $41,620. **Pop below poverty level:** 5.5%.

Unemployment: 5.2%. **Median home value:** $81,600. **Median travel time to work:** 20.4 minutes.

All statistics are based on the 2000 Census except the dollar figures given for per capita income, which are based on 1999 estimates.

JACKSON COUNTY

PO Box 318   **Ph:** 812-358-6116
Brownstown, IN 47220   **Fax:** 812-358-6187

In south-central IN, south of Columbus; established Dec 18, 1815 (prior to statehood) from Washington County. **Name Origin:** For Andrew Jackson (1767-1845), seventh U.S. president.

Area (sq mi): 513.75 (land 509.31; water 4.44).

Pop: 41,335 (White 95.1%; Black or African American 0.5%; Hispanic or Latino 2.7%; Asian 0.8%; Other 2.5%). **Foreign born:** 2.4%. **Median age:** 35.8. **State rank:** 34. **Pop change 1990-2000:** +9.6%.

Income: per capita $18,400; median household $39,401. **Pop below poverty level:** 8.5%.

Unemployment: 4.2%. **Median home value:** $87,500. **Median travel time to work:** 21.4 minutes.

JASPER COUNTY

Courthouse 115 W Washington St
Suite 204   **Ph:** 219-866-4926
Rensselaer, IN 47978   **Fax:** 219-866-4940

In northwestern IN, southeast of Gary; established Feb 7,1835 from Indian lands. **Name Origin:** For Sgt. William Jasper (1750-79), Revolutionary War soldier from SC.

Area (sq mi): 561.22 (land 559.87; water 1.36).

Pop: 30,043 (White 96.3%; Black or African American 0.3%; Hispanic or Latino 2.4%; Asian 0.2%; Other 1.5%). **Foreign born:** 1.5%. **Median age:** 35. **State rank:** 53. **Pop change 1990-2000:** +20.4%.

Income: per capita $19,012; median household $43,369. **Pop below poverty level:** 6.7%.

Unemployment: 5.5%. **Median home value:** $105,700. **Median travel time to work:** 27.3 minutes.

JAY COUNTY

120 Court St 2nd Fl   **Ph:** 260-726-6920
Portland, IN 47371   **Fax:** 260-726-6922
www.co.jay.in.us

On central eastern border of IN, northeast of Muncie; established Feb 7, 1835 from Randolph County. **Name Origin:** For John Jay (1745-1829), first Chief Justice of the U.S. Supreme Court (1789-95), and governor of NY (1795-1801).

Area (sq mi): 383.82 (land 383.64; water 0.18).

Pop: 21,806 (White 96.9%; Black or African American 0.3%; Hispanic or Latino 1.8%; Asian 0.3%; Other 1.7%). **Foreign born:** 1.5%. **Median age:** 36.7. **State rank:** 68. **Pop change 1990-2000:** +1.4%.

Income: per capita $16,686; median household $35,700. **Pop below poverty level:** 9.1%.

Unemployment: 6.5%. **Median home value:** $62,500. **Median travel time to work:** 22.3 minutes.

JEFFERSON COUNTY

300 E Main St Courthouse Rm 203   **Ph:** 812-265-8922
Madison, IN 47250   **Fax:** 812-265-8950
www.indico.net/counties/JEFFERSON/

On southeastern border of IN, southeast of Columbus; established Nov 23, 1810 (prior to statehood) from Indian lands. **Name Origin:** For Thomas Jefferson (1743-1826), U.S. patriot and statesman; third U.S. president.

Area (sq mi): 362.94 (land 361.37; water 1.58).

Pop: 31,705 (White 95.6%; Black or African American 1.5%; Hispanic or Latino 1%; Asian 0.6%; Other 1.7%). **Foreign born:** 1.2%. **Median age:** 36.6. **State rank:** 51. **Pop change 1990-2000:** +6.4%.

Income: per capita $17,412; median household $38,189. **Pop below poverty level:** 9.6%.

Unemployment: 4.7%. **Median home value:** $85,800. **Median travel time to work:** 21.9 minutes.

JENNINGS COUNTY

PO Box 385   **Ph:** 812-352-3070
Vernon, IN 47282   **Fax:** 812-352-3076

In southeastern IN, southeast of Columbus; established Dec 27, 1816 from Indian lands. **Name Origin:** For Jonathan Jennings (1784-1834), U.S. representative from IN (1809-16; 1822-31) and first governor (1816-22).

Area (sq mi): 378.35 (land 377.22; water 1.13).

Pop: 27,554 (White 97.1%; Black or African American 0.7%; Hispanic or Latino 0.7%; Asian 0.3%; Other 1.5%). **Foreign born:** 0.7%. **Median age:** 34.6. **State rank:** 56. **Pop change 1990-2000:** +16.5%.

Income: per capita $17,059; median household $39,402. **Pop below poverty level:** 9.2%.

Unemployment: 4.9%. **Median home value:** $81,900. **Median travel time to work:** 25.2 minutes.

JOHNSON COUNTY

5 E Jefferson St   **Ph:** 317-736-3708
Franklin, IN 46131   **Fax:** 317-736-3749
www.co.johnson.in.us

In central IN, south of Indianapolis; established Dec 31, 1822 from Indian lands. **Name Origin:** For John Johnson, a judge of the first IN supreme court.

Area (sq mi): 321.56 (land 320.19; water 1.36).

Pop: 115,209 (White 96.2%; Black or African American 0.8%; Hispanic or Latino 1.4%; Asian 0.8%; Other 1.4%). **Foreign born:** 1.7%. **Median age:** 34.9. **State rank:** 13. **Pop change 1990-2000:** +30.8%.

Income: per capita $22,976; median household $52,693. **Pop below poverty level:** 5.6%.

Unemployment: 2.4%. **Median home value:** $122,500. **Median travel time to work:** 24.7 minutes.

Please see sample entry on inside front cover for detailed information about the statistics presented with each county listing.

KNOX COUNTY
101 N 7th St   **Ph:** 812-885-2521
Vincennes, IN 47591   **Fax:** 812-895-4929
www.accessknoxcounty.com

On the southwest border of IN; organized Jun 20, 1790 (prior to statehood) from Northwest Territory. **Name Origin:** For Gen. Henry Knox (1750-1806), Revolutionary War officer and first U.S. secretary of war (1785-94).

Area (sq mi): 524.06 (land 515.83; water 8.22).

Pop: 39,256 (White 96%; Black or African American 1.9%; Hispanic or Latino 0.8%; Asian 0.5%; Other 1.2%). **Foreign born:** 1.1%. **Median age:** 36.7. **State rank:** 38. **Pop change 1990-2000:** -1.6%.

Income: per capita $16,085; median household $31,362. **Pop below poverty level:** 16%.

Unemployment: 3.3%. **Median home value:** $63,600. **Median travel time to work:** 18.3 minutes.

KOSCIUSKO COUNTY
121 N Lake St   **Ph:** 574-372-2334
Warsaw, IN 46580   **Fax:** 574-372-2338

In north-central IN, south of Elkhart; established Feb 7, 1835 from Indian lands. **Name Origin:** For Thaddeus Kosciusko (1746-1817), Polish soldier who fought with the Americans during the Revolutionary War.

Area (sq mi): 554.34 (land 537.5; water 16.84).

Pop: 74,057 (White 92.9%; Black or African American 0.6%; Hispanic or Latino 5%; Asian 0.6%; Other 4.3%). **Foreign born:** 2.9%. **Median age:** 35.1. **State rank:** 19. **Pop change 1990-2000:** +13.4%.

Income: per capita $19,806; median household $43,939. **Pop below poverty level:** 6.4%.

Unemployment: 4.7%. **Median home value:** $95,500. **Median travel time to work:** 20 minutes.

LAGRANGE COUNTY
105 N Detroit St   **Ph:** 260-499-6368
LaGrange, IN 46761   **Fax:** 260-463-2187
www.lagrangecounty.com

On the northeastern border of IN, east of Elkhart; organized Feb 2, 1832 from unorganized territory in Elkhart County. **Name Origin:** For the country home near Paris of the Marquis de Lafayette (1757-1834) who fought with the Americans during the Revolutionary War, from French 'the barn.'

Area (sq mi): 386.72 (land 379.56; water 7.15).

Pop: 34,909 (White 95.7%; Black or African American 0.2%; Hispanic or Latino 3.1%; Asian 0.3%; Other 2.7%). **Foreign born:** 2.1%. **Median age:** 29.5. **State rank:** 44. **Pop change 1990-2000:** +18.4%.

Income: per capita $16,481; median household $42,848. **Pop below poverty level:** 7.7%.

Unemployment: 6%. **Median home value:** $99,800. **Median travel time to work:** 21.4 minutes.

LAKE COUNTY
2293 N Main St   **Ph:** 219-755-3440
Crown Point, IN 46307   **Fax:** 219-755-3520
www.lakecountyin.com

In the northwest corner of IN; established Jan 28, 1836 from Porter and Newton counties. **Name Origin:** For its location on the southern shore of Lake Michigan.

Area (sq mi): 626.34 (land 496.98; water 129.36).

Pop: 484,564 (White 60.6%; Black or African American 25.3%; Hispanic or Latino 12.2%; Asian 0.8%; Other 7.2%). **Foreign born:** 5.3%. **Median age:** 35.9. **State rank:** 2. **Pop change 1990-2000:** +1.9%.

Income: per capita $19,639; median household $41,829. **Pop below poverty level:** 12.2%.

Unemployment: 5.5%. **Median home value:** $97,500. **Median travel time to work:** 27.1 minutes.

LAPORTE COUNTY
813 Lincolnway   **Ph:** 574-326-6808
La Porte, IN 46350   **Fax:** 574-326-5615
www.lc-link.org

On the northwestern border of IN, west of South Bend; organized Jan 9, 1832 from Indian lands. **Name Origin:** French 'the port' or 'the door,' referring to a natural opening through the forest that served as a gateway to the north.

Area (sq mi): 613.04 (land 598.24; water 14.8).

Pop: 110,106 (White 84.8%; Black or African American 10.1%; Hispanic or Latino 3.1%; Asian 0.5%; Other 3.1%). **Foreign born:** 2.5%. **Median age:** 37.1. **State rank:** 14. **Pop change 1990-2000:** +2.8%.

Income: per capita $18,913; median household $41,430. **Pop below poverty level:** 8.7%.

Unemployment: 4.9%. **Median home value:** $93,500. **Median travel time to work:** 22 minutes.

LAWRENCE COUNTY
916 15th St Rm 31   **Ph:** 812-275-7543
Bedford, IN 47421   **Fax:** 812-277-2024

In south-central IN, south of Bloomington; organized Jan 7, 1818 from Orange County. **Name Origin:** For Capt. James Lawrence (1781-1813), U.S. naval officer in the war with Barbary pirates near Trilpoli and commander of the U.S.S. *Chesapeake* in the War of 1812, who said, 'Don't give up the ship!'

Area (sq mi): 452.07 (land 448.83; water 3.24).

Pop: 45,922 (White 97.4%; Black or African American 0.4%; Hispanic or Latino 0.9%; Asian 0.3%; Other 1.4%). **Foreign born:** 0.9%. **Median age:** 38.2. **State rank:** 31. **Pop change 1990-2000:** +7.2%.

Income: per capita $17,653; median household $36,280. **Pop below poverty level:** 9.8%.

Unemployment: 8.1%. **Median home value:** $75,400. **Median travel time to work:** 25.2 minutes.

All statistics are based on the 2000 Census except the dollar figures given for per capita income, which are based on 1999 estimates.

MADISON COUNTY

16 E 9th St
Anderson, IN 46016

Ph: 765-641-9419
Fax: 765-648-1375

In central IN, west of Muncie; organized Jan 4, 1823 from Fayette County. **Name Origin:** For James Madison (1751-1836), fourth U.S. president.

Area (sq mi): 452.91 (land 452.13; water 0.78).

Pop: 133,358 (White 89.1%; Black or African American 7.9%; Hispanic or Latino 1.5%; Asian 0.4%; Other 1.8%). **Foreign born:** 1.2%. **Median age:** 37.4. **State rank:** 10. **Pop change 1990-2000:** +2.1%.

Income: per capita $20,090; median household $38,925. **Pop below poverty level:** 9.3%.

Unemployment: 4.6%. **Median home value:** $81,600. **Median travel time to work:** 23.3 minutes.

MARION COUNTY

200 E Washington St City County Bldg
Indianapolis, IN 46204
www.indygov.org/county

Ph: 317-327-3200
Fax: 317-327-3893

In central IN, southwest of Muncie; established Dec 31, 1821 from Ohio County. **Name Origin:** For Gen. Francis Marion (c.1732-95), SC soldier and legislator, known as 'The Swamp Fox' for his tactics during the Revolutionary War.

Area (sq mi): 403.04 (land 396.25; water 6.79).

Pop: 860,454 (White 68.9%; Black or African American 24.2%; Hispanic or Latino 3.9%; Asian 1.4%; Other 3.9%). **Foreign born:** 4.6%. **Median age:** 33.6. **State rank:** 1. **Pop change 1990-2000:** +7.9%.

Income: per capita $21,789; median household $40,421. **Pop below poverty level:** 11.4%.

Unemployment: 3.8%. **Median home value:** $99,000. **Median travel time to work:** 23 minutes.

MARSHALL COUNTY

112 W Jefferson St
Plymouth, IN 46563
www.co.marshall.in.us

Ph: 574-935-8510
Fax: 574-936-4863

In north-central IN, south of South Bend, established Feb 7, 1835 from Indian lands. **Name Origin:** For John Marshall (1755-1835), fourth Chief Justice of the U.S. Supreme Court (1801-35).

Area (sq mi): 449.92 (land 444.27; water 5.65).

Pop: 45,128 (White 92.5%; Black or African American 0.3%; Hispanic or Latino 5.9%; Asian 0.3%; Other 3.8%). **Foreign born:** 4.4%. **Median age:** 35.5. **State rank:** 32. **Pop change 1990-2000:** +7%.

Income: per capita $18,427; median household $42,581. **Pop below poverty level:** 6.8%.

Unemployment: 4.5%. **Median home value:** $88,100. **Median travel time to work:** 21.8 minutes.

MARTIN COUNTY

PO Box 120
Shoals, IN 47581

Ph: 812-247-3651
Fax: 812-247-2791

In southwestern IN, southwest of Bloomington; organized Jan 17, 1820 from Indian lands. **Name Origin:** For Maj. John Preston Martin (1811-62), U.S. representative from KY (1845-47).

Area (sq mi): 340.53 (land 336.14; water 4.39).

Pop: 10,369 (White 98.6%; Black or African American 0.2%; Hispanic or Latino 0.4%; Asian 0.1%; Other 0.7%). **Foreign born:** 0.3%. **Median age:** 38.5. **State rank:** 87. **Pop change 1990-2000:** +0%.

Income: per capita $17,054; median household $36,411. **Pop below poverty level:** 11.2%.

Unemployment: 5.1%. **Median home value:** $64,200. **Median travel time to work:** 27.7 minutes.

MIAMI COUNTY

PO Box 184
Peru, IN 46970

Ph: 765-472-3901
Fax: 765-472-1778

In north-central IN, north of Kokomo; established Feb 2, 1832 from Cass County. **Name Origin:** For the Miami Indians, an Algonquin tribe. Origin of the name is uncertain; probably from Ojibway *oumaumeg* 'people of the peninsula' or Delaware *we-mi-a-mik* 'all friends.'

Area (sq mi): 377.36 (land 375.62; water 1.74).

Pop: 36,082 (White 93%; Black or African American 3%; Hispanic or Latino 1.3%; Asian 0.3%; Other 3%). **Foreign born:** 1%. **Median age:** 36.6. **State rank:** 41. **Pop change 1990-2000:** -2.2%.

Income: per capita $17,726; median household $39,184. **Pop below poverty level:** 8%.

Unemployment: 6.4%. **Median home value:** $71,100. **Median travel time to work:** 22.1 minutes.

MONROE COUNTY

301 N College Ave
Bloomington, IN 47404
www.co.monroe.in.us

Ph: 812-349-2612
Fax: 812-349-2610

In central IN, west of Columbus; organized Jan 14, 1818 from Orange County. **Name Origin:** For James Monroe (1758-1831), fifth U.S. president.

Area (sq mi): 411.32 (land 394.35; water 16.97).

Pop: 120,563 (White 89.8%; Black or African American 3%; Hispanic or Latino 1.9%; Asian 3.4%; Other 2.8%). **Foreign born:** 5.4%. **Median age:** 27.6. **State rank:** 11. **Pop change 1990-2000:** +10.6%.

Income: per capita $18,534; median household $33,311. **Pop below poverty level:** 18.9%.

Unemployment: 3.1%. **Median home value:** $113,100. **Median travel time to work:** 18.2 minutes.

MONTGOMERY COUNTY

PO Box 768
Crawfordsville, IN 47933

Ph: 765-364-6430
Fax: 765-364-6355

In west-central IN, south of Lafayette; organized Mar 1, 1823 from

Please see sample entry on inside front cover for detailed information about the statistics presented with each county listing.

177

Indian lands. **Name Origin:** For Gen. Richard Montgomery (1738-75), American Revolutionary War officer who captured Montreal, Canada.

Area (sq mi): 505.34 (land 504.51; water 0.83).

Pop: 37,629 (White 96.3%; Black or African American 0.8%; Hispanic or Latino 1.6%; Asian 0.4%; Other 2%). **Foreign born:** 1.5%. **Median age:** 36.6. **State rank:** 40. **Pop change 1990-2000:** +9.3%.

Income: per capita $18,938; median household $41,297. **Pop below poverty level:** 8.3%.

Unemployment: 3.9%. **Median home value:** $88,800. **Median travel time to work:** 20.4 minutes.

MORGAN COUNTY
PO Box 1556 **Ph:** 765-342-1025
Martinsville, IN 46151 **Fax:** 765-342-1111

In central IN, southwest of Indianapolis; organized Feb 15, 1823 from Indian lands. **Name Origin:** For Gen. Daniel Morgan (1736-1802), an officer in the Revolutionary War and U.S. representative from VA (1797-99).

Area (sq mi): 409.39 (land 406.47; water 2.92).

Pop: 66,689 (White 98.1%; Black or African American 0.1%; Hispanic or Latino 0.7%; Asian 0.2%; Other 1.1%). **Foreign born:** 0.9%. **Median age:** 36. **State rank:** 24. **Pop change 1990-2000:** +19.3%.

Income: per capita $20,657; median household $47,739. **Pop below poverty level:** 6.6%.

Unemployment: 3.1%. **Median home value:** $116,200. **Median travel time to work:** 28.3 minutes.

NEWTON COUNTY
PO Box 49 **Ph:** 219-474-6081
Kentland, IN 47951 **Fax:** 219-474-5749

In northwestern IN, south of Gary; organized Feb 7, 1857 from Jasper County. **Name Origin:** For Sgt. John Newton (1752-80), a soldier under Gen. Francis Marion (1732?-95) in the Revolutionary War, who saved several colonial patriots from execution by surprising and capturing the British soldiers guarding them.

Area (sq mi): 403.53 (land 401.85; water 1.68).

Pop: 14,566 (White 95.8%; Black or African American 0.2%; Hispanic or Latino 2.9%; Asian 0.2%; Other 2.3%). **Foreign born:** 2.3%. **Median age:** 37.3. **State rank:** 82. **Pop change 1990-2000:** +7.5%.

Income: per capita $17,755; median household $40,944. **Pop below poverty level:** 6.9%.

Unemployment: 5.2%. **Median home value:** $87,500. **Median travel time to work:** 29.4 minutes.

NOBLE COUNTY
101 N Orange St **Ph:** 260-636-2736
Albion, IN 46701 **Fax:** 260-636-3053

In northeastern IN, southeast of Elkhart; established Feb 7, 1835 from Elkhart County. **Name Origin:** For either James Noble (1785-1831), U.S. senator from IN (1816-31), or for Moah Noble, governor of IN (1831-37) when the county was established.

Area (sq mi): 417.61 (land 411.11; water 6.5).

Pop: 46,275 (White 91.2%; Black or African American 0.4%; Hispanic or Latino 7.1%; Asian 0.4%; Other 5.1%). **Foreign born:** 4.9%. **Median age:** 33.3. **State rank:** 28. **Pop change 1990-2000:** +22.2%.

Income: per capita $17,896; median household $42,700. **Pop below poverty level:** 7.9%.

Unemployment: 6.7%. **Median home value:** $88,600. **Median travel time to work:** 21.2 minutes.

OHIO COUNTY
413 Main St **Ph:** 812-438-2610
Rising Sun, IN 47040 **Fax:** 812-438-1215

On the southeastern border of IN, southwest of Cincinnati, OH; organized Jan 4, 1844 from Dearborn County. **Name Origin:** For the Ohio River, which forms the eastern border of the county.

Area (sq mi): 87.47 (land 86.72; water 0.75).

Pop: 5,623 (White 98.4%; Black or African American 0.5%; Hispanic or Latino 0.4%; Asian 0.1%; Other 0.7%). **Foreign born:** 0.1%. **Median age:** 38.4. **State rank:** 92. **Pop change 1990-2000:** +5.8%.

Income: per capita $19,627; median household $41,348. **Pop below poverty level:** 7.1%.

Unemployment: 3.5%. **Median home value:** $97,100. **Median travel time to work:** 27.3 minutes.

ORANGE COUNTY
1 Court St **Ph:** 812-723-2649
Paoli, IN 47454 **Fax:** 812-723-0239

In south-central IN, south of Bloomington; established Dec 26, 1815 (prior to statehood) from Crawford and Washington counties. **Name Origin:** For Orange County, NC, former home of many early settlers.

Area (sq mi): 408.2 (land 399.52; water 8.68).

Pop: 19,306 (White 97.5%; Black or African American 0.6%; Hispanic or Latino 0.6%; Asian 0.2%; Other 1.2%). **Foreign born:** 0.8%. **Median age:** 37.5. **State rank:** 74. **Pop change 1990-2000:** +4.9%.

Income: per capita $16,717; median household $31,564. **Pop below poverty level:** 12.4%.

Unemployment: 9.1%. **Median home value:** $63,500. **Median travel time to work:** 25.2 minutes.

OWEN COUNTY
County Courthouse **Ph:** 812-829-5000
Spencer, IN 47460 **Fax:** 812-829-5004
www.owencounty.org

In west-central IN, northwest of Bloomington; established Dec 21, 1818 from Indian lands. **Name Origin:** For Col. Abraham Owen (?-1811), killed in the Battle of Tippecanoe.

Area (sq mi): 387.83 (land 385.18; water 2.65).

Pop: 21,786 (White 97.7%; Black or African American 0.3%; Hispanic or Latino 0.8%; Asian 0.2%; Other 1.4%). **Foreign born:**

All statistics are based on the 2000 Census except the dollar figures given for per capita income, which are based on 1999 estimates.

0.4%. **Median age:** 37.6. **State rank:** 69. **Pop change 1990-2000:** +26.1%.

Income: per capita $16,884; median household $36,529. **Pop below poverty level:** 9.4%.

Unemployment: 4.7%. **Median home value:** $84,600. **Median travel time to work:** 33.6 minutes.

PARKE COUNTY

116 W High St Rm 204   **Ph:** 765-569-5132
Rockville, IN 47872   **Fax:** 765-569-4037

In west-central IN, north of Terre Haute; organized Jan 9, 1821 from Indian lands. **Name Origin:** For Benjamin Parke (1777-1835), attorney general of IN Territory (1804-08), IN legislator, and judge of the U.S. District Court of IN (1817-35).

Area (sq mi): 450.1 (land 444.77; water 5.32).

Pop: 17,241 (White 96.1%; Black or African American 2.1%; Hispanic or Latino 0.6%; Asian 0.2%; Other 1.1%). **Foreign born:** 0.5%. **Median age:** 38.9. **State rank:** 78. **Pop change 1990-2000:** +11.9%.

Income: per capita $16,986; median household $35,724. **Pop below poverty level:** 11.5%.

Unemployment: 4.7%. **Median home value:** $64,900. **Median travel time to work:** 27.5 minutes.

PERRY COUNTY

County Courthouse 2219 Payne St   **Ph:** 812-547-3741
Tell City, IN 47586   **Fax:** 812-547-9782
www.perrycountyin.org

On the south-central border of IN; organized Sept 7, 1814 (prior to statehood) from Harrison and Warrick counties. **Name Origin:** For Oliver Hazard Perry (1785-1819), U.S. naval officer during the War of 1812, famous for the message, 'We have met the enemy and they are ours.'

Area (sq mi): 386.34 (land 381.39; water 4.95).

Pop: 18,899 (White 97.1%; Black or African American 1.4%; Hispanic or Latino 0.7%; Asian 0.1%; Other 0.8%). **Foreign born:** 0.4%. **Median age:** 38. **State rank:** 75. **Pop change 1990-2000:** -1.1%.

Income: per capita $16,673; median household $36,246. **Pop below poverty level:** 9.4%.

Unemployment: 6%. **Median home value:** $71,200. **Median travel time to work:** 24.8 minutes.

PIKE COUNTY

801 Main St   **Ph:** 812-354-6025
Petersburg, IN 47567   **Fax:** 812-354-3500

In southwestern IN, northeast of Evansville; established Dec 21, 1816 from Indian lands. **Name Origin:** For Zebulon Montgomery Pike (1779-1813), U.S. army officer and discoverer of Pikes Peak in CO.

Area (sq mi): 341.08 (land 336.18; water 4.91).

Pop: 12,837 (White 98.7%; Black or African American 0.1%; Hispanic or Latino 0.6%; Asian 0.1%; Other 0.6%). **Foreign born:**

0.6%. **Median age:** 38.8. **State rank:** 85. **Pop change 1990-2000:** +2.6%.

Income: per capita $16,217; median household $34,759. **Pop below poverty level:** 8%.

Unemployment: 4.1%. **Median home value:** $59,300. **Median travel time to work:** 26.1 minutes.

PORTER COUNTY

155 Indiana Ave   **Ph:** 219-465-3445
Valparaiso, IN 46383   **Fax:** 219-465-3592
www.co.porter.in.us

On the northwestern border of IN, east of Gary, bordered on north by Lake Michigan; established Feb 7, 1835 from Indian lands. **Name Origin:** For Commodore David Porter (1780-1843), naval hero in the War of 1812 and U.S. minister to Turkey (1839).

Area (sq mi): 521.61 (land 418.11; water 103.5).

Pop: 146,798 (White 92.2%; Black or African American 0.9%; Hispanic or Latino 4.8%; Asian 0.9%; Other 2.8%). **Foreign born:** 3%. **Median age:** 36.3. **State rank:** 9. **Pop change 1990-2000:** +13.9%.

Income: per capita $23,957; median household $53,100. **Pop below poverty level:** 5.9%.

Unemployment: 4%. **Median home value:** $127,000. **Median travel time to work:** 25.9 minutes.

POSEY COUNTY

126 E 3rd St   **Ph:** 812-838-1300
Mount Vernon, IN 47620

In the southwestern corner of IN, west of Evansville; organized Sept 7, 1814 (prior to statehood) from Knox County. **Name Origin:** For Gen. Thomas Posey (1750-1818), officer in the American Revolution, LA legislator (1805-06), U.S. senator from LA (1812-13), and IN territorial governor (1813-16).

Area (sq mi): 419.45 (land 408.5; water 10.95).

Pop: 27,061 (White 97.7%; Black or African American 0.9%; Hispanic or Latino 0.4%; Asian 0.2%; Other 1.1%). **Foreign born:** 0.5%. **Median age:** 37.4. **State rank:** 59. **Pop change 1990-2000:** +4.2%.

Income: per capita $19,516; median household $44,209. **Pop below poverty level:** 7.4%.

Unemployment: 3.1%. **Median home value:** $89,800. **Median travel time to work:** 23 minutes.

PULASKI COUNTY

112 E Main St Rm 230   **Ph:** 574-946-3313
Winamac, IN 46996   **Fax:** 574-946-4953

In northwestern IN, southwest of South Bend; established Feb 7, 1835 from Cass County. **Name Origin:** For Count Casimir Pulaski (1747-79), Polish soldier who fought for America during the Revolutionary War.

Area (sq mi): 434.57 (land 433.68; water 0.89).

Pop: 13,755 (White 96.6%; Black or African American 0.9%; Hispanic or Latino 1.4%; Asian 0.2%; Other 1.3%). **Foreign born:** 0.8%. **Median age:** 37.8. **State rank:** 84. **Pop change 1990-2000:** +8.8%.

Please see sample entry on inside front cover for detailed information about the statistics presented with each county listing.

Income: per capita $16,835; median household $35,422. **Pop below poverty level:** 8.3%.

Unemployment: 6.1%. **Median home value:** $72,500. **Median travel time to work:** 23.4 minutes.

PUTNAM COUNTY
1 Courthouse Sq Rm 20   **Ph:** 765-653-5513
Greencastle, IN 46135   **Fax:** 765-653-5992

In west-central IN, west of Indianapolis; established Dec 31, 1821 from Indian lands. **Name Origin:** For Gen. Israel Putnam (1718-90), Revolutionary War officer and American commander at the Battle of Bunker Hill.

Area (sq mi): 482.58 (land 480.31; water 2.27).

Pop: 36,019 (White 94.3%; Black or African American 2.9%; Hispanic or Latino 1.1%; Asian 0.5%; Other 1.6%). **Foreign born:** 1.1%. **Median age:** 35.1. **State rank:** 42. **Pop change 1990-2000:** +18.8%.

Income: per capita $17,163; median household $38,882. **Pop below poverty level:** 8%.

Unemployment: 3%. **Median home value:** $94,300. **Median travel time to work:** 25.6 minutes.

RANDOLPH COUNTY
County Courthouse 100 S Main St
PO Box 230   **Ph:** 765-584-7207
Winchester, IN 47394   **Fax:** 765-584-2958

On the east-central border of IN, east of Muncie; organized Jan 10, 1818 from Wayne County. **Name Origin:** For either Thomas Randolph (?-1811), attorney-general of IN Territory killed at the Battle of Tippecanoe, or for Randolph County, NC, former home of many early settlers.

Area (sq mi): 453.23 (land 452.83; water 0.39).

Pop: 27,401 (White 97.5%; Black or African American 0.3%; Hispanic or Latino 1.2%; Asian 0.2%; Other 1.5%). **Foreign born:** 0.7%. **Median age:** 38.2. **State rank:** 57. **Pop change 1990-2000:** +0.9%.

Income: per capita $16,954; median household $34,544. **Pop below poverty level:** 11.1%.

Unemployment: 6.6%. **Median home value:** $64,600. **Median travel time to work:** 23.3 minutes.

RIPLEY COUNTY
PO Box 177   **Ph:** 812-689-6115
Versailles, IN 47042   **Fax:** 812-689-6000
www.ripleycounty.com

In southeastern IN, east of Columbus; established Dec 27, 1816 from Indian lands. **Name Origin:** For Gen. Eleazar Wheelock Ripley (1782-1839), officer in the War of 1812, MA legislator, and U.S. representative from LA (1835-39).

Area (sq mi): 447.91 (land 446.36; water 1.55).

Pop: 26,523 (White 97.9%; Black or African American 0%; Hispanic or Latino 0.9%; Asian 0.4%; Other 1.2%). **Foreign born:** 0.7%. **Median age:** 35.7. **State rank:** 61. **Pop change 1990-2000:** +7.7%.

Income: per capita $17,559; median household $41,426. **Pop below poverty level:** 7.5%.

Unemployment: 3.5%. **Median home value:** $94,900. **Median travel time to work:** 26.3 minutes.

RUSH COUNTY
101 E 2nd St County Courthouse   **Ph:** 765-932-2077
Rushville, IN 46173   **Fax:** 765-938-1163

In east-central IN, southeast of Indianapolis; established Dec 31, 1821 from Franklin County. **Name Origin:** For Benjamin Rush (1745-1813), surgeon general in the Continental Army and a signer of the Declaration of Independence.

Area (sq mi): 408.62 (land 408.28; water 0.34).

Pop: 18,261 (White 97.4%; Black or African American 0.6%; Hispanic or Latino 0.5%; Asian 0.5%; Other 1.2%). **Foreign born:** 0.3%. **Median age:** 36.9. **State rank:** 76. **Pop change 1990-2000:** +0.7%.

Income: per capita $17,997; median household $38,152. **Pop below poverty level:** 7.3%.

Unemployment: 3.7%. **Median home value:** $82,300. **Median travel time to work:** 25.4 minutes.

SAINT JOSEPH COUNTY
101 S Main St   **Ph:** 574-235-9635
South Bend, IN 46601   **Fax:** 574-235-9838

On the central northern border of IN; organized Jan 29, 1830 from Indian lands. **Name Origin:** For the Saint Joseph River, which runs through the county.

Area (sq mi): 460.97 (land 457.34; water 3.63).

Pop: 265,559 (White 80.5%; Black or African American 11.5%; Hispanic or Latino 4.7%; Asian 1.3%; Other 5%). **Foreign born:** 4.6%. **Median age:** 34.4. **State rank:** 4. **Pop change 1990-2000:** +7.5%.

Income: per capita $19,756; median household $40,420. **Pop below poverty level:** 10.4%.

Unemployment: 4.6%. **Median home value:** $85,700. **Median travel time to work:** 20.2 minutes.

SCOTT COUNTY
1 E McClain Ave Suite 120   **Ph:** 812-752-4769
Scottsburg, IN 47170   **Fax:** 812-752-5459
www.greatscottindiana.org

On the southeastern border of IN, north of Louisville, KY; organized Jan 12, 1820 from Clark and Jackson counties. **Name Origin:** For Gen. Charles Scott (1739-1813), an officer in the Revolutionary War; governor of KY (1808-12).

Area (sq mi): 192.73 (land 190.39; water 2.34).

Pop: 22,960 (White 98.2%; Black or African American 0%; Hispanic or Latino 1%; Asian 0.2%; Other 1.1%). **Foreign born:** 0.4%. **Median age:** 35.1. **State rank:** 66. **Pop change 1990-2000:** +9.4%.

Income: per capita $16,065; median household $34,656. **Pop below poverty level:** 13.1%.

Unemployment: 4.9%. **Median home value:** $76,900. **Median travel time to work:** 25.3 minutes.

All statistics are based on the 2000 Census except the dollar figures given for per capita income, which are based on 1999 estimates.

SHELBY COUNTY

25 W Polk St
Shelbyville, IN 46176

Ph: 317-392-6330
Fax: 317-392-6393

In central IN, southeast of Indianapolis; established Dec 31, 1821 from Indian lands. **Name Origin:** For Gen. Isaac Shelby (1750-1826), officer in the Revolutionary War, NC legislator, and first governor of KY (1792-96; 1812-16).

Area (sq mi): 413.11 (land 412.64; water 0.47).

Pop: 43,445 (White 96.7%; Black or African American 0.8%; Hispanic or Latino 1.1%; Asian 0.6%; Other 1.4%). **Foreign born:** 1.6%. **Median age:** 36.2. **State rank:** 33. **Pop change 1990-2000:** +7.8%.

Income: per capita $20,324; median household $43,649. **Pop below poverty level:** 7.6%.

Unemployment: 3.7%. **Median home value:** $98,600. **Median travel time to work:** 21.8 minutes.

SPENCER COUNTY

PO Box 12
Rockport, IN 47635
www.spencerco.org

Ph: 812-649-6027
Fax: 812-649-6030

On the southwestern border of IN, east of Evansville; organized Jan 10, 1818 from Warrick County. **Name Origin:** For Captain Spier (Spear?) Spencer (?-1811), a KY officer killed at the Battle of Tippecanoe.

Area (sq mi): 401.23 (land 398.69; water 2.55).

Pop: 20,391 (White 97.1%; Black or African American 0.6%; Hispanic or Latino 1.5%; Asian 0.2%; Other 1.4%). **Foreign born:** 0.9%. **Median age:** 37.3. **State rank:** 72. **Pop change 1990-2000:** +4.6%.

Income: per capita $18,000; median household $42,451. **Pop below poverty level:** 6.9%.

Unemployment: 4.7%. **Median home value:** $85,100. **Median travel time to work:** 28 minutes.

STARKE COUNTY

53 E Washington St County Courthouse
Knox, IN 46534

Ph: 574-772-9128
Fax: 574-772-9169

In northwestern IN, southwest of South Bend; established Feb 7, 1835 from Marshall County. **Name Origin:** For Gen. John Stark (1728-1822), an officer in the French and Indian Wars and the American Revolution; no reason known why spelling was altered.

Area (sq mi): 312.31 (land 309.31; water 3).

Pop: 23,556 (White 96.3%; Black or African American 0.2%; Hispanic or Latino 2.2%; Asian 0.2%; Other 1.9%). **Foreign born:** 2.6%. **Median age:** 37. **State rank:** 65. **Pop change 1990-2000:** +3.6%.

Income: per capita $16,466; median household $37,243. **Pop below poverty level:** 11.1%.

Unemployment: 7%. **Median home value:** $80,000. **Median travel time to work:** 28.9 minutes.

STEUBEN COUNTY

55 S Public Sq
Angola, IN 46703
www.co.steuben.in.us

Ph: 260-668-1000
Fax: 260-668-3702

In the northeastern corner of IN; established Feb 7, 1835 from Indian lands. **Name Origin:** For Friedrich Wilhelm, Baron von Steuben (1730-94), Prussian soldier named inspector general of the U.S. Continental Army (1778).

Area (sq mi): 322.48 (land 308.72; water 13.76).

Pop: 33,214 (White 96.1%; Black or African American 0.4%; Hispanic or Latino 2.1%; Asian 0.4%; Other 2%). **Foreign born:** 1.4%. **Median age:** 35.5. **State rank:** 48. **Pop change 1990-2000:** +21%.

Income: per capita $20,647; median household $44,089. **Pop below poverty level:** 6.7%.

Unemployment: 6.1%. **Median home value:** $106,200. **Median travel time to work:** 20.9 minutes.

SULLIVAN COUNTY

PO Box 370
Sullivan, IN 47882

Ph: 812-268-4657
Fax: 812-268-4870

On the west-central border of IN, south of Terre Haute; established Dec 30, 1816 from Knox County. **Name Origin:** For Gen. Daniel Sullivan (?-1779), killed during the Revolutionary War.

Area (sq mi): 454.04 (land 447.2; water 6.85).

Pop: 21,751 (White 93.7%; Black or African American 4.3%; Hispanic or Latino 0.8%; Asian 0.1%; Other 1.4%). **Foreign born:** 0.3%. **Median age:** 37.3. **State rank:** 70. **Pop change 1990-2000:** +14.5%.

Income: per capita $16,234; median household $32,976. **Pop below poverty level:** 10.9%.

Unemployment: 5.7%. **Median home value:** $58,900. **Median travel time to work:** 26.8 minutes.

SWITZERLAND COUNTY

212 W Main St County Courthouse
Vevay, IN 47043

Ph: 812-427-3302

In the southeastern corner of IN, southeast of Columbus; organized Sept 7, 1814 (prior to statehood) from Indian lands. **Name Origin:** For the European country, named by Swiss settlers.

Area (sq mi): 223.52 (land 221.18; water 2.34).

Pop: 9,065 (White 98.3%; Black or African American 0.2%; Hispanic or Latino 0.9%; Asian 0.1%; Other 0.9%). **Foreign born:** 0.5%. **Median age:** 36.8. **State rank:** 89. **Pop change 1990-2000:** +17.1%.

Income: per capita $17,466; median household $37,092. **Pop below poverty level:** 13.9%.

Unemployment: 4.7%. **Median home value:** $78,400. **Median travel time to work:** 33.6 minutes.

TIPPECANOE COUNTY

20 N 3rd St
Lafayette, IN 47901
www.co.tippecanoe.in.us

Ph: 765-423-9215
Fax: 765-423-9196

In west-central IN, west of Kokomo; organized Jan 20, 1826 from

Please see sample entry on inside front cover for detailed information about the statistics presented with each county listing.

Montgomery County. **Name Origin:** For the Tippecanoe River, itself named from Potawatomi *quit-te-pe-con-nac* 'buffalo fish,' which were plentiful in the river.

Area (sq mi): 503.07 (land 499.79; water 3.28).

Pop: 148,955 (White 86.4%; Black or African American 2.5%; Hispanic or Latino 5.3%; Asian 4.5%; Other 4.2%). **Foreign born:** 8.2%. **Median age:** 27.2. **State rank:** 8. **Pop change 1990-2000:** +14.1%.

Income: per capita $19,375; median household $38,652. **Pop below poverty level:** 15.4%.

Unemployment: 3.1%. **Median home value:** $112,200. **Median travel time to work:** 17.3 minutes.

TIPTON COUNTY

101 E Jefferson St   **Ph:** 765-675-2794
Tipton, IN 46072   **Fax:** 765-675-3194

In central IN, south of Kokoma; organized Jan 15, 1844 from Hamilton County. **Name Origin:** For Gen. John Tipton (1786-1839), IN legislator (1819-23), and U.S. senator (1832-39).

Area (sq mi): 260.41 (land 260.39; water 0.02).

Pop: 16,577 (White 97.7%; Black or African American 0.1%; Hispanic or Latino 1.2%; Asian 0.3%; Other 1.2%). **Foreign born:** 1%. **Median age:** 38.4. **State rank:** 80. **Pop change 1990-2000:** +2.8%.

Income: per capita $21,926; median household $48,546. **Pop below poverty level:** 5.1%.

Unemployment: 5.3%. **Median home value:** $88,300. **Median travel time to work:** 22.1 minutes.

UNION COUNTY

26 W Union St   **Ph:** 765-458-6121
Liberty, IN 47353   **Fax:** 765-458-5263

On the southeastern border of IN, south of Richmond; organized Jan 15, 1821 from Wayne County. **Name Origin:** As an expression of belief in the federal union of the states.

Area (sq mi): 165.25 (land 161.55; water 3.7).

Pop: 7,349 (White 98.5%; Black or African American 0.2%; Hispanic or Latino 0.3%; Asian 0.2%; Other 0.9%). **Foreign born:** 0.4%. **Median age:** 36.5. **State rank:** 91. **Pop change 1990-2000:** +5.3%.

Income: per capita $19,549; median household $36,672. **Pop below poverty level:** 9.7%.

Unemployment: 4.8%. **Median home value:** $82,600. **Median travel time to work:** 24.6 minutes.

VANDERBURGH COUNTY

1 NW ML King Jr Blvd   **Ph:** 812-435-5241
Evansville, IN 47708   **Fax:** 812-435-5995
www.vanderburghgov.org

On the southwestern border of IN; organized Jan 7, 1818 from Indian lands. **Name Origin:** For Henry Vanderburgh, officer in the Revolutionary War and judge of the first court in the IN Territory.

Area (sq mi): 235.74 (land 234.57; water 1.16).

Pop: 171,922 (White 88.7%; Black or African American 8.2%; Hispanic or Latino 1%; Asian 0.8%; Other 1.7%). **Foreign born:** 1.6%. **Median age:** 36.9. **State rank:** 7. **Pop change 1990-2000:** +4.2%.

Income: per capita $20,655; median household $36,823. **Pop below poverty level:** 11.2%.

Unemployment: 3.6%. **Median home value:** $82,400. **Median travel time to work:** 19 minutes.

VERMILLION COUNTY

PO Box 10   **Ph:** 765-492-3500
Newport, IN 47966   **Fax:** 765-492-5001

On the central western border of IN, north of Terre Haute; organized Jan 2, 1824 from Parke County. **Name Origin:** For the Big Vermilllion River, which runs across the northern part of the county. Shortened French literal transliteration *Vermillion Jaune* 'yellow red' of the Indian name *Osanamon*, suggesting vermilion paint, probably from the soil that colored the river.

Area (sq mi): 259.94 (land 256.89; water 3.05).

Pop: 16,788 (White 98%; Black or African American 0.3%; Hispanic or Latino 0.6%; Asian 0.1%; Other 1.2%). **Foreign born:** 0.8%. **Median age:** 38.9. **State rank:** 79. **Pop change 1990-2000:** +0.1%.

Income: per capita $18,579; median household $34,837. **Pop below poverty level:** 9.5%.

Unemployment: 5.9%. **Median home value:** $59,500. **Median travel time to work:** 22.7 minutes.

VIGO COUNTY

PO Box 8449   **Ph:** 812-462-3211
Terre Haute, IN 47808   **Fax:** 812-232-2921
www.vigocountyin.com

On the central western border of IN, northwest of Bloomington; organized Jan 21, 1818 from Indian lands. **Name Origin:** For Giuseppe Maria Francesco Vigo (1747-1836), also known as Col. Francis Vigo, a Mondovian-born fur trader who furnished funds and assistance to Revolutionary soldier George Rogers Clark (1752-1818).

Area (sq mi): 410.47 (land 403.29; water 7.17).

Pop: 105,848 (White 89.9%; Black or African American 6%; Hispanic or Latino 1.2%; Asian 1.2%; Other 2.1%). **Foreign born:** 2%. **Median age:** 34.9. **State rank:** 15. **Pop change 1990-2000:** -0.2%.

Income: per capita $17,620; median household $33,184. **Pop below poverty level:** 14.1%.

Unemployment: 5.4%. **Median home value:** $72,500. **Median travel time to work:** 18.7 minutes.

WABASH COUNTY

69 W Hill St   **Ph:** 260-563-0661
Wabash, IN 46992   **Fax:** 260-569-1352

In north-central IN, southwest of Ft. Wayne; established Feb 2, 1832 from Huntington County. **Name Origin:** For the Wabash River, which runs across the center of the county itself named from a Miami Indian word probably meaning 'pure white,' referring to a limestone bed in the river.

Area (sq mi): 421.07 (land 413.17; water 7.9).

All statistics are based on the 2000 Census except the dollar figures given for per capita income, which are based on 1999 estimates.

Pop: 34,960 (White 96.7%; Black or African American 0.4%; Hispanic or Latino 1.2%; Asian 0.4%; Other 1.8%). **Foreign born:** 0.7%. **Median age:** 37.5. **State rank:** 43. **Pop change 1990-2000:** -0.3%.

Income: per capita $18,192; median household $40,413. **Pop below poverty level:** 6.9%.

Unemployment: 5.8%. **Median home value:** $78,400. **Median travel time to work:** 19.1 minutes.

WARREN COUNTY

125 N Monroe St Suite 11	**Ph:** 765-762-3510
Williamsport, IN 47993	**Fax:** 765-762-7251

On the west-central border of IN, southwest of Lafayette; organized Jan 19, 1827 from Indian lands. **Name Origin:** For Dr. Joseph Warren (1741-75), Revolutionary War general and member of the Committee of Safety who dispatched Paul Revere (1735-1818) on his famous ride.

Area (sq mi): 366.6 (land 364.88; water 1.72).

Pop: 8,419 (White 98.8%; Black or African American 0.1%; Hispanic or Latino 0.4%; Asian 0.2%; Other 0.6%). **Foreign born:** 0.3%. **Median age:** 38.2. **State rank:** 90. **Pop change 1990-2000:** +3%.

Income: per capita $18,070; median household $41,825. **Pop below poverty level:** 6.5%.

Unemployment: 3.6%. **Median home value:** $74,100. **Median travel time to work:** 24.9 minutes.

WARRICK COUNTY

107 W Locust St	**Ph:** 812-897-6120
Boonville, IN 47601	**Fax:** 812-897-6189
www.indico.net/counties/WARRICK/	

On the southwestern border of IN, east of Evansville; organized Mar 9, 1813 (prior to statehood) from Indian lands. **Name Origin:** For Capt. Jacob Warrick (1773-1811), distinguished early settler and officer who died at the Battle of Tippecanoe.

Area (sq mi): 390.86 (land 384.07; water 6.79).

Pop: 52,383 (White 97%; Black or African American 1%; Hispanic or Latino 0.6%; Asian 0.6%; Other 0.8%). **Foreign born:** 1.3%. **Median age:** 37.3. **State rank:** 26. **Pop change 1990-2000:** +16.6%.

Income: per capita $21,893; median household $48,814. **Pop below poverty level:** 5.3%.

Unemployment: 3.2%. **Median home value:** $104,400. **Median travel time to work:** 23.5 minutes.

WASHINGTON COUNTY

99 Public Sq	**Ph:** 812-883-5748
Salem, IN 47167	**Fax:** 812-883-8108
co.washington.ia.us	

In south-central IN, northwest of Louisville, KY; established Dec 21, 1813 (prior to statehood) from Indian lands. **Name Origin:** For George Washington (1732-99), American patriot and first U.S. president.

Area (sq mi): 516.53 (land 514.42; water 2.12).

Pop: 27,223 (White 98.3%; Black or African American 0.1%; Hispanic or Latino 0.7%; Asian 0.2%; Other 0.9%). **Foreign born:** 0.5%. **Median age:** 35.8. **State rank:** 58. **Pop change 1990-2000:** +14.8%.

Income: per capita $16,748; median household $36,630. **Pop below poverty level:** 10.6%.

Unemployment: 6.9%. **Median home value:** $77,500. **Median travel time to work:** 28.4 minutes.

WAYNE COUNTY

401 E Main St	**Ph:** 765-973-9200
Richmond, IN 47374	**Fax:** 765-973-9321
www.co.wayne.in.us	

On the central-eastern border of IN, southeast of Muncie; established Nov 27, 1810 (prior to statehood) from Indian lands. **Name Origin:** For Gen. Anthony Wayne (1745-96), PA soldier and statesman, nicknamed 'Mad Anthony' for his daring during the Revolutionary War, but honored here mostly for his defeat of Miami Indian chief Little Turtle (c. 1752-1812) in the Battle of Fallen Timbers (1794).

Area (sq mi): 404.34 (land 403.57; water 0.78).

Pop: 71,097 (White 91.4%; Black or African American 5.1%; Hispanic or Latino 1.4%; Asian 0.5%; Other 2.3%). **Foreign born:** 1.5%. **Median age:** 37.7. **State rank:** 22. **Pop change 1990-2000:** -1.2%.

Income: per capita $17,727; median household $34,885. **Pop below poverty level:** 11.4%.

Unemployment: 5.1%. **Median home value:** $80,300. **Median travel time to work:** 18.4 minutes.

WELLS COUNTY

102 W Market St Rm 205	**Ph:** 260-824-6470
Bluffton, IN 46714	**Fax:** 260-824-6475

In northeastern IN, south of Ft. Wayne; established Feb 7, 1835 from Indian lands. **Name Origin:** For Capt. William Wells (1770?-1812), a white man adopted by Miami Indian Chief Little Turtle (c.1752-1812), who served with the Indians; he returned to the white men and served as Indian agent, then fought the Indians at the Battle of Tippecanoe (1811).

Area (sq mi): 370.41 (land 369.96; water 0.45).

Pop: 27,600 (White 97.4%; Black or African American 0.2%; Hispanic or Latino 1.4%; Asian 0.2%; Other 1.2%). **Foreign born:** 0.8%. **Median age:** 36.8. **State rank:** 55. **Pop change 1990-2000:** +6.4%.

Income: per capita $19,158; median household $43,934. **Pop below poverty level:** 5.9%.

Unemployment: 4.3%. **Median home value:** $87,900. **Median travel time to work:** 20.8 minutes.

WHITE COUNTY

PO Box 350	**Ph:** 574-583-7032
Monticello, IN 47960	**Fax:** 574-583-1532
www.mwprairienet.lib.in.us/White/index.html	

In northwestern IN, north of Lafayette; organized Feb 1, 1834 from

Please see sample entry on inside front cover for detailed information about the statistics presented with each county listing.

183

Carroll County. **Name Origin:** For Col. Isaac White (?-1811), killed at the Battle of Tippecanoe.

Area (sq mi): 508.8 (land 505.24; water 3.56).

Pop: 25,267 (White 93.3%; Black or African American 0.2%; Hispanic or Latino 5.3%; Asian 0.2%; Other 4.4%). **Foreign born:** 3.5%. **Median age:** 37.6. **State rank:** 63. **Pop change 1990-2000:** +8.6%.

Income: per capita $18,323; median household $40,707. **Pop below poverty level:** 7%.

Unemployment: 5.2%. **Median home value:** $86,200. **Median travel time to work:** 22.2 minutes.

WHITLEY COUNTY
101 W Van Buren St   **Ph:** 260-248-3102
Columbia City, IN 46725   **Fax:** 260-248-3137
www.indico.net/counties/WHITLEY/

In northeastern IN, west of Ft. Wayne, established Feb 7, 1835 from Huntington County. **Name Origin:** For Col. William Whitley (1749-1813), soldier in the War of 1812 who enlisted at the age of 63.

Area (sq mi): 337.9 (land 335.52; water 2.38).

Pop: 30,707 (White 97.8%; Black or African American 0.2%; Hispanic or Latino 0.9%; Asian 0.2%; Other 1.3%). **Foreign born:** 0.8%. **Median age:** 36.9. **State rank:** 52. **Pop change 1990-2000:** +11.1%.

Income: per capita $20,519; median household $45,503. **Pop below poverty level:** 4.9%.

Unemployment: 5.3%. **Median home value:** $96,000. **Median travel time to work:** 23.5 minutes.

All statistics are based on the 2000 Census except the dollar figures given for per capita income, which are based on 1999 estimates.

IOWA - Counties

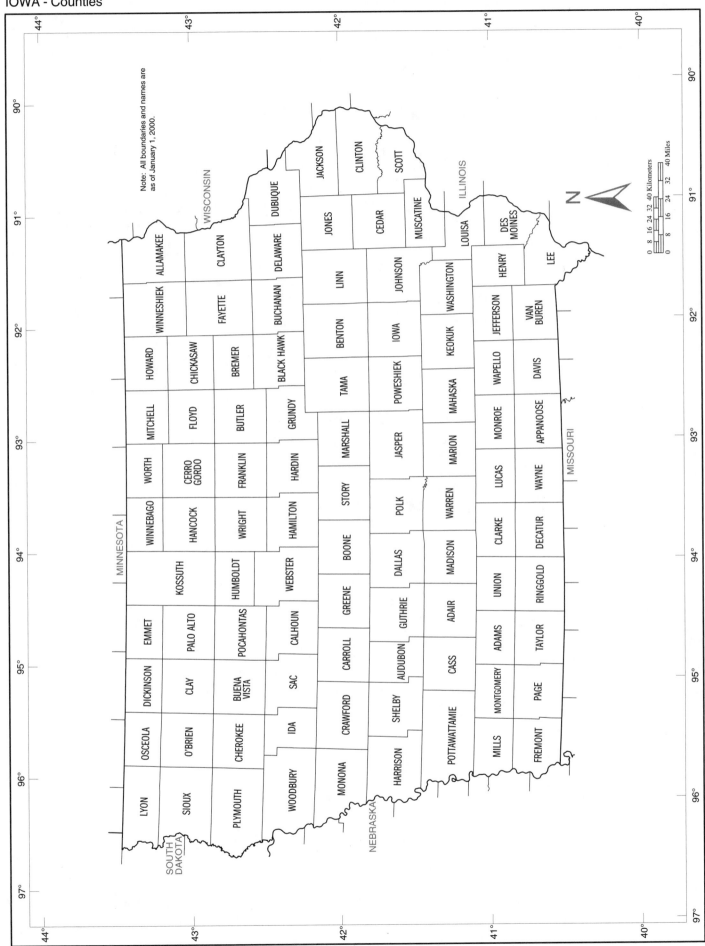

Note: All boundaries and names are as of January 1, 2000.

Iowa

IOWA STATE INFORMATION

www.state.ia.us **Ph:** 515-281-5011

Area (sq mi): 56,271.55 (land 55,869.36; water 402.2).

Pop: 2,926,324 (White 92.6%; Black or African American 2.1%; Hispanic or Latino 2.8%; Asian 1.3%; Other 2.7%). **Foreign born:** 3.1%. **Median age:** 36.6. **Pop change 1990-2000:** +5.4%.

Income: per capita $19,674; median household $39,469. **Pop below poverty level:** 9.1%.

Unemployment: 3.8%. **Median home value:** $82,500. **Median travel time to work:** 18.5 minutes.

ADAIR COUNTY

400 Public Sq **Ph:** 641-743-2546
Greenfield, IA 50849 **Fax:** 641-743-2565

In south-central IA, east of Council Bluffs; established Jan 15, 1851 from Cass County. **Name Origin:** For John Adair (1757-1840), governor of KY (1820-24).

Area (sq mi): 570.31 (land 569.3; water 1).

Pop: 8,243 (White 98.4%; Black or African American 0.1%; Hispanic or Latino 0.7%; Asian 0.2%; Other 0.8%). **Foreign born:** 0.7%. **Median age:** 41.8. **State rank:** 88. **Pop change 1990-2000:** -2%.

Income: per capita $17,262; median household $35,179. **Pop below poverty level:** 7.6%.

Unemployment: 2.3%. **Median home value:** $59,300. **Median travel time to work:** 19.9 minutes.

ADAMS COUNTY

PO Box 484 **Ph:** 641-322-4711
Corning, IA 50841 **Fax:** 641-322-4523
www.co.adams.ia.us

In southwestern IA, southeast of Council Bluffs; established Jan 15, 1851 from Taylor County. **Name Origin:** For John Adams (1735-1826), second U.S. president.

Area (sq mi): 425.41 (land 423.54; water 1.87).

Pop: 4,482 (White 98.5%; Black or African American 0.1%; Hispanic or Latino 0.6%; Asian 0.2%; Other 0.8%). **Foreign born:** 0.2%. **Median age:** 41.9. **State rank:** 99. **Pop change 1990-2000:** -7.9%.

Income: per capita $15,550; median household $30,453. **Pop below poverty level:** 9.3%.

Unemployment: 4.7%. **Median home value:** $46,500. **Median travel time to work:** 19.9 minutes.

ALLAMAKEE COUNTY

PO Box 248 **Ph:** 563-568-3318
Waukon, IA 52172 **Fax:** 563-568-6353
www.allamakeecounty.com

On the northeastern border of IA; county established Feb 20, 1847 from Clayton County. **Name Origin:** Combined form of an Indian trader's name, Allan Makee.

Area (sq mi): 658.71 (land 639.56; water 19.14).

Pop: 14,675 (White 95.3%; Black or African American 0.1%; Hispanic or Latino 3.5%; Asian 0.3%; Other 3.7%). **Foreign born:** 5.5%. **Median age:** 39.7. **State rank:** 56. **Pop change 1990-2000:** +5.9%.

Income: per capita $16,599; median household $33,967. **Pop below poverty level:** 9.6%.

Unemployment: 4.7%. **Median home value:** $68,100. **Median travel time to work:** 19.3 minutes.

APPANOOSE COUNTY

PO Box 400 **Ph:** 641-856-6101
Centerville, IA 52544 **Fax:** 641-856-2282

On the central-southern border of IA; established Feb 17, 1843 (prior to statehood) from Davis County. **Name Origin:** For a respected chief of the Sac and Fox tribes, prominent in IA and KS in the 1830s and 1840s. His name means 'chief when a child; prince.'

Area (sq mi): 516.35 (land 496.25; water 20.1).

Pop: 13,721 (White 97.5%; Black or African American 0.4%; Hispanic or Latino 1%; Asian 0.3%; Other 1.2%). **Foreign born:** 1%. **Median age:** 40.6. **State rank:** 60. **Pop change 1990-2000:** -0.2%.

Income: per capita $14,644; median household $28,612. **Pop below poverty level:** 14.5%.

Unemployment: 5%. **Median home value:** $45,400. **Median travel time to work:** 20.4 minutes.

AUDUBON COUNTY

318 Leroy St No 6 **Ph:** 712-563-4275
Audubon, IA 50025 **Fax:** 712-563-4276
www.auduboncounty.org

In west-central IA, east of Council Bluffs; established Jan 15, 1851 from Cass and Black Hawk counties. **Name Origin:** For John James Audubon (1785-1851), ornithologist and artist.

Please see sample entry on inside front cover for detailed information about the statistics presented with each county listing.

187

Area (sq mi): 443.58 (land 443.13; water 0.44).

Pop: 6,830 (White 98.7%; Black or African American 0.1%; Hispanic or Latino 0.5%; Asian 0.2%; Other 0.5%). **Foreign born:** 0.7%. **Median age:** 42.4. **State rank:** 96. **Pop change 1990-2000:** -6.9%.

Income: per capita $17,489; median household $32,215. **Pop below poverty level:** 7.7%.

Unemployment: 3.3%. **Median home value:** $48,700. **Median travel time to work:** 18.3 minutes.

BENTON COUNTY

PO Box 719   **Ph:** 319-472-2766
Vinton, IA 52349

In east-central IA, west of Grand Rapids; established Dec 21, 1837 (prior to statehood), from Indian lands. **Name Origin:** For Thomas Hart Benton (1782-1858), U.S. journalist and statesman; nicknamed 'Old Bullion' for championing the use of gold and silver currency rather than paper money.

Area (sq mi): 718.45 (land 716.39; water 2.06).

Pop: 25,308 (White 98.4%; Black or African American 0.2%; Hispanic or Latino 0.6%; Asian 0.2%; Other 0.7%). **Foreign born:** 0.6%. **Median age:** 37.2. **State rank:** 24. **Pop change 1990-2000:** +12.8%.

Income: per capita $18,891; median household $42,427. **Pop below poverty level:** 6.1%.

Unemployment: 3.6%. **Median home value:** $82,700. **Median travel time to work:** 25 minutes.

BLACK HAWK COUNTY

316 E 5th St   **Ph:** 319-833-3012
Waterloo, IA 50703   **Fax:** 319-833-3170
www.co.black-hawk.ia.us

In east-central IA, northwest of Cedar Rapids; established Feb 17, 1843 (prior to statehood) from Delaware County. **Name Origin:** For Black Hawk (1767-1838), famous Indian warrior and chief of the Sac and Fox tribes.

Area (sq mi): 571.91 (land 567.11; water 4.8).

Pop: 128,012 (White 87.7%; Black or African American 8%; Hispanic or Latino 1.8%; Asian 1%; Other 2.6%). **Foreign born:** 3.7%. **Median age:** 34.4. **State rank:** 4. **Pop change 1990-2000:** +3.4%.

Income: per capita $18,885; median household $37,266. **Pop below poverty level:** 13.1%.

Unemployment: 3.8%. **Median home value:** $77,000. **Median travel time to work:** 15.7 minutes.

BOONE COUNTY

201 State St   **Ph:** 515-433-0500
Boone, IA 50036   **Fax:** 515-432-8102
www.co.boone.ia.us

In central IA, northwest of Des Moines; established Jan 13, 1846 from Polk County. **Name Origin:** For Capt. Nathan Boone (1782-1863), son of Daniel; officer in the U.S. Dragoons and early explorer of IA.

Area (sq mi): 573.51 (land 571.46; water 2.05).

Pop: 26,224 (White 98.1%; Black or African American 0.4%; Hispanic or Latino 0.8%; Asian 0.2%; Other 0.9%). **Foreign born:** 0.8%. **Median age:** 38.6. **State rank:** 23. **Pop change 1990-2000:** +4.1%.

Income: per capita $19,943; median household $40,763. **Pop below poverty level:** 7.6%.

Unemployment: 2.9%. **Median home value:** $74,900. **Median travel time to work:** 20.9 minutes.

BREMER COUNTY

415 E Bremer Ave   **Ph:** 319-352-0130
Waverly, IA 50677   **Fax:** 319-352-0602
www.co.bremer.ia.us

In east-central IA, north of Waterloo; established Apr 29, 1851 from Winnebago Indian Reserve. **Name Origin:** For Frederika Bremer (1801-65), Swedish novelist, traveler, and early feminist.

Area (sq mi): 439.6 (land 437.9; water 1.7).

Pop: 23,325 (White 97.9%; Black or African American 0.5%; Hispanic or Latino 0.6%; Asian 0.5%; Other 0.8%). **Foreign born:** 1.2%. **Median age:** 38.1. **State rank:** 26. **Pop change 1990-2000:** +2.2%.

Income: per capita $19,199; median household $40,826. **Pop below poverty level:** 5.1%.

Unemployment: 2.8%. **Median home value:** $88,000. **Median travel time to work:** 19 minutes.

BUCHANAN COUNTY

PO Box 259   **Ph:** 319-334-2196
Independence, IA 50644   **Fax:** 319-334-7455
www.buchanancounty.com

In east-central IA, north of Cedar Rapids; established Dec 21, 1837 (prior to statehood), from Delaware County. **Name Origin:** For James Buchanan (1791-1868), fifteenth U.S. president.

Area (sq mi): 573.35 (land 571.26; water 2.09).

Pop: 21,093 (White 98%; Black or African American 0.3%; Hispanic or Latino 0.6%; Asian 0.4%; Other 0.9%). **Foreign born:** 0.9%. **Median age:** 36.4. **State rank:** 31. **Pop change 1990-2000:** +1.2%.

Income: per capita $18,405; median household $38,036. **Pop below poverty level:** 9.4%.

Unemployment: 4.4%. **Median home value:** $73,900. **Median travel time to work:** 23.2 minutes.

BUENA VISTA COUNTY

PO Box 1186   **Ph:** 712-749-2546
Storm Lake, IA 50588   **Fax:** 712-749-2700
www.co.buena-vista.ia.us

In west-central IA, northeast of Fort Dodge; established Jan 15, 1851 from Sac and Clay counties. **Name Origin:** For the Mexican town in Coahuila, site of Gen. Zachary Taylor's (1784-1850; twelfth U.S. president) final victory in the Mexican War (1847); Spanish for 'good view.'

Area (sq mi): 580.07 (land 574.78; water 5.28).

Pop: 20,411 (White 82.1%; Black or African American 0.4%; Hispanic or Latino 12.5%; Asian 4.3%; Other 7.3%). **Foreign born:**

All statistics are based on the 2000 Census except the dollar figures given for per capita income, which are based on 1999 estimates.

12.4%. **Median age:** 36.4. **State rank:** 33. **Pop change 1990-2000:** +2.2%.

Income: per capita $16,042; median household $35,300. **Pop below poverty level:** 10.5%.

Unemployment: 2.5%. **Median home value:** $64,900. **Median travel time to work:** 14.9 minutes.

BUTLER COUNTY

PO Box 307
Allison, IA 50602
www.butlercoiowa.org

Ph: 319-267-4300
Fax: 319-322-4387

In north-central IA, norhwest of Waterloo; established Jan 15, 1851 from Buchanan and Black Hawk counties. **Name Origin:** For Maj. William Orlando Butler (1791-1880), officer in the War of 1812 and Mexican-American War; U.S. representative from KY (1839-43).

Area (sq mi): 581.56 (land 580.38; water 1.18).

Pop: 15,305 (White 98.6%; Black or African American 0.1%; Hispanic or Latino 0.6%; Asian 0.2%; Other 0.8%). **Foreign born:** 0.9%. **Median age:** 41.3. **State rank:** 53. **Pop change 1990-2000:** -2.7%.

Income: per capita $17,036; median household $35,883. **Pop below poverty level:** 8%.

Unemployment: 5.3%. **Median home value:** $62,200. **Median travel time to work:** 22.3 minutes.

CALHOUN COUNTY

PO Box 273
Rockwell City, IA 50579

Ph: 712-297-8122
Fax: 712-297-5082

In central IA, west of Fort Dodge; established as Fox County Jan 15, 1851 from Greene County, name changed Jan 12, 1853. **Name Origin:** For John Caldwell Calhoun (1782-1850), U.S. statesman and proponent of Southern causes.

Area (sq mi): 572.29 (land 570.15; water 2.14).

Pop: 11,115 (White 97.6%; Black or African American 0.7%; Hispanic or Latino 0.9%; Asian 0.2%; Other 1%). **Foreign born:** 0.5%. **Median age:** 42.4. **State rank:** 74. **Pop change 1990-2000:** -3.4%.

Income: per capita $17,498; median household $33,286. **Pop below poverty level:** 10.1%.

Unemployment: 3.3%. **Median home value:** $54,700. **Median travel time to work:** 18.6 minutes.

CARROLL COUNTY

114 E 6th St
Carroll, IA 51401
www.co.carroll.ia.us

Ph: 712-792-4923
Fax: 712-792-9423

In west-central IA, west of Ames; established Jan 15, 1851 from Guthrie County. **Name Origin:** For Charles Carroll (1737-1832), a signer of the Declaration of Independence and U.S. senator from MD (1789-92).

Area (sq mi): 570.24 (land 569.31; water 0.92).

Pop: 21,421 (White 98.6%; Black or African American 0.2%; Hispanic or Latino 0.5%; Asian 0.3%; Other 0.6%). **Foreign born:** 0.6%. **Median age:** 38.7. **State rank:** 29. **Pop change 1990-2000:** +0%.

Income: per capita $18,595; median household $37,275. **Pop below poverty level:** 6.5%.

Unemployment: 2.6%. **Median home value:** $75,900. **Median travel time to work:** 14.4 minutes.

CASS COUNTY

5 W 7th St
Atlantic, IA 50022
www.nishna.net/tourism.html

Ph: 712-243-4570
Fax: 712-243-6660

In southwestern IA, east of Council Bluffs; established Jan 15, 1851 from Pottawattamie County. **Name Origin:** For Lewis Cass (1782-1866), OH legislator, governor of MI Territory (1813-31), U.S. secretary of war (1831-36), and U.S. secretary of state (1857-60).

Area (sq mi): 565.01 (land 564.33; water 0.68).

Pop: 14,684 (White 98.5%; Black or African American 0.2%; Hispanic or Latino 0.7%; Asian 0.1%; Other 0.7%). **Foreign born:** 0.8%. **Median age:** 41.6. **State rank:** 55. **Pop change 1990-2000:** -2.9%.

Income: per capita $17,067; median household $32,922. **Pop below poverty level:** 11.1%.

Unemployment: 4.5%. **Median home value:** $59,500. **Median travel time to work:** 18.9 minutes.

CEDAR COUNTY

400 Cedar St
Tipton, IA 52772
www.iowacity.com/cedarco/#cedar

Ph: 563-886-2101
Fax: 563-886-3594

In central-eastern IA, east of Iowa City; established Dec 21, 1837 (prior to statehood) from Wisconsin Territory. **Name Origin:** For the Red Cedar River that runs through the county.

Area (sq mi): 581.96 (land 579.52; water 2.44).

Pop: 18,187 (White 97.9%; Black or African American 0.2%; Hispanic or Latino 0.9%; Asian 0.3%; Other 1.1%). **Foreign born:** 0.7%. **Median age:** 39.2. **State rank:** 41. **Pop change 1990-2000:** +4.6%.

Income: per capita $19,200; median household $42,198. **Pop below poverty level:** 5.5%.

Unemployment: 3%. **Median home value:** $84,600. **Median travel time to work:** 24 minutes.

CERRO GORDO COUNTY

220 N Washington Ave
Mason City, IA 50401
www.co.cerro-gordo.ia.us

Ph: 641-421-3022
Fax: 641-421-3072

In north-central IA, northeast of Fort Dodge; established Jan 15, 1851 from Floyd County. **Name Origin:** For the city in Mexico, site of a Mexican War battle on Apr 18, 1847. Spanish 'fat hill' or 'big hill.'

Area (sq mi): 575.12 (land 568.33; water 6.8).

Pop: 46,447 (White 94.7%; Black or African American 0.8%; Hispanic or Latino 2.8%; Asian 0.7%; Other 2.3%). **Foreign born:** 1.4%. **Median age:** 39.3. **State rank:** 11. **Pop change 1990-2000:** -0.6%.

Please see sample entry on inside front cover for detailed information about the statistics presented with each county listing.

Income: per capita $19,184; median household $35,867. **Pop below poverty level:** 8.5%.

Unemployment: 3.5%. **Median home value:** $75,400. **Median travel time to work:** 15.2 minutes.

CHEROKEE COUNTY
520 W Main St PO Box F
Cherokee, IA 51012

Ph: 712-225-6744
Fax: 712-225-6749

In northwestern IA, northeast of Sioux City; established Jan 15, 1851 from Crawford County. **Name Origin:** For the Indian tribe of Iroquoian linguistic stock. Name may derive from Creek *tciloki* 'people of a different speech.'

Area (sq mi): 577.34 (land 577.15; water 0.18).

Pop: 13,035 (White 97.8%; Black or African American 0.3%; Hispanic or Latino 1%; Asian 0.4%; Other 1%). **Foreign born:** 0.9%. **Median age:** 41.7. **State rank:** 63. **Pop change 1990-2000:** -7.5%.

Income: per capita $17,934; median household $35,142. **Pop below poverty level:** 7.3%.

Unemployment: 2.8%. **Median home value:** $57,300. **Median travel time to work:** 16.4 minutes.

CHICKASAW COUNTY
PO Box 311
New Hampton, IA 50659

Ph: 641-394-2100
Fax: 641-394-5541

In northeastern IA, north of Waterloo; esablished Jan 15, 1851 from Fayette County. **Name Origin:** For the Indian tribe, closely connected with the Choctaw, and of Muskhogean linguistic stock; meaning of name unknown.

Area (sq mi): 505.48 (land 504.64; water 0.84).

Pop: 13,095 (White 98.5%; Black or African American 0.1%; Hispanic or Latino 0.6%; Asian 0.3%; Other 0.9%). **Foreign born:** 0.9%. **Median age:** 39.7. **State rank:** 62. **Pop change 1990-2000:** -1.5%.

Income: per capita $18,237; median household $37,649. **Pop below poverty level:** 8.3%.

Unemployment: 7.2%. **Median home value:** $71,200. **Median travel time to work:** 20.8 minutes.

CLARKE COUNTY
100 S Main St Courthouse
Osceola, IA 50213

Ph: 641-342-6096
Fax: 641-342-2463

In south-central IA, south of Des Moines, established Jan 13, 1846 from Lucas County. **Name Origin:** For James Clarke (1811-50), publisher of Burlington, IA, *Gazette* (1837), and last governor of IA Territory (1845-46).

Area (sq mi): 431.72 (land 431.12; water 0.6).

Pop: 9,133 (White 94.7%; Black or African American 0.1%; Hispanic or Latino 4%; Asian 0.4%; Other 2.9%). **Foreign born:** 2.5%. **Median age:** 38.6. **State rank:** 84. **Pop change 1990-2000:** +10.2%.

Income: per capita $16,409; median household $34,474. **Pop below poverty level:** 8.5%.

Unemployment: 4.2%. **Median home value:** $64,700. **Median travel time to work:** 23.3 minutes.

CLAY COUNTY
215 W 4th St
Spencer, IA 51301
www.co.clay.ia.us

Ph: 712-262-4335
Fax: 712-262-6042

In north-central IA, northwest of Fort Dodge; established Jan 15, 1851 from Indian lands. **Name Origin:** For Lt. Col. Henry Clay, Jr. (1807-47), son of the statesman (1777-1852); killed at the Battle of Buena Vista during the Mexican-American War.

Area (sq mi): 572.51 (land 568.89; water 3.63).

Pop: 17,372 (White 97.3%; Black or African American 0.2%; Hispanic or Latino 1.1%; Asian 0.8%; Other 0.9%). **Foreign born:** 1.8%. **Median age:** 39.4. **State rank:** 43. **Pop change 1990-2000:** -1.2%.

Income: per capita $19,451; median household $35,799. **Pop below poverty level:** 8.2%.

Unemployment: 3%. **Median home value:** $74,400. **Median travel time to work:** 14.2 minutes.

CLAYTON COUNTY
PO Box 418
Elkader, IA 52043

Ph: 563-245-2204
Fax: 563-245-1175

On northeastern border of IA, north of Dubuque; established Dec 21, 1837 (prior to statehood) from Dubuque County. **Name Origin:** For John Middleton Clayton (1796-1856), U.S. senator from DE and U.S. secretary of state (1849-50).

Area (sq mi): 792.81 (land 778.81; water 14).

Pop: 18,678 (White 98.4%; Black or African American 0.1%; Hispanic or Latino 0.8%; Asian 0.1%; Other 0.8%). **Foreign born:** 1.2%. **Median age:** 40.2. **State rank:** 39. **Pop change 1990-2000:** -2%.

Income: per capita $16,930; median household $34,068. **Pop below poverty level:** 8.6%.

Unemployment: 5.3%. **Median home value:** $66,400. **Median travel time to work:** 20.8 minutes.

CLINTON COUNTY
PO Box 2957
Clinton, IA 52733
www.clintoncountyiowa.com

Ph: 563-243-6210
Fax: 563-243-3655

On central eastern border, north of Davenport; established Dec 21,1837 (prior to statehood) from Dubuque County. **Name Origin:** For DeWitt Clinton (1769-1828), governor of NY (1817-23; 1825-28) and supporter of the Erie Canal.

Area (sq mi): 710.19 (land 694.98; water 15.21).

Pop: 50,149 (White 95.2%; Black or African American 1.9%; Hispanic or Latino 1.3%; Asian 0.6%; Other 1.6%). **Foreign born:** 1.4%. **Median age:** 38.2. **State rank:** 10. **Pop change 1990-2000:** -1.7%.

Income: per capita $17,724; median household $37,423. **Pop below poverty level:** 10.2%.

Unemployment: 4.6%. **Median home value:** $70,900. **Median travel time to work:** 19.6 minutes.

All statistics are based on the 2000 Census except the dollar figures given for per capita income, which are based on 1999 estimates.

CRAWFORD COUNTY

1202 Broadway
Denison, IA 51442

Ph: 712-263-2242
Fax: 712-263-5753

In west-central IA, northeast of Council Bluffs; established Jan 15, 1851 from Shelby County. **Name Origin:** For William Harris Crawford (1771-1834), U.S. senator from GA (1807-13), U.S. secretary of war (1815-16), and U.S. secretary of treasury (1816-25).

Area (sq mi): 714.99 (land 714.36; water 0.63).

Pop: 16,942 (White 89.4%; Black or African American 0.8%; Hispanic or Latino 8.7%; Asian 0.5%; Other 5.7%). **Foreign born:** 6.1%. **Median age:** 38.2. **State rank:** 46. **Pop change 1990-2000:** +1%.

Income: per capita $15,851; median household $33,922. **Pop below poverty level:** 11.1%.

Unemployment: 2.8%. **Median home value:** $58,200. **Median travel time to work:** 16.7 minutes.

DALLAS COUNTY

801 Court St
Adel, IA 50003
www.co.dallas.ia.us

Ph: 515-993-5814
Fax: 515-993-5820

In central IA, west of Des Moines; organized 1846 from Polk County. **Name Origin:** For George Mifflin Dallas (1792-1864), U.S. Minister to Great Britain (1856-61).

Area (sq mi): 591.73 (land 586.47; water 5.26).

Pop: 40,750 (White 92.4%; Black or African American 0.7%; Hispanic or Latino 5.4%; Asian 0.7%; Other 3.8%). **Foreign born:** 4%. **Median age:** 35.1. **State rank:** 14. **Pop change 1990-2000:** +37%.

Income: per capita $22,970; median household $48,528. **Pop below poverty level:** 5.6%.

Unemployment: 2.1%. **Median home value:** $108,000. **Median travel time to work:** 22 minutes.

DAVIS COUNTY

100 Courthouse Sq
Bloomfield, IA 52537

Ph: 641-664-2011
Fax: 641-664-2041

On southern border of IA, west of Burlington; established Feb 17, 1843 (prior to statehood) from Van Buren County. **Name Origin:** For Garrett Davis (1801-72), KY legislator and U.S. senator (1861-72).

Area (sq mi): 504.89 (land 503.24; water 1.65).

Pop: 8,541 (White 98%; Black or African American 0.2%; Hispanic or Latino 0.7%; Asian 0.2%; Other 1.2%). **Foreign born:** 0.4%. **Median age:** 38.5. **State rank:** 87. **Pop change 1990-2000:** +2.8%.

Income: per capita $15,127; median household $32,864. **Pop below poverty level:** 11.9%.

Unemployment: 3.5%. **Median home value:** $55,000. **Median travel time to work:** 24.9 minutes.

DECATUR COUNTY

207 N Main St
Leon, IA 50144

Ph: 641-446-4382
Fax: 641-446-7159

On central southern border of IA, south of Des Moines; organized 1846 from Appanoose County. **Name Origin:** For Stephen Decatur (1779-1820), U.S. naval officer during the War of 1812 and in actions against the Barbary pirates near Tripoli, who said '...may she always be in the right; but our country, right or wrong!'

Area (sq mi): 533.32 (land 531.8; water 1.52).

Pop: 8,689 (White 95.5%; Black or African American 1%; Hispanic or Latino 1.7%; Asian 0.6%; Other 1.9%). **Foreign born:** 2%. **Median age:** 36.4. **State rank:** 85. **Pop change 1990-2000:** +4.2%.

Income: per capita $14,209; median household $27,343. **Pop below poverty level:** 15.5%.

Unemployment: 4.4%. **Median home value:** $45,400. **Median travel time to work:** 22.2 minutes.

DELAWARE COUNTY

PO Box 527
Manchester, IA 52057

Ph: 563-927-4942
Fax: 563-927-3074

In eastern IA, west of Dubuque; established Dec 21, 1837 (prior to statehood) from Dubuque County. **Name Origin:** For the state, in appreciation of the services of John Middleton Clayton (1796-1856), U.S. senator from DE (1829-36; 1845-49; 1853-56) and U.S. secretary of state (1849-50).

Area (sq mi): 579.05 (land 577.85; water 1.19).

Pop: 18,404 (White 98.8%; Black or African American 0.1%; Hispanic or Latino 0.7%; Asian 0.1%; Other 0.5%). **Foreign born:** 0.6%. **Median age:** 37.1. **State rank:** 40. **Pop change 1990-2000:** +2%.

Income: per capita $17,327; median household $37,168. **Pop below poverty level:** 7.9%.

Unemployment: 4.6%. **Median home value:** $79,700. **Median travel time to work:** 21.3 minutes.

DES MOINES COUNTY

PO Box 158
Burlington, IA 52601
www.co.des-moines.ia.us

Ph: 319-753-8272
Fax: 319-753-8253

On southeastern border of IA; established Sep 6, 1834 (prior to statehood) from Wisconsin Territory. **Name Origin:** For the Des Moines River, which runs through the southeastern part of the state. From French *des* 'of the' and *moines*, a form of the Indian tribal name *Moingona* 'river of the mounds.' French name became *Riviere des Moines* 'river of the monks,' because the area was explored by Catholic missionaries. Also spelled De Moin, De Moyen, and Demoine.

Area (sq mi): 429.8 (land 416.15; water 13.65).

Pop: 42,351 (White 92.8%; Black or African American 3.6%; Hispanic or Latino 1.7%; Asian 0.6%; Other 2.1%). **Foreign born:** 1.6%. **Median age:** 38.9. **State rank:** 12. **Pop change 1990-2000:** -0.6%.

Income: per capita $19,701; median household $36,790. **Pop below poverty level:** 10.7%.

Unemployment: 4.9%. **Median home value:** $70,100. **Median travel time to work:** 16 minutes.

Please see sample entry on inside front cover for detailed information about the statistics presented with each county listing.

DICKINSON COUNTY

1802 Hill Ave
Spirit Lake, IA 51360
www.co.dickinson.ia.us

Ph: 712-336-3356
Fax: 712-336-2677

On the northern border of IA; established Jan 15, 1851 from Kossuth County. **Name Origin:** For Daniel Stevens Dickinson (1800-66), U.S. senator from NY (1844-51).

Area (sq mi): 403.69 (land 381.06; water 22.63).

Pop: 16,424 (White 98.4%; Black or African American 0.2%; Hispanic or Latino 0.7%; Asian 0.2%; Other 0.7%). **Foreign born:** 0.7%. **Median age:** 43.3. **State rank:** 49. **Pop change 1990-2000:** +10.2%.

Income: per capita $21,929; median household $39,020. **Pop below poverty level:** 6%.

Unemployment: 2.8%. **Median home value:** $96,800. **Median travel time to work:** 15.5 minutes.

DUBUQUE COUNTY

720 Central Ave
Dubuque, IA 52001
www.dubuquecounty.org

Ph: 563-589-4418

On the eastern border of IA, northeast of Cedar Rapids; established Sep 6, 1834 (prior to statehood) from Wisconsin Territory. The present boundaries were established in 1837. **Name Origin:** For Julien Dubuque (1762-1810), a French-Canadian and the first permanent white settler in Iowa (1785); he negotiated an agreement in 1788 with the Fox Indians so he could work lead mines in the IA region.

Area (sq mi): 616.56 (land 608.16; water 8.41).

Pop: 89,143 (White 96.5%; Black or African American 0.9%; Hispanic or Latino 1.2%; Asian 0.6%; Other 1.5%). **Foreign born:** 1.9%. **Median age:** 36.5. **State rank:** 7. **Pop change 1990-2000:** +3.2%.

Income: per capita $19,600; median household $39,582. **Pop below poverty level:** 7.8%.

Unemployment: 4.3%. **Median home value:** $93,300. **Median travel time to work:** 15.5 minutes.

EMMET COUNTY

609 1st Ave N
Estherville, IA 51334
www.emmet.org/pmc

Ph: 712-362-4261
Fax: 712-362-7454

On central northern border of IA, northwest of Fort Dodge; established Jan 15, 1851 from Kossuth and Dickinson counties. **Name Origin:** For Robert W. Emmet (1778-1803), Irish patriot executed by the English for revolutionary acts. Places were named for him during a time when leaders of rebellions were honored by Americans.

Area (sq mi): 402.38 (land 395.74; water 6.63).

Pop: 11,027 (White 94.5%; Black or African American 0.2%; Hispanic or Latino 4.3%; Asian 0.3%; Other 2.1%). **Foreign born:** 2.3%. **Median age:** 39.6. **State rank:** 75. **Pop change 1990-2000:** -4.7%.

Income: per capita $16,619; median household $33,305. **Pop below poverty level:** 8.2%.

Unemployment: 3.8%. **Median home value:** $53,000. **Median travel time to work:** 16.8 minutes.

FAYETTE COUNTY

PO Box 458
West Union, IA 52175

Ph: 563-422-5694
Fax: 563-422-3137

In northeastern IA, northeast of Waterloo; established Dec 21, 1837 (prior to statehood) from Clayton County. **Name Origin:** For the Marquis de Lafayette (1757-1834), French statesman and soldier who fought with the Americans during the Revolutionary War.

Area (sq mi): 731.45 (land 730.92; water 0.52).

Pop: 22,008 (White 96.9%; Black or African American 0.5%; Hispanic or Latino 1.5%; Asian 0.4%; Other 1.3%). **Foreign born:** 1.1%. **Median age:** 39.4. **State rank:** 28. **Pop change 1990-2000:** +0.8%.

Income: per capita $17,271; median household $32,453. **Pop below poverty level:** 10.8%.

Unemployment: 5.3%. **Median home value:** $58,300. **Median travel time to work:** 18.3 minutes.

FLOYD COUNTY

101 S Main St
Charles City, IA 50616

Ph: 641-257-6122
Fax: 641-257-6125

In north-central IA, northwest of Waterloo; established Jan 15, 1851 from Chickasaw County. **Name Origin:** For Sgt. Charles Floyd (?-1804), a member of the Lewis and Clark expedition (1803-6). He is buried on the banks of the Missouri River; his is the first recorded death and burial of a white man in IA. Some claim for William Floyd (1734-1821), a signer of the Declaration of Independence.

Area (sq mi): 501.31 (land 500.56; water 0.74).

Pop: 16,900 (White 97.4%; Black or African American 0.2%; Hispanic or Latino 1.3%; Asian 0.4%; Other 1.2%). **Foreign born:** 1.1%. **Median age:** 40.3. **State rank:** 47. **Pop change 1990-2000:** -0.9%.

Income: per capita $17,091; median household $35,237. **Pop below poverty level:** 9.3%.

Unemployment: 4.9%. **Median home value:** $64,700. **Median travel time to work:** 18.4 minutes.

FRANKLIN COUNTY

PO Box 28
Hampton, IA 50441

Ph: 641-456-5626
Fax: 641-456-5628

In central IA, northwest of Waterloo; established Jan 15, 1851 from Chickasaw County. **Name Origin:** For Benjamin Franklin (1706-90), U.S. patriot, diplomat, and statesman.

Area (sq mi): 583.01 (land 582.44; water 0.57).

Pop: 10,704 (White 93.4%; Black or African American 0.1%; Hispanic or Latino 6%; Asian 0.2%; Other 4.8%). **Foreign born:** 4.4%. **Median age:** 41.3. **State rank:** 77. **Pop change 1990-2000:** -5.8%.

Income: per capita $18,767; median household $36,042. **Pop below poverty level:** 8%.

Unemployment: 3.4%. **Median home value:** $55,200. **Median travel time to work:** 17.2 minutes.

All statistics are based on the 2000 Census except the dollar figures given for per capita income, which are based on 1999 estimates.

FREMONT COUNTY

PO Box 549   **Ph:** 712-374-2232
Sidney, IA 51652   **Fax:** 712-374-3330

On southwestern border of IA, south of Council Bluffs; established Feb 24, 1847 from Pottawattamie County. **Name Origin:** For John Charles Fremont (1813-90), soldier and explorer who led five expeditions to the West, U.S. senator from CA (1850-51), and governor of the AZ Territory (1878-83).

Area (sq mi): 516.76 (land 511.08; water 5.68).

Pop: 8,010 (White 96.9%; Black or African American 0%; Hispanic or Latino 2.2%; Asian 0.2%; Other 1.7%). **Foreign born:** 1.7%. **Median age:** 41.2. **State rank:** 90. **Pop change 1990-2000:** -2.6%.

Income: per capita $18,081; median household $38,345. **Pop below poverty level:** 9.5%.

Unemployment: 2.6%. **Median home value:** $64,400. **Median travel time to work:** 21.9 minutes.

GREENE COUNTY

114 N Chestnut St   **Ph:** 515-386-2516
Jefferson, IA 50129   **Fax:** 515-386-2321
www.jeffersoniowa.com

In central IA, west of Ames; established Jan 15, 1851 from Dallas County. **Name Origin:** For Gen. Nathanael Greene (1742-86), hero of the Revolutionary War, quartermaster general (1778-80), and commander of the Army of the South (1780).

Area (sq mi): 571.13 (land 568.41; water 2.72).

Pop: 10,366 (White 97.4%; Black or African American 0.1%; Hispanic or Latino 1.7%; Asian 0.2%; Other 1.5%). **Foreign born:** 1.2%. **Median age:** 41. **State rank:** 79. **Pop change 1990-2000:** +3.2%.

Income: per capita $16,866; median household $33,883. **Pop below poverty level:** 8.1%.

Unemployment: 4%. **Median home value:** $51,800. **Median travel time to work:** 19.4 minutes.

GRUNDY COUNTY

706 G Ave   **Ph:** 319-824-5229
Grundy Center, IA 50638   **Fax:** 319-824-3447

In central IA, west of Waterloo; established Jan 15, 1851 from Black Hawk County. **Name Origin:** For Felix Grundy (1777-1840) of KY, U.S. senator from TN (1829-38; 1839-40) and U.S. attorney general (1838-39).

Area (sq mi): 502.55 (land 502.51; water 0.03).

Pop: 12,369 (White 98.6%; Black or African American 0.1%; Hispanic or Latino 0.6%; Asian 0.3%; Other 0.7%). **Foreign born:** 0.8%. **Median age:** 40.8. **State rank:** 64. **Pop change 1990-2000:** +2.8%.

Income: per capita $19,142; median household $39,396. **Pop below poverty level:** 4.6%.

Unemployment: 2.3%. **Median home value:** $72,500. **Median travel time to work:** 20.6 minutes.

GUTHRIE COUNTY

200 N 5th St   **Ph:** 641-747-3415
Guthrie Center, IA 50115   **Fax:** 641-747-2420

In west-central IA, west of Des Moines, established Jan 15, 1851 from Jackson County. **Name Origin:** For Capt. Edwin Guthrie (?-1847), army officer from IA killed during the Mexican War.

Area (sq mi): 593.06 (land 590.6; water 2.46).

Pop: 11,353 (White 98%; Black or African American 0.1%; Hispanic or Latino 1.1%; Asian 0.1%; Other 1.1%). **Foreign born:** 1.2%. **Median age:** 41.9. **State rank:** 73. **Pop change 1990-2000:** +3.8%.

Income: per capita $19,726; median household $36,495. **Pop below poverty level:** 8%.

Unemployment: 3%. **Median home value:** $61,800. **Median travel time to work:** 26.7 minutes.

HAMILTON COUNTY

2300 Superior St   **Ph:** 515-832-9510
Webster City, IA 50595   **Fax:** 515-832-9514
www.hamiltoncounty.org

In central IA, north of Ames; established Dec 22, 1856 from Webster County. **Name Origin:** For William H. Hamilton, president of the IA senate (1856-57) at the time the county was established.

Area (sq mi): 577.44 (land 576.68; water 0.76).

Pop: 16,438 (White 96.1%; Black or African American 0.2%; Hispanic or Latino 1.4%; Asian 1.5%; Other 1.6%). **Foreign born:** 2.1%. **Median age:** 39.1. **State rank:** 48. **Pop change 1990-2000:** +2.3%.

Income: per capita $18,801; median household $38,658. **Pop below poverty level:** 6.3%.

Unemployment: 3%. **Median home value:** $70,500. **Median travel time to work:** 15.9 minutes.

HANCOCK COUNTY

PO Box 70   **Ph:** 641-923-2532
Garner, IA 50438   **Fax:** 641-923-3521

In north-central IA, west of Mason City; established Jan 15, 1851 from Wright County. **Name Origin:** For John Hancock (1737-93), noted signer of the Declaration of Independence, governor of MA (1780-85; 1787-93), and statesman.

Area (sq mi): 573.14 (land 571.11; water 2.03).

Pop: 12,100 (White 96.7%; Black or African American 0.1%; Hispanic or Latino 2.5%; Asian 0.3%; Other 1.9%). **Foreign born:** 2.2%. **Median age:** 39.7. **State rank:** 67. **Pop change 1990-2000:** -4.3%.

Income: per capita $17,957; median household $37,703. **Pop below poverty level:** 6%.

Unemployment: 2.3%. **Median home value:** $59,600. **Median travel time to work:** 17.6 minutes.

HARDIN COUNTY

1215 Edgington Ave County Courthouse   **Ph:** 641-939-8109
Eldora, IA 50627   **Fax:** 641-939-8245
www.co.hardin.ia.us

In central IA, east of Fort Dodge; established Jan 15, 1851 from

Please see sample entry on inside front cover for detailed information about the statistics presented with each county listing.

Black Hawk County. **Name Origin:** For Gen. John J. Hardin (1810-47), officer in the Black Hawk War and U.S. representative from IL (1843-45). He was killed at the Battle of Buena Vista in the Mexican-American War.

Area (sq mi): 569.93 (land 569.26; water 0.68).

Pop: 18,812 (White 96.1%; Black or African American 0.6%; Hispanic or Latino 2.4%; Asian 0.3%; Other 1.8%). **Foreign born:** 1.7%. **Median age:** 40.6. **State rank:** 38. **Pop change 1990-2000:** -1.5%.

Income: per capita $17,537; median household $35,429. **Pop below poverty level:** 8%.

Unemployment: 3.4%. **Median home value:** $57,200. **Median travel time to work:** 17.5 minutes.

HARRISON COUNTY

111 N 2nd Ave   **Ph:** 712-644-2665
Logan, IA 51546   **Fax:** 712-644-2615
www.harrisoncountyia.org

On central western border of IA, north of Council Bluffs; established Jan 15, 1851 from Pottawattamie County. **Name Origin:** For William Henry Harrison (1773-1841), ninth U.S. president.

Area (sq mi): 700.93 (land 696.72; water 4.2).

Pop: 15,666 (White 98.2%; Black or African American 0.1%; Hispanic or Latino 0.7%; Asian 0.2%; Other 1%). **Foreign born:** 0.8%. **Median age:** 38.9. **State rank:** 52. **Pop change 1990-2000:** +6.4%.

Income: per capita $17,662; median household $38,141. **Pop below poverty level:** 7.1%.

Unemployment: 3.8%. **Median home value:** $74,900. **Median travel time to work:** 27.3 minutes.

HENRY COUNTY

PO Box 176   **Ph:** 319-385-2632
Mount Pleasant, IA 52641   **Fax:** 319-385-4144

In southeastern IA, west of Burlington; established Dec 7, 1836 (prior to statehood) from Wisconsin Territory. **Name Origin:** For Col. Henry Dodge (1782-1867), officer in the Black Hawk War; governor of WI Territory (1836-41; 1845-48), and U.S. senator from WI (1848-57).

Area (sq mi): 436.68 (land 434.44; water 2.24).

Pop: 20,336 (White 94.2%; Black or African American 1.5%; Hispanic or Latino 1.3%; Asian 1.9%; Other 1.8%). **Foreign born:** 1.8%. **Median age:** 37.1. **State rank:** 34. **Pop change 1990-2000:** +5.8%.

Income: per capita $18,192; median household $39,087. **Pop below poverty level:** 8.8%.

Unemployment: 3.8%. **Median home value:** $76,700. **Median travel time to work:** 17.2 minutes.

HOWARD COUNTY

137 N Elm St County Courthouse   **Ph:** 563-547-2661
Cresco, IA 52136   **Fax:** 563-547-3605
www.crescoia.com/howardcounty/index.html

On northern border of IA, north of Waterloo; established Jan 15,

1851 from Chickasaw and Floyd counties. **Name Origin:** For Tilghman Ashurst Howard (1797-1844), TN legislator, U.S. representative from IN (1839-40), and TX patriot.

Area (sq mi): 473.76 (land 473.4; water 0.36).

Pop: 9,932 (White 98.6%; Black or African American 0.1%; Hispanic or Latino 0.6%; Asian 0.2%; Other 0.7%). **Foreign born:** 0.4%. **Median age:** 39.5. **State rank:** 82. **Pop change 1990-2000:** +1.3%.

Income: per capita $17,842; median household $34,641. **Pop below poverty level:** 9.3%.

Unemployment: 3.1%. **Median home value:** $59,500. **Median travel time to work:** 19.2 minutes.

HUMBOLDT COUNTY

PO Box 100   **Ph:** 515-332-1571
Dakota City, IA 50529   **Fax:** 515-332-1738

In north-central IA, north of Fort Dodge; established Jan 15, 1851 from Webster County. **Name Origin:** For Alexander von Humboldt (1769-1859), German explorer and naturalist.

Area (sq mi): 435.73 (land 434.41; water 1.31).

Pop: 10,381 (White 98.1%; Black or African American 0.1%; Hispanic or Latino 1%; Asian 0.2%; Other 1.1%). **Foreign born:** 1.4%. **Median age:** 41.3. **State rank:** 78. **Pop change 1990-2000:** -3.5%.

Income: per capita $18,300; median household $38,201. **Pop below poverty level:** 8.3%.

Unemployment: 3.1%. **Median home value:** $71,700. **Median travel time to work:** 18.8 minutes.

IDA COUNTY

401 Moorehead St   **Ph:** 712-364-2626
Ida Grove, IA 51445   **Fax:** 712-364-2746

In western IA, east of Sioux City; established Jan 15, 1851 from Cherokee County. **Name Origin:** For Mt. Ida of Greek myth; either the one in Crete or the one near ancient Troy (in present-day Turkey). The name was suggested by Eliphalet Price to connect the old classic civilization of Europe with the new civilization of the plains. Other sources say the county is named for the first white child born in the community (July 19, 1856), Ida Smith, daughter of Edwin Smith, a trapper.

Area (sq mi): 432.23 (land 431.71; water 0.52).

Pop: 7,837 (White 98.7%; Black or African American 0.1%; Hispanic or Latino 0.5%; Asian 0.2%; Other 0.7%). **Foreign born:** 0.2%. **Median age:** 41.5. **State rank:** 92. **Pop change 1990-2000:** -6.3%.

Income: per capita $18,675; median household $34,805. **Pop below poverty level:** 8.8%.

Unemployment: 2.7%. **Median home value:** $55,500. **Median travel time to work:** 15.7 minutes.

IOWA COUNTY

PO Box 266   **Ph:** 319-642-3914
Marengo, IA 52301

In east-central IA, west of Iowa City; established Feb 17, 1843

All statistics are based on the 2000 Census except the dollar figures given for per capita income, which are based on 1999 estimates.

(prior to statehood) from Washington County. **Name Origin:** For the Iowa River.

Area (sq mi): 587.35 (land 586.45; water 0.9).

Pop: 15,671 (White 98.2%; Black or African American 0.2%; Hispanic or Latino 1%; Asian 0.3%; Other 0.9%). **Foreign born:** 0.8%. **Median age:** 38.8. **State rank:** 51. **Pop change 1990-2000:** +7.1%.

Income: per capita $18,884; median household $41,222. **Pop below poverty level:** 5%.

Unemployment: 1.9%. **Median home value:** $85,600. **Median travel time to work:** 21.7 minutes.

JACKSON COUNTY
201 W Platt St   **Ph:** 563-652-3144
Maquoketa, IA 52060   **Fax:** 563-652-6975

On central eastern border of IA, south of Dubuque; established Dec 21, 1837 (prior to statehood) from Wisconsin Territory. **Name Origin:** For Andrew Jackson (1767-1845), seventh U.S. president.

Area (sq mi): 649.75 (land 636.09; water 13.66).

Pop: 20,296 (White 98.5%; Black or African American 0.1%; Hispanic or Latino 0.6%; Asian 0.1%; Other 0.8%). **Foreign born:** 0.7%. **Median age:** 39.1. **State rank:** 35. **Pop change 1990-2000:** +1.7%.

Income: per capita $17,329; median household $34,529. **Pop below poverty level:** 10.3%.

Unemployment: 5.7%. **Median home value:** $76,500. **Median travel time to work:** 21.9 minutes.

JASPER COUNTY
PO Box 944   **Ph:** 641-792-7016
Newton, IA 50208   **Fax:** 641-792-1053

In central IA, east of Des Moines; established Jan 13, 1846 from Mahaska County. **Name Origin:** For Sgt. Willliam Jasper (1750-79), Revolutionary War soldier from SC.

Area (sq mi): 732.93 (land 729.99; water 2.94).

Pop: 37,213 (White 96.9%; Black or African American 0.8%; Hispanic or Latino 1%; Asian 0.4%; Other 1.2%). **Foreign born:** 1.5%. **Median age:** 38.5. **State rank:** 19. **Pop change 1990-2000:** +6.9%.

Income: per capita $19,622; median household $41,683. **Pop below poverty level:** 6.5%.

Unemployment: 2.8%. **Median home value:** $82,500. **Median travel time to work:** 19.5 minutes.

JEFFERSON COUNTY
51 E Briggs Ave   **Ph:** 641-472-2840
Fairfield, IA 52556

In southeastern IA, east of Ottumwa; established Jan 21, 1839 (prior to statehnood) from Indian lands. **Name Origin:** For Thomas Jefferson (1743-1826), U.S. patriot, statesman, and third U.S. president.

Area (sq mi): 436.72 (land 435.34; water 1.38).

Pop: 16,181 (White 94.7%; Black or African American 0.6%; Hispanic or Latino 1.8%; Asian 1.7%; Other 1.6%). **Foreign born:** 4%. **Median age:** 41.1. **State rank:** 50. **Pop change 1990-2000:** -0.8%.

Income: per capita $19,579; median household $33,851. **Pop below poverty level:** 10.9%.

Unemployment: 5.1%. **Median home value:** $72,500. **Median travel time to work:** 14.1 minutes.

JOHNSON COUNTY
913 S Dubuque St Suite 201   **Ph:** 319-356-6000
Iowa City, IA 52240   **Fax:** 319-356-6036
www.co.johnson.ia.us

In east-central IA, south of Cedar Rapids, established Dec 21, 1837 (prior to statehood) from Des Moines County. **Name Origin:** For Col. Richard Mentor Johnson (1780-1850), officer in the War of 1812, U.S. senator from KY (1819-29), and U.S. vice president (1837-41).

Area (sq mi): 623.35 (land 614.48; water 8.87).

Pop: 111,006 (White 88.8%; Black or African American 2.9%; Hispanic or Latino 2.5%; Asian 4.1%; Other 2.8%). **Foreign born:** 6.4%. **Median age:** 28.4. **State rank:** 5. **Pop change 1990-2000:** +15.5%.

Income: per capita $22,220; median household $40,060. **Pop below poverty level:** 15%.

Unemployment: 2.4%. **Median home value:** $131,500. **Median travel time to work:** 17.7 minutes.

JONES COUNTY
PO Box 19   **Ph:** 319-462-4341
Anamosa, IA 52205
www.co.jones.ia.us

In eastern IA, east of Cedar Rapids, established Dec 21, 1837 (prior to statehood) from Wisconsin Territory. **Name Origin:** For George Wallace Jones (1804-96), surveyor of public lands for WI and IA territories and U.S. senator from IA (1848-59).

Area (sq mi): 576.7 (land 575.31; water 1.39).

Pop: 20,221 (White 96%; Black or African American 1.8%; Hispanic or Latino 1.1%; Asian 0.2%; Other 1.3%). **Foreign born:** 0.8%. **Median age:** 38.5. **State rank:** 36. **Pop change 1990-2000:** +4%.

Income: per capita $17,816; median household $37,449. **Pop below poverty level:** 8.6%.

Unemployment: 4%. **Median home value:** $80,400. **Median travel time to work:** 24.5 minutes.

KEOKUK COUNTY
101 S Main St Courthouse   **Ph:** 641-622-2210
Sigourney, IA 52591   **Fax:** 641-622-2171

In south-central IA, north of Ottumwa; established Dec 21, 1837 (prior to statehood) from Washington County. **Name Origin:** For Keokuk (c. 1780-1848), the chief of the Sac and Fox Indians at the time the first settlers arrived. His name was originally *Kiyokaga* 'he who moves around alert.'

Area (sq mi): 579.94 (land 579.19; water 0.75).

Pop: 11,400 (White 98.8%; Black or African American 0.1%; Hispanic or Latino 0.5%; Asian 0.2%; Other 0.7%). **Foreign born:** 0.4%. **Median age:** 40. **State rank:** 72. **Pop change 1990-2000:** -1.9%.

Please see sample entry on inside front cover for detailed information about the statistics presented with each county listing.

Income: per capita $17,120; median household $34,025. **Pop below poverty level:** 10.1%.

Unemployment: 5.1%. **Median home value:** $51,900. **Median travel time to work:** 25.2 minutes.

KOSSUTH COUNTY
114 W State St   **Ph:** 515-295-2718
Algona, IA 50511

On central northern border of IA, north of Fort Dodge; established Jan 15, 1851 from Webster County. **Name Origin:** For Lajos Kossuth (1802-94), Hungarian resistance leader against Austrian domination who was enthusiastically acclaimed on a visit to the U.S. Named at a time when revolutionaries were celebrated in the U.S.

Area (sq mi): 974.39 (land 973.01; water 1.38).

Pop: 17,163 (White 98.3%; Black or African American 0.1%; Hispanic or Latino 0.8%; Asian 0.3%; Other 0.7%). **Foreign born:** 0.9%. **Median age:** 41.3. **State rank:** 44. **Pop change 1990-2000:** -7.7%.

Income: per capita $16,598; median household $34,562. **Pop below poverty level:** 10.2%.

Unemployment: 3.1%. **Median home value:** $54,300. **Median travel time to work:** 16.7 minutes.

LEE COUNTY
PO Box 190   **Ph:** 319-372-6557
Fort Madison, IA 52627   **Fax:** 319-372-7033
www.leecounty.org

On southeasternmost border of IA; established Dec 7, 1836 (prior to statehood) from Des Moines County. **Name Origin:** Probably for Albert Miller Lea (1807-90), a surveyor of the Des Moines River who mapped the Iowa District, or for Charles Lee, an official of the New York Land Company, which had extensive landholdings in the area.

Area (sq mi): 538.77 (land 517.39; water 21.37).

Pop: 38,052 (White 93%; Black or African American 2.8%; Hispanic or Latino 2.4%; Asian 0.4%; Other 2.6%). **Foreign born:** 1.1%. **Median age:** 39.5. **State rank:** 18. **Pop change 1990-2000:** -1.6%.

Income: per capita $18,430; median household $36,193. **Pop below poverty level:** 9.7%.

Unemployment: 6.9%. **Median home value:** $60,300. **Median travel time to work:** 16.8 minutes.

LINN COUNTY
930 1st St SW   **Ph:** 319-892-5005
Cedar Rapids, IA 52404   **Fax:** 319-892-5009
www.co.linn.ia.us

In east-central IA, north of Iowa City; established Dec 21, 1837 (prior to statehood) from Wisconsin Territory. **Name Origin:** For Lewis Fields Linn (1795-1843), U.S. senator from MO (1833-43).

Area (sq mi): 724.55 (land 717.44; water 7.1).

Pop: 191,701 (White 93.1%; Black or African American 2.6%; Hispanic or Latino 1.4%; Asian 1.4%; Other 2.1%). **Foreign born:** 2.6%. **Median age:** 35.2. **State rank:** 2. **Pop change 1990-2000:** +13.6%.

Income: per capita $22,977; median household $46,206. **Pop below poverty level:** 6.5%.

Unemployment: 2.8%. **Median home value:** $99,400. **Median travel time to work:** 17.8 minutes.

LOUISA COUNTY
117 S Main St   **Ph:** 319-523-4541
Wapello, IA 52653   **Fax:** 319-523-4542

On southeastern border of IA, north of Burlington; established Dec 7, 1836 (prior to statehood) from Des Moines County. **Name Origin:** For Louisa Massey, pioneer heroine who shot and wounded her brother's murderer. Some sources claim Louisa, queen of Denmark (1724-51), youngest daughter of George II of England.

Area (sq mi): 417.64 (land 401.92; water 15.73).

Pop: 12,183 (White 86.4%; Black or African American 0.3%; Hispanic or Latino 12.6%; Asian 0.2%; Other 5.7%). **Foreign born:** 6.8%. **Median age:** 35.9. **State rank:** 66. **Pop change 1990-2000:** +5.1%.

Income: per capita $17,644; median household $39,086. **Pop below poverty level:** 9.3%.

Unemployment: 3.8%. **Median home value:** $66,600. **Median travel time to work:** 23.5 minutes.

LUCAS COUNTY
916 Braden St   **Ph:** 641-774-4421
Chariton, IA 50049   **Fax:** 641-774-8669

In south-central IA, southeast of Des Moines; established Jan 13, 1846 from Monroe County. **Name Origin:** For Col. Robert Lucas (1781-1853), governor of OH (1832-36) and first territorial governor of IA (1838-41).

Area (sq mi): 434.17 (land 430.55; water 3.63).

Pop: 9,422 (White 98%; Black or African American 0.1%; Hispanic or Latino 0.9%; Asian 0.3%; Other 1.1%). **Foreign born:** 0.7%. **Median age:** 39.9. **State rank:** 83. **Pop change 1990-2000:** +3.9%.

Income: per capita $15,341; median household $30,876. **Pop below poverty level:** 13.7%.

Unemployment: 3.7%. **Median home value:** $50,900. **Median travel time to work:** 25.6 minutes.

LYON COUNTY
206 S 2nd Ave   **Ph:** 712-472-2623
Rock Rapids, IA 51246   **Fax:** 712-472-2422

On northwestern border of IA; established as Buncombe County Jan 15, 1851 from Woodbury County; name changed Sep 11, 1862. **Name Origin:** For Gen. Nathaniel Lyon (1818-61), Union commander in the Civil War who helped preserve MO for the Union when it seemed likely to join the Confederacy. He was killed leading the First Iowa Infantry at the Battle of Wilson Creek, MO.

Area (sq mi): 587.63 (land 587.5; water 0.13).

Pop: 11,763 (White 98.9%; Black or African American 0.1%; Hispanic or Latino 0.4%; Asian 0.2%; Other 0.6%). **Foreign born:** 0.9%. **Median age:** 38.1. **State rank:** 69. **Pop change 1990-2000:** -1.6%.

All statistics are based on the 2000 Census except the dollar figures given for per capita income, which are based on 1999 estimates.

Income: per capita $16,081; median household $36,878. **Pop below poverty level:** 7%.

Unemployment: 2.7%. **Median home value:** $64,000. **Median travel time to work:** 18.4 minutes.

MADISON COUNTY

PO Box 152   **Ph:** 515-462-4451
Winterset, IA 50273   **Fax:** 515-462-9825
www.madisoncounty.com

In south-central IA, southwest of Des Moines; established Feb 14, 1844 (prior to statehood) from Polk County. **Name Origin:** For James Madison (1751-1836), fourth U.S. president.

Area (sq mi): 562.3 (land 561.14; water 1.16).

Pop: 14,019 (White 98.2%; Black or African American 0.1%; Hispanic or Latino 0.7%; Asian 0.2%; Other 1.2%). **Foreign born:** 0.6%. **Median age:** 37.9. **State rank:** 59. **Pop change 1990-2000:** +12.3%.

Income: per capita $19,357; median household $41,845. **Pop below poverty level:** 6.7%.

Unemployment: 3.6%. **Median home value:** $87,700. **Median travel time to work:** 27.2 minutes.

MAHASKA COUNTY

106 S 1st St Mahaska Courthouse   **Ph:** 641-673-7786
Oskaloosa, IA 52577   **Fax:** 641-672-1256
www.co.mahaska.ia.us

In south-central IA, northwest of Ottumwa; established Feb 17, 1843 (prior to statehood) from Indian lands. **Name Origin:** For Mahaska (1784-1834), a chief of the Iowa tribe, whose name means 'white cloud.' the county seat was named for one of his wives.

Area (sq mi): 573.4 (land 570.87; water 2.53).

Pop: 22,335 (White 96.7%; Black or African American 0.6%; Hispanic or Latino 0.9%; Asian 0.9%; Other 1.3%). **Foreign born:** 1.6%. **Median age:** 37.2. **State rank:** 27. **Pop change 1990-2000:** +3.8%.

Income: per capita $18,232; median household $37,314. **Pop below poverty level:** 9.8%.

Unemployment: 3.4%. **Median home value:** $68,100. **Median travel time to work:** 18.9 minutes.

MARION COUNTY

PO Box 497   **Ph:** 641-828-2207
Knoxville, IA 50138   **Fax:** 641-828-7580
www.marioncountyiowa.com

In south-central IA, southeast of Des Moines; established Jun 10, 1845 (prior to statehood) from Washington County. **Name Origin:** For Gen. Francis Marion (c. 1732-95), SC soldier and legislator, known as 'The Swamp Fox' for his tactics during the Revolutionary War.

Area (sq mi): 570.53 (land 554.21; water 16.32).

Pop: 32,052 (White 96.9%; Black or African American 0.4%; Hispanic or Latino 0.8%; Asian 1%; Other 1%). **Foreign born:** 1.7%. **Median age:** 37.2. **State rank:** 21. **Pop change 1990-2000:** +6.8%.

Income: per capita $18,717; median household $42,401. **Pop below poverty level:** 7.6%.

Unemployment: 3.3%. **Median home value:** $88,300. **Median travel time to work:** 19.7 minutes.

MARSHALL COUNTY

County Courthouse   **Ph:** 641-754-6300
Marshalltown, IA 50158   **Fax:** 641-754-6321
www.co.marshall.ia.us

In central IA, east of Ames; established Jan 13, 1846 from Jasper County. **Name Origin:** For John Marshall (1755-1835), Chief Justice of the U.S. Supreme Court (1801-35).

Area (sq mi): 573.02 (land 572.32; water 0.7).

Pop: 39,311 (White 88.1%; Black or African American 0.9%; Hispanic or Latino 9%; Asian 0.8%; Other 7.8%). **Foreign born:** 6.6%. **Median age:** 38.6. **State rank:** 17. **Pop change 1990-2000:** +2.7%.

Income: per capita $19,176; median household $38,268. **Pop below poverty level:** 10.2%.

Unemployment: 2.9%. **Median home value:** $71,200. **Median travel time to work:** 17.1 minutes.

MILLS COUNTY

418 Sharp St County Courthouse   **Ph:** 712-527-4880
Glenwood, IA 51534   **Fax:** 712-527-4936
www.millscoia.us

On southwestern border of IA, south of Council Bluffs; established Jan 15, 1851 from Pottawattamie County. **Name Origin:** For Maj. Frederick D. Mills (?-1847), IA officer killed at San Antonio Garita during the Mexican-American War.

Area (sq mi): 439.67 (land 436.53; water 3.13).

Pop: 14,547 (White 97.2%; Black or African American 0.3%; Hispanic or Latino 1.2%; Asian 0.3%; Other 1.5%). **Foreign born:** 1%. **Median age:** 38.1. **State rank:** 57. **Pop change 1990-2000:** +10.2%.

Income: per capita $18,736; median household $42,428. **Pop below poverty level:** 8.3%.

Unemployment: 2.8%. **Median home value:** $92,900. **Median travel time to work:** 23.5 minutes.

MITCHELL COUNTY

508 State St   **Ph:** 641-732-3726
Osage, IA 50461   **Fax:** 641-732-3728

On the central northern border of IA, northeast of Mason City; established Jan 15, 1851 from Chickasaw County. **Name Origin:** Named by Irish settlers for John Mitchel (1815-75), Irish journalist and nationalist who was imprisoned for helping to lead revolt against Britain and escaped to the U.S. in 1853.

Area (sq mi): 469.4 (land 468.92; water 0.47).

Pop: 10,874 (White 98.9%; Black or African American 0.2%; Hispanic or Latino 0.6%; Asian 0.2%; Other 0.4%). **Foreign born:** 0.5%. **Median age:** 40.6. **State rank:** 76. **Pop change 1990-2000:** -0.5%.

Income: per capita $16,809; median household $34,843. **Pop below poverty level:** 10.7%.

Please see sample entry on inside front cover for detailed information about the statistics presented with each county listing.

Unemployment: 2.8%. **Median home value:** $66,500. **Median travel time to work:** 19.3 minutes.

MONONA COUNTY

610 Iowa Ave　　　　**Ph:** 712-423-2491
Onawa, IA 51040　　　**Fax:** 712-423-2744

On central western border of IA, south of Sioux City; established in Jan 15, 1851 from Harrison County. **Name Origin:** Possibly the name of a legendary Indian girl who leaped into the Mississippi River when she believed that her lover had been killed; or the name of an Indian divinity; or Ottawa for 'beautiful land.'

Area (sq mi): 698.85 (land 693.12; water 5.73).

Pop: 10,020 (White 97.9%; Black or African American 0.1%; Hispanic or Latino 0.7%; Asian 0.1%; Other 1.5%). **Foreign born:** 0.4%. **Median age:** 43. **State rank:** 81. **Pop change 1990-2000:** -0.1%.

Income: per capita $17,477; median household $33,235. **Pop below poverty level:** 9.4%.

Unemployment: 3.7%. **Median home value:** $54,400. **Median travel time to work:** 22.8 minutes.

MONROE COUNTY

10 Benton Ave E　　　**Ph:** 641-932-5212
Albia, IA 52531　　　**Fax:** 641-932-3245

In south-central IA, west of Ottumwa; established as Kishkekosh County Feb 17, 1843 (prior to statehood) from Wapello County. Name changed Jan 19, 1846. **Name Origin:** For James Monroe (1758-1831), fifth U.S. president.

Area (sq mi): 434.11 (land 433.41; water 0.7).

Pop: 8,016 (White 98.1%; Black or African American 0.2%; Hispanic or Latino 0.5%; Asian 0.4%; Other 1%). **Foreign born:** 0.6%. **Median age:** 39.7. **State rank:** 89. **Pop change 1990-2000:** -1.2%.

Income: per capita $17,155; median household $34,877. **Pop below poverty level:** 9%.

Unemployment: 4.2%. **Median home value:** $52,400. **Median travel time to work:** 24.4 minutes.

MONTGOMERY COUNTY

PO Box 469　　　　**Ph:** 712-623-4986
Red Oak, IA 51566　　**Fax:** 712-623-4987

In southwestern IA, southeast of Council Bluffs; established Jan 15, 1851 from Polk County. **Name Origin:** For Gen. Richard Montgomery (1736-75), American Revolutionary War officer who captured Montreal, Canada.

Area (sq mi): 424.81 (land 423.88; water 0.93).

Pop: 11,771 (White 97.6%; Black or African American 0.1%; Hispanic or Latino 1.3%; Asian 0.2%; Other 1.4%). **Foreign born:** 1.2%. **Median age:** 40.4. **State rank:** 68. **Pop change 1990-2000:** -2.5%.

Income: per capita $16,373; median household $33,214. **Pop below poverty level:** 9.1%.

Unemployment: 5.1%. **Median home value:** $55,900. **Median travel time to work:** 17.6 minutes.

MUSCATINE COUNTY

401 E 3rd St　　　　**Ph:** 563-263-5821
Muscatine, IA 52761　**Fax:** 563-263-7248
www.co.muscatine.ia.us

On eastern border of IA, west of Davenport; established Dec 7, 1836 (prior to statehood) from Des Moines County. **Name Origin:** Variant name for the Mascouten tribe of the Potawatomie Indians. Meaning of the name is uncertain, but locally believed to be 'burning island.'

Area (sq mi): 449.07 (land 438.67; water 10.4).

Pop: 41,722 (White 85.7%; Black or African American 0.7%; Hispanic or Latino 11.9%; Asian 0.8%; Other 7.8%). **Foreign born:** 5.9%. **Median age:** 36.1. **State rank:** 13. **Pop change 1990-2000:** +4.5%.

Income: per capita $19,625; median household $41,803. **Pop below poverty level:** 8.9%.

Unemployment: 3.7%. **Median home value:** $84,700. **Median travel time to work:** 17.3 minutes.

O'BRIEN COUNTY

PO Box 340　　　　**Ph:** 712-957-3045
Primghar, IA 51245　**Fax:** 712-957-3946
www.obriencounty.com

In northwestern IA; established Jan 15, 1851 from Cherokee County. **Name Origin:** For William Smith O'Brien (1803-64), leader of the Irish rebellion of 1848.

Area (sq mi): 573.25 (land 573.08; water 0.17).

Pop: 15,102 (White 96.8%; Black or African American 0.3%; Hispanic or Latino 1.8%; Asian 0.5%; Other 1.2%). **Foreign born:** 2%. **Median age:** 40.7. **State rank:** 54. **Pop change 1990-2000:** -2.2%.

Income: per capita $17,281; median household $35,758. **Pop below poverty level:** 7.3%.

Unemployment: 2.4%. **Median home value:** $58,300. **Median travel time to work:** 16.9 minutes.

OSCEOLA COUNTY

300 7th St　　　　**Ph:** 712-754-2241
Sibley, IA 51249　　**Fax:** 712-754-3743
www.osceolacountyia.com

On the northwestern border of IA; established Jan 15, 1851 from Woodbury County. **Name Origin:** For Osceola (c. 1804-38), Seminole leader during the early years of the Second Seminole War (1835-37). Name, also spelled *Ashi Vaholo Yahola*, means 'black drink hallower.'

Area (sq mi): 399.48 (land 398.77; water 0.71).

Pop: 7,003 (White 97.3%; Black or African American 0.1%; Hispanic or Latino 1.8%; Asian 0.2%; Other 1.6%). **Foreign born:** 1.2%. **Median age:** 39.7. **State rank:** 94. **Pop change 1990-2000:** -3.6%.

Income: per capita $16,463; median household $34,274. **Pop below poverty level:** 7%.

Unemployment: 3.1%. **Median home value:** $53,400. **Median travel time to work:** 15.6 minutes.

All statistics are based on the 2000 Census except the dollar figures given for per capita income, which are based on 1999 estimates.

PAGE COUNTY

PO Box 263   **Ph:** 712-542-3214
Clarinda, IA 51632   **Fax:** 712-542-5460

On southwestern border of IA; established Feb 14, 1847 from Pottawattamie County. **Name Origin:** For Capt. John Page (?-1846), killed at the Battle of Palo Alto during the Mexican-American War.

Area (sq mi): 535.35 (land 534.82; water 0.52).

Pop: 16,976 (White 95.2%; Black or African American 1.7%; Hispanic or Latino 1.6%; Asian 0.5%; Other 1.8%). **Foreign born:** 1%. **Median age:** 40.2. **State rank:** 45. **Pop change 1990-2000:** +0.6%.

Income: per capita $16,670; median household $35,466. **Pop below poverty level:** 12.5%.

Unemployment: 4.8%. **Median home value:** $60,000. **Median travel time to work:** 14.8 minutes.

PALO ALTO COUNTY

PO Box 387   **Ph:** 712-852-3603
Emmetsburg, IA 50536   **Fax:** 712-852-2274

In north-central IA, northwest of Fort Dodge; established Jan 15, 1851 from Kossuth County. **Name Origin:** From Spanish *palo* 'stick,' and *alto* 'tall' or 'high.' For a small town in Texas, the scene of the first battle (1846) of the Mexican War.

Area (sq mi): 569.4 (land 563.83; water 5.57).

Pop: 10,147 (White 98.1%; Black or African American 0.1%; Hispanic or Latino 0.8%; Asian 0.3%; Other 1%). **Foreign born:** 0.9%. **Median age:** 40.7. **State rank:** 80. **Pop change 1990-2000:** -4.9%.

Income: per capita $17,733; median household $32,409. **Pop below poverty level:** 10.6%.

Unemployment: 3.9%. **Median home value:** $53,500. **Median travel time to work:** 15.5 minutes.

PLYMOUTH COUNTY

215 4th Ave SE   **Ph:** 712-546-6100
Le Mars, IA 51031   **Fax:** 712-546-5784

On northwestern border of IA, north of Sioux City; established Jan 15, 1851 from Woodbury County. **Name Origin:** For Plymouth, Devonshire, England, from which the Mayflower sailed for America in 1620, or to honor Plymouth, MA, the landing site of the pilgrims.

Area (sq mi): 863.96 (land 863.56; water 0.39).

Pop: 24,849 (White 97.4%; Black or African American 0.3%; Hispanic or Latino 1.3%; Asian 0.3%; Other 1.3%). **Foreign born:** 1.2%. **Median age:** 37.8. **State rank:** 25. **Pop change 1990-2000:** +6.2%.

Income: per capita $19,442; median household $41,638. **Pop below poverty level:** 6%.

Unemployment: 3%. **Median home value:** $88,200. **Median travel time to work:** 19.1 minutes.

POCAHONTAS COUNTY

99 Court Sq County Courthouse   **Ph:** 712-335-4208
Pocahontas, IA 50574   **Fax:** 712-335-5045

In north-central IA, northwest of Fort Dodge; established Jan 15, 1851 from Humboldt and Greene counties. **Name Origin:** For Pocahontas (Matoaka c. 1595-1617), daughter of chief Powhatan, who prevented the execution of Capt. John Smith (c. 1580-1631).

Area (sq mi): 579.13 (land 577.7; water 1.42).

Pop: 8,662 (White 98%; Black or African American 0.2%; Hispanic or Latino 0.9%; Asian 0.2%; Other 1.1%). **Foreign born:** 0.9%. **Median age:** 42.5. **State rank:** 86. **Pop change 1990-2000:** -9.1%.

Income: per capita $17,006; median household $33,362. **Pop below poverty level:** 9.1%.

Unemployment: 3.8%. **Median home value:** $40,400. **Median travel time to work:** 18.3 minutes.

POLK COUNTY

5th & Mulbury Sts   **Ph:** 515-286-3772
Des Moines, IA 50309   **Fax:** 515-323-5250
www.co.polk.ia.us

In south-central IA, south of Ames; established Jan 17, 1846 from Indian lands. **Name Origin:** For James Knox Polk (1795-1849), eleventh U.S. president.

Area (sq mi): 591.9 (land 569.35; water 22.55).

Pop: 374,601 (White 86.4%; Black or African American 4.8%; Hispanic or Latino 4.4%; Asian 2.6%; Other 4.3%). **Foreign born:** 5.9%. **Median age:** 34.4. **State rank:** 1. **Pop change 1990-2000:** +14.5%.

Income: per capita $23,654; median household $46,116. **Pop below poverty level:** 7.9%.

Unemployment: 2.6%. **Median home value:** $103,100. **Median travel time to work:** 18.2 minutes.

POTTAWATTAMIE COUNTY

PO Box 476   **Ph:** 712-328-5604
Council Bluffs, IA 51502
www.pottcounty.com

On southwestern border of IA; established Jan 15, 1848 from Indian lands. **Name Origin:** For the Potawatomie Indian tribe of Algonquian linguistic stock; name means 'people of the place of fire.'

Area (sq mi): 959.94 (land 954.26; water 5.68).

Pop: 87,704 (White 94.3%; Black or African American 0.8%; Hispanic or Latino 3.3%; Asian 0.5%; Other 2.8%). **Foreign born:** 2%. **Median age:** 36.5. **State rank:** 8. **Pop change 1990-2000:** +6.1%.

Income: per capita $19,275; median household $40,089. **Pop below poverty level:** 8.4%.

Unemployment: 3%. **Median home value:** $84,900. **Median travel time to work:** 20.2 minutes.

POWESHIEK COUNTY

PO Box 218   **Ph:** 641-623-5644
Montezuma, IA 50171   **Fax:** 641-623-5320

In central IA, east of Iowa City; established Feb 17, 1843 (prior to statehood) from Keokuk, Iowa, Johnson, and Mahaska counties. **Name Origin:** For a Sac and Fox chief, properly *Pawishika* 'he who shakes (something off himself).' He was chief during the Black Hawk War (1832); on behalf of his tribe he signed the Treaty of Fort Armstrong at Rock Island, IL.

Please see sample entry on inside front cover for detailed information about the statistics presented with each county listing.

Area (sq mi): 586.17 (land 585.03; water 1.14).

Pop: 18,815 (White 96.2%; Black or African American 0.5%; Hispanic or Latino 1.2%; Asian 1.1%; Other 1.6%). Foreign born: 2.1%. Median age: 38.4. State rank: 37. Pop change 1990-2000: -1.1%.

Income: per capita $18,629; median household $37,836. Pop below poverty level: 9.8%.

Unemployment: 3.6%. Median home value: $81,600. Median travel time to work: 16.3 minutes.

RINGGOLD COUNTY
109 W Madison St   Ph: 641-464-3234
Mount Ayr, IA 50854   Fax: 641-464-2478

On central-southern border of IA, southwest of Des Moines; established Feb 24, 1847 from Taylor County. Name Origin: For Maj. Samuel Ringgold (1800-1846), officer in the Seminole War and the Mexican-American War, he died at the Battle of Palo Alto.

Area (sq mi): 538.92 (land 537.67; water 1.26).

Pop: 5,469 (White 98.8%; Black or African American 0.1%; Hispanic or Latino 0.2%; Asian 0.2%; Other 0.6%). Foreign born: 0.5%. Median age: 43.2. State rank: 98. Pop change 1990-2000: +0.9%.

Income: per capita $15,023; median household $29,110. Pop below poverty level: 14.3%.

Unemployment: 3%. Median home value: $45,000. Median travel time to work: 22 minutes.

SAC COUNTY
PO Box 368   Ph: 712-662-7791
Sac City, IA 50583   Fax: 712-662-7978
www.saccounty.org

In west-central IA, southwest of Fort Dodge; established Jan 15, 1851 from Greene County. Name Origin: An Indian tribal name meaning 'outlet.' Also spelled Sauk.

Area (sq mi): 578.38 (land 575.82; water 2.56).

Pop: 11,529 (White 98%; Black or African American 0.3%; Hispanic or Latino 1%; Asian 0.1%; Other 1.1%). Foreign born: 1.3%. Median age: 42.1. State rank: 71. Pop change 1990-2000: -6.5%.

Income: per capita $16,902; median household $32,874. Pop below poverty level: 9.9%.

Unemployment: 2.9%. Median home value: $50,000. Median travel time to work: 16.8 minutes.

SCOTT COUNTY
416 W 4th St   Ph: 563-326-8647
Davenport, IA 52801
www.co.scott.ia.us

On central eastern border of IA; established Dec 21, 1837 (prior to statehood) from Wisconsin Territory. Name Origin: For Gen. Winfield Scott (1786-1866), officer in the War of 1812 and the Mexican-American War; general in chief of the U.S. Army (1841-61).

Area (sq mi): 468.17 (land 457.93; water 10.24).

Pop: 158,668 (White 86.6%; Black or African American 6.1%; Hispanic or Latino 4.1%; Asian 1.6%; Other 3.7%). Foreign born:

3.1%. Median age: 35.4. State rank: 3. Pop change 1990-2000: +5.1%.

Income: per capita $21,310; median household $42,701. Pop below poverty level: 10.5%.

Unemployment: 3.5%. Median home value: $92,400. Median travel time to work: 18.4 minutes.

SHELBY COUNTY
PO Box 431   Ph: 712-755-5543
Harlan, IA 51537   Fax: 712-755-2667
www.shco.org

In western IA, northeast of Council Bluffs; established Jan 15, 1851 from Cass County. Name Origin: For Gen. Isaac Shelby (1750-1826), officer in the Revolutionary War, NC legislator, and governor of KY (1792-96; 1812-16).

Area (sq mi): 591.37 (land 590.83; water 0.54).

Pop: 13,173 (White 98.2%; Black or African American 0.1%; Hispanic or Latino 0.7%; Asian 0.3%; Other 1%). Foreign born: 0.6%. Median age: 40.5. State rank: 61. Pop change 1990-2000: -0.4%.

Income: per capita $16,969; median household $37,442. Pop below poverty level: 6%.

Unemployment: 2.7%. Median home value: $73,800. Median travel time to work: 18.3 minutes.

SIOUX COUNTY
PO Box 47   Ph: 712-737-2286
Orange City, IA 51041   Fax: 712-737-8908
www.siouxcounty.org

On the northwestern border of IA, north of Sioux City, established Jan 13, 1851 from Plymouth County. Name Origin: For the Indian tribe, sometimes known as the Dakotas. Name is French form of Ojibway nadouessioux 'snakes' or 'enemies.'

Area (sq mi): 768.58 (land 767.88; water 0.7).

Pop: 31,589 (White 96.2%; Black or African American 0.2%; Hispanic or Latino 2.6%; Asian 0.6%; Other 1.8%). Foreign born: 2.9%. Median age: 32.8. State rank: 22. Pop change 1990-2000: +5.6%.

Income: per capita $16,532; median household $40,536. Pop below poverty level: 6.4%.

Unemployment: 2.7%. Median home value: $84,700. Median travel time to work: 13 minutes.

STORY COUNTY
PO Box 408   Ph: 515-382-7410
Nevada, IA 50201
www.storycounty.com

In central IA, north of Des Moines; established Jan 13, 1846 from Jasper, Polk, and Boone counties. Name Origin: For Joseph Story (1779-1845), MA legislator and associate justice of the Supreme Court (1811-45).

Area (sq mi): 573.7 (land 572.86; water 0.84).

Pop: 79,981 (White 90.3%; Black or African American 1.8%; Hispanic or Latino 1.5%; Asian 5.1%; Other 1.9%). Foreign born:

All statistics are based on the 2000 Census except the dollar figures given for per capita income, which are based on 1999 estimates.

6.9%. **Median age:** 26.5. **State rank:** 9. **Pop change 1990-2000:** +7.7%.

Income: per capita $19,949; median household $40,442. **Pop below poverty level:** 14.1%.

Unemployment: 2.5%. **Median home value:** $115,800. **Median travel time to work:** 16.9 minutes.

TAMA COUNTY

PO Box 306   **Ph:** 641-484-3721
Toledo, IA 52342   **Fax:** 641-484-6403
www.tamacounty.org

In central IA, west of Cedar Rapids; established Feb 17, 1843 (prior to statehood) from Boone and Benton counties. **Name Origin:** For either a Fox Indian chief or for the wife of Chief Poweshiek. Meaning is uncertain; has been interpreted as 'beautiful,' 'lovely' or 'pleasant' when referring to a woman, or 'a bear with a voice that makes the rocks tremble' when applied to a man. A nearby Mesquaki Indian suggested that the name derives from *tewaime*, associated with the sound of thunder.

Area (sq mi): 722.37 (land 721.3; water 1.07).

Pop: 18,103 (White 89.2%; Black or African American 0.3%; Hispanic or Latino 3.8%; Asian 0.2%; Other 9.2%). **Foreign born:** 2%. **Median age:** 39.1. **State rank:** 42. **Pop change 1990-2000:** +3.9%.

Income: per capita $17,097; median household $37,419. **Pop below poverty level:** 10.5%.

Unemployment: 3.6%. **Median home value:** $64,200. **Median travel time to work:** 20.7 minutes.

TAYLOR COUNTY

405 Jefferson St County Courthouse   **Ph:** 712-523-2095
Bedford, IA 50833   **Fax:** 712-523-2936

On southern border of IA; established Feb 24, 1847 from Page County. **Name Origin:** For Zachary Taylor (1784-1850), twelfth U.S. president.

Area (sq mi): 534.83 (land 533.95; water 0.87).

Pop: 6,958 (White 95.3%; Black or African American 0%; Hispanic or Latino 3.8%; Asian 0.3%; Other 2%). **Foreign born:** 2%. **Median age:** 41.6. **State rank:** 95. **Pop change 1990-2000:** -2.2%.

Income: per capita $15,082; median household $31,297. **Pop below poverty level:** 12.1%.

Unemployment: 4.3%. **Median home value:** $37,900. **Median travel time to work:** 20.2 minutes.

UNION COUNTY

300 N Pine St   **Ph:** 641-782-7315
Creston, IA 50801   **Fax:** 641-782-8241

In south-central IA, southwest of Des Moines; established Jan 15, 1851 from Clarke County. **Name Origin:** Probably for the union of the states.

Area (sq mi): 425.95 (land 424.39; water 1.57).

Pop: 12,309 (White 97.8%; Black or African American 0.2%; Hispanic or Latino 1%; Asian 0.3%; Other 1.1%). **Foreign born:** 0.9%. **Median age:** 40.1. **State rank:** 65. **Pop change 1990-2000:** -3.5%.

Income: per capita $16,690; median household $31,905. **Pop below poverty level:** 11.4%.

Unemployment: 3.5%. **Median home value:** $55,600. **Median travel time to work:** 16.4 minutes.

VAN BUREN COUNTY

PO Box 475   **Ph:** 319-293-3129
Keosauqua, IA 52565   **Fax:** 319-293-6404
www.800-tourvbc.com

On the southeastern border of IA, west of Burlington; established Dec 7, 1836 (prior to statehood) from Des Moines County. **Name Origin:** For Martin Van Buren (1782-1862), eighth U.S. president.

Area (sq mi): 490.55 (land 484.82; water 5.73).

Pop: 7,809 (White 98.1%; Black or African American 0.1%; Hispanic or Latino 0.8%; Asian 0.3%; Other 1.1%). **Foreign born:** 0.6%. **Median age:** 40.8. **State rank:** 93. **Pop change 1990-2000:** +1.7%.

Income: per capita $15,748; median household $31,094. **Pop below poverty level:** 12.7%.

Unemployment: 4.6%. **Median home value:** $43,100. **Median travel time to work:** 23.9 minutes.

WAPELLO COUNTY

101 W 4th St   **Ph:** 641-683-0060
Ottumwa, IA 52501   **Fax:** 641-683-0064

In south-central IA; established Feb 17, 1843 (prior to statehood) from Indian lands. **Name Origin:** For Wapello (1787-1842), a Fox Indian chief who figured prominently in the signing of several treaties. Variously translated as 'light,' 'dawn,' and 'he of the morning.' It may be just a birth-time designation, for which the last translation would be correct.

Area (sq mi): 435.98 (land 431.81; water 4.17).

Pop: 36,051 (White 95.3%; Black or African American 0.9%; Hispanic or Latino 2.2%; Asian 0.6%; Other 2.2%). **Foreign born:** 1.9%. **Median age:** 39.2. **State rank:** 20. **Pop change 1990-2000:** +1%.

Income: per capita $16,500; median household $32,188. **Pop below poverty level:** 13.2%.

Unemployment: 4.6%. **Median home value:** $50,100. **Median travel time to work:** 19.1 minutes.

WARREN COUNTY

PO Box 379   **Ph:** 515-961-1033
Indianola, IA 50125   **Fax:** 515-961-1071
www.co.warren.ia.us

In south-central IA, south of Des Moines; established Jan 13, 1846 from Polk County. **Name Origin:** For Dr. Joseph Warren (1741-75), Revolutionary War patriot and member of the Committee of Safety who sent Paul Revere (1735-1818) on his famous ride.

Area (sq mi): 573.21 (land 571.64; water 1.56).

Pop: 40,671 (White 97.5%; Black or African American 0.3%; Hispanic or Latino 1.1%; Asian 0.4%; Other 1.3%). **Foreign born:** 1.1%. **Median age:** 36. **State rank:** 15. **Pop change 1990-2000:** +12.9%.

Please see sample entry on inside front cover for detailed information about the statistics presented with each county listing.

Income: per capita $20,558; median household $50,349. **Pop below poverty level:** 5.1%.

Unemployment: 2.3%. **Median home value:** $102,000. **Median travel time to work:** 25.8 minutes.

WASHINGTON COUNTY
PO Box 391
Washington, IA 52353

Ph: 319-653-7741
Fax: 319-653-7787

In southeastern IA, south of Iowa City; established Jan 16, 1837 (prior to statehood) from Wisconsin Territory. **Name Origin:** For George Washington (1732-1799), American patriot and first U.S. president.

Area (sq mi): 570.77 (land 568.71; water 2.06).

Pop: 20,670 (White 96%; Black or African American 0.3%; Hispanic or Latino 2.7%; Asian 0.2%; Other 2.4%). **Foreign born:** 1.5%. **Median age:** 38.8. **State rank:** 32. **Pop change 1990-2000:** +5.4%.

Income: per capita $18,221; median household $39,103. **Pop below poverty level:** 7.6%.

Unemployment: 2.7%. **Median home value:** $83,600. **Median travel time to work:** 21.6 minutes.

WAYNE COUNTY
PO Box 424
Corydon, IA 50060

Ph: 641-872-2264
Fax: 641-872-2431

On the central southern border of IA; established Jan 16, 1846 from Appanoose County. **Name Origin:** For Gen. Anthony Wayne (1745-96), PA soldier and statesman, nicknamed 'Mad Anthony' for his daring during the Revolutionary War.

Area (sq mi): 527.08 (land 525.6; water 1.48).

Pop: 6,730 (White 98.3%; Black or African American 0.1%; Hispanic or Latino 0.7%; Asian 0.1%; Other 1%). **Foreign born:** 0.6%. **Median age:** 43. **State rank:** 97. **Pop change 1990-2000:** -4.8%.

Income: per capita $15,613; median household $29,380. **Pop below poverty level:** 14%.

Unemployment: 3.4%. **Median home value:** $35,600. **Median travel time to work:** 21.6 minutes.

WEBSTER COUNTY
701 Central Ave
Fort Dodge, IA 50501
www.webstercountyia.org

Ph: 515-574-3719
Fax: 515-574-3714

In central IA, northwest of Ames; established Jan 12, 1853 from Yell and Risley counties, both of which were organized in 1851 and abolished in 1853. **Name Origin:** For Daniel Webster (1782-1852), U.S. statesman and orator from MA.

Area (sq mi): 718.05 (land 715.23; water 2.82).

Pop: 40,235 (White 92.4%; Black or African American 3.4%; Hispanic or Latino 2.3%; Asian 0.7%; Other 2.5%). **Foreign born:** 2%. **Median age:** 37.7. **State rank:** 16. **Pop change 1990-2000:** -0.3%.

Income: per capita $17,857; median household $35,334. **Pop below poverty level:** 10%.

Unemployment: 3.4%. **Median home value:** $66,000. **Median travel time to work:** 16 minutes.

WINNEBAGO COUNTY
126 S Clark St
Forest City, IA 50436

Ph: 641-582-3412

On the central northern border of IA, northwest of Mason City; established Feb 20, 1847 from Kossuth County. **Name Origin:** For the Indian tribe of Siouan linguistic stock; their name is thought to mean 'fish eaters.'

Area (sq mi): 401.57 (land 400.47; water 1.1).

Pop: 11,723 (White 96.4%; Black or African American 0.2%; Hispanic or Latino 2%; Asian 0.7%; Other 1.7%). **Foreign born:** 1.8%. **Median age:** 39.8. **State rank:** 70. **Pop change 1990-2000:** -3.3%.

Income: per capita $18,494; median household $38,381. **Pop below poverty level:** 8.4%.

Unemployment: 2.8%. **Median home value:** $61,200. **Median travel time to work:** 14.8 minutes.

WINNESHIEK COUNTY
201 W Main St
Decorah, IA 52101

Ph: 563-382-2469
Fax: 563-382-0603

On the central northern border of IA, northwest of Mason City; established Feb 20, 1847 from Indian lands. **Name Origin:** For the younger (1812-72?) of two chiefs of the Winnebago tribe with the same name; he took part in the Black Hawk War. Name probably formed from *Winne* for Winnebago and *shiek* 'leader.'

Area (sq mi): 689.88 (land 689.61; water 0.27).

Pop: 21,310 (White 97.4%; Black or African American 0.5%; Hispanic or Latino 0.8%; Asian 0.8%; Other 0.8%). **Foreign born:** 2.1%. **Median age:** 35.7. **State rank:** 30. **Pop change 1990-2000:** +2.2%.

Income: per capita $17,047; median household $38,908. **Pop below poverty level:** 8%.

Unemployment: 3.5%. **Median home value:** $86,000. **Median travel time to work:** 15.9 minutes.

WOODBURY COUNTY
620 Douglas St
Sioux City, IA 51101
www.woodbury-ia.com

Ph: 712-279-6611
Fax: 712-279-6021

On the western border of IA; established Jan 15, 1851 from Indian lands. **Name Origin:** For Levi Woodbury (1789-1851), governor of NH (1823-24), U.S. senator (1825-31; 1841-45), U.S. secretary of the navy (1831-34), U.S. secretary of the treasury (1834-41), and U.S. Supreme Court Justice (1845-51).

Area (sq mi): 877.39 (land 872.59; water 4.79).

Pop: 103,877 (White 83.6%; Black or African American 2%; Hispanic or Latino 9.1%; Asian 2.4%; Other 8.1%). **Foreign born:** 7.2%. **Median age:** 34.2. **State rank:** 6. **Pop change 1990-2000:** +5.7%.

Income: per capita $18,771; median household $38,509. **Pop below poverty level:** 10.3%.

Unemployment: 3.3%. **Median home value:** $76,400. **Median travel time to work:** 17.6 minutes.

All statistics are based on the 2000 Census except the dollar figures given for per capita income, which are based on 1999 estimates.

WORTH COUNTY

1000 Central Ave   **Ph:** 641-324-2840
Northwood, IA 50459   **Fax:** 641-324-2360

On the central northern border of IA, north of Mason City; established Jan 15, 1851 from Mitchell County. **Name Origin:** For Gen. William Jenkins Worth (1794-1849), officer in the War of 1812, Seminole War, and Mexican-American War; cited by Congress for bravery.

Area (sq mi): 401.71 (land 400; water 1.71).

Pop: 7,909 (White 97.3%; Black or African American 0.3%; Hispanic or Latino 1.6%; Asian 0.1%; Other 1.2%). **Foreign born:** 1.1%. **Median age:** 40.7. **State rank:** 91. **Pop change 1990-2000:** -1%.

Income: per capita $16,952; median household $36,444. **Pop below poverty level:** 8.3%.

Unemployment: 3.6%. **Median home value:** $55,900. **Median travel time to work:** 20 minutes.

WRIGHT COUNTY

PO Box 147   **Ph:** 515-532-2771
Clarion, IA 50525   **Fax:** 515-532-2669
www.wrightcounty.org

In north-central IA, northeast of Fort Dodge; established Jan 15, 1851 from Webster County. **Name Origin:** For Joseph Albert Wright (1810-67), IN legislator, governor (1849-57) and U.S. senator (1862-63). Also for Silas Wright (1795-1847), U.S. senator from NY (1833-44) and governor (1844-46).

Area (sq mi): 582.54 (land 580.72; water 1.82).

Pop: 14,334 (White 94.1%; Black or African American 0.2%; Hispanic or Latino 4.9%; Asian 0.2%; Other 3.7%). **Foreign born:** 3%. **Median age:** 41.4. **State rank:** 58. **Pop change 1990-2000:** +0.5%.

Income: per capita $18,247; median household $36,197. **Pop below poverty level:** 7%.

Unemployment: 3.2%. **Median home value:** $52,500. **Median travel time to work:** 16 minutes.

Please see sample entry on inside front cover for detailed information about the statistics presented with each county listing.

KANSAS - Counties

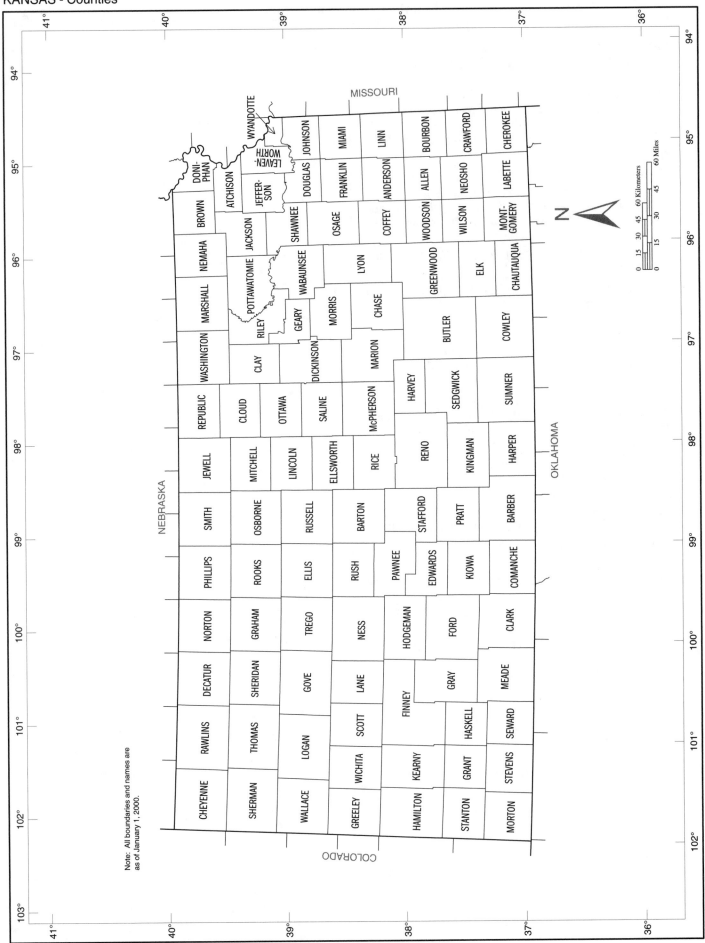

Note: All boundaries and names are as of January 1, 2000.

U.S. Census Bureau, Census 2000

Kansas

KANSAS STATE INFORMATION

www.accesskansas.org   **Ph:** 785-296-0111

Area (sq mi): 82,276.84 (land 81,814.88; water 461.96).

Pop: 2,688,418 (White 83.1%; Black or African American 5.7%; Hispanic or Latino 7%; Asian 1.7%; Other 6.4%). **Foreign born:** 5%. **Median age:** 35.2. **Pop change 1990-2000:** +8.5%.

Income: per capita $20,506; median household $40,624. **Pop below poverty level:** 9.9%.

Unemployment: 4.7%. **Median home value:** $83,500. **Median travel time to work:** 19 minutes.

ALLEN COUNTY

1 N Washington St   **Ph:** 620-365-1407
Iola, KS 66749   **Fax:** 620-365-1441
www.allencounty.org

In southeastern KS, southeast of Emporia; original county; organized Aug 30, 1855 (prior to statehood). **Name Origin:** For William Allen (1803-79), U.S. senator from OH (1837-49) and governor (1874-76).

Area (sq mi): 505.18 (land 503.01; water 2.18).

Pop: 14,385 (White 94%; Black or African American 1.6%; Hispanic or Latino 1.9%; Asian 0.3%; Other 3.4%). **Foreign born:** 0.9%. **Median age:** 38.8. **State rank:** 35. **Pop change 1990-2000:** -1.7%.

Income: per capita $15,640; median household $31,481. **Pop below poverty level:** 14.9%.

Unemployment: 7.4%. **Median home value:** $40,900. **Median travel time to work:** 17.4 minutes.

ANDERSON COUNTY

100 E 4th Ave   **Ph:** 785-448-6841
Garnett, KS 66032   **Fax:** 785-448-5621

In eastern KS, southeast of Emporia; original county; organized Aug 25, 1855 (prior to statehood). **Name Origin:** For Joseph C. Anderson, a member of the first KS territorial legislature.

Area (sq mi): 584.29 (land 582.92; water 1.38).

Pop: 8,110 (White 96.9%; Black or African American 0.3%; Hispanic or Latino 1.1%; Asian 0.2%; Other 1.9%). **Foreign born:** 0.6%. **Median age:** 39.6. **State rank:** 51. **Pop change 1990-2000:** +3.9%.

Income: per capita $16,458; median household $33,244. **Pop below poverty level:** 12.8%.

Unemployment: 5.9%. **Median home value:** $49,300. **Median travel time to work:** 25.5 minutes.

ATCHISON COUNTY

423 N 5th St   **Ph:** 913-367-1653
Atchison, KS 66002   **Fax:** 913-367-0227

On the northeastern border of KS, northwest of Kansas City; original county; organized Aug 25, 1855 (prior to statehood). **Name Origin:** For the town of Atchison, which was named for David Rice Atchison (1807-86), MO statesman and U.S. senator (1843-55).

Area (sq mi): 435.04 (land 432.34; water 2.7).

Pop: 16,774 (White 90.4%; Black or African American 5.3%; Hispanic or Latino 1.9%; Asian 0.3%; Other 2.8%). **Foreign born:** 0.7%. **Median age:** 36.2. **State rank:** 32. **Pop change 1990-2000:** -0.9%.

Income: per capita $15,207; median household $34,355. **Pop below poverty level:** 13.3%.

Unemployment: 5%. **Median home value:** $56,500. **Median travel time to work:** 19.4 minutes.

BARBER COUNTY

120 E Washington Ave   **Ph:** 620-886-3961
Medicine Lodge, KS 67104   **Fax:** 620-886-5425

On the central-southern border of KS, southwest of Wichita; organized as Barbour County Feb 26, 1867 from Harper County; spelling changed Mar 1, 1883. **Name Origin:** As a memorial to Thomas W. Barber (?-1855), a Free State martyr, murdered near Lawrence, KS.

Area (sq mi): 1136.21 (land 1134.11; water 2.1).

Pop: 5,307 (White 96.2%; Black or African American 0.4%; Hispanic or Latino 2%; Asian 0.1%; Other 2.5%). **Foreign born:** 0.5%. **Median age:** 42.6. **State rank:** 70. **Pop change 1990-2000:** -9.7%.

Income: per capita $16,627; median household $33,407. **Pop below poverty level:** 10.1%.

Unemployment: 3.3%. **Median home value:** $33,000. **Median travel time to work:** 14.3 minutes.

BARTON COUNTY

1400 Main St Suite 202   **Ph:** 620-793-1835
Great Bend, KS 67530   **Fax:** 620-793-1990
www.bartoncounty.org

In central KS, southwest of Salina; organized Feb 26, 1867 from Ellsworth County. **Name Origin:** For Clara Barton (1821-1912), Civil War nurse and first president (1881) of the American Red Cross. The only KS county named for a woman.

Please see sample entry on inside front cover for detailed information about the statistics presented with each county listing.

Area (sq mi): 900.46 (land 894; water 6.46).

Pop: 28,205 (White 89%; Black or African American 1.1%; Hispanic or Latino 8.3%; Asian 0.2%; Other 5.6%). **Foreign born:** 4.4%. **Median age:** 38.6. **State rank:** 20. **Pop change 1990-2000:** -4%.

Income: per capita $16,695; median household $32,176. **Pop below poverty level:** 12.9%.

Unemployment: 2.7%. **Median home value:** $55,500. **Median travel time to work:** 16.7 minutes.

BOURBON COUNTY
210 S National Ave   **Ph:** 620-223-3800
Fort Scott, KS 66701   **Fax:** 620-223-5832
www.bourboncountyks.org

On the southeastern border of KS; original county; organized Aug 25, 1855 (prior to statehood). **Name Origin:** For Bourbon County, KY, former home of Samuel A. Willliams, a member of the first KS legislature.

Area (sq mi): 638.82 (land 637.09; water 1.73).

Pop: 15,379 (White 93.3%; Black or African American 3.1%; Hispanic or Latino 1.3%; Asian 0.4%; Other 2.4%). **Foreign born:** 0.7%. **Median age:** 38. **State rank:** 34. **Pop change 1990-2000:** +2.8%.

Income: per capita $16,393; median household $31,199. **Pop below poverty level:** 13.5%.

Unemployment: 4.7%. **Median home value:** $46,200. **Median travel time to work:** 19.5 minutes.

BROWN COUNTY
601 Oregon St   **Ph:** 785-742-2581
Hiawatha, KS 66434   **Fax:** 785-742-3255

On the northeastern border of KS, west of Saint Joseph; original county; organized Aug 30, 1855 (prior to statehood). **Name Origin:** For either Orville H. Browne, a member of the 1855 KS territorial legislature, or for Albert Gallatin Browne (1813-80), governor of MS (1844-48). The e was dropped in 1857 when the county was named.

Area (sq mi): 572.2 (land 570.67; water 1.52).

Pop: 10,724 (White 86.1%; Black or African American 1.6%; Hispanic or Latino 2.3%; Asian 0.2%; Other 11.3%). **Foreign born:** 1.3%. **Median age:** 39.8. **State rank:** 40. **Pop change 1990-2000:** -3.6%.

Income: per capita $15,163; median household $31,971. **Pop below poverty level:** 12.9%.

Unemployment: 6.2%. **Median home value:** $50,800. **Median travel time to work:** 17.6 minutes.

BUTLER COUNTY
205 W Central Ave   **Ph:** 316-322-4239
El Dorado, KS 67042   **Fax:** 316-321-1011
www.bucoks.com

In east-central KS, east of Wichita; original county, organized Aug 25, 1855 (prior to statehood). **Name Origin:** For Andrew Pickens Butler (1796-1857), SC legislator; jurist, and U.S. senator (1846-57).

Area (sq mi): 1446.42 (land 1427.85; water 18.57).

Pop: 59,482 (White 93.6%; Black or African American 1.4%; Hispanic or Latino 2.2%; Asian 0.4%; Other 3.3%). **Foreign born:** 1.3%. **Median age:** 35.9. **State rank:** 9. **Pop change 1990-2000:** +17.6%.

Income: per capita $20,150; median household $45,474. **Pop below poverty level:** 7.3%.

Unemployment: 3.8%. **Median home value:** $83,900. **Median travel time to work:** 22.9 minutes.

CHASE COUNTY
PO Box 529   **Ph:** 620-273-6423
Cottonwood Falls, KS 66845   **Fax:** 620-273-6617

In east-central KS, west of Emporia; organized Feb 11, 1859 (prior to statehood) from Butler County. **Name Origin:** For Salmon Portland Chase (1808-73), U.S. senator from OH (1849-53), governor of OH (1855-59), and chief justice of the U.S. Supreme Court (1864-73).

Area (sq mi): 778.01 (land 775.89; water 2.12).

Pop: 3,030 (White 96%; Black or African American 1%; Hispanic or Latino 1.7%; Asian 0.1%; Other 2%). **Foreign born:** 1.1%. **Median age:** 40.3. **State rank:** 93. **Pop change 1990-2000:** +0.3%.

Income: per capita $17,422; median household $32,656. **Pop below poverty level:** 8.6%.

Unemployment: 4.3%. **Median home value:** $39,800. **Median travel time to work:** 25.1 minutes.

CHAUTAUQUA COUNTY
215 N Chautauqua St   **Ph:** 620-725-5800
Sedan, KS 67361   **Fax:** 620-725-5802

On the southern border of KS, west of Joplin, MO; organized Mar 3, 1875 (prior to statehood) from Howard County, which was organized in 1855 (named Godfrey and changed to Seward in 1867) and abolished at the time of its division into Chautauqua and Elk counties. **Name Origin:** For Chautauqua County, NY, former home of many settlers.

Area (sq mi): 644.83 (land 641.69; water 3.14).

Pop: 4,359 (White 93%; Black or African American 0.3%; Hispanic or Latino 1.4%; Asian 0.1%; Other 5.7%). **Foreign born:** 0.8%. **Median age:** 44.7. **State rank:** 77. **Pop change 1990-2000:** -1.1%.

Income: per capita $16,280; median household $28,717. **Pop below poverty level:** 12.2%.

Unemployment: 5.3%. **Median home value:** $26,200. **Median travel time to work:** 26.7 minutes.

CHEROKEE COUNTY
PO Box 14   **Ph:** 620-429-2042
Columbus, KS 66725   **Fax:** 620-429-1042

On the southeastern border of KS, west of Joplin, MO; organized as McGee County. **Name Origin:** For the Indian tribe of Iroquoian linguistic stock. Name may derive from Creek *tciloki* 'people of a different speech.' Originally for A.M. McGee, a noted proslavery leader.

Area (sq mi): 590.96 (land 587.12; water 3.85).

All statistics are based on the 2000 Census except the dollar figures given for per capita income, which are based on 1999 estimates.

Pop: 22,605 (White 91.6%; Black or African American 0.6%; Hispanic or Latino 1.3%; Asian 0.2%; Other 6.9%). **Foreign born:** 0.8%. **Median age:** 37. **State rank:** 26. **Pop change 1990-2000:** +5.8%.

Income: per capita $14,710; median household $30,505. **Pop below poverty level:** 14.3%.

Unemployment: 6.8%. **Median home value:** $46,900. **Median travel time to work:** 20 minutes.

CHEYENNE COUNTY

PO Box 985   **Ph:** 785-332-8800
Saint Francis, KS 67756   **Fax:** 785-332-8825

On northwestern border of KS; organized Mar 20, 1873 from Kirwin Land District. **Name Origin:** For the Cheyenne Indians, a Dakota tribe of Algonquian linguistic stock; name means 'red talkers.'

Area (sq mi): 1020.84 (land 1019.88; water 0.95).

Pop: 3,165 (White 96.4%; Black or African American 0.1%; Hispanic or Latino 2.6%; Asian 0.3%; Other 1.6%). **Foreign born:** 2.5%. **Median age:** 44.2. **State rank:** 90. **Pop change 1990-2000:** -2.4%.

Income: per capita $17,862; median household $30,599. **Pop below poverty level:** 9.4%.

Unemployment: 1.9%. **Median home value:** $48,500. **Median travel time to work:** 14.5 minutes.

CLARK COUNTY

913 Highland St   **Ph:** 620-635-2813
Ashland, KS 67831   **Fax:** 620-635-2393

On the central southern border of KS, south of Dodge City; first established Feb 16, 1867; abolished in 1883; recreated in 1885. **Name Origin:** For Capt. Charles F. Clarke (?-1862), Union officer in the Civil War. The *e* was dropped in naming the county.

Area (sq mi): 977.2 (land 974.68; water 2.52).

Pop: 2,390 (White 94.1%; Black or African American 0.3%; Hispanic or Latino 4%; Asian 0.1%; Other 3.9%). **Foreign born:** 2.8%. **Median age:** 42.1. **State rank:** 100. **Pop change 1990-2000:** -1.2%.

Income: per capita $17,795; median household $33,857. **Pop below poverty level:** 12.7%.

Unemployment: 1.7%. **Median home value:** $42,600. **Median travel time to work:** 14.1 minutes.

CLAY COUNTY

PO Box 98   **Ph:** 785-632-2552
Clay Center, KS 67432   **Fax:** 785-632-5856
www.claycountyks.org

In north-central KS, west of Manhattan; original county, organized Feb 27, 1857 (prior to statehood). **Name Origin:** For Henry Clay (1777-1852), U.S. senator from KY, known as the 'Great Pacificator' for his advocacy of compromise to avert national crises.

Area (sq mi): 655.44 (land 643.84; water 11.6).

Pop: 8,822 (White 97.2%; Black or African American 0.6%; Hispanic or Latino 0.8%; Asian 0.1%; Other 1.6%). **Foreign born:** 1%. **Median age:** 41.3. **State rank:** 47. **Pop change 1990-2000:** -3.7%.

Income: per capita $17,939; median household $33,965. **Pop below poverty level:** 10.1%.

Unemployment: 3.9%. **Median home value:** $52,900. **Median travel time to work:** 20 minutes.

CLOUD COUNTY

811 Washington St   **Ph:** 785-243-8110
Concordia, KS 66901   **Fax:** 785-243-8123
www.dustdevil.com/towns/concordia/courthouse

In north-central KS, north of Salina; organized as Shirley County Feb 27, 1860 (prior to statehood) from unorganized territory; name changed Feb 26, 1867. **Name Origin:** Named by John B. Rupe, a county representative, for William F. Cloud, an officer in the Kansas Volunteers. Originally named as a joke for Jane Shirley, 'a notorious Leavenworth prostitute' known 'to all the boys.'

Area (sq mi): 718.47 (land 715.63; water 2.84).

Pop: 10,268 (White 98%; Black or African American 0.3%; Hispanic or Latino 0.6%; Asian 0.3%; Other 1.1%). **Foreign born:** 1.4%. **Median age:** 41.4. **State rank:** 43. **Pop change 1990-2000:** -6.8%.

Income: per capita $17,536; median household $31,758. **Pop below poverty level:** 10.8%.

Unemployment: 3.4%. **Median home value:** $42,400. **Median travel time to work:** 14.6 minutes.

COFFEY COUNTY

110 S 6th St   **Ph:** 620-364-2191
Burlington, KS 66839   **Fax:** 620-364-8975
www.coffeycountyks.org

In eastern KS, east of Emporia; organized Aug 25, 1855 (prior to statehood) from Kiowa County. **Name Origin:** For Col. Asbury M. Coffey, a Confederate officer and settler from MO; first known white man in KS; served as a member of the Bogus Legislature in 1855.

Area (sq mi): 654.57 (land 629.75; water 24.82).

Pop: 8,865 (White 96.3%; Black or African American 0.2%; Hispanic or Latino 1.5%; Asian 0.3%; Other 2.4%). **Foreign born:** 0.8%. **Median age:** 39.2. **State rank:** 46. **Pop change 1990-2000:** +5.5%.

Income: per capita $18,337; median household $37,839. **Pop below poverty level:** 6.6%.

Unemployment: 6.5%. **Median home value:** $60,700. **Median travel time to work:** 19.1 minutes.

COMANCHE COUNTY

PO Box 776   **Ph:** 620-582-2361
Coldwater, KS 67029   **Fax:** 620-582-2426

On the central southern border of KS, southeast of Dodge City; organized Feb 26, 1875 from Kiowa County. **Name Origin:** For the Indian tribe of Shoshoean linguistic stock; the meaning of the name is unknown.

Area (sq mi): 789.7 (land 788.31; water 1.39).

Pop: 1,967 (White 96.9%; Black or African American 0.1%; Hispanic or Latino 1.8%; Asian 0.1%; Other 2%). **Foreign born:** 1.1%. **Median age:** 46.9. **State rank:** 103. **Pop change 1990-2000:** -15%.

Please see sample entry on inside front cover for detailed information about the statistics presented with each county listing.

Income: per capita $17,037; median household $29,415. **Pop below poverty level:** 10.2%.

Unemployment: 1.5%. **Median home value:** $29,700. **Median travel time to work:** 13.5 minutes.

COWLEY COUNTY
311 E 9th St
Winfield, KS 67156
www.cowleycounty.org

Ph: 620-221-5400
Fax: 620-221-5498

On the southern border of KS, southeast of Wichita; organized Feb 13, 1867. **Name Origin:** For Lt. Matthew Cowley (?-1864), a Union officer.

Area (sq mi): 1132.6 (land 1126.24; water 6.37).

Pop: 36,291 (White 88.4%; Black or African American 2.7%; Hispanic or Latino 3.6%; Asian 1.5%; Other 5.7%). **Foreign born:** 2.5%. **Median age:** 37. **State rank:** 13. **Pop change 1990-2000:** -1.7%.

Income: per capita $17,509; median household $34,406. **Pop below poverty level:** 12.9%.

Unemployment: 4.1%. **Median home value:** $54,100. **Median travel time to work:** 19.6 minutes.

CRAWFORD COUNTY
PO Box 249
Girard, KS 66743
www.crawfordcountykansas.org

Ph: 620-724-6115
Fax: 620-724-6007

On the southeastern border of KS; organized Feb 13, 1867 from Bourbon and Cherokee counties. **Name Origin:** For Col. Samuel J. Crawford (1835-1913), Union army officer and governor of KS (1865-68); he resigned to command a force to fight Indians.

Area (sq mi): 595.05 (land 592.91; water 2.14).

Pop: 38,242 (White 92.3%; Black or African American 1.8%; Hispanic or Latino 2.4%; Asian 1.1%; Other 3.7%). **Foreign born:** 2.7%. **Median age:** 33.8. **State rank:** 12. **Pop change 1990-2000:** +7.5%.

Income: per capita $16,245; median household $29,409. **Pop below poverty level:** 16%.

Unemployment: 5%. **Median home value:** $54,000. **Median travel time to work:** 16.9 minutes.

DECATUR COUNTY
PO Box 28
Oberlin, KS 67749

Ph: 785-475-8102
Fax: 785-475-8130

On the northwestern border of KS; organized Mar 6, 1873 from Norton County. **Name Origin:** For Stephen F. Decatur (1779-1820), U.S. naval officer during the War of 1812 and in actions against the Barbary pirates near Tripoli, who said '. . . may she always be in the right; but our country, right or wrong.'

Area (sq mi): 894.18 (land 893.55; water 0.63).

Pop: 3,472 (White 97.5%; Black or African American 0.5%; Hispanic or Latino 1%; Asian 0.1%; Other 1.5%). **Foreign born:** 1.2%. **Median age:** 44.3. **State rank:** 84. **Pop change 1990-2000:** -13.7%.

Income: per capita $16,348; median household $30,257. **Pop below poverty level:** 11.6%.

Unemployment: 2.3%. **Median home value:** $43,600. **Median travel time to work:** 16.7 minutes.

DICKINSON COUNTY
PO Box 248
Abilene, KS 67410
www.dkcoks.com

Ph: 785-263-3774
Fax: 785-263-2045

In central KS, east of Salina; original county; organized Feb 20, 1855 (prior to statehood). **Name Origin:** For Daniel Stevens Dickinson (1800-66), U.S. senator from NY (1844-51).

Area (sq mi): 852.12 (land 847.92; water 4.2).

Pop: 19,344 (White 95.2%; Black or African American 0.6%; Hispanic or Latino 2.3%; Asian 0.3%; Other 2.7%). **Foreign born:** 1.7%. **Median age:** 40. **State rank:** 28. **Pop change 1990-2000:** +2%.

Income: per capita $17,780; median household $35,975. **Pop below poverty level:** 7.5%.

Unemployment: 3.6%. **Median home value:** $62,800. **Median travel time to work:** 21.2 minutes.

DONIPHAN COUNTY
PO Box 278
Troy, KS 66087

Ph: 785-985-3513
Fax: 785-985-3723

On the northeastern border of KS, west of Saint Joseph, MO; original county; organized Aug 25, 1855 (prior to statehood). **Name Origin:** For Alexander Willliam Doniphan (1808-87), MO legislator and officer in the Mexican War.

Area (sq mi): 397.07 (land 392.18; water 4.89).

Pop: 8,249 (White 94.3%; Black or African American 2%; Hispanic or Latino 1.2%; Asian 0.3%; Other 2.9%). **Foreign born:** 0.8%. **Median age:** 36.8. **State rank:** 49. **Pop change 1990-2000:** +1.4%.

Income: per capita $14,849; median household $32,537. **Pop below poverty level:** 11.9%.

Unemployment: 9.9%. **Median home value:** $54,700. **Median travel time to work:** 21.5 minutes.

DOUGLAS COUNTY
111 E 11 St
Lawrence, KS 66044
www.douglas-county.com

Ph: 785-832-5132
Fax: 785-832-5174

In eastern KS, east of Topeka; original county; organized Aug 25, 1855 (prior to statehood). **Name Origin:** For Stephen Arnold Douglas (1813-61), U.S. orator and statesman.

Area (sq mi): 474.47 (land 456.87; water 17.6).

Pop: 99,962 (White 84.6%; Black or African American 4.2%; Hispanic or Latino 3.3%; Asian 3.1%; Other 6.6%). **Foreign born:** 5.2%. **Median age:** 26.6. **State rank:** 5. **Pop change 1990-2000:** +22.2%.

Income: per capita $19,952; median household $37,547. **Pop below poverty level:** 15.9%.

Unemployment: 4.4%. **Median home value:** $117,800. **Median travel time to work:** 19.4 minutes.

All statistics are based on the 2000 Census except the dollar figures given for per capita income, which are based on 1999 estimates.

EDWARDS COUNTY

312 Massachusetts Ave   **Ph:** 620-659-3000
Kinsley, KS 67547   **Fax:** 620-659-2583

In south-central KS, northeast of Dodge City; organized Mar 7, 1874 from Kiowa County. **Name Origin:** For W.C. and R.E. Edwards, prominent early KS settlers.

Area (sq mi): 622.1 (land 622.02; water 0.08).

Pop: 3,449 (White 89%; Black or African American 0.3%; Hispanic or Latino 9.7%; Asian 0.3%; Other 6.9%). **Foreign born:** 6.7%. **Median age:** 41. **State rank:** 86. **Pop change 1990-2000:** -8.9%.

Income: per capita $17,586; median household $30,530. **Pop below poverty level:** 10.4%.

Unemployment: 1.9%. **Median home value:** $36,300. **Median travel time to work:** 18.8 minutes.

ELK COUNTY

PO Box 606   **Ph:** 620-374-2490
Howard, KS 67349   **Fax:** 620-374-2771

In southeastern KS, southeast of Wichita; organized Mar 3, 1875 from Howard County, which was organized in 1855 (named Godfrey and changed to Seward in 1867) and abolished at the time of its division into Chautauqua and Elk counties. **Name Origin:** For the large North American deer, the elk or wapiti.

Area (sq mi): 650.36 (land 647.29; water 3.07).

Pop: 3,261 (White 94.5%; Black or African American 0.2%; Hispanic or Latino 2.2%; Asian 0.2%; Other 4.6%). **Foreign born:** 0.7%. **Median age:** 46. **State rank:** 89. **Pop change 1990-2000:** -2%.

Income: per capita $16,066; median household $27,267. **Pop below poverty level:** 13.8%.

Unemployment: 4.9%. **Median home value:** $24,700. **Median travel time to work:** 34 minutes.

ELLIS COUNTY

PO Box 720   **Ph:** 785-628-9410
Hays, KS 67601   **Fax:** 785-628-9413
www.ellisco.org

In central KS, west of Salina; organized Feb 26, 1867 from unorganized territory. **Name Origin:** For George Ellis (?-1854) KS infantryman killed during the Civil War.

Area (sq mi): 900.47 (land 899.97; water 0.5).

Pop: 27,507 (White 95.1%; Black or African American 0.7%; Hispanic or Latino 2.4%; Asian 0.8%; Other 2.4%). **Foreign born:** 2.3%. **Median age:** 32.7. **State rank:** 22. **Pop change 1990-2000:** +5.8%.

Income: per capita $18,259; median household $32,339. **Pop below poverty level:** 12.9%.

Unemployment: 2.6%. **Median home value:** $85,500. **Median travel time to work:** 13.8 minutes.

ELLSWORTH COUNTY

210 N Kansas St   **Ph:** 785-472-4161
Ellsworth, KS 67439   **Fax:** 785-472-3818

In central KS, west of Salina; organized Feb 26, 1867 from Saline County. **Name Origin:** For Lt. Allen Ellsworth, an officer in the Iowa Cavalry, who commanded the fort later named for him.

Area (sq mi): 723.44 (land 715.91; water 7.54).

Pop: 6,525 (White 91.2%; Black or African American 3.6%; Hispanic or Latino 3.6%; Asian 0.2%; Other 2.6%). **Foreign born:** 1.3%. **Median age:** 41.8. **State rank:** 60. **Pop change 1990-2000:** -0.9%.

Income: per capita $16,569; median household $35,772. **Pop below poverty level:** 7.2%.

Unemployment: 2.5%. **Median home value:** $43,400. **Median travel time to work:** 17.6 minutes.

FINNEY COUNTY

PO Box M   **Ph:** 620-272-3542
Garden City, KS 67846   **Fax:** 620-272-3599
www.finneycounty.org

In southwestern KS, northwest of Dodge City; organized as Sequoyah County Mar 6, 1873 from Arapahoe and Foote counties; name changed Feb 21, 1883; Garfield County was annexed to Finney County in 1893. **Name Origin:** For David W. Finney, lieutenant governor of KS (1861-65) and KS legislator.

Area (sq mi): 1302.62 (land 1301.77; water 0.84).

Pop: 40,523 (White 51.4%; Black or African American 1.3%; Hispanic or Latino 43.3%; Asian 2.9%; Other 26.9%). **Foreign born:** 22.7%. **Median age:** 28.1. **State rank:** 11. **Pop change 1990-2000:** +22.5%.

Income: per capita $15,377; median household $38,474. **Pop below poverty level:** 14.2%.

Unemployment: 9.6%. **Median home value:** $83,800. **Median travel time to work:** 15 minutes.

FORD COUNTY

100 Gunsmoke St   **Ph:** 620-227-4500
Dodge City, KS 67801   **Fax:** 620-227-4699
www.fordcounty.net

In southwestern KS, southeast of Garden City; organized Feb 26, 1867 from unorganized territory. **Name Origin:** For James Hobart Ford (?-1867), an officer in the Second Colorado cavalry during the Civil War.

Area (sq mi): 1099.29 (land 1098.5; water 0.79).

Pop: 32,458 (White 57.3%; Black or African American 1.6%; Hispanic or Latino 37.7%; Asian 2.1%; Other 21.5%). **Foreign born:** 22.5%. **Median age:** 29.9. **State rank:** 17. **Pop change 1990-2000:** +18.2%.

Income: per capita $15,721; median household $37,860. **Pop below poverty level:** 12.4%.

Unemployment: 2.7%. **Median home value:** $69,200. **Median travel time to work:** 15.1 minutes.

FRANKLIN COUNTY

315 S Main St   **Ph:** 785-229-3410
Ottawa, KS 66067   **Fax:** 785-229-3419
www.co.franklin.ks.us

In eastern KS, southwest of Olathe; original county; organized Aug

Please see sample entry on inside front cover for detailed information about the statistics presented with each county listing.

209

25, 1855 (prior to statehood). **Name Origin:** For Benjamin Franklin (1706-90), U.S. patriot, diplomat, and statesman.

Area (sq mi): 576.65 (land 573.85; water 2.8).

Pop: 24,784 (White 93.6%; Black or African American 1.2%; Hispanic or Latino 2.6%; Asian 0.3%; Other 3.4%). **Foreign born:** 1.3%. **Median age:** 36. **State rank:** 24. **Pop change 1990-2000:** +12.7%.

Income: per capita $17,311; median household $39,052. **Pop below poverty level:** 7.7%.

Unemployment: 5.3%. **Median home value:** $73,800. **Median travel time to work:** 25.1 minutes.

GEARY COUNTY

PO Box 927   **Ph:** 785-238-3912
Junction City, KS 66441   **Fax:** 785-238-5419

In east-central KS, south of Manhattan; organized as Davis County Aug 30, 1855 from Riley county; name changed Mar 7, 1889. **Name Origin:** For John White Geary (1819-73), territorial governor of KS (1856-57) and governor of PA (1867-73). Originally named by the pro-Southern legislature for Jefferson Davis, U.S. secretary of war (1853-57) and later president of the Confederacy.

Area (sq mi): 404.39 (land 384.69; water 19.7).

Pop: 27,947 (White 61.5%; Black or African American 22%; Hispanic or Latino 8.5%; Asian 3.2%; Other 10.7%). **Foreign born:** 7.3%. **Median age:** 29.1. **State rank:** 21. **Pop change 1990-2000:** -8.2%.

Income: per capita $16,199; median household $31,917. **Pop below poverty level:** 12.1%.

Unemployment: 7.1%. **Median home value:** $69,400. **Median travel time to work:** 17 minutes.

GOVE COUNTY

520 Washington St   **Ph:** 785-938-2300
Gove, KS 67736   **Fax:** 785-938-4486

In west-central KS, west of Hays; organized Mar 3, 1868 from Rooks County. **Name Origin:** For Capt. Grenville L. Gove (?-1864), Union army officer from KS.

Area (sq mi): 1071.47 (land 1071.38; water 0.09).

Pop: 3,068 (White 97.4%; Black or African American 0.1%; Hispanic or Latino 1.2%; Asian 0.1%; Other 1.9%). **Foreign born:** 0.5%. **Median age:** 42.6. **State rank:** 91. **Pop change 1990-2000:** -5%.

Income: per capita $17,852; median household $33,510. **Pop below poverty level:** 10.3%.

Unemployment: 1.6%. **Median home value:** $48,100. **Median travel time to work:** 14.3 minutes.

GRAHAM COUNTY

410 N Pomeroy St   **Ph:** 785-421-3453
Hill City, KS 67642   **Fax:** 785-421-6374

In north-central KS, northwest of Hays; organized Feb 26, 1867 from Rooks County. **Name Origin:** For Capt. John L. Graham (?-1863), a KS infantry officer killed at Chickamauga.

Area (sq mi): 898.67 (land 898.29; water 0.38).

Pop: 2,946 (White 94.7%; Black or African American 3.2%; Hispanic or Latino 0.8%; Asian 0.3%; Other 1.5%). **Foreign born:** 0.9%. **Median age:** 44.4. **State rank:** 95. **Pop change 1990-2000:** -16.9%.

Income: per capita $18,050; median household $31,286. **Pop below poverty level:** 11.5%.

Unemployment: 2.3%. **Median home value:** $41,300. **Median travel time to work:** 16.9 minutes.

GRANT COUNTY

108 S Glenn St   **Ph:** 620-356-1335
Ulysses, KS 67880   **Fax:** 620-356-3081
www.grantcoks.org

In southwestern KS; organized Mar 6, 1873 from Finney and Kearny counties. **Name Origin:** For Ulysses Simpson Grant (1822-85), Civil War general and eighteenth U.S. president.

Area (sq mi): 575.04 (land 574.86; water 0.18).

Pop: 7,909 (White 63.5%; Black or African American 0.2%; Hispanic or Latino 34.7%; Asian 0.4%; Other 22.5%). **Foreign born:** 12.3%. **Median age:** 31.4. **State rank:** 52. **Pop change 1990-2000:** +10.5%.

Income: per capita $17,072; median household $39,854. **Pop below poverty level:** 10.1%.

Unemployment: 2.7%. **Median home value:** $78,600. **Median travel time to work:** 15.3 minutes.

GRAY COUNTY

PO Box 487   **Ph:** 620-855-3618
Cimarron, KS 67835   **Fax:** 620-855-3107

In southwestern KS, west of Dodge City; organized Mar 5, 1887 from Finney and Ford counties. **Name Origin:** For Alfred Gray, teacher, lawyer, and secretary of the KS Board of Agriculture (1873-80).

Area (sq mi): 869.34 (land 868.9; water 0.44).

Pop: 5,904 (White 88.6%; Black or African American 0.2%; Hispanic or Latino 9.8%; Asian 0.1%; Other 7.5%). **Foreign born:** 9.5%. **Median age:** 33. **State rank:** 66. **Pop change 1990-2000:** +9.4%.

Income: per capita $18,632; median household $40,000. **Pop below poverty level:** 9.1%.

Unemployment: 2.3%. **Median home value:** $76,000. **Median travel time to work:** 17.2 minutes.

GREELEY COUNTY

PO Box 277   **Ph:** 620-376-4256
Tribune, KS 67879   **Fax:** 620-376-2294

On the central western border of KS; established Mar 6, 1873. **Name Origin:** For Horace Greeley (1811-72), editor of the *New York Tribune* and champion of westward expansion.

Area (sq mi): 778.01 (land 778.01; water 0).

Pop: 1,534 (White 87.2%; Black or African American 0.2%; Hispanic or Latino 11.5%; Asian 0.1%; Other 6.6%). **Foreign born:**

All statistics are based on the 2000 Census except the dollar figures given for per capita income, which are based on 1999 estimates.

8.5%. **Median age:** 38.6. **State rank:** 105. **Pop change 1990-2000:** -13.5%.

Income: per capita $19,974; median household $34,605. **Pop below poverty level:** 11.6%.

Unemployment: 3.6%. **Median home value:** $57,700. **Median travel time to work:** 15.8 minutes.

GREENWOOD COUNTY
311 N Main St   **Ph:** 620-583-8121
Eureka, KS 67045   **Fax:** 620-583-8124

In southeastern KS, east of Wichita; original county; organized Aug 25, 1855 (prior to statehood). **Name Origin:** For Alfred Burton Greenwood (1811-89), U.S. representative from AR (1853-59).

Area (sq mi): 1152.59 (land 1139.67; water 12.92).

Pop: 7,673 (White 95.8%; Black or African American 0.1%; Hispanic or Latino 1.7%; Asian 0.1%; Other 3.2%). **Foreign born:** 1%. **Median age:** 42.6. **State rank:** 53. **Pop change 1990-2000:** -2.2%.

Income: per capita $15,976; median household $30,169. **Pop below poverty level:** 12.5%.

Unemployment: 5.6%. **Median home value:** $35,300. **Median travel time to work:** 25.1 minutes.

HAMILTON COUNTY
PO Box 1167   **Ph:** 620-384-5629
Syracuse, KS 67878   **Fax:** 620-384-5853

On the western border of KS, west of Garden City; organized Mar 20, 1873 from unorganized territory. **Name Origin:** For Alexander Hamilton (1757-1804), first U.S. secretary of the treasury (1789-95).

Area (sq mi): 997.62 (land 996.49; water 1.13).

Pop: 2,670 (White 77.1%; Black or African American 0.5%; Hispanic or Latino 20.6%; Asian 0.6%; Other 17.3%). **Foreign born:** 13.5%. **Median age:** 37.6. **State rank:** 97. **Pop change 1990-2000:** +11.8%.

Income: per capita $16,484; median household $32,033. **Pop below poverty level:** 15.7%.

Unemployment: 1.8%. **Median home value:** $59,400. **Median travel time to work:** 17.3 minutes.

HARPER COUNTY
201 N Jennings Ave   **Ph:** 620-842-5555
Anthony, KS 67003   **Fax:** 620-842-3455
www.harpercounty.org

On the central southern border of KS, southwest of Wichita; established Feb 26, 1867 from Kingman County. **Name Origin:** For Sgt. Marion Harper (?-1863), soldier in the Kansas cavalry killed in the Civil War.

Area (sq mi): 802.95 (land 801.44; water 1.51).

Pop: 6,536 (White 96.7%; Black or African American 0.2%; Hispanic or Latino 1.1%; Asian 0.1%; Other 2.4%). **Foreign born:** 0.4%. **Median age:** 42.9. **State rank:** 59. **Pop change 1990-2000:** -8.3%.

Income: per capita $16,368; median household $29,776. **Pop below poverty level:** 11.6%.

Unemployment: 3.5%. **Median home value:** $44,100. **Median travel time to work:** 19.6 minutes.

HARVEY COUNTY
PO Box 687   **Ph:** 316-284-6840
Newton, KS 67114   **Fax:** 316-284-6856
www.harveycounty.com

In central KS, east of Hutchinson; organized Feb 29, 1872 from McPherson, Butler, and Sedgwick counties. **Name Origin:** For Capt. James Madison Harvey (1833-94), governor of KS (1869-73) and U.S. senator (1874-77).

Area (sq mi): 540.5 (land 539.33; water 1.17).

Pop: 32,869 (White 88.1%; Black or African American 1.6%; Hispanic or Latino 8%; Asian 0.5%; Other 6.8%). **Foreign born:** 3.7%. **Median age:** 37.6. **State rank:** 16. **Pop change 1990-2000:** +5.9%.

Income: per capita $18,715; median household $40,907. **Pop below poverty level:** 6.4%.

Unemployment: 3.4%. **Median home value:** $76,400. **Median travel time to work:** 18.2 minutes.

HASKELL COUNTY
PO Box 518   **Ph:** 620-675-2263
Sublette, KS 67877   **Fax:** 620-675-2681
www.haskellcounty.org

In southwestern KS; organized Mar 23, 1887 from Finney County. **Name Origin:** For Dudley Chase Haskell (1842-83), KS legislator and U.S. representative (1877-83).

Area (sq mi): 577.73 (land 577.37; water 0.36).

Pop: 4,307 (White 74%; Black or African American 0.2%; Hispanic or Latino 23.6%; Asian 0.6%; Other 14.1%). **Foreign born:** 13.4%. **Median age:** 30.8. **State rank:** 78. **Pop change 1990-2000:** +10.8%.

Income: per capita $17,349; median household $38,634. **Pop below poverty level:** 11.6%.

Unemployment: 2.4%. **Median home value:** $76,100. **Median travel time to work:** 15.6 minutes.

HODGEMAN COUNTY
PO Box 247   **Ph:** 620-357-6421
Jetmore, KS 67854   **Fax:** 620-357-6161

In southwest-central KS, north of Dodge City; organized Mar 6, 1873 from Indian lands. **Name Origin:** For Capt. Amos Hodgman (?-1863), Civil War officer. The *e* was mistakenly inserted when the county was named.

Area (sq mi): 860.24 (land 859.92; water 0.32).

Pop: 2,085 (White 95.5%; Black or African American 0.9%; Hispanic or Latino 2.7%; Asian 0%; Other 1.8%). **Foreign born:** 1%. **Median age:** 39.8. **State rank:** 102. **Pop change 1990-2000:** -4.2%.

Income: per capita $15,599; median household $35,994. **Pop below poverty level:** 11.5%.

Unemployment: 2.7%. **Median home value:** $45,000. **Median travel time to work:** 15.6 minutes.

Please see sample entry on inside front cover for detailed information about the statistics presented with each county listing.

JACKSON COUNTY

400 New York Ave 2nd Fl
Holton, KS 66436

Ph: 785-364-2891
Fax: 785-364-4204

In northeastern KS, north of Topeka; organized as Calhoun County Aug 30, 1855 (prior to statehood); name changed Feb 11, 1859. **Name Origin:** For Andrew Jackson (1767-1845), seventh U.S. president. Originally for John C. Calhoun (1782-1850), U.S. senator from SC.

Area (sq mi): 657.86 (land 655.59; water 2.27).

Pop: 12,657 (White 89.6%; Black or African American 0.5%; Hispanic or Latino 1.5%; Asian 0.2%; Other 9%). **Foreign born:** 0.5%. **Median age:** 37.4. **State rank:** 37. **Pop change 1990-2000:** +9.8%.

Income: per capita $18,606; median household $40,451. **Pop below poverty level:** 8.8%.

Unemployment: 3.7%. **Median home value:** $70,200. **Median travel time to work:** 27.5 minutes.

JEFFERSON COUNTY

PO Box 321
Oskaloosa, KS 66066
www.jfcountyks.com

Ph: 785-863-2272
Fax: 785-863-3135

In northeastern KS, east of Topeka; original county; organized Aug 25, 1855 (prior to statehood). **Name Origin:** For Thomas Jefferson (1743-1826), U.S. patriot and statesman; third U.S. president.

Area (sq mi): 556.94 (land 536.11; water 20.83).

Pop: 18,426 (White 96%; Black or African American 0.4%; Hispanic or Latino 1.3%; Asian 0.2%; Other 2.7%). **Foreign born:** 0.6%. **Median age:** 38. **State rank:** 29. **Pop change 1990-2000:** +15.9%.

Income: per capita $19,373; median household $45,535. **Pop below poverty level:** 6.7%.

Unemployment: 4.4%. **Median home value:** $83,100. **Median travel time to work:** 29.3 minutes.

JEWELL COUNTY

307 N Commercial St
Mankato, KS 66956

Ph: 785-378-4020
Fax: 785-378-4075

On central northern border of KS; organized Feb 26, 1867 from Mitchell County. **Name Origin:** For Lt. Col. Lewis R. Jewell (?-1862), officer in the Kansas cavalry killed during the Civil War.

Area (sq mi): 914.47 (land 909.18; water 5.29).

Pop: 3,791 (White 98.2%; Black or African American 0%; Hispanic or Latino 0.7%; Asian 0.1%; Other 1.1%). **Foreign born:** 0.9%. **Median age:** 46.2. **State rank:** 79. **Pop change 1990-2000:** -10.8%.

Income: per capita $16,644; median household $30,538. **Pop below poverty level:** 11.6%.

Unemployment: 1.7%. **Median home value:** $24,000. **Median travel time to work:** 16.8 minutes.

JOHNSON COUNTY

111 S Cherry St Suite 1200
Olathe, KS 66061
www.jocoks.com

Ph: 913-715-0775
Fax: 913-715-0800

On eastern border of KS, south of Kansas City; original county, organized Aug 25, 1855 (prior to statehood). **Name Origin:** For the Rev. Thomas Johnson (1802-65), assassinated missionary to the Shawnee Indians (1829-58).

Area (sq mi): 480.15 (land 476.78; water 3.37).

Pop: 451,086 (White 89%; Black or African American 2.6%; Hispanic or Latino 4%; Asian 2.8%; Other 3.3%). **Foreign born:** 5.7%. **Median age:** 35.2. **State rank:** 2. **Pop change 1990-2000:** +27%.

Income: per capita $30,919; median household $61,455. **Pop below poverty level:** 3.4%.

Unemployment: 3.4%. **Median home value:** $150,100. **Median travel time to work:** 20.2 minutes.

KEARNY COUNTY

PO Box 86
Lakin, KS 67860

Ph: 620-355-6422
Fax: 620-355-7382

In southwestern KS, west of Garden City; organized Mar 6, 1873 from Finney County. **Name Origin:** For Gen. Philip Kearny (1814-62), hero of the Mexican-American War and Civil War.

Area (sq mi): 871.5 (land 871.06; water 0.44).

Pop: 4,531 (White 71.1%; Black or African American 0.6%; Hispanic or Latino 26.6%; Asian 0.3%; Other 18.8%). **Foreign born:** 12.7%. **Median age:** 31.6. **State rank:** 75. **Pop change 1990-2000:** +12.5%.

Income: per capita $15,708; median household $40,149. **Pop below poverty level:** 11.7%.

Unemployment: 4.5%. **Median home value:** $77,500. **Median travel time to work:** 13.9 minutes.

KINGMAN COUNTY

130 Spruce St
Kingman, KS 67068

Ph: 620-532-2521
Fax: 620-532-2037

In south-central KS, west of Wichita; established Feb 29, 1872 from unorganized territory. **Name Origin:** For Samuel Austin Kingman (1822-?), KY legislator and Chief Justice of the KS Supreme Court (1866-77).

Area (sq mi): 866.7 (land 863.35; water 3.35).

Pop: 8,673 (White 96.5%; Black or African American 0.2%; Hispanic or Latino 1.4%; Asian 0.2%; Other 2.1%). **Foreign born:** 0.3%. **Median age:** 40.2. **State rank:** 48. **Pop change 1990-2000:** +4.6%.

Income: per capita $18,533; median household $37,790. **Pop below poverty level:** 10.6%.

Unemployment: 3.4%. **Median home value:** $56,800. **Median travel time to work:** 25.3 minutes.

KIOWA COUNTY

211 E Florida Ave
Greensburg, KS 67054

Ph: 620-723-3366
Fax: 620-723-3234

In south-central KS, southeast of Dodge City; established Feb 26, 1867 from Comanche and Edwards counties, abolished in 1875, and recreated in 1866 from Comanche and Edwards counties. **Name Origin:** For the Indian tribe of Tanoan linguistic stock; name means 'principal people.'

All statistics are based on the 2000 Census except the dollar figures given for per capita income, which are based on 1999 estimates.

Area (sq mi): 722.62 (land 722.39; water 0.23).

Pop: 3,278 (White 96.2%; Black or African American 0.2%; Hispanic or Latino 2%; Asian 0.3%; Other 2.3%). **Foreign born:** 1.9%. **Median age:** 42.1. **State rank:** 88. **Pop change 1990-2000:** -10.4%.

Income: per capita $17,207; median household $31,576. **Pop below poverty level:** 10.8%.

Unemployment: 2.1%. **Median home value:** $44,200. **Median travel time to work:** 15.3 minutes.

LABETTE COUNTY
PO Box 387
Oswego, KS 67356
www.labettecounty.com

Ph: 620-795-2138
Fax: 620-795-2928

On the southeastern border of KS, west of Joplin, MO; organized Feb 7, 1867 from Neosho County. **Name Origin:** For the creek, which runs through the county, named La Bette, possibly for a Pierre Labette who lived near the mouth of the stream. An 1836 map names it *La Bete*, French for 'the beast.'

Area (sq mi): 653.3 (land 648.82; water 4.48).

Pop: 22,835 (White 87.8%; Black or African American 4.7%; Hispanic or Latino 3.1%; Asian 0.3%; Other 5.7%). **Foreign born:** 1%. **Median age:** 37.9. **State rank:** 25. **Pop change 1990-2000:** -3.6%.

Income: per capita $15,525; median household $30,875. **Pop below poverty level:** 12.7%.

Unemployment: 5.6%. **Median home value:** $39,600. **Median travel time to work:** 16.8 minutes.

LANE COUNTY
PO Box 788
Dighton, KS 67839
trails.net/laneco/

Ph: 620-397-5356
Fax: 620-397-5419

In west-central KS, northeast of Garden City; organized Mar 6, 1873 from Finney County. **Name Origin:** For Col. James Henry Lane (1814-66), officer in the Mexican-American War, U.S. representative from IN (1853-55), and first U.S. senator from KS (1861-66).

Area (sq mi): 717.43 (land 717.22; water 0.21).

Pop: 2,155 (White 97%; Black or African American 0%; Hispanic or Latino 1.4%; Asian 0.1%; Other 2.1%). **Foreign born:** 0.5%. **Median age:** 41.6. **State rank:** 101. **Pop change 1990-2000:** -9.3%.

Income: per capita $18,606; median household $36,047. **Pop below poverty level:** 8.2%.

Unemployment: 3.9%. **Median home value:** $48,500. **Median travel time to work:** 15.7 minutes.

LEAVENWORTH COUNTY
300 Walnut St
Leavenworth, KS 66048
www.leavenworthcounty.org

Ph: 913-684-0400
Fax: 913-684-0406

On the northeastern border of KS, north of Kansas City; original county; organized Aug 25, 1855 (prior to statehood). **Name Origin:** For Fort Leavenworth, the state's first fort, named for Gen. Henry Leavenworth (1783-1834), officer in the War of 1812 who later fought the Indians.

Area (sq mi): 468.33 (land 463.27; water 5.06).

Pop: 68,691 (White 82%; Black or African American 10.4%; Hispanic or Latino 3.8%; Asian 1.1%; Other 4.2%). **Foreign born:** 2.7%. **Median age:** 35.6. **State rank:** 6. **Pop change 1990-2000:** +6.7%.

Income: per capita $20,292; median household $48,114. **Pop below poverty level:** 6.7%.

Unemployment: 5.3%. **Median home value:** $96,900. **Median travel time to work:** 22.4 minutes.

LINCOLN COUNTY
216 E Lincoln Ave
Lincoln, KS 67455

Ph: 785-524-4757
Fax: 785-524-5008

In north-central KS, northwest of Salina; organized Feb 26, 1867 from Ellsworth County. **Name Origin:** For Abraham Lincoln (1809-65), sixteenth U.S. president.

Area (sq mi): 719.94 (land 718.87; water 1.07).

Pop: 3,578 (White 97.6%; Black or African American 0.1%; Hispanic or Latino 1%; Asian 0.1%; Other 1.6%). **Foreign born:** 0.5%. **Median age:** 43.7. **State rank:** 81. **Pop change 1990-2000:** -2.1%.

Income: per capita $15,788; median household $30,893. **Pop below poverty level:** 9.7%.

Unemployment: 2.9%. **Median home value:** $33,900. **Median travel time to work:** 18.1 minutes.

LINN COUNTY
PO Box 350
Mound City, KS 66056

Ph: 913-795-2660
Fax: 913-795-2004

On the eastern border of KS, south of Kansas City; original county; organized Aug 25, 1855 (prior to statehood). **Name Origin:** For Lewis Fields Linn (1795-1843), U.S. senator from MO (1833-43).

Area (sq mi): 606.29 (land 598.67; water 7.62).

Pop: 9,570 (White 96.9%; Black or African American 0.6%; Hispanic or Latino 0.9%; Asian 0.1%; Other 1.8%). **Foreign born:** 0.3%. **Median age:** 40.8. **State rank:** 45. **Pop change 1990-2000:** +15.9%.

Income: per capita $17,009; median household $35,906. **Pop below poverty level:** 11%.

Unemployment: 9.6%. **Median home value:** $56,100. **Median travel time to work:** 34.3 minutes.

LOGAN COUNTY
710 W 2nd St
Oakley, KS 67748

Ph: 785-672-4244
Fax: 785-672-3341

In western KS, northwest of Garden City; organized as Saint John County Mar 4, 1881 from Wallace County; name changed Feb 24, 1887. **Name Origin:** For Gen. John Alexander Logan (1826-86), officer in the Mexican-American War and Civil War, U.S. senator from IL (1871-77; 1879-86).

Area (sq mi): 1073.09 (land 1072.99; water 0.11).

Pop: 3,046 (White 96.2%; Black or African American 0.6%; Hispanic or Latino 1.6%; Asian 0.2%; Other 2.5%). **Foreign born:** 0.6%. **Median age:** 40.7. **State rank:** 92. **Pop change 1990-2000:** -1.1%.

Please see sample entry on inside front cover for detailed information about the statistics presented with each county listing.

213

Income: per capita $17,294; median household $32,131. **Pop below poverty level:** 7.3%.

Unemployment: 2.5%. **Median home value:** $55,000. **Median travel time to work:** 15.4 minutes.

LYON COUNTY

430 Commercial St   **Ph:** 620-341-3243
Emporia, KS 66801   **Fax:** 620-341-3415
www.lyoncounty.org

In east-central KS, northeast of Wichita; established as Breckinridge County Feb 17, 1857 (prior to statehood) from Madison County (which was abolished at the time it was divided between Lyon and Greenwood counties); name changed Feb 5, 1862. **Name Origin:** For Gen. Nathaniel Lyon (1818-61), Union commander in the Civil War who helped preserve MO for the Union when it seemed likely to join the Confederacy.

Area (sq mi): 855.14 (land 850.87; water 4.27).

Pop: 35,935 (White 77.3%; Black or African American 2.3%; Hispanic or Latino 16.7%; Asian 2%; Other 12.5%). **Foreign born:** 9%. **Median age:** 30.9. **State rank:** 15. **Pop change 1990-2000:** +3.5%.

Income: per capita $15,724; median household $32,819. **Pop below poverty level:** 14.5%.

Unemployment: 4.8%. **Median home value:** $67,900. **Median travel time to work:** 15.9 minutes.

MARION COUNTY

PO Box 219   **Ph:** 620-382-2185
Marion, KS 66861   **Fax:** 620-382-3420

In central KS, north of Wichita; established Aug 25, 1855 (prior to statehood) from Chase County. **Name Origin:** For Gen. Francis Marion (c. 1732-95), SC soldier and legislator, known as 'The Swamp Fox' for his tactics during the Revolutionary War.

Area (sq mi): 953.54 (land 943.11; water 10.43).

Pop: 13,361 (White 96%; Black or African American 0.5%; Hispanic or Latino 1.9%; Asian 0.2%; Other 2.2%). **Foreign born:** 1.1%. **Median age:** 41. **State rank:** 36. **Pop change 1990-2000:** +3.7%.

Income: per capita $16,100; median household $34,500. **Pop below poverty level:** 8.3%.

Unemployment: 2.6%. **Median home value:** $52,300. **Median travel time to work:** 20.1 minutes.

MARSHALL COUNTY

1201 Broadway   **Ph:** 785-562-5361
Marysville, KS 66508   **Fax:** 785-562-5262

On the northern border of KS, north of Manhattan; original county; organized Aug 25, 1855 (prior to statehood). **Name Origin:** For Francis J. Marshall, local businessman and member of the first KS territorial legislature. County seat was named for his wife.

Area (sq mi): 904.36 (land 902.53; water 1.83).

Pop: 10,965 (White 97.7%; Black or African American 0.2%; Hispanic or Latino 0.8%; Asian 0.2%; Other 1.5%). **Foreign born:** 1.1%. **Median age:** 41.7. **State rank:** 38. **Pop change 1990-2000:** -6.3%.

Income: per capita $17,090; median household $32,089. **Pop below poverty level:** 9.2%.

Unemployment: 3.5%. **Median home value:** $46,200. **Median travel time to work:** 17.3 minutes.

McPHERSON COUNTY

PO Box 425   **Ph:** 620-241-3656
McPherson, KS 67460   **Fax:** 620-241-1168

In central KS, north of Hutchinson; organized Feb 26, 1867 from unorganized territory. **Name Origin:** For Gen. James Birdseye McPherson (1828-64), commander of the Union Army of the Tennessee during the Civil War.

Area (sq mi): 901.24 (land 899.71; water 1.52).

Pop: 29,554 (White 95.6%; Black or African American 0.8%; Hispanic or Latino 1.9%; Asian 0.3%; Other 2.4%). **Foreign born:** 0.6%. **Median age:** 38.1. **State rank:** 18. **Pop change 1990-2000:** +8.4%.

Income: per capita $18,921; median household $41,138. **Pop below poverty level:** 6.6%.

Unemployment: 3%. **Median home value:** $82,700. **Median travel time to work:** 14.6 minutes.

MEADE COUNTY

PO Box 278   **Ph:** 620-873-8700
Meade, KS 67864   **Fax:** 620-873-8713

On the southern border of KS, southwest of Dodge City; organized Jan 8, 1873 from unorganized territory. **Name Origin:** For Gen. George Gordon Meade (1815-72), officer in the Mexican-American War and Civil War; commander of the Union army that defeated Gen. Robert E. Lee (1807-70) at Gettysburg.

Area (sq mi): 979.66 (land 978.42; water 1.24).

Pop: 4,631 (White 86.8%; Black or African American 0.4%; Hispanic or Latino 10.9%; Asian 0.2%; Other 8.2%). **Foreign born:** 8.9%. **Median age:** 36.1. **State rank:** 73. **Pop change 1990-2000:** +9%.

Income: per capita $16,824; median household $36,761. **Pop below poverty level:** 9.3%.

Unemployment: 2.1%. **Median home value:** $52,900. **Median travel time to work:** 17.7 minutes.

MIAMI COUNTY

201 S Pearl St Suite 102   **Ph:** 913-294-3976
Paola, KS 66071   **Fax:** 913-294-9544
www.miamicountyks.org

On the eastern border of KS, south of Olathe; organized as Lykins County Aug 25, 1855 (prior to statehood); name changed Jun 3, 1861. **Name Origin:** For the Miami Indians, an Algonquin tribe. Origin of name uncertain; probably from Ojibway *oumaumeg* 'people of the peninsula' or from Delaware *we-mi-a-mik* 'all friends.'

Area (sq mi): 590.15 (land 576.72; water 13.43).

Pop: 28,351 (White 95%; Black or African American 1.5%; Hispanic or Latino 1.6%; Asian 0.2%; Other 2.3%). **Foreign born:** 0.6%. **Median age:** 36.7. **State rank:** 19. **Pop change 1990-2000:** +20.8%.

All statistics are based on the 2000 Census except the dollar figures given for per capita income, which are based on 1999 estimates.

Income: per capita $21,408; median household $46,665. **Pop below poverty level:** 5.5%.

Unemployment: 4.2%. **Median home value:** $106,300. **Median travel time to work:** 28.6 minutes.

MITCHELL COUNTY

PO Box 190   **Ph:** 785-738-3652
Beloit, KS 67420   **Fax:** 785-738-5524

In north-central KS, northwest of Salina; organized Feb 26, 1867 from Kirwin Land District. **Name Origin:** For Capt. William D. Mitchell (?-1865), Union officer killed at Battle of Monroe's Cross Roads, NC.

Area (sq mi): 718.62 (land 699.82; water 18.8).

Pop: 6,932 (White 97.1%; Black or African American 0.5%; Hispanic or Latino 0.9%; Asian 0.3%; Other 1.5%). **Foreign born:** 0.3%. **Median age:** 41.1. **State rank:** 56. **Pop change 1990-2000:** -3.8%.

Income: per capita $17,653; median household $33,385. **Pop below poverty level:** 9.5%.

Unemployment: 2.4%. **Median home value:** $55,600. **Median travel time to work:** 12.3 minutes.

MONTGOMERY COUNTY

PO Box 446   **Ph:** 620-330-1200
Independence, KS 67301   **Fax:** 620-330-1202

On the southeastern border of KS, west of Joplin, MO; organized Feb 26, 1867 from Labette County. **Name Origin:** For either James M. Montgomery (1814-71), abolitionist and preacher, a nephew or more distant relative of Gen. Richard Montgomery (1738-75), officer in the American Revolution, or for Gen. Richard Montgomery himself.

Area (sq mi): 651.4 (land 645.2; water 6.19).

Pop: 36,252 (White 84.5%; Black or African American 6.1%; Hispanic or Latino 3.1%; Asian 0.5%; Other 7.6%). **Foreign born:** 1.3%. **Median age:** 39.2. **State rank:** 14. **Pop change 1990-2000:** -6.6%.

Income: per capita $16,421; median household $30,997. **Pop below poverty level:** 12.6%.

Unemployment: 6.5%. **Median home value:** $44,400. **Median travel time to work:** 16.4 minutes.

MORRIS COUNTY

501 W Main St   **Ph:** 620-767-5518
Council Grove, KS 66846   **Fax:** 620-767-6861

In east-central KS, northwest of Emporia; organized as Wise County Aug 30, 1855 (prior to statehood) from Madison County; name changed Feb 11, 1859. **Name Origin:** For Thomas Morris (1766-1844), opponent of slavery and U.S. senator from OH (1833-39).

Area (sq mi): 702.84 (land 697.38; water 5.46).

Pop: 6,104 (White 96.2%; Black or African American 0.3%; Hispanic or Latino 2.2%; Asian 0.2%; Other 1.9%). **Foreign born:** 1.5%. **Median age:** 42. **State rank:** 63. **Pop change 1990-2000:** -1.5%.

Income: per capita $18,491; median household $32,163. **Pop below poverty level:** 9%.

Unemployment: 3.5%. **Median home value:** $48,400. **Median travel time to work:** 21.6 minutes.

MORTON COUNTY

PO Box 1116   **Ph:** 620-697-2157
Elkhart, KS 67950   **Fax:** 620-697-2159
www.mtcoks.com

In the southwestern corner of KS; organized Feb 18, 1886 from Stanton County. **Name Origin:** For Oliver Hazard Perry Throck Morton (1823-77), jurist, IN governor (1861-67), and U.S. senator (1867-77).

Area (sq mi): 729.94 (land 729.92; water 0.02).

Pop: 3,496 (White 82.7%; Black or African American 0.2%; Hispanic or Latino 14.1%; Asian 1.1%; Other 10.3%). **Foreign born:** 9.5%. **Median age:** 36.2. **State rank:** 83. **Pop change 1990-2000:** +0.5%.

Income: per capita $17,076; median household $37,232. **Pop below poverty level:** 10.5%.

Unemployment: 2.4%. **Median home value:** $67,700. **Median travel time to work:** 13.7 minutes.

NEMAHA COUNTY

PO Box 186   **Ph:** 785-336-3570
Seneca, KS 66538   **Fax:** 785-336-3373

On northern border of KS, west of Saint Joseph, MO; original county; organized Aug 25, 1855 (prior to statehood). **Name Origin:** For the Nemaha River, itself named from the Oto Indian *nimaha* 'muddy water.'

Area (sq mi): 719.4 (land 717.99; water 1.41).

Pop: 10,717 (White 97.9%; Black or African American 0.5%; Hispanic or Latino 0.7%; Asian 0.1%; Other 1.1%). **Foreign born:** 0.4%. **Median age:** 39.1. **State rank:** 41. **Pop change 1990-2000:** +2.6%.

Income: per capita $17,121; median household $34,296. **Pop below poverty level:** 9.1%.

Unemployment: 3.3%. **Median home value:** $58,200. **Median travel time to work:** 15.4 minutes.

NEOSHO COUNTY

PO Box 138   **Ph:** 620-244-3811
Erie, KS 66733   **Fax:** 620-244-3810

In southeastern KS, west of Pittsburgh; organized as Dorn County Aug 25, 1855 (prior to statehood) from Labette County. **Name Origin:** Osage Indian 'cold, clear water' or 'main river,' unclear which river is referred to.

Area (sq mi): 578.02 (land 571.75; water 6.27).

Pop: 16,997 (White 93.4%; Black or African American 0.9%; Hispanic or Latino 2.9%; Asian 0.3%; Other 4%). **Foreign born:** 0.7%. **Median age:** 38.4. **State rank:** 31. **Pop change 1990-2000:** -0.2%.

Income: per capita $16,539; median household $32,167. **Pop below poverty level:** 13%.

Please see sample entry on inside front cover for detailed information about the statistics presented with each county listing.

Unemployment: 5.8%. **Median home value:** $44,900. **Median travel time to work:** 16.3 minutes.

NESS COUNTY

202 W Sycamore St	**Ph:** 785-798-2401
Ness City, KS 67560	**Fax:** 785-798-3829

In west-central KS, north of Dodge City; established Feb 26, 1867. **Name Origin:** For Noah V. Ness (?-1864), a corporal in the Kansas cavalry killed in the Civil War, and the only corporal to be so honored in KS.

Area (sq mi): 1075 (land 1074.75; water 0.26).

Pop: 3,454 (White 97.5%; Black or African American 0.1%; Hispanic or Latino 1.5%; Asian 0.1%; Other 1.6%). **Foreign born:** 0.9%. **Median age:** 43.9. **State rank:** 85. **Pop change 1990-2000:** -14.4%.

Income: per capita $17,787; median household $32,340. **Pop below poverty level:** 8.7%.

Unemployment: 1.8%. **Median home value:** $40,600. **Median travel time to work:** 16.1 minutes.

NORTON COUNTY

PO Box 70	**Ph:** 785-877-5720
Norton, KS 67654	**Fax:** 785-877-5722

On the central northern border of KS; established as Oro County 1859 (prior to statehood) from unorganized territory; name changed to Norton Feb 26, 1867; changed to Billings Mar 6, 1873; changed back to Norton Feb 19, 1874. **Name Origin:** For Orloff Norton (?-1864), Kansas army officer killed during a skirmish at Cane Hill, AR. Previously for N. H. Billings, a member of the KS legislature.

Area (sq mi): 881.39 (land 877.84; water 3.55).

Pop: 5,953 (White 92.1%; Black or African American 4%; Hispanic or Latino 2.4%; Asian 0.4%; Other 2.1%). **Foreign born:** 0.6%. **Median age:** 40.1. **State rank:** 65. **Pop change 1990-2000:** +0.1%.

Income: per capita $16,835; median household $31,050. **Pop below poverty level:** 10.5%.

Unemployment: 1.6%. **Median home value:** $46,800. **Median travel time to work:** 12.7 minutes.

OSAGE COUNTY

PO Box 226	**Ph:** 785-828-4812
Lyndon, KS 66451	**Fax:** 785-828-4749

In eastern KS, south of Topeka; original county, organized as Weller County Aug 30, 1855 (prior to statehood); name changed Feb 11, 1859. **Name Origin:** For the Osage Indians, a tribe of Siouan linguistic stock. Name is a corruption of their name in their own language, *Wazhazhe*, meaning unknown.

Area (sq mi): 719.23 (land 703.5; water 15.72).

Pop: 16,712 (White 96.4%; Black or African American 0.2%; Hispanic or Latino 1.5%; Asian 0.2%; Other 2.4%). **Foreign born:** 0.6%. **Median age:** 38.9. **State rank:** 33. **Pop change 1990-2000:** +9.6%.

Income: per capita $17,691; median household $37,928. **Pop below poverty level:** 8.4%.

Unemployment: 4.7%. **Median home value:** $67,600. **Median travel time to work:** 30.1 minutes.

OSBORNE COUNTY

PO Box 160	**Ph:** 785-346-2431
Osborne, KS 67473	**Fax:** 785-346-5252

In north-central KS, northeast of Hays; organized Feb 26, 1867 from Mitchell County. **Name Origin:** For Vincent B. Osborne (?-1865), Kansas soldier and lawyer. The geodetic center of the U.S. is in this county.

Area (sq mi): 894.28 (land 892.39; water 1.89).

Pop: 4,452 (White 98.3%; Black or African American 0.1%; Hispanic or Latino 0.4%; Asian 0.2%; Other 1.1%). **Foreign born:** 0.7%. **Median age:** 44. **State rank:** 76. **Pop change 1990-2000:** -8.5%.

Income: per capita $16,236; median household $29,145. **Pop below poverty level:** 10.4%.

Unemployment: 3.1%. **Median home value:** $32,000. **Median travel time to work:** 15.3 minutes.

OTTAWA COUNTY

307 N Concord St Suite 130	**Ph:** 785-392-2279
Minneapolis, KS 67467	**Fax:** 785-392-3605
www.ottawacounty.org	

In north-central KS, north of Salina; established Feb 27, 1860 (prior to statehood) from Saline County. **Name Origin:** For the Ottawa Indians of Algonquian linguistic stock. Tribal name derived from *Kadawe* 'to trade,' for their ability as intertribal traders and barterers.

Area (sq mi): 721.9 (land 721.11; water 0.79).

Pop: 6,163 (White 96.9%; Black or African American 0.5%; Hispanic or Latino 1.3%; Asian 0.1%; Other 1.8%). **Foreign born:** 0.7%. **Median age:** 40.1. **State rank:** 62. **Pop change 1990-2000:** +9.4%.

Income: per capita $17,663; median household $38,009. **Pop below poverty level:** 8.6%.

Unemployment: 3.5%. **Median home value:** $58,900. **Median travel time to work:** 23.4 minutes.

PAWNEE COUNTY

715 Broadway	**Ph:** 620-285-3721
Larned, KS 67550	**Fax:** 620-285-3802

In central KS, west of Great Bend; established Feb 26, 1867 from Rush and Stafford counties. **Name Origin:** For an Indian tribe of Caddoan linguistic stock. Name may mean 'horn' for the shape of their hair lock; Osages called them *Pa-in* 'long-haired,' they called themselves 'civilized people.'

Area (sq mi): 754.56 (land 754.17; water 0.38).

Pop: 7,233 (White 88.8%; Black or African American 5%; Hispanic or Latino 4.2%; Asian 0.6%; Other 3.5%). **Foreign born:** 1.4%. **Median age:** 40.5. **State rank:** 55. **Pop change 1990-2000:** -4.3%.

Income: per capita $17,584; median household $35,175. **Pop below poverty level:** 11.8%.

All statistics are based on the 2000 Census except the dollar figures given for per capita income, which are based on 1999 estimates.

Unemployment: 1.7%. **Median home value:** $48,800. **Median travel time to work:** 15.3 minutes.

PHILLIPS COUNTY

301 State St   **Ph:** 785-543-6825
Phillipsburg, KS 67661   **Fax:** 785-543-6827
www.phillipscounty.org

On the central northern border of KS; established Feb 26, 1867 from Kirwin Land District. **Name Origin:** Either for William A. Phillips (?-1856), a free-state man murdered at Leavenworth by a proslaver, or for a 'gallant private soldier of the Union army.'

Area (sq mi): 894.81 (land 886.23; water 8.58).

Pop: 6,001 (White 97.8%; Black or African American 0.2%; Hispanic or Latino 0.7%; Asian 0.4%; Other 1%). **Foreign born:** 0.4%. **Median age:** 42.5. **State rank:** 64. **Pop change 1990-2000:** -8.9%.

Income: per capita $17,121; median household $35,013. **Pop below poverty level:** 10%.

Unemployment: 2%. **Median home value:** $48,200. **Median travel time to work:** 13.8 minutes.

POTTAWATOMIE COUNTY

PO Box 187   **Ph:** 785-457-3314
Westmoreland, KS 66549   **Fax:** 785-457-3507
www.pottcounty.org

In northeastern KS, east of Manhattan; organized Feb 20, 1857 (prior to statehood) from Indian lands. **Name Origin:** For the Potawatomie Indian tribe of Algonquian linguistic stock. Name means 'people of the place of the fire.'

Area (sq mi): 862.07 (land 844.24; water 17.83).

Pop: 18,209 (White 94.9%; Black or African American 0.7%; Hispanic or Latino 2.3%; Asian 0.3%; Other 2.7%). **Foreign born:** 1%. **Median age:** 35.9. **State rank:** 30. **Pop change 1990-2000:** +12.9%.

Income: per capita $17,785; median household $40,176. **Pop below poverty level:** 9.7%.

Unemployment: 3.3%. **Median home value:** $81,100. **Median travel time to work:** 22.1 minutes.

PRATT COUNTY

PO Box 885   **Ph:** 620-672-4115
Pratt, KS 67124   **Fax:** 620-672-9541
www.prattcounty.org

In south-central KS, west of Wichita; established Feb 26, 1867. The county was fradulently organized with no bona fide settlers at the time. Official recognition was given in 1879. **Name Origin:** For Lt. Caleb Pratt (?-1861), Union officer killed at battle of Wilson's Creek, MO.

Area (sq mi): 735.76 (land 734.99; water 0.76).

Pop: 9,647 (White 94.3%; Black or African American 1%; Hispanic or Latino 3.1%; Asian 0.5%; Other 3.2%). **Foreign born:** 1.2%. **Median age:** 40.2. **State rank:** 44. **Pop change 1990-2000:** -0.6%.

Income: per capita $17,906; median household $35,529. **Pop below poverty level:** 9.4%.

Unemployment: 2%. **Median home value:** $56,600. **Median travel time to work:** 13.1 minutes.

RAWLINS COUNTY

607 Main St   **Ph:** 785-626-3351
Atwood, KS 67730   **Fax:** 785-626-9019

On the northwestern border of KS; organized Mar 20, 1873 from Kirwin Land District. **Name Origin:** For Gen. John Aaron Rawlins (1831-69), officer in the Civil War and U.S. secretary of war under Grant (1869).

Area (sq mi): 1069.72 (land 1069.62; water 0.11).

Pop: 2,966 (White 98%; Black or African American 0.3%; Hispanic or Latino 0.8%; Asian 0.1%; Other 1.1%). **Foreign born:** 0.4%. **Median age:** 45.4. **State rank:** 94. **Pop change 1990-2000:** -12.9%.

Income: per capita $17,161; median household $32,105. **Pop below poverty level:** 12.5%.

Unemployment: 2.5%. **Median home value:** $41,300. **Median travel time to work:** 14.6 minutes.

RENO COUNTY

206 W 1st St   **Ph:** 620-694-2934
Hutchinson, KS 67501   **Fax:** 620-694-2534
www.rngov.reno.ks.us

In south-central KS, northwest of Wichita; established Feb 26, 1867 from Sedgwick County. **Name Origin:** For Gen. Jesse Lee Reno (1823-62), officer in the Mexican-American War and the Civil War.

Area (sq mi): 1271.25 (land 1254.42; water 16.84).

Pop: 64,790 (White 89.2%; Black or African American 2.9%; Hispanic or Latino 5.7%; Asian 0.4%; Other 5.1%). **Foreign born:** 2%. **Median age:** 38.2. **State rank:** 7. **Pop change 1990-2000:** +3.8%.

Income: per capita $18,520; median household $35,510. **Pop below poverty level:** 10.9%.

Unemployment: 4.3%. **Median home value:** $66,600. **Median travel time to work:** 17.6 minutes.

REPUBLIC COUNTY

1815 M St   **Ph:** 785-527-5691
Belleville, KS 66935   **Fax:** 785-527-2668
www.nckcn.com/repco

On the central northern border of KS, north of Salina; established Feb 27, 1860 (prior to statehood) from Washington and Cloud counties. **Name Origin:** For the Republican River, which first enters KS in this county; named for the valley that was home of the Pawnee Republic, a division of the Pawnee Tribe. Also, possibly for the Pawnee Republic.

Area (sq mi): 720.31 (land 716.38; water 3.93).

Pop: 5,835 (White 98%; Black or African American 0.3%; Hispanic or Latino 0.9%; Asian 0.2%; Other 1%). **Foreign born:** 0.8%. **Median age:** 45.7. **State rank:** 67. **Pop change 1990-2000:** -10%.

Income: per capita $17,433; median household $30,494. **Pop below poverty level:** 9.1%.

Unemployment: 2.3%. **Median home value:** $35,300. **Median travel time to work:** 16.3 minutes.

Please see sample entry on inside front cover for detailed information about the statistics presented with each county listing.

RICE COUNTY

101 W Commercial St
Lyons, KS 67554

Ph: 620-257-2232
Fax: 620-257-3039

In central KS, north of Hutchinson; organized Feb 26, 1867 from Reno County. **Name Origin:** For Gen. Samuel Allen Rice (1828-64), attorney and Union officer in the Civil War.

Area (sq mi): 728.3 (land 726.58; water 1.72).

Pop: 10,761 (White 91.4%; Black or African American 1.2%; Hispanic or Latino 5.6%; Asian 0.3%; Other 3.8%). **Foreign born:** 2.2%. **Median age:** 37.6. **State rank:** 39. **Pop change 1990-2000:** +1.4%.

Income: per capita $16,064; median household $35,671. **Pop below poverty level:** 10.7%.

Unemployment: 3.5%. **Median home value:** $42,900. **Median travel time to work:** 17.1 minutes.

RILEY COUNTY

110 Courthouse Plaza
Manhattan, KS 66502
www.co.riley.ks.us

Ph: 785-537-6300
Fax: 785-537-6394

In east-central KS, northwest of Topeka; organized Aug 25, 1855 (prior to statehood) from Wabaunsee County. **Name Origin:** For Fort Riley, named for Gen. Bennett Riley (1787-1853), professional soldier and territorial governor of CA (1848).

Area (sq mi): 622.11 (land 609.55; water 12.55).

Pop: 62,843 (White 82.7%; Black or African American 6.9%; Hispanic or Latino 4.6%; Asian 3.2%; Other 5.1%). **Foreign born:** 6.1%. **Median age:** 23.9. **State rank:** 8. **Pop change 1990-2000:** -6.4%.

Income: per capita $16,349; median household $32,042. **Pop below poverty level:** 20.6%.

Unemployment: 3.7%. **Median home value:** $93,700. **Median travel time to work:** 14.9 minutes.

ROOKS COUNTY

115 N Walnut St
Stockton, KS 67669
www.rookscounty.net

Ph: 785-425-6391
Fax: 785-425-6015

In north-central KS, north of Hays; established Feb 26, 1867 from Kirwin Land District. **Name Origin:** For John Calvin Rooks (?-1862), soldier who died of wounds received at the Battle of Prairie Grove, AR.

Area (sq mi): 895.36 (land 888.34; water 7.02).

Pop: 5,685 (White 96.5%; Black or African American 1.1%; Hispanic or Latino 1.1%; Asian 0.2%; Other 1.5%). **Foreign born:** 0.2%. **Median age:** 40.5. **State rank:** 68. **Pop change 1990-2000:** -5.9%.

Income: per capita $15,588; median household $30,457. **Pop below poverty level:** 9.8%.

Unemployment: 2.8%. **Median home value:** $38,300. **Median travel time to work:** 15.5 minutes.

RUSH COUNTY

PO Box 220
La Crosse, KS 67548

Ph: 785-222-2731
Fax: 785-222-3559

In central KS, south of Hays; established Feb 26, 1867 from unorganized territory. **Name Origin:** For Capt. Alexander Rush (?-1864), killed in action at Jenkins Ferry, AR.

Area (sq mi): 718.42 (land 718.21; water 0.21).

Pop: 3,551 (White 97.7%; Black or African American 0.3%; Hispanic or Latino 1%; Asian 0.1%; Other 1.1%). **Foreign born:** 0.5%. **Median age:** 44.6. **State rank:** 82. **Pop change 1990-2000:** -7.6%.

Income: per capita $18,033; median household $31,268. **Pop below poverty level:** 9.7%.

Unemployment: 2.3%. **Median home value:** $32,200. **Median travel time to work:** 18 minutes.

RUSSELL COUNTY

PO Box 113
Russell, KS 67665

Ph: 785-483-4641
Fax: 785-483-5725

In central KS, west of Salina; organized Feb 26, 1867 from Ellsworth County. **Name Origin:** For Capt. Avra P. Russell (?-1862), Union army officer who died of wounds received at Prairie Grove, AR.

Area (sq mi): 898.98 (land 884.68; water 14.3).

Pop: 7,370 (White 97%; Black or African American 0.5%; Hispanic or Latino 0.9%; Asian 0.3%; Other 1.6%). **Foreign born:** 0.7%. **Median age:** 44.1. **State rank:** 54. **Pop change 1990-2000:** -5.9%.

Income: per capita $17,073; median household $29,284. **Pop below poverty level:** 12%.

Unemployment: 4.5%. **Median home value:** $41,100. **Median travel time to work:** 15.9 minutes.

SALINE COUNTY

PO Box 5040
Salina, KS 67402
www.co.saline.ks.us

Ph: 785-309-5820
Fax: 785-309-5826

In central KS, southwest of Manhattan; original county; organized Feb 15, 1860 (prior to statehood). **Name Origin:** For the Saline River, which flows through the county.

Area (sq mi): 721.28 (land 719.61; water 1.67).

Pop: 53,597 (White 87%; Black or African American 3.1%; Hispanic or Latino 6%; Asian 1.7%; Other 5.9%). **Foreign born:** 4%. **Median age:** 36.1. **State rank:** 10. **Pop change 1990-2000:** +8.7%.

Income: per capita $19,073; median household $37,308. **Pop below poverty level:** 8.8%.

Unemployment: 3.5%. **Median home value:** $85,300. **Median travel time to work:** 14.8 minutes.

SCOTT COUNTY

303 Court St
Scott City, KS 67871

Ph: 620-872-2420
Fax: 620-872-7145

In western KS, north of Garden City; organized Mar 20, 1873 from Finney County. **Name Origin:** For Gen. Winfield Scott (1786-1866), officer in the War of 1812 and the Mexican-American War, general

All statistics are based on the 2000 Census except the dollar figures given for per capita income, which are based on 1999 estimates.

in chief of the U.S. Army (1841-61) and commander of the Union armies at the beginning of the Civil War.

Area (sq mi): 717.64 (land 717.52; water 0.12).

Pop: 5,120 (White 92.7%; Black or African American 0.1%; Hispanic or Latino 6.3%; Asian 0.1%; Other 4.3%). **Foreign born:** 2.6%. **Median age:** 39.2. **State rank:** 71. **Pop change 1990-2000:** -3.2%.

Income: per capita $20,443; median household $40,534. **Pop below poverty level:** 5.1%.

Unemployment: 1.8%. **Median home value:** $72,100. **Median travel time to work:** 14 minutes.

SEDGWICK COUNTY
525 N Main St Rm 211   **Ph:** 316-383-7666
Wichita, KS 67203   **Fax:** 316-383-7660
www.sedgwick.ks.us

In south-central KS, southeast of Hutchinson; organized Feb 26, 1867 from Butler County. **Name Origin:** For Gen. John Sedgwick (1813-64), Indian fighter and Union officer in the Civil War.

Area (sq mi): 1009.41 (land 999.38; water 10.03).

Pop: 452,869 (White 76.4%; Black or African American 9.1%; Hispanic or Latino 8%; Asian 3.3%; Other 8.2%). **Foreign born:** 6.6%. **Median age:** 33.6. **State rank:** 1. **Pop change 1990-2000:** +12.2%.

Income: per capita $20,907; median household $42,485. **Pop below poverty level:** 9.5%.

Unemployment: 4.2%. **Median home value:** $83,600. **Median travel time to work:** 18.7 minutes.

SEWARD COUNTY
415 N Washington Ave Suite 109   **Ph:** 620-626-3200
Liberal, KS 67901   **Fax:** 620-626-3211

On the southern border of KS, southwest of Dodge City; organized as Godfrey County Mar 26, 1873 from Indian lands; name changed to Seward Jun 3, 1861; changed to Howard 1867. In 1873 the name Seward was given to a new county in the present location. **Name Origin:** For William Henry Seward (1801-72), U.S. secretary of state (1861-69), renowned for negotiating the purchase of Alaska (1867).

Area (sq mi): 640.51 (land 639.52; water 0.99).

Pop: 22,510 (White 49.4%; Black or African American 3.8%; Hispanic or Latino 42.1%; Asian 2.9%; Other 28%). **Foreign born:** 27.4%. **Median age:** 29. **State rank:** 27. **Pop change 1990-2000:** +20.1%.

Income: per capita $15,059; median household $36,752. **Pop below poverty level:** 16.9%.

Unemployment: 3.5%. **Median home value:** $72,400. **Median travel time to work:** 14.8 minutes.

SHAWNEE COUNTY
200 SE 7th St   **Ph:** 785-233-8200
Topeka, KS 66603   **Fax:** 785-291-4959
www.co.shawnee.ks.us

In northeastern KS, west of Lawrence; original county; organized

Aug 25, 1855 (prior to statehood). **Name Origin:** For the Indian tribe of Algonquian linguistic stock. Name means 'southerner.'

Area (sq mi): 556.32 (land 549.82; water 6.5).

Pop: 169,871 (White 79.9%; Black or African American 9%; Hispanic or Latino 7.3%; Asian 1%; Other 7.1%). **Foreign born:** 2.7%. **Median age:** 37.1. **State rank:** 3. **Pop change 1990-2000:** +5.5%.

Income: per capita $20,904; median household $40,988. **Pop below poverty level:** 9.6%.

Unemployment: 4.1%. **Median home value:** $81,600. **Median travel time to work:** 18 minutes.

SHERIDAN COUNTY
PO Box 899   **Ph:** 785-675-3361
Hoxie, KS 67740   **Fax:** 785-675-3487

In northwestern KS, southwest of Norton; organized Mar 20, 1873 from unorganized territory. **Name Origin:** For Gen. Philip Henry Sheridan (1831-88), Union officer during the Civil War and commander in chief of the U.S. army (1883-88).

Area (sq mi): 896.61 (land 896.36; water 0.25).

Pop: 2,813 (White 97.9%; Black or African American 0.1%; Hispanic or Latino 1.5%; Asian 0.1%; Other 1.2%). **Foreign born:** 0.4%. **Median age:** 41.5. **State rank:** 96. **Pop change 1990-2000:** -7.6%.

Income: per capita $16,299; median household $33,547. **Pop below poverty level:** 15.7%.

Unemployment: 1.7%. **Median home value:** $56,000. **Median travel time to work:** 12.8 minutes.

SHERMAN COUNTY
813 Broadway Rm 102   **Ph:** 785-899-4800
Goodland, KS 67735   **Fax:** 785-899-4844

On the northwestern border of KS; organized Mar 20, 1873 from Kirwin Land District. **Name Origin:** For Gen. William Tecumseh Sherman (1820-91), officer in the Mexican-American War and the Civil War, leader of the 'march to the sea' through the Southern states; remembered for the statement 'War is hell.'

Area (sq mi): 1056.01 (land 1055.8; water 0.21).

Pop: 6,760 (White 90%; Black or African American 0.4%; Hispanic or Latino 8.4%; Asian 0.2%; Other 5.6%). **Foreign born:** 1.8%. **Median age:** 37.8. **State rank:** 58. **Pop change 1990-2000:** -2.4%.

Income: per capita $16,761; median household $32,684. **Pop below poverty level:** 12.9%.

Unemployment: 2.4%. **Median home value:** $63,900. **Median travel time to work:** 13.2 minutes.

SMITH COUNTY
218 S Grant St   **Ph:** 785-282-5110
Smith Center, KS 66967   **Fax:** 785-282-6257

On the central northern border of KS; established Feb 26, 1867 from unorganized territory. **Name Origin:** For Maj. J. Nelson Smith (?-1864), Union officer killed at the battle of Little Blue, MO.

Area (sq mi): 896.53 (land 895.43; water 1.1).

Please see sample entry on inside front cover for detailed information about the statistics presented with each county listing.

Pop: 4,536 (White 98.4%; Black or African American 0.1%; Hispanic or Latino 0.7%; Asian 0%; Other 1%). **Foreign born:** 0.6%. **Median age:** 46. **State rank:** 74. **Pop change 1990-2000:** -10.7%.

Income: per capita $14,983; median household $28,486. **Pop below poverty level:** 10.7%.

Unemployment: 1.9%. **Median home value:** $37,400. **Median travel time to work:** 15.4 minutes.

STAFFORD COUNTY
209 N Broadway St   **Ph:** 620-549-3509
Saint John, KS 67576   **Fax:** 620-549-3481
www.staffordcounty.org

In south-central KS, west of Hutchinson; established Feb 26, 1867 from unorganized territory. **Name Origin:** For Capt. Lewis Stafford (?-1863), Union army officer killed at Young's Point, LA.

Area (sq mi): 794.72 (land 792.05; water 2.67).

Pop: 4,789 (White 93%; Black or African American 0.1%; Hispanic or Latino 5.4%; Asian 0.1%; Other 4.8%). **Foreign born:** 3.6%. **Median age:** 41. **State rank:** 72. **Pop change 1990-2000:** -10.7%.

Income: per capita $16,409; median household $31,107. **Pop below poverty level:** 11.8%.

Unemployment: 2.3%. **Median home value:** $34,400. **Median travel time to work:** 17.8 minutes.

STANTON COUNTY
PO Box 190   **Ph:** 620-492-2140
Johnson, KS 67855   **Fax:** 620-492-2688

On the southwestern border of KS, southwest of Garden City; created Mar 6, 1873, later abolished and made part of Hamilton County; in 1887 Stanton County was reorganized from Hamilton County. **Name Origin:** For Edwin McMasters Stanton (1814-69), U.S. Attorney General (1860-61) and U.S. Secretary of War under Abraham Lincoln and Andrew Johnson (1862-68).

Area (sq mi): 680.06 (land 680; water 0.06).

Pop: 2,406 (White 74%; Black or African American 0.6%; Hispanic or Latino 23.7%; Asian 0.2%; Other 14.8%). **Foreign born:** 12.7%. **Median age:** 33.8. **State rank:** 99. **Pop change 1990-2000:** +3.1%.

Income: per capita $18,043; median household $40,172. **Pop below poverty level:** 14.9%.

Unemployment: 2.1%. **Median home value:** $73,400. **Median travel time to work:** 16.2 minutes.

STEVENS COUNTY
200 E 6th St   **Ph:** 620-544-2541
Hugoton, KS 67951   **Fax:** 620-544-4094

On the southwestern border of KS; organized Mar 6, 1873 from Indian lands. **Name Origin:** For Thaddeus Stevens (1792-1868), U.S. representative from PA (1849-53; 1859-68) who strongly opposed slavery.

Area (sq mi): 727.71 (land 727.53; water 0.18).

Pop: 5,463 (White 75.5%; Black or African American 0.9%; Hispanic or Latino 21.7%; Asian 0.2%; Other 15.8%). **Foreign born:** 12%. **Median age:** 33.6. **State rank:** 69. **Pop change 1990-2000:** +8.2%.

Income: per capita $17,814; median household $41,830. **Pop below poverty level:** 10.3%.

Unemployment: 2.8%. **Median home value:** $79,000. **Median travel time to work:** 12.5 minutes.

SUMNER COUNTY
501 N Washington Ave   **Ph:** 620-326-3395
Wellington, KS 67152   **Fax:** 620-326-2116
co.sumner.ks.us

On the central southern border of KS, south of Wichita; organized Feb 26, 1867 from Cowley County. **Name Origin:** For Charles Sumner (1811-74), a founder (1848) of the Free-Soil Party and U.S. senator from MA (1851-74); he was physically beaten on the floor of the Senate for his anti-slavery stand.

Area (sq mi): 1184.78 (land 1181.81; water 2.98).

Pop: 25,946 (White 92.8%; Black or African American 0.7%; Hispanic or Latino 3.6%; Asian 0.2%; Other 4.6%). **Foreign born:** 0.8%. **Median age:** 37.6. **State rank:** 23. **Pop change 1990-2000:** +0.4%.

Income: per capita $18,305; median household $39,415. **Pop below poverty level:** 9.5%.

Unemployment: 4.1%. **Median home value:** $62,100. **Median travel time to work:** 22.6 minutes.

THOMAS COUNTY
300 N Court Ave   **Ph:** 785-462-4500
Colby, KS 67701   **Fax:** 785-462-4512

In northwestern KS; organized Mar 6, 1873 from Kirwin Land District; reorganized Oct 8, 1895 with territory annexed from Logan County. **Name Origin:** For Gen. George Henry Thomas (1816-70), Union commander of the Army of the Cumberland.

Area (sq mi): 1074.9 (land 1074.78; water 0.11).

Pop: 8,180 (White 96.4%; Black or African American 0.4%; Hispanic or Latino 1.8%; Asian 0.3%; Other 2.2%). **Foreign born:** 0.4%. **Median age:** 35.3. **State rank:** 50. **Pop change 1990-2000:** -0.9%.

Income: per capita $19,028; median household $37,034. **Pop below poverty level:** 9.7%.

Unemployment: 2%. **Median home value:** $75,500. **Median travel time to work:** 11.7 minutes.

TREGO COUNTY
216 N Main St   **Ph:** 785-743-5773
WaKeeney, KS 67672   **Fax:** 785-743-2461

In west-central KS, west of Hays; established Feb 26, 1867. **Name Origin:** For Capt. Edgar P. Trego (?-1863), Union army officer killed at Chickamauga, TN.

Area (sq mi): 899.02 (land 888.29; water 10.73).

Pop: 3,319 (White 97.3%; Black or African American 0.2%; Hispanic or Latino 0.8%; Asian 0.5%; Other 1.7%). **Foreign born:** 0.5%. **Median age:** 43.5. **State rank:** 87. **Pop change 1990-2000:** -10.2%.

Income: per capita $16,239; median household $29,677. **Pop below poverty level:** 12.3%.

All statistics are based on the 2000 Census except the dollar figures given for per capita income, which are based on 1999 estimates.

Unemployment: 2.2%. **Median home value:** $47,400. **Median travel time to work:** 16.4 minutes.

UNITED GOVERNMENT OF WYANDOTTE COUNTY/KANSAS CITY

701 N 7th St
Kansas City, KS 66101
www.wycokck.org

Ph: 913-573-5260
Fax: 913-321-0237

On northeastern border of KS, east of Topeka; original county; organized Jan 29, 1859 (prior to statehood). **Name Origin:** For the Wyandotte Indians, a tribe of Iroquoian linguistic stock. Name is thought to mean 'islanders' or 'those who live on a peninsula' from their original home on islands in the Saint Lawrence River and on a peninsula.

Area (sq mi): 155.69 (land 151.39; water 4.3).

Pop: 157,882 (White 51.6%; Black or African American 28.3%; Hispanic or Latino 16%; Asian 1.6%; Other 11.8%). **Foreign born:** 9.5%. **Median age:** 32.5. **State rank:** 4. **Pop change 1990-2000:** -2.5%.

Income: per capita $16,005; median household $33,784. **Pop below poverty level:** 16.5%.

Unemployment: 8.3%. **Median home value:** $54,300. **Median travel time to work:** 21.5 minutes.

WABAUNSEE COUNTY

PO Box 278
Alma, KS 66401

Ph: 785-765-3414
Fax: 785-765-3704

In east-central KS, west of Topeka; organized as Richardson County Aug 30, 1855 (prior to statehood); name changed Feb 11, 1859. **Name Origin:** For Wabaunsee (1760-1845), a Potawatomi chief. Meaning of the name is uncertain: possibly 'dawn of day'; others not sufficiently documented or satisfactory are 'he lives through the winter,' 'daylight,' and 'boggy day.'

Area (sq mi): 799.8 (land 797.38; water 2.41).

Pop: 6,885 (White 96.3%; Black or African American 0.5%; Hispanic or Latino 1.9%; Asian 0.1%; Other 2.2%). **Foreign born:** 0.7%. **Median age:** 39.5. **State rank:** 57. **Pop change 1990-2000:** +4.3%.

Income: per capita $17,704; median household $41,710. **Pop below poverty level:** 7.3%.

Unemployment: 3.6%. **Median home value:** $62,600. **Median travel time to work:** 29.4 minutes.

WALLACE COUNTY

PO Box 70
Sharon Springs, KS 67758

Ph: 785-852-4282
Fax: 785-852-4783

On central western border of KS; organized Mar 2, 1868 from Indian lands. **Name Origin:** For Gen. William Harvey Lamb Wallace (?-1862), Union officer in the Civil War who died of wounds received at Shiloh, TN.

Area (sq mi): 914.05 (land 913.99; water 0.05).

Pop: 1,749 (White 92.8%; Black or African American 0.6%; Hispanic or Latino 4.8%; Asian 0.2%; Other 4.6%). **Foreign born:** 2.2%. **Median age:** 39.5. **State rank:** 104. **Pop change 1990-2000:** -4%.

Income: per capita $17,016; median household $33,000. **Pop below poverty level:** 16.1%.

Unemployment: 3%. **Median home value:** $45,700. **Median travel time to work:** 18.7 minutes.

WASHINGTON COUNTY

214 C St
Washington, KS 66968

Ph: 785-325-2974
Fax: 785-325-2830

On the northern border of KS; northwest of Manhattan; original county; established Feb 20, 1857 (prior to statehood). **Name Origin:** For George Washington (1732-99), American patriot and first U.S. president.

Area (sq mi): 898.84 (land 898.46; water 0.38).

Pop: 6,483 (White 98.4%; Black or African American 0.1%; Hispanic or Latino 0.6%; Asian 0%; Other 0.9%). **Foreign born:** 0.5%. **Median age:** 43.6. **State rank:** 61. **Pop change 1990-2000:** -8.3%.

Income: per capita $15,515; median household $29,363. **Pop below poverty level:** 10.1%.

Unemployment: 3.1%. **Median home value:** $32,200. **Median travel time to work:** 18.6 minutes.

WICHITA COUNTY

PO Box 968
Leoti, KS 67861

Ph: 620-375-2731
Fax: 620-375-4350

In western KS, northwest of Garden City; organized Mar 6, 1873 from Indian lands. **Name Origin:** For the Wichita Indians, one of the more important tribes of Caddoan linguistic stock. Name is translated 'man,' or from Choctaw *owa chito* 'big hunt.'

Area (sq mi): 718.54 (land 718.52; water 0.02).

Pop: 2,531 (White 80%; Black or African American 0.1%; Hispanic or Latino 18.4%; Asian 0.1%; Other 13.6%). **Foreign born:** 8%. **Median age:** 36.7. **State rank:** 98. **Pop change 1990-2000:** -8.2%.

Income: per capita $16,720; median household $33,462. **Pop below poverty level:** 14.8%.

Unemployment: 3.2%. **Median home value:** $55,300. **Median travel time to work:** 13 minutes.

WILSON COUNTY

615 Madison St
Fredonia, KS 66736

Ph: 620-378-2186
Fax: 620-378-3841

In southeastern KS, south of Iola; original county; organized Aug 25, 1855 (prior to statehood). **Name Origin:** For Hiero T. Wilson (1806-?), army officer, settler, and merchant.

Area (sq mi): 574.97 (land 573.81; water 1.17).

Pop: 10,332 (White 95.9%; Black or African American 0.4%; Hispanic or Latino 1.7%; Asian 0.3%; Other 2.6%). **Foreign born:** 0.6%. **Median age:** 40.6. **State rank:** 42. **Pop change 1990-2000:** +0.4%.

Income: per capita $14,910; median household $29,747. **Pop below poverty level:** 11.3%.

Unemployment: 5.4%. **Median home value:** $37,700. **Median travel time to work:** 16.4 minutes.

Please see sample entry on inside front cover for detailed information about the statistics presented with each county listing.

WOODSON COUNTY

105 W Rutledge St
Yates Center, KS 66783
www.woodsoncounty.net

Ph: 620-625-2179
Fax: 620-625-8670

In southeastern KS, east of Wichita; original county; organized Aug 25, 1855 (prior to statehood). **Name Origin:** For Daniel Woodson, secretary of KS Territory (1854-57).

Area (sq mi): 505.45 (land 500.61; water 4.85).

Pop: 3,788 (White 96.2%; Black or African American 0.8%; Hispanic or Latino 1.4%; Asian 0.1%; Other 2.2%). **Foreign born:** 0.8%. **Median age:** 44.1. **State rank:** 80. **Pop change 1990-2000:** -8%.

Income: per capita $14,283; median household $25,335. **Pop below poverty level:** 13.2%.

Unemployment: 7.7%. **Median home value:** $34,300. **Median travel time to work:** 21.7 minutes.

All statistics are based on the 2000 Census except the dollar figures given for per capita income, which are based on 1999 estimates.

KENTUCKY - Counties

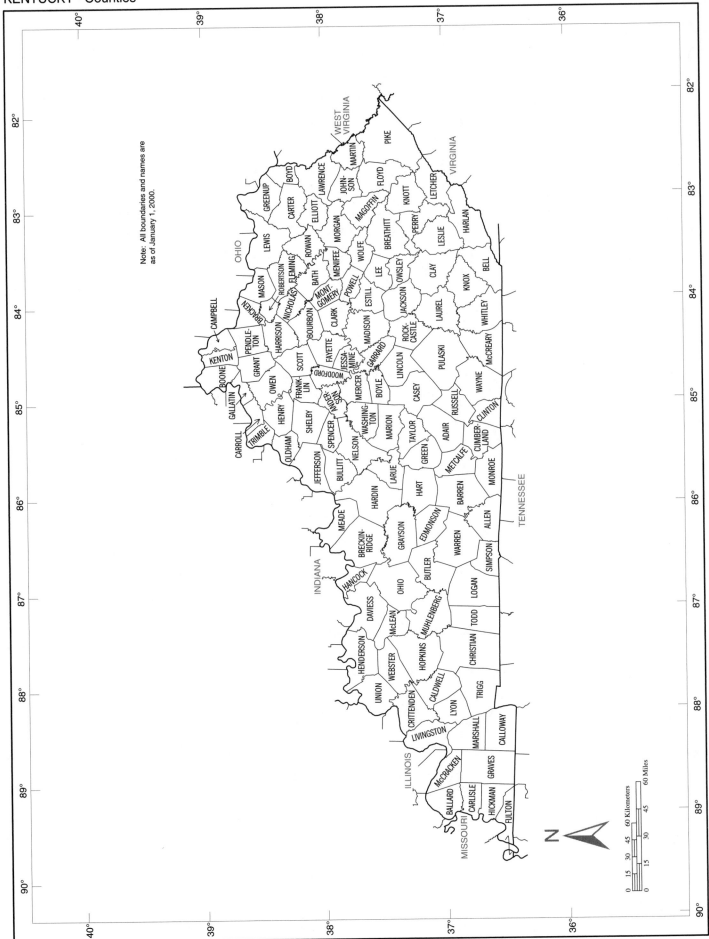

Note: All boundaries and names are as of January 1, 2000.

U.S. Census Bureau, Census 2000

Kentucky

KENTUCKY STATE INFORMATION

www.kentucky.gov   **Ph:** 502-564-2500

Area (sq mi): 40,409.02 (land 39,728.18; water 680.85).

Pop: 4,041,769 (White 89.3%; Black or African American 7.3%; Hispanic or Latino 1.5%; Asian 0.7%; Other 1.9%). **Foreign born:** 2%. **Median age:** 35.9. **Pop change 1990-2000:** +9.7%.

Income: per capita $18,093; median household $33,672. **Pop below poverty level:** 15.8%.

Unemployment: 5.3%. **Median home value:** $86,700. **Median travel time to work:** 23.5 minutes.

ADAIR COUNTY

424 Public Sq   **Ph:** 270-384-2801
Columbia, KY 42728   **Fax:** 270-384-4805
columbia-adaircounty.com

On central southern border of KY, southeast of Bowling Green; established Dec 11, 1802 from Green County. **Name Origin:** For John Adair (1757-1840), governor of KY (1820-24).

Area (sq mi): 412.23 (land 406.84; water 5.39).

Pop: 17,244 (White 95.5%; Black or African American 2.6%; Hispanic or Latino 0.8%; Asian 0.3%; Other 1.2%). **Foreign born:** 0.6%. **Median age:** 36.9. **State rank:** 63. **Pop change 1990-2000:** +12.3%.

Income: per capita $14,931; median household $24,055. **Pop below poverty level:** 24%.

Unemployment: 4.9%. **Median home value:** $60,800. **Median travel time to work:** 25 minutes.

ALLEN COUNTY

201 W Main St Rm 6   **Ph:** 270-237-3706
Scottsville, KY 42164   **Fax:** 270-237-9206

On central southern border of KY, southeast of Bowling Green; organized Jan 11, 1815 from Warren and Barren counties. **Name Origin:** For John Allen, army officer killed in IN territory.

Area (sq mi): 352.04 (land 346.12; water 5.92).

Pop: 17,800 (White 97.2%; Black or African American 1.1%; Hispanic or Latino 0.8%; Asian 0.1%; Other 1.3%). **Foreign born:** 0.8%. **Median age:** 36.2. **State rank:** 60. **Pop change 1990-2000:** +21.7%.

Income: per capita $14,506; median household $31,238. **Pop below poverty level:** 17.3%.

Unemployment: 7.3%. **Median home value:** $69,300. **Median travel time to work:** 26.3 minutes.

ANDERSON COUNTY

151 S Main St   **Ph:** 502-839-3041
Lawrenceburg, KY 40342   **Fax:** 502-839-3043

In north-central KY, west of Lexington; organized Jan 16, 1827 from Franklin, Mercer, and Washington counties. **Name Origin:** For Richard Clough Anderson, Jr. (1788-1826), KY legislator, U.S. representative (1817-21), and U.S. Minister to Colombia (1823).

Area (sq mi): 204.28 (land 202.67; water 1.61).

Pop: 19,111 (White 96%; Black or African American 2.3%; Hispanic or Latino 0.8%; Asian 0.1%; Other 1%). **Foreign born:** 0.9%. **Median age:** 35.5. **State rank:** 56. **Pop change 1990-2000:** +31.2%.

Income: per capita $18,621; median household $45,433. **Pop below poverty level:** 7.5%.

Unemployment: 5.4%. **Median home value:** $89,500. **Median travel time to work:** 26.6 minutes.

BALLARD COUNTY

PO Box 145   **Ph:** 270-335-5168
Wickliffe, KY 42087   **Fax:** 270-335-3081
www.ballardconet.com

On western border, west of Paducah; organized Feb 15, 1842 from McCracken and Hickman counties. **Name Origin:** For Maj. Bland W. Ballard (1759-1853), professional Indian fighter and scout, army officer, and KY legislator.

Area (sq mi): 273.6 (land 251.16; water 22.44).

Pop: 8,286 (White 94.9%; Black or African American 2.9%; Hispanic or Latino 0.6%; Asian 0.2%; Other 1.6%). **Foreign born:** 0.8%. **Median age:** 39.6. **State rank:** 105. **Pop change 1990-2000:** +4.9%.

Income: per capita $19,035; median household $32,130. **Pop below poverty level:** 13.6%.

Unemployment: 7.4%. **Median home value:** $58,800. **Median travel time to work:** 23.7 minutes.

BARREN COUNTY

117 N Public Sq Suite 1A   **Ph:** 270-651-3783
Glasgow, KY 42141   **Fax:** 270-651-1083

In south-central KY, east of Bowling Green; established Feb 20, 1798 from Warren and Green counties. **Name Origin:** Descriptive of the treeless prairie. It is believed the Indians burned off the growth to facilitate buffalo hunting.

Please see sample entry on inside front cover for detailed information about the statistics presented with each county listing.

Area (sq mi): 499.93 (land 490.97; water 8.96).

Pop: 38,033 (White 93.8%; Black or African American 4.1%; Hispanic or Latino 0.9%; Asian 0.4%; Other 1.1%). **Foreign born:** 1.2%. **Median age:** 38. **State rank:** 23. **Pop change 1990-2000:** +11.9%.

Income: per capita $16,816; median household $31,240. **Pop below poverty level:** 15.6%.

Unemployment: 5.5%. **Median home value:** $77,900. **Median travel time to work:** 19.9 minutes.

BATH COUNTY
PO Box 609   **Ph:** 606-674-2613
Owingsville, KY 40360   **Fax:** 606-674-9526

In north-central KY, east of Lexington; organized Jan 15, 1811 from Montgomery County. **Name Origin:** For the hot springs in the area.

Area (sq mi): 283.94 (land 279.46; water 4.48).

Pop: 11,085 (White 96.5%; Black or African American 1.8%; Hispanic or Latino 0.8%; Asian 0%; Other 1.3%). **Foreign born:** 0.7%. **Median age:** 37.4. **State rank:** 95. **Pop change 1990-2000:** +14.4%.

Income: per capita $15,326; median household $26,018. **Pop below poverty level:** 21.9%.

Unemployment: 7.6%. **Median home value:** $65,000. **Median travel time to work:** 28.7 minutes.

BELL COUNTY
PO Box 157   **Ph:** 606-337-6143
Pineville, KY 40977   **Fax:** 606-337-5415

On southeastern border of KY, west of Harlan; organized as Josh Bell County Feb 28, 1867 from Knox and Harlan counties; name shortened 1872. **Name Origin:** For Joshua Fry Bell (1811-70), KY legislator and U.S. representative (1845-47).

Area (sq mi): 361.35 (land 360.77; water 0.58).

Pop: 30,060 (White 95.6%; Black or African American 2.4%; Hispanic or Latino 0.6%; Asian 0.3%; Other 1.1%). **Foreign born:** 0.7%. **Median age:** 37. **State rank:** 36. **Pop change 1990-2000:** -4.6%.

Income: per capita $11,526; median household $19,057. **Pop below poverty level:** 31.1%.

Unemployment: 8.8%. **Median home value:** $52,500. **Median travel time to work:** 24.8 minutes.

BOONE COUNTY
2950 E Washington St   **Ph:** 859-334-3642
Burlington, KY 41005   **Fax:** 859-334-2193
www.boonecountyky.org

In northwestern KY, southwest of Cincinnati, OH; established Dec 13, 1798 from Campbell County. **Name Origin:** For Daniel Boone (1734?-1820), U.S. frontiersman and KY pioneer.

Area (sq mi): 256.96 (land 246.26; water 10.7).

Pop: 85,991 (White 94%; Black or African American 1.5%; Hispanic or Latino 2%; Asian 1.3%; Other 1.9%). **Foreign born:** 3%. **Median age:** 33.4. **State rank:** 8. **Pop change 1990-2000:** +49.3%.

Income: per capita $23,535; median household $53,593. **Pop below poverty level:** 5.6%.

Unemployment: 4.1%. **Median home value:** $131,800. **Median travel time to work:** 24.4 minutes.

BOURBON COUNTY
301 Main St Suite 106   **Ph:** 859-987-2142
Paris, KY 40361   **Fax:** 859-987-5660

In north-central KY, northeast of Lexington; organized May 1, 1786 (prior to statehood) from Fayette County. **Name Origin:** For the French royal family that ruled in France, Spain, and Naples from the latter 1500s until the 1900s.

Area (sq mi): 291.66 (land 291.43; water 0.23).

Pop: 19,360 (White 89.3%; Black or African American 6.9%; Hispanic or Latino 2.6%; Asian 0.1%; Other 2.5%). **Foreign born:** 2%. **Median age:** 37.6. **State rank:** 55. **Pop change 1990-2000:** +0.6%.

Income: per capita $18,335; median household $35,038. **Pop below poverty level:** 14%.

Unemployment: 4.2%. **Median home value:** $84,500. **Median travel time to work:** 25.5 minutes.

BOYD COUNTY
PO Box 523   **Ph:** 606-739-5116
Catlettsburg, KY 41129   **Fax:** 606-739-6357

On eastern border of KY; organized Feb 15, 1860 from Carter, Lawrence, and Greenup counties. **Name Origin:** For Linn Boyd (1800-59), KY legislator, U.S. representative (1835-37; 1839-55), and Speaker of the House (1851-55).

Area (sq mi): 161.82 (land 160.17; water 1.65).

Pop: 49,752 (White 95.1%; Black or African American 2.5%; Hispanic or Latino 1.1%; Asian 0.3%; Other 1.2%). **Foreign born:** 1.1%. **Median age:** 39.7. **State rank:** 16. **Pop change 1990-2000:** -2.7%.

Income: per capita $18,212; median household $32,749. **Pop below poverty level:** 15.5%.

Unemployment: 6.6%. **Median home value:** $68,800. **Median travel time to work:** 20.6 minutes.

BOYLE COUNTY
321 W Main St Rm 123   **Ph:** 859-238-1110
Danville, KY 40422   **Fax:** 859-238-1114
www.danville-ky.com

In central KY, southwest of Lexington; organized Feb 15, 1842 from Lincoln and Mercer counties (having the same county seat as the now-abolished Kentucky County, which was organized in 1776 from Fincastle County, VA). **Name Origin:** For John Boyle (1774-1835), KY legislator, U.S. representative (1803-09), and U.S. judge for District of KY (1826-35).

Area (sq mi): 182.99 (land 181.9; water 1.09).

Pop: 27,697 (White 87%; Black or African American 9.7%; Hispanic or Latino 1.4%; Asian 0.6%; Other 1.9%). **Foreign born:** 1.8%. **Median age:** 36.9. **State rank:** 38. **Pop change 1990-2000:** +8%.

Income: per capita $18,288; median household $35,241. **Pop below poverty level:** 11.9%.

All statistics are based on the 2000 Census except the dollar figures given for per capita income, which are based on 1999 estimates.

Unemployment: 5.1%. **Median home value:** $86,400. **Median travel time to work:** 18.7 minutes.

BRACKEN COUNTY

PO Box 147　　　　　　　　　　　　　**Ph:** 606-735-2952
Brooksville, KY 41004　　　　　　　**Fax:** 606-735-2863

On northeastern border of KY, southeast of Cincinnati, OH; established Dec 14, 1796 from Campbell and Mason counties. **Name Origin:** For two creeks in the county, Big and Little Bracken, named for William Bracken, an early settler.

Area (sq mi): 208.89 (land 203.22; water 5.67).

Pop: 8,279 (White 98.2%; Black or African American 0.6%; Hispanic or Latino 0.5%; Asian 0.1%; Other 0.9%). **Foreign born:** 0.3%. **Median age:** 36.8. **State rank:** 106. **Pop change 1990-2000:** +6.6%.

Income: per capita $16,478; median household $34,823. **Pop below poverty level:** 10.8%.

Unemployment: 4.8%. **Median home value:** $69,000. **Median travel time to work:** 37.4 minutes.

BREATHITT COUNTY

1137 Main St　　　　　　　　　　　　**Ph:** 606-666-3810
Jackson, KY 41339　　　　　　　　　**Fax:** 606-666-3807
www.breathittcounty.com

In southeastern KY; organized Feb 8, 1839 from Estill, Clay, and Perry counties. **Name Origin:** For John Breathitt (1786-1834), KY governor (1832-34).

Area (sq mi): 495.29 (land 495.19; water 0.09).

Pop: 16,100 (White 98.1%; Black or African American 0.4%; Hispanic or Latino 0.7%; Asian 0.3%; Other 0.6%). **Foreign born:** 0.4%. **Median age:** 35.9. **State rank:** 69. **Pop change 1990-2000:** +2.5%.

Income: per capita $11,044; median household $19,155. **Pop below poverty level:** 33.2%.

Unemployment: 10%. **Median home value:** $46,500. **Median travel time to work:** 33.6 minutes.

BRECKINRIDGE COUNTY

PO Box 538　　　　　　　　　　　　　**Ph:** 270-756-2246
Hardinsburg, KY 40143　　　　　　　**Fax:** 270-756-1569

On western border of KY, southwest of Louisville; established Dec 9, 1799 from Hardin County. **Name Origin:** For John Breckinridge (1760-1806), U.S. senator from KY (1801-05) and U.S. attorney general (1805-06).

Area (sq mi): 585.53 (land 572.41; water 13.12).

Pop: 18,648 (White 95.4%; Black or African American 2.9%; Hispanic or Latino 0.7%; Asian 0.1%; Other 1.2%). **Foreign born:** 0.5%. **Median age:** 38.5. **State rank:** 57. **Pop change 1990-2000:** +14.3%.

Income: per capita $15,402; median household $30,554. **Pop below poverty level:** 15.8%.

Unemployment: 8.4%. **Median home value:** $64,600. **Median travel time to work:** 32.7 minutes.

BULLITT COUNTY

PO Box 6　　　　　　　　　　　　　　**Ph:** 502-543-2513
Shepherdsville, KY 40165　　　　　　**Fax:** 502-543-9121
www.bullittcounty.org

On western border of KY, south of Louisville; established Dec 13, 1796 from Jefferson and Nelson counties. **Name Origin:** For Alexander Scott Bullitt (1761-1816), first president of the KY senate (1792-99) and first lieutenant-governor (1800-08).

Area (sq mi): 300.2 (land 299.08; water 1.12).

Pop: 61,236 (White 97.7%; Black or African American 0.4%; Hispanic or Latino 0.6%; Asian 0.3%; Other 1.3%). **Foreign born:** 0.6%. **Median age:** 34.5. **State rank:** 13. **Pop change 1990-2000:** +28.7%.

Income: per capita $18,339; median household $45,106. **Pop below poverty level:** 7.9%.

Unemployment: 4.2%. **Median home value:** $105,100. **Median travel time to work:** 25.9 minutes.

BUTLER COUNTY

PO Box 449　　　　　　　　　　　　　**Ph:** 270-526-5676
Morgantown, KY 42261　　　　　　　**Fax:** 270-526-2658

In western KY, north of Bowling Green; organized Jan 18, 1810 from Logan and Ohio counties. **Name Origin:** For Maj. Gen. Richard Butler (1743-91), officer and Indian commissioner after the American Revolution.

Area (sq mi): 431.52 (land 428.08; water 3.44).

Pop: 13,010 (White 97.5%; Black or African American 0.5%; Hispanic or Latino 1%; Asian 0.2%; Other 1.4%). **Foreign born:** 1.8%. **Median age:** 36.3. **State rank:** 86. **Pop change 1990-2000:** +15.7%.

Income: per capita $14,617; median household $29,405. **Pop below poverty level:** 16%.

Unemployment: 6.9%. **Median home value:** $59,900. **Median travel time to work:** 27.7 minutes.

CALDWELL COUNTY

100 E Market St Rm 3　　　　　　　　**Ph:** 270-365-6754
Princeton, KY 42445　　　　　　　　**Fax:** 270-365-7447

In western KY, northwest of Hopkinsville; organized Jan 31, 1809 from Livingston County. **Name Origin:** For Gen. John Caldwell (?-1804), soldier, member of the KY conventions (1787-89), and legislator.

Area (sq mi): 348.18 (land 346.98; water 1.2).

Pop: 13,060 (White 93.7%; Black or African American 4.8%; Hispanic or Latino 0.6%; Asian 0.2%; Other 1.1%). **Foreign born:** 0.5%. **Median age:** 41.2. **State rank:** 85. **Pop change 1990-2000:** -1.3%.

Income: per capita $16,264; median household $28,686. **Pop below poverty level:** 15.9%.

Unemployment: 5%. **Median home value:** $53,600. **Median travel time to work:** 23.6 minutes.

Please see sample entry on inside front cover for detailed information about the statistics presented with each county listing.

227

CALLOWAY COUNTY

101 S 5th St 2nd Fl   **Ph:** 270-753-3923
Murray, KY 42071   **Fax:** 270-759-9611

On southwestern border of KY, southeast of Paducah; established Dec 19, 1821 from Hickman County. **Name Origin:** For Col. Richard Calloway (?-1780), one of the founders, with Daniel Boone (1734?-1820) of Boonesborough.

Area (sq mi): 410.79 (land 386.25; water 24.53).

Pop: 34,177 (White 92.7%; Black or African American 3.6%; Hispanic or Latino 1.4%; Asian 1.3%; Other 1.6%). **Foreign born:** 2.7%. **Median age:** 34.5. **State rank:** 28. **Pop change 1990-2000:** +11.2%.

Income: per capita $16,566; median household $30,134. **Pop below poverty level:** 16.6%.

Unemployment: 5.2%. **Median home value:** $83,100. **Median travel time to work:** 17.9 minutes.

CAMPBELL COUNTY

340 York St   **Ph:** 859-292-3845
Newport, KY 41071   **Fax:** 859-292-0615
www.campbellcountyky.org

On northeastern tip of KY, southeast of Cincinnati, OH; established Dec 17, 1794 from Scott, Harrison, and Mason counties. **Name Origin:** Probably for George Washington Campbell (1769-1848), U.S. senator from TN (1811-14; 1815-18).

Area (sq mi): 159.43 (land 151.55; water 7.87).

Pop: 88,616 (White 96.1%; Black or African American 1.6%; Hispanic or Latino 0.9%; Asian 0.5%; Other 1.3%). **Foreign born:** 1.4%. **Median age:** 35.2. **State rank:** 7. **Pop change 1990-2000:** +5.7%.

Income: per capita $20,637; median household $41,903. **Pop below poverty level:** 9.3%.

Unemployment: 4.4%. **Median home value:** $101,000. **Median travel time to work:** 23.9 minutes.

CARLISLE COUNTY

PO Box 176   **Ph:** 270-628-3233
Bardwell, KY 42023   **Fax:** 270-628-0191

On western border of KY, southwest of Paducah; organized Apr 3, 1886 from Ballard County. **Name Origin:** For John Griffin Carlisle (1835-1910), KY legislator, U.S. senator (1890-93), and U.S. secretary of the treasury (1893-97).

Area (sq mi): 199.02 (land 192.49; water 6.54).

Pop: 5,351 (White 97.3%; Black or African American 1%; Hispanic or Latino 0.8%; Asian 0.1%; Other 1.2%). **Foreign born:** 0.2%. **Median age:** 39.5. **State rank:** 117. **Pop change 1990-2000:** +2.2%.

Income: per capita $16,276; median household $30,087. **Pop below poverty level:** 13.1%.

Unemployment: 6.1%. **Median home value:** $49,400. **Median travel time to work:** 28.2 minutes.

CARROLL COUNTY

440 Main St Courthouse   **Ph:** 502-732-7005
Carrollton, KY 41008   **Fax:** 502-732-7007

On northwestern border of KY, northeast of Louisville; organized Feb 9, 1838 from Gallatin County. **Name Origin:** For Charles Carroll (1737-1832), signer of the Declaration of Independence, U.S. senator from MD (1789-92), and founder of the Baltimore and Ohio Railroad.

Area (sq mi): 137.27 (land 130.09; water 7.18).

Pop: 10,155 (White 93.4%; Black or African American 1.9%; Hispanic or Latino 3.2%; Asian 0.2%; Other 2.6%). **Foreign born:** 1.9%. **Median age:** 35.9. **State rank:** 98. **Pop change 1990-2000:** +9.3%.

Income: per capita $17,057; median household $35,925. **Pop below poverty level:** 14.9%.

Unemployment: 7%. **Median home value:** $79,900. **Median travel time to work:** 19.5 minutes.

CARTER COUNTY

300 W Main St Rm 232   **Ph:** 606-474-5188
Grayson, KY 41143   **Fax:** 606-474-6883

In northeastern KY, southwest of Ashland; organized Feb 9, 1838 from Greenup and Lawrence counties. **Name Origin:** For Col. William Grayson Carter, a KY state senator.

Area (sq mi): 412.15 (land 410.6; water 1.55).

Pop: 26,889 (White 98.5%; Black or African American 0.1%; Hispanic or Latino 0.6%; Asian 0.1%; Other 0.7%). **Foreign born:** 0.4%. **Median age:** 35.8. **State rank:** 39. **Pop change 1990-2000:** +10.5%.

Income: per capita $13,442; median household $26,427. **Pop below poverty level:** 22.3%.

Unemployment: 14.7%. **Median home value:** $57,100. **Median travel time to work:** 32.8 minutes.

CASEY COUNTY

PO Box 306   **Ph:** 606-787-6154
Liberty, KY 42539

In south-central KY, southwest of Lexington; established Nov 14, 1806 from Lincoln County. **Name Origin:** For Col. William Casey, a pioneer settler from VA.

Area (sq mi): 445.73 (land 445.61; water 0.12).

Pop: 15,447 (White 97.5%; Black or African American 0.3%; Hispanic or Latino 1.3%; Asian 0.1%; Other 1.4%). **Foreign born:** 1.2%. **Median age:** 37.8. **State rank:** 72. **Pop change 1990-2000:** +8.7%.

Income: per capita $12,867; median household $21,580. **Pop below poverty level:** 25.5%.

Unemployment: 8.7%. **Median home value:** $49,500. **Median travel time to work:** 29.5 minutes.

All statistics are based on the 2000 Census except the dollar figures given for per capita income, which are based on 1999 estimates.

CHRISTIAN COUNTY
511 S Main St
Hopkinsville, KY 42240
www.christiancounty.org

Ph: 270-887-4105
Fax: 270-885-5925

On southwestern border of KY, west of Bowling Green; established Dec 13, 1796 from Logan County. **Name Origin:** For William Christian (1743-86), attorney and legislator, brother-in-law of Patrick Henry (1736-99).

Area (sq mi): 724.01 (land 721.32; water 2.69).

Pop: 72,265 (White 68.1%; Black or African American 23.7%; Hispanic or Latino 4.8%; Asian 0.9%; Other 5.4%). **Foreign born:** 2.5%. **Median age:** 27.9. **State rank:** 9. **Pop change 1990-2000:** +4.8%.

Income: per capita $14,611; median household $31,177. **Pop below poverty level:** 15%.

Unemployment: 7.2%. **Median home value:** $72,500. **Median travel time to work:** 17.9 minutes.

CLARK COUNTY
34 S Main St Rm 103
Winchester, KY 40391

Ph: 859-745-0200
Fax: 859-737-5678

In central KY, east of Lexington; established Dec 6, 1792 from Bourbon and Fayette counties. **Name Origin:** For George Rogers Clark (1752-1818), general in the American Revolution and frontiersman in the Northwest Territory.

Area (sq mi): 255.16 (land 254.31; water 0.85).

Pop: 33,144 (White 93%; Black or African American 4.8%; Hispanic or Latino 1.2%; Asian 0.2%; Other 1.4%). **Foreign born:** 1%. **Median age:** 36.8. **State rank:** 31. **Pop change 1990-2000:** +12.4%.

Income: per capita $19,170; median household $39,946. **Pop below poverty level:** 10.6%.

Unemployment: 5.5%. **Median home value:** $93,700. **Median travel time to work:** 25.6 minutes.

CLAY COUNTY
79 Hwy 80 Suite 3
Manchester, KY 40962

Ph: 606-598-3663
Fax: 606-598-4047

In southeastern KY; established Dec 2, 1806 from Madison, Knox, and Floyd counties. **Name Origin:** For Gen. Green Clay (1757-1826), pioneer surveyor, officer in War of 1812, and KY legislator.

Area (sq mi): 471.08 (land 471.01; water 0.07).

Pop: 24,556 (White 93%; Black or African American 4.8%; Hispanic or Latino 1.4%; Asian 0.1%; Other 1.1%). **Foreign born:** 0.7%. **Median age:** 34.6. **State rank:** 43. **Pop change 1990-2000:** +12.9%.

Income: per capita $9,716; median household $16,271. **Pop below poverty level:** 39.7%.

Unemployment: 6.8%. **Median home value:** $43,800. **Median travel time to work:** 31.2 minutes.

CLINTON COUNTY
County Courthouse 100 S Croff St
Albany, KY 42602

Ph: 606-387-5943
Fax: 606-387-5258

On central southern border of KY; organized Feb 20, 1836 from Wayne and Cumberland counties. **Name Origin:** For De Witt Clinton (1769-1828), governor of NY, and supporter of the Erie Canal.

Area (sq mi): 205.54 (land 197.46; water 8.09).

Pop: 9,634 (White 98.1%; Black or African American 0.1%; Hispanic or Latino 1.2%; Asian 0%; Other 0.7%). **Foreign born:** 0.8%. **Median age:** 39. **State rank:** 102. **Pop change 1990-2000:** +5.5%.

Income: per capita $13,286; median household $19,563. **Pop below poverty level:** 25.8%.

Unemployment: 5.1%. **Median home value:** $50,200. **Median travel time to work:** 21 minutes.

CRITTENDEN COUNTY
107 S Main St
Marion, KY 42064

Ph: 270-965-4200
Fax: 270-965-4572

On southwestern border of KY, northeast of Paducah; organized Jan 26, 1842 from Livingston County. **Name Origin:** For John Jordan Crittenden (1787-1863), U.S. senator from KY (1817-19; 1835-41; 1842-48; 1855-61), governor (1848-50), and U.S. Attorney General (1841; 1850-53).

Area (sq mi): 370.95 (land 362.14; water 8.81).

Pop: 9,384 (White 97.9%; Black or African American 0.7%; Hispanic or Latino 0.5%; Asian 0.1%; Other 0.9%). **Foreign born:** 0.4%. **Median age:** 40.1. **State rank:** 103. **Pop change 1990-2000:** +2%.

Income: per capita $15,262; median household $29,060. **Pop below poverty level:** 19.1%.

Unemployment: 10.8%. **Median home value:** $48,300. **Median travel time to work:** 28.5 minutes.

CUMBERLAND COUNTY
601 Courthouse Sq Rm 6
Burkesville, KY 42717

Ph: 270-864-3726
Fax: 270-864-5884

On central southern border of KY; established Dec 14, 1798 from Green County. **Name Origin:** For the Cumberland River that flows through the county.

Area (sq mi): 310.85 (land 305.82; water 5.02).

Pop: 7,147 (White 95%; Black or African American 3.4%; Hispanic or Latino 0.6%; Asian 0%; Other 1.3%). **Foreign born:** 0.3%. **Median age:** 40.1. **State rank:** 112. **Pop change 1990-2000:** +5.4%.

Income: per capita $12,643; median household $21,572. **Pop below poverty level:** 23.8%.

Unemployment: 7%. **Median home value:** $50,300. **Median travel time to work:** 24.3 minutes.

DAVIESS COUNTY
PO Box 609
Owensboro, KY 42302
www.daviessky.org

Ph: 270-685-8434
Fax: 270-686-7111

On northwestern border of KY, east of Henderson; organized Jan 14, 1815 from Ohio County. **Name Origin:** For Joseph Hamilton Davies (1774-1811), VA soldier and jurist, unsuccessful in his attempt to indict Aaron Burr (1756-1836) for treason.

Area (sq mi): 476.27 (land 462.39; water 13.88).

Please see sample entry on inside front cover for detailed information about the statistics presented with each county listing.

Pop: 91,545 (White 93.2%; Black or African American 4.3%; Hispanic or Latino 0.9%; Asian 0.4%; Other 1.4%). **Foreign born:** 1%. **Median age:** 36.8. **State rank:** 6. **Pop change 1990-2000:** +5%.

Income: per capita $18,739; median household $36,813. **Pop below poverty level:** 12.3%.

Unemployment: 5.4%. **Median home value:** $81,800. **Median travel time to work:** 19.5 minutes.

EDMONSON COUNTY

PO Box 830   **Ph:** 270-597-2624
Brownsville, KY 42210   **Fax:** 270-597-9714

In central KY, northeast of Bowling Green; organized 1825 from Hart, Warren, and Grayson counties. **Name Origin:** For Capt. John Edmonson (1764-1813), an American officer in the War of 1812, killed at the Frenchtown Battle on the River Raisin, MI.

Area (sq mi): 308.01 (land 302.62; water 5.39).

Pop: 11,644 (White 98%; Black or African American 0.6%; Hispanic or Latino 0.6%; Asian 0.1%; Other 1%). **Foreign born:** 0.4%. **Median age:** 38. **State rank:** 93. **Pop change 1990-2000:** +12.4%.

Income: per capita $14,480; median household $25,413. **Pop below poverty level:** 18.4%.

Unemployment: 6.2%. **Median home value:** $63,700. **Median travel time to work:** 33.9 minutes.

ELLIOTT COUNTY

PO Box 788   **Ph:** 606-738-5238
Sandy Hook, KY 41171   **Fax:** 606-738-6962

In eastern KY, southwest of Ashland; organized Jan 26, 1869 from Lawrence, Morgan, and Carter counties. **Name Origin:** For John Milton Elliott (1820-79), KY legislator, U.S. representative (1853-59), and justice of the KY Court of Appeals (1876-79). Some claim his father, John Lisle Elliott, a KY legislator.

Area (sq mi): 235.2 (land 233.96; water 1.24).

Pop: 6,748 (White 98.6%; Black or African American 0%; Hispanic or Latino 0.6%; Asian 0%; Other 0.9%). **Foreign born:** 0.2%. **Median age:** 37. **State rank:** 115. **Pop change 1990-2000:** +4.5%.

Income: per capita $12,067; median household $21,014. **Pop below poverty level:** 25.9%.

Unemployment: 12.4%. **Median home value:** $54,800. **Median travel time to work:** 48.7 minutes.

ESTILL COUNTY

PO Box 59   **Ph:** 606-723-5156
Irvine, KY 403361098   **Fax:** 606-723-5108

In east-central KY, southeast of Lexington; organized Jan 27, 1808 from Madison and Clark counties. **Name Origin:** For Capt. James Estill (1750-92), soldier and early pioneer who established Fort Estill in 1781.

Area (sq mi): 255.7 (land 253.93; water 1.76).

Pop: 15,307 (White 98.7%; Black or African American 0.1%; Hispanic or Latino 0.5%; Asian 0%; Other 0.8%). **Foreign born:** 0.3%. **Median age:** 36.7. **State rank:** 73. **Pop change 1990-2000:** +4.7%.

Income: per capita $12,285; median household $23,318. **Pop below poverty level:** 26.4%.

Unemployment: 6.8%. **Median home value:** $50,200. **Median travel time to work:** 34.9 minutes.

FAYETTE COUNTY

162 E Main St   **Ph:** 859-253-3344
Lexington, KY 40507   **Fax:** 859-231-9619
www.lfucg.com

In central KY, south of Cincinnati, OH; organized May 1, 1780 (prior to statehood) from Kentucky County. In 1974 the county and its seat were combined and given an 'urban-county government.' **Name Origin:** For the Marquis de Lafayette (1757-1834), French statesman and soldier who fought with the Americans during the Revolutionary War.

Area (sq mi): 285.52 (land 284.52; water 1).

Pop: 260,512 (White 79.1%; Black or African American 13.5%; Hispanic or Latino 3.3%; Asian 2.5%; Other 3%). **Foreign born:** 5.9%. **Median age:** 33. **State rank:** 2. **Pop change 1990-2000:** +15.6%.

Income: per capita $23,109; median household $39,813. **Pop below poverty level:** 12.9%.

Unemployment: 3%. **Median home value:** $110,800. **Median travel time to work:** 19.3 minutes.

FLEMING COUNTY

201 Court Sq   **Ph:** 606-845-7571
Flemingsburg, KY 41041   **Fax:** 606-845-1312
www.flemingcounty.org

In northeastern KY, northeast of Lexington; organized Feb 10, 1798 from Mason County. **Name Origin:** For Col. John Fleming (1760-94), early settler and army officer.

Area (sq mi): 351.47 (land 350.84; water 0.62).

Pop: 13,792 (White 96.9%; Black or African American 1.4%; Hispanic or Latino 0.7%; Asian 0.2%; Other 1.1%). **Foreign born:** 0.2%. **Median age:** 36.3. **State rank:** 80. **Pop change 1990-2000:** +12.2%.

Income: per capita $14,214; median household $27,990. **Pop below poverty level:** 18.6%.

Unemployment: 5.3%. **Median home value:** $63,600. **Median travel time to work:** 26 minutes.

FLOYD COUNTY

PO Box 1089   **Ph:** 606-886-3816
Prestonsburg, KY 41653   **Fax:** 606-886-8089
www.kymtnnet.org/floyd.html

In southeastern KY; established Dec 13, 1799 from Fleming, Mason, and Montgomery counties. **Name Origin:** For John Floyd (1783-1837), governor of VA (1830-34).

Area (sq mi): 395.46 (land 394.29; water 1.16).

Pop: 42,441 (White 97.3%; Black or African American 1.3%; Hispanic or Latino 0.6%; Asian 0.2%; Other 0.7%). **Foreign born:** 0.6%. **Median age:** 36.7. **State rank:** 21. **Pop change 1990-2000:** -2.6%.

Income: per capita $12,442; median household $21,168. **Pop below poverty level:** 30.3%.

All statistics are based on the 2000 Census except the dollar figures given for per capita income, which are based on 1999 estimates.

Unemployment: 6.4%. **Median home value:** $53,100. **Median travel time to work:** 25.8 minutes.

FRANKLIN COUNTY
PO Box 338   **Ph:** 502-875-8702
Frankfort, KY 40602   **Fax:** 502-875-8718

In north-central KY, northwest of Lexington; established Dec 7, 1794 from Woodford, Mercer, and Shelby counties. **Name Origin:** For Benjamin Franklin (1706-90), U.S. patriot, diplomat, and statesman.

Area (sq mi): 212.11 (land 210.46; water 1.65).

Pop: 47,687 (White 87.4%; Black or African American 9.4%; Hispanic or Latino 1.1%; Asian 0.7%; Other 1.9%). **Foreign born:** 1.9%. **Median age:** 37. **State rank:** 17. **Pop change 1990-2000:** +8.9%.

Income: per capita $21,229; median household $40,011. **Pop below poverty level:** 10.7%.

Unemployment: 2.9%. **Median home value:** $91,600. **Median travel time to work:** 18.2 minutes.

FULTON COUNTY
PO Box 126   **Ph:** 270-236-2727
Hickman, KY 42050   **Fax:** 270-236-2522

On southwestern border of KY, southwest of Paducah; organized Jan 15, 1845 from Hickman County. **Name Origin:** For Robert Fulton (1765-1815), builder of the *Clermont*, the first commercially successful steamboat.

Area (sq mi): 230.55 (land 208.95; water 21.6).

Pop: 7,752 (White 74.8%; Black or African American 23.2%; Hispanic or Latino 0.7%; Asian 0.3%; Other 1.3%). **Foreign born:** 0.4%. **Median age:** 38.5. **State rank:** 111. **Pop change 1990-2000:** -6.3%.

Income: per capita $14,309; median household $24,382. **Pop below poverty level:** 23.1%.

Unemployment: 7.2%. **Median home value:** $40,500. **Median travel time to work:** 18.6 minutes.

GALLATIN COUNTY
PO Box 1309   **Ph:** 859-567-5411
Warsaw, KY 41095   **Fax:** 859-567-5444

On northwestern border of KY, southwest of Cincinnati, OH; established Dec 4, 1798 from Franklin and Shelby counties. **Name Origin:** For Albert Gallatin (1761-1849), Swiss-born U.S. statesman and diplomat, and U.S. secretary of the treasury (1801-14).

Area (sq mi): 104.67 (land 98.81; water 5.87).

Pop: 7,870 (White 96.1%; Black or African American 1.6%; Hispanic or Latino 1%; Asian 0.2%; Other 1.5%). **Foreign born:** 0.4%. **Median age:** 34.6. **State rank:** 110. **Pop change 1990-2000:** +45.9%.

Income: per capita $16,416; median household $36,422. **Pop below poverty level:** 13.4%.

Unemployment: 5.8%. **Median home value:** $87,100. **Median travel time to work:** 30.3 minutes.

GARRARD COUNTY
15 Public Sq County Courthouse   **Ph:** 859-792-3071
Lancaster, KY 40444   **Fax:** 859-792-6751

In central KY, south of Lexington; organized Jun 1, 1797 from Madison, Lincoln, and Mercer counties. **Name Origin:** For James Garrard (1749-1822), KY legislator and governor (1796-1804).

Area (sq mi): 233.88 (land 231.21; water 2.67).

Pop: 14,792 (White 95%; Black or African American 3.1%; Hispanic or Latino 1.3%; Asian 0%; Other 1.1%). **Foreign born:** 1.6%. **Median age:** 37.1. **State rank:** 75. **Pop change 1990-2000:** +27.7%.

Income: per capita $16,915; median household $34,284. **Pop below poverty level:** 14.7%.

Unemployment: 4.5%. **Median home value:** $81,300. **Median travel time to work:** 31.8 minutes.

GRANT COUNTY
101 N Main St Rm 15   **Ph:** 859-824-3321
Williamstown, KY 41097   **Fax:** 859-824-3367
www.grantco.org

In north-central KY, south of Covington; organized Feb 12, 1820 from Pendleton County. **Name Origin:** For a member of the locally prominent Grant family, which included John Grant (1754-1826), pioneer salt producer; his brother, Samuel (1762-89), surveyor, and another brother, Squire (1769-1833), a surveyor and KY legislator.

Area (sq mi): 260.79 (land 259.93; water 0.86).

Pop: 22,384 (White 97.7%; Black or African American 0.3%; Hispanic or Latino 1%; Asian 0.3%; Other 1.1%). **Foreign born:** 1%. **Median age:** 32.7. **State rank:** 51. **Pop change 1990-2000:** +42.2%.

Income: per capita $16,776; median household $38,438. **Pop below poverty level:** 11.1%.

Unemployment: 6.7%. **Median home value:** $93,100. **Median travel time to work:** 31.5 minutes.

GRAVES COUNTY
County Courthouse 101 E South St Suite 2   **Ph:** 270-247-1676
Mayfield, KY 42066   **Fax:** 270-247-1274

On southwestern border of KY, south of Paducah; established Dec 19, 1823 from Hickman County. **Name Origin:** For Col. Benjamin Franklin Graves (1771-1813), an officer during the War of 1812 killed at the Frenchtown Battle on the River Raisin, MI.

Area (sq mi): 556.46 (land 555.59; water 0.87).

Pop: 37,028 (White 91.7%; Black or African American 4.4%; Hispanic or Latino 2.4%; Asian 0.2%; Other 2.6%). **Foreign born:** 2.1%. **Median age:** 38.1. **State rank:** 25. **Pop change 1990-2000:** +10.4%.

Income: per capita $16,834; median household $30,874. **Pop below poverty level:** 16.4%.

Unemployment: 7.3%. **Median home value:** $63,600. **Median travel time to work:** 23.3 minutes.

GRAYSON COUNTY
10 Public Sq   **Ph:** 270-259-3201
Leitchfield, KY 42754   **Fax:** 270-259-9264

In west-central KY, north of Bowling Green; organized Jan 25,

Please see sample entry on inside front cover for detailed information about the statistics presented with each county listing.

231

1810 from Hardin and Ohio counties. **Name Origin:** For Col. Robert Grayson, aide to George Washington (1732-99).

Area (sq mi): 510.85 (land 503.68; water 7.17).

Pop: 24,053 (White 97.7%; Black or African American 0.5%; Hispanic or Latino 0.8%; Asian 0.1%; Other 1.1%). **Foreign born:** 0.6%. **Median age:** 37.5. **State rank:** 44. **Pop change 1990-2000:** +14.3%.

Income: per capita $14,759; median household $27,639. **Pop below poverty level:** 18.1%.

Unemployment: 8.8%. **Median home value:** $65,600. **Median travel time to work:** 27.3 minutes.

GREEN COUNTY
203 W Court St   **Ph:** 270-932-5386
Greensburg, KY 42743   **Fax:** 270-932-6241

In south-central KY, southwest of Lexington; established Dec 20, 1792 from Lincoln and Nelson counties. **Name Origin:** For Gen. Nathanael Greene (1742-86), Revolutionary War officer and quartermaster general (1778-80). The missing e not explained.

Area (sq mi): 288.78 (land 288.66; water 0.12).

Pop: 11,518 (White 95.5%; Black or African American 2.6%; Hispanic or Latino 0.9%; Asian 0.1%; Other 1.1%). **Foreign born:** 0.7%. **Median age:** 40. **State rank:** 94. **Pop change 1990-2000:** +11.1%.

Income: per capita $16,107; median household $25,463. **Pop below poverty level:** 18.4%.

Unemployment: 7.6%. **Median home value:** $52,500. **Median travel time to work:** 29.9 minutes.

GREENUP COUNTY
PO Box 686   **Ph:** 606-473-7394
Greenup, KY 41144   **Fax:** 606-473-5354

In northeastern KY, northwest of Ashland; established Dec 12, 1803 from Mason County. **Name Origin:** For Col. Christopher Greenup (c.1750-1818), U.S. representative from KY (1792-97) and governor (1804-08).

Area (sq mi): 354.51 (land 346.11; water 8.41).

Pop: 36,891 (White 97.7%; Black or African American 0.6%; Hispanic or Latino 0.6%; Asian 0.4%; Other 0.9%). **Foreign born:** 0.6%. **Median age:** 39.2. **State rank:** 26. **Pop change 1990-2000:** +0.4%.

Income: per capita $17,137; median household $32,142. **Pop below poverty level:** 14.1%.

Unemployment: 6%. **Median home value:** $67,500. **Median travel time to work:** 25.3 minutes.

HANCOCK COUNTY
PO Box 146   **Ph:** 270-927-6117
Hawesville, KY 42348   **Fax:** 270-927-8639

On northwestern border of KY, east of Owensboro; organized Jan 3, 1829 from Breckinridge, Ohio, and Daviess counties. **Name Origin:** For John Hancock (1737-93), noted signer of the Declaration of Independence, governor of MA (1780-85; 1787-93), and statesman.

Area (sq mi): 198.92 (land 188.8; water 10.12).

Pop: 8,392 (White 97.4%; Black or African American 0.8%; Hispanic or Latino 0.8%; Asian 0.2%; Other 1.1%). **Foreign born:** 0.8%. **Median age:** 35.9. **State rank:** 104. **Pop change 1990-2000:** +6.7%.

Income: per capita $16,623; median household $36,914. **Pop below poverty level:** 13.6%.

Unemployment: 7.5%. **Median home value:** $71,800. **Median travel time to work:** 22.8 minutes.

HARDIN COUNTY
PO Box 1030   **Ph:** 270-765-2171
Elizabethtown, KY 42702   **Fax:** 270-769-2682

In north-central KY, southeast of Louisville; established Dec 15, 1792 from Nelson County. **Name Origin:** For Gen. John Hardin (1753-92), Revolutionary War officer and Indian fighter with George Rogers Clark (1752-1818) in the trans-Ohio campaigns; killed while on a peace mission to the Miami Indians.

Area (sq mi): 629.86 (land 627.98; water 1.88).

Pop: 94,174 (White 80.5%; Black or African American 11.9%; Hispanic or Latino 3.4%; Asian 1.8%; Other 4.3%). **Foreign born:** 4.5%. **Median age:** 33.5. **State rank:** 4. **Pop change 1990-2000:** +5.5%.

Income: per capita $17,487; median household $37,744. **Pop below poverty level:** 10%.

Unemployment: 6.4%. **Median home value:** $88,300. **Median travel time to work:** 23 minutes.

HARLAN COUNTY
PO Box 670   **Ph:** 606-573-3636
Harlan, KY 40831   **Fax:** 606-573-0064

On the southeastern border of KY; organized Jan 28, 1819 from Floyd and Knox counties. **Name Origin:** For Maj. Silas Harlan (?-1782), an officer in the Revolutionary War.

Area (sq mi): 467.97 (land 467.2; water 0.78).

Pop: 33,202 (White 95.1%; Black or African American 2.6%; Hispanic or Latino 0.7%; Asian 0.3%; Other 1.6%). **Foreign born:** 0.6%. **Median age:** 37.8. **State rank:** 30. **Pop change 1990-2000:** -9.2%.

Income: per capita $11,585; median household $18,665. **Pop below poverty level:** 32.5%.

Unemployment: 8.7%. **Median home value:** $43,000. **Median travel time to work:** 27 minutes.

HARRISON COUNTY
313 Oddville Ave   **Ph:** 859-234-7130
Cynthiana, KY 41031   **Fax:** 859-234-8049

In north-central KY, south of Covington; established Dec 21, 1793 from Bourbon and Scott counties. **Name Origin:** For Col. Benjamin Harrison, a Bourbon County representative in the KY legislature when the county was formed in 1793.

Area (sq mi): 309.88 (land 309.68; water 0.2).

Pop: 17,983 (White 95.2%; Black or African American 2.5%; Hispanic or Latino 1.2%; Asian 0.1%; Other 1.7%). **Foreign born:**

1.2%. **Median age:** 37.1. **State rank:** 59. **Pop change 1990-2000:** +10.7%.

Income: per capita $17,478; median household $36,210. **Pop below poverty level:** 12%.

Unemployment: 7.2%. **Median home value:** $83,100. **Median travel time to work:** 26.9 minutes.

HART COUNTY

PO Box 277
Munfordville, KY 42765
www.hartcounty.com

Ph: 270-524-2751
Fax: 270-524-0458

In central KY, northeast of Bowling Green; organized Jan 28, 1819 from Hardin and Barren counties. **Name Origin:** For Nathaniel G.T. Hart (1784-1813), lawyer, merchant, and officer in the War of 1812.

Area (sq mi): 417.91 (land 415.93; water 1.98).

Pop: 17,445 (White 92%; Black or African American 6.2%; Hispanic or Latino 0.9%; Asian 0.1%; Other 1.1%). **Foreign born:** 0.6%. **Median age:** 36.9. **State rank:** 62. **Pop change 1990-2000:** +17.2%.

Income: per capita $13,495; median household $25,378. **Pop below poverty level:** 22.4%.

Unemployment: 5.7%. **Median home value:** $60,100. **Median travel time to work:** 26.6 minutes.

HENDERSON COUNTY

PO Box 374
Henderson, KY 42419
www.go-henderson.com

Ph: 270-826-3906
Fax: 270-826-9677

On the northwestern border of KY, west of Owensboro; established Dec 21, 1798 from Christian County. **Name Origin:** For Richard Henderson (1734-85), who backed Daniel Boone's (c.1734-1820) explorations and founded the Transylvania Company.

Area (sq mi): 467.24 (land 440.12; water 27.11).

Pop: 44,829 (White 90.7%; Black or African American 7.1%; Hispanic or Latino 1%; Asian 0.3%; Other 1.5%). **Foreign born:** 1.1%. **Median age:** 37.2. **State rank:** 20. **Pop change 1990-2000:** +4.1%.

Income: per capita $18,470; median household $35,892. **Pop below poverty level:** 12.3%.

Unemployment: 5.7%. **Median home value:** $76,600. **Median travel time to work:** 19.8 minutes.

HENRY COUNTY

PO Box 615
New Castle, KY 40050

Ph: 502-845-5705
Fax: 502-845-5708

In northwestern KY, northeast of Louisville; established Dec 14, 1798 from Shelby County. **Name Origin:** For Patrick Henry (1736-99), patriot, governor of VA (1776-79; 1784-86), and statesman, famous for proclaiming, 'Give me liberty or give me death.'

Area (sq mi): 291.11 (land 289.32; water 1.79).

Pop: 15,060 (White 93.2%; Black or African American 3.3%; Hispanic or Latino 2.3%; Asian 0.3%; Other 2.4%). **Foreign born:** 1.4%. **Median age:** 37.3. **State rank:** 74. **Pop change 1990-2000:** +17.4%.

Income: per capita $17,846; median household $37,263. **Pop below poverty level:** 13.7%.

Unemployment: 4.4%. **Median home value:** $82,100. **Median travel time to work:** 30.9 minutes.

HICKMAN COUNTY

110 E Clay St County Courthouse
Clinton, KY 42031

Ph: 270-653-2131
Fax: 270-653-4248

On southwestern border of KY, southwest of Paducah; established Dec 19, 1821 from Caldwell and Livingston counties. **Name Origin:** For Capt. Paschal Hickman (?-1813), Army officer. The county comprised the entire KY portion of the Jackson Purchase, bought from the Chickasaw Indians in 1818.

Area (sq mi): 252.94 (land 244.44; water 8.49).

Pop: 5,262 (White 87.7%; Black or African American 9.9%; Hispanic or Latino 1%; Asian 0.1%; Other 1.7%). **Foreign born:** 0.6%. **Median age:** 40.9. **State rank:** 118. **Pop change 1990-2000:** -5.5%.

Income: per capita $17,279; median household $31,615. **Pop below poverty level:** 17.4%.

Unemployment: 6.2%. **Median home value:** $49,200. **Median travel time to work:** 24.2 minutes.

HOPKINS COUNTY

10 S Main St
Madisonville, KY 42431

Ph: 270-821-7361
Fax: 270-825-7000

In western KY, south of Henderson; established Dec 9, 1806 from Henderson County. **Name Origin:** For Gen. Samuel Hopkins (1753-1819), officer in the American Revolution and War of 1812, KY legislator, and US. representative (1813-15).

Area (sq mi): 554.23 (land 550.56; water 3.67).

Pop: 46,519 (White 91.5%; Black or African American 6.2%; Hispanic or Latino 0.9%; Asian 0.3%; Other 1.5%). **Foreign born:** 0.6%. **Median age:** 38.3. **State rank:** 18. **Pop change 1990-2000:** +0.9%.

Income: per capita $17,382; median household $30,868. **Pop below poverty level:** 16.5%.

Unemployment: 7%. **Median home value:** $57,200. **Median travel time to work:** 22 minutes.

JACKSON COUNTY

PO Box 700
McKee, KY 40447

Ph: 606-287-7800
Fax: 606-287-4505

In south-central KY, southeast of Lexington; organized Feb 2, 1858 from Madison, Owsley, Estill, Laurel, Clay, and Rockcastle counties. **Name Origin:** For Andrew Jackson (1767-1845), seventh U.S. president.

Area (sq mi): 346.57 (land 346.33; water 0.24).

Pop: 13,495 (White 98.7%; Black or African American 0.1%; Hispanic or Latino 0.5%; Asian 0%; Other 0.7%). **Foreign born:** 0.4%. **Median age:** 34.9. **State rank:** 81. **Pop change 1990-2000:** +12.9%.

Income: per capita $10,711; median household $20,177. **Pop below poverty level:** 30.2%.

Unemployment: 7%. **Median home value:** $48,300. **Median travel time to work:** 35 minutes.

Please see sample entry on inside front cover for detailed information about the statistics presented with each county listing.

JEFFERSON COUNTY
527 W Jefferson St
Louisville, KY 40202
www.co.jefferson.ky.us

Ph: 502-574-5700
Fax: 502-574-5566

On the northwestern border of KY, west of Lexington; organized May 1, 1780 (prior to statehood) from Kentucky County. **Name Origin:** For Thomas Jefferson (1743-1826), U.S. patriot and statesman; third U.S. president.

Area (sq mi): 398.58 (land 385.09; water 13.49).

Pop: 693,604 (White 76.4%; Black or African American 18.9%; Hispanic or Latino 1.8%; Asian 1.4%; Other 2.3%). **Foreign born:** 3.4%. **Median age:** 36.7. **State rank:** 1. **Pop change 1990-2000:** +4.3%.

Income: per capita $22,352; median household $39,457. **Pop below poverty level:** 12.4%.

Unemployment: 4.8%. **Median home value:** $103,000. **Median travel time to work:** 21.9 minutes.

JESSAMINE COUNTY
101 N Main St
Nicholasville, KY 40356

Ph: 859-885-4161
Fax: 859-885-5837

In central KY, south of Lexington; established Dec 19, 1798 from Fayette County. **Name Origin:** For the Jessamine Creek and the jasmine (jessamine) flowers on its banks. The legend that it was named for Jessamine Douglass, daughter of an early settler, is baseless.

Area (sq mi): 174.45 (land 173.13; water 1.32).

Pop: 39,041 (White 93.7%; Black or African American 3.1%; Hispanic or Latino 1.3%; Asian 0.6%; Other 1.8%). **Foreign born:** 1.8%. **Median age:** 32.9. **State rank:** 22. **Pop change 1990-2000:** +28%.

Income: per capita $18,842; median household $40,096. **Pop below poverty level:** 10.5%.

Unemployment: 2.8%. **Median home value:** $102,100. **Median travel time to work:** 24.1 minutes.

JOHNSON COUNTY
230 Court St
Paintsville, KY 41240

Ph: 606-789-2557
Fax: 606-789-2559

In eastern KY, south of Ashland; organized Feb 2, 1843 from Lawrence, Floyd, and Morgan counties. **Name Origin:** For Richard Mentor Johnson (1780-1850), U.S. vice president under Van Buren (1837-41).

Area (sq mi): 263.94 (land 261.54; water 2.4).

Pop: 23,445 (White 98.2%; Black or African American 0.3%; Hispanic or Latino 0.6%; Asian 0.3%; Other 0.8%). **Foreign born:** 0.5%. **Median age:** 37.4. **State rank:** 45. **Pop change 1990-2000:** +0.8%.

Income: per capita $14,051; median household $24,911. **Pop below poverty level:** 26.6%.

Unemployment: 6.2%. **Median home value:** $64,700. **Median travel time to work:** 26.2 minutes.

KENTON COUNTY
PO Box 1109
Covington, KY 41012
www.kentoncounty.org

Ph: 859-491-0702

On central northern border of KY, south of Cincinnati, OH; organized Jan 29, 1840 from Campbell County. **Name Origin:** For Simon Kenton (1755-1836), KY scout and Indian fighter.

Area (sq mi): 164.38 (land 161.97; water 2.42).

Pop: 151,464 (White 93.3%; Black or African American 3.8%; Hispanic or Latino 1.1%; Asian 0.6%; Other 1.5%). **Foreign born:** 1.6%. **Median age:** 34.5. **State rank:** 3. **Pop change 1990-2000:** +6.6%.

Income: per capita $22,085; median household $43,906. **Pop below poverty level:** 9%.

Unemployment: 4.6%. **Median home value:** $105,600. **Median travel time to work:** 22.9 minutes.

KNOTT COUNTY
PO Box 446
Hindman, KY 41822

Ph: 606-785-5651
Fax: 606-785-0996

In southeastern KY; organized May 5, 1884 from Floyd, Letcher, Perry, and Breathitt counties. **Name Origin:** For James Proctor Knott (1830-1911), KY legislator, U.S. representative (1867-71; 1875-83), and governor (1883-87).

Area (sq mi): 353.01 (land 352.19; water 0.82).

Pop: 17,649 (White 97.8%; Black or African American 0.7%; Hispanic or Latino 0.6%; Asian 0.2%; Other 0.8%). **Foreign born:** 0.4%. **Median age:** 35.9. **State rank:** 61. **Pop change 1990-2000:** -1.4%.

Income: per capita $11,297; median household $20,373. **Pop below poverty level:** 31.1%.

Unemployment: 6.1%. **Median home value:** $46,500. **Median travel time to work:** 29.4 minutes.

KNOX COUNTY
PO Box 173
Barbourville, KY 40906

Ph: 606-546-8915
Fax: 606-546-6196

In southeastern KY, west of Harlan; established Dec 19, 1799 from Lincoln County. **Name Origin:** For Gen. Henry Knox (1750-1806), Revolutionary War officer and first U.S. secretary of war (1785-95).

Area (sq mi): 387.71 (land 387.66; water 0.04).

Pop: 31,795 (White 97.4%; Black or African American 0.8%; Hispanic or Latino 0.6%; Asian 0.2%; Other 1.2%). **Foreign born:** 0.4%. **Median age:** 35.3. **State rank:** 34. **Pop change 1990-2000:** +7.1%.

Income: per capita $10,660; median household $18,294. **Pop below poverty level:** 34.8%.

Unemployment: 6.2%. **Median home value:** $59,400. **Median travel time to work:** 24.6 minutes.

LARUE COUNTY
209 W High St
Hodgenville, KY 42748

Ph: 270-358-3544
Fax: 270-358-4528

In central western KY, south of Louisville; organized Mar 4, 1843

All statistics are based on the 2000 Census except the dollar figures given for per capita income, which are based on 1999 estimates.

from Hardin County. **Name Origin:** For John LaRue, maternal grandfather of John LaRue Helm, a KY governor.

Area (sq mi): 263.72 (land 263.2; water 0.53).

Pop: 13,373 (White 94%; Black or African American 3.5%; Hispanic or Latino 1%; Asian 0.2%; Other 1.6%). **Foreign born:** 0.4%. **Median age:** 38.2. **State rank:** 82. **Pop change 1990-2000:** +14.5%.

Income: per capita $15,865; median household $32,056. **Pop below poverty level:** 15.4%.

Unemployment: 5%. **Median home value:** $72,100. **Median travel time to work:** 27.2 minutes.

LAUREL COUNTY

101 S Main St Rm 203   **Ph:** 606-864-5158
London, KY 40741   **Fax:** 606-864-7369

In south-central KY; established Dec 12, 1825 from Rockcastle, Knox, Clay, and Whitley counties. **Name Origin:** For the Laurel River, named for the abundant mountain laurel (*Kalmia latifolia*) trees on its banks.

Area (sq mi): 443.74 (land 435.67; water 8.07).

Pop: 52,715 (White 97.2%; Black or African American 0.6%; Hispanic or Latino 0.6%; Asian 0.3%; Other 1.4%). **Foreign born:** 0.8%. **Median age:** 35.5. **State rank:** 15. **Pop change 1990-2000:** +21.4%.

Income: per capita $14,165; median household $27,015. **Pop below poverty level:** 21.3%.

Unemployment: 5.5%. **Median home value:** $77,300. **Median travel time to work:** 22.5 minutes.

LAWRENCE COUNTY

122 S Main Cross St   **Ph:** 606-638-4108
Louisa, KY 41230   **Fax:** 606-638-0638

On eastern border of KY, south of Ashland; established Dec 14, 1821 from Floyd and Greenup counties. **Name Origin:** For Capt. James Lawrence (1781-1813), U.S. Navy commander in the War of 1812 who said, 'Don't give up the ship!'

Area (sq mi): 420.12 (land 418.78; water 1.35).

Pop: 15,569 (White 98.6%; Black or African American 0.1%; Hispanic or Latino 0.4%; Asian 0.1%; Other 1%). **Foreign born:** 0.1%. **Median age:** 36.5. **State rank:** 71. **Pop change 1990-2000:** +11.2%.

Income: per capita $12,008; median household $21,610. **Pop below poverty level:** 30.7%.

Unemployment: 10.1%. **Median home value:** $56,300. **Median travel time to work:** 36 minutes.

LEE COUNTY

PO Box 551   **Ph:** 606-464-4115
Beattyville, KY 41311   **Fax:** 606-464-4102

In east-central KY, southeast of Lexington; organized Jan 29, 1870 from Owsley, Breathitt, Estill, and Wolfe counties. **Name Origin:** Traditionally for Robert E. Lee (1807-70), American general and commander-in-chief of the Confederate forces during the Civil War. Others claim it was named for Lee County, VA, former home of many early settlers.

Area (sq mi): 211.22 (land 209.86; water 1.36).

Pop: 7,916 (White 94.9%; Black or African American 3.8%; Hispanic or Latino 0.4%; Asian 0.1%; Other 1.1%). **Foreign born:** 0.2%. **Median age:** 37.4. **State rank:** 109. **Pop change 1990-2000:** +6.7%.

Income: per capita $13,325; median household $18,544. **Pop below poverty level:** 30.4%.

Unemployment: 7.1%. **Median home value:** $52,300. **Median travel time to work:** 35.4 minutes.

LESLIE COUNTY

PO Box 619   **Ph:** 606-672-3200
Hyden, KY 41749   **Fax:** 606-672-7373

In southeastern KY; organized Mar 29, 1878 from Clay, Harlan, and Perry counties. **Name Origin:** For Preston Hopkins Leslie (1819-1907), KY legislator and governor (1871-75); territorial governor of MT (1887-89), and U.S. district attorney for MT (1894-98).

Area (sq mi): 404.36 (land 404.03; water 0.33).

Pop: 12,401 (White 98.6%; Black or African American 0.1%; Hispanic or Latino 0.6%; Asian 0.1%; Other 0.6%). **Foreign born:** 0.2%. **Median age:** 36.4. **State rank:** 89. **Pop change 1990-2000:** -9.1%.

Income: per capita $10,429; median household $18,546. **Pop below poverty level:** 32.7%.

Unemployment: 4.7%. **Median home value:** $36,900. **Median travel time to work:** 33.5 minutes.

LETCHER COUNTY

156 Main St Suite 102   **Ph:** 606-633-2432
Whitesburg, KY 41858   **Fax:** 606-632-9282

On southeastern border of KY; organized Mar 3, 1842 from Harlan and Perry counties. **Name Origin:** For Robert Perkins Letcher (1788-1861), U.S. representative from KY (1823-33; 1834-35), governor (1840-44), and U.S. Minister to Mexico (1849-52).

Area (sq mi): 339.12 (land 339.04; water 0.07).

Pop: 25,277 (White 98.3%; Black or African American 0.5%; Hispanic or Latino 0.4%; Asian 0.3%; Other 0.5%). **Foreign born:** 0.4%. **Median age:** 37.9. **State rank:** 42. **Pop change 1990-2000:** -6.4%.

Income: per capita $11,984; median household $21,110. **Pop below poverty level:** 27.1%.

Unemployment: 6.4%. **Median home value:** $39,500. **Median travel time to work:** 25.9 minutes.

LEWIS COUNTY

514 2nd St   **Ph:** 606-796-2722
Vanceburg, KY 41179   **Fax:** 606-796-0822

On northeastern border of KY, west of Ashland; established Dec 2, 1806 from Mason County. **Name Origin:** For Meriwether Lewis (1774-1809), co-leader of the Lewis and Clark Expedition (1804-06).

Area (sq mi): 495.7 (land 484.49; water 11.21).

Pop: 14,092 (White 98.6%; Black or African American 0.2%; Hispanic or Latino 0.4%; Asian 0%; Other 0.8%). **Foreign born:** 0.1%. **Median age:** 35.9. **State rank:** 78. **Pop change 1990-2000:** +8.2%.

Please see sample entry on inside front cover for detailed information about the statistics presented with each county listing.

Income: per capita $12,031; median household $22,208. **Pop below poverty level:** 28.5%.

Unemployment: 12.9%. **Median home value:** $44,700. **Median travel time to work:** 35.7 minutes.

LINCOLN COUNTY

102 E Main St County Courthouse   **Ph:** 606-365-4570
Stanford, KY 40484   **Fax:** 606-365-4572

In south-central KY, south of Lexington; organized May 1, 1780 (prior to statehood) from Kentucky County. **Name Origin:** For Gen. Benjamin Lincoln (1733-1810), Revolutionary War officer, U.S. secretary of war (1781-83), and lt. gov. of MA (1788).

Area (sq mi): 336.47 (land 336.26; water 0.21).

Pop: 23,361 (White 95.7%; Black or African American 2.5%; Hispanic or Latino 0.9%; Asian 0.1%; Other 1.2%). **Foreign born:** 0.7%. **Median age:** 36. **State rank:** 46. **Pop change 1990-2000:** +16.5%.

Income: per capita $13,602; median household $26,542. **Pop below poverty level:** 21.1%.

Unemployment: 6.5%. **Median home value:** $65,100. **Median travel time to work:** 26.9 minutes.

LIVINGSTON COUNTY

335 Court St   **Ph:** 270-928-2162
Smithland, KY 42081   **Fax:** 270-928-2162

On northwestern border of KY, east of Paducah; established Dec 13, 1798 from Christian County. **Name Origin:** For Robert R. Livingston (1746-1813), NY patriot, statesman, and a drafter of the Declaration of Independence.

Area (sq mi): 342.2 (land 316.08; water 26.12).

Pop: 9,804 (White 98%; Black or African American 0.1%; Hispanic or Latino 0.8%; Asian 0%; Other 1.3%). **Foreign born:** 0.2%. **Median age:** 39.8. **State rank:** 101. **Pop change 1990-2000:** +8.2%.

Income: per capita $17,072; median household $31,776. **Pop below poverty level:** 10.3%.

Unemployment: 7%. **Median home value:** $58,200. **Median travel time to work:** 25.9 minutes.

LOGAN COUNTY

229 W 3rd St PO Box 358   **Ph:** 270-726-6061
Russellville, KY 42276   **Fax:** 270-726-4355

On the southern border of KY, west of Bowling Green; organized Jun 28, 1792 from Lincoln County. **Name Origin:** For Benjamin Logan (c.1743-1802), VA patriot and soldier active in the West during the American Revolution.

Area (sq mi): 557.1 (land 555.68; water 1.41).

Pop: 26,573 (White 90%; Black or African American 7.6%; Hispanic or Latino 1.1%; Asian 0.2%; Other 1.5%). **Foreign born:** 0.8%. **Median age:** 37. **State rank:** 40. **Pop change 1990-2000:** +8.8%.

Income: per capita $15,962; median household $32,474. **Pop below poverty level:** 15.5%.

Unemployment: 8.7%. **Median home value:** $67,100. **Median travel time to work:** 23.2 minutes.

LYON COUNTY

PO Box 310   **Ph:** 270-388-2331
Eddyville, KY 42038   **Fax:** 270-388-0634

In western KY, east of Paducah; organized Jan 14, 1854 from Caldwell County. **Name Origin:** For Chittenden Lyon (1787-1842), U.S. representative from KY (1827-35).

Area (sq mi): 256.42 (land 215.7; water 40.71).

Pop: 8,080 (White 91.6%; Black or African American 6.7%; Hispanic or Latino 0.7%; Asian 0.2%; Other 1.2%). **Foreign born:** 0.8%. **Median age:** 41.5. **State rank:** 108. **Pop change 1990-2000:** +22%.

Income: per capita $16,016; median household $31,694. **Pop below poverty level:** 12.7%.

Unemployment: 5.5%. **Median home value:** $80,700. **Median travel time to work:** 22.6 minutes.

MADISON COUNTY

101 W Main St   **Ph:** 859-624-4703
Richmond, KY 40475   **Fax:** 859-623-3071

In central KY, southeast of Lexington; established Oct 17, 1785 (prior to statehood) from Lincoln County. **Name Origin:** For James Madison (1751-1836), fourth U.S. president.

Area (sq mi): 443.11 (land 440.68; water 2.42).

Pop: 70,872 (White 92.4%; Black or African American 4.4%; Hispanic or Latino 1%; Asian 0.7%; Other 1.8%). **Foreign born:** 1.5%. **Median age:** 30.7. **State rank:** 10. **Pop change 1990-2000:** +23.2%.

Income: per capita $16,790; median household $32,861. **Pop below poverty level:** 16.8%.

Unemployment: 4.3%. **Median home value:** $93,500. **Median travel time to work:** 23.5 minutes.

MAGOFFIN COUNTY

PO Box 430   **Ph:** 606-349-2313
Salyersville, KY 41465   **Fax:** 606-349-2109

In east-central KY; organized Feb 22, 1860 from Floyd, Johnson, and Morgan counties. **Name Origin:** For Beriah Magoffin (1815-85), KY legislator and governor (1859-62).

Area (sq mi): 309.44 (land 309.44; water 0.01).

Pop: 13,332 (White 98.9%; Black or African American 0.2%; Hispanic or Latino 0.4%; Asian 0.1%; Other 0.5%). **Foreign born:** 0.2%. **Median age:** 34.3. **State rank:** 83. **Pop change 1990-2000:** +2%.

Income: per capita $10,685; median household $19,421. **Pop below poverty level:** 36.6%.

Unemployment: 12.6%. **Median home value:** $55,600. **Median travel time to work:** 38.5 minutes.

MARION COUNTY

120 W Main St Suite 3   **Ph:** 270-692-2651
Lebanon, KY 40033   **Fax:** 270-692-9811

In west-central KY, southwest of Lexington; organized Jan 25, 1834 from Washington County. **Name Origin:** For Gen. Francis Marion (c.1732-95), SC soldier and legislator, known as 'The Swamp Fox' for his tactics during the Revolutionary War.

All statistics are based on the 2000 Census except the dollar figures given for per capita income, which are based on 1999 estimates.

Area (sq mi): 346.86 (land 346.39; water 0.47).

Pop: 18,212 (White 88.8%; Black or African American 9.1%; Hispanic or Latino 0.8%; Asian 0.4%; Other 1.3%). **Foreign born:** 1.2%. **Median age:** 35.4. **State rank:** 58. **Pop change 1990-2000:** +10.4%.

Income: per capita $14,472; median household $30,387. **Pop below poverty level:** 18.6%.

Unemployment: 5.6%. **Median home value:** $70,300. **Median travel time to work:** 24.4 minutes.

MARSHALL COUNTY

1101 Main St   **Ph:** 270-527-4740
Benton, KY 42025   **Fax:** 270-527-4738

In western KY, southeast of Paducah; organized Feb 12, 1842 from Calloway County. **Name Origin:** For John Marshall (1755-1835), American jurist; fourth Chief Justice of the U.S. Supreme Court (1801-35).

Area (sq mi): 340.32 (land 304.89; water 35.43).

Pop: 30,125 (White 98.1%; Black or African American 0.1%; Hispanic or Latino 0.8%; Asian 0.1%; Other 1.2%). **Foreign born:** 0.8%. **Median age:** 40.9. **State rank:** 35. **Pop change 1990-2000:** +10.7%.

Income: per capita $18,069; median household $35,573. **Pop below poverty level:** 9.5%.

Unemployment: 7.4%. **Median home value:** $82,800. **Median travel time to work:** 22.3 minutes.

MARTIN COUNTY

PO Box 460   **Ph:** 606-298-2810
Inez, KY 41224   **Fax:** 606-298-0143
www.kymtnnet.org/martin.html

On the eastern border of KY, south of Ashland; organized May 10, 1870 from Johnson, Pike, Floyd, and Lawrence counties. **Name Origin:** For John Preston Martin (1811-62), KY legislator and U.S. representative (1845-47).

Area (sq mi): 230.81 (land 230.7; water 0.11).

Pop: 12,578 (White 98.7%; Black or African American 0%; Hispanic or Latino 0.6%; Asian 0.1%; Other 0.7%). **Foreign born:** 0.1%. **Median age:** 34.1. **State rank:** 88. **Pop change 1990-2000:** +0.4%.

Income: per capita $10,650; median household $18,279. **Pop below poverty level:** 37%.

Unemployment: 6.4%. **Median home value:** $62,100. **Median travel time to work:** 29.8 minutes.

MASON COUNTY

PO Box 234   **Ph:** 606-564-3341
Maysville, KY 41056   **Fax:** 606-564-8979

On the northeastern border of KY, northeast of Lexington; established Nov 5, 1788 (prior to statehood) from Bourbon County. **Name Origin:** For George Mason (1725-92), author of the VA Declaration of Rights (1776), which served as the model for the American Bill of Rights.

Area (sq mi): 246.6 (land 241.11; water 5.49).

Pop: 16,800 (White 90.5%; Black or African American 7.2%; Hispanic or Latino 1%; Asian 0.4%; Other 1.6%). **Foreign born:** 1.4%. **Median age:** 38.1. **State rank:** 65. **Pop change 1990-2000:** +0.8%.

Income: per capita $16,589; median household $30,195. **Pop below poverty level:** 16.8%.

Unemployment: 4.3%. **Median home value:** $71,900. **Median travel time to work:** 21.5 minutes.

McCRACKEN COUNTY

PO Box 609   **Ph:** 270-444-4700
Paducah, KY 42002   **Fax:** 270-444-4704
www.co.mccracken.ky.us

On southwestern border of KY; established Dec 17, 1824 from Hickman County. **Name Origin:** For Capt. Virgil McCracken (?-1813), a soldier killed during the War of 1812 at the Frenchtown Battle on the River Raisin, MI.

Area (sq mi): 268.08 (land 251.02; water 17.05).

Pop: 65,514 (White 86.2%; Black or African American 10.9%; Hispanic or Latino 1.1%; Asian 0.5%; Other 1.9%). **Foreign born:** 0.9%. **Median age:** 39.2. **State rank:** 12. **Pop change 1990-2000:** +4.2%.

Income: per capita $19,533; median household $33,865. **Pop below poverty level:** 15.1%.

Unemployment: 4.5%. **Median home value:** $84,300. **Median travel time to work:** 17.8 minutes.

McCREARY COUNTY

PO Box 699   **Ph:** 606-376-2411
Whitley City, KY 42653   **Fax:** 606-376-3898

On the southern border of KY, south of Lexington; organized Mar 12, 1912 from Pulaski, Wayne, and Whitley counties. **Name Origin:** For Lt. Col. James Bennett McCreary (1838-1918), KY legislator, governor (1875-79; 1911-15), and U.S. senator (1903-09).

Area (sq mi): 430.64 (land 427.7; water 2.94).

Pop: 17,080 (White 97.6%; Black or African American 0.6%; Hispanic or Latino 0.6%; Asian 0%; Other 1.3%). **Foreign born:** 0.5%. **Median age:** 34.2. **State rank:** 64. **Pop change 1990-2000:** +9.5%.

Income: per capita $9,896; median household $19,348. **Pop below poverty level:** 32.2%.

Unemployment: 11.8%. **Median home value:** $46,300. **Median travel time to work:** 28.2 minutes.

McLEAN COUNTY

PO Box 57   **Ph:** 270-273-3082
Calhoun, KY 42327   **Fax:** 270-273-5084

In western KY, south of Owensboro; organized Feb 6, 1854 from Daviess, Ohio, and Muhlenberg counties. **Name Origin:** For Capt. Alney McLean (1779-1841), U.S. representative from KY (1815-17; 1819-21) and district court judge (1821-41).

Area (sq mi): 256.17 (land 254.3; water 1.88).

Pop: 9,938 (White 98.1%; Black or African American 0.4%; Hispanic or Latino 0.8%; Asian 0%; Other 1%). **Foreign born:** 0.7%. **Median age:** 38.1. **State rank:** 100. **Pop change 1990-2000:** +3.2%.

Please see sample entry on inside front cover for detailed information about the statistics presented with each county listing.

Income: per capita $16,046; median household $29,675. **Pop below poverty level:** 16%.

Unemployment: 7.1%. **Median home value:** $58,200. **Median travel time to work:** 30.1 minutes.

MEADE COUNTY

PO Box 614   **Ph:** 270-422-2152
Brandenburg, KY 40108   **Fax:** 270-422-2158

On the northwestern border of KY, southwest of Louisville; established Dec 17, 1823 from Breckinridge and Hardin counties. **Name Origin:** For Capt. James Meade (?-1813), an officer in the War of 1812 killed at the Frenchtown Battle on the River Raisin, MI.

Area (sq mi): 324.22 (land 308.51; water 15.71).

Pop: 26,349 (White 91.3%; Black or African American 4.1%; Hispanic or Latino 2.2%; Asian 0.5%; Other 2.9%). **Foreign born:** 2%. **Median age:** 32.2. **State rank:** 41. **Pop change 1990-2000:** +9%.

Income: per capita $16,000; median household $36,966. **Pop below poverty level:** 11.3%.

Unemployment: 5.8%. **Median home value:** $85,500. **Median travel time to work:** 31.1 minutes.

MENIFEE COUNTY

PO Box 123   **Ph:** 606-768-3512
Frenchburg, KY 40322   **Fax:** 606-768-6738

In east-central KY, east of Lexington; organized Mar 10, 1869 from Montgomery, Bath, Wolfe, Morgan, and Powell counties. **Name Origin:** For Richard Hickman Menefee (1809-41), KY Commonwealth attorney, legislator, and U.S. representative (1837-39). Spelling evidently changed when county was named.

Area (sq mi): 206.03 (land 203.9; water 2.13).

Pop: 6,556 (White 96.9%; Black or African American 1.4%; Hispanic or Latino 1.1%; Asian 0%; Other 0.9%). **Foreign born:** 0.4%. **Median age:** 36.3. **State rank:** 116. **Pop change 1990-2000:** +28.8%.

Income: per capita $11,399; median household $22,064. **Pop below poverty level:** 29.6%.

Unemployment: 7.9%. **Median home value:** $54,500. **Median travel time to work:** 36.1 minutes.

MERCER COUNTY

PO Box 426   **Ph:** 859-734-6310
Harrodsburg, KY 40330   **Fax:** 859-734-6309

In central KY, southwest of Lexington; established Oct 17, 1785 (prior to statehood) from Lincoln County. **Name Origin:** For Gen. Hugh Mercer (1721-77), Revolutionary War officer and physician.

Area (sq mi): 253.11 (land 250.92; water 2.2).

Pop: 20,817 (White 93.4%; Black or African American 3.7%; Hispanic or Latino 1.3%; Asian 0.5%; Other 1.8%). **Foreign born:** 1.7%. **Median age:** 38.2. **State rank:** 53. **Pop change 1990-2000:** +8.7%.

Income: per capita $17,972; median household $35,555. **Pop below poverty level:** 12.9%.

Unemployment: 5.3%. **Median home value:** $83,800. **Median travel time to work:** 24 minutes.

METCALFE COUNTY

PO Box 25   **Ph:** 270-432-4821
Edmonton, KY 42129   **Fax:** 270-432-5176

In south-central KY, east of Bowling Green; organized Feb 1, 1860 from Adair, Monroe, Cumberland, Barren, and Green counties. **Name Origin:** For Capt. Thomas Metcalfe (1780-1855), KY legislator, governor (1828-32), and U.S. senator (1848-49).

Area (sq mi): 290.96 (land 290.9; water 0.07).

Pop: 10,037 (White 96.8%; Black or African American 1.6%; Hispanic or Latino 0.5%; Asian 0.1%; Other 0.9%). **Foreign born:** 0.2%. **Median age:** 37.7. **State rank:** 99. **Pop change 1990-2000:** +12%.

Income: per capita $13,236; median household $23,540. **Pop below poverty level:** 23.6%.

Unemployment: 5%. **Median home value:** $52,600. **Median travel time to work:** 26.7 minutes.

MONROE COUNTY

PO Box 188   **Ph:** 270-487-5471
Tompkinsville, KY 42167   **Fax:** 270-487-5976

On southern border of KY, southeast of Bowling Green; organized Jan 19, 1820 from Barren and Cumberland counties. **Name Origin:** For James Monroe (1758-1831), fifth U.S. president.

Area (sq mi): 332.11 (land 330.81; water 1.3).

Pop: 11,756 (White 95.1%; Black or African American 2.8%; Hispanic or Latino 1.4%; Asian 0%; Other 1.6%). **Foreign born:** 1.4%. **Median age:** 38.2. **State rank:** 92. **Pop change 1990-2000:** +3.1%.

Income: per capita $14,365; median household $22,356. **Pop below poverty level:** 23.4%.

Unemployment: 12.9%. **Median home value:** $57,600. **Median travel time to work:** 23.3 minutes.

MONTGOMERY COUNTY

PO Box 414   **Ph:** 859-498-8700
Mount Sterling, KY 40353   **Fax:** 859-498-8729

In central KY, east of Lexington; established May 1, 1797 (prior to statehood) from Clark County. **Name Origin:** For Gen. Richard Montgomery (1736-75), American Revolutionary War officer who captured Montreal, Canada.

Area (sq mi): 198.8 (land 198.59; water 0.21).

Pop: 22,554 (White 94.3%; Black or African American 3.5%; Hispanic or Latino 1.1%; Asian 0.1%; Other 1.3%). **Foreign born:** 0.5%. **Median age:** 36. **State rank:** 50. **Pop change 1990-2000:** +15.3%.

Income: per capita $16,701; median household $31,746. **Pop below poverty level:** 15.2%.

Unemployment: 6.4%. **Median home value:** $82,100. **Median travel time to work:** 25.1 minutes.

MORGAN COUNTY

PO Box 26   **Ph:** 606-743-3949
West Liberty, KY 41472   **Fax:** 606-743-2111

In eastern KY, east of Lexington; established Dec 7, 1822 from

All statistics are based on the 2000 Census except the dollar figures given for per capita income, which are based on 1999 estimates.

Floyd and Bath counties. **Name Origin:** For Gen. Daniel Morgan (1736-1802), an officer in the Revolutionary War and U.S. representative from VA (1797-99).

Area (sq mi): 383.73 (land 381.26; water 2.47).

Pop: 13,948 (White 94.1%; Black or African American 4.4%; Hispanic or Latino 0.6%; Asian 0.2%; Other 0.9%). **Foreign born:** 0.7%. **Median age:** 35.8. **State rank:** 79. **Pop change 1990-2000:** +19.7%.

Income: per capita $12,657; median household $21,869. **Pop below poverty level:** 27.2%.

Unemployment: 10%. **Median home value:** $55,400. **Median travel time to work:** 33.2 minutes.

MUHLENBERG COUNTY

PO Box 525
Greenville, KY 42345

Ph: 270-338-1441
Fax: 270-338-1774

In west-central KY, northeast of Hopkinsville; established Dec 14, 1798 from Christian and Logan counties. **Name Origin:** For Gen. John Peter Gabriel Muhlenberg (1746-1807), an officer in the Revolutionary War, Lutheran minister, and U.S. representative from PA (1789-91; 1793-95; 1799-1801).

Area (sq mi): 479.43 (land 474.72; water 4.71).

Pop: 31,839 (White 93.7%; Black or African American 4.6%; Hispanic or Latino 0.7%; Asian 0.1%; Other 1%). **Foreign born:** 0.3%. **Median age:** 38.7. **State rank:** 33. **Pop change 1990-2000:** +1.7%.

Income: per capita $14,798; median household $28,566. **Pop below poverty level:** 19.7%.

Unemployment: 10.3%. **Median home value:** $58,200. **Median travel time to work:** 24.3 minutes.

NELSON COUNTY

PO Box 312
Bardstown, KY 40004

Ph: 502-348-1820
Fax: 502-348-1822

In west-central KY, southeast of Louisville; established Oct 18, 1784 (prior to statehood) from Jefferson County. **Name Origin:** For Thomas Nelson (1738-89), member of the Continental Congress, a signer of the Declaration of Independence, and governor of VA (1781).

Area (sq mi): 424.07 (land 422.63; water 1.45).

Pop: 37,477 (White 92.3%; Black or African American 5.5%; Hispanic or Latino 1.1%; Asian 0.5%; Other 1.1%). **Foreign born:** 1.2%. **Median age:** 34.9. **State rank:** 24. **Pop change 1990-2000:** +26.1%.

Income: per capita $18,120; median household $39,010. **Pop below poverty level:** 12.2%.

Unemployment: 7%. **Median home value:** $87,100. **Median travel time to work:** 26.5 minutes.

NICHOLAS COUNTY

PO Box 227
Carlisle, KY 40311

Ph: 859-289-3730
Fax: 859-289-3705

In north-central KY, northeast of Lexington; established Dec 18, 1799 from Bourbon and Mason counties. **Name Origin:** For Col. George Nicholas (1754-99), officer in the Revolutionary War and

first attorney general of KY. He is considered the 'Father of the KY Constitution' for his part in drafting it.

Area (sq mi): 196.85 (land 196.61; water 0.24).

Pop: 6,813 (White 98%; Black or African American 0.8%; Hispanic or Latino 0.5%; Asian 0.1%; Other 0.6%). **Foreign born:** 0.5%. **Median age:** 38.4. **State rank:** 114. **Pop change 1990-2000:** +1.3%.

Income: per capita $15,880; median household $29,886. **Pop below poverty level:** 13.2%.

Unemployment: 8.8%. **Median home value:** $62,000. **Median travel time to work:** 33.8 minutes.

OHIO COUNTY

PO Box 85
Hartford, KY 42347

Ph: 270-298-4423
Fax: 270-298-4425

In west-central KY, south of Owensboro; established Dec 17, 1798 from Hardin County. **Name Origin:** For the Ohio River which originally formed its northern border.

Area (sq mi): 596.73 (land 593.79; water 2.94).

Pop: 22,916 (White 97.2%; Black or African American 0.7%; Hispanic or Latino 1%; Asian 0.2%; Other 1.3%). **Foreign born:** 0.7%. **Median age:** 37.5. **State rank:** 49. **Pop change 1990-2000:** +8.6%.

Income: per capita $15,317; median household $29,557. **Pop below poverty level:** 17.3%.

Unemployment: 7.9%. **Median home value:** $56,600. **Median travel time to work:** 28.6 minutes.

OLDHAM COUNTY

100 W Jefferson St
LaGrange, KY 40031
www.oldhamcounty.net

Ph: 502-222-9311
Fax: 502-222-3208

On the northwestern border of KY, north of Louisville; organized Dec 16, 1823 from Jefferson, Shelby, and Henry counties. **Name Origin:** For Col. William Oldham (?-1791), officer in the American Revolution, killed in a battle with Indians.

Area (sq mi): 196.54 (land 189.19; water 7.36).

Pop: 46,178 (White 92.9%; Black or African American 4.2%; Hispanic or Latino 1.3%; Asian 0.4%; Other 1.8%). **Foreign born:** 1.6%. **Median age:** 36.7. **State rank:** 19. **Pop change 1990-2000:** +38.8%.

Income: per capita $25,374; median household $63,229. **Pop below poverty level:** 4.1%.

Unemployment: 2.5%. **Median home value:** $158,600. **Median travel time to work:** 26.1 minutes.

OWEN COUNTY

100 N Thomas St
Owenton, KY 40359

Ph: 502-484-3405
Fax: 502-484-1004

In northern KY, northwest of Lexington; organized Feb 6, 1819 from Scott, Gallatin, and Franklin counties. **Name Origin:** For Abraham Owen (?-1811), officer killed at the Battle of Tippecanoe.

Area (sq mi): 354.16 (land 352.14; water 2.02).

Please see sample entry on inside front cover for detailed information about the statistics presented with each county listing.

Pop: 10,547 (White 96.6%; Black or African American 1.1%; Hispanic or Latino 1%; Asian 0.2%; Other 1.7%). **Foreign born:** 0.7%. **Median age:** 37.5. **State rank:** 97. **Pop change 1990-2000:** +16.7%.

Income: per capita $15,521; median household $33,310. **Pop below poverty level:** 15.5%.

Unemployment: 4.2%. **Median home value:** $72,800. **Median travel time to work:** 32.3 minutes.

OWSLEY COUNTY
PO Box 500   **Ph:** 606-593-5735
Booneville, KY 41314   **Fax:** 606-593-5737

In southeast KY, southeast of Lexington; organized Jan 23, 1843 from Clay, Estill, and Breathitt counties. **Name Origin:** For William Owsley (1782-1862), judge of the KY Court of Appeals, and governor (1844-48).

Area (sq mi): 198.09 (land 198.09; water 0).

Pop: 4,858 (White 98.5%; Black or African American 0.1%; Hispanic or Latino 0.7%; Asian 0%; Other 0.6%). **Foreign born:** 0.1%. **Median age:** 38.2. **State rank:** 119. **Pop change 1990-2000:** -3.5%.

Income: per capita $10,742; median household $15,805. **Pop below poverty level:** 45.4%.

Unemployment: 5.7%. **Median home value:** $40,800. **Median travel time to work:** 28.7 minutes.

PENDLETON COUNTY
233 Main St   **Ph:** 859-654-4321
Falmouth, KY 41040   **Fax:** 859-654-5047
www.pendletoncountyky.org

In northern KY, south of Covington; established Dec 4, 1787 from Campbell and Bracken counties. **Name Origin:** For Edmund Pendleton (1721-1803), member of the Continental Congress (1774-75), active in establishment of state of VA, and president of the VA supreme court of appeals (1779-1803).

Area (sq mi): 281.87 (land 280.54; water 1.33).

Pop: 14,390 (White 98.1%; Black or African American 0.5%; Hispanic or Latino 0.7%; Asian 0.1%; Other 1%). **Foreign born:** 0.5%. **Median age:** 34.5. **State rank:** 76. **Pop change 1990-2000:** +19.6%.

Income: per capita $16,551; median household $38,125. **Pop below poverty level:** 11.4%.

Unemployment: 5.3%. **Median home value:** $77,700. **Median travel time to work:** 35.1 minutes.

PERRY COUNTY
PO Box 150   **Ph:** 606-436-4614
Hazard, KY 41702   **Fax:** 606-439-0557

In southeastern KY; established Nov 2, 1820 from Clay and Floyd counties. **Name Origin:** For Oliver Hazard Perry (1785-1819), U.S. naval officer during the War of 1812, famous for the message, 'We have met the enemy and they are ours.'

Area (sq mi): 342.64 (land 342.15; water 0.49).

Pop: 29,390 (White 96.9%; Black or African American 1.6%; Hispanic or Latino 0.5%; Asian 0.5%; Other 0.5%). **Foreign born:** 0.6%. **Median age:** 36.3. **State rank:** 37. **Pop change 1990-2000:** -2.9%.

Income: per capita $12,224; median household $22,089. **Pop below poverty level:** 29.1%.

Unemployment: 6.1%. **Median home value:** $52,500. **Median travel time to work:** 23.2 minutes.

PIKE COUNTY
PO Box 631   **Ph:** 606-432-6240
Pikeville, KY 41502   **Fax:** 606-432-6222

On the central eastern border of KY; established Dec 19, 1821 from Floyd County. **Name Origin:** For Gen. Zebulon Montgomery Pike (1779-1813), U.S. army officer and discoverer of Pikes Peak in CO.

Area (sq mi): 788.84 (land 787.69; water 1.15).

Pop: 68,736 (White 97.9%; Black or African American 0.5%; Hispanic or Latino 0.7%; Asian 0.4%; Other 0.8%). **Foreign born:** 0.4%. **Median age:** 37.1. **State rank:** 11. **Pop change 1990-2000:** -5.3%.

Income: per capita $14,005; median household $23,930. **Pop below poverty level:** 23.4%.

Unemployment: 4.6%. **Median home value:** $65,900. **Median travel time to work:** 27.1 minutes.

POWELL COUNTY
PO Box 548   **Ph:** 606-663-6444
Stanton, KY 40380   **Fax:** 606-663-6406

In east-central KY, southeast of Lexington; organized Jan 7, 1852 from Montgomery, Clark, and Estill counties. **Name Origin:** For Lazarus Whitehead Powell (1812-67), governor of KY (1851-55), U.S. commissioner to UT (1858), and U.S. senator from KY (1859-65).

Area (sq mi): 180.2 (land 180.14; water 0.07).

Pop: 13,237 (White 98%; Black or African American 0.6%; Hispanic or Latino 0.7%; Asian 0.1%; Other 0.8%). **Foreign born:** 0.2%. **Median age:** 34.8. **State rank:** 84. **Pop change 1990-2000:** +13.3%.

Income: per capita $13,060; median household $25,515. **Pop below poverty level:** 23.5%.

Unemployment: 8.5%. **Median home value:** $63,000. **Median travel time to work:** 28.9 minutes.

PULASKI COUNTY
PO Box 724   **Ph:** 606-679-2042
Somerset, KY 42502   **Fax:** 606-678-0073

In south-central KY, south of Lexington; established Dec 10, 1798 from Lincoln and Green counties. **Name Origin:** For Count Casimir Pulaski (1747-79), Polish soldier who fought for America during the Revolutionary War.

Area (sq mi): 677.05 (land 661.6; water 15.45).

Pop: 56,217 (White 96.9%; Black or African American 1.1%; Hispanic or Latino 0.8%; Asian 0.4%; Other 1.1%). **Foreign born:** 0.8%. **Median age:** 38.5. **State rank:** 14. **Pop change 1990-2000:** +13.6%.

Income: per capita $15,352; median household $27,370. **Pop below poverty level:** 19.1%.

Unemployment: 7.4%. **Median home value:** $74,100. **Median travel time to work:** 22.5 minutes.

All statistics are based on the 2000 Census except the dollar figures given for per capita income, which are based on 1999 estimates.

ROBERTSON COUNTY

PO Box 75   **Ph:** 606-724-5212
Mount Olivet, KY 41064   **Fax:** 606-724-5022

In north-central KY, southeast of Covington; organized Feb 11, 1867 from Nicholas, Harrison, Bracken, and Mason counties. **Name Origin:** For George Robertson (1790-1874), U.S. representative from KY (1817-21) and chief justice of KY Court of Appeals (1829-34).

Area (sq mi): 100.11 (land 100.07; water 0.04).

Pop: 2,266 (White 98.5%; Black or African American 0%; Hispanic or Latino 0.9%; Asian 0%; Other 1.3%). **Foreign born:** 0.5%. **Median age:** 39.5. **State rank:** 120. **Pop change 1990-2000:** +6.7%.

Income: per capita $13,404; median household $30,581. **Pop below poverty level:** 22.2%.

Unemployment: 5%. **Median home value:** $58,500. **Median travel time to work:** 37.8 minutes.

ROCKCASTLE COUNTY

205 E Main St Box 6   **Ph:** 606-256-2831
Mount Vernon, KY 40456   **Fax:** 606-256-4302

In south-central KY, southeast of Lexington; organized Jan 8, 1810 from Lincoln, Pulaski, Madison, and Knox counties. **Name Origin:** For the Rockcastle River, which flows along the southeastern border of the county; named for the castle-like rock formations along its banks.

Area (sq mi): 318.06 (land 317.53; water 0.54).

Pop: 16,582 (White 98.3%; Black or African American 0.1%; Hispanic or Latino 0.6%; Asian 0.1%; Other 0.8%). **Foreign born:** 0%. **Median age:** 36.3. **State rank:** 66. **Pop change 1990-2000:** +12%.

Income: per capita $12,337; median household $23,475. **Pop below poverty level:** 23.1%.

Unemployment: 8%. **Median home value:** $57,000. **Median travel time to work:** 28.4 minutes.

ROWAN COUNTY

627 E Main St 2nd Fl   **Ph:** 606-784-5212
Morehead, KY 40351   **Fax:** 606-784-2923

In northeastern KY, northeast of Lexington; organized Mar 15, 1856 from Fleming and Morgan counties. **Name Origin:** For John Rowan (1773-1843), judge of the KY Court of Appeals (1819-21) and U.S. senator (1825-31).

Area (sq mi): 286.25 (land 280.82; water 5.43).

Pop: 22,094 (White 95.3%; Black or African American 1.6%; Hispanic or Latino 1.1%; Asian 0.9%; Other 1.6%). **Foreign born:** 1.4%. **Median age:** 29.8. **State rank:** 52. **Pop change 1990-2000:** +8.6%.

Income: per capita $13,888; median household $28,055. **Pop below poverty level:** 21.3%.

Unemployment: 6.4%. **Median home value:** $80,000. **Median travel time to work:** 24.4 minutes.

RUSSELL COUNTY

410 Monument Sq Rm 103   **Ph:** 270-343-2125
Jamestown, KY 42629   **Fax:** 270-343-4700

In south-central KY, southwest of Lexington; established Dec 14, 1825 from Wayne, Adair, and Cumberland counties. **Name Origin:** For William Russell (1758-1825), VA soldier and statesman; served in legislatures of VA and KY.

Area (sq mi): 282.82 (land 253.53; water 29.29).

Pop: 16,315 (White 97.7%; Black or African American 0.6%; Hispanic or Latino 0.9%; Asian 0.1%; Other 0.9%). **Foreign born:** 1%. **Median age:** 39.9. **State rank:** 68. **Pop change 1990-2000:** +10.9%.

Income: per capita $13,183; median household $22,042. **Pop below poverty level:** 24.3%.

Unemployment: 8.8%. **Median home value:** $62,000. **Median travel time to work:** 22.5 minutes.

SCOTT COUNTY

PO Box 973   **Ph:** 502-863-7850
Georgetown, KY 40324   **Fax:** 502-863-7852

In north-central KY, north of Lexington; organized Jun 22, 1792 from Woodford County. **Name Origin:** For Gen. Charles Scott (1739-1813), career soldier and governor of KY (1808-12).

Area (sq mi): 285.3 (land 284.72; water 0.57).

Pop: 33,061 (White 91.2%; Black or African American 5.4%; Hispanic or Latino 1.6%; Asian 0.5%; Other 2.2%). **Foreign born:** 1.9%. **Median age:** 32.4. **State rank:** 32. **Pop change 1990-2000:** +38.5%.

Income: per capita $21,490; median household $47,081. **Pop below poverty level:** 8.8%.

Unemployment: 3.3%. **Median home value:** $107,900. **Median travel time to work:** 21.7 minutes.

SHELBY COUNTY

501 Main St   **Ph:** 502-633-1220
Shelbyville, KY 40065   **Fax:** 502-633-7623
www.shelbyvilleky.com

In northwestern KY, east of Louisville; organized Jun 23, 1792 from Jefferson County. **Name Origin:** For Gen. Isaac Shelby (1750-1826), officer in the Revolutionary War, NC legislator, and governor of KY (1792-96; 1812-16).

Area (sq mi): 385.65 (land 384.19; water 1.46).

Pop: 33,337 (White 84.9%; Black or African American 8.8%; Hispanic or Latino 4.5%; Asian 0.4%; Other 4.1%). **Foreign born:** 3.9%. **Median age:** 35.9. **State rank:** 29. **Pop change 1990-2000:** +34.3%.

Income: per capita $20,195; median household $45,534. **Pop below poverty level:** 9.9%.

Unemployment: 4.3%. **Median home value:** $114,600. **Median travel time to work:** 24.7 minutes.

SIMPSON COUNTY

PO Box 268   **Ph:** 270-586-8161
Franklin, KY 42135   **Fax:** 270-586-6464

On southern border of KY, south of Bowling Green; organized Jan

Please see sample entry on inside front cover for detailed information about the statistics presented with each county listing.

28, 1819 from Logan, Warren, and Allen counties. **Name Origin:** For Capt. James Simpson (?-1812), KY legislator, killed in action during the War of 1812.

Area (sq mi): 236.19 (land 236.19; water 0).

Pop: 16,405 (White 87.3%; Black or African American 10.2%; Hispanic or Latino 0.9%; Asian 0.5%; Other 1.5%). **Foreign born:** 1.2%. **Median age:** 35.9. **State rank:** 67. **Pop change 1990-2000:** +8.3%.

Income: per capita $17,150; median household $36,432. **Pop below poverty level:** 11.6%.

Unemployment: 6.3%. **Median home value:** $81,400. **Median travel time to work:** 20.6 minutes.

SPENCER COUNTY
2 W Main St   **Ph:** 502-477-3215
Taylorsville, KY 40071   **Fax:** 502-477-3216

In northwestern KY, southeast of Louisville; organized Jan 7, 1824 from Nelson, Shelby, and Bullitt counties. **Name Origin:** For Capt. Spier (Spear) Spencer (?-1811), KY officer killed at the Battle of Tippecanoe.

Area (sq mi): 191.8 (land 185.9; water 5.89).

Pop: 11,766 (White 96.7%; Black or African American 1.1%; Hispanic or Latino 1.1%; Asian 0.1%; Other 1.3%). **Foreign born:** 1.2%. **Median age:** 35.1. **State rank:** 91. **Pop change 1990-2000:** +73%.

Income: per capita $19,848; median household $47,042. **Pop below poverty level:** 8.8%.

Unemployment: 5.2%. **Median home value:** $122,400. **Median travel time to work:** 32.6 minutes.

TAYLOR COUNTY
203 N Court St Suite 5   **Ph:** 270-465-6677
Campbellsville, KY 42718   **Fax:** 270-789-1144

In west-central KY, southeast of Bowling Green; organized Jan 13, 1848 from Green County. **Name Origin:** For Zachary Taylor (1784-1850), twelfth U.S. president.

Area (sq mi): 277.05 (land 269.83; water 7.22).

Pop: 22,927 (White 93.1%; Black or African American 5.1%; Hispanic or Latino 0.8%; Asian 0.2%; Other 1.1%). **Foreign born:** 1.3%. **Median age:** 38.1. **State rank:** 48. **Pop change 1990-2000:** +8.4%.

Income: per capita $15,162; median household $28,089. **Pop below poverty level:** 17.5%.

Unemployment: 6.3%. **Median home value:** $70,700. **Median travel time to work:** 22 minutes.

TODD COUNTY
PO Box 307   **Ph:** 270-265-2363
Elkton, KY 42220   **Fax:** 270-265-2588

On the southern border of KY, east of Hopkinsville; established Dec 30, 1819 from Logan and Christian counties. **Name Origin:** For John Blair Todd (1814-72), governor of the Dakota Territory (1869-71).

Area (sq mi): 376.97 (land 376.35; water 0.62).

Pop: 11,971 (White 88.6%; Black or African American 8.8%; Hispanic or Latino 1.7%; Asian 0.2%; Other 1.8%). **Foreign born:** 1.3%. **Median age:** 35.9. **State rank:** 90. **Pop change 1990-2000:** +9.4%.

Income: per capita $15,462; median household $29,718. **Pop below poverty level:** 17.2%.

Unemployment: 9.4%. **Median home value:** $58,300. **Median travel time to work:** 23.4 minutes.

TRIGG COUNTY
PO Box 1310   **Ph:** 270-522-6661
Cadiz, KY 42211   **Fax:** 270-522-6662

On the southern border of KY, west of Hopkinsville; organized Jan 27, 1820 from Christian and Caldwell counties. **Name Origin:** For Col. Stephen Trigg (?-1782), an officer killed in action against Indians at Blue Licks.

Area (sq mi): 481.13 (land 443.12; water 38.01).

Pop: 12,597 (White 87.7%; Black or African American 9.8%; Hispanic or Latino 0.9%; Asian 0.3%; Other 1.6%). **Foreign born:** 0.8%. **Median age:** 40.5. **State rank:** 87. **Pop change 1990-2000:** +21.6%.

Income: per capita $17,184; median household $33,002. **Pop below poverty level:** 12.3%.

Unemployment: 5.7%. **Median home value:** $74,300. **Median travel time to work:** 26.2 minutes.

TRIMBLE COUNTY
PO Box 262   **Ph:** 502-255-7174
Bedford, KY 40006   **Fax:** 502-255-7045

On the northwestern border of KY, northeast of Louisville; established Feb 9, 1837 from Gallatin, Oldham, and Henry counties. **Name Origin:** For Robert Trimble (1777-1828), KY jurist and associate justice of the U.S. Supreme Court (1826-28).

Area (sq mi): 156.23 (land 148.85; water 7.38).

Pop: 8,125 (White 97.2%; Black or African American 0.3%; Hispanic or Latino 1.4%; Asian 0.1%; Other 1.8%). **Foreign born:** 1.1%. **Median age:** 35.7. **State rank:** 107. **Pop change 1990-2000:** +33.4%.

Income: per capita $16,354; median household $36,192. **Pop below poverty level:** 13.6%.

Unemployment: 7.9%. **Median home value:** $82,500. **Median travel time to work:** 30.7 minutes.

UNION COUNTY
PO Box 119   **Ph:** 270-389-1334
Morganfield, KY 42437   **Fax:** 270-389-9135

On northwestern border of KY, southwest of Henderson; organized Jan 15, 1811 from Henderson County. **Name Origin:** Allegedly for the united desire of the residents to form a new county.

Area (sq mi): 363.43 (land 345.1; water 18.33).

Pop: 15,637 (White 84.4%; Black or African American 12.9%; Hispanic or Latino 1.6%; Asian 0.1%; Other 2%). **Foreign born:** 1.4%. **Median age:** 34.5. **State rank:** 70. **Pop change 1990-2000:** -5.6%.

All statistics are based on the 2000 Census except the dollar figures given for per capita income, which are based on 1999 estimates.

Income: per capita $17,465; median household $35,018. **Pop below poverty level:** 17.7%.

Unemployment: 7%. **Median home value:** $59,400. **Median travel time to work:** 23.1 minutes.

WARREN COUNTY
PO Box 478   **Ph:** 270-842-9416
Bowling Green, KY 42102   **Fax:** 270-843-5315

In southwest KY, northeast of Hopkinsville; established Dec 14, 1796 from Logan County. **Name Origin:** For Gen. Joseph Warren (1741-75), Revolutionary War patriot and member of the Committee of Safety who dispatched Paul Revere (1735-1818) on his famous ride.

Area (sq mi): 547.69 (land 545.21; water 2.48).

Pop: 92,522 (White 85.8%; Black or African American 8.6%; Hispanic or Latino 2.7%; Asian 1.4%; Other 3%). **Foreign born:** 4.3%. **Median age:** 32.3. **State rank:** 5. **Pop change 1990-2000:** +20.7%.

Income: per capita $18,847; median household $36,151. **Pop below poverty level:** 15.4%.

Unemployment: 4.6%. **Median home value:** $100,400. **Median travel time to work:** 19.6 minutes.

WASHINGTON COUNTY
PO Box 446   **Ph:** 859-336-5425
Springfield, KY 40069   **Fax:** 859-336-5408

In west-central KY, southwest of Lexington; organized Jun 22, 1792 from Nelson County; the first county formed after KY became a state. **Name Origin:** For George Washington (1732-99), American patriot and first U.S. president.

Area (sq mi): 301.52 (land 300.59; water 0.93).

Pop: 10,916 (White 89.6%; Black or African American 7.5%; Hispanic or Latino 1.6%; Asian 0.3%; Other 1.6%). **Foreign born:** 0.7%. **Median age:** 37.1. **State rank:** 96. **Pop change 1990-2000:** +4.5%.

Income: per capita $15,722; median household $33,136. **Pop below poverty level:** 13.5%.

Unemployment: 6.2%. **Median home value:** $72,000. **Median travel time to work:** 25.9 minutes.

WAYNE COUNTY
PO Box 565   **Ph:** 606-348-6661
Monticello, KY 42633   **Fax:** 606-348-8303

On the southern border of KY, south of Lexington; established Dec 18, 1800 from Pulaski and Cumberland counties. **Name Origin:** For Gen. Anthony Wayne (1745-96), PA soldier and statesman, nicknamed 'Mad Anthony' for his daring during the Revolutionary War.

Area (sq mi): 484.2 (land 459.4; water 24.8).

Pop: 19,923 (White 96.2%; Black or African American 1.5%; Hispanic or Latino 1.5%; Asian 0.1%; Other 1.5%). **Foreign born:** 1.3%. **Median age:** 36.6. **State rank:** 54. **Pop change 1990-2000:** +14.1%.

Income: per capita $12,601; median household $20,863. **Pop below poverty level:** 29.4%.

Unemployment: 8.9%. **Median home value:** $55,400. **Median travel time to work:** 22.2 minutes.

WEBSTER COUNTY
PO Box 155   **Ph:** 270-639-5042
Dixon, KY 42409   **Fax:** 270-639-7009

In western KY, south of Henderson; organized Feb 29, 1860 from Hopkins, Union, and Henderson counties. **Name Origin:** For Daniel Webster (1782-1852), U.S. statesman and orator from MA.

Area (sq mi): 335.68 (land 334.75; water 0.93).

Pop: 14,120 (White 92.7%; Black or African American 4.7%; Hispanic or Latino 1.9%; Asian 0.1%; Other 1.7%). **Foreign born:** 1.9%. **Median age:** 37.8. **State rank:** 77. **Pop change 1990-2000:** +1.2%.

Income: per capita $15,657; median household $31,529. **Pop below poverty level:** 15.4%.

Unemployment: 7%. **Median home value:** $45,800. **Median travel time to work:** 26.4 minutes.

WHITLEY COUNTY
PO Box 8   **Ph:** 606-549-6002
Williamsburg, KY 40769   **Fax:** 606-549-2790

On the southeastern border of KY; organized Jan 17, 1818 from Knox County. **Name Origin:** For William Whitley (1749-1813), soldier believed by some to be the one who killed Shawnee Chief Tecumseh (1768-1813).

Area (sq mi): 445.15 (land 440.15; water 4.99).

Pop: 35,865 (White 97.8%; Black or African American 0.3%; Hispanic or Latino 0.7%; Asian 0.2%; Other 1.1%). **Foreign born:** 0.7%. **Median age:** 35.4. **State rank:** 27. **Pop change 1990-2000:** +7.6%.

Income: per capita $12,777; median household $22,075. **Pop below poverty level:** 26.4%.

Unemployment: 6.2%. **Median home value:** $62,100. **Median travel time to work:** 25.1 minutes.

WOLFE COUNTY
PO Box 400   **Ph:** 606-668-3515
Campton, KY 41301   **Fax:** 606-668-3492
wolfe.archland.com

In eastern KY, southeast of Lexington; organized Mar 5, 1860 from Breathitt, Morgan, Powell, and Owsley counties. **Name Origin:** For Nathaniel Wolfe (1810-65), KY legislator (1853-55; 1859-63).

Area (sq mi): 222.86 (land 222.78; water 0.08).

Pop: 7,065 (White 98.8%; Black or African American 0.2%; Hispanic or Latino 0.5%; Asian 0%; Other 0.5%). **Foreign born:** 0.7%. **Median age:** 36.4. **State rank:** 113. **Pop change 1990-2000:** +8.6%.

Income: per capita $10,321; median household $19,310. **Pop below poverty level:** 35.9%.

Unemployment: 9.4%. **Median home value:** $45,300. **Median travel time to work:** 33.8 minutes.

Please see sample entry on inside front cover for detailed information about the statistics presented with each county listing.

WOODFORD COUNTY

103 S Main St County Courthouse
Versailles, KY 40383

Ph: 859-873-3421
Fax: 859-873-0196

In central KY, west of Lexington; established Nov 12, 1788 (prior to statehood) from Fayette County; the last county formed while KY was still part of VA. **Name Origin:** For William Woodford (1735-1780), Revolutionary War general

Area (sq mi): 191.98 (land 190.68; water 1.3).

Pop: 23,208 (White 90.2%; Black or African American 5.4%; Hispanic or Latino 3%; Asian 0.3%; Other 2.1%). **Foreign born:** 2.7%. **Median age:** 37.1. **State rank:** 47. **Pop change 1990-2000:** +16.3%.

Income: per capita $22,839; median household $49,491. **Pop below poverty level:** 7.3%.

Unemployment: 3.4%. **Median home value:** $117,100. **Median travel time to work:** 21.4 minutes.

LOUISIANA - Parishes

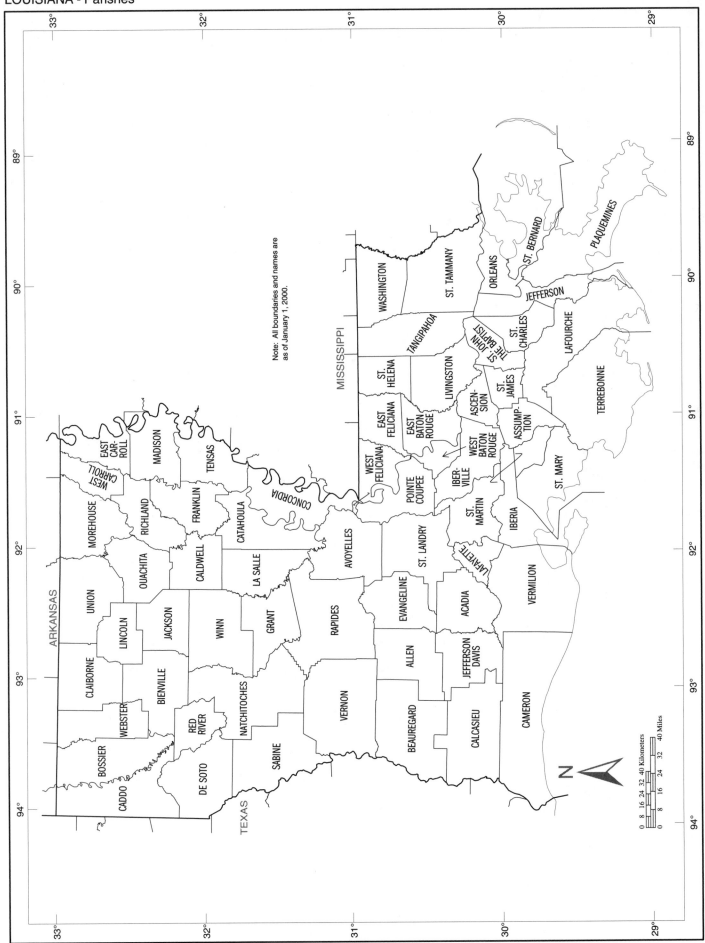

Note: All boundaries and names are
as of January 1, 2000.

MISSISSIPPI

ARKANSAS

TEXAS

WASHINGTON

ST. TAMMANY

ORLEANS

ST. BERNARD

PLAQUEMINES

JEFFERSON

TANGIPAHOA

LAFOURCHE

ST. CHARLES

ST. JOHN THE BAPTIST

ST. HELENA

LIVINGSTON

ST. JAMES

TERREBONNE

EAST FELICIANA

EAST BATON ROUGE

ASCENSION

ASSUMPTION

WEST BATON ROUGE

WEST FELICIANA

IBERVILLE

POINTE COUPEE

ST. MARY

EAST CARROLL

MADISON

TENSAS

WEST CARROLL

CONCORDIA

ST. MARTIN

IBERIA

MOREHOUSE

RICHLAND

FRANKLIN

CATAHOULA

AVOYELLES

ST. LANDRY

LAFAYETTE

OUACHITA

CALDWELL

LA SALLE

VERMILION

UNION

RAPIDES

EVANGELINE

ACADIA

LINCOLN

JACKSON

WINN

GRANT

CLAIBORNE

BIENVILLE

ALLEN

JEFFERSON DAVIS

WEBSTER

RED RIVER

NATCHITOCHES

VERNON

BEAUREGARD

CALCASIEU

CAMERON

BOSSIER

CADDO

DE SOTO

SABINE

0 8 16 24 32 40 Kilometers
0 8 16 24 32 40 Miles

N

Louisiana

LOUISIANA STATE INFORMATION

www.state.la.us   **Ph:** 225-342-6600

Area (sq mi): 51839.7 (land 43,561.85; water 8277.85).

Pop: 4,468,976 (White 62.5%; Black or African American 32.5%; Hispanic or Latino 2.4%; Asian 1.2%; Other 2.4%). **Foreign born:** 2.6%. **Median age:** 34. **Pop change 1990-2000:** +5.9%.

Income: per capita $16,912; median household $32,566. **Pop below poverty level:** 19.6%.

Unemployment: 5.3%. **Median home value:** $85,000. **Median travel time to work:** 25.7 minutes.

ACADIA PARISH

N Parkson Court Cir 3rd Fl   **Ph:** 337-788-8800
Crowley, LA 70526   **Fax:** 337-788-2421

In south-central LA, west of Lafayette; organized 1886 from Saint Landry Parish. **Name Origin:** French *Acadie*, an area in northeastern Canada and ME, former home of present-day Cajuns, descendants of France settlers displaced by English troops. Their journey is subject of Henry Wadsworth Longfellow's (1807-82) poem, 'Evangeline.'

Area (sq mi): 657.62 (land 655.28; water 2.33).

Pop: 58,861 (White 80.1%; Black or African American 18.2%; Hispanic or Latino 0.9%; Asian 0.2%; Other 0.9%). **Foreign born:** 0.4%. **Median age:** 33.7. **State rank:** 19. **Pop change 1990-2000:** +5.3%.

Income: per capita $13,424; median household $26,684. **Pop below poverty level:** 24.5%.

Unemployment: 6.1%. **Median home value:** $61,700. **Median travel time to work:** 29.9 minutes.

ALLEN PARISH

PO Box G   **Ph:** 337-639-4396
Oberlin, LA 70655   **Fax:** 337-639-4326

In south-central LA, northeast of Lake Charles; established Jun 12, 1912 from Calcasieu Parish. **Name Origin:** For Henry Watkins Allen (1820-66), Confederate general and governor of LA (1864-65).

Area (sq mi): 765.67 (land 764.5; water 1.17).

Pop: 25,440 (White 68.1%; Black or African American 24.6%; Hispanic or Latino 4.5%; Asian 0.6%; Other 2.9%). **Foreign born:** 0.6%. **Median age:** 34.8. **State rank:** 38. **Pop change 1990-2000:** +19.9%.

Income: per capita $13,101; median household $27,777. **Pop below poverty level:** 19.9%.

Unemployment: 6.7%. **Median home value:** $58,100. **Median travel time to work:** 27.8 minutes.

ASCENSION PARISH

PO Box 1659   **Ph:** 225-621-5709
Gonzales, LA 70707   **Fax:** 225-621-5704
www.ascensionparish.net

In eastern LA, southeast of Baton Rouge; organized Mar 31, 1807 (prior to statehood) from Acadia Parish. **Name Origin:** For the Feast of the Ascension of Jesus Christ usually observed by Christians of the fortieth day after Easter.

Area (sq mi): 302.88 (land 291.53; water 11.35).

Pop: 76,627 (White 76.2%; Black or African American 20.3%; Hispanic or Latino 2.5%; Asian 0.3%; Other 2%). **Foreign born:** 1.8%. **Median age:** 32. **State rank:** 16. **Pop change 1990-2000:** +31.6%.

Income: per capita $17,858; median household $44,288. **Pop below poverty level:** 12.9%.

Unemployment: 6.5%. **Median home value:** $103,800. **Median travel time to work:** 26.3 minutes.

ASSUMPTION PARISH

PO Box 249   **Ph:** 985-369-6653
Napoleonville, LA 70390   **Fax:** 985-369-2032

In southeastern LA, south of Baton Rouge; organized Mar 31, 1807 (prior to statehood) from Lafourche Parish. **Name Origin:** For the Feast of the Assumption of the Virgin Mary observed by Christians on August 15.

Area (sq mi): 364.55 (land 338.68; water 25.87).

Pop: 23,388 (White 66.6%; Black or African American 31.5%; Hispanic or Latino 1.2%; Asian 0.2%; Other 1.1%). **Foreign born:** 0.8%. **Median age:** 34.2. **State rank:** 40. **Pop change 1990-2000:** +2.8%.

Income: per capita $14,008; median household $31,168. **Pop below poverty level:** 21.8%.

Unemployment: 8%. **Median home value:** $78,800. **Median travel time to work:** 29.1 minutes.

AVOYELLES PARISH

312 N Main St Courthouse Bldg Suite D   **Ph:** 318-253-9208
Marksville, LA 71351   **Fax:** 318-253-4614

In east-central LA, east of Alexandria; original Parish; organized Mar 31, 1807 (prior to statehood). **Name Origin:** For the Indian tribe. The name probably means 'flint people.'

Area (sq mi): 865.67 (land 832.44; water 33.24).

Please see sample entry on inside front cover for detailed information about the statistics presented with each county listing.

247

Pop: 41,481 (White 67.9%; Black or African American 29.5%; Hispanic or Latino 1%; Asian 0.2%; Other 1.9%). **Foreign born:** 0.5%. **Median age:** 35.2. **State rank:** 29. **Pop change 1990-2000:** +5.9%.

Income: per capita $12,146; median household $23,851. **Pop below poverty level:** 25.9%.

Unemployment: 8.3%. **Median home value:** $54,800. **Median travel time to work:** 31.8 minutes.

BEAUREGARD PARISH

PO Box 100   **Ph:** 337-463-8595
DeRidder, LA 70634   **Fax:** 337-462-3916

On southwestern border of LA, north of Lake Charles; organized Jun 12, 1912 from Calcasieu Parish. **Name Origin:** For Pierre Gustave Toutant Beauregard (1818-93), superintendent at West Point who resigned to join the Confederate army (1861); he was the general who directed the bombardment of Fort Sumter and battles of Bull Run and Shiloh.

Area (sq mi): 1165.99 (land 1160.09; water 5.9).

Pop: 32,986 (White 83.4%; Black or African American 12.9%; Hispanic or Latino 1.4%; Asian 0.6%; Other 2.2%). **Foreign born:** 1.1%. **Median age:** 35.5. **State rank:** 33. **Pop change 1990-2000:** +9.7%.

Income: per capita $15,514; median household $32,582. **Pop below poverty level:** 15.6%.

Unemployment: 7.4%. **Median home value:** $64,800. **Median travel time to work:** 31.4 minutes.

BIENVILLE PARISH

100 Courthouse Dr Rm 100   **Ph:** 318-263-2123
Arcadia, LA 71001   **Fax:** 318-263-7426
www.bienvilleparish.org

In north-central LA, southeast of Shreveport; organized Mar 14, 1848 from Claiborne Parish. **Name Origin:** For Jean Baptiste Le Moyne, Sieur de Bienville (1680-1765?), founder of New Orleans (1718) and governor of the French colony of Louisiana (1701-13; 1718-26; 1733-43).

Area (sq mi): 821.77 (land 810.64; water 11.13).

Pop: 15,752 (White 54.6%; Black or African American 43.8%; Hispanic or Latino 0.9%; Asian 0.2%; Other 1.2%). **Foreign born:** 0.4%. **Median age:** 38. **State rank:** 52. **Pop change 1990-2000:** -1.4%.

Income: per capita $12,471; median household $23,663. **Pop below poverty level:** 26.1%.

Unemployment: 11.1%. **Median home value:** $46,700. **Median travel time to work:** 32.9 minutes.

BOSSIER PARISH

204 Burt Blvd 2nd Fl   **Ph:** 318-965-2336
Benton, LA 71006   **Fax:** 318-965-2713
www.mybossier.com

On the northwestern border of panhandle of LA, north of Shreveport; organized Feb 24, 1843 from Claiborne Parish. **Name Origin:** For Pierre Evariste Jean Baptiste Bossier (1797-1844), LA legislator and U.S. representative (1843-44).

Area (sq mi): 866.93 (land 839.25; water 27.68).

Pop: 98,310 (White 72.9%; Black or African American 20.8%; Hispanic or Latino 3.1%; Asian 1.3%; Other 3.3%). **Foreign born:** 2.5%. **Median age:** 33.8. **State rank:** 12. **Pop change 1990-2000:** +14.2%.

Income: per capita $18,119; median household $39,203. **Pop below poverty level:** 13.7%.

Unemployment: 5.5%. **Median home value:** $87,600. **Median travel time to work:** 22.4 minutes.

CADDO PARISH

505 Travis St 8th Fl   **Ph:** 318-226-6900
Shreveport, LA 711015476   **Fax:** 318-429-7630
www.caddo.org

On northwestern border of panhandle of LA; organized Jan 18, 1838 from Natchitoches Parish. **Name Origin:** For name of a group of tribes of Caddoan linguistic stock. Derived from one of the tribal groups, the Kadohadacho ('real chiefs') Confederacy.

Area (sq mi): 936.9 (land 881.99; water 54.91).

Pop: 252,161 (White 52.2%; Black or African American 44.6%; Hispanic or Latino 1.5%; Asian 0.7%; Other 1.8%). **Foreign born:** 1.5%. **Median age:** 35.1. **State rank:** 4. **Pop change 1990-2000:** +1.6%.

Income: per capita $17,839; median household $31,467. **Pop below poverty level:** 21.1%.

Unemployment: 6.4%. **Median home value:** $75,100. **Median travel time to work:** 21 minutes.

CALCASIEU PARISH

PO Box 1030   **Ph:** 337-437-3550
Lake Charles, LA 70602   **Fax:** 337-437-3350
www.cppj.net

On southwestern border of LA; organized Mar 24, 1840 from Saint Landry Parish. **Name Origin:** Said to be from Atakapan 'crying eagle,' the name of an Indian chief.

Area (sq mi): 1094.34 (land 1071.12; water 23.22).

Pop: 183,577 (White 72.8%; Black or African American 24%; Hispanic or Latino 1.3%; Asian 0.6%; Other 1.7%). **Foreign born:** 1.4%. **Median age:** 34.5. **State rank:** 7. **Pop change 1990-2000:** +9.2%.

Income: per capita $17,710; median household $35,372. **Pop below poverty level:** 15.4%.

Unemployment: 6.1%. **Median home value:** $80,500. **Median travel time to work:** 20.4 minutes.

CALDWELL PARISH

PO Box 1737   **Ph:** 318-649-2681
Columbia, LA 71418   **Fax:** 318-649-5930

In north-central LA, south of Monroe; organized Mar 6, 1838 from Catahoula and Ouachita parishes. **Name Origin:** For Matthew Caldwell, a pioneer from NC.

Area (sq mi): 540.72 (land 529.42; water 11.3).

Pop: 10,560 (White 79.5%; Black or African American 17.9%; Hispanic or Latino 1.5%; Asian 0.1%; Other 1.6%). **Foreign born:**

All statistics are based on the 2000 Census except the dollar figures given for per capita income, which are based on 1999 estimates.

248

0.6%. **Median age:** 36.7. **State rank:** 59. **Pop change 1990-2000:** +7.6%.

Income: per capita $13,884; median household $26,972. **Pop below poverty level:** 21.2%.

Unemployment: 9.2%. **Median home value:** $53,800. **Median travel time to work:** 36.8 minutes.

CAMERON PARISH

PO Box 549   **Ph:** 337-775-5316
Cameron, LA 70631   **Fax:** 337-775-7172
www.cameronparish.net

On the southwestern border of LA, south of Lake Charles; organized Mar 15, 1870 from Calcasieu and Vermilion parishes. **Name Origin:** For Robert Alexander Cameron, a Confederate soldier active in LA politics after the Civil War; or possibly for Simon Cameron (1799-1889), U.S. senator from PA (1845-49; 1857-61; 1867-77) and secretary of war (1861-62).

Area (sq mi): 1931.6 (land 1312.96; water 618.63).

Pop: 9,991 (White 92.5%; Black or African American 3.9%; Hispanic or Latino 2.2%; Asian 0.4%; Other 2%). **Foreign born:** 1.6%. **Median age:** 35. **State rank:** 61. **Pop change 1990-2000:** +7.9%.

Income: per capita $15,348; median household $34,232. **Pop below poverty level:** 12.3%.

Unemployment: 5.9%. **Median home value:** $59,600. **Median travel time to work:** 26.3 minutes.

CATAHOULA PARISH

PO Box 654   **Ph:** 318-744-5497
Harrisonburg, LA 71340   **Fax:** 318-744-5488

In northeastern LA, northeast of Alexandria; organized Mar 23, 1808 (prior to statehood) from Rapides Parish. **Name Origin:** From an Indian name of uncertain origin. Three derivations have been suggested: for the Etacoulow River 'River of the Great Spirit,' now called Little River, which runs through the parish; from Choctaw *okkattahoola* 'beautiful white water,' or Choctaw-French combination 'lake people.'

Area (sq mi): 739.43 (land 703.65; water 35.78).

Pop: 10,920 (White 71.3%; Black or African American 27.1%; Hispanic or Latino 0.9%; Asian 0.1%; Other 1%). **Foreign born:** 0.1%. **Median age:** 36.7. **State rank:** 58. **Pop change 1990-2000:** -1.3%.

Income: per capita $12,608; median household $22,528. **Pop below poverty level:** 28.1%.

Unemployment: 11.1%. **Median home value:** $48,800. **Median travel time to work:** 38.3 minutes.

CLAIBORNE PARISH

512 E Main St PO Box 330   **Ph:** 318-927-9601
Homer, LA 71040   **Fax:** 318-927-2345

On the central northern border of the LA panhandle, northeast of Shreveport; organized Mar 13, 1828 from Natchitoches Parish. **Name Origin:** For William Charles Cole Claiborne (1775-1817), governor of the Mississippi Territory (1801-05), of the Orleans Territory (1804-12), and of LA (1812-16).

Area (sq mi): 767.55 (land 754.65; water 12.9).

Pop: 16,851 (White 51.5%; Black or African American 47.4%; Hispanic or Latino 0.8%; Asian 0.1%; Other 0.7%). **Foreign born:** 0.4%. **Median age:** 37.7. **State rank:** 51. **Pop change 1990-2000:** -3.2%.

Income: per capita $13,825; median household $25,344. **Pop below poverty level:** 26.5%.

Unemployment: 8.1%. **Median home value:** $55,400. **Median travel time to work:** 25.9 minutes.

CONCORDIA PARISH

PO Box 790   **Ph:** 318-336-4204
Vidalia, LA 71373   **Fax:** 318-336-8777

On the central eastern border of LA, west of Natchez, MS; original colony, organized Apr 10, 1807 (prior to statehood). **Name Origin:** For either Concordia, the Roman goddess of peace and harmony, or a Latinized form of *concord* 'harmony.'

Area (sq mi): 748.68 (land 695.91; water 52.77).

Pop: 20,247 (White 60.1%; Black or African American 37.7%; Hispanic or Latino 1.5%; Asian 0.2%; Other 1.3%). **Foreign born:** 1.3%. **Median age:** 36.9. **State rank:** 48. **Pop change 1990-2000:** -2.8%.

Income: per capita $11,966; median household $22,742. **Pop below poverty level:** 29.1%.

Unemployment: 12.8%. **Median home value:** $55,600. **Median travel time to work:** 26.5 minutes.

DE SOTO PARISH

PO Box 1206   **Ph:** 318-872-3110
Mansfield, LA 71052   **Fax:** 318-872-4202

On the western border, south of Shreveport; organized Apr 1, 1843 from Natchitoches Parish. **Name Origin:** For Hernando de Soto (c.1500-42), Spanish explorer of southern U.S.

Area (sq mi): 894.49 (land 877.2; water 17.29).

Pop: 25,494 (White 55.3%; Black or African American 42.2%; Hispanic or Latino 1.6%; Asian 0.1%; Other 1.8%). **Foreign born:** 1%. **Median age:** 36.3. **State rank:** 37. **Pop change 1990-2000:** +0.6%.

Income: per capita $13,606; median household $28,252. **Pop below poverty level:** 25.1%.

Unemployment: 9.5%. **Median home value:** $58,100. **Median travel time to work:** 30.1 minutes.

EAST BATON ROUGE PARISH

1755 Florida St   **Ph:** 225-389-3129
Baton Rouge, LA 70821   **Fax:** 225-389-3118
www.ci.baton-rouge.la.us

In eastern LA, northwest of New Orleans; organized 1810 (prior to statehood) from Spanish West Florida. **Name Origin:** For its location. The city and the parish share a joint mayor-council form of government.

Area (sq mi): 470.54 (land 455.43; water 15.11).

Pop: 412,852 (White 55.1%; Black or African American 40.1%; Hispanic or Latino 1.8%; Asian 2.1%; Other 1.6%). **Foreign born:** 3.7%. **Median age:** 31.5. **State rank:** 3. **Pop change 1990-2000:** +8.6%.

Please see sample entry on inside front cover for detailed information about the statistics presented with each county listing.

Income: per capita $19,790; median household $37,224. **Pop below poverty level:** 17.9%.

Unemployment: 5%. **Median home value:** $98,800. **Median travel time to work:** 23.2 minutes.

EAST CARROLL PARISH
400 1st St   **Ph:** 318-559-2399
Lake Providence, LA 71254
www.eastcarroll.net

On the northeastern border of the LA panhandle; organized Mar 28, 1877 from Carroll Parish. **Name Origin:** From the division of Carroll Parish into two parishes, East and West. Originally for Charles Carroll (1737-1832), signer of the Declaration of Independence and U.S. senator from MD (1789-92).

Area (sq mi): 442.45 (land 421.44; water 21.01).

Pop: 9,421 (White 31.1%; Black or African American 67.3%; Hispanic or Latino 1.2%; Asian 0.3%; Other 0.9%). **Foreign born:** 0.9%. **Median age:** 30.9. **State rank:** 63. **Pop change 1990-2000:** -3%.

Income: per capita $9,629; median household $20,723. **Pop below poverty level:** 40.5%.

Unemployment: 18.6%. **Median home value:** $35,900. **Median travel time to work:** 20.4 minutes.

EAST FELICIANA PARISH
PO Box 599   **Ph:** 225-683-5145
Clinton, LA 70722   **Fax:** 225-683-3556

On the northeastern border of LA, north of Baton Rouge; organized Feb 17, 1824 from Feliciana Parish. **Name Origin:** From the division of Feliciana Parish into two parishes: East and West. Name is Spanish for 'happiness,' or possibly for Felicite, the wife of a colonial governor.

Area (sq mi): 455.69 (land 453.4; water 2.29).

Pop: 21,360 (White 51.4%; Black or African American 47.1%; Hispanic or Latino 0.7%; Asian 0.2%; Other 0.9%). **Foreign born:** 0.6%. **Median age:** 35.8. **State rank:** 44. **Pop change 1990-2000:** +11.2%.

Income: per capita $15,428; median household $31,631. **Pop below poverty level:** 23%.

Unemployment: 6.6%. **Median home value:** $76,600. **Median travel time to work:** 32.4 minutes.

EVANGELINE PARISH
PO Drawer 347   **Ph:** 337-363-5671
Ville Platte, LA 70586 **Fax:** 337-363-5780

In south-central LA, northwest of Lafayette; established Jun 15, 1910 from Saint Landry Parish. **Name Origin:** For the heroine of Henry Wadsworth Longfellow's (1807-82) poem of the same name.

Area (sq mi): 679.61 (land 664.27; water 15.34).

Pop: 35,434 (White 69.8%; Black or African American 28.6%; Hispanic or Latino 1%; Asian 0.1%; Other 0.9%). **Foreign born:** 0.6%. **Median age:** 33.7. **State rank:** 31. **Pop change 1990-2000:** +6.5%.

Income: per capita $11,432; median household $20,532. **Pop below poverty level:** 32.2%.

Unemployment: 6.6%. **Median home value:** $53,000. **Median travel time to work:** 32.7 minutes.

FRANKLIN PARISH
PO Box 1564   **Ph:** 318-435-5133
Winnsboro, LA 71295 **Fax:** 318-435-5134

In northeastern LA, southeast of Monroe; organized Mar 1, 1843 from Catahoula, Ouachita, and Madison parishes. **Name Origin:** For Benjamin Franklin (1706-90), U.S. patriot, diplomat, and statesman.

Area (sq mi): 635.43 (land 623.61; water 11.82).

Pop: 21,263 (White 66.8%; Black or African American 31.6%; Hispanic or Latino 0.8%; Asian 0.2%; Other 1%). **Foreign born:** 0.6%. **Median age:** 35.9. **State rank:** 45. **Pop change 1990-2000:** -5%.

Income: per capita $12,675; median household $22,964. **Pop below poverty level:** 28.4%.

Unemployment: 9.9%. **Median home value:** $48,700. **Median travel time to work:** 32.5 minutes.

GRANT PARISH
PO Box 263   **Ph:** 318-627-3246
Colfax, LA 71417   **Fax:** 318-627-3201

In central LA, north of Alexandria; organized Mar 4, 1869 from Rapides and Winn parishes. **Name Origin:** For Ulysses S. Grant (1822-85), Civil War general and eighteenth U.S. president.

Area (sq mi): 664.56 (land 645.11; water 19.45).

Pop: 18,698 (White 84.8%; Black or African American 11.9%; Hispanic or Latino 1.1%; Asian 0.1%; Other 2.6%). **Foreign born:** 0.5%. **Median age:** 35.5. **State rank:** 49. **Pop change 1990-2000:** +6.7%.

Income: per capita $14,410; median household $29,622. **Pop below poverty level:** 21.5%.

Unemployment: 9.4%. **Median home value:** $58,500. **Median travel time to work:** 38.6 minutes.

IBERIA PARISH
PO Box 12010   **Ph:** 337-365-7282
New Iberia, LA 70562 **Fax:** 337-365-0737

On the central southern border of LA, southeast of Lafayette; organized Oct 30, 1868 from Saint Martin and Saint Mary parishes. **Name Origin:** For the European peninsula containing present-day Spain and Portugal.

Area (sq mi): 1030.86 (land 575.13; water 455.73).

Pop: 73,266 (White 64.3%; Black or African American 30.8%; Hispanic or Latino 1.5%; Asian 1.9%; Other 2.1%). **Foreign born:** 2%. **Median age:** 33.3. **State rank:** 17. **Pop change 1990-2000:** +7.3%.

Income: per capita $14,145; median household $31,204. **Pop below poverty level:** 23.6%.

Unemployment: 5.7%. **Median home value:** $75,500. **Median travel time to work:** 24 minutes.

All statistics are based on the 2000 Census except the dollar figures given for per capita income, which are based on 1999 estimates.

IBERVILLE PARISH

PO Box 423   **Ph:** 225-687-5160
Plaquemine, LA 70764   **Fax:** 225-687-5260
www.parish.iberville.la.us

In south-central LA, west of Baton Rouge; organized 1807 (prior to statehood). **Name Origin:** For Pierre le Moyne, Sieur d'Iberville (1661-1706), French-Canadian naval officer who explored the Mississippi River delta and founded French colonies at present-day Biloxi and Mobile; governor of LA (1703).

Area (sq mi): 652.84 (land 618.64; water 34.2).

Pop: 33,320 (White 48.6%; Black or African American 49.7%; Hispanic or Latino 1%; Asian 0.3%; Other 0.8%). **Foreign born:** 0.7%. **Median age:** 34.4. **State rank:** 32. **Pop change 1990-2000:** +7.3%.

Income: per capita $13,272; median household $29,039. **Pop below poverty level:** 23.1%.

Unemployment: 8.6%. **Median home value:** $76,700. **Median travel time to work:** 26.6 minutes.

JACKSON PARISH

PO Box 730   **Ph:** 318-259-2424
Jonesboro, LA 71251   **Fax:** 318-395-0386

In north-central LA, southwest of Monroe; organized Feb 27, 1845 from Claiborne, Ouachita, and Union parishes. **Name Origin:** For Andrew Jackson (1767-1845), seventh U.S. president.

Area (sq mi): 580.34 (land 569.75; water 10.59).

Pop: 15,397 (White 70.7%; Black or African American 27.9%; Hispanic or Latino 0.6%; Asian 0.2%; Other 0.9%). **Foreign born:** 0.4%. **Median age:** 37.6. **State rank:** 53. **Pop change 1990-2000:** -2%.

Income: per capita $15,354; median household $28,352. **Pop below poverty level:** 19.8%.

Unemployment: 9%. **Median home value:** $53,100. **Median travel time to work:** 24.5 minutes.

JEFFERSON DAVIS PARISH

PO Box 799   **Ph:** 337-824-8340
Jennings, LA 70546

In southwestern LA, east of Lake Charles; organized Jun 12, 1912 from Calcasieu Parish. **Name Origin:** For Jefferson Davis (1808-89), president of the Confederate States of America (1862-65).

Area (sq mi): 658.58 (land 652.31; water 6.26).

Pop: 31,435 (White 80%; Black or African American 17.8%; Hispanic or Latino 1%; Asian 0.2%; Other 1.4%). **Foreign born:** 0.6%. **Median age:** 34.5. **State rank:** 34. **Pop change 1990-2000:** +2.3%.

Income: per capita $13,398; median household $27,736. **Pop below poverty level:** 20.9%.

Unemployment: 6.8%. **Median home value:** $60,500. **Median travel time to work:** 30.8 minutes.

JEFFERSON PARISH

PO Box 9   **Ph:** 504-364-2600
Gretna, LA 70054   **Fax:** 504-364-2636
www.jeffparish.net

In southeastern LA bordered on the north by Lake Pontchartrain

and on the south by the Gulf of Mexico; organized Feb 11, 1825 from Orleans Parish. **Name Origin:** For Thomas Jefferson (1743-1826), U.S. patriot and statesman; third U.S. president.

Area (sq mi): 642.41 (land 306.52; water 335.89).

Pop: 455,466 (White 65.4%; Black or African American 22.9%; Hispanic or Latino 7.1%; Asian 3.1%; Other 4.1%). **Foreign born:** 7.5%. **Median age:** 35.9. **State rank:** 2. **Pop change 1990-2000:** +1.6%.

Income: per capita $19,953; median household $38,435. **Pop below poverty level:** 13.7%.

Unemployment: 4.3%. **Median home value:** $105,300. **Median travel time to work:** 25 minutes.

LA SALLE PARISH

PO Box 1288   **Ph:** 318-992-2101
Jena, LA 71342   **Fax:** 318-992-2103

In east-central LA, northeast of Alexandria; organized Jul 3, 1908 from Catahoula Parish. **Name Origin:** For Robert Cavelier (1643-87), Sieur de La Salle, French adventurer and explorer who claimed the land west of the Mississippi River for France.

Area (sq mi): 662.36 (land 623.83; water 38.54).

Pop: 14,282 (White 85.6%; Black or African American 12.2%; Hispanic or Latino 0.8%; Asian 0.2%; Other 1.4%). **Foreign born:** 0.6%. **Median age:** 36.4. **State rank:** 55. **Pop change 1990-2000:** +4.5%.

Income: per capita $14,033; median household $28,189. **Pop below poverty level:** 18.7%.

Unemployment: 7.2%. **Median home value:** $53,200. **Median travel time to work:** 36.3 minutes.

LAFAYETTE CONSOLIDATED GOVERNMENT

PO Box 2009   **Ph:** 337-233-0150
Lafayette, LA 70502   **Fax:** 337-919-6392
www.lafayettegov.org

In south-central LA, west of Baton Rouge; organized Jan 17, 1823 from Attakapas and Saint Martin parishes. **Name Origin:** For the Mauquis de Lafayette (1757-1834), French statesman and soldier who fought with the Americans during the Revolutionary War.

Area (sq mi): 270.29 (land 269.83; water 0.46).

Pop: 190,503 (White 72.3%; Black or African American 23.8%; Hispanic or Latino 1.7%; Asian 1.1%; Other 1.7%). **Foreign born:** 2.5%. **Median age:** 32.4. **State rank:** 6. **Pop change 1990-2000:** +15.6%.

Income: per capita $19,371; median household $36,518. **Pop below poverty level:** 15.7%.

Unemployment: 3.9%. **Median home value:** $100,500. **Median travel time to work:** 23.8 minutes.

LAFOURCHE PARISH

PO Box 5548   **Ph:** 985-446-8427
Thibodaux, LA 70302   **Fax:** 985-446-8459
www.lapage.com/parishes/lafou.htm

In southeastern LA, southwest of New Orleans; organized 1807

Please see sample entry on inside front cover for detailed information about the statistics presented with each county listing.

(prior to statehood). **Name Origin:** For Bayou Lafourche, which runs the length of the county; from French 'the fork.'

Area (sq mi): 1472.19 (land 1084.68; water 387.51).

Pop: 89,974 (White 82.2%; Black or African American 12.6%; Hispanic or Latino 1.4%; Asian 0.7%; Other 3.9%). **Foreign born:** 1.5%. **Median age:** 34.1. **State rank:** 14. **Pop change 1990-2000:** +4.8%.

Income: per capita $15,809; median household $34,910. **Pop below poverty level:** 16.5%.

Unemployment: 3.8%. **Median home value:** $78,900. **Median travel time to work:** 26.8 minutes.

LINCOLN PARISH

100 W Texas Ave   **Ph:** 318-251-5150
Ruston, LA 71270   **Fax:** 318-251-5149
www.lincolnparish.org

In north-central LA, west of Monroe; organized Feb 27, 1873 from Bienville, Jackson, and Union parishes. **Name Origin:** For Abraham Lincoln (1809-65), sixteenth U.S. president.

Area (sq mi): 472.27 (land 471.38; water 0.89).

Pop: 42,509 (White 56.9%; Black or African American 39.8%; Hispanic or Latino 1.2%; Asian 1.3%; Other 1.5%). **Foreign born:** 2.1%. **Median age:** 26.5. **State rank:** 27. **Pop change 1990-2000:** +1.8%.

Income: per capita $14,313; median household $26,977. **Pop below poverty level:** 26.5%.

Unemployment: 4.6%. **Median home value:** $79,800. **Median travel time to work:** 18.6 minutes.

LIVINGSTON PARISH

20180 Iowa St   **Ph:** 225-686-2266
Livingston, LA 70754   **Fax:** 225-686-7079
www.lapage.com/parishes/livin.htm

On eastern border of LA, east of Baton Rouge; organized Feb 10, 1832 from Saint Helena Parish. **Name Origin:** For Robert R. Livingston (1746-1813), NY patriot, statesman, and a drafter of the Declaration of Independence.

Area (sq mi): 702.84 (land 648.02; water 54.82).

Pop: 91,814 (White 93.5%; Black or African American 4.2%; Hispanic or Latino 1.1%; Asian 0.2%; Other 1.3%). **Foreign born:** 0.8%. **Median age:** 32.8. **State rank:** 13. **Pop change 1990-2000:** +30.2%.

Income: per capita $16,282; median household $38,887. **Pop below poverty level:** 11.4%.

Unemployment: 6.1%. **Median home value:** $96,100. **Median travel time to work:** 33.1 minutes.

MADISON PARISH

PO Box 1710   **Ph:** 318-574-0655
Tallulah, LA 71282   **Fax:** 318-574-3961

On the northeastern border of LA, west of Vicksburg, MS; organized Jan 19, 1838 from Concordia Parish. **Name Origin:** For James Madison (1751-1836), fourth U.S. president.

Area (sq mi): 650.53 (land 624.09; water 26.45).

Pop: 13,728 (White 37.1%; Black or African American 60.3%; Hispanic or Latino 2.1%; Asian 0.2%; Other 1.6%). **Foreign born:** 0.5%. **Median age:** 29.8. **State rank:** 56. **Pop change 1990-2000:** +10.2%.

Income: per capita $10,114; median household $20,509. **Pop below poverty level:** 36.7%.

Unemployment: 11.5%. **Median home value:** $46,900. **Median travel time to work:** 22.5 minutes.

MOREHOUSE PARISH

PO Box 1543   **Ph:** 318-281-3343
Bastrop, LA 71221   **Fax:** 318-281-3775

On the northern border of the LA panhandle, northeast of Monroe; organized Mar 25, 1844 from Ouachita Territory. **Name Origin:** For Abraham Morehouse (?-1813), colonizer and representative to the legislature of the Territory of Orleans.

Area (sq mi): 805.2 (land 794.25; water 10.95).

Pop: 31,021 (White 55.5%; Black or African American 43.4%; Hispanic or Latino 0.7%; Asian 0.2%; Other 0.6%). **Foreign born:** 0.4%. **Median age:** 35.6. **State rank:** 35. **Pop change 1990-2000:** -2.9%.

Income: per capita $13,197; median household $25,124. **Pop below poverty level:** 26.8%.

Unemployment: 12.2%. **Median home value:** $50,400. **Median travel time to work:** 24.9 minutes.

NATCHITOCHES PARISH

PO Box 799   **Ph:** 318-352-2714
Natchitoches, LA 71458   **Fax:** 318-357-2208

In west-central LA, northwest of Alexandria; organized 1807 (prior to statehood). **Name Origin:** For the Indian tribe, from a Caddoan word translated variously as 'chinquapin eaters,' 'chestnut eaters,' 'pawpaw eaters,' or 'pawpaws.'

Area (sq mi): 1299.3 (land 1255.45; water 43.85).

Pop: 39,080 (White 57.2%; Black or African American 38.4%; Hispanic or Latino 1.4%; Asian 0.4%; Other 3.3%). **Foreign born:** 1.5%. **Median age:** 30.2. **State rank:** 30. **Pop change 1990-2000:** +6.5%.

Income: per capita $13,743; median household $25,722. **Pop below poverty level:** 26.5%.

Unemployment: 6.7%. **Median home value:** $70,400. **Median travel time to work:** 24.8 minutes.

ORLEANS PARISH

1300 Perdido St Rm 9-E-06   **Ph:** 504-565-6570
New Orleans, LA 70112   **Fax:** 504-565-7255
www.nocitycouncil.com

In southeastern LA, southeast of Baton Rouge; organized 1807 (prior to statehood). **Name Origin:** For the city of France, former home of many early settlers.

Area (sq mi): 350.21 (land 180.56; water 169.66).

Pop: 484,674 (White 26.6%; Black or African American 67.3%;

All statistics are based on the 2000 Census except the dollar figures given for per capita income, which are based on 1999 estimates.

Hispanic or Latino 3.1%; Asian 2.3%; Other 2.4%). **Foreign born:** 4.2%. **Median age:** 33.1. **State rank:** 1. **Pop change 1990-2000:** -2.5%.

Income: per capita $17,258; median household $27,133. **Pop below poverty level:** 27.9%.

Unemployment: 5.9%. **Median home value:** $87,300. **Median travel time to work:** 25.7 minutes.

OUACHITA PARISH

PO Box 1862   **Ph:** 318-327-1444
Monroe, LA 71210   **Fax:** 318-327-1462
www.oppj.org

In north-central LA; organized 1807 (prior to statehood). **Name Origin:** For the Ouachita River, which runs through the parish; named for an Indian tribe of the Natchitoches Confederacy; meaning of the name is unclear.

Area (sq mi): 632.7 (land 610.53; water 22.17).

Pop: 147,250 (White 63.8%; Black or African American 33.6%; Hispanic or Latino 1.2%; Asian 0.6%; Other 1.2%). **Foreign born:** 1%. **Median age:** 32.3. **State rank:** 8. **Pop change 1990-2000:** +3.6%.

Income: per capita $17,084; median household $32,047. **Pop below poverty level:** 20.7%.

Unemployment: 5.5%. **Median home value:** $80,000. **Median travel time to work:** 20.4 minutes.

PLAQUEMINES PARISH

PO Box 40   **Ph:** 504-392-4969
Belle Chasse, LA 70037

On southeastern border of LA, south of New Orleans; organized Mar 31, 1807 (prior to statehood) from Orleans Parish. **Name Origin:** A French rendering of Illinois Indian *piakimin* 'persimmon' for the many trees.

Area (sq mi): 2428.54 (land 844.56; water 1583.98).

Pop: 26,757 (White 68.8%; Black or African American 23.4%; Hispanic or Latino 1.6%; Asian 2.6%; Other 4.2%). **Foreign born:** 2.8%. **Median age:** 33.7. **State rank:** 36. **Pop change 1990-2000:** +4.6%.

Income: per capita $15,937; median household $38,173. **Pop below poverty level:** 18%.

Unemployment: 5.1%. **Median home value:** $110,100. **Median travel time to work:** 26.4 minutes.

POINTE COUPEE PARISH

PO Box 86   **Ph:** 225-638-9596
New Roads, LA 70760   **Fax:** 225-638-9590
www.pcpolicejury.org

In south-central LA, northwest of Baton Rouge; organized 1807 (prior to statehood). **Name Origin:** From French 'cut-off point,' descriptive of a point where the Mississippi River cut a new channel.

Area (sq mi): 590.68 (land 557.34; water 33.34).

Pop: 22,763 (White 60.3%; Black or African American 37.8%; Hispanic or Latino 1.1%; Asian 0.3%; Other 1.1%). **Foreign born:**

0.9%. **Median age:** 36.7. **State rank:** 42. **Pop change 1990-2000:** +1%.

Income: per capita $15,387; median household $30,618. **Pop below poverty level:** 23.1%.

Unemployment: 8.7%. **Median home value:** $80,100. **Median travel time to work:** 31.2 minutes.

RAPIDES PARISH

PO Box 952   **Ph:** 318-473-8153
Alexandria, LA 71309   **Fax:** 318-473-4667
www.rppj.com

In central LA; organized 1807 (prior to statehood). **Name Origin:** French for the 'rapids,' on the Red River, which runs through the parish.

Area (sq mi): 1361.96 (land 1322.54; water 39.42).

Pop: 126,337 (White 65.7%; Black or African American 30.4%; Hispanic or Latino 1.4%; Asian 0.9%; Other 2.1%). **Foreign born:** 1.6%. **Median age:** 35.5. **State rank:** 9. **Pop change 1990-2000:** -4%.

Income: per capita $16,088; median household $29,856. **Pop below poverty level:** 20.5%.

Unemployment: 6%. **Median home value:** $74,000. **Median travel time to work:** 23.6 minutes.

RED RIVER PARISH

PO Box 485   **Ph:** 318-932-6741
Coushatta, LA 71019   **Fax:** 318-932-3126

In west-central LA, southeast of Shreveport; organized 1871 from Caddo, Bossier, Bienville, Natchitoches, and De Soto parishes. **Name Origin:** For the river, which runs through the county.

Area (sq mi): 402.08 (land 389.29; water 12.79).

Pop: 9,622 (White 57.6%; Black or African American 40.9%; Hispanic or Latino 1%; Asian 0.1%; Other 1.1%). **Foreign born:** 0.4%. **Median age:** 34.6. **State rank:** 62. **Pop change 1990-2000:** +2.5%.

Income: per capita $12,119; median household $23,153. **Pop below poverty level:** 29.9%.

Unemployment: 10.6%. **Median home value:** $48,500. **Median travel time to work:** 31 minutes.

RICHLAND PARISH

708 Julia St   **Ph:** 318-728-2061
Rayville, LA 71269   **Fax:** 318-728-7004

In northeastern LA, east of Monroe; organized Mar 11, 1852 from Ouachita, Carroll, Franklin, and Morehouse parishes. **Name Origin:** Descriptive of the fertile soil.

Area (sq mi): 564.51 (land 558.45; water 6.05).

Pop: 20,981 (White 60.4%; Black or African American 38%; Hispanic or Latino 1.1%; Asian 0.2%; Other 0.8%). **Foreign born:** 0.5%. **Median age:** 35.8. **State rank:** 47. **Pop change 1990-2000:** +1.7%.

Income: per capita $12,479; median household $23,668. **Pop below poverty level:** 27.9%.

Please see sample entry on inside front cover for detailed information about the statistics presented with each county listing.

Unemployment: 10.5%. **Median home value:** $55,400. **Median travel time to work:** 27.3 minutes.

SABINE PARISH

400 S Capitol St   **Ph:** 318-256-6223
Many, LA 71449   **Fax:** 318-256-9037

On the western border of LA, south of Shreveport; organized Mar 7, 1843 from Natchitoches Parish. **Name Origin:** For the Sabine River, which forms the parish's western border.

Area (sq mi): 1011.51 (land 865.27; water 146.25).

Pop: 23,459 (White 71.3%; Black or African American 16.9%; Hispanic or Latino 2.7%; Asian 0.1%; Other 10.3%). **Foreign born:** 1%. **Median age:** 38.2. **State rank:** 39. **Pop change 1990-2000:** +3.6%.

Income: per capita $15,199; median household $26,655. **Pop below poverty level:** 21.5%.

Unemployment: 7.2%. **Median home value:** $61,400. **Median travel time to work:** 35.4 minutes.

SAINT BERNARD PARISH

8201 W Judge Perez Dr   **Ph:** 504-277-6371
Chalmette, LA 70043   **Fax:** 504-278-4329
www.st-bernard.la.us

On the northeastern border of LA, east of New Orleans; organized Mar 31, 1807 (prior to statehood) from Orleans Parish. **Name Origin:** For Don Bernardo de Galvez (1746-86), Spanish colonial governor who supplied American forces during the American Revolution.

Area (sq mi): 1793.75 (land 465.04; water 1328.71).

Pop: 67,229 (White 84.4%; Black or African American 7.6%; Hispanic or Latino 5.1%; Asian 1.3%; Other 2.7%). **Foreign born:** 3%. **Median age:** 36.6. **State rank:** 18. **Pop change 1990-2000:** +0.9%.

Income: per capita $16,718; median household $35,939. **Pop below poverty level:** 13.1%.

Unemployment: 5.9%. **Median home value:** $85,200. **Median travel time to work:** 29.3 minutes.

SAINT CHARLES PARISH

15045 River Rd   **Ph:** 985-783-5000
Hahnville, LA 70057   **Fax:** 985-783-2067
www.st-charles.la.us

In southeastern LA, southwest of New Orleans; organized Mar 31, 1807 (prior to statehood) from German Coast Parish. **Name Origin:** For Saint Charles Borromeo (1538-84), founder of the order of the Oblates of Saint Ambrose.

Area (sq mi): 410.16 (land 283.64; water 126.52).

Pop: 48,072 (White 70.5%; Black or African American 25.2%; Hispanic or Latino 2.8%; Asian 0.6%; Other 1.8%). **Foreign born:** 2.5%. **Median age:** 34.2. **State rank:** 24. **Pop change 1990-2000:** +13.3%.

Income: per capita $19,054; median household $45,139. **Pop below poverty level:** 11.4%.

Unemployment: 5.6%. **Median home value:** $104,200. **Median travel time to work:** 26.5 minutes.

SAINT HELENA PARISH

PO Box 308   **Ph:** 225-222-4514
Greensburg, LA 70441   **Fax:** 225-222-3443

On the northern border of LA, northeast of Baton Rouge; organized Oct 27, 1810 (prior to statehood) from Feliciana Parish. **Name Origin:** For Saint Helena (c.250-330), mother of Constantine the Great.

Area (sq mi): 409.46 (land 408.36; water 1.09).

Pop: 10,525 (White 46.2%; Black or African American 52.4%; Hispanic or Latino 1%; Asian 0.1%; Other 0.9%). **Foreign born:** 0.3%. **Median age:** 35. **State rank:** 60. **Pop change 1990-2000:** +6.6%.

Income: per capita $12,318; median household $24,970. **Pop below poverty level:** 26.8%.

Unemployment: 6.7%. **Median home value:** $71,400. **Median travel time to work:** 35.7 minutes.

SAINT JAMES PARISH

PO Box 63   **Ph:** 225-562-2270
Convent, LA 70723   **Fax:** 225-562-2383
www.stjamesla.com

In southeastern LA, southeast of Baton Rouge; original parish, organized Mar 31, 1807 (prior to statehood). **Name Origin:** For James the Apostle, disciple of Jesus Christ.

Area (sq mi): 257.79 (land 246.13; water 11.66).

Pop: 21,216 (White 49.7%; Black or African American 49.4%; Hispanic or Latino 0.6%; Asian 0%; Other 0.6%). **Foreign born:** 0.2%. **Median age:** 34. **State rank:** 46. **Pop change 1990-2000:** +1.6%.

Income: per capita $14,381; median household $35,277. **Pop below poverty level:** 20.7%.

Unemployment: 11.5%. **Median home value:** $81,500. **Median travel time to work:** 25.4 minutes.

SAINT JOHN THE BAPTIST PARISH

1801 W Airline Hwy   **Ph:** 985-652-9569
LaPlace, LA 70068   **Fax:** 985-652-4131
www.sjbparish.com

On the southeastern border of LA, west of New Orleans; organized Mar 31, 1807 (prior to statehood) from German Coast Parish. **Name Origin:** For the saint who baptized Jesus, his cousin.

Area (sq mi): 347.84 (land 218.9; water 128.94).

Pop: 43,044 (White 51%; Black or African American 44.8%; Hispanic or Latino 2.9%; Asian 0.5%; Other 2.2%). **Foreign born:** 2.3%. **Median age:** 32. **State rank:** 26. **Pop change 1990-2000:** +7.6%.

Income: per capita $15,445; median household $39,456. **Pop below poverty level:** 16.7%.

Unemployment: 8.2%. **Median home value:** $83,500. **Median travel time to work:** 27.8 minutes.

SAINT LANDRY PARISH

PO Box 750   **Ph:** 337-942-5606
Opelousas, LA 70571   **Fax:** 337-948-7265
www.slpolicejury.org

In south-central LA, north of Lafayette; organized Mar 31, 1807

All statistics are based on the 2000 Census except the dollar figures given for per capita income, which are based on 1999 estimates.

(prior to statehood) from Opelousas Parish. **Name Origin:** For Saint Landry (or Landri or Landericus; ?-656), bishop of Paris (650-656).

Area (sq mi): 938.83 (land 928.65; water 10.18).

Pop: 87,700 (White 56.1%; Black or African American 42.1%; Hispanic or Latino 0.9%; Asian 0.2%; Other 1.1%). **Foreign born:** 0.5%. **Median age:** 34.6. **State rank:** 15. **Pop change 1990-2000:** +9.2%.

Income: per capita $12,042; median household $22,855. **Pop below poverty level:** 29.3%.

Unemployment: 7.5%. **Median home value:** $59,600. **Median travel time to work:** 28.6 minutes.

SAINT MARTIN PARISH

PO Box 308　　　　　　　　　　**Ph:** 337-394-2210
Saint Martinville, LA 70582　　**Fax:** 337-394-7772
stmartinparish-la.org

In south-central LA, east of Lafayette; organized 1815 from Attakapas County. **Name Origin:** For Saint Martin (c.315-399), bishop of Tours.

Area (sq mi): 816.46 (land 739.85; water 76.6).

Pop: 48,583 (White 65.5%; Black or African American 32%; Hispanic or Latino 0.8%; Asian 0.9%; Other 1.2%). **Foreign born:** 0.9%. **Median age:** 33.4. **State rank:** 23. **Pop change 1990-2000:** +10.5%.

Income: per capita $13,619; median household $30,701. **Pop below poverty level:** 21.5%.

Unemployment: 8%. **Median home value:** $71,800. **Median travel time to work:** 30 minutes.

SAINT MARY PARISH

PO Box 1231　　　　　　　　　**Ph:** 337-828-4100
Franklin, LA 70538　　　　　　**Fax:** 337-828-2509
www.parish.st-mary.la.us

On the central southern border of LA, southeast of New Iberia; organized Apr 17, 1811 (prior to statehood) from Attakapas Parish. **Name Origin:** For the Virgin Mary, the mother of Jesus.

Area (sq mi): 1118.83 (land 612.79; water 506.04).

Pop: 53,500 (White 61.8%; Black or African American 31.8%; Hispanic or Latino 2.2%; Asian 1.6%; Other 3.8%). **Foreign born:** 2%. **Median age:** 34.3. **State rank:** 21. **Pop change 1990-2000:** -7.9%.

Income: per capita $13,399; median household $28,072. **Pop below poverty level:** 23.6%.

Unemployment: 8.5%. **Median home value:** $74,200. **Median travel time to work:** 18.8 minutes.

SAINT TAMMANY PARISH

PO Box 1090　　　　　　　　　**Ph:** 985-898-2430
Covington, LA 70434
www.stpgov.org

On the southeastern border of LA, east of Baton Rouge; organized Oct 27, 1810 (prior to statehood) from Feliciana Parish. **Name Origin:** For a celebrated Delaware Indian chief who lived in the

1600s; from *Tamanend*, possibly 'friendly' or 'affable.' His admirers claimed him as their 'patron saint' during the American Revolution.

Area (sq mi): 1124.08 (land 854.15; water 269.93).

Pop: 191,268 (White 85.3%; Black or African American 9.9%; Hispanic or Latino 2.5%; Asian 0.7%; Other 2.3%). **Foreign born:** 2.4%. **Median age:** 36.3. **State rank:** 5. **Pop change 1990-2000:** +32.4%.

Income: per capita $22,514; median household $47,883. **Pop below poverty level:** 9.7%.

Unemployment: 4.3%. **Median home value:** $123,900. **Median travel time to work:** 32.1 minutes.

TANGIPAHOA PARISH

PO Box 215　　　　　　　　　　**Ph:** 985-748-3211
Amite, LA 70422　　　　　　　**Fax:** 985-748-7576
www.tangicouncil.com

On the northern border of LA, east of Baton Rouge; organized Mar 6, 1869 from Livingston, Saint Tammany, Saint Helena, and Washington parishes. **Name Origin:** For the Indian tribe, which has since disappeared. The name is probably from Choctaw *tanchapi* 'cornstalk' or 'cob,' and *ayua* 'gather': 'corn gatherers.'

Area (sq mi): 823.12 (land 790.24; water 32.88).

Pop: 100,588 (White 68.9%; Black or African American 28.4%; Hispanic or Latino 1.5%; Asian 0.4%; Other 1.5%). **Foreign born:** 0.8%. **Median age:** 32.3. **State rank:** 11. **Pop change 1990-2000:** +17.4%.

Income: per capita $14,461; median household $29,412. **Pop below poverty level:** 22.7%.

Unemployment: 8.5%. **Median home value:** $85,400. **Median travel time to work:** 29.5 minutes.

TENSAS PARISH

PO Box 78　　　　　　　　　　**Ph:** 318-766-3921
Saint Joseph, LA 71366　　　　**Fax:** 318-766-3926

On the northeastern border of LA, north of Natchez, MS; organized Mar 17, 1843 from Concordia Parish. **Name Origin:** For the Taensa Indian tribe, which lived in the area. The origin and meaning of the name have been lost.

Area (sq mi): 641.2 (land 602.48; water 38.72).

Pop: 6,618 (White 42.9%; Black or African American 55.4%; Hispanic or Latino 1.3%; Asian 0.1%; Other 1%). **Foreign born:** 1.2%. **Median age:** 37.3. **State rank:** 64. **Pop change 1990-2000:** -6.8%.

Income: per capita $12,622; median household $19,799. **Pop below poverty level:** 36.3%.

Unemployment: 9%. **Median home value:** $45,300. **Median travel time to work:** 26.6 minutes.

TERREBONNE PARISH

PO Box 1569　　　　　　　　　**Ph:** 985-872-0466
Houma, LA 70361　　　　　　　**Fax:** 985-868-5143
www.terrebonneparish.com

On the southern border of LA, southwest of New Orleans; organized Mar 22, 1822 from Lafourche Parish. **Name Origin:** From the French for 'good land.'

Please see sample entry on inside front cover for detailed information about the statistics presented with each county listing.

255

Area (sq mi): 2079.9 (land 1254.93; water 824.97).

Pop: 104,503 (White 73.2%; Black or African American 17.8%; Hispanic or Latino 1.6%; Asian 0.8%; Other 7.3%). **Foreign born:** 1.5%. **Median age:** 33. **State rank:** 10. **Pop change 1990-2000:** +7.8%.

Income: per capita $16,051; median household $35,235. **Pop below poverty level:** 19.1%.

Unemployment: 3.8%. **Median home value:** $80,500. **Median travel time to work:** 25.2 minutes.

UNION PARISH
100 E Bayou St Suite 105　　　　**Ph:** 318-368-3055
Farmerville, LA 71241　　　　　**Fax:** 318-368-3861

On the central northern border of the LA panhandle, north of Monroe; organized Mar 13, 1839 from Ouachita Parish. **Name Origin:** For the union of the United States.

Area (sq mi): 905.28 (land 877.6; water 27.68).

Pop: 22,803 (White 69.2%; Black or African American 27.9%; Hispanic or Latino 2%; Asian 0.3%; Other 2%). **Foreign born:** 1.2%. **Median age:** 37.3. **State rank:** 41. **Pop change 1990-2000:** +10.2%.

Income: per capita $14,819; median household $29,061. **Pop below poverty level:** 18.6%.

Unemployment: 5.9%. **Median home value:** $63,900. **Median travel time to work:** 30.8 minutes.

VERMILION PARISH
County Courthouse 100 N State St Suite 101　**Ph:** 337-898-1992
Abbeville, LA 70510　　　　　　**Fax:** 337-898-9803

On the central southern border of LA, south of Lafayette; organized Mar 25, 1844 from Lafayette Parish. **Name Origin:** For the red clay soil.

Area (sq mi): 1538.31 (land 1173.78; water 364.53).

Pop: 53,807 (White 81.8%; Black or African American 14.2%; Hispanic or Latino 1.4%; Asian 1.8%; Other 1.4%). **Foreign born:** 2%. **Median age:** 35.1. **State rank:** 20. **Pop change 1990-2000:** +7.5%.

Income: per capita $14,201; median household $29,500. **Pop below poverty level:** 22.1%.

Unemployment: 6.4%. **Median home value:** $68,000. **Median travel time to work:** 29.4 minutes.

VERNON PARISH
PO Box 40　　　　　　　　**Ph:** 337-238-1384
Leesville, LA 71496　　　　　**Fax:** 337-238-9902

On the central western border of LA, southwest of Alexandria; organized Mar 30, 1871 from Natchitoches, Rapides, and Sabine parishes. **Name Origin:** For Mount Vernon, the home of George Washington (1732-99) in VA.

Area (sq mi): 1341.51 (land 1328.41; water 13.1).

Pop: 52,531 (White 71.4%; Black or African American 17.1%; Hispanic or Latino 5.9%; Asian 1.6%; Other 7.7%). **Foreign born:** 4.1%. **Median age:** 28.3. **State rank:** 22. **Pop change 1990-2000:** -15.2%.

Income: per capita $14,036; median household $31,216. **Pop below poverty level:** 15.3%.

Unemployment: 6.2%. **Median home value:** $66,900. **Median travel time to work:** 24 minutes.

WASHINGTON PARISH
909 Pearl St　　　　　　　**Ph:** 985-839-7825
Franklinton, LA 70438　　　　**Fax:** 985-839-7828

On the northeastern border of LA, northeast of Baton Rouge; organized Mar 6, 1819 from Saint Tammany Parish. **Name Origin:** For George Washington (1732-99), American patriot and first U.S. president.

Area (sq mi): 675.97 (land 669.57; water 6.4).

Pop: 43,926 (White 66.9%; Black or African American 31.5%; Hispanic or Latino 0.8%; Asian 0.2%; Other 0.8%). **Foreign born:** 0.4%. **Median age:** 36.1. **State rank:** 25. **Pop change 1990-2000:** +1.7%.

Income: per capita $12,915; median household $24,264. **Pop below poverty level:** 24.7%.

Unemployment: 8.4%. **Median home value:** $54,200. **Median travel time to work:** 32.6 minutes.

WEBSTER PARISH
PO Box 370　　　　　　　**Ph:** 318-371-0366
Minden, LA 71058　　　　　**Fax:** 318-371-0226

On the northwestern border of the LA panhandle, northeast of Shreveport; organized Feb 27, 1871 from Bossier, Claiborne, and Bienville parishes. **Name Origin:** For Daniel Webster (1782-1852), U.S. statesman and orator from MA.

Area (sq mi): 615.07 (land 595.22; water 19.85).

Pop: 41,831 (White 65.1%; Black or African American 32.8%; Hispanic or Latino 0.9%; Asian 0.2%; Other 1.4%). **Foreign born:** 0.7%. **Median age:** 38.1. **State rank:** 28. **Pop change 1990-2000:** -0.4%.

Income: per capita $15,203; median household $28,408. **Pop below poverty level:** 20.2%.

Unemployment: 8.4%. **Median home value:** $57,200. **Median travel time to work:** 26.7 minutes.

WEST BATON ROUGE PARISH
PO Box 757　　　　　　　**Ph:** 225-383-4755
Port Allen, LA 70767　　　　**Fax:** 225-387-0218
www.wbrcouncil.org

In east-central LA, west of Baton Rouge; organized Mar 31, 1807 (prior to statehood) from Baton Rouge Parish. **Name Origin:** From the division of Baton Rouge Parish into two parishes: East and West.

Area (sq mi): 203.62 (land 191.2; water 12.42).

Pop: 21,601 (White 62%; Black or African American 35.5%; Hispanic or Latino 1.4%; Asian 0.2%; Other 1.5%). **Foreign born:** 0.9%. **Median age:** 34. **State rank:** 43. **Pop change 1990-2000:** +11.2%.

Income: per capita $15,773; median household $37,117. **Pop below poverty level:** 17%.

All statistics are based on the 2000 Census except the dollar figures given for per capita income, which are based on 1999 estimates.

Unemployment: 5.7%. **Median home value:** $87,400. **Median travel time to work:** 21.2 minutes.

WEST CARROLL PARISH

PO Box 1078   **Ph:** 318-428-3281
Oak Grove, LA 71263   **Fax:** 318-428-9896
www.westcarrollweb.com

On the northeastern border of the LA panhandle, northeast of Monroe; organized Mar 28, 1877 from Carroll Parish. **Name Origin:** From the division of Carroll Parish into two parishes: East and West.

Area (sq mi): 360.32 (land 359.4; water 0.92).

Pop: 12,314 (White 79.1%; Black or African American 18.9%; Hispanic or Latino 1.3%; Asian 0.1%; Other 1.1%). **Foreign born:** 0.3%. **Median age:** 37.2. **State rank:** 57. **Pop change 1990-2000:** +1.8%.

Income: per capita $12,302; median household $24,637. **Pop below poverty level:** 23.4%.

Unemployment: 15%. **Median home value:** $48,200. **Median travel time to work:** 26.5 minutes.

WEST FELICIANA PARISH

PO Box 1921   **Ph:** 225-635-3864
Saint Francisville, LA 70775

On the northern border of LA, northwest of Baton Rouge; organized Feb 17, 1824 from Feliciana Parish. **Name Origin:** From the divison of Feliciana Parish into two parishes: East and West.

Area (sq mi): 426.01 (land 406; water 20.01).

Pop: 15,111 (White 48.1%; Black or African American 50.5%; Hispanic or Latino 1%; Asian 0.2%; Other 0.6%). **Foreign born:** 0.5%. **Median age:** 36.6. **State rank:** 54. **Pop change 1990-2000:** +17%.

Income: per capita $16,201; median household $39,667. **Pop below poverty level:** 19.9%.

Unemployment: 6.3%. **Median home value:** $107,500. **Median travel time to work:** 28.4 minutes.

WINN PARISH

PO Box 951   **Ph:** 318-628-5824
Winnfield, LA 71483   **Fax:** 318-628-7336

In north-central LA, southwest of Monroe; organized 1852 from Natchitoches, Catahoula, and Rapides parishes. **Name Origin:** For Walter O. Winn, a prominent lawyer and citizen.

Area (sq mi): 956.91 (land 950.49; water 6.43).

Pop: 16,894 (White 65.7%; Black or African American 32%; Hispanic or Latino 0.9%; Asian 0.2%; Other 1.6%). **Foreign born:** 0.5%. **Median age:** 36.2. **State rank:** 50. **Pop change 1990-2000:** +3.8%.

Income: per capita $11,794; median household $25,462. **Pop below poverty level:** 21.5%.

Unemployment: 7.2%. **Median home value:** $43,000. **Median travel time to work:** 28.3 minutes.

Please see sample entry on inside front cover for detailed information about the statistics presented with each county listing.

MAINE - Counties

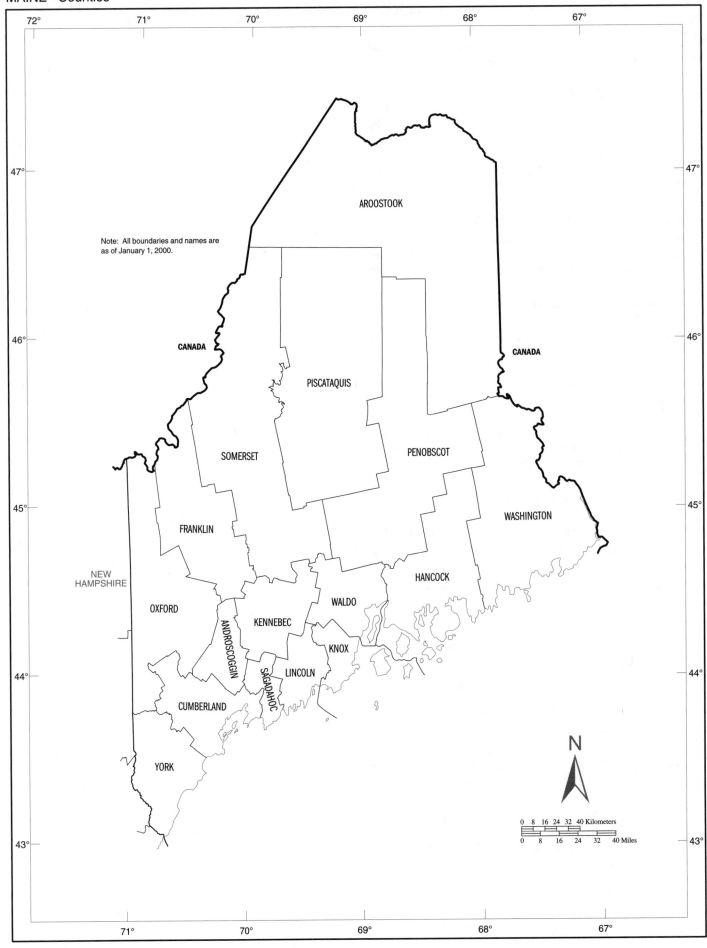

Note: All boundaries and names are as of January 1, 2000.

CANADA

CANADA

AROOSTOOK

PISCATAQUIS

SOMERSET

PENOBSCOT

FRANKLIN

WASHINGTON

NEW HAMPSHIRE

OXFORD

HANCOCK

WALDO

KENNEBEC

ANDROSCOGGIN

KNOX

SAGADAHOC

LINCOLN

CUMBERLAND

YORK

N

| 0 | 8 | 16 | 24 | 32 | 40 Kilometers |
| 0 | 8 | 16 | 24 | 32 | 40 Miles |

Maine

MAINE STATE INFORMATION

www.maine.gov   **Ph:** 207-624-9494

Area (sq mi): 35,384.65 (land 30,861.55; water 4523.1).

Pop: 1,274,923 (White 96.5%; Black or African American 0.5%; Hispanic or Latino 0.7%; Asian 0.7%; Other 1.8%). **Foreign born:** 2.9%. **Median age:** 38.6. **Pop change 1990-2000:** +3.8%.

Income: per capita $19,533; median household $37,240. **Pop below poverty level:** 10.9%.

Unemployment: 4.6%. **Median home value:** $98,700. **Median travel time to work:** 22.7 minutes.

ANDROSCOGGIN COUNTY

2 Turner St   **Ph:** 207-784-8390
Auburn, ME 04210   **Fax:** 207-782-5367
www.androscoggincounty.com

In southern ME, southwest of Augusta; organized Mar 18, 1854 from Cumberland, Oxford, and Kennebec counties. **Name Origin:** For the river, from an Abnaki Indian name meaning either 'place where fish are cured,' 'fishing place for alewives.' or 'fish spearing.'

Area (sq mi): 497.23 (land 470.27; water 26.95).

Pop: 103,793 (White 96.4%; Black or African American 0.7%; Hispanic or Latino 1%; Asian 0.6%; Other 1.8%). **Foreign born:** 2.6%. **Median age:** 37.2. **State rank:** 5. **Pop change 1990-2000:** -1.4%.

Income: per capita $18,734; median household $35,793. **Pop below poverty level:** 11.1%.

Unemployment: 4.1%. **Median home value:** $89,900. **Median travel time to work:** 23.3 minutes.

AROOSTOOK COUNTY

144 Sweden St Suite 101   **Ph:** 207-498-8125
Caribou, ME 04736
www.aroostook.me.us

In northern ME, bordered on west and northwest by Quebec, Canada, and on the northeast and east by New Brunswick, Canada. Organized Mar 16, 1839 from Washington and Penobscot counties. **Name Origin:** For the Aroostook River, which runs through the county; from Micmac Indian 'clear river.'

Area (sq mi): 6828.79 (land 6671.54; water 157.25).

Pop: 73,938 (White 96.4%; Black or African American 0.4%; Hispanic or Latino 0.6%; Asian 0.5%; Other 2.4%). **Foreign born:** 5.8%. **Median age:** 40.7. **State rank:** 6. **Pop change 1990-2000:** -15%.

Income: per capita $15,033; median household $28,837. **Pop below poverty level:** 14.3%.

Unemployment: 4.4%. **Median home value:** $60,200. **Median travel time to work:** 18.3 minutes.

CUMBERLAND COUNTY

142 Federal St Rm 102   **Ph:** 207-871-8380
Portland, ME 04101   **Fax:** 207-871-8292
www.cumberlandcounty.org

In southern ME, south of Lewiston; organized May 28, 1760 (prior to statehood) from York County. **Name Origin:** For William Augustus, Duke of Cumberland (1721-65), British general and second son of King George II (1683-1760).

Area (sq mi): 1216.89 (land 835.51; water 381.38).

Pop: 265,612 (White 95.2%; Black or African American 1.1%; Hispanic or Latino 1%; Asian 1.4%; Other 1.7%). **Foreign born:** 3.8%. **Median age:** 37.6. **State rank:** 1. **Pop change 1990-2000:** +9.2%.

Income: per capita $23,949; median household $44,048. **Pop below poverty level:** 7.9%.

Unemployment: 2.3%. **Median home value:** $131,200. **Median travel time to work:** 22 minutes.

FRANKLIN COUNTY

140 Main St   **Ph:** 207-778-6614
Farmington, ME 04938   **Fax:** 207-778-5899

On northwestern border of ME, northwest of Augusta; organized Mar 20, 1838 from Cumberland County. **Name Origin:** For Benjamin Franklin (1706-90), U.S. patriot, diplomat, and statesman.

Area (sq mi): 1744.31 (land 1697.81; water 46.5).

Pop: 29,467 (White 97.6%; Black or African American 0.2%; Hispanic or Latino 0.5%; Asian 0.4%; Other 1.4%). **Foreign born:** 1.6%. **Median age:** 38.2. **State rank:** 15. **Pop change 1990-2000:** +1.6%.

Income: per capita $15,796; median household $31,459. **Pop below poverty level:** 14.6%.

Unemployment: 6.4%. **Median home value:** $78,300. **Median travel time to work:** 23.2 minutes.

HANCOCK COUNTY

50 State St   **Ph:** 207-667-9542
Ellsworth, ME 04605   **Fax:** 207-667-1412
www.co.hancock.me.us

In eastern ME, on the Atlantic Coast; organized Jun 25, 1789

Please see sample entry on inside front cover for detailed information about the statistics presented with each county listing.

(prior to statehood) from Lincoln County. **Name Origin:** For John Hancock (1737-93), president of the Continental Congress (1775-77), noted signer of the Declaration of Independence, and governor of MA (1780-85; 1787-93).

Area (sq mi): 2351.03 (land 1587.7; water 763.33).

Pop: 51,791 (White 97.2%; Black or African American 0.3%; Hispanic or Latino 0.6%; Asian 0.4%; Other 1.7%). **Foreign born:** 2.3%. **Median age:** 40.7. **State rank:** 8. **Pop change 1990-2000:** +10.3%.

Income: per capita $19,809; median household $35,811. **Pop below poverty level:** 10.2%.

Unemployment: 4.5%. **Median home value:** $108,600. **Median travel time to work:** 22.4 minutes.

KENNEBEC COUNTY

125 State St	**Ph:** 207-622-0971
Augusta, ME 04330	**Fax:** 207-623-4083

In south-central ME, southwest of Bangor; organized Feb 20, 1799 (prior to statehood) from Lincoln County. **Name Origin:** For part of the Kennebec River; from an Abnaki Indian word probably meaning 'long, quiet water.'

Area (sq mi): 951.18 (land 867.58; water 83.6).

Pop: 117,114 (White 97%; Black or African American 0.3%; Hispanic or Latino 0.7%; Asian 0.6%; Other 1.6%). **Foreign born:** 2.2%. **Median age:** 38.7. **State rank:** 4. **Pop change 1990-2000:** +1%.

Income: per capita $18,520; median household $36,498. **Pop below poverty level:** 11.1%.

Unemployment: 4%. **Median home value:** $87,200. **Median travel time to work:** 22.6 minutes.

KNOX COUNTY

62 Union St	**Ph:** 207-594-0420
Rockland, ME 04841	**Fax:** 207-594-0445
knoxcounty.midcoast.com	

On Atlantic coast of ME, east of Augusta; organized Mar 9, 1860 from Lincoln and Waldo counties. **Name Origin:** For Gen. Henry Knox (1750-1806), officer in the Revolutionary War, and first U.S. secretary of war (1785-95).

Area (sq mi): 1142.1 (land 365.67; water 776.43).

Pop: 39,618 (White 97.9%; Black or African American 0.2%; Hispanic or Latino 0.6%; Asian 0.4%; Other 1.1%). **Foreign born:** 2.1%. **Median age:** 41.4. **State rank:** 10. **Pop change 1990-2000:** +9.1%.

Income: per capita $19,981; median household $36,774. **Pop below poverty level:** 10.1%.

Unemployment: 2.9%. **Median home value:** $112,200. **Median travel time to work:** 18.9 minutes.

LINCOLN COUNTY

PO Box 249	**Ph:** 207-882-6311
Wiscasset, ME 04578	**Fax:** 207-882-4320
www.co.lincoln.me.us	

On Atlantic coast of ME, south of Augusta; organized May 28, 1760

(prior to statehood) from York County. **Name Origin:** For either Enoch Lincoln (1788-1829), governor of ME (1827-29), or for Gen. Benjamin Lincoln (1733-1810), officer in the Revolutionary War, U.S. secretary of war (1781-83), and lt. gov. of MA (1788).

Area (sq mi): 699.81 (land 455.99; water 243.82).

Pop: 33,616 (White 98.1%; Black or African American 0.2%; Hispanic or Latino 0.5%; Asian 0.4%; Other 1%). **Foreign born:** 2%. **Median age:** 42.6. **State rank:** 14. **Pop change 1990-2000:** +10.7%.

Income: per capita $20,760; median household $38,686. **Pop below poverty level:** 10.1%.

Unemployment: 2.9%. **Median home value:** $119,900. **Median travel time to work:** 23.4 minutes.

OXFORD COUNTY

PO Box 179	**Ph:** 207-743-6359
South Paris, ME 04281	

On western border of ME and NH, west of Lewiston; organized Mar 4, 1805 (prior to starthood) from York and Cumberland counties. **Name Origin:** For Oxford, MA; named by David Leonard, an early settler who came from there.

Area (sq mi): 2175.26 (land 2078; water 97.26).

Pop: 54,755 (White 97.9%; Black or African American 0.2%; Hispanic or Latino 0.5%; Asian 0.4%; Other 1.2%). **Foreign born:** 1.8%. **Median age:** 40.2. **State rank:** 7. **Pop change 1990-2000:** +4.1%.

Income: per capita $16,945; median household $33,435. **Pop below poverty level:** 11.8%.

Unemployment: 6%. **Median home value:** $82,800. **Median travel time to work:** 25.9 minutes.

PENOBSCOT COUNTY

97 Hammond St	**Ph:** 207-942-8535
Bangor, ME 04401	**Fax:** 207-945-6027

In east-central ME; organized Feb 15, 1816 (prior to statehood) from Hancock County. **Name Origin:** For the Penobscot River, which flows through the county; from an Indian word *penobskeag* 'rocky place' or 'river of rocks.'

Area (sq mi): 3556.14 (land 3395.73; water 160.41).

Pop: 144,919 (White 96.2%; Black or African American 0.5%; Hispanic or Latino 0.6%; Asian 0.7%; Other 2.2%). **Foreign born:** 2.5%. **Median age:** 37.2. **State rank:** 3. **Pop change 1990-2000:** -1.1%.

Income: per capita $17,801; median household $34,274. **Pop below poverty level:** 13.7%.

Unemployment: 4.1%. **Median home value:** $82,400. **Median travel time to work:** 20.7 minutes.

PISCATAQUIS COUNTY

159 E Main St	**Ph:** 207-564-2161
Dover-Foxcroft, ME 04426	**Fax:** 207-564-3022

In central ME, north of Bangor; organized 1838 from Penobscot and Somerset counties. **Name Origin:** For the Piscataquis River, which runs through it; from an Abnaki Indian word probably meaning 'divided tidal river.'

All statistics are based on the 2000 Census except the dollar figures given for per capita income, which are based on 1999 estimates.

Area (sq mi): 4377.36 (land 3966.22; water 411.14).

Pop: 17,235 (White 97.5%; Black or African American 0.2%; Hispanic or Latino 0.5%; Asian 0.3%; Other 1.6%). **Foreign born:** 1.9%. **Median age:** 42.1. **State rank:** 16. **Pop change 1990-2000:** -7.6%.

Income: per capita $14,374; median household $28,250. **Pop below poverty level:** 14.8%.

Unemployment: 6.7%. **Median home value:** $62,300. **Median travel time to work:** 22.1 minutes.

SAGADAHOC COUNTY

PO Box 246   **Ph:** 207-443-8200
Bath, ME 04530   **Fax:** 207-443-8213

On Atlantic coast of ME, east of Portland; organized Apr 4, 1854 from Lincoln County. **Name Origin:** From an Abnaki Indian word probably meaning 'land of the mouth,' or 'mouth of the river,' for its location at the confluence of the Androscoggin and Kennebec rivers where they meet the Atlantic.

Area (sq mi): 370.19 (land 253.9; water 116.29).

Pop: 35,214 (White 95.9%; Black or African American 0.9%; Hispanic or Latino 1.1%; Asian 0.6%; Other 2%). **Foreign born:** 2.4%. **Median age:** 38. **State rank:** 12. **Pop change 1990-2000:** +5%.

Income: per capita $20,378; median household $41,908. **Pop below poverty level:** 8.6%.

Unemployment: 3.2%. **Median home value:** $110,200. **Median travel time to work:** 22.5 minutes.

SOMERSET COUNTY

County Courthouse   **Ph:** 207-474-9861
Skowhegan, ME 04976   **Fax:** 207-474-7405

In west-central ME and north to the border with Quebec, Canada; organized Mar 1, 1809 (prior to statehood) from Kennebec County. **Name Origin:** For Somerset county in England.

Area (sq mi): 4095.37 (land 3926.5; water 168.87).

Pop: 50,888 (White 97.7%; Black or African American 0.2%; Hispanic or Latino 0.5%; Asian 0.3%; Other 1.4%). **Foreign born:** 1.7%. **Median age:** 38.9. **State rank:** 9. **Pop change 1990-2000:** +2.3%.

Income: per capita $15,474; median household $30,731. **Pop below poverty level:** 14.9%.

Unemployment: 7.6%. **Median home value:** $70,100. **Median travel time to work:** 24.2 minutes.

WALDO COUNTY

PO Box D   **Ph:** 207-338-1710
Belfast, ME 04915   **Fax:** 207-338-6360

On central Atlantic coast of ME, southwest of Bangor; organized Feb 7, 1827 from Hancock County. **Name Origin:** For Gen. Samuel Waldo (1695-1759), an officer in the French and Indian Wars, and promoter of settlement in the area that became Maine.

Area (sq mi): 852.74 (land 729.73; water 123.01).

Pop: 36,280 (White 97.5%; Black or African American 0.2%; Hispanic or Latino 0.6%; Asian 0.2%; Other 1.7%). **Foreign born:**

1.7%. **Median age:** 39.3. **State rank:** 11. **Pop change 1990-2000:** +9.9%.

Income: per capita $17,438; median household $33,986. **Pop below poverty level:** 13.9%.

Unemployment: 4%. **Median home value:** $90,100. **Median travel time to work:** 26.4 minutes.

WASHINGTON COUNTY

PO Box 297   **Ph:** 207-255-3127
Machias, ME 04654   **Fax:** 207-255-3313

On Atlantic coast in extreme eastern ME, east of Bangor; organized Jun 25, 1789 (prior to statehood) from Lincoln County. **Name Origin:** For George Washington (1732-99), American patriot and first U.S. president.

Area (sq mi): 3254.91 (land 2568.48; water 686.44).

Pop: 33,941 (White 93.2%; Black or African American 0.3%; Hispanic or Latino 0.8%; Asian 0.3%; Other 5.9%). **Foreign born:** 4.1%. **Median age:** 40.5. **State rank:** 13. **Pop change 1990-2000:** -3.9%.

Income: per capita $14,119; median household $25,869. **Pop below poverty level:** 19%.

Unemployment: 8.1%. **Median home value:** $68,700. **Median travel time to work:** 19.2 minutes.

YORK COUNTY

45 Kennebunk Rd PO Box 399   **Ph:** 207-324-1571
Alfred, ME 04002   **Fax:** 207-324-9494
www.co.york.me.us

At southwestern tip of ME along Atlantic coast and NH border, southwest of Portland; original county (formerly Yorkshire County, MA), organized Nov 20, 1652 (prior to statehood). **Name Origin:** For James, Duke of York and Albany (1633-1701), later James II of England.

Area (sq mi): 1271.34 (land 990.92; water 280.43).

Pop: 186,742 (White 97.1%; Black or African American 0.4%; Hispanic or Latino 0.7%; Asian 0.7%; Other 1.2%). **Foreign born:** 2.8%. **Median age:** 38.5. **State rank:** 2. **Pop change 1990-2000:** +13.5%.

Income: per capita $21,225; median household $43,630. **Pop below poverty level:** 8.2%.

Unemployment: 3.6%. **Median home value:** $122,600. **Median travel time to work:** 25.8 minutes.

Please see sample entry on inside front cover for detailed information about the statistics presented with each county listing.

261

MARYLAND - Counties and Independent City

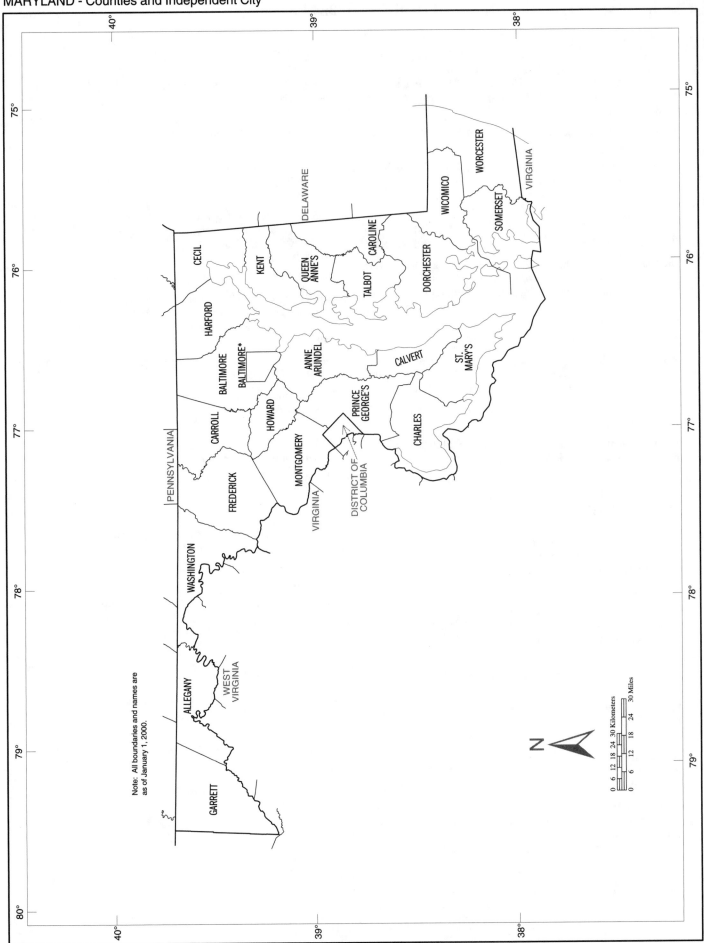

Note: All boundaries and names are
as of January 1, 2000.

Maryland

MARYLAND STATE INFORMATION

www.maryland.gov   **Ph:** 410-333-3098

Area (sq mi): 12,406.68 (land 9773.82; water 2632.86).

Pop: 5,296,486 (White 62.1%; Black or African American 27.9%; Hispanic or Latino 4.3%; Asian 4%; Other 4.1%). **Foreign born:** 9.8%. **Median age:** 36. **Pop change 1990-2000:** +10.8%.

Income: per capita $25,614; median household $52,868. **Pop below poverty level:** 8.5%.

Unemployment: 4%. **Median home value:** $146,000. **Median travel time to work:** 31.2 minutes.

ALLEGANY COUNTY

701 Kelly Rd   **Ph:** 301-777-5911
Cumberland, MD 21502   **Fax:** 301-777-5819
www.allconet.org

On northwestern border of panhandle of MD; organized Dec 25, 1789 from Washington County. **Name Origin:** For the Allegheny Mountains (using a variant spelling), which cross through the county.

Area (sq mi): 429.82 (land 425.42; water 4.4).

Pop: 74,930 (White 92.5%; Black or African American 5.3%; Hispanic or Latino 0.8%; Asian 0.5%; Other 1.1%). **Foreign born:** 1.2%. **Median age:** 39.1. **State rank:** 15. **Pop change 1990-2000:** +0%.

Income: per capita $16,780; median household $30,821. **Pop below poverty level:** 14.8%.

Unemployment: 7.6%. **Median home value:** $71,100. **Median travel time to work:** 22.6 minutes.

ANNE ARUNDEL COUNTY

PO Box 71   **Ph:** 443-481-1000
Annapolis, MD 21404
www.co.anne-arundel.md.us

In east-central MD, south of Baltimore; original county, organized 1650. **Name Origin:** For Anne Arundel, daughter of Lord Thomas Arundell of Wardour and wife of Cecilius Calvert, Lord Baltimore (1605-75).

Area (sq mi): 587.9 (land 415.94; water 171.96).

Pop: 489,656 (White 79.8%; Black or African American 13.6%; Hispanic or Latino 2.6%; Asian 2.3%; Other 3%). **Foreign born:** 4.7%. **Median age:** 36. **State rank:** 5. **Pop change 1990-2000:** +14.6%.

Income: per capita $27,578; median household $61,768. **Pop below poverty level:** 5.1%.

Unemployment: 3.2%. **Median home value:** $159,300. **Median travel time to work:** 28.9 minutes.

BALTIMORE (INDEPENDENT CITY)

100 N Holliday St   **Ph:** 410-396-3100
Baltimore, MD 21202   **Fax:** 410-576-9425
www.ci.baltimore.md.us

In northern MD on Patapsco River, upper Chesapeake Bay, 41 mi. northeast of Washington, DC. Founded 1729; incorporated 1796. Distinct from and independent of Baltimore County since 1851, with the same political power as a county. **Name Origin:** For the barony of Baltimore in Ireland, source of the hereditary title Lord Baltimore of the Calvert family, proprietors of the colony of MD.

Area (sq mi): 92.08 (land 80.8; water 11.27).

Pop: 651,154 (White 31%; Black or African American 64.3%; Hispanic or Latino 1.7%; Asian 1.5%; Other 2.5%). **Foreign born:** 4.6%. **Median age:** 35. **State rank:** 4. **Pop change 1990-2000:** -11.5%.

Income: per capita $16,978; median household $30,078. **Pop below poverty level:** 22.9%.

Unemployment: 4.4%. **Median home value:** $69,100. **Median travel time to work:** 31.1 minutes.

BALTIMORE COUNTY

401 Bosley Ave   **Ph:** 410-887-2697
Towson, MD 21204   **Fax:** 410-887-3062
www.co.ba.md.us

On central northern border of MD, north of Annapolis; original county, legal origin not known, but was in existence by Jan 12, 1659. Baltimore City was made indlependent of the county in 1851. **Name Origin:** For the barony of Baltimore in Ireland, source of the hereditary title Lord Baltimore of the Calvert family, proprietors of the colony of MD.

Area (sq mi): 682.03 (land 598.59; water 83.44).

Pop: 754,292 (White 73.4%; Black or African American 20.1%; Hispanic or Latino 1.8%; Asian 3.2%; Other 2.3%). **Foreign born:** 7.1%. **Median age:** 37.7. **State rank:** 3. **Pop change 1990-2000:** +9%.

Income: per capita $26,167; median household $50,667. **Pop below poverty level:** 6.5%.

Unemployment: 4.4%. **Median home value:** $127,300. **Median travel time to work:** 27.6 minutes.

Please see sample entry on inside front cover for detailed information about the statistics presented with each county listing.

CALVERT COUNTY

175 Main St   **Ph:** 410-535-1600
Prince Frederick, MD 20678   **Fax:** 410-535-9572
www.co.cal.md.us

In south-central MD, south of Annapolis; original county, organized as Patuxent County in 1654; name changed in 1658. **Name Origin:** For the family name of the Lords Baltimore, proprietors of MD.

Area (sq mi): 345.09 (land 215.17; water 129.91).

Pop: 74,563 (White 83%; Black or African American 13.1%; Hispanic or Latino 1.5%; Asian 0.9%; Other 2.1%). **Foreign born:** 2.2%. **Median age:** 35.9. **State rank:** 16. **Pop change 1990-2000:** +45.1%.

Income: per capita $25,410; median household $65,945. **Pop below poverty level:** 4.4%.

Unemployment: 2.5%. **Median home value:** $169,200. **Median travel time to work:** 39.8 minutes.

CAROLINE COUNTY

109 Market St   **Ph:** 410-479-0660
Denton, MD 21629   **Fax:** 410-479-4060
www.carolinemd.org

On eastern border of MD, southwest of Dover, DE; organized Jun 15, 1773 (prior to statehood) from Dorchester and Queen Anne's counties. **Name Origin:** For Caroline Calvert Eden, sister of Frederick Calvert, 6th Baron Baltimore and the last proprietor of MD.

Area (sq mi): 326.06 (land 320.14; water 5.92).

Pop: 29,772 (White 80.7%; Black or African American 14.8%; Hispanic or Latino 2.7%; Asian 0.5%; Other 3%). **Foreign born:** 2.5%. **Median age:** 37. **State rank:** 22. **Pop change 1990-2000:** +10.1%.

Income: per capita $17,275; median household $38,832. **Pop below poverty level:** 11.7%.

Unemployment: 5.1%. **Median home value:** $101,700. **Median travel time to work:** 30.4 minutes.

CARROLL COUNTY

225 N Center St Rm 300   **Ph:** 410-386-2400
Westminster, MD 21157   **Fax:** 410-848-0003
www.ccgov.carr.org

On central northern border of MD, northwest of Baltimore; organized Jun 19, 1836 from Baltimore and Frederick counties. **Name Origin:** For Charles Carroll (1737-1832), signer of the Declaration of Independence, U.S. senator from MD, and founder of the Baltimore and Ohio Railroad.

Area (sq mi): 452.4 (land 449.13; water 3.27).

Pop: 150,897 (White 95.1%; Black or African American 2.3%; Hispanic or Latino 1%; Asian 0.8%; Other 1.2%). **Foreign born:** 2%. **Median age:** 36.9. **State rank:** 9. **Pop change 1990-2000:** +22.3%.

Income: per capita $23,829; median household $60,021. **Pop below poverty level:** 3.8%.

Unemployment: 2.8%. **Median home value:** $162,500. **Median travel time to work:** 34.1 minutes.

CECIL COUNTY

129 E Main St Rm 108   **Ph:** 410-996-5375
Elkton, MD 21921   **Fax:** 410-392-6032
www.ccmagazine.org/cecilcounty.htm

On northeastern border of MD, west of Wilmington, DE; organized 1674 from Baltimore and Kent counties. **Name Origin:** For Cecilius Calvert, 2nd Lord Baltimore (1605-75), founder and first proprietor of the colony of MD, though he never visited it.

Area (sq mi): 417.88 (land 348.13; water 69.75).

Pop: 85,951 (White 92.5%; Black or African American 3.9%; Hispanic or Latino 1.5%; Asian 0.7%; Other 2%). **Foreign born:** 1.8%. **Median age:** 35.5. **State rank:** 13. **Pop change 1990-2000:** +20.5%.

Income: per capita $21,384; median household $50,510. **Pop below poverty level:** 7.2%.

Unemployment: 5.7%. **Median home value:** $132,300. **Median travel time to work:** 28.2 minutes.

CHARLES COUNTY

PO Box 2150   **Ph:** 301-645-0600
La Plata, MD 20646   **Fax:** 301-645-0560
www.charlescounty.org

In southwestern MD, south of Alexandria, VA; original county, organized 1658. **Name Origin:** For Charles Calvert, 3rd Baron Baltimore (1637-1715), second proprietor of the colony of MD; the son of Cecilius Calvert (1606-75) and Anne Arundell.

Area (sq mi): 643.22 (land 461; water 182.22).

Pop: 120,546 (White 67.3%; Black or African American 26.1%; Hispanic or Latino 2.3%; Asian 1.8%; Other 3.7%). **Foreign born:** 2.9%. **Median age:** 34.6. **State rank:** 11. **Pop change 1990-2000:** +19.2%.

Income: per capita $24,285; median household $62,199. **Pop below poverty level:** 5.5%.

Unemployment: 2.6%. **Median home value:** $153,000. **Median travel time to work:** 39.3 minutes.

DORCHESTER COUNTY

PO Box 26   **Ph:** 410-228-1700
Cambridge, MD 21613   **Fax:** 410-228-9641
www.commissioners.net

In south-central MD, west of Salisbury; original county whose legal origin is unknown, but it was in existence by Feb 16,1668-69. **Name Origin:** For Richard Sackville II, 5th Earl of Dorset (1622-77), friend of the Calvert family.

Area (sq mi): 982.92 (land 557.54; water 425.38).

Pop: 30,674 (White 68.8%; Black or African American 28.4%; Hispanic or Latino 1.3%; Asian 0.7%; Other 1.5%). **Foreign born:** 2%. **Median age:** 40.7. **State rank:** 20. **Pop change 1990-2000:** +1.4%.

Income: per capita $18,929; median household $34,077. **Pop below poverty level:** 13.8%.

Unemployment: 9.3%. **Median home value:** $92,300. **Median travel time to work:** 25.2 minutes.

All statistics are based on the 2000 Census except the dollar figures given for per capita income, which are based on 1999 estimates.

FREDERICK COUNTY

12 E Church St
Frederick, MD 21701
www.co.frederick.md.us

Ph: 301-694-1100
Fax: 301-694-1849

On northwestern border of MD, southeast of Hagerstown; organized Jun 10, 1748 from Baltimore and Prince George's counties. **Name Origin:** For Frederick Calvert, 6th Baron Baltimore (1731-71), fifth and last proprietor of the colony of MD.

Area (sq mi): 667.34 (land 662.88; water 4.46).

Pop: 195,277 (White 88.1%; Black or African American 6.4%; Hispanic or Latino 2.4%; Asian 1.7%; Other 2.6%). **Foreign born:** 4%. **Median age:** 35.6. **State rank:** 8. **Pop change 1990-2000:** +30%.

Income: per capita $25,404; median household $60,276. **Pop below poverty level:** 4.5%.

Unemployment: 2.8%. **Median home value:** $160,200. **Median travel time to work:** 31.9 minutes.

GARRETT COUNTY

203 S 4th St Rm 207
Oakland, MD 21550
www.garrettcounty.org

Ph: 301-334-8970
Fax: 301-334-5000

On northwestern border of the panhandle of MD, west of Cumberland; organized Apr 1, 1872 from Allegany County; the last county to be formed in MD. **Name Origin:** For John Work Garrett (1820-84), president of the Baltimore and Ohio railroad (1858-84).

Area (sq mi): 655.9 (land 647.96; water 7.94).

Pop: 29,846 (White 98.4%; Black or African American 0.4%; Hispanic or Latino 0.4%; Asian 0.2%; Other 0.6%). **Foreign born:** 0.8%. **Median age:** 38.3. **State rank:** 21. **Pop change 1990-2000:** +6.1%.

Income: per capita $16,219; median household $32,238. **Pop below poverty level:** 13.3%.

Unemployment: 7.7%. **Median home value:** $86,400. **Median travel time to work:** 24.8 minutes.

HARFORD COUNTY

220 S Main St
Bel Air, MD 21014
www.co.ha.md.us

Ph: 410-838-6000
Fax: 410-879-3564

On northern border of MD, northeast of Baltimore; organized 1773 (prior to statehood) from Baltimore County. **Name Origin:** For Henry Harford (c. 1759-1834), an illegitimate son of Frederick Calvert (1731-71), 6th Lord Baltimore, and the last proprietor of the colony of MD.

Area (sq mi): 526.72 (land 440.35; water 86.37).

Pop: 218,590 (White 85.8%; Black or African American 9.3%; Hispanic or Latino 1.9%; Asian 1.5%; Other 2.5%). **Foreign born:** 3.4%. **Median age:** 36.2. **State rank:** 7. **Pop change 1990-2000:** +20%.

Income: per capita $24,232; median household $57,234. **Pop below poverty level:** 4.9%.

Unemployment: 3.9%. **Median home value:** $149,800. **Median travel time to work:** 31.6 minutes.

HOWARD COUNTY

3430 Courthouse Dr
Ellicott City, MD 21043
www.co.ho.md.us

Ph: 410-313-2011
Fax: 410-313-3051

In north-central MD, west of Baltimore; organized as Howard District in1838 from Anne Arundel County; formed as county May 13, 1851. **Name Origin:** For John Eager Howard (1752-1827), member of the Continental Congress (1784-88), MD governor (1788-91), and U.S. senator (1796-1803).

Area (sq mi): 253.55 (land 252.04; water 1.51).

Pop: 247,842 (White 72.6%; Black or African American 14.4%; Hispanic or Latino 3%; Asian 7.7%; Other 3.5%). **Foreign born:** 11.3%. **Median age:** 35.5. **State rank:** 6. **Pop change 1990-2000:** +32.3%.

Income: per capita $32,402; median household $74,167. **Pop below poverty level:** 3.9%.

Unemployment: 2.6%. **Median home value:** $206,300. **Median travel time to work:** 30.2 minutes.

KENT COUNTY

400 High St
Chestertown, MD 21620
www.kentcounty.com

Ph: 410-778-7435
Fax: 410-778-7482

On northeastern border of MD, northwest of Dover, MD; original county, organized Dec 16, 1642. **Name Origin:** For the county in England.

Area (sq mi): 414.31 (land 279.43; water 134.87).

Pop: 19,197 (White 78.4%; Black or African American 17.4%; Hispanic or Latino 2.8%; Asian 0.5%; Other 2.3%). **Foreign born:** 2.9%. **Median age:** 41.3. **State rank:** 24. **Pop change 1990-2000:** +7.6%.

Income: per capita $21,573; median household $39,869. **Pop below poverty level:** 13%.

Unemployment: 4.1%. **Median home value:** $115,500. **Median travel time to work:** 24.6 minutes.

MONTGOMERY COUNTY

101 Monroe St
Rockville, MD 20850
www.co.mo.md.us

Ph: 240-777-2500
Fax: 240-777-2517

On central western border of MD, north of Washington, D.C.; organized Sept 6, 1776 (prior to statehood) from Frederick County. Added territory (Takoma Park city) from Prince George's County effective July 1, 1997. **Name Origin:** For Gen. Richard Montgomery (1736-75), an officer in the Revolutionary War.

Area (sq mi): 507.14 (land 495.52; water 11.63).

Pop: 873,341 (White 59.5%; Black or African American 15.1%; Hispanic or Latino 11.5%; Asian 11.3%; Other 8.7%). **Foreign born:** 26.7%. **Median age:** 36.8. **State rank:** 1. **Pop change 1990-2000:** +15.4%.

Income: per capita $35,684; median household $71,551. **Pop below poverty level:** 5.4%.

Unemployment: 2.3%. **Median home value:** $221,800. **Median travel time to work:** 32.8 minutes.

Please see sample entry on inside front cover for detailed information about the statistics presented with each county listing.

PRINCE GEORGE'S COUNTY

14741 Governor Oden Bowie Dr **Ph:** 301-952-3600
Upper Marlboro, MD 20772 **Fax:** 301-952-4862
www.goprincegeorgescounty.com

In central MD, east of Washington, D.C.; organized May 20, 1695 from Charles and Calvert counties. Lost territory (Takoma Park city) to Montgomery County effective July 1, 1997. **Name Origin:** For Prince George of Denmark (1653-1708), husband of Queen Anne of England (1665-1714).

Area (sq mi): 498.45 (land 485.43; water 13.01).

Pop: 801,515 (White 24.3%; Black or African American 62.7%; Hispanic or Latino 7.1%; Asian 3.9%; Other 6.4%). **Foreign born:** 13.8%. **Median age:** 33.3. **State rank:** 2. **Pop change 1990-2000:** +9.9%.

Income: per capita $23,360; median household $55,256. **Pop below poverty level:** 7.7%.

Unemployment: 4.1%. **Median home value:** $145,600. **Median travel time to work:** 35.9 minutes.

QUEEN ANNE'S COUNTY

107 N Liberty St **Ph:** 410-758-4098
Centreville, MD 21617 **Fax:** 410-758-1170
www.qac.org

On eastern border of MD, west of Dover, DE; organized 1706 from Talbot County. **Name Origin:** For Anne (1665-1714), queen of Great Britain and Ireland (1702-14).

Area (sq mi): 509.79 (land 372.21; water 137.58).

Pop: 40,563 (White 88.4%; Black or African American 8.8%; Hispanic or Latino 1.1%; Asian 0.6%; Other 1.5%). **Foreign born:** 2.4%. **Median age:** 38.8. **State rank:** 18. **Pop change 1990-2000:** +19.5%.

Income: per capita $26,364; median household $57,037. **Pop below poverty level:** 6.3%.

Unemployment: 3.3%. **Median home value:** $160,000. **Median travel time to work:** 33.6 minutes.

SAINT MARY'S COUNTY

PO Box 676 **Ph:** 301-475-4567
Leonardtown, MD 20650 **Fax:** 301-475-4470
www.co.saint-marys.md.us

On southern border of MD, bounded by the Potomac River on the west, the Patuxent River on the east, and Chesapeake Bay on the south; the first original county, organized 1637. **Name Origin:** For Mary, the mother of Jesus Christ. The ships Ark and Dove, carrying colonists, landed on Saint Clement's Island on Mar 25, 1634, the Feast of the Annunciation of Mary.

Area (sq mi): 764.5 (land 361.25; water 403.25).

Pop: 86,211 (White 80.4%; Black or African American 13.9%; Hispanic or Latino 2%; Asian 1.8%; Other 2.7%). **Foreign born:** 2.8%. **Median age:** 34.2. **State rank:** 12. **Pop change 1990-2000:** +13.5%.

Income: per capita $22,662; median household $54,706. **Pop below poverty level:** 7.2%.

Unemployment: 2.8%. **Median home value:** $150,000. **Median travel time to work:** 29.2 minutes.

SOMERSET COUNTY

11916 Somerset Ave Rm 111 **Ph:** 410-651-0320
Princess Anne, MD 21853 **Fax:** 410-651-0366

On southern border of MD, southwest of Salisbury; original county; organized Aug 22, 1666. **Name Origin:** For Mary Somerset, sister-in-law of Cecilius Calvert (1605-75), 2nd Lord Baltimore.

Area (sq mi): 610.78 (land 327.21; water 283.56).

Pop: 24,747 (White 55.8%; Black or African American 41.1%; Hispanic or Latino 1.3%; Asian 0.5%; Other 2.1%). **Foreign born:** 2.5%. **Median age:** 36.5. **State rank:** 23. **Pop change 1990-2000:** +5.6%.

Income: per capita $15,965; median household $29,903. **Pop below poverty level:** 20.1%.

Unemployment: 7.5%. **Median home value:** $81,100. **Median travel time to work:** 25.1 minutes.

TALBOT COUNTY

11 N Washington St County Courthouse **Ph:** 410-770-8010
Easton, MD 21601 **Fax:** 410-770-8007
www.co.talbot.md.us

In east-central MD, southeast of Annapolis; in existence by Feb 18, 1661-62, organized from Kent County. **Name Origin:** For Grace Talbot, daughter of George Calvert (1580?-1632), 1st Lord Baltimore, and sister of Cecilius Calvert, first proprietor of the colony of MD.

Area (sq mi): 476.77 (land 269.14; water 207.64).

Pop: 33,812 (White 81.2%; Black or African American 15.4%; Hispanic or Latino 1.8%; Asian 0.8%; Other 1.9%). **Foreign born:** 3.3%. **Median age:** 43.3. **State rank:** 19. **Pop change 1990-2000:** +10.7%.

Income: per capita $28,164; median household $43,532. **Pop below poverty level:** 8.3%.

Unemployment: 3.1%. **Median home value:** $149,200. **Median travel time to work:** 22.4 minutes.

WASHINGTON COUNTY

100 W Washington St **Ph:** 240-313-2200
Hagerstown, MD 21740 **Fax:** 240-313-2201
pilot.wash.lib.md.us/washco

On central northern border of MD; organized Sept 6, 1776 from Frederick County. **Name Origin:** For George Washington (1732-99), American patriot and first U.S. president.

Area (sq mi): 467.55 (land 458.14; water 9.41).

Pop: 131,923 (White 89.1%; Black or African American 7.8%; Hispanic or Latino 1.2%; Asian 0.8%; Other 1.7%). **Foreign born:** 1.9%. **Median age:** 37.4. **State rank:** 10. **Pop change 1990-2000:** +8.7%.

Income: per capita $20,062; median household $40,617. **Pop below poverty level:** 9.5%.

Unemployment: 4.1%. **Median home value:** $115,000. **Median travel time to work:** 25.1 minutes.

All statistics are based on the 2000 Census except the dollar figures given for per capita income, which are based on 1999 estimates.

WICOMICO COUNTY

PO Box 870
Salisbury, MD 21803
www.wicomicocounty.org

Ph: 410-548-4801
Fax: 410-548-4803

In southeastern MD, north of Princess Anne; organized Aug 17, 1867 from Somerset and Worcester counties. **Name Origin:** For the Wicomico River, which flows through it. Possibly for a Nanticoke Indian village near its banks named *wicko-mekee*, possibly 'where houses are being built,' or 'pleasant place of dwelling.'

Area (sq mi): 399.79 (land 377.17; water 22.62).

Pop: 84,644 (White 71.5%; Black or African American 23.3%; Hispanic or Latino 2.2%; Asian 1.7%; Other 2.3%). **Foreign born:** 3.9%. **Median age:** 35.8. **State rank:** 14. **Pop change 1990-2000:** +13.9%.

Income: per capita $19,171; median household $39,035. **Pop below poverty level:** 12.8%.

Unemployment: 5.4%. **Median home value:** $94,500. **Median travel time to work:** 20.9 minutes.

WORCESTER COUNTY

1 W Market St County Courthouse Suite 1103
Snow Hill, MD 21863
www.co.worcester.md.us

Ph: 410-632-1194
Fax: 410-632-3131

On southeastern border of MD, on Atlantic Ocean; organized Oct 29, 1742 from Somerset County. **Name Origin:** For Edward Somerset, Earl of Worcester (c.1601-67), son-in-law of George Calvert (1580?-1632).

Area (sq mi): 694.73 (land 473.24; water 221.49).

Pop: 46,543 (White 80.4%; Black or African American 16.7%; Hispanic or Latino 1.3%; Asian 0.6%; Other 1.6%). **Foreign born:** 2.7%. **Median age:** 43. **State rank:** 17. **Pop change 1990-2000:** +32.9%.

Income: per capita $22,505; median household $40,650. **Pop below poverty level:** 9.6%.

Unemployment: 9.9%. **Median home value:** $121,500. **Median travel time to work:** 23.3 minutes.

Please see sample entry on inside front cover for detailed information about the statistics presented with each county listing.

267

MASSACHUSETTS - Counties

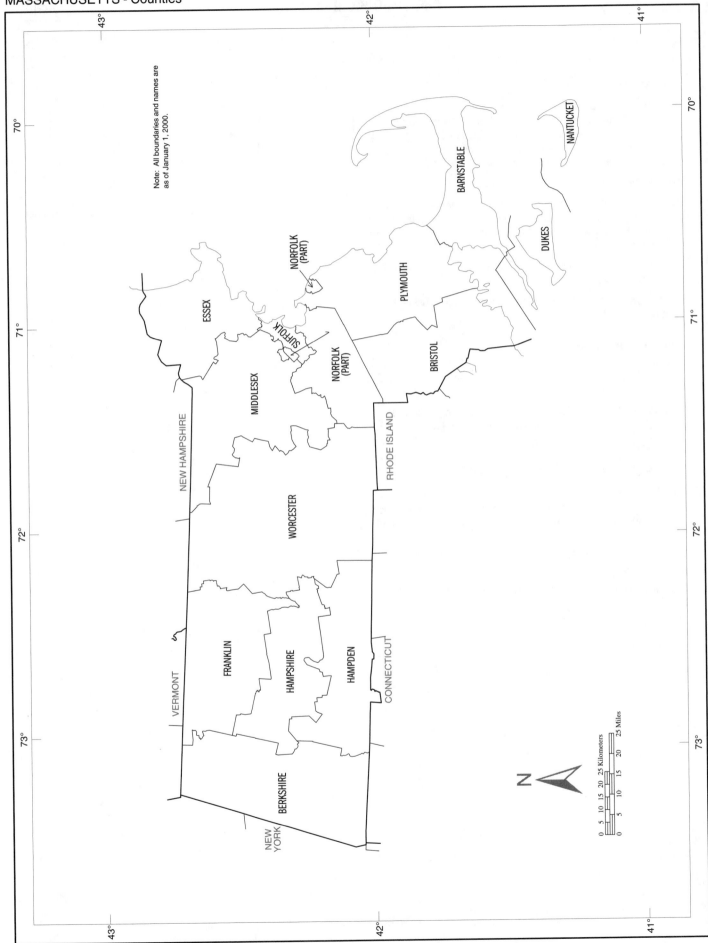

Note: All boundaries and names are as of January 1, 2000.

NEW HAMPSHIRE

ESSEX

MIDDLESEX

NORFOLK (PART)

SUFFOLK

NORFOLK (PART)

BARNSTABLE

NANTUCKET

DUKES

PLYMOUTH

BRISTOL

RHODE ISLAND

WORCESTER

VERMONT

FRANKLIN

HAMPSHIRE

HAMPDEN

CONNECTICUT

BERKSHIRE

NEW YORK

N

0 5 10 15 20 25 Kilometers
0   5   10   15   20   25 Miles

Massachusetts

MASSACHUSETTS STATE INFORMATION

www.mass.gov   **Ph:** 866-888-2808

Area (sq mi): 10,554.57 (land 7840.02; water 2714.55).

Pop: 6,349,097 (White 81.9%; Black or African American 5.4%; Hispanic or Latino 6.8%; Asian 3.8%; Other 6.2%). **Foreign born:** 12.2%. **Median age:** 36.5. **Pop change 1990-2000:** +5.5%.

Income: per capita $25,952; median household $50,502. **Pop below poverty level:** 9.3%.

Unemployment: 5.2%. **Median home value:** $185,700. **Median travel time to work:** 27 minutes.

BARNSTABLE COUNTY

3195 Main St Box 427   **Ph:** 508-362-2511
Barnstable, MA 02630   **Fax:** 508-362-4136
www.barnstablecounty.org

Coextensive with Cape Cod, in southeastern MA; organized Jun 2, 1685 from Old Plymouth Colony. **Name Origin:** For Barnstaple, Devonshire, England. Original meaning was 'Bearda's staple or post,' or 'post to which a warship was moored.' Folk etymology changed it to -*stable*.

Area (sq mi): 1305.62 (land 395.51; water 910.1).

Pop: 222,230 (White 93.4%; Black or African American 1.8%; Hispanic or Latino 1.3%; Asian 0.6%; Other 3.4%). **Foreign born:** 4.9%. **Median age:** 44.6. **State rank:** 9. **Pop change 1990-2000:** +19.1%.

Income: per capita $25,318; median household $45,933. **Pop below poverty level:** 6.9%.

Unemployment: 3.9%. **Median home value:** $178,800. **Median travel time to work:** 24.1 minutes.

BERKSHIRE COUNTY

76 East St   **Ph:** 413-499-1940
Pittsfield, MA 01201   **Fax:** 413-499-0213

On western border of MA, bordered on north by VT, by NY on west, and by CT on south; organized April 21, 1761 from Hampshire County. **Name Origin:** For the county in England.

Area (sq mi): 946.27 (land 931.32; water 14.95).

Pop: 134,953 (White 94.1%; Black or African American 2%; Hispanic or Latino 1.7%; Asian 1%; Other 1.9%). **Foreign born:** 3.7%. **Median age:** 40.5. **State rank:** 11. **Pop change 1990-2000:** -3.2%.

Income: per capita $21,807; median household $39,047. **Pop below poverty level:** 9.5%.

Unemployment: 3.7%. **Median home value:** $116,800. **Median travel time to work:** 19.2 minutes.

BRISTOL COUNTY

9 Court St   **Ph:** 508-824-9681
Taunton, MA 02780   **Fax:** 508-821-1570

On southwestern border of MA with RI; organized Jun 2, 1685 from Old Plymouth Colony. **Name Origin:** For Bristol, Gloucestershire and Somerset, England.

Area (sq mi): 691.19 (land 556; water 135.19).

Pop: 534,678 (White 89.4%; Black or African American 2%; Hispanic or Latino 3.6%; Asian 1.3%; Other 5.6%). **Foreign born:** 11.7%. **Median age:** 36.7. **State rank:** 6. **Pop change 1990-2000:** +5.6%.

Income: per capita $20,978; median household $43,496. **Pop below poverty level:** 10%.

Unemployment: 4.8%. **Median home value:** $151,500. **Median travel time to work:** 25.6 minutes.

DUKES COUNTY

PO Box 190   **Ph:** 508-696-3840
Edgartown, MA 02539   **Fax:** 508-696-3841
www.dukescounty.org

Southeast of New Bedford; includes islands of Martha's Vineyard, Chappaquiddick, Elizabeth, and Noman's Land. Organized Jun 22, 1695 from Martha's Vineyard. **Name Origin:** For James II (1633-1701), Duke of York and Albany, administrator of the colonies at the time of naming.

Area (sq mi): 490.95 (land 103.78; water 387.18).

Pop: 14,987 (White 90%; Black or African American 2.4%; Hispanic or Latino 1%; Asian 0.5%; Other 6.5%). **Foreign born:** 6.3%. **Median age:** 40.7. **State rank:** 13. **Pop change 1990-2000:** +28.8%.

Income: per capita $26,472; median household $45,559. **Pop below poverty level:** 7.3%.

Unemployment: 3.3%. **Median home value:** $304,000. **Median travel time to work:** 16.5 minutes.

ESSEX COUNTY

36 Federal St County Administration Bldg
1st Fl   **Ph:** 978-741-0200
Salem, MA 01970

On northeastern border of MA, north of Boston; original county, organized May 10, 1643. **Name Origin:** For the county of Essex, England.

Please see sample entry on inside front cover for detailed information about the statistics presented with each county listing.

269

Area (sq mi): 828.53 (land 500.67; water 327.86).

Pop: 723,419 (White 83.1%; Black or African American 2.6%; Hispanic or Latino 11%; Asian 2.3%; Other 8.5%). **Foreign born:** 11.3%. **Median age:** 37.5. **State rank:** 3. **Pop change 1990-2000:** +8%.

Income: per capita $26,358; median household $51,576. **Pop below poverty level:** 8.9%.

Unemployment: 4.1%. **Median home value:** $220,000. **Median travel time to work:** 27.1 minutes.

FRANKLIN COUNTY
425 Main St PO Box 1573   **Ph:** 413-774-5535
Greenfield, MA 01302   **Fax:** 413-774-4770
www.co.franklin.ma.us

On northern border of MA, north of Northampton; organized Jun 24, 1811 from Hampshire County. **Name Origin:** For Benjamin Franklin (1706-90), U.S. patriot, diplomat, and statesman.

Area (sq mi): 724.74 (land 702.03; water 22.71).

Pop: 71,535 (White 94.4%; Black or African American 0.9%; Hispanic or Latino 2%; Asian 1%; Other 2.6%). **Foreign born:** 3.6%. **Median age:** 39.5. **State rank:** 12. **Pop change 1990-2000:** +2.1%.

Income: per capita $20,672; median household $40,768. **Pop below poverty level:** 9.4%.

Unemployment: 3.2%. **Median home value:** $119,000. **Median travel time to work:** 23.7 minutes.

HAMPDEN COUNTY
50 State St   **Ph:** 413-748-8600
Springfield, MA 01103   **Fax:** 413-787-4841

On southern border of MA, south of Northampton; organized Feb 25, 1812 from Hampshire County. **Name Origin:** For John Hampden (1594-1643), English statesman influential in the establishment of Puritan colonies in North America.

Area (sq mi): 634.12 (land 618.4; water 15.71).

Pop: 456,228 (White 74.4%; Black or African American 8.1%; Hispanic or Latino 15.2%; Asian 1.3%; Other 11.5%). **Foreign born:** 7.2%. **Median age:** 36.4. **State rank:** 8. **Pop change 1990-2000:** +0%.

Income: per capita $19,541; median household $39,718. **Pop below poverty level:** 14.7%.

Unemployment: 4.3%. **Median home value:** $117,400. **Median travel time to work:** 21.8 minutes.

HAMPSHIRE COUNTY
99 Main St Rm 205   **Ph:** 413-584-0557
Northampton, MA 01060   **Fax:** 413-584-1465

In west-central MA, north of Springfield, organized May 7, 1662 from Middlesex County. **Name Origin:** Named by Capt. John Mason (1586-1635) for the county of Hampshire, England.

Area (sq mi): 545.44 (land 529.03; water 16.41).

Pop: 152,251 (White 89.5%; Black or African American 2%; Hispanic or Latino 3.4%; Asian 3.4%; Other 3.6%). **Foreign born:** 6.6%. **Median age:** 34.4. **State rank:** 10. **Pop change 1990-2000:** +3.9%.

Income: per capita $21,685; median household $46,098. **Pop below poverty level:** 9.4%.

Unemployment: 2.5%. **Median home value:** $142,400. **Median travel time to work:** 21.9 minutes.

MIDDLESEX COUNTY
40 Thorndike St   **Ph:** 617-494-4300
Cambridge, MA 02141

In northern MA, west and northwest of Boston; bounded on north by NH and on the south by Massachusetts Bay. Original county, organized May 10, 1643. **Name Origin:** For an ancient county in England, most of which became part of Greater London in 1965.

Area (sq mi): 847.54 (land 823.46; water 24.08).

Pop: 1,465,396 (White 83.6%; Black or African American 3.4%; Hispanic or Latino 4.6%; Asian 6.3%; Other 4.5%). **Foreign born:** 15.2%. **Median age:** 36.4. **State rank:** 1. **Pop change 1990-2000:** +4.8%.

Income: per capita $31,199; median household $60,821. **Pop below poverty level:** 6.5%.

Unemployment: 3.1%. **Median home value:** $247,900. **Median travel time to work:** 27.4 minutes.

NANTUCKET COUNTY
16 Broad St   **Ph:** 508-228-7216
Nantucket, MA 02554   **Fax:** 508-325-5313

Coextensive with Nantucket Island, south of Cape Cod, MA; original county, organized Jun 22, 1695. **Name Origin:** From an Indian word of uncertain meaning. An early map marks the island as *Natocok*, which may mean 'far away.' Others suggest the root *Nantuck* means 'the sandy, sterile soil tempted no one.'

Area (sq mi): 303.64 (land 47.81; water 255.83).

Pop: 9,520 (White 86.9%; Black or African American 8.3%; Hispanic or Latino 2.2%; Asian 0.6%; Other 3.2%). **Foreign born:** 8%. **Median age:** 36.7. **State rank:** 14. **Pop change 1990-2000:** +58.4%.

Income: per capita $31,314; median household $55,522. **Pop below poverty level:** 7.5%.

Unemployment: 1.5%. **Median home value:** $577,500. **Median travel time to work:** 9.5 minutes.

NORFOLK COUNTY
614 High St   **Ph:** 781-461-6105
Dedham, MA 02026   **Fax:** 781-326-6480
www.norfolkcounty.org

In eastern MA, south of Boston; organized Mar 26, 1793 from Suffolk County. **Name Origin:** For the county in England.

Area (sq mi): 443.94 (land 399.58; water 44.35).

Pop: 650,308 (White 87.9%; Black or African American 3.2%; Hispanic or Latino 1.8%; Asian 5.5%; Other 2.3%). **Foreign born:** 11.8%. **Median age:** 38.1. **State rank:** 5. **Pop change 1990-2000:** +5.6%.

Income: per capita $32,484; median household $63,432. **Pop below poverty level:** 4.6%.

Unemployment: 2.8%. **Median home value:** $230,400. **Median travel time to work:** 30 minutes.

All statistics are based on the 2000 Census except the dollar figures given for per capita income, which are based on 1999 estimates.

PLYMOUTH COUNTY

Court St
Plymouth, MA 02360
www.plymouth-1620.com

Ph: 508-747-6911
Fax: 508-830-0676

In southeastern MA, northeast of New Bedford; organized Jun 2, 1685 from Old Plymouth Colony. **Name Origin:** For Plymouth, Devonshire, England, from which the *Mayflower* sailed for America.

Area (sq mi): 1093.39 (land 660.85; water 432.54).

Pop: 472,822 (White 87.6%; Black or African American 4.6%; Hispanic or Latino 2.4%; Asian 0.9%; Other 5.8%). **Foreign born:** 6.3%. **Median age:** 36.8. **State rank:** 7. **Pop change 1990-2000:** +8.6%.

Income: per capita $24,789; median household $55,615. **Pop below poverty level:** 6.6%.

Unemployment: 3.5%. **Median home value:** $179,200. **Median travel time to work:** 32.3 minutes.

SUFFOLK COUNTY

55 Pemberton Sq Government Ctr
Boston, MA 02108

Ph: 617-725-8000

In eastern MA, on Massachusetts Bay; original county, organized May 10, 1643. **Name Origin:** For the county in England.

Area (sq mi): 120.19 (land 58.52; water 61.68).

Pop: 689,807 (White 52.1%; Black or African American 22.2%; Hispanic or Latino 15.5%; Asian 7%; Other 13.1%). **Foreign born:** 25.5%. **Median age:** 31.7. **State rank:** 4. **Pop change 1990-2000:** +3.9%.

Income: per capita $22,766; median household $39,355. **Pop below poverty level:** 19%.

Unemployment: 4.1%. **Median home value:** $187,300. **Median travel time to work:** 29 minutes.

WORCESTER COUNTY

2 Main St County Courthouse
Worcester, MA 01608

Ph: 508-798-7737
Fax: 508-798-7741

In central MA, having its northern border with NH, its southern border with CT; organized Apr 2, 1731 from Middlesex and Suffolk counties. **Name Origin:** For either the town of Worcester or the county of Worcestershire, both in England.

Area (sq mi): 1579.02 (land 1513.06; water 65.95).

Pop: 750,963 (White 86.5%; Black or African American 2.7%; Hispanic or Latino 6.8%; Asian 2.6%; Other 5%). **Foreign born:** 7.9%. **Median age:** 36.3. **State rank:** 2. **Pop change 1990-2000:** +5.8%.

Income: per capita $22,983; median household $47,874. **Pop below poverty level:** 9.2%.

Unemployment: 4.1%. **Median home value:** $146,000. **Median travel time to work:** 25.8 minutes.

Please see sample entry on inside front cover for detailed information about the statistics presented with each county listing.

271

MICHIGAN - Counties

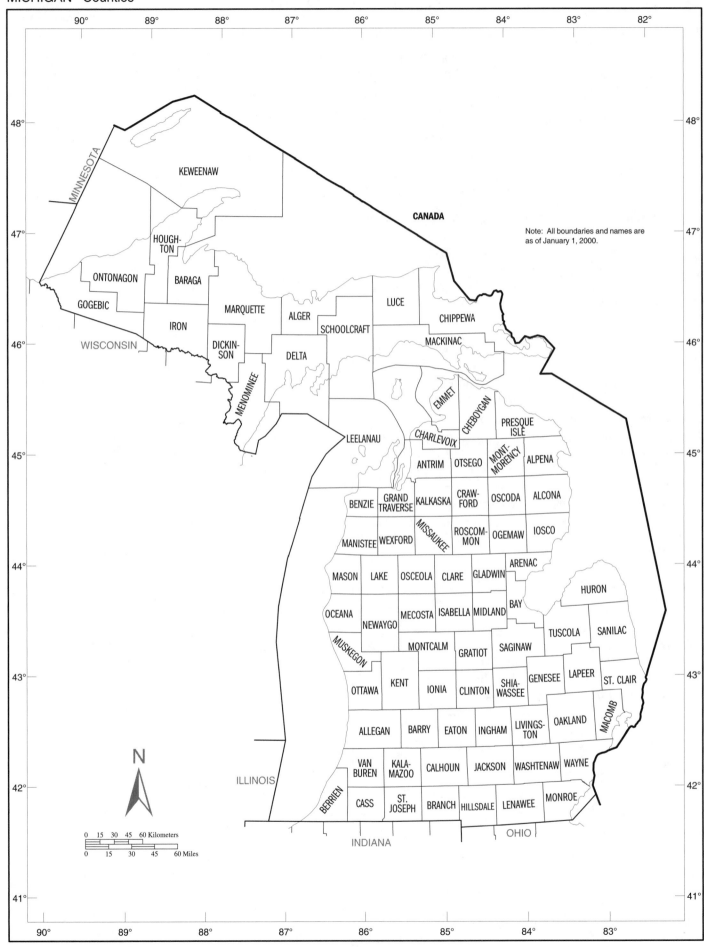

Michigan

MICHIGAN STATE INFORMATION

www.michigan.gov   **Ph:** 517-373-1837

Area (sq mi): 96,716.11 (land 56,803.82; water 39,912.28).

Pop: 9,938,444 (White 78.6%; Black or African American 14.2%; Hispanic or Latino 3.3%; Asian 1.8%; Other 3.8%). **Foreign born:** 5.3%. **Median age:** 35.5. **Pop change 1990-2000:** +6.9%.

Income: per capita $22,168; median household $44,667. **Pop below poverty level:** 10.5%.

Unemployment: 6.2%. **Median home value:** $115,600. **Median travel time to work:** 24.1 minutes.

ALCONA COUNTY

PO Box 308   **Ph:** 989-724-5374
Harrisville, MI 48740   **Fax:** 989-724-5838

On the northeastern coast of MI on Lake Huron; established as Neewaygo County Apr 1, 1840 from Alpena County; name changed Mar 8, 1843. **Name Origin:** A local coinage, said to mean 'beautiful plains.'

Area (sq mi): 1790.54 (land 674.43; water 1116.1).

Pop: 11,719 (White 97.4%; Black or African American 0.2%; Hispanic or Latino 0.7%; Asian 0.2%; Other 1.6%). **Foreign born:** 1.5%. **Median age:** 49. **State rank:** 74. **Pop change 1990-2000:** +15.5%.

Income: per capita $17,653; median household $31,362. **Pop below poverty level:** 12.6%.

Unemployment: 10.2%. **Median home value:** $83,700. **Median travel time to work:** 27.5 minutes.

ALGER COUNTY

PO Box 538   **Ph:** 906-387-2076
Munising, MI 49862   **Fax:** 906-387-2156

On the north-central coast of the Upper Peninsula of MI, on Lake Superior, established Mar 17, 1885, from Schoolcraft County. **Name Origin:** For Gen. Russell Alexander Alger (1836-1907), governor of MI (1885-87), U.S. secretary of war (1897-99), and U.S. senator from MI (1902-07).

Area (sq mi): 5049.08 (land 917.83; water 4131.25).

Pop: 9,862 (White 87.5%; Black or African American 6.1%; Hispanic or Latino 1%; Asian 0.3%; Other 5.7%). **Foreign born:** 1%. **Median age:** 41.2. **State rank:** 77. **Pop change 1990-2000:** +9.9%.

Income: per capita $18,210; median household $35,892. **Pop below poverty level:** 10.3%.

Unemployment: 6%. **Median home value:** $75,900. **Median travel time to work:** 19.8 minutes.

ALLEGAN COUNTY

113 Chestnut St   **Ph:** 269-673-0205
Allegan, MI 49010   **Fax:** 269-673-0367
www.allegancounty.org

On the southwestern coast of MI, bordered on the west by Lake Michigan; established Mar 2, 1831 (prior to statehood) from Kalamazoo County. **Name Origin:** Named for the Allegan (Alleghen) Indian tribe by Henry Rowe Schoolcraft (1793-1864), explorer, MI legislator, author, and superintendent of Indian Affairs for MI (1836-41).

Area (sq mi): 1833.3 (land 827.46; water 1005.83).

Pop: 105,665 (White 91%; Black or African American 1.3%; Hispanic or Latino 5.7%; Asian 0.6%; Other 4.6%). **Foreign born:** 2.9%. **Median age:** 35.2. **State rank:** 19. **Pop change 1990-2000:** +16.7%.

Income: per capita $19,918; median household $45,813. **Pop below poverty level:** 7.3%.

Unemployment: 4.6%. **Median home value:** $115,500. **Median travel time to work:** 23.4 minutes.

ALPENA COUNTY

720 W Chisholm St   **Ph:** 989-356-0930
Alpena, MI 49707   **Fax:** 989-354-9648
www.alpenacounty.org

On the northeastern coast of MI, bordered on the east by Lake Huron; established as Anamickee County Apr 1, 1840 from Presque Isle County; name changed Mar 8, 1843. **Name Origin:** From an Indian word probably meaning 'partridge' or 'partridge country.' Originally named for the Chippewa chief.

Area (sq mi): 1695 (land 574.15; water 1120.85).

Pop: 31,314 (White 97.8%; Black or African American 0.2%; Hispanic or Latino 0.6%; Asian 0.3%; Other 1.2%). **Foreign born:** 1.2%. **Median age:** 40.4. **State rank:** 47. **Pop change 1990-2000:** +2.3%.

Income: per capita $17,566; median household $34,177. **Pop below poverty level:** 10.5%.

Unemployment: 8.7%. **Median home value:** $78,100. **Median travel time to work:** 17 minutes.

ANTRIM COUNTY

PO Box 520   **Ph:** 231-533-6353
Bellaire, MI 49615   **Fax:** 231-533-6935
www.antrimcounty.org

Please see sample entry on inside front cover for detailed information about the statistics presented with each county listing.

273

On the northwest coast of MI; established as Meegisee County Apr 1, 1840 from Mackinac County; name changed Mar 8, 1843. **Name Origin:** For the county in Ireland.

Area (sq mi): 601.9 (land 476.94; water 124.97).

Pop: 23,110 (White 96.2%; Black or African American 0.2%; Hispanic or Latino 1.2%; Asian 0.2%; Other 2.7%). **Foreign born:** 1.5%. **Median age:** 41.1. **State rank:** 62. **Pop change 1990-2000:** +27.1%.

Income: per capita $19,485; median household $38,107. **Pop below poverty level:** 9%.

Unemployment: 7.5%. **Median home value:** $110,000. **Median travel time to work:** 23 minutes.

ARENAC COUNTY

PO Box 747
Standish, MI 48658

Ph: 989-846-4626

On the east coast of MI on Saginaw Bay; established Mar 2, 1831 (prior to statehood). **Name Origin:** Name coined by Henry Rowe Schoolcraft (1793-1864), author, explorer, MI legislator, and superintendent of Indian Affairs for MI (1836-41), meaning 'sandy place' from Spanish *arena* 'sand' and *-ac* 'place of.'

Area (sq mi): 680.81 (land 366.84; water 313.97).

Pop: 17,269 (White 94.4%; Black or African American 1.8%; Hispanic or Latino 1.4%; Asian 0.3%; Other 2.4%). **Foreign born:** 1.1%. **Median age:** 40.1. **State rank:** 66. **Pop change 1990-2000:** +15.7%.

Income: per capita $16,300; median household $32,805. **Pop below poverty level:** 13.9%.

Unemployment: 9.1%. **Median home value:** $77,700. **Median travel time to work:** 28.3 minutes.

BARAGA COUNTY

16 N 3rd St
L'Anse, MI 49946

Ph: 906-524-6183
Fax: 906-524-6186

On the north coast of the Upper Peninsula of MI on Keweenaw Bay; established Feb 19, 1875 from Houghton County. **Name Origin:** For the Rev. Frederic Baraga (1797-1868), Slovenian-born Roman Catholic missionary to the Ojibways who became a bishop in 1853. He established schools for the Chippewa and Ottawa (1830-68).

Area (sq mi): 1068.85 (land 904; water 164.85).

Pop: 8,746 (White 78.3%; Black or African American 5%; Hispanic or Latino 0.9%; Asian 0.3%; Other 16.1%). **Foreign born:** 0.8%. **Median age:** 39. **State rank:** 80. **Pop change 1990-2000:** +10%.

Income: per capita $15,860; median household $33,673. **Pop below poverty level:** 11.1%.

Unemployment: 9.5%. **Median home value:** $67,100. **Median travel time to work:** 17.8 minutes.

BARRY COUNTY

220 W State St
Hastings, MI 49058
www.barrycounty.org

Ph: 269-948-4810
Fax: 269-945-0209

In southwestern MI, northeast of Kalamazoo; established Oct 29, 1829 (prior to statehood) from Eaton County. **Name Origin:** For

William Taylor Barry (1784-1835), KY legislator, U.S. senator (1814-16), and U.S. Postmaster General (1829-35).

Area (sq mi): 576.9 (land 556.14; water 20.77).

Pop: 56,755 (White 96.5%; Black or African American 0.2%; Hispanic or Latino 1.5%; Asian 0.3%; Other 2.1%). **Foreign born:** 0.8%. **Median age:** 36.9. **State rank:** 34. **Pop change 1990-2000:** +13.4%.

Income: per capita $20,636; median household $46,820. **Pop below poverty level:** 5.5%.

Unemployment: 4.3%. **Median home value:** $107,100. **Median travel time to work:** 26.9 minutes.

BAY COUNTY

515 Center Ave
Bay City, MI 48708
www.co.bay.mi.us

Ph: 989-895-4280
Fax: 989-895-4284

On the east coast of MI, north of Saginaw; established Feb 27, 1857 from Saginaw and Midland counties. **Name Origin:** For its location at the head of Saginaw Bay.

Area (sq mi): 630.91 (land 444.25; water 186.66).

Pop: 110,157 (White 92.7%; Black or African American 1.3%; Hispanic or Latino 3.9%; Asian 0.5%; Other 3.2%). **Foreign born:** 1.4%. **Median age:** 38.4. **State rank:** 18. **Pop change 1990-2000:** -1.4%.

Income: per capita $19,698; median household $38,646. **Pop below poverty level:** 9.7%.

Unemployment: 5.6%. **Median home value:** $84,900. **Median travel time to work:** 21.8 minutes.

BENZIE COUNTY

PO Box 377
Beulah, MI 49617

Ph: 231-882-9671
Fax: 231-882-5941

On the northwestern coast of MI, bordered on west by Lake Michigan; established Feb 27, 1863 from Manistee and Grand Traverse counties. **Name Origin:** Origin uncertain; perhaps a variant of the French name for the Betsie river, *Aux Bec Scies* 'sawbill' a species of duck. Americans corrupted it to *Betsie*, then to *Benzie* for the county.

Area (sq mi): 859.64 (land 321.31; water 538.32).

Pop: 15,998 (White 95.4%; Black or African American 0.3%; Hispanic or Latino 1.5%; Asian 0.2%; Other 3.2%). **Foreign born:** 1.7%. **Median age:** 40.8. **State rank:** 68. **Pop change 1990-2000:** +31.1%.

Income: per capita $18,524; median household $37,350. **Pop below poverty level:** 7%.

Unemployment: 6.7%. **Median home value:** $107,400. **Median travel time to work:** 25.4 minutes.

BERRIEN COUNTY

811 Port St
Saint Joseph, MI 49085
www.berriencounty.org

Ph: 269-983-7111
Fax: 269-982-8642

In the southwestern corner of MI, bordered on west by Lake Michigan; established Oct 29, 1829 (prior to statehood) from Indian

All statistics are based on the 2000 Census except the dollar figures given for per capita income, which are based on 1999 estimates.

lands. **Name Origin:** For Col. John Macpherson Berrien (1781-1856), U.S. senator from GA (1825-29; 1841-52) and U.S. attorney general (1829-31).

Area (sq mi): 1581.38 (land 571; water 1010.39).

Pop: 162,453 (White 78.1%; Black or African American 15.9%; Hispanic or Latino 3%; Asian 1.1%; Other 3.1%). **Foreign born:** 4.9%. **Median age:** 37.4. **State rank:** 13. **Pop change 1990-2000:** +0.7%.

Income: per capita $19,952; median household $38,567. **Pop below poverty level:** 12.7%.

Unemployment: 5.7%. **Median home value:** $94,700. **Median travel time to work:** 20 minutes.

BRANCH COUNTY

31 Division St	**Ph:** 517-279-4301
Coldwater, MI 49036	**Fax:** 517-278-4130
www.co.branch.mi.us	

On the south-central border of MI; established Oct 29, 1829 (prior to statehood) from Saint Joseph County. **Name Origin:** For John Branch (1782-1863), NC governor (1817-20), U.S. secretary of the navy (1829-31), and governor of FL Territory (1844-45).

Area (sq mi): 519.49 (land 507.41; water 12.08).

Pop: 45,787 (White 92%; Black or African American 2.6%; Hispanic or Latino 3%; Asian 0.4%; Other 3.6%). **Foreign born:** 2.6%. **Median age:** 36.7. **State rank:** 38. **Pop change 1990-2000:** +10.3%.

Income: per capita $17,552; median household $38,760. **Pop below poverty level:** 9.3%.

Unemployment: 5.7%. **Median home value:** $85,000. **Median travel time to work:** 21.6 minutes.

CALHOUN COUNTY

315 W Green St	**Ph:** 269-781-0730
Marshall, MI 49068	**Fax:** 269-781-0721
www.calhoun-mi.com	

In south-central MI, east of Kalamazoo; established Oct. 29, 1829 (prior to statehood) from Indian lands. **Name Origin:** For John Caldwell Calhoun (1782-1850), U.S. statesman and proponent of Southern causes.

Area (sq mi): 718.44 (land 708.72; water 9.72).

Pop: 137,985 (White 82.4%; Black or African American 10.9%; Hispanic or Latino 3.2%; Asian 1.1%; Other 4%). **Foreign born:** 2.4%. **Median age:** 36.4. **State rank:** 17. **Pop change 1990-2000:** +1.5%.

Income: per capita $19,230; median household $38,918. **Pop below poverty level:** 11.3%.

Unemployment: 5.4%. **Median home value:** $81,000. **Median travel time to work:** 20.1 minutes.

CASS COUNTY

PO Box 355	**Ph:** 269-445-3701
Cassopolis, MI 49031	
casscountymi.org	

On the southwestern border of MI, southwest of Kalamazoo; established Oct 29, 1829 (prior to statehood) from Indian lands. **Name**

Origin: For Gen. Lewis Cass (1782-1866), OH legislator, governor of MI Territory (1813-31), U.S. secretary of war (1831-36), and U.S. secretary of state (1857-60).

Area (sq mi): 508.46 (land 492.18; water 16.29).

Pop: 51,104 (White 88.2%; Black or African American 6.1%; Hispanic or Latino 2.4%; Asian 0.5%; Other 4.1%). **Foreign born:** 1.9%. **Median age:** 38.5. **State rank:** 35. **Pop change 1990-2000:** +3.3%.

Income: per capita $19,474; median household $41,264. **Pop below poverty level:** 9.9%.

Unemployment: 5.2%. **Median home value:** $91,800. **Median travel time to work:** 24.2 minutes.

CHARLEVOIX COUNTY

203 Antrim St	**Ph:** 231-547-7200
Charlevoix, MI 49720	**Fax:** 231-547-7217
www.charlevoixcounty.org	

On the northwestern coast of MI, bordered on west by Lake Michigan; established as Reshkauko County Apr 1, 1840; name changed Mar 8, 1843. **Name Origin:** For Pierre Francois Xavier de Charlevoix (1682-1761), French Jesuit explorer and writer who traveled from the Great Lakes down the Illinois and Mississippi rivers to New Orleans (1720-22).

Area (sq mi): 1390.76 (land 416.84; water 973.92).

Pop: 26,090 (White 95.8%; Black or African American 0.2%; Hispanic or Latino 1%; Asian 0.2%; Other 3.2%). **Foreign born:** 1.4%. **Median age:** 39.1. **State rank:** 55. **Pop change 1990-2000:** +21.5%.

Income: per capita $20,130; median household $39,788. **Pop below poverty level:** 8%.

Unemployment: 6.8%. **Median home value:** $112,700. **Median travel time to work:** 19.8 minutes.

CHEBOYGAN COUNTY

PO Box 70	**Ph:** 231-627-8808
Cheboygan, MI 49721	**Fax:** 231-627-8453

On the north coast of MI; established Apr 1, 1840 from Antrim County. **Name Origin:** For the Cheboygan River; the name is Algonquian but the meaning is in dispute.

Area (sq mi): 885.23 (land 715.6; water 169.63).

Pop: 26,448 (White 94.3%; Black or African American 0.2%; Hispanic or Latino 0.8%; Asian 0.2%; Other 4.6%). **Foreign born:** 1.2%. **Median age:** 41.3. **State rank:** 54. **Pop change 1990-2000:** +23.6%.

Income: per capita $18,088; median household $33,417. **Pop below poverty level:** 12.2%.

Unemployment: 11.2%. **Median home value:** $94,500. **Median travel time to work:** 23 minutes.

CHIPPEWA COUNTY

319 Court St	**Ph:** 906-635-6300
Sault Sainte Marie, MI 49783	**Fax:** 906-635-6851
users.lighthouse.net/chippewa/	

On the northeast coast of the Upper Peninsula of MI on Whitefish Bay; established Dec 22, 1826 (prior to statehood) from Mackinac

Please see sample entry on inside front cover for detailed information about the statistics presented with each county listing.

275

County. **Name Origin:** For the Ojibway Indians of Algonquian linguistic stock. The name means 'puckered' and probably refers to the seam in their moccasins.

Area (sq mi): 2697.98 (land 1561.06; water 1136.92).

Pop: 38,543 (White 75.2%; Black or African American 5.5%; Hispanic or Latino 1.6%; Asian 0.5%; Other 18.1%). **Foreign born:** 3%. **Median age:** 36.2. **State rank:** 42. **Pop change 1990-2000:** +11.4%.

Income: per capita $15,858; median household $34,464. **Pop below poverty level:** 12.8%.

Unemployment: 7.8%. **Median home value:** $77,300. **Median travel time to work:** 17.7 minutes.

CLARE COUNTY

225 W Main St
Harrison, MI 48625
www.clarecountychamber.com

Ph: 989-539-7131
Fax: 989-539-6616

In central MI, northwest of Midland; established as Kaykakee County Apr 1, 1840 from Isabella County; name changed Mar 8, 1843. **Name Origin:** For the county in Ireland. Originally for the Indian chief, Kaykakee 'pigeon hawk' who had signed the Treaty of 1826.

Area (sq mi): 575.22 (land 566.8; water 8.42).

Pop: 31,252 (White 96.7%; Black or African American 0.3%; Hispanic or Latino 1.1%; Asian 0.3%; Other 2%). **Foreign born:** 1.1%. **Median age:** 40.5. **State rank:** 48. **Pop change 1990-2000:** +25.2%.

Income: per capita $15,922; median household $28,845. **Pop below poverty level:** 16%.

Unemployment: 8.9%. **Median home value:** $70,500. **Median travel time to work:** 28.3 minutes.

CLINTON COUNTY

PO Box 69
Saint Johns, MI 48879
www.clinton-county.org

Ph: 989-224-5140
Fax: 989-224-5102

In central MI, north of Lansing; established Mar 2, 1831 (prior to statehood) from Shiawassee County. **Name Origin:** For DeWitt Clinton (1769-1828), governor of NY (1817-21; 1825-28) and supporter of the Erie Canal.

Area (sq mi): 574.57 (land 571.46; water 3.12).

Pop: 64,753 (White 94.8%; Black or African American 0.6%; Hispanic or Latino 2.6%; Asian 0.5%; Other 2.4%). **Foreign born:** 1.2%. **Median age:** 36.7. **State rank:** 27. **Pop change 1990-2000:** +11.9%.

Income: per capita $22,913; median household $52,806. **Pop below poverty level:** 4.6%.

Unemployment: 2.8%. **Median home value:** $120,500. **Median travel time to work:** 24.2 minutes.

CRAWFORD COUNTY

200 W Michigan Ave
Grayling, MI 49738
www.crawfordco.org

Ph: 989-344-3206
Fax: 989-344-3223

In north-central MI; established Apr 1, 1840 as Shawano County;

name changed Mar 8, 1843. **Name Origin:** For Col. William Crawford (1732-82), VA officer in the Revolutionary War, Indian fighter, and surveyor.

Area (sq mi): 563.37 (land 558.12; water 5.25).

Pop: 14,273 (White 95.7%; Black or African American 1.5%; Hispanic or Latino 1%; Asian 0.3%; Other 1.9%). **Foreign born:** 1.3%. **Median age:** 40.6. **State rank:** 71. **Pop change 1990-2000:** +16.4%.

Income: per capita $16,903; median household $33,364. **Pop below poverty level:** 12.7%.

Unemployment: 6.8%. **Median home value:** $79,500. **Median travel time to work:** 21.3 minutes.

DELTA COUNTY

310 Ludington St
Escanaba, MI 49829
www.deltami.org

Ph: 906-789-5105
Fax: 906-789-5196

On the Upper Peninsula of MI on Green Bay; established Mar 9, 1843 from Schoolcraft County. **Name Origin:** For the Greek letter, which the shape of the county resembles.

Area (sq mi): 1991.58 (land 1170.03; water 821.56).

Pop: 38,520 (White 95.5%; Black or African American 0.1%; Hispanic or Latino 0.5%; Asian 0.3%; Other 3.7%). **Foreign born:** 1%. **Median age:** 40.4. **State rank:** 43. **Pop change 1990-2000:** +2%.

Income: per capita $18,667; median household $35,511. **Pop below poverty level:** 9.5%.

Unemployment: 7.3%. **Median home value:** $80,000. **Median travel time to work:** 18.8 minutes.

DICKINSON COUNTY

PO Box 609
Iron Mountain, MI 49801

Ph: 906-774-0988
Fax: 906-774-4660

On the south-central border of the Upper Peninsula of MI, south of Ishpeming; established May 21, 1891 from Marquette County. **Name Origin:** For Donald McDonald Dickinson (1846-1917), U.S. postmaster-general (1887-89).

Area (sq mi): 777.12 (land 766.34; water 10.78).

Pop: 27,472 (White 97.5%; Black or African American 0.1%; Hispanic or Latino 0.7%; Asian 0.4%; Other 1.4%). **Foreign born:** 1.1%. **Median age:** 40. **State rank:** 51. **Pop change 1990-2000:** +2.4%.

Income: per capita $18,516; median household $34,825. **Pop below poverty level:** 9.1%.

Unemployment: 5.1%. **Median home value:** $64,600. **Median travel time to work:** 15.7 minutes.

EATON COUNTY

1045 Independence Blvd
Charlotte, MI 48813
www.co.eaton.mi.us

Ph: 517-543-7500

In south-central MI, east of Lansing; established Oct 29, 1829. **Name Origin:** For John Henry Eaton (1790-1856), U.S. senator from TN (1818-29), U.S. secretary of War (1829-31), and governor of FL Territory (1834-36).

All statistics are based on the 2000 Census except the dollar figures given for per capita income, which are based on 1999 estimates.

Area (sq mi): 579.02 (land 576.41; water 2.61).

Pop: 103,655 (White 88.7%; Black or African American 5.3%; Hispanic or Latino 3.2%; Asian 1.1%; Other 3.3%). **Foreign born:** 2.2%. **Median age:** 36.4. **State rank:** 20. **Pop change 1990-2000:** +11.6%.

Income: per capita $22,411; median household $49,588. **Pop below poverty level:** 5.8%.

Unemployment: 3.2%. **Median home value:** $113,700. **Median travel time to work:** 22.4 minutes.

EMMET COUNTY
200 Division St
Petoskey, MI 49770
www.co.emmet.mi.us

Ph: 231-348-1744
Fax: 231-348-0602

On the northwest coast of MI, bordered on west by Lake Michigan; established as Tonedagana County Apr 1, 1840 from Mackinac County; name changed Mar 8, 1843. **Name Origin:** For Robert W. Emmet (1778-1803), Irish rebel executed by the British; named for him during a time when rebel leaders were honored by Americans.

Area (sq mi): 882.26 (land 467.82; water 414.44).

Pop: 31,437 (White 93.8%; Black or African American 0.5%; Hispanic or Latino 0.9%; Asian 0.4%; Other 4.8%). **Foreign born:** 1.7%. **Median age:** 38.9. **State rank:** 46. **Pop change 1990-2000:** +25.5%.

Income: per capita $21,070; median household $40,222. **Pop below poverty level:** 7.4%.

Unemployment: 7.1%. **Median home value:** $131,500. **Median travel time to work:** 19.1 minutes.

GENESEE COUNTY
900 S Saginaw St Rm 202
Flint, MI 48502
www.co.genesee.mi.us

Ph: 810-257-3282
Fax: 810-257-3464

In east-central MI, northeast of Lansing; organized Mar 28, 1835 (prior to statehood) from Oakland County. **Name Origin:** For Genesee County, NY, former home of many early settlers; from Iroquoian 'beautiful valley.'

Area (sq mi): 649.34 (land 639.64; water 9.7).

Pop: 436,141 (White 74.1%; Black or African American 20.4%; Hispanic or Latino 2.3%; Asian 0.8%; Other 3.6%). **Foreign born:** 2.1%. **Median age:** 35. **State rank:** 5. **Pop change 1990-2000:** +1.3%.

Income: per capita $20,883; median household $41,951. **Pop below poverty level:** 13.1%.

Unemployment: 7.6%. **Median home value:** $95,000. **Median travel time to work:** 25.6 minutes.

GLADWIN COUNTY
401 W Cedar Ave
Gladwin, MI 48624

Ph: 989-426-7351
Fax: 989-426-6917

In east-central MI, north of Midland; established Mar 2, 1831 (prior to statehood) from unorganized territory. **Name Origin:** For Gen. Henry Gladwin (1729-91), British soldier during the French and Indian War and defender of Detroit against Chief Pontiac.

Area (sq mi): 516.43 (land 506.8; water 9.63).

Pop: 26,023 (White 97.1%; Black or African American 0.1%; Hispanic or Latino 1%; Asian 0.3%; Other 2%). **Foreign born:** 1.3%. **Median age:** 42.3. **State rank:** 56. **Pop change 1990-2000:** +18.8%.

Income: per capita $16,614; median household $32,019. **Pop below poverty level:** 13.8%.

Unemployment: 8.6%. **Median home value:** $86,800. **Median travel time to work:** 29.5 minutes.

GOGEBIC COUNTY
200 N Moore St
Bessemer, MI 49911

Ph: 906-663-4518
Fax: 906-663-4660

On the southwest border of the Upper Peninsula of MI; organized Feb 7, 1887 from Ontonagon County. **Name Origin:** From Ojibway *agogebic*, of uncertain origin, though *bic* translates to 'lake'; also possibly 'trembling ground.'

Area (sq mi): 1476.43 (land 1101.86; water 374.57).

Pop: 17,370 (White 93.8%; Black or African American 1.8%; Hispanic or Latino 0.9%; Asian 0.2%; Other 3.7%). **Foreign born:** 1.3%. **Median age:** 42.9. **State rank:** 65. **Pop change 1990-2000:** -3.8%.

Income: per capita $16,169; median household $27,405. **Pop below poverty level:** 14.4%.

Unemployment: 7.3%. **Median home value:** $39,700. **Median travel time to work:** 17.3 minutes.

GRAND TRAVERSE COUNTY
400 Boardman Ave
Traverse City, MI 49684
www.grandtraverse.org

Ph: 231-922-4760
Fax: 231-922-4658

On the northwest coast of MI on Grand Traverse Bay; organized as Omeena County Apr 1, 1840; name changed Apr 17, 1851. **Name Origin:** From French *Le Grand Traverse* 'the long crossing,' for the trail across the foot of Traverse Bay.

Area (sq mi): 601.13 (land 465.07; water 136.06).

Pop: 77,654 (White 95.6%; Black or African American 0.4%; Hispanic or Latino 1.5%; Asian 0.5%; Other 2.5%). **Foreign born:** 2.1%. **Median age:** 37.7. **State rank:** 24. **Pop change 1990-2000:** +20.8%.

Income: per capita $22,111; median household $43,169. **Pop below poverty level:** 5.9%.

Unemployment: 5%. **Median home value:** $130,400. **Median travel time to work:** 20.5 minutes.

GRATIOT COUNTY
County Courthouse 214 E Center St
PO Box 437
Ithaca, MI 48847
www.gratiotcounty.org

Ph: 989-875-5215
Fax: 989-875-5284

In central MI, north of Lansing; established Mar 2, 1831 from Saginaw County. **Name Origin:** For Gen. Charles Gratiot (1786-1855), U.S. army officer who built Ft. Gratiot at Port Huron (1814); chief engineer of U.S. Army (1828-38).

Area (sq mi): 571.61 (land 570.13; water 1.48).

Please see sample entry on inside front cover for detailed information about the statistics presented with each county listing.

Pop: 42,285 (White 89.9%; Black or African American 3.7%; Hispanic or Latino 4.4%; Asian 0.3%; Other 3.9%). **Foreign born:** 1.2%. **Median age:** 35.6. **State rank:** 40. **Pop change 1990-2000:** +8.5%.

Income: per capita $17,118; median household $37,262. **Pop below poverty level:** 10.3%.

Unemployment: 5.5%. **Median home value:** $75,300. **Median travel time to work:** 22.7 minutes.

HILLSDALE COUNTY

29 N Howell St **Ph:** 517-437-3391
Hillsdale, MI 49242 **Fax:** 517-437-3392
www.co.hillsdale.mi.us

On the south-central border of MI, southeast of Kalamazoo; established Oct 29, 1829 (prior to statehood) from Lenawee County. **Name Origin:** For its topography of hills and dales.

Area (sq mi): 607.14 (land 598.84; water 8.3).

Pop: 46,527 (White 96.8%; Black or African American 0.4%; Hispanic or Latino 1.2%; Asian 0.3%; Other 1.7%). **Foreign born:** 1.1%. **Median age:** 36.5. **State rank:** 37. **Pop change 1990-2000:** +7.1%.

Income: per capita $18,255; median household $40,396. **Pop below poverty level:** 8.2%.

Unemployment: 6.5%. **Median home value:** $85,800. **Median travel time to work:** 23.6 minutes.

HOUGHTON COUNTY

401 E Houghton Ave **Ph:** 906-482-1150
Houghton, MI 49931 **Fax:** 906-483-0364

On the northwest coast of the Upper Peninsula of MI; organized Mar 19, 1845 from Marquette, Schoolcraft, and Ontonagon counties. **Name Origin:** For Douglas Houghton (1809-45), professor and pioneer state geologist (1834-41).

Area (sq mi): 1501.56 (land 1011.72; water 489.84).

Pop: 36,016 (White 95.1%; Black or African American 0.9%; Hispanic or Latino 0.7%; Asian 1.8%; Other 1.7%). **Foreign born:** 2.7%. **Median age:** 34. **State rank:** 45. **Pop change 1990-2000:** +1.6%.

Income: per capita $15,078; median household $28,817. **Pop below poverty level:** 16.8%.

Unemployment: 5.9%. **Median home value:** $54,800. **Median travel time to work:** 15.6 minutes.

HURON COUNTY

250 E Huron Ave Rm 305 **Ph:** 989-269-8242
Bad Axe, MI 48413 **Fax:** 989-269-6152

On the east coast of MI on Saginaw Bay; organized Apr 1, 1840 from Sanilac and Tuscola counties. **Name Origin:** For the Huron Indians (later known as Wyandots), a tribe of Iroquoian linguistic stock; from a French word for 'rough,' probably because they were formidable opponents.

Area (sq mi): 2136.47 (land 836.52; water 1299.95).

Pop: 36,079 (White 96.8%; Black or African American 0.2%; Hispanic or Latino 1.6%; Asian 0.4%; Other 1.4%). **Foreign born:**

1.4%. **Median age:** 41.2. **State rank:** 44. **Pop change 1990-2000:** +3.2%.

Income: per capita $17,851; median household $35,315. **Pop below poverty level:** 10.2%.

Unemployment: 8.2%. **Median home value:** $78,000. **Median travel time to work:** 20.6 minutes.

INGHAM COUNTY

PO Box 179 **Ph:** 517-676-7204
Mason, MI 48854 **Fax:** 517-676-7254
www.ingham.org

In south-central MI; established Oct 29, 1829 (prior to statehood) from unorganized territory. **Name Origin:** For Samuel Delucenna Ingham (1779-1860), U.S. representative from PA (1813-18; 1822-29) and U.S. secretary of the treasury (1829-31).

Area (sq mi): 560.94 (land 559.19; water 1.75).

Pop: 279,320 (White 76.9%; Black or African American 10.9%; Hispanic or Latino 5.8%; Asian 3.7%; Other 6%). **Foreign born:** 6.3%. **Median age:** 30.4. **State rank:** 7. **Pop change 1990-2000:** -0.9%.

Income: per capita $21,079; median household $40,774. **Pop below poverty level:** 14.6%.

Unemployment: 3.6%. **Median home value:** $98,400. **Median travel time to work:** 20.1 minutes.

IONIA COUNTY

100 Main St **Ph:** 616-527-5322
Ionia, MI 48846 **Fax:** 616-527-8201
www.ioniacounty.org

In central MI, east of Grand Rapids; established Mar 2, 1831 (prior to statehood) from unorganized territory. **Name Origin:** For the ancient province in Greece.

Area (sq mi): 580.23 (land 573.21; water 7.02).

Pop: 61,518 (White 90.6%; Black or African American 4.6%; Hispanic or Latino 2.8%; Asian 0.3%; Other 3.1%). **Foreign born:** 1.2%. **Median age:** 32.9. **State rank:** 31. **Pop change 1990-2000:** +7.9%.

Income: per capita $17,451; median household $43,074. **Pop below poverty level:** 8.7%.

Unemployment: 5.7%. **Median home value:** $94,400. **Median travel time to work:** 27.6 minutes.

IOSCO COUNTY

PO Box 778 **Ph:** 989-362-4212
Tawas City, MI 48764 **Fax:** 989-984-1002
iosco.m33access.com

On the east-central coast of MI bordered on east by Lake Huron; organized as Kanotin County Apr 1, 1840 from unorganized territory; name changed Mar 8, 1843. **Name Origin:** From an Indian word meaning 'shining water' or 'water of light.'

Area (sq mi): 1890.77 (land 549.11; water 1341.66).

Pop: 27,339 (White 96.3%; Black or African American 0.4%; Hispanic or Latino 1%; Asian 0.5%; Other 2.3%). **Foreign born:** 1.3%. **Median age:** 44.2. **State rank:** 52. **Pop change 1990-2000:** -9.5%.

All statistics are based on the 2000 Census except the dollar figures given for per capita income, which are based on 1999 estimates.

Income: per capita $17,115; median household $31,321. **Pop below poverty level:** 12.7%.

Unemployment: 10.6%. **Median home value:** $77,100. **Median travel time to work:** 21.8 minutes.

IRON COUNTY

2 S 6th St
Crystal Falls, MI 49920
www.iron.org

Ph: 906-875-3221
Fax: 906-875-6775

On the southwest border of the Upper Peninsula of MI; established Apr 3, 1885 from Marquette and Menominee counties. **Name Origin:** For the iron mines in the area.

Area (sq mi): 1211.02 (land 1166.36; water 44.67).

Pop: 13,138 (White 95.9%; Black or African American 1.1%; Hispanic or Latino 0.6%; Asian 0.2%; Other 2.4%). **Foreign born:** 1.1%. **Median age:** 45.4. **State rank:** 72. **Pop change 1990-2000:** -0.3%.

Income: per capita $16,506; median household $28,560. **Pop below poverty level:** 11.3%.

Unemployment: 6.5%. **Median home value:** $47,500. **Median travel time to work:** 20.2 minutes.

ISABELLA COUNTY

200 N Main St
Mount Pleasant, MI 48858
www.isabellacounty.org

Ph: 989-772-0911
Fax: 989-773-7431

In central MI, west of Midland; organized Mar 2, 1831 (prior to statehood) from unorganized territory. **Name Origin:** For Isabella (1451-1504), queen of Spain who financed Christopher Columbus's expeditions.

Area (sq mi): 577.75 (land 574.27; water 3.48).

Pop: 63,351 (White 90.4%; Black or African American 1.9%; Hispanic or Latino 2.2%; Asian 1.4%; Other 5.2%). **Foreign born:** 2.3%. **Median age:** 25.1. **State rank:** 29. **Pop change 1990-2000:** +16%.

Income: per capita $16,242; median household $34,262. **Pop below poverty level:** 20.4%.

Unemployment: 3.3%. **Median home value:** $91,800. **Median travel time to work:** 18.2 minutes.

JACKSON COUNTY

312 S Jackson St 1st Fl
Jackson, MI 49201
www.co.jackson.mi.us

Ph: 517-788-4265
Fax: 517-788-4601

In south-central MI, west of Ann Arbor, established Oct 29, 1829 (prior to statehood) from Washtenaw County. **Name Origin:** For Andrew Jackson (1767-1845), seventh U.S. president.

Area (sq mi): 723.76 (land 706.6; water 17.17).

Pop: 158,422 (White 87.4%; Black or African American 7.9%; Hispanic or Latino 2.2%; Asian 0.5%; Other 2.9%). **Foreign born:** 1.7%. **Median age:** 36.6. **State rank:** 14. **Pop change 1990-2000:** +5.8%.

Income: per capita $20,171; median household $43,171. **Pop below poverty level:** 9%.

Unemployment: 5.3%. **Median home value:** $96,900. **Median travel time to work:** 23.1 minutes.

KALAMAZOO COUNTY

201 W Kalamazoo Ave
Kalamazoo, MI 49007
www.kalcounty.com

Ph: 269-383-8840
Fax: 269-384-8143

In southwest MI, south of Grand Rapids; organized Oct 29, 1829 (prior to statehood) from Saint Joseph County. **Name Origin:** From Algonquian, *ke-kala-mazoo*, meaning uncertain, interpreted as connected with 'smoke,' 'beautiful water,' 'otters,' or 'boiling water.'

Area (sq mi): 580.18 (land 561.86; water 18.32).

Pop: 238,603 (White 83.5%; Black or African American 9.7%; Hispanic or Latino 2.6%; Asian 1.8%; Other 3.9%). **Foreign born:** 4%. **Median age:** 32.7. **State rank:** 8. **Pop change 1990-2000:** +6.8%.

Income: per capita $21,739; median household $42,022. **Pop below poverty level:** 12%.

Unemployment: 4.2%. **Median home value:** $108,000. **Median travel time to work:** 19.7 minutes.

KALKASKA COUNTY

PO Box 10
Kalkaska, MI 49646

Ph: 231-258-3300
Fax: 231-258-3337

In north-central MI, east of Traverse City; established as Wabassee County Apr 1, 1840 from Crawford County; name changed Mar 8, 1843. **Name Origin:** From an Indian word of uncertain origin and meaning, although some sources suggest that it is from a Chippewa word meaning 'burned over.'

Area (sq mi): 570.76 (land 561.02; water 9.75).

Pop: 16,571 (White 96.9%; Black or African American 0.2%; Hispanic or Latino 0.9%; Asian 0.2%; Other 2%). **Foreign born:** 0.8%. **Median age:** 38. **State rank:** 67. **Pop change 1990-2000:** +22.8%.

Income: per capita $16,309; median household $36,072. **Pop below poverty level:** 10.5%.

Unemployment: 9.1%. **Median home value:** $85,100. **Median travel time to work:** 28.2 minutes.

KENT COUNTY

300 Monroe Ave NW
Grand Rapids, MI 49503
www.co.kent.mi.us/

Ph: 616-336-3550
Fax: 616-336-2885

In west-central MI, east of Muskegon; established Mar 2, 1831 (prior to statehood) from unorganized territory. **Name Origin:** For James Kent (1763-1847), chief justice of the NY supreme court (1804-14).

Area (sq mi): 872.18 (land 856.17; water 16.01).

Pop: 574,335 (White 80.3%; Black or African American 8.9%; Hispanic or Latino 7%; Asian 1.9%; Other 6.1%). **Foreign born:** 6.6%. **Median age:** 32.5. **State rank:** 4. **Pop change 1990-2000:** +14.7%.

Income: per capita $21,629; median household $45,980. **Pop below poverty level:** 8.9%.

Unemployment: 5%. **Median home value:** $115,100. **Median travel time to work:** 20.7 minutes.

Please see sample entry on inside front cover for detailed information about the statistics presented with each county listing.

KEWEENAW COUNTY

HCR 1 Box 607
Eagle River, MI 49950

Ph: 906-337-2229
Fax: 906-337-2795

On northernmost tip of the Upper Peninsula of MI on Lake Superior; organized Mar 11, 1861 from Houghton County. **Name Origin:** From Ojibway (or Potawatomi), probably 'to cross a point,' or 'portage,' variant of Kewaunee.

Area (sq mi): 5965.96 (land 540.97; water 5424.98).

Pop: 2,301 (White 94.6%; Black or African American 3.5%; Hispanic or Latino 0.8%; Asian 0.1%; Other 1.4%). **Foreign born:** 1%. **Median age:** 44.9. **State rank:** 83. **Pop change 1990-2000:** +35.3%.

Income: per capita $16,769; median household $28,140. **Pop below poverty level:** 12.7%.

Unemployment: 9.9%. **Median home value:** $44,100. **Median travel time to work:** 21.3 minutes.

LAKE COUNTY

800 10th St
Baldwin, MI 49304

Ph: 231-745-4641
Fax: 231-745-2241

In west-central MI, north of Grand Rapids; established as Aishcum County Apr 1, 1840; name changed Mar 8, 1843. **Name Origin:** Possibly for Lake Michigan.

Area (sq mi): 574.6 (land 567.44; water 7.17).

Pop: 11,333 (White 83.9%; Black or African American 11.2%; Hispanic or Latino 1.7%; Asian 0.2%; Other 4%). **Foreign born:** 1%. **Median age:** 43.1. **State rank:** 75. **Pop change 1990-2000:** +32%.

Income: per capita $14,457; median household $26,622. **Pop below poverty level:** 19.4%.

Unemployment: 9.2%. **Median home value:** $61,300. **Median travel time to work:** 30.6 minutes.

LAPEER COUNTY

255 Clay St
Lapeer, MI 48446
www.county.lapeer.org

Ph: 810-667-0356
Fax: 810-667-0362

In east-central MI, east of Flint; established Sept 10, 1822 (prior to statehood) from Oakland and Saint Clair counties. **Name Origin:** From the local spelling of French *la pierre* 'the stone' or 'flint', probably a transliteration of an Indian name for the Flint River, for its rocky bed.

Area (sq mi): 663.08 (land 654.2; water 8.88).

Pop: 87,904 (White 94.4%; Black or African American 0.8%; Hispanic or Latino 3.1%; Asian 0.4%; Other 2.7%). **Foreign born:** 2.2%. **Median age:** 35.9. **State rank:** 22. **Pop change 1990-2000:** +17.6%.

Income: per capita $21,462; median household $51,717. **Pop below poverty level:** 5.4%.

Unemployment: 6.7%. **Median home value:** $134,600. **Median travel time to work:** 35.3 minutes.

LEELANAU COUNTY

PO Box 467
Leland, MI 49654
www.leelanaucounty.com

Ph: 231-256-9824
Fax: 231-256-8295

On the northwest coast of MI, bordered on the west by Lake Michigan; established Apr 1, 1840. **Name Origin:** For an Indian maid, supposedly, whose name means 'delight of life.' Named at the suggestion of Henry Rowe Schoolcraft (1793-1864), author, explorer, MI legislator, and superintendent of Indian Affairs for MI (1836-41).

Area (sq mi): 2532.38 (land 348.47; water 2183.91).

Pop: 21,119 (White 92%; Black or African American 0.2%; Hispanic or Latino 3.3%; Asian 0.2%; Other 6%). **Foreign born:** 2.2%. **Median age:** 42.6. **State rank:** 64. **Pop change 1990-2000:** +27.8%.

Income: per capita $24,686; median household $47,062. **Pop below poverty level:** 5.4%.

Unemployment: 3.4%. **Median home value:** $165,400. **Median travel time to work:** 22.6 minutes.

LENAWEE COUNTY

425 N Main St
Adrian, MI 49221
www.lenawee.mi.us

Ph: 517-264-4606
Fax: 517-264-4790

On the southern border of MI, southwest of Ann Arbor; established Sep 10, 1822 (prior to statehood) from Indian lands. **Name Origin:** Origin uncertain; perhaps from an Indian word meaning 'man'.

Area (sq mi): 761.31 (land 750.5; water 10.81).

Pop: 98,890 (White 89.2%; Black or African American 2.1%; Hispanic or Latino 7%; Asian 0.5%; Other 4.9%). **Foreign born:** 1.6%. **Median age:** 36.4. **State rank:** 21. **Pop change 1990-2000:** +8.1%.

Income: per capita $20,186; median household $45,739. **Pop below poverty level:** 6.7%.

Unemployment: 5.5%. **Median home value:** $109,500. **Median travel time to work:** 25 minutes.

LIVINGSTON COUNTY

200 E Grand River Ave
Howell, MI 48843
www.co.livingston.mi.us

Ph: 517-546-0500
Fax: 517-546-4354

In south-central MI, southwest of Flint; established Mar 21, 1833 (prior to statehood) from Shiawassee County. **Name Origin:** For Edward Livingston (1764-1836), NY legislator, LA legislator and U.S. senator (1829-31), and U.S. secretary of state (1831-33).

Area (sq mi): 585.43 (land 568.4; water 17.03).

Pop: 156,951 (White 96.3%; Black or African American 0.5%; Hispanic or Latino 1.2%; Asian 0.6%; Other 1.8%). **Foreign born:** 3%. **Median age:** 36.2. **State rank:** 15. **Pop change 1990-2000:** +35.7%.

Income: per capita $28,069; median household $67,400. **Pop below poverty level:** 3.4%.

Unemployment: 3.1%. **Median home value:** $187,500. **Median travel time to work:** 31 minutes.

All statistics are based on the 2000 Census except the dollar figures given for per capita income, which are based on 1999 estimates.

LUCE COUNTY

407 W Harrie St   **Ph:** 906-293-5521
Newberry, MI 49868   **Fax:** 906-293-0050

On the northern coast of the Upper Peninsula of MI on Lake Superior; established Mar 1, 1887 from Chippewa County. **Name Origin:** For Cyrus Gray Luce (1824-1905), MI legislator, member of MI Constitutional Convention (1867), and governor (1887-96).

Area (sq mi): 1911.89 (land 903.08; water 1008.8).

Pop: 7,024 (White 82.4%; Black or African American 7.5%; Hispanic or Latino 1.8%; Asian 0.4%; Other 9.2%). **Foreign born:** 1.1%. **Median age:** 38.6. **State rank:** 82. **Pop change 1990-2000:** +21.9%.

Income: per capita $16,828; median household $32,031. **Pop below poverty level:** 14.9%.

Unemployment: 6.9%. **Median home value:** $67,800. **Median travel time to work:** 18.5 minutes.

MACKINAC COUNTY

100 S Marley St   **Ph:** 906-643-7300
Saint Ignace, MI 49781   **Fax:** 906-643-7302

On the southeast coast of the Upper Peninsula of MI bordering Lakes Michigan and Huron; original county; established as Michilimackinac County Oct 26, 1818 (prior to statehood); name changed Mar 9, 1843. **Name Origin:** For Mackinac Island, from Ojibway *Michilimackinak* 'island of the large turtle.'

Area (sq mi): 2100.55 (land 1021.58; water 1078.96).

Pop: 11,943 (White 79.6%; Black or African American 0.2%; Hispanic or Latino 0.9%; Asian 0.3%; Other 19.4%). **Foreign born:** 1.2%. **Median age:** 42.8. **State rank:** 73. **Pop change 1990-2000:** +11.9%.

Income: per capita $17,777; median household $33,356. **Pop below poverty level:** 10.5%.

Unemployment: 9.3%. **Median home value:** $91,800. **Median travel time to work:** 22.5 minutes.

MACOMB COUNTY

40 N Main St 1st Fl   **Ph:** 586-469-5120
Mount Clemens, MI 48043   **Fax:** 586-783-8184
www.co.macomb.mi.us

On the southeast coast of MI, north of Detroit; original county; established Jan 15, 1818 (prior to statehood). **Name Origin:** For Alexander Macomb (1782-1841), officer in the War of 1812 and commanding general of the U.S. Army (1835-41).

Area (sq mi): 569.78 (land 480.44; water 89.34).

Pop: 788,149 (White 91.6%; Black or African American 2.7%; Hispanic or Latino 1.6%; Asian 2.1%; Other 2.5%). **Foreign born:** 8.8%. **Median age:** 36.9. **State rank:** 3. **Pop change 1990-2000:** +9.9%.

Income: per capita $24,446; median household $52,102. **Pop below poverty level:** 5.6%.

Unemployment: 5%. **Median home value:** $139,200. **Median travel time to work:** 26.2 minutes.

MANISTEE COUNTY

415 3rd St   **Ph:** 231-723-3331
Manistee, MI 49660   **Fax:** 231-723-1492
www.manisteecounty.net

On the northwest coast of MI, bordered on west by Lake Michigan; established Apr 1, 1840. **Name Origin:** For the Manistee River, which runs through it; from an Ojibway word possibly meaning 'sound of the winds,' 'lost river,' 'spirit of the woods,' 'crooked river,' or 'red river.'

Area (sq mi): 1280.77 (land 543.61; water 737.16).

Pop: 24,527 (White 92.9%; Black or African American 1.6%; Hispanic or Latino 2.6%; Asian 0.3%; Other 3.8%). **Foreign born:** 1.3%. **Median age:** 41.5. **State rank:** 59. **Pop change 1990-2000:** +15.3%.

Income: per capita $17,204; median household $34,208. **Pop below poverty level:** 10.3%.

Unemployment: 7.1%. **Median home value:** $77,400. **Median travel time to work:** 20.9 minutes.

MARQUETTE COUNTY

234 W Baraga Ave   **Ph:** 906-225-8330
Marquette, MI 49855   **Fax:** 906-228-1572
www.co.marquette.mi.us

On the north coast of the Upper Peninsula of MI on Lake Superior; organized Mar 9, 1843 from Schoolcraft County. **Name Origin:** For Jacques Marquette (1637-75), known as Pere Marquette, French Jesuit missionary and explorer with Louis Joliet (1645-1700).

Area (sq mi): 3425.17 (land 1821.05; water 1604.12).

Pop: 64,634 (White 94.7%; Black or African American 1.3%; Hispanic or Latino 0.7%; Asian 0.5%; Other 3%). **Foreign born:** 1.4%. **Median age:** 37.5. **State rank:** 28. **Pop change 1990-2000:** -8.8%.

Income: per capita $18,070; median household $35,548. **Pop below poverty level:** 10.9%.

Unemployment: 6%. **Median home value:** $77,200. **Median travel time to work:** 17.7 minutes.

MASON COUNTY

304 E Ludington Ave   **Ph:** 231-843-8202
Ludington, MI 49431   **Fax:** 231-843-1972

On the west-central coast of MI bordered on west by Lake Michigan; established as Notiopekago County Apr 1, 1840 from Ionia County; name changed Mar 8, 1843. **Name Origin:** For Stevens Thomson Mason (1811-43), secretary and acting governor of MI Territory (1831-35) and first state governor (1835-38).

Area (sq mi): 1241.86 (land 495.17; water 746.7).

Pop: 28,274 (White 94%; Black or African American 0.7%; Hispanic or Latino 3%; Asian 0.3%; Other 3.1%). **Foreign born:** 1.6%. **Median age:** 40.4. **State rank:** 50. **Pop change 1990-2000:** +10.7%.

Income: per capita $17,713; median household $34,704. **Pop below poverty level:** 11%.

Unemployment: 11.4%. **Median home value:** $81,500. **Median travel time to work:** 18.9 minutes.

Please see sample entry on inside front cover for detailed information about the statistics presented with each county listing.

MECOSTA COUNTY

400 Elm St   **Ph:** 231-592-0787
Big Rapids, MI 49307   **Fax:** 231-592-0193

In central MI, northeast of Grand Rapids; established Apr 1, 1840 from Newaygo and Osceola counties. **Name Origin:** For the Potawatomi chief whose name means 'bear cub.'

Area (sq mi): 571.1 (land 555.69; water 15.41).

Pop: 40,553 (White 91.9%; Black or African American 3.6%; Hispanic or Latino 1.3%; Asian 0.9%; Other 2.8%). **Foreign born:** 1.9%. **Median age:** 31.9. **State rank:** 41. **Pop change 1990-2000:** +8.7%.

Income: per capita $16,372; median household $33,849. **Pop below poverty level:** 16.1%.

Unemployment: 5.3%. **Median home value:** $90,100. **Median travel time to work:** 24.4 minutes.

MENOMINEE COUNTY

839 10th Ave   **Ph:** 906-863-9968
Menominee, MI 49858   **Fax:** 906-863-8839

On the south-central coast of the Upper Peninsula of MI on Green Bay; established as Bleecker County Mar 19, 1863 from Marquette County; name changed Mar 19, 1863. **Name Origin:** For the Menominee Indians, a tribe of Algonquian linguistic stock; name means 'wild rice people.'

Area (sq mi): 1337.99 (land 1043.52; water 294.47).

Pop: 25,326 (White 95.8%; Black or African American 0.1%; Hispanic or Latino 0.8%; Asian 0.2%; Other 3.5%). **Foreign born:** 0.9%. **Median age:** 40.4. **State rank:** 58. **Pop change 1990-2000:** +1.6%.

Income: per capita $16,909; median household $32,888. **Pop below poverty level:** 11.5%.

Unemployment: 6.6%. **Median home value:** $63,400. **Median travel time to work:** 19.7 minutes.

MIDLAND COUNTY

220 W Ellsworth St   **Ph:** 989-832-6739
Midland, MI 48640   **Fax:** 989-832-6680
www.co.midland.mi.us

In central MI, east of Bay City; established Mar 2, 1831 (prior to statehood) from Saginaw County. **Name Origin:** For its location in the geographic center of the state.

Area (sq mi): 527.89 (land 521.19; water 6.7).

Pop: 82,874 (White 94.5%; Black or African American 1%; Hispanic or Latino 1.6%; Asian 1.5%; Other 1.9%). **Foreign born:** 3.2%. **Median age:** 36.3. **State rank:** 23. **Pop change 1990-2000:** +9.5%.

Income: per capita $23,383; median household $45,674. **Pop below poverty level:** 8.4%.

Unemployment: 4%. **Median home value:** $101,800. **Median travel time to work:** 21.1 minutes.

MISSAUKEE COUNTY

PO Box 800   **Ph:** 231-839-4967
Lake City, MI 49651   **Fax:** 231-839-3684

In north-central MI, east of Cadillac; established Apr 1, 1840 from unorganized territory. **Name Origin:** For an Ottawa chief.

Area (sq mi): 573.82 (land 566.75; water 7.08).

Pop: 14,478 (White 96.9%; Black or African American 0.2%; Hispanic or Latino 1.2%; Asian 0.2%; Other 2.1%). **Foreign born:** 1%. **Median age:** 37.7. **State rank:** 69. **Pop change 1990-2000:** +19.2%.

Income: per capita $16,072; median household $35,224. **Pop below poverty level:** 10.7%.

Unemployment: 8%. **Median home value:** $78,700. **Median travel time to work:** 24.8 minutes.

MONROE COUNTY

106 E 1st St   **Ph:** 734-240-7020
Monroe, MI 48161   **Fax:** 734-240-7266
www.co.monroe.mi.us

In the southeast corner of MI bordered on east by Lake Erie; original county; established Jul 14, 1817 (prior to statehood). **Name Origin:** For James Monroe (1758-1831), fifth U.S. president.

Area (sq mi): 680.03 (land 551.1; water 128.93).

Pop: 145,945 (White 94.1%; Black or African American 1.9%; Hispanic or Latino 2.1%; Asian 0.5%; Other 2.2%). **Foreign born:** 1.9%. **Median age:** 36. **State rank:** 16. **Pop change 1990-2000:** +9.2%.

Income: per capita $22,458; median household $51,743. **Pop below poverty level:** 7%.

Unemployment: 4.3%. **Median home value:** $132,000. **Median travel time to work:** 24 minutes.

MONTCALM COUNTY

PO Box 368   **Ph:** 989-831-7339
Stanton, MI 48888   **Fax:** 989-831-7474

In central MI, northeast of Grand Rapids; established Mar 2, 1831 (prior to statehood) from Isabella County. **Name Origin:** For Louis Joseph de Montcalm (1712-59), commander of French troops against the British in Canada.

Area (sq mi): 720.98 (land 708.04; water 12.94).

Pop: 61,266 (White 93.5%; Black or African American 2.2%; Hispanic or Latino 2.3%; Asian 0.3%; Other 2.7%). **Foreign born:** 1.1%. **Median age:** 35.6. **State rank:** 32. **Pop change 1990-2000:** +15.5%.

Income: per capita $16,183; median household $37,218. **Pop below poverty level:** 10.9%.

Unemployment: 7.8%. **Median home value:** $84,900. **Median travel time to work:** 28.2 minutes.

MONTMORENCY COUNTY

PO Box 789   **Ph:** 989-785-8013
Atlanta, MI 49709   **Fax:** 989-785-8014

In northeast MI, west of Alpena; established as Chenoquet County Apr 1, 1840 from Alpena County; name changed Mar 8, 1843. **Name**

All statistics are based on the 2000 Census except the dollar figures given for per capita income, which are based on 1999 estimates.

Origin: For Count Raymond de Montmorency (1806-89), a French officer who helped the colonies against England during the Revolutionary War.

Area (sq mi): 562.44 (land 547.63; water 14.81).

Pop: 10,315 (White 97.9%; Black or African American 0.2%; Hispanic or Latino 0.6%; Asian 0.1%; Other 1.3%). **Foreign born:** 1.3%. **Median age:** 47. **State rank:** 76. **Pop change 1990-2000:** +15.4%.

Income: per capita $16,493; median household $30,005. **Pop below poverty level:** 12.8%.

Unemployment: 12.8%. **Median home value:** $76,900. **Median travel time to work:** 24.7 minutes.

MUSKEGON COUNTY

990 Terrace St   **Ph:** 231-724-6211
Muskegon, MI 49442   **Fax:** 231-724-6673
www.co.muskegon.mi.us

On the west-central coast of MI, bordered on west by Lake Michigan; established Jan 7, 1859 from Newaygo County. **Name Origin:** For the Muskegon River, from an Ojibway word meaning 'marshy river.'

Area (sq mi): 1459.3 (land 509.12; water 950.18).

Pop: 170,200 (White 79.5%; Black or African American 14.2%; Hispanic or Latino 3.5%; Asian 0.4%; Other 4.1%). **Foreign born:** 1.9%. **Median age:** 35.5. **State rank:** 11. **Pop change 1990-2000:** +7.1%.

Income: per capita $17,967; median household $38,008. **Pop below poverty level:** 11.4%.

Unemployment: 6.9%. **Median home value:** $85,900. **Median travel time to work:** 20.8 minutes.

NEWAYGO COUNTY

1087 Newell St   **Ph:** 231-689-7200
White Cloud, MI 49349   **Fax:** 231-689-7205

In west-central MI, north of Grand Rapids; established Apr 1, 1840 from unorganized territory. **Name Origin:** For the Ojibway Indian chief, signer of the Saginaw Treaty of 1819.

Area (sq mi): 861.39 (land 842.37; water 19.03).

Pop: 47,874 (White 93%; Black or African American 1.1%; Hispanic or Latino 3.9%; Asian 0.3%; Other 3.7%). **Foreign born:** 1.8%. **Median age:** 36.4. **State rank:** 36. **Pop change 1990-2000:** +25.3%.

Income: per capita $16,976; median household $37,130. **Pop below poverty level:** 11.6%.

Unemployment: 8.2%. **Median home value:** $88,700. **Median travel time to work:** 31 minutes.

OAKLAND COUNTY

1200 N Telegraph Rd   **Ph:** 248-858-1000
Pontiac, MI 48341   **Fax:** 248-858-1572
www.co.oakland.mi.us

In southeast MI, northwest of Detroit; original county; established Jan 12, 1819 (prior to statehood). **Name Origin:** For the abundant oak trees in the area.

Area (sq mi): 908 (land 872.51; water 35.49).

Pop: 1,194,156 (White 81.4%; Black or African American 10.1%; Hispanic or Latino 2.4%; Asian 4.1%; Other 3%). **Foreign born:** 10%. **Median age:** 36.7. **State rank:** 2. **Pop change 1990-2000:** +10.2%.

Income: per capita $32,534; median household $61,907. **Pop below poverty level:** 5.5%.

Unemployment: 3.9%. **Median home value:** $181,200. **Median travel time to work:** 26.5 minutes.

OCEANA COUNTY

PO Box 653   **Ph:** 231-873-4328
Hart, MI 49420   **Fax:** 231-873-1391
www.co.oceana.mi.us

On the west-central coast of MI, bordered on west by Lake Michigan; established Mar 2, 1831 (prior to statehood) from Newaygo County. **Name Origin:** For its long shoreline on the 'fresh water ocean' of Lake Michigan.

Area (sq mi): 1306.73 (land 540.46; water 766.27).

Pop: 26,873 (White 85.8%; Black or African American 0.3%; Hispanic or Latino 11.6%; Asian 0.2%; Other 9%). **Foreign born:** 4.4%. **Median age:** 36.9. **State rank:** 53. **Pop change 1990-2000:** +19.7%.

Income: per capita $15,878; median household $35,307. **Pop below poverty level:** 14.7%.

Unemployment: 8.2%. **Median home value:** $82,500. **Median travel time to work:** 24.4 minutes.

OGEMAW COUNTY

806 W Houghton Ave   **Ph:** 989-345-0215
West Branch, MI 48661   **Fax:** 989-345-7223

In northeast MI, north of Bay City; established Apr 1, 1840. **Name Origin:** The Chippewa word for 'chief.'

Area (sq mi): 574.63 (land 564.3; water 10.33).

Pop: 21,645 (White 96.6%; Black or African American 0.1%; Hispanic or Latino 1.2%; Asian 0.4%; Other 1.9%). **Foreign born:** 1.3%. **Median age:** 42.3. **State rank:** 63. **Pop change 1990-2000:** +15.9%.

Income: per capita $15,768; median household $30,474. **Pop below poverty level:** 14%.

Unemployment: 8.3%. **Median home value:** $72,900. **Median travel time to work:** 24.8 minutes.

ONTONAGON COUNTY

725 Greenland Rd   **Ph:** 906-884-4255
Ontonagon, MI 49953   **Fax:** 906-884-2916

On the northwest coast of the Upper Peninsula of MI; established Mar 9, 1843 from Michilimacknac and Chippewa counties. **Name Origin:** For the Ontonagon River, which runs through it; from Ojibway *onagan* 'dish' or 'bowl,' from the shape of the river's mouth.

Area (sq mi): 3741.45 (land 1311.53; water 2429.92).

Pop: 7,818 (White 96.8%; Black or African American 0%; Hispanic or Latino 0.7%; Asian 0.2%; Other 2.6%). **Foreign born:** 1.4%. **Median age:** 45.9. **State rank:** 81. **Pop change 1990-2000:** -11.7%.

Please see sample entry on inside front cover for detailed information about the statistics presented with each county listing.

Income: per capita $16,695; median household $29,552. **Pop below poverty level:** 10.4%.

Unemployment: 9.2%. **Median home value:** $41,400. **Median travel time to work:** 21.7 minutes.

OSCEOLA COUNTY

301 W Upton Ave
Reed City, MI 49677

Ph: 231-832-3261
Fax: 231-832-6149

In central MI, south of Cadillac; established as Unwattin County Apr 1, 1840; name changed Mar 8, 1843. **Name Origin:** For the Seminole chief (c. 1804-38) who led the second Seminole War against the U.S.

Area (sq mi): 573.1 (land 565.98; water 7.12).

Pop: 23,197 (White 96.8%; Black or African American 0.3%; Hispanic or Latino 1%; Asian 0.2%; Other 1.9%). **Foreign born:** 1.2%. **Median age:** 37.6. **State rank:** 61. **Pop change 1990-2000:** +15.1%.

Income: per capita $15,632; median household $34,102. **Pop below poverty level:** 12.7%.

Unemployment: 8%. **Median home value:** $70,000. **Median travel time to work:** 23.2 minutes.

OSCODA COUNTY

PO Box 399
Mio, MI 48647

Ph: 989-826-1109
Fax: 989-826-1136

In northeast MI, southwest of Alpena; established Apr 1, 1840 from unorganized territory. **Name Origin:** 'Pebbly prairie' from *ossin* 'stone' and *muskoda* 'prairie,' coined by Henry Rowe Schoolcraft (1793-1864), author, explorer, MI legislator, and superintendent of Indian Affairs for MI (1836-41).

Area (sq mi): 571.57 (land 565; water 6.57).

Pop: 9,418 (White 97.3%; Black or African American 0.1%; Hispanic or Latino 0.9%; Asian 0.1%; Other 2%). **Foreign born:** 1.5%. **Median age:** 43.7. **State rank:** 78. **Pop change 1990-2000:** +20.1%.

Income: per capita $15,697; median household $28,228. **Pop below poverty level:** 14.6%.

Unemployment: 11%. **Median home value:** $67,300. **Median travel time to work:** 23.5 minutes.

OTSEGO COUNTY

225 W Main St
Gaylord, MI 49735

Ph: 989-732-6484
Fax: 989-732-1562

In north-central MI, southeast of Petoskey; established as Okkuddo County Apr 1, 1840; name changed Mar 8, 1843. **Name Origin:** Probably for Otsego County, NY, home of some early settlers; from Iroquoian 'rock site' or 'place of the rock.'

Area (sq mi): 525.98 (land 514.54; water 11.44).

Pop: 23,301 (White 97%; Black or African American 0.2%; Hispanic or Latino 0.8%; Asian 0.3%; Other 2%). **Foreign born:** 1.6%. **Median age:** 37.7. **State rank:** 60. **Pop change 1990-2000:** +29.8%.

Income: per capita $19,810; median household $40,876. **Pop below poverty level:** 6.8%.

Unemployment: 6.2%. **Median home value:** $102,500. **Median travel time to work:** 18.4 minutes.

OTTAWA COUNTY

414 Washington St
Grand Haven, MI 49417
www.co.ottawa.mi.us

Ph: 616-846-8312
Fax: 616-846-8138

On the west-central coast of MI bordered on west by Lake Michigan; established Mar 2, 1831 (prior to statehood). **Name Origin:** For the Ottawa Indians, a tribe of Algonquian linguistic stock whose name is derived from *adawe* 'to trade.'

Area (sq mi): 1631.97 (land 565.65; water 1066.32).

Pop: 238,314 (White 88.6%; Black or African American 1%; Hispanic or Latino 7%; Asian 2.1%; Other 5.4%). **Foreign born:** 4.9%. **Median age:** 32.3. **State rank:** 9. **Pop change 1990-2000:** +26.9%.

Income: per capita $21,676; median household $52,347. **Pop below poverty level:** 5.5%.

Unemployment: 4.3%. **Median home value:** $133,000. **Median travel time to work:** 19.4 minutes.

PRESQUE ISLE COUNTY

PO Box 110
Rogers City, MI 49779

Ph: 989-734-3288
Fax: 989-734-7635

On the northeast coast of MI, bordered on east by Lake Huron; established Apr 1, 1840 from unorganized territory. **Name Origin:** French 'almost an island,' i.e., a peninsula.

Area (sq mi): 2572.75 (land 660.07; water 1912.68).

Pop: 14,411 (White 97.7%; Black or African American 0.3%; Hispanic or Latino 0.5%; Asian 0.2%; Other 1.5%). **Foreign born:** 1.2%. **Median age:** 45.1. **State rank:** 70. **Pop change 1990-2000:** +4.9%.

Income: per capita $17,363; median household $31,656. **Pop below poverty level:** 10.3%.

Unemployment: 11.1%. **Median home value:** $77,800. **Median travel time to work:** 23.9 minutes.

ROSCOMMON COUNTY

500 Lake St
Roscommon, MI 48653
www.roscommoncounty.net

Ph: 989-275-5923
Fax: 989-275-8640

In central MI, east of Cadillac; established as Mikenauk County Apr 1, 1840; name changed Mar 8, 1843. **Name Origin:** For the county in Ireland.

Area (sq mi): 579.84 (land 521.4; water 58.44).

Pop: 25,469 (White 97.4%; Black or African American 0.3%; Hispanic or Latino 0.8%; Asian 0.2%; Other 1.4%). **Foreign born:** 1.7%. **Median age:** 47.2. **State rank:** 57. **Pop change 1990-2000:** +28.8%.

Income: per capita $17,837; median household $30,029. **Pop below poverty level:** 12.4%.

Unemployment: 7.6%. **Median home value:** $78,900. **Median travel time to work:** 24.2 minutes.

All statistics are based on the 2000 Census except the dollar figures given for per capita income, which are based on 1999 estimates.

SAGINAW COUNTY
111 S Michigan Ave
Saginaw, MI 48602
www.saginawcounty.com

Ph: 989-790-5251
Fax: 989-790-5254

In central MI, northwest of Flint; established Sep 10, 1822 (prior to statehood) from unorganized territory. **Name Origin:** For the Saginaw River, which runs through it; from Ojibway 'the place of the Sac [Indians].'

Area (sq mi): 815.78 (land 808.93; water 6.85).

Pop: 210,039 (White 72.4%; Black or African American 18.6%; Hispanic or Latino 6.7%; Asian 0.8%; Other 5.3%). **Foreign born:** 2%. **Median age:** 36.3. **State rank:** 10. **Pop change 1990-2000:** -0.9%.

Income: per capita $19,438; median household $38,637. **Pop below poverty level:** 13.9%.

Unemployment: 5.9%. **Median home value:** $85,200. **Median travel time to work:** 21.6 minutes.

SAINT CLAIR COUNTY
201 McMorran Blvd Rm 204
Port Huron, MI 48060
www.saintclaircounty.org

Ph: 810-985-2200
Fax: 810-985-4796

On the southeast coast of Michigan, northeast of Detroit, bordered on east by the Saint Clair River, original county, established Mar 28, 1820 (prior to statehood). **Name Origin:** For Gen. Arthur Saint Clair (1736?-1818), an officer in the French and Indian War and the Revolutionary War, president of the Continental Congress (1787), and governor of the Northwest Territory (1788-1802).

Area (sq mi): 836.63 (land 724.37; water 112.26).

Pop: 164,235 (White 93.7%; Black or African American 2.1%; Hispanic or Latino 2.2%; Asian 0.4%; Other 2.5%). **Foreign born:** 2.7%. **Median age:** 36.4. **State rank:** 12. **Pop change 1990-2000:** +12.8%.

Income: per capita $21,582; median household $46,313. **Pop below poverty level:** 7.8%.

Unemployment: 6.9%. **Median home value:** $125,200. **Median travel time to work:** 28.7 minutes.

SAINT JOSEPH COUNTY
PO Box 189
Centreville, MI 49032

Ph: 269-467-5602
Fax: 269-467-5628

On the southern border of MI, south of Kalamazoo; established Oct 29, 1829 (prior to statehood) from Indian lands. **Name Origin:** For the spouse of the Virgin Mary.

Area (sq mi): 521.15 (land 503.72; water 17.43).

Pop: 62,422 (White 91.3%; Black or African American 2.6%; Hispanic or Latino 4%; Asian 0.6%; Other 3.4%). **Foreign born:** 3.4%. **Median age:** 35.6. **State rank:** 30. **Pop change 1990-2000:** +6%.

Income: per capita $18,247; median household $40,355. **Pop below poverty level:** 11.3%.

Unemployment: 6.8%. **Median home value:** $85,000. **Median travel time to work:** 20.8 minutes.

SANILAC COUNTY
60 W Sanilac Rd
Sandusky, MI 48471

Ph: 810-648-3212
Fax: 810-648-5466

On the east-central coast of MI bordered on the east by Lake Huron; established Sep 10, 1822 (prior to statehood). **Name Origin:** For the Wyandot chief who is the main character in Henry Whiting's poem 'Sannilac.' The name was spelled with only one 'n' in the proclamation by Gov. Lewis Cass (1782-1866) that announced the formation of the county.

Area (sq mi): 1590.22 (land 963.8; water 626.42).

Pop: 44,547 (White 95.4%; Black or African American 0.3%; Hispanic or Latino 2.8%; Asian 0.3%; Other 2.6%). **Foreign born:** 1.6%. **Median age:** 37.8. **State rank:** 39. **Pop change 1990-2000:** +11.6%.

Income: per capita $17,089; median household $36,870. **Pop below poverty level:** 10.4%.

Unemployment: 8.3%. **Median home value:** $88,900. **Median travel time to work:** 28.1 minutes.

SCHOOLCRAFT COUNTY
300 Walnut St Rm 164
Manistique, MI 49854

Ph: 906-341-3618
Fax: 906-341-5680

On the south-central coast of the Upper Peninsula of MI, on Lake Michigan; established Mar 9, 1843 from Michilimackinac and Chippewa counties. **Name Origin:** For Henry Rowe Schoolcraft (1793-1864), explorer, MI legislator, author, and superintendent of Indian Affairs for MI (1836-41).

Area (sq mi): 1883.69 (land 1178.11; water 705.58).

Pop: 8,903 (White 88.1%; Black or African American 1.6%; Hispanic or Latino 0.9%; Asian 0.4%; Other 9.3%). **Foreign born:** 1%. **Median age:** 41.4. **State rank:** 79. **Pop change 1990-2000:** +7.2%.

Income: per capita $17,137; median household $31,140. **Pop below poverty level:** 12.2%.

Unemployment: 9%. **Median home value:** $64,900. **Median travel time to work:** 20.8 minutes.

SHIAWASSEE COUNTY
208 N Shiawassee St
Corunna, MI 48817
www.co.shiawassee.mi.us

Ph: 989-743-2242
Fax: 989-743-2241

In south-central MI, west of Flint; established Sep 10, 1822 (prior to statehood) from Indian lands. **Name Origin:** For the Shiawassee River, which runs through it; from Algonquian 'the water straight ahead' or 'river that twists about.'

Area (sq mi): 540.73 (land 538.73; water 2).

Pop: 71,687 (White 96.3%; Black or African American 0.2%; Hispanic or Latino 1.8%; Asian 0.3%; Other 2.2%). **Foreign born:** 1.2%. **Median age:** 36.4. **State rank:** 26. **Pop change 1990-2000:** +2.7%.

Income: per capita $19,229; median household $42,553. **Pop below poverty level:** 7.8%.

Unemployment: 6%. **Median home value:** $95,900. **Median travel time to work:** 27.6 minutes.

Please see sample entry on inside front cover for detailed information about the statistics presented with each county listing.

TUSCOLA COUNTY

440 N State St
Caro, MI 48723
www.tuscolacounty.org

Ph: 989-672-3780
Fax: 989-672-4266

In east MI, northeast of Flint; established Apr 1, 1840 from Sanilac County. **Name Origin:** Name coined by Henry Rowe Schoolcraft (1793-1864), author, explorer, MI legislator, and superintendent of Indian Affairs for MI (1836-41); means either 'warrior prairie' or 'level lands.'

Area (sq mi): 913.82 (land 812.43; water 101.39).

Pop: 58,266 (White 94.7%; Black or African American 1.1%; Hispanic or Latino 2.3%; Asian 0.3%; Other 2.6%). **Foreign born:** 1.1%. **Median age:** 37. **State rank:** 33. **Pop change 1990-2000:** +5%.

Income: per capita $17,985; median household $40,174. **Pop below poverty level:** 8.2%.

Unemployment: 7.9%. **Median home value:** $87,100. **Median travel time to work:** 30.3 minutes.

VAN BUREN COUNTY

219 E Paw Paw St Suite 201
Paw Paw, MI 49079

Ph: 269-657-8253
Fax: 269-657-2547

On the southwest coast of MI, bordered on west by Lake Michigan; established Oct 29, 1829 (prior to statehood) from unorganized territory. **Name Origin:** For Martin Van Buren (1782-1862), eighth U.S. president.

Area (sq mi): 1090.19 (land 610.86; water 479.33).

Pop: 76,263 (White 84.5%; Black or African American 5.2%; Hispanic or Latino 7.4%; Asian 0.3%; Other 6.5%). **Foreign born:** 3.5%. **Median age:** 36.6. **State rank:** 25. **Pop change 1990-2000:** +8.9%.

Income: per capita $17,878; median household $39,365. **Pop below poverty level:** 11.1%.

Unemployment: 6%. **Median home value:** $94,200. **Median travel time to work:** 23.6 minutes.

WASHTENAW COUNTY

PO Box 8645
Ann Arbor, MI 48107
www.ewashtenaw.org

Ph: 734-222-6850
Fax: 734-222-6715

In southeast MI, west of Detroit; original county; established Sept 10, 1822 (prior to statehood). **Name Origin:** For the small stream running through the county; from an Ojibway word meaning 'on the river' or 'far off.'

Area (sq mi): 722.53 (land 709.94; water 12.59).

Pop: 322,895 (White 75.9%; Black or African American 12.3%; Hispanic or Latino 2.7%; Asian 6.3%; Other 4%). **Foreign born:** 10.3%. **Median age:** 31.3. **State rank:** 6. **Pop change 1990-2000:** +14.1%.

Income: per capita $27,173; median household $51,990. **Pop below poverty level:** 11.1%.

Unemployment: 2.4%. **Median home value:** $174,300. **Median travel time to work:** 22.2 minutes.

WAYNE COUNTY

211 City-County Bldg
Detroit, MI 48226
www.co.wayne.mi.us

Ph: 313-224-6262
Fax: 313-224-5364

In southeastern MI bordered on the east by the Detroit River and Lake Saint Clair; original colony; established Nov 21, 1815 (prior to statehood). **Name Origin:** For Gen. Anthony Wayne (1745-96), PA soldier and statesman, nicknamed 'Mad Anthony' for his daring during the Revolutionary War.

Area (sq mi): 672.2 (land 614.15; water 58.05).

Pop: 2,061,162 (White 49.9%; Black or African American 42.2%; Hispanic or Latino 3.7%; Asian 1.7%; Other 4.5%). **Foreign born:** 6.7%. **Median age:** 34. **State rank:** 1. **Pop change 1990-2000:** -2.4%.

Income: per capita $20,058; median household $40,776. **Pop below poverty level:** 16.4%.

Unemployment: 5.8%. **Median home value:** $99,400. **Median travel time to work:** 25.8 minutes.

WEXFORD COUNTY

437 E Division St
Cadillac, MI 49601
www.wexfordcounty.org

Ph: 231-779-9453
Fax: 231-779-0292

In northwest MI, south of Traverse City; established as Kautawaubet County Apr 1, 1840 from unorganized territory; name changed Mar 8, 1843. **Name Origin:** For the county in Ireland.

Area (sq mi): 575.84 (land 565.49; water 10.35).

Pop: 30,484 (White 96.7%; Black or African American 0.2%; Hispanic or Latino 1%; Asian 0.4%; Other 2%). **Foreign born:** 1.8%. **Median age:** 37.3. **State rank:** 49. **Pop change 1990-2000:** +15.6%.

Income: per capita $17,144; median household $35,363. **Pop below poverty level:** 10.3%.

Unemployment: 10.2%. **Median home value:** $79,900. **Median travel time to work:** 20.9 minutes.

All statistics are based on the 2000 Census except the dollar figures given for per capita income, which are based on 1999 estimates.

MINNESOTA - Counties

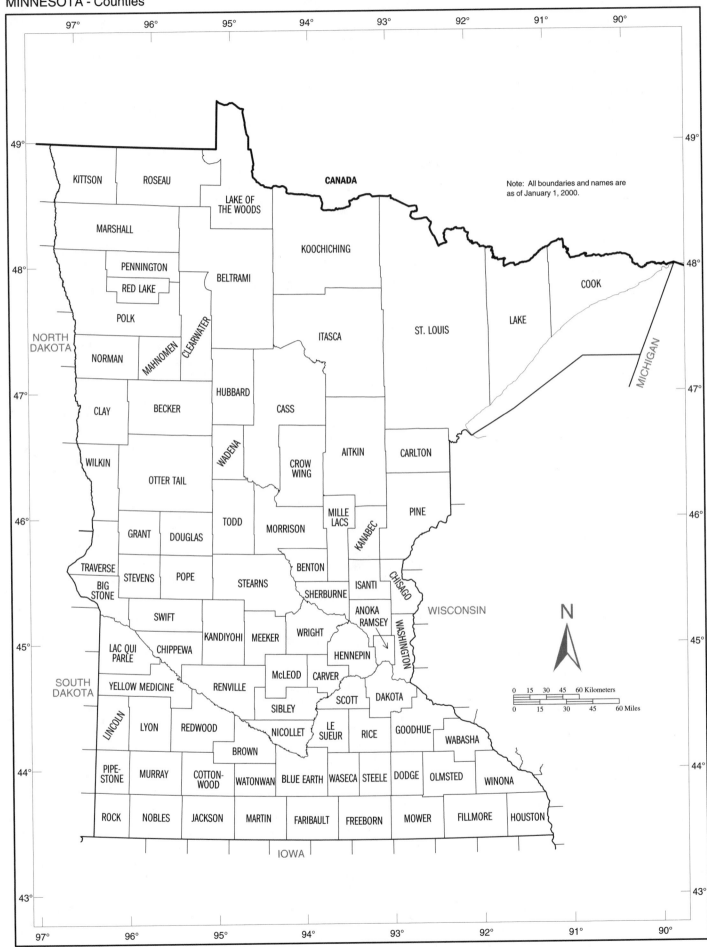

Note: All boundaries and names are as of January 1, 2000.

U.S. Census Bureau, Census 2000

Minnesota

MINNESOTA STATE INFORMATION

www.state.mn.us   **Ph:** 651-296-6013

Area (sq mi): 86,938.87 (land 79,610.08; water 7328.79).

Pop: 4,919,479 (White 88.2%; Black or African American 3.5%; Hispanic or Latino 2.9%; Asian 2.9%; Other 4.1%). **Foreign born:** 5.3%. **Median age:** 35.4. **Pop change 1990-2000:** +12.4%.

Income: per capita $23,198; median household $47,111. **Pop below poverty level:** 7.9%.

Unemployment: 4.3%. **Median home value:** $122,400. **Median travel time to work:** 21.9 minutes.

AITKIN COUNTY

209 2nd St NW   **Ph:** 218-927-7350
Aitkin, MN 56431   **Fax:** 218-927-4535
www.co.aitkin.mn.us

In east-central MN, west of Duluth; established May 23, 1857 (prior to statehood) from Cass and Itasca counties. **Name Origin:** For William Alexander Aitkin (c. 1787-1851), a local fur trader.

Area (sq mi): 1995.31 (land 1819.3; water 176.01).

Pop: 15,301 (White 96.1%; Black or African American 0.2%; Hispanic or Latino 0.6%; Asian 0.2%; Other 3.2%). **Foreign born:** 0.9%. **Median age:** 46.5. **State rank:** 57. **Pop change 1990-2000:** +23.1%.

Income: per capita $17,848; median household $31,139. **Pop below poverty level:** 11.6%.

Unemployment: 7.5%. **Median home value:** $93,200. **Median travel time to work:** 25.2 minutes.

ANOKA COUNTY

325 E Main St   **Ph:** 763-421-4760
Anoka, MN 55303   **Fax:** 763-422-6919
www.co.anoka.mn.us

In east-central MN, north of Minneapolis; established May 23, 1857 (prior to statehood) from Hennepin County; annexed Manomin County in 1869. **Name Origin:** For the town of the same name; from Siouan 'the other side' or 'both sides'; the town is on both sides of the Rum River.

Area (sq mi): 446.26 (land 423.61; water 22.65).

Pop: 298,084 (White 92.8%; Black or African American 1.6%; Hispanic or Latino 1.7%; Asian 1.7%; Other 3%). **Foreign born:** 3.6%. **Median age:** 33.7. **State rank:** 4. **Pop change 1990-2000:** +22.3%.

Income: per capita $23,297; median household $57,754. **Pop below poverty level:** 4.2%.

Unemployment: 3.3%. **Median home value:** $131,300. **Median travel time to work:** 27.3 minutes.

BECKER COUNTY

913 Lake Ave   **Ph:** 218-846-7301
Detroit Lakes, MN 56502   **Fax:** 218-846-7257
www.co.becker.mn.us

In west-central MN, east of Fargo, ND; established Mar 18, 1858 from Indian lands. **Name Origin:** For Gen. George Loomis Becker (1829-1904), lawyer, MN legislator, and land commissioner of the Saint Paul and Pacific Railroad.

Area (sq mi): 1445.11 (land 1310.42; water 134.69).

Pop: 30,000 (White 89%; Black or African American 0.2%; Hispanic or Latino 0.8%; Asian 0.4%; Other 10%). **Foreign born:** 1%. **Median age:** 39.4. **State rank:** 34. **Pop change 1990-2000:** +7.6%.

Income: per capita $17,085; median household $34,797. **Pop below poverty level:** 12.2%.

Unemployment: 6.1%. **Median home value:** $87,400. **Median travel time to work:** 23.1 minutes.

BELTRAMI COUNTY

619 Beltrami Ave NW Courthouse   **Ph:** 218-759-4120
Bemidji, MN 56601   **Fax:** 218-759-4209
www.co.beltrami.mn.us

In north-central MN, east of Grand Forks, ND; established Feb 28, 1866 from unorganized territory. **Name Origin:** For Giacomo Constantino Beltrami (1779-1855), an Italian who, under the anglicized name James Constantine, explored the sources of the Mississippi River and wrote *A Pilgrimage in Europe and America, Leading to the Discovery of the Sources of the Mississippi and Bloody River.*

Area (sq mi): 3055.59 (land 2505.27; water 550.32).

Pop: 39,650 (White 76.3%; Black or African American 0.4%; Hispanic or Latino 1%; Asian 0.6%; Other 22.4%). **Foreign born:** 1.8%. **Median age:** 31.5. **State rank:** 23. **Pop change 1990-2000:** +15.3%.

Income: per capita $15,497; median household $33,392. **Pop below poverty level:** 17.6%.

Unemployment: 4.9%. **Median home value:** $79,800. **Median travel time to work:** 19.4 minutes.

BENTON COUNTY

615 Hwy 23   **Ph:** 320-968-5205
Foley, MN 56329   **Fax:** 320-968-5353
www.co.benton.mn.us

In east-central MN, northeast of Saint Cloud; original county;

established Oct 27, 1849 (prior to statehood). **Name Origin:** For Thomas Hart Benton (1782-1858), U.S. journalist and statesman; nicknamed 'Old Bullion' for championing the use of gold and silver currency rather than paper money.

Area (sq mi): 413 (land 408.28; water 4.72).

Pop: 34,226 (White 95.7%; Black or African American 0.8%; Hispanic or Latino 0.9%; Asian 1.1%; Other 1.8%). **Foreign born:** 2.1%. **Median age:** 31.9. **State rank:** 26. **Pop change 1990-2000:** +13.4%.

Income: per capita $19,008; median household $41,968. **Pop below poverty level:** 7.1%.

Unemployment: 4.4%. **Median home value:** $99,100. **Median travel time to work:** 21.1 minutes.

BIG STONE COUNTY

20 SE 2nd St   **Ph:** 320-839-2537
Ortonville, MN 56278   **Fax:** 320-839-2537
www.bigstonecounty.org

On central western border of MN; established Feb 20, 1862 from Pierce County (which was abolished the same year). **Name Origin:** For Big Stone Lake in the western part of the county.

Area (sq mi): 527.88 (land 496.95; water 30.93).

Pop: 5,820 (White 98.3%; Black or African American 0.2%; Hispanic or Latino 0.3%; Asian 0.4%; Other 0.9%). **Foreign born:** 0.8%. **Median age:** 43.6. **State rank:** 81. **Pop change 1990-2000:** -7.4%.

Income: per capita $15,708; median household $30,721. **Pop below poverty level:** 12%.

Unemployment: 4.2%. **Median home value:** $41,900. **Median travel time to work:** 15.7 minutes.

BLUE EARTH COUNTY

PO Box 0347   **Ph:** 507-389-8100
Mankato, MN 56002   **Fax:** 507-389-8437
www.co.blue-earth.mn.us

In south-central MN, west of Rochester; established Mar 5, 1853 (prior to statehood) from unorganized territory. **Name Origin:** For the Blue Earth River, which runs through it; a transliteration of the Nankato name for the color of the earth in the river, used as a pigment by the Sisseton Sioux.

Area (sq mi): 765.9 (land 752.36; water 13.54).

Pop: 55,941 (White 94.1%; Black or African American 1.2%; Hispanic or Latino 1.8%; Asian 1.8%; Other 2.1%). **Foreign born:** 2.9%. **Median age:** 29.9. **State rank:** 15. **Pop change 1990-2000:** +3.5%.

Income: per capita $18,712; median household $38,940. **Pop below poverty level:** 12.9%.

Unemployment: 2.7%. **Median home value:** $98,200. **Median travel time to work:** 17 minutes.

BROWN COUNTY

PO Box 248   **Ph:** 507-233-6660
New Ulm, MN 56073   **Fax:** 507-359-1430
www.co.brown.mn.us

In south-central MN, west of Mankato; established Feb 20, 1855

(prior to statehood) from Nicollet County. **Name Origin:** For Joseph Renshaw Brown (1805-70), a trader with the Sioux Indians, publisher, and MN legislator.

Area (sq mi): 618.6 (land 610.86; water 7.74).

Pop: 26,911 (White 96.9%; Black or African American 0.1%; Hispanic or Latino 2%; Asian 0.4%; Other 1.6%). **Foreign born:** 1.3%. **Median age:** 38.4. **State rank:** 37. **Pop change 1990-2000:** -0.3%.

Income: per capita $19,535; median household $39,800. **Pop below poverty level:** 6.4%.

Unemployment: 4.3%. **Median home value:** $85,400. **Median travel time to work:** 14.5 minutes.

CARLTON COUNTY

PO Box 190   **Ph:** 218-384-4281
Carlton, MN 55718   **Fax:** 218-384-9182
www.co.carlton.mn.us

On central-eastern border of MN, south of Duluth; established May 23, 1857 (prior to statehood) from Pine County. **Name Origin:** For Reuben B. Carlton (1812-62), farmer and blacksmith for Ojibway Indians and MN state legislator.

Area (sq mi): 875.23 (land 860.33; water 14.9).

Pop: 31,671 (White 91.3%; Black or African American 1%; Hispanic or Latino 0.8%; Asian 0.4%; Other 6.9%). **Foreign born:** 1.6%. **Median age:** 38.4. **State rank:** 31. **Pop change 1990-2000:** +8.2%.

Income: per capita $18,073; median household $40,021. **Pop below poverty level:** 7.9%.

Unemployment: 5.8%. **Median home value:** $85,400. **Median travel time to work:** 21.2 minutes.

CARVER COUNTY

606 E 4th St   **Ph:** 952-361-1500
Chaska, MN 55318   **Fax:** 952-361-1491
www.co.carver.mn.us

In south-central MN, east of Minneapolis, established Feb 20, 1855 (prior to statehood) from Hennepin County. **Name Origin:** For Capt. Jonathan Carver (1710-80), an officer in the French and Indian War, explorer, and author.

Area (sq mi): 376.15 (land 357.04; water 19.11).

Pop: 70,205 (White 94.4%; Black or African American 0.6%; Hispanic or Latino 2.6%; Asian 1.6%; Other 1.9%). **Foreign born:** 3.4%. **Median age:** 33.9. **State rank:** 11. **Pop change 1990-2000:** +46.5%.

Income: per capita $28,486; median household $65,540. **Pop below poverty level:** 3.5%.

Unemployment: 3%. **Median home value:** $170,200. **Median travel time to work:** 25.6 minutes.

CASS COUNTY

PO Box 3000   **Ph:** 218-547-7200
Walker, MN 56484   **Fax:** 218-547-1904
www.co.cass.mn.us

In central MN, northwest of Duluth; original county; established Mar 31, 1851 (prior to statehood). **Name Origin:** For Gen. Lewis

All statistics are based on the 2000 Census except the dollar figures given for per capita income, which are based on 1999 estimates.

Cass (1782-1866), OH legislator, governor of MI Territory (1813-31), U.S. secretary of war (1831-36), and U.S. secretary of state (1857-60). Formerly called Van Buren.

Area (sq mi): 2414.21 (land 2017.6; water 396.61).

Pop: 27,150 (White 86.1%; Black or African American 0.1%; Hispanic or Latino 0.8%; Asian 0.3%; Other 13.1%). **Foreign born:** 0.8%. **Median age:** 42.2. **State rank:** 36. **Pop change 1990-2000:** +24.6%.

Income: per capita $17,189; median household $34,332. **Pop below poverty level:** 13.6%.

Unemployment: 6.2%. **Median home value:** $105,900. **Median travel time to work:** 21.9 minutes.

CHIPPEWA COUNTY

629 N 11th St
Montevideo, MN 56265
www.co.chippewa.mn.us

Ph: 320-269-7447
Fax: 320-269-7412

In west-central MN, southwest of Saint Cloud; established Feb 20, 1862 from Pierce County, which was abolished in 1862. **Name Origin:** For the Chippewa (more properly Ojibway) Indians, a tribe of Algonquian linguistic stock. The name probably means 'puckered,' and refers to the seam in their moccasins.

Area (sq mi): 587.83 (land 582.8; water 5.02).

Pop: 13,088 (White 95.9%; Black or African American 0.2%; Hispanic or Latino 1.9%; Asian 0.3%; Other 2.7%). **Foreign born:** 1.4%. **Median age:** 40.5. **State rank:** 62. **Pop change 1990-2000:** -1.1%.

Income: per capita $18,039; median household $35,582. **Pop below poverty level:** 8.6%.

Unemployment: 5.7%. **Median home value:** $62,200. **Median travel time to work:** 15.3 minutes.

CHISAGO COUNTY

313 N Main St Rm 174
Center City, MN 55012
www.co.chisago.mn.us

Ph: 651-213-1300
Fax: 651-213-0359

On the central eastern border of MN, northeast of Minneapolis; established Sep 1, 1851 (prior to statehood) from Washington County. **Name Origin:** For Chisago Lake, largest in the county; from Ojibway *kichi* 'large' and *saga* 'fair' or 'beautiful.' The first syllable was omitted and a clerical error changed *a* to *o*.

Area (sq mi): 442.49 (land 417.63; water 24.86).

Pop: 41,101 (White 96.4%; Black or African American 0.5%; Hispanic or Latino 1.2%; Asian 0.7%; Other 1.6%). **Foreign born:** 1.2%. **Median age:** 34.3. **State rank:** 22. **Pop change 1990-2000:** +34.7%.

Income: per capita $21,013; median household $52,012. **Pop below poverty level:** 5.1%.

Unemployment: 4.7%. **Median home value:** $132,500. **Median travel time to work:** 31.9 minutes.

CLAY COUNTY

PO Box 280
Moorhead, MN 56560
www.co.clay.mn.us

Ph: 218-299-5002
Fax: 218-299-5195

On the central western border of MN; established as Breckenridge County Mar 9, 1862; name changed later in 1862. **Name Origin:** For Henry Clay (1777-1852), U.S. senator from KY, known as the 'Great Pacificator' for his advocacy of compromise to avert national crises.

Area (sq mi): 1052.74 (land 1045.24; water 7.49).

Pop: 51,229 (White 92.4%; Black or African American 0.5%; Hispanic or Latino 3.7%; Asian 0.9%; Other 4.6%). **Foreign born:** 2.6%. **Median age:** 32.3. **State rank:** 17. **Pop change 1990-2000:** +1.6%.

Income: per capita $17,557; median household $37,889. **Pop below poverty level:** 13.2%.

Unemployment: 2.7%. **Median home value:** $85,400. **Median travel time to work:** 17.4 minutes.

CLEARWATER COUNTY

213 Main Ave N
Bagley, MN 56621
www.co.clearwater.mn.us

Ph: 218-694-6520
Fax: 218-694-6244

In north-central MN, east of Grand Forks, ND; established Dec 2, 1902 from Beltrami County. **Name Origin:** For Clearwater River and Lake, which are partly within the county.

Area (sq mi): 1029.79 (land 994.71; water 35.08).

Pop: 8,423 (White 89.1%; Black or African American 0.2%; Hispanic or Latino 0.8%; Asian 0.2%; Other 10.3%). **Foreign born:** 0.9%. **Median age:** 39.7. **State rank:** 75. **Pop change 1990-2000:** +1.4%.

Income: per capita $15,694; median household $30,517. **Pop below poverty level:** 15.1%.

Unemployment: 11.6%. **Median home value:** $51,300. **Median travel time to work:** 23.9 minutes.

COOK COUNTY

PO Box 1150
Grand Marais, MN 55604
www.co.cook.mn.us

Ph: 218-387-3000
Fax: 218-387-3007

On the northeastern border of MN; established Mar 9, 1874 from Lake County. **Name Origin:** For Maj. Michael Cook (1828-64), an officer in the Civil War and MN legislator. Some claim John Cook (?-1872), killed by Ojibway Indians.

Area (sq mi): 3339.72 (land 1450.6; water 1889.11).

Pop: 5,168 (White 89.2%; Black or African American 0.3%; Hispanic or Latino 0.8%; Asian 0.3%; Other 10%). **Foreign born:** 2.7%. **Median age:** 44. **State rank:** 84. **Pop change 1990-2000:** +33.6%.

Income: per capita $21,775; median household $36,640. **Pop below poverty level:** 10.1%.

Unemployment: 4.6%. **Median home value:** $107,700. **Median travel time to work:** 18.2 minutes.

Please see sample entry on inside front cover for detailed information about the statistics presented with each county listing.

COTTONWOOD COUNTY

900 3rd Ave
Windom, MN 56101

Ph: 507-831-1905

In southwestern MN, southwest of Mankato; established May 23, 1857 (prior to statehood) from Brown County. **Name Origin:** For the Cottonwood River, which runs through the county; itself named for the poplar trees along its banks, which have cotton-like tufts on the seeds.

Area (sq mi): 648.91 (land 639.99; water 8.91).

Pop: 12,167 (White 94.6%; Black or African American 0.3%; Hispanic or Latino 2.2%; Asian 1.6%; Other 2.7%). **Foreign born:** 2.2%. **Median age:** 41.7. **State rank:** 63. **Pop change 1990-2000:** -4.2%.

Income: per capita $16,647; median household $31,943. **Pop below poverty level:** 11.7%.

Unemployment: 3.9%. **Median home value:** $50,600. **Median travel time to work:** 14 minutes.

CROW WING COUNTY

326 Laurel St
Brainerd, MN 56401
www.co.crow-wing.mn.us

Ph: 218-824-1000

In central MN, north of Saint Cloud; established May 23, 1857 (prior to statehood) from Cass and Aitkin counties. **Name Origin:** For the Crow Wing river, which forms the southwestern border of the county; the Ojibway called the river *Kagiwigwan* or *Gagagiwgwuni* 'crow wing' or 'raven feather.'

Area (sq mi): 1156.56 (land 996.57; water 160).

Pop: 55,099 (White 97.2%; Black or African American 0.3%; Hispanic or Latino 0.7%; Asian 0.3%; Other 1.8%). **Foreign born:** 1.2%. **Median age:** 39.4. **State rank:** 16. **Pop change 1990-2000:** +24.5%.

Income: per capita $19,174; median household $37,589. **Pop below poverty level:** 9.8%.

Unemployment: 4.6%. **Median home value:** $107,500. **Median travel time to work:** 20.5 minutes.

DAKOTA COUNTY

1560 Hwy 55
Hastings, MN 55033
www.co.dakota.mn.us

Ph: 651-437-3191
Fax: 651-438-4405

On the southeastern border of MN, south of Saint Paul; original county; established Oct 27, 1849 (prior to statehood); originally spelled Dakotah. **Name Origin:** For the Dakota (also known as Sioux) Indians of Siouan linguistic stock.

Area (sq mi): 586.33 (land 569.58; water 16.75).

Pop: 355,904 (White 90%; Black or African American 2.3%; Hispanic or Latino 2.9%; Asian 2.9%; Other 3.5%). **Foreign born:** 5.1%. **Median age:** 33.7. **State rank:** 3. **Pop change 1990-2000:** +29.3%.

Income: per capita $27,008; median household $61,863. **Pop below poverty level:** 3.6%.

Unemployment: 2.8%. **Median home value:** $152,400. **Median travel time to work:** 22.8 minutes.

DODGE COUNTY

22 6th St E
Mantorville, MN 55955
www.co.dodge.mn.us

Ph: 507-635-6239
Fax: 507-635-6265

In southeastern MN, west of Rochester; established Feb 20, 1855 (prior to statehood) from Olmstead County. **Name Origin:** For Gen. Henry Dodge (1782-1867), officer in the War of 1812 and the Black Hawk War, governor of WI Territory (1836-41; 1845-48), and U.S. senator (1848-57); also for his son, Augustus Caesar Dodge (1812-83), U.S. senator from IA (1848-55) and U.S. Minister to Spain (1855-59).

Area (sq mi): 439.63 (land 439.5; water 0.12).

Pop: 17,731 (White 95.7%; Black or African American 0.2%; Hispanic or Latino 3%; Asian 0.4%; Other 2.8%). **Foreign born:** 2.5%. **Median age:** 34.8. **State rank:** 51. **Pop change 1990-2000:** +12.7%.

Income: per capita $19,259; median household $47,437. **Pop below poverty level:** 5.8%.

Unemployment: 4%. **Median home value:** $97,100. **Median travel time to work:** 22.6 minutes.

DOUGLAS COUNTY

305 8th Ave W
Alexandria, MN 56308
www.co.douglas.mn.us

Ph: 320-762-2381
Fax: 320-762-2389

In west-central MN, northwest of Saint Cloud; established Mar 8, 1858 from Todd County. **Name Origin:** For Stephen Arnold Douglas (1813-61), U.S. orator and statesman.

Area (sq mi): 719.94 (land 634.32; water 85.62).

Pop: 32,821 (White 98.2%; Black or African American 0.2%; Hispanic or Latino 0.6%; Asian 0.4%; Other 0.9%). **Foreign born:** 0.9%. **Median age:** 39.7. **State rank:** 28. **Pop change 1990-2000:** +14.5%.

Income: per capita $18,850; median household $37,703. **Pop below poverty level:** 8.5%.

Unemployment: 3.7%. **Median home value:** $102,300. **Median travel time to work:** 17.2 minutes.

FARIBAULT COUNTY

PO Box 130
Blue Earth, MN 56013
www.co.faribault.mn.us

Ph: 507-526-6277
Fax: 507-526-3054

On the central southern border of MN, south of Mankato; established Feb 20, 1855 (prior to statehood) from Blue Earth County. **Name Origin:** For Jean Baptiste Faribault (1774-1860), a French-Canadian fur trader in the Northwest Territory who had great influence with the Sioux.

Area (sq mi): 721.61 (land 713.63; water 7.98).

Pop: 16,181 (White 95.2%; Black or African American 0.2%; Hispanic or Latino 3.5%; Asian 0.4%; Other 2.3%). **Foreign born:** 1.6%. **Median age:** 42.4. **State rank:** 55. **Pop change 1990-2000:** -4.5%.

Income: per capita $17,193; median household $34,440. **Pop below poverty level:** 8.6%.

Unemployment: 4.3%. **Median home value:** $50,300. **Median travel time to work:** 19.4 minutes.

All statistics are based on the 2000 Census except the dollar figures given for per capita income, which are based on 1999 estimates.

FILLMORE COUNTY

PO Box 436   **Ph:** 507-765-3356
Preston, MN 55965   **Fax:** 507-765-4571
www.co.fillmore.mn.us

On the southeastern border of MN, southeast of Rochester; original county; established Mar 5, 1853 (prior to statehood). **Name Origin:** For Millard Fillmore (1800-74), thirteenth U.S. president.

Area (sq mi): 862.15 (land 861.25; water 0.9).

Pop: 21,122 (White 98.6%; Black or African American 0.2%; Hispanic or Latino 0.5%; Asian 0.1%; Other 0.8%). **Foreign born:** 0.8%. **Median age:** 39.8. **State rank:** 46. **Pop change 1990-2000:** +1.7%.

Income: per capita $17,067; median household $36,651. **Pop below poverty level:** 10.1%.

Unemployment: 4.1%. **Median home value:** $74,400. **Median travel time to work:** 25 minutes.

FREEBORN COUNTY

PO Box 1147   **Ph:** 507-377-5116
Albert Lea, MN 56007   **Fax:** 507-377-5109
www.co.freeborn.mn.us

On the southern border of MN, southwest of Rochester; established Feb 20, 1855 (prior to statehood) from Blue Earth and Rice counties. **Name Origin:** For William Freeborn (1816-1900), MN territorial legislator (1854-57)

Area (sq mi): 722.63 (land 707.64; water 14.99).

Pop: 32,584 (White 92.3%; Black or African American 0.2%; Hispanic or Latino 6.3%; Asian 0.5%; Other 4%). **Foreign born:** 3.1%. **Median age:** 40.4. **State rank:** 29. **Pop change 1990-2000:** -1.4%.

Income: per capita $18,325; median household $36,964. **Pop below poverty level:** 8.4%.

Unemployment: 4.5%. **Median home value:** $71,400. **Median travel time to work:** 18.1 minutes.

GOODHUE COUNTY

509 W 5th St   **Ph:** 651-385-3000
Red Wing, MN 55066   **Fax:** 651-385-3004
www.co.goodhue.mn.us

In southeastern MN, southeast of Saint Paul; established Mar 5, 1853 (prior to statehood) from Wabasha County. **Name Origin:** For James Madison Goodhue (1810-52), lawyer and prominent editor of the first newspaper in the MN Territory.

Area (sq mi): 780.44 (land 758.27; water 22.17).

Pop: 44,127 (White 96.1%; Black or African American 0.6%; Hispanic or Latino 1.1%; Asian 0.6%; Other 2.2%). **Foreign born:** 1.2%. **Median age:** 38.1. **State rank:** 19. **Pop change 1990-2000:** +8.4%.

Income: per capita $21,934; median household $46,972. **Pop below poverty level:** 5.7%.

Unemployment: 3.5%. **Median home value:** $116,000. **Median travel time to work:** 21.3 minutes.

GRANT COUNTY

PO Box 1007 County Courthouse   **Ph:** 218-685-4825
Elbow Lake, MN 56531   **Fax:** 218-685-4319

In west-central MN, southeast of Fargo, ND; established Mar 6, 1868 from Stearns County. **Name Origin:** For Ulysses S. Grant (1822-85), Civil War general and eighteenth U.S. president.

Area (sq mi): 575.18 (land 546.41; water 28.77).

Pop: 6,289 (White 98.1%; Black or African American 0.2%; Hispanic or Latino 0.5%; Asian 0.2%; Other 1.3%). **Foreign born:** 0.7%. **Median age:** 42.5. **State rank:** 80. **Pop change 1990-2000:** +0.7%.

Income: per capita $17,131; median household $33,775. **Pop below poverty level:** 8.4%.

Unemployment: 6.8%. **Median home value:** $52,900. **Median travel time to work:** 19 minutes.

HENNEPIN COUNTY

300 S 6th St   **Ph:** 612-348-3000
Minneapolis, MN 55487
www.co.hennepin.mn.us

In east-central MN, west of Saint Paul; original county; established Mar 6, 1852 (prior to statehood). **Name Origin:** For Louis Hennepin (1640-1701), Franciscan missionary and explorer (with La Salle) who named the Falls of Saint Anthony in the Mississippi River at present-day Minneapolis.

Area (sq mi): 606.38 (land 556.62; water 49.77).

Pop: 1,116,200 (White 78.9%; Black or African American 9%; Hispanic or Latino 4.1%; Asian 4.8%; Other 5.7%). **Foreign born:** 9.9%. **Median age:** 34.9. **State rank:** 1. **Pop change 1990-2000:** +8.1%.

Income: per capita $28,789; median household $51,711. **Pop below poverty level:** 8.3%.

Unemployment: 3.2%. **Median home value:** $143,400. **Median travel time to work:** 22.2 minutes.

HOUSTON COUNTY

304 S Marshall St   **Ph:** 507-725-5806
Caledonia, MN 55921   **Fax:** 507-725-5550
www.geocities.com/houstoncountymn/HC.html

In the southeastern corner of MN, southeast of Rochester; established Feb 23, 1854 (prior to statehood) from Fillmore County. **Name Origin:** For Samuel Houston (1793-1863), governor of TN (1827-29), president of the Republic of Texas (1836-38; 1841-44), U.S. senator from TX (1846-59), and TX governor (1859-61).

Area (sq mi): 568.91 (land 558.41; water 10.5).

Pop: 19,718 (White 98.1%; Black or African American 0.3%; Hispanic or Latino 0.6%; Asian 0.4%; Other 0.8%). **Foreign born:** 1.1%. **Median age:** 38.8. **State rank:** 48. **Pop change 1990-2000:** +6.6%.

Income: per capita $18,826; median household $40,680. **Pop below poverty level:** 6.5%.

Unemployment: 3.8%. **Median home value:** $88,600. **Median travel time to work:** 20.7 minutes.

Please see sample entry on inside front cover for detailed information about the statistics presented with each county listing.

HUBBARD COUNTY

301 Court Ave County Courthouse   **Ph:** 218-732-3196
Park Rapids, MN 56470   **Fax:** 218-732-3645
www.co.hubbard.mn.us

In north-central MN, northeast of Fargo, ND; established Feb 26, 1883 from Cass County. **Name Origin:** For Gen. Lucius Frederick Hubbard (1836-1913), an officer in the Civil War and the Spanish-American War, MN legislator and governor (1882-87).

Area (sq mi): 999.39 (land 922.46; water 76.93).

Pop: 18,376 (White 95.9%; Black or African American 0.2%; Hispanic or Latino 0.7%; Asian 0.3%; Other 3.2%). **Foreign born:** 1.1%. **Median age:** 41.8. **State rank:** 50. **Pop change 1990-2000:** +23%.

Income: per capita $18,115; median household $35,321. **Pop below poverty level:** 9.7%.

Unemployment: 5.5%. **Median home value:** $97,300. **Median travel time to work:** 20.7 minutes.

ISANTI COUNTY

555 18th Ave SW   **Ph:** 763-689-3859
Cambridge, MN 55008   **Fax:** 763-689-8226
www.co.isanti.mn.us

In central-eastern MN, north of Minneapolis; established Feb 13, 1857 (prior to statehood) from Anoka County. **Name Origin:** For the Izaty or Santee Indians, a tribe of the Dakotas who inhabited the area. Also spelled *Issati*. The name means 'knife' or perhaps 'ones who make knives.'

Area (sq mi): 451.87 (land 439.07; water 12.81).

Pop: 31,287 (White 97.1%; Black or African American 0.3%; Hispanic or Latino 0.8%; Asian 0.4%; Other 1.7%). **Foreign born:** 1.3%. **Median age:** 35.7. **State rank:** 33. **Pop change 1990-2000:** +20.7%.

Income: per capita $20,348; median household $50,127. **Pop below poverty level:** 5.7%.

Unemployment: 4.7%. **Median home value:** $110,700. **Median travel time to work:** 32.6 minutes.

ITASCA COUNTY

123 NE 4th St   **Ph:** 218-327-2847
Grand Rapids, MN 55744   **Fax:** 218-327-2848
www.co.itasca.mn.us

In north-central MN, west of Hibbing; original county; established Oct 27, 1850 (prior to statehood). **Name Origin:** For Itasca Lake; name coined by explorer and ethnologist Henry Rowe Schoolcraft (1793-1864), who thought the lake was the 'true source' of the Mississippi River. From Latin: the last part of *veritas* 'truth' and first part of @itcaput 'head.'

Area (sq mi): 2927.78 (land 2665.06; water 262.72).

Pop: 43,992 (White 94.3%; Black or African American 0.2%; Hispanic or Latino 0.6%; Asian 0.3%; Other 4.9%). **Foreign born:** 1.3%. **Median age:** 41.1. **State rank:** 20. **Pop change 1990-2000:** +7.7%.

Income: per capita $17,717; median household $36,234. **Pop below poverty level:** 10.6%.

Unemployment: 7.1%. **Median home value:** $81,700. **Median travel time to work:** 22 minutes.

JACKSON COUNTY

PO Box 226   **Ph:** 507-847-2763
Jackson, MN 56143   **Fax:** 507-847-4718

On southern border of MN, southwest of Mankato; established May 23, 1857 (prior to statehood) from unorganized lands. **Name Origin:** For Henry Jackson (1811-57), an early merchant in Saint Paul (1842), first postmaster (1846-49), and territorial legislator. There is also a debatable claim that the county was named for Andrew Jackson.

Area (sq mi): 719.46 (land 701.69; water 17.76).

Pop: 11,268 (White 96.2%; Black or African American 0.1%; Hispanic or Latino 1.9%; Asian 1.4%; Other 1.5%). **Foreign born:** 1.5%. **Median age:** 40.8. **State rank:** 66. **Pop change 1990-2000:** -3.5%.

Income: per capita $17,499; median household $36,746. **Pop below poverty level:** 8.6%.

Unemployment: 3.3%. **Median home value:** $56,800. **Median travel time to work:** 15.7 minutes.

KANABEC COUNTY

18 N Vine St   **Ph:** 320-679-6466
Mora, MN 55051   **Fax:** 320-679-9994

In east-central MN, north of Minneapolis; established Mar 13, 1858 from Pine County. **Name Origin:** For the meandering Snake River, which flows through the county; from the Ojibway word for 'snake.'

Area (sq mi): 533.38 (land 524.93; water 8.45).

Pop: 14,996 (White 96.6%; Black or African American 0.2%; Hispanic or Latino 0.9%; Asian 0.4%; Other 2.1%). **Foreign born:** 0.9%. **Median age:** 38. **State rank:** 58. **Pop change 1990-2000:** +17.1%.

Income: per capita $17,741; median household $38,520. **Pop below poverty level:** 9.5%.

Unemployment: 8.2%. **Median home value:** $90,400. **Median travel time to work:** 31.3 minutes.

KANDIYOHI COUNTY

PO Box 936   **Ph:** 320-231-6202
Willmar, MN 56201   **Fax:** 320-231-6263
www.co.kandiyohi.mn.us

In south-central MN, west of Minneapollis; established Mar 20, 1858 from Meeker County, annexed Monongalia County in Nov 1870. **Name Origin:** From Siouan 'place where the buffalo fish arrive,' the Indian name for several lakes at the source of the Crow River where the fish *Ictiobus cyprinella*, *I. urus* and *I. bubalus* go to spawn.

Area (sq mi): 861.97 (land 796.06; water 65.92).

Pop: 41,203 (White 90.3%; Black or African American 0.5%; Hispanic or Latino 8%; Asian 0.4%; Other 5.5%). **Foreign born:** 3.8%. **Median age:** 36.9. **State rank:** 21. **Pop change 1990-2000:** +6.3%.

Income: per capita $19,627; median household $39,772. **Pop below poverty level:** 9.2%.

All statistics are based on the 2000 Census except the dollar figures given for per capita income, which are based on 1999 estimates.

Unemployment: 3.7%. **Median home value:** $90,400. **Median travel time to work:** 17.9 minutes.

KITTSON COUNTY

PO Box 848
Hallock, MN 56728

Ph: 218-843-2655
Fax: 218-843-2656

In the northwestern corner of MN, north of Grand Forks, ND; established as Pembina County Apr 24, 1879 from unorganized lands; name changed Mar 9, 1878. **Name Origin:** For Norman Wolfred Kittson (1814-88), fur trader, territorial legislator (1851-55), and mayor of Saint Paul (1858).

Area (sq mi): 1103.51 (land 1097.08; water 6.43).

Pop: 5,285 (White 97.3%; Black or African American 0.2%; Hispanic or Latino 1.3%; Asian 0.2%; Other 1.6%). **Foreign born:** 2%. **Median age:** 42.4. **State rank:** 82. **Pop change 1990-2000:** -8.4%.

Income: per capita $16,525; median household $32,515. **Pop below poverty level:** 10.2%.

Unemployment: 6.2%. **Median home value:** $39,400. **Median travel time to work:** 19.5 minutes.

KOOCHICHING COUNTY

715 4th St
International Falls, MN 56649
www.co.koochiching.mn.us

Ph: 218-283-6220

On the central-northern border of MN; established Dec 19, 1906 from Itasca County. **Name Origin:** Origin uncertain, but evidence points to a Cree Indian word meaning 'rainy lake,' descriptive of the mists from the nearby International Falls on Rainy River.

Area (sq mi): 3154.32 (land 3102.36; water 51.96).

Pop: 14,355 (White 95.7%; Black or African American 0.2%; Hispanic or Latino 0.6%; Asian 0.2%; Other 3.6%). **Foreign born:** 5.9%. **Median age:** 41.5. **State rank:** 59. **Pop change 1990-2000:** -11.9%.

Income: per capita $19,167; median household $36,262. **Pop below poverty level:** 12.1%.

Unemployment: 6.1%. **Median home value:** $65,400. **Median travel time to work:** 15.5 minutes.

LAC QUI PARLE COUNTY

600 6th St
Madison, MN 56256
www.mnhs.org/places/sites/lpm/index.html

Ph: 320-598-7444
Fax: 320-598-3125

On the southwestern border of MN; organized 1863 north of the Minnesota River, disestablished in 1868, then recreated Mar 6, 1871 south of the river. **Name Origin:** French 'talking lake,' probably a transliteration of Siouan *mde* 'lake,' *iye* 'speaks,' and *dan*, a diminutive suffix. Origin uncertain, but possibly for echoes reflected from surrounding cliffs.

Area (sq mi): 778.05 (land 764.87; water 13.19).

Pop: 8,067 (White 98.7%; Black or African American 0.2%; Hispanic or Latino 0.3%; Asian 0.3%; Other 0.7%). **Foreign born:** 1%. **Median age:** 43.4. **State rank:** 76. **Pop change 1990-2000:** -9.6%.

Income: per capita $17,399; median household $32,626. **Pop below poverty level:** 8.5%.

Unemployment: 4.3%. **Median home value:** $43,100. **Median travel time to work:** 17.5 minutes.

LAKE COUNTY

601 3rd Ave
Two Harbors, MN 55616
www.lakecnty.com

Ph: 218-834-8300
Fax: 218-834-8360

On the northeastern border of MN, northeast of Duluth; established Mar 1, 1856 (prior to statehood); name changed from Doty County. **Name Origin:** For Lake Superior, which forms its eastern border.

Area (sq mi): 2990.82 (land 2099.16; water 891.66).

Pop: 11,058 (White 97.7%; Black or African American 0.1%; Hispanic or Latino 0.6%; Asian 0.2%; Other 1.7%). **Foreign born:** 1.7%. **Median age:** 42.9. **State rank:** 69. **Pop change 1990-2000:** +6.2%.

Income: per capita $19,761; median household $40,402. **Pop below poverty level:** 7.4%.

Unemployment: 5.2%. **Median home value:** $71,300. **Median travel time to work:** 21.4 minutes.

LAKE OF THE WOODS COUNTY

PO Box 808
Baudette, MN 56623
www.co.lake-of-the-woods.mn.us

Ph: 218-634-2836
Fax: 218-634-2509

On the central northern border of MN; established Nov 28, 1922 from Beltrami County; the latest county formed. **Name Origin:** For the Lake of the Woods in Canada, which forms its northern border.

Area (sq mi): 1775.05 (land 1296.7; water 478.35).

Pop: 4,522 (White 96.7%; Black or African American 0.3%; Hispanic or Latino 0.6%; Asian 0.2%; Other 2.2%). **Foreign born:** 2.9%. **Median age:** 41.6. **State rank:** 85. **Pop change 1990-2000:** +10.9%.

Income: per capita $16,976; median household $32,861. **Pop below poverty level:** 9.8%.

Unemployment: 4.5%. **Median home value:** $74,000. **Median travel time to work:** 17.4 minutes.

LE SUEUR COUNTY

88 South Pk
Le Center, MN 56057
www.co.le-sueur.mn.us

Ph: 507-357-2251
Fax: 507-357-6375

In south-central MN, north of Mankato; established Mar 5, 1853 (prior to statehood) from unorganized lands. **Name Origin:** For Pierre Charles Le Sueur (1657-1702?), French-Canadian fur trader and explorer of the upper Mississippi River and its tributaries.

Area (sq mi): 473.86 (land 448.5; water 25.36).

Pop: 25,426 (White 94.8%; Black or African American 0.1%; Hispanic or Latino 3.9%; Asian 0.3%; Other 3%). **Foreign born:** 1.8%. **Median age:** 37.3. **State rank:** 39. **Pop change 1990-2000:** +9.4%.

Income: per capita $20,151; median household $45,933. **Pop below poverty level:** 6.9%.

Unemployment: 4.7%. **Median home value:** $105,600. **Median travel time to work:** 22.5 minutes.

Please see sample entry on inside front cover for detailed information about the statistics presented with each county listing.

LINCOLN COUNTY

319 N Rebecca St   **Ph:** 507-694-1529
Ivanhoe, MN 56142   **Fax:** 507-694-1198
www.co.lincoln.mn.us

On the southwestern border of MN; established Mar 1, 1866 from Lyon County. **Name Origin:** For Abraham Lincoln (1809-65), sixteenth U.S. president.

Area (sq mi): 548.44 (land 537.03; water 11.41).

Pop: 6,429 (White 98.4%; Black or African American 0%; Hispanic or Latino 0.9%; Asian 0.2%; Other 0.9%). **Foreign born:** 0.7%. **Median age:** 43. **State rank:** 79. **Pop change 1990-2000:** -6.7%.

Income: per capita $16,009; median household $31,607. **Pop below poverty level:** 9.7%.

Unemployment: 3.7%. **Median home value:** $43,700. **Median travel time to work:** 18.3 minutes.

LYON COUNTY

607 W Main St   **Ph:** 507-537-6728
Marshall, MN 56258   **Fax:** 507-537-6091
www.lyonco.org

In southwestern MN; established Mar 6, 1868 from Yellow Medicine County. **Name Origin:** For Gen. Nathaniel Lyon (1818-61), officer in the Seminole War and the Mexican-American War; as a Union commander in the Civil War, he helped preserve MO for the Union.

Area (sq mi): 721.46 (land 714.17; water 7.29).

Pop: 25,425 (White 91.8%; Black or African American 1.5%; Hispanic or Latino 4%; Asian 1.7%; Other 3.2%). **Foreign born:** 4.5%. **Median age:** 34. **State rank:** 40. **Pop change 1990-2000:** +2.6%.

Income: per capita $18,013; median household $38,996. **Pop below poverty level:** 10.1%.

Unemployment: 3.7%. **Median home value:** $81,000. **Median travel time to work:** 13.5 minutes.

MAHNOMEN COUNTY

PO Box 379   **Ph:** 218-935-5669
Mahnomen, MN 56557   **Fax:** 218-935-5946

In west-central MN, northeast of Fargo, ND; established Dec 27, 1906 from Norman County. **Name Origin:** The Ojibway word meaning 'wild rice,' which grows abundantly in the region.

Area (sq mi): 582.99 (land 556.14; water 26.85).

Pop: 5,190 (White 62.7%; Black or African American 0.1%; Hispanic or Latino 0.9%; Asian 0.1%; Other 37%). **Foreign born:** 1.3%. **Median age:** 38.2. **State rank:** 83. **Pop change 1990-2000:** +2.9%.

Income: per capita $13,438; median household $30,053. **Pop below poverty level:** 16.7%.

Unemployment: 7.3%. **Median home value:** $53,100. **Median travel time to work:** 21.5 minutes.

MARSHALL COUNTY

208 E Colvin Ave   **Ph:** 218-745-4851
Warren, MN 56762   **Fax:** 218-745-5089

In northwestern MN, north of Grand Forks, ND; established Feb

25, 1879 from Kittson County. **Name Origin:** For Gen. William Rainey Marshall (1825-96), MN businessman and governor (1866-70).

Area (sq mi): 1812.79 (land 1772.24; water 40.55).

Pop: 10,155 (White 96%; Black or African American 0.1%; Hispanic or Latino 2.9%; Asian 0.2%; Other 2.5%). **Foreign born:** 1.9%. **Median age:** 40.5. **State rank:** 70. **Pop change 1990-2000:** -7.6%.

Income: per capita $16,317; median household $34,804. **Pop below poverty level:** 9.8%.

Unemployment: 8.8%. **Median home value:** $50,500. **Median travel time to work:** 23.2 minutes.

MARTIN COUNTY

201 Lake Ave Suite 201   **Ph:** 507-238-3211
Fairmont, MN 56031   **Fax:** 507-238-3259
www.co.martin.mn.us

On the central southern border of MN, southwest of Mankato; established May 23, 1857 (prior to statehood) from Faribault County. **Name Origin:** Either for Henry Martin (1829-1908), CT speculator with large holdings in the area, or for Morgan Lewis Martin (1805-87), U.S. representative from WI Territory who introduced the bill for the organization of the Territory of MN.

Area (sq mi): 729.56 (land 709.34; water 20.21).

Pop: 21,802 (White 96.8%; Black or African American 0.3%; Hispanic or Latino 1.9%; Asian 0.4%; Other 2.1%). **Foreign born:** 1.4%. **Median age:** 41.5. **State rank:** 44. **Pop change 1990-2000:** -4.9%.

Income: per capita $18,529; median household $34,810. **Pop below poverty level:** 10.5%.

Unemployment: 4.1%. **Median home value:** $62,200. **Median travel time to work:** 15.8 minutes.

McLEOD COUNTY

830 11th St E   **Ph:** 320-864-5551
Glencoe, MN 55336   **Fax:** 320-864-5905
www.co.mcleod.mn.us

In south-central MN, west of Minneapolis; established Mar 1, 1856 (prior to statehood) from Carver County. **Name Origin:** For Martin McLeod (1813-60), fur trader, MN territorial legislator (1849-53), and a founder of Glencoe.

Area (sq mi): 505.67 (land 491.91; water 13.76).

Pop: 34,898 (White 94.9%; Black or African American 0.2%; Hispanic or Latino 3.6%; Asian 0.6%; Other 2.7%). **Foreign born:** 2.2%. **Median age:** 35.6. **State rank:** 25. **Pop change 1990-2000:** +9%.

Income: per capita $20,137; median household $45,953. **Pop below poverty level:** 4.8%.

Unemployment: 3.8%. **Median home value:** $104,800. **Median travel time to work:** 20.1 minutes.

MEEKER COUNTY

325 N Sibley Ave   **Ph:** 320-693-5230
Litchfield, MN 55355   **Fax:** 320-693-5254
www.co.meeker.mn.us

In south-central MN, northwest of Minneapolis; established Feb

All statistics are based on the 2000 Census except the dollar figures given for per capita income, which are based on 1999 estimates.

23, 1856 (prior to statehood) from Wright County. **Name Origin:** For Bradley B. Meeker (1813-73), associate justice of the MN supreme court (1849-53).

Area (sq mi): 645.08 (land 608.54; water 36.54).

Pop: 22,644 (White 96.7%; Black or African American 0.2%; Hispanic or Latino 2.2%; Asian 0.4%; Other 2.1%). **Foreign born:** 0.8%. **Median age:** 38.3. **State rank:** 42. **Pop change 1990-2000:** +8.6%.

Income: per capita $18,628; median household $40,908. **Pop below poverty level:** 7.1%.

Unemployment: 6.6%. **Median home value:** $89,200. **Median travel time to work:** 23.8 minutes.

MILLE LACS COUNTY
635 2nd St SE   **Ph:** 320-983-8313
Milaca, MN 56353   **Fax:** 320-983-8384
www.co.mille-lacs.mn.us

In east-central MN, northeast of Saint Cloud; established May 23, 1857 (prior to statehood) from Kanabec County. **Name Origin:** For Mille Lacs Lake in the northern part of the county; French 'thousand lakes.'

Area (sq mi): 681.77 (land 574.47; water 107.3).

Pop: 22,330 (White 93%; Black or African American 0.3%; Hispanic or Latino 1%; Asian 0.2%; Other 6%). **Foreign born:** 1.1%. **Median age:** 38. **State rank:** 43. **Pop change 1990-2000:** +19.6%.

Income: per capita $17,656; median household $36,977. **Pop below poverty level:** 9.6%.

Unemployment: 7%. **Median home value:** $91,000. **Median travel time to work:** 27.1 minutes.

MORRISON COUNTY
213 SE 1st Ave   **Ph:** 320-632-2941
Little Falls, MN 56345   **Fax:** 320-632-0294
www.co.morrison.mn.us

In central MN, north of Saint Cloud; established Feb 25, 1856 (prior to statehood) from Benton and Stearns counties. **Name Origin:** For the Morrison brothers; William (1785-1866), fur trader and explorer, and Allen (1803-77), fur trader and representative in the first territorial legislature.

Area (sq mi): 1153.32 (land 1124.5; water 28.82).

Pop: 31,712 (White 98.1%; Black or African American 0.2%; Hispanic or Latino 0.6%; Asian 0.3%; Other 1%). **Foreign born:** 1%. **Median age:** 36.9. **State rank:** 30. **Pop change 1990-2000:** +7.1%.

Income: per capita $16,566; median household $37,047. **Pop below poverty level:** 11.1%.

Unemployment: 6.8%. **Median home value:** $82,800. **Median travel time to work:** 24.6 minutes.

MOWER COUNTY
201 1st St NE   **Ph:** 507-437-9535
Austin, MN 55912   **Fax:** 507-437-9471
www.co.mower.mn.us

On the southeastern border of MN, south of Rochester; established Feb 20, 1855 (prior to statehood) from Fillmore County. **Name**

Origin: For John Mower (1815-79), MN territorial and state legislator (1854-55; 1874-75).

Area (sq mi): 711.71 (land 711.5; water 0.21).

Pop: 38,603 (White 93%; Black or African American 0.6%; Hispanic or Latino 4.3%; Asian 1.5%; Other 3.3%). **Foreign born:** 3.6%. **Median age:** 38.9. **State rank:** 24. **Pop change 1990-2000:** +3.3%.

Income: per capita $19,795; median household $36,654. **Pop below poverty level:** 9.2%.

Unemployment: 3%. **Median home value:** $71,400. **Median travel time to work:** 18.7 minutes.

MURRAY COUNTY
PO Box 57   **Ph:** 507-836-6148
Slayton, MN 56172   **Fax:** 507-836-8904
www.murray-countymn.com

In southwestern MN, southwest of Mankato; established May 23, 1857 from Lyon County. **Name Origin:** For William Pitt Murray (1825-1910), MN legislator and Saint Paul city attorney (1876-89).

Area (sq mi): 719.52 (land 704.43; water 15.09).

Pop: 9,165 (White 97.4%; Black or African American 0.1%; Hispanic or Latino 1.5%; Asian 0.2%; Other 1.3%). **Foreign born:** 1.4%. **Median age:** 42.4. **State rank:** 74. **Pop change 1990-2000:** -5.1%.

Income: per capita $17,936; median household $34,966. **Pop below poverty level:** 8.3%.

Unemployment: 5%. **Median home value:** $50,900. **Median travel time to work:** 20.1 minutes.

NICOLLET COUNTY
501 S Minnesota Ave   **Ph:** 507-931-6800
Saint Peter, MN 56082   **Fax:** 507-931-9220
www.co.nicollet.mn.us

In south-central MN, northwest of Mankato; established Mar 5, 1853 (prior to statehood) from unorganized lands. **Name Origin:** For Joseph Nicholas Nicollet (1786-1843), French explorer who mapped area of MN, ND and SD; author of *Map of the Hydrographical Basin of the Upper Mississippi River*.

Area (sq mi): 466.95 (land 452.29; water 14.65).

Pop: 29,771 (White 95.4%; Black or African American 0.8%; Hispanic or Latino 1.8%; Asian 1.1%; Other 1.7%). **Foreign born:** 2.7%. **Median age:** 32.6. **State rank:** 35. **Pop change 1990-2000:** +6%.

Income: per capita $20,517; median household $46,170. **Pop below poverty level:** 7.5%.

Unemployment: 2.6%. **Median home value:** $113,400. **Median travel time to work:** 15.1 minutes.

NOBLES COUNTY
PO Box 547   **Ph:** 507-372-8263
Worthington, MN 56187   **Fax:** 507-372-4994
www.co.nobles.mn.us

On the southwestern border of MN, southwest of Mankato; established May 23, 1857 (prior to statehood) from Jackson County. **Name Origin:** For William H. Nobles (1816-76), MN Territory

Please see sample entry on inside front cover for detailed information about the statistics presented with each county listing.

297

legislator (1854;1856); discovered Nobles Pass through the Rocky Mountains.

Area (sq mi): 722.33 (land 715.39; water 6.94).

Pop: 20,832 (White 82.7%; Black or African American 1.1%; Hispanic or Latino 11.2%; Asian 4%; Other 8.4%). **Foreign born:** 9%. **Median age:** 37.5. **State rank:** 47. **Pop change 1990-2000:** +3.7%.

Income: per capita $16,987; median household $35,684. **Pop below poverty level:** 11.7%.

Unemployment: 3.6%. **Median home value:** $61,400. **Median travel time to work:** 15.8 minutes.

NORMAN COUNTY

PO Box 266   **Ph:** 218-784-2101
Ada, MN 56510   **Fax:** 218-784-4531
www.co.norman.mn.us

On the northwestern border of MN, north of Fargo, ND; established Feb 17, 1881 from Polk County. **Name Origin:** For the many Norwegians, known locally as Normans (Norsemen), living in the area and serving in the state legislature when the county was formed.

Area (sq mi): 876.82 (land 876.27; water 0.55).

Pop: 7,442 (White 93.5%; Black or African American 0.1%; Hispanic or Latino 3.1%; Asian 0.3%; Other 4.2%). **Foreign born:** 1.9%. **Median age:** 40.9. **State rank:** 77. **Pop change 1990-2000:** -6.7%.

Income: per capita $15,895; median household $32,535. **Pop below poverty level:** 10.3%.

Unemployment: 4.7%. **Median home value:** $43,600. **Median travel time to work:** 20.9 minutes.

OLMSTED COUNTY

151 4th St SE   **Ph:** 507-285-8115
Rochester, MN 55904   **Fax:** 507-287-2693
www.co.olmsted.mn.us

In southeastern MN, southeast of Mankato; established Feb 20, 1855 (prior to statehood) from unorganized lands. **Name Origin:** For David Olmsted (1822-61), president of the first MN territorial legislature (1849-50) and first mayor of Saint Paul. Some claim S. Baldwin Olmstead (1810-78), a member of the territorial council (1854-55) when the county was formed.

Area (sq mi): 654.5 (land 653.01; water 1.49).

Pop: 124,277 (White 89%; Black or African American 2.7%; Hispanic or Latino 2.4%; Asian 4.3%; Other 2.7%). **Foreign born:** 7.9%. **Median age:** 35. **State rank:** 8. **Pop change 1990-2000:** +16.7%.

Income: per capita $24,939; median household $51,316. **Pop below poverty level:** 6.4%.

Unemployment: 2.5%. **Median home value:** $117,000. **Median travel time to work:** 16.3 minutes.

OTTER TAIL COUNTY

121 W Junius Ave   **Ph:** 218-739-2271
Fergus Falls, MN 56537   **Fax:** 218-998-8438
www.co.ottertail.mn.us

In west-central MN, southeast of Fargo, ND; established Mar 18,

1858 from Pembina and Cass counties. **Name Origin:** For Otter Tail lake and river. The lake was named by the Ojibway *nigigwanowe* 'otter tail,' referring to the shape of the lake.

Area (sq mi): 2224.91 (land 1979.71; water 245.2).

Pop: 57,159 (White 96.5%; Black or African American 0.3%; Hispanic or Latino 1.7%; Asian 0.4%; Other 2.1%). **Foreign born:** 2%. **Median age:** 41.1. **State rank:** 13. **Pop change 1990-2000:** +12.7%.

Income: per capita $18,014; median household $35,395. **Pop below poverty level:** 10.1%.

Unemployment: 4.6%. **Median home value:** $84,000. **Median travel time to work:** 19.4 minutes.

PENNINGTON COUNTY

PO Box 616   **Ph:** 218-681-4011
Thief River Falls, MN 56701   **Fax:** 218-681-1235

In northwestern MN, east of Grand Forks, ND; established Nov 23, 1910 from Red Lake County. **Name Origin:** For Edmund Pennington (1848-1926), president of the Saint Paul and Sault Sainte Marie Railroad.

Area (sq mi): 618.34 (land 616.54; water 1.8).

Pop: 13,584 (White 96.4%; Black or African American 0.2%; Hispanic or Latino 1.2%; Asian 0.6%; Other 2.1%). **Foreign born:** 1.6%. **Median age:** 37.9. **State rank:** 61. **Pop change 1990-2000:** +2.1%.

Income: per capita $17,346; median household $34,216. **Pop below poverty level:** 11.1%.

Unemployment: 5.1%. **Median home value:** $63,300. **Median travel time to work:** 14.9 minutes.

PINE COUNTY

315 6th St   **Ph:** 320-629-5600
Pine City, MN 55063   **Fax:** 320-629-5762
www.pinecounty.com

On the central eastern border of MN, northeast of Saint Paul; established Mar 1, 1856 (prior to statehood) from unorganized lands; annexed Buchanan County in 1861. **Name Origin:** For the extensive forests of red (Norway) and white pine, and possibly for the Pine lakes and river in the county.

Area (sq mi): 1434.57 (land 1411.04; water 23.52).

Pop: 26,530 (White 93.1%; Black or African American 1.3%; Hispanic or Latino 1.8%; Asian 0.3%; Other 4%). **Foreign born:** 1.1%. **Median age:** 38.4. **State rank:** 38. **Pop change 1990-2000:** +24.8%.

Income: per capita $17,445; median household $37,379. **Pop below poverty level:** 11.3%.

Unemployment: 8%. **Median home value:** $89,700. **Median travel time to work:** 30.2 minutes.

PIPESTONE COUNTY

416 S Hiawatha Ave   **Ph:** 507-825-6740
Pipestone, MN 56164   **Fax:** 507-825-6741
www.mncounties.org/pipestone/

On the southwestern border of MN; established mistakenly as Rock County May 23, 1857 (prior to statehood) from Murray County;

All statistics are based on the 2000 Census except the dollar figures given for per capita income, which are based on 1999 estimates.

name changed Feb 20, 1862. **Name Origin:** For the red stone (catlinite) quarried by Indians to make pipe bowls.

Area (sq mi): 466.15 (land 465.89; water 0.26).

Pop: 9,895 (White 96.4%; Black or African American 0.2%; Hispanic or Latino 0.7%; Asian 0.5%; Other 2.7%). **Foreign born:** 1.4%. **Median age:** 40.2. **State rank:** 72. **Pop change 1990-2000:** -5.7%.

Income: per capita $16,450; median household $31,909. **Pop below poverty level:** 9.5%.

Unemployment: 3.4%. **Median home value:** $49,000. **Median travel time to work:** 15.2 minutes.

POLK COUNTY

612 N Broadway Suite 301   **Ph:** 218-281-2332
Crookston, MN 56716   **Fax:** 218-281-2204
www.co.polk.mn.us

In northwestern MN, east of Grand Forks, ND; established Jul 20, 1858 from Indian lands. **Name Origin:** For James Knox Polk (1795-1849), eleventh U.S. president.

Area (sq mi): 1997.81 (land 1970.37; water 27.44).

Pop: 31,369 (White 92.4%; Black or African American 0.3%; Hispanic or Latino 4.8%; Asian 0.3%; Other 5.2%). **Foreign born:** 2.2%. **Median age:** 38.2. **State rank:** 32. **Pop change 1990-2000:** -3.5%.

Income: per capita $17,279; median household $35,105. **Pop below poverty level:** 10.9%.

Unemployment: 4.3%. **Median home value:** $75,000. **Median travel time to work:** 16.5 minutes.

POPE COUNTY

130 E Minnesota Ave   **Ph:** 320-634-5705
Glenwood, MN 56334   **Fax:** 320-634-3087
www.mncounties.org/pope/

In west-central MN, west of Saint Cloud; established Feb 20, 1862 from Pierce County, which was abolished the same year. **Name Origin:** For explorer Gen. John Pope (1822-92), career army officer in the Mexican-American War and the Civil War.

Area (sq mi): 717.29 (land 670.14; water 47.15).

Pop: 11,236 (White 98.6%; Black or African American 0.2%; Hispanic or Latino 0.5%; Asian 0.1%; Other 0.9%). **Foreign born:** 0.9%. **Median age:** 42.1. **State rank:** 67. **Pop change 1990-2000:** +4.6%.

Income: per capita $19,032; median household $35,633. **Pop below poverty level:** 8.8%.

Unemployment: 4%. **Median home value:** $74,100. **Median travel time to work:** 18 minutes.

RAMSEY COUNTY

15 W Kellogg Blvd Rm 250   **Ph:** 651-266-8000
Saint Paul, MN 55102   **Fax:** 651-266-8039
www.co.ramsey.mn.us

In east-central MN, west of Minneapolis; original county; established Oct 27, 1849 (prior to statehood). **Name Origin:** For Alexander Ramsey (1815-1903), PA legislator, first MN territorial governor

(1849-53), state governor (1860-63), U.S. senator (1863-75), and U.S. secretary of war (1879-81).

Area (sq mi): 170.13 (land 155.78; water 14.36).

Pop: 511,035 (White 75.3%; Black or African American 7.6%; Hispanic or Latino 5.3%; Asian 8.8%; Other 6.3%). **Foreign born:** 10.6%. **Median age:** 33.7. **State rank:** 2. **Pop change 1990-2000:** +5.2%.

Income: per capita $23,536; median household $45,722. **Pop below poverty level:** 10.6%.

Unemployment: 3.3%. **Median home value:** $126,400. **Median travel time to work:** 21.2 minutes.

RED LAKE COUNTY

PO Box 367   **Ph:** 218-253-2598
Red Lake Falls, MN 56750   **Fax:** 218-253-4894

In northwestern MN, southeast of Grand Forks, ND; established Dec 24, 1896 from Polk County. **Name Origin:** For the Red Lake River, which flows through it; from a translation of the Ojibway word meaning 'red', referring to the color of the lake when the setting sun is reflected in it.

Area (sq mi): 432.51 (land 432.43; water 0.08).

Pop: 4,299 (White 97.3%; Black or African American 0.2%; Hispanic or Latino 0.3%; Asian 0.1%; Other 2.2%). **Foreign born:** 1.1%. **Median age:** 40.4. **State rank:** 86. **Pop change 1990-2000:** -5%.

Income: per capita $15,372; median household $32,052. **Pop below poverty level:** 10.8%.

Unemployment: 9.6%. **Median home value:** $43,200. **Median travel time to work:** 21.2 minutes.

REDWOOD COUNTY

PO Box 130 3rd & Jefferson Courthouse Sq   **Ph:** 507-637-4013
Redwood Falls, MN 56283   **Fax:** 507-637-4072
www.co.redwood.mn.us

In southwestern MN, northwest of Mankato; established Feb 6, 1862 from Brown County. **Name Origin:** For the Redwood River, which flows through it; from a Dakota phrase *chan sha ayapi* 'wood-red-on the river,' which may refer to the red bark taken from a shrub, which the Indians dried and mixed with smoking tobacco; the red cedar trees lining the banks; or spots of red paint found on trees, marking an ancient trail for a war party.

Area (sq mi): 881.24 (land 879.73; water 1.51).

Pop: 16,815 (White 94.4%; Black or African American 0.1%; Hispanic or Latino 1.1%; Asian 0.3%; Other 4.6%). **Foreign born:** 0.7%. **Median age:** 39.5. **State rank:** 53. **Pop change 1990-2000:** -2.5%.

Income: per capita $18,903; median household $37,352. **Pop below poverty level:** 7.7%.

Unemployment: 4.1%. **Median home value:** $57,900. **Median travel time to work:** 16.4 minutes.

Please see sample entry on inside front cover for detailed information about the statistics presented with each county listing.

RENVILLE COUNTY

500 E DePue Ave 3rd Fl   **Ph:** 320-523-3680
Olivia, MN 56277   **Fax:** 320-523-3689
www.co.renville.mn.us

In south-central MN, southwest of Minneapolis; established Feb 20, 1855 (prior to statehood) from unorganized lands. **Name Origin:** For Joseph Renville (1779?-1846), captain in the British Army during the War of 1812, fur trader, and assistant to missionaries to the Sioux.

Area (sq mi): 987.22 (land 982.92; water 4.3).

Pop: 17,154 (White 93.8%; Black or African American 0.1%; Hispanic or Latino 5.1%; Asian 0.2%; Other 4%). **Foreign born:** 2.1%. **Median age:** 39.7. **State rank:** 52. **Pop change 1990-2000:** -2.9%.

Income: per capita $17,770; median household $37,652. **Pop below poverty level:** 8.8%.

Unemployment: 6%. **Median home value:** $57,700. **Median travel time to work:** 18.8 minutes.

RICE COUNTY

320 NW 3rd St   **Ph:** 507-332-6101
Faribault, MN 55021   **Fax:** 507-332-5999
www.co.rice.mn.us

In south-central MN, south of Minneapolis; established Mar 5, 1853 (prior to statehood) from Nobles County. **Name Origin:** For Henry Mower Rice (1817-94), MN territorial delegate to Congress (1853-57) and one of its first two U.S. senators (1858-63).

Area (sq mi): 516.13 (land 497.57; water 18.56).

Pop: 56,665 (White 90.5%; Black or African American 1.3%; Hispanic or Latino 5.5%; Asian 1.5%; Other 3.6%). **Foreign born:** 4.8%. **Median age:** 32.9. **State rank:** 14. **Pop change 1990-2000:** +15.2%.

Income: per capita $19,695; median household $48,651. **Pop below poverty level:** 6.9%.

Unemployment: 3.7%. **Median home value:** $123,600. **Median travel time to work:** 20.2 minutes.

ROCK COUNTY

PO Box 745   **Ph:** 507-283-5020
Luverne, MN 56156   **Fax:** 507-283-5017
www.co.rock.mn.us

In the southwestern corner of MN; established mistakenly as Pipestone County May 23, 1857 (prior to statehood) from Nobles County; name changed Feb 20, 1862. **Name Origin:** For the Rock River, which runs through the county; named for the outcrop of quartzite about 3 sq. mi. in area and rising 175 ft. above this prairie region; now called 'the Mound.'

Area (sq mi): 482.84 (land 482.61; water 0.23).

Pop: 9,721 (White 96.7%; Black or African American 0.5%; Hispanic or Latino 1.3%; Asian 0.6%; Other 1.5%). **Foreign born:** 1.1%. **Median age:** 39.9. **State rank:** 73. **Pop change 1990-2000:** -0.9%.

Income: per capita $17,411; median household $38,102. **Pop below poverty level:** 8%.

Unemployment: 2.4%. **Median home value:** $68,500. **Median travel time to work:** 19 minutes.

ROSEAU COUNTY

606 5th Ave SW Rm 20   **Ph:** 218-463-2541
Roseau, MN 56751   **Fax:** 218-463-1889

On the northern border of MN, northeast of Grand Forks, ND; established Dec 31, 1894 from Kittson County. **Name Origin:** For Roseau lake and river, both in the northern part of the county; from French 'reed,' from a translation of an Ojibway word that refers to the coarse grass (Phragmites communis) growing along the banks.

Area (sq mi): 1678.33 (land 1662.51; water 15.82).

Pop: 16,338 (White 95.6%; Black or African American 0.1%; Hispanic or Latino 0.4%; Asian 1.7%; Other 2.2%). **Foreign born:** 2.8%. **Median age:** 35.3. **State rank:** 54. **Pop change 1990-2000:** +8.7%.

Income: per capita $17,053; median household $39,852. **Pop below poverty level:** 6.6%.

Unemployment: 4%. **Median home value:** $76,300. **Median travel time to work:** 17.5 minutes.

SAINT LOUIS COUNTY

100 North 5th Ave W Rm 214   **Ph:** 218-726-2380
Duluth, MN 55802   **Fax:** 218-725-5060
www.co.st-louis.mn.us

On the northeastern border of MN, bordered on the southeast by Lake Superior; established Mar 3, 1855 (prior to statehood) from Lake County (then called Doty County). **Name Origin:** For the Saint Louis River, which flows through the county; itself named for Louis IX of France (1215-70), who participated in the Sixth Crusade (1248-54) and was canonized in 1297.

Area (sq mi): 6859.91 (land 6225.16; water 634.75).

Pop: 200,528 (White 94.4%; Black or African American 0.8%; Hispanic or Latino 0.8%; Asian 0.7%; Other 3.5%). **Foreign born:** 1.9%. **Median age:** 39. **State rank:** 6. **Pop change 1990-2000:** +1.2%.

Income: per capita $18,982; median household $36,306. **Pop below poverty level:** 12.1%.

Unemployment: 5.5%. **Median home value:** $75,000. **Median travel time to work:** 19.4 minutes.

SCOTT COUNTY

200 4th Ave W   **Ph:** 952-445-7750
Shakopee, MN 55379   **Fax:** 952-496-8257
www.co.scott.mn.us

In south-central MN, south of Minneapolis; established Mar 5, 1853 (prior to statehood) from Dakota County. **Name Origin:** For Gen. Winfield Scott (1786-1866), officer in the War of 1812 and the Mexican-American War; general in chief of the U.S. Army (1841-61) and commander of the Union armies at the beginning of the Civil War.

Area (sq mi): 368.56 (land 356.68; water 11.88).

Pop: 89,498 (White 92.4%; Black or African American 0.9%; Hispanic or Latino 2.7%; Asian 2.2%; Other 3.2%). **Foreign born:** 4%. **Median age:** 32.7. **State rank:** 10. **Pop change 1990-2000:** +54.7%.

Income: per capita $26,418; median household $66,612. **Pop below poverty level:** 3.4%.

All statistics are based on the 2000 Census except the dollar figures given for per capita income, which are based on 1999 estimates.

Unemployment: 3.4%. **Median home value:** $157,300. **Median travel time to work:** 24.3 minutes.

SHERBURNE COUNTY

13880 Hwy 10   **Ph:** 763-241-2860
Elk River, MN 55330   **Fax:** 763-241-2816
www.co.sherburne.mn.us

In east-central MN, southeast of Saint Cloud; established Feb 25, 1856 (prior to statehood) from Anoka County. **Name Origin:** For Moses Sherburne (1808-68), associate justice of the MN Territory supreme court (1853-57) and active in the formation of the state.

Area (sq mi): 451 (land 436.3; water 14.7).

Pop: 64,417 (White 96.1%; Black or African American 0.9%; Hispanic or Latino 1.1%; Asian 0.6%; Other 1.7%). **Foreign born:** 1.5%. **Median age:** 31.4. **State rank:** 12. **Pop change 1990-2000:** +53.6%.

Income: per capita $21,322; median household $57,014. **Pop below poverty level:** 4.4%.

Unemployment: 4%. **Median home value:** $137,500. **Median travel time to work:** 29.9 minutes.

SIBLEY COUNTY

PO Box 867   **Ph:** 507-237-4051
Gaylord, MN 55334   **Fax:** 507-237-4062
www.co.sibley.mn.us

In south-central MN, southwest of Minneapolis; established Mar 5, 1853 (prior to statehood) from unorganized lands. **Name Origin:** For Henry Hastings Sibley (1811-91), delegate to the U.S. Congress from WI territory (1848-49) and from MN Territory (1849-53), and first governor of MN (1858-60).

Area (sq mi): 600.41 (land 588.65; water 11.76).

Pop: 15,356 (White 93.4%; Black or African American 0.1%; Hispanic or Latino 5.4%; Asian 0.3%; Other 4%). **Foreign born:** 2.6%. **Median age:** 37.3. **State rank:** 56. **Pop change 1990-2000:** +6.9%.

Income: per capita $18,004; median household $41,458. **Pop below poverty level:** 8.1%.

Unemployment: 5.1%. **Median home value:** $80,700. **Median travel time to work:** 24.1 minutes.

STEARNS COUNTY

705 Courthouse Sq Rm 121   **Ph:** 320-656-3601
Saint Cloud, MN 56303   **Fax:** 320-656-6393
www.co.stearns.mn.us

In central MN, northwest of Minneapolis; established Feb 20, 1855 (prior to statehood) from unorganized lands. **Name Origin:** For Charles Thomas Stearns (1807-98), territorial legislator (1854-55). In the original bill, the county was to be named for Isaac Ingalls Stevens (1818-62), first territorial governor of WA and surveyor for the Northern Pacific Railway, but apparently a clerical error was made and allowed to stand.

Area (sq mi): 1389.93 (land 1344.52; water 45.41).

Pop: 133,166 (White 95.2%; Black or African American 0.8%; Hispanic or Latino 1.4%; Asian 1.6%; Other 1.6%). **Foreign born:** 2.4%. **Median age:** 31.6. **State rank:** 7. **Pop change 1990-2000:** +12.1%.

Income: per capita $19,211; median household $42,426. **Pop below poverty level:** 8.7%.

Unemployment: 4%. **Median home value:** $100,300. **Median travel time to work:** 19.3 minutes.

STEELE COUNTY

PO Box 487   **Ph:** 507-444-7700
Owatonna, MN 55060   **Fax:** 507-444-7491
www.co.steele.mn.us

In southeastern MN, west of Rochester; established Feb 20, 1855 (prior to statehood) from unorganized territory. **Name Origin:** For Franklin Steele (1813-80), prominent civic leader and member of the first board of regents of the University of Minnesota.

Area (sq mi): 432.16 (land 429.55; water 2.62).

Pop: 33,680 (White 93.3%; Black or African American 1.1%; Hispanic or Latino 3.8%; Asian 0.8%; Other 2.8%). **Foreign born:** 3.5%. **Median age:** 35.7. **State rank:** 27. **Pop change 1990-2000:** +9.6%.

Income: per capita $20,328; median household $46,106. **Pop below poverty level:** 6.2%.

Unemployment: 3.8%. **Median home value:** $102,300. **Median travel time to work:** 16.3 minutes.

STEVENS COUNTY

PO Box 530   **Ph:** 320-589-7287
Morris, MN 56267   **Fax:** 320-589-7288
www.co.stevens.mn.us

In west-central MN, west of Saint Cloud; established Feb 20, 1862 from Pierce County, which was abolished the same year. **Name Origin:** For Gen. Isaac Ingalls Stevens (1818-62), an officer in the Mexican-American War and the Civil War, first governor of WA Territory (1853-57) and surveyor for the Northern Pacific Railway.

Area (sq mi): 575.24 (land 562.06; water 13.17).

Pop: 10,053 (White 95.8%; Black or African American 0.9%; Hispanic or Latino 0.9%; Asian 0.9%; Other 2.1%). **Foreign born:** 1.7%. **Median age:** 33.9. **State rank:** 71. **Pop change 1990-2000:** -5.5%.

Income: per capita $17,569; median household $37,267. **Pop below poverty level:** 13.6%.

Unemployment: 2.8%. **Median home value:** $67,100. **Median travel time to work:** 13 minutes.

SWIFT COUNTY

PO Box 110   **Ph:** 320-843-2744
Benson, MN 56215   **Fax:** 320-843-4124
www.swiftcounty.com

In west-central MN, southwest of Saint Cloud; established Feb 18, 1870 from Chippewa County. **Name Origin:** For Henry Adoniram Swift (1823-69), MN legislator and governor (1863-64).

Area (sq mi): 752.35 (land 743.53; water 8.82).

Pop: 11,956 (White 89.7%; Black or African American 2.7%; Hispanic or Latino 2.7%; Asian 1.4%; Other 5.2%). **Foreign born:** 1.2%. **Median age:** 39.3. **State rank:** 64. **Pop change 1990-2000:** +11.5%.

Please see sample entry on inside front cover for detailed information about the statistics presented with each county listing.

Income: per capita $16,360; median household $34,820. **Pop below poverty level:** 8.4%.

Unemployment: 4.4%. **Median home value:** $58,200. **Median travel time to work:** 17.2 minutes.

TODD COUNTY

215 1st Ave S   **Ph:** 320-732-4469
Long Prairie, MN 56347   **Fax:** 320-732-4001
www.co.todd.mn.us

In central MN, northwest of Saint Cloud; established Feb 20, 1855 (prior to statehood) from Stearns County. **Name Origin:** For John Blair Smith Todd (1814-72), army officer in the Seminole Wars, the Mexican-American War, and the Civil War; delegate to Congress for Dakota (1861-65), and Dakota Territory lawyer and legislator.

Area (sq mi): 979.34 (land 942.02; water 37.32).

Pop: 24,426 (White 96.6%; Black or African American 0.1%; Hispanic or Latino 1.9%; Asian 0.3%; Other 2%). **Foreign born:** 1.8%. **Median age:** 38.5. **State rank:** 41. **Pop change 1990-2000:** +4.5%.

Income: per capita $15,658; median household $32,281. **Pop below poverty level:** 12.9%.

Unemployment: 6.1%. **Median home value:** $64,400. **Median travel time to work:** 23.2 minutes.

TRAVERSE COUNTY

PO Box 428   **Ph:** 320-563-4242
Wheaton, MN 56296   **Fax:** 320-563-4424

On the central western border of MN, south of Fargo, ND; established Feb 20, 1862 from Wilkin County (then called Toombs County). **Name Origin:** For Lake Traverse on the southwestern border of the county; from the French *lac travers*, a translation of the Siouan name *Mdehdakinyan* 'lake lying crosswise' [to Big Stone and Lac Qui Parle lakes].

Area (sq mi): 585.96 (land 574.09; water 11.87).

Pop: 4,134 (White 95.5%; Black or African American 0%; Hispanic or Latino 1.2%; Asian 0.3%; Other 3.3%). **Foreign born:** 0.7%. **Median age:** 42.9. **State rank:** 87. **Pop change 1990-2000:** -7.4%.

Income: per capita $16,378; median household $30,617. **Pop below poverty level:** 12%.

Unemployment: 5.3%. **Median home value:** $34,100. **Median travel time to work:** 13.2 minutes.

WABASHA COUNTY

625 Jefferson Ave   **Ph:** 651-565-2648
Wabasha, MN 55981   **Fax:** 651-565-2774
www.co.wabasha.mn.us

On the southeastern border of MN, north of Rochester; original county; established Oct 27, 1849 (prior to statehood); originally spelled Wabashaw. **Name Origin:** The name of hereditary Sioux chiefs. The name of the chiefs has been transliterated as *Wapashaw* and is said to mean 'red leaf,' 'red hat,' or 'red battle-standard.' The origin of the latter is probably a decoration or red uniform given by the British to one of the chiefs.

Area (sq mi): 549.83 (land 525.01; water 24.82).

Pop: 21,610 (White 97%; Black or African American 0.2%; Hispanic

or Latino 1.7%; Asian 0.4%; Other 1.3%). **Foreign born:** 2%. **Median age:** 38. **State rank:** 45. **Pop change 1990-2000:** +9.5%.

Income: per capita $19,664; median household $42,117. **Pop below poverty level:** 6%.

Unemployment: 3.4%. **Median home value:** $95,000. **Median travel time to work:** 23.7 minutes.

WADENA COUNTY

415 S Jefferson St   **Ph:** 218-631-7634
Wadena, MN 56482   **Fax:** 218-631-7635
www.co.wadena.mn.us

In central MN, northwest of Saint Cloud; established Jun 11, 1858 from Cass and Todd counties. **Name Origin:** For the Wadena trading post on the trail from Crow Wing to Otter Tail City; from an archaic Ojibway word meaning 'a little round hill,' possibly a reference to the Crow Wing bluffs, but also a common Ojibway personal name.

Area (sq mi): 543 (land 535.02; water 7.98).

Pop: 13,713 (White 97.3%; Black or African American 0.5%; Hispanic or Latino 0.9%; Asian 0.2%; Other 1.5%). **Foreign born:** 1%. **Median age:** 39.9. **State rank:** 60. **Pop change 1990-2000:** +4.2%.

Income: per capita $15,146; median household $30,651. **Pop below poverty level:** 14.1%.

Unemployment: 5.7%. **Median home value:** $56,900. **Median travel time to work:** 19.3 minutes.

WASECA COUNTY

307 N State St   **Ph:** 507-835-0610
Waseca, MN 56093   **Fax:** 507-835-0633
www.co.waseca.mn.us

In south-central MN, southeast of Mankato; established Feb 27, 1857 (prior to statehood) from Steele County. **Name Origin:** From Dakota 'rich,' referring either to provisions or the fertile soil.

Area (sq mi): 432.81 (land 423.25; water 9.56).

Pop: 19,526 (White 93.2%; Black or African American 2.3%; Hispanic or Latino 2.9%; Asian 0.5%; Other 2.6%). **Foreign born:** 1.3%. **Median age:** 36.3. **State rank:** 49. **Pop change 1990-2000:** +8%.

Income: per capita $18,631; median household $42,440. **Pop below poverty level:** 6.5%.

Unemployment: 4%. **Median home value:** $87,700. **Median travel time to work:** 17.6 minutes.

WASHINGTON COUNTY

14949 62nd St N   **Ph:** 651-430-6001
Stillwater, MN 55082   **Fax:** 651-430-6017
www.co.washington.mn.us

On the central eastern border of MN, east of Saint Paul; original county; established Oct 27, 1849 (prior to statehood). **Name Origin:** For George Washington (1732-99), American patriot and first U.S. president.

Area (sq mi): 423.16 (land 391.7; water 31.46).

Pop: 201,130 (White 92.5%; Black or African American 1.8%; Hispanic or Latino 1.9%; Asian 2.1%; Other 2.4%). **Foreign born:**

3.4%. **Median age:** 35.1. **State rank:** 5. **Pop change 1990-2000:** +37.9%.

Income: per capita $28,148; median household $66,305. **Pop below poverty level:** 2.9%.

Unemployment: 2.6%. **Median home value:** $156,200. **Median travel time to work:** 24.6 minutes.

WATONWAN COUNTY
PO Box 518   **Ph:** 507-375-1236
Saint James, MN 56081   **Fax:** 507-375-5010

In south-central MN, southwest of Mankato; established Feb 25, 1860 from Brown County. **Name Origin:** For the Watonwan River, whose head steams flow through the county; probably from a Dakota word meaning 'where fish bait can be found' or 'where fish abound.'

Area (sq mi): 439.92 (land 434.51; water 5.4).

Pop: 11,876 (White 82.9%; Black or African American 0.4%; Hispanic or Latino 15.2%; Asian 0.9%; Other 10.2%). **Foreign born:** 8%. **Median age:** 38.6. **State rank:** 65. **Pop change 1990-2000:** +1.7%.

Income: per capita $16,413; median household $35,441. **Pop below poverty level:** 9.8%.

Unemployment: 3.6%. **Median home value:** $56,600. **Median travel time to work:** 17.7 minutes.

WILKIN COUNTY
PO Box 219   **Ph:** 218-643-7172
Breckenridge, MN 56520   **Fax:** 218-643-7167
www.co.wilkin.mn.us

On the central western border of MN, south of Fargo, ND; established Mar 8, 1858 from Cass County; name changed from Toombs County to Andy Johnson County in 1863 and from Andy Johnson County to present name Mar 6, 1868. **Name Origin:** For Col. Alexander Wilkin (1820-64), an officer in the Union army killed at the Battle of Tupelo. Originally for Robert Toombs (1810-85), U.S. senator from GA (1853-61), who became the Confederate secretary of state and thus angered the local residents. Changed to honor the seventeenth U.S. president, Andrew Johnson (1808-75), but his subsequent political stands also angered them.

Area (sq mi): 751.63 (land 751.43; water 0.2).

Pop: 7,138 (White 96.8%; Black or African American 0.2%; Hispanic or Latino 1.5%; Asian 0.2%; Other 1.9%). **Foreign born:** 0.7%. **Median age:** 38.1. **State rank:** 78. **Pop change 1990-2000:** -5%.

Income: per capita $16,873; median household $38,093. **Pop below poverty level:** 8.1%.

Unemployment: 3.4%. **Median home value:** $64,100. **Median travel time to work:** 18.3 minutes.

WINONA COUNTY
177 Main St   **Ph:** 507-457-6350
Winona, MN 55987   **Fax:** 507-454-9365

On the southeastern border of MN, east of Rochester; established Feb 23, 1854 (prior to statehood) from unorganized lands. **Name Origin:** For the town that became the county seat, which was named for a Dakota Indian woman active in the removal of the Winnebagos from IA to MN. Name was also popularized by H.L. Gordon's poem, 'Winona' (1881).

Area (sq mi): 641.59 (land 626.3; water 15.29).

Pop: 49,985 (White 95.1%; Black or African American 0.8%; Hispanic or Latino 1.4%; Asian 1.9%; Other 1.5%). **Foreign born:** 2.7%. **Median age:** 32.8. **State rank:** 18. **Pop change 1990-2000:** +4.5%.

Income: per capita $18,077; median household $38,700. **Pop below poverty level:** 12%.

Unemployment: 3.5%. **Median home value:** $95,800. **Median travel time to work:** 17 minutes.

WRIGHT COUNTY
10 NW 2nd St Rm 203   **Ph:** 763-682-3900
Buffalo, MN 55313   **Fax:** 763-682-6178
www.co.wright.mn.us

In east-central MN, northwest of Minneapolis; established Feb 20, 1855 (prior to statehood). **Name Origin:** For Silas Wright (1795-1847), NY governor (1845-47) and friend of a member of the county organization committee; his name was chosen 'as a compromise after a somewhat animated discussion.'

Area (sq mi): 714.39 (land 660.75; water 53.63).

Pop: 89,986 (White 97.2%; Black or African American 0.3%; Hispanic or Latino 1.1%; Asian 0.4%; Other 1.5%). **Foreign born:** 1.1%. **Median age:** 33.1. **State rank:** 9. **Pop change 1990-2000:** +31%.

Income: per capita $21,844; median household $53,945. **Pop below poverty level:** 4.7%.

Unemployment: 4%. **Median home value:** $135,300. **Median travel time to work:** 29.1 minutes.

YELLOW MEDICINE COUNTY
415 9th Ave   **Ph:** 320-564-3325
Granite Falls, MN 56241   **Fax:** 320-564-4435

On the southwestern border of MN; established Mar 6, 1871 from Redwood County. **Name Origin:** For the Yellow Medicine River, which flows through it; from a translation of the Siouan name for moonseed, *Menispermum canadense*, a medicinal plant that grows abundantly in the area.

Area (sq mi): 763.39 (land 757.96; water 5.43).

Pop: 11,080 (White 95.4%; Black or African American 0.1%; Hispanic or Latino 1.8%; Asian 0.2%; Other 3.6%). **Foreign born:** 1.2%. **Median age:** 40.4. **State rank:** 68. **Pop change 1990-2000:** -5.2%.

Income: per capita $17,120; median household $34,393. **Pop below poverty level:** 10.4%.

Unemployment: 6.1%. **Median home value:** $52,400. **Median travel time to work:** 16.8 minutes.

Please see sample entry on inside front cover for detailed information about the statistics presented with each county listing.

303

MISSISSIPPI - Counties

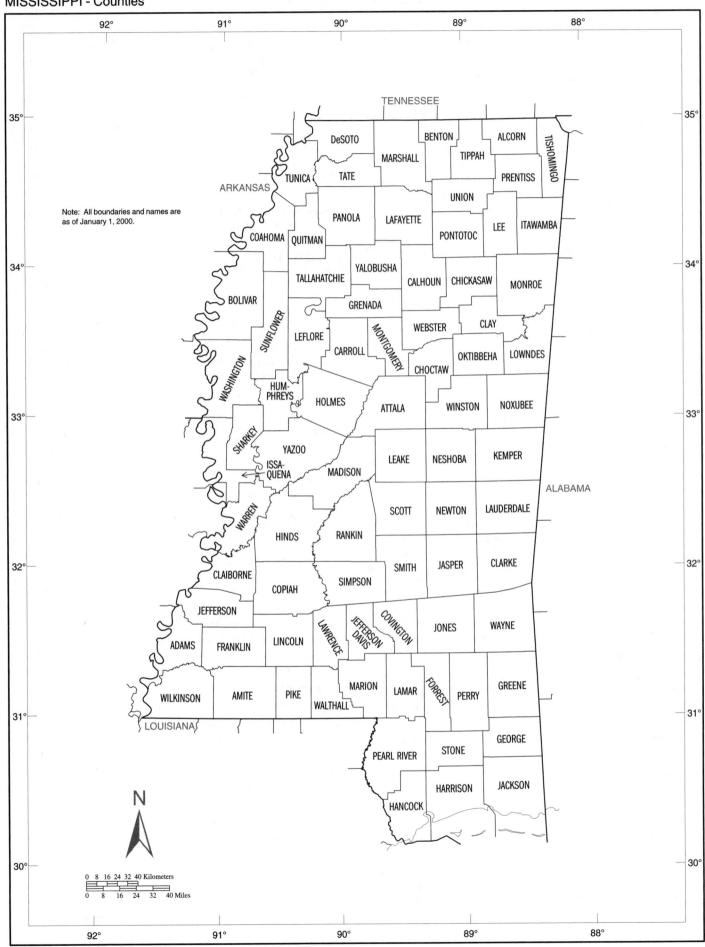

TENNESSEE

ARKANSAS

Note: All boundaries and names are as of January 1, 2000.

ALABAMA

LOUISIANA

N

0 8 16 24 32 40 Kilometers

0 8 16 24 32 40 Miles

DeSOTO
BENTON
ALCORN
TISHOMINGO
MARSHALL
TIPPAH
TUNICA
TATE
PRENTISS
UNION
PANOLA
LAFAYETTE
PONTOTOC
LEE
ITAWAMBA
COAHOMA
QUITMAN
YALOBUSHA
TALLAHATCHIE
CALHOUN
CHICKASAW
MONROE
BOLIVAR
GRENADA
SUNFLOWER
LEFLORE
WEBSTER
CLAY
CARROLL
MONTGOMERY
OKTIBBEHA
LOWNDES
WASHINGTON
CHOCTAW
HUM-PHREYS
HOLMES
ATTALA
WINSTON
NOXUBEE
SHARKEY
YAZOO
KEMPER
ISSA-QUENA
LEAKE
NESHOBA
MADISON
WARREN
SCOTT
NEWTON
LAUDERDALE
HINDS
RANKIN
CLAIBORNE
SMITH
JASPER
CLARKE
COPIAH
SIMPSON
JEFFERSON
COVINGTON
JONES
WAYNE
LAWRENCE
JEFFERSON DAVIS
ADAMS
FRANKLIN
LINCOLN
MARION
LAMAR
FORREST
PERRY
GREENE
WILKINSON
AMITE
PIKE
WALTHALL
GEORGE
PEARL RIVER
STONE
HARRISON
JACKSON
HANCOCK

Mississippi

MISSISSIPPI STATE INFORMATION

www.mississippi.gov **Ph:** 601-359-1000

Area (sq mi): 48,430.19 (land 46,906.96; water 1523.24).

Pop: 2,844,658 (White 60.7%; Black or African American 36.3%; Hispanic or Latino 1.4%; Asian 0.7%; Other 1.6%). **Foreign born:** 1.4%. **Median age:** 33.8. **Pop change 1990-2000:** +10.5%.

Income: per capita $15,853; median household $31,330. **Pop below poverty level:** 19.9%.

Unemployment: 6.4%. **Median home value:** $71,400. **Median travel time to work:** 24.6 minutes.

ADAMS COUNTY

PO Box 1006 **Ph:** 601-446-6684
Natchez, MS 39121 **Fax:** 601-445-7913

On the southwestern border of MS; organized Apr 2, 1799 (prior to statehood) from Natchez District. **Name Origin:** For John Adams (1735-1826), second U.S. president.

Area (sq mi): 486.25 (land 460.26; water 25.99).

Pop: 34,340 (White 45.7%; Black or African American 52.8%; Hispanic or Latino 0.8%; Asian 0.2%; Other 0.9%). **Foreign born:** 1.4%. **Median age:** 38.1. **State rank:** 26. **Pop change 1990-2000:** -2.9%.

Income: per capita $15,778; median household $25,234. **Pop below poverty level:** 25.9%.

Unemployment: 6.9%. **Median home value:** $60,200. **Median travel time to work:** 21.9 minutes.

ALCORN COUNTY

PO Box 69 **Ph:** 662-286-7700
Corinth, MS 38835 **Fax:** 662-286-7706

On the northeastern border of MS, southeast of Memphis, TN; organized Apr 15, 1870 from Tippah, Tishomingo, and Wilkinson counties. **Name Origin:** For James Lusk Alcorn (1816-94), MS governor (1870-71) and U.S. senator (1871-77).

Area (sq mi): 401.35 (land 399.89; water 1.46).

Pop: 34,558 (White 86.7%; Black or African American 11.1%; Hispanic or Latino 1.3%; Asian 0.2%; Other 1.4%). **Foreign born:** 1%. **Median age:** 37.6. **State rank:** 24. **Pop change 1990-2000:** +8.9%.

Income: per capita $15,418; median household $29,041. **Pop below poverty level:** 16.6%.

Unemployment: 5.5%. **Median home value:** $62,100. **Median travel time to work:** 20.8 minutes.

AMITE COUNTY

PO Box 680 **Ph:** 601-657-8022
Liberty, MS 39645 **Fax:** 601-657-8288

On the southwestern border of MS, southeast of Natchez; organized Feb 24, 1809 (prior to statehood) from Wilkinson County. **Name Origin:** Adapted from *amitie*, the French word for 'friendship.'

Area (sq mi): 731.64 (land 729.6; water 2.04).

Pop: 13,599 (White 56.2%; Black or African American 42.7%; Hispanic or Latino 0.8%; Asian 0.1%; Other 0.8%). **Foreign born:** 0.4%. **Median age:** 38.3. **State rank:** 62. **Pop change 1990-2000:** +2%.

Income: per capita $14,048; median household $26,033. **Pop below poverty level:** 22.6%.

Unemployment: 4.1%. **Median home value:** $54,100. **Median travel time to work:** 36.1 minutes.

ATTALA COUNTY

230 W Washington St **Ph:** 662-289-2921
Kosciusko, MS 39090 **Fax:** 662-289-7662

In central MS, southwest of Columbus; organized Dec 23, 1833 from Choctaw cession. **Name Origin:** Either from Cherokee *otale* 'mountain,' or *Attala*, an Indian heroine.

Area (sq mi): 737.1 (land 735.13; water 1.97).

Pop: 19,661 (White 57.8%; Black or African American 40%; Hispanic or Latino 1.4%; Asian 0.3%; Other 1.4%). **Foreign born:** 0.8%. **Median age:** 37.3. **State rank:** 49. **Pop change 1990-2000:** +6.4%.

Income: per capita $13,782; median household $24,794. **Pop below poverty level:** 21.8%.

Unemployment: 8%. **Median home value:** $49,900. **Median travel time to work:** 28.6 minutes.

BENTON COUNTY

PO Box 218 **Ph:** 662-224-6300
Ashland, MS 38603 **Fax:** 662-224-6303

On the central northern border of MS, southeast of Memphis, TN; organized Jul 21, 1870 from Marshall and Tippah counties. **Name Origin:** For Thomas Hart Benton (1782-1858), U.S. journalist and statesman; nicknamed 'Old Bullion' for championing the use of gold and silver currency rather than paper money.

Area (sq mi): 408.65 (land 406.79; water 1.86).

Pop: 8,026 (White 61.5%; Black or African American 36.8%; Hispanic or Latino 1%; Asian 0%; Other 1.5%). **Foreign born:** 0.7%. **Median age:** 35.6. **State rank:** 80. **Pop change 1990-2000:** -0.2%.

Please see sample entry on inside front cover for detailed information about the statistics presented with each county listing.

305

Income: per capita $12,212; median household $24,149. **Pop below poverty level:** 23.2%.

Unemployment: 6.3%. **Median home value:** $55,500. **Median travel time to work:** 32.9 minutes.

BOLIVAR COUNTY

200 Court St   **Ph:** 662-846-5877
Cleveland, MS 38732   **Fax:** 662-846-5880
www.co.bolivar.ms.us

On the northwestern border of MS, north of Greenville; organized Feb 9, 1836 from Choctaw cession. **Name Origin:** For Simon Bolivar (1783-1830), Venezuelan leader of South American revolt against Spanish rule; known as 'the Liberator' and 'George Washington to South America.'

Area (sq mi): 905.76 (land 876.28; water 29.47).

Pop: 40,633 (White 32.9%; Black or African American 65.1%; Hispanic or Latino 1.2%; Asian 0.5%; Other 1.2%). **Foreign born:** 0.5%. **Median age:** 29.8. **State rank:** 17. **Pop change 1990-2000:** -3%.

Income: per capita $12,088; median household $23,428. **Pop below poverty level:** 33.3%.

Unemployment: 7.3%. **Median home value:** $57,200. **Median travel time to work:** 19.7 minutes.

CALHOUN COUNTY

PO Box 8   **Ph:** 662-412-3117
Pittsboro, MS 38951   **Fax:** 662-412-3128

In north-central MS, northwest of Columbus; organized Mar 8, 1852 from Chickasaw, Lafayette, and Yalobusha counties. **Name Origin:** For John Caldwell Calhoun (1782-1850), U.S. statesman and champion of Southern causes.

Area (sq mi): 587.97 (land 586.54; water 1.43).

Pop: 15,069 (White 68.6%; Black or African American 28.7%; Hispanic or Latino 2.1%; Asian 0.1%; Other 1.8%). **Foreign born:** 1.6%. **Median age:** 37.4. **State rank:** 58. **Pop change 1990-2000:** +1.1%.

Income: per capita $15,106; median household $27,113. **Pop below poverty level:** 18.1%.

Unemployment: 10.4%. **Median home value:** $46,500. **Median travel time to work:** 24.9 minutes.

CARROLL COUNTY

PO Box 60   **Ph:** 662-237-9274
Carrollton, MS 38917   **Fax:** 662-237-9642

In north-central MS, east of Greenville; organized Dec 23, 1833 from Choctaw cession. **Name Origin:** For Charles Carroll (1737-1832), signer of the Declaration of Independence, U.S. senator from MD (1789-92), and founder of the Baltimore and Ohio Railroad.

Area (sq mi): 634.54 (land 627.73; water 6.81).

Pop: 10,769 (White 62.3%; Black or African American 36.6%; Hispanic or Latino 0.7%; Asian 0.2%; Other 0.6%). **Foreign born:** 0.8%. **Median age:** 38.1. **State rank:** 71. **Pop change 1990-2000:** +16.6%.

Income: per capita $15,744; median household $28,878. **Pop below poverty level:** 16%.

Unemployment: 6.9%. **Median home value:** $57,800. **Median travel time to work:** 30.9 minutes.

CHICKASAW COUNTY

County Courthouse 1 Pinson Sq   **Ph:** 662-456-2513
Houston, MS 38851   **Fax:** 662-456-5295

In east-central MS, northwest of Columbus; organized Feb 9, 1836 from Chickasaw cession of 1832. **Name Origin:** For the Indian tribe, closely connected with the Choctaw, of Muskhogean linguistic stock; meaning of name unknown.

Area (sq mi): 504.27 (land 501.56; water 2.71).

Pop: 19,440 (White 56%; Black or African American 41.3%; Hispanic or Latino 2.3%; Asian 0.2%; Other 1.7%). **Foreign born:** 1.3%. **Median age:** 34.4. **State rank:** 50. **Pop change 1990-2000:** +7.5%.

Income: per capita $13,279; median household $26,364. **Pop below poverty level:** 20%.

Unemployment: 14.5%. **Median home value:** $51,400. **Median travel time to work:** 23.3 minutes.

CHOCTAW COUNTY

PO Box 250   **Ph:** 662-285-6329
Ackerman, MS 39735   **Fax:** 662-285-3444

In east-central MS, west of Columbus; organized Dec 23, 1833 from Chickasaw cession of 1832. **Name Origin:** For the Indian tribe of Muskhogean linguistic stock; meaning of name unknown.

Area (sq mi): 419.81 (land 419.1; water 0.71).

Pop: 9,758 (White 67.8%; Black or African American 30.7%; Hispanic or Latino 0.8%; Asian 0.1%; Other 1.1%). **Foreign born:** 0.3%. **Median age:** 36.9. **State rank:** 76. **Pop change 1990-2000:** +7.6%.

Income: per capita $13,474; median household $27,020. **Pop below poverty level:** 24.7%.

Unemployment: 12%. **Median home value:** $55,300. **Median travel time to work:** 26.9 minutes.

CLAIBORNE COUNTY

410 Main St   **Ph:** 601-437-5841
Port Gibson, MS 39150   **Fax:** 601-437-4543

On the southwestern border of MS, south of Vicksburg; organized Jan 27, 1802 (prior to statehood) from Jefferson County. **Name Origin:** For William Charles Cole Claiborne (1775-1817), governor of the Mississippi Territory (1801-05), of the Orleans Territory (1804-12), and of LA (1812-16).

Area (sq mi): 501.36 (land 486.77; water 14.59).

Pop: 11,831 (White 15.1%; Black or African American 84.1%; Hispanic or Latino 0.8%; Asian 0.1%; Other 0.6%). **Foreign born:** 0.6%. **Median age:** 25.6. **State rank:** 69. **Pop change 1990-2000:** +4.1%.

Income: per capita $11,244; median household $22,615. **Pop below poverty level:** 32.4%.

All statistics are based on the 2000 Census except the dollar figures given for per capita income, which are based on 1999 estimates.

Unemployment: 9.4%. **Median home value:** $48,200. **Median travel time to work:** 30.7 minutes.

CLARKE COUNTY
PO Box 689   **Ph:** 601-776-2126
Quitman, MS 39355   **Fax:** 601-776-1001

On the central eastern border of MS, south of Meridian; organized Dec 10, 1812 (prior to statehood) from Choctaw cession. **Name Origin:** For Joshua G. Clarke, first chancellor of MS.

Area (sq mi): 693.41 (land 691.27; water 2.14).

Pop: 17,955 (White 64.1%; Black or African American 34.8%; Hispanic or Latino 0.7%; Asian 0.1%; Other 0.6%). **Foreign born:** 0.3%. **Median age:** 36.8. **State rank:** 55. **Pop change 1990-2000:** +3.7%.

Income: per capita $14,288; median household $26,610. **Pop below poverty level:** 23%.

Unemployment: 9.4%. **Median home value:** $53,600. **Median travel time to work:** 31.3 minutes.

CLAY COUNTY
PO Box 815   **Ph:** 662-494-3124
West Point, MS 39773   **Fax:** 662-492-4059

In east-central MS, northwest of Columbus; established as Colfax County May 12, 1871 from Chickasaw, Oktibbeha, and Lowndes counties; name changed Apr 10, 1876. **Name Origin:** For Henry Clay (1777-1852), U.S. senator from KY, known as the 'Great Pacificator' for his advocacy of compromise to avert national crises.

Area (sq mi): 416.02 (land 408.56; water 7.46).

Pop: 21,979 (White 42.5%; Black or African American 56.3%; Hispanic or Latino 0.9%; Asian 0.2%; Other 0.7%). **Foreign born:** 0.5%. **Median age:** 33.9. **State rank:** 42. **Pop change 1990-2000:** +4.1%.

Income: per capita $14,512; median household $27,372. **Pop below poverty level:** 23.5%.

Unemployment: 10.3%. **Median home value:** $60,900. **Median travel time to work:** 21.7 minutes.

COAHOMA COUNTY
PO Box 98   **Ph:** 662-624-3000
Clarksdale, MS 38614   **Fax:** 662-624-3040

On the northwestern border of MS, north of Greenville; organized Feb 9, 1836 from Chickasaw cession of 1836. **Name Origin:** For Sweet Coahoma, known also as Coahoma Sheriff, daughter of the last Choctaw in the area. The name means 'red panther.'

Area (sq mi): 583.14 (land 554.15; water 28.99).

Pop: 30,622 (White 29.1%; Black or African American 69.2%; Hispanic or Latino 0.9%; Asian 0.5%; Other 1%). **Foreign born:** 0.9%. **Median age:** 30.5. **State rank:** 29. **Pop change 1990-2000:** -3.3%.

Income: per capita $12,558; median household $22,338. **Pop below poverty level:** 35.9%.

Unemployment: 8.3%. **Median home value:** $51,200. **Median travel time to work:** 24 minutes.

COPIAH COUNTY
PO Box 507   **Ph:** 601-894-3021
Hazlehurst, MS 39083   **Fax:** 601-894-3026

In southwestern MS, southwest of Jackson; organized Jan 21, 1823 from Hinds County. **Name Origin:** From an Indian word, said to mean 'panther,' but uncertain. It is believed locally to mean 'clear water.'

Area (sq mi): 779.38 (land 776.6; water 2.78).

Pop: 28,757 (White 47.4%; Black or African American 51%; Hispanic or Latino 1.2%; Asian 0.2%; Other 1.1%). **Foreign born:** 0.8%. **Median age:** 34. **State rank:** 30. **Pop change 1990-2000:** +4.2%.

Income: per capita $12,408; median household $26,358. **Pop below poverty level:** 25.1%.

Unemployment: 6.2%. **Median home value:** $54,800. **Median travel time to work:** 29.3 minutes.

COVINGTON COUNTY
PO Box 1679   **Ph:** 601-765-4242
Collins, MS 39428   **Fax:** 601-765-1056

In south-central MS, west of Laurel; organized Feb 5, 1819 from Lawrence and Wayne counties. **Name Origin:** For Leonard Wales Covington (1768-1813), general in the War of 1812.

Area (sq mi): 414.94 (land 413.79; water 1.15).

Pop: 19,407 (White 63.1%; Black or African American 35.6%; Hispanic or Latino 0.8%; Asian 0.1%; Other 0.9%). **Foreign born:** 0.6%. **Median age:** 33.8. **State rank:** 51. **Pop change 1990-2000:** +17.4%.

Income: per capita $14,506; median household $26,669. **Pop below poverty level:** 23.5%.

Unemployment: 4.5%. **Median home value:** $55,000. **Median travel time to work:** 29.5 minutes.

DESOTO COUNTY
365 Losher St   **Ph:** 662-429-1460
Hernando, MS 38632   **Fax:** 662-429-4116
www.desotoms.com

In the northwestern corner of MS, south of Memphis, TN; organized Feb 9, 1836 from Indian lands. **Name Origin:** For Hernando De Soto (c.1500-42), Spanish explorer of southern U.S.

Area (sq mi): 496.77 (land 477.86; water 18.91).

Pop: 107,199 (White 84.7%; Black or African American 11.4%; Hispanic or Latino 2.3%; Asian 0.6%; Other 2.2%). **Foreign born:** 1.9%. **Median age:** 33.7. **State rank:** 5. **Pop change 1990-2000:** +57.9%.

Income: per capita $20,468; median household $48,206. **Pop below poverty level:** 7.1%.

Unemployment: 2.7%. **Median home value:** $103,100. **Median travel time to work:** 25.8 minutes.

Please see sample entry on inside front cover for detailed information about the statistics presented with each county listing.

FORREST COUNTY

630 N Main St   **Ph:** 601-582-3213
Hattiesburg, MS 39401   **Fax:** 601-545-6065
www.co.forrest.ms.us

In southeastern MS, southwest of Laurel; organized Apr 19, 1906 from Perry County. **Name Origin:** For Nathan Bedford Forrest (1821-77), Confederate general often quoted as saying 'Get there fustest with the mostest.'

Area (sq mi): 470.17 (land 466.58; water 3.59).

Pop: 72,604 (White 63.7%; Black or African American 33.6%; Hispanic or Latino 1.3%; Asian 0.7%; Other 1.4%). **Foreign born:** 2%. **Median age:** 29.7. **State rank:** 9. **Pop change 1990-2000:** +6.3%.

Income: per capita $15,160; median household $27,420. **Pop below poverty level:** 22.5%.

Unemployment: 3.4%. **Median home value:** $69,100. **Median travel time to work:** 21.6 minutes.

FRANKLIN COUNTY

PO Box 297   **Ph:** 601-384-2330
Meadville, MS 39653   **Fax:** 601-384-5864

In southwestern MS, east of Natchez; organized Dec 21, 1809 (prior to statehood) from Adams County. **Name Origin:** For Benjamin Franklin (1706-90), patriot, diplomat, and statesman.

Area (sq mi): 566.74 (land 564.6; water 2.14).

Pop: 8,448 (White 62.6%; Black or African American 36.3%; Hispanic or Latino 0.5%; Asian 0.1%; Other 0.8%). **Foreign born:** 0.3%. **Median age:** 37. **State rank:** 79. **Pop change 1990-2000:** +0.8%.

Income: per capita $13,643; median household $24,885. **Pop below poverty level:** 24.1%.

Unemployment: 8.2%. **Median home value:** $47,300. **Median travel time to work:** 32.7 minutes.

GEORGE COUNTY

355 Cox St Suite A   **Ph:** 601-947-4801
Lucedale, MS 39452   **Fax:** 601-947-1300

On the southeastern border of MS, north of Pascagoula; organized Mar 16, 1810 (prior to statehood) from Greene and Jackson counties. **Name Origin:** For Gen. James Zachariah George (1826-97), Confederate army officer and U.S. senator from MS (1881-97).

Area (sq mi): 483.63 (land 478.29; water 5.34).

Pop: 19,144 (White 88.7%; Black or African American 8.8%; Hispanic or Latino 1.6%; Asian 0.2%; Other 1.6%). **Foreign born:** 1.3%. **Median age:** 33.3. **State rank:** 53. **Pop change 1990-2000:** +14.8%.

Income: per capita $14,337; median household $34,730. **Pop below poverty level:** 16.7%.

Unemployment: 9.2%. **Median home value:** $66,500. **Median travel time to work:** 36.6 minutes.

GREENE COUNTY

PO Box 610   **Ph:** 601-394-2377
Leakesville, MS 39451   **Fax:** 601-394-4445

On the southeastern border of MS, east of Hattiesburg; organized Dec 9, 1811 (prior to statehood) from Amite, Franklin, and Wayne counties. **Name Origin:** For Gen. Nathanael Greene (1742-86), hero of the Revolutionary War, quartermaster general (1778-80), and commander of the Army of the South (1780).

Area (sq mi): 718.69 (land 712.82; water 5.87).

Pop: 13,299 (White 72.5%; Black or African American 26.2%; Hispanic or Latino 0.8%; Asian 0.1%; Other 0.9%). **Foreign born:** 0.3%. **Median age:** 32.4. **State rank:** 63. **Pop change 1990-2000:** +30.1%.

Income: per capita $11,868; median household $28,336. **Pop below poverty level:** 19.6%.

Unemployment: 8.6%. **Median home value:** $57,900. **Median travel time to work:** 42.1 minutes.

GRENADA COUNTY

PO Drawer 1208   **Ph:** 662-226-1821
Grenada, MS 38902   **Fax:** 662-227-2860

In north-central MS, northwest of Columbus; organized May 9, 1870 from Carroll and Tallahatchie counties. **Name Origin:** Believed to have been named for the island in the West Indies, chosen when the towns of Pittsburg and Tullohoma united after some years of rivalry. There is also a theory that it is a form of Granada, Spain.

Area (sq mi): 449.38 (land 421.79; water 27.58).

Pop: 23,263 (White 57.7%; Black or African American 40.9%; Hispanic or Latino 0.6%; Asian 0.3%; Other 0.7%). **Foreign born:** 1%. **Median age:** 35.7. **State rank:** 40. **Pop change 1990-2000:** +7.9%.

Income: per capita $13,786; median household $27,385. **Pop below poverty level:** 20.9%.

Unemployment: 6.9%. **Median home value:** $68,300. **Median travel time to work:** 20.1 minutes.

HANCOCK COUNTY

PO Box 550   **Ph:** 228-467-5404
Bay Saint Louis, MS 39520   **Fax:** 228-467-3159

In the southwestern corner of MS, west of Gulfport; organized Dec 18, 1812 (prior to statehood) from Mobile District. **Name Origin:** For John Hancock (1737-93), noted signer of the Declaration of Independence, governor of MA (1780-85; 1787-93), and statesman.

Area (sq mi): 552.53 (land 476.88; water 75.65).

Pop: 42,967 (White 88.9%; Black or African American 6.8%; Hispanic or Latino 1.8%; Asian 0.9%; Other 2%). **Foreign born:** 1.4%. **Median age:** 38.5. **State rank:** 15. **Pop change 1990-2000:** +35.3%.

Income: per capita $17,748; median household $35,202. **Pop below poverty level:** 14.4%.

Unemployment: 3.3%. **Median home value:** $92,500. **Median travel time to work:** 32.5 minutes.

HARRISON COUNTY

PO Drawer CC   **Ph:** 228-865-4036
Gulfport, MS 39502   **Fax:** 228-868-1480
www.co.harrison.ms.us

On the southern border of MS, west of Pascagoula; organized Feb 5, 1841 from Hancock and Jackson counties. **Name Origin:** For William Henry Harrison (1773-1841), ninth U.S. president.

All statistics are based on the 2000 Census except the dollar figures given for per capita income, which are based on 1999 estimates.

Area (sq mi): 976.15 (land 580.98; water 395.17).

Pop: 189,601 (White 71.8%; Black or African American 21.1%; Hispanic or Latino 2.6%; Asian 2.6%; Other 3.2%). **Foreign born:** 3.6%. **Median age:** 33.9. **State rank:** 2. **Pop change 1990-2000:** +14.7%.

Income: per capita $18,024; median household $35,624. **Pop below poverty level:** 14.6%.

Unemployment: 3.8%. **Median home value:** $87,200. **Median travel time to work:** 21.8 minutes.

HINDS COUNTY

316 S President St   **Ph:** 601-968-6501
Jackson, MS 39205   **Fax:** 601-968-6794
www.co.hinds.ms.us

In west-central MS, east of Vicksburg; organized Feb 12, 1821 from Choctaw cession. **Name Origin:** For Gen. Thomas Hinds (1780-1840), officer during the War of 1812 and U.S. representative from MS (1828-31).

Area (sq mi): 877.35 (land 869.18; water 8.16).

Pop: 250,800 (White 37%; Black or African American 61.1%; Hispanic or Latino 0.8%; Asian 0.6%; Other 0.9%). **Foreign born:** 1.1%. **Median age:** 31.9. **State rank:** 1. **Pop change 1990-2000:** -1.4%.

Income: per capita $17,785; median household $33,991. **Pop below poverty level:** 19.9%.

Unemployment: 4.2%. **Median home value:** $73,100. **Median travel time to work:** 21.6 minutes.

HOLMES COUNTY

PO Box 239   **Ph:** 662-834-2508
Lexington, MS 39095   **Fax:** 662-834-3020

In central MS, north of Jackson; organized Feb 19, 1833 from Yazoo County. **Name Origin:** For David Holmes (1769-1832), U.S. representative from VA (1797-1809), MS territorial governor (1809-17), state governor (1817-20; 1826), and U.S. senator (1820-25).

Area (sq mi): 764.18 (land 756; water 8.18).

Pop: 21,609 (White 20.3%; Black or African American 78.7%; Hispanic or Latino 0.9%; Asian 0.2%; Other 0.7%). **Foreign born:** 0.3%. **Median age:** 29.7. **State rank:** 44. **Pop change 1990-2000:** +0%.

Income: per capita $10,683; median household $17,235. **Pop below poverty level:** 41.1%.

Unemployment: 18%. **Median home value:** $44,900. **Median travel time to work:** 29.1 minutes.

HUMPHREYS COUNTY

PO Box 547   **Ph:** 662-247-1740
Belzoni, MS 39038   **Fax:** 662-247-0101

In west-central MS, southeast of Greenville; organized Mar 28, 1918 from Holmes, Washington, Yazoo, and Sunflower counties. **Name Origin:** For Benjamin Grubb Humphreys (1808-82), general in the Confederate army, MS legislator, and governor (1865-66).

Area (sq mi): 431.16 (land 418.09; water 13.07).

Pop: 11,206 (White 26.8%; Black or African American 71.5%; Hispanic or Latino 1.5%; Asian 0.3%; Other 1%). **Foreign born:** 0.8%. **Median age:** 30.5. **State rank:** 70. **Pop change 1990-2000:** -7.6%.

Income: per capita $10,926; median household $20,566. **Pop below poverty level:** 38.2%.

Unemployment: 12.8%. **Median home value:** $49,600. **Median travel time to work:** 19.6 minutes.

ISSAQUENA COUNTY

PO Box 27   **Ph:** 662-873-2761
Mayersville, MS 39113   **Fax:** 662-873-2061

On the central western border of MS, north of Vicksburg; organized Jan 23, 1844 from Washington County. **Name Origin:** From the Choctaw word probably meaning 'deer's head.'

Area (sq mi): 441.36 (land 413.06; water 28.3).

Pop: 2,274 (White 36.1%; Black or African American 62.8%; Hispanic or Latino 0.4%; Asian 0%; Other 0.9%). **Foreign born:** 0.2%. **Median age:** 33.1. **State rank:** 82. **Pop change 1990-2000:** +19.1%.

Income: per capita $10,581; median household $19,936. **Pop below poverty level:** 33.2%.

Unemployment: 17.7%. **Median home value:** $58,600. **Median travel time to work:** 23.4 minutes.

ITAWAMBA COUNTY

PO Box 776   **Ph:** 662-862-3421
Fulton, MS 38843   **Fax:** 662-862-3421

On the northeastern border of MS, north of Columbus; organized Feb 9, 1836 from Indian lands. **Name Origin:** For the personal name of an Indian chief; meaning uncertain.

Area (sq mi): 540.42 (land 532.31; water 8.11).

Pop: 22,770 (White 92%; Black or African American 6.5%; Hispanic or Latino 1%; Asian 0.2%; Other 0.8%). **Foreign born:** 0.6%. **Median age:** 36.2. **State rank:** 41. **Pop change 1990-2000:** +13.8%.

Income: per capita $14,956; median household $31,156. **Pop below poverty level:** 14%.

Unemployment: 4.7%. **Median home value:** $58,600. **Median travel time to work:** 27.2 minutes.

JACKSON COUNTY

PO Box 998   **Ph:** 228-769-3089
Pascagoula, MS 39568   **Fax:** 228-769-3348
www.co.jackson.ms.us

In the southeastern corner of MS, east of Biloxi; organized Dec 18, 1812 (prior to statehood) from Mobile District. **Name Origin:** For Andrew Jackson (1767-1845), seventh U.S. president.

Area (sq mi): 1043.3 (land 726.9; water 316.4).

Pop: 131,420 (White 74.2%; Black or African American 20.9%; Hispanic or Latino 2.1%; Asian 1.6%; Other 2.1%). **Foreign born:** 2.7%. **Median age:** 34.7. **State rank:** 3. **Pop change 1990-2000:** +14%.

Income: per capita $17,768; median household $39,118. **Pop below poverty level:** 12.7%.

Please see sample entry on inside front cover for detailed information about the statistics presented with each county listing.

Unemployment: 4.8%. **Median home value:** $80,300. **Median travel time to work:** 23.7 minutes.

JASPER COUNTY

PO Box 1047
Bay Springs, MS 39422

Ph: 601-764-3368
Fax: 601-764-3999

In east-central MS, north of Laurel; organized Dec 23, 1833 from Indian lands. **Name Origin:** For Sgt. William Jasper (1750-79), American Revolutionary War soldier from SC.

Area (sq mi): 677.44 (land 676; water 1.44).

Pop: 18,149 (White 46.2%; Black or African American 52.9%; Hispanic or Latino 0.6%; Asian 0.1%; Other 0.6%). **Foreign born:** 0.3%. **Median age:** 35.1. **State rank:** 54. **Pop change 1990-2000:** +6%.

Income: per capita $12,889; median household $24,441. **Pop below poverty level:** 22.7%.

Unemployment: 4.8%. **Median home value:** $51,200. **Median travel time to work:** 27.8 minutes.

JEFFERSON COUNTY

PO Box 145
Fayette, MS 39069

Ph: 601-786-3021
Fax: 601-786-6009

On the southwestern border of MS, north of Natchez; organized Apr 2, 1799 (prior to statehood) from Pickering County. **Name Origin:** For Thomas Jefferson (1743-1826), U.S. patriot and statesman; third U.S. president.

Area (sq mi): 527.19 (land 519.39; water 7.81).

Pop: 9,740 (White 13%; Black or African American 86.5%; Hispanic or Latino 0.7%; Asian 0.1%; Other 0.3%). **Foreign born:** 0.3%. **Median age:** 32.4. **State rank:** 77. **Pop change 1990-2000:** +12.6%.

Income: per capita $9,709; median household $18,447. **Pop below poverty level:** 36%.

Unemployment: 17.3%. **Median home value:** $48,700. **Median travel time to work:** 33 minutes.

JEFFERSON DAVIS COUNTY

PO Box 1137
Prentiss, MS 39474

Ph: 601-792-4204
Fax: 601-792-2894

In south-central MS, northwest of Hattiesburg; organized Mar 31, 1906 from Covington and Lawrence counties. **Name Origin:** For Jefferson Davis (1808-89), president of the Confederate States of America (1862-65).

Area (sq mi): 409.1 (land 408.41; water 0.7).

Pop: 13,962 (White 41.4%; Black or African American 57.4%; Hispanic or Latino 0.8%; Asian 0.2%; Other 0.8%). **Foreign born:** 0.3%. **Median age:** 35. **State rank:** 60. **Pop change 1990-2000:** -0.6%.

Income: per capita $11,974; median household $21,834. **Pop below poverty level:** 28.2%.

Unemployment: 10.6%. **Median home value:** $47,700. **Median travel time to work:** 37.2 minutes.

JONES COUNTY

PO Box 1468
Laurel, MS 39441

Ph: 601-428-0527

In east-central MS, north of Hattiesburg; organized Jan 24, 1826 from Covington and Wayne counties. **Name Origin:** For John Paul Jones (1747-92), commander of the *Bonhomme Richard* in its victory over the British ship *Serapis* during the American Revolution. He later served as an admiral in the Russian Navy.

Area (sq mi): 699.73 (land 693.82; water 5.91).

Pop: 64,958 (White 70.7%; Black or African American 26.3%; Hispanic or Latino 2%; Asian 0.3%; Other 2.3%). **Foreign born:** 2%. **Median age:** 35.8. **State rank:** 10. **Pop change 1990-2000:** +4.7%.

Income: per capita $14,820; median household $28,786. **Pop below poverty level:** 19.8%.

Unemployment: 3.3%. **Median home value:** $59,000. **Median travel time to work:** 22.7 minutes.

KEMPER COUNTY

PO Box 188
De Kalb, MS 39328

Ph: 601-743-2460
Fax: 601-743-2789

On the central eastern border of MS, north of Meridian; organized Dec 23, 1833 from Indian lands. **Name Origin:** For Reuben Kemper (?-1827), hero of the Florida and Mexican Wars.

Area (sq mi): 767 (land 766.13; water 0.87).

Pop: 10,453 (White 38.9%; Black or African American 58.1%; Hispanic or Latino 0.7%; Asian 0.1%; Other 2.8%). **Foreign born:** 0.4%. **Median age:** 35.2. **State rank:** 72. **Pop change 1990-2000:** +0.9%.

Income: per capita $11,985; median household $23,998. **Pop below poverty level:** 26%.

Unemployment: 8.9%. **Median home value:** $48,400. **Median travel time to work:** 33.5 minutes.

LAFAYETTE COUNTY

PO Box 1240
Oxford, MS 38655

Ph: 662-234-7563
Fax: 662-234-5038

In north-central MS, southeast of Memphis, TN; organized Feb 9, 1836 from Chickasaw cession of 1832. **Name Origin:** For the Marquis de Lafayette (1757-1834), French statesman and soldier who fought with Ameicans during the Revolutionary War.

Area (sq mi): 679.29 (land 631.11; water 48.17).

Pop: 38,744 (White 71.3%; Black or African American 25%; Hispanic or Latino 1.1%; Asian 1.7%; Other 1.4%). **Foreign born:** 2.4%. **Median age:** 26.9. **State rank:** 20. **Pop change 1990-2000:** +21.7%.

Income: per capita $16,406; median household $28,517. **Pop below poverty level:** 21.3%.

Unemployment: 2.2%. **Median home value:** $101,100. **Median travel time to work:** 19 minutes.

All statistics are based on the 2000 Census except the dollar figures given for per capita income, which are based on 1999 estimates.

LAMAR COUNTY

PO Box 247   **Ph:** 601-794-8504
Purvis, MS 39475   **Fax:** 601-794-3903
www.lamarcounty.com

In south-central MS, west of Hattiesburg; organized Feb 19, 1904 from Marion and Pearl River counties. **Name Origin:** For Lucius Quintus Cincinnatus Lamar (1825-93), U.S. statesman and a justice of the U.S. Supreme Court (1888-93).

Area (sq mi): 500.49 (land 497.07; water 3.42).

Pop: 39,070 (White 84.7%; Black or African American 12.9%; Hispanic or Latino 1.1%; Asian 0.7%; Other 1.1%). **Foreign born:** 1.1%. **Median age:** 32.6. **State rank:** 18. **Pop change 1990-2000:** +28.4%.

Income: per capita $18,849; median household $37,628. **Pop below poverty level:** 13.3%.

Unemployment: 2.6%. **Median home value:** $93,000. **Median travel time to work:** 25.1 minutes.

LAUDERDALE COUNTY

PO Box 1587   **Ph:** 601-482-9714
Meridian, MS 39301   **Fax:** 601-486-4943
www.lauderdalecounty.org

On the central eastern border of MS, south of Columbus; organized Dec 23, 1833 from Choctaw cession. **Name Origin:** For Col. James Lauderdale (?-1814), soldier killed at the Battle of New Orleans during the War of 1812.

Area (sq mi): 715.28 (land 703.51; water 11.77).

Pop: 78,161 (White 59.6%; Black or African American 38.2%; Hispanic or Latino 1.1%; Asian 0.5%; Other 1.1%). **Foreign born:** 0.7%. **Median age:** 35. **State rank:** 6. **Pop change 1990-2000:** +3.4%.

Income: per capita $16,026; median household $30,768. **Pop below poverty level:** 20.8%.

Unemployment: 5.2%. **Median home value:** $67,600. **Median travel time to work:** 21.3 minutes.

LAWRENCE COUNTY

PO Box 821   **Ph:** 601-587-7162
Monticello, MS 39654   **Fax:** 601-587-0767

In south-central MS, south of Jackson; organized Dec 22, 1814 (prior to statehood) from Marion County. **Name Origin:** For Capt. James Lawrence (1781-1813), U.S. Navy commander in War of 1812 who said, 'Don't give up the ship!'

Area (sq mi): 435.73 (land 430.63; water 5.11).

Pop: 13,258 (White 66.6%; Black or African American 32.1%; Hispanic or Latino 0.7%; Asian 0.3%; Other 0.7%). **Foreign born:** 0.6%. **Median age:** 35.8. **State rank:** 64. **Pop change 1990-2000:** +6.4%.

Income: per capita $14,469; median household $28,495. **Pop below poverty level:** 19.6%.

Unemployment: 9.3%. **Median home value:** $56,400. **Median travel time to work:** 36.7 minutes.

LEAKE COUNTY

PO Box 72   **Ph:** 601-267-7372
Carthage, MS 39051   **Fax:** 601-267-6137

In central MS, northeast of Jackson; organized Dec 23, 1833 from Choctaw cession of 1830. **Name Origin:** For Walter Leake (1762-1825), VA legislator, judge of the MS Territory (1807), U.S. senator from MS (1817-20), and governor (1822-25).

Area (sq mi): 585.39 (land 582.71; water 2.68).

Pop: 20,940 (White 55.5%; Black or African American 37.4%; Hispanic or Latino 2.1%; Asian 0.1%; Other 6.3%). **Foreign born:** 1.4%. **Median age:** 34.8. **State rank:** 46. **Pop change 1990-2000:** +13.6%.

Income: per capita $13,365; median household $27,055. **Pop below poverty level:** 23.3%.

Unemployment: 5.4%. **Median home value:** $53,000. **Median travel time to work:** 32.6 minutes.

LEE COUNTY

PO Box 7127   **Ph:** 662-841-9100
Tupelo, MS 38802   **Fax:** 662-680-6091

In northeastern MS, north of Columbus; organized Oct 26, 1866 from Itawamba and Pontotoc counties. **Name Origin:** For Robert E. Lee (1807-70), American general and commander in chief of the Confederate forces during the Civil War.

Area (sq mi): 453.14 (land 449.59; water 3.55).

Pop: 75,755 (White 73.1%; Black or African American 24.5%; Hispanic or Latino 1.2%; Asian 0.5%; Other 1.2%). **Foreign born:** 1.1%. **Median age:** 34.6. **State rank:** 7. **Pop change 1990-2000:** +15.5%.

Income: per capita $18,956; median household $36,165. **Pop below poverty level:** 13.4%.

Unemployment: 4.5%. **Median home value:** $85,500. **Median travel time to work:** 19.3 minutes.

LEFLORE COUNTY

306 W Market St   **Ph:** 662-453-1041
Greenwood, MS 38930   **Fax:** 662-455-7965

In west-central MS, northeast of Greenville; organized Mar 15, 1871 from Carroll and Sunflower counties. **Name Origin:** For Greenwood LeFlore (1800-65), leader of a prominent Choctaw family of French ancestry, landowner, and legislator.

Area (sq mi): 606.35 (land 591.93; water 14.42).

Pop: 37,947 (White 29.6%; Black or African American 67.7%; Hispanic or Latino 1.9%; Asian 0.6%; Other 1.6%). **Foreign born:** 1.1%. **Median age:** 30.1. **State rank:** 22. **Pop change 1990-2000:** +1.6%.

Income: per capita $12,553; median household $21,518. **Pop below poverty level:** 34.8%.

Unemployment: 10%. **Median home value:** $56,800. **Median travel time to work:** 18 minutes.

Please see sample entry on inside front cover for detailed information about the statistics presented with each county listing.

LINCOLN COUNTY

PO Box 555   **Ph:** 601-835-3479
Brookhaven, MS 39602   **Fax:** 601-835-3423

In southwestern MS, east of Natchez; organized Apr 7, 1870 from Amite, Pike, Lawrence, and Franklin counties. **Name Origin:** For Abraham Lincoln (1809-65), sixteenth U.S. president.

Area (sq mi): 588.17 (land 585.71; water 2.47).

Pop: 33,166 (White 68.9%; Black or African American 29.7%; Hispanic or Latino 0.7%; Asian 0.2%; Other 0.8%). **Foreign born:** 0.6%. **Median age:** 35.8. **State rank:** 28. **Pop change 1990-2000:** +9.5%.

Income: per capita $13,961; median household $27,279. **Pop below poverty level:** 19.2%.

Unemployment: 4.9%. **Median home value:** $64,400. **Median travel time to work:** 30.5 minutes.

LOWNDES COUNTY

505 2nd Ave N   **Ph:** 662-329-5888
Columbus, MS 39701   **Fax:** 662-329-5870

On the central eastern border of MS, north of Meridian; organized Jan 30, 1830 from Monroe County. **Name Origin:** For William Jones Lowndes (1782-1822), SC legislator and U.S. representative (1811-22).

Area (sq mi): 516.45 (land 502.3; water 14.15).

Pop: 61,586 (White 56%; Black or African American 41.6%; Hispanic or Latino 1.1%; Asian 0.5%; Other 1.5%). **Foreign born:** 1.3%. **Median age:** 32.7. **State rank:** 12. **Pop change 1990-2000:** +3.8%.

Income: per capita $16,514; median household $32,123. **Pop below poverty level:** 21.3%.

Unemployment: 7.2%. **Median home value:** $74,700. **Median travel time to work:** 21.1 minutes.

MADISON COUNTY

PO Box 404   **Ph:** 601-859-1177
Canton, MS 39046   **Fax:** 601-859-5875
www.madison-co.com

In central MS, north of Jackson; organized Jan 29, 1828 from Yazoo County. **Name Origin:** For James Madison (1751-1836), fourth U.S. president.

Area (sq mi): 741.97 (land 717.11; water 24.86).

Pop: 74,674 (White 59.7%; Black or African American 37.5%; Hispanic or Latino 1%; Asian 1.3%; Other 0.9%). **Foreign born:** 1.7%. **Median age:** 33.4. **State rank:** 8. **Pop change 1990-2000:** +38.8%.

Income: per capita $23,469; median household $46,970. **Pop below poverty level:** 14%.

Unemployment: 3.2%. **Median home value:** $117,000. **Median travel time to work:** 24.5 minutes.

MARION COUNTY

250 Broad St Suite 2   **Ph:** 601-736-2691
Columbia, MS 39429   **Fax:** 601-444-0206

On the central southern border of MS, west of Hattiesburg; organized Dec 9, 1811 (prior to statehood) from Amite, Wayne, and Franklin counties. **Name Origin:** For Gen. Francis Marion (c.1732-95), SC soldier and legislator, known as 'The Swamp Fox' for his tactics during the Revolutionary War.

Area (sq mi): 548.58 (land 542.34; water 6.24).

Pop: 25,595 (White 66.7%; Black or African American 31.9%; Hispanic or Latino 0.6%; Asian 0.2%; Other 0.9%). **Foreign born:** 0.8%. **Median age:** 35.1. **State rank:** 36. **Pop change 1990-2000:** +0.2%.

Income: per capita $12,301; median household $24,555. **Pop below poverty level:** 24.8%.

Unemployment: 5.3%. **Median home value:** $57,600. **Median travel time to work:** 34.8 minutes.

MARSHALL COUNTY

PO Box 219   **Ph:** 662-252-4431
Holly Springs, MS 38635   **Fax:** 662-252-0004

On central northern border of MS, southeast of Memphis, TN; organized Feb 9, 1836 from Indian lands. **Name Origin:** For John Marshall (1755-1835), American jurist; fourth Chief Justice of the U.S. Supreme Court (1801-35).

Area (sq mi): 709.8 (land 706.33; water 3.47).

Pop: 34,993 (White 47.9%; Black or African American 50.4%; Hispanic or Latino 1.2%; Asian 0.1%; Other 1.2%). **Foreign born:** 1%. **Median age:** 33.9. **State rank:** 23. **Pop change 1990-2000:** +15.3%.

Income: per capita $14,028; median household $28,756. **Pop below poverty level:** 21.9%.

Unemployment: 7.7%. **Median home value:** $67,400. **Median travel time to work:** 30.8 minutes.

MONROE COUNTY

PO Box 578   **Ph:** 662-369-8143
Aberdeen, MS 39730   **Fax:** 662-369-7928

On the central eastern border of MS, north of Columbus; organized Feb 9, 1821 from Chickasaw cession of 1821. **Name Origin:** For James Monroe (1758-1831), fifth U.S. president.

Area (sq mi): 772.04 (land 764.17; water 7.87).

Pop: 38,014 (White 68%; Black or African American 30.8%; Hispanic or Latino 0.7%; Asian 0.2%; Other 0.7%). **Foreign born:** 0.6%. **Median age:** 35.7. **State rank:** 21. **Pop change 1990-2000:** +3.9%.

Income: per capita $14,072; median household $30,307. **Pop below poverty level:** 17.2%.

Unemployment: 10.7%. **Median home value:** $64,200. **Median travel time to work:** 25.7 minutes.

MONTGOMERY COUNTY

PO Box 71   **Ph:** 662-283-2333
Winona, MS 38967   **Fax:** 662-283-2233

In central MS, west of Columbus; organized May 13, 1871 from Carroll and Choctaw counties. **Name Origin:** For Gen. Richard Montgomery (1736-75), American Revolutionary War officer who captured Montreal, Canada.

Area (sq mi): 407.86 (land 406.85; water 1.02).

All statistics are based on the 2000 Census except the dollar figures given for per capita income, which are based on 1999 estimates.

Pop: 12,189 (White 53.9%; Black or African American 45%; Hispanic or Latino 0.8%; Asian 0.3%; Other 0.6%). **Foreign born:** 0.2%. **Median age:** 37.3. **State rank:** 67. **Pop change 1990-2000:** -1.6%.

Income: per capita $14,040; median household $25,270. **Pop below poverty level:** 24.3%.

Unemployment: 9.6%. **Median home value:** $51,000. **Median travel time to work:** 25.4 minutes.

NESHOBA COUNTY
401 Beacon St Suite 107   **Ph:** 601-656-3581
Philadelphia, MS 39350   **Fax:** 601-650-3280

In east-central MS, northwest of Meridian; organized Dec 23, 1833 from Choctaw cession in 1830. **Name Origin:** Choctaw, probably 'wolf,' but debatable.

Area (sq mi): 571.64 (land 570; water 1.64).

Pop: 28,684 (White 64.9%; Black or African American 19.3%; Hispanic or Latino 1.2%; Asian 0.2%; Other 14.9%). **Foreign born:** 0.8%. **Median age:** 34.7. **State rank:** 31. **Pop change 1990-2000:** +15.7%.

Income: per capita $14,964; median household $28,300. **Pop below poverty level:** 21%.

Unemployment: 4.8%. **Median home value:** $55,800. **Median travel time to work:** 24.1 minutes.

NEWTON COUNTY
PO Box 68   **Ph:** 601-635-2368
Decatur, MS 39327

In east-central MS, west of Meridian; organized Feb 25, 1836 from Neshoba County. **Name Origin:** For Sir Isaac Newton (1642-1727), English mathematician and natural philosopher, formulator of the law of gravitation.

Area (sq mi): 579.58 (land 578.03; water 1.55).

Pop: 21,838 (White 64.5%; Black or African American 30.4%; Hispanic or Latino 0.9%; Asian 0.2%; Other 4.4%). **Foreign born:** 0.5%. **Median age:** 35.1. **State rank:** 43. **Pop change 1990-2000:** +7.6%.

Income: per capita $14,008; median household $28,735. **Pop below poverty level:** 19.9%.

Unemployment: 5.7%. **Median home value:** $54,300. **Median travel time to work:** 24.1 minutes.

NOXUBEE COUNTY
PO Box 147   **Ph:** 662-726-4243
Macon, MS 39341

On the central eastern border of MS, south of Columbus; organized Dec 23, 1833 for Choctaw cession in 1830. **Name Origin:** For the Noxubee River, which runs through it; from Choctaw probably 'stinking water.'

Area (sq mi): 700.05 (land 694.79; water 5.26).

Pop: 12,548 (White 29.2%; Black or African American 69.3%; Hispanic or Latino 1.1%; Asian 0.1%; Other 1.2%). **Foreign born:** 1%. **Median age:** 32.3. **State rank:** 66. **Pop change 1990-2000:** -0.4%.

Income: per capita $12,018; median household $22,330. **Pop below poverty level:** 32.8%.

Unemployment: 11.3%. **Median home value:** $46,800. **Median travel time to work:** 23.3 minutes.

OKTIBBEHA COUNTY
101 E Main St   **Ph:** 662-323-5834
Starkville, MS 39759   **Fax:** 662-338-1065
www.eda.co.oktibbeha.ms.us

In east-central MS, west of Columbus; organized Dec 23, 1833 from Choctaw cession 1830. **Name Origin:** For Choctaw, locally believed to mean 'pure water.'

Area (sq mi): 461.9 (land 457.71; water 4.19).

Pop: 42,902 (White 58.2%; Black or African American 37.4%; Hispanic or Latino 1.1%; Asian 2.5%; Other 1.4%). **Foreign born:** 3.3%. **Median age:** 24.8. **State rank:** 16. **Pop change 1990-2000:** +11.8%.

Income: per capita $14,998; median household $24,899. **Pop below poverty level:** 28.2%.

Unemployment: 3.1%. **Median home value:** $89,400. **Median travel time to work:** 17.5 minutes.

PANOLA COUNTY
151 Public Sq   **Ph:** 662-563-6205
Batesville, MS 38606   **Fax:** 662-563-6277

In northwestern MS, south of Memphis, TN; organized Feb 9, 1836 from Indian lands. **Name Origin:** From the Choctaw word probably meaning 'cotton.'

Area (sq mi): 705.13 (land 684.2; water 20.94).

Pop: 34,274 (White 50.2%; Black or African American 48.4%; Hispanic or Latino 1.1%; Asian 0.2%; Other 1%). **Foreign born:** 0.6%. **Median age:** 33. **State rank:** 27. **Pop change 1990-2000:** +14.3%.

Income: per capita $13,075; median household $26,785. **Pop below poverty level:** 25.3%.

Unemployment: 10.2%. **Median home value:** $57,700. **Median travel time to work:** 27.2 minutes.

PEARL RIVER COUNTY
PO Box 431   **Ph:** 601-795-2237
Poplarville, MS 39470   **Fax:** 601-795-3093

In south-central MS, northwest of Biloxi; organized Feb 22, 1890 from Hancock and Marion counties. **Name Origin:** For the river, which flows through the county.

Area (sq mi): 818.93 (land 811.33; water 7.6).

Pop: 48,621 (White 84.7%; Black or African American 12.2%; Hispanic or Latino 1.4%; Asian 0.3%; Other 1.9%). **Foreign born:** 1.2%. **Median age:** 35.9. **State rank:** 14. **Pop change 1990-2000:** +25.6%.

Income: per capita $15,160; median household $30,912. **Pop below poverty level:** 18.4%.

Unemployment: 3.4%. **Median home value:** $76,500. **Median travel time to work:** 36.4 minutes.

Please see sample entry on inside front cover for detailed information about the statistics presented with each county listing.

PERRY COUNTY

PO Box 198   **Ph:** 601-964-8398
New Augusta, MS 39462   **Fax:** 601-964-8746

In southeastern MS, southeast of Hattiesburg; organized Feb 3, 1820 from Greene County. **Name Origin:** For Oliver Hazard Perry (1785-1819), U.S. naval officer during the War of 1812, famous for the message, 'We have met the enemy and they are ours.'

Area (sq mi): 650.2 (land 647.18; water 3.02).

Pop: 12,138 (White 75.7%; Black or African American 22.6%; Hispanic or Latino 1%; Asian 0.1%; Other 1.1%). **Foreign born:** 0.5%. **Median age:** 33.5. **State rank:** 68. **Pop change 1990-2000:** +11.7%.

Income: per capita $12,837; median household $27,189. **Pop below poverty level:** 22%.

Unemployment: 6.8%. **Median home value:** $56,100. **Median travel time to work:** 36.1 minutes.

PIKE COUNTY

PO Box 309   **Ph:** 601-783-3363
Magnolia, MS 39652   **Fax:** 601-783-5982

On the central southern border of MS; organized Dec 9, 1815 (prior to statehood) from Marion County. **Name Origin:** For Zebulon Montgomery Pike (1779-1813), U.S. army officer and discoverer of Pikes Peak in CO.

Area (sq mi): 410.78 (land 408.89; water 1.89).

Pop: 38,940 (White 51%; Black or African American 47.5%; Hispanic or Latino 0.7%; Asian 0.3%; Other 0.9%). **Foreign born:** 0.9%. **Median age:** 35.2. **State rank:** 19. **Pop change 1990-2000:** +5.6%.

Income: per capita $14,040; median household $24,562. **Pop below poverty level:** 25.3%.

Unemployment: 5.9%. **Median home value:** $59,700. **Median travel time to work:** 26.4 minutes.

PONTOTOC COUNTY

PO Box 209   **Ph:** 662-489-3900
Pontotoc, MS 38863   **Fax:** 662-489-3940

In north-central MS, northwest of Columbus; organized Feb 9, 1836 from Chickasaw cession. **Name Origin:** From the Chickasaw term probably meaning 'cattails growing on the prairie.'

Area (sq mi): 500.99 (land 497.35; water 3.64).

Pop: 26,726 (White 83.6%; Black or African American 14%; Hispanic or Latino 1.8%; Asian 0.1%; Other 1.5%). **Foreign born:** 1.1%. **Median age:** 34.8. **State rank:** 35. **Pop change 1990-2000:** +20.2%.

Income: per capita $15,658; median household $32,055. **Pop below poverty level:** 13.8%.

Unemployment: 5.1%. **Median home value:** $66,400. **Median travel time to work:** 23.3 minutes.

PRENTISS COUNTY

PO Box 477   **Ph:** 662-728-8151
Booneville, MS 38829   **Fax:** 662-728-2007

In northeastern MS, south of Corinth; organized Apr 15, 1870 from

Tishomingo County. **Name Origin:** For Seargeant Smith Prentiss (1808-50), MS legislator and U.S. representative (1838-39).

Area (sq mi): 418.24 (land 414.93; water 3.32).

Pop: 25,556 (White 85.5%; Black or African American 12.9%; Hispanic or Latino 0.7%; Asian 0.2%; Other 1.1%). **Foreign born:** 0.4%. **Median age:** 35. **State rank:** 37. **Pop change 1990-2000:** +9.8%.

Income: per capita $14,131; median household $28,446. **Pop below poverty level:** 16.5%.

Unemployment: 4.7%. **Median home value:** $56,400. **Median travel time to work:** 22.8 minutes.

QUITMAN COUNTY

230 Chestnut St County Courthouse   **Ph:** 662-326-2661
Marks, MS 38646   **Fax:** 662-326-8004

In northwestern MS, southwest of Memphis, TN; organized Feb 1, 1877 from Panola and Coahoma counties. **Name Origin:** For John Anthony Quitman (1799-1858), tenth and sixteenth governor of MS (1835-36; 1850-51) and U.S. representative (1855-58).

Area (sq mi): 406.49 (land 404.84; water 1.66).

Pop: 10,117 (White 30.3%; Black or African American 68.6%; Hispanic or Latino 0.5%; Asian 0.2%; Other 0.7%). **Foreign born:** 0.2%. **Median age:** 31.8. **State rank:** 75. **Pop change 1990-2000:** -3.6%.

Income: per capita $10,817; median household $20,636. **Pop below poverty level:** 33.1%.

Unemployment: 11.6%. **Median home value:** $37,100. **Median travel time to work:** 27.8 minutes.

RANKIN COUNTY

PO Box 1599   **Ph:** 601-825-1466
Brandon, MS 39043   **Fax:** 601-825-1465
www.rankincounty.org

In central MS, east of Jackson; organized Feb 4, 1828 from Hinds County. **Name Origin:** For Christopher Rankin (1788-1826), MS legislator and U.S. representative (1819-26).

Area (sq mi): 806.09 (land 774.52; water 31.57).

Pop: 115,327 (White 80.3%; Black or African American 17.1%; Hispanic or Latino 1.3%; Asian 0.7%; Other 1.2%). **Foreign born:** 1.6%. **Median age:** 34.6. **State rank:** 4. **Pop change 1990-2000:** +32.3%.

Income: per capita $20,412; median household $44,946. **Pop below poverty level:** 9.5%.

Unemployment: 2.5%. **Median home value:** $98,600. **Median travel time to work:** 25.5 minutes.

SCOTT COUNTY

PO Box 630   **Ph:** 601-469-1922
Forest, MS 39074   **Fax:** 601-469-5180

In central MS, east of Jackson; organized Dec 23, 1833 from Choctaw cession in 1832. **Name Origin:** For Abram M. Scott (?-1833), governor of MS (1832-33).

Area (sq mi): 610.38 (land 609.08; water 1.3).

All statistics are based on the 2000 Census except the dollar figures given for per capita income, which are based on 1999 estimates.

Pop: 28,423 (White 54.7%; Black or African American 38.9%; Hispanic or Latino 5.8%; Asian 0.2%; Other 3.7%). **Foreign born:** 4.2%. **Median age:** 33.8. **State rank:** 32. **Pop change 1990-2000:** +17.8%.

Income: per capita $14,013; median household $26,686. **Pop below poverty level:** 20.7%.

Unemployment: 4.5%. **Median home value:** $48,200. **Median travel time to work:** 27.2 minutes.

SHARKEY COUNTY
PO Box 218   **Ph:** 662-873-2755
Rolling Fork, MS 39159   **Fax:** 662-873-6045

In central western MS, north of Vicksburg; organized Mar 29, 1876 from Warren, Washington, and Issaquena counties. **Name Origin:** For William Lewis Sharkey (1798-1873), MS legislator, circuit court judge (1832), and provisional governor (1865).

Area (sq mi): 434.88 (land 427.71; water 7.17).

Pop: 6,580 (White 29%; Black or African American 69.3%; Hispanic or Latino 1.3%; Asian 0.3%; Other 1.1%). **Foreign born:** 0.4%. **Median age:** 30.8. **State rank:** 81. **Pop change 1990-2000:** -6.9%.

Income: per capita $11,396; median household $22,285. **Pop below poverty level:** 38.3%.

Unemployment: 13%. **Median home value:** $49,300. **Median travel time to work:** 24.2 minutes.

SIMPSON COUNTY
PO Box 367   **Ph:** 601-847-2626
Mendenhall, MS 39114   **Fax:** 601-847-7004

In south-central MS, south of Jackson; organized Jan 23, 1824 from Copiah County. **Name Origin:** For Josiah Simpson, a judge in the Mississippi Territory.

Area (sq mi): 590.53 (land 588.73; water 1.8).

Pop: 27,639 (White 64%; Black or African American 34.3%; Hispanic or Latino 1.2%; Asian 0.1%; Other 1.2%). **Foreign born:** 0.9%. **Median age:** 35. **State rank:** 34. **Pop change 1990-2000:** +15.4%.

Income: per capita $13,344; median household $28,343. **Pop below poverty level:** 21.6%.

Unemployment: 4.3%. **Median home value:** $58,800. **Median travel time to work:** 32.8 minutes.

SMITH COUNTY
PO Box 517   **Ph:** 601-782-4751
Raleigh, MS 39153   **Fax:** 601-782-4007

In east-central MS, southeast of Jackson; organized Dec 23, 1833 from Indian lands. **Name Origin:** For a David Smith; other information has been lost.

Area (sq mi): 637.27 (land 635.89; water 1.38).

Pop: 16,182 (White 75.8%; Black or African American 23.1%; Hispanic or Latino 0.6%; Asian 0.1%; Other 0.7%). **Foreign born:** 0.5%. **Median age:** 35.6. **State rank:** 56. **Pop change 1990-2000:** +9.4%.

Income: per capita $14,752; median household $30,840. **Pop below poverty level:** 16.9%.

Unemployment: 5.3%. **Median home value:** $58,400. **Median travel time to work:** 29.7 minutes.

STONE COUNTY
PO Drawer 7   **Ph:** 601-928-5266
Wiggins, MS 39577   **Fax:** 601-928-6464
www.stonecounty.com

In southeastern MS, north of Gulfport; organized Apr 3, 1916 from Harrison County. **Name Origin:** For Col. John Marshall Stone (1830-1900), acting governor (1876-82) and governor (1890-96).

Area (sq mi): 448.07 (land 445.37; water 2.71).

Pop: 13,622 (White 78.7%; Black or African American 19.2%; Hispanic or Latino 1.2%; Asian 0.2%; Other 1.2%). **Foreign born:** 1%. **Median age:** 33.6. **State rank:** 61. **Pop change 1990-2000:** +26.7%.

Income: per capita $14,693; median household $30,495. **Pop below poverty level:** 17.5%.

Unemployment: 5.5%. **Median home value:** $71,100. **Median travel time to work:** 33 minutes.

SUNFLOWER COUNTY
PO Box 988   **Ph:** 662-887-4703
Indianola, MS 38751   **Fax:** 662-887-7054

In west-central MS, northeast of Greenville; organized Feb 15, 1844 from Bolivar County. **Name Origin:** For the Sunflower River, which runs through the county.

Area (sq mi): 707.22 (land 693.79; water 13.43).

Pop: 34,369 (White 28.5%; Black or African American 69.9%; Hispanic or Latino 1.3%; Asian 0.4%; Other 0.9%). **Foreign born:** 0.6%. **Median age:** 30.2. **State rank:** 25. **Pop change 1990-2000:** +4.6%.

Income: per capita $11,365; median household $24,970. **Pop below poverty level:** 30%.

Unemployment: 12.7%. **Median home value:** $50,000. **Median travel time to work:** 20.6 minutes.

TALLAHATCHIE COUNTY
PO Box 350   **Ph:** 662-647-5551
Charleston, MS 38921   **Fax:** 662-647-8490

In north-central MS, northeast of Greenville; organized Dec 23, 1833 from Indian lands. **Name Origin:** For the Tallahatchie River, which runs through it; possibly from Cree *talwa* 'town,' and *hachi* 'river': 'river town.'

Area (sq mi): 652.08 (land 643.92; water 8.16).

Pop: 14,903 (White 39.4%; Black or African American 59.4%; Hispanic or Latino 0.9%; Asian 0.4%; Other 0.6%). **Foreign born:** 0.5%. **Median age:** 33.3. **State rank:** 59. **Pop change 1990-2000:** -2%.

Income: per capita $10,749; median household $22,229. **Pop below poverty level:** 32.2%.

Unemployment: 12.2%. **Median home value:** $42,300. **Median travel time to work:** 30.5 minutes.

Please see sample entry on inside front cover for detailed information about the statistics presented with each county listing.

TATE COUNTY

PO Box 309   **Ph:** 662-562-5661
Senatobia, MS 38668   **Fax:** 662-560-6205

In northwestern MS, south of Memphis, TN; organized Apr 15, 1873 from DeSoto, Marshall, and Tunica counties. **Name Origin:** Named by T.S. Tate, an early settler, for his family.

Area (sq mi): 410.95 (land 404.48; water 6.47).

Pop: 25,370 (White 67.4%; Black or African American 31%; Hispanic or Latino 0.9%; Asian 0.1%; Other 1%). **Foreign born:** 0.2%. **Median age:** 34.2. **State rank:** 38. **Pop change 1990-2000:** +18.4%.

Income: per capita $16,154; median household $35,836. **Pop below poverty level:** 13.5%.

Unemployment: 4.8%. **Median home value:** $80,000. **Median travel time to work:** 31.1 minutes.

TIPPAH COUNTY

PO Box 99   **Ph:** 662-837-7374
Ripley, MS 38663   **Fax:** 662-837-7148

On the northern border of MS; organized Feb 9, 1836 from Chickasaw cession. **Name Origin:** For the wife of a Chickasaw chief; name is thought to mean 'cut-off.'

Area (sq mi): 459.97 (land 457.91; water 2.07).

Pop: 20,826 (White 81.1%; Black or African American 15.9%; Hispanic or Latino 2.1%; Asian 0.1%; Other 2.1%). **Foreign born:** 1.9%. **Median age:** 35.9. **State rank:** 47. **Pop change 1990-2000:** +6.7%.

Income: per capita $14,041; median household $29,300. **Pop below poverty level:** 16.9%.

Unemployment: 6%. **Median home value:** $57,200. **Median travel time to work:** 25.3 minutes.

TISHOMINGO COUNTY

1008 Battleground Dr   **Ph:** 662-423-7010
Iuka, MS 38852   **Fax:** 662-423-7005

On northeastern corner of MS; organized Feb 9, 1836 from Chickasaw cession, divided in 1870 into Alcorn, Prentiss, and Tishomingo counties. **Name Origin:** For Tishomingo (1733?-1837?), last full-blooded war chief of the Chickasaw Indians. Name means 'assistant chief': at this time he was the principal leader next to Ishtehotopa, the Chickasaw king.

Area (sq mi): 444.54 (land 424.12; water 20.41).

Pop: 19,163 (White 94.3%; Black or African American 3.1%; Hispanic or Latino 1.8%; Asian 0.1%; Other 1.9%). **Foreign born:** 1%. **Median age:** 39.1. **State rank:** 52. **Pop change 1990-2000:** +8.4%.

Income: per capita $15,395; median household $28,315. **Pop below poverty level:** 14.1%.

Unemployment: 7.4%. **Median home value:** $60,200. **Median travel time to work:** 24.9 minutes.

TUNICA COUNTY

PO Box 217   **Ph:** 662-363-2451
Tunica, MS 38676   **Fax:** 662-357-5934
www.tunicacounty.com

On the northwestern border of MS, southwest of Memphis, TN;

organized Feb 9, 1836 by the Treaty of Pontotoc from Chickasaw cession of 1832. **Name Origin:** For a tribe of Tunican linguistic stock located on the lower Yazoo River in MS. Their name probably means 'the people' or 'those who are the people.'

Area (sq mi): 480.78 (land 454.81; water 25.97).

Pop: 9,227 (White 26.9%; Black or African American 70.2%; Hispanic or Latino 2.5%; Asian 0.4%; Other 1.9%). **Foreign born:** 0.9%. **Median age:** 30.6. **State rank:** 78. **Pop change 1990-2000:** +13%.

Income: per capita $11,978; median household $23,270. **Pop below poverty level:** 33.1%.

Unemployment: 5.5%. **Median home value:** $56,800. **Median travel time to work:** 19.7 minutes.

UNION COUNTY

PO Box 847   **Ph:** 662-534-1900
New Albany, MS 38652   **Fax:** 662-534-1907

In north-central MS, northwest of Tupelo; organized Jul 7, 1870 from Pontotoc and Tippah counties. **Name Origin:** Possibly for its establishment from parts of two counties or for the union of the north and south following the Civil War.

Area (sq mi): 416.87 (land 415.43; water 1.44).

Pop: 25,362 (White 82.7%; Black or African American 14.9%; Hispanic or Latino 1.6%; Asian 0.2%; Other 1.4%). **Foreign born:** 1.8%. **Median age:** 35.6. **State rank:** 39. **Pop change 1990-2000:** +14.8%.

Income: per capita $15,700; median household $32,682. **Pop below poverty level:** 12.6%.

Unemployment: 4.2%. **Median home value:** $68,300. **Median travel time to work:** 22.4 minutes.

WALTHALL COUNTY

PO Box 351   **Ph:** 601-876-4947
Tylertown, MS 39667   **Fax:** 601-876-6026

On the central southern border of MS, west of Hattiesburg; organized Mar 16, 1910 from Marion and Pike counties. **Name Origin:** For Gen. Edward Cary Walthall (1831-98), Confederate army officer and U.S. senator from MS (1885-86; 1895-98).

Area (sq mi): 404.44 (land 403.82; water 0.62).

Pop: 15,156 (White 54.2%; Black or African American 44.1%; Hispanic or Latino 1.3%; Asian 0.2%; Other 1.1%). **Foreign born:** 0.5%. **Median age:** 35.1. **State rank:** 57. **Pop change 1990-2000:** +5.6%.

Income: per capita $12,563; median household $22,945. **Pop below poverty level:** 27.8%.

Unemployment: 6.7%. **Median home value:** $60,500. **Median travel time to work:** 32.6 minutes.

WARREN COUNTY

PO Box 351   **Ph:** 601-636-4415
Vicksburg, MS 39181   **Fax:** 601-630-8016

On the central western border of MS, west of Jackson; organized Dec 22, 1809 (prior to statehood) from Natchez District. **Name Origin:** For Gen. Joseph Warren (1741-75), Revolutionary War

All statistics are based on the 2000 Census except the dollar figures given for per capita income, which are based on 1999 estimates.

316

patriot and member of the Committee of Safety who dispatched Paul Revere (1735-1818) on his famous ride.

Area (sq mi): 618.76 (land 586.61; water 32.15).

Pop: 49,644 (White 54.5%; Black or African American 43.2%; Hispanic or Latino 1%; Asian 0.6%; Other 1.2%). **Foreign born:** 1.2%. **Median age:** 34.8. **State rank:** 13. **Pop change 1990-2000:** +3.7%.

Income: per capita $17,527; median household $35,056. **Pop below poverty level:** 18.7%.

Unemployment: 4%. **Median home value:** $79,100. **Median travel time to work:** 21 minutes.

WASHINGTON COUNTY

PO Box 309   **Ph:** 662-332-1595
Greenville, MS 38702   **Fax:** 662-334-2725

On the central western border of MS, north of Vicksburg; organized Jan 29, 1827 from Warren and Yazoo counties. **Name Origin:** For George Washington (1732-99), American patriot and first U.S. president.

Area (sq mi): 761.26 (land 723.99; water 37.27).

Pop: 62,977 (White 33.7%; Black or African American 64.6%; Hispanic or Latino 0.8%; Asian 0.5%; Other 0.9%). **Foreign born:** 0.8%. **Median age:** 31.5. **State rank:** 11. **Pop change 1990-2000:** -7.3%.

Income: per capita $13,430; median household $25,757. **Pop below poverty level:** 29.2%.

Unemployment: 11.2%. **Median home value:** $55,400. **Median travel time to work:** 17.2 minutes.

WAYNE COUNTY

609 Azalea Dr County Courthouse   **Ph:** 601-735-2873
Waynesboro, MS 39367   **Fax:** 601-735-6224

On the central eastern border of MS, east of Laurel; organized Dec 21, 1809 (prior to statehood) from Washington County. **Name Origin:** For Gen. Anthony Wayne (1745-96), PA soldier and statesman, nicknamed 'Mad Anthony' for his daring during the Revolutionary War.

Area (sq mi): 813.5 (land 810.32; water 3.18).

Pop: 21,216 (White 61.1%; Black or African American 38%; Hispanic or Latino 0.6%; Asian 0.2%; Other 0.5%). **Foreign born:** 0.3%. **Median age:** 33.8. **State rank:** 45. **Pop change 1990-2000:** +8.7%.

Income: per capita $12,757; median household $25,918. **Pop below poverty level:** 25.4%.

Unemployment: 7.6%. **Median home value:** $54,400. **Median travel time to work:** 30.8 minutes.

WEBSTER COUNTY

PO Box 398   **Ph:** 662-258-4131
Walthall, MS 39771   **Fax:** 662-258-6657

In east-central MS, west of Columbus; organized as Sumner County Apr 6, 1874 from Montgomery County; name changed Jan 20, 1882. Originally named for an early settler. **Name Origin:** For Daniel Webster (1782-1852), U.S. statesman and orator from MA.

Area (sq mi): 423.34 (land 422.49; water 0.85).

Pop: 10,294 (White 76.9%; Black or African American 20.9%; Hispanic or Latino 1.7%; Asian 0.2%; Other 1.3%). **Foreign born:** 0.5%. **Median age:** 37.3. **State rank:** 74. **Pop change 1990-2000:** +0.7%.

Income: per capita $14,109; median household $28,834. **Pop below poverty level:** 18.7%.

Unemployment: 10.9%. **Median home value:** $55,600. **Median travel time to work:** 28.8 minutes.

WILKINSON COUNTY

PO Box 516   **Ph:** 601-888-4381
Woodville, MS 39669   **Fax:** 601-888-6776

On the southwestern border of MS, south of Natchez; organized Jan 30, 1802 (prior to statehood) from Adams County. **Name Origin:** For James Wilkinson (1757-1825), officer under Washington, negotiator for the Louisiana Purchase, and first governor of the Louisiana Territory.

Area (sq mi): 687.66 (land 676.7; water 10.95).

Pop: 10,312 (White 31.1%; Black or African American 68.2%; Hispanic or Latino 0.4%; Asian 0%; Other 0.6%). **Foreign born:** 0.1%. **Median age:** 35. **State rank:** 73. **Pop change 1990-2000:** +6.6%.

Income: per capita $10,868; median household $18,929. **Pop below poverty level:** 37.7%.

Unemployment: 8.7%. **Median home value:** $43,800. **Median travel time to work:** 34.1 minutes.

WINSTON COUNTY

PO Box 69   **Ph:** 662-773-3631
Louisville, MS 39339   **Fax:** 662-773-8814

In east-central MS, northwest of Meridian; organized Dec 23, 1833 from Indian lands. **Name Origin:** For Louis Winston (?-1824), judge on the MS supreme court (1821).

Area (sq mi): 610.11 (land 606.97; water 3.14).

Pop: 20,160 (White 54.7%; Black or African American 43.2%; Hispanic or Latino 1.2%; Asian 0.1%; Other 1.5%). **Foreign born:** 1.1%. **Median age:** 36.3. **State rank:** 48. **Pop change 1990-2000:** +3.7%.

Income: per capita $14,548; median household $28,256. **Pop below poverty level:** 23.7%.

Unemployment: 13.2%. **Median home value:** $56,700. **Median travel time to work:** 26.1 minutes.

YALOBUSHA COUNTY

PO Box 664   **Ph:** 662-473-2091
Water Valley, MS 38965   **Fax:** 662-473-3622

In north-central MS; organized Dec 23, 1833 from Choctaw cession in 1830. **Name Origin:** For the Yalobusha River, which flows through a nearby county; from Choctaw, probably 'tadpole-place.'

Area (sq mi): 495 (land 467.12; water 27.88).

Pop: 13,051 (White 60%; Black or African American 38.7%; Hispanic or Latino 1%; Asian 0.1%; Other 0.8%). **Foreign born:** 0.4%. **Median age:** 37.7. **State rank:** 65. **Pop change 1990-2000:** +8.5%.

Please see sample entry on inside front cover for detailed information about the statistics presented with each county listing.

Income: per capita $14,953; median household $26,315. **Pop below poverty level:** 21.8%.

Unemployment: 7.5%. **Median home value:** $51,600. **Median travel time to work:** 26 minutes.

YAZOO COUNTY

211 E Broadway   **Ph:** 662-746-2661
Yazoo City, MS 39194   **Fax:** 662-746-3893

In west-central MS, north of Jackson; organized 1823 from Hinds County. **Name Origin:** For the Yazoo River, which forms its western border; named for the Indian tribe that inhabited the lower part of the river. The meaning and origin of the name are unknown.

Area (sq mi): 934.12 (land 919.48; water 14.64).

Pop: 28,149 (White 41.1%; Black or African American 54%; Hispanic or Latino 4.4%; Asian 0.4%; Other 0.9%). **Foreign born:** 3.9%. **Median age:** 33.7. **State rank:** 33. **Pop change 1990-2000:** +10.4%.

Income: per capita $12,062; median household $24,795. **Pop below poverty level:** 31.9%.

Unemployment: 8%. **Median home value:** $54,700. **Median travel time to work:** 26.3 minutes.

All statistics are based on the 2000 Census except the dollar figures given for per capita income, which are based on 1999 estimates.

MISSOURI - Counties and Independent City

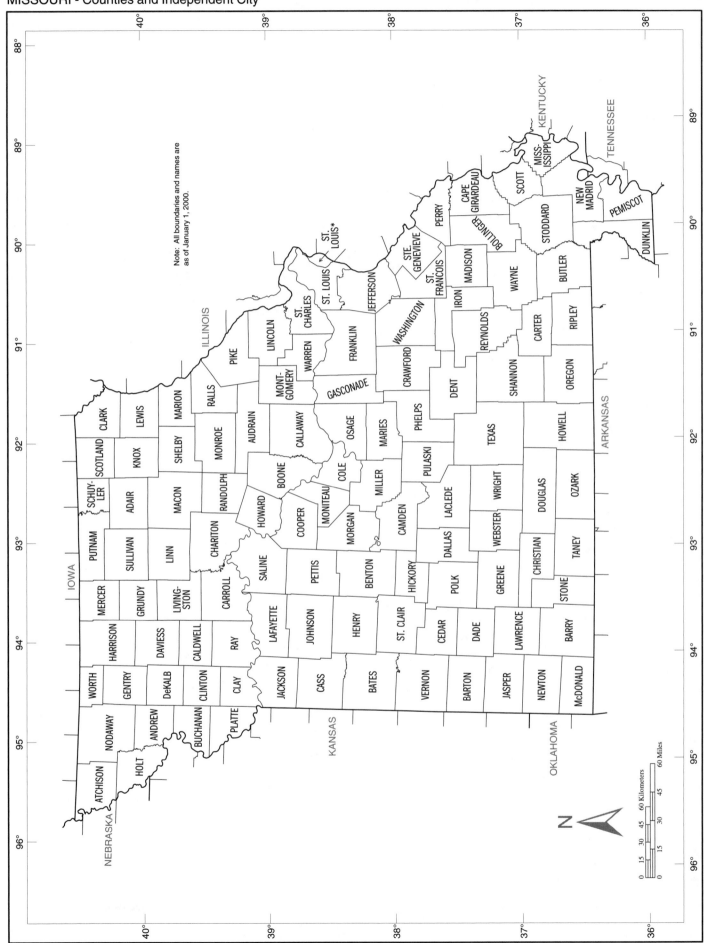

Note: All boundaries and names are as of January 1, 2000.

Missouri

MISSOURI STATE INFORMATION

www.missouri.gov **Ph:** 573-751-2000

Area (sq mi): 69,704.31 (land 68,885.93; water 818.39).

Pop: 5,595,211 (White 83.8%; Black or African American 11.2%; Hispanic or Latino 2.1%; Asian 1.1%; Other 2.8%). **Foreign born:** 2.7%. **Median age:** 36.1. **Pop change 1990-2000:** +9.3%.

Income: per capita $19,936; median household $37,934. **Pop below poverty level:** 11.7%.

Unemployment: 5.1%. **Median home value:** $89,900. **Median travel time to work:** 23.8 minutes.

ADAIR COUNTY

106 W Washington St County Courthouse **Ph:** 660-665-3350
Kirksville, MO 63501 **Fax:** 660-785-3233

In north-central MO; organized Jan 29, 1841 from Macon County. **Name Origin:** For John Adair (1757-1840), governor of KY (1820-24).

Area (sq mi): 569.32 (land 567; water 2.31).

Pop: 24,977 (White 95%; Black or African American 1.2%; Hispanic or Latino 1.3%; Asian 1.4%; Other 1.6%). **Foreign born:** 2%. **Median age:** 27.9. **State rank:** 41. **Pop change 1990-2000:** +1.6%.

Income: per capita $15,484; median household $26,677. **Pop below poverty level:** 23.3%.

Unemployment: 3.5%. **Median home value:** $73,900. **Median travel time to work:** 14.7 minutes.

ANDREW COUNTY

PO Box 206 **Ph:** 816-324-3624
Savannah, MO 64485 **Fax:** 816-324-6154

On northwestern border of MO, north of Saint Joseph; organized Jan 29, 1841 from Platte Purchase. **Name Origin:** For either Andrew Jackson, seventh U.S. president, or Andrew Jackson Davis, a distinguished lawyer from Saint Louis.

Area (sq mi): 436.5 (land 435.18; water 1.32).

Pop: 16,492 (White 97.8%; Black or African American 0.4%; Hispanic or Latino 0.8%; Asian 0.2%; Other 1%). **Foreign born:** 0.6%. **Median age:** 37.8. **State rank:** 65. **Pop change 1990-2000:** +12.7%.

Income: per capita $19,375; median household $40,688. **Pop below poverty level:** 8.2%.

Unemployment: 4.6%. **Median home value:** $89,000. **Median travel time to work:** 25.2 minutes.

ATCHISON COUNTY

PO Box 280 **Ph:** 660-744-2707
Rock Port, MO 64482 **Fax:** 660-744-5705

At the northwestern tip of MO, northwest of Saint Joseph; established Feb 3, 1843 from Holt County. **Name Origin:** For David Rice Atchison (1807-86), MO statesman and U.S. senator (1843-55)

Area (sq mi): 547.36 (land 544.72; water 2.64).

Pop: 6,430 (White 96.6%; Black or African American 2.1%; Hispanic or Latino 0.7%; Asian 0.1%; Other 0.8%). **Foreign born:** 0.3%. **Median age:** 41.7. **State rank:** 107. **Pop change 1990-2000:** -13.8%.

Income: per capita $16,956; median household $30,959. **Pop below poverty level:** 11.6%.

Unemployment: 3.1%. **Median home value:** $49,800. **Median travel time to work:** 18.9 minutes.

AUDRAIN COUNTY

101 N Jefferson St Rm 101 **Ph:** 573-473-5820
Mexico, MO 65265 **Fax:** 573-581-2380
www.audrain-county.org

In east-central MO, northeast of Columbia; established Jan 12, 1831 from Pike, Callaway, and Ralls counties. **Name Origin:** For James H. Audrain (1782-1831), MO legislator.

Area (sq mi): 696.79 (land 693.1; water 3.69).

Pop: 25,853 (White 90.6%; Black or African American 7.2%; Hispanic or Latino 0.7%; Asian 0.3%; Other 1.4%). **Foreign born:** 0.7%. **Median age:** 38. **State rank:** 40. **Pop change 1990-2000:** +9.6%.

Income: per capita $16,441; median household $32,057. **Pop below poverty level:** 14.8%.

Unemployment: 4%. **Median home value:** $62,400. **Median travel time to work:** 18.3 minutes.

BARRY COUNTY

700 Main St Suite 2 **Ph:** 417-847-2561
Cassville, MO 65625 **Fax:** 417-847-5311

On the southwestern border of MO, southwest of Springfield; organized Jan 5, 1835 from Greene County. **Name Origin:** For William Taylor Barry (1784-1835), KY legislator, U.S. senator (1814-16), and U.S. Postmaster General (1829-35).

Area (sq mi): 790.89 (land 779.06; water 11.83).

Pop: 34,010 (White 92.6%; Black or African American 0.1%; Hispanic or Latino 5%; Asian 0.3%; Other 5.6%). **Foreign born:** 3.5%. **Median age:** 38.2. **State rank:** 31. **Pop change 1990-2000:** +23.5%.

Please see sample entry on inside front cover for detailed information about the statistics presented with each county listing.

321

Income: per capita $14,980; median household $28,906. **Pop below poverty level:** 16.6%.

Unemployment: 4.6%. **Median home value:** $70,600. **Median travel time to work:** 23.2 minutes.

BARTON COUNTY
1004 Gulf St   **Ph:** 417-682-3529
Lamar, MO 64759   **Fax:** 417-682-4100

On the southwestern border of MO, north of Joplin; organized Dec 12, 1855 from Jasper County. **Name Origin:** For David Barton (1788-1837), MO jurist, legislator, and U.S. senator (1821-31).

Area (sq mi): 596.72 (land 594.25; water 2.47).

Pop: 12,541 (White 96.3%; Black or African American 0.3%; Hispanic or Latino 0.9%; Asian 0.3%; Other 2.4%). **Foreign born:** 0.7%. **Median age:** 37.3. **State rank:** 79. **Pop change 1990-2000:** +10.9%.

Income: per capita $13,987; median household $29,275. **Pop below poverty level:** 13%.

Unemployment: 3.5%. **Median home value:** $55,800. **Median travel time to work:** 19.1 minutes.

BATES COUNTY
1 N Delaware St   **Ph:** 660-679-3371
Butler, MO 64730   **Fax:** 660-679-9922
www.batescounty.net

On the central western border of MO, south of Kansas City; organized Jan 29, 1841 from Cooper County. **Name Origin:** For Frederick Bates (1777-1825), secretary of LA Territory (1806), governor of MO Territory (1809-10), and state governor (1824-25).

Area (sq mi): 851.37 (land 848.47; water 2.9).

Pop: 16,653 (White 96.8%; Black or African American 0.6%; Hispanic or Latino 1.1%; Asian 0.2%; Other 1.9%). **Foreign born:** 0.9%. **Median age:** 38.4. **State rank:** 64. **Pop change 1990-2000:** +10.8%.

Income: per capita $15,477; median household $30,731. **Pop below poverty level:** 14.5%.

Unemployment: 6.1%. **Median home value:** $58,000. **Median travel time to work:** 31.8 minutes.

BENTON COUNTY
PO Box 1238   **Ph:** 660-438-7326
Warsaw, MO 65355   **Fax:** 660-438-3275

In west-central MO, southwest of Jefferson City; organized Jan 3, 1835 from Cooper County. **Name Origin:** For Thomas Hart Benton (1782-1858), U.S. journalist and statesman; nicknamed 'Old Bullion' for championing the use of gold and silver currency rather than paper money.

Area (sq mi): 752.48 (land 705.51; water 46.97).

Pop: 17,180 (White 97.3%; Black or African American 0.1%; Hispanic or Latino 0.9%; Asian 0.1%; Other 1.7%). **Foreign born:** 0.7%. **Median age:** 46.3. **State rank:** 62. **Pop change 1990-2000:** +24%.

Income: per capita $15,457; median household $26,646. **Pop below poverty level:** 15.7%.

Unemployment: 8%. **Median home value:** $65,700. **Median travel time to work:** 27.2 minutes.

BOLLINGER COUNTY
PO Box 110 County Courthouse   **Ph:** 573-238-1900
Marble Hill, MO 63764   **Fax:** 573-238-4511

In southeastern MO, west of Cape Girardeau; organized Mar 1, 1851 from Cape Girardeau, Madison, Stoddard, and Wayne counties. **Name Origin:** For Col. George Frederick Bollinger (1770-1842), who led German settlers into MO in 1800.

Area (sq mi): 621.2 (land 620.74; water 0.46).

Pop: 12,029 (White 97.4%; Black or African American 0.2%; Hispanic or Latino 0.6%; Asian 0.2%; Other 1.7%). **Foreign born:** 0.4%. **Median age:** 37.9. **State rank:** 81. **Pop change 1990-2000:** +13.3%.

Income: per capita $13,641; median household $30,462. **Pop below poverty level:** 13.8%.

Unemployment: 7.2%. **Median home value:** $58,400. **Median travel time to work:** 33.8 minutes.

BOONE COUNTY
801 E Walnut St   **Ph:** 573-886-4295
Columbia, MO 65201   **Fax:** 573-886-4300
www.co.boone.mo.us

In central MO, north of Jefferson City; organized Nov 16, 1820 (prior to statehood) from Howard County. **Name Origin:** For Daniel Boone (1734?-1820), U.S. frontiersman and KY pioneer.

Area (sq mi): 691.31 (land 685.43; water 5.88).

Pop: 135,454 (White 84.4%; Black or African American 8.5%; Hispanic or Latino 1.8%; Asian 3%; Other 3%). **Foreign born:** 4.5%. **Median age:** 29.5. **State rank:** 8. **Pop change 1990-2000:** +20.5%.

Income: per capita $19,844; median household $37,485. **Pop below poverty level:** 14.5%.

Unemployment: 1.8%. **Median home value:** $107,400. **Median travel time to work:** 17.8 minutes.

BUCHANAN COUNTY
411 Jules St   **Ph:** 816-271-1411
Saint Joseph, MO 64501   **Fax:** 816-271-1535
www.co.buchanan.mo.us

On the northwestern border of MO, northwest of Kansas City; organized Dec 31, 1838 from Platte Purchase. **Name Origin:** For James Buchanan (1791-1868), fifteenth U.S. president.

Area (sq mi): 414.57 (land 409.73; water 4.84).

Pop: 85,998 (White 91.2%; Black or African American 4.4%; Hispanic or Latino 2.4%; Asian 0.4%; Other 2.4%). **Foreign born:** 1.1%. **Median age:** 36.1. **State rank:** 11. **Pop change 1990-2000:** +3.5%.

Income: per capita $17,882; median household $34,704. **Pop below poverty level:** 12.2%.

Unemployment: 5.3%. **Median home value:** $72,700. **Median travel time to work:** 18.3 minutes.

All statistics are based on the 2000 Census except the dollar figures given for per capita income, which are based on 1999 estimates.

BUTLER COUNTY

100 N Main St Courthouse Rm 202 **Ph:** 573-686-8050
Poplar Bluff, MO 63901 **Fax:** 573-686-8066

On the southeastern border of MO, southwest of Cape Girardeau; organized Feb 27, 1849 from Wayne County. **Name Origin:** For Maj. William Orlando Butler (1791-1880), officer in the War of 1812 and Mexican- American War, U.S. representative from KY (1839-43).

Area (sq mi): 698.97 (land 697.54; water 1.43).

Pop: 40,867 (White 91.6%; Black or African American 5.2%; Hispanic or Latino 1%; Asian 0.4%; Other 2.3%). **Foreign born:** 1.4%. **Median age:** 38.7. **State rank:** 21. **Pop change 1990-2000:** +5.4%.

Income: per capita $15,721; median household $27,228. **Pop below poverty level:** 18.6%.

Unemployment: 6%. **Median home value:** $59,400. **Median travel time to work:** 19.4 minutes.

CALDWELL COUNTY

PO Box 67 **Ph:** 816-586-2571
Kingston, MO 64650 **Fax:** 816-586-3600

In northwestern MO, east of Saint Joseph; organized Dec 29, 1836 from Ray County. **Name Origin:** For Matthew Caldwell, an officer of the KY Volunteers in the War of 1812, or for Gen. John Caldwell (?-1804), KY Indian fighter and legislator.

Area (sq mi): 429.72 (land 429.34; water 0.38).

Pop: 8,969 (White 98%; Black or African American 0.1%; Hispanic or Latino 0.7%; Asian 0.1%; Other 1.2%). **Foreign born:** 0.4%. **Median age:** 38.8. **State rank:** 94. **Pop change 1990-2000:** +7%.

Income: per capita $15,343; median household $31,240. **Pop below poverty level:** 11.9%.

Unemployment: 6.1%. **Median home value:** $53,800. **Median travel time to work:** 33.4 minutes.

CALLAWAY COUNTY

10 E 5th St **Ph:** 573-642-0730
Fulton, MO 65251 **Fax:** 573-642-7181
callaway.county.missouri.org

In east-central MO, east of Columbia; organized Nov 25, 1820 (prior to statehood) from Howard, Boone, and Montgomery counties. **Name Origin:** For Capt. James Callaway (1783-1815), grandson of Daniel Boone, killed in a battle with Indians.

Area (sq mi): 847.03 (land 838.84; water 8.19).

Pop: 40,766 (White 91.2%; Black or African American 5.7%; Hispanic or Latino 0.9%; Asian 0.5%; Other 2%). **Foreign born:** 1.1%. **Median age:** 34.7. **State rank:** 22. **Pop change 1990-2000:** +24.3%.

Income: per capita $17,005; median household $39,110. **Pop below poverty level:** 8.5%.

Unemployment: 3.5%. **Median home value:** $85,800. **Median travel time to work:** 23.1 minutes.

CAMDEN COUNTY

1 Court Cir Suite 8 **Ph:** 573-346-4440
Camdenton, MO 65020 **Fax:** 573-346-5181

In central MO, southwest of Jefferson City; organized Jan 29, 1841 as Kinderhook County from Pulaski, Morgan, and Benton counties; name changed Feb 23, 1843. **Name Origin:** For Charles Pratt (1714-94), 1st Earl of Camden, English statesman who supported the American colonies before the Revolutionary War.

Area (sq mi): 708.86 (land 655.14; water 53.71).

Pop: 37,051 (White 97%; Black or African American 0.3%; Hispanic or Latino 0.9%; Asian 0.3%; Other 1.7%). **Foreign born:** 1.4%. **Median age:** 45.2. **State rank:** 29. **Pop change 1990-2000:** +34.8%.

Income: per capita $20,197; median household $35,840. **Pop below poverty level:** 11.4%.

Unemployment: 6%. **Median home value:** $124,300. **Median travel time to work:** 23.3 minutes.

CAPE GIRARDEAU COUNTY

1 Barton Sq **Ph:** 573-243-3547
Jackson, MO 63755 **Fax:** 573-204-2418

On the southeastern border of MO, original county; organized Oct 1, 1812 (prior to statehood). **Name Origin:** For Jean Girardot, a French naval officer stationed at Kaskaskia, IL (1704-20), later a trading-post operator. No explanation for the spelling variance.

Area (sq mi): 586.29 (land 578.62; water 7.67).

Pop: 68,693 (White 91.6%; Black or African American 5.3%; Hispanic or Latino 0.9%; Asian 0.7%; Other 1.8%). **Foreign born:** 1.3%. **Median age:** 35.2. **State rank:** 15. **Pop change 1990-2000:** +11.5%.

Income: per capita $18,593; median household $36,458. **Pop below poverty level:** 11.1%.

Unemployment: 3.9%. **Median home value:** $94,700. **Median travel time to work:** 18.6 minutes.

CARROLL COUNTY

8 S Main Suite 6 **Ph:** 660-542-0615
Carrollton, MO 64633 **Fax:** 660-542-0621

In north-central MO, northeast of Kansas City; organized Jan 2, 1833 from Ray County. **Name Origin:** For Charles Carroll (1737-1832), a signer of the Declaration of Independence, U.S. senator from MD (1789-92), and founder of the Baltimore and Ohio Railroad.

Area (sq mi): 702.3 (land 694.72; water 7.57).

Pop: 10,285 (White 96.4%; Black or African American 1.7%; Hispanic or Latino 0.7%; Asian 0.1%; Other 1.2%). **Foreign born:** 0.4%. **Median age:** 40. **State rank:** 88. **Pop change 1990-2000:** -4.3%.

Income: per capita $15,522; median household $30,643. **Pop below poverty level:** 13.7%.

Unemployment: 4.9%. **Median home value:** $48,900. **Median travel time to work:** 26.5 minutes.

CARTER COUNTY

PO Box 517 **Ph:** 573-323-4527
Van Buren, MO 63965 **Fax:** 573-323-4527

In southeastern MO, southwest of Cape Girardeau; organized Mar 10, 1859 from Ripley, Reynolds, Shannon, and Oregon counties. **Name Origin:** For Zimri A. Carter, a settler from SC in 1812.

Please see sample entry on inside front cover for detailed information about the statistics presented with each county listing.

Area (sq mi): 509.02 (land 507.58; water 1.44).

Pop: 5,941 (White 95.7%; Black or African American 0.1%; Hispanic or Latino 1.2%; Asian 0.1%; Other 3.1%). **Foreign born:** 0.3%. **Median age:** 38.9. **State rank:** 108. **Pop change 1990-2000:** +7.7%.

Income: per capita $13,349; median household $22,863. **Pop below poverty level:** 25.2%.

Unemployment: 6.5%. **Median home value:** $51,900. **Median travel time to work:** 28.1 minutes.

CASS COUNTY
102 E Wall St   **Ph:** 816-380-8100
Harrisonville, MO 64701   **Fax:** 816-380-8101
www.casscounty.com

On the central western border of MO, south of Kansas City; organized as Van Buren County Mar 3, 1835 from Jackson County; name changed in 1849. **Name Origin:** For Gen. Lewis Cass (1782-1866), OH legislator, governor of MI Territory (1813-31), U.S. secretary of war (1831-36), and U.S. secretary of state (1857-60).

Area (sq mi): 702.67 (land 698.99; water 3.68).

Pop: 82,092 (White 94.1%; Black or African American 1.4%; Hispanic or Latino 2.2%; Asian 0.5%; Other 2.5%). **Foreign born:** 1.6%. **Median age:** 35.8. **State rank:** 12. **Pop change 1990-2000:** +28.7%.

Income: per capita $21,073; median household $49,562. **Pop below poverty level:** 5.8%.

Unemployment: 3.6%. **Median home value:** $104,200. **Median travel time to work:** 29.2 minutes.

CEDAR COUNTY
PO Box 665   **Ph:** 417-276-6700
Stockton, MO 65785   **Fax:** 417-276-5001

In southwestern MO, northwest of Springfield; organized Feb 14, 1845 from Dade and Saint Clair counties. **Name Origin:** For the many cedar trees found by early settlers.

Area (sq mi): 498.51 (land 475.93; water 22.57).

Pop: 13,733 (White 96%; Black or African American 0.3%; Hispanic or Latino 1.1%; Asian 0.5%; Other 2.6%). **Foreign born:** 1.3%. **Median age:** 42.2. **State rank:** 73. **Pop change 1990-2000:** +13.6%.

Income: per capita $14,356; median household $26,694. **Pop below poverty level:** 17.4%.

Unemployment: 5%. **Median home value:** $57,900. **Median travel time to work:** 24.7 minutes.

CHARITON COUNTY
306 S Cherry St   **Ph:** 660-288-3273
Keytesville, MO 65261   **Fax:** 660-288-3403

In north-central MO, northwest of Columbia; organized Nov 16, 1820 (prior to statehood) from Howard County. **Name Origin:** For a French fur trader, probably Jean Chariton, who was also called Joseph or John Chorette. During the 1700s he established a trading post on the north bank of the Missouri River in what is now IA.

Area (sq mi): 768.25 (land 755.87; water 12.38).

Pop: 8,438 (White 95.6%; Black or African American 3.2%; Hispanic or Latino 0.6%; Asian 0.1%; Other 0.7%). **Foreign born:** 0.6%. **Median age:** 42.5. **State rank:** 98. **Pop change 1990-2000:** -8.3%.

Income: per capita $15,515; median household $32,285. **Pop below poverty level:** 11.6%.

Unemployment: 6.7%. **Median home value:** $43,800. **Median travel time to work:** 23.4 minutes.

CHRISTIAN COUNTY
100 W Church St Rm 206   **Ph:** 417-581-6360
Ozark, MO 65721   **Fax:** 417-581-8331

In southwestern MO, south of Springfield; organized Mar 8, 1859 from Taney, Greene, and Webster counties. **Name Origin:** For Col. William Christian (1743-86), army officer, Indian fighter, and legislator; brother-in-law of Revolutionary leader Patrick Henry (1736-99).

Area (sq mi): 564.05 (land 563.16; water 0.89).

Pop: 54,285 (White 96.5%; Black or African American 0.3%; Hispanic or Latino 1.3%; Asian 0.3%; Other 2.1%). **Foreign born:** 0.9%. **Median age:** 34.5. **State rank:** 17. **Pop change 1990-2000:** +66.3%.

Income: per capita $18,422; median household $38,085. **Pop below poverty level:** 9.1%.

Unemployment: 3.9%. **Median home value:** $97,900. **Median travel time to work:** 25.1 minutes.

CLARK COUNTY
111 E Court St   **Ph:** 660-727-3283
Kahoka, MO 63445   **Fax:** 660-727-1051

On the northeastern tip of MO; organized Dec 16, 1836 from Lewis County. **Name Origin:** For William Clark (1770-1838), explorer and co-leader of the Lewis and Clark Expedition (1803-06).

Area (sq mi): 511.9 (land 507.31; water 4.59).

Pop: 7,416 (White 98.4%; Black or African American 0.1%; Hispanic or Latino 0.7%; Asian 0.1%; Other 1%). **Foreign born:** 0.2%. **Median age:** 39.2. **State rank:** 102. **Pop change 1990-2000:** -1.7%.

Income: per capita $15,988; median household $29,457. **Pop below poverty level:** 14.1%.

Unemployment: 7.3%. **Median home value:** $51,300. **Median travel time to work:** 28.1 minutes.

CLAY COUNTY
1 Courthouse Sq   **Ph:** 816-792-7733
Liberty, MO 64068   **Fax:** 816-792-7777

In west-central MO, north of Kansas City; organized Jun 2, 1822 from Ray County. **Name Origin:** For Henry Clay (1777-1852), U.S. senator from KY, known as the 'Great Pacificator' for his advocacy of compromise to avert national crises.

Area (sq mi): 408.86 (land 396.35; water 12.52).

Pop: 184,006 (White 90.5%; Black or African American 2.7%; Hispanic or Latino 3.6%; Asian 1.3%; Other 3.6%). **Foreign born:** 2.9%. **Median age:** 35. **State rank:** 7. **Pop change 1990-2000:** +19.9%.

All statistics are based on the 2000 Census except the dollar figures given for per capita income, which are based on 1999 estimates.

Income: per capita $23,144; median household $48,347. **Pop below poverty level:** 5.5%.

Unemployment: 3.1%. **Median home value:** $104,900. **Median travel time to work:** 22.4 minutes.

CLINTON COUNTY
PO Box 245   **Ph:** 816-539-3713
Plattsburg, MO 64477   **Fax:** 816-539-3072
www.co.clinton.mo.us

In west-central MO, north of Kansas City; organized Jan 2, 1833 from Clay and Ray counties. **Name Origin:** For DeWitt Clinton (1769-1828), governor of NY (1817-21; 1825-28) and supporter of the Erie Canal.

Area (sq mi): 423.47 (land 418.76; water 4.71).

Pop: 18,979 (White 95.8%; Black or African American 1.5%; Hispanic or Latino 1.1%; Asian 0.2%; Other 1.7%). **Foreign born:** 0.5%. **Median age:** 37.7. **State rank:** 57. **Pop change 1990-2000:** +14.4%.

Income: per capita $19,056; median household $41,629. **Pop below poverty level:** 9.3%.

Unemployment: 3.7%. **Median home value:** $86,400. **Median travel time to work:** 30 minutes.

COLE COUNTY
311 High St   **Ph:** 573-634-9106
Jefferson City, MO 65101   **Fax:** 573-681-9678
www.colecounty.org

In central MO, south of Columbia; organized Nov 16, 1820 (prior to statehood) from Cooper county. **Name Origin:** For Capt. Stephen Cole (?-1822), an Indian fighter.

Area (sq mi): 399.08 (land 391.44; water 7.64).

Pop: 71,397 (White 86.4%; Black or African American 9.9%; Hispanic or Latino 1.3%; Asian 0.9%; Other 2%). **Foreign born:** 2.2%. **Median age:** 35.5. **State rank:** 14. **Pop change 1990-2000:** +12.3%.

Income: per capita $20,739; median household $42,924. **Pop below poverty level:** 8.7%.

Unemployment: 2.9%. **Median home value:** $97,200. **Median travel time to work:** 17.4 minutes.

COOPER COUNTY
200 Main St   **Ph:** 660-882-2114
Boonville, MO 65233   **Fax:** 660-882-5645

In central MO, west of Columbia; organized Dec 17, 1818 (prior to statehood) from Howard County. **Name Origin:** For Sarshel Cooper (?-1814), an early settler.

Area (sq mi): 570.22 (land 565.03; water 5.19).

Pop: 16,670 (White 88.6%; Black or African American 9%; Hispanic or Latino 0.9%; Asian 0.2%; Other 1.8%). **Foreign born:** 0.6%. **Median age:** 35.2. **State rank:** 63. **Pop change 1990-2000:** +12.4%.

Income: per capita $15,648; median household $35,313. **Pop below poverty level:** 10.7%.

Unemployment: 4.8%. **Median home value:** $74,200. **Median travel time to work:** 22.4 minutes.

CRAWFORD COUNTY
PO Box AS   **Ph:** 573-775-2376
Steelville, MO 65565   **Fax:** 573-775-3066

In east-central MO, southwest of Saint Louis; organized Jan 23, 1829 from Gasconade County. **Name Origin:** For William Harris Crawford (1772-1834), U.S. senator from GA (1807-13), U.S. Secretary of War (1815-16), and U.S. Secretary of Treasury (1816-25).

Area (sq mi): 743.79 (land 742.52; water 1.27).

Pop: 22,804 (White 97.7%; Black or African American 0.1%; Hispanic or Latino 0.8%; Asian 0.1%; Other 1.4%). **Foreign born:** 1.2%. **Median age:** 37.9. **State rank:** 49. **Pop change 1990-2000:** +18.9%.

Income: per capita $14,825; median household $30,860. **Pop below poverty level:** 16.3%.

Unemployment: 6.4%. **Median home value:** $66,100. **Median travel time to work:** 29.2 minutes.

DADE COUNTY
County Courthouse   **Ph:** 417-637-2724
Greenfield, MO 65661   **Fax:** 417-637-1006

In southwestern MO, northwest of Springfield; organized Jan 29, 1841 from Polk and Barry counties. **Name Origin:** For Francis Langhorne Dade (1793-1835), officer killed in the Seminole War (1835-42).

Area (sq mi): 506.3 (land 490.34; water 15.96).

Pop: 7,923 (White 96.8%; Black or African American 0.3%; Hispanic or Latino 0.8%; Asian 0.1%; Other 2.2%). **Foreign born:** 1%. **Median age:** 41.7. **State rank:** 101. **Pop change 1990-2000:** +6.4%.

Income: per capita $14,254; median household $29,097. **Pop below poverty level:** 13.4%.

Unemployment: 4.5%. **Median home value:** $54,500. **Median travel time to work:** 27.8 minutes.

DALLAS COUNTY
PO Box 436   **Ph:** 417-345-2632
Buffalo, MO 65622   **Fax:** 417-345-5321

In south-central MO, northeast of Springfield; organized as Niangua County Jan 29, 1841 from Polk County; name changed Dec 16, 1844. **Name Origin:** For George Mifflin Dallas (1792-1864), U.S. senator from PA (1831-33), U.S. vice president (1845-49), and U.S. Minister to Russia (1837-39) and Great Britain (1856-61).

Area (sq mi): 542.83 (land 541.54; water 1.29).

Pop: 15,661 (White 96.8%; Black or African American 0.1%; Hispanic or Latino 0.9%; Asian 0.1%; Other 2.4%). **Foreign born:** 0.5%. **Median age:** 37.9. **State rank:** 67. **Pop change 1990-2000:** +23.8%.

Income: per capita $15,106; median household $27,346. **Pop below poverty level:** 17.9%.

Unemployment: 7%. **Median home value:** $72,300. **Median travel time to work:** 32 minutes.

Please see sample entry on inside front cover for detailed information about the statistics presented with each county listing.

DAVIESS COUNTY

102 N Main St   **Ph:** 660-663-2641
Gallatin, MO 64640   **Fax:** 660-663-3376

In north-central MO, northeast of Saint Joseph; organized Dec 29, 1836 from Ray County. **Name Origin:** For Col. Joseph Hamilton Daviess (1774-1811), VA soldier and jurist who unsuccessfully attempted to indict Aaron Burr for treason (1806). According to Jacob Piatt Dunn, 'The Colonel's name was Daveiss and he always wrote it that way', however, the name is sometimes spelled 'Daviess' in biographical entries and in places named for him.

Area (sq mi): 569.07 (land 566.97; water 2.11).

Pop: 8,016 (White 98.3%; Black or African American 0%; Hispanic or Latino 0.7%; Asian 0.1%; Other 1.2%). **Foreign born:** 0.2%. **Median age:** 38.9. **State rank:** 100. **Pop change 1990-2000:** +1.9%.

Income: per capita $15,953; median household $30,855. **Pop below poverty level:** 15.2%.

Unemployment: 5.1%. **Median home value:** $56,700. **Median travel time to work:** 29.2 minutes.

DEKALB COUNTY

PO Box 248   **Ph:** 816-449-5402
Maysville, MO 64469   **Fax:** 816-449-2440

In northwestern MO, east of Saint Joseph; organized Feb 25, 1845 from Clinton County. **Name Origin:** For Johann, Baron de Kalb (1721-1780), German-born French soldier who fought with the Americans during the Revolutionary War.

Area (sq mi): 425.77 (land 424.2; water 1.57).

Pop: 11,597 (White 88.4%; Black or African American 8.9%; Hispanic or Latino 1.1%; Asian 0.2%; Other 1.9%). **Foreign born:** 1%. **Median age:** 37.7. **State rank:** 83. **Pop change 1990-2000:** +16.4%.

Income: per capita $12,687; median household $31,654. **Pop below poverty level:** 10.8%.

Unemployment: 2.8%. **Median home value:** $64,800. **Median travel time to work:** 26.8 minutes.

DENT COUNTY

400 N Main St   **Ph:** 573-729-4144
Salem, MO 65560   **Fax:** 573-729-6106

In south-central MO, northwest of Cape Girardeau; organized Feb 10, 1851 from Shannon and Crawford counties. **Name Origin:** For Lewis Dent (1808-80), landowner and MO legislator.

Area (sq mi): 754.51 (land 753.54; water 0.97).

Pop: 14,927 (White 96.6%; Black or African American 0.4%; Hispanic or Latino 0.8%; Asian 0.2%; Other 2.3%). **Foreign born:** 0.6%. **Median age:** 39.6. **State rank:** 69. **Pop change 1990-2000:** +8.9%.

Income: per capita $14,463; median household $27,193. **Pop below poverty level:** 17.2%.

Unemployment: 8.8%. **Median home value:** $61,000. **Median travel time to work:** 24.4 minutes.

DOUGLAS COUNTY

PO Box 398   **Ph:** 417-683-4714
Ava, MO 65608   **Fax:** 417-683-1017

In south-central MO, southeast of Springfield; organized Oct 29, 1857 from Ozark County. **Name Origin:** For Stephen Arnold Douglas (1813-61), U.S. orator and statesman.

Area (sq mi): 814.6 (land 814.53; water 0.07).

Pop: 13,084 (White 96.4%; Black or African American 0.1%; Hispanic or Latino 0.8%; Asian 0.2%; Other 2.8%). **Foreign born:** 0.9%. **Median age:** 40.1. **State rank:** 77. **Pop change 1990-2000:** +10.2%.

Income: per capita $13,785; median household $25,918. **Pop below poverty level:** 17.5%.

Unemployment: 10.1%. **Median home value:** $54,100. **Median travel time to work:** 31 minutes.

DUNKLIN COUNTY

PO Box 188   **Ph:** 573-888-1374
Kennett, MO 63857   **Fax:** 573-888-2832

On the southern border of MO, southwest of Cape Girardeau; organized Feb 14, 1845 from Stoddard County. **Name Origin:** For Daniel Dunklin (1790-1844), governor of MO (1833-36) and surveyor-general of MO, IL, and AR.

Area (sq mi): 547.11 (land 545.62; water 1.49).

Pop: 33,155 (White 87.4%; Black or African American 8.7%; Hispanic or Latino 2.5%; Asian 0.3%; Other 2.4%). **Foreign born:** 1.5%. **Median age:** 37.8. **State rank:** 32. **Pop change 1990-2000:** +0.1%.

Income: per capita $13,561; median household $24,878. **Pop below poverty level:** 24.5%.

Unemployment: 7.3%. **Median home value:** $48,500. **Median travel time to work:** 20.7 minutes.

FRANKLIN COUNTY

300 E Main St Rm 201   **Ph:** 636-583-6355
Union, MO 63084   **Fax:** 636-583-7320

In central-eastern MO, west of Saint Louis; organized Dec 11, 1818 (prior to statehood) from Saint Louis County. **Name Origin:** For Benjamin Franklin (1706-90), U.S. patriot, diplomat, and statesman.

Area (sq mi): 930.65 (land 922.81; water 7.84).

Pop: 93,807 (White 97%; Black or African American 0.9%; Hispanic or Latino 0.7%; Asian 0.3%; Other 1.3%). **Foreign born:** 0.8%. **Median age:** 35.8. **State rank:** 10. **Pop change 1990-2000:** +16.4%.

Income: per capita $19,705; median household $43,474. **Pop below poverty level:** 7%.

Unemployment: 5.5%. **Median home value:** $96,400. **Median travel time to work:** 29.2 minutes.

GASCONADE COUNTY

119 E 1st St Rm 2   **Ph:** 573-486-5427
Hermann, MO 65041   **Fax:** 573-486-8893

In east-central MO, west of Saint Louis; organized Nov 25, 1820

All statistics are based on the 2000 Census except the dollar figures given for per capita income, which are based on 1999 estimates.

(prior to statehood) from Franklin County. **Name Origin:** For the Gasconade River, which runs through it. It is believed that French residents of Saint Louis gave this name to the river and general area for the bragging of the inhabitants when they went to Saint Louis; an allusion to the residents of the French province of Gascony, supposed to be boastful.

Area (sq mi): 526.09 (land 520.67; water 5.43).

Pop: 15,342 (White 98.4%; Black or African American 0.1%; Hispanic or Latino 0.4%; Asian 0.2%; Other 1%). **Foreign born:** 0.5%. **Median age:** 40.3. **State rank:** 68. **Pop change 1990-2000:** +9.5%.

Income: per capita $17,319; median household $35,047. **Pop below poverty level:** 9.5%.

Unemployment: 5.3%. **Median home value:** $70,500. **Median travel time to work:** 29.1 minutes.

GENTRY COUNTY
200 W Clay St   **Ph:** 660-726-3618
Albany, MO 64402   **Fax:** 660-726-4102

In northwestern MO, northeast of Saint Joseph; established Feb 12, 1841 from Clinton County. **Name Origin:** For Richard Gentry (1788-1837), officer in the Black Hawk War who died fighting the Seminoles in Florida.

Area (sq mi): 491.81 (land 491.52; water 0.29).

Pop: 6,861 (White 98%; Black or African American 0.1%; Hispanic or Latino 0.6%; Asian 0.2%; Other 1.2%). **Foreign born:** 0.6%. **Median age:** 40.2. **State rank:** 104. **Pop change 1990-2000:** +0.2%.

Income: per capita $15,879; median household $28,750. **Pop below poverty level:** 12%.

Unemployment: 3.9%. **Median home value:** $47,200. **Median travel time to work:** 24.4 minutes.

GREENE COUNTY
940 N Boonville Ave   **Ph:** 417-868-4055
Springfield, MO 65802   **Fax:** 417-868-4170
www.greenecountymo.org

In south-central MO, northeast of Joplin; organized Jan 2, 1833 from Wayne and Crawford counties. **Name Origin:** For Gen. Nathanael Greene (1742-1786), hero of the Revolutionary War, quartermaster general (1778-80), and commander of the Army of the South.

Area (sq mi): 677.8 (land 674.97; water 2.82).

Pop: 240,391 (White 92.5%; Black or African American 2.3%; Hispanic or Latino 1.8%; Asian 1.1%; Other 3.2%). **Foreign born:** 1.9%. **Median age:** 35.1. **State rank:** 5. **Pop change 1990-2000:** +15.6%.

Income: per capita $19,185; median household $34,157. **Pop below poverty level:** 12.1%.

Unemployment: 3.3%. **Median home value:** $88,200. **Median travel time to work:** 19.2 minutes.

GRUNDY COUNTY
700 Main St   **Ph:** 660-359-6305
Trenton, MO 64683   **Fax:** 660-359-6786

In north-central MO, northeast of Saint Joseph; organized Jan 29,

1841 from Livingston and Ray counties. **Name Origin:** For Felix Grundy (1777-1840), chief justice of KY supreme court, U.S. senator from TN (1829-38; 1839-40), and U.S. Attorney General (1838-39).

Area (sq mi): 437.98 (land 435.82; water 2.16).

Pop: 10,432 (White 96.7%; Black or African American 0.4%; Hispanic or Latino 1.6%; Asian 0.2%; Other 1.8%). **Foreign born:** 1.4%. **Median age:** 41.3. **State rank:** 86. **Pop change 1990-2000:** -1%.

Income: per capita $15,432; median household $27,333. **Pop below poverty level:** 15.8%.

Unemployment: 4%. **Median home value:** $42,500. **Median travel time to work:** 19.6 minutes.

HARRISON COUNTY
PO Box 525   **Ph:** 660-425-6424
Bethany, MO 64424   **Fax:** 660-425-3772

On the central northern border of MO, northeast of Saint Joseph; organized Feb 14, 1845 from Daviess and Ray counties. **Name Origin:** For Albert Galliton Harrison (1800-39), U.S. representative from MO (1835-39).

Area (sq mi): 726.45 (land 725.13; water 1.32).

Pop: 8,850 (White 97.8%; Black or African American 0.1%; Hispanic or Latino 1%; Asian 0.1%; Other 1.4%). **Foreign born:** 1%. **Median age:** 41.7. **State rank:** 97. **Pop change 1990-2000:** +4.5%.

Income: per capita $14,192; median household $28,707. **Pop below poverty level:** 13.5%.

Unemployment: 3.3%. **Median home value:** $41,500. **Median travel time to work:** 22.4 minutes.

HENRY COUNTY
100 W Franklin St   **Ph:** 660-885-6963
Clinton, MO 64735   **Fax:** 660-885-8456

In west-central MO, southeast of Kansas City; organized as Rives County Dec 13, 1834 from Lafayette County; name changed Feb 15, 1841. **Name Origin:** For Patrick Henry (1736-99), patriot, governor of VA (1776-79; 1784-86), and statesman, famous for proclaiming 'Give me liberty or give me death.'

Area (sq mi): 732.55 (land 702.48; water 30.07).

Pop: 21,997 (White 96.2%; Black or African American 1%; Hispanic or Latino 0.9%; Asian 0.2%; Other 2.1%). **Foreign born:** 0.8%. **Median age:** 40. **State rank:** 50. **Pop change 1990-2000:** +9.7%.

Income: per capita $16,468; median household $30,949. **Pop below poverty level:** 14.3%.

Unemployment: 5.8%. **Median home value:** $64,200. **Median travel time to work:** 25.4 minutes.

HICKORY COUNTY
PO Box 3   **Ph:** 417-745-6450
Hermitage, MO 65668   **Fax:** 417-745-6057

In west-central MO, north of Springfield; organized Feb 14, 1845 from Benton and Polk counties. **Name Origin:** For 'Old Hickory,' the nickname of Andrew Jackson (1767-1845), seventh U.S. president.

Please see sample entry on inside front cover for detailed information about the statistics presented with each county listing.

Area (sq mi): 411.74 (land 398.63; water 13.11).

Pop: 8,940 (White 97%; Black or African American 0.1%; Hispanic or Latino 0.8%; Asian 0.1%; Other 2.3%). **Foreign born:** 1%. **Median age:** 49.7. **State rank:** 95. **Pop change 1990-2000:** +21.9%.

Income: per capita $13,536; median household $25,346. **Pop below poverty level:** 19.7%.

Unemployment: 8.7%. **Median home value:** $62,600. **Median travel time to work:** 33.2 minutes.

HOLT COUNTY
PO Box 437   **Ph:** 660-446-3303
Oregon, MO 64473   **Fax:** 660-446-3328

On northwestern border of MO, northwest of Saint Joseph; organized as Nodaway County Jan 29, 1841 from Platte Purchase; name changed Feb 15, 1841. **Name Origin:** For David Rice Holt (1803-40), MO legislator.

Area (sq mi): 469.05 (land 461.87; water 7.18).

Pop: 5,351 (White 98.2%; Black or African American 0.1%; Hispanic or Latino 0.4%; Asian 0.1%; Other 1.3%). **Foreign born:** 0.4%. **Median age:** 41.8. **State rank:** 109. **Pop change 1990-2000:** -11.3%.

Income: per capita $15,876; median household $29,461. **Pop below poverty level:** 13%.

Unemployment: 4.3%. **Median home value:** $50,100. **Median travel time to work:** 23.1 minutes.

HOWARD COUNTY
1 Courthouse Sq   **Ph:** 660-248-2284
Fayette, MO 65248   **Fax:** 660-248-1075

In north-central MO, northwest of Columbia; organized Jan 13, 1816 (prior to statehood) from Saint Louis and Saint Charles counties. **Name Origin:** For Gen. Benjamin Howard (1760-1814), KY legislator and U.S. representative (1807-10), governor of LA Territory (1810-12), and commander of the Eighth Military Department, territory west of the Mississippi River.

Area (sq mi): 470.55 (land 465.74; water 4.82).

Pop: 10,212 (White 90.7%; Black or African American 6.8%; Hispanic or Latino 0.9%; Asian 0.1%; Other 1.9%). **Foreign born:** 1%. **Median age:** 36.7. **State rank:** 89. **Pop change 1990-2000:** +6%.

Income: per capita $15,198; median household $31,614. **Pop below poverty level:** 11.6%.

Unemployment: 4.9%. **Median home value:** $59,500. **Median travel time to work:** 25.3 minutes.

HOWELL COUNTY
1 Courthouse   **Ph:** 417-256-2591
West Plains, MO 65775   **Fax:** 417-256-2512

On the central southern border of MO; organized Mar 2, 1857 from Oregon County. **Name Origin:** For Thomas Jefferson Howell, MO legislator; or for James Howell, a prominent citizen; or for Josiah Howell.

Area (sq mi): 928.33 (land 927.74; water 0.59).

Pop: 37,238 (White 95.7%; Black or African American 0.3%; Hispanic or Latino 1.2%; Asian 0.4%; Other 2.9%). **Foreign born:**

1.3%. **Median age:** 38.2. **State rank:** 28. **Pop change 1990-2000:** +18.4%.

Income: per capita $13,959; median household $25,628. **Pop below poverty level:** 18.7%.

Unemployment: 4.8%. **Median home value:** $67,700. **Median travel time to work:** 20.1 minutes.

IRON COUNTY
PO Box 42   **Ph:** 573-546-2912
Ironton, MO 63650   **Fax:** 573-546-6499
www.ironcounty.org

In southeastern MO, northwest of Cape Girardeau; organized Feb 17, 1857 from Madison, Saint Francois, Wayne, Washington, and Reynolds counties. **Name Origin:** For the rich iron deposits.

Area (sq mi): 552.05 (land 551.34; water 0.71).

Pop: 10,697 (White 96.4%; Black or African American 1.6%; Hispanic or Latino 0.6%; Asian 0.1%; Other 1.5%). **Foreign born:** 0.4%. **Median age:** 39.7. **State rank:** 84. **Pop change 1990-2000:** -0.3%.

Income: per capita $14,227; median household $26,080. **Pop below poverty level:** 19%.

Unemployment: 8%. **Median home value:** $51,800. **Median travel time to work:** 28.1 minutes.

JACKSON COUNTY
415 E 12th St   **Ph:** 816-881-3000
Kansas City, MO 64106   **Fax:** 816-881-3133
www.co.jackson.mo.us

On central western border of MO; organized Dec 15, 1826 from Lafayette County. **Name Origin:** For Andrew Jackson (1767-1845), seventh U.S. president.

Area (sq mi): 616.41 (land 604.84; water 11.57).

Pop: 654,880 (White 67.7%; Black or African American 23.3%; Hispanic or Latino 5.4%; Asian 1.3%; Other 5.4%). **Foreign born:** 4.3%. **Median age:** 35.2. **State rank:** 2. **Pop change 1990-2000:** +3.4%.

Income: per capita $20,788; median household $39,277. **Pop below poverty level:** 11.9%.

Unemployment: 4.9%. **Median home value:** $85,000. **Median travel time to work:** 23.6 minutes.

JASPER COUNTY
302 S Main St Rm 102   **Ph:** 417-358-0416
Carthage, MO 64836   **Fax:** 417-358-0415

On the southwestern border of MO, west of Springfield; organized Jan 29, 1841 from Barry County. **Name Origin:** For Sgt. William Jasper (1750-79), Revolutionary War soldier from SC.

Area (sq mi): 641.32 (land 639.73; water 1.59).

Pop: 104,686 (White 91.1%; Black or African American 1.5%; Hispanic or Latino 3.5%; Asian 0.7%; Other 5.2%). **Foreign born:** 2.6%. **Median age:** 34.9. **State rank:** 9. **Pop change 1990-2000:** +15.7%.

Income: per capita $16,227; median household $31,323. **Pop below poverty level:** 14.5%.

All statistics are based on the 2000 Census except the dollar figures given for per capita income, which are based on 1999 estimates.

Unemployment: 4.1%. **Median home value:** $67,700. **Median travel time to work:** 17.8 minutes.

JEFFERSON COUNTY

PO Box 100 **Ph:** 636-797-5478
Hillsboro, MO 63050 **Fax:** 636-797-5360
www.jeffcomo.org

On the central eastern border of MO, south of Saint Louis; organized Dec 8, 1818 (prior to statehood) from Saint Genevieve and Saint Louis counties. **Name Origin:** For Thomas Jefferson (1743-1826), U.S. patriot and statesman, third U.S. president.

Area (sq mi): 664.09 (land 656.8; water 7.29).

Pop: 198,099 (White 96.8%; Black or African American 0.7%; Hispanic or Latino 1%; Asian 0.4%; Other 1.4%). **Foreign born:** 1%. **Median age:** 34.9. **State rank:** 6. **Pop change 1990-2000:** +15.6%.

Income: per capita $19,435; median household $46,338. **Pop below poverty level:** 6.8%.

Unemployment: 4.8%. **Median home value:** $99,200. **Median travel time to work:** 31.1 minutes.

JOHNSON COUNTY

300 N Holden St County Courthouse **Ph:** 660-747-6161
Warrensburg, MO 64093 **Fax:** 660-747-9332

In west-central MO, southeast of Kansas City; organized Dec 13, 1834 from Lafayette County. **Name Origin:** For Col. Richard Mentor Johnson (1781-1850), officer in the War of 1812, U.S. senator from KY (1819-29), and U.S. vice president under Van Buren (1837-41).

Area (sq mi): 833.03 (land 830.44; water 2.59).

Pop: 48,258 (White 88.7%; Black or African American 4.3%; Hispanic or Latino 2.9%; Asian 1.4%; Other 4.1%). **Foreign born:** 3%. **Median age:** 28.5. **State rank:** 19. **Pop change 1990-2000:** +13.5%.

Income: per capita $16,037; median household $35,391. **Pop below poverty level:** 14.9%.

Unemployment: 3.6%. **Median home value:** $86,500. **Median travel time to work:** 22.5 minutes.

KNOX COUNTY

107 N 4th St **Ph:** 660-397-2184
Edina, MO 63537 **Fax:** 660-397-3331

In northeastern MO, north of Columbia; organized Feb 14, 1845 from Scotland County. **Name Origin:** For Gen. Henry Knox (1750-1806), Revolutionary War officer and first U.S. Secretary of War (1785-95).

Area (sq mi): 506.77 (land 505.71; water 1.07).

Pop: 4,361 (White 98.1%; Black or African American 0.1%; Hispanic or Latino 0.6%; Asian 0.1%; Other 1.3%). **Foreign born:** 0.3%. **Median age:** 41.6. **State rank:** 112. **Pop change 1990-2000:** -2.7%.

Income: per capita $13,075; median household $27,124. **Pop below poverty level:** 18%.

Unemployment: 4.5%. **Median home value:** $37,800. **Median travel time to work:** 23.4 minutes.

LACLEDE COUNTY

200 N Adams Ave **Ph:** 417-532-5471
Lebanon, MO 65536 **Fax:** 417-588-9288
laclede.county.missouri.org

In south-central MO, northeast of Springfield; organized Feb 24, 1849 from Pulaski, Wright, and Camden counties. **Name Origin:** For Pierre Laclede Liguest (1724-78), French fur trader who established the site of Saint Louis (Dec 1763).

Area (sq mi): 768 (land 765.85; water 2.14).

Pop: 32,513 (White 96.3%; Black or African American 0.4%; Hispanic or Latino 1.2%; Asian 0.3%; Other 2.2%). **Foreign born:** 0.9%. **Median age:** 36.6. **State rank:** 34. **Pop change 1990-2000:** +19.7%.

Income: per capita $15,572; median household $29,562. **Pop below poverty level:** 14.3%.

Unemployment: 6.5%. **Median home value:** $73,000. **Median travel time to work:** 20.7 minutes.

LAFAYETTE COUNTY

1001 Main St **Ph:** 660-259-4315
Lexington, MO 64067 **Fax:** 660-259-6109

In west-central MO, east of Kansas City; organized as Lillard County Nov 16, 1820 (prior to statehood) from Cooper County; name changed Feb 16, 1825. **Name Origin:** For Marquis de Lafayette (1757-1834), French statesman and soldier who fought with the Americans during the Revolutionary War.

Area (sq mi): 638.86 (land 629.31; water 9.55).

Pop: 32,960 (White 94.9%; Black or African American 2.3%; Hispanic or Latino 1.2%; Asian 0.2%; Other 1.9%). **Foreign born:** 0.7%. **Median age:** 37.9. **State rank:** 33. **Pop change 1990-2000:** +6%.

Income: per capita $18,493; median household $38,235. **Pop below poverty level:** 8.8%.

Unemployment: 4.4%. **Median home value:** $74,400. **Median travel time to work:** 28.3 minutes.

LAWRENCE COUNTY

1 Courthouse Sq Suite 101 **Ph:** 417-466-2638
Mount Vernon, MO 65712 **Fax:** 417-466-4995

In southwestern MO, west of Springfield; organized Feb 14, 1845 from Dade and Barry counties. **Name Origin:** For Capt. James Lawrence (1781-1813), U.S. naval officer in the war with Barbary pirates near Tripoli and commander of the U.S.S. Chesapeake in the War of 1812, who said, 'Don't give up the ship!'

Area (sq mi): 613.38 (land 613.08; water 0.3).

Pop: 35,204 (White 94.3%; Black or African American 0.3%; Hispanic or Latino 3.4%; Asian 0.2%; Other 3.9%). **Foreign born:** 2.3%. **Median age:** 36.9. **State rank:** 30. **Pop change 1990-2000:** +16.4%.

Income: per capita $15,399; median household $31,239. **Pop below poverty level:** 14.1%.

Unemployment: 4.9%. **Median home value:** $65,500. **Median travel time to work:** 23.6 minutes.

Please see sample entry on inside front cover for detailed information about the statistics presented with each county listing.

LEWIS COUNTY

PO Box 67
Monticello, MO 63457

Ph: 573-767-5205
Fax: 573-767-8245

On the northeastern border of MO, northeast of Columbia; organized Jan 2, 1833 from Marion County. **Name Origin:** For Meriwether Lewis (1774-1809), co-leader of the Lewis and Clark Expedition (1804-06).

Area (sq mi): 510.85 (land 505.01; water 5.85).

Pop: 10,494 (White 95.6%; Black or African American 2.5%; Hispanic or Latino 0.7%; Asian 0.2%; Other 1.3%). **Foreign born:** 0.6%. **Median age:** 36. **State rank:** 85. **Pop change 1990-2000:** +2.6%.

Income: per capita $14,746; median household $30,651. **Pop below poverty level:** 16.1%.

Unemployment: 4.1%. **Median home value:** $52,400. **Median travel time to work:** 22.9 minutes.

LINCOLN COUNTY

201 Main St
Troy, MO 63379

Ph: 636-528-6300
Fax: 636-528-5528

On the central eastern border of MO, north of Saint Louis; organized Dec 14, 1818 (prior to statehood) from Saint Charles County. **Name Origin:** For Gen. Benjamin Lincoln (1733-1810), Revolutionary War officer, U.S. Secretary of War (1781-83), and Lt. Gov. of MA (1788).

Area (sq mi): 640.41 (land 630.49; water 9.92).

Pop: 38,944 (White 95.5%; Black or African American 1.7%; Hispanic or Latino 1.1%; Asian 0.2%; Other 1.9%). **Foreign born:** 0.6%. **Median age:** 34.5. **State rank:** 27. **Pop change 1990-2000:** +34.8%.

Income: per capita $17,149; median household $42,592. **Pop below poverty level:** 8.3%.

Unemployment: 5.1%. **Median home value:** $102,200. **Median travel time to work:** 31.3 minutes.

LINN COUNTY

108 N High St
Linneus, MO 64653

Ph: 660-895-5417
Fax: 660-895-5527

In north-central MO, east of Saint Joseph; organized Jan 6, 1837 from Chariton County. **Name Origin:** For Lewis Fields Linn (1795-1843), U.S. senator from MO (1833-43).

Area (sq mi): 621.46 (land 620.35; water 1.11).

Pop: 13,754 (White 97.5%; Black or African American 0.6%; Hispanic or Latino 0.8%; Asian 0.1%; Other 1.4%). **Foreign born:** 0.6%. **Median age:** 40.3. **State rank:** 72. **Pop change 1990-2000:** -0.9%.

Income: per capita $15,378; median household $28,242. **Pop below poverty level:** 14.9%.

Unemployment: 9.2%. **Median home value:** $42,200. **Median travel time to work:** 20.8 minutes.

LIVINGSTON COUNTY

700 Webster St
Chillicothe, MO 64601

Ph: 660-646-2293
Fax: 660-646-6139

In north-central MO, east of Saint Joseph; organized Jan 6, 1837 from Carroll County. **Name Origin:** For Edward Livingston (1764-1836), NY legislator, LA legislator and U.S. senator (1829-31), and U.S. Secretary of State (1831-33).

Area (sq mi): 538.48 (land 534.52; water 3.95).

Pop: 14,558 (White 95.6%; Black or African American 2.3%; Hispanic or Latino 0.6%; Asian 0.3%; Other 1.4%). **Foreign born:** 0.4%. **Median age:** 39.7. **State rank:** 71. **Pop change 1990-2000:** -0.2%.

Income: per capita $16,685; median household $32,290. **Pop below poverty level:** 12.4%.

Unemployment: 3.6%. **Median home value:** $61,400. **Median travel time to work:** 18.2 minutes.

MACON COUNTY

PO Box 96
Macon, MO 63552

Ph: 660-385-2913
Fax: 660-385-7203

In north-central MO, northwest of Columbia; organized Jan 6, 1837 from Randolph and Chariton counties. **Name Origin:** For Nathaniel Macon (1757-1837), Revolutionary War soldier, NC legislator, U.S. representative (1791-1815), U.S. senator (1815-28), and president of the NC constitutional convention (1835).

Area (sq mi): 812.53 (land 803.77; water 8.76).

Pop: 15,762 (White 95.6%; Black or African American 2.2%; Hispanic or Latino 0.8%; Asian 0.2%; Other 1.4%). **Foreign born:** 0.3%. **Median age:** 40.1. **State rank:** 66. **Pop change 1990-2000:** +2.7%.

Income: per capita $16,189; median household $30,195. **Pop below poverty level:** 12.5%.

Unemployment: 10.3%. **Median home value:** $55,900. **Median travel time to work:** 21.3 minutes.

MADISON COUNTY

1 Courthouse Sq
Fredericktown, MO 63645

Ph: 573-783-2176
Fax: 573-783-5351

In southeastern MO, northwest of Cape Girardeau; organized Dec 14, 1818 (prior to statehood) from Sainte Genevieve and Cape Girardeau counties. **Name Origin:** For James Madison (1751-1836), fourth U.S. president.

Area (sq mi): 497.6 (land 496.73; water 0.87).

Pop: 11,800 (White 97.9%; Black or African American 0.1%; Hispanic or Latino 0.6%; Asian 0.3%; Other 1.3%). **Foreign born:** 0.8%. **Median age:** 39.1. **State rank:** 82. **Pop change 1990-2000:** +6%.

Income: per capita $13,215; median household $25,601. **Pop below poverty level:** 17.2%.

Unemployment: 8.3%. **Median home value:** $54,800. **Median travel time to work:** 29.5 minutes.

All statistics are based on the 2000 Census except the dollar figures given for per capita income, which are based on 1999 estimates.

MARIES COUNTY

PO Box 205
Vienna, MO 65582

Ph: 573-422-3388
Fax: 573-422-3269

In east-central MO, southwest of Saint Louis; established Mar 2, 1855 from Osage and Pulaski counties. **Name Origin:** For the Maries River, which runs through it; a corruption of French *marais* 'swamp.'

Area (sq mi): 529.97 (land 527.73; water 2.25).

Pop: 8,903 (White 96.7%; Black or African American 0.3%; Hispanic or Latino 1.2%; Asian 0.1%; Other 2.1%). **Foreign born:** 0.8%. **Median age:** 38.5. **State rank:** 96. **Pop change 1990-2000:** +11.6%.

Income: per capita $15,662; median household $31,925. **Pop below poverty level:** 13.1%.

Unemployment: 5.1%. **Median home value:** $64,400. **Median travel time to work:** 33.7 minutes.

MARION COUNTY

100 S Main St
Palmyra, MO 63461

Ph: 573-769-2549
Fax: 573-769-4312

On the northeastern border of MO, north of Saint Louis; established Dec 14, 1822 from Ralls County. **Name Origin:** For Gen. Francis Marion (c. 1732-95), SC soldier and legislator, known as 'The Swamp Fox' for his tactics in the Carolina swamps during the Revolutionary War.

Area (sq mi): 444.05 (land 438.07; water 5.97).

Pop: 28,289 (White 92.7%; Black or African American 4.6%; Hispanic or Latino 0.9%; Asian 0.3%; Other 1.9%). **Foreign born:** 0.8%. **Median age:** 37.1. **State rank:** 38. **Pop change 1990-2000:** +2.2%.

Income: per capita $16,964; median household $31,774. **Pop below poverty level:** 12.1%.

Unemployment: 5.5%. **Median home value:** $66,600. **Median travel time to work:** 16.7 minutes.

McDONALD COUNTY

PO Box 665
Pineville, MO 64856

Ph: 417-223-4717
Fax: 417-223-7519

In southwestern corner of MO, south of Joplin; organized Mar 3, 1849 from Newton County. **Name Origin:** For Sgt. Alexander McDonald, a soldier in the American Revolution.

Area (sq mi): 539.7 (land 539.51; water 0.19).

Pop: 21,681 (White 84.6%; Black or African American 0.2%; Hispanic or Latino 9.4%; Asian 0.1%; Other 10%). **Foreign born:** 5.6%. **Median age:** 34.3. **State rank:** 52. **Pop change 1990-2000:** +28%.

Income: per capita $13,175; median household $27,010. **Pop below poverty level:** 20.7%.

Unemployment: 5.2%. **Median home value:** $55,800. **Median travel time to work:** 27.3 minutes.

MERCER COUNTY

802 Main St County Courthouse
Princeton, MO 64673

Ph: 660-748-3425
Fax: 660-748-3180

On the central northern border of MO, northeast of Saint Joseph; organized Feb 14, 1845 from Grundy and Livingston counties. **Name Origin:** For Lt. Col. John Francis Mercer (1759-1821), officer in the Revolutionary War, MD legislator, and governor of MD (1801-13); or possibly for Gen. Hugh Mercer (1721-77), Revolutionary War officer and physician.

Area (sq mi): 455.18 (land 454.18; water 1).

Pop: 3,757 (White 98.6%; Black or African American 0.2%; Hispanic or Latino 0.3%; Asian 0%; Other 1.2%). **Foreign born:** 0.4%. **Median age:** 42.4. **State rank:** 114. **Pop change 1990-2000:** +0.9%.

Income: per capita $15,140; median household $29,640. **Pop below poverty level:** 13.3%.

Unemployment: 3.6%. **Median home value:** $32,300. **Median travel time to work:** 24.8 minutes.

MILLER COUNTY

PO Box 12
Tuscumbia, MO 65082

Ph: 573-369-2731
Fax: 573-369-2910

In central MO, south of Jefferson City; organized Feb 6, 1837 from Cole and Pulaski counties. **Name Origin:** For Col. John Miller (1781-1846), officer in the War of 1812, governor of MO (1825-32), and U.S. representative (1837-43).

Area (sq mi): 599.94 (land 592.26; water 7.69).

Pop: 23,564 (White 97.3%; Black or African American 0.3%; Hispanic or Latino 1%; Asian 0.1%; Other 1.6%). **Foreign born:** 0.7%. **Median age:** 37.2. **State rank:** 45. **Pop change 1990-2000:** +13.8%.

Income: per capita $15,144; median household $30,977. **Pop below poverty level:** 14.2%.

Unemployment: 6.6%. **Median home value:** $69,900. **Median travel time to work:** 25 minutes.

MISSISSIPPI COUNTY

PO Box 369
Charleston, MO 63834

Ph: 573-683-2146
Fax: 573-683-6091

On the southeastern border of MO, south of Cape Girardeau; established Feb 14, 1845 from Scott County. **Name Origin:** For its location on the Mississippi River.

Area (sq mi): 428.91 (land 413.16; water 15.75).

Pop: 13,427 (White 77.5%; Black or African American 20.5%; Hispanic or Latino 1%; Asian 0.1%; Other 1.4%). **Foreign born:** 0.5%. **Median age:** 37.3. **State rank:** 75. **Pop change 1990-2000:** -7%.

Income: per capita $13,038; median household $23,012. **Pop below poverty level:** 23.7%.

Unemployment: 9.1%. **Median home value:** $47,000. **Median travel time to work:** 19.7 minutes.

MONITEAU COUNTY

200 E Main St
California, MO 65018

Ph: 573-796-4661
Fax: 573-796-3082

In central MO, west of Jefferson City; organized Feb 14, 1845 from

Please see sample entry on inside front cover for detailed information about the statistics presented with each county listing.

Cole and Morgan counties, annexed small part of Morgan County in 1881. **Name Origin:** A French transliteration of an Algonquian word meaning 'God spirit' or 'great spirit.'

Area (sq mi): 418.85 (land 416.52; water 2.33).

Pop: 14,827 (White 91.4%; Black or African American 3.8%; Hispanic or Latino 2.9%; Asian 0.3%; Other 3.2%). **Foreign born:** 1.6%. **Median age:** 35.9. **State rank:** 70. **Pop change 1990-2000:** +20.6%.

Income: per capita $16,609; median household $37,168. **Pop below poverty level:** 9.9%.

Unemployment: 4.1%. **Median home value:** $69,900. **Median travel time to work:** 24.4 minutes.

MONROE COUNTY

300 N Main St Rm 204   **Ph:** 660-327-5106
Paris, MO 65275   **Fax:** 660-327-1019

In northeastern MO, northeast of Columbia; organized Jan 6, 1831 from Ralls County. **Name Origin:** For James Monroe (1758-1831), fifth U.S. president.

Area (sq mi): 670.23 (land 645.98; water 24.24).

Pop: 9,311 (White 94.2%; Black or African American 3.8%; Hispanic or Latino 0.6%; Asian 0.1%; Other 1.4%). **Foreign born:** 0.5%. **Median age:** 39.4. **State rank:** 93. **Pop change 1990-2000:** +2.3%.

Income: per capita $14,695; median household $30,871. **Pop below poverty level:** 11.9%.

Unemployment: 7.4%. **Median home value:** $55,300. **Median travel time to work:** 25.1 minutes.

MONTGOMERY COUNTY

211 E 3rd St   **Ph:** 573-564-3357
Montgomery City, MO 63361   **Fax:** 573-564-8088

In east-central MO, northwest of Saint Louis; organized Dec 14, 1818 (prior to statehood) from Saint Charles County. **Name Origin:** For Gen. Richard Montgomery (1736-75), American Revolutionary War officer who captured Montreal, Canada.

Area (sq mi): 540.34 (land 537.46; water 2.88).

Pop: 12,136 (White 95.6%; Black or African American 2%; Hispanic or Latino 0.8%; Asian 0.3%; Other 1.7%). **Foreign born:** 1.2%. **Median age:** 39.4. **State rank:** 80. **Pop change 1990-2000:** +6.9%.

Income: per capita $15,092; median household $32,772. **Pop below poverty level:** 11.8%.

Unemployment: 5.9%. **Median home value:** $59,300. **Median travel time to work:** 27.7 minutes.

MORGAN COUNTY

100 E Newton St   **Ph:** 573-378-5436
Versailles, MO 65084   **Fax:** 573-378-5991

In central MO, west of Jefferson City; organized Jan 5, 1833 from Cooper County. **Name Origin:** For Gen. Daniel Morgan (1736-1802), an officer in the Revolutionary War and U.S. representative from VA (1797-99).

Area (sq mi): 613.89 (land 597.41; water 16.48).

Pop: 19,309 (White 96.8%; Black or African American 0.5%; Hispanic or Latino 0.8%; Asian 0.1%; Other 2%). **Foreign born:** 1%. **Median age:** 42.6. **State rank:** 56. **Pop change 1990-2000:** +24%.

Income: per capita $15,950; median household $30,659. **Pop below poverty level:** 16.2%.

Unemployment: 7%. **Median home value:** $79,500. **Median travel time to work:** 25.3 minutes.

NEW MADRID COUNTY

PO Box 68   **Ph:** 573-748-2524
New Madrid, MO 63869   **Fax:** 573-748-9269

On the southeastern border of MO, south of Cape Girardeau; original county; organized Oct 1, 1812 (prior to statehood). **Name Origin:** For the city, named for the capital of Spain. Originally called *Nuevo Madrid* by Col. George Morgan, who founded the city in 1788.

Area (sq mi): 698.02 (land 678.01; water 20.01).

Pop: 19,760 (White 82.7%; Black or African American 15.4%; Hispanic or Latino 0.9%; Asian 0.1%; Other 1.3%). **Foreign born:** 0.3%. **Median age:** 37.4. **State rank:** 55. **Pop change 1990-2000:** -5.6%.

Income: per capita $14,204; median household $26,826. **Pop below poverty level:** 22.1%.

Unemployment: 7.9%. **Median home value:** $48,100. **Median travel time to work:** 18.1 minutes.

NEWTON COUNTY

PO Box 488   **Ph:** 417-451-8220
Neosho, MO 64850   **Fax:** 417-451-7434

On the southwestern border of MO, south of Joplin; organized Dec 30, 1838 from Barry County. **Name Origin:** For Sgt. John Newton (1752-80); soldier under Gen. Francis Marion in the Revolutionary War, who saved several colonial patriots from execution by surprising and capturing the British soldiers guarding them.

Area (sq mi): 626.66 (land 626.42; water 0.24).

Pop: 52,636 (White 92.4%; Black or African American 0.6%; Hispanic or Latino 2.2%; Asian 0.3%; Other 5.8%). **Foreign born:** 1.4%. **Median age:** 37.1. **State rank:** 18. **Pop change 1990-2000:** +18.4%.

Income: per capita $17,502; median household $35,041. **Pop below poverty level:** 11.6%.

Unemployment: 5.1%. **Median home value:** $74,200. **Median travel time to work:** 21.8 minutes.

NODAWAY COUNTY

PO Box 218   **Ph:** 660-582-2251
Maryville, MO 64468   **Fax:** 660-582-5282

On the northwestern border of MO, north of Saint Joseph; established Jan 29, 1841 from Andrew County. **Name Origin:** A Potawatomi Indian word whose meaning is unclear, possibly 'placid.'

Area (sq mi): 877.75 (land 876.62; water 1.13).

Pop: 21,912 (White 96.1%; Black or African American 1.3%; Hispanic or Latino 0.7%; Asian 0.9%; Other 1.1%). **Foreign born:**

All statistics are based on the 2000 Census except the dollar figures given for per capita income, which are based on 1999 estimates.

1.4%. **Median age:** 30.2. **State rank:** 51. **Pop change 1990-2000:** +0.9%.

Income: per capita $15,384; median household $31,781. **Pop below poverty level:** 16.5%.

Unemployment: 1.9%. **Median home value:** $71,100. **Median travel time to work:** 16.3 minutes.

OREGON COUNTY

PO Box 324   **Ph:** 417-778-7475
Alton, MO 65606   **Fax:** 417-778-7488

On the central southern border of MO, southwest of Cape Giradeau; organized Feb 14, 1845 from Ripley County. **Name Origin:** For OR Territory, named during the dispute with Great Britain over its possession.

Area (sq mi): 791.59 (land 791.4; water 0.18).

Pop: 10,344 (White 93.7%; Black or African American 0.1%; Hispanic or Latino 1.1%; Asian 0.1%; Other 5.2%). **Foreign born:** 0.7%. **Median age:** 41. **State rank:** 87. **Pop change 1990-2000:** +9.2%.

Income: per capita $12,812; median household $22,359. **Pop below poverty level:** 22%.

Unemployment: 4.4%. **Median home value:** $45,900. **Median travel time to work:** 27.9 minutes.

OSAGE COUNTY

PO Box 826   **Ph:** 573-897-2139
Linn, MO 65051   **Fax:** 573-897-4741

In east-central MO, west of Saint Louis; organized Jan 29, 1841 from Gasconade County. **Name Origin:** For the Osage Indians, a tribe of Siouan linguistic stock. Name is a corruption of their name in their language, *Wazhazhe*, meaning unknown.

Area (sq mi): 613.41 (land 606.11; water 7.3).

Pop: 13,062 (White 98.2%; Black or African American 0.2%; Hispanic or Latino 0.6%; Asian 0.1%; Other 1.1%). **Foreign born:** 0.5%. **Median age:** 36.1. **State rank:** 78. **Pop change 1990-2000:** +8.7%.

Income: per capita $17,245; median household $39,565. **Pop below poverty level:** 8.3%.

Unemployment: 5.1%. **Median home value:** $81,400. **Median travel time to work:** 28 minutes.

OZARK COUNTY

PO Box 416   **Ph:** 417-679-3516
Gainesville, MO 65655   **Fax:** 417-679-3209

On the central southern border of MO, southeast of Springfield; organized Jan 29, 1841 from Taney County. **Name Origin:** For the Ozark Mountains, whose name derives from the anglicized phonetic spelling of French *aux arcs* or *aux Arks* 'in the country of the Arkansas Indians.'

Area (sq mi): 755.07 (land 742.15; water 12.92).

Pop: 9,542 (White 96.9%; Black or African American 0.1%; Hispanic or Latino 0.9%; Asian 0.1%; Other 2.2%). **Foreign born:** 1%. **Median age:** 43.6. **State rank:** 92. **Pop change 1990-2000:** +11%.

Income: per capita $14,133; median household $25,861. **Pop below poverty level:** 21.6%.

Unemployment: 5.9%. **Median home value:** $62,600. **Median travel time to work:** 29.5 minutes.

PEMISCOT COUNTY

610 Ward Ave   **Ph:** 573-333-4203
Caruthersville, MO 63830   **Fax:** 573-333-0440

On southeastern tip of MO, south of Cape Girardeau; organized Feb 19, 1851 from New Madrid County. **Name Origin:** From an Indian name of uncertain origin and meaning 'at the long place,' 'running beside,' and 'liquid mud' have been suggested.

Area (sq mi): 512.41 (land 493.08; water 19.33).

Pop: 20,047 (White 71.1%; Black or African American 26.2%; Hispanic or Latino 1.6%; Asian 0.3%; Other 1.7%). **Foreign born:** 0.9%. **Median age:** 34.4. **State rank:** 54. **Pop change 1990-2000:** -8.5%.

Income: per capita $12,968; median household $21,911. **Pop below poverty level:** 30.4%.

Unemployment: 9.4%. **Median home value:** $44,200. **Median travel time to work:** 18.3 minutes.

PERRY COUNTY

321 N Main St Suite 2   **Ph:** 573-547-4242
Perryville, MO 63775   **Fax:** 573-547-7367
www.perryvillemo.com/county/

On the southeastern border of MO, north of Cape Girardeau; organized Nov 16, 1820 (prior to statehood) from Sainte Genevieve County. **Name Origin:** For Oliver Hazard Perry (1785-1819), U.S. naval officer who won the Battle of Lake Erie during the War of 1812, famous for the message, 'We have met the enemy and they are ours.'

Area (sq mi): 484.28 (land 474.67; water 9.61).

Pop: 18,132 (White 97.8%; Black or African American 0.2%; Hispanic or Latino 0.5%; Asian 0.6%; Other 0.9%). **Foreign born:** 1.1%. **Median age:** 36.8. **State rank:** 59. **Pop change 1990-2000:** +8.9%.

Income: per capita $16,554; median household $36,632. **Pop below poverty level:** 9%.

Unemployment: 3.5%. **Median home value:** $80,000. **Median travel time to work:** 22.3 minutes.

PETTIS COUNTY

415 S Ohio St   **Ph:** 660-826-5395
Sedalia, MO 65301   **Fax:** 660-827-8637

In west-central MO, southwest of Columbia; organized Jan 26, 1833 from Saline and Cooper counties. **Name Origin:** For Spencer Darwin Pettis (1802-31), U.S. representative from MO (1829-31) killed in a duel with Maj. Thomas Biddle.

Area (sq mi): 686.34 (land 684.82; water 1.52).

Pop: 39,403 (White 90.9%; Black or African American 3%; Hispanic or Latino 3.9%; Asian 0.4%; Other 4.6%). **Foreign born:** 2.9%. **Median age:** 36.4. **State rank:** 26. **Pop change 1990-2000:** +11.2%.

Please see sample entry on inside front cover for detailed information about the statistics presented with each county listing.

Income: per capita $16,251; median household $31,822. **Pop below poverty level:** 12.8%.

Unemployment: 6.2%. **Median home value:** $66,400. **Median travel time to work:** 18.9 minutes.

PHELPS COUNTY
200 N Main St
Rolla, MO 65401
www.phelpscounty.org

Ph: 573-364-1891
Fax: 573-364-0436

In south-central MO, southwest of Saint Louis; organized Nov 13, 1857 from Crawford County. **Name Origin:** For John Smith Phelps (1814-86), MO legislator, U.S. representative (1845-63), and governor (1876-80).

Area (sq mi): 674.28 (land 672.85; water 1.43).

Pop: 39,825 (White 92.6%; Black or African American 1.5%; Hispanic or Latino 1.2%; Asian 2.4%; Other 3%). **Foreign born:** 4%. **Median age:** 34.9. **State rank:** 24. **Pop change 1990-2000:** +13%.

Income: per capita $16,084; median household $29,378. **Pop below poverty level:** 16.4%.

Unemployment: 3.5%. **Median home value:** $74,800. **Median travel time to work:** 19.1 minutes.

PIKE COUNTY
115 W Main St
Bowling Green, MO 63334

Ph: 573-324-2412
Fax: 573-324-5154

On the central eastern border of MO, north of Saint Louis; organized Dec 14, 1818 (prior to statehood) from Saint Charles County. **Name Origin:** For Zebulon Montgomery Pike (1779-1813), U.S. army officer and discoverer of Pikes Peak, CO.

Area (sq mi): 684.81 (land 672.82; water 11.99).

Pop: 18,351 (White 87.8%; Black or African American 9.2%; Hispanic or Latino 1.6%; Asian 0.2%; Other 2.1%). **Foreign born:** 1.6%. **Median age:** 37.7. **State rank:** 58. **Pop change 1990-2000:** +14.9%.

Income: per capita $14,462; median household $32,373. **Pop below poverty level:** 15.5%.

Unemployment: 5.6%. **Median home value:** $63,400. **Median travel time to work:** 24.6 minutes.

PLATTE COUNTY
415 3rd St
Platte City, MO 64079
www.co.platte.mo.us

Ph: 816-858-2232
Fax: 816-858-3363

On the northwestern border of MO, northwest of Kansas City; organized Dec 31, 1838 from Platte Purchase. **Name Origin:** For the Platte River, which runs through it; French 'flat' or 'still.'

Area (sq mi): 427.22 (land 420.33; water 6.89).

Pop: 73,781 (White 89.8%; Black or African American 3.5%; Hispanic or Latino 3%; Asian 1.5%; Other 3.6%). **Foreign born:** 3.7%. **Median age:** 35.9. **State rank:** 13. **Pop change 1990-2000:** +27.5%.

Income: per capita $26,356; median household $55,849. **Pop below poverty level:** 4.8%.

Unemployment: 2.8%. **Median home value:** $126,700. **Median travel time to work:** 23 minutes.

POLK COUNTY
102 E Broadway
Bolivar, MO 65613

Ph: 417-326-4031
Fax: 417-326-3525

In south-central MO, north of Springfield; organized Jan 5, 1835 from Greene and Laclede counties. **Name Origin:** For James Knox Polk (1795-1849), eleventh U.S. president.

Area (sq mi): 642.46 (land 637.2; water 5.26).

Pop: 26,992 (White 96.4%; Black or African American 0.5%; Hispanic or Latino 1.3%; Asian 0.2%; Other 2.1%). **Foreign born:** 1.5%. **Median age:** 35. **State rank:** 39. **Pop change 1990-2000:** +23.7%.

Income: per capita $13,645; median household $29,656. **Pop below poverty level:** 16.3%.

Unemployment: 4.3%. **Median home value:** $77,000. **Median travel time to work:** 25.3 minutes.

PULASKI COUNTY
301 Historic 66 E Suite 101
Waynesville, MO 65583

Ph: 573-774-4701
Fax: 573-774-5601

In south-central MO, northeast of Springfield; organized Jan 19, 1833 from Crawford County. **Name Origin:** For Count Casimir Pulaski (1747-79), Polish soldier who fought for America during the Revolutionary War.

Area (sq mi): 551.41 (land 547.02; water 4.39).

Pop: 41,165 (White 75.8%; Black or African American 12%; Hispanic or Latino 5.8%; Asian 2.3%; Other 7.4%). **Foreign born:** 4.8%. **Median age:** 28.5. **State rank:** 20. **Pop change 1990-2000:** -0.3%.

Income: per capita $14,586; median household $34,247. **Pop below poverty level:** 10.3%.

Unemployment: 6.3%. **Median home value:** $78,300. **Median travel time to work:** 18.8 minutes.

PUTNAM COUNTY
Rm 204 County Courthouse
Unionville, MO 63565

Ph: 660-947-2674
Fax: 660-947-4214

On the central northern border of MO; established Feb 22, 1843 from Adair, Sullivan, and Linn counties, annexed Dodge County in 1853. **Name Origin:** For Gen. Israel Putnam (1718-90), Revolutionary War officer and American commander at the Battle of Bunker Hill.

Area (sq mi): 519.66 (land 517.9; water 1.76).

Pop: 5,223 (White 98.7%; Black or African American 0.1%; Hispanic or Latino 0.6%; Asian 0.1%; Other 0.7%). **Foreign born:** 0.5%. **Median age:** 41.9. **State rank:** 110. **Pop change 1990-2000:** +2.8%.

Income: per capita $14,647; median household $26,282. **Pop below poverty level:** 16%.

Unemployment: 4%. **Median home value:** $44,500. **Median travel time to work:** 26.7 minutes.

All statistics are based on the 2000 Census except the dollar figures given for per capita income, which are based on 1999 estimates.

RALLS COUNTY

PO Box 400
New London, MO 63459

Ph: 573-985-7111
Fax: 573-985-6100

On northeastern border of MO; northeast of Columbia; organized Nov 16, 1820 (prior to statehood) from Pike County. **Name Origin:** For Daniel Ralls (1785-1820) a MO legislator who died the year the county was formed.

Area (sq mi): 483.82 (land 471; water 12.82).

Pop: 9,626 (White 97.6%; Black or African American 1.1%; Hispanic or Latino 0.4%; Asian 0.1%; Other 0.8%). **Foreign born:** 0.3%. **Median age:** 39.3. **State rank:** 91. **Pop change 1990-2000:** +13.6%.

Income: per capita $16,456; median household $37,094. **Pop below poverty level:** 8.7%.

Unemployment: 5.7%. **Median home value:** $67,400. **Median travel time to work:** 21.5 minutes.

RANDOLPH COUNTY

110 S Main St
Huntsville, MO 65259

Ph: 660-277-4717
Fax: 660-277-3246

In north-central MO, north of Columbia; organized Jan 22, 1829 from Chariton and Ralls counties. **Name Origin:** For John Randolph (1773-1833), VA statesman and U.S. Minister to Russia (1830).

Area (sq mi): 487.65 (land 482.32; water 5.33).

Pop: 24,663 (White 89.9%; Black or African American 7%; Hispanic or Latino 1.1%; Asian 0.4%; Other 2%). **Foreign born:** 1.3%. **Median age:** 37.2. **State rank:** 42. **Pop change 1990-2000:** +1.2%.

Income: per capita $15,010; median household $31,464. **Pop below poverty level:** 12.5%.

Unemployment: 6%. **Median home value:** $49,300. **Median travel time to work:** 21.1 minutes.

RAY COUNTY

100 W Main St County Courthouse
Richmond, MO 64085

Ph: 816-776-4502
Fax: 816-776-4512

In west-central MO, northeast of Kansas City; organized Nov 16, 1820 (prior to statehood) from Howard County. **Name Origin:** For John Ray, a MO legislator when the county was named.

Area (sq mi): 573.57 (land 569.47; water 4.11).

Pop: 23,354 (White 95.8%; Black or African American 1.5%; Hispanic or Latino 1.1%; Asian 0.2%; Other 1.9%). **Foreign born:** 0.4%. **Median age:** 37.1. **State rank:** 46. **Pop change 1990-2000:** +6.3%.

Income: per capita $18,685; median household $41,886. **Pop below poverty level:** 6.8%.

Unemployment: 4.3%. **Median home value:** $81,000. **Median travel time to work:** 32.7 minutes.

REYNOLDS COUNTY

PO Box 10
Centerville, MO 63633

Ph: 573-648-2494
Fax: 573-648-2296

In southeastern MO, west of Cape Girardeau; organized Feb 25, 1845 from Shannon County. **Name Origin:** For Thomas Reynolds (1796-1844), IL legislator, MO legislator, and governor (1840-440.

Area (sq mi): 814.41 (land 811.2; water 3.21).

Pop: 6,689 (White 95.2%; Black or African American 0.5%; Hispanic or Latino 0.8%; Asian 0.2%; Other 3.6%). **Foreign born:** 0.4%. **Median age:** 40.7. **State rank:** 106. **Pop change 1990-2000:** +0.4%.

Income: per capita $13,065; median household $25,867. **Pop below poverty level:** 20.1%.

Unemployment: 9.2%. **Median home value:** $47,200. **Median travel time to work:** 28 minutes.

RIPLEY COUNTY

County Courthouse 100 Courthouse Sq
Doniphan, MO 63935

Ph: 573-996-3215
Fax: 573-996-5014

On the southeastern border of MO, southwest of Cape Girardeau; organized Jan 5, 1833 from Wayne County. **Name Origin:** For Gen. Eleazar Wheelock Ripley (1782-1839), officer in the War of 1812, MA legislator, and U.S. representative from LA (1835-39).

Area (sq mi): 631.66 (land 629.47; water 2.2).

Pop: 13,509 (White 96.4%; Black or African American 0%; Hispanic or Latino 1%; Asian 0.2%; Other 2.6%). **Foreign born:** 1.1%. **Median age:** 39.4. **State rank:** 74. **Pop change 1990-2000:** +9.8%.

Income: per capita $12,889; median household $22,761. **Pop below poverty level:** 22%.

Unemployment: 7.4%. **Median home value:** $49,100. **Median travel time to work:** 25.4 minutes.

SAINT CHARLES COUNTY

201 N 2nd St
Saint Charles, MO 63301
www.win.org/county/sccg.htm

Ph: 636-949-7550
Fax: 636-949-7552

On central eastern border of MO, north of Saint Louis; original county; organized Oct 1, 1812 (prior to statehood). **Name Origin:** For Saint Carlo Borromeo (1538-84), archbishop of Milan and founder of the religious order of the Oblates of Saint Ambrose.

Area (sq mi): 592.35 (land 560.42; water 31.93).

Pop: 283,883 (White 93.8%; Black or African American 2.7%; Hispanic or Latino 1.5%; Asian 0.9%; Other 1.8%). **Foreign born:** 2.1%. **Median age:** 34.3. **State rank:** 4. **Pop change 1990-2000:** +33.3%.

Income: per capita $23,592; median household $57,258. **Pop below poverty level:** 4%.

Unemployment: 3.3%. **Median home value:** $126,200. **Median travel time to work:** 26.4 minutes.

SAINT CLAIR COUNTY

655 2nd St
Osceola, MO 64776

Ph: 417-646-2315
Fax: 417-646-8080

In west-central MO, northwest of Springfield; organized Jan 29, 1841 from Rives County. **Name Origin:** For Gen. Arthur Saint Clair (1736?-1818), an officer in the French and Indian War and the Revolutionary War, president of the Continental Congress (1787), and governor of the Northwest Territory (1788-1802).

Area (sq mi): 701.9 (land 676.66; water 25.25).

Please see sample entry on inside front cover for detailed information about the statistics presented with each county listing.

Pop: 9,652 (White 96.7%; Black or African American 0.2%; Hispanic or Latino 1%; Asian 0.1%; Other 2.2%). **Foreign born:** 0.7%. **Median age:** 43.9. **State rank:** 90. **Pop change 1990-2000:** +14.1%.

Income: per capita $14,025; median household $25,321. **Pop below poverty level:** 19.6%.

Unemployment: 5.6%. **Median home value:** $48,500. **Median travel time to work:** 32.3 minutes.

SAINT FRANCOIS COUNTY

1 N Washington St Rm 206   **Ph:** 573-756-5411
Farmington, MO 63640   **Fax:** 573-756-2817

In southeastern MO, south of Saint Louis; established Dec 19, 1821 from Sainte Genevieve, Jefferson, and Washington counties. **Name Origin:** For the Saint Francois Mountains, part of which are in the county; French for Saint Francis.

Area (sq mi): 452.4 (land 449.46; water 2.94).

Pop: 55,641 (White 95.7%; Black or African American 2%; Hispanic or Latino 0.8%; Asian 0.3%; Other 1.5%). **Foreign born:** 0.9%. **Median age:** 37.2. **State rank:** 16. **Pop change 1990-2000:** +13.8%.

Income: per capita $15,273; median household $31,199. **Pop below poverty level:** 14.9%.

Unemployment: 7.3%. **Median home value:** $68,200. **Median travel time to work:** 27.6 minutes.

SAINT LOUIS (INDEPENDENT CITY)

1200 Market St   **Ph:** 314-622-3201
Saint Louis, MO 63103   **Fax:** 314-622-4061
stlouis.missouri.org

On the central-eastern border of MO on the Mississippi River, 11 mi. below its confluence with the Missouri River; chartered as a city 1822. **Name Origin:** For Louis IX (1214-70), crusader king of France, canonized in 1297.

Area (sq mi): 66.15 (land 61.92; water 4.23).

Pop: 348,189 (White 42.9%; Black or African American 51.2%; Hispanic or Latino 2%; Asian 2%; Other 3%). **Foreign born:** 5.6%. **Median age:** 33.7. **State rank:** 3. **Pop change 1990-2000:** -12.2%.

Income: per capita $16,108; median household $27,156. **Pop below poverty level:** 24.6%.

Unemployment: 8.2%. **Median home value:** $63,900. **Median travel time to work:** 25.1 minutes.

SAINT LOUIS COUNTY

41 S Central Ave   **Ph:** 314-615-5432
Clayton, MO 63105   **Fax:** 314-615-7890
www.co.st-louis.mo.us

On the central-eastern border of MO on the Mississippi River, 11 mi. below its confluence with the Missouri River. Organized 1812; original county. **Name Origin:** For Louis IX (1214-70), crusader king of France, canonized in 1297.

Area (sq mi): 523.69 (land 507.81; water 15.89).

Pop: 1,016,315 (White 76%; Black or African American 19%; Hispanic or Latino 1.4%; Asian 2.2%; Other 2%). **Foreign born:** 4.2%. **Median age:** 37.5. **State rank:** 1. **Pop change 1990-2000:** +2.3%.

Income: per capita $27,595; median household $50,532. **Pop below poverty level:** 6.9%.

Unemployment: 3.9%. **Median home value:** $116,600. **Median travel time to work:** 24 minutes.

SAINTE GENEVIEVE COUNTY

55 S 3rd St   **Ph:** 573-883-5589
Sainte Genevieve, MO 63670   **Fax:** 573-883-5312

On southeastern border of MO, south of Saint Louis; original county; organized Oct 1, 1812 (prior to statehood). **Name Origin:** For the city, the oldest white settlement in MO; itself named for Sainte Genevieve (c. 422-c. 500), French nun and patron saint of Paris.

Area (sq mi): 508.94 (land 502.39; water 6.55).

Pop: 17,842 (White 97.5%; Black or African American 0.7%; Hispanic or Latino 0.7%; Asian 0.2%; Other 1.1%). **Foreign born:** 0.6%. **Median age:** 37.7. **State rank:** 61. **Pop change 1990-2000:** +11.3%.

Income: per capita $17,283; median household $39,200. **Pop below poverty level:** 8.2%.

Unemployment: 5.2%. **Median home value:** $83,700. **Median travel time to work:** 25.9 minutes.

SALINE COUNTY

Rm 202 County Courthouse   **Ph:** 660-886-3331
Marshall, MO 65340   **Fax:** 660-886-2603

In central MO, east of Kansas City; organized Nov 25, 1820 (prior to statehood) from Cooper County. **Name Origin:** French 'salt spring' or 'lick.'

Area (sq mi): 764.59 (land 755.55; water 9.04).

Pop: 23,756 (White 88.1%; Black or African American 5.4%; Hispanic or Latino 4.4%; Asian 0.4%; Other 4.2%). **Foreign born:** 3.5%. **Median age:** 37.2. **State rank:** 44. **Pop change 1990-2000:** +1%.

Income: per capita $16,132; median household $32,743. **Pop below poverty level:** 13.2%.

Unemployment: 5.2%. **Median home value:** $59,700. **Median travel time to work:** 17.1 minutes.

SCHUYLER COUNTY

PO Box 187   **Ph:** 660-457-3842
Lancaster, MO 63548   **Fax:** 660-457-3016

On the northeastern border of MO; organized Feb 14, 1845 from Adair County. **Name Origin:** For Gen. Philip John Schuyler (1733-1804), an officer in the Revolutionary War, member of the Continental Congress (1775-77; 1778-81), and U.S. senator from NY (1789-91; 1797-98).

Area (sq mi): 308.16 (land 307.87; water 0.29).

Pop: 4,170 (White 98%; Black or African American 0%; Hispanic or Latino 0.6%; Asian 0.2%; Other 1.3%). **Foreign born:** 0.4%. **Median age:** 40.8. **State rank:** 113. **Pop change 1990-2000:** -1.6%.

Income: per capita $15,850; median household $27,385. **Pop below poverty level:** 17%.

All statistics are based on the 2000 Census except the dollar figures given for per capita income, which are based on 1999 estimates.

Unemployment: 5.3%. **Median home value:** $38,500. **Median travel time to work:** 25 minutes.

SCOTLAND COUNTY

County Courthouse 117 S Market St
Suite 100   **Ph:** 660-465-7027
Memphis, MO 63555   **Fax:** 660-465-8673

On the northeastern border of MO; organized Jan 29, 1841 from Clark, Lewis and Shelby counties. **Name Origin:** For the country, the former home of early settlers.

Area (sq mi): 439.25 (land 438.47; water 0.79).

Pop: 4,983 (White 98.1%; Black or African American 0.2%; Hispanic or Latino 0.8%; Asian 0.1%; Other 0.9%). **Foreign born:** 0.3%. **Median age:** 37.4. **State rank:** 111. **Pop change 1990-2000:** +3.3%.

Income: per capita $14,474; median household $27,409. **Pop below poverty level:** 16.8%.

Unemployment: 4.3%. **Median home value:** $43,300. **Median travel time to work:** 21.9 minutes.

SCOTT COUNTY

PO Box 188   **Ph:** 573-545-3549
Benton, MO 63736   **Fax:** 573-545-3540

On the southeastern border of MO, south of Cape Girardeau; established Dec 28, 1821 from New Madrid County. **Name Origin:** For John Scott (1785-1861), lawyer and U.S. representative from MO (1821-27).

Area (sq mi): 426.04 (land 421.01; water 5.03).

Pop: 40,422 (White 87.1%; Black or African American 10.5%; Hispanic or Latino 1.1%; Asian 0.2%; Other 1.6%). **Foreign born:** 0.6%. **Median age:** 36. **State rank:** 23. **Pop change 1990-2000:** +2.7%.

Income: per capita $15,620; median household $31,352. **Pop below poverty level:** 16.1%.

Unemployment: 5.9%. **Median home value:** $68,200. **Median travel time to work:** 19.1 minutes.

SHANNON COUNTY

PO Box 187   **Ph:** 573-226-3414
Eminence, MO 65466   **Fax:** 573-226-5321

In south-central MO, east of Springfield; organized Jan 29, 1841 from Ripley County. **Name Origin:** For George F. 'Peg-leg' Shannon (1785-1836), a member of the Lewis and Clark expedition.

Area (sq mi): 1003.99 (land 1003.83; water 0.15).

Pop: 8,324 (White 94.5%; Black or African American 0.2%; Hispanic or Latino 0.9%; Asian 0%; Other 4.7%). **Foreign born:** 0.5%. **Median age:** 38.8. **State rank:** 99. **Pop change 1990-2000:** +9.3%.

Income: per capita $11,492; median household $20,878. **Pop below poverty level:** 26.9%.

Unemployment: 6.6%. **Median home value:** $41,400. **Median travel time to work:** 26.1 minutes.

SHELBY COUNTY

PO Box 186   **Ph:** 573-633-2181
Shelbyville, MO 63469   **Fax:** 573-633-1004

In northeastern MO, northeast of Columbia; organized Jan 2, 1835 from Marion County. **Name Origin:** For Gen. Isaac Shelby (1750-1826), officer in the Revolutionary War, NC legislator, and governor of KY (1792-96; 1812-16).

Area (sq mi): 502.43 (land 500.93; water 1.49).

Pop: 6,799 (White 97.5%; Black or African American 1%; Hispanic or Latino 0.6%; Asian 0.1%; Other 1.1%). **Foreign born:** 0.8%. **Median age:** 40.4. **State rank:** 105. **Pop change 1990-2000:** -2.1%.

Income: per capita $15,632; median household $29,448. **Pop below poverty level:** 16.3%.

Unemployment: 6.8%. **Median home value:** $44,000. **Median travel time to work:** 20.5 minutes.

STODDARD COUNTY

PO Box 110   **Ph:** 573-568-3339
Bloomfield, MO 63825   **Fax:** 573-568-2194

In southeastern MO, southwest of Cape Girardeau; organized Jun 21, 1835 from Cape Girardeau County. **Name Origin:** For Capt. Amos Stoddard (1762-1813), an officer in the Revolutionary War and acting governor of LA Territory (1804-05).

Area (sq mi): 828.94 (land 827.12; water 1.82).

Pop: 29,705 (White 96.9%; Black or African American 0.9%; Hispanic or Latino 0.8%; Asian 0.1%; Other 1.6%). **Foreign born:** 0.5%. **Median age:** 39.1. **State rank:** 36. **Pop change 1990-2000:** +2.8%.

Income: per capita $14,656; median household $26,987. **Pop below poverty level:** 16.5%.

Unemployment: 7%. **Median home value:** $57,200. **Median travel time to work:** 21.1 minutes.

STONE COUNTY

PO Box 45   **Ph:** 417-357-6127
Galena, MO 65656   **Fax:** 417-357-6861

On the southwestern border of MO, south of Springfield; organized Feb 10, 1851 from Taney County. **Name Origin:** For either William Stone, a prominent judge, or John W. Stone, an early settler.

Area (sq mi): 510.91 (land 463.22; water 47.68).

Pop: 28,658 (White 97%; Black or African American 0.1%; Hispanic or Latino 1%; Asian 0.2%; Other 2.1%). **Foreign born:** 1.1%. **Median age:** 44.1. **State rank:** 37. **Pop change 1990-2000:** +50.2%.

Income: per capita $18,036; median household $32,637. **Pop below poverty level:** 12.8%.

Unemployment: 9.9%. **Median home value:** $102,700. **Median travel time to work:** 30.1 minutes.

SULLIVAN COUNTY

109 N Main St   **Ph:** 660-265-3786
Milan, MO 63556   **Fax:** 660-265-3724

In north-central MO; organized Feb 14, 1845 from Linn County. **Name Origin:** For either James Sullivan, a prominent local resident, or for Sullivan County, TN, which was named for Gen. John

---

Please see sample entry on inside front cover for detailed information about the statistics presented with each county listing.

Sullivan (1740-95), Revolutionary War officer, member of the Continental Congress, chief executive and governor (1786-87, 1789) of NH.

Area (sq mi): 651.43 (land 650.95; water 0.48).

Pop: 7,219 (White 90.2%; Black or African American 0.1%; Hispanic or Latino 8.8%; Asian 0.1%; Other 4.7%). **Foreign born:** 5.8%. **Median age:** 38.9. **State rank:** 103. **Pop change 1990-2000:** +14.1%.

Income: per capita $13,392; median household $26,107. **Pop below poverty level:** 16.5%.

Unemployment: 3.6%. **Median home value:** $37,700. **Median travel time to work:** 21.2 minutes.

TANEY COUNTY
PO Box 156   **Ph:** 417-546-7201
Forsyth, MO 656530156   **Fax:** 417-546-2519
www.co.taney.mo.us

On southwestern border of MO, south of Springfield; organized Jan 6, 1837 from Greene County. **Name Origin:** For Roger Brooke Taney (1777-1864), Chief Justice of the U.S. Supreme Court (1836-64), who wrote the decision in the Dred Scott Case.

Area (sq mi): 651.48 (land 632.36; water 19.12).

Pop: 39,703 (White 94.8%; Black or African American 0.3%; Hispanic or Latino 2.4%; Asian 0.3%; Other 3.1%). **Foreign born:** 2%. **Median age:** 38.8. **State rank:** 25. **Pop change 1990-2000:** +55.3%.

Income: per capita $17,267; median household $30,898. **Pop below poverty level:** 12.4%.

Unemployment: 7.9%. **Median home value:** $93,500. **Median travel time to work:** 21.7 minutes.

TEXAS COUNTY
210 N Grand Ave   **Ph:** 417-967-2112
Houston, MO 65483   **Fax:** 417-967-3837

In south-central MO, east of Springfield; organized as Ashley County Feb 17, 1843 from Shannon and Wright counties; name changed Feb 14, 1845. **Name Origin:** Probably in honor of the admission of the state of TX.

Area (sq mi): 1179.24 (land 1178.54; water 0.7).

Pop: 23,003 (White 95.8%; Black or African American 0.2%; Hispanic or Latino 1%; Asian 0.3%; Other 3%). **Foreign born:** 0.8%. **Median age:** 40.4. **State rank:** 48. **Pop change 1990-2000:** +7.1%.

Income: per capita $13,799; median household $24,545. **Pop below poverty level:** 21.4%.

Unemployment: 7.1%. **Median home value:** $61,000. **Median travel time to work:** 27.2 minutes.

VERNON COUNTY
100 W Cherry St   **Ph:** 417-448-2500
Nevada, MO 64772   **Fax:** 417-667-6035
www.vernoncountymo.org

On central western border of MO, north of Joplin; organized Feb 17, 1851 from Bates County. **Name Origin:** For Col. Miles Vernon (1786-1866), veteran of the Battle of New Orleans and MO legislator.

Area (sq mi): 837.04 (land 833.95; water 3.09).

Pop: 20,454 (White 96.5%; Black or African American 0.6%; Hispanic or Latino 0.8%; Asian 0.3%; Other 2.1%). **Foreign born:** 1.3%. **Median age:** 37.1. **State rank:** 53. **Pop change 1990-2000:** +7.4%.

Income: per capita $15,047; median household $30,021. **Pop below poverty level:** 14.9%.

Unemployment: 3.8%. **Median home value:** $58,500. **Median travel time to work:** 20.9 minutes.

WARREN COUNTY
104 W Main St   **Ph:** 636-456-3331
Warrenton, MO 63383   **Fax:** 636-456-1801

In east-central MO, west of Saint Louis; organized Jan 5, 1833 from Montgomery County. **Name Origin:** For Gen. Joseph Warren (1741-75), Revolutionary War patriot and member of the Committee of Safety who dispatched Paul Revere (1735-1818) on his famous ride (1775).

Area (sq mi): 437.74 (land 431.31; water 6.43).

Pop: 24,525 (White 95.1%; Black or African American 1.9%; Hispanic or Latino 1.3%; Asian 0.2%; Other 1.8%). **Foreign born:** 1.5%. **Median age:** 37.4. **State rank:** 43. **Pop change 1990-2000:** +25.6%.

Income: per capita $19,690; median household $41,016. **Pop below poverty level:** 8.6%.

Unemployment: 5.1%. **Median home value:** $108,600. **Median travel time to work:** 29.4 minutes.

WASHINGTON COUNTY
102 N Missouri St   **Ph:** 573-438-4901
Potosi, MO 63664   **Fax:** 573-438-4038

In east-central MO, southwest of Saint Louis; organized Aug 21, 1813 (prior to statehood) from Sainte Genevieve County. **Name Origin:** For George Washington (1732-99), American patriot and first U.S. president.

Area (sq mi): 762.46 (land 759.59; water 2.87).

Pop: 23,344 (White 94.9%; Black or African American 2.5%; Hispanic or Latino 0.7%; Asian 0.1%; Other 2%). **Foreign born:** 0.7%. **Median age:** 35.2. **State rank:** 47. **Pop change 1990-2000:** +14.5%.

Income: per capita $12,934; median household $27,112. **Pop below poverty level:** 20.8%.

Unemployment: 8.7%. **Median home value:** $57,600. **Median travel time to work:** 36.5 minutes.

WAYNE COUNTY
109 Walnut St County Courthouse   **Ph:** 573-224-3011
Greenville, MO 63944   **Fax:** 573-224-5609

In southeastern MO, southwest of Cape Giradeau; organized Dec 11, 1818 (prior to statehood) from Cape Girardeau and Lawrence counties. **Name Origin:** For Gen. Anthony Wayne (1745-96), PA soldier and statesman, nicknamed 'Mad Anthony' for his daring during the Revolutionary War.

Area (sq mi): 774.09 (land 761.03; water 13.05).

All statistics are based on the 2000 Census except the dollar figures given for per capita income, which are based on 1999 estimates.

Pop: 13,259 (White 97.3%; Black or African American 0.2%; Hispanic or Latino 0.5%; Asian 0.1%; Other 2.1%). **Foreign born:** 0.3%. **Median age:** 42.5. **State rank:** 76. **Pop change 1990-2000:** +14.9%.

Income: per capita $13,434; median household $24,007. **Pop below poverty level:** 21.9%.

Unemployment: 11.6%. **Median home value:** $44,700. **Median travel time to work:** 33.3 minutes.

WEBSTER COUNTY

101 S Crittenden St
County Courthouse Rm 11   **Ph:** 417-468-2223
Marshfield, MO 65706   **Fax:** 417-468-5307

In south-central MO, east of Springfield; organized Mar 3, 1855 from Greene County. **Name Origin:** For Daniel Webster (1782-1852), U.S. statesman and orator from MA.

Area (sq mi): 593.69 (land 593.32; water 0.37).

Pop: 31,045 (White 95.4%; Black or African American 1.2%; Hispanic or Latino 1.3%; Asian 0.3%; Other 2.4%). **Foreign born:** 0.8%. **Median age:** 34.6. **State rank:** 35. **Pop change 1990-2000:** +30.7%.

Income: per capita $14,502; median household $31,929. **Pop below poverty level:** 14.8%.

Unemployment: 4.4%. **Median home value:** $80,900. **Median travel time to work:** 29 minutes.

WORTH COUNTY

PO Box 450   **Ph:** 660-564-2219
Grant City, MO 64456   **Fax:** 660-564-2432

On the northwestern border of MO, northeast of Saint Joseph; organized Feb 8, 1861 from Gentry County. **Name Origin:** For Gen. William Jenkins Worth (1794-1849), officer in the War of 1812, Seminole War, and the Mexican-American War; cited by Congress for bravery.

Area (sq mi): 266.75 (land 266.52; water 0.23).

Pop: 2,382 (White 98.7%; Black or African American 0.2%; Hispanic or Latino 0.3%; Asian 0.1%; Other 0.7%). **Foreign born:** 0.2%. **Median age:** 41.9. **State rank:** 115. **Pop change 1990-2000:** -2.4%.

Income: per capita $14,367; median household $27,471. **Pop below poverty level:** 14.3%.

Unemployment: 5%. **Median home value:** $27,200. **Median travel time to work:** 24.7 minutes.

WRIGHT COUNTY

PO Box 98   **Ph:** 417-741-6661
Hartville, MO 65667   **Fax:** 417-741-6142

In south-central MO, east of Springfield; organized Jan 29, 1841 from Pulaski County. **Name Origin:** For Silas Wright (1795-1847), NY governor (1844-46), U.S. representative, and senator (1833-45).

Area (sq mi): 683.18 (land 682.13; water 1.05).

Pop: 17,955 (White 97.1%; Black or African American 0.3%; Hispanic or Latino 0.8%; Asian 0.1%; Other 2%). **Foreign born:** 0.9%. **Median age:** 37.7. **State rank:** 60. **Pop change 1990-2000:** +7.1%.

Income: per capita $13,135; median household $24,691. **Pop below poverty level:** 21.7%.

Unemployment: 9.3%. **Median home value:** $57,000. **Median travel time to work:** 26.6 minutes.

Please see sample entry on inside front cover for detailed information about the statistics presented with each county listing.

MONTANA - Counties

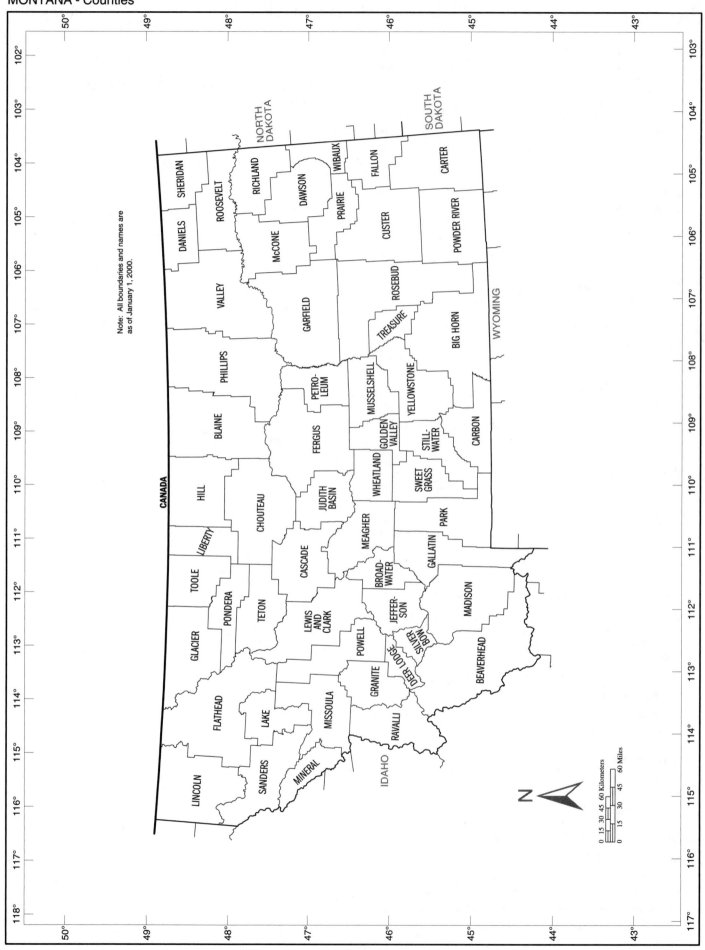

Note: All boundaries and names are
as of January 1, 2000.

CANADA

NORTH DAKOTA

SOUTH DAKOTA

WYOMING

IDAHO

SHERIDAN

DANIELS

ROOSEVELT

RICHLAND

DAWSON

WIBAUX

FALLON

CARTER

McCONE

PRAIRIE

CUSTER

POWDER RIVER

VALLEY

GARFIELD

ROSEBUD

TREASURE

BIG HORN

PHILLIPS

PETRO-
LEUM

MUSSELSHELL

YELLOWSTONE

BLAINE

FERGUS

GOLDEN
VALLEY

STILL-
WATER

CARBON

HILL

JUDITH
BASIN

WHEATLAND

SWEET
GRASS

CHOUTEAU

MEAGHER

PARK

LIBERTY

CASCADE

BROAD-
WATER

GALLATIN

TOOLE

PONDERA

TETON

LEWIS
AND
CLARK

JEFFER-
SON

MADISON

GLACIER

POWELL

DEER LODGE

SILVER BOW

BEAVERHEAD

GRANITE

FLATHEAD

LAKE

MISSOULA

RAVALLI

SANDERS

MINERAL

LINCOLN

N

0 15 30 45 60 Kilometers
0 15 30 45 60 Miles

Montana

MONTANA STATE INFORMATION

www.state.mt.us   **Ph:** 406-444-2511

Area (sq mi): 14,7042.4 (land 145,552.43; water 1489.96).

Pop: 902,195 (White 89.5%; Black or African American 0.3%; Hispanic or Latino 2%; Asian 0.5%; Other 8.6%). **Foreign born:** 1.8%. **Median age:** 37.5. **Pop change 1990-2000:** +12.9%.

Income: per capita $17,151; median household $33,024. **Pop below poverty level:** 14.6%.

Unemployment: 4.2%. **Median home value:** $99,500. **Median travel time to work:** 17.7 minutes.

ANACONDA-DEER LODGE COUNTY

800 S Main St   **Ph:** 406-563-4060
Anaconda, MT 59711   **Fax:** 406-563-4001

In southwestern MT, west of Butte; original county; organized Feb 2, 1865 (prior to statehood). **Name Origin:** Descriptive of the area where deer came to the salt licks.

Area (sq mi): 741.16 (land 736.98; water 4.19).

Pop: 9,417 (White 94.7%; Black or African American 0.2%; Hispanic or Latino 1.6%; Asian 0.4%; Other 3.6%). **Foreign born:** 1.4%. **Median age:** 42.3. **State rank:** 22. **Pop change 1990-2000:** -8.4%.

Income: per capita $15,580; median household $26,305. **Pop below poverty level:** 15.8%.

Unemployment: 6.8%. **Median home value:** $70,700. **Median travel time to work:** 21.1 minutes.

BEAVERHEAD COUNTY

2 S Pacific St   **Ph:** 406-683-5245
Dillon, MT 59725   **Fax:** 406-683-3769

On the southwestern border of MT, south of Butte; original county; organized Feb 2, 1865 (prior to statehood); annexed part of Madison County in 1911. **Name Origin:** For the Beaverhead River, which contains a rock formation that the Indians thought resembled a beaver's head.

Area (sq mi): 5572.04 (land 5542.31; water 29.73).

Pop: 9,202 (White 94.4%; Black or African American 0.2%; Hispanic or Latino 2.7%; Asian 0.2%; Other 3.8%). **Foreign born:** 1.6%. **Median age:** 37.6. **State rank:** 24. **Pop change 1990-2000:** +9.2%.

Income: per capita $15,621; median household $28,962. **Pop below poverty level:** 17.1%.

Unemployment: 3.3%. **Median home value:** $89,200. **Median travel time to work:** 14.4 minutes.

BIG HORN COUNTY

121 W 3rd St   **Ph:** 406-665-9735
Hardin, MT 59034   **Fax:** 406-665-9738

On the central southern border of MT, south of Billings; organized Jan 13, 1913 from Rosebud and Yellowstone counties. **Name Origin:** For the Big Horn and Little Big Horn rivers that flow through it; the rivers named for the great droves of bighorn sheep on the hillsides.

Area (sq mi): 5014.65 (land 4994.81; water 19.84).

Pop: 12,671 (White 35.2%; Black or African American 0%; Hispanic or Latino 3.7%; Asian 0.2%; Other 63.2%). **Foreign born:** 0.8%. **Median age:** 29.8. **State rank:** 14. **Pop change 1990-2000:** +11.8%.

Income: per capita $10,792; median household $27,684. **Pop below poverty level:** 29.2%.

Unemployment: 16.8%. **Median home value:** $61,400. **Median travel time to work:** 20.8 minutes.

BLAINE COUNTY

400 Ohio St   **Ph:** 406-357-3250
Chinook, MT 59523   **Fax:** 406-357-2199

On the central northern border of MT, northeast of Great Falls; organized Feb 29, 1912 from Chouteau County. **Name Origin:** For James Gillespie Blaine (1830-93), U.S. representative from ME (1863-76), U.S. senator (1876-81), and U.S. secretary of state (1881; 1889-92).

Area (sq mi): 4238.92 (land 4226.18; water 12.74).

Pop: 7,009 (White 52.4%; Black or African American 0.2%; Hispanic or Latino 1%; Asian 0.1%; Other 47.1%). **Foreign born:** 1.4%. **Median age:** 34.4. **State rank:** 29. **Pop change 1990-2000:** +4.2%.

Income: per capita $12,101; median household $25,247. **Pop below poverty level:** 28.1%.

Unemployment: 5.6%. **Median home value:** $56,800. **Median travel time to work:** 16.1 minutes.

BROADWATER COUNTY

515 Broadway   **Ph:** 406-266-3443
Townsend, MT 59644   **Fax:** 406-266-3674

In west-central MT, east of Helena; organized Feb 9, 1895 from Jefferson and Meagher counties. **Name Origin:** For Col. Charles

A. Broadwater (1840-92), miner, businessman, president of the Montana Central Railroad, and local resort proprietor.

Area (sq mi): 1238.94 (land 1191.35; water 47.59).

Pop: 4,385 (White 96.1%; Black or African American 0.3%; Hispanic or Latino 1.3%; Asian 0.1%; Other 2.6%). **Foreign born:** 1.4%. **Median age:** 41.3. **State rank:** 37. **Pop change 1990-2000:** +32.2%.

Income: per capita $16,237; median household $32,689. **Pop below poverty level:** 10.8%.

Unemployment: 4.3%. **Median home value:** $85,500. **Median travel time to work:** 22.7 minutes.

BUTTE-SILVER BOW COUNTY

155 W Granite St   **Ph:** 406-497-6200
Butte, MT 59703   **Fax:** 406-497-6358
www.co.silverbow.mt.us

In southwestern MT, southwest of Helena; organized Feb 16, 1881 (prior to statehood) from Deer Lodge County. **Name Origin:** For Silver Bow Creek, which runs through the county; named by prospectors who saw the sun shining 'like a silver bow' on its waters.

Area (sq mi): 718.97 (land 718.31; water 0.66).

Pop: 34,606 (White 93.7%; Black or African American 0.2%; Hispanic or Latino 2.7%; Asian 0.4%; Other 4.1%). **Foreign born:** 1.6%. **Median age:** 38.9. **State rank:** 8. **Pop change 1990-2000:** +2%.

Income: per capita $17,009; median household $30,402. **Pop below poverty level:** 14.9%.

Unemployment: 5.1%. **Median home value:** $74,900. **Median travel time to work:** 14.3 minutes.

CARBON COUNTY

PO Box 887   **Ph:** 406-446-1220
Red Lodge, MT 59068   **Fax:** 406-446-2640

On the central southern border of MT, southwest of Billings; organized Mar 4, 1895 from Park and Yellowstone counties. **Name Origin:** For the abundant coal deposits within its borders.

Area (sq mi): 2062.19 (land 2047.99; water 14.2).

Pop: 9,552 (White 96.2%; Black or African American 0.3%; Hispanic or Latino 1.8%; Asian 0.4%; Other 2.3%). **Foreign born:** 1.6%. **Median age:** 41.9. **State rank:** 21. **Pop change 1990-2000:** +18.2%.

Income: per capita $17,204; median household $32,139. **Pop below poverty level:** 11.6%.

Unemployment: 4.6%. **Median home value:** $101,700. **Median travel time to work:** 28.1 minutes.

CARTER COUNTY

PO Box 315   **Ph:** 406-775-8749
Ekalaka, MT 59324   **Fax:** 406-775-8750

In the southeastern corner of MT; organized Feb 22, 1917 from Fallon County. **Name Origin:** For Thomas Henry Carter (1854-1911), first U.S. senator from MT (1895-1901; 1905-11).

Area (sq mi): 3348.29 (land 3339.57; water 8.73).

Pop: 1,360 (White 98.5%; Black or African American 0.1%; Hispanic or Latino 0.6%; Asian 0.1%; Other 1.2%). **Foreign born:** 1%. **Median age:** 41.8. **State rank:** 50. **Pop change 1990-2000:** -9.5%.

Income: per capita $13,280; median household $26,313. **Pop below poverty level:** 18.1%.

Unemployment: 2.3%. **Median home value:** $34,600. **Median travel time to work:** 22.5 minutes.

CASCADE COUNTY

PO Box 2867   **Ph:** 406-454-6800
Great Falls, MT 59403   **Fax:** 406-454-6802
www.co.cascade.mt.us

In central MT, northeast of Helena; organized Sep 12, 1887 (prior to statehood) from Chouteau and Meagher counties. **Name Origin:** For the falls in the Missouri River, which runs through the northern part of the county.

Area (sq mi): 2711.65 (land 2697.9; water 13.75).

Pop: 80,357 (White 89.5%; Black or African American 1.1%; Hispanic or Latino 2.4%; Asian 0.8%; Other 7.4%). **Foreign born:** 2.4%. **Median age:** 36.7. **State rank:** 3. **Pop change 1990-2000:** +3.4%.

Income: per capita $17,566; median household $32,971. **Pop below poverty level:** 13.5%.

Unemployment: 4.5%. **Median home value:** $92,500. **Median travel time to work:** 15.9 minutes.

CHOUTEAU COUNTY

PO Box 459   **Ph:** 406-622-5151
Fort Benton, MT 59442   **Fax:** 406-622-3012

In north-central MT, north of Great Falls; original county; organized Feb 2, 1865 (prior to statehood). **Name Origin:** For the Chouteau family, whose members included Auguste (1749-1829) and Pierre (1758-1849), fur traders.

Area (sq mi): 3997 (land 3973.24; water 23.76).

Pop: 5,970 (White 83.9%; Black or African American 0.1%; Hispanic or Latino 0.7%; Asian 0.2%; Other 15.6%). **Foreign born:** 1.9%. **Median age:** 39.3. **State rank:** 33. **Pop change 1990-2000:** +9.5%.

Income: per capita $14,851; median household $29,150. **Pop below poverty level:** 20.5%.

Unemployment: 3.1%. **Median home value:** $69,000. **Median travel time to work:** 19.7 minutes.

CUSTER COUNTY

1010 Main St   **Ph:** 406-874-3343
Miles City, MT 59301

In southeastern MT; original county; organized as Big Horn County Feb 2, 1865 (prior to statehood); name changed Feb 16, 1877. **Name Origin:** For Gen. George Armstrong Custer (1839-76), U.S. army officer defeated at the Battle of Little Bighorn (1876).

Area (sq mi): 3793.22 (land 3783.13; water 10.09).

Pop: 11,696 (White 96%; Black or African American 0.1%; Hispanic

All statistics are based on the 2000 Census except the dollar figures given for per capita income, which are based on 1999 estimates.

or Latino 1.5%; Asian 0.3%; Other 2.7%). **Foreign born:** 1.4%. **Median age:** 39.3. **State rank:** 16. **Pop change 1990-2000:** +0%.

Income: per capita $15,876; median household $30,000. **Pop below poverty level:** 15.1%.

Unemployment: 3.7%. **Median home value:** $63,100. **Median travel time to work:** 11.9 minutes.

DANIELS COUNTY

PO Box 247
Scobey, MT 59263   **Ph:** 406-487-5561

On the northeastern border of MT; organized Aug 30, 1920 from Sheridan and Valley counties. **Name Origin:** For Mansfield A. Daniels, an early rancher and storekeeper.

Area (sq mi): 1426.52 (land 1426.09; water 0.43).

Pop: 2,017 (White 95.7%; Black or African American 0%; Hispanic or Latino 1.6%; Asian 0.2%; Other 3.7%). **Foreign born:** 4.7%. **Median age:** 47. **State rank:** 46. **Pop change 1990-2000:** -11%.

Income: per capita $16,055; median household $27,306. **Pop below poverty level:** 16.9%.

Unemployment: 2.8%. **Median home value:** $45,100. **Median travel time to work:** 12.5 minutes.

DAWSON COUNTY

207 W Bell St   **Ph:** 406-377-3058
Glendive, MT 59330   **Fax:** 406-377-2022

In central eastern MT; original county, organized Jan 15, 1869 (prior to statehood). **Name Origin:** For Maj. Andrew Dawson, commander of Fort Benton for the American Fur Company.

Area (sq mi): 2383.13 (land 2373.14; water 9.99).

Pop: 9,059 (White 97%; Black or African American 0.3%; Hispanic or Latino 0.9%; Asian 0.1%; Other 2.1%). **Foreign born:** 1.1%. **Median age:** 41. **State rank:** 25. **Pop change 1990-2000:** -4.7%.

Income: per capita $15,368; median household $31,393. **Pop below poverty level:** 14.9%.

Unemployment: 2.7%. **Median home value:** $62,700. **Median travel time to work:** 13.1 minutes.

FALLON COUNTY

PO Box 1521   **Ph:** 406-778-7114
Baker, MT 59313   **Fax:** 406-778-2815

On southeastern border of MT; organized Dec 9, 1913 from Custer County. **Name Origin:** For Benjamin O'Fallon (1793-1842), army officer, Indian agent, and nephew of the explorer William Clark (1770-1838).

Area (sq mi): 1623.02 (land 1620.33; water 2.69).

Pop: 2,837 (White 98.3%; Black or African American 0.1%; Hispanic or Latino 0.4%; Asian 0.4%; Other 0.9%). **Foreign born:** 1%. **Median age:** 41.1. **State rank:** 41. **Pop change 1990-2000:** -8.6%.

Income: per capita $16,014; median household $29,944. **Pop below poverty level:** 12.5%.

Unemployment: 2.6%. **Median home value:** $48,000. **Median travel time to work:** 14.9 minutes.

FERGUS COUNTY

712 W Main St   **Ph:** 406-538-5119
Lewistown, MT 59457   **Fax:** 406-538-9023
www.co.fergus.mt.us

In central MT, northwest of Billings; organized Mar 12, 1885 (prior to statehood) from Meagher County. Its county seat is in the exact center of MT. **Name Origin:** For James Fergus (1813-97), cattleman, miner, and a MT territorial legislator.

Area (sq mi): 4350.36 (land 4339.17; water 11.2).

Pop: 11,893 (White 96.7%; Black or African American 0.1%; Hispanic or Latino 0.8%; Asian 0.2%; Other 2.7%). **Foreign born:** 1%. **Median age:** 42.4. **State rank:** 15. **Pop change 1990-2000:** -1.6%.

Income: per capita $15,808; median household $30,409. **Pop below poverty level:** 15.4%.

Unemployment: 5.8%. **Median home value:** $70,600. **Median travel time to work:** 16.4 minutes.

FLATHEAD COUNTY

800 S Main St   **Ph:** 406-758-5503
Kalispell, MT 59901   **Fax:** 406-758-5861
www.co.flathead.mt.us

On the northwestern border of MT, north of Missoula; organized Feb 6, 1893 from Missoula County; annexed part of Deer Lodge County before 1900. **Name Origin:** For the Salish or Flathead Indians of the Catawba group; there is no evidence that they flattened the heads of their infants, as some other tribes did. It has been suggested the name comes from their home at the 'flat' head of the Columbia River rather than in the deep canyons below.

Area (sq mi): 5256.45 (land 5098.34; water 158.11).

Pop: 74,471 (White 95.4%; Black or African American 0.2%; Hispanic or Latino 1.4%; Asian 0.5%; Other 3.1%). **Foreign born:** 2.1%. **Median age:** 39. **State rank:** 4. **Pop change 1990-2000:** +25.8%.

Income: per capita $18,112; median household $34,466. **Pop below poverty level:** 13%.

Unemployment: 5.9%. **Median home value:** $125,600. **Median travel time to work:** 19 minutes.

GALLATIN COUNTY

311 W Main St Rm 204   **Ph:** 406-582-3050
Bozeman, MT 59715
www.co.gallatin.mt.us

On the southwestern border of MT, east of Butte; original county; organized Feb 2, 1865 (prior to statehood). Annexed populated portion of deleted Yellowstone National Park (county equivalent) effective November 7, 1997. **Name Origin:** For the Gallatin River, which flows through the county; itself named by Lewis and Clark in 1805 for Abraham Alfonse Albert Gallatin (1761-1849), U.S. secretary of the treasury (1802-14) at the time.

Area (sq mi): 2631.84 (land 2605.84; water 26).

Pop: 67,831 (White 95.3%; Black or African American 0.2%; Hispanic or Latino 1.5%; Asian 0.9%; Other 2.7%). **Foreign born:** 2.7%. **Median age:** 30.7. **State rank:** 5. **Pop change 1990-2000:** +34.4%.

Please see sample entry on inside front cover for detailed information about the statistics presented with each county listing.

343

Income: per capita $19,074; median household $38,120. **Pop below poverty level:** 12.8%.

Unemployment: 2.5%. **Median home value:** $143,000. **Median travel time to work:** 17 minutes.

GARFIELD COUNTY

PO Box 8   **Ph:** 406-557-6254
Jordan, MT 59337   **Fax:** 406-557-2625

In east-central MT, northeast of Billings; organized Feb 7, 1919 from Valley and McCone counties. **Name Origin:** For James Abram Garfield (1831-81), twentieth U.S. president.

Area (sq mi): 4847.54 (land 4668.06; water 179.48).

Pop: 1,279 (White 98.8%; Black or African American 0.1%; Hispanic or Latino 0.4%; Asian 0.1%; Other 0.7%). **Foreign born:** 1.1%. **Median age:** 41.6. **State rank:** 51. **Pop change 1990-2000:** -19.5%.

Income: per capita $13,930; median household $25,917. **Pop below poverty level:** 21.5%.

Unemployment: 2.2%. **Median home value:** $34,700. **Median travel time to work:** 13.2 minutes.

GLACIER COUNTY

512 E Main St   **Ph:** 406-873-5063
Cut Bank, MT 59427   **Fax:** 406-873-2125

On the northwestern border of MT, northwest of Great Falls, bordering Alberta province, Canada and Glacier National Park; organized Feb 17, 1919 from Flathead and Teton counties. **Name Origin:** For Glacier National Park on the county's western border.

Area (sq mi): 3037.11 (land 2994.72; water 42.39).

Pop: 13,247 (White 35.3%; Black or African American 0.1%; Hispanic or Latino 1.2%; Asian 0.1%; Other 64.5%). **Foreign born:** 2.1%. **Median age:** 30.6. **State rank:** 13. **Pop change 1990-2000:** +9.3%.

Income: per capita $11,597; median household $27,921. **Pop below poverty level:** 27.3%.

Unemployment: 11.1%. **Median home value:** $60,900. **Median travel time to work:** 14.9 minutes.

GOLDEN VALLEY COUNTY

107 Kemp St   **Ph:** 406-568-2231
Ryegate, MT 59074   **Fax:** 406-568-2598

In south-central MT, northwest of Billings; organized Oct 4, 1920 from Musselshell and Sweet Grass counties. **Name Origin:** For the rich soil and plentiful streams.

Area (sq mi): 1176.4 (land 1175.3; water 1.1).

Pop: 1,042 (White 97.9%; Black or African American 0%; Hispanic or Latino 1.2%; Asian 0.1%; Other 0.8%). **Foreign born:** 2.6%. **Median age:** 41.5. **State rank:** 54. **Pop change 1990-2000:** +14.3%.

Income: per capita $13,573; median household $27,308. **Pop below poverty level:** 25.8%.

Unemployment: 4.7%. **Median home value:** $47,700. **Median travel time to work:** 29.2 minutes.

GRANITE COUNTY

220 N Sansome St PO Box 925   **Ph:** 406-859-3771
Philipsburg, MT 59858   **Fax:** 406-859-3817

In west-central MT, northwest of Butte; organized Mar 2, 1893 from Deer Lodge County. **Name Origin:** For the Granite Mountain Silver Mine, itself named for the granite rock within the mine.

Area (sq mi): 1733.11 (land 1727.44; water 5.67).

Pop: 2,830 (White 95.3%; Black or African American 0%; Hispanic or Latino 1.3%; Asian 0.1%; Other 3.6%). **Foreign born:** 1%. **Median age:** 42.8. **State rank:** 42. **Pop change 1990-2000:** +11.1%.

Income: per capita $16,636; median household $27,813. **Pop below poverty level:** 16.8%.

Unemployment: 7.7%. **Median home value:** $78,300. **Median travel time to work:** 26.4 minutes.

HILL COUNTY

315 4th St   **Ph:** 406-265-5481
Havre, MT 59501   **Fax:** 406-265-3693
co.hill.mt.us

On the central northern border of MT, northeast of Great Falls; organized Feb 28, 1912 from Chouteau County. **Name Origin:** For James Jerome Hill (1838-1916), president and developer of the Great Northern Railroad.

Area (sq mi): 2916.05 (land 2896.36; water 19.69).

Pop: 16,673 (White 79.1%; Black or African American 0.1%; Hispanic or Latino 1.2%; Asian 0.4%; Other 20%). **Foreign born:** 2%. **Median age:** 34.5. **State rank:** 11. **Pop change 1990-2000:** -5.6%.

Income: per capita $14,935; median household $30,781. **Pop below poverty level:** 18.4%.

Unemployment: 4.1%. **Median home value:** $80,500. **Median travel time to work:** 12.5 minutes.

JEFFERSON COUNTY

PO Box H   **Ph:** 406-225-4020
Boulder, MT 59632   **Fax:** 406-225-4149
www.co.jefferson.mt.us

In west-central MT, east of Butte; original county, organized Feb 2, 1865 (prior to statehood). **Name Origin:** For the Jefferson River, which forms part of the county's southern border; itself named by Lewis and Clark for Thomas Jefferson (1743-1826), third U.S. president.

Area (sq mi): 1658.83 (land 1656.64; water 2.19).

Pop: 10,049 (White 95.2%; Black or African American 0.1%; Hispanic or Latino 1.5%; Asian 0.4%; Other 3.5%). **Foreign born:** 1%. **Median age:** 40.2. **State rank:** 19. **Pop change 1990-2000:** +26.6%.

Income: per capita $18,250; median household $41,506. **Pop below poverty level:** 9%.

Unemployment: 4.4%. **Median home value:** $128,700. **Median travel time to work:** 22.4 minutes.

JUDITH BASIN COUNTY

PO Box 427   **Ph:** 406-566-2277
Stanford, MT 59479   **Fax:** 406-566-2211

In central MT, southeast of Great Falls; organized Dec 10, 1920

All statistics are based on the 2000 Census except the dollar figures given for per capita income, which are based on 1999 estimates.

from Fergus and Cascade counties. **Name Origin:** For the basin of the Judith River, which flows through the county; named by Meriwether Lewis (1774-1809) for his cousin, Judith Hancock, who later married Lt. William Clark (1770-1838).

Area (sq mi): 1870.71 (land 1869.85; water 0.86).

Pop: 2,329 (White 98.2%; Black or African American 0%; Hispanic or Latino 0.6%; Asian 0.1%; Other 1.2%). **Foreign born:** 1.4%. **Median age:** 42. **State rank:** 43. **Pop change 1990-2000:** +2.1%.

Income: per capita $14,291; median household $29,241. **Pop below poverty level:** 21.1%.

Unemployment: 3.7%. **Median home value:** $56,700. **Median travel time to work:** 17.5 minutes.

LAKE COUNTY

106 4th Ave E   **Ph:** 406-883-7208
Polson, MT 59860   **Fax:** 406-883-7283
www.lakecounty-mt.org

In northwestern MT, north of Missoula; organized May 11, 1923 from Flathead and Missoula counties. **Name Origin:** For Flathead Lake, which comprises most of the northern part of the county.

Area (sq mi): 1653.72 (land 1493.77; water 159.95).

Pop: 26,507 (White 70.6%; Black or African American 0.1%; Hispanic or Latino 2.5%; Asian 0.3%; Other 28.2%). **Foreign born:** 1.6%. **Median age:** 38.2. **State rank:** 9. **Pop change 1990-2000:** +26%.

Income: per capita $15,173; median household $28,740. **Pop below poverty level:** 18.7%.

Unemployment: 8.6%. **Median home value:** $117,200. **Median travel time to work:** 18.4 minutes.

LEWIS & CLARK COUNTY

316 N Park Ave   **Ph:** 406-447-8200
Helena, MT 59624   **Fax:** 406-447-8330
www.co.lewis-clark.mt.us

Area (sq mi): 3497.56 (land 3460.96; water 36.6).

Pop: 55,716 (White 94.4%; Black or African American 0.2%; Hispanic or Latino 1.5%; Asian 0.5%; Other 4.1%). **Foreign born:** 1.6%. **Median age:** 38. **State rank:** 6. **Pop change 1990-2000:** +17.3%.

Income: per capita $18,763; median household $37,360. **Pop below poverty level:** 10.9%.

Unemployment: 4.3%. **Median home value:** $112,200. **Median travel time to work:** 16.7 minutes.

LIBERTY COUNTY

PO Box 459   **Ph:** 406-759-5365
Chester, MT 59522   **Fax:** 406-759-5395

On the central northern border of MT, north of Great Falls; organized Feb 11, 1920 from Chouteau and Hill counties. **Name Origin:** For the inhabitants' 'freedom' from Hill County.

Area (sq mi): 1447.19 (land 1429.76; water 17.44).

Pop: 2,158 (White 99.1%; Black or African American 0%; Hispanic or Latino 0.2%; Asian 0.3%; Other 0.5%). **Foreign born:** 1.4%. **Median age:** 41.5. **State rank:** 45. **Pop change 1990-2000:** -6%.

Income: per capita $14,882; median household $30,284. **Pop below poverty level:** 20.3%.

Unemployment: 2.9%. **Median home value:** $58,800. **Median travel time to work:** 16.1 minutes.

LINCOLN COUNTY

512 California Ave   **Ph:** 406-293-7781
Libby, MT 59923   **Fax:** 406-293-8577
www.lincolncountymt.us/

On the northwestern corner of MT; organized Mar 9, 1909 from Flathead County. **Name Origin:** For Abraham Lincoln (1809-65), sixteenth U.S. president.

Area (sq mi): 3675.11 (land 3612.67; water 62.44).

Pop: 18,837 (White 95.1%; Black or African American 0.1%; Hispanic or Latino 1.4%; Asian 0.3%; Other 3.5%). **Foreign born:** 1.4%. **Median age:** 42.1. **State rank:** 10. **Pop change 1990-2000:** +7.8%.

Income: per capita $13,923; median household $26,754. **Pop below poverty level:** 19.2%.

Unemployment: 11.3%. **Median home value:** $82,600. **Median travel time to work:** 17.6 minutes.

MADISON COUNTY

PO Box 185   **Ph:** 406-843-4230
Virginia City, MT 59755   **Fax:** 406-843-5207

In southwestern MT, southeast of Butte; original county; organized Feb 2, 1865 (prior to statehood). **Name Origin:** For the Madison River, which flows through the county; itself named by Lewis and Clark for James Madison (1751-1836), then secretary of state (1801-09), later fourth U.S. president.

Area (sq mi): 3602.85 (land 3586.54; water 16.31).

Pop: 6,851 (White 96%; Black or African American 0%; Hispanic or Latino 1.9%; Asian 0.3%; Other 2.7%). **Foreign born:** 1.4%. **Median age:** 43.4. **State rank:** 30. **Pop change 1990-2000:** +14.4%.

Income: per capita $16,944; median household $30,233. **Pop below poverty level:** 12.1%.

Unemployment: 3.4%. **Median home value:** $104,500. **Median travel time to work:** 22.4 minutes.

McCONE COUNTY

PO Box 199   **Ph:** 406-485-3505
Circle, MT 59215   **Fax:** 406-485-2689

In east-central MT; organized Feb 20, 1919 from Dawson and Richland counties. **Name Origin:** For George McCone, a MT state legislator.

Area (sq mi): 2682.77 (land 2642.53; water 40.25).

Pop: 1,977 (White 96.3%; Black or African American 0.3%; Hispanic or Latino 1%; Asian 0.3%; Other 2.5%). **Foreign born:** 0.7%. **Median age:** 42.4. **State rank:** 47. **Pop change 1990-2000:** -13.1%.

Income: per capita $15,162; median household $29,718. **Pop below poverty level:** 16.8%.

Unemployment: 2.3%. **Median home value:** $42,600. **Median travel time to work:** 15.1 minutes.

Please see sample entry on inside front cover for detailed information about the statistics presented with each county listing.

MEAGHER COUNTY

PO Box 309   **Ph:** 406-547-3612
White Sulphur Springs, MT 59645   **Fax:** 406-547-3388

In central MT, east of Helena; original county; organized Nov 16, 1867 (prior to statehood) from Chouteau and Gallatin counties; annexed part of Fergus County in 1911. **Name Origin:** For Thomas Francis Meagher (1823-67), Irish revolutionary tried for sedition and banished to Tasmania. He escaped to New York Cilty, where he practiced law. He became a brigadier general in the Civil War and led the 'Irish Brigade.' He was acting governor of MT Territory (1865-66).

Area (sq mi): 2394.83 (land 2391.82; water 3.02).

Pop: 1,932 (White 96.8%; Black or African American 0%; Hispanic or Latino 1.5%; Asian 0.2%; Other 2.7%). **Foreign born:** 1.8%. **Median age:** 42.8. **State rank:** 48. **Pop change 1990-2000:** +6.2%.

Income: per capita $15,019; median household $29,375. **Pop below poverty level:** 18.9%.

Unemployment: 5.9%. **Median home value:** $72,100. **Median travel time to work:** 16.6 minutes.

MINERAL COUNTY

PO Box 550   **Ph:** 406-822-3520
Superior, MT 59872   **Fax:** 406-822-3579

On the central western border of MT, west of Missoula; organized Aug 7, 1914 from Missoula County. **Name Origin:** For its many mines.

Area (sq mi): 1223.38 (land 1219.82; water 3.56).

Pop: 3,884 (White 93.6%; Black or African American 0.2%; Hispanic or Latino 1.6%; Asian 0.5%; Other 4.7%). **Foreign born:** 1.5%. **Median age:** 41.1. **State rank:** 39. **Pop change 1990-2000:** +17.2%.

Income: per capita $15,166; median household $27,143. **Pop below poverty level:** 15.8%.

Unemployment: 8.2%. **Median home value:** $88,300. **Median travel time to work:** 22.6 minutes.

MISSOULA COUNTY

200 W Broadway St   **Ph:** 406-523-4780
Missoula, MT 59802   **Fax:** 406-523-4899
www.co.missoula.mt.us

In west-central MT; original county; organized Feb 2, 1865 (prior to statehood). **Name Origin:** From a Salish (Flathead) Indian word whose meaning is in dispute; possibly 'feared water,' 'at the stream of surprise and ambush,' or 'river of awe'; believed to refer to Hell Gate Canyon where Blackfeet Indians ambushed the Salish.

Area (sq mi): 2618.34 (land 2597.97; water 20.37).

Pop: 95,802 (White 93.1%; Black or African American 0.3%; Hispanic or Latino 1.6%; Asian 1%; Other 4.7%). **Foreign born:** 2.3%. **Median age:** 33.2. **State rank:** 2. **Pop change 1990-2000:** +21.8%.

Income: per capita $17,808; median household $34,454. **Pop below poverty level:** 14.8%.

Unemployment: 3.6%. **Median home value:** $136,500. **Median travel time to work:** 17.5 minutes.

MUSSELSHELL COUNTY

506 Main St   **Ph:** 406-323-1104
Roundup, MT 59072   **Fax:** 406-323-3303

In south-central MT, north of Billings; organized Feb 11, 1911 from Fergus, Yellowstone, and Meagher counties. **Name Origin:** For the Musselshell River, which forms part of the county's eastern border, the river was named for the mussel shells found on its banks.

Area (sq mi): 1870.91 (land 1867.15; water 3.76).

Pop: 4,497 (White 95.9%; Black or African American 0.1%; Hispanic or Latino 1.6%; Asian 0.2%; Other 2.9%). **Foreign born:** 2%. **Median age:** 43.2. **State rank:** 36. **Pop change 1990-2000:** +9.5%.

Income: per capita $15,389; median household $25,527. **Pop below poverty level:** 19.9%.

Unemployment: 6.6%. **Median home value:** $54,600. **Median travel time to work:** 25 minutes.

PARK COUNTY

414 E Callender St   **Ph:** 406-222-4110
Livingston, MT 59047   **Fax:** 406-222-4199
www.parkcounty.org

On the southern border of MT, east of Bozeman; organized Feb 23, 1887 (prior to statehood) from Gallatin County. Annexed unpopulated portion of deleted Yellowstone National Park (county equivalent) effective November 7, 1997. **Name Origin:** For Yellowstone National Park, which is on the county's southern border.

Area (sq mi): 2813.59 (land 2802.41; water 11.18).

Pop: 15,694 (White 95.5%; Black or African American 0.4%; Hispanic or Latino 1.8%; Asian 0.4%; Other 2.6%). **Foreign born:** 2.7%. **Median age:** 40.6. **State rank:** 12. **Pop change 1990-2000:** +7.8%.

Income: per capita $17,704; median household $31,739. **Pop below poverty level:** 11.4%.

Unemployment: 4.7%. **Median home value:** $97,900. **Median travel time to work:** 21.3 minutes.

PETROLEUM COUNTY

PO Box 226   **Ph:** 406-429-5311
Winnett, MT 59087   **Fax:** 406-429-6328

In central MT, north of Billings; organized Feb 22, 1925 from Fergus County. **Name Origin:** For the petroleum production in the Cat Creek fields.

Area (sq mi): 1674.01 (land 1653.9; water 20.11).

Pop: 493 (White 98.2%; Black or African American 0%; Hispanic or Latino 1.2%; Asian 0%; Other 0.8%). **Foreign born:** 0.6%. **Median age:** 41.1. **State rank:** 56. **Pop change 1990-2000:** -5%.

Income: per capita $15,986; median household $24,107. **Pop below poverty level:** 23.2%.

Unemployment: 2.4%. **Median home value:** $58,300. **Median travel time to work:** 11.7 minutes.

All statistics are based on the 2000 Census except the dollar figures given for per capita income, which are based on 1999 estimates.

PHILLIPS COUNTY

PO Box 360   **Ph:** 406-654-2423
Malta, MT 59538   **Fax:** 406-654-2429

On central northern border of MT; organized Feb 5, 1915 from Blaine and Valley counties. **Name Origin:** For Benjamin D. Phillips, a local landowner and prominent citizen.

Area (sq mi): 5212.17 (land 5139.57; water 72.6).

Pop: 4,601 (White 88.8%; Black or African American 0.2%; Hispanic or Latino 1.2%; Asian 0.3%; Other 10.1%). **Foreign born:** 1%. **Median age:** 40.8. **State rank:** 35. **Pop change 1990-2000:** -10.9%.

Income: per capita $15,058; median household $28,702. **Pop below poverty level:** 18.3%.

Unemployment: 4.4%. **Median home value:** $60,700. **Median travel time to work:** 14.3 minutes.

PONDERA COUNTY

20 4th Ave SW   **Ph:** 406-278-4000
Conrad, MT 59425   **Fax:** 406-278-4070
www.ponderacountymontana.org

In northwest-central MT, northwest of Great Falls; organized Feb 17, 1919 from Chouteau and Teton counties. **Name Origin:** From French #it1pend d'oreille 'hanging ear,' first applied to a lake in ID, thought to resemble an earlobe. To avoid confusion with the lake and town, name was changed to Pondera.

Area (sq mi): 1639.85 (land 1624.7; water 15.16).

Pop: 6,424 (White 83.2%; Black or African American 0.1%; Hispanic or Latino 0.8%; Asian 0.1%; Other 16.1%). **Foreign born:** 1.6%. **Median age:** 38.6. **State rank:** 32. **Pop change 1990-2000:** -0.1%.

Income: per capita $14,276; median household $30,464. **Pop below poverty level:** 18.8%.

Unemployment: 4.2%. **Median home value:** $70,500. **Median travel time to work:** 15.8 minutes.

POWDER RIVER COUNTY

PO Box 270   **Ph:** 406-436-2657
Broadus, MT 59317   **Fax:** 406-436-2151

On the southeastern border of MT, southeast of Billings; organized Mar 7, 1919 from Custer County. **Name Origin:** For the river, which runs diagonally through the county; the river's name comes either from the fine black sand resembling gunpowder that is found along its banks, or from an incident when a group of soldiers were attacked by Indians, and one yelled 'hide the powder!'

Area (sq mi): 3297.94 (land 3297.18; water 0.76).

Pop: 1,858 (White 97%; Black or African American 0%; Hispanic or Latino 0.6%; Asian 0.1%; Other 2.5%). **Foreign born:** 0.6%. **Median age:** 42.1. **State rank:** 49. **Pop change 1990-2000:** -11.1%.

Income: per capita $15,351; median household $28,398. **Pop below poverty level:** 12.9%.

Unemployment: 1.9%. **Median home value:** $59,800. **Median travel time to work:** 13.2 minutes.

POWELL COUNTY

409 Missouri Ave   **Ph:** 406-846-3680
Deer Lodge, MT 59722   **Fax:** 406-846-2784

In west-central MT, west of Helena; organized Jan 31, 1901 from Deer Lodge County. **Name Origin:** For John Wesley Powell (1834-1902), geologist and explorer of the Grand Canyon (1870), director of the U.S. Geological Survey, and first head of the U.S. Bureau of Reclamation.

Area (sq mi): 2332.68 (land 2325.94; water 6.74).

Pop: 7,180 (White 91.5%; Black or African American 0.5%; Hispanic or Latino 1.9%; Asian 0.4%; Other 6.5%). **Foreign born:** 0.6%. **Median age:** 39.7. **State rank:** 28. **Pop change 1990-2000:** +8.5%.

Income: per capita $13,816; median household $30,625. **Pop below poverty level:** 12.6%.

Unemployment: 4.8%. **Median home value:** $73,500. **Median travel time to work:** 22.3 minutes.

PRAIRIE COUNTY

PO Box 125   **Ph:** 406-635-5575
Terry, MT 59349   **Fax:** 406-635-5576

In east-central MT, north of Miles City; organized Feb 5, 1915 from Custer, Dawson, and Fallon counties. **Name Origin:** For the topography of most of the eastern half of the state.

Area (sq mi): 1742.56 (land 1736.55; water 6).

Pop: 1,199 (White 97.7%; Black or African American 0%; Hispanic or Latino 0.7%; Asian 0.2%; Other 1.9%). **Foreign born:** 1.2%. **Median age:** 48.9. **State rank:** 52. **Pop change 1990-2000:** -13.3%.

Income: per capita $14,422; median household $25,451. **Pop below poverty level:** 17.2%.

Unemployment: 4.6%. **Median home value:** $36,500. **Median travel time to work:** 13.6 minutes.

RAVALLI COUNTY

215 S 4th St Suite C   **Ph:** 406-375-6212
Hamilton, MT 59840   **Fax:** 406-375-6326
www.co.ravalli.mt.us

On the central western border of MT, west of Butte; organized Feb 16, 1893 from Missoula County. **Name Origin:** For Father Anthony Ravalli (1812-84), Jesuit missionary to the Salish (Flathead) Indians at Saint Mary's Mission, Stevensville, MT, the first white settlement in MT.

Area (sq mi): 2400.32 (land 2394.21; water 6.11).

Pop: 36,070 (White 95.5%; Black or African American 0.1%; Hispanic or Latino 1.9%; Asian 0.3%; Other 2.8%). **Foreign born:** 1.7%. **Median age:** 41.1. **State rank:** 7. **Pop change 1990-2000:** +44.2%.

Income: per capita $17,935; median household $31,992. **Pop below poverty level:** 13.8%.

Unemployment: 4.6%. **Median home value:** $133,400. **Median travel time to work:** 23 minutes.

Please see sample entry on inside front cover for detailed information about the statistics presented with each county listing.

RICHLAND COUNTY

201 W Main St   **Ph:** 406-433-1708
Sidney, MT 59270   **Fax:** 406-482-3731
www.richland.org

On the northeastern border of MT; organized May 27, 1914 from Dawson County. **Name Origin:** Promotional, to attract new visitors.

Area (sq mi): 2103.02 (land 2084.09; water 18.93).

Pop: 9,667 (White 95.4%; Black or African American 0.1%; Hispanic or Latino 2.2%; Asian 0.2%; Other 3.1%). **Foreign born:** 1.4%. **Median age:** 39.2. **State rank:** 20. **Pop change 1990-2000:** -9.8%.

Income: per capita $16,006; median household $32,110. **Pop below poverty level:** 12.2%.

Unemployment: 4.9%. **Median home value:** $61,000. **Median travel time to work:** 13.5 minutes.

ROOSEVELT COUNTY

400 2nd Ave S   **Ph:** 406-653-6200
Wolf Point, MT 59201   **Fax:** 406-653-6202

On the northeastern border of MT; organized Feb 18, 1919 from Sheridan County. **Name Origin:** For Theodore Roosevelt (1858-1919), twenty-sixth U.S. president.

Area (sq mi): 2369.65 (land 2355.6; water 14.05).

Pop: 10,620 (White 40.8%; Black or African American 0%; Hispanic or Latino 1.2%; Asian 0.4%; Other 58.6%). **Foreign born:** 0.9%. **Median age:** 32.3. **State rank:** 17. **Pop change 1990-2000:** -3.4%.

Income: per capita $11,347; median household $24,834. **Pop below poverty level:** 32.4%.

Unemployment: 7.2%. **Median home value:** $47,400. **Median travel time to work:** 11.7 minutes.

ROSEBUD COUNTY

1200 Main St   **Ph:** 406-356-7318
Forsyth, MT 59327   **Fax:** 406-356-7551

In south-central MT, east of Billling; organized Feb 11, 1901 from Custer County. **Name Origin:** For Rosebud Creek, which runs through the county; named for the profusion of wild roses along its banks.

Area (sq mi): 5026.94 (land 5012.37; water 14.57).

Pop: 9,383 (White 63.5%; Black or African American 0.2%; Hispanic or Latino 2.3%; Asian 0.3%; Other 35.1%). **Foreign born:** 1.1%. **Median age:** 34.5. **State rank:** 23. **Pop change 1990-2000:** -10.7%.

Income: per capita $15,032; median household $35,898. **Pop below poverty level:** 22.4%.

Unemployment: 7.1%. **Median home value:** $66,700. **Median travel time to work:** 16 minutes.

SANDERS COUNTY

PO Box 519   **Ph:** 406-827-6942
Thompson Falls, MT 59873   **Fax:** 406-827-4388
www.co.sanders.mt.us

On the northwestern border of MT, northwest of Missoula; organized Feb 5, 1907 from Missoula County. **Name Origin:** For Wilbur

Fisk Sanders (1834-1905), officer in the Civil War and U.S. senator from MT (1890-93).

Area (sq mi): 2790.03 (land 2762.17; water 27.86).

Pop: 10,227 (White 90.9%; Black or African American 0.1%; Hispanic or Latino 1.6%; Asian 0.3%; Other 7.6%). **Foreign born:** 2%. **Median age:** 44.2. **State rank:** 18. **Pop change 1990-2000:** +18%.

Income: per capita $14,593; median household $26,852. **Pop below poverty level:** 17.2%.

Unemployment: 8.3%. **Median home value:** $82,900. **Median travel time to work:** 22.3 minutes.

SHERIDAN COUNTY

100 W Laurel Ave   **Ph:** 406-765-2310
Plentywood, MT 59254   **Fax:** 406-765-2609
www.co.sheridan.mt.us

In the northeastern corner of MT; organized Mar 4, 1913 from Valley County. **Name Origin:** For Gen. Philip Henry Sheridan (1831-88), Union officer during the Civil War and commander in chief of the U.S. army (1883-88).

Area (sq mi): 1706.3 (land 1676.58; water 29.73).

Pop: 4,105 (White 96.4%; Black or African American 0.1%; Hispanic or Latino 1.1%; Asian 0.3%; Other 2.6%). **Foreign born:** 1.9%. **Median age:** 45.1. **State rank:** 38. **Pop change 1990-2000:** -13.3%.

Income: per capita $16,038; median household $29,518. **Pop below poverty level:** 14.7%.

Unemployment: 3.2%. **Median home value:** $45,800. **Median travel time to work:** 12.8 minutes.

STILLWATER COUNTY

PO Box 149   **Ph:** 406-322-8000
Columbus, MT 59019   **Fax:** 406-322-8007

In south-central MT, west of Billlings; organized Mar 24, 1913 from Carbon, Sweet Grass, and Yellowstone counties. **Name Origin:** For the Stillwater River, which runs through the county.

Area (sq mi): 1804.61 (land 1795.09; water 9.52).

Pop: 8,195 (White 95.9%; Black or African American 0.1%; Hispanic or Latino 2%; Asian 0.2%; Other 2.8%). **Foreign born:** 1.5%. **Median age:** 40.8. **State rank:** 26. **Pop change 1990-2000:** +25.4%.

Income: per capita $18,468; median household $39,205. **Pop below poverty level:** 9.8%.

Unemployment: 3.1%. **Median home value:** $102,200. **Median travel time to work:** 28.5 minutes.

SWEET GRASS COUNTY

PO Box 888   **Ph:** 406-932-5152
Big Timber, MT 59011   **Fax:** 406-932-5177

In south-central MT, west of Billings; organized Mar 5, 1895 from Meagher, Park, and Yellowstone counties. **Name Origin:** For the abundant fragrant grass of the genus *Glyceria*, at the suggestion of Mrs. Paul Van Cleve, Sr.

Area (sq mi): 1862 (land 1855.08; water 6.92).

All statistics are based on the 2000 Census except the dollar figures given for per capita income, which are based on 1999 estimates.

Pop: 3,609 (White 96.1%; Black or African American 0.1%; Hispanic or Latino 1.5%; Asian 0.3%; Other 2.6%). **Foreign born:** 1.7%. **Median age:** 41.2. **State rank:** 40. **Pop change 1990-2000:** +14.4%.

Income: per capita $17,880; median household $32,422. **Pop below poverty level:** 11.4%.

Unemployment: 2.6%. **Median home value:** $97,800. **Median travel time to work:** 20.8 minutes.

TETON COUNTY

PO Box 610   **Ph:** 406-466-2151
Choteau, MT 59422   **Fax:** 406-466-2138
www.tetoncomt.org

In west-central MT, northwest of Great Falls; organized Feb 7, 1893 from Chouteau County. **Name Origin:** For the Teton River and Teton Peak in the Teton Mountains or for the Teton Indian tribe.

Area (sq mi): 2292.58 (land 2272.61; water 19.97).

Pop: 6,445 (White 95.6%; Black or African American 0.2%; Hispanic or Latino 1.1%; Asian 0.1%; Other 3.4%). **Foreign born:** 1.5%. **Median age:** 40. **State rank:** 31. **Pop change 1990-2000:** +2.8%.

Income: per capita $14,635; median household $30,197. **Pop below poverty level:** 16.6%.

Unemployment: 3.5%. **Median home value:** $74,700. **Median travel time to work:** 19.2 minutes.

TOOLE COUNTY

226 1st St S   **Ph:** 406-434-5121
Shelby, MT 59474   **Fax:** 406-434-2467

On the central northern border of MT, north of Great Falls; organized May 7, 1914 from Hill and Teton counties. **Name Origin:** For Joseph Kemp Toole (1851-1929), governor of MT (1889-93; 1901-08).

Area (sq mi): 1945.86 (land 1910.95; water 34.91).

Pop: 5,267 (White 93.3%; Black or African American 0.2%; Hispanic or Latino 1.2%; Asian 0.3%; Other 5.6%). **Foreign born:** 3.6%. **Median age:** 39.1. **State rank:** 34. **Pop change 1990-2000:** +4.4%.

Income: per capita $14,731; median household $30,169. **Pop below poverty level:** 12.9%.

Unemployment: 2.7%. **Median home value:** $60,700. **Median travel time to work:** 14.2 minutes.

TREASURE COUNTY

PO Box 392   **Ph:** 406-342-5547
Hysham, MT 59038   **Fax:** 406-342-5445

In south-central MT, northeast of Billings; organized Feb 7, 1919 from Rosebud County. **Name Origin:** For the nickname of MT, the 'Treasure State.'

Area (sq mi): 984.11 (land 978.86; water 5.24).

Pop: 861 (White 95.6%; Black or African American 0.1%; Hispanic or Latino 1.5%; Asian 0.3%; Other 3.1%). **Foreign born:** 0.8%. **Median age:** 41.8. **State rank:** 55. **Pop change 1990-2000:** -1.5%.

Income: per capita $14,392; median household $29,830. **Pop below poverty level:** 14.7%.

Unemployment: 3.2%. **Median home value:** $40,700. **Median travel time to work:** 18.3 minutes.

VALLEY COUNTY

501 Court Sq Box 2   **Ph:** 406-228-6220
Glasgow, MT 59230   **Fax:** 406-228-9027

On the northern border of MT with the province of Saskatchewan, Canada; organized Feb 6, 1893 from Dawson County. **Name Origin:** For the Milk and Missouri river valleys.

Area (sq mi): 5061.98 (land 4921; water 140.98).

Pop: 7,675 (White 87.8%; Black or African American 0.1%; Hispanic or Latino 0.8%; Asian 0.2%; Other 11.5%). **Foreign born:** 1.1%. **Median age:** 41.7. **State rank:** 27. **Pop change 1990-2000:** -6.8%.

Income: per capita $16,246; median household $30,979. **Pop below poverty level:** 13.5%.

Unemployment: 3.5%. **Median home value:** $59,400. **Median travel time to work:** 12.6 minutes.

WHEATLAND COUNTY

PO Box 1903   **Ph:** 406-632-4891
Harlowton, MT 59036   **Fax:** 406-632-4880

In south-central MT, northwest of Billings; organized Feb 22, 1917 from Meagher and Sweet Grass counties. **Name Origin:** For the major crop in the area.

Area (sq mi): 1428.29 (land 1423.09; water 5.19).

Pop: 2,259 (White 96.4%; Black or African American 0.1%; Hispanic or Latino 1.1%; Asian 0.2%; Other 2.7%). **Foreign born:** 2.9%. **Median age:** 41.4. **State rank:** 44. **Pop change 1990-2000:** +0.6%.

Income: per capita $11,954; median household $24,492. **Pop below poverty level:** 20.4%.

Unemployment: 3.5%. **Median home value:** $53,100. **Median travel time to work:** 18.8 minutes.

WIBAUX COUNTY

PO Box 292   **Ph:** 406-796-2484
Wibaux, MT 59353   **Fax:** 406-796-2625

On the central eastern border of MT; organized Aug 17, 1914 from Dawson, Fallon, and Richland counties. **Name Origin:** For Pierre Wibaux, a Huguenot immigrant who owned one of the largest herds of cattle in MT.

Area (sq mi): 890.09 (land 889.31; water 0.78).

Pop: 1,068 (White 97.8%; Black or African American 0.2%; Hispanic or Latino 0.4%; Asian 0.2%; Other 1.6%). **Foreign born:** 1.4%. **Median age:** 42.3. **State rank:** 53. **Pop change 1990-2000:** -10.3%.

Income: per capita $16,121; median household $28,224. **Pop below poverty level:** 15.3%.

Unemployment: 2.6%. **Median home value:** $37,500. **Median travel time to work:** 19.5 minutes.

Please see sample entry on inside front cover for detailed information about the statistics presented with each county listing.

YELLOWSTONE COUNTY

217 N 27th St Rm 401   **Ph:** 406-256-2785
Billings, MT 59101   **Fax:** 406-256-2736
www.co.yellowstone.mt.us

In south-central MT; organized Feb 26, 1883 from Custer County.
Name Origin: For the Yellowstone River, which flows through the
county.

Area (sq mi): 2649.05 (land 2635.15; water 13.9).

Pop: 129,352 (White 91%; Black or African American 0.4%; Hispanic or Latino 3.7%; Asian 0.5%; Other 6.3%). **Foreign born:**
1.4%. **Median age:** 36.9. **State rank:** 1. **Pop change 1990-2000:**
+14%.

Income: per capita $19,303; median household $36,727. **Pop below
poverty level:** 11.1%.

Unemployment: 3.3%. **Median home value:** $101,900. **Median
travel time to work:** 17.9 minutes.

NEBRASKA - Counties

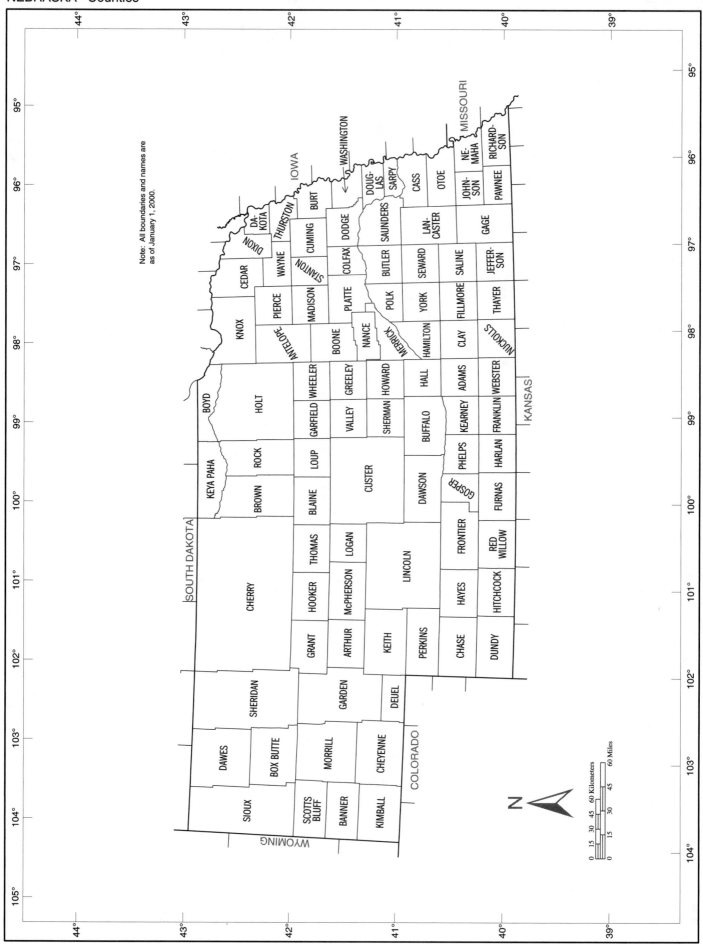

Note: All boundaries and names are as of January 1, 2000.

Nebraska

NEBRASKA STATE INFORMATION

www.nebraska.gov   **Ph:** 402-471-2311

Area (sq mi): 77,353.73 (land 76,872.41; water 481.31).

Pop: 1,711,263 (White 87.3%; Black or African American 4%; Hispanic or Latino 5.5%; Asian 1.3%; Other 5.1%). **Foreign born:** 4.4%. **Median age:** 35.3. **Pop change 1990-2000:** +8.4%.

Income: per capita $19,613; median household $39,250. **Pop below poverty level:** 9.7%.

Unemployment: 3.3%. **Median home value:** $88,000. **Median travel time to work:** 18 minutes.

ADAMS COUNTY

PO Box 2067   **Ph:** 402-461-7104
Hastings, NE 68902   **Fax:** 402-461-7185
www.adamscounty.org

In south-central NE, south of Grand Island; organized Feb 16, 1867 from Clay County. **Name Origin:** For John Adams (1735-1826), second U.S. president.

Area (sq mi): 564.16 (land 563.41; water 0.76).

Pop: 31,151 (White 92.2%; Black or African American 0.6%; Hispanic or Latino 4.6%; Asian 1.6%; Other 3.2%). **Foreign born:** 4.4%. **Median age:** 36.5. **State rank:** 11. **Pop change 1990-2000:** +5.2%.

Income: per capita $18,308; median household $37,160. **Pop below poverty level:** 9.3%.

Unemployment: 2.8%. **Median home value:** $77,200. **Median travel time to work:** 15.5 minutes.

ANTELOPE COUNTY

501 Main St   **Ph:** 402-887-4410
Neligh, NE 68756   **Fax:** 402-887-4719
www.co.antelope.ne.us

In east-central NE, southwest of Sioux City, IA; organized Jun 15, 1871 from Pierce County. **Name Origin:** The bill for establishment of the county was introduced by Leander Gerrard who once shot an antelope for food while on the trail of Indians.

Area (sq mi): 858.43 (land 857.06; water 1.37).

Pop: 7,452 (White 98.5%; Black or African American 0.1%; Hispanic or Latino 0.7%; Asian 0.1%; Other 1.1%). **Foreign born:** 0.4%. **Median age:** 40.6. **State rank:** 43. **Pop change 1990-2000:** -6.4%.

Income: per capita $14,601; median household $30,114. **Pop below poverty level:** 13.6%.

Unemployment: 3.8%. **Median home value:** $44,600. **Median travel time to work:** 18.6 minutes.

ARTHUR COUNTY

PO Box 126   **Ph:** 308-764-2203
Arthur, NE 69121   **Fax:** 308-764-2216

In west-central NE, northwest of North Platte; county approved Mar 31, 1887 from unattached lands; formed Jun 7, 1913. **Name Origin:** For Chester A. Arthur (1830-86), twenty-first U.S. presidesnt.

Area (sq mi): 718.32 (land 715.37; water 2.95).

Pop: 444 (White 95.7%; Black or African American 0%; Hispanic or Latino 1.4%; Asian 0.7%; Other 2.9%). **Foreign born:** 0.7%. **Median age:** 40.3. **State rank:** 93. **Pop change 1990-2000:** -3.9%.

Income: per capita $15,810; median household $27,375. **Pop below poverty level:** 13.8%.

Unemployment: 3.4%. **Median home value:** $44,300. **Median travel time to work:** 18.7 minutes.

BANNER COUNTY

204 State St PO Box 67   **Ph:** 308-436-5265
Harrisburg, NE 69345   **Fax:** 308-436-4180
www.co.banner.ne.us

On the southwestern border of NE, south of Scottsbluff; organized Nov 6, 1888 from Cheyenne County. **Name Origin:** Named by the citizens who wanted the county to be the 'banner county' of the state.

Area (sq mi): 746.37 (land 746.22; water 0.15).

Pop: 819 (White 93.9%; Black or African American 0.1%; Hispanic or Latino 5.6%; Asian 0.1%; Other 3.9%). **Foreign born:** 0.9%. **Median age:** 39.9. **State rank:** 85. **Pop change 1990-2000:** -3.9%.

Income: per capita $17,149; median household $31,339. **Pop below poverty level:** 13.6%.

Unemployment: 1.7%. **Median home value:** $45,800. **Median travel time to work:** 24.1 minutes.

BLAINE COUNTY

Lincoln Ave Bldg 1   **Ph:** 308-547-2222
Brewster, NE 68821   **Fax:** 308-547-2228
www.nol.org/blaine/

In central NE, northeast of North Platte; organized Mar 5, 1885 from Custer County. **Name Origin:** For James Gillespie Blaine (1830-93), U.S. representative from ME (1863-76), U.S. senator (1876-81), and U.S. secretary of state (1881; 1889-92).

Please see sample entry on inside front cover for detailed information about the statistics presented with each county listing.

353

Area (sq mi): 714.34 (land 710.74; water 3.59).

Pop: 583 (White 98.8%; Black or African American 0%; Hispanic or Latino 0.2%; Asian 0%; Other 1%). **Foreign born:** 0.3%. **Median age:** 39.8. **State rank:** 91. **Pop change 1990-2000:** -13.6%.

Income: per capita $12,323; median household $25,278. **Pop below poverty level:** 19.4%.

Unemployment: 1.6%. **Median home value:** $22,500. **Median travel time to work:** 20.9 minutes.

BOONE COUNTY
222 S 4th St   **Ph:** 402-395-2055
Albion, NE 68620   **Fax:** 402-395-6592
www.co.boone.ne.us

In east-central NE, northeast of Grand Island; organized Mar 28, 1871 from Platte County. **Name Origin:** For Daniel Boone (1734?-1820), U.S. frontiersman and KY pioneer.

Area (sq mi): 687.25 (land 686.69; water 0.56).

Pop: 6,259 (White 98.8%; Black or African American 0%; Hispanic or Latino 0.9%; Asian 0%; Other 0.6%). **Foreign born:** 0.9%. **Median age:** 39.9. **State rank:** 51. **Pop change 1990-2000:** -6.1%.

Income: per capita $15,831; median household $31,444. **Pop below poverty level:** 10.4%.

Unemployment: 3.5%. **Median home value:** $50,700. **Median travel time to work:** 16.4 minutes.

BOX BUTTE COUNTY
PO Box 678   **Ph:** 308-762-6565
Alliance, NE 69301   **Fax:** 308-762-2867
www.co.box-butte.ne.us

In northwestern NE, northeast of Scottsbluff; organized Nov 2, 1886 from Dawes County. **Name Origin:** Descriptive of the rectangular-shaped butte near Alliance.

Area (sq mi): 1077.84 (land 1075.29; water 2.54).

Pop: 12,158 (White 87.7%; Black or African American 0.4%; Hispanic or Latino 7.6%; Asian 0.5%; Other 8.3%). **Foreign born:** 3.1%. **Median age:** 38.2. **State rank:** 22. **Pop change 1990-2000:** -7.4%.

Income: per capita $18,407; median household $39,366. **Pop below poverty level:** 10.7%.

Unemployment: 4.4%. **Median home value:** $71,700. **Median travel time to work:** 14.5 minutes.

BOYD COUNTY
PO Box 26   **Ph:** 402-775-2391
Butte, NE 68722   **Fax:** 402-775-2146

On the northern border of NE; organized Mar 20, 1891 from Holt County. **Name Origin:** For James E. Boyd (1834-1906), NE governor (1891; 1892-93).

Area (sq mi): 544.59 (land 540.05; water 4.54).

Pop: 2,438 (White 98.8%; Black or African American 0%; Hispanic or Latino 0.1%; Asian 0.2%; Other 1%). **Foreign born:** 0.4%. **Median age:** 43.8. **State rank:** 74. **Pop change 1990-2000:** -14%.

Income: per capita $13,840; median household $26,075. **Pop below poverty level:** 15.2%.

Unemployment: 3.8%. **Median home value:** $22,500. **Median travel time to work:** 15.2 minutes.

BROWN COUNTY
148 W 4th St   **Ph:** 402-387-2705
Ainsworth, NE 69210   **Fax:** 402-387-0918
www.co.brown.ne.us

In north-central NE; organized Feb 19, 1883 from unorganized territory. **Name Origin:** Possibly for two state legislators named Brown who sponsored the bill for organization of the county.

Area (sq mi): 1225.08 (land 1221.28; water 3.8).

Pop: 3,525 (White 98.1%; Black or African American 0%; Hispanic or Latino 0.8%; Asian 0.3%; Other 1%). **Foreign born:** 0.7%. **Median age:** 43.1. **State rank:** 67. **Pop change 1990-2000:** -3.6%.

Income: per capita $15,924; median household $28,356. **Pop below poverty level:** 11.1%.

Unemployment: 3.4%. **Median home value:** $42,700. **Median travel time to work:** 13.4 minutes.

BUFFALO COUNTY
PO Box 1270   **Ph:** 308-236-1226
Kearney, NE 68848   **Fax:** 308-233-3649
www.co.buffalo.ne.us

In south-central NE, west of Grand Island; original county; organized Mar 14, 1855 (prior to statehood); not officially recognized until Jan 20, 1870. **Name Origin:** For the former feeding grounds of the buffalo.

Area (sq mi): 975.27 (land 967.99; water 7.28).

Pop: 42,259 (White 93%; Black or African American 0.5%; Hispanic or Latino 4.7%; Asian 0.7%; Other 3.5%). **Foreign born:** 2.6%. **Median age:** 30. **State rank:** 5. **Pop change 1990-2000:** +12.9%.

Income: per capita $17,510; median household $36,782. **Pop below poverty level:** 11.2%.

Unemployment: 3%. **Median home value:** $91,300. **Median travel time to work:** 15.6 minutes.

BURT COUNTY
PO Box 87   **Ph:** 402-374-2955
Tekamah, NE 68061   **Fax:** 402-374-2956

On the central eastern border of NE, north of Omaha; original county; organized Feb 18, 1855 (prior to statehood). **Name Origin:** For Francis Burt (1807-54), SC legislator, editor, and first territorial governor of NE (1854).

Area (sq mi): 497.1 (land 492.77; water 4.33).

Pop: 7,791 (White 96.8%; Black or African American 0.2%; Hispanic or Latino 1.3%; Asian 0.2%; Other 2%). **Foreign born:** 1.1%. **Median age:** 42.2. **State rank:** 41. **Pop change 1990-2000:** -1%.

Income: per capita $16,654; median household $33,954. **Pop below poverty level:** 8.9%.

Unemployment: 4.3%. **Median home value:** $59,700. **Median travel time to work:** 22.9 minutes.

All statistics are based on the 2000 Census except the dollar figures given for per capita income, which are based on 1999 estimates.

BUTLER COUNTY

PO Box 289   **Ph:** 402-367-7430
David City, NE 68632   **Fax:** 402-367-3329
www.co.butler.ne.us

In east-central NE, west of Omaha; organized Jun 26, 1856 from unorganized territory. **Name Origin:** For David Butler (1829-91), first governor of NE (1867-71).

Area (sq mi): 584.41 (land 583.59; water 0.82).

Pop: 8,767 (White 97.6%; Black or African American 0.1%; Hispanic or Latino 1.7%; Asian 0.1%; Other 1.4%). **Foreign born:** 0.9%. **Median age:** 38.8. **State rank:** 37. **Pop change 1990-2000:** +1.9%.

Income: per capita $16,394; median household $36,331. **Pop below poverty level:** 8.2%.

Unemployment: 3.5%. **Median home value:** $62,900. **Median travel time to work:** 23.9 minutes.

CASS COUNTY

346 Main St   **Ph:** 402-296-9300
Plattsmouth, NE 68048   **Fax:** 402-296-9332
www.cassne.org

On the southeastern border of NE, northeast of Lincoln; original county; organized Mar 7, 1855 (prior to statehood). **Name Origin:** For Gen. Lewis Cass (1782-1866), OH legislator, military and civil governor of MI Territory (1813-31), U.S. secretary of war (1831-36), and U.S. secretary of state (1857-60).

Area (sq mi): 566.21 (land 559.18; water 7.03).

Pop: 24,334 (White 96.9%; Black or African American 0.2%; Hispanic or Latino 1.5%; Asian 0.3%; Other 1.6%). **Foreign born:** 1.2%. **Median age:** 36.9. **State rank:** 13. **Pop change 1990-2000:** +14.1%.

Income: per capita $20,156; median household $46,515. **Pop below poverty level:** 5.2%.

Unemployment: 3.1%. **Median home value:** $95,400. **Median travel time to work:** 27 minutes.

CEDAR COUNTY

101 S Broadway   **Ph:** 402-254-7411
Hartington, NE 68739   **Fax:** 402-254-7410
www.co.cedar.ne.us

On the northeastern border of NE, west of Sioux City, IA; original county; organized Feb 12, 1855 (prior to statehood). **Name Origin:** For the cedar trees that are abundant locally.

Area (sq mi): 745.81 (land 740.23; water 5.59).

Pop: 9,615 (White 98.9%; Black or African American 0.1%; Hispanic or Latino 0.4%; Asian 0%; Other 0.8%). **Foreign born:** 0.4%. **Median age:** 38.8. **State rank:** 31. **Pop change 1990-2000:** -5.1%.

Income: per capita $15,514; median household $33,435. **Pop below poverty level:** 9.1%.

Unemployment: 2.5%. **Median home value:** $55,200. **Median travel time to work:** 17.5 minutes.

CHASE COUNTY

PO Box 1299   **Ph:** 308-882-5266
Imperial, NE 69033   **Fax:** 308-882-5390
www.co.chase.ne.us

On the southwestern border of NE, southwest of North Platte; organized Apr 24, 1886 from Keith County. **Name Origin:** For Champion S. Chase (?-1898), mayor of Omaha, NE, and first attorney general of NE.

Area (sq mi): 897.63 (land 894.5; water 3.14).

Pop: 4,068 (White 95.9%; Black or African American 0.2%; Hispanic or Latino 3.4%; Asian 0.2%; Other 1.8%). **Foreign born:** 1.4%. **Median age:** 42.1. **State rank:** 62. **Pop change 1990-2000:** -7.1%.

Income: per capita $17,490; median household $32,351. **Pop below poverty level:** 9.6%.

Unemployment: 2.2%. **Median home value:** $56,900. **Median travel time to work:** 12.9 minutes.

CHERRY COUNTY

PO Box 120   **Ph:** 402-376-2771
Valentine, NE 69201   **Fax:** 402-376-3095
www.co.cherry.ne.us

On the central northern border of NE; organized Feb 23, 1883 from unorganized territory. Claims to be the largest county in the U.S. **Name Origin:** For Lt. Samuel A. Cherry (?-1881), an army officer.

Area (sq mi): 6009.54 (land 5960.52; water 49.02).

Pop: 6,148 (White 93.8%; Black or African American 0.1%; Hispanic or Latino 0.9%; Asian 0.4%; Other 5.3%). **Foreign born:** 0.7%. **Median age:** 39.4. **State rank:** 53. **Pop change 1990-2000:** -2.5%.

Income: per capita $15,943; median household $29,268. **Pop below poverty level:** 12.3%.

Unemployment: 1.8%. **Median home value:** $63,300. **Median travel time to work:** 12.4 minutes.

CHEYENNE COUNTY

PO Box 217   **Ph:** 308-254-2141
Sidney, NE 69162   **Fax:** 308-254-4293
www.co.cheyenne.ne.us

On the southwestern border of NE, west of North Platte; organized Jun 6, 1871 from Lincoln County. **Name Origin:** For the Cheyenne Indians who once lived in the area.

Area (sq mi): 1196.45 (land 1196.34; water 0.11).

Pop: 9,830 (White 93.9%; Black or African American 0.1%; Hispanic or Latino 4.5%; Asian 0.4%; Other 3.2%). **Foreign born:** 0.9%. **Median age:** 38.7. **State rank:** 29. **Pop change 1990-2000:** +3.5%.

Income: per capita $17,437; median household $33,438. **Pop below poverty level:** 10%.

Unemployment: 2.1%. **Median home value:** $56,500. **Median travel time to work:** 15.5 minutes.

Please see sample entry on inside front cover for detailed information about the statistics presented with each county listing.

CLAY COUNTY

111 W Fairfield St
Clay Center, NE 68933

Ph: 402-762-3463
Fax: 402-762-3506

In south-central NE, southeast of Grand Island; original county, organized Mar 7, 1855 (prior to statehood). According to Thorndale and Dollarhide's *Map Guide to the U.S. Federal Censuses, 1790-1920*, area originally called Clay County is now part of Lancaster and Gage counties, while present-day Clay county occupies area which was unattached in 1860. **Name Origin:** For Henry Clay (1777-1852), U.S. senator from KY, known as the 'Great Pacificator' for his advocacy of compromise to avert national crises.

Area (sq mi): 573.53 (land 573.03; water 0.49).

Pop: 7,039 (White 95.6%; Black or African American 0.2%; Hispanic or Latino 3.5%; Asian 0.3%; Other 1.9%). **Foreign born:** 2.6%. **Median age:** 39.9. **State rank:** 45. **Pop change 1990-2000:** -1.2%.

Income: per capita $16,870; median household $34,259. **Pop below poverty level:** 10.4%.

Unemployment: 2.7%. **Median home value:** $50,900. **Median travel time to work:** 19.9 minutes.

COLFAX COUNTY

411 E 11th St
Schuyler, NE 68661
www.nol.org/colfax

Ph: 402-352-8504
Fax: 402-352-8515

In east-central NE, northwest of Omaha; organized Feb 15, 1869 from Platte County. **Name Origin:** For Schuyler Colfax (1823-85), U.S. vice president under Ulysses S. Grant (1869-73).

Area (sq mi): 418.58 (land 413.14; water 5.44).

Pop: 10,441 (White 73%; Black or African American 0.1%; Hispanic or Latino 26.2%; Asian 0.2%; Other 17.9%). **Foreign born:** 18.2%. **Median age:** 35. **State rank:** 26. **Pop change 1990-2000:** +14.2%.

Income: per capita $15,148; median household $35,849. **Pop below poverty level:** 10.8%.

Unemployment: 2.5%. **Median home value:** $57,800. **Median travel time to work:** 18.6 minutes.

CUMING COUNTY

200 S Lincoln St
West Point, NE 68788
www.co.cuming.ne.us

Ph: 402-372-6002
Fax: 402-372-6013

In east-central NE; northwest of Omaha; organized Mar 16, 1855 from Burt County. **Name Origin:** For Thomas B. Cuming (?-1858), acting governor of NE Territory (1854-55; 1857-58).

Area (sq mi): 574.54 (land 572; water 2.54).

Pop: 10,203 (White 93.6%; Black or African American 0.1%; Hispanic or Latino 5.5%; Asian 0.2%; Other 3.8%). **Foreign born:** 3.8%. **Median age:** 39.2. **State rank:** 27. **Pop change 1990-2000:** +0.9%.

Income: per capita $16,443; median household $33,186. **Pop below poverty level:** 9%.

Unemployment: 2.1%. **Median home value:** $66,000. **Median travel time to work:** 15.5 minutes.

CUSTER COUNTY

431 S 10th St
Broken Bow, NE 68822
www.co.custer.ne.us

Ph: 308-872-5701
Fax: 308-872-2811

In south-central NE, east of North Platte; organized as Kountze County Feb 17, 1877 from unorganized territory. **Name Origin:** For Gen. George Armstrong Custer (1839-76), U.S. army officer and Indian fighter.

Area (sq mi): 2576.08 (land 2575.71; water 0.37).

Pop: 11,793 (White 98%; Black or African American 0.1%; Hispanic or Latino 0.9%; Asian 0.2%; Other 1.2%). **Foreign born:** 0.4%. **Median age:** 41.3. **State rank:** 23. **Pop change 1990-2000:** -3.9%.

Income: per capita $16,171; median household $30,677. **Pop below poverty level:** 12.4%.

Unemployment: 1.9%. **Median home value:** $45,100. **Median travel time to work:** 17.7 minutes.

DAKOTA COUNTY

1601 Broadway
Dakota City, NE 68731
www.sscdc.net/county/

Ph: 402-987-2126
Fax: 402-494-9228

On the northeastern border of NE, south of Sioux City, IA; original county, organized Mar 7, 1855. **Name Origin:** For the Dakota (also called the Sioux) Indian tribe.

Area (sq mi): 267.39 (land 263.8; water 3.6).

Pop: 20,253 (White 70.9%; Black or African American 0.6%; Hispanic or Latino 22.6%; Asian 3.1%; Other 17.5%). **Foreign born:** 15.6%. **Median age:** 31.4. **State rank:** 15. **Pop change 1990-2000:** +21%.

Income: per capita $16,125; median household $38,834. **Pop below poverty level:** 11.4%.

Unemployment: 2.8%. **Median home value:** $81,200. **Median travel time to work:** 17.3 minutes.

DAWES COUNTY

451 Main St
Chadron, NE 69337
www.co.dawes.ne.us

Ph: 308-432-0100
Fax: 308-432-5179

On the northwestern border of NE, northeast of Scottsbluff; organized Feb 19, 1885 from Sioux County. **Name Origin:** For James William Dawes (1845-87), governor of NE (1883-87).

Area (sq mi): 1400.86 (land 1396.24; water 4.62).

Pop: 9,060 (White 92.4%; Black or African American 0.8%; Hispanic or Latino 2.4%; Asian 0.3%; Other 5.6%). **Foreign born:** 2.2%. **Median age:** 30.6. **State rank:** 35. **Pop change 1990-2000:** +0.4%.

Income: per capita $16,353; median household $29,476. **Pop below poverty level:** 18.9%.

Unemployment: 3.9%. **Median home value:** $55,200. **Median travel time to work:** 13.3 minutes.

All statistics are based on the 2000 Census except the dollar figures given for per capita income, which are based on 1999 estimates.

DAWSON COUNTY

PO Box 370   **Ph:** 308-324-2127
Lexington, NE 68850   **Fax:** 308-324-6106
www.dawsoncountyne.net

In south-central NE, west of Grand Island; organized Jan 11, 1860 from Buffalo County. **Name Origin:** For Jacob Dawson, first postmaster of Lancaster (now Lincoln).

Area (sq mi): 1019.3 (land 1012.92; water 6.37).

Pop: 24,365 (White 72.8%; Black or African American 0.3%; Hispanic or Latino 25.4%; Asian 0.7%; Other 16.7%). **Foreign born:** 15.9%. **Median age:** 34.3. **State rank:** 12. **Pop change 1990-2000:** +22.2%.

Income: per capita $15,973; median household $36,132. **Pop below poverty level:** 10.8%.

Unemployment: 3.2%. **Median home value:** $64,100. **Median travel time to work:** 14 minutes.

DEUEL COUNTY

PO Box 327   **Ph:** 308-874-3308
Chappell, NE 69129   **Fax:** 308-874-3472
www.co.deuel.ne.us

On the southern border of NE, west of North Platte; organized Jan 1889 from Cheyenne County. **Name Origin:** For Henry (or Harry) Porter Deuel (1836-1914), an early settler of Omaha and later a local railroad official.

Area (sq mi): 440.79 (land 439.89; water 0.9).

Pop: 2,098 (White 96%; Black or African American 0%; Hispanic or Latino 2.7%; Asian 0.4%; Other 2.2%). **Foreign born:** 0.9%. **Median age:** 43.5. **State rank:** 78. **Pop change 1990-2000:** -6.2%.

Income: per capita $17,891; median household $32,981. **Pop below poverty level:** 9.1%.

Unemployment: 2.8%. **Median home value:** $48,300. **Median travel time to work:** 18 minutes.

DIXON COUNTY

PO Box 395   **Ph:** 402-755-2881
Ponca, NE 68770   **Fax:** 402-755-2632
www.co.dixon.ne.us

On the northeastern border of NE, west of Sioux City, IA; original county, organized Dec 1858 (prior to statehood) from Dakota County. **Name Origin:** For an early settler.

Area (sq mi): 482.72 (land 476.39; water 6.33).

Pop: 6,339 (White 93.5%; Black or African American 0%; Hispanic or Latino 5.5%; Asian 0.3%; Other 5.1%). **Foreign born:** 3.4%. **Median age:** 38.7. **State rank:** 50. **Pop change 1990-2000:** +3.2%.

Income: per capita $15,350; median household $34,201. **Pop below poverty level:** 10%.

Unemployment: 2.9%. **Median home value:** $58,100. **Median travel time to work:** 22.8 minutes.

DODGE COUNTY

435 N Park Ave Rm 102   **Ph:** 402-727-2767
Fremont, NE 68025   **Fax:** 402-727-2764

In east-central NE, northwest of Omaha; original county, organized Mar 6, 1855 (prior to statehood). **Name Origin:** For Augustus Caesar Dodge (1812-83), son of Henry Dodge. First U.S. senator from IA (1848-55) and an active supporter of the Kansas-Nebraska bill.

Area (sq mi): 543.92 (land 534.39; water 9.53).

Pop: 36,160 (White 94.3%; Black or African American 0.4%; Hispanic or Latino 3.9%; Asian 0.5%; Other 3.2%). **Foreign born:** 2.8%. **Median age:** 37.9. **State rank:** 7. **Pop change 1990-2000:** +4.8%.

Income: per capita $17,757; median household $37,188. **Pop below poverty level:** 8.6%.

Unemployment: 3.6%. **Median home value:** $83,400. **Median travel time to work:** 19.7 minutes.

DOUGLAS COUNTY

1819 Farnum St   **Ph:** 402-444-7000
Omaha, NE 68183   **Fax:** 402-444-6456
www.co.douglas.ne.us

On the eastern border of NE, west of Council Bluffs, IA; original county; organized 1854 (prior to statehood). **Name Origin:** For Stephen Arnold Douglas (1813-61), U.S. orator and statesman.

Area (sq mi): 339.6 (land 330.98; water 8.62).

Pop: 463,585 (White 78.2%; Black or African American 11.5%; Hispanic or Latino 6.7%; Asian 1.7%; Other 5.9%). **Foreign born:** 5.9%. **Median age:** 33.6. **State rank:** 1. **Pop change 1990-2000:** +11.3%.

Income: per capita $22,879; median household $43,209. **Pop below poverty level:** 9.8%.

Unemployment: 3.4%. **Median home value:** $100,800. **Median travel time to work:** 18.6 minutes.

DUNDY COUNTY

PO Box 506   **Ph:** 308-423-2058
Benkelman, NE 69021

On the southern border of NE, west of McCook; organized Feb 27, 1873 from unorganized territory. **Name Origin:** For Elmer S. Dundy (1830-96), NE territorial legislator and jurist of the U.S. circuit court.

Area (sq mi): 920.79 (land 919.86; water 0.93).

Pop: 2,292 (White 94.7%; Black or African American 0%; Hispanic or Latino 3.2%; Asian 0.5%; Other 2.5%). **Foreign born:** 1.9%. **Median age:** 43.5. **State rank:** 75. **Pop change 1990-2000:** -11.2%.

Income: per capita $15,786; median household $27,010. **Pop below poverty level:** 13.6%.

Unemployment: 2%. **Median home value:** $32,600. **Median travel time to work:** 14.4 minutes.

FILLMORE COUNTY

PO Box 307   **Ph:** 402-759-4931
Geneva, NE 68361   **Fax:** 402-759-4307
www.fillmorecounty.org

In southeastern NE, southwest of Lincoln; established Jan 26, 1856 from unorganized territory, organized 1871. **Name Origin:** For Millard Fillmore (1800-74), thirteenth U.S. president.

Please see sample entry on inside front cover for detailed information about the statistics presented with each county listing.

357

Area (sq mi): 576.62 (land 576.46; water 0.16).

Pop: 6,634 (White 97.1%; Black or African American 0.2%; Hispanic or Latino 1.7%; Asian 0.1%; Other 1.9%). **Foreign born:** 0.8%. **Median age:** 41.4. **State rank:** 47. **Pop change 1990-2000:** -6.6%.

Income: per capita $17,465; median household $35,162. **Pop below poverty level:** 7.8%.

Unemployment: 2.7%. **Median home value:** $51,300. **Median travel time to work:** 15.7 minutes.

FRANKLIN COUNTY

PO Box 146   **Ph:** 308-425-6202
Franklin, NE 68939   **Fax:** 308-425-6093

On central southern border of NE, southwest of Grand Island; organized Mar 9, 1871 from Kearney County. **Name Origin:** For Benjamin Franklin (1706-90), U.S. patriot, diplomat, and statesman.

Area (sq mi): 576.11 (land 575.92; water 0.19).

Pop: 3,574 (White 98.7%; Black or African American 0%; Hispanic or Latino 0.6%; Asian 0.1%; Other 0.7%). **Foreign born:** 0.6%. **Median age:** 42.8. **State rank:** 66. **Pop change 1990-2000:** -9.2%.

Income: per capita $15,390; median household $29,304. **Pop below poverty level:** 13.2%.

Unemployment: 2.5%. **Median home value:** $33,100. **Median travel time to work:** 20.9 minutes.

FRONTIER COUNTY

PO Box 40   **Ph:** 308-367-8641
Stockville, NE 69042   **Fax:** 308-367-8730
www.co.frontier.ne.us

In south-central NE, south of North Platter; organized Jan 17, 1872 from unorganized territory. **Name Origin:** For its location on the NE frontier at the time of naming.

Area (sq mi): 980.06 (land 974.55; water 5.51).

Pop: 3,099 (White 98%; Black or African American 0.1%; Hispanic or Latino 1%; Asian 0.3%; Other 1.4%). **Foreign born:** 1%. **Median age:** 38.5. **State rank:** 71. **Pop change 1990-2000:** -0.1%.

Income: per capita $16,648; median household $33,038. **Pop below poverty level:** 12.2%.

Unemployment: 2.1%. **Median home value:** $54,800. **Median travel time to work:** 18 minutes.

FURNAS COUNTY

PO Box 387   **Ph:** 308-268-4145
Beaver City, NE 68926   **Fax:** 308-268-3205

On the central southern border of NE, east of McCook; organized Feb 27, 1873 from unorganized territory. **Name Origin:** For Col. Robert Wilkinson Furnas (1824-1905), an officer in the Civil War and governor of NE (1873-75).

Area (sq mi): 720.51 (land 718.09; water 2.42).

Pop: 5,324 (White 97.6%; Black or African American 0.1%; Hispanic or Latino 1.1%; Asian 0.2%; Other 1.5%). **Foreign born:** 0.3%. **Median age:** 43.5. **State rank:** 57. **Pop change 1990-2000:** -4.1%.

Income: per capita $17,223; median household $30,498. **Pop below poverty level:** 10.6%.

Unemployment: 1.9%. **Median home value:** $37,300. **Median travel time to work:** 15.7 minutes.

GAGE COUNTY

PO Box 429   **Ph:** 402-223-1300
Beatrice, NE 68310   **Fax:** 402-223-1371
www.state.ne.us/gage/

On the southern border of NE, south of Lincoln; original county; organized Mar 16, 1855 (prior to statehood). **Name Origin:** For William D. Gage (1803-85). Methodist minister and a local official.

Area (sq mi): 859.94 (land 855.29; water 4.65).

Pop: 22,993 (White 97.2%; Black or African American 0.3%; Hispanic or Latino 0.9%; Asian 0.3%; Other 1.7%). **Foreign born:** 0.7%. **Median age:** 39.9. **State rank:** 14. **Pop change 1990-2000:** +0.9%.

Income: per capita $17,190; median household $34,908. **Pop below poverty level:** 8.7%.

Unemployment: 2.7%. **Median home value:** $68,600. **Median travel time to work:** 18.6 minutes.

GARDEN COUNTY

PO Box 486   **Ph:** 308-772-3924
Oshkosh, NE 69154   **Fax:** 308-772-0124
www.co.garden.ne.us

In west-central NE, southeast of Scottsbluff; organized Nov 2, 1909 from Devel County. **Name Origin:** Named by John T. and William R. Twiford, the developers who thought it would become the 'garden spot of the west.'

Area (sq mi): 1731 (land 1704.4; water 26.6).

Pop: 2,292 (White 97.3%; Black or African American 0.1%; Hispanic or Latino 1.4%; Asian 0.3%; Other 1.3%). **Foreign born:** 0.9%. **Median age:** 45.6. **State rank:** 76. **Pop change 1990-2000:** -6.8%.

Income: per capita $15,414; median household $26,458. **Pop below poverty level:** 14.8%.

Unemployment: 3.1%. **Median home value:** $44,300. **Median travel time to work:** 14.1 minutes.

GARFIELD COUNTY

PO Box 218   **Ph:** 308-346-4161
Burwell, NE 68823

In east-central NE, northwest of Grand Island; organized Nov 8, 1881 from Wheeler County. **Name Origin:** For James Abram Garfield (1831-81), twentieth U.S. president.

Area (sq mi): 571.34 (land 570.03; water 1.31).

Pop: 1,902 (White 98.2%; Black or African American 0%; Hispanic or Latino 1%; Asian 0.1%; Other 1.2%). **Foreign born:** 0.7%. **Median age:** 45.9. **State rank:** 79. **Pop change 1990-2000:** -11.2%.

Income: per capita $14,368; median household $27,407. **Pop below poverty level:** 12.6%.

Unemployment: 1.8%. **Median home value:** $38,200. **Median travel time to work:** 16.5 minutes.

All statistics are based on the 2000 Census except the dollar figures given for per capita income, which are based on 1999 estimates.

GOSPER COUNTY

507 Smith Ave PO Box 136   **Ph:** 308-785-2611
Elwood, NE 68937   **Fax:** 308-785-2300

In south-central NE, organized Aug 29, 1873 from unorganized territory. **Name Origin:** For John J. Gosper, NE secretary of state (1873-75).

Area (sq mi): 462.74 (land 458.18; water 4.57).

Pop: 2,143 (White 98%; Black or African American 0%; Hispanic or Latino 1.3%; Asian 0.2%; Other 0.9%). **Foreign born:** 0.5%. **Median age:** 43.4. **State rank:** 77. **Pop change 1990-2000:** +11.2%.

Income: per capita $17,957; median household $36,827. **Pop below poverty level:** 7.9%.

Unemployment: 2.2%. **Median home value:** $67,900. **Median travel time to work:** 18.7 minutes.

GRANT COUNTY

105 E Harrison St PO Box 139   **Ph:** 308-458-2488
Hyannis, NE 69350   **Fax:** 308-458-2780

In west-central NE, northwest of North Platte; organized Mar 31, 1888 from unorganized territory. In 1870 a 'paper' county called Grant covered parts of present-day Lincoln, Frontier, Red Willow, Furnas, Gosper, Dawson, Hayes, and Hitchcock counties, much of which was known as Shorter County in 1860. **Name Origin:** For Ulysses Simpson Grant (1822-85), Civil War general and eighteenth U.S. president.

Area (sq mi): 783.23 (land 776.22; water 7).

Pop: 747 (White 98.3%; Black or African American 0%; Hispanic or Latino 1.3%; Asian 0.3%; Other 0.9%). **Foreign born:** 1.1%. **Median age:** 39.9. **State rank:** 88. **Pop change 1990-2000:** -2.9%.

Income: per capita $14,815; median household $34,821. **Pop below poverty level:** 9.7%.

Unemployment: 1.7%. **Median home value:** $27,500. **Median travel time to work:** 18.7 minutes.

GREELEY COUNTY

PO Box 287   **Ph:** 308-428-3625
Greeley, NE 68842   **Fax:** 308-428-3022

In east-central NE, north of Grand Island; organized Mar 1, 1871 from Boone County. **Name Origin:** For Horace Greeley (1811-72), editor who championed westward expansion.

Area (sq mi): 570.71 (land 569.85; water 0.85).

Pop: 2,714 (White 97.9%; Black or African American 0.7%; Hispanic or Latino 0.8%; Asian 0.1%; Other 1.4%). **Foreign born:** 0.7%. **Median age:** 41.7. **State rank:** 73. **Pop change 1990-2000:** -9.7%.

Income: per capita $13,731; median household $28,375. **Pop below poverty level:** 14.6%.

Unemployment: 3%. **Median home value:** $36,600. **Median travel time to work:** 18.6 minutes.

HALL COUNTY

121 S Pine St   **Ph:** 308-385-5080
Grand Island, NE 68801   **Fax:** 308-385-5184
www.hcgi.org

In south-central NE, west of Lincoln; original county; organized Nov 4, 1858 (prior to statehood). **Name Origin:** For Augustus Hall (1814-61), U.S. representative from IA (1855-57) and chief justice of NE Territory (1858-61).

Area (sq mi): 552.22 (land 546.4; water 5.83).

Pop: 53,534 (White 83.7%; Black or African American 0.4%; Hispanic or Latino 14%; Asian 1.1%; Other 9.8%). **Foreign born:** 8.3%. **Median age:** 35.6. **State rank:** 4. **Pop change 1990-2000:** +9.4%.

Income: per capita $17,386; median household $36,972. **Pop below poverty level:** 12%.

Unemployment: 2.9%. **Median home value:** $83,700. **Median travel time to work:** 15.2 minutes.

HAMILTON COUNTY

1111 13th St Suite 1   **Ph:** 402-694-3443
Aurora, NE 68818   **Fax:** 402-694-2396
www.co.hamilton.ne.us

In south-central NE, east of Grand Island; organized Feb 16, 1867 from York County. **Name Origin:** For Alexander Hamilton (1757-1804), first U.S. secretary of treasury (1789-95).

Area (sq mi): 546.77 (land 543.68; water 3.09).

Pop: 9,403 (White 98%; Black or African American 0.2%; Hispanic or Latino 1.1%; Asian 0.2%; Other 1.2%). **Foreign born:** 0.4%. **Median age:** 38.1. **State rank:** 33. **Pop change 1990-2000:** +6.1%.

Income: per capita $17,590; median household $40,277. **Pop below poverty level:** 7.5%.

Unemployment: 1.9%. **Median home value:** $78,200. **Median travel time to work:** 17.3 minutes.

HARLAN COUNTY

PO Box 698   **Ph:** 308-928-2173
Alma, NE 68920   **Fax:** 308-928-2079

On the central southern border of NE, southwest of Kearney; organized Jun 3, 1871 from Lincoln County. **Name Origin:** For either Thomas Harlan, a local official, or for his uncle, James Harlan (1820-99), U.S. senator from IA (1855-65; 1867-73) and U.S. secretary of the interior (1865-66).

Area (sq mi): 574.18 (land 552.78; water 21.4).

Pop: 3,786 (White 98.5%; Black or African American 0.1%; Hispanic or Latino 0.8%; Asian 0.1%; Other 0.9%). **Foreign born:** 0.3%. **Median age:** 44.5. **State rank:** 65. **Pop change 1990-2000:** -0.6%.

Income: per capita $15,618; median household $30,679. **Pop below poverty level:** 10.1%.

Unemployment: 2.4%. **Median home value:** $43,100. **Median travel time to work:** 17.5 minutes.

Please see sample entry on inside front cover for detailed information about the statistics presented with each county listing.

HAYES COUNTY

PO Box 370   **Ph:** 308-286-3413
Hayes Center, NE 69032   **Fax:** 308-286-3208
www.geocities.com/hayes_county/

In south-central NE, southwest of North Platte; organized Feb 19, 1877 from unorganized territory. **Name Origin:** For Rutherford Birchard Hayes (1822-93), nineteenth U.S. president.

Area (sq mi): 713.33 (land 713.11; water 0.22).

Pop: 1,068 (White 96.4%; Black or African American 0.2%; Hispanic or Latino 2.5%; Asian 0.3%; Other 2.4%). **Foreign born:** 2%. **Median age:** 42.5. **State rank:** 82. **Pop change 1990-2000:** -12.6%.

Income: per capita $14,099; median household $26,667. **Pop below poverty level:** 18.4%.

Unemployment: 2.4%. **Median home value:** $31,800. **Median travel time to work:** 17.4 minutes.

HITCHCOCK COUNTY

PO Box 248   **Ph:** 308-334-5646
Trenton, NE 69044   **Fax:** 308-334-5398
www.co.hitchcock.ne.us

On the central southern border of NE, south of North Platte; organized Feb 27, 1873 from unorganized territory. **Name Origin:** For Phineas Warrener Hitchcock (1831-81), U.S. senator from NE (1871-77).

Area (sq mi): 718.57 (land 710.03; water 8.54).

Pop: 3,111 (White 97.4%; Black or African American 0.1%; Hispanic or Latino 1.4%; Asian 0.1%; Other 1.4%). **Foreign born:** 1.2%. **Median age:** 43.6. **State rank:** 70. **Pop change 1990-2000:** -17%.

Income: per capita $14,804; median household $28,287. **Pop below poverty level:** 14.9%.

Unemployment: 3.1%. **Median home value:** $38,000. **Median travel time to work:** 20.7 minutes.

HOLT COUNTY

PO Box 329   **Ph:** 402-336-1762
O'Neill, NE 68763   **Fax:** 402-336-1762
www.co.holt.ne.us

In north-central NE; organized Jan 9, 1862 from Elkhorn County. **Name Origin:** For Joseph Holt (1807-94), U.S. Postmaster General (1859-61); secretary of war (1861), and judge advocate general for the U.S. army (1862-75).

Area (sq mi): 2417.65 (land 2412.66; water 4.99).

Pop: 11,551 (White 98.5%; Black or African American 0%; Hispanic or Latino 0.7%; Asian 0.2%; Other 1%). **Foreign born:** 0.8%. **Median age:** 40.5. **State rank:** 24. **Pop change 1990-2000:** -8.3%.

Income: per capita $15,256; median household $30,738. **Pop below poverty level:** 13%.

Unemployment: 3%. **Median home value:** $59,700. **Median travel time to work:** 15.5 minutes.

HOOKER COUNTY

PO Box 184   **Ph:** 308-546-2244
Mullen, NE 69152   **Fax:** 308-546-2490
www.co.hooker.ne.us

In west-central NE, northwest of North Platte; organized Mar 29, 1889 from unorganized territory. **Name Origin:** For Joseph Hooker (1814-79), famous Union general during the Civil War.

Area (sq mi): 721.51 (land 721.17; water 0.34).

Pop: 783 (White 97.8%; Black or African American 0%; Hispanic or Latino 1%; Asian 0.1%; Other 1.1%). **Foreign born:** 0%. **Median age:** 45.3. **State rank:** 86. **Pop change 1990-2000:** -1.3%.

Income: per capita $15,513; median household $27,868. **Pop below poverty level:** 6.9%.

Unemployment: 3.1%. **Median home value:** $41,300. **Median travel time to work:** 15 minutes.

HOWARD COUNTY

PO Box 25   **Ph:** 308-754-4343
Saint Paul, NE 68873   **Fax:** 308-754-4125

In east-central NE, north of Grand Island; organized Mar 1, 1871 from Hall County. **Name Origin:** For Gen. Oliver Otis Howard (1830-1909), Union officer in the Seminole War and the Civil War; president of Howard University (1869-73). Others believe it was for Howard Paul, son of an early settler, whose family founded Saint Paul, the county seat.

Area (sq mi): 575.74 (land 569.47; water 6.27).

Pop: 6,567 (White 98%; Black or African American 0.3%; Hispanic or Latino 1%; Asian 0.1%; Other 0.8%). **Foreign born:** 0.8%. **Median age:** 38.1. **State rank:** 48. **Pop change 1990-2000:** +8.5%.

Income: per capita $15,535; median household $33,305. **Pop below poverty level:** 11.7%.

Unemployment: 2.8%. **Median home value:** $66,100. **Median travel time to work:** 22.2 minutes.

JEFFERSON COUNTY

411 4th St   **Ph:** 402-729-2323
Fairbury, NE 68352   **Fax:** 402-729-2016
www.co.jefferson.ne.us

On the southern border of NE, southwest of Lincoln. Organized 1864; combined with Jones County 1867; both counties dissolved 1871 and eastern part (Jones County) named Jefferson. Original Jones County probably established Jan 26, 1856. Jefferson County attached to Gage County for judicial purposes between 1857 and 1864. **Name Origin:** For Thomas Jefferson (1743-1826), U.S. patriot and statesman; third U.S. president.

Area (sq mi): 575.5 (land 573.01; water 2.48).

Pop: 8,333 (White 97.7%; Black or African American 0.1%; Hispanic or Latino 1.3%; Asian 0.2%; Other 1.3%). **Foreign born:** 0.4%. **Median age:** 42.9. **State rank:** 38. **Pop change 1990-2000:** -4.9%.

Income: per capita $18,380; median household $32,629. **Pop below poverty level:** 8.9%.

Unemployment: 4.7%. **Median home value:** $42,100. **Median travel time to work:** 18.6 minutes.

All statistics are based on the 2000 Census except the dollar figures given for per capita income, which are based on 1999 estimates.

JOHNSON COUNTY

PO Box 416   **Ph:** 402-335-6300
Tecumseh, NE 68450   **Fax:** 402-335-6311
www.co.johnson.ne.us

In southeastern NE, southeast of Lincoln; original county; organized Mar 2, 1855 (prior to statehood). **Name Origin:** For Col. Richard Mentor Johnson (1781-1850), officer in the War of 1812, U.S. senator from KY (1819-29), and U.S. vice president under Van Buren (1837-41).

Area (sq mi): 376.82 (land 376.13; water 0.69).

Pop: 4,488 (White 92.8%; Black or African American 0.1%; Hispanic or Latino 2.9%; Asian 2.7%; Other 3.7%). **Foreign born:** 4.3%. **Median age:** 42.4. **State rank:** 60. **Pop change 1990-2000:** -4%.

Income: per capita $16,437; median household $32,460. **Pop below poverty level:** 8.9%.

Unemployment: 3.2%. **Median home value:** $51,300. **Median travel time to work:** 24 minutes.

KEARNEY COUNTY

PO Box 339   **Ph:** 308-832-2723
Minden, NE 68959   **Fax:** 308-832-2729

In south-central NE, southwest of Grand Island; original county; organized Jan 10, 1860 (prior to statehood). **Name Origin:** For Fort Kearny, itself named for Gen. Stephen Watts Kearny (1794-1848), officer in the War of 1812 and the Mexican-American War. The *e* in the last syllable was added in 1857, reason unknown.

Area (sq mi): 516.13 (land 516.03; water 0.11).

Pop: 6,882 (White 96.8%; Black or African American 0.2%; Hispanic or Latino 2.3%; Asian 0.2%; Other 1.8%). **Foreign born:** 1.6%. **Median age:** 38.7. **State rank:** 46. **Pop change 1990-2000:** +3.8%.

Income: per capita $18,118; median household $39,247. **Pop below poverty level:** 8.5%.

Unemployment: 2.3%. **Median home value:** $77,600. **Median travel time to work:** 18.5 minutes.

KEITH COUNTY

PO Box 149   **Ph:** 308-284-4726
Ogallala, NE 69153   **Fax:** 308-284-6277
www.co.keith.ne.us

In west-central NE, west of North Platte; organized May 3, 1873 from Lincoln County. **Name Origin:** For either Morrill C. Keith, the grandfather of NE governor Keith Morrill (1917-19), or John Keith, a prominent citizen of North Platte.

Area (sq mi): 1109.77 (land 1061.26; water 48.51).

Pop: 8,875 (White 94.5%; Black or African American 0.1%; Hispanic or Latino 4.2%; Asian 0.2%; Other 3%). **Foreign born:** 1.7%. **Median age:** 41.1. **State rank:** 36. **Pop change 1990-2000:** +3.4%.

Income: per capita $17,421; median household $32,325. **Pop below poverty level:** 9.3%.

Unemployment: 2.9%. **Median home value:** $69,300. **Median travel time to work:** 16.4 minutes.

KEYA PAHA COUNTY

PO Box 349   **Ph:** 402-497-3791
Springview, NE 68778   **Fax:** 402-497-3799
www.co.keya-paha.ne.us

On the central northern border of NE; organized Nov 4, 1884 from Brown County. **Name Origin:** For the Keya Paha River, which flows through the northeastern part of the county. From Dakota Indian *keya* 'turtle' and *paha* 'hill,' for a turtle-shaped hill.

Area (sq mi): 774.17 (land 773.29; water 0.89).

Pop: 983 (White 95.7%; Black or African American 0%; Hispanic or Latino 3.9%; Asian 0%; Other 0.6%). **Foreign born:** 2.2%. **Median age:** 41.9. **State rank:** 83. **Pop change 1990-2000:** -4.5%.

Income: per capita $11,860; median household $24,911. **Pop below poverty level:** 26.9%.

Unemployment: 1.3%. **Median home value:** $28,200. **Median travel time to work:** 18.2 minutes.

KIMBALL COUNTY

114 E 3rd St   **Ph:** 308-235-2241
Kimball, NE 69145   **Fax:** 308-235-3654
www.co.kimball.ne.us

In the southwestern corner of NE, south of Scottsbluff; organized Nov 6, 1888 from Cheyenne County. **Name Origin:** For Thomas Lord Kimball (1831-99), vice president of the Union Pacific Railroad.

Area (sq mi): 952.31 (land 951.72; water 0.58).

Pop: 4,089 (White 94.5%; Black or African American 0.2%; Hispanic or Latino 3.3%; Asian 0.1%; Other 2.7%). **Foreign born:** 0.7%. **Median age:** 42.8. **State rank:** 61. **Pop change 1990-2000:** -0.5%.

Income: per capita $17,525; median household $30,586. **Pop below poverty level:** 11.1%.

Unemployment: 2.2%. **Median home value:** $49,400. **Median travel time to work:** 15.7 minutes.

KNOX COUNTY

PO Box 166   **Ph:** 402-288-4282
Center, NE 68724   **Fax:** 402-288-5605
www.co.knox.ne.us

On the northeastern border of NE, northwest of Sioux City, IA. Original county; organized as L'Eau Qui Court County, Feb 10, 1857 (prior to statehood); name changed to Emmett County; then to present name Feb 21, 1873. **Name Origin:** For Gen. Henry Knox (1750-1806), Revolutionary War officer and first U.S. secretary of war (1785-95).

Area (sq mi): 1139.65 (land 1108.12; water 31.53).

Pop: 9,374 (White 91.3%; Black or African American 0.1%; Hispanic or Latino 0.9%; Asian 0.2%; Other 8%). **Foreign born:** 1%. **Median age:** 43. **State rank:** 34. **Pop change 1990-2000:** -1.7%.

Income: per capita $13,971; median household $27,564. **Pop below poverty level:** 15.6%.

Unemployment: 3.6%. **Median home value:** $42,100. **Median travel time to work:** 17.3 minutes.

Please see sample entry on inside front cover for detailed information about the statistics presented with each county listing.

LANCASTER COUNTY

555 S 10th St   **Ph:** 402-441-7481
Lincoln, NE 68508   **Fax:** 402-441-8728
www.co.lancaster.ne.us

In southeastern NE, southwest of Omaha; original county, organized Mar 6, 1855 (prior to statehood). **Name Origin:** For Lancaster County, PA, former home of many settlers.

Area (sq mi): 846.71 (land 838.88; water 7.83).

Pop: 250,291 (White 88.7%; Black or African American 2.8%; Hispanic or Latino 3.4%; Asian 2.9%; Other 4.3%). **Foreign born:** 5.4%. **Median age:** 32. **State rank:** 2. **Pop change 1990-2000:** +17.2%.

Income: per capita $21,265; median household $41,850. **Pop below poverty level:** 9.5%.

Unemployment: 2.8%. **Median home value:** $105,900. **Median travel time to work:** 17.8 minutes.

LINCOLN COUNTY

301 N Jeffers St   **Ph:** 308-534-4350
North Platte, NE 69101   **Fax:** 308-535-3527
www.co.lincoln.ne.us

In south-central NE, north of McCook; organized as Shorter County Jan 7, 1860 (prior to statehood) from unorganized territory (contained the 'paper' counties of Grant and Jackson in 1870); name changed 1866. **Name Origin:** For Abraham Lincoln (1809-65), sixteenth U.S. president.

Area (sq mi): 2575.1 (land 2563.98; water 11.12).

Pop: 34,632 (White 92.6%; Black or African American 0.5%; Hispanic or Latino 5.4%; Asian 0.4%; Other 4.4%). **Foreign born:** 1.2%. **Median age:** 37.8. **State rank:** 9. **Pop change 1990-2000:** +6.5%.

Income: per capita $18,696; median household $36,568. **Pop below poverty level:** 9.7%.

Unemployment: 3.5%. **Median home value:** $78,200. **Median travel time to work:** 16 minutes.

LOGAN COUNTY

317 Main St   **Ph:** 308-636-2311
Stapleton, NE 69163
www.co.logan.ne.us

In central NE, north of North Platte; organized Feb 24, 1885 from Custer County. **Name Origin:** For Gen. John Alexander Logan (1826-86), officer in the Mexican-American War and Civil War; U.S. senator from IL (1871-77; 1879-86).

Area (sq mi): 571.15 (land 570.68; water 0.46).

Pop: 774 (White 97.7%; Black or African American 0.1%; Hispanic or Latino 0.9%; Asian 0%; Other 1.3%). **Foreign born:** 0.3%. **Median age:** 41.8. **State rank:** 87. **Pop change 1990-2000:** -11.8%.

Income: per capita $14,937; median household $33,125. **Pop below poverty level:** 10.5%.

Unemployment: 2.3%. **Median home value:** $51,700. **Median travel time to work:** 24.1 minutes.

LOUP COUNTY

408 4th St   **Ph:** 308-942-3135
Taylor, NE 68879   **Fax:** 308-942-6015
www.co.loup.ne.us

In central NE, northeast of North Platte; organized as Taylor County Mar 6, 1855 from unorganized territory (prior to statehood); name changed Jul 23, 1883. **Name Origin:** For the Loup River, which flows through the county; itself named for the Pawnee Loup Indians. Name is French translation of Pawnee *skidi* 'wolf.'

Area (sq mi): 571.02 (land 569.71; water 1.31).

Pop: 712 (White 97.8%; Black or African American 0%; Hispanic or Latino 1.7%; Asian 0.1%; Other 1%). **Foreign born:** 1%. **Median age:** 42.9. **State rank:** 90. **Pop change 1990-2000:** +4.2%.

Income: per capita $12,427; median household $26,250. **Pop below poverty level:** 17.7%.

Unemployment: 1.9%. **Median home value:** $27,500. **Median travel time to work:** 24.6 minutes.

MADISON COUNTY

PO Box 290   **Ph:** 402-454-3311
Madison, NE 68748   **Fax:** 402-454-6682
www.co.madison.ne.us

In east-central NE, northwest of Omaha; organized Dec 1867 from Platte County. **Name Origin:** For either James Madison (1751-1836), fourth U.S. president, or for Madison County, WI, former home of early German settlers.

Area (sq mi): 575.05 (land 572.57; water 2.49).

Pop: 35,226 (White 88.3%; Black or African American 0.9%; Hispanic or Latino 8.6%; Asian 0.4%; Other 7.3%). **Foreign born:** 5.5%. **Median age:** 35. **State rank:** 8. **Pop change 1990-2000:** +7.9%.

Income: per capita $16,804; median household $35,807. **Pop below poverty level:** 11.2%.

Unemployment: 3.6%. **Median home value:** $80,100. **Median travel time to work:** 13.7 minutes.

MCPHERSON COUNTY

PO Box 122   **Ph:** 308-587-2363
Tryon, NE 69167   **Fax:** 308-587-2363

In central NE, north of North Platte; boundaries set Mar 31, 1887 from Lincoln and Keith counties. **Name Origin:** For Gen. James Birdseye McPherson (1828-64), commander of the Union army in Tennessee during the Civil War.

Area (sq mi): 860.02 (land 858.98; water 1.04).

Pop: 533 (White 97.2%; Black or African American 0%; Hispanic or Latino 1.5%; Asian 0.4%; Other 1.7%). **Foreign born:** 0%. **Median age:** 40.6. **State rank:** 92. **Pop change 1990-2000:** -2.4%.

Income: per capita $13,055; median household $25,750. **Pop below poverty level:** 16.2%.

Unemployment: 1%. **Median home value:** $40,900. **Median travel time to work:** 28.9 minutes.

All statistics are based on the 2000 Census except the dollar figures given for per capita income, which are based on 1999 estimates.

MERRICK COUNTY

PO Box 27

Central City, NE 68826

Ph: 308-946-2881

Fax: 308-946-2332

In east-central NE, northeast of Grand Island; original county; organized Nov 4, 1858 (prior to statehood). **Name Origin:** For Elvira Merrick De Puy, wife of Rep. Henry W. De Puy, who introduced the bill for the county's establishment.

Area (sq mi): 494.72 (land 484.88; water 9.85).

Pop: 8,204 (White 97.2%; Black or African American 0.2%; Hispanic or Latino 2%; Asian 0.2%; Other 1.3%). **Foreign born:** 1%. **Median age:** 39.2. **State rank:** 39. **Pop change 1990-2000:** +2%.

Income: per capita $15,958; median household $34,961. **Pop below poverty level:** 8.9%.

Unemployment: 2.5%. **Median home value:** $62,700. **Median travel time to work:** 20.7 minutes.

MORRILL COUNTY

PO Box 610

Bridgeport, NE 69336

www.co.morrill.ne.us

Ph: 308-262-0860

Fax: 308-262-1469

In western NE, east of Scottsbluff; organized Nov 3, 1908 from Cheyenne County. **Name Origin:** For Charles Henry Morrill, regent of the University of Nebraska (1890-1903).

Area (sq mi): 1429.81 (land 1423.75; water 6.06).

Pop: 5,440 (White 88.6%; Black or African American 0.1%; Hispanic or Latino 10.1%; Asian 0.2%; Other 6%). **Foreign born:** 3.8%. **Median age:** 39.5. **State rank:** 56. **Pop change 1990-2000:** +0.3%.

Income: per capita $14,725; median household $30,235. **Pop below poverty level:** 14.7%.

Unemployment: 2.8%. **Median home value:** $49,500. **Median travel time to work:** 20.7 minutes.

NANCE COUNTY

209 Esther St

Fullerton, NE 68638

www.co.nance.ne.us

Ph: 308-536-2331

Fax: 308-536-2742

In east-central NE, northeast of Grand Island; organized Feb 4, 1879 from Merrick County, encompassing the entire former Pawnee Reservation. **Name Origin:** For Albinus Nance (1848-1911), governor of NE (1879-83).

Area (sq mi): 448.04 (land 441.32; water 6.73).

Pop: 4,038 (White 97.9%; Black or African American 0%; Hispanic or Latino 1.1%; Asian 0%; Other 1.5%). **Foreign born:** 0.8%. **Median age:** 40.1. **State rank:** 64. **Pop change 1990-2000:** -5.5%.

Income: per capita $16,886; median household $31,267. **Pop below poverty level:** 13.1%.

Unemployment: 4.1%. **Median home value:** $45,500. **Median travel time to work:** 21.2 minutes.

NEMAHA COUNTY

1824 'N' St

Auburn, NE 68305

www.co.nemaha.ne.us

Ph: 402-274-4285

Fax: 402-274-4389

On the southeastern border of NE, southeast of Lincoln; original county, organized Mar 7, 1855 (prior to statehood). **Name Origin:** For the Nemaha River, which flows through the county; itself named from the Otoe Indian word *nimaha* 'murky water.'

Area (sq mi): 411.89 (land 409.3; water 2.58).

Pop: 7,576 (White 97.1%; Black or African American 0.4%; Hispanic or Latino 1%; Asian 0.6%; Other 1.4%). **Foreign born:** 0.8%. **Median age:** 39.4. **State rank:** 42. **Pop change 1990-2000:** -5.1%.

Income: per capita $17,004; median household $32,588. **Pop below poverty level:** 12.6%.

Unemployment: 3.5%. **Median home value:** $58,200. **Median travel time to work:** 17 minutes.

NUCKOLLS COUNTY

PO Box 366

Nelson, NE 68961

Ph: 402-225-4361

Fax: 402-225-4301

On the southern border of NE, southeast of Grand Island; organized Jun 27, 1871 from unorganized territory; a county originally named Nuckolls is now Thayer County. **Name Origin:** For Stephen Friel Nuckolls (1825-79), pioneer, NE territorial legislator (1859), and U.S. representative from WY (1869-71).

Area (sq mi): 575.96 (land 575.3; water 0.66).

Pop: 5,057 (White 98.5%; Black or African American 0%; Hispanic or Latino 1%; Asian 0.2%; Other 0.9%). **Foreign born:** 0.6%. **Median age:** 44.1. **State rank:** 58. **Pop change 1990-2000:** -12.6%.

Income: per capita $15,608; median household $28,958. **Pop below poverty level:** 11.2%.

Unemployment: 2.5%. **Median home value:** $33,000. **Median travel time to work:** 16.8 minutes.

OTOE COUNTY

PO Box 249

Nebraska City, NE 68410

www.co.otoe.ne.us

Ph: 402-873-9500

Fax: 402-873-9506

On the southeastern border of NE, southeast of Lincoln; original county; organized Mar 2, 1855 (prior to statehood). **Name Origin:** For the Indian tribe of Siouan linguistic stock; meaning uncertain, but said to be 'lechers,' either as 'lovers' or in the pejorative sense. The name seems to be a shortened version of a Siouan or possibly French name.

Area (sq mi): 619.09 (land 615.69; water 3.4).

Pop: 15,396 (White 96.3%; Black or African American 0.3%; Hispanic or Latino 2.4%; Asian 0.2%; Other 1.9%). **Foreign born:** 1.4%. **Median age:** 39.5. **State rank:** 19. **Pop change 1990-2000:** +8%.

Income: per capita $17,752; median household $37,302. **Pop below poverty level:** 8.1%.

Unemployment: 3.4%. **Median home value:** $78,000. **Median travel time to work:** 20.3 minutes.

Please see sample entry on inside front cover for detailed information about the statistics presented with each county listing.

PAWNEE COUNTY
PO Box 431   **Ph:** 402-852-2962
Pawnee City, NE 68420
www.co.pawnee.ne.us

In southeastern NE, southeast of Lincoln; original county; organized Mar 6, 1855 (prior to statehood). **Name Origin:** For the Indian tribe of Caddoan linguistic stock. The name may mean 'horn,' for the shape of their forelock; they called themselves 'civilized people.'

Area (sq mi): 432.95 (land 431.57; water 1.38).

Pop: 3,087 (White 98.5%; Black or African American 0%; Hispanic or Latino 0.7%; Asian 0.3%; Other 0.8%). **Foreign born:** 0.4%. **Median age:** 45.9. **State rank:** 72. **Pop change 1990-2000:** -6.9%.

Income: per capita $16,687; median household $29,000. **Pop below poverty level:** 11%.

Unemployment: 2.9%. **Median home value:** $30,300. **Median travel time to work:** 21.8 minutes.

PERKINS COUNTY
PO Box 156   **Ph:** 308-352-4643
Grant, NE 69140   **Fax:** 308-352-2455
www.co.perkins.ne.us

In west-central NE, west of North Platte; organized Nov 8, 1887 from Keith County. **Name Origin:** For Charles Elliott Perkins (1807-1907), president of the Chicago, Burlington, and Quincy Railroad. Locally it is also said to be for Joseph Perkins, an early resident.

Area (sq mi): 884.27 (land 883.18; water 1.1).

Pop: 3,200 (White 96.6%; Black or African American 0%; Hispanic or Latino 2.3%; Asian 0.2%; Other 2%). **Foreign born:** 1.4%. **Median age:** 40.7. **State rank:** 69. **Pop change 1990-2000:** -5%.

Income: per capita $17,830; median household $34,205. **Pop below poverty level:** 13.6%.

Unemployment: 1.9%. **Median home value:** $52,200. **Median travel time to work:** 15.1 minutes.

PHELPS COUNTY
PO Box 404   **Ph:** 308-995-4469
Holdrege, NE 68949   **Fax:** 308-995-4368

In south-central NE, southwest of Grand Island; organized Feb 11, 1873 from unorganized territory. **Name Origin:** For Capt. William Phelps (1808-?), an early settler and former Missouri River steamboat captain.

Area (sq mi): 540.6 (land 539.97; water 0.64).

Pop: 9,747 (White 96.6%; Black or African American 0.1%; Hispanic or Latino 2.3%; Asian 0.3%; Other 1.8%). **Foreign born:** 0.8%. **Median age:** 39.4. **State rank:** 30. **Pop change 1990-2000:** +0.3%.

Income: per capita $19,044; median household $37,319. **Pop below poverty level:** 8.9%.

Unemployment: 2.3%. **Median home value:** $71,400. **Median travel time to work:** 15.5 minutes.

PIERCE COUNTY
111 W Court St Rm 1   **Ph:** 402-329-4225
Pierce, NE 68767   **Fax:** 402-329-6439
www.co.pierce.ne.us

In northeast NE, southwest of Sioux City, IA; organized Jan 26, 1856 from Madison County. **Name Origin:** For Franklin Pierce (1804-69), fourteenth U.S. president.

Area (sq mi): 575.27 (land 573.93; water 1.34).

Pop: 7,857 (White 98.2%; Black or African American 0.1%; Hispanic or Latino 0.7%; Asian 0.2%; Other 1.1%). **Foreign born:** 0.8%. **Median age:** 37.9. **State rank:** 40. **Pop change 1990-2000:** +0.4%.

Income: per capita $15,980; median household $32,239. **Pop below poverty level:** 11.8%.

Unemployment: 3%. **Median home value:** $59,900. **Median travel time to work:** 19.7 minutes.

PLATTE COUNTY
2610 14th St   **Ph:** 402-563-4904
Columbus, NE 68601   **Fax:** 402-564-4164
www.co.platte.ne.us

In east-central NE, northwest of Omaha; original county; organized as Loup County Jan 26, 1856 (prior to statehood); name changed 1859. **Name Origin:** For the Platte River, which forms part of its southern border; from French for 'flat' or 'still.'

Area (sq mi): 689.08 (land 678.07; water 11.01).

Pop: 31,662 (White 92%; Black or African American 0.4%; Hispanic or Latino 6.5%; Asian 0.4%; Other 5%). **Foreign born:** 4.1%. **Median age:** 35.8. **State rank:** 10. **Pop change 1990-2000:** +6.2%.

Income: per capita $18,064; median household $39,359. **Pop below poverty level:** 7.7%.

Unemployment: 3.7%. **Median home value:** $80,800. **Median travel time to work:** 14.3 minutes.

POLK COUNTY
PO Box 276   **Ph:** 402-747-5431
Osceola, NE 68651   **Fax:** 402-747-2656

In east-central NE, west of Omaha; boundaries established Jan 26, 1856 (prior to statehood) from Butler County. **Name Origin:** For James Knox Polk (1795-1849), eleventh U.S. president.

Area (sq mi): 440.72 (land 438.84; water 1.88).

Pop: 5,639 (White 98.3%; Black or African American 0%; Hispanic or Latino 1.1%; Asian 0.1%; Other 1%). **Foreign born:** 0.8%. **Median age:** 41.6. **State rank:** 55. **Pop change 1990-2000:** -0.6%.

Income: per capita $17,934; median household $37,819. **Pop below poverty level:** 5.8%.

Unemployment: 2.9%. **Median home value:** $57,800. **Median travel time to work:** 19.8 minutes.

RED WILLOW COUNTY
502 Norris Ave   **Ph:** 308-345-1552
McCook, NE 69001   **Fax:** 308-345-4460
www.co.red-willow.ne.us

On the central southern border of NE, south of North Platte;

All statistics are based on the 2000 Census except the dollar figures given for per capita income, which are based on 1999 estimates.

organized Feb 27, 1873 from unorganized territory. **Name Origin:** For Red Willow Creek, which runs through the county; a mistranslation of the Dakota term for 'Red Dogwood Creek,' for the trees that grow there.

Area (sq mi): 718.06 (land 716.65; water 1.4).

Pop: 11,448 (White 96.3%; Black or African American 0.2%; Hispanic or Latino 2.5%; Asian 0.2%; Other 2.1%). **Foreign born:** 1.2%. **Median age:** 39.9. **State rank:** 25. **Pop change 1990-2000:** -2.2%.

Income: per capita $16,303; median household $32,293. **Pop below poverty level:** 9.6%.

Unemployment: 2.2%. **Median home value:** $58,900. **Median travel time to work:** 12 minutes.

RICHARDSON COUNTY

1700 Stone St   **Ph:** 402-245-2911
Falls City, NE 68355   **Fax:** 402-245-2946
www.co.richardson.ne.us

In the southeastern corner of NE, southeast of Lincoln; original county; organized Mar 7, 1855 (prior to statehood). **Name Origin:** For Maj. William A. Richardson (1811-75), officer in the Mexican-American War, U.S. senator from IL (1863-65), and governor of NE Territory (1858).

Area (sq mi): 555.95 (land 553.26; water 2.7).

Pop: 9,531 (White 95.1%; Black or African American 0.2%; Hispanic or Latino 1%; Asian 0.1%; Other 4%). **Foreign born:** 1.2%. **Median age:** 41.4. **State rank:** 32. **Pop change 1990-2000:** -4.1%.

Income: per capita $16,460; median household $29,884. **Pop below poverty level:** 10.1%.

Unemployment: 5.3%. **Median home value:** $38,900. **Median travel time to work:** 19.5 minutes.

ROCK COUNTY

400 State St   **Ph:** 402-684-3933
Bassett, NE 68714   **Fax:** 402-684-2741
www.co.rock.ne.us

In north-central NE; organized Nov 6, 1888 from Brown County. **Name Origin:** For the rocky soil.

Area (sq mi): 1011.85 (land 1008.46; water 3.4).

Pop: 1,756 (White 98.8%; Black or African American 0%; Hispanic or Latino 0.5%; Asian 0.2%; Other 0.9%). **Foreign born:** 0.3%. **Median age:** 43.5. **State rank:** 80. **Pop change 1990-2000:** -13%.

Income: per capita $14,350; median household $25,795. **Pop below poverty level:** 21.8%.

Unemployment: 3.8%. **Median home value:** $37,800. **Median travel time to work:** 15.2 minutes.

SALINE COUNTY

PO Box 865   **Ph:** 402-821-2374
Wilber, NE 68465   **Fax:** 402-821-3381
www.co.saline.ne.us

In southeastern NE, southwest of Lincoln; organized Feb 18, 1867 from Gage and Lancaster counties. **Name Origin:** In the unfounded

belief that extensive salt springs or deposits could be found within its boundaries.

Area (sq mi): 576.06 (land 575.34; water 0.73).

Pop: 13,843 (White 90.3%; Black or African American 0.4%; Hispanic or Latino 6.6%; Asian 1.7%; Other 4.9%). **Foreign born:** 6%. **Median age:** 36.4. **State rank:** 21. **Pop change 1990-2000:** +8.9%.

Income: per capita $16,287; median household $35,914. **Pop below poverty level:** 9.4%.

Unemployment: 2.8%. **Median home value:** $69,000. **Median travel time to work:** 19.2 minutes.

SARPY COUNTY

1210 Golden Gate Dr Suite 1118   **Ph:** 402-593-2105
Papillion, NE 68046   **Fax:** 402-593-4360
www.co.sarpy.ne.us

On the central eastern border of NE, south of Omaha; organized Feb 7, 1857 from Douglas County. **Name Origin:** For Col. Peter A. Sarpy (1805-65), an early settler, trader and quartermaster for NE volunteer regiment (1855).

Area (sq mi): 247.28 (land 240.52; water 6.76).

Pop: 122,595 (White 87.1%; Black or African American 4.4%; Hispanic or Latino 4.4%; Asian 1.9%; Other 4.6%). **Foreign born:** 3.7%. **Median age:** 31.5. **State rank:** 3. **Pop change 1990-2000:** +19.5%.

Income: per capita $21,985; median household $53,804. **Pop below poverty level:** 4.2%.

Unemployment: 2.5%. **Median home value:** $112,100. **Median travel time to work:** 19.4 minutes.

SAUNDERS COUNTY

PO Box 61   **Ph:** 402-443-8101
Wahoo, NE 68066   **Fax:** 402-443-5010
www.co.saunders.ne.us

In east-central NE, west of Omaha; organized as Calhoun County Jan 26, 1856 (prior to statehood); name changed Jan 8, 1862. **Name Origin:** For Alvin Saunders (1817-99), NE Territory governor (1861-67) and U.S. senator from NE (1877-83).

Area (sq mi): 758.82 (land 753.9; water 4.92).

Pop: 19,830 (White 97.9%; Black or African American 0.1%; Hispanic or Latino 1%; Asian 0.2%; Other 1.1%). **Foreign born:** 1.2%. **Median age:** 38. **State rank:** 16. **Pop change 1990-2000:** +8.4%.

Income: per capita $18,392; median household $42,173. **Pop below poverty level:** 6.6%.

Unemployment: 3.3%. **Median home value:** $87,800. **Median travel time to work:** 24.2 minutes.

SCOTTS BLUFF COUNTY

1825 10th St   **Ph:** 308-436-6600
Gering, NE 69341   **Fax:** 308-436-3178
www.scottsbluffcounty.org

On western border of NE; organized Nov 6, 1888 from Cheyenne County. **Name Origin:** For the prominent bluff on the North Platte River, named for Hiram Scott, a member of the Bonneville expedition of 1832, who died there.

Please see sample entry on inside front cover for detailed information about the statistics presented with each county listing.

Area (sq mi): 745.5 (land 739.27; water 6.22).

Pop: 36,951 (White 79.7%; Black or African American 0.3%; Hispanic or Latino 17.2%; Asian 0.6%; Other 11.5%). **Foreign born:** 4.1%. **Median age:** 38.4. **State rank:** 6. **Pop change 1990-2000:** +2.6%.

Income: per capita $17,355; median household $32,016. **Pop below poverty level:** 14.5%.

Unemployment: 4%. **Median home value:** $71,500. **Median travel time to work:** 14.9 minutes.

SEWARD COUNTY

PO Box 190   **Ph:** 402-643-2883
Seward, NE 68434   **Fax:** 402-643-9243
connectseward.org/cgov/

In east-central NE, west of Lincoln; organized as Greene County Jan 26, 1856 (prior to statehood) from Lancaster County; name changed Jan 3, 1862 when Gen. Greene of Missouri joined the Confederacy. **Name Origin:** For William Henry Seward (1801-72), U.S. secretary of state (1861-69) who negotiated the purchase of Alaska (1867).

Area (sq mi): 575.73 (land 574.75; water 0.97).

Pop: 16,496 (White 97.5%; Black or African American 0.3%; Hispanic or Latino 1.1%; Asian 0.3%; Other 1.3%). **Foreign born:** 1.7%. **Median age:** 35.7. **State rank:** 18. **Pop change 1990-2000:** +6.8%.

Income: per capita $18,379; median household $42,700. **Pop below poverty level:** 7%.

Unemployment: 3.2%. **Median home value:** $88,100. **Median travel time to work:** 19.9 minutes.

SHERIDAN COUNTY

PO Box 39   **Ph:** 308-327-2633
Rushville, NE 69360   **Fax:** 308-327-2712

On the northern border of NE, northeast of Scottsbluff; organized Feb 25, 1885 from Sioux County. **Name Origin:** For Gen. Philip Henry Sheridan (1831-88), Union officer during the Civil War and commander in chief of the U.S. army (1883-88).

Area (sq mi): 2469.99 (land 2441.04; water 28.95).

Pop: 6,198 (White 87.6%; Black or African American 0.1%; Hispanic or Latino 1.5%; Asian 0.1%; Other 11.6%). **Foreign born:** 0.7%. **Median age:** 42. **State rank:** 52. **Pop change 1990-2000:** -8.2%.

Income: per capita $14,844; median household $29,484. **Pop below poverty level:** 13.2%.

Unemployment: 2.7%. **Median home value:** $41,700. **Median travel time to work:** 17.3 minutes.

SHERMAN COUNTY

PO Box 456   **Ph:** 308-745-1513
Loup City, NE 68853   **Fax:** 308-745-1820
www.co.sherman.ne.us

In central NE, northwest of Grand Island; organized Mar 1, 1871 from Buffalo County. **Name Origin:** For Gen. William Tecumseh Sherman (1820-91), officer in the Mexican-American War and the

Civil War, remembered for his 'march to the sea' through the South.

Area (sq mi): 571.63 (land 565.84; water 5.78).

Pop: 3,318 (White 98%; Black or African American 0.1%; Hispanic or Latino 1%; Asian 0.2%; Other 1.1%). **Foreign born:** 0.4%. **Median age:** 43.3. **State rank:** 68. **Pop change 1990-2000:** -10.8%.

Income: per capita $14,064; median household $28,646. **Pop below poverty level:** 12.9%.

Unemployment: 2.7%. **Median home value:** $38,000. **Median travel time to work:** 24.7 minutes.

SIOUX COUNTY

PO Box 158   **Ph:** 308-668-2443
Harrison, NE 69346   **Fax:** 308-668-2443
www.co.sioux.ne.us

On the northwestern border of NE, north of Scottsbluff; organized Feb 19, 1877 from unorganized territory. **Name Origin:** For the Sioux Indian tribe, also known as the Dakotas.

Area (sq mi): 2067.32 (land 2066.59; water 0.73).

Pop: 1,475 (White 96.5%; Black or African American 0%; Hispanic or Latino 2.3%; Asian 0.2%; Other 2.2%). **Foreign born:** 1.3%. **Median age:** 41.5. **State rank:** 81. **Pop change 1990-2000:** -4.8%.

Income: per capita $15,999; median household $29,851. **Pop below poverty level:** 15.4%.

Unemployment: 1.3%. **Median home value:** $42,600. **Median travel time to work:** 23 minutes.

STANTON COUNTY

PO Box 347   **Ph:** 402-439-2222
Stanton, NE 68779   **Fax:** 402-439-2200
www.co.stanton.ne.us

In east-central NE, west of Norfolk; organized Jan 10, 1862 from Dodge County; previously called Izard County. **Name Origin:** For Edwin McMasters Stanton (1814-69), U.S. secretary of war under Abraham Lincoln and Andrew Johnson (1862-68).

Area (sq mi): 431.06 (land 429.83; water 1.23).

Pop: 6,455 (White 96%; Black or African American 0.4%; Hispanic or Latino 2.3%; Asian 0.1%; Other 2.8%). **Foreign born:** 1.2%. **Median age:** 35.9. **State rank:** 49. **Pop change 1990-2000:** +3.4%.

Income: per capita $15,511; median household $36,676. **Pop below poverty level:** 6.8%.

Unemployment: 2.9%. **Median home value:** $67,200. **Median travel time to work:** 19.1 minutes.

THAYER COUNTY

PO Box 208   **Ph:** 402-768-6126
Hebron, NE 68370   **Fax:** 402-768-2129

On the southern border of NE, southwest of Lincoln; organized as Jefferson County 1867; name changed 1871. **Name Origin:** For Gen. John Milton Thayer (1820-1906), an officer in the Civil War, U.S. senator from NE (1867-71), and governor (1887-92).

Area (sq mi): 575.3 (land 574.55; water 0.75).

Pop: 6,055 (White 98.1%; Black or African American 0%; Hispanic

All statistics are based on the 2000 Census except the dollar figures given for per capita income, which are based on 1999 estimates.

or Latino 1%; Asian 0.1%; Other 1.2%). **Foreign born:** 0.8%. **Median age:** 44.1. **State rank:** 54. **Pop change 1990-2000:** -8.7%.

Income: per capita $17,043; median household $30,740. **Pop below poverty level:** 10.7%.

Unemployment: 2.6%. **Median home value:** $38,800. **Median travel time to work:** 14.4 minutes.

THOMAS COUNTY
PO Box 226   **Ph:** 308-645-2261
Thedford, NE 69166   **Fax:** 308-645-2623

In central NE, north of North Platte; organized Mar 31, 1887 from Blaine County. **Name Origin:** For Gen. George Henry Thomas (1816-70), Union commander of the Army of the Cumberland.

Area (sq mi): 713.65 (land 712.86; water 0.79).

Pop: 729 (White 98.8%; Black or African American 0%; Hispanic or Latino 0.8%; Asian 0%; Other 0.6%). **Foreign born:** 1.6%. **Median age:** 44.2. **State rank:** 89. **Pop change 1990-2000:** -14.3%.

Income: per capita $15,335; median household $27,292. **Pop below poverty level:** 14.3%.

Unemployment: 5.7%. **Median home value:** $34,300. **Median travel time to work:** 15.1 minutes.

THURSTON COUNTY
PO Box G   **Ph:** 402-385-2343
Pender, NE 68047   **Fax:** 402-385-3544

On the northeastern border of NE, south of Sioux City, IA; organized as Blackbird County Mar 7, 1865 from Burt County; name changed in 1889. **Name Origin:** For John Mellen Thurston (1847-1916), U.S. senator from NE (1895-1901), active in establishing the county. Originally named for either Chief Blackbird of the Omaha Indians, or Black Bird, for their mythological Thunder Bird.

Area (sq mi): 396.25 (land 393.81; water 2.44).

Pop: 7,171 (White 45.5%; Black or African American 0.2%; Hispanic or Latino 2.4%; Asian 0.1%; Other 54%). **Foreign born:** 1.6%. **Median age:** 29.8. **State rank:** 44. **Pop change 1990-2000:** +3.4%.

Income: per capita $10,951; median household $28,170. **Pop below poverty level:** 25.6%.

Unemployment: 7.5%. **Median home value:** $50,600. **Median travel time to work:** 18.6 minutes.

VALLEY COUNTY
125 S 15th St   **Ph:** 308-728-3700
Ord, NE 68862   **Fax:** 308-728-7725
www.co.valley.ne.us

In central NE, northwest of Grand Island; organized Mar 1, 1871 from unorganized territory. **Name Origin:** For the North Loup River valley, which comprises the county.

Area (sq mi): 570.51 (land 568.11; water 2.41).

Pop: 4,647 (White 97.5%; Black or African American 0.2%; Hispanic or Latino 1.6%; Asian 0.1%; Other 1.6%). **Foreign born:** 1.1%. **Median age:** 43.5. **State rank:** 59. **Pop change 1990-2000:** -10.1%.

Income: per capita $14,996; median household $27,926. **Pop below poverty level:** 12.8%.

Unemployment: 2.8%. **Median home value:** $45,000. **Median travel time to work:** 15.1 minutes.

WASHINGTON COUNTY
PO Box 466   **Ph:** 402-426-6822
Blair, NE 68008   **Fax:** 402-426-6825

On the central eastern border of NE, north of Omaha; original county; organized Feb 22, 1855 (prior to statehood). **Name Origin:** For George Washington (1732-99), American patriot and first U.S. president.

Area (sq mi): 393.76 (land 390.49; water 3.27).

Pop: 18,780 (White 97.5%; Black or African American 0.3%; Hispanic or Latino 1.1%; Asian 0.3%; Other 1.2%). **Foreign born:** 1.6%. **Median age:** 37.1. **State rank:** 17. **Pop change 1990-2000:** +13.1%.

Income: per capita $21,055; median household $48,500. **Pop below poverty level:** 6%.

Unemployment: 2.6%. **Median home value:** $114,300. **Median travel time to work:** 22.8 minutes.

WAYNE COUNTY
PO Box 248   **Ph:** 402-375-2288
Wayne, NE 68787   **Fax:** 402-375-2288
county.waynene.org

In northeastern NE, southwest of Sioux City, IA; organized 1870 from Thurston County. **Name Origin:** For Gen. Anthony Wayne (1745-96), PA soldier and statesman, nicknamed 'Mad Anthony' for his daring during the Revolutionary War.

Area (sq mi): 443.48 (land 443.43; water 0.05).

Pop: 9,851 (White 96.2%; Black or African American 0.9%; Hispanic or Latino 1.5%; Asian 0.3%; Other 1.9%). **Foreign born:** 1.7%. **Median age:** 27.9. **State rank:** 28. **Pop change 1990-2000:** +5.2%.

Income: per capita $14,644; median household $32,366. **Pop below poverty level:** 14.5%.

Unemployment: 3.4%. **Median home value:** $76,700. **Median travel time to work:** 15.5 minutes.

WEBSTER COUNTY
PO Box 250   **Ph:** 402-746-2716
Red Cloud, NE 68970   **Fax:** 402-746-2710
www.co.webster.ne.us

On the central southern border of NE, south of Grand Island; organized Feb 16, 1867 (prior to statehood) from unorganized territory. **Name Origin:** For Daniel Webster (1782-1852), U.S. statesman and orator from MA.

Area (sq mi): 575.02 (land 574.89; water 0.13).

Pop: 4,061 (White 97.8%; Black or African American 0.1%; Hispanic or Latino 0.5%; Asian 0.5%; Other 1.3%). **Foreign born:** 1.3%. **Median age:** 44.2. **State rank:** 63. **Pop change 1990-2000:** -5.1%.

Please see sample entry on inside front cover for detailed information about the statistics presented with each county listing.

Income: per capita $16,802; median household $30,026. **Pop below poverty level:** 11.2%.

Unemployment: 2.5%. **Median home value:** $38,300. **Median travel time to work:** 20.7 minutes.

WHEELER COUNTY

PO Box 127   **Ph:** 308-654-3235
Bartlett, NE 68622   **Fax:** 308-654-3470

In north-central NE, north of Grand Island; organized Feb 17, 1877 from Boone County. **Name Origin:** For Daniel H. Wheeler (1834-?), a state official.

Area (sq mi): 575.57 (land 575.17; water 0.41).

Pop: 886 (White 99.1%; Black or African American 0%; Hispanic or Latino 0.6%; Asian 0%; Other 0.9%). **Foreign born:** 0%. **Median age:** 40.4. **State rank:** 84. **Pop change 1990-2000:** -6.5%.

Income: per capita $14,355; median household $26,771. **Pop below poverty level:** 20.9%.

Unemployment: 2.9%. **Median home value:** $35,000. **Median travel time to work:** 18.3 minutes.

YORK COUNTY

510 Lincoln Ave   **Ph:** 402-362-7759
York, NE 68467   **Fax:** 402-362-2651
www.nol.org/york/

In south-central NE, west of Lincoln; original county; boundaries defined Mar 13, 1855 (prior to statehood). **Name Origin:** Either for York, England, named by Alfred D. Jones. Or for York County, PA, former home of early settlers.

Area (sq mi): 576.02 (land 575.66; water 0.36).

Pop: 14,598 (White 96.3%; Black or African American 1%; Hispanic or Latino 1.4%; Asian 0.5%; Other 1.8%). **Foreign born:** 1.7%. **Median age:** 38.8. **State rank:** 20. **Pop change 1990-2000:** +1.2%.

Income: per capita $17,670; median household $37,093. **Pop below poverty level:** 8.5%.

Unemployment: 2%. **Median home value:** $74,900. **Median travel time to work:** 13.1 minutes.

All statistics are based on the 2000 Census except the dollar figures given for per capita income, which are based on 1999 estimates.

NEVADA - Counties and Independent City

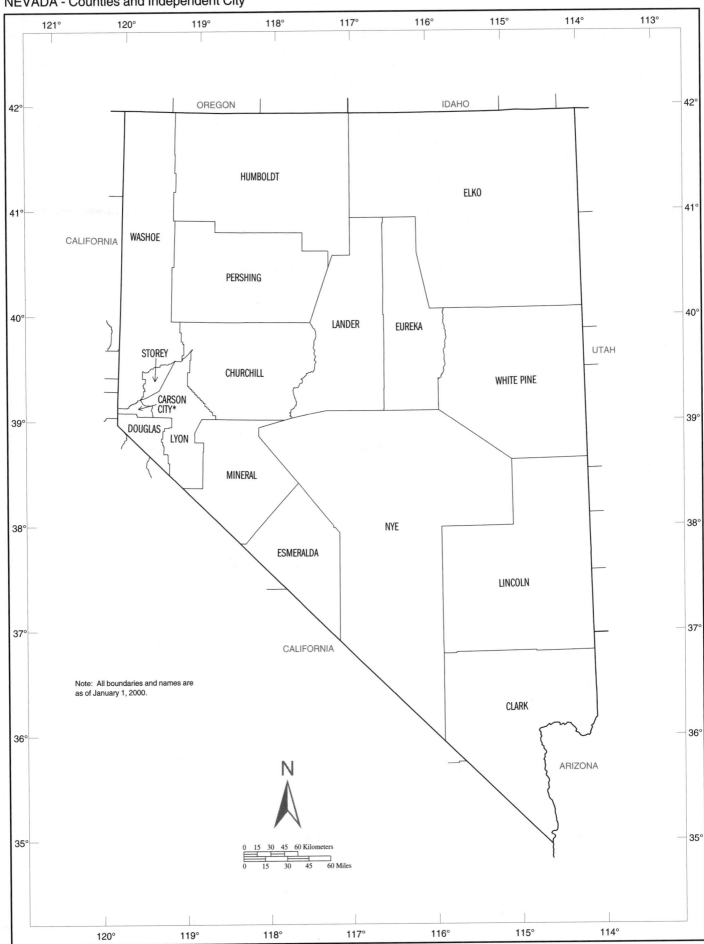

121° 120° 119° 118° 117° 116° 115° 114° 113°

OREGON

IDAHO

42°

HUMBOLDT

ELKO

41°

CALIFORNIA

WASHOE

PERSHING

40°

LANDER   EUREKA

UTAH

STOREY

CHURCHILL

WHITE PINE

CARSON
CITY*

DOUGLAS

LYON

39°

MINERAL

NYE

38°

ESMERALDA

LINCOLN

CALIFORNIA

Note: All boundaries and names are
as of January 1, 2000.

37°

CLARK

36°

ARIZONA

N

35°

0 15 30 45 60 Kilometers

0 15 30 45 60 Miles

120° 119° 118° 117° 116° 115° 114°

U.S. Census Bureau, Census 2000

Nevada

NEVADA STATE INFORMATION

silver.state.nv.us Ph: 775-687-5000

Area (sq mi): 110,560.71 (land 109,825.99; water 734.71).

Pop: 1,998,257 (White 65.2%; Black or African American 6.8%; Hispanic or Latino 19.7%; Asian 4.5%; Other 13.5%). **Foreign born:** 15.8%. **Median age:** 35. **Pop change 1990-2000:** +66.3%.

Income: per capita $21,989; median household $44,581. **Pop below poverty level:** 10.5%.

Unemployment: 5%. **Median home value:** $142,000. **Median travel time to work:** 23.3 minutes.

CARSON CITY (INDEPENDENT CITY)

201 N Carson St Ph: 775-887-2100
Carson City, NV 89701 Fax: 775-887-2286
www.carson-city.nv.us

In western NV near the Carson River and Lake Tahoe, 28 mi. south of Reno. Laid out 1858 by Maj. William M. Omsby; county seat since 1861; independent city 1969; state capital. City government consolidated with county. **Name Origin:** For frontiersman Christopher 'Kit' Carson (1809-68). Previously called Eagle Station.

Area (sq mi): 155.66 (land 143.35; water 12.31).

Pop: 52,457 (White 78.5%; Black or African American 1.8%; Hispanic or Latino 14.2%; Asian 1.8%; Other 11.1%). **Foreign born:** 9.9%. **Median age:** 38.7. **State rank:** 3. **Pop change 1990-2000:** +29.7%.

Income: per capita $20,943; median household $41,809. **Pop below poverty level:** 10%.

Unemployment: 5.5%. **Median home value:** $147,500. **Median travel time to work:** 17.7 minutes.

CHURCHILL COUNTY

155 N Taylor St Suite 153 Ph: 775-423-5136
Fallon, NV 89406 Fax: 775-423-0717
www.churchillcounty.org

In west-central NV, east of Reno; original county, organized Nov 25, 1861 (prior to statehood). **Name Origin:** For Fort Churchill, which was named for either Charles C. Churchill, an officer of the Third U.S. Artillery Regiment, or possibly Gen. Sylvester Churchill (1783-1862), an officer in the War of 1812 and the Mexican-American War.

Area (sq mi): 5023.38 (land 4929.08; water 94.3).

Pop: 23,982 (White 79.9%; Black or African American 1.6%; Hispanic or Latino 8.7%; Asian 2.7%; Other 11.5%). **Foreign born:**
6%. **Median age:** 34.7. **State rank:** 8. **Pop change 1990-2000:** +33.7%.

Income: per capita $19,264; median household $40,808. **Pop below poverty level:** 8.7%.

Unemployment: 8.7%. **Median home value:** $117,100. **Median travel time to work:** 20.7 minutes.

CLARK COUNTY

200 S 3rd St Ph: 702-455-4277
Las Vegas, NV 89155 Fax: 702-386-9104
www.co.clark.nv.us

In the southeastern corner of NV; organized Feb 5, 1908 from Lincoln County. **Name Origin:** For William Andrews Clark (1839-1925), U.S. senator from MT (1899-1900; 1901-07).

Area (sq mi): 8090.66 (land 7910.34; water 180.32).

Pop: 1,375,765 (White 60.2%; Black or African American 9.1%; Hispanic or Latino 22%; Asian 5.3%; Other 14.1%). **Foreign born:** 18%. **Median age:** 34.4. **State rank:** 1. **Pop change 1990-2000:** +85.5%.

Income: per capita $21,785; median household $44,616. **Pop below poverty level:** 10.8%.

Unemployment: 5.5%. **Median home value:** $139,500. **Median travel time to work:** 24.3 minutes.

DOUGLAS COUNTY

PO Box 218 Ph: 775-782-9020
Minden, NV 89423 Fax: 775-782-9016
www.co.douglas.nv.us

On the southwestern border of NV, south of Reno; original county; organized Nov 25, 1861 (prior to statehood). **Name Origin:** For Stephen Arnold Douglas (1813-61), U.S. orator and statesman.

Area (sq mi): 737.65 (land 709.85; water 27.8).

Pop: 41,259 (White 87.8%; Black or African American 0.3%; Hispanic or Latino 7.4%; Asian 1.3%; Other 6.6%). **Foreign born:** 5.7%. **Median age:** 41.7. **State rank:** 5. **Pop change 1990-2000:** +49.3%.

Income: per capita $27,288; median household $51,849. **Pop below poverty level:** 7.3%.

Unemployment: 4.8%. **Median home value:** $181,800. **Median travel time to work:** 23.5 minutes.

Please see sample entry on inside front cover for detailed information about the statistics presented with each county listing.

ELKO COUNTY

569 Court St
Elko, NV 89801

Ph: 775-738-5398
Fax: 775-753-8535

On the northeastern border of NV; organized Mar 5, 1869 from Lander County. **Name Origin:** For the town; meaning of name is undetermined, possibly *elk* plus *-o*, a typical railroad name. It has been suggested that the town was named for elk (the animal) or that the word is an Indian term meaning 'first white woman.'

Area (sq mi): 17,202.94 (land 17,179.03; water 23.91).

Pop: 45,291 (White 72.4%; Black or African American 0.6%; Hispanic or Latino 19.7%; Asian 0.7%; Other 16.7%). **Foreign born:** 10.2%. **Median age:** 31.2. **State rank:** 4. **Pop change 1990-2000:** +35.1%.

Income: per capita $18,482; median household $48,383. **Pop below poverty level:** 8.9%.

Unemployment: 6%. **Median home value:** $123,100. **Median travel time to work:** 25.2 minutes.

ESMERALDA COUNTY

PO Box 547
Goldfield, NV 89013

Ph: 775-485-6367
Fax: 775-485-6376

On the central southern border of NV with CA; original county; organized Nov 25, 1861 (prior to statehood). **Name Origin:** For the Esmeralda Mining District, from Spanish 'emerald,' for the stones found there.

Area (sq mi): 3589 (land 3588.5; water 0.5).

Pop: 971 (White 80.4%; Black or African American 0.1%; Hispanic or Latino 10.2%; Asian 0%; Other 17.8%). **Foreign born:** 6.5%. **Median age:** 45.1. **State rank:** 17. **Pop change 1990-2000:** -27.8%.

Income: per capita $18,971; median household $33,203. **Pop below poverty level:** 15.3%.

Unemployment: 8.2%. **Median home value:** $75,600. **Median travel time to work:** 21.9 minutes.

EUREKA COUNTY

PO Box 677
Eureka, NV 89316
www.co.eureka.nv.us

Ph: 775-237-5262
Fax: 775-237-6015

In east-central NV; organized Mar 1, 1873 from Lander County. **Name Origin:** For the Eureka Mining District, from Greek 'I have found it.'

Area (sq mi): 4179.96 (land 4175.68; water 4.28).

Pop: 1,651 (White 84.9%; Black or African American 0.4%; Hispanic or Latino 9.6%; Asian 0.8%; Other 9.6%). **Foreign born:** 7.8%. **Median age:** 38.3. **State rank:** 16. **Pop change 1990-2000:** +6.7%.

Income: per capita $18,629; median household $41,417. **Pop below poverty level:** 12.6%.

Unemployment: 3.6%. **Median home value:** $89,200. **Median travel time to work:** 18.2 minutes.

HUMBOLDT COUNTY

50 W 5th St County Courthouse Rm 205
Winnemucca, NV 89445
www.humboldt-county-nv.net

Ph: 775-623-6300
Fax: 775-623-6302

On the northern border of NV; original county; organized Nov 25, 1861 (prior to statehood). **Name Origin:** For the Little Humboldt River, which runs through the county; named for Alexander von Humboldt (1769-1859), German explorer and naturalist.

Area (sq mi): 9657.87 (land 9647.91; water 9.96).

Pop: 16,106 (White 74.4%; Black or African American 0.5%; Hispanic or Latino 18.9%; Asian 0.6%; Other 15.7%). **Foreign born:** 10.4%. **Median age:** 33.4. **State rank:** 9. **Pop change 1990-2000:** +25.4%.

Income: per capita $19,539; median household $47,147. **Pop below poverty level:** 9.7%.

Unemployment: 6.1%. **Median home value:** $117,400. **Median travel time to work:** 26.2 minutes.

LANDER COUNTY

315 S Humboldt St
Battle Mountain, NV 89820

Ph: 775-635-5738
Fax: 775-635-5761

In central NV; organized Dec 19, 1862 (prior to statehood). Originally encompassed a third of the state and was called 'Great East' and later 'mother of counties.' **Name Origin:** For Gen. Frederick William Lander (1822-62), Union army officer, surveyor, and Indian agent.

Area (sq mi): 5519.47 (land 5493.63; water 25.84).

Pop: 5,794 (White 75.7%; Black or African American 0.2%; Hispanic or Latino 18.5%; Asian 0.3%; Other 15%). **Foreign born:** 9.6%. **Median age:** 34.1. **State rank:** 12. **Pop change 1990-2000:** -7.5%.

Income: per capita $16,998; median household $46,067. **Pop below poverty level:** 12.5%.

Unemployment: 9.6%. **Median home value:** $82,400. **Median travel time to work:** 23.6 minutes.

LINCOLN COUNTY

PO Box 90
Pioche, NV 89043
www.co.lincoln.nv.us

Ph: 775-962-5390
Fax: 775-962-5180

On the southeast border of NV, north of Las Vegas; organized Feb 25, 1866. **Name Origin:** For Abraham Lincoln (1809-65), sixteenth U.S.president.

Area (sq mi): 10,636.77 (land 10,633.61; water 3.17).

Pop: 4,165 (White 89.1%; Black or African American 1.8%; Hispanic or Latino 5.3%; Asian 0.3%; Other 6.4%). **Foreign born:** 3.5%. **Median age:** 38.8. **State rank:** 14. **Pop change 1990-2000:** +10.3%.

Income: per capita $17,326; median household $31,979. **Pop below poverty level:** 16.5%.

Unemployment: 7.2%. **Median home value:** $80,300. **Median travel time to work:** 20.2 minutes.

All statistics are based on the 2000 Census except the dollar figures given for per capita income, which are based on 1999 estimates.

LYON COUNTY

27 S Main St   **Ph:** 775-463-6503
Yerington, NV 89447   **Fax:** 775-463-6533
www.lyon-county.org

In southwestern NV, southeast of Reno; original county; organized Nov 25, 1861 (prior to statehood). **Name Origin:** For either Gen. Nathaniel Lyon (1818-61), an officer in the Seminole War, Mexican-American War, and Civil War, or for Capt. Robert Lyon, a hero of the Indian Wars.

Area (sq mi): 2016.4 (land 1993.69; water 22.71).

Pop: 34,501 (White 83.4%; Black or African American 0.7%; Hispanic or Latino 11%; Asian 0.6%; Other 10%). **Foreign born:** 6%. **Median age:** 38.2. **State rank:** 6. **Pop change 1990-2000:** +72.5%.

Income: per capita $18,543; median household $40,699. **Pop below poverty level:** 10.4%.

Unemployment: 7.2%. **Median home value:** $119,200. **Median travel time to work:** 28 minutes.

MINERAL COUNTY

PO Box 1450   **Ph:** 775-945-2446
Hawthorne, NV 89415   **Fax:** 775-945-0706

On the southwestern border of NV with CA, southeast of Reno; organized Feb 10, 1911 from Esmeralda County. **Name Origin:** For the profusion of various minerals in the area.

Area (sq mi): 3812.97 (land 3756.4; water 56.56).

Pop: 5,071 (White 70.1%; Black or African American 4.8%; Hispanic or Latino 8.4%; Asian 0.8%; Other 20.6%). **Foreign born:** 2.4%. **Median age:** 42.9. **State rank:** 13. **Pop change 1990-2000:** -21.7%.

Income: per capita $16,952; median household $32,891. **Pop below poverty level:** 15.2%.

Unemployment: 8.6%. **Median home value:** $59,500. **Median travel time to work:** 16.9 minutes.

NYE COUNTY

PO Box 1031   **Ph:** 775-482-8127
Tonopah, NV 89049   **Fax:** 775-482-8133
www.co.nye.nv.us

In south-central NV; organized Feb 16, 1864 from Esmeralda County; largest county in NV. **Name Origin:** For James Warren Nye (1814-76), NY statesman, governor of NV Territory (1861-64), and U.S. senator from NV (1864-73).

Area (sq mi): 18,158.73 (land 18,146.66; water 12.07).

Pop: 32,485 (White 84.7%; Black or African American 1.2%; Hispanic or Latino 8.4%; Asian 0.8%; Other 8.4%). **Foreign born:** 5%. **Median age:** 42.9. **State rank:** 7. **Pop change 1990-2000:** +82.7%.

Income: per capita $17,962; median household $36,024. **Pop below poverty level:** 10.7%.

Unemployment: 6.6%. **Median home value:** $122,100. **Median travel time to work:** 28.6 minutes.

PERSHING COUNTY

PO Box 820   **Ph:** 775-273-2208
Lovelock, NV 89419   **Fax:** 775-273-3015

In west-central NV northeast of Reno; organized Mar 18, 1919 from Humboldt County. **Name Origin:** For Gen. John Joseph 'Black Jack' Pershing (1860-1948), an officer who served in Cuba, the Philippines, and Manchuria; commander in chief of the American Expeditionary Force (1917-18) during WWI, and U.S. army chief of staff (1921-24).

Area (sq mi): 6067.55 (land 6036.56; water 30.99).

Pop: 6,693 (White 69.7%; Black or African American 5.3%; Hispanic or Latino 19.3%; Asian 0.6%; Other 16.3%). **Foreign born:** 7%. **Median age:** 34.4. **State rank:** 11. **Pop change 1990-2000:** +54.4%.

Income: per capita $16,589; median household $40,670. **Pop below poverty level:** 11.4%.

Unemployment: 4.7%. **Median home value:** $82,200. **Median travel time to work:** 22.8 minutes.

STOREY COUNTY

PO Box D   **Ph:** 775-847-0968
Virginia City, NV 89440   **Fax:** 775-847-0949

In southwestern NV, east of Reno; original county; organized Nov 25, 1861 (prior to statehood). **Name Origin:** For Capt. Edward Faris Storey (?-1860), army officer killed by Paiute Indians at Pyramid Lake.

Area (sq mi): 263.8 (land 263.45; water 0.34).

Pop: 3,399 (White 90%; Black or African American 0.3%; Hispanic or Latino 5.1%; Asian 1%; Other 5.6%). **Foreign born:** 2.2%. **Median age:** 44.5. **State rank:** 15. **Pop change 1990-2000:** +34.6%.

Income: per capita $23,642; median household $45,490. **Pop below poverty level:** 5.8%.

Unemployment: 3.9%. **Median home value:** $134,800. **Median travel time to work:** 29.4 minutes.

WASHOE COUNTY

PO Box 30083   **Ph:** 775-328-3260
Reno, NV 89520   **Fax:** 775-328-3582
www.co.washoe.nv.us

On the western border of NV; original county; organized Nov 25, 1861 (prior to statehood); in 1883 annexed Roop County (called Lake County until 1862), which was also an original county. **Name Origin:** For the Washo or Washiu Indian tribe in northwestern NV and adjacent areas of CA. Their name has been translated as 'person,' 'tall bunch grass,' and 'rye grass.' The first seems most probable.

Area (sq mi): 6551.32 (land 6342.27; water 209.05).

Pop: 339,486 (White 73%; Black or African American 2.1%; Hispanic or Latino 16.6%; Asian 4.3%; Other 13.3%). **Foreign born:** 14.1%. **Median age:** 35.6. **State rank:** 2. **Pop change 1990-2000:** +33.3%.

Income: per capita $24,277; median household $45,815. **Pop below poverty level:** 10%.

Unemployment: 4.1%. **Median home value:** $161,600. **Median travel time to work:** 19.2 minutes.

Please see sample entry on inside front cover for detailed information about the statistics presented with each county listing.

WHITE PINE COUNTY
953 Campton St
Ely, NV 89301
www.co.white-pine.nv.us

Ph: 775-289-2341
Fax: 775-289-2544

On the central eastern border of NV; organized Mar 2, 1869 from Lander County. **Name Origin:** For the White Pine Mining District, itself named for the area's many pine trees.

Area (sq mi): 8896.6 (land 8875.98; water 20.62).

Pop: 9,181 (White 79.5%; Black or African American 4.1%; Hispanic or Latino 11%; Asian 0.8%; Other 8.7%). **Foreign born:** 2.9%. **Median age:** 37.7. **State rank:** 10. **Pop change 1990-2000:** -0.9%.

Income: per capita $18,309; median household $36,688. **Pop below poverty level:** 11%.

Unemployment: 4.5%. **Median home value:** $70,000. **Median travel time to work:** 18.3 minutes.

All statistics are based on the 2000 Census except the dollar figures given for per capita income, which are based on 1999 estimates.

NEW HAMPSHIRE - Counties

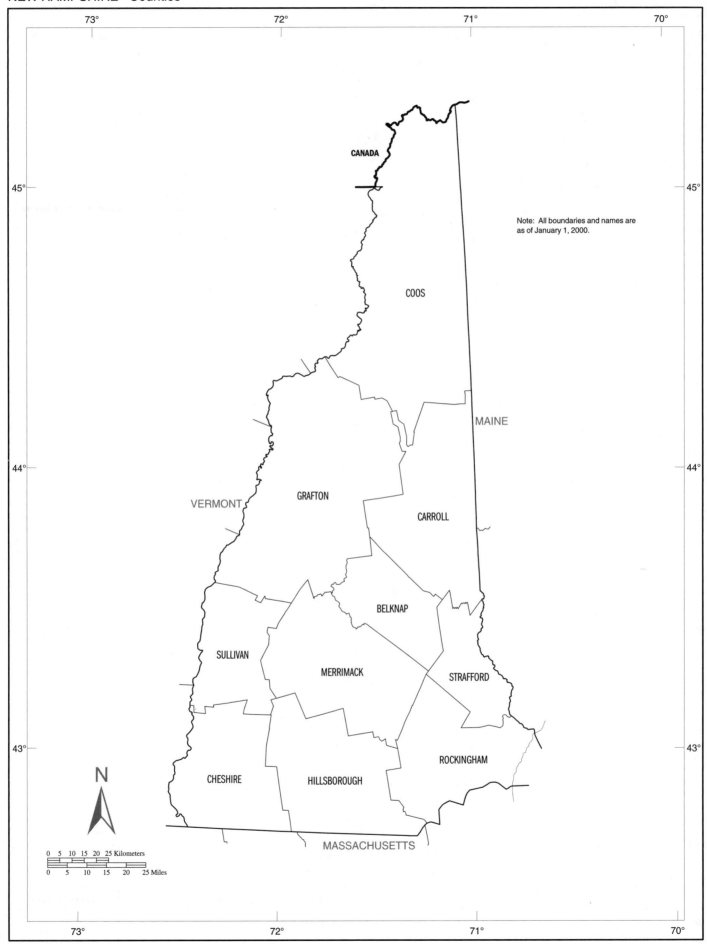

73°   72°   71°   70°

45°

CANADA

COOS

Note: All boundaries and names are as of January 1, 2000.

MAINE

44°

VERMONT

GRAFTON

CARROLL

BELKNAP

SULLIVAN

MERRIMACK

STRAFFORD

43°

CHESHIRE

HILLSBOROUGH

ROCKINGHAM

MASSACHUSETTS

N

0 5 10 15 20 25 Kilometers
0   5   10   15   20   25 Miles

73°   72°   71°   70°

45°

44°

43°

U.S. Census Bureau, Census 2000

New Hampshire

NEW HAMPSHIRE STATE INFORMATION
www.state.nh.us   **Ph:** 603-271-1110

Area (sq mi): 9349.94 (land 8968.1; water 381.84).

Pop: 1,235,786 (White 95.1%; Black or African American 0.7%; Hispanic or Latino 1.7%; Asian 1.3%; Other 1.9%). **Foreign born:** 4.4%. **Median age:** 37.1. **Pop change 1990-2000:** +11.4%.

Income: per capita $23,844; median household $49,467. **Pop below poverty level:** 6.5%.

Unemployment: 4.4%. **Median home value:** $133,300. **Median travel time to work:** 25.3 minutes.

BELKNAP COUNTY
34 County Dr   **Ph:** 603-527-5400
Laconia, NH 03246   **Fax:** 603-527-5409
www.belknapcounty.org

In east-central NH, north of Concord; organized Dec 22, 1840 from Strafford County. **Name Origin:** For Jeremy Belknap (1744-98), clergyman and historian, author of *History of New Hampshire* (1784-92) and *American Biography* (1794-98).

Area (sq mi): 468.55 (land 401.29; water 67.26).

Pop: 56,325 (White 97.1%; Black or African American 0.3%; Hispanic or Latino 0.7%; Asian 0.6%; Other 1.6%). **Foreign born:** 2.5%. **Median age:** 40.1. **State rank:** 7. **Pop change 1990-2000:** +14.4%.

Income: per capita $22,758; median household $43,605. **Pop below poverty level:** 6.1%.

Unemployment: 3%. **Median home value:** $109,600. **Median travel time to work:** 24.8 minutes.

CARROLL COUNTY
PO Box 152   **Ph:** 603-539-2428
Ossipee, NH 03864   **Fax:** 603-539-4287

On central eastern border of NH, north of Laconia; organized Dec 22, 1840 from Strafford, Coos, and Grafton counties. **Name Origin:** For Charles Carroll (1737-1832), signer of the Declaration of Independence, U.S. senator from MD, and founder of the Baltimore and Ohio Railroad.

Area (sq mi): 992.24 (land 933.8; water 58.44).

Pop: 43,666 (White 97.9%; Black or African American 0.2%; Hispanic or Latino 0.5%; Asian 0.4%; Other 1.3%). **Foreign born:** 2.4%. **Median age:** 42.5. **State rank:** 8. **Pop change 1990-2000:** +23.3%.

Income: per capita $21,931; median household $39,990. **Pop below poverty level:** 7.9%.

Unemployment: 3.1%. **Median home value:** $119,900. **Median travel time to work:** 26 minutes.

CHESHIRE COUNTY
12 Court St   **Ph:** 603-352-6902
Keene, NH 03431
www.co.cheshire.nh.us

In southwestern corner of NH, west of Manchester; original county, organized Apr 29, 1769. **Name Origin:** For Cheshire county in England, site of one of the estates of the Wentworths; named by NH Gov. John Wentworth (1737-1820) on its establishment.

Area (sq mi): 729.15 (land 707.4; water 21.75).

Pop: 73,825 (White 97.3%; Black or African American 0.4%; Hispanic or Latino 0.7%; Asian 0.5%; Other 1.4%). **Foreign born:** 2.2%. **Median age:** 37.6. **State rank:** 6. **Pop change 1990-2000:** +5.3%.

Income: per capita $20,685; median household $42,382. **Pop below poverty level:** 8%.

Unemployment: 3.2%. **Median home value:** $105,300. **Median travel time to work:** 22.3 minutes.

COOS COUNTY
55 School St Suite 301   **Ph:** 603-788-4900
Lancaster, NH 03584

In northern NH; organized Dec 24, 1803 from Grafton County. **Name Origin:** From the Pennacook Indian word *cohos* 'pine tree' or 'place where pines grow.'

Area (sq mi): 1831.44 (land 1800.39; water 31.06).

Pop: 33,111 (White 97.7%; Black or African American 0.1%; Hispanic or Latino 0.6%; Asian 0.4%; Other 1.5%). **Foreign born:** 4%. **Median age:** 41.5. **State rank:** 10. **Pop change 1990-2000:** -4.9%.

Income: per capita $17,218; median household $33,593. **Pop below poverty level:** 10%.

Unemployment: 5.5%. **Median home value:** $70,500. **Median travel time to work:** 19.3 minutes.

GRAFTON COUNTY
3801 Dartmouth College Hwy **Ph:** 603-787-6941
North Haverhill, NH 03774 **Fax:** 603-787-2345

On central western border of NH; original county, organized Apr 29, 1769. **Name Origin:** For Augustus Henry Fitzroy (1735-1811),

Please see sample entry on inside front cover for detailed information about the statistics presented with each county listing.

377

3rd Duke of Grafton, an English parliamentarian who supported American colonial interests.

Area (sq mi): 1750.08 (land 1713.33; water 36.75).

Pop: 81,743 (White 95.1%; Black or African American 0.5%; Hispanic or Latino 1.1%; Asian 1.7%; Other 2%). **Foreign born:** 3.9%. **Median age:** 37. **State rank:** 5. **Pop change 1990-2000:** +9.1%.

Income: per capita $22,227; median household $41,962. **Pop below poverty level:** 8.6%.

Unemployment: 2.1%. **Median home value:** $109,500. **Median travel time to work:** 21.3 minutes.

HILLSBOROUGH COUNTY
300 Chestnut St Rm 139   **Ph:** 603-627-5600
Manchester, NH 03101   **Fax:** 603-627-5603
www.hillsboroughcountynh.org

On central southern border of NH, south of Concord; original county, organized Apr 29, 1769. **Name Origin:** For Wills Hill (1718-93), 1st Earl of Hillsborough, English secretary of state for the colonies (1768-72). Also spelled *Hillsboro*. Some also note that one of the original grantees of land was Col. John Hill of MA.

Area (sq mi): 892.2 (land 876.36; water 15.84).

Pop: 380,841 (White 92.3%; Black or African American 1.3%; Hispanic or Latino 3.2%; Asian 2%; Other 2.7%). **Foreign born:** 6.8%. **Median age:** 35.9. **State rank:** 1. **Pop change 1990-2000:** +13.3%.

Income: per capita $25,198; median household $53,384. **Pop below poverty level:** 6.3%.

Unemployment: 3.8%. **Median home value:** $139,100. **Median travel time to work:** 25.5 minutes.

MERRIMACK COUNTY
4 Court St Suite 2   **Ph:** 603-228-0331
Concord, NH 03301   **Fax:** 603-224-2665

In south-central NH, north of Manchester; organized Jul 1, 1823 from Rickingham and Hillsborough counties. **Name Origin:** For the Merrimack River, which bisects the county.

Area (sq mi): 956.49 (land 934.43; water 22.06).

Pop: 136,225 (White 96.4%; Black or African American 0.5%; Hispanic or Latino 1%; Asian 0.9%; Other 1.4%). **Foreign born:** 3.2%. **Median age:** 37.7. **State rank:** 3. **Pop change 1990-2000:** +13.5%.

Income: per capita $23,208; median household $48,522. **Pop below poverty level:** 5.9%.

Unemployment: 2.7%. **Median home value:** $117,900. **Median travel time to work:** 24.3 minutes.

ROCKINGHAM COUNTY
10 Rt 125   **Ph:** 603-642-5256
Brentwood, NH 03833
www.co.rockingham.nh.us

On southeastern border of NH, southeast of Concord; original county, organized Apr 29, 1769. **Name Origin:** For Charles Watson-Wentworth, Marquis of Rockingham (1730-82), British statesman, prime minister, and cousin of the NH Wentworths, largely responsible for repeal of the Stamp Act.

Area (sq mi): 793.96 (land 694.96; water 99).

Pop: 277,359 (White 96.1%; Black or African American 0.6%; Hispanic or Latino 1.2%; Asian 1.1%; Other 1.5%). **Foreign born:** 3.7%. **Median age:** 37.2. **State rank:** 2. **Pop change 1990-2000:** +12.8%.

Income: per capita $26,656; median household $58,150. **Pop below poverty level:** 4.5%.

Unemployment: 4.3%. **Median home value:** $164,900. **Median travel time to work:** 28.6 minutes.

STRAFFORD COUNTY
PO Box 799   **Ph:** 603-742-1458
Dover, NH 03821   **Fax:** 603-743-4407

On southeastern border of NH, south of Portsmouth; original county, organized Apr 29, 1769. **Name Origin:** For William Wentworth (1722-91), 4th Earl of Strafford, cousin of John Wentworth (1737-1820), governor of NH at the time of its establishment.

Area (sq mi): 383.91 (land 368.76; water 15.15).

Pop: 112,233 (White 95.7%; Black or African American 0.6%; Hispanic or Latino 1%; Asian 1.4%; Other 1.6%). **Foreign born:** 3.4%. **Median age:** 34.4. **State rank:** 4. **Pop change 1990-2000:** +7.7%.

Income: per capita $20,479; median household $44,803. **Pop below poverty level:** 9.2%.

Unemployment: 3.1%. **Median home value:** $121,000. **Median travel time to work:** 24.1 minutes.

SULLIVAN COUNTY
14 Main St   **Ph:** 603-863-2560
Newport, NH 03773   **Fax:** 603-863-9314

On southwestern border of NH, north of Keene; organized Jul 5, 1827 from Cheshire County. **Name Origin:** For Gen. John Sullivan (1740-95), officer in the Revolutionary War, member of the Continental Congress, chief executive of NH (1786-87), and governor (1789).

Area (sq mi): 551.92 (land 537.38; water 14.54).

Pop: 40,458 (White 97.6%; Black or African American 0.2%; Hispanic or Latino 0.5%; Asian 0.4%; Other 1.3%). **Foreign born:** 2.9%. **Median age:** 40. **State rank:** 9. **Pop change 1990-2000:** +4.8%.

Income: per capita $21,319; median household $40,938. **Pop below poverty level:** 8.5%.

Unemployment: 2.2%. **Median home value:** $91,900. **Median travel time to work:** 23.2 minutes.

All statistics are based on the 2000 Census except the dollar figures given for per capita income, which are based on 1999 estimates.

NEW JERSEY - Counties

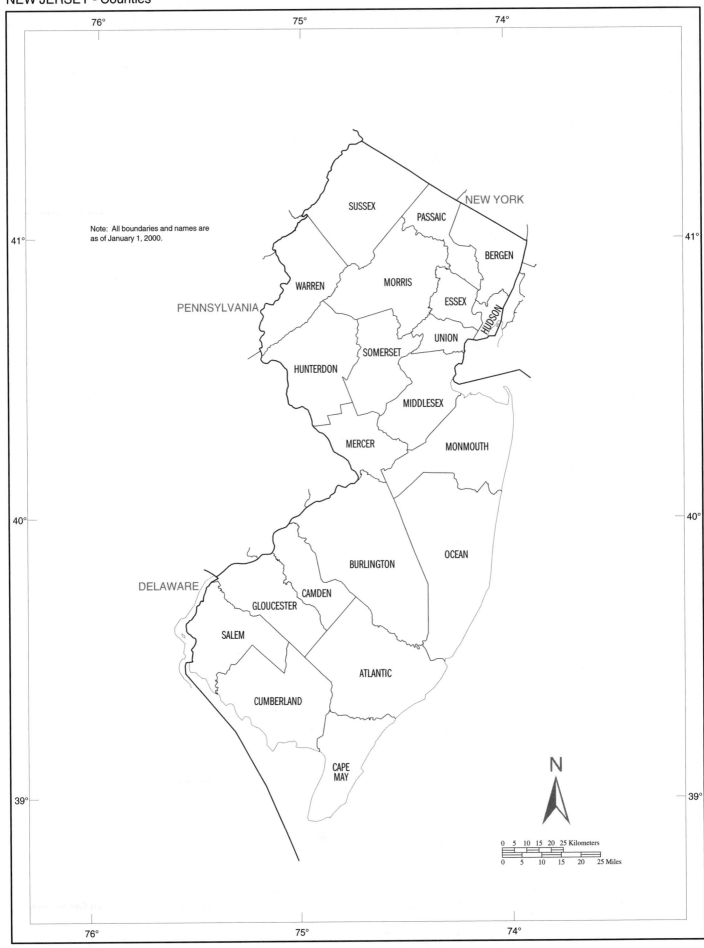

Note: All boundaries and names are as of January 1, 2000.

PENNSYLVANIA

NEW YORK

DELAWARE

SUSSEX

PASSAIC

BERGEN

WARREN

MORRIS

ESSEX

HUDSON

UNION

SOMERSET

HUNTERDON

MIDDLESEX

MERCER

MONMOUTH

OCEAN

BURLINGTON

CAMDEN

GLOUCESTER

SALEM

ATLANTIC

CUMBERLAND

CAPE
MAY

N

0 5 10 15 20 25 Kilometers

0 5 10 15 20 25 Miles

New Jersey

NEW JERSEY STATE INFORMATION

www.newjersey.gov   **Ph:** 609-292-2121

Area (sq mi): 8721.3 (land 7417.34; water 1303.96).

Pop: 8,414,350 (White 66%; Black or African American 13.6%; Hispanic or Latino 13.3%; Asian 5.7%; Other 8.1%). **Foreign born:** 17.5%. **Median age:** 36.7. **Pop change 1990-2000:** +8.9%.

Income: per capita $27,006; median household $55,146. **Pop below poverty level:** 8.5%.

Unemployment: 5.5%. **Median home value:** $170,800. **Median travel time to work:** 30 minutes.

ATLANTIC COUNTY

5901 Main St   **Ph:** 609-641-7867
Mays Landing, NJ 08330   **Fax:** 609-625-4738
www.aclink.org

In southern NJ on Atlantic coast, east of Vineland; organized Feb 7, 1837 from Gloucester County. **Name Origin:** For the Atlantic Ocean.

Area (sq mi): 671.45 (land 561.07; water 110.37).

Pop: 252,552 (White 63.9%; Black or African American 17.6%; Hispanic or Latino 12.2%; Asian 5.1%; Other 9%). **Foreign born:** 11.8%. **Median age:** 37. **State rank:** 15. **Pop change 1990-2000:** +12.6%.

Income: per capita $21,034; median household $43,933. **Pop below poverty level:** 10.5%.

Unemployment: 5.4%. **Median home value:** $122,000. **Median travel time to work:** 23.7 minutes.

BERGEN COUNTY

1 Bergen County Plaza Rm 580   **Ph:** 201-336-7300
Hackensack, NJ 07601
www.co.bergen.nj.us

In northeastern NJ bordering on NY, north of Jersey City; original county, organized Mar 7, 1683. **Name Origin:** Named by early Dutch settlers for the town of Bergen-op-zoom, North Brabant, Netherlands.

Area (sq mi): 246.8 (land 234.17; water 12.63).

Pop: 884,118 (White 72.3%; Black or African American 5.3%; Hispanic or Latino 10.3%; Asian 10.7%; Other 5.7%). **Foreign born:** 25.1%. **Median age:** 39.1. **State rank:** 1. **Pop change 1990-2000:** +7.1%.

Income: per capita $33,638; median household $65,241. **Pop below poverty level:** 5%.

Unemployment: 3.6%. **Median home value:** $250,300. **Median travel time to work:** 29.7 minutes.

BURLINGTON COUNTY

PO Box 6000   **Ph:** 609-265-5020
Mount Holly, NJ 08060   **Fax:** 609-265-5022
www.co.burlington.nj.us

In central NJ, east of Philadelphia, original county, organzed May 17, 1694. **Name Origin:** For Bridlington, Yorkshire, England. The alternate spelling reflects the pronunciation used in England.

Area (sq mi): 819.43 (land 804.57; water 14.86).

Pop: 423,394 (White 76.3%; Black or African American 15.1%; Hispanic or Latino 4.2%; Asian 2.7%; Other 3.8%). **Foreign born:** 6.3%. **Median age:** 37.1. **State rank:** 11. **Pop change 1990-2000:** +7.2%.

Income: per capita $26,339; median household $58,608. **Pop below poverty level:** 4.7%.

Unemployment: 3.2%. **Median home value:** $137,400. **Median travel time to work:** 28.2 minutes.

CAMDEN COUNTY

520 Market St Rm 102   **Ph:** 856-225-5300
Camden, NJ 08102   **Fax:** 856-225-5316
www.co.camden.nj.us

On central western border of NJ, east of Philadelphia, organized Mar 13, 1844 from Gloucester County. **Name Origin:** For the city of Camden.

Area (sq mi): 227.58 (land 222.3; water 5.28).

Pop: 508,932 (White 67.8%; Black or African American 18.1%; Hispanic or Latino 9.7%; Asian 3.7%; Other 7.3%). **Foreign born:** 6.9%. **Median age:** 35.8. **State rank:** 8. **Pop change 1990-2000:** +1.2%.

Income: per capita $22,354; median household $48,097. **Pop below poverty level:** 10.4%.

Unemployment: 4.1%. **Median home value:** $111,200. **Median travel time to work:** 27.9 minutes.

CAPE MAY COUNTY

7 N Main St PO Box 5000   **Ph:** 609-465-1010
Cape May Court House, NJ 08210   **Fax:** 609-465-8625
www.beachcomber.com/Capemay/tourism.html

On southern tip of NJ, south of Atlantic City; organized Nov 12, 1692 from Cumberland County. **Name Origin:** For the cape, whose name commemorates Cornelis Jacobsen Mey, Dutch captain who explored the Atlantic coast of North America from Long Island to Cape May in 1612-14.

Area (sq mi): 620.28 (land 255.19; water 365.09).

Pop: 102,326 (White 90%; Black or African American 5.1%; Hispanic or Latino 3.3%; Asian 0.6%; Other 2.7%). **Foreign born:** 3.2%. **Median age:** 42.3. **State rank:** 20. **Pop change 1990-2000:** +7.6%.

Income: per capita $24,172; median household $41,591. **Pop below poverty level:** 8.6%.

Unemployment: 8.2%. **Median home value:** $137,600. **Median travel time to work:** 23.2 minutes.

CUMBERLAND COUNTY
60 W Broad St   **Ph:** 856-451-8000
Bridgeton, NJ 08302   **Fax:** 856-455-1410
www.co.cumberland.nj.us

In southern NJ, on Delaware Bay; organized Jan 19, 1748 from Salem County. **Name Origin:** For William Augustus, Duke of Cumberland (1721-65), British general and second son of King George II (1683-1760).

Area (sq mi): 676.59 (land 489.3; water 187.29).

Pop: 146,438 (White 58.4%; Black or African American 20.2%; Hispanic or Latino 19%; Asian 1%; Other 13.1%). **Foreign born:** 6.2%. **Median age:** 35.6. **State rank:** 16. **Pop change 1990-2000:** +6.1%.

Income: per capita $17,376; median household $39,150. **Pop below poverty level:** 15%.

Unemployment: 7.5%. **Median home value:** $91,200. **Median travel time to work:** 23.1 minutes.

ESSEX COUNTY
465 ML King Jr Blvd Rm 245   **Ph:** 973-621-4920
Newark, NJ 07102   **Fax:** 973-621-2537
www.co.essex.nj.us

In northeastern NJ, west of New York City; original county, organized Mar 7, 1683. **Name Origin:** For the county of Essex, England.

Area (sq mi): 129.56 (land 126.27; water 3.29).

Pop: 793,633 (White 37.6%; Black or African American 41.2%; Hispanic or Latino 15.4%; Asian 3.7%; Other 10.6%). **Foreign born:** 21.2%. **Median age:** 34.7. **State rank:** 2. **Pop change 1990-2000:** +2%.

Income: per capita $24,943; median household $44,944. **Pop below poverty level:** 15.6%.

Unemployment: 5.4%. **Median home value:** $208,400. **Median travel time to work:** 31.2 minutes.

GLOUCESTER COUNTY
1 N Broad St Rm 101   **Ph:** 856-853-3237
Woodbury, NJ 08096   **Fax:** 856-853-3327
www.co.gloucester.nj.us

In southwestern NJ, southeast of Philadelphia; original county, organized May 26, 1686. **Name Origin:** For Henry, Duke of Gloucester (1639-60), third son of Charles I (1600-49), king of England.

Area (sq mi): 336.92 (land 324.72; water 12.2).

Pop: 254,673 (White 85.7%; Black or African American 9.1%; Hispanic or Latino 2.6%; Asian 1.5%; Other 2.4%). **Foreign born:** 3.4%. **Median age:** 36.1. **State rank:** 14. **Pop change 1990-2000:** +10.7%.

Income: per capita $22,708; median household $54,273. **Pop below poverty level:** 6.2%.

Unemployment: 3.9%. **Median home value:** $120,100. **Median travel time to work:** 28 minutes.

HUDSON COUNTY
583 Newark Ave Brennan Courthouse   **Ph:** 201-795-6112
Jersey City, NJ 07306   **Fax:** 201-795-2581
www.hudsoncountynj.org

In northeastern NJ, across the Hudson River from New York City; organized Feb 22, 1840 from Bergen County. **Name Origin:** For the Hudson River.

Area (sq mi): 62.43 (land 46.69; water 15.74).

Pop: 608,975 (White 35.3%; Black or African American 13.5%; Hispanic or Latino 39.8%; Asian 9.4%; Other 21.6%). **Foreign born:** 38.5%. **Median age:** 33.6. **State rank:** 5. **Pop change 1990-2000:** +10.1%.

Income: per capita $21,154; median household $40,293. **Pop below poverty level:** 15.5%.

Unemployment: 6.2%. **Median home value:** $150,300. **Median travel time to work:** 32.6 minutes.

HUNTERDON COUNTY
71 Main St   **Ph:** 908-788-1221
Flemington, NJ 08822   **Fax:** 908-782-4068
www.co.hunterdon.nj.us

In central NJ along the Delaware River, northwest of Trenton; organized Mar 13, 1714 from Burlington County. **Name Origin:** For Robert Hunter (?-1734), colonial governor of New York and East and West Jersey (1710-19).

Area (sq mi): 437.76 (land 429.94; water 7.82).

Pop: 121,989 (White 92.2%; Black or African American 2.2%; Hispanic or Latino 2.8%; Asian 1.9%; Other 1.9%). **Foreign born:** 6.3%. **Median age:** 38.8. **State rank:** 18. **Pop change 1990-2000:** +13.2%.

Income: per capita $36,370; median household $79,888. **Pop below poverty level:** 2.6%.

Unemployment: 2.1%. **Median home value:** $245,000. **Median travel time to work:** 33.5 minutes.

MERCER COUNTY
PO Box 8068   **Ph:** 609-989-6470
Trenton, NJ 08650   **Fax:** 609-989-1111
www.mercercounty.org

In central NJ along the Delaware River, northeast of Philadelphia; organized Feb 22, 1838 from Hunterdon and Middlesex counties. **Name Origin:** For Gen. Hugh Mercer (1721-77), Revolutionary War officer and physician.

Area (sq mi): 228.84 (land 225.93; water 2.91).

All statistics are based on the 2000 Census except the dollar figures given for per capita income, which are based on 1999 estimates.

Pop: 350,761 (White 64.2%; Black or African American 19.8%; Hispanic or Latino 9.7%; Asian 4.9%; Other 6.8%). **Foreign born:** 13.9%. **Median age:** 36. **State rank:** 12. **Pop change 1990-2000:** +7.7%.

Income: per capita $27,914; median household $56,613. **Pop below poverty level:** 8.6%.

Unemployment: 3.4%. **Median home value:** $147,400. **Median travel time to work:** 27.1 minutes.

MIDDLESEX COUNTY
1 JFK Sq   **Ph:** 732-745-3040
New Brunswick, NJ 08901   **Fax:** 732-745-3092
co.middlesex.nj.us

In northern NJ, southwest of Newark; original county, organized Mar 1, 1683. **Name Origin:** For the ancient county in England (most of which is now part of Greater London).

Area (sq mi): 322.51 (land 309.72; water 12.79).

Pop: 750,162 (White 61.9%; Black or African American 9.1%; Hispanic or Latino 13.6%; Asian 13.9%; Other 8.5%). **Foreign born:** 24.2%. **Median age:** 35.7. **State rank:** 3. **Pop change 1990-2000:** +11.7%.

Income: per capita $26,535; median household $61,446. **Pop below poverty level:** 6.6%.

Unemployment: 3.7%. **Median home value:** $168,500. **Median travel time to work:** 31.5 minutes.

MONMOUTH COUNTY
Market Yard   **Ph:** 732-431-7324
Freehold, NJ 07728   **Fax:** 732-409-7566
www.co.monmouth.nj.us

In central NJ on Lower New York Bay and the Atlantic Ocean, south of Jersey City; original county, organized Mar 7, 1683. **Name Origin:** For Monmouthshire, a county in England.

Area (sq mi): 665.12 (land 471.94; water 193.18).

Pop: 615,301 (White 80.6%; Black or African American 8.1%; Hispanic or Latino 6.2%; Asian 4%; Other 3.5%). **Foreign born:** 10.4%. **Median age:** 37.7. **State rank:** 4. **Pop change 1990-2000:** +11.2%.

Income: per capita $31,149; median household $64,271. **Pop below poverty level:** 6.3%.

Unemployment: 3.6%. **Median home value:** $203,100. **Median travel time to work:** 34.8 minutes.

MORRIS COUNTY
PO Box 315   **Ph:** 973-285-6120
Morristown, NJ 07963   **Fax:** 973-285-5231
www.co.morris.nj.us

In north-central NJ, west of Newark; organized Mar 15, 1739 from Hunterdon County. **Name Origin:** For Lewis Morris (1671-1746), chief justice of the superior court of NY and NJ (1692) and first governor the colony of NJ (1738-46).

Area (sq mi): 481.29 (land 468.99; water 12.29).

Pop: 470,212 (White 82%; Black or African American 2.8%; Hispanic or Latino 7.8%; Asian 6.3%; Other 3.7%). **Foreign born:**

15.4%. **Median age:** 37.8. **State rank:** 10. **Pop change 1990-2000:** +11.6%.

Income: per capita $36,964; median household $77,340. **Pop below poverty level:** 3.9%.

Unemployment: 2.9%. **Median home value:** $257,400. **Median travel time to work:** 29.4 minutes.

OCEAN COUNTY
118 Washington St   **Ph:** 732-929-2018
Toms River, NJ 08753   **Fax:** 732-349-4336
www.co.ocean.nj.us

In central NJ, north of Atlantic City; organized Feb 15, 1850 from Monmouth County. **Name Origin:** For its location on the Atlantic coast.

Area (sq mi): 915.88 (land 636.28; water 279.6).

Pop: 510,916 (White 89.9%; Black or African American 3%; Hispanic or Latino 5%; Asian 1.3%; Other 2.6%). **Foreign born:** 6.5%. **Median age:** 41. **State rank:** 7. **Pop change 1990-2000:** +17.9%.

Income: per capita $23,054; median household $46,443. **Pop below poverty level:** 7%.

Unemployment: 4.1%. **Median home value:** $131,300. **Median travel time to work:** 32.4 minutes.

PASSAIC COUNTY
401 Grand St   **Ph:** 973-225-3632
Paterson, NJ 07505   **Fax:** 973-754-1920
www.passaiccountynj.org

In northern NJ on the NY border, northwest of Newark; organized Feb 7, 1837 from Bergen and Sussex counties. **Name Origin:** For the Passaic River; its name is from a Delaware Indian term *passaic* or *passajeek*, variously translated as 'peace' or 'valley.'

Area (sq mi): 197.05 (land 185.29; water 11.76).

Pop: 489,049 (White 51.5%; Black or African American 13.2%; Hispanic or Latino 30%; Asian 3.7%; Other 20.6%). **Foreign born:** 26.6%. **Median age:** 34.8. **State rank:** 9. **Pop change 1990-2000:** +7.9%.

Income: per capita $21,370; median household $49,210. **Pop below poverty level:** 12.3%.

Unemployment: 5.7%. **Median home value:** $190,600. **Median travel time to work:** 26.4 minutes.

SALEM COUNTY
PO Box 18   **Ph:** 856-935-7510
Salem, NJ 08079   **Fax:** 856-935-8882

In southwestern NJ along Delaware River, east of Wilmington, DE; original county, organized May 17, 1694. **Name Origin:** Anglicization of Hebrew *shalom* 'peace.'

Area (sq mi): 372.57 (land 337.88; water 34.69).

Pop: 64,285 (White 79.6%; Black or African American 14.8%; Hispanic or Latino 3.9%; Asian 0.6%; Other 3.5%). **Foreign born:** 2.5%. **Median age:** 38. **State rank:** 21. **Pop change 1990-2000:** -1.5%.

Income: per capita $20,874; median household $45,573. **Pop below poverty level:** 9.5%.

Please see sample entry on inside front cover for detailed information about the statistics presented with each county listing.

Unemployment: 4.6%. **Median home value:** $105,200. **Median travel time to work:** 24.6 minutes.

SOMERSET COUNTY
20 Grove St   **Ph:** 908-231-7006
Somerville, NJ 08876   **Fax:** 908-253-8853
www.co.somerset.nj.us

In north-central NJ, southwest of Newark, organized May 14, 1688 from Middlesex County. **Name Origin:** For Somersetshire, the county in England.

Area (sq mi): 305.05 (land 304.69; water 0.36).

Pop: 297,490 (White 74.1%; Black or African American 7.5%; Hispanic or Latino 8.7%; Asian 8.4%; Other 4.6%). **Foreign born:** 18.1%. **Median age:** 37.2. **State rank:** 13. **Pop change 1990-2000:** +23.8%.

Income: per capita $37,970; median household $76,933. **Pop below poverty level:** 3.8%.

Unemployment: 2.7%. **Median home value:** $235,000. **Median travel time to work:** 30.1 minutes.

SUSSEX COUNTY
4 Park Pl   **Ph:** 973-579-0900
Newton, NJ 07860   **Fax:** 973-383-7493
www.sussex.nj.us

In northwestern NJ on border with PA and NY, northwest of Newark; organized May 16, 1753 from Morris County. **Name Origin:** For the county of Sussex, England.

Area (sq mi): 535.99 (land 521.26; water 14.73).

Pop: 144,166 (White 93.4%; Black or African American 1%; Hispanic or Latino 3.3%; Asian 1.2%; Other 1.9%). **Foreign born:** 5.7%. **Median age:** 37.1. **State rank:** 17. **Pop change 1990-2000:** +10.1%.

Income: per capita $26,992; median household $65,266. **Pop below poverty level:** 4%.

Unemployment: 3.6%. **Median home value:** $157,700. **Median travel time to work:** 38.3 minutes.

UNION COUNTY
2 Broad St Rm 115   **Ph:** 908-527-4999
Elizabeth, NJ 07207   **Fax:** 908-558-2589
www.unioncountynj.org

In northeastern NJ, south of Newark; organized Mar 19, 1857 from Essex County. **Name Origin:** As an expression of belief in the federal union of the states; also in the hope that citizens of Elizabeth and Newark would settle their differences.

Area (sq mi): 105.46 (land 103.29; water 2.17).

Pop: 522,541 (White 54.2%; Black or African American 20.8%; Hispanic or Latino 19.7%; Asian 3.8%; Other 9.8%). **Foreign born:** 25.1%. **Median age:** 36.6. **State rank:** 6. **Pop change 1990-2000:** +5.8%.

Income: per capita $26,992; median household $55,339. **Pop below poverty level:** 8.4%.

Unemployment: 4.5%. **Median home value:** $188,800. **Median travel time to work:** 28.7 minutes.

WARREN COUNTY
413 2nd St   **Ph:** 908-475-6211
Belvidere, NJ 07823   **Fax:** 908-475-6208
www.co.warren.nj.us

On northwestern border of NJ, east of Easton, PA; organized Nov 20, 1824 from Sussex County. **Name Origin:** For Joseph Warren (1741-75), the Revolutionary War patriot and member of the Continental Congress who dispatched Paul Revere (1735-1818) on his famous ride.

Area (sq mi): 362.75 (land 357.87; water 4.89).

Pop: 102,437 (White 92.2%; Black or African American 1.9%; Hispanic or Latino 3.7%; Asian 1.2%; Other 2.3%). **Foreign born:** 5.8%. **Median age:** 37.6. **State rank:** 19. **Pop change 1990-2000:** +11.8%.

Income: per capita $25,728; median household $56,100. **Pop below poverty level:** 5.4%.

Unemployment: 3.6%. **Median home value:** $155,500. **Median travel time to work:** 33.3 minutes.

All statistics are based on the 2000 Census except the dollar figures given for per capita income, which are based on 1999 estimates.

NEW MEXICO - Counties

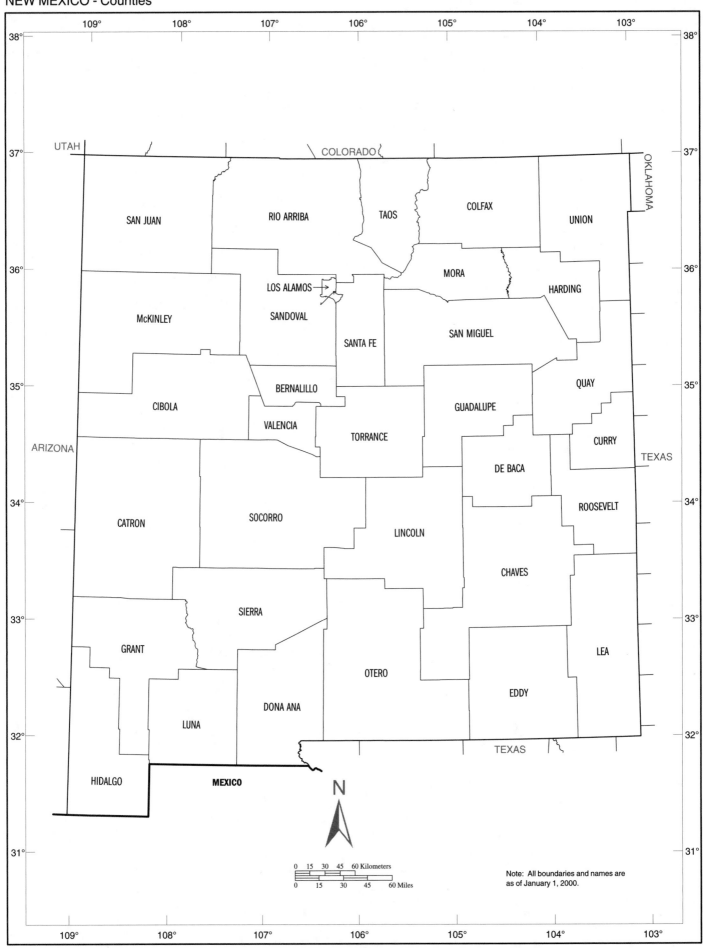

New Mexico

NEW MEXICO STATE INFORMATION

www.state.nm.us   **Ph:** 800-825-6639

Area (sq mi): 121,589.48 (land 121,355.53; water 233.96).

Pop: 1,819,046 (White 44.7%; Black or African American 1.9%; Hispanic or Latino 42.1%; Asian 1.1%; Other 30.2%). **Foreign born:** 8.2%. **Median age:** 34.6. **Pop change 1990-2000:** +20.1%.

Income: per capita $17,261; median household $34,133. **Pop below poverty level:** 18.4%.

Unemployment: 5.8%. **Median home value:** $108,100. **Median travel time to work:** 21.9 minutes.

BERNALILLO COUNTY

1 Civic Plaza NW 10th Fl   **Ph:** 505-768-4000
Albuquerque, NM 87102   **Fax:** 505-768-4329
www.bernco.gov

In west-central NM, southwest of Santa Fe, original county; organized Jan 8, 1852 (prior to statehood); annexed Santa Ana County 1876. **Name Origin:** Spanish for 'little Bernal,' possibly for a young member of the Gonzales-Bernal family who lived in the area as early as 1680. It may also have been named for Fray Juan Bernal, a friend of one of the community leaders.

Area (sq mi): 1168.65 (land 1166.03; water 2.62).

Pop: 556,678 (White 48.3%; Black or African American 2.8%; Hispanic or Latino 42%; Asian 1.9%; Other 24.6%). **Foreign born:** 8.6%. **Median age:** 35. **State rank:** 1. **Pop change 1990-2000:** +15.8%.

Income: per capita $20,790; median household $38,788. **Pop below poverty level:** 13.7%.

Unemployment: 3.5%. **Median home value:** $128,300. **Median travel time to work:** 21.3 minutes.

CATRON COUNTY

PO Box 507   **Ph:** 505-533-6423
Reserve, NM 87830   **Fax:** 505-533-6433
totalwebgov.org/catroncountynm/

On the central western border of NM, southwest of Albuquerque; organized Feb 25, 1921 from Socorro County. **Name Origin:** For Thomas Benton Catron (1840-1921), Confederate officer during the Civil War and U.S. senator from NM (1912-17).

Area (sq mi): 6929.03 (land 6927.81; water 1.22).

Pop: 3,543 (White 75.8%; Black or African American 0.3%; Hispanic or Latino 19.2%; Asian 0.7%; Other 11.3%). **Foreign born:**
1.6%. **Median age:** 47.8. **State rank:** 31. **Pop change 1990-2000:** +38.2%.

Income: per capita $13,951; median household $23,892. **Pop below poverty level:** 24.5%.

Unemployment: 6.8%. **Median home value:** $82,000. **Median travel time to work:** 25 minutes.

CHAVES COUNTY

PO Box 580   **Ph:** 505-624-6614
Roswell, NM 88202   **Fax:** 505-624-6523

In southeastern NM, northeast of Las Cruces; organized Feb 24, 1889 from Lincoln County (prior to statehood). **Name Origin:** For Lt. Col. Jose Francisco Chaves (1833-1904), an officer during the Civil War and U.S. representative from NM (1865-67; 1869-71).

Area (sq mi): 6075.07 (land 6070.86; water 4.21).

Pop: 61,382 (White 52.1%; Black or African American 2%; Hispanic or Latino 43.8%; Asian 0.5%; Other 25.5%). **Foreign born:** 11.2%. **Median age:** 35.2. **State rank:** 9. **Pop change 1990-2000:** +6.1%.

Income: per capita $14,990; median household $28,513. **Pop below poverty level:** 21.3%.

Unemployment: 5.8%. **Median home value:** $61,000. **Median travel time to work:** 17.1 minutes.

CIBOLA COUNTY

515 W High Ave   **Ph:** 505-287-9431
Grants, NM 870202526   **Fax:** 505-285-5434

On the central western border of NM, west of Albuquerque; organized Jun 19, 1981 from Valencia County. **Name Origin:** For the Cibola National Forest, part of which is within the county. Origin and meaning of name unknown; possibly a transliteration of Zuni Indian *shiwina*, the name for their tribal range; or possibly from Isleta Indian *sibulada* 'buffalo.'

Area (sq mi): 4541.71 (land 4539.21; water 2.5).

Pop: 25,595 (White 24.7%; Black or African American 1%; Hispanic or Latino 33.4%; Asian 0.4%; Other 59%). **Foreign born:** 2.3%. **Median age:** 33.1. **State rank:** 17. **Pop change 1990-2000:** +7.6%.

Income: per capita $11,731; median household $27,774. **Pop below poverty level:** 24.8%.

Unemployment: 5.6%. **Median home value:** $62,600. **Median travel time to work:** 23.5 minutes.

Please see sample entry on inside front cover for detailed information about the statistics presented with each county listing.

COLFAX COUNTY

PO Box 159   **Ph:** 505-445-5551
Raton, NM 87740   **Fax:** 505-445-4031

On the northern border of NM, northeast of Santa Fe; organized Jan 25, 1869 from Mora County (prior to statehood). **Name Origin:** For Schuyler Colfax (1823-85), U.S. vice president under Ulysses S. Grant (1869-73).

Area (sq mi): 3768.05 (land 3756.79; water 11.26).

Pop: 14,189 (White 49.9%; Black or African American 0.3%; Hispanic or Latino 47.5%; Asian 0.3%; Other 17.9%). **Foreign born:** 2.2%. **Median age:** 40.8. **State rank:** 24. **Pop change 1990-2000:** +9.8%.

Income: per capita $16,418; median household $30,744. **Pop below poverty level:** 14.8%.

Unemployment: 5.1%. **Median home value:** $76,600. **Median travel time to work:** 16.5 minutes.

CURRY COUNTY

700 N Main St Suite 7   **Ph:** 505-763-5591
Clovis, NM 88101   **Fax:** 505-763-4232
www.currycounty.org

On the central eastern border of NM, southeast of Albuquerque; organized Feb 25, 1909 from Quay and Roosevelt counties (prior to statehood). **Name Origin:** For Capt. George Curry (1863-1947), an officer in the Spanish-American War, NM territorial governor (1907-11), and U.S. representative (1912-13).

Area (sq mi): 1407.67 (land 1405.95; water 1.72).

Pop: 45,044 (White 58.7%; Black or African American 6.9%; Hispanic or Latino 30.4%; Asian 1.8%; Other 18.9%). **Foreign born:** 5.9%. **Median age:** 30.8. **State rank:** 12. **Pop change 1990-2000:** +6.7%.

Income: per capita $15,049; median household $28,917. **Pop below poverty level:** 19%.

Unemployment: 3.2%. **Median home value:** $64,700. **Median travel time to work:** 15.6 minutes.

DEBACA COUNTY

PO Box 347   **Ph:** 505-355-2601
Fort Sumner, NM 88119   **Fax:** 505-355-2441

In east-central NM, west of Clovis; organized Feb 28, 1917 from Chaves, Guadalupe, and Roosevelt counties. **Name Origin:** For Ezequiel Cabeza de Baca (1864-1917), lt. governor (1911-16) and governor (1917) who died after six weeks in office.

Area (sq mi): 2333.83 (land 2324.87; water 8.96).

Pop: 2,240 (White 62.8%; Black or African American 0%; Hispanic or Latino 35.3%; Asian 0.2%; Other 15.6%). **Foreign born:** 3.7%. **Median age:** 43.8. **State rank:** 32. **Pop change 1990-2000:** -0.5%.

Income: per capita $14,065; median household $25,441. **Pop below poverty level:** 17.7%.

Unemployment: 4.7%. **Median home value:** $45,800. **Median travel time to work:** 16.8 minutes.

DOÑA ANA COUNTY

180 W Amador Ave   **Ph:** 505-647-7200
Las Cruces, NM 88001   **Fax:** 505-647-7224
www.co.dona-ana.nm.us

On the central southern border of NM, south of Albuquerque; original county; organized Jan 9, 1852 (prior to statehood); annexed Arizona County 1861. **Name Origin:** For either Dona Ana Robledo, a woman famous for charity in the 1600s, or for Dona Ana Maria Nina de Cordova, a girl captured during an Apache raid and never seen again.

Area (sq mi): 3814.62 (land 3807.18; water 7.44).

Pop: 174,682 (White 32.5%; Black or African American 1.6%; Hispanic or Latino 63.4%; Asian 0.8%; Other 29.9%). **Foreign born:** 18.7%. **Median age:** 30.2. **State rank:** 2. **Pop change 1990-2000:** +28.9%.

Income: per capita $13,999; median household $29,808. **Pop below poverty level:** 25.4%.

Unemployment: 6.7%. **Median home value:** $90,900. **Median travel time to work:** 21.3 minutes.

EDDY COUNTY

101 W Greene St Suite 225   **Ph:** 505-887-9511
Carlsbad, NM 88220   **Fax:** 505-887-1039
www.carlsbadnm.com/ecourt

On the southern border of NM, east of Las Cruces; organized Feb 25, 1889 from Lincoln County (prior to statehood). **Name Origin:** For Charles B. Eddy, rancher, promoter of the Carlsbad Irrigation Project, and railroad builder.

Area (sq mi): 4197.57 (land 4182.02; water 15.55).

Pop: 51,658 (White 57.7%; Black or African American 1.6%; Hispanic or Latino 38.8%; Asian 0.4%; Other 21.7%). **Foreign born:** 5.3%. **Median age:** 36.4. **State rank:** 11. **Pop change 1990-2000:** +6.3%.

Income: per capita $15,823; median household $31,998. **Pop below poverty level:** 17.2%.

Unemployment: 5.1%. **Median home value:** $64,200. **Median travel time to work:** 18.3 minutes.

GRANT COUNTY

201 N Cooper St 3rd Fl   **Ph:** 505-538-9581
Silver City, NM 88061   **Fax:** 505-538-3518

On the western border of NM, northwest of Las Cruces; organized Jan 30, 1868 from Socorro County (prior to statehood). **Name Origin:** For Ulysses Simpson Grant (1822-85), Civil War general and eighteenth U.S. president.

Area (sq mi): 3967.5 (land 3965.88; water 1.62).

Pop: 31,002 (White 48.5%; Black or African American 0.5%; Hispanic or Latino 48.8%; Asian 0.3%; Other 23.5%). **Foreign born:** 3.3%. **Median age:** 38.8. **State rank:** 14. **Pop change 1990-2000:** +12%.

Income: per capita $14,597; median household $29,134. **Pop below poverty level:** 18.7%.

Unemployment: 6.8%. **Median home value:** $87,900. **Median travel time to work:** 19.1 minutes.

All statistics are based on the 2000 Census except the dollar figures given for per capita income, which are based on 1999 estimates.

GUADALUPE COUNTY
420 Parker Ave Suite 1   **Ph:** 505-472-3791
Santa Rosa, NM 88435   **Fax:** 505-472-3735

In east-central NM, east of Albuquerque; organized Feb 26, 1891 from Lincoln and San Miguel counties (prior to statehood). **Name Origin:** For Our Lady of Guadalupe, patron saint of Mexico.

Area (sq mi): 3031.58 (land 3030.37; water 1.2).

Pop: 4,680 (White 15.5%; Black or African American 1.3%; Hispanic or Latino 81.2%; Asian 0.5%; Other 44%). **Foreign born:** 4%. **Median age:** 37.5. **State rank:** 29. **Pop change 1990-2000:** +12.6%.

Income: per capita $11,241; median household $24,783. **Pop below poverty level:** 21.6%.

Unemployment: 8.7%. **Median home value:** $52,100. **Median travel time to work:** 17.6 minutes.

HARDING COUNTY
PO Box 1002   **Ph:** 505-673-2301
Mosquero, NM 87733   **Fax:** 505-673-2922

In northeastern NM, northeast of Santa Fe; organized Mar 4, 1921 from Mora and Union counties. **Name Origin:** For Warren Gamaliel Harding (1865-1923), twenty-ninth U.S. president.

Area (sq mi): 2125.95 (land 2125.34; water 0.61).

Pop: 810 (White 52.8%; Black or African American 0.4%; Hispanic or Latino 44.9%; Asian 0%; Other 15.3%). **Foreign born:** 2.5%. **Median age:** 48.7. **State rank:** 33. **Pop change 1990-2000:** -17.9%.

Income: per capita $16,240; median household $26,111. **Pop below poverty level:** 16.3%.

Unemployment: 3.3%. **Median home value:** $27,300. **Median travel time to work:** 21.1 minutes.

HIDALGO COUNTY
300 Shakespeare St   **Ph:** 505-542-9213
Lordsburg, NM 88045   **Fax:** 505-542-3193

In the southwestern corner of NM, southwest of Las Cruces; organized Feb 25, 1919 from Grant County. **Name Origin:** Probably for the Treaty of Guadalupe Hidalgo, which ended the Mexican War; others claim for Miguel Hidalgo y Costilla (1753-1811), leader of the Mexican war for independence from Spain.

Area (sq mi): 3445.91 (land 3445.63; water 0.28).

Pop: 5,932 (White 42.7%; Black or African American 0.4%; Hispanic or Latino 56%; Asian 0.3%; Other 15.6%). **Foreign born:** 11.1%. **Median age:** 34.8. **State rank:** 27. **Pop change 1990-2000:** -0.4%.

Income: per capita $12,431; median household $24,819. **Pop below poverty level:** 27.3%.

Unemployment: 8.7%. **Median home value:** $53,900. **Median travel time to work:** 22.6 minutes.

LEA COUNTY
100 N Main St Suite 11   **Ph:** 505-396-8521
Lovington, NM 88260   **Fax:** 505-396-5684
www.leacounty.net

In the southeastern corner of NM, east of Roswell; organized Mar

7, 1917 from Chaves and Eddy counties. **Name Origin:** For Gen. Joseph C. Lea (?-1904), Confederate officer in the Civil War, 'father of [the town of] Roswell,' and founder of the New Mexico Military Institute there.

Area (sq mi): 4394.02 (land 4392.96; water 1.06).

Pop: 55,511 (White 54%; Black or African American 4.4%; Hispanic or Latino 39.6%; Asian 0.4%; Other 28.1%). **Foreign born:** 11.3%. **Median age:** 33.1. **State rank:** 10. **Pop change 1990-2000:** -0.5%.

Income: per capita $14,184; median household $29,799. **Pop below poverty level:** 21.1%.

Unemployment: 3.2%. **Median home value:** $50,100. **Median travel time to work:** 18.7 minutes.

LINCOLN COUNTY
PO Box 338   **Ph:** 505-648-2331
Carrizozo, NM 88301   **Fax:** 505-648-2576

In south-central NM, west of Roswell; organized Jan 16, 1869 (prior to statehood). **Name Origin:** For Abraham Lincoln (1809-65), sixteenth U.S. president.

Area (sq mi): 4831.25 (land 4830.97; water 0.28).

Pop: 19,411 (White 70.9%; Black or African American 0.4%; Hispanic or Latino 25.6%; Asian 0.3%; Other 15.9%). **Foreign born:** 6.1%. **Median age:** 43.8. **State rank:** 19. **Pop change 1990-2000:** +58.9%.

Income: per capita $19,338; median household $33,886. **Pop below poverty level:** 14.9%.

Unemployment: 4.1%. **Median home value:** $108,400. **Median travel time to work:** 20.9 minutes.

LOS ALAMOS COUNTY
2300 Trinity Dr Rm 230   **Ph:** 505-662-8080
Los Alamos, NM 87544   **Fax:** 505-662-8079
www.lac-nm.us

In north-central NM, northwest of Santa Fe; organized Mar 16, 1949 from Sandoval and Santa Fe counties. Site of the Manhattan Project that produced the first atomic bomb. **Name Origin:** For its county seat, itself named for the Los Alamos School for Boys, established 1925 by Ashley Pond; form Spanish 'poplars' or 'cotton-woods.'

Area (sq mi): 109.35 (land 109.35; water 0).

Pop: 18,343 (White 82.1%; Black or African American 0.4%; Hispanic or Latino 11.7%; Asian 3.8%; Other 5.6%). **Foreign born:** 6.7%. **Median age:** 40.8. **State rank:** 20. **Pop change 1990-2000:** +1.3%.

Income: per capita $34,646; median household $78,993. **Pop below poverty level:** 2.9%.

Unemployment: 1%. **Median home value:** $228,300. **Median travel time to work:** 15.2 minutes.

LUNA COUNTY
PO Box 1838   **Ph:** 505-546-0491
Deming, NM 88031   **Fax:** 505-546-4708

On the southern border of NM, west of Las Cruces; organized Mar 16, 1901 from Dona Ana and Grant counties (prior to statehood).

Please see sample entry on inside front cover for detailed information about the statistics presented with each county listing.

389

Name Origin: For Don Salomon Luna, a sheep rancher and a leader of the Republican party in the state.

Area (sq mi): 2965.28 (land 2965.09; water 0.19).

Pop: 25,016 (White 39.7%; Black or African American 0.9%; Hispanic or Latino 57.7%; Asian 0.3%; Other 24.4%). **Foreign born:** 19.5%. **Median age:** 36.7. **State rank:** 18. **Pop change 1990-2000:** +38.1%.

Income: per capita $11,218; median household $20,784. **Pop below poverty level:** 32.9%.

Unemployment: 23.7%. **Median home value:** $66,000. **Median travel time to work:** 17.9 minutes.

McKINLEY COUNTY
PO Box 1268　　　　　　　　**Ph:** 505-863-6866
Gallup, NM 87305　　　　　　**Fax:** 505-863-1419

On the northwestern border of NM, west of Santa Fe; organized Feb 23, 1899 from Bernalillo, Valencia, and San Juan counties. **Name Origin:** For William McKinley (1843-1901), twenty-fifth U.S. president.

Area (sq mi): 5455.22 (land 5448.72; water 6.49).

Pop: 74,798 (White 11.9%; Black or African American 0.4%; Hispanic or Latino 12.4%; Asian 0.5%; Other 82.7%). **Foreign born:** 1.8%. **Median age:** 26.9. **State rank:** 6. **Pop change 1990-2000:** +23.3%.

Income: per capita $9,872; median household $25,005. **Pop below poverty level:** 36.1%.

Unemployment: 6.1%. **Median home value:** $57,000. **Median travel time to work:** 24.2 minutes.

MORA COUNTY
PO Box 360　　　　　　　　　**Ph:** 505-387-2448
Mora, NM 87732　　　　　　　**Fax:** 505-387-9023

In east-central NM, northeast of Santa Fe; organized Feb 1, 1860 from San Miguel County (prior to statehood). **Name Origin:** Either from personal and family names of early settlers, such as Mora Pineda and Garcia de la Mora, or possibly from the Spanish word meaning 'blackberry' or 'mulberry,' referring to the abundance of fruit locally.

Area (sq mi): 1933.48 (land 1931.1; water 2.38).

Pop: 5,180 (White 16.9%; Black or African American 0.1%; Hispanic or Latino 81.6%; Asian 0.1%; Other 40.9%). **Foreign born:** 1.7%. **Median age:** 39.6. **State rank:** 28. **Pop change 1990-2000:** +21.5%.

Income: per capita $12,340; median household $24,518. **Pop below poverty level:** 25.4%.

Unemployment: 12.2%. **Median home value:** $75,900. **Median travel time to work:** 35.1 minutes.

OTERO COUNTY
1000 New York Ave Rm 101　　　**Ph:** 505-437-7427
Alamogordo, NM 88310　　　　　**Fax:** 505-443-2904
www.co.otero.nm.us

On the central southern border of NM, east of Las Cruces; organized Jan 30, 1899 from Dona Ana and Lincoln counties. **Name Origin:**

For Miguel Antonio Otero (1859-1944), territorial governor of New Mexico (1896-1906).

Area (sq mi): 6627.43 (land 6626.5; water 0.93).

Pop: 62,298 (White 55.7%; Black or African American 3.9%; Hispanic or Latino 32.2%; Asian 1.2%; Other 21.2%). **Foreign born:** 11.1%. **Median age:** 33.8. **State rank:** 8. **Pop change 1990-2000:** +20%.

Income: per capita $14,345; median household $30,861. **Pop below poverty level:** 19.3%.

Unemployment: 5.4%. **Median home value:** $78,800. **Median travel time to work:** 20.9 minutes.

QUAY COUNTY
PO Box 1246　　　　　　　　　**Ph:** 505-461-2112
Tucumcari, NM 88401

On the central eastern border of NM; organized Jan 28, 1903 (prior to statehood). **Name Origin:** For Lt. Col. Matthew S. Quay (1833-1904), U.S. senator from PA (1887-99; 1901-04) who was active in establishing the area.

Area (sq mi): 2881.8 (land 2874.93; water 6.87).

Pop: 10,155 (White 58.6%; Black or African American 0.8%; Hispanic or Latino 38%; Asian 0.8%; Other 16.2%). **Foreign born:** 3.4%. **Median age:** 41.5. **State rank:** 26. **Pop change 1990-2000:** -6.2%.

Income: per capita $14,938; median household $24,894. **Pop below poverty level:** 20.9%.

Unemployment: 4.4%. **Median home value:** $54,000. **Median travel time to work:** 15.1 minutes.

RIO ARRIBA COUNTY
PO Box 127　　　　　　　　　**Ph:** 505-588-7255
Tierra Amarilla, NM 87575　　　**Fax:** 505-588-7810

On the central northern border of NM, northwest of Santa Fe; original county; organized Jan 9, 1852 (prior to statehood). **Name Origin:** Spanish 'upper river,' the Spanish designation for the upper Rio Grande in NM.

Area (sq mi): 5896.1 (land 5857.63; water 38.47).

Pop: 41,190 (White 13.6%; Black or African American 0.3%; Hispanic or Latino 72.9%; Asian 0.1%; Other 42.9%). **Foreign born:** 3.7%. **Median age:** 34.5. **State rank:** 13. **Pop change 1990-2000:** +19.9%.

Income: per capita $14,263; median household $29,429. **Pop below poverty level:** 20.3%.

Unemployment: 6.6%. **Median home value:** $107,500. **Median travel time to work:** 28.1 minutes.

ROOSEVELT COUNTY
County Courthouse 109 W 1st St　**Ph:** 505-356-8562
Portales, NM 88130　　　　　　**Fax:** 505-356-3560
www.rooseveltcounty.com

On the central eastern border of NM, south of Clovis; organized Feb 28, 1903 from Chaves and Guadalupe counties (prior to statehood). **Name Origin:** For Theodore Roosevelt (1858-1919), twenty-sixth U.S. president.

All statistics are based on the 2000 Census except the dollar figures given for per capita income, which are based on 1999 estimates.

Area (sq mi): 2454.87 (land 2448.5; water 6.37).

Pop: 18,018 (White 62.7%; Black or African American 1.7%; Hispanic or Latino 33.3%; Asian 0.6%; Other 23.7%). **Foreign born:** 6.2%. **Median age:** 29.5. **State rank:** 22. **Pop change 1990-2000:** +7.9%.

Income: per capita $14,185; median household $26,586. **Pop below poverty level:** 22.7%.

Unemployment: 2.8%. **Median home value:** $54,900. **Median travel time to work:** 16.7 minutes.

SAN JUAN COUNTY
PO Box 550   **Ph:** 505-334-9471
Aztec, NM 87410   **Fax:** 505-334-3635
www.co.san-juan.nm.us

On the northwestern border of NM; organized Jan 24, 1887 from Rio Arriba County (prior to statehood). **Name Origin:** For the San Juan River, which flows through the county; Spanish for Saint John (the Baptist).

Area (sq mi): 5538.36 (land 5514.02; water 24.35).

Pop: 113,801 (White 46.5%; Black or African American 0.4%; Hispanic or Latino 15%; Asian 0.3%; Other 46.5%). **Foreign born:** 2.4%. **Median age:** 31. **State rank:** 4. **Pop change 1990-2000:** +24.2%.

Income: per capita $14,282; median household $33,762. **Pop below poverty level:** 21.5%.

Unemployment: 6.1%. **Median home value:** $91,300. **Median travel time to work:** 23.8 minutes.

SAN MIGUEL COUNTY
County Courthouse 500 W National St
Suite 100   **Ph:** 505-425-9333
Las Vegas, NM 87701   **Fax:** 505-425-7019
www.sandovalcounty.com

In east-central NM, east of Santa Fe; original county; organized Jan 9, 1852 (prior to statehood). **Name Origin:** For the town of San Miguel del Bado, Spanish 'Saint Michael of the ford,' a river crossing on the Pecos River on the Old Santa Fe Trail.

Area (sq mi): 4735.63 (land 4717.04; water 18.59).

Pop: 30,126 (White 18.9%; Black or African American 0.8%; Hispanic or Latino 78%; Asian 0.5%; Other 42.4%). **Foreign born:** 2.5%. **Median age:** 35.1. **State rank:** 15. **Pop change 1990-2000:** +17%.

Income: per capita $13,268; median household $26,524. **Pop below poverty level:** 24.4%.

Unemployment: 6.4%. **Median home value:** $90,100. **Median travel time to work:** 23.6 minutes.

SANDOVAL COUNTY
PO Box 40   **Ph:** 505-867-7572
Bernalillo, NM 87004   **Fax:** 505-771-8610
www.sandovalcounty.com

In north-central NM, west of Santa Fe; organized Mar 10, 1903 from Rio Arriba County (prior to statehood). **Name Origin:** For

the Sandoval family, descendants of Juan de Dios Sandoval Martinez, who came to the area in 1692.

Area (sq mi): 3714.32 (land 3709.34; water 4.98).

Pop: 89,908 (White 50.3%; Black or African American 1.7%; Hispanic or Latino 29.4%; Asian 1%; Other 32.3%). **Foreign born:** 4.3%. **Median age:** 35.1. **State rank:** 5. **Pop change 1990-2000:** +42%.

Income: per capita $19,174; median household $44,949. **Pop below poverty level:** 12.1%.

Unemployment: 3.9%. **Median home value:** $115,400. **Median travel time to work:** 28.1 minutes.

SANTA FE COUNTY
PO Box 276   **Ph:** 505-986-6200
Santa Fe, NM 87504   **Fax:** 505-995-2740
www.co.santa-fe.nm.us

In north-central NM, northeast of Albuquerque; original county; organized Jan 9, 1852 (prior to statehood). **Name Origin:** For the capital of NM and the county seat; Spanish 'Holy Faith.'

Area (sq mi): 1910.79 (land 1909.19; water 1.6).

Pop: 129,292 (White 45.5%; Black or African American 0.6%; Hispanic or Latino 49%; Asian 0.9%; Other 25%). **Foreign born:** 10.1%. **Median age:** 37.9. **State rank:** 3. **Pop change 1990-2000:** +30.7%.

Income: per capita $23,594; median household $42,207. **Pop below poverty level:** 12%.

Unemployment: 2.6%. **Median home value:** $189,400. **Median travel time to work:** 22.1 minutes.

SIERRA COUNTY
100 N Date St   **Ph:** 505-894-6215
Truth or Consequences, NM 87901   **Fax:** 505-894-9548

In west-central NM, northwest of Las Cruces; organized Apr 3, 1884 from Socorro County (prior to statehood). **Name Origin:** For the Sierra de los Caballos Range, Spanish 'saw' for the shape of the mountains, thus 'saw-toothed mountain of the horses.' The county may have been named for the Sierra family, whose members included Nicholas de la Sierra.

Area (sq mi): 4236.3 (land 4180.23; water 56.07).

Pop: 13,270 (White 70.5%; Black or African American 0.5%; Hispanic or Latino 26.3%; Asian 0.2%; Other 12.4%). **Foreign born:** 6.6%. **Median age:** 48.9. **State rank:** 25. **Pop change 1990-2000:** +33.9%.

Income: per capita $15,023; median household $24,152. **Pop below poverty level:** 20.9%.

Unemployment: 3.8%. **Median home value:** $77,800. **Median travel time to work:** 20.1 minutes.

SOCORRO COUNTY
210 Park St   **Ph:** 505-835-0589
Socorro, NM 87801   **Fax:** 505-835-4629

In west-central NM, south of Albuquerque; original county; organized Jul 1850 (prior to statehood). **Name Origin:** Name given to

Please see sample entry on inside front cover for detailed information about the statistics presented with each county listing.

the Piro Indian pueblo of Teypana in 1598 by Juan de Onate (1550?-1630) because 'they gave us much corn.' Spanish 'aid, help, succor, assistance.'

Area (sq mi): 6648.71 (land 6646.4; water 2.31).

Pop: 18,078 (White 37.6%; Black or African American 0.6%; Hispanic or Latino 48.7%; Asian 1.1%; Other 35.4%). **Foreign born:** 6.4%. **Median age:** 32.4. **State rank:** 21. **Pop change 1990-2000:** +22.4%.

Income: per capita $12,826; median household $23,439. **Pop below poverty level:** 31.7%.

Unemployment: 6.1%. **Median home value:** $80,900. **Median travel time to work:** 20.9 minutes.

TAOS COUNTY

105 Albright St Suite D   **Ph:** 505-751-8654
Taos, NM 87571   **Fax:** 505-751-8637

On the central northern border of NM; north of Santa Fe; original county; organized Jan 9, 1852 (prior to statehood). **Name Origin:** A Spanish transliteration for a town of the Tewa Pueblos, located in what is now Taos County. From either *tuota* 'red willow place,' or *tuatah* 'at the village.'

Area (sq mi): 2204.62 (land 2203.17; water 1.45).

Pop: 29,979 (White 33.8%; Black or African American 0.4%; Hispanic or Latino 57.9%; Asian 0.4%; Other 35.5%). **Foreign born:** 4.1%. **Median age:** 39.5. **State rank:** 16. **Pop change 1990-2000:** +29.7%.

Income: per capita $16,103; median household $26,762. **Pop below poverty level:** 20.9%.

Unemployment: 9.7%. **Median home value:** $150,400. **Median travel time to work:** 21.5 minutes.

TORRANCE COUNTY

PO Box 767   **Ph:** 505-384-2221
Estancia, NM 87016   **Fax:** 505-384-4080
www.torrancecounty.org

In central NM, southeast of Albuquerque; organized Mar 16, 1903 (prior to statehood). **Name Origin:** For the town of Torrance, itself named for Francis J. Torrance, a New Mexico Central Railroad promoter.

Area (sq mi): 3345.81 (land 3344.81; water 1).

Pop: 16,911 (White 57.2%; Black or African American 1.7%; Hispanic or Latino 37.2%; Asian 0.3%; Other 24.1%). **Foreign born:** 4.2%. **Median age:** 34.8. **State rank:** 23. **Pop change 1990-2000:** +64.4%.

Income: per capita $14,134; median household $30,446. **Pop below poverty level:** 19%.

Unemployment: 4.6%. **Median home value:** $82,800. **Median travel time to work:** 36.3 minutes.

UNION COUNTY

PO Box 430   **Ph:** 505-374-9491
Clayton, NM 88415   **Fax:** 505-374-2763

In the northeastern corner of NM; organized Feb 13, 1893 from

Colfax, Mora, and San Miguel counties (prior to statehood). **Name Origin:** For the union of the three counties.

Area (sq mi): 3830.79 (land 3830; water 0.79).

Pop: 4,174 (White 62.7%; Black or African American 0%; Hispanic or Latino 35.1%; Asian 0.3%; Other 19.3%). **Foreign born:** 2.2%. **Median age:** 39.9. **State rank:** 30. **Pop change 1990-2000:** +1.2%.

Income: per capita $14,700; median household $28,080. **Pop below poverty level:** 18.1%.

Unemployment: 2.5%. **Median home value:** $49,800. **Median travel time to work:** 20 minutes.

VALENCIA COUNTY

PO Box 969   **Ph:** 505-866-2073
Los Lunas, NM 87031   **Fax:** 505-866-2023
www.co.valencia.nm.us

In west-central NM, south of Albuquerque; original county; organized Jan 9, 1852 (prior to statehood). **Name Origin:** Either for the town, itself named for Juan de Valencia, a seventeenth-century Spanish settler, or for the seventeenth-century home of Francisco de Valencia, a Spanish official.

Area (sq mi): 1068.21 (land 1067.63; water 0.58).

Pop: 66,152 (White 39.4%; Black or African American 1.3%; Hispanic or Latino 55%; Asian 0.4%; Other 31.9%). **Foreign born:** 6.4%. **Median age:** 33.8. **State rank:** 7. **Pop change 1990-2000:** +46.2%.

Income: per capita $14,747; median household $34,099. **Pop below poverty level:** 16.8%.

Unemployment: 4.1%. **Median home value:** $108,300. **Median travel time to work:** 30.7 minutes.

All statistics are based on the 2000 Census except the dollar figures given for per capita income, which are based on 1999 estimates.

NEW YORK - Counties

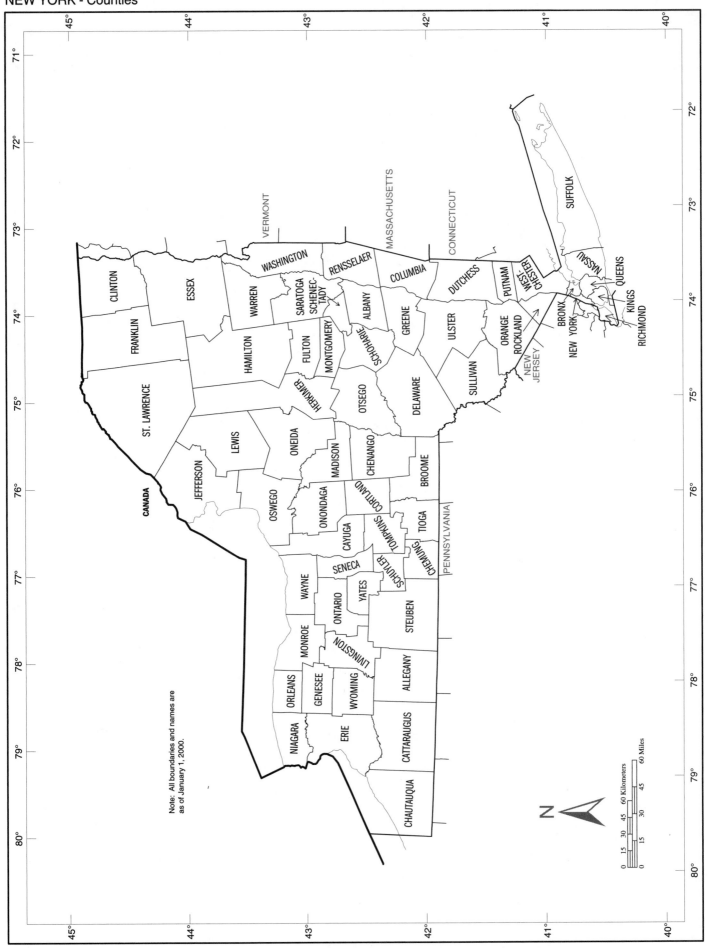

Note: All boundaries and names are as of January 1, 2000.

New York

NEW YORK STATE INFORMATION

www.state.ny.us   **Ph:** 518-474-2121

Area (sq mi): 54,556 (land 47,213.79; water 7342.22).

Pop: 18,976,457 (White 62%; Black or African American 15.9%; Hispanic or Latino 15.1%; Asian 5.5%; Other 10.6%). **Foreign born:** 20.4%. **Median age:** 35.9. **Pop change 1990-2000:** +5.5%.

Income: per capita $23,389; median household $43,393. **Pop below poverty level:** 14.6%.

Unemployment: 6.3%. **Median home value:** $148,700. **Median travel time to work:** 31.7 minutes.

ALBANY COUNTY

112 State St Rm 200   **Ph:** 518-447-7040
Albany, NY 12207   **Fax:** 518-447-5589
www.albanycounty.com

In east-central NY, southeast of Schenectady; original county, organized Nov 1, 1683. **Name Origin:** For James Stuart, Duke of York and Albany (1633-1701), who later became James II, king of England.

Area (sq mi): 533.21 (land 523.45; water 9.76).

Pop: 294,565 (White 81.8%; Black or African American 11.1%; Hispanic or Latino 3.1%; Asian 2.7%; Other 3%). **Foreign born:** 6.5%. **Median age:** 36.8. **State rank:** 13. **Pop change 1990-2000:** +0.7%.

Income: per capita $23,345; median household $42,935. **Pop below poverty level:** 10.6%.

Unemployment: 2.6%. **Median home value:** $116,300. **Median travel time to work:** 20.3 minutes.

ALLEGANY COUNTY

7 Court St County Courthouse   **Ph:** 585-268-9270
Belmont, NY 14813   **Fax:** 585-268-9446
www.co.allegany.ny.us

In southwestern NY, southeast of Buffalo; organized Apr 7, 1806 from Genesee County. **Name Origin:** For the Allegheny River, with a variant spelling.

Area (sq mi): 1034.42 (land 1030.22; water 4.2).

Pop: 49,927 (White 96.6%; Black or African American 0.7%; Hispanic or Latino 0.9%; Asian 0.7%; Other 1.6%). **Foreign born:** 1.8%. **Median age:** 35. **State rank:** 49. **Pop change 1990-2000:** -1.1%.

Income: per capita $14,975; median household $32,106. **Pop below poverty level:** 15.5%.

Unemployment: 5.7%. **Median home value:** $50,400. **Median travel time to work:** 21.8 minutes.

BRONX COUNTY

851 Grand Concourse   **Ph:** 718-590-3500
Bronx, NY 10451   **Fax:** 718-590-3537

Established Apr 19, 1912 from New York County. The county is coterminous with the borough of the Bronx, part of New York City. The only borough of New York City that is not on an island. **Name Origin:** For Jonas Bronck or Bronk (?-1643), the first European settler north of the Harlem River. His farm was called 'Broncksland.' the borough is usually called 'The Bronx.'

Area (sq mi): 57.43 (land 42.03; water 15.4).

Pop: 1,332,650 (White 14.5%; Black or African American 35.6%; Hispanic or Latino 48.4%; Asian 3%; Other 31.5%). **Foreign born:** 29%. **Median age:** 31.2. **State rank:** 6. **Pop change 1990-2000:** +10.7%.

Income: per capita $13,959; median household $27,611. **Pop below poverty level:** 30.7%.

Unemployment: 7.4%. **Median home value:** $190,400. **Median travel time to work:** 43 minutes.

BROOME COUNTY

PO Box 2062   **Ph:** 607-778-2451
Binghamton, NY 13902   **Fax:** 607-778-2243
www.gobroomecounty.com

On central southern border of NY, southeast of Ithaca; organized Mar 28, 1806 from Tioga County. **Name Origin:** For John Broome (1738-1810), member of the NY constitutional convention (1777) and lieutenant governor (1804-10).

Area (sq mi): 715.46 (land 706.82; water 8.64).

Pop: 200,536 (White 90.4%; Black or African American 3.3%; Hispanic or Latino 2%; Asian 2.8%; Other 2.6%). **Foreign born:** 5.3%. **Median age:** 38.2. **State rank:** 19. **Pop change 1990-2000:** -5.5%.

Income: per capita $19,168; median household $35,347. **Pop below poverty level:** 12.8%.

Unemployment: 4.2%. **Median home value:** $75,800. **Median travel time to work:** 18.9 minutes.

CATTARAUGUS COUNTY

303 Court St   **Ph:** 716-938-9111
Little Valley, NY 14755   **Fax:** 716-938-6009
www.co.cattaraugus.ny.us

On southwestern border of NY, south of Buffalo; organized Mar

Please see sample entry on inside front cover for detailed information about the statistics presented with each county listing.

395

11, 1808 from Genesee County. **Name Origin:** For the Cattaraugus Creek, which forms its northern border; probably from Seneca 'bad smelling shore.'

Area (sq mi): 1322.25 (land 1309.85; water 12.4).

Pop: 83,955 (White 94%; Black or African American 1.1%; Hispanic or Latino 0.9%; Asian 0.5%; Other 3.8%). **Foreign born:** 1.4%. **Median age:** 37.4. **State rank:** 33. **Pop change 1990-2000:** -0.3%.

Income: per capita $15,959; median household $33,404. **Pop below poverty level:** 13.7%.

Unemployment: 6.7%. **Median home value:** $60,800. **Median travel time to work:** 21.7 minutes.

CAYUGA COUNTY
160 Genesee St   **Ph:** 315-253-1271
Auburn, NY 13021
www.co.cayuga.ny.us

On central northern border of NY, east of Rochester; organized Mar 8, 1799 from Onondaga County. **Name Origin:** For the Cayuga Indians, one of the Five Nations of the Iroquois.

Area (sq mi): 863.64 (land 693.18; water 170.46).

Pop: 81,963 (White 92.4%; Black or African American 4%; Hispanic or Latino 2%; Asian 0.4%; Other 2.2%). **Foreign born:** 2.3%. **Median age:** 37.3. **State rank:** 34. **Pop change 1990-2000:** -0.4%.

Income: per capita $18,003; median household $37,487. **Pop below poverty level:** 11.1%.

Unemployment: 4.9%. **Median home value:** $75,300. **Median travel time to work:** 22 minutes.

CHAUTAUQUA COUNTY
3 N Erie St Gerace Office Bldg   **Ph:** 716-753-4211
Mayville, NY 14757   **Fax:** 716-753-4756
www.chautco.com

In southwestern corner of NY, southwest of Buffalo; organized Mar 11, 1808 from Genesee County. **Name Origin:** For Lake Chautauqua, which is in the middle of the county; its name is a contraction of Seneca Indian words of uncertain origin and meaning; possibly 'where the fish was taken out.'

Area (sq mi): 1500.02 (land 1062.05; water 437.97).

Pop: 139,750 (White 91.9%; Black or African American 2.2%; Hispanic or Latino 4.2%; Asian 0.4%; Other 3.3%). **Foreign born:** 1.9%. **Median age:** 37.9. **State rank:** 23. **Pop change 1990-2000:** -1.5%.

Income: per capita $16,840; median household $33,458. **Pop below poverty level:** 13.8%.

Unemployment: 5.4%. **Median home value:** $64,000. **Median travel time to work:** 18.4 minutes.

CHEMUNG COUNTY
PO Box 588   **Ph:** 607-737-2920
Elmira, NY 14902   **Fax:** 607-737-2897
www.chemungcounty.com

On central southern border of NY, southwest of Syracuse; organized Mar 29, 1836 from Tioga County. **Name Origin:** For a former

Seneca village near the town of Chemung. The name means 'big horn.'

Area (sq mi): 410.79 (land 408.17; water 2.62).

Pop: 91,070 (White 90.2%; Black or African American 5.8%; Hispanic or Latino 1.8%; Asian 0.8%; Other 2.3%). **Foreign born:** 2.2%. **Median age:** 37.9. **State rank:** 32. **Pop change 1990-2000:** -4.3%.

Income: per capita $18,264; median household $36,415. **Pop below poverty level:** 13%.

Unemployment: 5.3%. **Median home value:** $67,200. **Median travel time to work:** 19.3 minutes.

CHENANGO COUNTY
5 Court St   **Ph:** 607-337-1450
Norwich, NY 13815   **Fax:** 607-337-1455

In south-central NY, southeast of Ithaca; organized Mar 15, 1798 from Herkimer and Tioga counties. **Name Origin:** From an Onondaga Indian word probably meaning 'bull thistle.'

Area (sq mi): 898.7 (land 894.36; water 4.34).

Pop: 51,401 (White 96.9%; Black or African American 0.8%; Hispanic or Latino 1.1%; Asian 0.3%; Other 1.2%). **Foreign born:** 1.7%. **Median age:** 38.4. **State rank:** 47. **Pop change 1990-2000:** -0.7%.

Income: per capita $16,427; median household $33,679. **Pop below poverty level:** 14.4%.

Unemployment: 5.1%. **Median home value:** $62,700. **Median travel time to work:** 26.3 minutes.

CLINTON COUNTY
137 Margaret St Suite 208   **Ph:** 518-565-4600
Plattsburgh, NY 12901   **Fax:** 518-565-4616
www.co.clinton.ny.us

In northeastern corner of NY, northwest of Burlington, VT; organized Mar 7, 1788 (prior to statehood) from Washington County. **Name Origin:** For George Clinton (1739-1812), first governor of NY (1777-95).

Area (sq mi): 1117.61 (land 1038.95; water 78.67).

Pop: 79,894 (White 92.3%; Black or African American 3.6%; Hispanic or Latino 2.5%; Asian 0.7%; Other 2.4%). **Foreign born:** 4.5%. **Median age:** 35.7. **State rank:** 35. **Pop change 1990-2000:** -7.1%.

Income: per capita $17,946; median household $37,028. **Pop below poverty level:** 13.9%.

Unemployment: 4.2%. **Median home value:** $84,200. **Median travel time to work:** 20.2 minutes.

COLUMBIA COUNTY
56 Warren St County Courthouse   **Ph:** 518-828-3339
Hudson, NY 12534   **Fax:** 518-828-5299

On central eastern border of NY, southeast of Albany; organized Apr 4, 1786 (prior to statehood) from Albany County. **Name Origin:** Feminine form of Columbus, a poetic and honorific reference to Christopher Columbus (1451-1506) and America.

All statistics are based on the 2000 Census except the dollar figures given for per capita income, which are based on 1999 estimates.

Area (sq mi): 648.27 (land 635.73; water 12.54).

Pop: 63,094 (White 90.9%; Black or African American 4.5%; Hispanic or Latino 2.5%; Asian 0.8%; Other 2.5%). **Foreign born:** 4.4%. **Median age:** 40.5. **State rank:** 41. **Pop change 1990-2000:** +0.2%.

Income: per capita $22,265; median household $41,915. **Pop below poverty level:** 9%.

Unemployment: 2.7%. **Median home value:** $111,800. **Median travel time to work:** 26.1 minutes.

CORTLAND COUNTY
60 Central Ave   **Ph:** 607-753-5021
Cortland, NY 13045   **Fax:** 607-758-5500
www.cortland-co.org

In south-central NY, south of Syracuse; organized Apr 8, 1808 from Onondaga County. **Name Origin:** For Pierre Van Cortland, Jr. (1762-1848), NY legislator, U.S. representative (1811-13), and banker.

Area (sq mi): 501.52 (land 499.65; water 1.87).

Pop: 48,599 (White 96.2%; Black or African American 0.9%; Hispanic or Latino 1.2%; Asian 0.4%; Other 1.8%). **Foreign born:** 2.2%. **Median age:** 34.2. **State rank:** 51. **Pop change 1990-2000:** -0.7%.

Income: per capita $16,622; median household $34,364. **Pop below poverty level:** 15.5%.

Unemployment: 6%. **Median home value:** $74,700. **Median travel time to work:** 21.1 minutes.

DELAWARE COUNTY
PO Box 426   **Ph:** 607-746-2123
Delhi, NY 13753   **Fax:** 607-746-6924
www.co.delaware.ny.us

In south-central NY, east of Binghamton; organized Mar 10, 1797 from Ulster and Otsego counties. **Name Origin:** For the Delaware River, whose two main branches flow through the county.

Area (sq mi): 1468.04 (land 1446.37; water 21.67).

Pop: 48,055 (White 95.1%; Black or African American 1.2%; Hispanic or Latino 2%; Asian 0.5%; Other 1.8%). **Foreign born:** 3.4%. **Median age:** 41.4. **State rank:** 53. **Pop change 1990-2000:** +1.8%.

Income: per capita $17,357; median household $32,461. **Pop below poverty level:** 12.9%.

Unemployment: 4.3%. **Median home value:** $74,200. **Median travel time to work:** 24 minutes.

DUTCHESS COUNTY
22 Market St   **Ph:** 845-486-2120
Poughkeepsie, NY 12601
www.co.dutchess.ny.us

In southeastern NY, north of NYC, original county, organized Nov 1, 1683. **Name Origin:** For Mary (1658-1718), Duchess of York, wife of James, Duke of York and Albany, later James II, king of England; spelling is 17th-century variant of *duchess*.

Area (sq mi): 825.38 (land 801.59; water 23.78).

Pop: 280,150 (White 80.3%; Black or African American 9.3%; Hispanic or Latino 6.4%; Asian 2.5%; Other 4.5%). **Foreign born:** 8.4%. **Median age:** 36.7. **State rank:** 15. **Pop change 1990-2000:** +8%.

Income: per capita $23,940; median household $53,086. **Pop below poverty level:** 7.5%.

Unemployment: 3.2%. **Median home value:** $154,200. **Median travel time to work:** 29.8 minutes.

ERIE COUNTY
25 Delaware Ave   **Ph:** 716-858-8785
Buffalo, NY 14202   **Fax:** 716-858-6550
www.erie.gov

On central western border of NY on Lake Erie, south of Niagara Falls; organized Apr 2, 1821 from Niagara County. **Name Origin:** For the Erie Indian tribe of Iroquoian linguistic stock, who lived along the southern shore of Lake Erie.

Area (sq mi): 1226.89 (land 1044.21; water 182.68).

Pop: 950,265 (White 80.8%; Black or African American 13%; Hispanic or Latino 3.3%; Asian 1.5%; Other 3.3%). **Foreign born:** 4.5%. **Median age:** 38. **State rank:** 7. **Pop change 1990-2000:** -1.9%.

Income: per capita $20,357; median household $38,567. **Pop below poverty level:** 12.2%.

Unemployment: 5.1%. **Median home value:** $90,800. **Median travel time to work:** 21.3 minutes.

ESSEX COUNTY
PO Box 247   **Ph:** 518-873-3600
Elizabethtown, NY 12932   **Fax:** 518-873-3548
www.co.essex.ny.us

On northeastern border of NY, southwest of Burlington, VT; organized Mar 1, 1799 from Clinton County. **Name Origin:** For the county of Essex, England.

Area (sq mi): 1916.5 (land 1796.8; water 119.7).

Pop: 38,851 (White 93.6%; Black or African American 2.8%; Hispanic or Latino 2.2%; Asian 0.4%; Other 2%). **Foreign born:** 3.4%. **Median age:** 39.4. **State rank:** 56. **Pop change 1990-2000:** +4.6%.

Income: per capita $18,194; median household $34,823. **Pop below poverty level:** 11.6%.

Unemployment: 5.3%. **Median home value:** $77,100. **Median travel time to work:** 20.7 minutes.

FRANKLIN COUNTY
355 W Main St PO Box 70   **Ph:** 518-481-1681
Malone, NY 12953   **Fax:** 518-483-9143
www.adirondacklakes.org

On northeastern border of NY, south of Montreal, prov. of Quebec, Canada; organized Mar 11, 1808 from Clinton County. **Name Origin:** For Benjamin Franklin (1706-90), U.S. patriot, diplomat, and statesman.

Area (sq mi): 1697.44 (land 1631.49; water 65.95).

Please see sample entry on inside front cover for detailed information about the statistics presented with each county listing.

397

Pop: 51,134 (White 82.6%; Black or African American 6.6%; Hispanic or Latino 4%; Asian 0.4%; Other 9%). **Foreign born:** 3.7%. **Median age:** 36.3. **State rank:** 48. **Pop change 1990-2000:** +9.9%.

Income: per capita $15,888; median household $31,517. **Pop below poverty level:** 14.6%.

Unemployment: 7%. **Median home value:** $62,600. **Median travel time to work:** 19.1 minutes.

FULTON COUNTY
223 W Main St   **Ph:** 518-736-5555
Johnstown, NY 12095   **Fax:** 518-762-3839
www.fultoncountyny.org

In east-central NY, east of Utica; organized Apr 18, 1838 from Montgomery County. **Name Origin:** For Robert Fulton (1765-1815), developer of the *Clermont*, the first commercially successful steamboat.

Area (sq mi): 532.9 (land 496.17; water 36.73).

Pop: 55,073 (White 95.1%; Black or African American 1.8%; Hispanic or Latino 1.6%; Asian 0.5%; Other 1.7%). **Foreign born:** 1.9%. **Median age:** 38.6. **State rank:** 45. **Pop change 1990-2000:** +1.6%.

Income: per capita $16,844; median household $33,663. **Pop below poverty level:** 12.5%.

Unemployment: 4.8%. **Median home value:** $67,400. **Median travel time to work:** 22.4 minutes.

GENESEE COUNTY
7 Main St   **Ph:** 585-344-2550
Batavia, NY 14020   **Fax:** 585-344-8582
www.co.genesee.ny.us

In northwestern NY, southeast of Rochester; organized Mar 30, 1802 from Ontario County. **Name Origin:** From the Iroquoian word probably meaning 'beautiful valley.'

Area (sq mi): 495.33 (land 494.11; water 1.22).

Pop: 60,370 (White 94.1%; Black or African American 2.1%; Hispanic or Latino 1.5%; Asian 0.5%; Other 2.7%). **Foreign born:** 2.2%. **Median age:** 37.4. **State rank:** 44. **Pop change 1990-2000:** +0.5%.

Income: per capita $18,498; median household $40,542. **Pop below poverty level:** 7.6%.

Unemployment: 5%. **Median home value:** $83,200. **Median travel time to work:** 22.4 minutes.

GREENE COUNTY
PO Box 446   **Ph:** 518-943-2050
Catskill, NY 12414   **Fax:** 518-943-2146
www.greene-ny.com

In southeastern NY, southwest of Albany; organized Mar 25, 1800 from Albany and Ulster counties. **Name Origin:** For Gen,. Nathanael Greene (1742-86), hero of the Revolutionary War; quartermaster general (1778-80).

Area (sq mi): 658.13 (land 647.75; water 10.38).

Pop: 48,195 (White 88.5%; Black or African American 5.5%; Hispanic or Latino 4.3%; Asian 0.5%; Other 3.2%). **Foreign born:**

6.4%. **Median age:** 39.1. **State rank:** 52. **Pop change 1990-2000:** +7.7%.

Income: per capita $18,931; median household $36,493. **Pop below poverty level:** 12.2%.

Unemployment: 4.4%. **Median home value:** $92,400. **Median travel time to work:** 29.1 minutes.

HAMILTON COUNTY
PO Box 204 Rt 8   **Ph:** 518-548-7111
Lake Pleasant, NY 12108   **Fax:** 518-548-9740

In north-central NY, northeast of Utica; organized Apr 12, 1816 from Montgomery County. **Name Origin:** For Alexander Hamilton (1757-1804), first U.S. secretary of the treasury (1789-95).

Area (sq mi): 1807.81 (land 1720.39; water 87.41).

Pop: 5,379 (White 97.1%; Black or African American 0.4%; Hispanic or Latino 1.1%; Asian 0.1%; Other 1.8%). **Foreign born:** 1.5%. **Median age:** 45.4. **State rank:** 62. **Pop change 1990-2000:** +1.9%.

Income: per capita $18,643; median household $32,287. **Pop below poverty level:** 10.4%.

Unemployment: 5.4%. **Median home value:** $86,700. **Median travel time to work:** 22.8 minutes.

HERKIMER COUNTY
109 Mary St Suite 1111   **Ph:** 315-867-1129
Herkimer, NY 13350   **Fax:** 315-866-4396

In north-central NY, east of Utica; organized Feb 16, 1791 from Montgomery County. **Name Origin:** For Gen. Nicholas Herkimer (1728-77), Revolutionary War officer and patriot, fatally wounded at the Battle of Oriskany. An earlier name was German Flats, for German settlers.

Area (sq mi): 1458.35 (land 1411.25; water 47.1).

Pop: 64,427 (White 97.3%; Black or African American 0.5%; Hispanic or Latino 0.9%; Asian 0.4%; Other 1.2%). **Foreign born:** 2%. **Median age:** 39. **State rank:** 38. **Pop change 1990-2000:** -2.1%.

Income: per capita $16,141; median household $32,924. **Pop below poverty level:** 12.5%.

Unemployment: 4.7%. **Median home value:** $67,500. **Median travel time to work:** 21.9 minutes.

JEFFERSON COUNTY
175 Arsenal St   **Ph:** 315-785-3081
Watertown, NY 13601   **Fax:** 315-785-5145
www.co.jefferson.ny.us

On central western border of NY on Lake Ontario; organized Mar 28, 1805 from Oneida County. **Name Origin:** For Thomas Jefferson (1743-1826), U.S. patriot and statesman; third U.S. president.

Area (sq mi): 1857.08 (land 1272.2; water 584.88).

Pop: 111,738 (White 87.2%; Black or African American 5.8%; Hispanic or Latino 4.2%; Asian 0.9%; Other 4.5%). **Foreign born:** 3.7%. **Median age:** 32.5. **State rank:** 26. **Pop change 1990-2000:** +0.7%.

Income: per capita $16,202; median household $34,006. **Pop below poverty level:** 13.3%.

All statistics are based on the 2000 Census except the dollar figures given for per capita income, which are based on 1999 estimates.

Unemployment: 8.1%. **Median home value:** $68,200. **Median travel time to work:** 18.4 minutes.

KINGS COUNTY

360 Adams St   **Ph:** 718-643-7037
Brooklyn, NY 11201

On the southwestern end of Long Island, east of Manhattan Island; original county, organized Nov 1, 1683. The county is coterminous with the borough of Brooklyn, part of New York City. **Name Origin:** For Charles II (1630-85), king of England.

Area (sq mi): 96.9 (land 70.61; water 26.29).

Pop: 2,465,326 (White 34.7%; Black or African American 36.4%; Hispanic or Latino 19.8%; Asian 7.5%; Other 14.9%). **Foreign born:** 37.8%. **Median age:** 33.1. **State rank:** 1. **Pop change 1990-2000:** +7.2%.

Income: per capita $16,775; median household $32,135. **Pop below poverty level:** 25.1%.

Unemployment: 6.7%. **Median home value:** $224,100. **Median travel time to work:** 43.2 minutes.

LEWIS COUNTY

PO Box 232   **Ph:** 315-376-5333
Lowville, NY 13367   **Fax:** 315-376-3768
lewiscountyny.org

In north-central NY, east of Syracuse; organized Mar 28, 1805 from Oneida County. **Name Origin:** For Morgan Lewis (1754-1844), officer in the Revolutionary War and the War of 1812, NY legislator, and governor (1804-07).

Area (sq mi): 1289.89 (land 1275.42; water 14.47).

Pop: 26,944 (White 97.8%; Black or African American 0.4%; Hispanic or Latino 0.6%; Asian 0.2%; Other 1.3%). **Foreign born:** 1.1%. **Median age:** 36.8. **State rank:** 59. **Pop change 1990-2000:** +0.6%.

Income: per capita $14,971; median household $34,361. **Pop below poverty level:** 13.2%.

Unemployment: 8.6%. **Median home value:** $63,600. **Median travel time to work:** 21 minutes.

LIVINGSTON COUNTY

6 Court St Rm 201   **Ph:** 585-243-7010
Geneseo, NY 14454
www.co.livingston.state.ny.us

In western NY, south of Rochester; organized Feb 23, 1821 from Genesee and Ontario counties. **Name Origin:** For Robert R. Livingston (1746-1813), NY patriot, statesman, and a drafter of the Declaration of Independence.

Area (sq mi): 640.44 (land 632.13; water 8.32).

Pop: 64,328 (White 92.9%; Black or African American 3%; Hispanic or Latino 2.3%; Asian 0.8%; Other 2.1%). **Foreign born:** 2.6%. **Median age:** 35.3. **State rank:** 39. **Pop change 1990-2000:** +3.1%.

Income: per capita $18,062; median household $42,066. **Pop below poverty level:** 10.4%.

Unemployment: 4.6%. **Median home value:** $88,800. **Median travel time to work:** 25.3 minutes.

MADISON COUNTY

PO Box 668   **Ph:** 315-366-2261
Wampsville, NY 13163   **Fax:** 315-366-2615
www.madisoncounty.org

In central NY, east of Syracuse; organized Mar 21, 1806 from Chenango County. **Name Origin:** For James Madison (1751-1836), U.S. secretary of state at the time of the county's creation, later fourth U.S. president.

Area (sq mi): 661.54 (land 655.86; water 5.69).

Pop: 69,441 (White 95.9%; Black or African American 1.3%; Hispanic or Latino 1.1%; Asian 0.6%; Other 1.6%). **Foreign born:** 2.2%. **Median age:** 36.1. **State rank:** 37. **Pop change 1990-2000:** +0.5%.

Income: per capita $19,105; median household $40,184. **Pop below poverty level:** 9.8%.

Unemployment: 5%. **Median home value:** $81,500. **Median travel time to work:** 22.6 minutes.

MONROE COUNTY

39 W Main St Rm 101   **Ph:** 585-428-5151
Rochester, NY 14614   **Fax:** 585-428-5447
www.monroecounty.gov

On northwestern border of NY on Lake Ontario; organized Feb 23, 1821 from Genesee and Ontario counties. **Name Origin:** For James Monroe (1758-1831), fifth U.S. president, in office at the time of the county's creation.

Area (sq mi): 1365.61 (land 659.29; water 706.31).

Pop: 735,343 (White 77.1%; Black or African American 13.7%; Hispanic or Latino 5.3%; Asian 2.4%; Other 4.6%). **Foreign born:** 7.3%. **Median age:** 36.1. **State rank:** 9. **Pop change 1990-2000:** +3%.

Income: per capita $22,821; median household $44,891. **Pop below poverty level:** 11.2%.

Unemployment: 4.4%. **Median home value:** $98,700. **Median travel time to work:** 19.6 minutes.

MONTGOMERY COUNTY

PO Box 1500   **Ph:** 518-853-3431
Fonda, NY 12068   **Fax:** 518-853-8220
www.co.montgomery.ny.us

In south-central NY, northwest of Albany; organized as Tryon County Mar 12, 1772 (prior to statehood) from Albany County; name changed Apr 2, 1784. **Name Origin:** For Gen. Richard Montgomery (1736-75), Revolutionary War officer.

Area (sq mi): 410.32 (land 404.82; water 5.51).

Pop: 49,708 (White 90.7%; Black or African American 1.2%; Hispanic or Latino 6.9%; Asian 0.5%; Other 3.4%). **Foreign born:** 3.2%. **Median age:** 39.7. **State rank:** 50. **Pop change 1990-2000:** -4.4%.

Income: per capita $17,005; median household $32,128. **Pop below poverty level:** 12%.

Unemployment: 5.7%. **Median home value:** $67,600. **Median travel time to work:** 23.3 minutes.

Please see sample entry on inside front cover for detailed information about the statistics presented with each county listing.

NASSAU COUNTY
240 Old Country Rd   **Ph:** 516-571-2664
Mineola, NY 11501   **Fax:** 516-742-4099
www.co.nassau.ny.us

On the western end of Long Island, east of Manhattan Island; organized Apr 27, 1898 from Queens County. **Name Origin:** For the duchy in Germany associated with the House of Orange, hence with William, Prince of Orange (1650-1702), later William III, King of England.

Area (sq mi): 453.08 (land 286.69; water 166.39).

Pop: 1,334,544 (White 74%; Black or African American 10.1%; Hispanic or Latino 10%; Asian 4.7%; Other 5.9%). **Foreign born:** 17.9%. **Median age:** 38.5. **State rank:** 5. **Pop change 1990-2000:** +3.7%.

Income: per capita $32,151; median household $72,030. **Pop below poverty level:** 5.2%.

Unemployment: 3.1%. **Median home value:** $242,300. **Median travel time to work:** 34.3 minutes.

NEW YORK COUNTY
60 Centre St   **Ph:** 212-374-8359
New York, NY 10007

Primarily on Manhattan Island at the southeastern tip of NY, west of Long Island; original county, organized Nov 1, 1683. The county is coterminous with the borough of Manhattan, part of New York City. **Name Origin:** Named in 1664 when Col. Richard Nicolls seized the Dutch territories for King Charles II of England, who granted them to his brother, James (1633-1701), Duke of York and Albany, later James II, King of England. Lands east of the Hudson River were called Yorkshire, later New York. Called Nieuw Amsterdam by the Dutch.

Area (sq mi): 33.77 (land 22.96; water 10.81).

Pop: 1,537,195 (White 45.8%; Black or African American 17.4%; Hispanic or Latino 27.2%; Asian 9.4%; Other 18.8%). **Foreign born:** 29.4%. **Median age:** 35.7. **State rank:** 3. **Pop change 1990-2000:** +3.3%.

Income: per capita $42,922; median household $47,030. **Pop below poverty level:** 20%.

Unemployment: 6%. **Median home value:** $1,000,001. **Median travel time to work:** 30.5 minutes.

NIAGARA COUNTY
PO Box 461   **Ph:** 716-439-7022
Lockport, NY 14095   **Fax:** 716-439-7066
www.niagaracounty.com

In northwestern corner of NY on Lake Ontario; organized Mar 11, 1808 from Genesee County. **Name Origin:** For the Niagara River, which forms its western border.

Area (sq mi): 1139.83 (land 522.95; water 616.89).

Pop: 219,846 (White 90%; Black or African American 6.1%; Hispanic or Latino 1.3%; Asian 0.6%; Other 2.5%). **Foreign born:** 3.9%. **Median age:** 38.2. **State rank:** 17. **Pop change 1990-2000:** -0.4%.

Income: per capita $19,219; median household $38,136. **Pop below poverty level:** 10.6%.

Unemployment: 6.6%. **Median home value:** $82,600. **Median travel time to work:** 20.1 minutes.

ONEIDA COUNTY
800 Park Ave   **Ph:** 315-798-5790
Utica, NY 13501   **Fax:** 315-798-5790
www.co.oneida.ny.us

In central NY, northeast of Syracuse; organized May 15, 1798 from Herkimer County. **Name Origin:** For the Oneida Indian tribe of Iroquoian linguistic stock; one of the Five Nations of the Iroquois. The name probably means 'stone people,' perhaps in praise of their bravery.

Area (sq mi): 1257.11 (land 1212.7; water 44.41).

Pop: 235,469 (White 88.6%; Black or African American 5.7%; Hispanic or Latino 3.2%; Asian 1.2%; Other 2.8%). **Foreign born:** 5.2%. **Median age:** 38.2. **State rank:** 16. **Pop change 1990-2000:** -6.1%.

Income: per capita $18,516; median household $35,909. **Pop below poverty level:** 13%.

Unemployment: 4.6%. **Median home value:** $76,500. **Median travel time to work:** 20.1 minutes.

ONONDAGA COUNTY
401 Montgomery St Rm 200   **Ph:** 315-435-2226
Syracuse, NY 13202   **Fax:** 315-435-3455
www.co.onondaga.ny.us

In north-central NY, southwest of Rome; organized Mar 5, 1794. **Name Origin:** For the lake, named for the Onondaga Indian tribe, one of the Five Nations of the Iroquois; name probably means 'hill people.'

Area (sq mi): 805.69 (land 780.29; water 25.4).

Pop: 458,336 (White 83.7%; Black or African American 9.4%; Hispanic or Latino 2.4%; Asian 2.1%; Other 3.8%). **Foreign born:** 5.7%. **Median age:** 36.3. **State rank:** 10. **Pop change 1990-2000:** -2.3%.

Income: per capita $21,336; median household $40,847. **Pop below poverty level:** 12.2%.

Unemployment: 4.2%. **Median home value:** $85,400. **Median travel time to work:** 19.3 minutes.

ONTARIO COUNTY
20 Ontario St   **Ph:** 585-396-4200
Canandaigua, NY 14424   **Fax:** 585-393-2951
www.co.ontario.ny.us

In west-central NY, southeast of Rochester, organized Jan 27, 1789 from Montgomery County. **Name Origin:** For Lake Ontario.

Area (sq mi): 662.43 (land 644.38; water 18.05).

Pop: 100,224 (White 94%; Black or African American 2.1%; Hispanic or Latino 2.1%; Asian 0.7%; Other 2.2%). **Foreign born:** 2.7%. **Median age:** 37.9. **State rank:** 27. **Pop change 1990-2000:** +5.4%.

Income: per capita $21,533; median household $44,579. **Pop below poverty level:** 7.3%.

All statistics are based on the 2000 Census except the dollar figures given for per capita income, which are based on 1999 estimates.

Unemployment: 4.3%. **Median home value:** $94,100. **Median travel time to work:** 23.2 minutes.

ORANGE COUNTY

255 Main St   **Ph:** 845-291-2700
Goshen, NY 10924   **Fax:** 845-291-2724
www.co.orange.ny.us

In southeastern NY, southwest of Poughkeepsie; original county, organized Nov 1, 1683. **Name Origin:** For William of Orange (1650-1702), later William III, king of England.

Area (sq mi): 838.55 (land 816.34; water 22.21).

Pop: 341,367 (White 77.6%; Black or African American 8.1%; Hispanic or Latino 11.6%; Asian 1.5%; Other 6.7%). **Foreign born:** 8.4%. **Median age:** 34.7. **State rank:** 12. **Pop change 1990-2000:** +11%.

Income: per capita $21,597; median household $52,058. **Pop below poverty level:** 10.5%.

Unemployment: 3.6%. **Median home value:** $144,500. **Median travel time to work:** 32.5 minutes.

ORLEANS COUNTY

3 S Main St   **Ph:** 585-589-5334
Albion, NY 14411   **Fax:** 585-589-0181
www.orleansny.com

On northwestern border of NY, on Lake Ontario, west of Rochester; organized Nov 12, 1824 from Genesee County. **Name Origin:** For the French city of Orleans

Area (sq mi): 817.47 (land 391.4; water 426.07).

Pop: 44,171 (White 87.3%; Black or African American 7.3%; Hispanic or Latino 3.9%; Asian 0.3%; Other 3.2%). **Foreign born:** 2.7%. **Median age:** 36.2. **State rank:** 54. **Pop change 1990-2000:** +5.6%.

Income: per capita $16,457; median household $37,972. **Pop below poverty level:** 10.8%.

Unemployment: 5.5%. **Median home value:** $72,600. **Median travel time to work:** 25.7 minutes.

OSWEGO COUNTY

46 E Bridge St   **Ph:** 315-349-8385
Oswego, NY 13126   **Fax:** 315-349-8383
www.co.oswego.ny.us/

In northwestern NY on Lake Ontario, north of Syracuse; organized Mar 1, 1816 from Oneida and Onondage counties. **Name Origin:** For the Oswego River, which runs through its western part; from Iroquoian *osh-we-go*, probably 'outpouring,' in reference to the mouth of the Oswego River where it empties into Lake Ontario, also translated 'the place where the valley widens.'

Area (sq mi): 1312.18 (land 953.3; water 358.88).

Pop: 122,377 (White 96.5%; Black or African American 0.6%; Hispanic or Latino 1.3%; Asian 0.4%; Other 1.8%). **Foreign born:** 1.6%. **Median age:** 35. **State rank:** 24. **Pop change 1990-2000:** +0.5%.

Income: per capita $16,853; median household $36,598. **Pop below poverty level:** 14%.

Unemployment: 6.5%. **Median home value:** $74,200. **Median travel time to work:** 24.4 minutes.

OTSEGO COUNTY

PO Box 710   **Ph:** 607-547-4275
Cooperstown, NY 13326   **Fax:** 607-547-7544
www.otsegocounty.com

In south-central NY, south of Utica; organized Feb 16, 1791 from Montgomery County. **Name Origin:** Iroquoian 'rock site' or 'place of the rock.'

Area (sq mi): 1015.1 (land 1002.8; water 12.31).

Pop: 61,676 (White 94.6%; Black or African American 1.7%; Hispanic or Latino 1.9%; Asian 0.6%; Other 1.8%). **Foreign born:** 2.3%. **Median age:** 37.1. **State rank:** 42. **Pop change 1990-2000:** +1.9%.

Income: per capita $16,806; median household $33,444. **Pop below poverty level:** 14.9%.

Unemployment: 4.3%. **Median home value:** $75,900. **Median travel time to work:** 22.4 minutes.

PUTNAM COUNTY

40 Gleneida Ave   **Ph:** 845-225-3641
Carmel, NY 10512   **Fax:** 845-228-0231
www.putnamcountyny.com

In southeastern NY, southeast of Poughkeepsie; organized Jun 12, 1812 from Dutchess County. **Name Origin:** For Israel Putnam (1718-90), MA general and American commander at the Battle of Bunker Hill.

Area (sq mi): 246.25 (land 231.28; water 14.97).

Pop: 95,745 (White 89.8%; Black or African American 1.6%; Hispanic or Latino 6.2%; Asian 1.2%; Other 3.2%). **Foreign born:** 8.8%. **Median age:** 37.4. **State rank:** 30. **Pop change 1990-2000:** +14.1%.

Income: per capita $30,127; median household $72,279. **Pop below poverty level:** 4.4%.

Unemployment: 2.7%. **Median home value:** $206,900. **Median travel time to work:** 38.4 minutes.

QUEENS COUNTY

88-11 Sutphin Blvd   **Ph:** 718-520-3136
Jamaica, NY 11435   **Fax:** 718-520-4731

In western end of Long Island, east of Brooklyn; original county, organized Nov 1, 1683. The county is coterminous with the borough of Queens, part of New York City. Includes the following areas; Astoria, Bay Ridge, Flushing, Forest Hills, Howard Beach, Jackson Heights, and Ozone Park. **Name Origin:** For Queen Catharine of Braganza (1638-1705), wife of King Charles II of England.

Area (sq mi): 178.28 (land 109.24; water 69.04).

Pop: 2,229,379 (White 32.9%; Black or African American 20%; Hispanic or Latino 25%; Asian 17.6%; Other 18.4%). **Foreign born:** 46.1%. **Median age:** 35.4. **State rank:** 2. **Pop change 1990-2000:** +14.2%.

Income: per capita $19,222; median household $42,439. **Pop below poverty level:** 14.6%.

Please see sample entry on inside front cover for detailed information about the statistics presented with each county listing.

Unemployment: 5.1%. **Median home value:** $212,600. **Median travel time to work:** 42.2 minutes.

RENSSELAER COUNTY

1600 7th Ave   **Ph:** 518-270-2700
Troy, NY 12180   **Fax:** 518-270-2961
www.rensco.com

On central eastern border of NY, east of Albany; organized Feb 7, 1791 from Albany County. **Name Origin:** For Kiliaen Van Rensselaer (1595-1644), one of the early patrons of the Dutch New Netherlands territories and a founder of the Dutch West India Company. Much of the territory of the county had been granted him by patent in 1630.

Area (sq mi): 665.39 (land 653.96; water 11.43).

Pop: 152,538 (White 90.2%; Black or African American 4.7%; Hispanic or Latino 2.1%; Asian 1.7%; Other 2.4%). **Foreign born:** 3.7%. **Median age:** 36.7. **State rank:** 21. **Pop change 1990-2000:** -1.2%.

Income: per capita $21,095; median household $42,905. **Pop below poverty level:** 9.5%.

Unemployment: 3.8%. **Median home value:** $102,900. **Median travel time to work:** 23.7 minutes.

RICHMOND COUNTY

130 Stuyvesant Pl   **Ph:** 718-390-5393
Staten Island, NY 10301   **Fax:** 718-390-5269

Coterminous with Staten Island in New York Bay between Long Island and New Jersey; original county, organized Nov 1, 1683. The county is coterminous with the borough of Staten Island, part of New York City. **Name Origin:** For Charles Lennox (1672-1723), first Duke of Richmond, son of King Charles II of England (1630-85).

Area (sq mi): 102.5 (land 58.48; water 44.02).

Pop: 443,728 (White 71.3%; Black or African American 9.7%; Hispanic or Latino 12.1%; Asian 5.7%; Other 7%). **Foreign born:** 16.4%. **Median age:** 35.9. **State rank:** 11. **Pop change 1990-2000:** +17.1%.

Income: per capita $23,905; median household $55,039. **Pop below poverty level:** 10%.

Unemployment: 4.8%. **Median home value:** $209,100. **Median travel time to work:** 43.9 minutes.

ROCKLAND COUNTY

11 New Hempstead Rd   **Ph:** 845-638-5100
New City, NY 10956   **Fax:** 845-638-5675
www.co.rockland.ny.us

In southeastern NY, northwest of NYC; organized Feb 23, 1798 from Orange County. **Name Origin:** For the rugged land and the Palisades on the Hudson River, which form its eastern border.

Area (sq mi): 199.34 (land 174.22; water 25.12).

Pop: 286,753 (White 71.7%; Black or African American 11%; Hispanic or Latino 10.2%; Asian 5.5%; Other 6.6%). **Foreign born:** 19.1%. **Median age:** 36.2. **State rank:** 14. **Pop change 1990-2000:** +8%.

Income: per capita $28,082; median household $67,971. **Pop below poverty level:** 9.5%.

Unemployment: 3.1%. **Median home value:** $242,500. **Median travel time to work:** 32.6 minutes.

SAINT LAWRENCE COUNTY

48 Court St   **Ph:** 315-379-2237
Canton, NY 13617   **Fax:** 315-379-2302
www.co.st-lawrence.ny.us

On northwestern border of NY, north of Watertown; organized Mar 3, 1802 from Clinton, Montgomery, and Herkimer counties. **Name Origin:** For the Saint Lawrence River, which forms its western boundary.

Area (sq mi): 2821.48 (land 2685.6; water 135.88).

Pop: 111,931 (White 93.6%; Black or African American 2.4%; Hispanic or Latino 1.8%; Asian 0.7%; Other 2.4%). **Foreign born:** 3.4%. **Median age:** 35.4. **State rank:** 25. **Pop change 1990-2000:** +0%.

Income: per capita $15,728; median household $32,356. **Pop below poverty level:** 16.9%.

Unemployment: 7.6%. **Median home value:** $60,200. **Median travel time to work:** 20.2 minutes.

SARATOGA COUNTY

40 McMaster St   **Ph:** 518-885-5381
Ballston Spa, NY 12020   **Fax:** 518-884-4726
www.co.saratoga.ny.us

In east-central NY, north of Albany; organized Feb 7, 1791 from Albany County. **Name Origin:** Of Indian origin; possibly from Mohawk word meaning 'springs from the hillside', or from Iroquois for 'beaver place.'

Area (sq mi): 843.71 (land 811.84; water 31.87).

Pop: 200,635 (White 95.1%; Black or African American 1.4%; Hispanic or Latino 1.4%; Asian 1%; Other 1.6%). **Foreign born:** 3.1%. **Median age:** 36.9. **State rank:** 18. **Pop change 1990-2000:** +10.7%.

Income: per capita $23,945; median household $49,460. **Pop below poverty level:** 5.7%.

Unemployment: 3%. **Median home value:** $120,400. **Median travel time to work:** 25 minutes.

SCHENECTADY COUNTY

620 State St   **Ph:** 518-388-4222
Schenectady, NY 12305
govt.co.schenectady.ny.us

In east-central NY, northwest of Albany; organized Mar 7, 1809 from Albany County. **Name Origin:** For the city, its county seat.

Area (sq mi): 209.62 (land 206.1; water 3.52).

Pop: 146,555 (White 86.3%; Black or African American 6.8%; Hispanic or Latino 3.2%; Asian 2%; Other 3.4%). **Foreign born:** 5.3%. **Median age:** 38.6. **State rank:** 22. **Pop change 1990-2000:** -1.8%.

Income: per capita $21,992; median household $41,739. **Pop below poverty level:** 10.9%.

Unemployment: 3%. **Median home value:** $94,500. **Median travel time to work:** 21.8 minutes.

All statistics are based on the 2000 Census except the dollar figures given for per capita income, which are based on 1999 estimates.

SCHOHARIE COUNTY

PO Box 429   **Ph:** 518-295-8347
Schoharie, NY 12157   **Fax:** 518-295-8482

In south-central NY, west of Albany; organized Apr 6, 1795 from Albany and Otsego counties. **Name Origin:** For the Schoharie Creek, which runs through it; from Iroquoian for 'driftwood.' Variants include: *skoharle, towasschoher, shoary, skohary*, and *schughhorre*.

Area (sq mi): 626.36 (land 622.02; water 4.34).

Pop: 31,582 (White 95.3%; Black or African American 1.3%; Hispanic or Latino 1.9%; Asian 0.4%; Other 1.7%). **Foreign born:** 2.4%. **Median age:** 38. **State rank:** 58. **Pop change 1990-2000:** -0.9%.

Income: per capita $17,778; median household $36,585. **Pop below poverty level:** 11.4%.

Unemployment: 4.2%. **Median home value:** $82,500. **Median travel time to work:** 28.5 minutes.

SCHUYLER COUNTY

105 9th St   **Ph:** 607-535-8133
Watkins Glen, NY 14891   **Fax:** 607-535-8130
www.lightlink.com/schco/

In north-central NY, southeast of Rochester; organized Apr 17, 1854 from Tompkins, Steuben, and Chemung counties. **Name Origin:** For Gen. Philip John Schuyler (1733-1804), an officer in the Revolutionary War, NY legislator, and U.S. senator (1789-91; 1797-98).

Area (sq mi): 342.22 (land 328.71; water 13.51).

Pop: 19,224 (White 95.8%; Black or African American 1.5%; Hispanic or Latino 1.2%; Asian 0.3%; Other 1.8%). **Foreign born:** 1.2%. **Median age:** 38.8. **State rank:** 61. **Pop change 1990-2000:** +3%.

Income: per capita $17,039; median household $36,010. **Pop below poverty level:** 11.8%.

Unemployment: 6.7%. **Median home value:** $68,400. **Median travel time to work:** 25.4 minutes.

SENECA COUNTY

1 DiPronio Dr   **Ph:** 315-539-1800
Waterloo, NY 13165   **Fax:** 315-539-9479
www.co.seneca.ny.us

In north-central NY, southeast of Rochester; organized Mar 24, 1804 from Cayuga County. **Name Origin:** For the Seneca Indians, one of the Five Nations of the Iroquois.

Area (sq mi): 390.51 (land 324.91; water 65.6).

Pop: 33,342 (White 94%; Black or African American 2.3%; Hispanic or Latino 2%; Asian 0.7%; Other 2%). **Foreign born:** 2.4%. **Median age:** 38.2. **State rank:** 57. **Pop change 1990-2000:** -1%.

Income: per capita $17,630; median household $37,140. **Pop below poverty level:** 11.5%.

Unemployment: 4.4%. **Median home value:** $72,400. **Median travel time to work:** 22.5 minutes.

STEUBEN COUNTY

3 E Pulteny Sq   **Ph:** 607-776-9631
Bath, NY 14810   **Fax:** 607-776-7158
www.steubencony.org

On central southern border of NY, south of Rochester; organized Mar 17, 1796 from Ontario County. **Name Origin:** For Baron Friedrich Wilhelm von Steuben (1730-94), Prussian soldier and inspector general of the Continental Army during the American Revolution.

Area (sq mi): 1404.1 (land 1392.64; water 11.45).

Pop: 98,726 (White 95.9%; Black or African American 1.4%; Hispanic or Latino 0.8%; Asian 0.9%; Other 1.3%). **Foreign born:** 1.9%. **Median age:** 38.2. **State rank:** 28. **Pop change 1990-2000:** -0.4%.

Income: per capita $18,197; median household $35,479. **Pop below poverty level:** 13.2%.

Unemployment: 5.7%. **Median home value:** $66,200. **Median travel time to work:** 21.6 minutes.

SUFFOLK COUNTY

PO Box 6100   **Ph:** 631-853-4000
Hauppauge, NY 11788   **Fax:** 631-853-4818
www.co.suffolk.ny.us

On eastern end of Long Island, NY; original county, organized Nov 1, 1683. **Name Origin:** For Suffolk County, England.

Area (sq mi): 2373.07 (land 912.2; water 1460.87).

Pop: 1,419,369 (White 78.8%; Black or African American 6.9%; Hispanic or Latino 10.5%; Asian 2.4%; Other 6.1%). **Foreign born:** 11.2%. **Median age:** 36.5. **State rank:** 4. **Pop change 1990-2000:** +7.4%.

Income: per capita $26,577; median household $65,288. **Pop below poverty level:** 6%.

Unemployment: 3.5%. **Median home value:** $185,200. **Median travel time to work:** 31.8 minutes.

SULLIVAN COUNTY

100 North St   **Ph:** 845-794-3000
Monticello, NY 12701   **Fax:** 845-794-6928
www.co.sullivan.ny.us

In south-central NY, west of Poughkeepsie; organized Mar 27, 1809 from Ulster County. **Name Origin:** For Gen. John Sullivan (1740-95), Revolutionary War officer, member of the Continental Congress (1780-81), and president of NH (1786, 1787, 1789).

Area (sq mi): 996.85 (land 969.71; water 27.14).

Pop: 73,966 (White 80.1%; Black or African American 8.5%; Hispanic or Latino 9.2%; Asian 1.1%; Other 5.1%). **Foreign born:** 7.9%. **Median age:** 38.8. **State rank:** 36. **Pop change 1990-2000:** +6.8%.

Income: per capita $18,892; median household $36,998. **Pop below poverty level:** 16.3%.

Unemployment: 4.9%. **Median home value:** $93,300. **Median travel time to work:** 29.3 minutes.

Please see sample entry on inside front cover for detailed information about the statistics presented with each county listing.

TIOGA COUNTY

PO Box 307
Owego, NY 13827
www.tiogacountyny.com

Ph: 607-687-0562
Fax: 607-687-3240

On central southern border of NY, south of Ithaca; organized Feb 16, 1791 from Montgomery County. **Name Origin:** For the Iroquoian town on the Susquehanna River near Athens, PA, just south of the county line; from Iroquoian probably meaning 'place between two points' or 'at the forks.'

Area (sq mi): 522.91 (land 518.69; water 4.21).

Pop: 51,784 (White 96.9%; Black or African American 0.5%; Hispanic or Latino 1%; Asian 0.6%; Other 1.3%). **Foreign born:** 1.7%. **Median age:** 38. **State rank:** 46. **Pop change 1990-2000:** -1.1%.

Income: per capita $18,673; median household $40,266. **Pop below poverty level:** 8.4%.

Unemployment: 4.2%. **Median home value:** $77,400. **Median travel time to work:** 24.8 minutes.

TOMPKINS COUNTY

320 N Tioga St
Ithaca, NY 14850
www.co.tompkins.ny.us

Ph: 607-274-5431
Fax: 607-274-5445

In south-central NY, northeast of Elmira; organized Apr 7, 1817 from Cayuga and Seneca counties. **Name Origin:** For Daniel D. Tompkins (1774-1825), associate justice of the NY supreme court (1804-07), governor (1807-17) and U.S. vice president (1817-25).

Area (sq mi): 491.63 (land 476.05; water 15.57).

Pop: 96,501 (White 83.8%; Black or African American 3.6%; Hispanic or Latino 3.1%; Asian 7.2%; Other 3.7%). **Foreign born:** 10.5%. **Median age:** 28.6. **State rank:** 29. **Pop change 1990-2000:** +2.6%.

Income: per capita $19,659; median household $37,272. **Pop below poverty level:** 17.6%.

Unemployment: 2.6%. **Median home value:** $101,600. **Median travel time to work:** 17.8 minutes.

ULSTER COUNTY

PO Box 1800
Kingston, NY 12402
www.co.ulster.ny.us

Ph: 845-340-3288
Fax: 845-340-3299

In southeastern NY, west of Poughkeepsie; original county, organized Nov 1, 1683. **Name Origin:** For Ulster, Ireland, the earldom of the Duke of York, specifically honoring James Stuart (1633-1701), later James II, king of England.

Area (sq mi): 1160.76 (land 1126.48; water 34.28).

Pop: 177,749 (White 85.5%; Black or African American 5.4%; Hispanic or Latino 6.2%; Asian 1.2%; Other 4.5%). **Foreign born:** 5.9%. **Median age:** 38.2. **State rank:** 20. **Pop change 1990-2000:** +7.5%.

Income: per capita $20,846; median household $42,551. **Pop below poverty level:** 11.4%.

Unemployment: 3.5%. **Median home value:** $113,100. **Median travel time to work:** 26.9 minutes.

WARREN COUNTY

1340 State Rt 9
Lake George, NY 12845
www.co.warren.ny.us

Ph: 518-761-6429
Fax: 518-761-6551

In northeastern NY, north of Saratoga; organized Mar 12, 1813 from Washington County. **Name Origin:** For Joseph Warren (1741-75), Revolutionary War patriot and member of the Continental Congress who dispatched Paul Revere (1735-1818) on his famous ride.

Area (sq mi): 931.66 (land 869.29; water 62.37).

Pop: 63,303 (White 96.8%; Black or African American 0.6%; Hispanic or Latino 1%; Asian 0.5%; Other 1.3%). **Foreign born:** 2.4%. **Median age:** 39. **State rank:** 40. **Pop change 1990-2000:** +6.9%.

Income: per capita $20,727; median household $39,198. **Pop below poverty level:** 9.7%.

Unemployment: 4.8%. **Median home value:** $97,500. **Median travel time to work:** 21.4 minutes.

WASHINGTON COUNTY

383 Broadway Bldg A
Fort Edward, NY 12828

Ph: 518-746-2170
Fax: 518-746-2166

On central eastern border of NY, east of Glens Falls; organized as Charlotte County Mar 12, 1772 (prior to statehood) from Albany County. **Name Origin:** For George Washington (1732-99), American patriot and first U.S. president. Name changed Apr 2, 1784 from Charlotte, which had been given to honor the wife of King George III of England (1738-1820).

Area (sq mi): 845.84 (land 835.44; water 10.4).

Pop: 61,042 (White 94%; Black or African American 2.9%; Hispanic or Latino 2%; Asian 0.3%; Other 1.8%). **Foreign born:** 1.9%. **Median age:** 37.5. **State rank:** 43. **Pop change 1990-2000:** +2.9%.

Income: per capita $17,958; median household $37,668. **Pop below poverty level:** 9.4%.

Unemployment: 3.9%. **Median home value:** $77,400. **Median travel time to work:** 24.4 minutes.

WAYNE COUNTY

26 Church St
Lyons, NY 14489
www.co.wayne.ny.us

Ph: 315-946-5400
Fax: 315-946-5407

On central western border of NY on Lake Ontario, east of Rochester; organized Apr 11, 1823 from Ontario and Seneca counties. **Name Origin:** For Gen. Anthony Wayne (1745-1796), PA soldier and statesman, nicknamed 'Mad Anthony' for his daring during the American Revolution.

Area (sq mi): 1384.14 (land 604.21; water 779.93).

Pop: 93,765 (White 92.5%; Black or African American 3.2%; Hispanic or Latino 2.4%; Asian 0.5%; Other 2.5%). **Foreign born:** 2.3%. **Median age:** 36.9. **State rank:** 31. **Pop change 1990-2000:** +5.2%.

Income: per capita $19,258; median household $44,157. **Pop below poverty level:** 8.6%.

Unemployment: 5.3%. **Median home value:** $85,700. **Median travel time to work:** 24.6 minutes.

All statistics are based on the 2000 Census except the dollar figures given for per capita income, which are based on 1999 estimates.

WESTCHESTER COUNTY

110 Dr ML King Jr Blvd   **Ph:** 914-995-3080
White Plains, NY 10601
www.co.westchester.ny.us

In southwestern NY, north of New York City; original county, organized Nov 1, 1683. **Name Origin:** For the town and county of Chester in England.

Area (sq mi): 500.08 (land 432.82; water 67.26).

Pop: 923,459 (White 64.1%; Black or African American 14.2%; Hispanic or Latino 15.6%; Asian 4.5%; Other 9.9%). **Foreign born:** 22.2%. **Median age:** 37.6. **State rank:** 8. **Pop change 1990-2000:** +5.6%.

Income: per capita $36,726; median household $63,582. **Pop below poverty level:** 8.8%.

Unemployment: 3.5%. **Median home value:** $325,800. **Median travel time to work:** 32.7 minutes.

WYOMING COUNTY

143 N Main St   **Ph:** 585-786-8810
Warsaw, NY 14569   **Fax:** 585-786-3703

In northwestern NY, southeast of Buffalo, organized May 19, 1841 from Genesee County. **Name Origin:** From an Indian word *maughwauwame* 'large meadows,' originally applied to a valley in northeastern PA, but made famous in the popular poem 'Gertrude of Wyoming,' published in 1809 by British poet Thomas Campbell (1777-1844).

Area (sq mi): 596.44 (land 592.91; water 3.53).

Pop: 43,424 (White 90.6%; Black or African American 5.5%; Hispanic or Latino 2.9%; Asian 0.4%; Other 2.3%). **Foreign born:** 2.3%. **Median age:** 36.7. **State rank:** 55. **Pop change 1990-2000:** +2.2%.

Income: per capita $17,248; median household $39,895. **Pop below poverty level:** 8.4%.

Unemployment: 5.4%. **Median home value:** $74,000. **Median travel time to work:** 25.6 minutes.

YATES COUNTY

417 Liberty St   **Ph:** 315-536-5120
Penn Yan, NY 14527   **Fax:** 315-536-5545
www.yatesny.com

In northwestern NY, southeast of Rochester; organized Feb 5, 1823 from Ontario County. **Name Origin:** For Joseph Christopher Yates (1768-1837), NY supreme court justice (1808-22) and governor (1823-24) at the time of the county's creation.

Area (sq mi): 375.76 (land 338.24; water 37.52).

Pop: 24,621 (White 97.4%; Black or African American 0.6%; Hispanic or Latino 0.9%; Asian 0.3%; Other 1.2%). **Foreign born:** 2.3%. **Median age:** 37.9. **State rank:** 60. **Pop change 1990-2000:** +7.9%.

Income: per capita $16,781; median household $34,640. **Pop below poverty level:** 13.1%.

Unemployment: 3.5%. **Median home value:** $75,600. **Median travel time to work:** 23.6 minutes.

Please see sample entry on inside front cover for detailed information about the statistics presented with each county listing.

NORTH CAROLINA - Counties

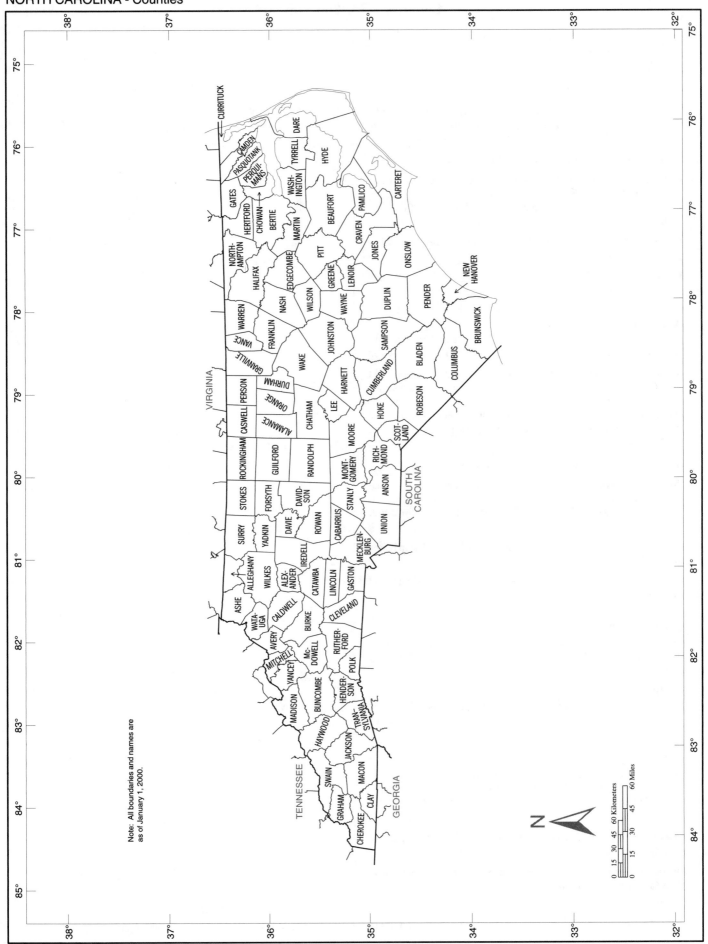

Note: All boundaries and names are as of January 1, 2000.

N

0 15 30 45 60 Kilometers
0 15 30 45 60 Miles

North Carolina

NORTH CAROLINA STATE INFORMATION

www.ncgov.com   **Ph:** 919-733-1110

Area (sq mi): 53,818.51 (land 48,710.88; water 5107.63).

Pop: 8,049,313 (White 70.2%; Black or African American 21.6%; Hispanic or Latino 4.7%; Asian 1.4%; Other 4.8%). **Foreign born:** 5.3%. **Median age:** 35.3. **Pop change 1990-2000:** +21.4%.

Income: per capita $20,307; median household $39,184. **Pop below poverty level:** 12.3%.

Unemployment: 6%. **Median home value:** $108,300. **Median travel time to work:** 24 minutes.

ALAMANCE COUNTY

124 W Elm St   **Ph:** 336-228-1312
Graham, NC 27253   **Fax:** 336-570-6788
www.alamance-nc.com

In north-central NC, west of Durham; organized Jan 29, 1849 from Orange County. **Name Origin:** For Great Alamance Creek, which flows through the county, from an Indian word of uncertain meaning; or for the Battle of Alamance (May 6, 1771).

Area (sq mi): 434.77 (land 429.99; water 4.78).

Pop: 130,800 (White 72.5%; Black or African American 18.8%; Hispanic or Latino 6.8%; Asian 0.9%; Other 4.8%). **Foreign born:** 6.3%. **Median age:** 36.3. **State rank:** 15. **Pop change 1990-2000:** +20.9%.

Income: per capita $19,391; median household $39,168. **Pop below poverty level:** 11.1%.

Unemployment: 5.7%. **Median home value:** $107,200. **Median travel time to work:** 21.6 minutes.

ALEXANDER COUNTY

255 Liledoun Rd   **Ph:** 828-632-9332
Taylorsville, NC 28681   **Fax:** 828-632-0059
www.co.alexander.nc.us

In west-central NC, northwest of Charlotte; established Jan 15, 1847 from Iredell, Caldwell, and Wilks counties. **Name Origin:** For William Julius Alexander (1797-1857), NC legislator.

Area (sq mi): 263.14 (land 260.18; water 2.95).

Pop: 33,603 (White 91%; Black or African American 4.6%; Hispanic or Latino 2.5%; Asian 1%; Other 2.2%). **Foreign born:** 2.4%. **Median age:** 36.6. **State rank:** 65. **Pop change 1990-2000:** +22%.

Income: per capita $18,507; median household $38,684. **Pop below poverty level:** 8.5%.

Unemployment: 6.2%. **Median home value:** $95,600. **Median travel time to work:** 22.9 minutes.

ALLEGHANY COUNTY

PO Box 61   **Ph:** 336-372-8949
Sparta, NC 28675   **Fax:** 336-372-4899

On the northwestern border of NC, northwest of Winston-Salem; organized 1859 from Ashe County. **Name Origin:** For the Allegheny River, with a variant spelling.

Area (sq mi): 235.52 (land 234.65; water 0.87).

Pop: 10,677 (White 93%; Black or African American 1.2%; Hispanic or Latino 5%; Asian 0.2%; Other 3%). **Foreign born:** 4.1%. **Median age:** 43. **State rank:** 93. **Pop change 1990-2000:** +11.3%.

Income: per capita $17,691; median household $29,244. **Pop below poverty level:** 17.2%.

Unemployment: 8.5%. **Median home value:** $89,700. **Median travel time to work:** 24.1 minutes.

ANSON COUNTY

Courthouse Rm 30   **Ph:** 704-694-2796
Wadesboro, NC 28170   **Fax:** 704-694-7015
www.co.anson.nc.us

On the central-southern border of NC, southeast of Charlotte; organized Mar 17, 1749 (prior to statehood) from Bladen County. **Name Origin:** For George, Lord Anson (1697-1762), British admiral assigned to protect the Carolina coast from pirates.

Area (sq mi): 537.13 (land 531.57; water 5.56).

Pop: 25,275 (White 49.2%; Black or African American 48.6%; Hispanic or Latino 0.8%; Asian 0.6%; Other 1.2%). **Foreign born:** 0.7%. **Median age:** 36.6. **State rank:** 73. **Pop change 1990-2000:** +7.7%.

Income: per capita $14,853; median household $29,849. **Pop below poverty level:** 17.8%.

Unemployment: 10.4%. **Median home value:** $64,300. **Median travel time to work:** 27.5 minutes.

ASHE COUNTY

150 Government Cir Suite 3100   **Ph:** 336-246-5641
Jefferson, NC 28640   **Fax:** 336-246-4276
www.ashechamber.com

In the northwest corner of NC; organized Nov 18, 1799 from Wilkes County. **Name Origin:** For Samuel Ashe (1725-1813), NC legislator, chief justice of NC (1777-95), and governor (1795-98).

Area (sq mi): 426.78 (land 426.13; water 0.65).

Please see sample entry on inside front cover for detailed information about the statistics presented with each county listing.

407

Pop: 24,384 (White 96.1%; Black or African American 0.7%; Hispanic or Latino 2.4%; Asian 0.2%; Other 2%). **Foreign born:** 1.9%. **Median age:** 42.1. **State rank:** 74. **Pop change 1990-2000:** +9.8%.

Income: per capita $16,429; median household $28,824. **Pop below poverty level:** 13.5%.

Unemployment: 9.3%. **Median home value:** $91,600. **Median travel time to work:** 26.6 minutes.

AVERY COUNTY

PO Box 115   **Ph:** 828-733-2900
Newland, NC 28657   **Fax:** 828-733-8410
www.averyco.com/gov

On the northwestern border of NC, northeast of Asheville; organized Feb 23, 1911 from Mitchell, Caldwell, and Watauga counties. **Name Origin:** For Col. Waightstill Avery (1745-1821), Revolutionary War officer, NC legislator, and attorney general (1777-79).

Area (sq mi): 247.21 (land 247; water 0.2).

Pop: 17,167 (White 93%; Black or African American 3.5%; Hispanic or Latino 2.4%; Asian 0.2%; Other 2.3%). **Foreign born:** 2.6%. **Median age:** 38.4. **State rank:** 86. **Pop change 1990-2000:** +15.5%.

Income: per capita $15,176; median household $30,627. **Pop below poverty level:** 15.3%.

Unemployment: 4.6%. **Median home value:** $88,000. **Median travel time to work:** 22.9 minutes.

BEAUFORT COUNTY

PO Box 1027   **Ph:** 252-946-0079
Washington, NC 27889   **Fax:** 252-946-7722
www.co.beaufort.nc.us

On central eastern border of NC, east of Goldsboro; organized as Pamptecough Precinct Dec 3, 1705 (prior to statehood) from Bath County, which was organized in 1696 and abolished in 1739; name changed about 1712. **Name Origin:** For Henry Somerset (1684-1714), Duke of Beaufort, a Lord Proprietor of the colony of SC. Originally for the Pamptecough (Pamlico) River.

Area (sq mi): 958.69 (land 827.97; water 130.72).

Pop: 44,958 (White 66.8%; Black or African American 29%; Hispanic or Latino 3.2%; Asian 0.2%; Other 2.3%). **Foreign born:** 2.6%. **Median age:** 40.2. **State rank:** 53. **Pop change 1990-2000:** +6.3%.

Income: per capita $16,722; median household $31,066. **Pop below poverty level:** 19.5%.

Unemployment: 9.6%. **Median home value:** $81,900. **Median travel time to work:** 25.4 minutes.

BERTIE COUNTY

106 Dundee St   **Ph:** 252-794-5300
Windsor, NC 27983   **Fax:** 252-794-5327
www.co.bertie.nc.us

In northeastern NC, east of Rocky Mount; organized 1722 (prior to statehood) from Chowan County. **Name Origin:** For James (1673-1735) and Henry (1675-1735) Bertie, brothers who were Lords Proprietor of the colony of North Carolina.

Area (sq mi): 741.22 (land 699.19; water 42.03).

Pop: 19,773 (White 36%; Black or African American 62.3%; Hispanic or Latino 1%; Asian 0.1%; Other 1.2%). **Foreign born:** 0.7%. **Median age:** 38.6. **State rank:** 80. **Pop change 1990-2000:** -3%.

Income: per capita $14,096; median household $25,177. **Pop below poverty level:** 23.5%.

Unemployment: 8.6%. **Median home value:** $59,200. **Median travel time to work:** 28.5 minutes.

BLADEN COUNTY

166 E Broad St Rm 105   **Ph:** 910-862-6700
Elizabethtown, NC 28337   **Fax:** 910-862-6767

In south-central NC, southeast of Fayetteville; organized 1734 (prior to statehood) from New Hanover County. **Name Origin:** For Martin Bladen (1680-1746), English soldier and commissioner of trade and plantations (1717-46).

Area (sq mi): 887.13 (land 874.94; water 12.19).

Pop: 32,278 (White 55.9%; Black or African American 37.9%; Hispanic or Latino 3.7%; Asian 0.1%; Other 4.7%). **Foreign born:** 2.3%. **Median age:** 37.9. **State rank:** 67. **Pop change 1990-2000:** +12.6%.

Income: per capita $14,735; median household $26,877. **Pop below poverty level:** 21%.

Unemployment: 7.4%. **Median home value:** $65,200. **Median travel time to work:** 26.9 minutes.

BRUNSWICK COUNTY

PO Box 249   **Ph:** 910-253-2000
Bolivia, NC 28422   **Fax:** 910-253-2022
www.co.brunswick.nc.us

On the southeastern border of NC, west of Wilmington; organized 1764 (prior to statehood) from New Hanover and Bladen counties. **Name Origin:** For the German city and duchy; the Duke of Brunswick was one of the titles of the British royal house of Hanover.

Area (sq mi): 1050.01 (land 854.79; water 195.21).

Pop: 73,143 (White 81.1%; Black or African American 14.4%; Hispanic or Latino 2.7%; Asian 0.3%; Other 3%). **Foreign born:** 2.9%. **Median age:** 42.2. **State rank:** 34. **Pop change 1990-2000:** +43.5%.

Income: per capita $19,857; median household $35,888. **Pop below poverty level:** 12.6%.

Unemployment: 5.4%. **Median home value:** $127,400. **Median travel time to work:** 24.6 minutes.

BUNCOMBE COUNTY

1 Oak Plaza   **Ph:** 828-250-4100
Asheville, NC 28801   **Fax:** 828-255-5461
www.buncombecounty.org

In southwestern NC; organized Dec 5, 1791 from Burke and Rutherford counties (in 1812 annexed Walton County, which was formed in 1803 from Indian lands). **Name Origin:** For Col. Edward Buncombe (1742-78), a NC officer in the Revolutionary War who died while a prisoner of the British.

Area (sq mi): 659.8 (land 655.99; water 3.81).

Pop: 206,330 (White 87.6%; Black or African American 7.5%; Hispanic or Latino 2.8%; Asian 0.7%; Other 2.7%). **Foreign born:**

All statistics are based on the 2000 Census except the dollar figures given for per capita income, which are based on 1999 estimates.

3.9%. **Median age:** 38.9. **State rank:** 7. **Pop change 1990-2000:** +18%.

Income: per capita $20,384; median household $36,666. **Pop below poverty level:** 11.4%.

Unemployment: 3.6%. **Median home value:** $119,600. **Median travel time to work:** 21.1 minutes.

BURKE COUNTY

PO Box 219
Morganton, NC 28680
www.co.burke.nc.us

Ph: 828-439-4340
Fax: 828-438-2782

In southwestern NC, northeast of Asheville; organized Apr 8, 1777 (prior to statehood) from Rowan County. **Name Origin:** For Dr. Thomas Burke (1747-83), member of the Continental Congress (1776-81) and NC governor (1781-82).

Area (sq mi): 514.89 (land 506.72; water 8.17).

Pop: 89,148 (White 84.9%; Black or African American 6.7%; Hispanic or Latino 3.6%; Asian 3.5%; Other 3.8%). **Foreign born:** 4.8%. **Median age:** 36.9. **State rank:** 29. **Pop change 1990-2000:** +17.7%.

Income: per capita $17,397; median household $35,629. **Pop below poverty level:** 10.7%.

Unemployment: 6.6%. **Median home value:** $85,900. **Median travel time to work:** 21 minutes.

CABARRUS COUNTY

PO Box 707
Concord, NC 28026
www.co.cabarrus.nc.us

Ph: 704-920-2100
Fax: 704-920-2820

In west-central NC, northeast of Charlotte; organized Nov 15, 1791 from Mecklenburg County. **Name Origin:** For Stephen Cabarrus (1754-1808), NC legislator and speaker of the NC House of Commons.

Area (sq mi): 364.98 (land 364.39; water 0.59).

Pop: 131,063 (White 80.9%; Black or African American 12.2%; Hispanic or Latino 5.1%; Asian 0.9%; Other 3.6%). **Foreign born:** 4.7%. **Median age:** 35.4. **State rank:** 14. **Pop change 1990-2000:** +32.5%.

Income: per capita $21,121; median household $46,140. **Pop below poverty level:** 7.1%.

Unemployment: 4.8%. **Median home value:** $118,200. **Median travel time to work:** 27 minutes.

CALDWELL COUNTY

PO Box 2200
Lenoir, NC 28645
www.co.caldwell.nc.us

Ph: 828-757-1300
Fax: 828-757-1295

In northwestern NC, northwest of Charlotte; organized Jan 11, 1841 from Burke and Wilkes counties. **Name Origin:** For Joseph Caldwell (1773-1835), first president of the University of North Carolina (1804-12; 1817-35).

Area (sq mi): 474.29 (land 471.6; water 2.7).

Pop: 77,415 (White 90.8%; Black or African American 5.5%; Hispanic or Latino 2.5%; Asian 0.4%; Other 2.4%). **Foreign born:**

1.9%. **Median age:** 37.5. **State rank:** 31. **Pop change 1990-2000:** +9.5%.

Income: per capita $17,353; median household $35,739. **Pop below poverty level:** 10.7%.

Unemployment: 6.7%. **Median home value:** $86,700. **Median travel time to work:** 21.6 minutes.

CAMDEN COUNTY

PO Box 190
Camden, NC 27921

Ph: 252-335-4691
Fax: 252-333-1603

On northeastern border of NC, east of Elizabeth City; organized Apr 8, 1777 (prior to statehood) from Pasquotank County. **Name Origin:** For Charles Pratt (1716-94), Earl of Camden, English jurist and political leader who supported the American colonies before the Revolutionary War.

Area (sq mi): 305.7 (land 240.68; water 65.02).

Pop: 6,885 (White 80.1%; Black or African American 17.3%; Hispanic or Latino 0.7%; Asian 0.6%; Other 1.5%). **Foreign born:** 0.7%. **Median age:** 39.1. **State rank:** 98. **Pop change 1990-2000:** +16.6%.

Income: per capita $18,681; median household $39,493. **Pop below poverty level:** 10.1%.

Unemployment: 3.3%. **Median home value:** $103,100. **Median travel time to work:** 32.4 minutes.

CARTERET COUNTY

Courthouse Sq
Beaufort, NC 28516
www.co.carteret.nc.us

Ph: 252-728-8400
Fax: 252-728-2092

On the central eastern shore of NC, east of Jacksonville; organized 1722 (prior to statehood) from Craven County. **Name Origin:** For John Carteret (1690-1763), later Earl Granville, a lord proprietor of the Carolinas.

Area (sq mi): 1340.53 (land 519.84; water 820.68).

Pop: 59,383 (White 89.3%; Black or African American 7%; Hispanic or Latino 1.7%; Asian 0.5%; Other 2.2%). **Foreign born:** 2%. **Median age:** 42.3. **State rank:** 41. **Pop change 1990-2000:** +13%.

Income: per capita $21,260; median household $38,344. **Pop below poverty level:** 10.7%.

Unemployment: 4.9%. **Median home value:** $123,900. **Median travel time to work:** 23 minutes.

CASWELL COUNTY

PO Box 790
Yanceyville, NC 27379

Ph: 336-694-4171
Fax: 336-694-7338

On the central northern border of NC, northwest of Durham; organized Apr 8, 1777 (prior to statehood) from Orange County. **Name Origin:** For Gen. Richard Caswell (1729-89), Revolutionary War officer; first and fifth governor of NC (1775-79; 1784-87).

Area (sq mi): 428.43 (land 424.67; water 3.76).

Pop: 23,501 (White 60.6%; Black or African American 36.5%; Hispanic or Latino 1.8%; Asian 0.2%; Other 2.3%). **Foreign born:** 1.6%. **Median age:** 38.2. **State rank:** 76. **Pop change 1990-2000:** +13.6%.

Please see sample entry on inside front cover for detailed information about the statistics presented with each county listing.

Income: per capita $16,470; median household $35,018. **Pop below poverty level:** 14.4%.

Unemployment: 5.4%. **Median home value:** $80,800. **Median travel time to work:** 30.6 minutes.

CATAWBA COUNTY

PO Box 389   **Ph:** 828-465-8201
Newton, NC 28658   **Fax:** 828-465-8392
www.co.catawba.nc.us

In west-central NC, northwest of Charlotte; organized Dec 12, 1842 from Lincoln County. **Name Origin:** For the Catawba Indians of Siouan linguistic stock who lived in the area and were recognized as the most powerful tribe; origin of name unknown.

Area (sq mi): 413.51 (land 399.97; water 13.54).

Pop: 141,685 (White 82.1%; Black or African American 8.4%; Hispanic or Latino 5.6%; Asian 2.9%; Other 3.8%). **Foreign born:** 6.5%. **Median age:** 36.1. **State rank:** 12. **Pop change 1990-2000:** +19.7%.

Income: per capita $20,358; median household $40,536. **Pop below poverty level:** 9.1%.

Unemployment: 6.7%. **Median home value:** $103,000. **Median travel time to work:** 20.7 minutes.

CHATHAM COUNTY

PO Box 369   **Ph:** 919-542-3240
Pittsboro, NC 27312   **Fax:** 919-542-1402
www.co.chatham.nc.us

In north-central NC, southwest of Durham; established Apr 1, 1771 (prior to statehood) from Orange County. **Name Origin:** For William Pitt (the Elder; 1708-78), 1st Earl of Chatham, known as 'the Great Commoner,' for his support of the American colonies before the Revolutionary War.

Area (sq mi): 709.05 (land 682.85; water 26.19).

Pop: 49,329 (White 71.6%; Black or African American 17.1%; Hispanic or Latino 9.6%; Asian 0.6%; Other 7.3%). **Foreign born:** 8.7%. **Median age:** 38.8. **State rank:** 47. **Pop change 1990-2000:** +27.3%.

Income: per capita $23,355; median household $42,851. **Pop below poverty level:** 9.7%.

Unemployment: 3.2%. **Median home value:** $127,200. **Median travel time to work:** 27.3 minutes.

CHEROKEE COUNTY

75 Peachtree St   **Ph:** 828-837-5527
Murphy, NC 28906   **Fax:** 828-837-9684
www.cherokeecounty-nc.org

In the southwestern corner of NC, southwest of Asheville; organized Jan 4, 1839 from Macon County. **Name Origin:** For the Indian tribe of Iroquoian linguistic stock. Name may derive from Creek *tciloki* 'people of a different speech.'

Area (sq mi): 466.68 (land 455.19; water 11.49).

Pop: 24,298 (White 94.1%; Black or African American 1.6%; Hispanic or Latino 1.2%; Asian 0.3%; Other 3.2%). **Foreign born:**

1.2%. **Median age:** 44. **State rank:** 75. **Pop change 1990-2000:** +20.5%.

Income: per capita $15,814; median household $27,992. **Pop below poverty level:** 15.3%.

Unemployment: 8.1%. **Median home value:** $86,000. **Median travel time to work:** 24.1 minutes.

CHOWAN COUNTY

115 E King St   **Ph:** 252-482-8431
Edenton, NC 27932   **Fax:** 252-482-0126
www.co.chowan.nc.us

In northeastern NC on Albemarle Sound; organized as Shaftsbury Precinct of Albemarle County in 1668 (prior to statehood); name changed about 1681. **Name Origin:** For the Chowan River, which forms its western border; itself named for the Chowanoc, an Algonquian Indian tribe, probably 'those in the south.' Originally for Anthony Ashley Cooper (1621-83), Earl of Shaftsbury, an original lord proprietor of Carolina.

Area (sq mi): 233.31 (land 172.64; water 60.67).

Pop: 14,526 (White 59.9%; Black or African American 37.5%; Hispanic or Latino 1.5%; Asian 0.3%; Other 1.6%). **Foreign born:** 0.9%. **Median age:** 39.8. **State rank:** 88. **Pop change 1990-2000:** +7.6%.

Income: per capita $15,027; median household $30,928. **Pop below poverty level:** 17.6%.

Unemployment: 5.1%. **Median home value:** $85,200. **Median travel time to work:** 27.4 minutes.

CLAY COUNTY

PO Box 506   **Ph:** 828-389-8334
Hayesville, NC 28904   **Fax:** 828-389-3329

On the southwestern border of NC, southwest of Asheville; organized Feb 20, 1861 from Cherokee County. **Name Origin:** For Henry Clay (1777-1852), U.S. senator from KY, known as the 'Great Pacificator' for his advocacy of compromise to avert national crises.

Area (sq mi): 220.6 (land 214.7; water 5.89).

Pop: 8,775 (White 97.3%; Black or African American 0.8%; Hispanic or Latino 0.8%; Asian 0.1%; Other 1.1%). **Foreign born:** 1.2%. **Median age:** 46.7. **State rank:** 96. **Pop change 1990-2000:** +22.6%.

Income: per capita $18,221; median household $31,397. **Pop below poverty level:** 11.4%.

Unemployment: 4%. **Median home value:** $99,800. **Median travel time to work:** 26.2 minutes.

CLEVELAND COUNTY

PO Box 1210   **Ph:** 704-484-4800
Shelby, NC 28151   **Fax:** 704-484-4930
www.co.cleveland.nc.us

On the southern border of NC, west of Charlotte; organized as Cleaveland County Jan 11, 1841 from Rutherford and Lincoln counties. Present spelling adopted in 1887. **Name Origin:** For Col. Benjamin Cleaveland (1738-1806), a hero of the Battle of King's Mountain (1780).

All statistics are based on the 2000 Census except the dollar figures given for per capita income, which are based on 1999 estimates.

Area (sq mi): 468.6 (land 464.63; water 3.97).

Pop: 96,287 (White 76.2%; Black or African American 20.9%; Hispanic or Latino 1.5%; Asian 0.7%; Other 1.6%). **Foreign born:** 1.7%. **Median age:** 36.5. **State rank:** 24. **Pop change 1990-2000:** +13.7%.

Income: per capita $17,395; median household $35,283. **Pop below poverty level:** 13.3%.

Unemployment: 11.4%. **Median home value:** $83,200. **Median travel time to work:** 23.5 minutes.

COLUMBUS COUNTY
PO Box 1587   **Ph:** 910-641-3000
Whiteville, NC 28472   **Fax:** 910-641-3027

On southeastern border of NC, west of Wilmington; organized Dec 15, 1808 from Bladen and Brunswick counties. **Name Origin:** For explorer Christopher Columbus (1451-1506).

Area (sq mi): 953.6 (land 936.8; water 16.8).

Pop: 54,749 (White 62.8%; Black or African American 30.9%; Hispanic or Latino 2.3%; Asian 0.2%; Other 5.4%). **Foreign born:** 1.4%. **Median age:** 36.9. **State rank:** 45. **Pop change 1990-2000:** +10.4%.

Income: per capita $14,415; median household $26,805. **Pop below poverty level:** 22.7%.

Unemployment: 9.5%. **Median home value:** $76,100. **Median travel time to work:** 27.1 minutes.

CRAVEN COUNTY
406 Craven St   **Ph:** 252-636-6600
New Bern, NC 28560
www.co.craven.nc.us

In central eastern NC, northeast of Jacksonville; organized Dec 3, 1705 (prior to statehood) as Archdale Precinct of Bath District, although there is evidence that an Archdale County had existed since 1696. Name changed 1712. **Name Origin:** Probably for William (1668-1711), 2nd Earl of Craven, who died the year before the name changed. Others claim the 1st Earl (1606-97), an original lord proprietor of Carolina, or the 3rd Earl, one of the proprietors when the name was changed. Originally named for John Archdale (1642?-1717), a lord proprietor and governor of Carolina (1694-96).

Area (sq mi): 774.14 (land 708.43; water 65.72).

Pop: 91,436 (White 68.3%; Black or African American 25.1%; Hispanic or Latino 4%; Asian 1%; Other 4%). **Foreign born:** 3.4%. **Median age:** 34.4. **State rank:** 26. **Pop change 1990-2000:** +12%.

Income: per capita $18,423; median household $35,966. **Pop below poverty level:** 13.1%.

Unemployment: 5.3%. **Median home value:** $96,600. **Median travel time to work:** 20.6 minutes.

CUMBERLAND COUNTY
PO Box 1829   **Ph:** 910-678-7700
Fayetteville, NC 28302   **Fax:** 910-678-7717
www.co.cumberland.nc.us

In south-central NC, south of Durham; organized Feb 19, 1754 (prior to statehood) from Bladen County. **Name Origin:** For William

Augustus (1721-65), Duke of Cumberland, British general and second son of George II.

Area (sq mi): 658.46 (land 652.72; water 5.74).

Pop: 302,963 (White 52.6%; Black or African American 34.9%; Hispanic or Latino 6.9%; Asian 1.9%; Other 8%). **Foreign born:** 5.3%. **Median age:** 29.6. **State rank:** 5. **Pop change 1990-2000:** +10.3%.

Income: per capita $17,376; median household $37,466. **Pop below poverty level:** 12.8%.

Unemployment: 5.4%. **Median home value:** $88,800. **Median travel time to work:** 21.9 minutes.

CURRITUCK COUNTY
153 Courthouse Rd PO Box 39   **Ph:** 252-232-2075
Currituck, NC 27929   **Fax:** 252-232-3551
www.co.currituck.nc.us

On the northeastern shore of NC, east of Elizabeth City; organized by 1668 (prior to statehood) as a precinct of Albemarle District. **Name Origin:** From an obscure Indian name, said to mean 'wild geese.'

Area (sq mi): 525.65 (land 261.7; water 263.95).

Pop: 18,190 (White 89.5%; Black or African American 7.2%; Hispanic or Latino 1.4%; Asian 0.4%; Other 2%). **Foreign born:** 1.4%. **Median age:** 38.3. **State rank:** 84. **Pop change 1990-2000:** +32.4%.

Income: per capita $19,908; median household $40,822. **Pop below poverty level:** 10.7%.

Unemployment: 2.8%. **Median home value:** $115,500. **Median travel time to work:** 35 minutes.

DARE COUNTY
PO Box 1000   **Ph:** 252-475-5800
Manteo, NC 27954   **Fax:** 252-473-1817
www.co.dare.nc.us

On the central eastern shore of NC on Pamlico Sound, east of Greenville; organized Feb 2, 1870 from Tyrrell, Hyde, and Currituck counties. **Name Origin:** For Virginia Dare, born (Aug 18, 1587) on Roanoke Island in the county, the first child of English parents to be born in the Americas.

Area (sq mi): 1561.51 (land 383.58; water 1177.93).

Pop: 29,967 (White 93.5%; Black or African American 2.7%; Hispanic or Latino 2.2%; Asian 0.4%; Other 2.2%). **Foreign born:** 2.5%. **Median age:** 40.4. **State rank:** 68. **Pop change 1990-2000:** +31.7%.

Income: per capita $23,614; median household $42,411. **Pop below poverty level:** 8%.

Unemployment: 6.4%. **Median home value:** $137,200. **Median travel time to work:** 19.9 minutes.

DAVIDSON COUNTY
PO Box 1067   **Ph:** 336-242-2200
Lexington, NC 27293   **Fax:** 336-248-8440
www.co.davidson.nc.us/dcinfo.htm

In west-central NC, south of Winston-Salem; organized 1822 from

Please see sample entry on inside front cover for detailed information about the statistics presented with each county listing.

411

Rowan County. **Name Origin:** For Gen. William Lee Davidson (1746-81), army officer killed during the Revolutionary War.

Area (sq mi): 566.77 (land 552.15; water 14.62).

Pop: 147,246 (White 85.7%; Black or African American 9.1%; Hispanic or Latino 3.2%; Asian 0.8%; Other 3%). **Foreign born:** 3.6%. **Median age:** 37.1. **State rank:** 11. **Pop change 1990-2000:** +16.2%.

Income: per capita $18,703; median household $38,640. **Pop below poverty level:** 10.1%.

Unemployment: 6.3%. **Median home value:** $98,600. **Median travel time to work:** 22.8 minutes.

DAVIE COUNTY

123 S Main St   **Ph:** 336-751-5513
Mocksville, NC 27028   **Fax:** 336-751-7408
www.co.davie.nc.us

In west-central NC, southwest of Winston-Salem; organized 1836 from Rowan County. **Name Origin:** For Gen. William Richardson Davie (1756-1820), Revolutionary War hero, NC governor (1798-99), and a founder of the University of NC.

Area (sq mi): 266.89 (land 265.18; water 1.7).

Pop: 34,835 (White 88.5%; Black or African American 6.8%; Hispanic or Latino 3.5%; Asian 0.3%; Other 2.4%). **Foreign born:** 3.4%. **Median age:** 38.4. **State rank:** 63. **Pop change 1990-2000:** +25%.

Income: per capita $21,359; median household $40,174. **Pop below poverty level:** 8.6%.

Unemployment: 5.1%. **Median home value:** $116,200. **Median travel time to work:** 23.9 minutes.

DUPLIN COUNTY

PO Box 189   **Ph:** 910-296-1686
Kenansville, NC 28349   **Fax:** 910-296-2310
www.duplincounty.org

In southeastern NC, south of Goldsboro; organized 1750 (prior to statehood) from New Hanover County. **Name Origin:** For Thomas Hay (1710-87), Lord Duplin, member of the Board of Trade and Plantations.

Area (sq mi): 819.11 (land 817.73; water 1.38).

Pop: 49,063 (White 55.2%; Black or African American 28.9%; Hispanic or Latino 15.1%; Asian 0.2%; Other 12.3%). **Foreign born:** 11.3%. **Median age:** 34.9. **State rank:** 48. **Pop change 1990-2000:** +22.7%.

Income: per capita $14,499; median household $29,890. **Pop below poverty level:** 19.4%.

Unemployment: 6.2%. **Median home value:** $74,800. **Median travel time to work:** 26.6 minutes.

DURHAM COUNTY

200 E Main St   **Ph:** 919-560-0000
Durham, NC 27701   **Fax:** 919-560-0020
www.co.durham.nc.us

In north-central NC, northwest of Raleigh; organized Feb 28, 1881 from Orange and Wake counties. **Name Origin:** For the city of Durham, the county seat.

Area (sq mi): 297.79 (land 290.32; water 7.47).

Pop: 223,314 (White 48.1%; Black or African American 39.5%; Hispanic or Latino 7.6%; Asian 3.3%; Other 6.3%). **Foreign born:** 10.9%. **Median age:** 32.2. **State rank:** 6. **Pop change 1990-2000:** +22.8%.

Income: per capita $23,156; median household $43,337. **Pop below poverty level:** 13.4%.

Unemployment: 3.8%. **Median home value:** $129,000. **Median travel time to work:** 21.2 minutes.

EDGECOMBE COUNTY

PO Box 10   **Ph:** 252-641-7833
Tarboro, NC 27886   **Fax:** 252-641-0456
www.edgecombe.cc.nc.us/County/

In east-central NC, northeast of Goldsboro; organized Apr 4, 1741 (prior to statehood) from Bertie County, although deeds began in 1732. **Name Origin:** For Richard Edgecumbe (1680-1758), later 1st Baron Edgecumbe, English statesman. Present spelling is now accepted.

Area (sq mi): 506.58 (land 505.03; water 1.55).

Pop: 55,606 (White 39.3%; Black or African American 57.5%; Hispanic or Latino 2.8%; Asian 0.1%; Other 2.4%). **Foreign born:** 2.1%. **Median age:** 36.2. **State rank:** 44. **Pop change 1990-2000:** -1.7%.

Income: per capita $14,435; median household $30,983. **Pop below poverty level:** 19.6%.

Unemployment: 9.6%. **Median home value:** $70,800. **Median travel time to work:** 21 minutes.

FORSYTH COUNTY

PO Box 20099   **Ph:** 336-761-2250
Winston-Salem, NC 27120   **Fax:** 336-761-2018
www.co.forsyth.nc.us

In north-central NC, west of Greensboro; organized Jan 6, 1849 from Stokes County. **Name Origin:** For Col. Benjamin Forsyth (c.1760-1814), NC legislator and army officer killed during the War of 1812.

Area (sq mi): 412.92 (land 409.6; water 3.32).

Pop: 306,067 (White 66.1%; Black or African American 25.6%; Hispanic or Latino 6.4%; Asian 1%; Other 4.9%). **Foreign born:** 6.5%. **Median age:** 36. **State rank:** 4. **Pop change 1990-2000:** +15.1%.

Income: per capita $23,023; median household $42,097. **Pop below poverty level:** 11%.

Unemployment: 4.2%. **Median home value:** $114,000. **Median travel time to work:** 21.2 minutes.

FRANKLIN COUNTY

113 Market St   **Ph:** 919-496-5994
Louisburg, NC 27549   **Fax:** 919-496-2683
www.co.franklin.nc.us

In north-central NC, northeast of Raleigh; organized 1779 (prior to statehood) from Bute County, which was discontinued at that

All statistics are based on the 2000 Census except the dollar figures given for per capita income, which are based on 1999 estimates.

time. **Name Origin:** For Benjamin Franklin (1706-90), U.S. patriot, diplomat, and statesman.

Area (sq mi): 494.59 (land 492.02; water 2.57).

Pop: 47,260 (White 64.2%; Black or African American 30%; Hispanic or Latino 4.4%; Asian 0.3%; Other 3.6%). **Foreign born:** 3.6%. **Median age:** 35.8. **State rank:** 51. **Pop change 1990-2000:** +29.8%.

Income: per capita $17,562; median household $38,968. **Pop below poverty level:** 12.6%.

Unemployment: 4.4%. **Median home value:** $101,800. **Median travel time to work:** 33.2 minutes.

GASTON COUNTY

PO Box 1578   **Ph:** 704-866-3100
Gastonia, NC 28053   **Fax:** 704-866-3147
www.co.gaston.nc.us

On the southern central border of NC, west of Charlotte; organized Dec 21, 1846 from Lincoln County. **Name Origin:** For William Gaston (1778-1844), NC legislator, U.S. representative (1813-17), and judge of the NC Supreme Court (1833-44).

Area (sq mi): 363.54 (land 356.21; water 7.33).

Pop: 190,365 (White 81.4%; Black or African American 13.9%; Hispanic or Latino 3%; Asian 1%; Other 2.2%). **Foreign born:** 3.3%. **Median age:** 36.2. **State rank:** 8. **Pop change 1990-2000:** +8.7%.

Income: per capita $19,225; median household $39,482. **Pop below poverty level:** 10.9%.

Unemployment: 8.1%. **Median home value:** $90,300. **Median travel time to work:** 24.6 minutes.

GATES COUNTY

PO Box 148   **Ph:** 252-357-1240
Gatesville, NC 27938   **Fax:** 252-357-0073

On the northeastern border of NC, northwest of Elizabeth City; organized 1779 (prior to statehood) from Chowan, Hertford, and Perquimans counties. **Name Origin:** For Gen. Horatio Gates (1728?-1806), Continental Army officer who defeated John Burgoyne (1722-92) at the Battle of Satatoga (1777).

Area (sq mi): 345.6 (land 340.61; water 5).

Pop: 10,516 (White 58.5%; Black or African American 39.2%; Hispanic or Latino 0.8%; Asian 0.2%; Other 1.4%). **Foreign born:** 1.1%. **Median age:** 38.1. **State rank:** 94. **Pop change 1990-2000:** +13%.

Income: per capita $15,963; median household $35,647. **Pop below poverty level:** 17%.

Unemployment: 3.5%. **Median home value:** $77,200. **Median travel time to work:** 37.7 minutes.

GRAHAM COUNTY

12 N Main St   **Ph:** 828-479-7973
Robbinsville, NC 28771   **Fax:** 828-479-6417

On the southwestern border of NC, southwest of Asheville; organized Jan 30, 1872 from Cherokee County. **Name Origin:** For

William Alexander Graham (1804-75), U.S. senator from NC (1840-43), governor (1845-49), and U.S. secretary of the navy (1850-52).

Area (sq mi): 301.6 (land 292.07; water 9.53).

Pop: 7,993 (White 91.4%; Black or African American 0.2%; Hispanic or Latino 0.8%; Asian 0.2%; Other 7.7%). **Foreign born:** 1.3%. **Median age:** 41.5. **State rank:** 97. **Pop change 1990-2000:** +11.1%.

Income: per capita $14,237; median household $26,645. **Pop below poverty level:** 19.5%.

Unemployment: 9.3%. **Median home value:** $76,100. **Median travel time to work:** 27.9 minutes.

GRANVILLE COUNTY

PO Box 906   **Ph:** 919-693-4761
Oxford, NC 27565   **Fax:** 919-690-1766
www.granvillecounty.org

On the central northern border of NC, north of Raleigh; organized Jun 28, 1746 (prior to statehood) from Edgecombe County. **Name Origin:** For John Carteret (1690-1763), Earl Granville, a lord proprietor who owned the district in which the new county was located.

Area (sq mi): 536.56 (land 531.12; water 5.45).

Pop: 48,498 (White 59.3%; Black or African American 34.9%; Hispanic or Latino 4%; Asian 0.4%; Other 4%). **Foreign born:** 4%. **Median age:** 36.2. **State rank:** 50. **Pop change 1990-2000:** +26.5%.

Income: per capita $17,118; median household $39,965. **Pop below poverty level:** 11.7%.

Unemployment: 6%. **Median home value:** $100,400. **Median travel time to work:** 27.4 minutes.

GREENE COUNTY

PO Box 675   **Ph:** 252-747-3505
Snow Hill, NC 28580   **Fax:** 252-747-2700
www.co.greene.nc.us

In east-central NC, northeast of Goldsboro; organized Nov 18, 1799 when Glasgow County was renamed Greene. **Name Origin:** For Gen. Nathanael Greene (1742-86), hero of the Revolutionary War, quartermaster general (1778-80), and commander of the Army of the South (1780). Originally for James Glasgow, NC secretary of state (1777-98), who became involved in land frauds.

Area (sq mi): 265.89 (land 265.4; water 0.49).

Pop: 18,974 (White 50.1%; Black or African American 41.2%; Hispanic or Latino 8%; Asian 0.1%; Other 6.8%). **Foreign born:** 4.9%. **Median age:** 35.5. **State rank:** 82. **Pop change 1990-2000:** +23.3%.

Income: per capita $15,452; median household $32,074. **Pop below poverty level:** 20.2%.

Unemployment: 6.3%. **Median home value:** $74,300. **Median travel time to work:** 27.6 minutes.

GUILFORD COUNTY

PO Box 3427   **Ph:** 336-641-3383
Greensboro, NC 27402   **Fax:** 336-641-6833
www.co.guilford.nc.us

In north-central NC, east of Winston-Salem; organized 1771 (prior to statehood) from Rowan and Orange counties. **Name Origin:**

Please see sample entry on inside front cover for detailed information about the statistics presented with each county listing.

For Francis North (1704-90), 1st Earl of Guilford and father of Frederick, Lord North (1732-92), who was the prime minister of England at the time of the American Revolution.

Area (sq mi): 657.7 (land 649.42; water 8.28).

Pop: 421,048 (White 62.9%; Black or African American 29.3%; Hispanic or Latino 3.8%; Asian 2.4%; Other 3.8%). **Foreign born:** 6.5%. **Median age:** 34.9. **State rank:** 3. **Pop change 1990-2000:** +21.2%.

Income: per capita $23,340; median household $42,618. **Pop below poverty level:** 10.6%.

Unemployment: 4.8%. **Median home value:** $116,900. **Median travel time to work:** 21.4 minutes.

HALIFAX COUNTY
PO Box 38   **Ph:** 252-583-1131
Halifax, NC 27839   **Fax:** 252-583-9921
www.halifaxnc.com

On the central northern border of NC, north of Rocky Mount; organized 1758 (prior to statehood) from Edgecombe County. **Name Origin:** For George Montagu (1716-71), second Earl of Halifax, president of the English Board of Trade, called the 'Father of the Colonies' for his strong support of trade with them.

Area (sq mi): 731.35 (land 725.36; water 5.99).

Pop: 57,370 (White 42.3%; Black or African American 52.6%; Hispanic or Latino 1%; Asian 0.5%; Other 4.3%). **Foreign born:** 1.1%. **Median age:** 37.2. **State rank:** 43. **Pop change 1990-2000:** +3.3%.

Income: per capita $13,810; median household $26,459. **Pop below poverty level:** 23.9%.

Unemployment: 11.1%. **Median home value:** $68,300. **Median travel time to work:** 24.2 minutes.

HARNETT COUNTY
PO Box 759   **Ph:** 910-893-7555
Lillington, NC 27546   **Fax:** 910-814-2662
www.harnett.org

In central NC, north of Fayetteville; organized Feb 7, 1855 from Cumberland County. **Name Origin:** For Cornelius Harnett (1723-81), patriot and member of the Continental Congress (1777-80).

Area (sq mi): 601.3 (land 595.01; water 6.29).

Pop: 91,025 (White 68.9%; Black or African American 22.5%; Hispanic or Latino 5.9%; Asian 0.6%; Other 5.8%). **Foreign born:** 4.6%. **Median age:** 32.5. **State rank:** 27. **Pop change 1990-2000:** +34.2%.

Income: per capita $16,775; median household $35,105. **Pop below poverty level:** 14.9%.

Unemployment: 6.9%. **Median home value:** $91,200. **Median travel time to work:** 29.2 minutes.

HAYWOOD COUNTY
215 N Main St   **Ph:** 828-452-6625
Waynesville, NC 28786   **Fax:** 828-452-6715
www.haywoodnc.org/government

On the southwestern border of NC, west of Asheville; organized

Dec 15, 1808 from Buncombe County. **Name Origin:** For John Haywood (1755-1827), NC state treasurer (1787-1827).

Area (sq mi): 554.62 (land 553.66; water 0.96).

Pop: 54,033 (White 96%; Black or African American 1.3%; Hispanic or Latino 1.4%; Asian 0.2%; Other 1.6%). **Foreign born:** 1.6%. **Median age:** 42.3. **State rank:** 46. **Pop change 1990-2000:** +15.1%.

Income: per capita $18,554; median household $33,922. **Pop below poverty level:** 11.5%.

Unemployment: 5.7%. **Median home value:** $99,100. **Median travel time to work:** 22.7 minutes.

HENDERSON COUNTY
100 N King St   **Ph:** 828-697-4808
Hendersonville, NC 28792   **Fax:** 828-692-9855
www.hendersoncountync.org

On the southwestern border of NC, south of Asheville; organized Dec 15, 1838 from Buncombe County. **Name Origin:** For Leonard Henderson (1772-1833), judge of the NC Supreme Court (1818-29) and chief justice (1829-33).

Area (sq mi): 375.04 (land 374; water 1.04).

Pop: 89,173 (White 89.8%; Black or African American 3.1%; Hispanic or Latino 5.5%; Asian 0.6%; Other 3.8%). **Foreign born:** 5.9%. **Median age:** 42.7. **State rank:** 28. **Pop change 1990-2000:** +28.7%.

Income: per capita $21,110; median household $38,109. **Pop below poverty level:** 9.7%.

Unemployment: 3.4%. **Median home value:** $130,100. **Median travel time to work:** 22.2 minutes.

HERTFORD COUNTY
PO Box 86   **Ph:** 252-358-7845
Winton, NC 27986   **Fax:** 252-358-0793
www.co.hertford.nc.us

On the northeastern border of NC, northeast of Rocky Mount; organized 1759 (prior to statehood) from Chowan, Bertie, and Northampton counties. **Name Origin:** For Francis Seymour Conway (1719-94), Earl (later Marquis) of Hertford, British statesman.

Area (sq mi): 360.42 (land 353.26; water 7.16).

Pop: 22,601 (White 37.1%; Black or African American 59.6%; Hispanic or Latino 1.6%; Asian 0.3%; Other 2.7%). **Foreign born:** 1.2%. **Median age:** 39.2. **State rank:** 77. **Pop change 1990-2000:** +0.3%.

Income: per capita $15,641; median household $26,422. **Pop below poverty level:** 18.3%.

Unemployment: 7.1%. **Median home value:** $61,700. **Median travel time to work:** 25.1 minutes.

HOKE COUNTY
PO Box 210   **Ph:** 910-875-8751
Raeford, NC 28376   **Fax:** 910-875-9222
www.hoke-raeford.com

In south-central NC, west of Fayetteville; organized Feb 7, 1911 from Cumberland and Robeson counties. **Name Origin:** For Gen.

All statistics are based on the 2000 Census except the dollar figures given for per capita income, which are based on 1999 estimates.

Robert F. Hoke (1837-1912), a Confederate Army officer and railway president.

Area (sq mi): 392.34 (land 391.21; water 1.12).

Pop: 33,646 (White 41.6%; Black or African American 37.6%; Hispanic or Latino 7.2%; Asian 0.8%; Other 17%). **Foreign born:** 5.8%. **Median age:** 30. **State rank:** 64. **Pop change 1990-2000:** +47.2%.

Income: per capita $13,635; median household $33,230. **Pop below poverty level:** 17.7%.

Unemployment: 8.1%. **Median home value:** $83,900. **Median travel time to work:** 26.4 minutes.

HYDE COUNTY
PO Box 188   **Ph:** 252-926-4400
Swanquarter, NC 27885   **Fax:** 252-926-3701

On the central eastern shore of NC on Pamlico Sound, northeast of Jacksonville; organized Dec 3, 1705 (prior to statehood) as Wickham Precinct of Bath District; name changed in 1712. **Name Origin:** Either for Edward Hyde (1661-1723), 3rd Earl of Clarendon, a colonial governor of NJ and NY (1701-08); or for Edward Hyde (1650-1712), deputy governor, acting governor, and governor of NC (1709-12). Originally for the manor home of the Archdale family in Buckinghamshire, England.

Area (sq mi): 1424 (land 612.8; water 811.2).

Pop: 5,826 (White 61.6%; Black or African American 35.1%; Hispanic or Latino 2.2%; Asian 0.4%; Other 1.9%). **Foreign born:** 2.3%. **Median age:** 39.7. **State rank:** 99. **Pop change 1990-2000:** +7.7%.

Income: per capita $13,164; median household $28,444. **Pop below poverty level:** 15.4%.

Unemployment: 6.8%. **Median home value:** $76,500. **Median travel time to work:** 21.5 minutes.

IREDELL COUNTY
PO Box 788   **Ph:** 704-878-3000
Statesville, NC 28687   **Fax:** 704-878-3032
www.co.iredell.nc.us

In west-central NC, north of Charlotte; organized Nov 3, 1788 (prior to statehood) from Rowan County. **Name Origin:** For James Iredell (1751-99), NC attorney general (1779), delegate to the Constitutional Convention of 1788, and associate justice of the U.S. Supreme Court (1790-99).

Area (sq mi): 597.01 (land 575.57; water 21.44).

Pop: 122,660 (White 80.7%; Black or African American 13.7%; Hispanic or Latino 3.4%; Asian 1.3%; Other 2.9%). **Foreign born:** 3.6%. **Median age:** 36.5. **State rank:** 20. **Pop change 1990-2000:** +32%.

Income: per capita $21,148; median household $41,920. **Pop below poverty level:** 8.2%.

Unemployment: 5.7%. **Median home value:** $116,100. **Median travel time to work:** 24.5 minutes.

JACKSON COUNTY
401 Grindstaff Cove Rd   **Ph:** 828-586-4055
Sylva, NC 28779   **Fax:** 828-586-7528

On the southwestern border of NC, southwest of Asheville; organized Jan 29, 1851 from Haywood and Macon counties. **Name Origin:** For Andrew Jackson (1767-1845), seventh U.S. president.

Area (sq mi): 494.5 (land 490.71; water 3.79).

Pop: 33,121 (White 84.8%; Black or African American 1.7%; Hispanic or Latino 1.7%; Asian 0.5%; Other 12.1%). **Foreign born:** 1.7%. **Median age:** 36.2. **State rank:** 66. **Pop change 1990-2000:** +23.4%.

Income: per capita $17,582; median household $32,552. **Pop below poverty level:** 15.1%.

Unemployment: 3.9%. **Median home value:** $106,700. **Median travel time to work:** 20.6 minutes.

JOHNSTON COUNTY
PO Box 297   **Ph:** 919-934-3191
Smithfield, NC 27577   **Fax:** 919-934-5857
www.co.johnston.nc.us

In east-central NC, southeast of Raleigh; organized 1746 (prior to statehood) from Craven County. **Name Origin:** For Gabriel Johnston (1699-1752), colonial governor of NC (1734-52).

Area (sq mi): 795.79 (land 791.85; water 3.94).

Pop: 121,965 (White 75.3%; Black or African American 15.7%; Hispanic or Latino 7.7%; Asian 0.3%; Other 5.9%). **Foreign born:** 5.9%. **Median age:** 34.2. **State rank:** 21. **Pop change 1990-2000:** +50%.

Income: per capita $18,788; median household $40,872. **Pop below poverty level:** 12.8%.

Unemployment: 3.5%. **Median home value:** $108,800. **Median travel time to work:** 31.3 minutes.

JONES COUNTY
PO Box 280   **Ph:** 252-448-7351
Trenton, NC 28585   **Fax:** 252-448-1072
www.co.jones.nc.us

In southeastern NC, north of Jacksonville; organized 1778 (prior to statehood) from Craven County. **Name Origin:** For Willie Jones (1740-1801), American Revolutionary leader and member of the Continental Congress (1780-81); he later opposed the adoption of the Constitution.

Area (sq mi): 473.32 (land 471.88; water 1.44).

Pop: 10,381 (White 60.3%; Black or African American 35.9%; Hispanic or Latino 2.7%; Asian 0.2%; Other 3%). **Foreign born:** 2.1%. **Median age:** 39.1. **State rank:** 95. **Pop change 1990-2000:** +10.3%.

Income: per capita $15,916; median household $30,882. **Pop below poverty level:** 16.9%.

Unemployment: 5.5%. **Median home value:** $75,100. **Median travel time to work:** 29.7 minutes.

Please see sample entry on inside front cover for detailed information about the statistics presented with each county listing.

LEE COUNTY
PO Box 4209   **Ph:** 919-708-4400
Sanford, NC 27331   **Fax:** 919-775-3483

In central NC, southwest of Raleigh; organized Mar 6, 1907 from Chatham and Moore counties. **Name Origin:** For Robert E. Lee (1807-70), American general and commander in chief of the Confederate forces during the Civil War.

Area (sq mi): 259.33 (land 257.26; water 2.07).

Pop: 49,040 (White 66.2%; Black or African American 20.5%; Hispanic or Latino 11.7%; Asian 0.7%; Other 8.8%). **Foreign born:** 9.5%. **Median age:** 35.9. **State rank:** 49. **Pop change 1990-2000:** +18.5%.

Income: per capita $19,147; median household $38,900. **Pop below poverty level:** 12.8%.

Unemployment: 6.1%. **Median home value:** $95,100. **Median travel time to work:** 24.1 minutes.

LENOIR COUNTY
PO Box 3289   **Ph:** 252-559-6450
Kinston, NC 28502   **Fax:** 252-559-6466
www.co.lenoir.nc.us

In east-central NC, southeast of Goldsboro; organized Dec 5, 1791 from Dobbs County, when Dobbs County was dissolved and divided between Glasgow and Lenoir counties. **Name Origin:** For Gen. William Lenoir (1751-1839), one of the heros of the Battle of Kings Mountain (1780) during the American Revolution and first president of the board of the University of NC.

Area (sq mi): 402.09 (land 399.85; water 2.24).

Pop: 59,648 (White 55.5%; Black or African American 40.4%; Hispanic or Latino 3.2%; Asian 0.3%; Other 2.9%). **Foreign born:** 2.7%. **Median age:** 38.1. **State rank:** 40. **Pop change 1990-2000:** +4.1%.

Income: per capita $16,744; median household $31,191. **Pop below poverty level:** 16.6%.

Unemployment: 8.1%. **Median home value:** $82,600. **Median travel time to work:** 23.8 minutes.

LINCOLN COUNTY
PO Box 8   **Ph:** 704-736-8471
Lincolnton, NC 28092   **Fax:** 704-736-8718
www.co.lincoln.nc.us

In southwestern NC, northwest of Charlotte; organized 1779 (prior to statehood) from Tyron County, which was organized in 1768 and abolished in 1779. **Name Origin:** For Gen. Benjamin Lincoln (1733-1810), Revolutionary War officer, U.S. secretary of war (1781-83), and lt. gov. of MA (1788).

Area (sq mi): 307.03 (land 298.79; water 8.24).

Pop: 63,780 (White 86.7%; Black or African American 6.4%; Hispanic or Latino 5.7%; Asian 0.3%; Other 3%). **Foreign born:** 4.8%. **Median age:** 36.4. **State rank:** 37. **Pop change 1990-2000:** +26.8%.

Income: per capita $18,877; median household $41,421. **Pop below poverty level:** 9.2%.

Unemployment: 7.6%. **Median home value:** $104,500. **Median travel time to work:** 27.1 minutes.

MACON COUNTY
5 W Main St   **Ph:** 828-349-2025
Franklin, NC 28734   **Fax:** 828-349-2400
www.maconnc.org

On the southwestern border of NC, southwest of Asheville; organized 1828 from Haywood County. **Name Origin:** For Nathaniel Macon (1757-1837), U.S. representative from NC (1791-1815), U.S. senator (1815-28), and president of the NC constitutional convention (1835).

Area (sq mi): 519.47 (land 516.47; water 3).

Pop: 29,811 (White 96%; Black or African American 1.2%; Hispanic or Latino 1.5%; Asian 0.4%; Other 1.2%). **Foreign born:** 2.6%. **Median age:** 45.2. **State rank:** 69. **Pop change 1990-2000:** +26.9%.

Income: per capita $18,642; median household $32,139. **Pop below poverty level:** 12.6%.

Unemployment: 3.8%. **Median home value:** $103,700. **Median travel time to work:** 20 minutes.

MADISON COUNTY
PO Box 579   **Ph:** 828-649-2531
Marshall, NC 28753   **Fax:** 828-649-2829

On the southwestern border of NC, north of Asheville; organized Jan 27, 1851 from Yancey and Buncombe counties. **Name Origin:** For James Madison (1751-1836), fourth U.S. president.

Area (sq mi): 451.59 (land 449.42; water 2.17).

Pop: 19,635 (White 96.8%; Black or African American 0.8%; Hispanic or Latino 1.4%; Asian 0.2%; Other 1.3%). **Foreign born:** 1.7%. **Median age:** 39.3. **State rank:** 81. **Pop change 1990-2000:** +15.8%.

Income: per capita $16,076; median household $30,985. **Pop below poverty level:** 15.4%.

Unemployment: 5.2%. **Median home value:** $94,600. **Median travel time to work:** 30.1 minutes.

MARTIN COUNTY
PO Box 668   **Ph:** 252-792-1901
Williamston, NC 27892   **Fax:** 252-792-7477

In east-central NC, northeast of Greenville; organized Mar 2, 1774 (prior to statehood) from Tyrell and Halifax counties. **Name Origin:** For Josiah Martin (1737-86), the last royal governor of NC (1771-75). The name was reinforced by the popularity of Alexander Martin, NC governor (1782-85; 1789-92).

Area (sq mi): 461.49 (land 461.17; water 0.32).

Pop: 25,593 (White 51.8%; Black or African American 45.4%; Hispanic or Latino 2.1%; Asian 0.2%; Other 1.8%). **Foreign born:** 1.5%. **Median age:** 38.7. **State rank:** 72. **Pop change 1990-2000:** +2.1%.

Income: per capita $15,102; median household $28,793. **Pop below poverty level:** 20.2%.

Unemployment: 8.2%. **Median home value:** $68,400. **Median travel time to work:** 24.3 minutes.

All statistics are based on the 2000 Census except the dollar figures given for per capita income, which are based on 1999 estimates.

McDOWELL COUNTY

60 E Court St   **Ph:** 828-652-7121
Marion, NC 28752   **Fax:** 828-659-3484
mcdowell.main.nc.us/~mcdowell/

In southwestern NC, east of Asheville; organized Dec 19, 1842 from Burke and Rutherford counties. **Name Origin:** For Maj. Joseph McDowell (1756-1801), a hero of the Battle of Kings Mountain (1780) during the Revolutionary War and U.S. representative from NC (1797-99).

Area (sq mi): 446.41 (land 441.68; water 4.73).

Pop: 42,151 (White 91%; Black or African American 4.2%; Hispanic or Latino 2.9%; Asian 0.9%; Other 2.7%). **Foreign born:** 2.7%. **Median age:** 38. **State rank:** 57. **Pop change 1990-2000:** +18.1%.

Income: per capita $16,109; median household $32,396. **Pop below poverty level:** 11.6%.

Unemployment: 8%. **Median home value:** $72,000. **Median travel time to work:** 25.3 minutes.

MECKLENBURG COUNTY

Charlotte-Mecklenburg Govt Ctr
600 E 4th St   **Ph:** 704-336-2472
Charlotte, NC 28202   **Fax:** 704-336-5887
www.co.mecklenburg.nc.us

On the central southern border of NC, east of Gastonia; organized Nov 3, 1762 (prior to statehood) from Anson County. **Name Origin:** For Mecklenburg-Strelitz, home of Princess Charlotte Sophia (1744-1818), wife of King George III (1738-1820) of England.

Area (sq mi): 546.22 (land 526.28; water 19.94).

Pop: 695,454 (White 61.1%; Black or African American 27.9%; Hispanic or Latino 6.5%; Asian 3.1%; Other 4.9%). **Foreign born:** 9.8%. **Median age:** 33.1. **State rank:** 1. **Pop change 1990-2000:** +36%.

Income: per capita $27,352; median household $50,579. **Pop below poverty level:** 9.2%.

Unemployment: 4.1%. **Median home value:** $141,800. **Median travel time to work:** 26 minutes.

MITCHELL COUNTY

PO Box 409   **Ph:** 828-688-2434
Bakersville, NC 28705   **Fax:** 828-688-4443
www.mitchellcounty.org

On the southwestern border of NC, northeast of Asheville; organized Feb 16, 1861 from Burke, Caldwell, Yancey, McDowell, and Watauga counties. **Name Origin:** For Elisha Mitchell (1793-1857), a professor at the University of North Carolina who was killed while exploring what is now called Mt. Mitchell.

Area (sq mi): 222.14 (land 221.43; water 0.71).

Pop: 15,687 (White 97%; Black or African American 0.2%; Hispanic or Latino 2%; Asian 0.2%; Other 1.7%). **Foreign born:** 1.5%. **Median age:** 42. **State rank:** 87. **Pop change 1990-2000:** +8.7%.

Income: per capita $15,933; median household $30,508. **Pop below poverty level:** 13.8%.

Unemployment: 10.2%. **Median home value:** $78,800. **Median travel time to work:** 24.9 minutes.

MONTGOMERY COUNTY

PO Box 527   **Ph:** 910-576-4211
Troy, NC 27371   **Fax:** 910-576-5020

In south-central NC, east of Charlotte; organized 1779 (prior to statehood) from Anson County. **Name Origin:** For Gen. Richard Montgomery (1736-75), American Revolutionary War officer who captured Montreal, Canada.

Area (sq mi): 501.64 (land 491.6; water 10.04).

Pop: 26,822 (White 65.3%; Black or African American 21.8%; Hispanic or Latino 10.4%; Asian 1.6%; Other 7.4%). **Foreign born:** 8%. **Median age:** 36.7. **State rank:** 71. **Pop change 1990-2000:** +14.9%.

Income: per capita $16,504; median household $32,903. **Pop below poverty level:** 15.4%.

Unemployment: 7.2%. **Median home value:** $77,200. **Median travel time to work:** 24.5 minutes.

MOORE COUNTY

PO Box 905   **Ph:** 910-947-6363
Carthage, NC 28327   **Fax:** 910-947-1874
www.co.moore.nc.us

In south-central NC, northwest of Fayetteville; organized Apr 18, 1784 (prior to statehood) from Cumberland County. **Name Origin:** For Capt. Alfred Moore (1755-1810), Revolutionary War officer, attorney general of NC (1782), and associate justice of the U.S. Supreme Court (1799-1804).

Area (sq mi): 705.67 (land 697.74; water 7.94).

Pop: 74,769 (White 78.7%; Black or African American 15.5%; Hispanic or Latino 4%; Asian 0.4%; Other 3.9%). **Foreign born:** 4.2%. **Median age:** 41.8. **State rank:** 32. **Pop change 1990-2000:** +26.7%.

Income: per capita $23,377; median household $41,240. **Pop below poverty level:** 11.4%.

Unemployment: 5%. **Median home value:** $131,100. **Median travel time to work:** 22.8 minutes.

NASH COUNTY

120 W Washington St Sutie 3072   **Ph:** 252-459-9800
Nashville, NC 27856   **Fax:** 252-459-9817
www.co.nash.nc.us

In east-central NC, northeast of Raleigh; organized Nov 15, 1777 (prior to statehood) from Edgecombe County. **Name Origin:** For Gen. Francis Nash (1742-77), Revolutionary War officer and NC legislator.

Area (sq mi): 542.69 (land 540.27; water 2.42).

Pop: 87,420 (White 61%; Black or African American 33.9%; Hispanic or Latino 3.4%; Asian 0.6%; Other 3.6%). **Foreign born:** 3%. **Median age:** 36.5. **State rank:** 30. **Pop change 1990-2000:** +14%.

Income: per capita $18,863; median household $37,147. **Pop below poverty level:** 13.4%.

Unemployment: 6.6%. **Median home value:** $95,800. **Median travel time to work:** 22.7 minutes.

Please see sample entry on inside front cover for detailed information about the statistics presented with each county listing.

NEW HANOVER COUNTY

320 Chestnut St Rm 502   **Ph:** 910-341-7184
Wilmington, NC 28401   **Fax:** 910-341-4027
www.co.new-hanover.nc.us

On the southeastern shore of NC, southwest of Jacksonville; organized Nov 27, 1729 from Craven County. **Name Origin:** For the British royal house of Hanover, which began with George I (1660-1727), Duke of Hannover. Anglicized to Hanover.

Area (sq mi): 327.92 (land 198.93; water 128.98).

Pop: 160,307 (White 78.9%; Black or African American 17%; Hispanic or Latino 2%; Asian 0.8%; Other 2.4%). **Foreign born:** 3.2%. **Median age:** 36.3. **State rank:** 9. **Pop change 1990-2000:** +33.3%.

Income: per capita $23,123; median household $40,172. **Pop below poverty level:** 13.1%.

Unemployment: 4.7%. **Median home value:** $135,600. **Median travel time to work:** 20.7 minutes.

NORTHAMPTON COUNTY

PO Box 808   **Ph:** 252-534-2501
Jackson, NC 27845   **Fax:** 252-534-1166
www.northamptonnc.com

On the northern border of NC, northeast of Rocky Mount; organized 1741 from Bertie County. **Name Origin:** For Northampton, England, or the British earl of Northampton.

Area (sq mi): 550.61 (land 536.48; water 14.13).

Pop: 22,086 (White 39%; Black or African American 59.4%; Hispanic or Latino 0.7%; Asian 0.1%; Other 1.4%). **Foreign born:** 0.7%. **Median age:** 40. **State rank:** 78. **Pop change 1990-2000:** +6.2%.

Income: per capita $15,413; median household $26,652. **Pop below poverty level:** 21.3%.

Unemployment: 9.5%. **Median home value:** $57,500. **Median travel time to work:** 27.2 minutes.

ONSLOW COUNTY

118 Old Bridge St   **Ph:** 910-347-4717
Jacksonville, NC 28540   **Fax:** 910-455-7878
www.co.onslow.nc.us

On the southeastern shore of NC, northeast of Wilmington; organized 1734 (prior to statehood) from New Hanover County. **Name Origin:** For Arthur Onslow (1691-1768), speaker of the House of Commons in England (1728-61).

Area (sq mi): 908.56 (land 766.82; water 141.74).

Pop: 150,355 (White 69.6%; Black or African American 18.5%; Hispanic or Latino 7.2%; Asian 1.7%; Other 7.7%). **Foreign born:** 4.1%. **Median age:** 25. **State rank:** 10. **Pop change 1990-2000:** +0.3%.

Income: per capita $14,853; median household $33,756. **Pop below poverty level:** 12.9%.

Unemployment: 4.5%. **Median home value:** $85,900. **Median travel time to work:** 21.2 minutes.

ORANGE COUNTY

106 E Margaret Ln   **Ph:** 919-732-8181
Hillsborough, NC 27278   **Fax:** 919-644-3043
www.co.orange.nc.us

In north-central NC, west of Durham; organized Mar 31, 1753 (prior to statehood) from Bladen, Granville, and Johnston counties. **Name Origin:** Said to be for William III of the House of Orange, but when the county was formed, William V (1748-1806) was Stadholder; it seems more likely to be named for the latter (grandson of George II of England) than for the former, who had been dead for fifty years.

Area (sq mi): 401.21 (land 399.84; water 1.37).

Pop: 118,227 (White 75.8%; Black or African American 13.8%; Hispanic or Latino 4.5%; Asian 4.1%; Other 4.1%). **Foreign born:** 9.1%. **Median age:** 30.4. **State rank:** 22. **Pop change 1990-2000:** +26%.

Income: per capita $24,873; median household $42,372. **Pop below poverty level:** 14.1%.

Unemployment: 2.2%. **Median home value:** $179,000. **Median travel time to work:** 22 minutes.

PAMLICO COUNTY

PO Box 776   **Ph:** 252-745-3133
Bayboro, NC 28515   **Fax:** 252-745-5514
www.co.pamlico.nc.us

On the central eastern shore of NC on Pamlico Sound, east of New Bern; organized Feb 8, 1872 from Craven and Beaufort counties. **Name Origin:** For Pamlico Sound.

Area (sq mi): 566.23 (land 336.94; water 229.29).

Pop: 12,934 (White 72.6%; Black or African American 24.6%; Hispanic or Latino 1.3%; Asian 0.4%; Other 1.8%). **Foreign born:** 1.8%. **Median age:** 42.9. **State rank:** 91. **Pop change 1990-2000:** +13.7%.

Income: per capita $18,005; median household $34,084. **Pop below poverty level:** 15.3%.

Unemployment: 4.5%. **Median home value:** $89,900. **Median travel time to work:** 28.9 minutes.

PASQUOTANK COUNTY

PO Box 39   **Ph:** 252-335-0865
Elizabeth City, NC 27907   **Fax:** 252-335-0866
www.co.pasquotank.nc.us

On the northeastern border of NC, on Albemarle Sound; organized 1668 (prior to statehood) as a precinct of Albemarle County. **Name Origin:** For the Pasquotank River, which forms its eastern border; from the Indian word *pask-etan-ki* 'where the current [of the stream] divides or forks.'

Area (sq mi): 289.44 (land 226.88; water 62.56).

Pop: 34,897 (White 56.4%; Black or African American 40%; Hispanic or Latino 1.2%; Asian 0.9%; Other 2.2%). **Foreign born:** 2.3%. **Median age:** 35.9. **State rank:** 62. **Pop change 1990-2000:** +11.5%.

Income: per capita $14,815; median household $30,444. **Pop below poverty level:** 18.4%.

All statistics are based on the 2000 Census except the dollar figures given for per capita income, which are based on 1999 estimates.

Unemployment: 4.5%. **Median home value:** $85,500. **Median travel time to work:** 22.8 minutes.

PENDER COUNTY

PO Box 5   **Ph:** 910-259-1200
Burgaw, NC 28425   **Fax:** 910-259-1402
www.pender-county.com

On the southeastern shore of NC, north of Wilmington; organized Feb 16, 1875 from New Hanover County. **Name Origin:** For Gen. William Dorsey Pender (1834-63), officer in the Confederate Army killed at the Battle of Gettysburg.

Area (sq mi): 932.64 (land 870.67; water 61.97).

Pop: 41,082 (White 71.7%; Black or African American 23.6%; Hispanic or Latino 3.6%; Asian 0.2%; Other 3.4%). **Foreign born:** 3.6%. **Median age:** 38.8. **State rank:** 58. **Pop change 1990-2000:** +42.4%.

Income: per capita $17,882; median household $35,902. **Pop below poverty level:** 13.6%.

Unemployment: 6.1%. **Median home value:** $113,400. **Median travel time to work:** 29.2 minutes.

PERQUIMANS COUNTY

PO Box 45   **Ph:** 252-426-8484
Hertford, NC 279440045
www.co.perquimans.nc.us

In northeastern NC on Albemarle Sound, west of Elizabeth City; organized 1679 (prior to statehood) as Berkeley Precinct of Albemarle County. **Name Origin:** For the Perquimans River, which runs through it, named for the Indian tribe who once lived along its banks.

Area (sq mi): 328.93 (land 247.17; water 81.76).

Pop: 11,368 (White 70.5%; Black or African American 28%; Hispanic or Latino 0.6%; Asian 0.2%; Other 0.9%). **Foreign born:** 0.7%. **Median age:** 42.2. **State rank:** 92. **Pop change 1990-2000:** +8.8%.

Income: per capita $15,728; median household $29,538. **Pop below poverty level:** 17.9%.

Unemployment: 4.9%. **Median home value:** $82,800. **Median travel time to work:** 33.1 minutes.

PERSON COUNTY

304 S Morgan St Rm 212   **Ph:** 336-597-1720
Roxboro, NC 27573   **Fax:** 336-599-1609
www.personcounty.net

On the central northern border of NC, north of Durham; organized Dec 5, 1791 from Caswell County. **Name Origin:** For Gen. Thomas Person (1733-1800), Revolutionary War officer and NC legislator.

Area (sq mi): 404.09 (land 392.31; water 11.78).

Pop: 35,623 (White 68.1%; Black or African American 28.2%; Hispanic or Latino 2.1%; Asian 0.1%; Other 2.9%). **Foreign born:** 1.3%. **Median age:** 38. **State rank:** 61. **Pop change 1990-2000:** +18%.

Income: per capita $18,709; median household $37,159. **Pop below poverty level:** 12%.

Unemployment: 7.9%. **Median home value:** $90,400. **Median travel time to work:** 29.7 minutes.

PITT COUNTY

1717 W 5th St   **Ph:** 252-902-2951
Greenville, NC 27834   **Fax:** 252-830-6311
www.co.pitt.nc.us/Pitt/

In east-central NC, northeast of Goldsboro; organized Apr 24, 1760 (prior to statehood) from Beaufort County. **Name Origin:** For William Pitt (1708-78), 1st Earl of Chatham, known as 'the Great Commoner' for his support of the American colonies before the Revolutionary War.

Area (sq mi): 654.77 (land 651.58; water 3.19).

Pop: 133,798 (White 61%; Black or African American 33.6%; Hispanic or Latino 3.2%; Asian 1.1%; Other 3.2%). **Foreign born:** 3.6%. **Median age:** 30.4. **State rank:** 13. **Pop change 1990-2000:** +24%.

Income: per capita $18,243; median household $32,868. **Pop below poverty level:** 20.3%.

Unemployment: 6.1%. **Median home value:** $96,800. **Median travel time to work:** 20.7 minutes.

POLK COUNTY

PO Box 308   **Ph:** 828-894-3301
Columbus, NC 28722   **Fax:** 828-894-2263
www.co.polk.nc.us

On the southwestern border, southeast of Asheville; organized 1855 from Rutherford and Henderson counties. **Name Origin:** For Col. William Polk (1785-1834), an officer in the American Revolution, NC legislator, and supervisor of internal revenue (1791-1808).

Area (sq mi): 238.6 (land 237.85; water 0.75).

Pop: 18,324 (White 90.1%; Black or African American 5.9%; Hispanic or Latino 3%; Asian 0.2%; Other 1.6%). **Foreign born:** 3.7%. **Median age:** 44.9. **State rank:** 83. **Pop change 1990-2000:** +27.1%.

Income: per capita $19,804; median household $36,259. **Pop below poverty level:** 10.1%.

Unemployment: 3.5%. **Median home value:** $112,000. **Median travel time to work:** 26.2 minutes.

RANDOLPH COUNTY

PO Box 4728   **Ph:** 336-318-6300
Asheboro, NC 27204   **Fax:** 336-318-6853
www.co.randolph.nc.us

In west-central NC, south of Greensboro; organized 1779 (prior to statehood) from Guilford County. **Name Origin:** For Peyton Randolph (1721?-75), member of the VA House of Burgesses (1748-49; 1752-75) and speaker (1766-75); president of the Continental Congress (1774-75).

Area (sq mi): 789.93 (land 787.36; water 2.57).

Pop: 130,454 (White 86%; Black or African American 5.6%; Hispanic or Latino 6.6%; Asian 0.6%; Other 4.5%). **Foreign born:** 5.7%. **Median age:** 36.2. **State rank:** 16. **Pop change 1990-2000:** +22.4%.

Income: per capita $18,236; median household $38,348. **Pop below poverty level:** 9.1%.

Please see sample entry on inside front cover for detailed information about the statistics presented with each county listing.

Unemployment: 5.4%. **Median home value:** $94,700. **Median travel time to work:** 23.6 minutes.

RICHMOND COUNTY

125 S Hancock Sr
Rockingham, NC 28379
www.co.richmond.nc.us

Ph: 910-997-8211
Fax: 910-997-8208

On the southern border of NC, west of Fayetteville; organized Oct 18, 1779 (prior to statehood) from Anson County. **Name Origin:** For Charles Lennox (1735-1806), third Duke of Richmond, British secretary of state who denounced British policy toward American colonies.

Area (sq mi): 479.58 (land 473.98; water 5.6).

Pop: 46,564 (White 63.4%; Black or African American 30.5%; Hispanic or Latino 2.8%; Asian 0.7%; Other 4%). **Foreign born:** 2.2%. **Median age:** 35.5. **State rank:** 52. **Pop change 1990-2000:** +4.6%.

Income: per capita $14,485; median household $28,830. **Pop below poverty level:** 19.6%.

Unemployment: 9.7%. **Median home value:** $59,300. **Median travel time to work:** 21.6 minutes.

ROBESON COUNTY

701 N Elm St
Lumberton, NC 28358
www.co.robeson.nc.us

Ph: 910-671-3022
Fax: 910-671-3010

On southern border of NC, south of Fayetteville; organized 1786 from Bladen County (prior to statehood). **Name Origin:** For Col. Thomas Robeson (1740-85), an officer in the American Revolution.

Area (sq mi): 951.03 (land 948.84; water 2.19).

Pop: 123,339 (White 30.8%; Black or African American 25.1%; Hispanic or Latino 4.9%; Asian 0.3%; Other 41.8%). **Foreign born:** 4.2%. **Median age:** 32. **State rank:** 19. **Pop change 1990-2000:** +17.3%.

Income: per capita $13,224; median household $28,202. **Pop below poverty level:** 22.8%.

Unemployment: 11.5%. **Median home value:** $66,100. **Median travel time to work:** 28.1 minutes.

ROCKINGHAM COUNTY

PO Box 206
Wentworth, NC 27375
www.co.rockingham.nc.us

Ph: 336-342-8101
Fax: 336-342-8105

On the central northern border of NC, north of Greensboro; organized Nov 19, 1785 (prior to statehood) from Guilford County. **Name Origin:** For Charles Watson Wentworth (1730-82), second Marquis of Rockingham, prime minister of England (1765-66; 1782), and supporter of independence for American colonies.

Area (sq mi): 572.33 (land 566.44; water 5.9).

Pop: 91,928 (White 76.2%; Black or African American 19.6%; Hispanic or Latino 3.1%; Asian 0.3%; Other 2.8%). **Foreign born:** 2.7%. **Median age:** 38.5. **State rank:** 25. **Pop change 1990-2000:** +6.8%.

Income: per capita $17,120; median household $33,784. **Pop below poverty level:** 12.8%.

Unemployment: 7.4%. **Median home value:** $81,400. **Median travel time to work:** 26.1 minutes.

ROWAN COUNTY

130 W Innes St
Salisbury, NC 28144
www.co.rowan.nc.us

Ph: 704-636-0361
Fax: 704-638-3092

In west-central NC, southwest of Winston-Salem; organized Mar 27, 1753 (prior to statehood) from Anson County. **Name Origin:** For Matthew Rowan (?-1760), NC legislator, justice of the peace, and acting governor when the county was established.

Area (sq mi): 523.86 (land 511.31; water 12.55).

Pop: 130,340 (White 78.1%; Black or African American 15.8%; Hispanic or Latino 4.1%; Asian 0.8%; Other 3.3%). **Foreign born:** 3.7%. **Median age:** 36.4. **State rank:** 17. **Pop change 1990-2000:** +17.8%.

Income: per capita $18,071; median household $37,494. **Pop below poverty level:** 10.6%.

Unemployment: 6.6%. **Median home value:** $95,200. **Median travel time to work:** 23.3 minutes.

RUTHERFORD COUNTY

289 N Main St
Rutherfordton, NC 28139
www.rutherfordgov.org

Ph: 828-287-6060
Fax: 828-287-6262

On the southwestern border of NC, southeast of Asheville; organized Apr 14, 1779 (prior to statehood) from Burke and Tryon counties, the latter organized in 1768 and abolished in 1779. **Name Origin:** For Gen. Griffith Rutherford (1731-1800), Indian fighter, member of the Provincial Congress, and Revolutionary War officer.

Area (sq mi): 565.9 (land 564.12; water 1.78).

Pop: 62,899 (White 85.8%; Black or African American 11.2%; Hispanic or Latino 1.8%; Asian 0.3%; Other 1.6%). **Foreign born:** 1.4%. **Median age:** 38.3. **State rank:** 38. **Pop change 1990-2000:** +10.5%.

Income: per capita $16,270; median household $31,122. **Pop below poverty level:** 13.9%.

Unemployment: 8.4%. **Median home value:** $77,600. **Median travel time to work:** 22.1 minutes.

SAMPSON COUNTY

435 Rowan Rd
Clinton, NC 28328
www.sampsonnc.com

Ph: 910-592-6308
Fax: 910-592-1945

In south-central NC, east of Fayetteville; organized Apr 18, 1784 (prior to statehood) from Duplin County. **Name Origin:** For Col. John Sampson (?-1784), advisor to Josiah Martin, the last royal governor.

Area (sq mi): 947.45 (land 945.45; water 2.01).

Pop: 60,161 (White 56.8%; Black or African American 29.9%; Hispanic or Latino 10.8%; Asian 0.3%; Other 10%). **Foreign born:** 7.1%. **Median age:** 35. **State rank:** 39. **Pop change 1990-2000:** +27.2%.

Income: per capita $14,976; median household $31,793. **Pop below poverty level:** 17.6%.

All statistics are based on the 2000 Census except the dollar figures given for per capita income, which are based on 1999 estimates.

Unemployment: 7.2%. **Median home value:** $76,700. **Median travel time to work:** 25.1 minutes.

SCOTLAND COUNTY
PO Box 489   **Ph:** 910-277-2406
Laurinburg, NC 28353   **Fax:** 910-277-2411
www.scotlandcounty.org

On the southern border of NC, southwest of Fayetteville; organized Feb 20, 1899 from Richmond County. **Name Origin:** For the country, former home of many early settlers.

Area (sq mi): 320.64 (land 319.14; water 1.5).

Pop: 35,998 (White 51.1%; Black or African American 37.3%; Hispanic or Latino 1.2%; Asian 0.5%; Other 10.7%). **Foreign born:** 1.3%. **Median age:** 34.6. **State rank:** 60. **Pop change 1990-2000:** +6.6%.

Income: per capita $15,693; median household $31,010. **Pop below poverty level:** 20.6%.

Unemployment: 10.1%. **Median home value:** $73,200. **Median travel time to work:** 22.4 minutes.

STANLY COUNTY
201 S 2nd St   **Ph:** 704-986-3600
Albemarle, NC 280015747   **Fax:** 704-983-3133
www.co.stanly.nc.us

In west-central NC, northeast of Charlotte; organized Jan 11, 1841 from Montgomery County. **Name Origin:** For John Stanly (1774-1834), NC legislator and U.S. representative (1801-03; 1809-11).

Area (sq mi): 404.26 (land 395.06; water 9.2).

Pop: 58,100 (White 83.7%; Black or African American 11.5%; Hispanic or Latino 2.1%; Asian 1.8%; Other 2%). **Foreign born:** 2.6%. **Median age:** 36.9. **State rank:** 42. **Pop change 1990-2000:** +12.2%.

Income: per capita $17,825; median household $36,898. **Pop below poverty level:** 10.7%.

Unemployment: 8.3%. **Median home value:** $87,700. **Median travel time to work:** 25.3 minutes.

STOKES COUNTY
PO Box 250   **Ph:** 336-593-9173
Danbury, NC 27016   **Fax:** 336-593-5459
www.co.stokes.nc.us

On the northern border of NC, north of Winston-Salem; organized Nov 2, 1798 from Surry County. **Name Origin:** For Col. John Stokes (1756-90), hero of the American Revolution, NC legislator, and district judge (1783).

Area (sq mi): 455.89 (land 451.84; water 4.05).

Pop: 44,711 (White 92.5%; Black or African American 4.7%; Hispanic or Latino 1.9%; Asian 0.2%; Other 1.7%). **Foreign born:** 1.5%. **Median age:** 37.2. **State rank:** 54. **Pop change 1990-2000:** +20.1%.

Income: per capita $18,130; median household $38,808. **Pop below poverty level:** 9.1%.

Unemployment: 5%. **Median home value:** $94,700. **Median travel time to work:** 30.7 minutes.

SURRY COUNTY
202 Kapp St   **Ph:** 336-386-3700
Dobson, NC 27017   **Fax:** 336-386-9879
www.co.surry.nc.us

On the northwestern border of NC, northwest of Winston-Salem; organized 1771 (prior to statehood) from Rowan County. **Name Origin:** For Surrey County in England, home of then-incumbent governor, William Tryon. Possibly influenced by similarity to *Saura*, the local Indian tribe. Spelling the name without the 'e' seems to have been a common colonial practice.

Area (sq mi): 537.79 (land 536.52; water 1.27).

Pop: 71,219 (White 88%; Black or African American 4.2%; Hispanic or Latino 6.5%; Asian 0.6%; Other 4.8%). **Foreign born:** 5.3%. **Median age:** 38. **State rank:** 35. **Pop change 1990-2000:** +15.4%.

Income: per capita $17,722; median household $33,046. **Pop below poverty level:** 12.4%.

Unemployment: 6.5%. **Median home value:** $87,500. **Median travel time to work:** 25.5 minutes.

SWAIN COUNTY
PO Box 1397   **Ph:** 828-488-2288
Bryson City, NC 28713   **Fax:** 828-488-9360
www.swaincounty.org

On the southwestern border of NC, west of Asheville; organized Feb 24, 1871 from Jackson and Macon counties. **Name Origin:** For David Lowrie Swain (1801-68), NC governor (1832-35) and president of the University of NC (1835-68).

Area (sq mi): 540.64 (land 528.1; water 12.54).

Pop: 12,968 (White 65.9%; Black or African American 1.7%; Hispanic or Latino 1.5%; Asian 0.2%; Other 31.8%). **Foreign born:** 1%. **Median age:** 38.8. **State rank:** 90. **Pop change 1990-2000:** +15.1%.

Income: per capita $14,647; median household $28,608. **Pop below poverty level:** 18.3%.

Unemployment: 11.2%. **Median home value:** $86,800. **Median travel time to work:** 20.8 minutes.

TRANSYLVANIA COUNTY
28 E Main St   **Ph:** 828-884-3100
Brevard, NC 28712   **Fax:** 828-884-3119
www.transylvaniacounty.org

On the southwestern border of NC, southwest of Asheville; organized Feb 15, 1861 from Jacksonville and Henderson counties. **Name Origin:** From Latin *trans* plus *sylva* 'across the woods.' The name may also echo that of the province of Transylvania, now in Rumania, but more probably it is literary or promotional name.

Area (sq mi): 380.56 (land 378.39; water 2.17).

Pop: 29,334 (White 93.1%; Black or African American 4.2%; Hispanic or Latino 1%; Asian 0.4%; Other 1.7%). **Foreign born:** 2.3%. **Median age:** 43.9. **State rank:** 70. **Pop change 1990-2000:** +14.9%.

Income: per capita $20,767; median household $38,587. **Pop below poverty level:** 9.5%.

Unemployment: 4.7%. **Median home value:** $122,300. **Median travel time to work:** 22.1 minutes.

Please see sample entry on inside front cover for detailed information about the statistics presented with each county listing.

TYRRELL COUNTY
108 S Water St PO Box 449   **Ph:** 252-796-1371
Columbia, NC 27925   **Fax:** 252-796-1188

In northeastern NC, on Albemarle Sound, south of Elizabeth City; organized 1729 (prior to statehood) from Chowan, Bertie, Currituck, and Pasquotank counties. **Name Origin:** For John Tyrrell (1685-1729), a lord proprietor of NC.

Area (sq mi): 600.3 (land 389.91; water 210.39).

Pop: 4,149 (White 55.5%; Black or African American 39.4%; Hispanic or Latino 3.6%; Asian 0.7%; Other 3.3%). **Foreign born:** 4%. **Median age:** 38.7. **State rank:** 100. **Pop change 1990-2000:** +7.6%.

Income: per capita $13,326; median household $25,684. **Pop below poverty level:** 23.3%.

Unemployment: 8.8%. **Median home value:** $59,000. **Median travel time to work:** 32.5 minutes.

UNION COUNTY
500 N Main St Rm 921   **Ph:** 704-283-3672
Monroe, NC 28112   **Fax:** 704-282-0121
www.co.union.nc.us

On the southern border of NC, southeast of Charlotte; organized Dec 19, 1842 from Mecklenburg and Anson counties. **Name Origin:** A compromise to a disagreement between Whigs and Democrats as to whether it should be named for Clay or Jackson; county was also a union of parts of two other counties.

Area (sq mi): 639.59 (land 637.37; water 2.22).

Pop: 123,677 (White 79.7%; Black or African American 12.5%; Hispanic or Latino 6.2%; Asian 0.6%; Other 4%). **Foreign born:** 5.7%. **Median age:** 34. **State rank:** 18. **Pop change 1990-2000:** +46.9%.

Income: per capita $21,978; median household $50,638. **Pop below poverty level:** 8.1%.

Unemployment: 3.8%. **Median home value:** $128,500. **Median travel time to work:** 29 minutes.

VANCE COUNTY
122 Young St Suite B   **Ph:** 919-492-0031
Henderson, NC 27536
www.vancecounty.org

On the central northern border of NC, northeast of Raleigh; organized Mar 5, 1881 from Franklin, Granville, and Warren counties. **Name Origin:** For Zebulon Baird Vance (1830-94), U.S. representative from NC (1858-61), governor (1862-65; 1877-79), and U.S. senator (1879-94).

Area (sq mi): 269.82 (land 253.52; water 16.31).

Pop: 42,954 (White 46.3%; Black or African American 48.3%; Hispanic or Latino 4.6%; Asian 0.4%; Other 3%). **Foreign born:** 3.4%. **Median age:** 35. **State rank:** 55. **Pop change 1990-2000:** +10.4%.

Income: per capita $15,897; median household $31,301. **Pop below poverty level:** 20.5%.

Unemployment: 10.3%. **Median home value:** $82,200. **Median travel time to work:** 23.6 minutes.

WAKE COUNTY
PO Box 550 Suite 1100   **Ph:** 919-856-6160
Raleigh, NC 27602   **Fax:** 919-856-6168
www.co.wake.nc.us

In north-central NC, east of Durham; organized 1771 (prior to statehood) from Cumberland, Johnston, and Orange counties. **Name Origin:** For Margaret Wake (1733-1819), wife of Gov. William Tryon (1729-88).

Area (sq mi): 857.26 (land 831.92; water 25.33).

Pop: 627,846 (White 69.9%; Black or African American 19.7%; Hispanic or Latino 5.4%; Asian 3.4%; Other 4.4%). **Foreign born:** 9.7%. **Median age:** 32.9. **State rank:** 2. **Pop change 1990-2000:** +48.3%.

Income: per capita $27,004; median household $54,988. **Pop below poverty level:** 7.8%.

Unemployment: 3.3%. **Median home value:** $162,900. **Median travel time to work:** 24.7 minutes.

WARREN COUNTY
PO Box 709   **Ph:** 252-257-3261
Warrenton, NC 27589   **Fax:** 252-257-5529

On the central northern border of NC, northeast of Raleigh; organized Apr 14, 1779 (prior to statehood) from Bute County, which was discontinued at that time. **Name Origin:** For Gen. Joseph Warren (1741-75), Revolutionary War patriot and member of the Committee of Safety who dispatched Paul Revere (1735-1818) on his famous ride.

Area (sq mi): 443.8 (land 428.7; water 15.09).

Pop: 19,972 (White 38.5%; Black or African American 54.5%; Hispanic or Latino 1.6%; Asian 0.1%; Other 6.5%). **Foreign born:** 2.3%. **Median age:** 39.7. **State rank:** 79. **Pop change 1990-2000:** +15.7%.

Income: per capita $14,716; median household $28,351. **Pop below poverty level:** 19.4%.

Unemployment: 10.3%. **Median home value:** $80,500. **Median travel time to work:** 30.4 minutes.

WASHINGTON COUNTY
PO Box 1007   **Ph:** 252-793-5823
Plymouth, NC 27962   **Fax:** 252-793-1183
www.washingtoncountygov.com

In east-central NC, on Albemarle Sound, southwest of Elizabeth City; organized 1799 from Tyrrell County. **Name Origin:** For George Washington (1732-99), American patriot and first U.S. president.

Area (sq mi): 424.39 (land 348.46; water 75.93).

Pop: 13,723 (White 47.8%; Black or African American 48.9%; Hispanic or Latino 2.3%; Asian 0.3%; Other 2.5%). **Foreign born:** 1.4%. **Median age:** 39.2. **State rank:** 89. **Pop change 1990-2000:** -2%.

Income: per capita $14,994; median household $28,865. **Pop below poverty level:** 21.8%.

Unemployment: 7.1%. **Median home value:** $69,400. **Median travel time to work:** 28.3 minutes.

All statistics are based on the 2000 Census except the dollar figures given for per capita income, which are based on 1999 estimates.

WATAUGA COUNTY

842 W King St Courthouse   **Ph:** 828-265-8000
Boone, NC 28607   **Fax:** 828-264-3230
www.wataugacounty.org

On the northeastern border of NC, northeast of Asheville; organized Jan 27, 1849 from Ashe, Caldwell, Wilkes, and Yancey counties. **Name Origin:** For the Watauga River, which runs through the county; from the Indian word probably meaning 'beautiful water.'

Area (sq mi): 312.73 (land 312.51; water 0.22).

Pop: 42,695 (White 95.4%; Black or African American 1.6%; Hispanic or Latino 1.5%; Asian 0.6%; Other 1.4%). **Foreign born:** 1.9%. **Median age:** 29.9. **State rank:** 56. **Pop change 1990-2000:** +15.5%.

Income: per capita $17,258; median household $32,611. **Pop below poverty level:** 17.9%.

Unemployment: 2.1%. **Median home value:** $139,300. **Median travel time to work:** 20.4 minutes.

WAYNE COUNTY

PO Box 227   **Ph:** 919-731-1435
Goldsboro, NC 27533   **Fax:** 919-731-1446
www.esn.net/waynecounty

In east-central NC, southeast of Raleigh; organized Oct 18, 1779 (prior to statehood) from Dobbs County. **Name Origin:** For Gen. Anthony Wayne (1745-96), PA soldier and statesman, nicknamed 'Mad Anthony' for his daring during the Revolutionary War.

Area (sq mi): 556.69 (land 552.57; water 4.12).

Pop: 113,329 (White 59.8%; Black or African American 33%; Hispanic or Latino 4.9%; Asian 1%; Other 4.8%). **Foreign born:** 4.2%. **Median age:** 34.8. **State rank:** 23. **Pop change 1990-2000:** +8.3%.

Income: per capita $17,010; median household $33,942. **Pop below poverty level:** 13.8%.

Unemployment: 5.4%. **Median home value:** $87,600. **Median travel time to work:** 21.5 minutes.

WILKES COUNTY

110 North St   **Ph:** 336-651-7300
Wilkesboro, NC 28697   **Fax:** 336-651-7546

In northwestern NC, northwest of Winston-Salem; organized Nov 15, 1777 (prior to statehood) from Surry County. **Name Origin:** For John Wilkes (1727-97), English political leader who supported American rights at the time of the Revolutionary War.

Area (sq mi): 759.93 (land 757.19; water 2.74).

Pop: 65,632 (White 91.4%; Black or African American 4.2%; Hispanic or Latino 3.4%; Asian 0.3%; Other 2.5%). **Foreign born:** 3%. **Median age:** 38.5. **State rank:** 36. **Pop change 1990-2000:** +10.5%.

Income: per capita $17,516; median household $34,258. **Pop below poverty level:** 11.9%.

Unemployment: 5.7%. **Median home value:** $89,200. **Median travel time to work:** 24 minutes.

WILSON COUNTY

PO Box 1728   **Ph:** 252-399-2810
Wilson, NC 27894   **Fax:** 252-237-4341
www.wilson-co.com

In east-central NC, north of Goldsboro; organized Feb 13, 1855 from Edgecombe, Johnston, Wayne, and Nash counties. **Name Origin:** For Louis Dicken Wilson (1789-1847), member of the NC General Assembly and an officer in the Mexican war.

Area (sq mi): 374.26 (land 371.09; water 3.17).

Pop: 73,814 (White 53.5%; Black or African American 39.3%; Hispanic or Latino 6%; Asian 0.4%; Other 4.4%). **Foreign born:** 4.9%. **Median age:** 36.2. **State rank:** 33. **Pop change 1990-2000:** +11.7%.

Income: per capita $17,102; median household $33,116. **Pop below poverty level:** 18.5%.

Unemployment: 8.3%. **Median home value:** $86,400. **Median travel time to work:** 21 minutes.

YADKIN COUNTY

PO Box 146   **Ph:** 336-679-4200
Yadkinville, NC 27055   **Fax:** 336-679-6005
www.yadkincounty.gov

In north-central NC, west of Winston-Salem; organized Dec 28, 1850 from Surry County. **Name Origin:** For the Yadkin River, which runs through it; meaning of the name is unknown.

Area (sq mi): 337.49 (land 335.55; water 1.94).

Pop: 36,348 (White 89.3%; Black or African American 3.4%; Hispanic or Latino 6.5%; Asian 0.2%; Other 3.9%). **Foreign born:** 4.4%. **Median age:** 37.6. **State rank:** 59. **Pop change 1990-2000:** +19.2%.

Income: per capita $18,576; median household $36,660. **Pop below poverty level:** 10%.

Unemployment: 4.9%. **Median home value:** $90,600. **Median travel time to work:** 27.5 minutes.

YANCEY COUNTY

110 Town Square Rm 11   **Ph:** 828-682-3971
Burnsville, NC 28714   **Fax:** 828-682-4301

On the northwestern border of NC, northeast of Asheville; organized 1833 from Buncombe and Burke counties. **Name Origin:** For Bartlett Yancey (1785-1828), U.S. representative from NC (1813-17) and presiding officer of the state senate (1817-27).

Area (sq mi): 313.11 (land 312.45; water 0.65).

Pop: 17,774 (White 95.8%; Black or African American 0.6%; Hispanic or Latino 2.7%; Asian 0.1%; Other 1.3%). **Foreign born:** 2.8%. **Median age:** 41.9. **State rank:** 85. **Pop change 1990-2000:** +15.3%.

Income: per capita $16,335; median household $29,674. **Pop below poverty level:** 15.8%.

Unemployment: 12.7%. **Median home value:** $93,000. **Median travel time to work:** 27 minutes.

Please see sample entry on inside front cover for detailed information about the statistics presented with each county listing.

NORTH DAKOTA - Counties

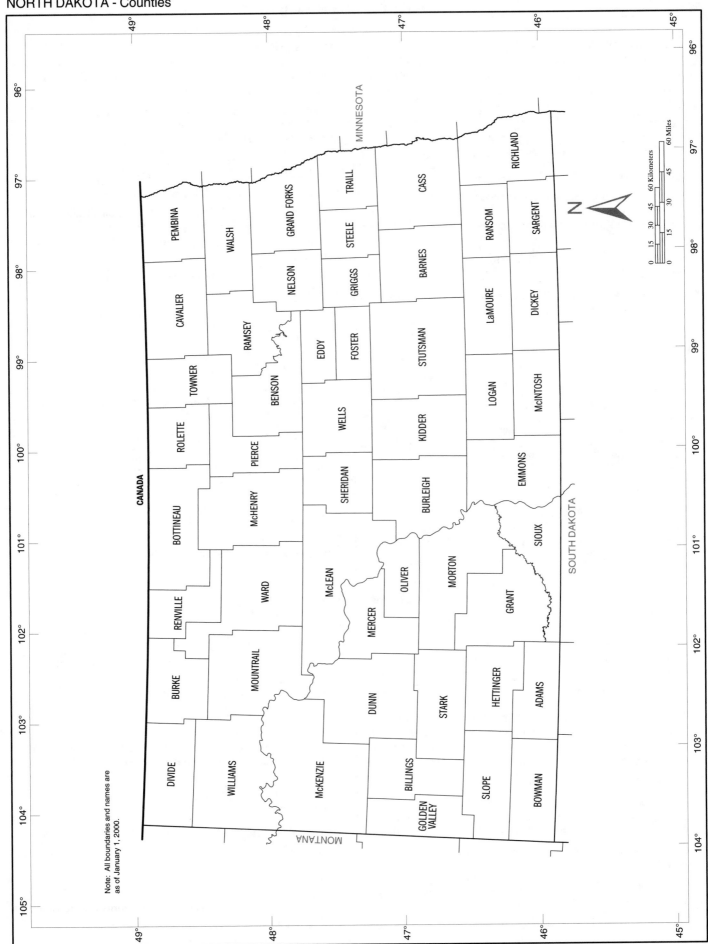

Note: All boundaries and names are as of January 1, 2000.

CANADA

MINNESOTA

SOUTH DAKOTA

MONTANA

DIVIDE

BURKE

RENVILLE

WILLIAMS

MOUNTRAIL

WARD

BOTTINEAU

McHENRY

PIERCE

ROLETTE

TOWNER

CAVALIER

PEMBINA

WALSH

BENSON

RAMSEY

GRAND FORKS

NELSON

McKENZIE

DUNN

MERCER

OLIVER

McLEAN

SHERIDAN

WELLS

EDDY

FOSTER

GRIGGS

STEELE

TRAILL

STUTSMAN

BARNES

CASS

KIDDER

BURLEIGH

LOGAN

LaMOURE

DICKEY

McINTOSH

EMMONS

MORTON

GRANT

SIOUX

RANSOM

SARGENT

RICHLAND

STARK

HETTINGER

ADAMS

BILLINGS

GOLDEN VALLEY

SLOPE

BOWMAN

N

60 Miles

60 Kilometers

45

30

15

0

15

30

45

0

U.S. Census Bureau, Census 2000

North Dakota

NORTH DAKOTA STATE INFORMATION
discovernd.com   **Ph:** 701-328-2000

Area (sq mi): 70,699.79 (land 68,975.93; water 1723.86).

Pop: 642,200 (White 91.7%; Black or African American 0.6%; Hispanic or Latino 1.2%; Asian 0.6%; Other 6.5%). **Foreign born:** 1.9%. **Median age:** 36.2. **Pop change 1990-2000:** +0.5%.

Income: per capita $17,769; median household $34,604. **Pop below poverty level:** 11.9%.

Unemployment: 3.5%. **Median home value:** $74,400. **Median travel time to work:** 15.8 minutes.

ADAMS COUNTY
602 Adams Ave   **Ph:** 701-567-2460
Hettinger, ND 58639   **Fax:** 701-567-2910

On the southwestern border of ND, south of Dickinson; organized Apr 24, 1907 from Hettinger County. **Name Origin:** For John Quincy Adams (1848-1919), land and townsite agent for the Chicago, Milwaukee and Saint Paul Railway whose main line to the Pacific coast was built through the area (1906-07). Adams was distantly related to the president of the same name.

Area (sq mi): 988.84 (land 987.91; water 0.92).

Pop: 2,593 (White 98.3%; Black or African American 0.5%; Hispanic or Latino 0.3%; Asian 0.2%; Other 0.7%). **Foreign born:** 1.5%. **Median age:** 45.6. **State rank:** 44. **Pop change 1990-2000:** -18.3%.

Income: per capita $18,425; median household $29,079. **Pop below poverty level:** 10.4%.

Unemployment: 2%. **Median home value:** $37,500. **Median travel time to work:** 12.6 minutes.

BARNES COUNTY
230 4th St NW Rm 202   **Ph:** 701-845-8500
Valley City, ND 58072   **Fax:** 701-845-8548
www.co.barnes.nd.us

In southeastern ND, west of Fargo; organized as Burbank County by the 1872-1873 territorial legislature (prior to statehood) from Cass County; renamed Jan 14, 1875. **Name Origin:** For Alanson H. Barnes (1818-90), judge of the federal district court (1872-81). Originally for John A. Burbank (1827-1905), governor of Dakota Territory (1869-73).

Area (sq mi): 1513.23 (land 1491.65; water 21.58).

Pop: 11,775 (White 97.5%; Black or African American 0.5%; Hispanic or Latino 0.5%; Asian 0.2%; Other 1.5%). **Foreign born:**

0.9%. **Median age:** 40.6. **State rank:** 13. **Pop change 1990-2000:** -6.1%.

Income: per capita $16,566; median household $31,166. **Pop below poverty level:** 10.8%.

Unemployment: 2.6%. **Median home value:** $57,600. **Median travel time to work:** 15.7 minutes.

BENSON COUNTY
PO Box 213   **Ph:** 701-473-5345
Minnewaukan, ND 58351   **Fax:** 701-473-5571

In east-central ND, east of Minot; organized Mar 9, 1883 (prior to statehood) from Ramsey County. **Name Origin:** For Bertil W. Benson, a Dakota Territory legislator at the time the county was organized.

Area (sq mi): 1439.27 (land 1380.6; water 58.68).

Pop: 6,964 (White 50.7%; Black or African American 0.1%; Hispanic or Latino 0.8%; Asian 0%; Other 49%). **Foreign born:** 0.5%. **Median age:** 31.4. **State rank:** 19. **Pop change 1990-2000:** -3.3%.

Income: per capita $11,509; median household $26,688. **Pop below poverty level:** 29.1%.

Unemployment: 7.5%. **Median home value:** $31,100. **Median travel time to work:** 18.4 minutes.

BILLINGS COUNTY
PO Box 138   **Ph:** 701-623-4491
Medora, ND 58645   **Fax:** 701-623-4896

In southwestern ND, west of Dickinson; organized Feb 10, 1879 (prior to statehood) from unorganized territory. **Name Origin:** For Frederick K. Billings (1823-90), president of the Northern Pacific Railroad (1879-81).

Area (sq mi): 1153.4 (land 1151.41; water 1.99).

Pop: 888 (White 98.4%; Black or African American 0%; Hispanic or Latino 0.3%; Asian 0%; Other 1.2%). **Foreign born:** 1%. **Median age:** 41.9. **State rank:** 52. **Pop change 1990-2000:** -19.9%.

Income: per capita $16,186; median household $32,667. **Pop below poverty level:** 12.8%.

Unemployment: 3.9%. **Median home value:** $56,500. **Median travel time to work:** 22.3 minutes.

BOTTINEAU COUNTY
314 W 5th St   **Ph:** 701-228-3983
Bottineau, ND 58318   **Fax:** 701-228-2336

On the central northern border of ND, northeast of Minot; organized Jan 4, 1873 (prior to statehood) from unorganized territory.

Please see sample entry on inside front cover for detailed information about the statistics presented with each county listing.

425

Name Origin: For Pierre Bottineau (c. 1814-95), a French-Canadian frontiersman, guide, and land speculator.

Area (sq mi): 1697.74 (land 1668.59; water 29.16).

Pop: 7,149 (White 97%; Black or African American 0.2%; Hispanic or Latino 0.5%; Asian 0.2%; Other 2.4%). **Foreign born:** 2.1%. **Median age:** 43.4. **State rank:** 18. **Pop change 1990-2000:** -10.8%.

Income: per capita $16,227; median household $29,853. **Pop below poverty level:** 10.7%.

Unemployment: 3.1%. **Median home value:** $43,600. **Median travel time to work:** 17.9 minutes.

BOWMAN COUNTY

PO Box 379   **Ph:** 701-523-3450
Bowman, ND 58623   **Fax:** 701-523-5443

In the southwestern corner of ND; organized Mar 8, 1883 (prior to statehood) from Billings County. Eliminated in 1903 for lack of settlement; reestablished Jun 10, 1907. **Name Origin:** Possibly for Edward M. Bowman, a Dakota Territory representative. Another source says that William Bowman was the territorial legislator, and Edward M. Bowman was an official of the Milwaukee Road Railroad that ran through the county.

Area (sq mi): 1166.99 (land 1162.05; water 4.95).

Pop: 3,242 (White 98.6%; Black or African American 0%; Hispanic or Latino 0.7%; Asian 0%; Other 1%). **Foreign born:** 0.4%. **Median age:** 43. **State rank:** 36. **Pop change 1990-2000:** -9.8%.

Income: per capita $17,662; median household $31,906. **Pop below poverty level:** 8.2%.

Unemployment: 1.9%. **Median home value:** $53,600. **Median travel time to work:** 12.9 minutes.

BURKE COUNTY

PO Box 219   **Ph:** 701-377-2718
Bowbells, ND 58721   **Fax:** 701-377-2020

On the northwestern border of ND, northwest of Minot; organized Jul 12, 1910 from Ward County. **Name Origin:** For John Burke (1859-1937), ND governor (1907-13), treasurer of the U.S. (1913-21), and justice of ND Supreme Court (1925-37).

Area (sq mi): 1129.26 (land 1103.53; water 25.73).

Pop: 2,242 (White 99%; Black or African American 0.1%; Hispanic or Latino 0.4%; Asian 0.1%; Other 0.4%). **Foreign born:** 1.5%. **Median age:** 47.5. **State rank:** 48. **Pop change 1990-2000:** -25.3%.

Income: per capita $14,026; median household $25,330. **Pop below poverty level:** 15.4%.

Unemployment: 2.5%. **Median home value:** $24,700. **Median travel time to work:** 18.5 minutes.

BURLEIGH COUNTY

PO Box 1055   **Ph:** 701-222-6761
Bismarck, ND 58502   **Fax:** 701-221-3756
www.co.burleigh.nd.us

In south-central ND; organized Jan 4, 1873 (prior to statehood) from Buffalo County, which was discontinued. **Name Origin:** For Walter Atwood Burleigh (1820-96), attorney, physician, Dakota Territory delegate to Congress (1865-69), and legislator.

Area (sq mi): 1668.04 (land 1633.09; water 34.95).

Pop: 69,416 (White 94.6%; Black or African American 0.3%; Hispanic or Latino 0.7%; Asian 0.4%; Other 4.3%). **Foreign born:** 1.5%. **Median age:** 35.9. **State rank:** 2. **Pop change 1990-2000:** +15.4%.

Income: per capita $20,436; median household $41,309. **Pop below poverty level:** 7.8%.

Unemployment: 2.2%. **Median home value:** $98,900. **Median travel time to work:** 15.1 minutes.

CASS COUNTY

PO Box 2806   **Ph:** 701-241-5601
Fargo, ND 58108   **Fax:** 701-241-5728
www.co.cass.nd.us

On the southeastern border of ND, south of Grand Forks; original county; organized Jan 4, 1873 (prior to statehood). **Name Origin:** For George W. Cass (1810-88), president of the Northern Pacific Railroad (1856).

Area (sq mi): 1767.91 (land 1765.23; water 2.68).

Pop: 123,138 (White 94.4%; Black or African American 0.8%; Hispanic or Latino 1.2%; Asian 1.3%; Other 2.8%). **Foreign born:** 3.2%. **Median age:** 31.3. **State rank:** 1. **Pop change 1990-2000:** +19.7%.

Income: per capita $20,889; median household $38,147. **Pop below poverty level:** 10.1%.

Unemployment: 1.5%. **Median home value:** $98,400. **Median travel time to work:** 15.7 minutes.

CAVALIER COUNTY

PO Box 469   **Ph:** 701-256-2229
Langdon, ND 58249   **Fax:** 701-256-2566

On the northeastern border of ND, northwest of Grand Forks; organized Jan 4, 1873 (prior to statehood) from Pembina County. **Name Origin:** For either Charles T. Cavileer (1818-1902), an early white settler and public official (with the spelling changed to seem French); or Rene Robert Cavalier, Sieur de la Salle (1643-87), the explorer.

Area (sq mi): 1510.14 (land 1488.46; water 21.68).

Pop: 4,831 (White 97.7%; Black or African American 0.1%; Hispanic or Latino 0.6%; Asian 0.1%; Other 1.6%). **Foreign born:** 2.5%. **Median age:** 45.2. **State rank:** 26. **Pop change 1990-2000:** -20.3%.

Income: per capita $15,817; median household $31,868. **Pop below poverty level:** 11.5%.

Unemployment: 2.9%. **Median home value:** $46,100. **Median travel time to work:** 12.7 minutes.

DICKEY COUNTY

PO Box 215   **Ph:** 701-349-3249
Ellendale, ND 58436   **Fax:** 701-349-4639

On the southern border of ND, southwest of Fargo; organized Mar 5, 1881 (prior to statehood) from La Moure County. **Name Origin:** For either Alfred M. Dickey (1846-1901), a homesteader in the

All statistics are based on the 2000 Census except the dollar figures given for per capita income, which are based on 1999 estimates.

county and lt. governor of ND (1889-90), or for George H. Dickey (1858-1923), an attorney and ND legislator.

Area (sq mi): 1141.66 (land 1131; water 10.66).

Pop: 5,757 (White 97%; Black or African American 0.1%; Hispanic or Latino 1.4%; Asian 0.5%; Other 1.6%). **Foreign born:** 1.6%. **Median age:** 40.7. **State rank:** 23. **Pop change 1990-2000:** -5.7%.

Income: per capita $15,846; median household $29,231. **Pop below poverty level:** 14.8%.

Unemployment: 2.2%. **Median home value:** $48,700. **Median travel time to work:** 15 minutes.

DIVIDE COUNTY
PO Box 49   **Ph:** 701-965-6831
Crosby, ND 58730   **Fax:** 701-965-6943

In the northwestern corner of ND; organized Dec 9, 1910 from Williams County. **Name Origin:** For the division of Williams County to form it, or possibly for the mountains that divide the county.

Area (sq mi): 1294.18 (land 1259.53; water 34.65).

Pop: 2,283 (White 98.6%; Black or African American 0%; Hispanic or Latino 0.6%; Asian 0.5%; Other 0.5%). **Foreign born:** 2.4%. **Median age:** 49. **State rank:** 46. **Pop change 1990-2000:** -21.2%.

Income: per capita $16,225; median household $30,089. **Pop below poverty level:** 14.6%.

Unemployment: 1.9%. **Median home value:** $31,000. **Median travel time to work:** 13.4 minutes.

DUNN COUNTY
PO Box 105   **Ph:** 701-573-4448
Manning, ND 58642   **Fax:** 701-573-4444

In west-central ND, north of Dickinson; organized Mar 9, 1883 (prior to statehood) from Howard County, which was discontinued. **Name Origin:** For John P. Dunn (1839-1917), early settler and mayor of Bismarck, ND.

Area (sq mi): 2082.25 (land 2009.6; water 72.65).

Pop: 3,600 (White 86.1%; Black or African American 0%; Hispanic or Latino 0.8%; Asian 0.1%; Other 13.3%). **Foreign born:** 0.7%. **Median age:** 40.9. **State rank:** 34. **Pop change 1990-2000:** -10.1%.

Income: per capita $14,624; median household $30,015. **Pop below poverty level:** 17.5%.

Unemployment: 3.6%. **Median home value:** $37,400. **Median travel time to work:** 19.2 minutes.

EDDY COUNTY
524 Central Ave   **Ph:** 701-947-2434
New Rockford, ND 58356   **Fax:** 701-947-2067

In east-central ND, west of Grand Forks; organized Mar 9, 1885 (prior to statehood) from Foster County. **Name Origin:** For Ezra B. Eddy (1830-85), founder of the First National Bank of Fargo.

Area (sq mi): 644.23 (land 630.12; water 14.11).

Pop: 2,757 (White 96.1%; Black or African American 0.1%; Hispanic or Latino 0.6%; Asian 0.1%; Other 3.5%). **Foreign born:** 0.4%. **Median age:** 43.8. **State rank:** 39. **Pop change 1990-2000:** -6.6%.

Income: per capita $15,941; median household $28,642. **Pop below poverty level:** 9.7%.

Unemployment: 4.8%. **Median home value:** $34,000. **Median travel time to work:** 16.6 minutes.

EMMONS COUNTY
PO Box 129   **Ph:** 701-254-4807
Linton, ND 58552   **Fax:** 701-254-4012

On the central southern border of ND, southeast of Bismarck; organized Feb 10, 1879 (prior to statehood) from unorganized territory. **Name Origin:** For James A. Emmons (1845-1919), steamboat captain, early settler, and merchant.

Area (sq mi): 1554.72 (land 1509.88; water 44.83).

Pop: 4,331 (White 98.3%; Black or African American 0%; Hispanic or Latino 1.2%; Asian 0.2%; Other 0.7%). **Foreign born:** 0.5%. **Median age:** 44.5. **State rank:** 30. **Pop change 1990-2000:** -10.3%.

Income: per capita $14,604; median household $26,119. **Pop below poverty level:** 20.1%.

Unemployment: 4.6%. **Median home value:** $37,000. **Median travel time to work:** 17.6 minutes.

FOSTER COUNTY
PO Box 257   **Ph:** 701-652-1001
Carrington, ND 58421   **Fax:** 701-652-2173

In east-central ND, southwest of Grand Forks; organized Jan 4, 1873 (prior to statehood) from Pembina County. **Name Origin:** For either James S. Foster, commissioner of immigration, or possibly his brother, George I. Foster. Both were prominent in Dakota territorial affairs.

Area (sq mi): 646.72 (land 635.2; water 11.52).

Pop: 3,759 (White 98.9%; Black or African American 0.1%; Hispanic or Latino 0.2%; Asian 0%; Other 0.9%). **Foreign born:** 1.5%. **Median age:** 40.5. **State rank:** 32. **Pop change 1990-2000:** -5.6%.

Income: per capita $17,928; median household $32,019. **Pop below poverty level:** 9.3%.

Unemployment: 2.8%. **Median home value:** $55,300. **Median travel time to work:** 12.3 minutes.

GOLDEN VALLEY COUNTY
150 1st Ave SE PO Box 9   **Ph:** 701-872-4352
Beach, ND 58621   **Fax:** 701-872-4383

On the southwestern border of ND, west of Dickinson; organized Nov 11, 1912 from Billings County. **Name Origin:** Descriptive, or for the Golden Valley Land and Cattle Company.

Area (sq mi): 1002.36 (land 1001.99; water 0.37).

Pop: 1,924 (White 97.2%; Black or African American 0%; Hispanic or Latino 1%; Asian 0.1%; Other 2.1%). **Foreign born:** 0.5%. **Median age:** 41.2. **State rank:** 50. **Pop change 1990-2000:** -8.7%.

Income: per capita $14,173; median household $29,967. **Pop below poverty level:** 15.3%.

Unemployment: 2.1%. **Median home value:** $40,600. **Median travel time to work:** 14.1 minutes.

Please see sample entry on inside front cover for detailed information about the statistics presented with each county listing.

GRAND FORKS COUNTY

124 S 4th St
Grand Forks, ND 58201

Ph: 701-780-8214
Fax: 701-795-3886

On the central border of ND; organized Jan 4, 1873 (prior to statehood) from Pembina County. **Name Origin:** For the village of Grand Forks, itself named for the forks of the Red River of the North and Red Lake River.

Area (sq mi): 1439.83 (land 1437.81; water 2.02).

Pop: 66,109 (White 92%; Black or African American 1.4%; Hispanic or Latino 2.1%; Asian 1%; Other 4.7%). **Foreign born:** 3.2%. **Median age:** 29.2. **State rank:** 3. **Pop change 1990-2000:** -6.5%.

Income: per capita $17,868; median household $35,785. **Pop below poverty level:** 12.3%.

Unemployment: 2.7%. **Median home value:** $92,800. **Median travel time to work:** 14.5 minutes.

GRANT COUNTY

102 2nd Ave
Carson, ND 58529

Ph: 701-622-3615
Fax: 701-622-3717

In south-central ND, southwest of Bismarck; organized Nov 25, 1916 from Morton County. **Name Origin:** For Ulysses Simpson Grant (1822-85), Civil War general and eighteenth U.S. president.

Area (sq mi): 1665.92 (land 1659.46; water 6.46).

Pop: 2,841 (White 96.7%; Black or African American 0%; Hispanic or Latino 0.6%; Asian 0.4%; Other 2.8%). **Foreign born:** 1.3%. **Median age:** 46.5. **State rank:** 38. **Pop change 1990-2000:** -19.9%.

Income: per capita $14,616; median household $23,165. **Pop below poverty level:** 20.3%.

Unemployment: 2.7%. **Median home value:** $23,500. **Median travel time to work:** 20.7 minutes.

GRIGGS COUNTY

PO Box 326
Cooperstown, ND 58425

Ph: 701-797-2772
Fax: 701-797-3587

In east-central ND, southwest of Grand Forks; organized Feb 18, 1881 (prior to statehood) from Foster County. **Name Origin:** For Alexander Griggs (1838-1903), a Red River pilot known as 'Captain,' closely identified with the earliest navigation on the Red River.

Area (sq mi): 716.17 (land 708.5; water 7.67).

Pop: 2,754 (White 99.1%; Black or African American 0%; Hispanic or Latino 0.4%; Asian 0.1%; Other 0.5%). **Foreign born:** 1%. **Median age:** 45.8. **State rank:** 40. **Pop change 1990-2000:** -16.6%.

Income: per capita $16,131; median household $29,572. **Pop below poverty level:** 10.1%.

Unemployment: 1.7%. **Median home value:** $36,000. **Median travel time to work:** 14.4 minutes.

HETTINGER COUNTY

PO Box 668
Mott, ND 58646

Ph: 701-824-2645
Fax: 701-824-2717

In southwestern ND, south of Dickinson; organized Mar 9, 1883 (prior to statehood) from Stark County. **Name Origin:** For Mathias K. Hettinger of IL; named by his son-in-law, Erastus A. Williams, a ND territorial legislator and county founder.

Area (sq mi): 1133.7 (land 1132.25; water 1.45).

Pop: 2,715 (White 98.7%; Black or African American 0.1%; Hispanic or Latino 0.2%; Asian 0.1%; Other 0.9%). **Foreign born:** 0.1%. **Median age:** 46.2. **State rank:** 42. **Pop change 1990-2000:** -21.2%.

Income: per capita $15,555; median household $29,209. **Pop below poverty level:** 14.8%.

Unemployment: 2.2%. **Median home value:** $30,300. **Median travel time to work:** 17.5 minutes.

KIDDER COUNTY

120 E Broadway Kidder County Courthouse
Steele, ND 58482

Ph: 701-475-2632
Fax: 701-475-2202

In central ND, east of Bismarck; organized Jan 4, 1873 (prior to statehood) from Buffalo County, which was discontinued. **Name Origin:** For Jefferson Parrish Kidder (1815-83), VT legislator and lieutenant governor, MN legislator (1863-64), and associate justice of the Dakota territorial supreme court (1865-76; 1879-83).

Area (sq mi): 1433.21 (land 1350.79; water 82.42).

Pop: 2,753 (White 98.9%; Black or African American 0.2%; Hispanic or Latino 0.6%; Asian 0.1%; Other 0.2%). **Foreign born:** 0.9%. **Median age:** 44.5. **State rank:** 41. **Pop change 1990-2000:** -17.4%.

Income: per capita $14,270; median household $25,389. **Pop below poverty level:** 19.8%.

Unemployment: 5.3%. **Median home value:** $33,400. **Median travel time to work:** 22.7 minutes.

LAMOURE COUNTY

PO Box 128
La Moure, ND 58458

Ph: 701-883-5301
Fax: 701-883-5304

In southeastern ND, southwest of Fargo; organized Jan 4, 1873 (prior to statehood) from Pembina County. **Name Origin:** For Judson LaMoure (1839-1918), pioneer, legislator, and commissioner of Dakota Territory (1890).

Area (sq mi): 1150.81 (land 1147.18; water 3.63).

Pop: 4,701 (White 98.9%; Black or African American 0%; Hispanic or Latino 0.6%; Asian 0.1%; Other 0.6%). **Foreign born:** 0.8%. **Median age:** 43.3. **State rank:** 27. **Pop change 1990-2000:** -12.7%.

Income: per capita $17,059; median household $29,707. **Pop below poverty level:** 14.7%.

Unemployment: 2.9%. **Median home value:** $34,600. **Median travel time to work:** 17.2 minutes.

LOGAN COUNTY

301 Broadway St
Napoleon, ND 58561

Ph: 701-754-2751
Fax: 701-754-2270

In south-central ND, southeast of Bismarck; organized Jan 4, 1873 (prior to statehood) from Buffalo County, which was discontinued. **Name Origin:** For Gen. John Alexander Logan (1826-86), officer in the Mexican-American War and Civil War; U.S. senator from IL (1871-77; 1879-86).

Area (sq mi): 1011.07 (land 992.64; water 18.43).

All statistics are based on the 2000 Census except the dollar figures given for per capita income, which are based on 1999 estimates.

Pop: 2,308 (White 98.6%; Black or African American 0.1%; Hispanic or Latino 0.7%; Asian 0.2%; Other 0.5%). **Foreign born:** 0.6%. **Median age:** 46.4. **State rank:** 45. **Pop change 1990-2000:** -18.9%.

Income: per capita $16,947; median household $27,986. **Pop below poverty level:** 15.1%.

Unemployment: 2.2%. **Median home value:** $30,200. **Median travel time to work:** 20.4 minutes.

McHENRY COUNTY
PO Box 117   **Ph:** 701-537-5729
Towner, ND 58788   **Fax:** 701-537-5969

In north-central ND, east of Minot; organized Jan 4, 1873 (prior to statehood) from Buffalo County, which was discontinued. **Name Origin:** For James McHenry, an early settler of Vermillion, SD.

Area (sq mi): 1911.71 (land 1874.09; water 37.62).

Pop: 5,987 (White 98.5%; Black or African American 0.1%; Hispanic or Latino 0.4%; Asian 0%; Other 1.2%). **Foreign born:** 1%. **Median age:** 43. **State rank:** 21. **Pop change 1990-2000:** -8.3%.

Income: per capita $15,140; median household $27,274. **Pop below poverty level:** 15.8%.

Unemployment: 5%. **Median home value:** $32,600. **Median travel time to work:** 24.6 minutes.

McINTOSH COUNTY
PO Box 179   **Ph:** 701-288-3450
Ashley, ND 58413   **Fax:** 701-288-3671

On the central southern border of ND, southeast of Bismarck; organized Mar 9, 1883 (prior to statehood) from Logan County. **Name Origin:** For either John J. McIntosh, a state legislator, or for Edward H. McIntosh (1922-1901), a Dakota territorial legislator.

Area (sq mi): 995.04 (land 975.19; water 19.84).

Pop: 3,390 (White 98.2%; Black or African American 0%; Hispanic or Latino 0.8%; Asian 0.3%; Other 0.8%). **Foreign born:** 0.8%. **Median age:** 51. **State rank:** 35. **Pop change 1990-2000:** -15.7%.

Income: per capita $15,018; median household $26,389. **Pop below poverty level:** 15.4%.

Unemployment: 2.2%. **Median home value:** $28,100. **Median travel time to work:** 13.7 minutes.

McKENZIE COUNTY
PO Box 524   **Ph:** 701-444-3452
Watford City, ND 58854   **Fax:** 701-444-3916

On the central western border of ND, southwest of Minot; organized Mar 9, 1883 (prior to statehood) from Howard County; which was discontinued. McKenzie County eliminated in 1891 for lack of settlement; present county formed 1905. **Name Origin:** For Alexander McKenzie (1851-1922), sheriff of Burleigh County and a powerful political leader.

Area (sq mi): 2860.89 (land 2742.02; water 118.87).

Pop: 5,737 (White 77%; Black or African American 0.1%; Hispanic or Latino 1%; Asian 0.1%; Other 22.5%). **Foreign born:** 1.4%. **Median age:** 39.5. **State rank:** 24. **Pop change 1990-2000:** -10.1%.

Income: per capita $14,732; median household $29,342. **Pop below poverty level:** 17.2%.

Unemployment: 2.6%. **Median home value:** $51,100. **Median travel time to work:** 19.8 minutes.

McLEAN COUNTY
PO Box 1108   **Ph:** 701-462-8541
Washburn, ND 58577   **Fax:** 701-462-8212
www.visitmcleancounty.com

In west-central ND, northwest of Bismarck; organized Mar 8, 1883 (prior to statehood) from Stevens County. **Name Origin:** For John A. McLean (1849-1916), first mayor of Bismarck, ND.

Area (sq mi): 2328.17 (land 2109.95; water 218.21).

Pop: 9,311 (White 92.3%; Black or African American 0%; Hispanic or Latino 0.9%; Asian 0.1%; Other 7.3%). **Foreign born:** 0.9%. **Median age:** 44.1. **State rank:** 14. **Pop change 1990-2000:** -11%.

Income: per capita $16,220; median household $32,337. **Pop below poverty level:** 13.5%.

Unemployment: 5.9%. **Median home value:** $48,400. **Median travel time to work:** 22.1 minutes.

MERCER COUNTY
PO Box 39   **Ph:** 701-745-3262
Stanton, ND 58571   **Fax:** 701-745-3710

In west-central ND, northwest of Bismarck; organized Jan 14, 1875 (prior to statehood) from original territory. **Name Origin:** For William Henry Harrison Mercer (1884-1901), an early rancher.

Area (sq mi): 1112.42 (land 1045.49; water 66.93).

Pop: 8,644 (White 95.8%; Black or African American 0%; Hispanic or Latino 0.4%; Asian 0.3%; Other 3.7%). **Foreign born:** 1.5%. **Median age:** 40.1. **State rank:** 15. **Pop change 1990-2000:** -11.9%.

Income: per capita $18,256; median household $42,269. **Pop below poverty level:** 7.5%.

Unemployment: 5.1%. **Median home value:** $62,500. **Median travel time to work:** 14.8 minutes.

MORTON COUNTY
210 2nd Ave NW   **Ph:** 701-667-3300
Mandan, ND 58554   **Fax:** 701-667-3453
www.mortoncountynd.org

In south-central ND, west of Bismarck; organized Jan 8, 1873 (prior to statehood) from original territory. **Name Origin:** For Oliver Hazard Perry Throck Morton (1823-77), jurist, IN governor (1861-67), and U.S. senator (1867-77).

Area (sq mi): 1945.28 (land 1926.27; water 19.01).

Pop: 25,303 (White 95.5%; Black or African American 0.2%; Hispanic or Latino 0.6%; Asian 0.3%; Other 3.8%). **Foreign born:** 0.9%. **Median age:** 37.4. **State rank:** 5. **Pop change 1990-2000:** +6.8%.

Income: per capita $17,202; median household $37,028. **Pop below poverty level:** 9.6%.

Unemployment: 3.3%. **Median home value:** $74,800. **Median travel time to work:** 19.1 minutes.

Please see sample entry on inside front cover for detailed information about the statistics presented with each county listing.

MOUNTRAIL COUNTY

PO Box 69
Stanley, ND 58784

Ph: 701-628-2915
Fax: 701-628-3975

In north-central ND, west of Minot; organized as Mountraille County Jan 4, 1873 (prior to statehood) from Ward County. Eliminated in 1891; reestablished with present spelling Jan 25, 1909. **Name Origin:** For 'Savage' Joseph Mountraille, prominent voyageur who carried the mail.

Area (sq mi): 1941.08 (land 1823.93; water 117.15).

Pop: 6,631 (White 65.7%; Black or African American 0.1%; Hispanic or Latino 1.3%; Asian 0.2%; Other 33.7%). **Foreign born:** 1.2%. **Median age:** 39.6. **State rank:** 20. **Pop change 1990-2000:** -5.6%.

Income: per capita $13,422; median household $27,098. **Pop below poverty level:** 19.3%.

Unemployment: 4.7%. **Median home value:** $39,700. **Median travel time to work:** 16.5 minutes.

NELSON COUNTY

PO Box 565
Lakota, ND 58344

Ph: 701-247-2462
Fax: 701-247-2412

In east-central ND, west of Grand Forks; organized Mar 9, 1883 (prior to statehood) from Foster and Grand Forks counties. **Name Origin:** For Nelson E. Nelson (1830-1913), a ND legislator at the time.

Area (sq mi): 1008.74 (land 981.62; water 27.12).

Pop: 3,715 (White 98.5%; Black or African American 0.1%; Hispanic or Latino 0.2%; Asian 0.3%; Other 1%). **Foreign born:** 1.7%. **Median age:** 47.2. **State rank:** 33. **Pop change 1990-2000:** -15.8%.

Income: per capita $16,320; median household $28,892. **Pop below poverty level:** 10.3%.

Unemployment: 4%. **Median home value:** $36,100. **Median travel time to work:** 21.8 minutes.

OLIVER COUNTY

PO Box 125
Center, ND 58530

Ph: 701-794-8777
Fax: 701-794-3476

In south-central ND, northwest of Bismarck; organized Mar 12, 1885 (prior to statehood) from Mercer County. **Name Origin:** For Harry S. Oliver (1855-1909), a Dakota Territory legislator.

Area (sq mi): 731.19 (land 723.52; water 7.67).

Pop: 2,065 (White 97.1%; Black or African American 0.1%; Hispanic or Latino 0.6%; Asian 0.1%; Other 2.2%). **Foreign born:** 0.3%. **Median age:** 42. **State rank:** 49. **Pop change 1990-2000:** -13.3%.

Income: per capita $16,271; median household $36,650. **Pop below poverty level:** 14.9%.

Unemployment: 4.9%. **Median home value:** $59,600. **Median travel time to work:** 23.1 minutes.

PEMBINA COUNTY

301 Dakota St W MD 6
Cavalier, ND 58220

Ph: 701-265-4275
Fax: 701-265-4876

In the northeast corner of ND; organized Jan 9, 1867 (prior to

statehood) from Indian lands. **Name Origin:** From Ojibway Indian *anepeminan* 'high bush cranberries,' which grew abundantly in the area.

Area (sq mi): 1121.74 (land 1118.75; water 2.99).

Pop: 8,585 (White 93.9%; Black or African American 0.2%; Hispanic or Latino 3.1%; Asian 0.2%; Other 4.1%). **Foreign born:** 3.8%. **Median age:** 41.6. **State rank:** 16. **Pop change 1990-2000:** -7.1%.

Income: per capita $18,692; median household $36,430. **Pop below poverty level:** 9.2%.

Unemployment: 5.1%. **Median home value:** $55,100. **Median travel time to work:** 16.6 minutes.

PIERCE COUNTY

240 SE 2nd St PO Box 258
Rugby, ND 58368

Ph: 701-776-6161
Fax: 701-776-5707

In north-central ND, east of Minot; organized Mar 11, 1887 (prior to statehood) from parts of Rolette, Bottineau, and McHenry counties and all of De Smet County; annexed part of Church County in 1891. **Name Origin:** For Lt. Col. Gilbert Ashville Pierce (1839-1901), officer in the Civil War, governor of Dakota Territory (1884-87), and U.S. senator from ND (1889-91).

Area (sq mi): 1082.16 (land 1017.82; water 64.34).

Pop: 4,675 (White 98.1%; Black or African American 0.1%; Hispanic or Latino 0.6%; Asian 0.3%; Other 1.1%). **Foreign born:** 1.2%. **Median age:** 42.9. **State rank:** 28. **Pop change 1990-2000:** -7.5%.

Income: per capita $14,055; median household $26,524. **Pop below poverty level:** 12.5%.

Unemployment: 3.3%. **Median home value:** $62,300. **Median travel time to work:** 14.8 minutes.

RAMSEY COUNTY

524 4th Ave Rm 4
Devils Lake, ND 58301

Ph: 701-662-7069
Fax: 701-662-7063

In east-central ND, northwest of Grand Forks; organized Jan 4, 1873 (prior to statehood) from Pembina County. **Name Origin:** For Alexander Ramsey (1815-1903), first governor of MN Territory, U.S. senator from MN (1863-75), and U.S. secretary of war (1879-81).

Area (sq mi): 1300.88 (land 1184.85; water 116.04).

Pop: 12,066 (White 92.1%; Black or African American 0.2%; Hispanic or Latino 0.5%; Asian 0.3%; Other 7.2%). **Foreign born:** 1.5%. **Median age:** 39.5. **State rank:** 12. **Pop change 1990-2000:** -4.8%.

Income: per capita $18,060; median household $35,600. **Pop below poverty level:** 12.6%.

Unemployment: 3.3%. **Median home value:** $63,500. **Median travel time to work:** 13.9 minutes.

RANSOM COUNTY

PO Box 668
Lisbon, ND 58054

Ph: 701-683-5823
Fax: 701-683-5827

In southeastern ND, southwest of Fargo; organized Jan 4, 1873

All statistics are based on the 2000 Census except the dollar figures given for per capita income, which are based on 1999 estimates.

(prior to statehood) from Pembina County. **Name Origin:** For Fort Ransom, built in 1867 and named for Gen. Thomas E.G. Ransom (1834-64), a Union officer from IL.

Area (sq mi): 864.13 (land 862.75; water 1.38).

Pop: 5,890 (White 97.6%; Black or African American 0.2%; Hispanic or Latino 0.8%; Asian 0.3%; Other 1.6%). **Foreign born:** 0.9%. **Median age:** 40.7. **State rank:** 22. **Pop change 1990-2000:** -0.5%.

Income: per capita $18,219; median household $37,672. **Pop below poverty level:** 8.8%.

Unemployment: 2.1%. **Median home value:** $56,100. **Median travel time to work:** 15.1 minutes.

RENVILLE COUNTY

205 Main St E   **Ph:** 701-756-6398
Mohall, ND 58761   **Fax:** 701-756-6398
www.renvillecounty.org

On the central northern border of ND, northwest of Minot; organized Jan 4, 1873 (prior to statehood) from Pembina County. Dissolved in 1891 for lack of settlement; present county created Jul 23, 1910. **Name Origin:** For Gabriel Renville, an early settler and trader.

Area (sq mi): 892.03 (land 874.77; water 17.27).

Pop: 2,610 (White 97.1%; Black or African American 0.2%; Hispanic or Latino 0.7%; Asian 0.5%; Other 1.6%). **Foreign born:** 1.5%. **Median age:** 43.6. **State rank:** 43. **Pop change 1990-2000:** -17.4%.

Income: per capita $16,478; median household $30,746. **Pop below poverty level:** 11%.

Unemployment: 1.9%. **Median home value:** $44,500. **Median travel time to work:** 19.1 minutes.

RICHLAND COUNTY

418 2nd Ave N   **Ph:** 701-671-1524
Wahpeton, ND 58075   **Fax:** 701-671-1512
www.richlandcounty.org

In the southeastern corner of ND, south of Fargo; original county; organized Jan 4, 1873 (prior to statehood). **Name Origin:** For Morgan T. Rich (1832-98), settler and founder of the city of Wahpeton.

Area (sq mi): 1445.73 (land 1436.71; water 9.02).

Pop: 17,998 (White 96.3%; Black or African American 0.3%; Hispanic or Latino 0.7%; Asian 0.2%; Other 2.5%). **Foreign born:** 1.1%. **Median age:** 35.4. **State rank:** 9. **Pop change 1990-2000:** -0.8%.

Income: per capita $16,339; median household $36,098. **Pop below poverty level:** 10.4%.

Unemployment: 2.9%. **Median home value:** $67,200. **Median travel time to work:** 18.8 minutes.

ROLETTE COUNTY

102 2nd Ave   **Ph:** 701-477-3816
Rolla, ND 58367   **Fax:** 701-477-5770
www.rolettecounty.com

On the central northern border of ND, northeast of Minot; organized Jan 4, 1873 (prior to statehood) from Buffalo County, which was discontinued. **Name Origin:** For Joseph Rolette (1820-71), pioneer and fur trader who opened a post for the American Fur Co.

Area (sq mi): 939.33 (land 902.45; water 36.88).

Pop: 13,674 (White 25%; Black or African American 0.1%; Hispanic or Latino 0.8%; Asian 0.1%; Other 74.7%). **Foreign born:** 1.3%. **Median age:** 28.9. **State rank:** 10. **Pop change 1990-2000:** +7.1%.

Income: per capita $10,873; median household $26,232. **Pop below poverty level:** 31%.

Unemployment: 10.7%. **Median home value:** $55,200. **Median travel time to work:** 15.8 minutes.

SARGENT COUNTY

PO Box 176   **Ph:** 701-724-6241
Forman, ND 58032   **Fax:** 701-724-6244

On the southeastern border of ND, southwest of Fargo; organized Mar 3, 1883 (prior to statehood) from Ransom County. **Name Origin:** For Gen. Homer E. Sargent, superintendent of the Northern Pacific Railroad Company and developer of the Red River Valley.

Area (sq mi): 867.09 (land 858.75; water 8.34).

Pop: 4,366 (White 98%; Black or African American 0%; Hispanic or Latino 0.7%; Asian 0%; Other 1.7%). **Foreign born:** 0.5%. **Median age:** 40.3. **State rank:** 29. **Pop change 1990-2000:** -4%.

Income: per capita $18,689; median household $37,213. **Pop below poverty level:** 8.2%.

Unemployment: 2.8%. **Median home value:** $44,800. **Median travel time to work:** 16.7 minutes.

SHERIDAN COUNTY

PO Box 409   **Ph:** 701-363-2207
McClusky, ND 58463   **Fax:** 701-363-2953

In central ND, northeast of Bismarck; organized Nov 1908 (prior to statehood) from McLean County. **Name Origin:** For Gen. Philip Henry Sheridan (1831-88), Union officer during the Civil War and commander in chief of the U.S. Army (1883-88).

Area (sq mi): 1005.78 (land 971.75; water 34.02).

Pop: 1,710 (White 98.9%; Black or African American 0.1%; Hispanic or Latino 0.4%; Asian 0%; Other 0.7%). **Foreign born:** 1.1%. **Median age:** 48.1. **State rank:** 51. **Pop change 1990-2000:** -20.4%.

Income: per capita $13,283; median household $24,450. **Pop below poverty level:** 21%.

Unemployment: 6.2%. **Median home value:** $23,900. **Median travel time to work:** 19.1 minutes.

SIOUX COUNTY

PO Box L   **Ph:** 701-854-3853
Fort Yates, ND 58538   **Fax:** 701-854-3854

On the central southern border of ND, south of Bismarck; organized

Please see sample entry on inside front cover for detailed information about the statistics presented with each county listing.

431

Sep 3, 1914 from the Standing Rock Indian Reservation. **Name Origin:** For the Sioux Indians, sometimes known as the Dakotas.

Area (sq mi): 1128.3 (land 1094.12; water 34.18).

Pop: 4,044 (White 14.3%; Black or African American 0%; Hispanic or Latino 1.6%; Asian 0%; Other 85.6%). **Foreign born:** 0.8%. **Median age:** 23.9. **State rank:** 31. **Pop change 1990-2000:** +7.5%.

Income: per capita $7,731; median household $22,483. **Pop below poverty level:** 39.2%.

Unemployment: 5.4%. **Median home value:** $48,000. **Median travel time to work:** 16.5 minutes.

SLOPE COUNTY
PO Box JJ **Ph:** 701-879-6275
Amidon, ND 58620 **Fax:** 701-879-6278

On the southwestern border of ND, southwest of Dickinson; organized Jan 14, 1915 from Billings County. **Name Origin:** For the Missouri Slope, a popular name for western ND, especially the area west of the Missouri River.

Area (sq mi): 1219.22 (land 1217.94; water 1.28).

Pop: 767 (White 99.6%; Black or African American 0%; Hispanic or Latino 0.1%; Asian 0%; Other 0.2%). **Foreign born:** 0.3%. **Median age:** 42.5. **State rank:** 53. **Pop change 1990-2000:** -15.4%.

Income: per capita $14,513; median household $24,667. **Pop below poverty level:** 16.9%.

Unemployment: 2.2%. **Median home value:** $23,900. **Median travel time to work:** 16.7 minutes.

STARK COUNTY
PO Box 130 **Ph:** 701-456-7630
Dickinson, ND 58602 **Fax:** 701-456-7634

In southwestern ND, west of Bismarck; organized Feb 10, 1879 (prior to statehood) from unorganized territory. **Name Origin:** For George Stark, vice president of the Northern Pacific Railroad Co.

Area (sq mi): 1340.46 (land 1338.16; water 2.3).

Pop: 22,636 (White 96.8%; Black or African American 0.2%; Hispanic or Latino 1%; Asian 0.2%; Other 2%). **Foreign born:** 0.8%. **Median age:** 36.9. **State rank:** 6. **Pop change 1990-2000:** -0.9%.

Income: per capita $15,929; median household $32,526. **Pop below poverty level:** 12.3%.

Unemployment: 2.8%. **Median home value:** $70,400. **Median travel time to work:** 14.1 minutes.

STEELE COUNTY
PO Box 296 **Ph:** 701-524-2152
Finley, ND 58230 **Fax:** 701-524-1325

In east-central ND, southwest of Grand Forks; organized Mar 8, 1883 (prior to statehood) from Traill County. **Name Origin:** For Edward H. Steele (1846-99), an officer of the Red River Land Co., which figured prominently in the establishment of the county.

Area (sq mi): 715.49 (land 712.36; water 3.13).

Pop: 2,258 (White 98.3%; Black or African American 0%; Hispanic or Latino 0.2%; Asian 0%; Other 1.6%). **Foreign born:** 0.3%. **Median age:** 41.4. **State rank:** 47. **Pop change 1990-2000:** -6.7%.

Income: per capita $17,601; median household $35,757. **Pop below poverty level:** 7.1%.

Unemployment: 1.2%. **Median home value:** $34,600. **Median travel time to work:** 19.3 minutes.

STUTSMAN COUNTY
511 2nd Ave SE **Ph:** 701-252-9035
Jamestown, ND 58401 **Fax:** 701-251-1603

In south-central ND, west of Fargo; organized Jan 4, 1873 (prior to statehood) from Pembina County. **Name Origin:** For Enos Stutsman (1926-74), member of the Dakota Council and a special agent of the U.S. Treasury Dept.

Area (sq mi): 2298.26 (land 2221.4; water 76.86).

Pop: 21,908 (White 97%; Black or African American 0.3%; Hispanic or Latino 0.9%; Asian 0.4%; Other 1.7%). **Foreign born:** 1%. **Median age:** 39.6. **State rank:** 7. **Pop change 1990-2000:** -1.5%.

Income: per capita $17,706; median household $33,848. **Pop below poverty level:** 10.4%.

Unemployment: 2.1%. **Median home value:** $66,600. **Median travel time to work:** 13.9 minutes.

TOWNER COUNTY
PO Box 517 **Ph:** 701-968-4340
Cando, ND 58324 **Fax:** 701-968-4344

On the central northern border of ND; organized Mar 8, 1883 (prior to statehood) from Rolette County. **Name Origin:** For Oscar M. Towner (1842-97), Dakota Territory legislator.

Area (sq mi): 1041.56 (land 1024.55; water 17).

Pop: 2,876 (White 97.3%; Black or African American 0.1%; Hispanic or Latino 0.2%; Asian 0.1%; Other 2.6%). **Foreign born:** 0.8%. **Median age:** 44. **State rank:** 37. **Pop change 1990-2000:** -20.7%.

Income: per capita $17,605; median household $32,740. **Pop below poverty level:** 8.9%.

Unemployment: 2.7%. **Median home value:** $42,200. **Median travel time to work:** 15.8 minutes.

TRAILL COUNTY
PO Box 805 **Ph:** 701-436-4458
Hillsboro, ND 58045 **Fax:** 701-436-4457

On the central eastern border of ND, south of Grand Forks; organized Jan 12, 1875 (prior to statehood) from Grand Forks County. **Name Origin:** For Walter J.S. Traill (1847-1933) of the Hudson Bay Company; he was a founder of the county.

Area (sq mi): 862.53 (land 861.89; water 0.65).

Pop: 8,477 (White 96.4%; Black or African American 0.1%; Hispanic or Latino 2.2%; Asian 0.2%; Other 2.4%). **Foreign born:** 1.4%. **Median age:** 39. **State rank:** 17. **Pop change 1990-2000:** -3.1%.

Income: per capita $18,014; median household $37,445. **Pop below poverty level:** 9.2%.

Unemployment: 3.2%. **Median home value:** $60,000. **Median travel time to work:** 17.5 minutes.

All statistics are based on the 2000 Census except the dollar figures given for per capita income, which are based on 1999 estimates.

WALSH COUNTY

600 Cooper Ave   **Ph:** 701-352-2851
Grafton, ND 58237   **Fax:** 701-352-3340

On the northeastern border of ND, north of Grand Forks; organized Feb 18, 1881 (prior to statehood) from Grand Forks and Pembina counties. **Name Origin:** For George H. Walsh (1868-1913), newspaper publisher and member of the ND legislative council (1881, 1883, 1885, 1889).

Area (sq mi): 1294.11 (land 1281.74; water 12.36).

Pop: 12,389 (White 92.3%; Black or African American 0.3%; Hispanic or Latino 5.7%; Asian 0.2%; Other 4.6%). **Foreign born:** 1.9%. **Median age:** 40.9. **State rank:** 11. **Pop change 1990-2000:** -10.5%.

Income: per capita $16,496; median household $33,845. **Pop below poverty level:** 10.9%.

Unemployment: 3.6%. **Median home value:** $52,100. **Median travel time to work:** 17.5 minutes.

WARD COUNTY

PO Box 5005   **Ph:** 701-857-6460
Minot, ND 58702   **Fax:** 701-857-6468
www.co.ward.nd.us

In north-central ND; organized Apr 14, 1885 (prior to statehood) from Renville County. **Name Origin:** For either J.P. Ward or Mark Ward (1844-1902), or both, members of the Dakota Territory legislature in 1885 when the county was formed.

Area (sq mi): 2056.25 (land 2012.88; water 43.36).

Pop: 58,795 (White 91.5%; Black or African American 2.2%; Hispanic or Latino 1.9%; Asian 0.8%; Other 4.6%). **Foreign born:** 2.1%. **Median age:** 32.4. **State rank:** 4. **Pop change 1990-2000:** +1.5%.

Income: per capita $16,926; median household $33,670. **Pop below poverty level:** 10.8%.

Unemployment: 2.9%. **Median home value:** $79,500. **Median travel time to work:** 14.5 minutes.

WELLS COUNTY

PO Box 155   **Ph:** 701-547-3122
Fessenden, ND 58438   **Fax:** 701-547-3840

In central ND, northeast of Bismarck; organized as Gingras County Jan 4, 1873 (prior to statehood) from Sheridan County; name changed Feb 26, 1881. **Name Origin:** For Edward Payson Wells (1847-1936), ND territorial legislator (1881), banker, and developer of the James River valley.

Area (sq mi): 1290.62 (land 1271.28; water 19.34).

Pop: 5,102 (White 98.9%; Black or African American 0.1%; Hispanic or Latino 0.3%; Asian 0.2%; Other 0.5%). **Foreign born:** 0.8%. **Median age:** 45.2. **State rank:** 25. **Pop change 1990-2000:** -13%.

Income: per capita $17,932; median household $31,894. **Pop below poverty level:** 13.5%.

Unemployment: 3.4%. **Median home value:** $38,700. **Median travel time to work:** 17 minutes.

WILLIAMS COUNTY

PO Box 2047   **Ph:** 701-577-4540
Williston, ND 58802   **Fax:** 701-577-4535

On the northwestern border of ND, west of Minot; established Jan 8, 1873 by absorbing both Buford and Flannery counties. Originally located south of the Missouri River, near present-day Dunn and Mercer counties; established in present location in 1892. **Name Origin:** For Erastus A. Williams (1850-1930), Dakota Territory legislator, ND surveyor general, and a founder of Hettinger County.

Area (sq mi): 2147.97 (land 2070.46; water 77.51).

Pop: 19,761 (White 92.3%; Black or African American 0.1%; Hispanic or Latino 0.9%; Asian 0.2%; Other 6.7%). **Foreign born:** 1.2%. **Median age:** 39.8. **State rank:** 8. **Pop change 1990-2000:** -6.5%.

Income: per capita $16,763; median household $31,491. **Pop below poverty level:** 11.9%.

Unemployment: 2.7%. **Median home value:** $56,100. **Median travel time to work:** 15.1 minutes.

OHIO - Counties

Note: All boundaries and names are as of January 1, 2000.

MICHIGAN

CANADA

WILLIAMS
FULTON
LUCAS
OTTAWA
LAKE
ASHTABULA

DEFIANCE
HENRY
WOOD
SANDUSKY
ERIE
CUYAHOGA
GEAUGA
TRUMBULL

PAULDING
PUTNAM
SENECA
HURON
LORAIN
MEDINA
SUMMIT
PORTAGE

VAN WERT
HANCOCK
WYANDOT
CRAWFORD
ASHLAND
MAHONING

ALLEN
HARDIN
MARION
RICHLAND
WAYNE
STARK
COLUMBIANA

MERCER
AUGLAIZE
MORROW
HOLMES
CARROLL

SHELBY
LOGAN
UNION
DELAWARE
KNOX
COSHOCTON
TUSCARAWAS
HARRISON
JEFFERSON

DARKE
MIAMI
CHAMPAIGN
LICKING
MUSKINGUM
GUERNSEY
BELMONT

CLARK
MADISON
FRANKLIN

PREBLE
MONTGOMERY
GREENE
FAIRFIELD
PERRY
NOBLE
MONROE

FAYETTE
PICKAWAY
MORGAN

BUTLER
WARREN
CLINTON
ROSS
HOCKING
WASHINGTON

HAMILTON
HIGHLAND
VINTON
ATHENS

CLERMONT
PIKE
JACKSON
MEIGS

BROWN
ADAMS
SCIOTO
GALLIA

WEST
VIRGINIA

LAWRENCE

KENTUCKY

INDIANA

PENNSYLVANIA

N

0 8 16 24 32 40 Kilometers
0 8 16 24 32 40 Miles

Ohio

OHIO STATE INFORMATION
www.ohio.gov   **Ph:** 614-466-2000

Area (sq mi): 44824.9 (land 40,948.38; water 3876.53).

Pop: 11,353,140 (White 84%; Black or African American 11.5%; Hispanic or Latino 1.9%; Asian 1.2%; Other 2.4%). **Foreign born:** 3%. **Median age:** 36.2. **Pop change 1990-2000:** +4.7%.

Income: per capita $21,003; median household $40,956. **Pop below poverty level:** 10.6%.

Unemployment: 5.5%. **Median home value:** $103,700. **Median travel time to work:** 22.9 minutes.

ADAMS COUNTY
110 W Main St Rm 25 County Courthouse   **Ph:** 937-544-2011
West Union, OH 45693   **Fax:** 937-544-8911

On the south-central border of OH; original county; organized Jul 10, 1797 (prior to statehood). **Name Origin:** For John Adams (1735-1826), second U.S. president.

Area (sq mi): 585.79 (land 583.91; water 1.88).

Pop: 27,330 (White 97.3%; Black or African American 0.2%; Hispanic or Latino 0.6%; Asian 0.1%; Other 1.9%). **Foreign born:** 0.2%. **Median age:** 36.3. **State rank:** 80. **Pop change 1990-2000:** +7.7%.

Income: per capita $14,515; median household $29,315. **Pop below poverty level:** 17.4%.

Unemployment: 9.3%. **Median home value:** $67,400. **Median travel time to work:** 36.8 minutes.

ALLEN COUNTY
PO Box 1243   **Ph:** 419-228-3700
Lima, OH 45802   **Fax:** 419-224-0183
www.allencountyohio.com

In west-central OH, north of Dayton; organized Feb 12, 1820 from Mercer County. **Name Origin:** For Ethan Allen (1738-89), leader of the Green Mountain Boys of VT in the Revolutionary War.

Area (sq mi): 406.88 (land 404.43; water 2.46).

Pop: 108,473 (White 84.2%; Black or African American 12.2%; Hispanic or Latino 1.4%; Asian 0.6%; Other 2.3%). **Foreign born:** 1%. **Median age:** 36.3. **State rank:** 26. **Pop change 1990-2000:** -1.2%.

Income: per capita $17,511; median household $37,048. **Pop below poverty level:** 12.1%.

Unemployment: 5.1%. **Median home value:** $81,800. **Median travel time to work:** 18.4 minutes.

ASHLAND COUNTY
142 W 2nd St   **Ph:** 419-289-0000
Ashland, OH 44805   **Fax:** 419-282-4240
www.ashlandcounty.org

In north-central OH, southwest of Akron; organized Feb 24, 1846 from the counties of Huron (Ruggles twp), Lorain (Sullivan and Trop twps), Richland (Vermillion, Montgomery, Orange, Green, Hanover, and parts of Monroe, Mifflin, and Clear Fork twps), and Wayne (Jackson, Perry, Mohican, and Lake twps). **Name Origin:** Named in 1822 for the home of Henry Clay (1777-1852) at Lexington, KY.

Area (sq mi): 426.85 (land 424.37; water 2.47).

Pop: 52,523 (White 97.1%; Black or African American 0.8%; Hispanic or Latino 0.6%; Asian 0.5%; Other 1.1%). **Foreign born:** 1.1%. **Median age:** 36.3. **State rank:** 48. **Pop change 1990-2000:** +10.6%.

Income: per capita $17,308; median household $39,179. **Pop below poverty level:** 9.5%.

Unemployment: 4.6%. **Median home value:** $95,900. **Median travel time to work:** 20.3 minutes.

ASHTABULA COUNTY
25 W Jefferson St   **Ph:** 440-576-3637
Jefferson, OH 44047   **Fax:** 440-576-2819
www.co.ashtabula.oh.us

In the northeastern corner of OH, bordered on north by Lake Erie; organized Jun 7, 1807 from Trumbull County. **Name Origin:** For the Ashtabula River, which runs through the northeastern part of the county; from an Algonquian name thought to mean 'fish river' or 'there are always enough moving,' possibly referring to the fish.

Area (sq mi): 1368.47 (land 702.44; water 666.03).

Pop: 102,728 (White 92.9%; Black or African American 3.2%; Hispanic or Latino 2.2%; Asian 0.3%; Other 2.5%). **Foreign born:** 1.6%. **Median age:** 37.6. **State rank:** 27. **Pop change 1990-2000:** +2.9%.

Income: per capita $16,814; median household $35,607. **Pop below poverty level:** 12.1%.

Unemployment: 6.5%. **Median home value:** $85,300. **Median travel time to work:** 23.9 minutes.

Please see sample entry on inside front cover for detailed information about the statistics presented with each county listing.

435

ATHENS COUNTY

PO Box 290   **Ph:** 740-592-3242
Athens, OH 45701   **Fax:** 740-592-3282
www.athenscountygovernment.com

In southeastern OH, southeast of Columbus; organized Mar 1, 1805 from Washington County. **Name Origin:** For Athens, Greece.

Area (sq mi): 508.54 (land 506.76; water 1.78).

Pop: 62,223 (White 92.8%; Black or African American 2.4%; Hispanic or Latino 1%; Asian 1.9%; Other 2.3%). **Foreign born:** 3.3%. **Median age:** 25.7. **State rank:** 41. **Pop change 1990-2000:** +4.5%.

Income: per capita $14,171; median household $27,322. **Pop below poverty level:** 27.4%.

Unemployment: 3.8%. **Median home value:** $84,300. **Median travel time to work:** 21.7 minutes.

AUGLAIZE COUNTY

201 Willipie St Suite G 11   **Ph:** 419-738-3612
Wapakoneta, OH 45895   **Fax:** 419-738-4713
www.auglaizecounty.org

In west-central OH, south of Lima; organized Feb 14, 1848 from Allen and Mercer counties. **Name Origin:** For the Auglaize River, which traverses it; from French 'at the stream' or 'at the lick,' with possible reference to a salt lick; or from an Indian word meaning 'fallen timbers.'

Area (sq mi): 401.72 (land 401.25; water 0.47).

Pop: 46,611 (White 97.7%; Black or African American 0.2%; Hispanic or Latino 0.7%; Asian 0.4%; Other 1.2%). **Foreign born:** 1.1%. **Median age:** 36.5. **State rank:** 51. **Pop change 1990-2000:** +4.5%.

Income: per capita $19,593; median household $43,367. **Pop below poverty level:** 6.2%.

Unemployment: 4.4%. **Median home value:** $90,600. **Median travel time to work:** 18.1 minutes.

BELMONT COUNTY

101 W Main St Courthouse   **Ph:** 740-695-2121
Saint Clairsville, OH 43950   **Fax:** 740-699-2156
www.belmontcountyohio.org

On the central eastern border of OH, west of Wheeling, WV; organized Sept 7, 1801 (prior to statehood) from Jefferson County. **Name Origin:** French 'beautiful mountain.'

Area (sq mi): 541.39 (land 537.35; water 4.04).

Pop: 70,226 (White 94.7%; Black or African American 3.6%; Hispanic or Latino 0.4%; Asian 0.3%; Other 1.1%). **Foreign born:** 1%. **Median age:** 40.9. **State rank:** 37. **Pop change 1990-2000:** -1.2%.

Income: per capita $16,221; median household $29,714. **Pop below poverty level:** 14.6%.

Unemployment: 4.1%. **Median home value:** $64,600. **Median travel time to work:** 23.5 minutes.

BROWN COUNTY

800 Mt Orab Pike   **Ph:** 937-378-3956
Georgetown, OH 45121   **Fax:** 937-378-6324

On the southwestern border of OH, east of Cincinnati; organized

Mar 1, 1818 from Adams and Clermont counties. **Name Origin:** For Gen. Jacob Jennings Brown (1775-1828), an officer in the War of 1812 and commander of the U.S. Army (1821-28).

Area (sq mi): 495.22 (land 491.76; water 3.46).

Pop: 42,285 (White 97.8%; Black or African American 0.9%; Hispanic or Latino 0.4%; Asian 0.1%; Other 0.9%). **Foreign born:** 0.4%. **Median age:** 35.4. **State rank:** 54. **Pop change 1990-2000:** +20.9%.

Income: per capita $17,100; median household $38,303. **Pop below poverty level:** 11.6%.

Unemployment: 6.4%. **Median home value:** $89,900. **Median travel time to work:** 35 minutes.

BUTLER COUNTY

315 High St   **Ph:** 513-887-3278
Hamilton, OH 45011   **Fax:** 513-887-3966
www.butlercountyohio.org

On the southwestern border of OH, north of Cincinnati; organized May 1, 1803 from Hamilton County. **Name Origin:** For Maj. Gen. Richard Butler (1743-91), an officer in the Revolutionary War, PA legislator, and Indian commissioner.

Area (sq mi): 470.2 (land 467.27; water 2.93).

Pop: 332,807 (White 90.5%; Black or African American 5.3%; Hispanic or Latino 1.4%; Asian 1.5%; Other 1.9%). **Foreign born:** 2.7%. **Median age:** 34.2. **State rank:** 8. **Pop change 1990-2000:** +14.2%.

Income: per capita $22,076; median household $47,885. **Pop below poverty level:** 8.7%.

Unemployment: 3.2%. **Median home value:** $123,200. **Median travel time to work:** 23 minutes.

CARROLL COUNTY

119 Public Sq   **Ph:** 330-627-4869
Carrollton, OH 44615   **Fax:** 330-627-6656
www.carrollcountyohio.net

In east-central OH, southeast of Canton; organized Jan 1, 1833 from Columbiana, Stark, Harrison, and Jefferson counties. **Name Origin:** For Charles Carroll (1737-1832), a signer of the Declaration of Independence, U.S. senator from MD (1789-92), and founder of the Baltimore and Ohio Railroad.

Area (sq mi): 399.01 (land 394.67; water 4.33).

Pop: 28,836 (White 97.8%; Black or African American 0.5%; Hispanic or Latino 0.5%; Asian 0.1%; Other 1.1%). **Foreign born:** 0.6%. **Median age:** 38.8. **State rank:** 76. **Pop change 1990-2000:** +8.7%.

Income: per capita $16,701; median household $35,509. **Pop below poverty level:** 11.4%.

Unemployment: 4.7%. **Median home value:** $89,700. **Median travel time to work:** 27.5 minutes.

CHAMPAIGN COUNTY

1512 S US Hwy 68   **Ph:** 937-484-1611
Urbana, OH 43078   **Fax:** 937-484-1609
www.co.champaign.oh.us

In west-central OH, west of Columbus; organized Mar 1, 1805 from

All statistics are based on the 2000 Census except the dollar figures given for per capita income, which are based on 1999 estimates.

436

Greene and Franklin counties. **Name Origin:** Variation of French *campagne* 'field' or 'plain,' referring to the flatness of the county.

Area (sq mi): 429.71 (land 428.56; water 1.15).

Pop: 38,890 (White 95.3%; Black or African American 2.3%; Hispanic or Latino 0.7%; Asian 0.3%; Other 1.7%). **Foreign born:** 0.7%. **Median age:** 37. **State rank:** 66. **Pop change 1990-2000:** +8%.

Income: per capita $19,542; median household $43,139. **Pop below poverty level:** 7.6%.

Unemployment: 4.6%. **Median home value:** $95,500. **Median travel time to work:** 25 minutes.

CLARK COUNTY
101 N Limestone St   **Ph:** 937-328-2458
Springfield, OH 45502   **Fax:** 937-328-2436
www.co.clark.oh.us

In west-central OH, west of Columbus; organized Mar 1, 1817 from Champaign, Madison and Greene counties. **Name Origin:** For Gen. George Rogers Clark (1752-1818), officer in the Revolutionary War and frontiersman in the Northwest Territory.

Area (sq mi): 403.56 (land 399.86; water 3.7).

Pop: 144,742 (White 87.6%; Black or African American 8.9%; Hispanic or Latino 1.2%; Asian 0.5%; Other 2.4%). **Foreign born:** 1.2%. **Median age:** 37.6. **State rank:** 19. **Pop change 1990-2000:** -1.9%.

Income: per capita $19,501; median household $40,340. **Pop below poverty level:** 10.7%.

Unemployment: 5.3%. **Median home value:** $90,500. **Median travel time to work:** 21.6 minutes.

CLERMONT COUNTY
101 E Main St   **Ph:** 513-732-7300
Batavia, OH 45103   **Fax:** 513-732-7826
www.co.clermont.oh.us

On the southwestern border of OH, east of Cincinnati; original county; organized Dec 6, 1800 (prior to statehood). **Name Origin:** For the province in France, former home of some early settlers; French 'clear mountain.'

Area (sq mi): 457.67 (land 451.99; water 5.68).

Pop: 177,977 (White 96.6%; Black or African American 0.9%; Hispanic or Latino 0.9%; Asian 0.6%; Other 1.4%). **Foreign born:** 1.6%. **Median age:** 34.8. **State rank:** 13. **Pop change 1990-2000:** +18.5%.

Income: per capita $22,370; median household $49,386. **Pop below poverty level:** 7.1%.

Unemployment: 3.9%. **Median home value:** $122,900. **Median travel time to work:** 28.2 minutes.

CLINTON COUNTY
46 S South St   **Ph:** 937-382-2103
Wilmington, OH 45177   **Fax:** 937-383-2884
www.co.clinton.oh.us

In southwestern OH, northeast of Cincinnati; organized Mar 1, 1810 from Highland County. **Name Origin:** For George Clinton

(1739-1812), first governor of NY and vice president of the U.S. (1805-12).

Area (sq mi): 412.29 (land 410.88; water 1.41).

Pop: 40,543 (White 95.6%; Black or African American 2.2%; Hispanic or Latino 0.7%; Asian 0.4%; Other 1.5%). **Foreign born:** 1%. **Median age:** 35.3. **State rank:** 61. **Pop change 1990-2000:** +14.5%.

Income: per capita $18,462; median household $40,467. **Pop below poverty level:** 8.6%.

Unemployment: 2.9%. **Median home value:** $96,800. **Median travel time to work:** 23.8 minutes.

COLUMBIANA COUNTY
105 S Market St   **Ph:** 330-424-7777
Lisbon, OH 44432   **Fax:** 330-424-3960

On the northeastern border of OH, east of Canton; organized May 1, 1803 from Jefferson and Washington counties. **Name Origin:** A variation of Columbus or Columbia, for Christopher Columbus (1451-1506). The ending '-iana' may be the feminine form, which was considered appropriate for place names, or it may refer to an unidentified person named Anne or Anna.

Area (sq mi): 535.18 (land 532.46; water 2.73).

Pop: 112,075 (White 95.5%; Black or African American 2.2%; Hispanic or Latino 1.2%; Asian 0.2%; Other 1.1%). **Foreign born:** 1.4%. **Median age:** 38.5. **State rank:** 23. **Pop change 1990-2000:** +3.5%.

Income: per capita $16,655; median household $34,226. **Pop below poverty level:** 11.5%.

Unemployment: 5.5%. **Median home value:** $79,800. **Median travel time to work:** 22.7 minutes.

COSHOCTON COUNTY
349 1/2 Main St   **Ph:** 740-622-1753
Coshocton, OH 43812   **Fax:** 740-622-4917
www.co.coshocton.oh.us

In central OH, southwest of Canton; organized Jan 31, 1810 from Muskingum County. **Name Origin:** From Delaware Indian *goschachgunk*, thought to mean 'union of waters,' referring to the confluence of the Tuscarawas and Muskingum rivers; 'crossing' or 'ford,' or 'black bear town.'

Area (sq mi): 567.58 (land 564.07; water 3.51).

Pop: 36,655 (White 97%; Black or African American 1.1%; Hispanic or Latino 0.6%; Asian 0.3%; Other 1.2%). **Foreign born:** 1%. **Median age:** 37.8. **State rank:** 67. **Pop change 1990-2000:** +3.5%.

Income: per capita $16,364; median household $34,701. **Pop below poverty level:** 9.1%.

Unemployment: 6%. **Median home value:** $79,300. **Median travel time to work:** 22.4 minutes.

CRAWFORD COUNTY
112 E Mansfield St   **Ph:** 419-562-5876
Bucyrus, OH 44820   **Fax:** 419-562-3491

In north-central OH, north of Columbus; organized Apr 1, 1820 from Old Indian Territory. **Name Origin:** For Col. William Crawford

Please see sample entry on inside front cover for detailed information about the statistics presented with each county listing.

437

(1732-82), VA officer in the Revolutionary War, Indian fighter, and surveyor.

Area (sq mi): 402.83 (land 402.11; water 0.72).

Pop: 46,966 (White 97.5%; Black or African American 0.6%; Hispanic or Latino 0.8%; Asian 0.3%; Other 1%). **Foreign born:** 0.5%. **Median age:** 38.2. **State rank:** 50. **Pop change 1990-2000:** -1.9%.

Income: per capita $17,466; median household $36,227. **Pop below poverty level:** 10.4%.

Unemployment: 6.9%. **Median home value:** $79,200. **Median travel time to work:** 20 minutes.

CUYAHOGA COUNTY
1219 Ontario St   **Ph:** 216-443-7000
Cleveland, OH 44114
www.cuyahoga.oh.us

On the northeastern border of OH, bordered on north by Lake Erie; organized Jun 7, 1808 from Geauga County. **Name Origin:** For the Cuyahoga River, which runs through it; from an Indian word, exact origin uncertain. Possibly from *Cayahaga* 'crooked,' or *Cuyahoganuk* 'lake river,' or the Iroquoian word for 'river.'

Area (sq mi): 1245.56 (land 458.49; water 787.07).

Pop: 1,393,978 (White 65.9%; Black or African American 27.4%; Hispanic or Latino 3.4%; Asian 1.8%; Other 3.4%). **Foreign born:** 6.4%. **Median age:** 37.3. **State rank:** 1. **Pop change 1990-2000:** -1.3%.

Income: per capita $22,272; median household $39,168. **Pop below poverty level:** 13.1%.

Unemployment: 4.6%. **Median home value:** $113,800. **Median travel time to work:** 24.4 minutes.

DARKE COUNTY
520 S Broadway St   **Ph:** 937-547-7370
Greenville, OH 45331   **Fax:** 937-547-7367
www.co.darke.oh.us

On the central western border of OH, northwest of Dayton; organized Jan 3, 1809 from Miami County. **Name Origin:** For Gen. William Darke (1736-1801), an officer in the French and Indian War and the Revolutionary War.

Area (sq mi): 600.29 (land 599.8; water 0.49).

Pop: 53,309 (White 97.6%; Black or African American 0.4%; Hispanic or Latino 0.9%; Asian 0.2%; Other 1.2%). **Foreign born:** 0.7%. **Median age:** 37.4. **State rank:** 46. **Pop change 1990-2000:** -0.6%.

Income: per capita $18,670; median household $39,307. **Pop below poverty level:** 8%.

Unemployment: 4.2%. **Median home value:** $91,100. **Median travel time to work:** 22.8 minutes.

DEFIANCE COUNTY
500 Court St Suite A   **Ph:** 419-782-4761
Defiance, OH 43512   **Fax:** 419-782-8449
www.defiance-county.com/

On the northwestern border of OH; organized Apr 7, 1845 from Williams, Henry, and Paulding counties. **Name Origin:** For Fort Defiance, built here 1794 by Gen. 'Mad Anthony' Wayne (1745-96), and which he described as being so strong that he 'defied hell and all her emissaries...' to take it.

Area (sq mi): 414.19 (land 411.16; water 3.03).

Pop: 39,500 (White 89.8%; Black or African American 1.8%; Hispanic or Latino 7.2%; Asian 0.4%; Other 5.3%). **Foreign born:** 1.5%. **Median age:** 36.5. **State rank:** 63. **Pop change 1990-2000:** +0.4%.

Income: per capita $19,667; median household $44,938. **Pop below poverty level:** 5.6%.

Unemployment: 5.1%. **Median home value:** $86,800. **Median travel time to work:** 19.2 minutes.

DELAWARE COUNTY
101 N Sandusky St   **Ph:** 740-833-2100
Delaware, OH 43015   **Fax:** 740-833-2099
www.co.delaware.oh.us

In central OH, north of Columbus; organized Apr 1, 1808 from Franklin County. **Name Origin:** For the Delaware Indians (also called Leni-Lenape), named for the Delaware Bay.

Area (sq mi): 455.97 (land 442.41; water 13.56).

Pop: 109,989 (White 93.6%; Black or African American 2.5%; Hispanic or Latino 1%; Asian 1.5%; Other 1.6%). **Foreign born:** 2.6%. **Median age:** 35.3. **State rank:** 25. **Pop change 1990-2000:** +64.3%.

Income: per capita $31,600; median household $67,258. **Pop below poverty level:** 3.8%.

Unemployment: 2.2%. **Median home value:** $190,400. **Median travel time to work:** 26.5 minutes.

ERIE COUNTY
323 Columbus Ave   **Ph:** 419-627-7705
Sandusky, OH 44870   **Fax:** 419-624-6873
www.co.erie.oh.us

On the north-central coast of OH, bordered on north by Lake Erie; organized Mar 15, 1838 from Huron and Sandusky counties. **Name Origin:** For Lake Erie.

Area (sq mi): 626.15 (land 254.88; water 371.27).

Pop: 79,551 (White 87.4%; Black or African American 8.6%; Hispanic or Latino 2.1%; Asian 0.4%; Other 2.3%). **Foreign born:** 1.5%. **Median age:** 39.5. **State rank:** 32. **Pop change 1990-2000:** +3.6%.

Income: per capita $21,530; median household $42,746. **Pop below poverty level:** 8.3%.

Unemployment: 4.7%. **Median home value:** $109,800. **Median travel time to work:** 18.8 minutes.

FAIRFIELD COUNTY
210 E Main St   **Ph:** 740-687-7190
Lancaster, OH 43130   **Fax:** 740-687-6048
www.co.fairfield.oh.us

In central OH, southeast of Columbus; organized Dec 9, 1800 (prior to statehood) from Franklin County. **Name Origin:** Descriptive name for the rich farmland in the area.

All statistics are based on the 2000 Census except the dollar figures given for per capita income, which are based on 1999 estimates.

Area (sq mi): 508.6 (land 505.11; water 3.49).

Pop: 122,759 (White 94.7%; Black or African American 2.7%; Hispanic or Latino 0.8%; Asian 0.7%; Other 1.4%). **Foreign born:** 1.3%. **Median age:** 36.2. **State rank:** 21. **Pop change 1990-2000:** +18.7%.

Income: per capita $21,671; median household $47,962. **Pop below poverty level:** 5.9%.

Unemployment: 2.8%. **Median home value:** $129,500. **Median travel time to work:** 27.7 minutes.

FAYETTE COUNTY
133 S Main St Suite 401   **Ph:** 740-335-0720
Washington Court House, OH 43160   **Fax:** 740-333-3530
www.fayette-co-oh.com

In central OH, east of Dayton; organized Mar 1, 1810 from Ross and Highland counties. **Name Origin:** For the Marquis de Lafayette (1757-1834), French statesman and soldier who fought with the Americans during the Revolutionary War.

Area (sq mi): 407.08 (land 406.58; water 0.5).

Pop: 28,433 (White 95%; Black or African American 2.1%; Hispanic or Latino 1.2%; Asian 0.5%; Other 2%). **Foreign born:** 0.9%. **Median age:** 37.5. **State rank:** 77. **Pop change 1990-2000:** +3.5%.

Income: per capita $18,063; median household $36,735. **Pop below poverty level:** 10.1%.

Unemployment: 3.6%. **Median home value:** $85,800. **Median travel time to work:** 24.4 minutes.

FRANKLIN COUNTY
369 S High St 23rd Fl   **Ph:** 614-462-3600
Columbus, OH 43215   **Fax:** 614-462-4325
www.co.franklin.oh.us

In central OH; organized Apr 30, 1803 from Ross County. **Name Origin:** For Benjamin Franklin (1706-90), author, inventor, founder of the Philadelphia Library, scientist, and statesman.

Area (sq mi): 543.32 (land 539.87; water 3.45).

Pop: 1,068,978 (White 74.4%; Black or African American 17.9%; Hispanic or Latino 2.3%; Asian 3.1%; Other 3.5%). **Foreign born:** 6%. **Median age:** 32.5. **State rank:** 2. **Pop change 1990-2000:** +11.2%.

Income: per capita $23,059; median household $42,734. **Pop below poverty level:** 11.6%.

Unemployment: 2.8%. **Median home value:** $116,200. **Median travel time to work:** 21.9 minutes.

FULTON COUNTY
152 S Fulton St Suite 270   **Ph:** 419-337-9255
Wauseon, OH 43567   **Fax:** 419-337-9285
www.fultoncountyoh.com

On the northwestern border of OH, west of Toledo; organized Apr 1, 1850 from Lucas, Henry, and Williams counties. **Name Origin:** For Robert Fulton (1765-1815), builder of the *Clermont*, the first commercially successful steamboat.

Area (sq mi): 407.32 (land 406.78; water 0.54).

Pop: 42,084 (White 92.7%; Black or African American 0.2%; Hispanic or Latino 5.8%; Asian 0.4%; Other 3.7%). **Foreign born:** 1.3%. **Median age:** 36.1. **State rank:** 55. **Pop change 1990-2000:** +9.3%.

Income: per capita $18,999; median household $44,074. **Pop below poverty level:** 5.4%.

Unemployment: 4.3%. **Median home value:** $108,300. **Median travel time to work:** 21.3 minutes.

GALLIA COUNTY
18 Locust St   **Ph:** 740-446-4374
Gallipolis, OH 45631   **Fax:** 740-446-4804
www.galliacounty.org

On the southeastern border of OH; organized Apr 30, 1803 from Washington County. **Name Origin:** For Gaul, the Latin name for France, chosen by French colonists.

Area (sq mi): 471.13 (land 468.78; water 2.36).

Pop: 31,069 (White 94.8%; Black or African American 2.7%; Hispanic or Latino 0.6%; Asian 0.4%; Other 1.6%). **Foreign born:** 0.8%. **Median age:** 37.4. **State rank:** 73. **Pop change 1990-2000:** +0.4%.

Income: per capita $15,183; median household $30,191. **Pop below poverty level:** 18.1%.

Unemployment: 5.6%. **Median home value:** $77,600. **Median travel time to work:** 28.1 minutes.

GEAUGA COUNTY
470 Center St Bldg 4   **Ph:** 440-285-2222
Chardon, OH 44024   **Fax:** 440-286-9177
www.co.geauga.oh.us

In northeastern OH, east of Cleveland; organized Mar 1, 1806 from Trumbull County. **Name Origin:** Meaning of name is unclear; possibly from Iroquoian *sheauga* 'raccoon,' or for an Indian chief.

Area (sq mi): 408.29 (land 403.66; water 4.63).

Pop: 90,895 (White 97%; Black or African American 1.2%; Hispanic or Latino 0.6%; Asian 0.4%; Other 0.9%). **Foreign born:** 2.8%. **Median age:** 38.7. **State rank:** 30. **Pop change 1990-2000:** +12%.

Income: per capita $27,944; median household $60,200. **Pop below poverty level:** 4.6%.

Unemployment: 3.2%. **Median home value:** $182,400. **Median travel time to work:** 27 minutes.

GREENE COUNTY
35 Green St   **Ph:** 937-562-5006
Xenia, OH 45385   **Fax:** 937-562-5331
www.co.greene.oh.us

In west-central OH, east of Dayton; organized May 1, 1803 from Hamilton and Ross counties. **Name Origin:** For Gen. Nathanael Greene (1742-86), hero of the Revolutionary War, quartermaster general (1778-80), and commander of the Army of the South (1780).

Area (sq mi): 416.21 (land 414.88; water 1.34).

Please see sample entry on inside front cover for detailed information about the statistics presented with each county listing.

Pop: 147,886 (White 88.5%; Black or African American 6.4%; Hispanic or Latino 1.2%; Asian 2%; Other 2.4%). **Foreign born:** 3.4%. **Median age:** 35.6. **State rank:** 17. **Pop change 1990-2000:** +8.2%.

Income: per capita $23,057; median household $48,656. **Pop below poverty level:** 8.5%.

Unemployment: 3.4%. **Median home value:** $121,200. **Median travel time to work:** 20.3 minutes.

GUERNSEY COUNTY
128 E 8th St Suite 101   **Ph:** 740-432-9200
Cambridge, OH 43725   **Fax:** 740-432-9359

In east-central OH, south of Canton; organized Mar 1, 1810 from Belmont County. **Name Origin:** For the British Island in the English Channel.

Area (sq mi): 528.29 (land 521.9; water 6.39).

Pop: 40,792 (White 95.9%; Black or African American 1.5%; Hispanic or Latino 0.6%; Asian 0.3%; Other 1.9%). **Foreign born:** 1.1%. **Median age:** 37.7. **State rank:** 60. **Pop change 1990-2000:** +4.5%.

Income: per capita $15,542; median household $30,110. **Pop below poverty level:** 16%.

Unemployment: 5.9%. **Median home value:** $65,500. **Median travel time to work:** 23.7 minutes.

HAMILTON COUNTY
138 E Court St   **Ph:** 513-946-4400
Cincinnati, OH 45202   **Fax:** 513-946-4444
www.hamilton-co.org

In the southwest corner of OH; original county; organized Jan 2, 1790 (prior to statehood). **Name Origin:** For Alexander Hamilton (1757-1804), first U.S. secretary of the treasury (1789-95).

Area (sq mi): 412.78 (land 407.36; water 5.42).

Pop: 845,303 (White 72.4%; Black or African American 23.4%; Hispanic or Latino 1.1%; Asian 1.6%; Other 2%). **Foreign born:** 3.4%. **Median age:** 35.5. **State rank:** 3. **Pop change 1990-2000:** -2.4%.

Income: per capita $24,053; median household $40,964. **Pop below poverty level:** 11.8%.

Unemployment: 3.6%. **Median home value:** $111,400. **Median travel time to work:** 23 minutes.

HANCOCK COUNTY
300 S Main St   **Ph:** 419-424-7037
Findlay, OH 45840
www.co.hancock.oh.us

In north-central OH, south of Toledo; organized Apr 1, 1820 from Indian lands. **Name Origin:** For John Hancock (1737-93), noted signer of the Declaration of Independence, governor of MA (1780-85; 1787-93), and statesman.

Area (sq mi): 533.6 (land 531.35; water 2.24).

Pop: 71,295 (White 93.6%; Black or African American 1.1%; Hispanic or Latino 3.1%; Asian 1.2%; Other 2.5%). **Foreign born:** 2%. **Median age:** 36. **State rank:** 36. **Pop change 1990-2000:** +8.8%.

Income: per capita $20,991; median household $43,856. **Pop below poverty level:** 7.5%.

Unemployment: 3.2%. **Median home value:** $100,400. **Median travel time to work:** 17.5 minutes.

HARDIN COUNTY
1 Courthouse Sq Suite 100   **Ph:** 419-674-2205
Kenton, OH 43326   **Fax:** 419-674-2272
www.co.hardin.oh.us

In west-central OH, northwest of Columbus; organized Apr 1, 1820 from Indian lands. **Name Origin:** For Gen. John Hardin (1753-92), Revolutionary War officer and Indian fighter with George Rogers Clark (1752-1818) in the trans-Ohio campaigns; killed while on a peace mission to the Miami Indians.

Area (sq mi): 470.54 (land 470.29; water 0.25).

Pop: 31,945 (White 97.1%; Black or African American 0.7%; Hispanic or Latino 0.8%; Asian 0.4%; Other 1.3%). **Foreign born:** 1%. **Median age:** 33.3. **State rank:** 71. **Pop change 1990-2000:** +2.7%.

Income: per capita $16,200; median household $34,440. **Pop below poverty level:** 13.2%.

Unemployment: 4.6%. **Median home value:** $73,800. **Median travel time to work:** 21.8 minutes.

HARRISON COUNTY
100 W Market St   **Ph:** 740-942-8861
Cadiz, OH 43907   **Fax:** 740-942-8860

In east-central OH, southeast of Canton; organized Feb 1, 1813 from Jefferson and Tuscarawas counties. **Name Origin:** For William Henry Harrison (1773-1841), ninth U.S. president.

Area (sq mi): 410.79 (land 403.53; water 7.26).

Pop: 15,856 (White 96.3%; Black or African American 2.2%; Hispanic or Latino 0.4%; Asian 0.1%; Other 1.2%). **Foreign born:** 0.5%. **Median age:** 41.1. **State rank:** 84. **Pop change 1990-2000:** -1.4%.

Income: per capita $16,479; median household $30,318. **Pop below poverty level:** 13.3%.

Unemployment: 4.7%. **Median home value:** $58,400. **Median travel time to work:** 28.8 minutes.

HENRY COUNTY
PO Box 546   **Ph:** 419-592-4876
Napoleon, OH 43545

In northwestern OH, southwest of Toledo; organized Feb 12, 1820 from Wood County. **Name Origin:** For Patrick Henry (1736-99), patriot, governor of VA (1776-79; 1784-86), and statesman, famous for proclaiming, 'Give me liberty or give me death.'

Area (sq mi): 419.98 (land 416.5; water 3.47).

Pop: 29,210 (White 93%; Black or African American 0.6%; Hispanic or Latino 5.4%; Asian 0.4%; Other 3.7%). **Foreign born:** 1.3%. **Median age:** 36.5. **State rank:** 75. **Pop change 1990-2000:** +0.4%.

Income: per capita $18,667; median household $42,657. **Pop below poverty level:** 7%.

Unemployment: 5.1%. **Median home value:** $86,800. **Median travel time to work:** 21.4 minutes.

All statistics are based on the 2000 Census except the dollar figures given for per capita income, which are based on 1999 estimates.

HIGHLAND COUNTY

114 Governor Foraker Pl   **Ph:** 937-393-1911
Hillsboro, OH 45133   **Fax:** 937-393-5850

In southwest OH; organized May 1, 1805 from Ross, Adams, and Clermont counties. **Name Origin:** For the terrain.

Area (sq mi): 557.84 (land 553.28; water 4.56).

Pop: 40,875 (White 96.6%; Black or African American 1.5%; Hispanic or Latino 0.5%; Asian 0.3%; Other 1.3%). **Foreign born:** 0.6%. **Median age:** 36.1. **State rank:** 59. **Pop change 1990-2000:** +14.4%.

Income: per capita $16,521; median household $35,313. **Pop below poverty level:** 11.8%.

Unemployment: 5.3%. **Median home value:** $82,100. **Median travel time to work:** 29.3 minutes.

HOCKING COUNTY

1 E Main St   **Ph:** 740-385-5195
Logan, OH 43138   **Fax:** 740-385-1105
www.co.hocking.oh.us

In central OH, southeast of Columbus; organized Jan 3, 1818 from Athens and Ross counties. **Name Origin:** For the Hocking River, which runs through it; from an anglicized Algonquian word whose meaning is uncertain, perhaps referred to cleared fields.

Area (sq mi): 423.6 (land 422.75; water 0.85).

Pop: 28,241 (White 97.2%; Black or African American 0.9%; Hispanic or Latino 0.4%; Asian 0.1%; Other 1.5%). **Foreign born:** 0.6%. **Median age:** 37.7. **State rank:** 78. **Pop change 1990-2000:** +10.6%.

Income: per capita $16,095; median household $34,261. **Pop below poverty level:** 13.5%.

Unemployment: 6.6%. **Median home value:** $83,300. **Median travel time to work:** 35.9 minutes.

HOLMES COUNTY

2 Court St   **Ph:** 330-674-0286
Millersburg, OH 44654   **Fax:** 330-674-0566

In central OH, southwest of Canton; organized Jan 20, 1824 from Coshocton County. **Name Origin:** For Maj. Andrew Hunter Holmes (?-1814), officer in the War of 1812.

Area (sq mi): 424.02 (land 422.99; water 1.03).

Pop: 38,943 (White 98.4%; Black or African American 0.3%; Hispanic or Latino 0.7%; Asian 0.1%; Other 0.6%). **Foreign born:** 0.7%. **Median age:** 28. **State rank:** 65. **Pop change 1990-2000:** +18.6%.

Income: per capita $14,197; median household $36,944. **Pop below poverty level:** 12.9%.

Unemployment: 2.6%. **Median home value:** $107,700. **Median travel time to work:** 21.6 minutes.

HURON COUNTY

County Courthouse 2 E Main St 2nd Fl   **Ph:** 419-668-5113
Norwalk, OH 44857   **Fax:** 419-663-4048
www.hccommissioners.com

In north-central OH, west of Akron; organized Feb 7, 1809 from

Indian lands. **Name Origin:** For the Huron Indians, a tribe of Iroquoian linguistic stock, later known as the Wyandot. Name from a French word for 'rough,' with a derogatory suffix, -on, probably indicating that they were formidable opponents.

Area (sq mi): 494.52 (land 492.69; water 1.83).

Pop: 59,487 (White 94.2%; Black or African American 1%; Hispanic or Latino 3.6%; Asian 0.3%; Other 2.8%). **Foreign born:** 1.9%. **Median age:** 34.9. **State rank:** 43. **Pop change 1990-2000:** +5.8%.

Income: per capita $18,133; median household $40,558. **Pop below poverty level:** 8.5%.

Unemployment: 7.2%. **Median home value:** $95,100. **Median travel time to work:** 20.2 minutes.

JACKSON COUNTY

275 Portsmouth St   **Ph:** 740-286-3301
Jackson, OH 45640   **Fax:** 740-286-4061

In south-central OH; organized Mar 1, 1816 from Pike County. **Name Origin:** For Andrew Jackson (1767-1845), seventh U.S. president.

Area (sq mi): 421.5 (land 420.28; water 1.22).

Pop: 32,641 (White 97.5%; Black or African American 0.6%; Hispanic or Latino 0.6%; Asian 0.2%; Other 1.3%). **Foreign born:** 1.1%. **Median age:** 36.3. **State rank:** 70. **Pop change 1990-2000:** +8%.

Income: per capita $14,789; median household $30,661. **Pop below poverty level:** 16.5%.

Unemployment: 7.2%. **Median home value:** $70,400. **Median travel time to work:** 28.3 minutes.

JEFFERSON COUNTY

301 Market St Courthouse   **Ph:** 740-283-8500
Steubenville, OH 43952   **Fax:** 740-283-8599

On east-central border of OH, southeast of Canton; original county; organized Jul 27, 1797 (prior to statehood). **Name Origin:** For Thomas Jefferson (1743-1826), U.S. patriot and statesman; third U.S. president.

Area (sq mi): 410.87 (land 409.61; water 1.27).

Pop: 73,894 (White 92.1%; Black or African American 5.7%; Hispanic or Latino 0.6%; Asian 0.3%; Other 1.5%). **Foreign born:** 1.3%. **Median age:** 41.6. **State rank:** 34. **Pop change 1990-2000:** -8%.

Income: per capita $16,476; median household $30,853. **Pop below poverty level:** 15.1%.

Unemployment: 5.3%. **Median home value:** $65,400. **Median travel time to work:** 22.2 minutes.

KNOX COUNTY

117 E High St Suite 161   **Ph:** 740-393-6703
Mount Vernon, OH 43050   **Fax:** 740-393-6705
www.knoxcountyohio.org

In central OH, northeast of Columbus; organized Mar 1, 1808 from Fairfield County. **Name Origin:** For Gen. Henry Knox (1750-1806), Revolutionary War officer and first U.S. secretary of war (1785-95).

Please see sample entry on inside front cover for detailed information about the statistics presented with each county listing.

Area (sq mi): 529.53 (land 527.12; water 2.41).

Pop: 54,500 (White 97.2%; Black or African American 0.7%; Hispanic or Latino 0.7%; Asian 0.3%; Other 1.3%). **Foreign born:** 1%. **Median age:** 36.5. **State rank:** 45. **Pop change 1990-2000:** +14.8%.

Income: per capita $17,695; median household $38,877. **Pop below poverty level:** 10.1%.

Unemployment: 3.7%. **Median home value:** $92,100. **Median travel time to work:** 25.8 minutes.

LAKE COUNTY
PO Box 490   **Ph:** 440-350-2500
Painesville, OH 44077
www.lakecountyohio.org

On the northeastern border of OH, bounded on the north by Lake Erie, organized Mar 6, 1840 from Geauga and Cuyahoga counties. **Name Origin:** For its location on Lake Erie.

Area (sq mi): 978.87 (land 228.21; water 750.65).

Pop: 227,511 (White 94.4%; Black or African American 2%; Hispanic or Latino 1.7%; Asian 0.9%; Other 1.7%). **Foreign born:** 4.3%. **Median age:** 38.6. **State rank:** 11. **Pop change 1990-2000:** +5.6%.

Income: per capita $23,160; median household $48,763. **Pop below poverty level:** 5.1%.

Unemployment: 4.2%. **Median home value:** $127,900. **Median travel time to work:** 22.9 minutes.

LAWRENCE COUNTY
PO Box 208   **Ph:** 740-533-4355
Ironton, OH 45638   **Fax:** 740-533-4383

On the southeastern border of OH; organized Dec 21, 1815 from Gallia County. **Name Origin:** For Capt. James Lawrence (1781-1813), U.S. naval officer in the war with Barbary pirates near Tripoli and commander of the U.S.S. *Chesapeake* in the War of 1812, who said, 'Don't give up the ship!'

Area (sq mi): 457.28 (land 454.96; water 2.32).

Pop: 62,319 (White 96.1%; Black or African American 2.1%; Hispanic or Latino 0.6%; Asian 0.2%; Other 1.2%). **Foreign born:** 0.5%. **Median age:** 37.6. **State rank:** 40. **Pop change 1990-2000:** +0.8%.

Income: per capita $14,678; median household $29,127. **Pop below poverty level:** 18.9%.

Unemployment: 5.2%. **Median home value:** $69,400. **Median travel time to work:** 24.1 minutes.

LICKING COUNTY
20 S 2nd St   **Ph:** 740-349-6000
Newark, OH 43055   **Fax:** 740-349-6114
www.lcounty.com

In central OH, east of Columbus; organized Mar 1, 1808 from Fairfield County. **Name Origin:** For the salt licks in the area.

Area (sq mi): 688.38 (land 686.5; water 1.88).

Pop: 145,491 (White 95.2%; Black or African American 2.1%; Hispanic or Latino 0.8%; Asian 0.6%; Other 1.7%). **Foreign born:**

1.1%. **Median age:** 36.6. **State rank:** 18. **Pop change 1990-2000:** +13.4%.

Income: per capita $20,581; median household $44,124. **Pop below poverty level:** 7.5%.

Unemployment: 3.6%. **Median home value:** $110,700. **Median travel time to work:** 24.8 minutes.

LOGAN COUNTY
117 E Columbus St   **Ph:** 937-599-7283
Bellefontaine, OH 43311   **Fax:** 937-599-7268
www.co.logan.oh.us

In west-central OH, northwest of Columbus; organized Mar 1, 1817 from Champaign County. **Name Origin:** For Gen. Benjamin Logan (c. 1743-1802), VA patriot and soldier active in the West during the Revolutionary War.

Area (sq mi): 466.78 (land 458.44; water 8.34).

Pop: 46,005 (White 95.7%; Black or African American 1.7%; Hispanic or Latino 0.7%; Asian 0.4%; Other 1.7%). **Foreign born:** 1.1%. **Median age:** 36.9. **State rank:** 52. **Pop change 1990-2000:** +8.7%.

Income: per capita $18,984; median household $41,479. **Pop below poverty level:** 9.3%.

Unemployment: 3%. **Median home value:** $88,300. **Median travel time to work:** 22 minutes.

LORAIN COUNTY
308 2nd St   **Ph:** 440-329-5536
Elyria, OH 44035   **Fax:** 440-329-5404

On the northern coast of OH, bordered on the north by Lake Erie; organized Dec 26, 1822 from Huron, Cuyahoga, and Medina counties. **Name Origin:** For the province of Lorraine, France, former home of early settlers.

Area (sq mi): 923.02 (land 492.5; water 430.52).

Pop: 284,664 (White 82.4%; Black or African American 8.5%; Hispanic or Latino 6.9%; Asian 0.6%; Other 5.4%). **Foreign born:** 2.6%. **Median age:** 36.5. **State rank:** 9. **Pop change 1990-2000:** +5%.

Income: per capita $21,054; median household $45,042. **Pop below poverty level:** 9%.

Unemployment: 5.6%. **Median home value:** $115,100. **Median travel time to work:** 22.8 minutes.

LUCAS COUNTY
1 Government Ctr Suite 800   **Ph:** 419-213-4500
Toledo, OH 43604   **Fax:** 419-213-4532
www.co.lucas.oh.us

On the northwest coast of OH, bordered on the north by Lake Erie, organized Jun 20, 1835 from Wood County. **Name Origin:** For Col. Robert Lucas (1781-1853), governor of OH (1832-36) and first territorial governor of IA (1838-41).

Area (sq mi): 595.88 (land 340.46; water 255.42).

Pop: 455,054 (White 75.4%; Black or African American 17%; Hispanic or Latino 4.5%; Asian 1.2%; Other 4.4%). **Foreign born:**

All statistics are based on the 2000 Census except the dollar figures given for per capita income, which are based on 1999 estimates.

442

3.2%. **Median age:** 35. **State rank:** 6. **Pop change 1990-2000:** -1.6%.

Income: per capita $20,518; median household $38,004. **Pop below poverty level:** 13.9%.

Unemployment: 5%. **Median home value:** $90,700. **Median travel time to work:** 20.5 minutes.

MADISON COUNTY

PO Box 618   **Ph:** 740-852-2972
London, OH 43140   **Fax:** 740-845-1660
www.co.madison.oh.us

In west-central OH, west of Columbus; organized Mar 1, 1810 from Fayette County. **Name Origin:** For James Madison (1751-1836), fourth U.S. president.

Area (sq mi): 466.18 (land 465.44; water 0.74).

Pop: 40,213 (White 91.4%; Black or African American 6.2%; Hispanic or Latino 0.7%; Asian 0.4%; Other 1.5%). **Foreign born:** 1.1%. **Median age:** 35.8. **State rank:** 62. **Pop change 1990-2000:** +8.5%.

Income: per capita $18,721; median household $44,212. **Pop below poverty level:** 7.8%.

Unemployment: 2.6%. **Median home value:** $104,300. **Median travel time to work:** 25.8 minutes.

MAHONING COUNTY

120 Market St   **Ph:** 330-740-2104
Youngstown, OH 445031710   **Fax:** 330-740-2105

On the northeastern border of OH, northeast of Canton; organized Feb 16, 1846 from Columbiana and Trumbull counties. **Name Origin:** From Delaware Indian *mahanoi* or *m'hoani* 'salt lick,' also spelled *Mahanoy*.

Area (sq mi): 423.38 (land 415.25; water 8.14).

Pop: 257,555 (White 79.6%; Black or African American 15.9%; Hispanic or Latino 3%; Asian 0.5%; Other 2.6%). **Foreign born:** 2.4%. **Median age:** 39.7. **State rank:** 10. **Pop change 1990-2000:** -2.7%.

Income: per capita $18,818; median household $35,248. **Pop below poverty level:** 12.5%.

Unemployment: 5.9%. **Median home value:** $79,700. **Median travel time to work:** 21.5 minutes.

MARION COUNTY

100 N Main St   **Ph:** 740-387-5871
Marion, OH 43302   **Fax:** 740-223-4279
www.co.marion.oh.us

In central OH, north of Columbus; organized Apr 1, 1820 from Crawford County. **Name Origin:** For Gen. Francis Marion (c. 1732-95), SC soldier and legislator, known as 'The Swamp Fox' for his tactics in the Carolina swamps during the Revolutionary War.

Area (sq mi): 404.15 (land 403.84; water 0.3).

Pop: 66,217 (White 91.5%; Black or African American 5.7%; Hispanic or Latino 1.1%; Asian 0.5%; Other 1.6%). **Foreign born:** 1.1%. **Median age:** 37.2. **State rank:** 38. **Pop change 1990-2000:** +3%.

Income: per capita $18,255; median household $38,709. **Pop below poverty level:** 9.7%.

Unemployment: 4.4%. **Median home value:** $78,500. **Median travel time to work:** 21.5 minutes.

MEDINA COUNTY

93 Public Sq   **Ph:** 330-725-9722
Medina, OH 44256
www.co.medina.oh.us

In north-central OH, northwest of Akron; organized Feb 18, 1812 from Portage County. **Name Origin:** Named for the city in Saudi Arabia to which Muhammad (c. 570-632), founder of Islam, fled from Mecca in 622.

Area (sq mi): 423.11 (land 421.55; water 1.57).

Pop: 151,095 (White 96.6%; Black or African American 0.9%; Hispanic or Latino 0.9%; Asian 0.6%; Other 1.2%). **Foreign born:** 3%. **Median age:** 36.6. **State rank:** 16. **Pop change 1990-2000:** +23.5%.

Income: per capita $24,251; median household $55,811. **Pop below poverty level:** 4.6%.

Unemployment: 3.9%. **Median home value:** $144,400. **Median travel time to work:** 26.4 minutes.

MEIGS COUNTY

PO Box 151   **Ph:** 740-992-5290
Pomeroy, OH 45769   **Fax:** 740-992-4429

On the southeastern border of OH; organized Jan 21, 1819 from Gallia and Athens counties. **Name Origin:** For Return Jonathan Meigs (1764-1824), OH governor (1810-14) and U.S. Postmaster General (1814-23).

Area (sq mi): 432.38 (land 429.42; water 2.95).

Pop: 23,072 (White 97.4%; Black or African American 0.7%; Hispanic or Latino 0.6%; Asian 0.1%; Other 1.5%). **Foreign born:** 0.2%. **Median age:** 38.6. **State rank:** 81. **Pop change 1990-2000:** +0.4%.

Income: per capita $13,848; median household $27,287. **Pop below poverty level:** 19.8%.

Unemployment: 8.7%. **Median home value:** $59,600. **Median travel time to work:** 31.8 minutes.

MERCER COUNTY

220 W Livingston St Rm A201   **Ph:** 419-586-3178
Celina, OH 45822   **Fax:** 419-586-1699
www.mercercountyohio.org

On the central-western border of OH, southwest of Lima; organized Feb 12, 1820 from Darke County. **Name Origin:** For Gen. Hugh Mercer (1721-77), Revolutionary War officer and physician.

Area (sq mi): 473.29 (land 463.27; water 10.03).

Pop: 40,924 (White 97.8%; Black or African American 0.1%; Hispanic or Latino 1.1%; Asian 0.3%; Other 1.2%). **Foreign born:** 0.8%. **Median age:** 35.7. **State rank:** 57. **Pop change 1990-2000:** +3.8%.

Income: per capita $18,531; median household $42,742. **Pop below poverty level:** 6.4%.

Please see sample entry on inside front cover for detailed information about the statistics presented with each county listing.

443

Unemployment: 5.8%. **Median home value:** $94,000. **Median travel time to work:** 19.9 minutes.

MIAMI COUNTY

201 W Main St   **Ph:** 937-332-6924
Troy, OH 45373   **Fax:** 937-339-9882
www.co.miami.oh.us

In west-central OH, north of Dayton; organized Mar 1, 1807 from Montgomery County. **Name Origin:** For the Miami Indians, an Algonquin Indian tribe. Origin of the name uncertain, probably from Ojibway *oumaumeg* 'people of the peninsula,' or from Delaware *we-mi-a-mik* 'all friends.'

Area (sq mi): 409.22 (land 407.04; water 2.18).

Pop: 98,868 (White 95.3%; Black or African American 2%; Hispanic or Latino 0.7%; Asian 0.8%; Other 1.5%). **Foreign born:** 1.5%. **Median age:** 37.7. **State rank:** 28. **Pop change 1990-2000:** +6.1%.

Income: per capita $21,669; median household $44,109. **Pop below poverty level:** 6.7%.

Unemployment: 4.3%. **Median home value:** $109,600. **Median travel time to work:** 20.1 minutes.

MONROE COUNTY

101 N Main St Rm 35   **Ph:** 740-472-5181
Woodsfield, OH 43793   **Fax:** 740-472-2526

On the central-eastern border of OH; organized Jan 29, 1813 from Belmont, Washington, and Guernsey counties. **Name Origin:** For James Monroe (1758-1831), fifth U.S. president.

Area (sq mi): 457.46 (land 455.54; water 1.92).

Pop: 15,180 (White 98.4%; Black or African American 0.3%; Hispanic or Latino 0.4%; Asian 0.1%; Other 1%). **Foreign born:** 0.3%. **Median age:** 40.8. **State rank:** 85. **Pop change 1990-2000:** -2%.

Income: per capita $15,096; median household $30,467. **Pop below poverty level:** 13.9%.

Unemployment: 6.6%. **Median home value:** $62,500. **Median travel time to work:** 30.8 minutes.

MONTGOMERY COUNTY

451 W 3rd St   **Ph:** 937-225-4000
Dayton, OH 45422   **Fax:** 937-496-7723
www.co.montgomery.oh.us

In west-central OH, north of Cincinnati; organized Mar 24, 1803 from Hamilton and Ross counties. **Name Origin:** For Gen. Richard Montgomery (1736-75), American Revolutionary War officer who captured Montreal, Canada.

Area (sq mi): 464.34 (land 461.68; water 2.67).

Pop: 559,062 (White 75.9%; Black or African American 19.9%; Hispanic or Latino 1.3%; Asian 1.3%; Other 2.2%). **Foreign born:** 2.5%. **Median age:** 36.4. **State rank:** 4. **Pop change 1990-2000:** -2.6%.

Income: per capita $21,743; median household $40,156. **Pop below poverty level:** 11.3%.

Unemployment: 4.3%. **Median home value:** $95,900. **Median travel time to work:** 21.2 minutes.

MORGAN COUNTY

19 E Main St   **Ph:** 740-962-4752
McConnelsville, OH 43756 **Fax:** 740-962-4522

In east-central OH, southeast of Columbus; organized Dec 29, 1817 from Washington County. **Name Origin:** For Gen. Daniel Morgan (1736-1802), an officer in the Revolutionary War and U.S. representative from VA (1797-99).

Area (sq mi): 421.86 (land 417.66; water 4.2).

Pop: 14,897 (White 93.4%; Black or African American 3.4%; Hispanic or Latino 0.4%; Asian 0.1%; Other 2.8%). **Foreign born:** 0.5%. **Median age:** 38.9. **State rank:** 86. **Pop change 1990-2000:** +5%.

Income: per capita $13,967; median household $28,868. **Pop below poverty level:** 18.4%.

Unemployment: 15%. **Median home value:** $66,800. **Median travel time to work:** 36.2 minutes.

MORROW COUNTY

48 E High St   **Ph:** 419-947-4085
Mount Gilead, OH 43338   **Fax:** 419-947-1860
www.co.morrow.oh.us

In central OH, north of Columbus; organized Mar 1, 1848 from Knox, Marion, Delaware, and Richland counties. **Name Origin:** For Jeremiah Morrow (1771-1852), OH legislator, U.S. senator (1813-19), and governor (1822-36).

Area (sq mi): 407.36 (land 406.22; water 1.13).

Pop: 31,628 (White 98%; Black or African American 0.3%; Hispanic or Latino 0.6%; Asian 0.1%; Other 1.2%). **Foreign born:** 0.5%. **Median age:** 36.5. **State rank:** 72. **Pop change 1990-2000:** +14%.

Income: per capita $17,830; median household $40,882. **Pop below poverty level:** 9%.

Unemployment: 6%. **Median home value:** $97,400. **Median travel time to work:** 30.4 minutes.

MUSKINGUM COUNTY

401 Main St   **Ph:** 740-455-7104
Zanesville, OH 43701

In central OH, east of Columbus; organized Mar 1, 1804 from Washington and Fairfield counties. **Name Origin:** For the Muskingum River, which flows through it; from Algonquian but the meaning is uncertain, possibly 'by the river.'

Area (sq mi): 672.59 (land 664.63; water 7.97).

Pop: 84,585 (White 93.5%; Black or African American 4%; Hispanic or Latino 0.5%; Asian 0.3%; Other 1.8%). **Foreign born:** 0.7%. **Median age:** 36.5. **State rank:** 31. **Pop change 1990-2000:** +3.1%.

Income: per capita $17,533; median household $35,185. **Pop below poverty level:** 12.9%.

Unemployment: 5.9%. **Median home value:** $83,300. **Median travel time to work:** 24.2 minutes.

All statistics are based on the 2000 Census except the dollar figures given for per capita income, which are based on 1999 estimates.

NOBLE COUNTY

County Courthouse Rm 210   **Ph:** 740-732-2969
Caldwell, OH 43724   **Fax:** 740-732-5702
www.noblecountyohio.com

In east-central OH, south of Canton; organized Apr 1, 1851 from Monroe, Morgan, Guernsey, and Washington counties. **Name Origin:** For James and Warren P. Noble, early settlers.

Area (sq mi): 404.59 (land 399; water 5.59).

Pop: 14,058 (White 92.2%; Black or African American 6.7%; Hispanic or Latino 0.4%; Asian 0.1%; Other 0.7%). **Foreign born:** 0.6%. **Median age:** 35.5. **State rank:** 87. **Pop change 1990-2000:** +24%.

Income: per capita $14,100; median household $32,940. **Pop below poverty level:** 11.4%.

Unemployment: 5.6%. **Median home value:** $63,700. **Median travel time to work:** 26.7 minutes.

OTTAWA COUNTY

315 Madison St   **Ph:** 419-734-6710
Port Clinton, OH 43452   **Fax:** 419-734-6898
www.co.ottawa.oh.us

On the northern coast of OH, bordered on the north by Lake Erie; organized Mar 6, 1840 from Erie, Sandusky, and Lucas counties. **Name Origin:** For the Ottawa Indians, a tribe of Algonquian linguistic stock. Tribal name is derived from *adawe* 'to trade,' for their ability as intertribal traders and barterers.

Area (sq mi): 585.12 (land 254.95; water 330.17).

Pop: 40,985 (White 94.6%; Black or African American 0.6%; Hispanic or Latino 3.7%; Asian 0.2%; Other 2.5%). **Foreign born:** 1.1%. **Median age:** 41. **State rank:** 56. **Pop change 1990-2000:** +2.4%.

Income: per capita $21,973; median household $44,224. **Pop below poverty level:** 5.9%.

Unemployment: 5.7%. **Median home value:** $113,000. **Median travel time to work:** 22.5 minutes.

PAULDING COUNTY

County Courthouse 115 N Williams St
Rm 104   **Ph:** 419-399-8210
Paulding, OH 45879   **Fax:** 419-399-8248

On the northwest coast of OH; organized Feb 12, 1820 from Indian lands. **Name Origin:** For John Paulding (1758-1818) of Peekskill, NY, one of the captors (1780) of British spy John Andre (1750-80) during the Revolutionary War.

Area (sq mi): 418.9 (land 416.26; water 2.64).

Pop: 20,293 (White 94.7%; Black or African American 1%; Hispanic or Latino 3%; Asian 0.2%; Other 3%). **Foreign born:** 0.6%. **Median age:** 36.5. **State rank:** 83. **Pop change 1990-2000:** -1%.

Income: per capita $18,062; median household $40,327. **Pop below poverty level:** 7.7%.

Unemployment: 5.2%. **Median home value:** $73,800. **Median travel time to work:** 24.6 minutes.

PERRY COUNTY

121 W Brown St PO Box 248 **Ph:** 740-342-2045
New Lexington, OH 43764 **Fax:** 740-342-5505

In central OH, southeast of Columbus; organized Mar 1, 1818 from Washington, Fairfield, and Muskingum counties. **Name Origin:** For Oliver Hazard Perry (1785-1819), U.S. naval officer during the War of 1812, famous for the message, 'We have met the enemy and they are ours.'

Area (sq mi): 412.59 (land 409.78; water 2.82).

Pop: 34,078 (White 98.2%; Black or African American 0.2%; Hispanic or Latino 0.4%; Asian 0.1%; Other 1.2%). **Foreign born:** 0.6%. **Median age:** 35. **State rank:** 69. **Pop change 1990-2000:** +8%.

Income: per capita $15,674; median household $34,383. **Pop below poverty level:** 11.8%.

Unemployment: 7.2%. **Median home value:** $72,500. **Median travel time to work:** 33.5 minutes.

PICKAWAY COUNTY

139 W Franklin St   **Ph:** 740-474-6093
Circleville, OH 43113   **Fax:** 740-474-8988

In central OH, south of Columbus; organized Jan 12, 1810 from Ross, Fairfield, and Franklin counties. **Name Origin:** A folk etymological form of *Piqua*, believed to be the name of the Shawnee subtribe to which Tecumseh (1768-1813) belonged. Name is thought to mean 'ashes,' referring to the myth that the first man of their tribe rose out of ashes.

Area (sq mi): 506.79 (land 501.91; water 4.88).

Pop: 52,727 (White 91.5%; Black or African American 6.4%; Hispanic or Latino 0.6%; Asian 0.2%; Other 1.4%). **Foreign born:** 0.7%. **Median age:** 36. **State rank:** 47. **Pop change 1990-2000:** +9.3%.

Income: per capita $17,478; median household $42,832. **Pop below poverty level:** 9.5%.

Unemployment: 3.5%. **Median home value:** $112,400. **Median travel time to work:** 26.7 minutes.

PIKE COUNTY

100 E 2nd St   **Ph:** 740-947-2715
Waverly, OH 45690   **Fax:** 740-947-1729

In south-central OH, south of Columbus; organized Jan 4, 1815 from Ross, Highland, and Scioto counties. **Name Origin:** For Gen. Zebulon Montgomery Pike (1779-1813), U.S. army officer and discoverer of Pikes Peak, CO.

Area (sq mi): 443.94 (land 441.49; water 2.46).

Pop: 27,695 (White 96.3%; Black or African American 0.9%; Hispanic or Latino 0.6%; Asian 0.2%; Other 2.2%). **Foreign born:** 0.6%. **Median age:** 35.3. **State rank:** 79. **Pop change 1990-2000:** +14.2%.

Income: per capita $16,093; median household $31,649. **Pop below poverty level:** 18.6%.

Unemployment: 8%. **Median home value:** $77,400. **Median travel time to work:** 29.6 minutes.

Please see sample entry on inside front cover for detailed information about the statistics presented with each county listing.

PORTAGE COUNTY

449 S Meridian St   **Ph:** 330-297-3600
Ravenna, OH 44266   **Fax:** 330-297-3610
www.co.portage.oh.us

In northeastern OH, east of Akron; organized Jun 7, 1807 from Trumbull and Jackson counties. **Name Origin:** For the portage of canoes or other craft between the Cuyahoga and Manhoning rivers.

Area (sq mi): 507.11 (land 492.39; water 14.72).

Pop: 152,061 (White 93.9%; Black or African American 3.2%; Hispanic or Latino 0.7%; Asian 0.8%; Other 1.6%). **Foreign born:** 2%. **Median age:** 34.4. **State rank:** 15. **Pop change 1990-2000:** +6.6%.

Income: per capita $20,428; median household $44,347. **Pop below poverty level:** 9.3%.

Unemployment: 4.1%. **Median home value:** $123,000. **Median travel time to work:** 25.1 minutes.

PREBLE COUNTY

101 E Main St   **Ph:** 937-456-8143
Eaton, OH 45320   **Fax:** 937-456-8114

On the southwestern border of OH, west of Dayton; organized Mar 1, 1808 from Montgomery and Butler counties. **Name Origin:** For Capt. Edward Preble (1761-1807), commander of the U.S.S. *Constitution*, which bombarded Tripoli in 1804 during the war against the Barbary pirates.

Area (sq mi): 426.33 (land 424.8; water 1.52).

Pop: 42,337 (White 98.2%; Black or African American 0.3%; Hispanic or Latino 0.4%; Asian 0.3%; Other 0.9%). **Foreign born:** 0.6%. **Median age:** 37.5. **State rank:** 53. **Pop change 1990-2000:** +5.5%.

Income: per capita $18,444; median household $42,093. **Pop below poverty level:** 6.1%.

Unemployment: 4.4%. **Median home value:** $93,500. **Median travel time to work:** 26.7 minutes.

PUTNAM COUNTY

245 E Main St Suite 101   **Ph:** 419-523-3656
Ottawa, OH 45875   **Fax:** 419-523-9213

In northwestern OH, north of Lima; organized Apr 1, 1820 from Indian Territory. **Name Origin:** For Gen. Israel Putnam, (1718-90), Revolutionary War officer and American commander at the Battle of Bunker Hill.

Area (sq mi): 484.23 (land 483.87; water 0.36).

Pop: 34,726 (White 94.8%; Black or African American 0.2%; Hispanic or Latino 4.4%; Asian 0.2%; Other 3.4%). **Foreign born:** 0.7%. **Median age:** 35. **State rank:** 68. **Pop change 1990-2000:** +2.7%.

Income: per capita $18,680; median household $46,426. **Pop below poverty level:** 5.6%.

Unemployment: 4%. **Median home value:** $93,300. **Median travel time to work:** 21.1 minutes.

RICHLAND COUNTY

50 Park Ave E   **Ph:** 419-774-5549
Mansfield, OH 44902   **Fax:** 419-774-5547
www.richlandcountygov.net

In north-central OH, west of Canton; organized Mar 1, 1808 from Knox County. **Name Origin:** For the fertile soil in the area.

Area (sq mi): 500.33 (land 496.88; water 3.45).

Pop: 128,852 (White 87.6%; Black or African American 9.4%; Hispanic or Latino 0.9%; Asian 0.5%; Other 1.9%). **Foreign born:** 1.8%. **Median age:** 37.7. **State rank:** 20. **Pop change 1990-2000:** +2.2%.

Income: per capita $18,582; median household $37,397. **Pop below poverty level:** 10.6%.

Unemployment: 5.2%. **Median home value:** $88,100. **Median travel time to work:** 20.2 minutes.

ROSS COUNTY

2 N Paint St Suite A   **Ph:** 740-702-3010
Chillicothe, OH 45601   **Fax:** 740-702-3018
www.co.ross.oh.us

In south-central OH, south of Columbus; original county; organized Aug 20, 1798 (prior to statehood). **Name Origin:** For James Ross (1762-1847), U.S. senator from PA (1794-1803).

Area (sq mi): 692.96 (land 688.41; water 4.55).

Pop: 73,345 (White 91.3%; Black or African American 6.2%; Hispanic or Latino 0.6%; Asian 0.4%; Other 1.7%). **Foreign born:** 0.7%. **Median age:** 36.9. **State rank:** 35. **Pop change 1990-2000:** +5.8%.

Income: per capita $17,569; median household $37,117. **Pop below poverty level:** 12%.

Unemployment: 5.1%. **Median home value:** $87,000. **Median travel time to work:** 25.9 minutes.

SANDUSKY COUNTY

100 N Park Ave   **Ph:** 419-334-6100
Fremont, OH 43420   **Fax:** 419-334-6104

In north-central OH, southeast of Toledo; organized Feb 12, 1820 from Huron County. **Name Origin:** For the Sandusky River, which flows through it. From a Wyandot word, now lost, which seems to have meant 'cold water' or 'pure water.'

Area (sq mi): 417.77 (land 409.18; water 8.59).

Pop: 61,792 (White 89%; Black or African American 2.7%; Hispanic or Latino 7%; Asian 0.3%; Other 4.8%). **Foreign born:** 1.3%. **Median age:** 37.3. **State rank:** 42. **Pop change 1990-2000:** -0.3%.

Income: per capita $19,239; median household $40,584. **Pop below poverty level:** 7.5%.

Unemployment: 5.1%. **Median home value:** $90,100. **Median travel time to work:** 19.4 minutes.

SCIOTO COUNTY

602 7th St Rm 205   **Ph:** 740-355-8218
Portsmouth, OH 45662   **Fax:** 740-354-2057
www.sciotocountyohio.com

On the southern border of OH; organized May 1, 1803 from Indian

---

All statistics are based on the 2000 Census except the dollar figures given for per capita income, which are based on 1999 estimates.

Territory. **Name Origin:** For the Scioto River, which flows through it; from an Iroquoian word of uncertain meaning, said by some scholars to be Wyandot 'deer.'

Area (sq mi): 616.07 (land 612.27; water 3.8).

Pop: 79,195 (White 94.5%; Black or African American 2.7%; Hispanic or Latino 0.6%; Asian 0.2%; Other 2.1%). **Foreign born:** 0.6%. **Median age:** 36.7. **State rank:** 33. **Pop change 1990-2000:** -1.4%.

Income: per capita $15,408; median household $28,008. **Pop below poverty level:** 19.3%.

Unemployment: 7%. **Median home value:** $63,400. **Median travel time to work:** 26 minutes.

SENECA COUNTY

81 Jefferson St   **Ph:** 419-447-4550
Tiffin, OH 44883   **Fax:** 419-447-0556

In north-central OH, southeast of Toledo; organized Feb 12, 1820 from Sandusky County. **Name Origin:** For the Seneca Indians, one of the Five Nations of the Iroquois; name probably means 'stony area.'

Area (sq mi): 552.37 (land 550.59; water 1.78).

Pop: 58,683 (White 93.4%; Black or African American 1.8%; Hispanic or Latino 3.4%; Asian 0.4%; Other 2.8%). **Foreign born:** 1.2%. **Median age:** 36.3. **State rank:** 44. **Pop change 1990-2000:** -1.8%.

Income: per capita $17,027; median household $38,037. **Pop below poverty level:** 9%.

Unemployment: 5.8%. **Median home value:** $81,300. **Median travel time to work:** 20.5 minutes.

SHELBY COUNTY

129 E Court St Suite 100   **Ph:** 937-498-7226
Sidney, OH 45365   **Fax:** 937-498-1293
www.co.shelby.oh.us

In west-central OH, north of Dayton; organized Jan 7, 1819 from Miami County. **Name Origin:** For Gen. Isaac Shelby (1750-1826), officer in the Revolutionary War, NC legislator, and governor of KY (1792-96; 1812-16).

Area (sq mi): 411.03 (land 409.27; water 1.76).

Pop: 47,910 (White 95.5%; Black or African American 1.5%; Hispanic or Latino 0.8%; Asian 1%; Other 1.5%). **Foreign born:** 1.4%. **Median age:** 34.8. **State rank:** 49. **Pop change 1990-2000:** +6.7%.

Income: per capita $20,255; median household $44,507. **Pop below poverty level:** 6.7%.

Unemployment: 4.1%. **Median home value:** $97,000. **Median travel time to work:** 17.4 minutes.

STARK COUNTY

200 W Tuscarawas St   **Ph:** 330-451-7432
Canton, OH 44702
www.co.stark.oh.us

In northeastern OH, south of Akron; organized Feb 13, 1808 from Indian Territory. **Name Origin:** For Gen. John Stark (1728-1822), officer in the French and Indian War and the Revolutionary War.

Area (sq mi): 580.91 (land 576.14; water 4.77).

Pop: 378,098 (White 89.7%; Black or African American 7.2%; Hispanic or Latino 0.9%; Asian 0.5%; Other 1.9%). **Foreign born:** 1.8%. **Median age:** 38.2. **State rank:** 7. **Pop change 1990-2000:** +2.9%.

Income: per capita $20,417; median household $39,824. **Pop below poverty level:** 9.2%.

Unemployment: 4%. **Median home value:** $100,300. **Median travel time to work:** 21.3 minutes.

SUMMIT COUNTY

175 S Main St   **Ph:** 330-643-2500
Akron, OH 44308   **Fax:** 330-643-2507
www.co.summit.oh.us

In northeastern OH, south of Cleveland; organized Mar 3, 1840 from Portage, Medina, and Stark counties. **Name Origin:** From the Greek 'summit,' because the highest point on the Ohio Canal is at the county seat, Akron.

Area (sq mi): 420.06 (land 412.72; water 7.34).

Pop: 542,899 (White 83%; Black or African American 13.2%; Hispanic or Latino 0.9%; Asian 1.4%; Other 1.9%). **Foreign born:** 3.3%. **Median age:** 37.2. **State rank:** 5. **Pop change 1990-2000:** +5.4%.

Income: per capita $22,842; median household $42,304. **Pop below poverty level:** 9.9%.

Unemployment: 4.3%. **Median home value:** $109,100. **Median travel time to work:** 22.4 minutes.

TRUMBULL COUNTY

160 High St NW 5th Fl
Administration Bldg   **Ph:** 330-675-2451
Warren, OH 44481   **Fax:** 330-675-2462
www.co.trumbull.oh.us

On the northeastern border of OH; organized Jul 10, 1800 from Jefferson County (prior to statehood). **Name Origin:** For Jonathan Trumbull (1740-1809), aide-de-camp to Gen. George Washington (1780-83), governor of CT (1798-1809), and son of the colonial governor of the same name.

Area (sq mi): 634.72 (land 616.48; water 18.24).

Pop: 225,116 (White 89.7%; Black or African American 7.9%; Hispanic or Latino 0.8%; Asian 0.5%; Other 1.4%). **Foreign born:** 1.8%. **Median age:** 39. **State rank:** 12. **Pop change 1990-2000:** -1.2%.

Income: per capita $19,188; median household $38,298. **Pop below poverty level:** 10.3%.

Unemployment: 6.3%. **Median home value:** $85,500. **Median travel time to work:** 21 minutes.

TUSCARAWAS COUNTY

125 E High Ave   **Ph:** 330-364-8811
New Philadelphia, OH 44663   **Fax:** 330-365-8811
www.co.tuscarawas.oh.us

In east-central OH, south of Canton; organized Mar 15, 1808 from Jefferson County. **Name Origin:** For the Tuscarawas River, which

Please see sample entry on inside front cover for detailed information about the statistics presented with each county listing.

447

flows through it; from an Indian word thought to mean 'open mouth.'

Area (sq mi): 571.48 (land 567.58; water 3.91).

Pop: 90,914 (White 97.4%; Black or African American 0.7%; Hispanic or Latino 0.7%; Asian 0.2%; Other 1.1%). **Foreign born:** 0.9%. **Median age:** 37.9. **State rank:** 29. **Pop change 1990-2000:** +8.1%.

Income: per capita $17,276; median household $35,489. **Pop below poverty level:** 9.4%.

Unemployment: 4.7%. **Median home value:** $88,100. **Median travel time to work:** 21.6 minutes.

UNION COUNTY
233 W 6th St   **Ph:** 937-645-3012
Marysville, OH 43040   **Fax:** 937-645-3002
www.co.union.oh.us

In central OH, northwest of Columbus; organized Apr 1, 1820 from Franklin, Madison, and Logan counties. **Name Origin:** For the union of parts of four counties.

Area (sq mi): 436.98 (land 436.65; water 0.33).

Pop: 40,909 (White 94.8%; Black or African American 2.8%; Hispanic or Latino 0.8%; Asian 0.5%; Other 1.4%). **Foreign born:** 1%. **Median age:** 34.5. **State rank:** 58. **Pop change 1990-2000:** +28%.

Income: per capita $20,577; median household $51,743. **Pop below poverty level:** 4.6%.

Unemployment: 2.7%. **Median home value:** $128,800. **Median travel time to work:** 23 minutes.

VAN WERT COUNTY
114 E Main St   **Ph:** 419-238-6159
Van Wert, OH 45891   **Fax:** 419-238-4528
vanwertcounty.org

On the western border of OH, west of Lima; organized Apr 1, 1820 from Indian Territory. **Name Origin:** For Isaac Van Wert (?-1828), a captor of John Andre (1750-80), a British spy, during the Revolutionary War.

Area (sq mi): 410.49 (land 410.09; water 0.4).

Pop: 29,659 (White 96.7%; Black or African American 0.7%; Hispanic or Latino 1.6%; Asian 0.2%; Other 1.7%). **Foreign born:** 0.7%. **Median age:** 37.6. **State rank:** 74. **Pop change 1990-2000:** -2.6%.

Income: per capita $18,293; median household $39,497. **Pop below poverty level:** 5.5%.

Unemployment: 5.6%. **Median home value:** $76,000. **Median travel time to work:** 19 minutes.

VINTON COUNTY
100 E Main St County Courthouse   **Ph:** 740-596-4571
McArthur, OH 45651   **Fax:** 740-596-4571
www.vintoncounty.com

In south-central OH; organized Mar 23, 1850 from Gallia, Athens, Ross, Hocking, Meigs, and Jackson counties. **Name Origin:** For Samuel Finley Vinton (1792-1862), U.S. representative from OH (1823-37; 1843-51).

Area (sq mi): 414.96 (land 414.08; water 0.88).

Pop: 12,806 (White 97.8%; Black or African American 0.4%; Hispanic or Latino 0.5%; Asian 0.1%; Other 1.6%). **Foreign born:** 0.3%. **Median age:** 35.5. **State rank:** 88. **Pop change 1990-2000:** +15.4%.

Income: per capita $13,731; median household $29,465. **Pop below poverty level:** 20%.

Unemployment: 11.7%. **Median home value:** $64,400. **Median travel time to work:** 37 minutes.

WARREN COUNTY
550 Justice Dr   **Ph:** 513-695-1370
Lebanon, OH 45036   **Fax:** 513-695-2990
www.co.warren.oh.us

In southwestern OH, northeast of Cincinnati; organized Mar 24, 1803 from Hamilton County. **Name Origin:** For Gen. Joseph Warren (1741-75), Revolutionary War patriot and member of the Committee of Safety, who dispatched Paul Revere (1735-1818) on his famous ride.

Area (sq mi): 407.14 (land 399.63; water 7.51).

Pop: 158,383 (White 94%; Black or African American 2.7%; Hispanic or Latino 1%; Asian 1.3%; Other 1.3%). **Foreign born:** 2.3%. **Median age:** 35.2. **State rank:** 14. **Pop change 1990-2000:** +39%.

Income: per capita $25,517; median household $57,952. **Pop below poverty level:** 4.2%.

Unemployment: 3.3%. **Median home value:** $142,200. **Median travel time to work:** 24.1 minutes.

WASHINGTON COUNTY
205 Putnam St   **Ph:** 740-373-6623
Marietta, OH 45750   **Fax:** 740-373-2085
www.co.washington.oh.us

On the southeastern border of OH; original county; organized Jul 27, 1788 (prior to statehood). **Name Origin:** For George Washington (1732-99), American patriot and first U.S. president.

Area (sq mi): 640.15 (land 635.15; water 5).

Pop: 63,251 (White 96.9%; Black or African American 0.9%; Hispanic or Latino 0.5%; Asian 0.4%; Other 1.2%). **Foreign born:** 0.6%. **Median age:** 39.1. **State rank:** 39. **Pop change 1990-2000:** +1.6%.

Income: per capita $18,082; median household $34,275. **Pop below poverty level:** 11.4%.

Unemployment: 3.8%. **Median home value:** $80,400. **Median travel time to work:** 22.5 minutes.

WAYNE COUNTY
428 W Liberty St   **Ph:** 330-287-5400
Wooster, OH 44691   **Fax:** 330-287-5407
www.wooster-wayne.com/county/

In north-central OH, west of Canton; original county; organized Aug 15, 1796 (prior to statehood). **Name Origin:** For Gen. Anthony Wayne (1745-96), PA soldier and statesman, nicknamed 'Mad Anthony' for his daring during the Revolutionary War.

Area (sq mi): 556.31 (land 555.36; water 0.96).

All statistics are based on the 2000 Census except the dollar figures given for per capita income, which are based on 1999 estimates.

Pop: 111,564 (White 96%; Black or African American 1.6%; Hispanic or Latino 0.8%; Asian 0.7%; Other 1.2%). **Foreign born:** 1.7%. **Median age:** 35.4. **State rank:** 24. **Pop change 1990-2000:** +10%.

Income: per capita $18,330; median household $41,538. **Pop below poverty level:** 8%.

Unemployment: 3.9%. **Median home value:** $108,100. **Median travel time to work:** 19.4 minutes.

WILLIAMS COUNTY

1 Courthouse Sq   **Ph:** 419-636-2059
Bryan, OH 43506   **Fax:** 419-636-0643
www.co.williams.oh.us

In the northwestern corner of OH; organized Feb 12, 1820 from Henry County. **Name Origin:** For David Williams, a captor of British spy John Andre (1750-80), in the Revolutionary War.

Area (sq mi): 423.05 (land 421.74; water 1.31).

Pop: 39,188 (White 95.3%; Black or African American 0.7%; Hispanic or Latino 2.7%; Asian 0.5%; Other 2.2%). **Foreign born:** 1%. **Median age:** 36.9. **State rank:** 64. **Pop change 1990-2000:** +6%.

Income: per capita $18,441; median household $40,735. **Pop below poverty level:** 6%.

Unemployment: 5.8%. **Median home value:** $85,700. **Median travel time to work:** 18 minutes.

WOOD COUNTY

PO Box 829   **Ph:** 419-354-9280
Bowling Green, OH 43402   **Fax:** 419-354-9241
www.co.wood.oh.us

In west-central OH, south of Toledo; organized Feb 12, 1820 from Indian lands. **Name Origin:** For Capt. Eleazer Derby Wood (1783-1814), an officer in the War of 1812 and builder of Fort Meigs.

Area (sq mi): 620.54 (land 617.32; water 3.22).

Pop: 121,065 (White 93.3%; Black or African American 1.3%; Hispanic or Latino 3.3%; Asian 1%; Other 2.9%). **Foreign born:** 2.4%. **Median age:** 32.6. **State rank:** 22. **Pop change 1990-2000:** +6.9%.

Income: per capita $21,284; median household $44,442. **Pop below poverty level:** 9.6%.

Unemployment: 3.5%. **Median home value:** $120,000. **Median travel time to work:** 20.1 minutes.

WYANDOT COUNTY

109 S Sandusky Ave County Courthouse   **Ph:** 419-294-1432
Upper Sandusky, OH 43351
www.co.wyandot.oh.us

In west-central OH; organized Feb 3, 1845 from Marion, Crawford, Hardin, and Hancock counties. **Name Origin:** For the Wyandot Indians, a tribe of Iroquoian linguistic stock. Name is thought to mean 'islanders' or 'those who live on a peninsula,' from their original home on island in the Saint Lawrence River and on a peninsula. Also spelled *Wyandotte*.

Area (sq mi): 407.62 (land 405.61; water 2.01).

Pop: 22,908 (White 97.3%; Black or African American 0.1%; Hispanic or Latino 1.5%; Asian 0.5%; Other 1.4%). **Foreign born:**

0.8%. **Median age:** 37.4. **State rank:** 82. **Pop change 1990-2000:** +2.9%.

Income: per capita $17,170; median household $38,839. **Pop below poverty level:** 5.5%.

Unemployment: 4.4%. **Median home value:** $82,300. **Median travel time to work:** 20 minutes.

Please see sample entry on inside front cover for detailed information about the statistics presented with each county listing.

OKLAHOMA - Counties

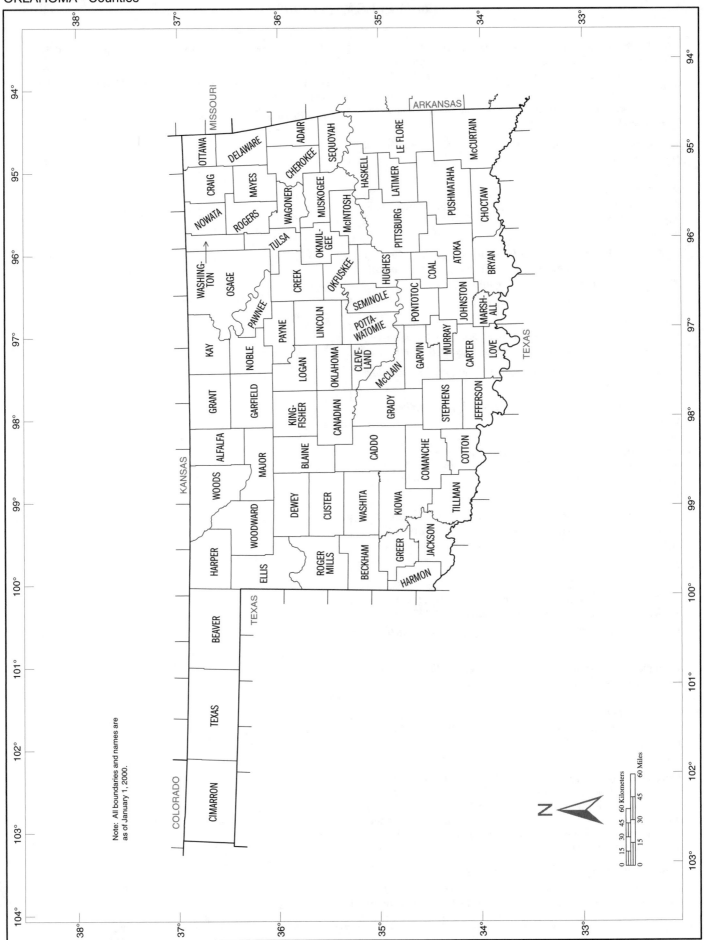

Note: All boundaries and names are as of January 1, 2000.

U.S. Census Bureau, Census 2000

Oklahoma

OKLAHOMA STATE INFORMATION

www.state.ok.us   **Ph:** 405-521-2011

Area (sq mi): 69,898.19 (land 68,667.06; water 1231.13).

Pop: 3,450,654 (White 74.1%; Black or African American 7.6%; Hispanic or Latino 5.2%; Asian 1.4%; Other 14.9%). **Foreign born:** 3.8%. **Median age:** 35.5. **Pop change 1990-2000:** +9.7%.

Income: per capita $17,646; median household $33,400. **Pop below poverty level:** 14.7%.

Unemployment: 5%. **Median home value:** $70,700. **Median travel time to work:** 21.7 minutes.

ADAIR COUNTY

PO Box 169   **Ph:** 918-696-7198
Stilwell, OK 74960   **Fax:** 918-696-2603

On the central eastern border of OK, east of Tulsa; organized Jul 16, 1907 from Cherokee lands. **Name Origin:** For either John Lynch Adair (1828-96) or members of a well-known Cherokee family.

Area (sq mi): 577.03 (land 575.67; water 1.36).

Pop: 21,038 (White 47.7%; Black or African American 0.2%; Hispanic or Latino 3.1%; Asian 0.1%; Other 51.2%). **Foreign born:** 1.4%. **Median age:** 33.2. **State rank:** 38. **Pop change 1990-2000:** +14.2%.

Income: per capita $11,185; median household $24,881. **Pop below poverty level:** 23.2%.

Unemployment: 4.8%. **Median home value:** $45,400. **Median travel time to work:** 25.8 minutes.

ALFALFA COUNTY

300 S Grand Ave   **Ph:** 580-596-3158
Cherokee, OK 73728

On the central northern border of OK, northwest of Enid; organized Nov 16, 1907 from Woods County. **Name Origin:** For William Henry 'Alfalfa Bill' Murray (1869-1956), U.S. representative from OK (1913-17) and governor (1931-35).

Area (sq mi): 881.44 (land 866.65; water 14.79).

Pop: 6,105 (White 88.4%; Black or African American 4.2%; Hispanic or Latino 2.9%; Asian 0.1%; Other 6.2%). **Foreign born:** 0.7%. **Median age:** 42.3. **State rank:** 67. **Pop change 1990-2000:** -4.8%.

Income: per capita $14,704; median household $30,259. **Pop below poverty level:** 13.7%.

Unemployment: 1.4%. **Median home value:** $29,000. **Median travel time to work:** 18.1 minutes.

ATOKA COUNTY

200 E Court St   **Ph:** 580-889-2643
Atoka, OK 74525   **Fax:** 580-889-2608

In south-central OK, southwest of McAlester; organized as Shappaway County Nov 16, 1907 from Choctaw lands. **Name Origin:** For Capt. Atoka, the Choctaw athlete who led a band of his people to OK during their removal from MS and AL. Originally for another noted Choctaw leader.

Area (sq mi): 990 (land 978.29; water 11.71).

Pop: 13,879 (White 75.4%; Black or African American 5.9%; Hispanic or Latino 1.4%; Asian 0.2%; Other 18.1%). **Foreign born:** 0.3%. **Median age:** 38.3. **State rank:** 48. **Pop change 1990-2000:** +8.6%.

Income: per capita $12,919; median household $24,752. **Pop below poverty level:** 19.8%.

Unemployment: 4%. **Median home value:** $43,800. **Median travel time to work:** 29.5 minutes.

BEAVER COUNTY

PO Box 338   **Ph:** 580-625-3151
Beaver, OK 73932   **Fax:** 580-625-3430

In the OK panhandle; original county; organized 1890 (prior to statehood) and comprising the entire panhandle. Present Beaver County was organized Nov 16, 1907 from the eastern third of the original county. **Name Origin:** For the Beaver River, which runs across the county.

Area (sq mi): 1817.58 (land 1814.36; water 3.22).

Pop: 5,857 (White 86.6%; Black or African American 0.3%; Hispanic or Latino 10.8%; Asian 0.1%; Other 6.9%). **Foreign born:** 5.5%. **Median age:** 39.3. **State rank:** 70. **Pop change 1990-2000:** -2.8%.

Income: per capita $17,905; median household $36,715. **Pop below poverty level:** 11.7%.

Unemployment: 2.7%. **Median home value:** $58,200. **Median travel time to work:** 21.1 minutes.

BECKHAM COUNTY

PO Box 67   **Ph:** 580-928-2457
Sayre, OK 73662   **Fax:** 580-928-2467

On the southwestern border of OK; organized Nov 16, 1907 from Greer and Roger Mills counties. **Name Origin:** For John Crepps

Please see sample entry on inside front cover for detailed information about the statistics presented with each county listing.

451

Wickliffe Beckham (1869-1940), KY governor (1900-07) and U.S. senator (1915-21).

Area (sq mi): 904.14 (land 901.83; water 2.31).

Pop: 19,799 (White 84.7%; Black or African American 5.5%; Hispanic or Latino 5.4%; Asian 0.4%; Other 7%). **Foreign born:** 1.6%. **Median age:** 36.6. **State rank:** 40. **Pop change 1990-2000:** +5.2%.

Income: per capita $14,488; median household $27,402. **Pop below poverty level:** 18.2%.

Unemployment: 2.7%. **Median home value:** $51,700. **Median travel time to work:** 18.4 minutes.

BLAINE COUNTY
200 N Weigle St   **Ph:** 580-623-5890
Watonga, OK 73772

In west-central OK, northwest of Oklahoma City; original county; organized as 'C' County in 1890; renamed in Nov 1892 (prior to statehood). **Name Origin:** For James Gillespie Blaine (1830-93), U.S. representative from ME (1863-76), U.S. senator (1876-81), and U.S. secretary of state (1881; 1889-92).

Area (sq mi): 938.88 (land 928.43; water 10.45).

Pop: 11,976 (White 73.7%; Black or African American 6.7%; Hispanic or Latino 6.6%; Asian 0.7%; Other 16.4%). **Foreign born:** 3.5%. **Median age:** 37.6. **State rank:** 51. **Pop change 1990-2000:** +4.4%.

Income: per capita $13,546; median household $28,356. **Pop below poverty level:** 16.9%.

Unemployment: 4.7%. **Median home value:** $41,900. **Median travel time to work:** 19.1 minutes.

BRYAN COUNTY
PO Box 1789   **Ph:** 580-924-2202
Durant, OK 74702   **Fax:** 580-924-2289

On the central southern border of OK; organized Nov 16, 1907 from Chickasaw lands. **Name Origin:** For William Jennings Bryan (1860-1925), U.S. representative from NE (1891-95), U.S. secretary of state (1913-15), and prosecuter in John Scopes' (1900-70) trial for teaching the theory of evolution (1925).

Area (sq mi): 943.43 (land 908.8; water 34.63).

Pop: 36,534 (White 78.9%; Black or African American 1.4%; Hispanic or Latino 2.6%; Asian 0.4%; Other 18.1%). **Foreign born:** 1.4%. **Median age:** 35.8. **State rank:** 26. **Pop change 1990-2000:** +13.9%.

Income: per capita $14,217; median household $27,888. **Pop below poverty level:** 18.4%.

Unemployment: 2.9%. **Median home value:** $55,900. **Median travel time to work:** 23.7 minutes.

CADDO COUNTY
PO Box 68   **Ph:** 405-247-6609
Anadarko, OK 73005   **Fax:** 405-247-6510

In west-central OK, west of Oklahoma City; original county; organized Aug 6, 1901 (prior to statehood). **Name Origin:** Name applied to a group of tribes of Caddoan linguistic stock, from Caddo Indian *kaadi* 'life' or 'chiefs.'

Area (sq mi): 1290.31 (land 1278.33; water 11.98).

Pop: 30,150 (White 64.1%; Black or African American 2.9%; Hispanic or Latino 6.3%; Asian 0.2%; Other 31.4%). **Foreign born:** 2.2%. **Median age:** 36. **State rank:** 32. **Pop change 1990-2000:** +2%.

Income: per capita $13,298; median household $27,347. **Pop below poverty level:** 21.7%.

Unemployment: 5.4%. **Median home value:** $44,300. **Median travel time to work:** 23.6 minutes.

CANADIAN COUNTY
PO Box 458   **Ph:** 405-262-1070
El Reno, OK 73036   **Fax:** 405-422-2411
www.canadiancounty.org/county/

In central OK, west of Oklahoma City; original county; organized 1890 (prior to statehood). **Name Origin:** For the Canadian River, which runs through it; known to the Osage as *Ne-sout-che-bra-ra*, probably named in honor of their homelands by French-Canadian explorers or traders.

Area (sq mi): 905.17 (land 899.71; water 5.45).

Pop: 87,697 (White 85%; Black or African American 2.2%; Hispanic or Latino 3.9%; Asian 2.4%; Other 8.4%). **Foreign born:** 3.2%. **Median age:** 35.4. **State rank:** 5. **Pop change 1990-2000:** +17.9%.

Income: per capita $19,691; median household $45,439. **Pop below poverty level:** 7.9%.

Unemployment: 3.1%. **Median home value:** $84,600. **Median travel time to work:** 22.9 minutes.

CARTER COUNTY
PO Box 1236   **Ph:** 580-223-8162
Ardmore, OK 73402
www.brightok.net/cartercounty/

In south-central OK, southeast of Lawton; organized Nov 16, 1907 from Chickasaw lands. **Name Origin:** For Charles David Carter (1868-1929), U.S. representative from OK (1907-27); or possibly for Benjamin Wisnor Carter, a Cherokee Indian, soldier in the Confederate army, and OK territorial judge.

Area (sq mi): 833.72 (land 823.79; water 9.93).

Pop: 45,621 (White 76.8%; Black or African American 7.6%; Hispanic or Latino 2.8%; Asian 0.6%; Other 13.8%). **Foreign born:** 1.3%. **Median age:** 38. **State rank:** 16. **Pop change 1990-2000:** +6.3%.

Income: per capita $15,511; median household $29,405. **Pop below poverty level:** 16.6%.

Unemployment: 4.2%. **Median home value:** $58,400. **Median travel time to work:** 23.7 minutes.

CHEROKEE COUNTY
213 W Delaware St Rm 200   **Ph:** 918-456-3171
Tahlequah, OK 74464   **Fax:** 918-458-6508

In central-eastern OK, southeast of Tulsa; organized Nov 16, 1907 from Indian lands. **Name Origin:** For the Cherokee Nation, a tribe of Iroquoian linguistic stock. Name may derive from Creek *tciloki* 'people of a different speech.'

All statistics are based on the 2000 Census except the dollar figures given for per capita income, which are based on 1999 estimates.

Area (sq mi): 776.4 (land 751.04; water 25.37).

Pop: 42,521 (White 55.2%; Black or African American 1.2%; Hispanic or Latino 4.1%; Asian 0.3%; Other 42.1%). **Foreign born:** 2.6%. **Median age:** 32.3. **State rank:** 21. **Pop change 1990-2000:** +24.9%.

Income: per capita $13,436; median household $26,536. **Pop below poverty level:** 22.9%.

Unemployment: 3.1%. **Median home value:** $67,100. **Median travel time to work:** 24.6 minutes.

CHOCTAW COUNTY

300 E Duke St   **Ph:** 580-326-3778
Hugo, OK 74743   **Fax:** 580-326-6787

On the southeastern border of OK; organized Nov 16, 1907 from Choctaw lands. **Name Origin:** For the Choctaw Nation, an Indian tribe of Muskhogean linguistic stock. Meaning of the name is unknown.

Area (sq mi): 800.68 (land 773.93; water 26.75).

Pop: 15,342 (White 67.8%; Black or African American 10.9%; Hispanic or Latino 1.6%; Asian 0.2%; Other 20.4%). **Foreign born:** 0.5%. **Median age:** 38.7. **State rank:** 44. **Pop change 1990-2000:** +0.3%.

Income: per capita $12,296; median household $22,743. **Pop below poverty level:** 24.3%.

Unemployment: 6.7%. **Median home value:** $41,500. **Median travel time to work:** 24.9 minutes.

CIMARRON COUNTY

Courthouse Sq PO Box 145   **Ph:** 580-544-2251
Boise City, OK 73933   **Fax:** 580-544-2251

In the OK panhandle; organized Nov 16, 1907 from Beaver County. **Name Origin:** For the Cimarron River, which flows across the northern part of the county. Meaning and application of the term are uncertain. The river may have been called in Spanish *el rio de los carneros cimarron* 'River of the Wild Sheep'; or it is possibly a Mexican-Apache word meaning 'wanderer.'

Area (sq mi): 1841.17 (land 1835.04; water 6.13).

Pop: 3,148 (White 81%; Black or African American 0.6%; Hispanic or Latino 15.4%; Asian 0.2%; Other 13.4%). **Foreign born:** 10.3%. **Median age:** 39.3. **State rank:** 77. **Pop change 1990-2000:** -4.6%.

Income: per capita $15,744; median household $30,625. **Pop below poverty level:** 17.6%.

Unemployment: 2.3%. **Median home value:** $37,000. **Median travel time to work:** 14.8 minutes.

CLEVELAND COUNTY

201 S Jones Ave Rm 204   **Ph:** 405-366-0240
Norman, OK 73069   **Fax:** 405-366-0229

In central OK, south of Oklahoma City; original county; organized 1890 (prior to statehood) from Cherokee lands. **Name Origin:** For Grover Cleveland (1837-1908), twenty-second and twenty-fourth U.S. president.

Area (sq mi): 558.34 (land 536.11; water 22.23).

Pop: 208,016 (White 81.5%; Black or African American 3.6%; Hispanic or Latino 4%; Asian 2.8%; Other 10%). **Foreign born:** 4.4%. **Median age:** 32.2. **State rank:** 3. **Pop change 1990-2000:** +19.4%.

Income: per capita $20,114; median household $41,846. **Pop below poverty level:** 10.6%.

Unemployment: 3.2%. **Median home value:** $88,500. **Median travel time to work:** 22.3 minutes.

COAL COUNTY

4 N Main St   **Ph:** 580-927-3122
Coalgate, OK 74538   **Fax:** 580-927-4003

In south-central OK, southeast of Ada; organized Nov 16, 1907 from Tobucksy County. **Name Origin:** For the chief economic product of the county.

Area (sq mi): 521.3 (land 518.22; water 3.07).

Pop: 6,031 (White 74.5%; Black or African American 0.4%; Hispanic or Latino 2.1%; Asian 0.3%; Other 24.1%). **Foreign born:** 1.6%. **Median age:** 38.1. **State rank:** 69. **Pop change 1990-2000:** +4.3%.

Income: per capita $12,013; median household $23,705. **Pop below poverty level:** 23.1%.

Unemployment: 6.8%. **Median home value:** $33,800. **Median travel time to work:** 24.3 minutes.

COMANCHE COUNTY

315 SW 5th St Suite 304   **Ph:** 580-355-5214
Lawton, OK 73501
www.comancheco.gen.ok.us

In south-central OK, southwest of Oklahoma City; organized Nov 16, 1907 from Cherokee lands. **Name Origin:** For the Comanche Indians of Shoshonean linguistic stock; name is believed to derive from Spanish *camino ancho* 'broad trail.'

Area (sq mi): 1083.82 (land 1069.35; water 14.48).

Pop: 114,996 (White 62%; Black or African American 19%; Hispanic or Latino 8.4%; Asian 2.1%; Other 13.7%). **Foreign born:** 5.4%. **Median age:** 30.1. **State rank:** 4. **Pop change 1990-2000:** +3.1%.

Income: per capita $15,728; median household $33,867. **Pop below poverty level:** 15.6%.

Unemployment: 3.3%. **Median home value:** $71,600. **Median travel time to work:** 16.9 minutes.

COTTON COUNTY

301 N Broadway   **Ph:** 580-875-3026
Walters, OK 73572   **Fax:** 580-875-3756

On the southern border of OK, south of Lawton; organized Aug 28, 1912 from Comanche County. **Name Origin:** For the principal agricultural product of the county.

Area (sq mi): 641.94 (land 636.64; water 5.31).

Pop: 6,614 (White 82.8%; Black or African American 2.9%; Hispanic or Latino 4.9%; Asian 0.1%; Other 12.3%). **Foreign born:** 1.5%. **Median age:** 38.6. **State rank:** 66. **Pop change 1990-2000:** -0.6%.

Please see sample entry on inside front cover for detailed information about the statistics presented with each county listing.

453

Income: per capita $14,626; median household $27,210. **Pop below poverty level:** 18.2%.

Unemployment: 4.1%. **Median home value:** $47,200. **Median travel time to work:** 25.3 minutes.

CRAIG COUNTY
PO Box 397   **Ph:** 918-256-2507
Vinita, OK 74301   **Fax:** 918-256-3617

On the northeastern border of OK, northeast of Tulsa; organized Nov 16, 1907 from Cherokee lands. **Name Origin:** For Granville Craig, a prominent Cherokee citizen.

Area (sq mi): 762.71 (land 761.03; water 1.68).

Pop: 14,950 (White 68.1%; Black or African American 3.1%; Hispanic or Latino 1.2%; Asian 0.2%; Other 28.2%). **Foreign born:** 0.5%. **Median age:** 39.3. **State rank:** 45. **Pop change 1990-2000:** +6%.

Income: per capita $16,539; median household $30,997. **Pop below poverty level:** 13.7%.

Unemployment: 3.6%. **Median home value:** $52,100. **Median travel time to work:** 23.2 minutes.

CREEK COUNTY
317 E Lee St Rm 100   **Ph:** 918-224-4084
Sapulpa, OK 74066

In east-central OK, southwest of Tulsa; organized Nov 16, 1907 from Cherokee lands. **Name Origin:** For the Creek Nation, a loose confederation of southeastern tribes of Muskhogean linguistic stock. The name is from 'Ochese Creek Indians.' applied to them by settlers in what is now TN. They were probably the Yuchi.

Area (sq mi): 969.77 (land 955.53; water 14.23).

Pop: 67,367 (White 81.4%; Black or African American 2.6%; Hispanic or Latino 1.9%; Asian 0.3%; Other 14.9%). **Foreign born:** 0.7%. **Median age:** 36.9. **State rank:** 9. **Pop change 1990-2000:** +10.6%.

Income: per capita $16,191; median household $33,168. **Pop below poverty level:** 13.5%.

Unemployment: 3.7%. **Median home value:** $67,400. **Median travel time to work:** 26 minutes.

CUSTER COUNTY
Broadway & B St   **Ph:** 580-323-1221
Arapaho, OK 73620

In west-central OK, west of Oklahoma City; original county; organized 1891 (prior to statehood). **Name Origin:** For Gen. George Armstrong Custer (1839-76), U.S. army officer and Indian fighter.

Area (sq mi): 1002 (land 986.51; water 15.49).

Pop: 26,142 (White 79.3%; Black or African American 2.9%; Hispanic or Latino 9%; Asian 0.9%; Other 14.8%). **Foreign born:** 3.4%. **Median age:** 32.7. **State rank:** 36. **Pop change 1990-2000:** -2.8%.

Income: per capita $15,584; median household $28,524. **Pop below poverty level:** 18.5%.

Unemployment: 3.4%. **Median home value:** $67,800. **Median travel time to work:** 15.7 minutes.

DELAWARE COUNTY
PO Box 309   **Ph:** 918-253-4520
Jay, OK 74346   **Fax:** 918-253-8352

On the northeastern border of OK, northeast of Tulsa; organized Nov 16, 1907 from Cherokee lands. **Name Origin:** For the Indian tribe, also known as Leni or Leni-Lenape, named for Thomas West (1577-1618), Lord Delaware (or De La Warr).

Area (sq mi): 792.33 (land 740.65; water 51.68).

Pop: 37,077 (White 69.4%; Black or African American 0.1%; Hispanic or Latino 1.8%; Asian 0.2%; Other 29.4%). **Foreign born:** 1.3%. **Median age:** 40.8. **State rank:** 25. **Pop change 1990-2000:** +32.1%.

Income: per capita $15,424; median household $27,996. **Pop below poverty level:** 18.3%.

Unemployment: 3.6%. **Median home value:** $81,900. **Median travel time to work:** 25.5 minutes.

DEWEY COUNTY
PO Box 368   **Ph:** 580-328-5361
Taloga, OK 73667   **Fax:** 580-328-5652

In west-central OK, southwest of Enid; original county; organized 1892 (prior to statehood). **Name Origin:** For George Dewey (1837-1917), who captured Manila (1898) during the Spanish-American War and was given the rank of Admiral of the Navy.

Area (sq mi): 1008.26 (land 1000.13; water 8.13).

Pop: 4,743 (White 90.6%; Black or African American 0.1%; Hispanic or Latino 2.7%; Asian 0.1%; Other 7.6%). **Foreign born:** 1.3%. **Median age:** 43. **State rank:** 72. **Pop change 1990-2000:** -14.6%.

Income: per capita $15,806; median household $28,172. **Pop below poverty level:** 15%.

Unemployment: 2.7%. **Median home value:** $38,000. **Median travel time to work:** 22.9 minutes.

ELLIS COUNTY
PO Box 197   **Ph:** 580-885-7301
Arnett, OK 73832   **Fax:** 580-885-7258

On the western border of OK, below the panhandle; organized Nov 16, 1907 from Day (which had been the northern part of Roger Mills County and was now abolished) and Woodward counties. **Name Origin:** For Albert H. Ellis, an OK constitutional convention delegate in 1907.

Area (sq mi): 1231.84 (land 1229.14; water 2.7).

Pop: 4,075 (White 94.8%; Black or African American 0%; Hispanic or Latino 2.6%; Asian 0.1%; Other 3.5%). **Foreign born:** 0.8%. **Median age:** 45.3. **State rank:** 73. **Pop change 1990-2000:** -9.4%.

Income: per capita $16,472; median household $27,951. **Pop below poverty level:** 12.5%.

Unemployment: 3.1%. **Median home value:** $34,000. **Median travel time to work:** 18.7 minutes.

All statistics are based on the 2000 Census except the dollar figures given for per capita income, which are based on 1999 estimates.

GARFIELD COUNTY

PO Box 1664   **Ph:** 580-237-0225
Enid, OK 73702   **Fax:** 580-249-5951

In north-central OK, southwest of Ponca City; original county; organized 1895 (prior to statehood). **Name Origin:** For James Abram Garfield (1831-81), twentieth U.S. president.

Area (sq mi): 1059.94 (land 1058.39; water 1.55).

Pop: 57,813 (White 86.9%; Black or African American 3.3%; Hispanic or Latino 4.1%; Asian 0.8%; Other 7.2%). **Foreign born:** 2.7%. **Median age:** 37.7. **State rank:** 11. **Pop change 1990-2000:** +1.9%.

Income: per capita $17,457; median household $33,006. **Pop below poverty level:** 13.9%.

Unemployment: 2.9%. **Median home value:** $58,800. **Median travel time to work:** 17.7 minutes.

GARVIN COUNTY

PO Box 926   **Ph:** 405-238-2772
Pauls Valley, OK 73075   **Fax:** 405-238-6283

In south-central OK, east of Ada; organized Nov 16, 1907 from Chickasaw lands. **Name Origin:** For Samuel J. Garvin, a leader of the Chickasaw Nation.

Area (sq mi): 813.66 (land 807.49; water 6.18).

Pop: 27,210 (White 83.4%; Black or African American 2.6%; Hispanic or Latino 3.4%; Asian 0.2%; Other 12.2%). **Foreign born:** 1.6%. **Median age:** 39. **State rank:** 35. **Pop change 1990-2000:** +2.3%.

Income: per capita $14,856; median household $28,070. **Pop below poverty level:** 15.9%.

Unemployment: 4.1%. **Median home value:** $45,400. **Median travel time to work:** 23.4 minutes.

GRADY COUNTY

326 Choctaw St   **Ph:** 405-224-7388
Chickasha, OK 73018   **Fax:** 405-222-4506

In south-central OK, southwest of Oklahoma City; organized Nov 16, 1907 from Caddo and Comanche counties. **Name Origin:** For Henry Woodfin Grady (1850-89), orator and editor of the *Atlanta Constitution* newspaper, whose writings and ideas helped alleviate the post-Civil War depression of the South.

Area (sq mi): 1105.3 (land 1100.96; water 4.34).

Pop: 45,516 (White 86.1%; Black or African American 3.1%; Hispanic or Latino 2.9%; Asian 0.3%; Other 9.2%). **Foreign born:** 1.1%. **Median age:** 36.5. **State rank:** 17. **Pop change 1990-2000:** +9%.

Income: per capita $15,846; median household $32,625. **Pop below poverty level:** 13.9%.

Unemployment: 3.6%. **Median home value:** $62,500. **Median travel time to work:** 26.9 minutes.

GRANT COUNTY

112 E Guthrie St PO Box 167   **Ph:** 580-395-2274
Medford, OK 73759

On the central northern border of OK, north of Enid; original county; organized 1895 (prior to statehood). **Name Origin:** For Ulysses S. Grant (1822-85), Civil War general and eighteenth U.S. president.

Area (sq mi): 1003.61 (land 1000.56; water 3.05).

Pop: 5,144 (White 94.3%; Black or African American 0.1%; Hispanic or Latino 1.8%; Asian 0.1%; Other 4.4%). **Foreign born:** 0.9%. **Median age:** 41.4. **State rank:** 71. **Pop change 1990-2000:** -9.6%.

Income: per capita $15,709; median household $28,977. **Pop below poverty level:** 13.7%.

Unemployment: 2.7%. **Median home value:** $36,300. **Median travel time to work:** 21.1 minutes.

GREER COUNTY

PO Box 207   **Ph:** 580-782-3664
Mangum, OK 73554   **Fax:** 580-782-3803

In southwestern OK, northwest of Lawton; original county; organized 1890 (prior to statehood). **Name Origin:** For John A. Greer, a lieutenant governor of TX.

Area (sq mi): 643.66 (land 639.36; water 4.3).

Pop: 6,061 (White 78.7%; Black or African American 8.8%; Hispanic or Latino 7.4%; Asian 0.3%; Other 9.5%). **Foreign born:** 1.5%. **Median age:** 40. **State rank:** 68. **Pop change 1990-2000:** -7.6%.

Income: per capita $14,053; median household $25,793. **Pop below poverty level:** 19.6%.

Unemployment: 3.1%. **Median home value:** $32,300. **Median travel time to work:** 17.8 minutes.

HARMON COUNTY

114 W Hollis St   **Ph:** 580-688-3658
Hollis, OK 73550   **Fax:** 580-688-9784

On the southwestern border of OK, west of Lawton; organized May 22, 1909 from Greer County. **Name Origin:** For Judson C. Harmon (1846-1927), U.S. Attorney General (1895-97) and governor of OH (1908-13).

Area (sq mi): 538.56 (land 537.82; water 0.74).

Pop: 3,283 (White 65.8%; Black or African American 9.8%; Hispanic or Latino 22.8%; Asian 0.2%; Other 17.3%). **Foreign born:** 3%. **Median age:** 39.9. **State rank:** 76. **Pop change 1990-2000:** -13.4%.

Income: per capita $13,464; median household $22,365. **Pop below poverty level:** 29.7%.

Unemployment: 3.9%. **Median home value:** $28,000. **Median travel time to work:** 14.6 minutes.

HARPER COUNTY

PO Box 369   **Ph:** 580-735-2870
Buffalo, OK 73834

On the northwestern border of OK, at eastern end of panhandle; organized Nov 16, 1905 from Woodward County. **Name Origin:** For Oscar G. Harper, an official at the OK constitutional convention (1906-07).

Please see sample entry on inside front cover for detailed information about the statistics presented with each county listing.

455

Area (sq mi): 1040.96 (land 1039; water 1.96).

Pop: 3,562 (White 92.9%; Black or African American 0%; Hispanic or Latino 5.6%; Asian 0.1%; Other 4%). **Foreign born:** 3.5%. **Median age:** 43.1. **State rank:** 74. **Pop change 1990-2000:** -12.3%.

Income: per capita $18,011; median household $33,705. **Pop below poverty level:** 10.2%.

Unemployment: 2.8%. **Median home value:** $37,900. **Median travel time to work:** 18.9 minutes.

HASKELL COUNTY

202 E Main St   **Ph:** 918-967-2884
Stigler, OK 74462   **Fax:** 918-967-2885

In east-central OK, south of Muskogee; organized Nov 16, 1907 from Choctaw lands. **Name Origin:** For Charles Nathaniel Haskell (1860-1933), member of the OK Constitutional Convention (1906-07) and first governor (1907-11).

Area (sq mi): 625.27 (land 577.03; water 48.24).

Pop: 11,792 (White 77.5%; Black or African American 0.6%; Hispanic or Latino 1.5%; Asian 0.3%; Other 20.8%). **Foreign born:** 0.8%. **Median age:** 38.6. **State rank:** 53. **Pop change 1990-2000:** +7.8%.

Income: per capita $13,775; median household $24,553. **Pop below poverty level:** 20.5%.

Unemployment: 4.7%. **Median home value:** $44,500. **Median travel time to work:** 28.7 minutes.

HUGHES COUNTY

200 N Broadway St Suite 7   **Ph:** 405-379-2746
Holdenville, OK 74848   **Fax:** 405-379-6739

In east-central OK, northeast of Ada; organized Nov 16, 1907 from Creek lands. **Name Origin:** For William C. Hughes, delegate to the OK Constitutional Convention (1906-07).

Area (sq mi): 814.64 (land 806.73; water 7.9).

Pop: 14,154 (White 71.8%; Black or African American 4.5%; Hispanic or Latino 2.5%; Asian 0.2%; Other 22.6%). **Foreign born:** 1.1%. **Median age:** 39.3. **State rank:** 46. **Pop change 1990-2000:** +8.7%.

Income: per capita $12,687; median household $22,621. **Pop below poverty level:** 21.9%.

Unemployment: 5%. **Median home value:** $32,600. **Median travel time to work:** 25 minutes.

JACKSON COUNTY

PO Box 515   **Ph:** 580-482-4070
Altus, OK 73522   **Fax:** 580-428-4472
www.intplsrv.net/jacksoncounty/

On the southwestern border of OK, west of Lawton; organized Nov 16, 1907 from Greer County. **Name Origin:** For Gen. Thomas J. 'Stonewall' Jackson (1824-63), Confederate officer who stood firm against the enemy 'like a stonewall.' Some claim Andrew Jackson (1767-1845), seventh U.S. president.

Area (sq mi): 804.15 (land 802.68; water 1.47).

Pop: 28,439 (White 71.5%; Black or African American 8%; Hispanic

or Latino 15.6%; Asian 1.2%; Other 14.6%). **Foreign born:** 4.7%. **Median age:** 33. **State rank:** 33. **Pop change 1990-2000:** -1.1%.

Income: per capita $15,454; median household $30,737. **Pop below poverty level:** 16.2%.

Unemployment: 2.8%. **Median home value:** $59,600. **Median travel time to work:** 14.4 minutes.

JEFFERSON COUNTY

220 N Main St Rm 103   **Ph:** 580-228-2029
Waurika, OK 73573   **Fax:** 580-228-3608

On the central southern border of OK, southeast of Lawton; organized Nov 16, 1907 from Comanche County. **Name Origin:** For Thomas Jefferson (1743-1826), U.S. patriot and statesman; third U.S. president.

Area (sq mi): 773.83 (land 758.75; water 15.07).

Pop: 6,818 (White 83.7%; Black or African American 0.7%; Hispanic or Latino 7%; Asian 1.1%; Other 11%). **Foreign born:** 3.6%. **Median age:** 40.4. **State rank:** 65. **Pop change 1990-2000:** -2.7%.

Income: per capita $12,899; median household $23,674. **Pop below poverty level:** 19.2%.

Unemployment: 3.7%. **Median home value:** $33,300. **Median travel time to work:** 27.5 minutes.

JOHNSTON COUNTY

403 W Main St   **Ph:** 580-371-3058
Tishomingo, OK 73460   **Fax:** 580-371-2174

In south-central OK, south of Ada; organized Nov 16, 1907 from Chickasaw lands. **Name Origin:** For Douglas H. Johnston (1856-1939), last governor for the Chickasaw nation, who remained in office until his death.

Area (sq mi): 658.29 (land 644.5; water 13.78).

Pop: 10,513 (White 75.4%; Black or African American 1.7%; Hispanic or Latino 2.5%; Asian 0.3%; Other 21.9%). **Foreign born:** 0.8%. **Median age:** 38. **State rank:** 59. **Pop change 1990-2000:** +4.8%.

Income: per capita $13,747; median household $24,592. **Pop below poverty level:** 22%.

Unemployment: 5%. **Median home value:** $40,000. **Median travel time to work:** 24.9 minutes.

KAY COUNTY

PO Box 450   **Ph:** 580-362-2537
Newkirk, OK 74647   **Fax:** 580-362-3300
www.courthouse.kay.ok.us/home.html

On the central northern border of OK, northeast of Enid; original county; organized as 'K' County 1895 (prior to statehood). **Name Origin:** For the letter *K*. The first seven counties of OK were originally numbered. The next fifteen were lettered (A-Q, except I and J). All later received names except 'K' County, which became Kay.

Area (sq mi): 945.12 (land 918.7; water 26.42).

Pop: 48,080 (White 82.5%; Black or African American 1.8%; Hispanic or Latino 4.3%; Asian 0.5%; Other 13.5%). **Foreign born:**

All statistics are based on the 2000 Census except the dollar figures given for per capita income, which are based on 1999 estimates.

2.3%. **Median age:** 38.1. **State rank:** 15. **Pop change 1990-2000:** +0%.

Income: per capita $16,643; median household $30,762. **Pop below poverty level:** 16%.

Unemployment: 5%. **Median home value:** $53,400. **Median travel time to work:** 16.1 minutes.

KINGFISHER COUNTY

101 S Main St Rm 3   **Ph:** 405-375-3887
Kingfisher, OK 73750   **Fax:** 405-375-6033
www.kingfisherco.com

In central OK, northwest of Oklahoma City; original county; organized 1890 (prior to statehood). **Name Origin:** For Kingfisher Creek, which runs through the county; itself named for King David Fisher (1819-63), who ran a stage and trading station on the Chisholm Trail.

Area (sq mi): 905.96 (land 903; water 2.96).

Pop: 13,926 (White 86.1%; Black or African American 1.6%; Hispanic or Latino 6.9%; Asian 0.2%; Other 10%). **Foreign born:** 4.1%. **Median age:** 38. **State rank:** 47. **Pop change 1990-2000:** +5.4%.

Income: per capita $18,167; median household $36,676. **Pop below poverty level:** 10.8%.

Unemployment: 2.6%. **Median home value:** $67,900. **Median travel time to work:** 22.5 minutes.

KIOWA COUNTY

PO Box 73   **Ph:** 580-726-5286
Hobart, OK 73651   **Fax:** 580-726-6033

In southwestern OK, northwest of Lawton; original county; organized 1891 (prior to statehood); re-formed from part of the original county in 1901. **Name Origin:** For the Indian tribe of Tanoan linguistic stock; name means 'principal people.'

Area (sq mi): 1030.66 (land 1014.56; water 16.1).

Pop: 10,227 (White 80.5%; Black or African American 4.7%; Hispanic or Latino 6.7%; Asian 0.3%; Other 11.5%). **Foreign born:** 1%. **Median age:** 40.9. **State rank:** 60. **Pop change 1990-2000:** -9.9%.

Income: per capita $14,231; median household $26,053. **Pop below poverty level:** 19.3%.

Unemployment: 3.1%. **Median home value:** $34,600. **Median travel time to work:** 18.3 minutes.

LATIMER COUNTY

109 N Central St   **Ph:** 918-465-2021
Wilburton, OK 74578   **Fax:** 918-465-3736

In east-central OK, east of McAlester; organized Nov 16, 1907 from Choctaw lands. **Name Origin:** For James S. Latimer, member of the OK Constitutional Convention (1906-07).

Area (sq mi): 729.12 (land 722.17; water 6.95).

Pop: 10,692 (White 72.5%; Black or African American 1%; Hispanic or Latino 1.5%; Asian 0.2%; Other 25.8%). **Foreign born:** 1.3%. **Median age:** 36.8. **State rank:** 57. **Pop change 1990-2000:** +3.5%.

Income: per capita $12,842; median household $23,962. **Pop below poverty level:** 22.7%.

Unemployment: 5.1%. **Median home value:** $46,800. **Median travel time to work:** 22.1 minutes.

LE FLORE COUNTY

PO Box 218   **Ph:** 918-647-5738
Poteau, OK 74953   **Fax:** 918-647-8930

On the eastern border of OK, east of McAlester; organized Nov 16, 1907 from Choctaw lands. **Name Origin:** For Greenwood LeFlore (1800-65), leader of a prominent Choctaw family of French ancestry, a landowner, and MS state legislator. He remained in MS when most of the tribe were moved to OK.

Area (sq mi): 1608.03 (land 1585.82; water 22.2).

Pop: 48,109 (White 78.4%; Black or African American 2.2%; Hispanic or Latino 3.8%; Asian 0.2%; Other 17.1%). **Foreign born:** 2.5%. **Median age:** 36.1. **State rank:** 14. **Pop change 1990-2000:** +11.2%.

Income: per capita $13,737; median household $27,278. **Pop below poverty level:** 19.1%.

Unemployment: 5.8%. **Median home value:** $51,600. **Median travel time to work:** 23.6 minutes.

LINCOLN COUNTY

PO Box 126   **Ph:** 405-258-1264
Chandler, OK 74834   **Fax:** 405-258-0439

In east-central OK, northeast of Oklahoma City; original county; organized Oct 1, 1891 (prior to statehood). **Name Origin:** For Abraham Lincoln (1809-65), sixteenth U.S. president.

Area (sq mi): 965.62 (land 957.74; water 7.88).

Pop: 32,080 (White 85.7%; Black or African American 2.5%; Hispanic or Latino 1.5%; Asian 0.2%; Other 10.8%). **Foreign born:** 0.8%. **Median age:** 37.5. **State rank:** 31. **Pop change 1990-2000:** +9.8%.

Income: per capita $14,890; median household $31,187. **Pop below poverty level:** 14.5%.

Unemployment: 4.4%. **Median home value:** $53,200. **Median travel time to work:** 31 minutes.

LOGAN COUNTY

301 E Harrison Ave Suite 102   **Ph:** 405-282-0266
Guthrie, OK 73044   **Fax:** 405-282-0267

In north-central OK, north of Oklahoma City; original county; organized as County No. 1 in 1891 (prior to statehood). **Name Origin:** For Gen. John Alexander Logan (1826-86), Civil War officer, U.S. senator from IL (1871-77; 1879-86), and national commander of the Grand Army of the Republic.

Area (sq mi): 748.92 (land 744.45; water 4.46).

Pop: 33,924 (White 80.3%; Black or African American 11%; Hispanic or Latino 2.9%; Asian 0.3%; Other 7%). **Foreign born:** 1.5%. **Median age:** 36.1. **State rank:** 29. **Pop change 1990-2000:** +16.9%.

Income: per capita $17,872; median household $36,784. **Pop below poverty level:** 12.9%.

Unemployment: 3.1%. **Median home value:** $74,100. **Median travel time to work:** 28.5 minutes.

Please see sample entry on inside front cover for detailed information about the statistics presented with each county listing.

LOVE COUNTY

405 W Main St Suite 203   **Ph:** 580-276-3059
Marietta, OK 73448

On the central southern border of OK; organized Nov 16, 1907 from Chickasaw lands. **Name Origin:** For a prominent Chickasaw family whose best-known member was Overton Love, a prominent judge of the Chickasaws.

Area (sq mi): 531.94 (land 515.38; water 16.56).

Pop: 8,831 (White 81.3%; Black or African American 2.2%; Hispanic or Latino 7%; Asian 0.3%; Other 13.4%). **Foreign born:** 3.2%. **Median age:** 39.4. **State rank:** 63. **Pop change 1990-2000:** +8.3%.

Income: per capita $16,648; median household $32,558. **Pop below poverty level:** 11.8%.

Unemployment: 4.7%. **Median home value:** $49,400. **Median travel time to work:** 26.8 minutes.

MAJOR COUNTY

PO Box 379   **Ph:** 580-227-4732
Fairview, OK 73737   **Fax:** 580-227-2736

In north-central OK, west of Enid; organized Nov 16, 1907 from Woods County. **Name Origin:** For John C. Major, member of the OK Constitutional Convention (1906-07).

Area (sq mi): 957.87 (land 956.76; water 1.11).

Pop: 7,545 (White 93.8%; Black or African American 0.2%; Hispanic or Latino 4%; Asian 0.1%; Other 4.7%). **Foreign born:** 2.1%. **Median age:** 41.6. **State rank:** 64. **Pop change 1990-2000:** -6.3%.

Income: per capita $17,272; median household $30,949. **Pop below poverty level:** 12%.

Unemployment: 2.6%. **Median home value:** $50,400. **Median travel time to work:** 20.1 minutes.

MARSHALL COUNTY

1 County Courthouse St Rm 106   **Ph:** 580-795-3165
Madill, OK 73446   **Fax:** 580-795-3165

On the central southern border of OK; organized Nov 16, 1907 from Chickasaw lands. **Name Origin:** For the maiden name of the mother of George A. Hendshaw, a member of the OK Constitutional Convention (1906-07).

Area (sq mi): 426.95 (land 371.11; water 55.84).

Pop: 13,184 (White 76.5%; Black or African American 1.8%; Hispanic or Latino 8.6%; Asian 0.2%; Other 20%). **Foreign born:** 5%. **Median age:** 41.3. **State rank:** 49. **Pop change 1990-2000:** +21.7%.

Income: per capita $14,982; median household $26,437. **Pop below poverty level:** 17.9%.

Unemployment: 4.2%. **Median home value:** $49,400. **Median travel time to work:** 23.6 minutes.

MAYES COUNTY

PO Box 97   **Ph:** 918-825-2426
Pryor, OK 74362   **Fax:** 918-825-3803

In northeastern OK, east of Tulsa; organized Nov 16, 1907 from Indian lands. **Name Origin:** For Chief Samuel Houston Mayes

(1845-1927), principal leader of the Cherokee Nation, also a prominent merchant and rancher.

Area (sq mi): 683.51 (land 656.14; water 27.37).

Pop: 38,369 (White 71.3%; Black or African American 0.3%; Hispanic or Latino 1.9%; Asian 0.3%; Other 27.2%). **Foreign born:** 1%. **Median age:** 37.2. **State rank:** 24. **Pop change 1990-2000:** +15%.

Income: per capita $15,350; median household $31,125. **Pop below poverty level:** 14.3%.

Unemployment: 4.9%. **Median home value:** $66,500. **Median travel time to work:** 25.7 minutes.

McCLAIN COUNTY

PO Box 629   **Ph:** 405-527-3360
Purcell, OK 73080

In south-central OK, south of Oklahoma City; organized Nov 16, 1907 from Chickasaw lands. **Name Origin:** For Charles M. McClain, a member of the OK Constitutional Convention (1906-07).

Area (sq mi): 580.13 (land 569.67; water 10.46).

Pop: 27,740 (White 85.3%; Black or African American 0.7%; Hispanic or Latino 4.9%; Asian 0.2%; Other 11.8%). **Foreign born:** 2.6%. **Median age:** 36.9. **State rank:** 34. **Pop change 1990-2000:** +21.7%.

Income: per capita $18,158; median household $37,275. **Pop below poverty level:** 10.5%.

Unemployment: 3.9%. **Median home value:** $77,200. **Median travel time to work:** 27.3 minutes.

McCURTAIN COUNTY

PO Box 1078   **Ph:** 580-286-2370
Idabel, OK 74745   **Fax:** 580-286-1040

In the southeastern corner of OK; organized Nov 16, 1907 from Choctaw lands. **Name Origin:** For a prominent Choctaw family, of which the father and his three sons each served as chief of the Choctaw Nation.

Area (sq mi): 1901.32 (land 1852.26; water 49.07).

Pop: 34,402 (White 69.5%; Black or African American 9.3%; Hispanic or Latino 3.1%; Asian 0.2%; Other 19.9%). **Foreign born:** 1.8%. **Median age:** 36. **State rank:** 28. **Pop change 1990-2000:** +2.9%.

Income: per capita $13,693; median household $24,162. **Pop below poverty level:** 24.7%.

Unemployment: 6.3%. **Median home value:** $44,500. **Median travel time to work:** 23.7 minutes.

McINTOSH COUNTY

PO Box 110   **Ph:** 918-689-2741
Eufaula, OK 74432   **Fax:** 918-689-3385

In east-central OK, southwest of Muskogee; organized Nov 16, 1907 from Indian lands. **Name Origin:** For a prominent Creek family, which included a number of prominent tribal chiefs.

Area (sq mi): 712.48 (land 620.01; water 92.48).

Pop: 19,456 (White 72%; Black or African American 4.1%; Hispanic

All statistics are based on the 2000 Census except the dollar figures given for per capita income, which are based on 1999 estimates.

or Latino 1.3%; Asian 0.1%; Other 23.1%). **Foreign born:** 0.5%. **Median age:** 44.1. **State rank:** 41. **Pop change 1990-2000:** +16%.

Income: per capita $16,410; median household $25,964. **Pop below poverty level:** 18.2%.

Unemployment: 5.8%. **Median home value:** $60,700. **Median travel time to work:** 27.5 minutes.

MURRAY COUNTY
PO Box 240   **Ph:** 580-622-3777
Sulphur, OK 73086   **Fax:** 580-622-6209

In south-central OK, north of Ardmore; organized Nov 16, 1907 from Chickasaw lands. **Name Origin:** For William Henry 'Alfalfa Bill' Murray (1869-1956), U.S. representative from OK (1913-17) and governor (1931-35).

Area (sq mi): 424.92 (land 418.25; water 6.67).

Pop: 12,623 (White 79.2%; Black or African American 1.9%; Hispanic or Latino 3.1%; Asian 0.3%; Other 17.1%). **Foreign born:** 2.8%. **Median age:** 39.8. **State rank:** 50. **Pop change 1990-2000:** +4.8%.

Income: per capita $16,084; median household $30,294. **Pop below poverty level:** 14.1%.

Unemployment: 4.9%. **Median home value:** $51,800. **Median travel time to work:** 21 minutes.

MUSKOGEE COUNTY
PO Box 1008   **Ph:** 918-682-7781
Muskogee, OK 74402   **Fax:** 918-682-8803

In east-cental OK, southeast of Tulsa; organized Nov 16, 1907 from Cherokee lands. **Name Origin:** For the Muscogee Creek Indians, a tribe of Muskhogean linguistic stock.

Area (sq mi): 838.99 (land 813.85; water 25.14).

Pop: 69,451 (White 62.8%; Black or African American 13.2%; Hispanic or Latino 2.7%; Asian 0.6%; Other 22.5%). **Foreign born:** 1.8%. **Median age:** 37. **State rank:** 7. **Pop change 1990-2000:** +2%.

Income: per capita $14,828; median household $28,438. **Pop below poverty level:** 17.9%.

Unemployment: 4.3%. **Median home value:** $57,700. **Median travel time to work:** 21.7 minutes.

NOBLE COUNTY
300 Courthouse Dr Rm 11   **Ph:** 580-336-2141
Perry, OK 73077   **Fax:** 580-336-2481

In north-central OK, east of Enid; organized as County 'P' 1897 (prior to statehood) from Indian lands. **Name Origin:** For Gen. John Willock Noble (1831-1912), U.S. district attorney for the eastern district of MO (1867) and U.S. secretary of the interior (1889-93).

Area (sq mi): 742.44 (land 731.9; water 10.54).

Pop: 11,411 (White 85.8%; Black or African American 1.6%; Hispanic or Latino 1.8%; Asian 0.3%; Other 11.6%). **Foreign born:** 1.1%. **Median age:** 38.3. **State rank:** 56. **Pop change 1990-2000:** +3.3%.

Income: per capita $17,022; median household $33,968. **Pop below poverty level:** 12.8%.

Unemployment: 4.5%. **Median home value:** $54,400. **Median travel time to work:** 19 minutes.

NOWATA COUNTY
229 N Maple St   **Ph:** 918-273-0175
Nowata, OK 74048   **Fax:** 918-273-1936

On the northeastern border of OK, northeast of Tulsa; organized Nov 16, 1907 from Cherokee lands. **Name Origin:** For the town of Nowata.

Area (sq mi): 580.87 (land 564.95; water 15.92).

Pop: 10,569 (White 71.9%; Black or African American 2.5%; Hispanic or Latino 1.2%; Asian 0.1%; Other 25.1%). **Foreign born:** 0.2%. **Median age:** 39. **State rank:** 58. **Pop change 1990-2000:** +5.8%.

Income: per capita $14,244; median household $29,470. **Pop below poverty level:** 14.1%.

Unemployment: 5.8%. **Median home value:** $41,100. **Median travel time to work:** 26.7 minutes.

OKFUSKEE COUNTY
PO Box 26   **Ph:** 918-623-0939
Okemah, OK 74859   **Fax:** 918-623-0635

In east-central OK, east of Oklahoma City; organized Nov 16, 1907 from Creek lands. **Name Origin:** For a Creek town in Cleburne County, AL, probably transferred by the Creek Indians; name possibly means 'point between streams' or 'promontory.'

Area (sq mi): 628.91 (land 624.76; water 4.15).

Pop: 11,814 (White 64.9%; Black or African American 10.4%; Hispanic or Latino 1.6%; Asian 0.1%; Other 24.1%). **Foreign born:** 1.7%. **Median age:** 38.6. **State rank:** 52. **Pop change 1990-2000:** +2.3%.

Income: per capita $12,746; median household $24,324. **Pop below poverty level:** 23%.

Unemployment: 4.7%. **Median home value:** $39,100. **Median travel time to work:** 27.1 minutes.

OKLAHOMA COUNTY
320 Robert S Kerr Ave   **Ph:** 405-270-0082
Oklahoma City, OK 73102   **Fax:** 405-713-7171
www.oklahomacounty.org

In central OK, north of Norman; original county; organized 1891 (prior to statehood). **Name Origin:** For Oklahoma City.

Area (sq mi): 718.31 (land 709.09; water 9.22).

Pop: 660,448 (White 67.1%; Black or African American 15%; Hispanic or Latino 8.7%; Asian 2.8%; Other 11.8%). **Foreign born:** 7.2%. **Median age:** 34.2. **State rank:** 1. **Pop change 1990-2000:** +10.1%.

Income: per capita $19,551; median household $35,063. **Pop below poverty level:** 15.3%.

Unemployment: 4.1%. **Median home value:** $75,800. **Median travel time to work:** 20.9 minutes.

Please see sample entry on inside front cover for detailed information about the statistics presented with each county listing.

OKMULGEE COUNTY

PO Box 904   **Ph:** 918-756-0788
Okmulgee, OK 74447   **Fax:** 918-758-1261

In east-central OK, south of Tulsa; organized Nov 16, 1907 from Creek lands. **Name Origin:** For a Creek town in Russell County, AL; from *oki mulgi* 'boiling waters,' probably referring to a spring.

Area (sq mi): 702.32 (land 696.97; water 5.34).

Pop: 39,685 (White 69%; Black or African American 10.2%; Hispanic or Latino 1.9%; Asian 0.2%; Other 19.8%). **Foreign born:** 0.7%. **Median age:** 36.9. **State rank:** 22. **Pop change 1990-2000:** +8.8%.

Income: per capita $14,065; median household $27,652. **Pop below poverty level:** 18.9%.

Unemployment: 6.8%. **Median home value:** $46,000. **Median travel time to work:** 27.3 minutes.

OSAGE COUNTY

PO Box 87   **Ph:** 918-287-3136
Pawhuska, OK 74056   **Fax:** 918-287-4979

On the central northern border of OK, northeast of Tulsa; organized Nov 16, 1907 from Osage Indian lands. **Name Origin:** For the Osage Indian tribe of Siouan linguistic stock from the area near the Osage River. The name is a French corruption of their tribal name, *Washazhe*, meaning unknown.

Area (sq mi): 2303.8 (land 2250.8; water 53).

Pop: 44,437 (White 66.1%; Black or African American 10.8%; Hispanic or Latino 2.1%; Asian 0.2%; Other 21.8%). **Foreign born:** 1%. **Median age:** 38.1. **State rank:** 18. **Pop change 1990-2000:** +6.7%.

Income: per capita $17,014; median household $34,477. **Pop below poverty level:** 13.2%.

Unemployment: 3.5%. **Median home value:** $63,500. **Median travel time to work:** 25.3 minutes.

OTTAWA COUNTY

102 E Central Ave Suite 203   **Ph:** 918-542-3332
Miami, OK 74354   **Fax:** 918-542-8260

On the northeastern border of OK, northeast of Tulsa; organized Nov 16, 1907 from Indian lands. **Name Origin:** For the Ottawa Indians, a tribe of Algonquian linguistic stock whose earliest known location was along the northern shore of Georgian Bay, Ont., Canada. The name is derived from Algonquian *adawe*, probably 'to trade.'

Area (sq mi): 484.73 (land 471.32; water 13.41).

Pop: 33,194 (White 72.9%; Black or African American 0.6%; Hispanic or Latino 3.2%; Asian 0.3%; Other 24.9%). **Foreign born:** 1.7%. **Median age:** 37.3. **State rank:** 30. **Pop change 1990-2000:** +8.6%.

Income: per capita $14,478; median household $27,507. **Pop below poverty level:** 16.6%.

Unemployment: 7.3%. **Median home value:** $47,200. **Median travel time to work:** 21.1 minutes.

PAWNEE COUNTY

500 Harrison St Rm 203   **Ph:** 918-762-3741
Pawnee, OK 74058   **Fax:** 918-762-3714

In north-central OK, northwest of Tulsa; organized as County 'Q' in 1892 (prior to statehood) from Indian lands. **Name Origin:** For the Pawnee Indian tribe of Caddoan linguistic stock. The name may mean 'horn,' for the shape in which they wore their hair lock. The Osages called them *Pa-in* 'long-haired'; they called themselves 'civilized people.'

Area (sq mi): 594.87 (land 569.44; water 25.43).

Pop: 16,612 (White 81.7%; Black or African American 0.7%; Hispanic or Latino 1.2%; Asian 0.2%; Other 16.7%). **Foreign born:** 0.6%. **Median age:** 38.5. **State rank:** 43. **Pop change 1990-2000:** +6.7%.

Income: per capita $15,261; median household $31,661. **Pop below poverty level:** 13%.

Unemployment: 4.9%. **Median home value:** $56,300. **Median travel time to work:** 30.6 minutes.

PAYNE COUNTY

315 W 6th St Suite 202   **Ph:** 405-747-8310
Stillwater, OK 74074   **Fax:** 405-747-8304
www.paynecounty.org

In north-central OK, west of Tulsa; original county; organized 1890 (prior to statehood), known as 'Old Oklahoma.' **Name Origin:** For David L. Payne (1836-84), active in the Oklahoma Boomer (land development) movement.

Area (sq mi): 697.13 (land 686.34; water 10.79).

Pop: 68,190 (White 83.3%; Black or African American 3.6%; Hispanic or Latino 2.1%; Asian 3%; Other 9%). **Foreign born:** 4.6%. **Median age:** 27.6. **State rank:** 8. **Pop change 1990-2000:** +10.9%.

Income: per capita $15,983; median household $28,733. **Pop below poverty level:** 20.3%.

Unemployment: 1.5%. **Median home value:** $79,700. **Median travel time to work:** 16.8 minutes.

PITTSBURG COUNTY

115 E Carl Albert Pkwy Suite 1A   **Ph:** 918-423-6865
McAlester, OK 74501   **Fax:** 918-423-7304

In east-central OK, southwest of Muskogee; organized Nov 16, 1907 from Tobucksy County. **Name Origin:** For Pittsburgh, PA.

Area (sq mi): 1377.85 (land 1305.94; water 71.91).

Pop: 43,953 (White 76.3%; Black or African American 4%; Hispanic or Latino 2.1%; Asian 0.3%; Other 18.5%). **Foreign born:** 1.1%. **Median age:** 39.4. **State rank:** 19. **Pop change 1990-2000:** +8.3%.

Income: per capita $15,494; median household $28,679. **Pop below poverty level:** 17.2%.

Unemployment: 4.2%. **Median home value:** $53,400. **Median travel time to work:** 20.6 minutes.

PONTOTOC COUNTY

PO Box 1425   **Ph:** 580-332-1425
Ada, OK 74820   **Fax:** 580-332-9509

In south-central OK, southeast of Oklahoma City; organized Nov

All statistics are based on the 2000 Census except the dollar figures given for per capita income, which are based on 1999 estimates.

16, 1907 from Choctaw lands. **Name Origin:** Of Chickasaw origin; the name of a chief, said to mean 'cattails growing on the prairie.'

Area (sq mi): 725.45 (land 719.64; water 5.82).

Pop: 35,143 (White 74.8%; Black or African American 2.1%; Hispanic or Latino 2.3%; Asian 0.5%; Other 21.7%). **Foreign born:** 1.2%. **Median age:** 35.7. **State rank:** 27. **Pop change 1990-2000:** +3%.

Income: per capita $14,664; median household $26,955. **Pop below poverty level:** 16.5%.

Unemployment: 3.9%. **Median home value:** $58,000. **Median travel time to work:** 18 minutes.

POTTAWATOMIE COUNTY
PO Box 576   **Ph:** 405-273-8222
Shawnee, OK 74802   **Fax:** 405-275-6898

In central OK, southeast of Oklahoma City; original county; organized as County 'B' in 1891 (prior to statehood); name changed in 1892. **Name Origin:** For the Potawatomie Indian tribe of Algonquian linguistic stock. The name probably means 'people of the place of the fire.'

Area (sq mi): 793.26 (land 787.7; water 5.57).

Pop: 65,521 (White 78.8%; Black or African American 2.9%; Hispanic or Latino 2.4%; Asian 0.6%; Other 16.6%). **Foreign born:** 1.1%. **Median age:** 35.5. **State rank:** 10. **Pop change 1990-2000:** +11.5%.

Income: per capita $15,972; median household $31,573. **Pop below poverty level:** 14.6%.

Unemployment: 5.2%. **Median home value:** $60,500. **Median travel time to work:** 25 minutes.

PUSHMATAHA COUNTY
304 SW 'B' St   **Ph:** 580-298-2512
Antlers, OK 74523   **Fax:** 580-298-5299

In southeastern OK, southeast of McAlester; organized Nov 16, 1907 from Indian lands. **Name Origin:** For the Pushmataha district of the Choctaw Nation, named for the noted Choctaw chief (c.1765-1824) who served with Andrew Jackson (1767-1845) and is buried in the Congressional Cemetery. The name may mean 'ready to be a sapling,' ie., now grown to be a young man; or 'qualified sapling,' indicating a rank to which he belonged.

Area (sq mi): 1422.78 (land 1397.31; water 25.47).

Pop: 11,667 (White 77.1%; Black or African American 0.8%; Hispanic or Latino 1.6%; Asian 0.1%; Other 21.2%). **Foreign born:** 0.5%. **Median age:** 40.1. **State rank:** 54. **Pop change 1990-2000:** +6.1%.

Income: per capita $12,864; median household $22,127. **Pop below poverty level:** 23.2%.

Unemployment: 6.6%. **Median home value:** $42,600. **Median travel time to work:** 26.8 minutes.

ROGER MILLS COUNTY
PO Box 708   **Ph:** 580-497-3365
Cheyenne, OK 73628   **Fax:** 580-497-3488

On the central western border of OK; original county; organized as County 'F' Apr 19, 1892; name changed Nov 1892; annexed part of Day County when the latter was abolished in 1907. **Name Origin:** For Col. Roger Quarles Mills (1832-1911), U.S. representative from TX (1873-92) and U.S. senator (1892-99).

Area (sq mi): 1146.46 (land 1141.87; water 4.58).

Pop: 3,436 (White 90.2%; Black or African American 0.3%; Hispanic or Latino 2.6%; Asian 0.1%; Other 7.9%). **Foreign born:** 0.7%. **Median age:** 41.7. **State rank:** 75. **Pop change 1990-2000:** -17.1%.

Income: per capita $16,821; median household $30,078. **Pop below poverty level:** 16.3%.

Unemployment: 1.9%. **Median home value:** $39,000. **Median travel time to work:** 24.7 minutes.

ROGERS COUNTY
219 S Missouri St   **Ph:** 918-341-2518
Claremore, OK 74017   **Fax:** 918-341-4529
www.rogerscounty.org

In northeastern OK, east of Tulsa; organized Nov 16, 1907 from Cherokee lands. **Name Origin:** For Clement V. Rogers, member of the OK Constitutional Convention (1906-07) and father of the humorist Will Rogers (1879-1935).

Area (sq mi): 711.44 (land 674.95; water 36.49).

Pop: 70,641 (White 79%; Black or African American 0.7%; Hispanic or Latino 1.8%; Asian 0.3%; Other 19.1%). **Foreign born:** 1.3%. **Median age:** 36.2. **State rank:** 6. **Pop change 1990-2000:** +28%.

Income: per capita $19,073; median household $44,471. **Pop below poverty level:** 8.6%.

Unemployment: 3%. **Median home value:** $94,100. **Median travel time to work:** 25.4 minutes.

SEMINOLE COUNTY
PO Box 1180   **Ph:** 405-257-2501
Wewoka, OK 74884   **Fax:** 405-257-6422

In central OK, east of Shawnee; organized Nov 16, 1907 from Seminole lands. **Name Origin:** For the Seminole Indians, a Muskhogean tribe from FL, forced to move to OK at the conclusion of the Seminole War (1835-42). The name is from Creek, probably 'the separate ones.'

Area (sq mi): 640.57 (land 632.51; water 8.06).

Pop: 24,894 (White 69.9%; Black or African American 5.6%; Hispanic or Latino 2.2%; Asian 0.2%; Other 23.4%). **Foreign born:** 1%. **Median age:** 38.1. **State rank:** 37. **Pop change 1990-2000:** -2%.

Income: per capita $13,956; median household $25,568. **Pop below poverty level:** 20.8%.

Unemployment: 5.7%. **Median home value:** $39,300. **Median travel time to work:** 23.7 minutes.

SEQUOYAH COUNTY
120 E Chickasaw Ave   **Ph:** 918-775-4516
Sallisaw, OK 74955

On central eastern border of OK, west of Fort Smith, AR; organized Nov 16, 1907 from Cherokee lands. **Name Origin:** From the Sequoyah District of the Cherokee Nation, named for the Indian chief

Please see sample entry on inside front cover for detailed information about the statistics presented with each county listing.

461

Sequoyah (c.1773-1843), who invented the Cherokee alphabet. He was also called George Guess.

Area (sq mi): 714.88 (land 673.82; water 41.06).

Pop: 38,972 (White 67.4%; Black or African American 1.9%; Hispanic or Latino 2%; Asian 0.2%; Other 29.7%). **Foreign born:** 0.7%. **Median age:** 36.4. **State rank:** 23. **Pop change 1990-2000:** +15.2%.

Income: per capita $13,405; median household $27,615. **Pop below poverty level:** 19.8%.

Unemployment: 5.3%. **Median home value:** $59,800. **Median travel time to work:** 27.4 minutes.

STEPHENS COUNTY

101 S 11th St   **Ph:** 580-255-4193
Duncan, OK 73533   **Fax:** 580-255-1771

In south-central OK, east of Lawton; organized Nov 16, 1907 from Comanche County. **Name Origin:** For John Hall Stephens (1847-1924), U.S. representative from TX (1897-1917) and strong advocate for OK statehood.

Area (sq mi): 891.12 (land 874.04; water 17.08).

Pop: 43,182 (White 86.2%; Black or African American 2.2%; Hispanic or Latino 4%; Asian 0.3%; Other 9%). **Foreign born:** 1.8%. **Median age:** 40.1. **State rank:** 20. **Pop change 1990-2000:** +2.1%.

Income: per capita $16,357; median household $30,709. **Pop below poverty level:** 14.6%.

Unemployment: 3.4%. **Median home value:** $54,500. **Median travel time to work:** 21.2 minutes.

TEXAS COUNTY

PO Box 197   **Ph:** 580-338-3233
Guymon, OK 73942   **Fax:** 580-338-4311
www.texascounty.org

In the central OK panhandle; organized Nov 16, 1907 from part of the old Beaver County. **Name Origin:** For the state.

Area (sq mi): 2048.81 (land 2037.16; water 11.66).

Pop: 20,107 (White 66.7%; Black or African American 0.7%; Hispanic or Latino 29.9%; Asian 0.6%; Other 22%). **Foreign born:** 16.9%. **Median age:** 30.4. **State rank:** 39. **Pop change 1990-2000:** +22.5%.

Income: per capita $15,692; median household $35,872. **Pop below poverty level:** 14.1%.

Unemployment: 2%. **Median home value:** $67,500. **Median travel time to work:** 16.6 minutes.

TILLMAN COUNTY

PO Box 992   **Ph:** 580-335-3421
Frederick, OK 73542   **Fax:** 580-335-3795

On the southwestern border of OK, southwest of Lawton; organized Nov 16, 1907 from Comanche County. **Name Origin:** For Benjamin Ryan Tillman (1847-1918), governor of SC (1890-94) and U.S. senator from SC (1895-1918), who was active in the formation of the state of OK.

Area (sq mi): 879.21 (land 871.97; water 7.25).

Pop: 9,287 (White 68.5%; Black or African American 9%; Hispanic or Latino 17.7%; Asian 0.3%; Other 16.4%). **Foreign born:** 4.3%. **Median age:** 38.9. **State rank:** 61. **Pop change 1990-2000:** -10.6%.

Income: per capita $14,270; median household $24,828. **Pop below poverty level:** 21.9%.

Unemployment: 4.7%. **Median home value:** $29,100. **Median travel time to work:** 20.9 minutes.

TULSA COUNTY

500 S Denver Ave   **Ph:** 918-596-5000
Tulsa, OK 74103   **Fax:** 918-596-5819
www.tulsacounty.org

In northeastern OK, northwest of Muskogee; organized Nov 16, 1907 from Creek lands. **Name Origin:** For Tulsa, a town at the time.

Area (sq mi): 587.02 (land 570.3; water 16.72).

Pop: 563,299 (White 72.5%; Black or African American 10.9%; Hispanic or Latino 6%; Asian 1.6%; Other 12.4%). **Foreign born:** 5.4%. **Median age:** 34.4. **State rank:** 2. **Pop change 1990-2000:** +11.9%.

Income: per capita $21,115; median household $38,213. **Pop below poverty level:** 11.6%.

Unemployment: 3.4%. **Median home value:** $87,000. **Median travel time to work:** 19.7 minutes.

WAGONER COUNTY

PO Box 156   **Ph:** 918-485-6171
Wagoner, OK 74467   **Fax:** 918-485-7709

In east-central OK, north of Muskogee; organized Nov 16, 1907 from Creek lands. **Name Origin:** For the city of Wagoner.

Area (sq mi): 590.99 (land 562.91; water 28.07).

Pop: 57,491 (White 78.9%; Black or African American 3.8%; Hispanic or Latino 2.5%; Asian 0.5%; Other 15.7%). **Foreign born:** 1.8%. **Median age:** 36.2. **State rank:** 12. **Pop change 1990-2000:** +20.1%.

Income: per capita $18,272; median household $41,744. **Pop below poverty level:** 8.9%.

Unemployment: 3%. **Median home value:** $89,800. **Median travel time to work:** 26.6 minutes.

WASHINGTON COUNTY

401 S Johnstone Ave Rm 100   **Ph:** 918-337-2840
Bartlesville, OK 74003   **Fax:** 918-337-2894
www.co.washington.ok.us

On the northern border of OK, north of Tulsa; organized Nov 16, 1907 from Cherokee lands. **Name Origin:** For George Washington (1732-99), American patriot and first U.S. president.

Area (sq mi): 424.15 (land 416.82; water 7.34).

Pop: 48,996 (White 79.9%; Black or African American 2.5%; Hispanic or Latino 2.6%; Asian 0.7%; Other 15.6%). **Foreign born:** 2%. **Median age:** 40.1. **State rank:** 13. **Pop change 1990-2000:** +1.9%.

Income: per capita $20,250; median household $35,816. **Pop below poverty level:** 11.9%.

All statistics are based on the 2000 Census except the dollar figures given for per capita income, which are based on 1999 estimates.

Unemployment: 3.3%. **Median home value:** $63,000. **Median travel time to work:** 20.1 minutes.

WASHITA COUNTY

PO Box 380   **Ph:** 580-832-2284
Cordell, OK 73632   **Fax:** 580-832-3526

In west-central OK, southwest of Oklahoma City; organized as County 'H' in 1892 (prior to statehood) from Indian lands; name changed later. **Name Origin:** For the Washita River, which runs through it. Name is believed to be from Choctaw *owa* and *chita* 'big hunt.'

Area (sq mi): 1009.07 (land 1003.35; water 5.73).

Pop: 11,508 (White 90.4%; Black or African American 0.4%; Hispanic or Latino 4.5%; Asian 0.3%; Other 7%). **Foreign born:** 1.6%. **Median age:** 39.2. **State rank:** 55. **Pop change 1990-2000:** +0.6%.

Income: per capita $15,528; median household $29,563. **Pop below poverty level:** 15.5%.

Unemployment: 3%. **Median home value:** $39,800. **Median travel time to work:** 21.2 minutes.

WOODS COUNTY

PO Box 386   **Ph:** 580-327-2126
Alva, OK 73717   **Fax:** 580-327-6200

On the northern border of OK, northwest of Enid; original county; organized as County 'M' in 1893 (prior to statehood); name changed later; re-formed Nov 16, 1907. **Name Origin:** For Lt. Col. Samuel N. Wood (?-1814), career army officer killed in the war of 1812. The letter *s* was a clerical error allowed to stand.

Area (sq mi): 1290.07 (land 1286.57; water 3.51).

Pop: 9,089 (White 91.9%; Black or African American 2.4%; Hispanic or Latino 2.4%; Asian 0.5%; Other 3.7%). **Foreign born:** 0.9%. **Median age:** 37.8. **State rank:** 62. **Pop change 1990-2000:** -0.2%.

Income: per capita $17,487; median household $28,927. **Pop below poverty level:** 15%.

Unemployment: 1.5%. **Median home value:** $46,300. **Median travel time to work:** 12.6 minutes.

WOODWARD COUNTY

1600 Main St Suite 9   **Ph:** 580-256-8097
Woodward, OK 73801   **Fax:** 580-254-6840

In northwestern OK, west of Enid; organized as County 'N' in 1893 from Indian lands; re-formed Nov 16, 1907. **Name Origin:** For the railroad station, itself named for Brinton W. Woodward, a director of the Santa Fe Railroad.

Area (sq mi): 1246.01 (land 1242.3; water 3.71).

Pop: 18,486 (White 90.3%; Black or African American 1.1%; Hispanic or Latino 4.8%; Asian 0.5%; Other 6.2%). **Foreign born:** 2.5%. **Median age:** 37.4. **State rank:** 42. **Pop change 1990-2000:** -2.6%.

Income: per capita $16,734; median household $33,581. **Pop below poverty level:** 12.5%.

Unemployment: 3.1%. **Median home value:** $61,100. **Median travel time to work:** 19.8 minutes.

Please see sample entry on inside front cover for detailed information about the statistics presented with each county listing.

OREGON - Counties

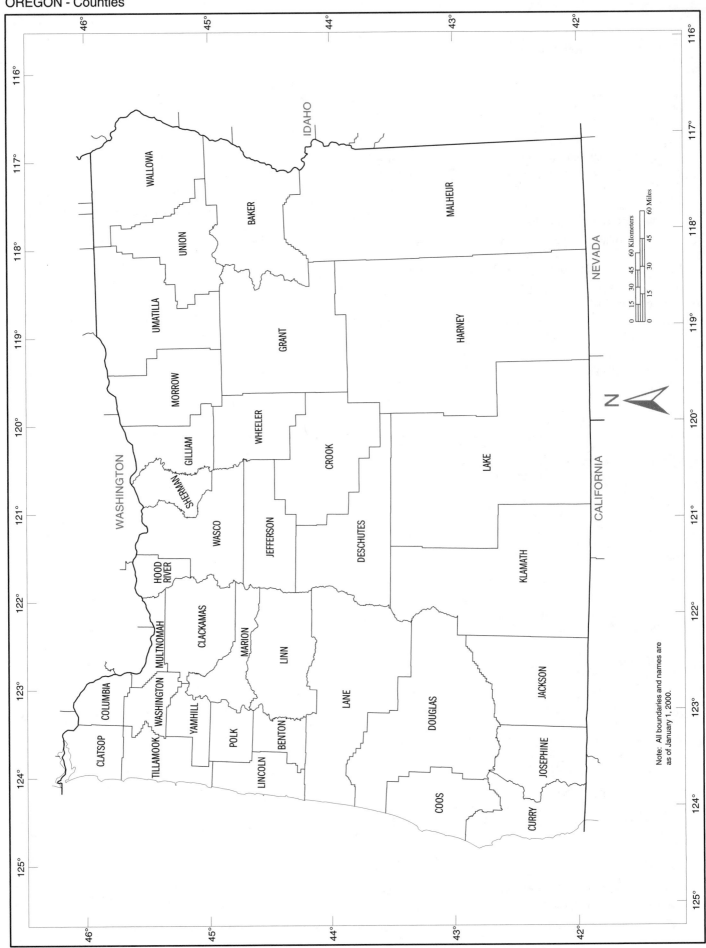

Note: All boundaries and names are as of January 1, 2000.

U.S. Census Bureau, Census 2000

Oregon

OREGON STATE INFORMATION

www.oregon.gov   **Ph:** 503-378-6500

Area (sq mi): 98,380.64 (land 95,996.79; water 2383.85).

Pop: 3,421,399 (White 83.5%; Black or African American 1.6%; Hispanic or Latino 8%; Asian 3%; Other 8.8%). **Foreign born:** 8.5%. **Median age:** 36.3. **Pop change 1990-2000:** +20.4%.

Income: per capita $20,940; median household $40,916. **Pop below poverty level:** 11.6%.

Unemployment: 7.5%. **Median home value:** $152,100. **Median travel time to work:** 22.2 minutes.

BAKER COUNTY

1995 3rd St Suite 150   **Ph:** 541-523-8207
Baker City, OR 97814   **Fax:** 541-523-8240
www.bakercounty.org

On the northeastern border of OR; organized Sep 22, 1862 from Wasco County. **Name Origin:** For Col. Edward Dickinson Baker (1811-61), officer in the Civil War, U.S. representative from IL (1845-47; 1849-51), and U.S. senator from OR (1860-61).

Area (sq mi): 3088.43 (land 3068.12; water 20.32).

Pop: 16,741 (White 94.6%; Black or African American 0.2%; Hispanic or Latino 2.3%; Asian 0.4%; Other 3.7%). **Foreign born:** 1.8%. **Median age:** 42.7. **State rank:** 28. **Pop change 1990-2000:** +9.3%.

Income: per capita $15,612; median household $30,367. **Pop below poverty level:** 14.7%.

Unemployment: 8.8%. **Median home value:** $84,700. **Median travel time to work:** 17 minutes.

BENTON COUNTY

PO Box 3020   **Ph:** 541-766-6800
Corvallis, OR 97339   **Fax:** 541-766-6893
www.co.benton.or.us

In west-central OR, north of Eugene; original county; organized Dec 23, 1847 (prior to statehood). **Name Origin:** For Thomas Hart Benton (1782-1858), U.S. journalist and statesman; nicknamed 'Old Bullion' for championing the use of gold and silver currency rather than paper money.

Area (sq mi): 678.97 (land 676.46; water 2.51).

Pop: 78,153 (White 86.8%; Black or African American 0.8%; Hispanic or Latino 4.7%; Asian 4.5%; Other 5.5%). **Foreign born:** 7.6%. **Median age:** 31.1. **State rank:** 11. **Pop change 1990-2000:** +10.4%.

Income: per capita $21,868; median household $41,897. **Pop below poverty level:** 14.6%.

Unemployment: 3%. **Median home value:** $169,800. **Median travel time to work:** 17.8 minutes.

CLACKAMAS COUNTY

104 11th St   **Ph:** 503-655-8551
Oregon City, OR 97045   **Fax:** 503-650-3035
www.co.clackamas.or.us

In northern OR, south of Portland; original county; organized Jul 5, 1843 (prior to statehood). **Name Origin:** For the Clackamas tribe of Chinook Indians; meaning of name is unknown.

Area (sq mi): 1879.01 (land 1868.17; water 10.83).

Pop: 338,391 (White 89.1%; Black or African American 0.7%; Hispanic or Latino 4.9%; Asian 2.5%; Other 5.7%). **Foreign born:** 7.1%. **Median age:** 37.5. **State rank:** 3. **Pop change 1990-2000:** +21.4%.

Income: per capita $25,973; median household $52,080. **Pop below poverty level:** 6.6%.

Unemployment: 4.5%. **Median home value:** $199,000. **Median travel time to work:** 26.2 minutes.

CLATSOP COUNTY

PO Box 178   **Ph:** 503-325-8511
Astoria, OR 97103   **Fax:** 503-325-9307
www.co.clatsop.or.us

In the northwestern corner of OR; original county; organized Jun 22, 1844 (prior to statehood) from the Tuality district. **Name Origin:** For the Clatsop Indian tribe of Chinook Indians, whose name means 'dried salmon.'

Area (sq mi): 1084.75 (land 827.23; water 257.52).

Pop: 35,630 (White 90.8%; Black or African American 0.5%; Hispanic or Latino 4.5%; Asian 1.2%; Other 5.1%). **Foreign born:** 4.2%. **Median age:** 40. **State rank:** 19. **Pop change 1990-2000:** +7%.

Income: per capita $19,515; median household $36,301. **Pop below poverty level:** 13.2%.

Unemployment: 5.2%. **Median home value:** $143,400. **Median travel time to work:** 19.5 minutes.

Please see sample entry on inside front cover for detailed information about the statistics presented with each county listing.

465

COLUMBIA COUNTY
County Courthouse 230 Strand St   **Ph:** 503-397-3796
Saint Helens, OR 97051   **Fax:** 503-397-7266
www.co.columbia.or.us

On the northwestern border of OR, northwest of Portland; organized Jan 16, 1854 (prior to statehood) from Washington County. **Name Origin:** For the Columbia River, which forms its northern and eastern borders.

Area (sq mi): 688.33 (land 656.72; water 31.61).

Pop: 43,560 (White 93.1%; Black or African American 0.2%; Hispanic or Latino 2.5%; Asian 0.6%; Other 4.7%). **Foreign born:** 1.8%. **Median age:** 37.7. **State rank:** 18. **Pop change 1990-2000:** +16%.

Income: per capita $20,078; median household $45,797. **Pop below poverty level:** 9.1%.

Unemployment: 7.8%. **Median home value:** $150,700. **Median travel time to work:** 29.3 minutes.

COOS COUNTY
250 N Baxter St   **Ph:** 541-396-3121
Coquille, OR 97423   **Fax:** 541-396-4861
www.co.coos.or.us

On the southwestern coast of OR, southwest of Eugene; organized Dec 22, 1853 (prior to statehood) from Umpqua and Jackson counties. **Name Origin:** For the Coos Bay Indian tribe, the name being interpreted as either 'take' or 'place of pines.'

Area (sq mi): 1806.38 (land 1600.48; water 205.9).

Pop: 62,779 (White 90.2%; Black or African American 0.3%; Hispanic or Latino 3.4%; Asian 0.9%; Other 6.9%). **Foreign born:** 2.7%. **Median age:** 43.1. **State rank:** 15. **Pop change 1990-2000:** +4.2%.

Income: per capita $17,547; median household $31,542. **Pop below poverty level:** 15%.

Unemployment: 8.2%. **Median home value:** $98,900. **Median travel time to work:** 19.9 minutes.

CROOK COUNTY
300 NE 3rd St Rm 23   **Ph:** 541-447-6553
Prineville, OR 97754   **Fax:** 541-416-2145
www.co.crook.or.us

In central OR; organized Oct 24, 1882 from Wasco and Grant counties. **Name Origin:** For Gen. George Crook (1829-90), army officer in the OR Territory (1852-60).

Area (sq mi): 2987.41 (land 2979.38; water 8.03).

Pop: 19,182 (White 91.4%; Black or African American 0%; Hispanic or Latino 5.6%; Asian 0.4%; Other 6.5%). **Foreign born:** 3.3%. **Median age:** 38.6. **State rank:** 26. **Pop change 1990-2000:** +35.9%.

Income: per capita $16,899; median household $35,186. **Pop below poverty level:** 11.3%.

Unemployment: 9.7%. **Median home value:** $100,000. **Median travel time to work:** 18.7 minutes.

CURRY COUNTY
PO Box 746   **Ph:** 541-247-3295
Gold Beach, OR 97444   **Fax:** 541-247-6440
www.co.curry.or.us

On the southwestern coast of OR; organized Dec 18, 1855 (prior to statehood) from Coos County. **Name Origin:** For George Law Curry (1820-78), governor of OR Territory (1853-59).

Area (sq mi): 1988.57 (land 1627.38; water 361.19).

Pop: 21,137 (White 90.9%; Black or African American 0.2%; Hispanic or Latino 3.6%; Asian 0.7%; Other 6.2%). **Foreign born:** 3.7%. **Median age:** 48.8. **State rank:** 24. **Pop change 1990-2000:** +9.4%.

Income: per capita $18,138; median household $30,117. **Pop below poverty level:** 12.2%.

Unemployment: 6%. **Median home value:** $148,000. **Median travel time to work:** 14.4 minutes.

DESCHUTES COUNTY
1130 NW Harriman St   **Ph:** 541-388-6570
Bend, OR 97701   **Fax:** 541-388-4752
www.co.deschutes.or.us

In central OR, east of Eugene; organized Dec 13, 1916 from Crook County. **Name Origin:** For the Deschutes River, which traverses the county; from French '[river] of the falls.'

Area (sq mi): 3054.77 (land 3018.15; water 36.61).

Pop: 115,367 (White 92.9%; Black or African American 0.2%; Hispanic or Latino 3.7%; Asian 0.7%; Other 4.3%). **Foreign born:** 2.8%. **Median age:** 38.3. **State rank:** 7. **Pop change 1990-2000:** +53.9%.

Income: per capita $21,767; median household $41,847. **Pop below poverty level:** 9.3%.

Unemployment: 6.4%. **Median home value:** $148,800. **Median travel time to work:** 18.7 minutes.

DOUGLAS COUNTY
PO Box 10   **Ph:** 541-440-4323
Roseburg, OR 97470   **Fax:** 541-440-4408
www.co.douglas.or.us

In southwestern OR, south of Eugene; organized Jan 7, 1852 (prior to statehood) from Umpqua County, which was organized in 1851 and whose remnant, after Coos County was broken off in 1855, was annexed to Douglas County in 1862. **Name Origin:** For Stephen Arnold Douglas (1813-61), U.S. orator and statesman.

Area (sq mi): 5133.83 (land 5036.62; water 97.21).

Pop: 100,399 (White 91.9%; Black or African American 0.2%; Hispanic or Latino 3.3%; Asian 0.6%; Other 5.3%). **Foreign born:** 2.1%. **Median age:** 41.2. **State rank:** 9. **Pop change 1990-2000:** +6.1%.

Income: per capita $16,581; median household $33,223. **Pop below poverty level:** 13.1%.

Unemployment: 9%. **Median home value:** $104,800. **Median travel time to work:** 20 minutes.

All statistics are based on the 2000 Census except the dollar figures given for per capita income, which are based on 1999 estimates.

GILLIAM COUNTY

221 S Oregon St   **Ph:** 541-384-2311
Condon, OR 97823   **Fax:** 541-384-2166

On the central northern border of OR; organized Feb 25, 1885 from Wasco County. **Name Origin:** For Col. Cornelius Gilliam (1798-1848), veteran of Indian wars and former county official in MT.

Area (sq mi): 1222.84 (land 1204.07; water 18.77).

Pop: 1,915 (White 96%; Black or African American 0.2%; Hispanic or Latino 1.8%; Asian 0.2%; Other 2.8%). **Foreign born:** 1.7%. **Median age:** 42.8. **State rank:** 35. **Pop change 1990-2000:** +11.5%.

Income: per capita $17,659; median household $33,611. **Pop below poverty level:** 9.1%.

Unemployment: 5.8%. **Median home value:** $71,000. **Median travel time to work:** 18.1 minutes.

GRANT COUNTY

201 S Humbolt St Suite 290   **Ph:** 541-575-1675
Canyon City, OR 97820   **Fax:** 541-575-2248

In northeastern OR; organized Oct 14, 1864. **Name Origin:** For Ulysses Simpson Grant (1822-85), Civil War general and eighteenth U.S. president.

Area (sq mi): 4529.32 (land 4528.6; water 0.71).

Pop: 7,935 (White 94.6%; Black or African American 0.1%; Hispanic or Latino 2.1%; Asian 0.2%; Other 4%). **Foreign born:** 1.4%. **Median age:** 41.7. **State rank:** 30. **Pop change 1990-2000:** +1%.

Income: per capita $16,794; median household $32,560. **Pop below poverty level:** 13.7%.

Unemployment: 10.3%. **Median home value:** $79,700. **Median travel time to work:** 18.7 minutes.

HARNEY COUNTY

450 N Buena Vista Ave   **Ph:** 541-573-6641
Burns, OR 97720   **Fax:** 541-573-8370
www.co.harney.or.us

In southeastern OR; organized Feb 25, 1889 from Grant County. **Name Origin:** For Gen. William Selby Harney (1800-89), officer in the Black Hawk War, Seminole War, and Mexican-American War; commander of department of OR who was instrumental in opening eastern OR for settlement.

Area (sq mi): 10,226.49 (land 10,134.33; water 92.16).

Pop: 7,609 (White 89.7%; Black or African American 0.1%; Hispanic or Latino 4.2%; Asian 0.5%; Other 7.5%). **Foreign born:** 2.1%. **Median age:** 39.8. **State rank:** 31. **Pop change 1990-2000:** +7.8%.

Income: per capita $16,159; median household $30,957. **Pop below poverty level:** 11.8%.

Unemployment: 14.1%. **Median home value:** $73,300. **Median travel time to work:** 14.8 minutes.

HOOD RIVER COUNTY

309 State St Rm 107   **Ph:** 541-386-3970
Hood River, OR 97031   **Fax:** 541-386-9392

On northwestern border of OR, east of Portland; organized Jun 23, 1908 from Wasco County. **Name Origin:** For the river and the town; the river was named for either Samuel Hood (1724-1816), or for Arthur William Acland Hood (1824-1901), admirals in the British Navy.

Area (sq mi): 533.56 (land 522.35; water 11.21).

Pop: 20,411 (White 70.7%; Black or African American 0.6%; Hispanic or Latino 25%; Asian 1.5%; Other 19.1%). **Foreign born:** 16.4%. **Median age:** 35.3. **State rank:** 25. **Pop change 1990-2000:** +20.8%.

Income: per capita $17,877; median household $38,326. **Pop below poverty level:** 14.2%.

Unemployment: 9.2%. **Median home value:** $152,400. **Median travel time to work:** 19.1 minutes.

JACKSON COUNTY

10 S Oakdale Ave Courthouse   **Ph:** 541-774-6035
Medford, OR 97501   **Fax:** 541-774-6455
www.co.jackson.or.us

On the southwestern border of OR; organized Jan 12, 1852 (prior to statehood) from the original Yamhill and Champoeg districts. **Name Origin:** For Andrew Jackson (1767-1845), seventh U.S. president.

Area (sq mi): 2801.77 (land 2785.19; water 16.57).

Pop: 181,269 (White 88.7%; Black or African American 0.4%; Hispanic or Latino 6.7%; Asian 0.9%; Other 7.1%). **Foreign born:** 4.9%. **Median age:** 39.2. **State rank:** 6. **Pop change 1990-2000:** +23.8%.

Income: per capita $19,498; median household $36,461. **Pop below poverty level:** 12.5%.

Unemployment: 6.3%. **Median home value:** $140,000. **Median travel time to work:** 18.9 minutes.

JEFFERSON COUNTY

66 SE 'D' St Suite C   **Ph:** 541-475-4451
Madras, OR 97741   **Fax:** 541-325-5018

In north-central OR; organized Dec 12, 1914 from Crook County. **Name Origin:** For Mount Jefferson on the county's western border, itself named for Thomas Jefferson (1743-1826), third U.S. president.

Area (sq mi): 1791.17 (land 1780.78; water 10.38).

Pop: 19,009 (White 64.9%; Black or African American 0.3%; Hispanic or Latino 17.7%; Asian 0.3%; Other 30.4%). **Foreign born:** 9.9%. **Median age:** 34.8. **State rank:** 27. **Pop change 1990-2000:** +39%.

Income: per capita $15,675; median household $35,853. **Pop below poverty level:** 14.6%.

Unemployment: 7.6%. **Median home value:** $105,500. **Median travel time to work:** 20.9 minutes.

JOSEPHINE COUNTY

PO Box 69   **Ph:** 541-474-5240
Grants Pass, OR 97528   **Fax:** 541-474-5246
www.co.josephine.or.us

On the southwestern border of OR, west of Jackson; organized Jan

Please see sample entry on inside front cover for detailed information about the statistics presented with each county listing.

22, 1856 from Jackson County. **Name Origin:** For either Josephine Rollins (1835-c.1911), daughter of the leader of a wagon train bound for California and first white woman to settle in the county, or for Josephine Creek, which was also named in her honor.

Area (sq mi): 1641.63 (land 1639.59; water 2.04).

Pop: 75,726 (White 91.4%; Black or African American 0.3%; Hispanic or Latino 4.3%; Asian 0.6%; Other 5.3%). **Foreign born:** 3.1%. **Median age:** 43.1. **State rank:** 12. **Pop change 1990-2000:** +20.9%.

Income: per capita $17,234; median household $31,229. **Pop below poverty level:** 15%.

Unemployment: 8.5%. **Median home value:** $128,700. **Median travel time to work:** 20 minutes.

KLAMATH COUNTY
305 Main St   **Ph:** 541-883-5134
Klamath Falls, OR 97601   **Fax:** 541-883-5165
www.co.klamath.or.us

On central southern border of OR; organized Oct 17, 1882 from Lake County. **Name Origin:** For the Klamath Indians; the name is probably from Chinook *tlamatl*, their name for the sister tribe of the Modocs; the meaning is unknown. Also spelled *Claminitt* and *Clammittee*.

Area (sq mi): 6135.75 (land 5944.19; water 191.56).

Pop: 63,775 (White 84.1%; Black or African American 0.6%; Hispanic or Latino 7.8%; Asian 0.8%; Other 11.2%). **Foreign born:** 4.8%. **Median age:** 38.2. **State rank:** 14. **Pop change 1990-2000:** +10.5%.

Income: per capita $16,719; median household $31,537. **Pop below poverty level:** 16.8%.

Unemployment: 9.5%. **Median home value:** $91,100. **Median travel time to work:** 17.2 minutes.

LAKE COUNTY
513 Center St   **Ph:** 541-947-6006
Lakeview, OR 97630   **Fax:** 541-947-6015

On central southern border of OR; organized Oct 24, 1874 from Jackson County. **Name Origin:** For the many lakes in the area.

Area (sq mi): 8358.47 (land 8135.75; water 222.71).

Pop: 7,422 (White 89.2%; Black or African American 0.1%; Hispanic or Latino 5.4%; Asian 0.7%; Other 8.2%). **Foreign born:** 3.4%. **Median age:** 42.7. **State rank:** 32. **Pop change 1990-2000:** +3.3%.

Income: per capita $16,136; median household $29,506. **Pop below poverty level:** 16.1%.

Unemployment: 10.4%. **Median home value:** $65,700. **Median travel time to work:** 16.1 minutes.

LANE COUNTY
125 E 8th Ave   **Ph:** 541-682-4203
Eugene, OR 97401   **Fax:** 541-682-4616
www.co.lane.or.us

On central-western coast of OR; organized Jan 28, 1851 (prior to statehood) from Linn and Benton counties. **Name Origin:** For Gen.

Joseph Lane (1801-81). OR territorial governor (1849-50; 1853) and first U.S. senator from OR (1859-61).

Area (sq mi): 4721.79 (land 4554; water 167.79).

Pop: 322,959 (White 88.6%; Black or African American 0.8%; Hispanic or Latino 4.6%; Asian 2%; Other 6.5%). **Foreign born:** 4.9%. **Median age:** 36.6. **State rank:** 4. **Pop change 1990-2000:** +14.2%.

Income: per capita $19,681; median household $36,942. **Pop below poverty level:** 14.4%.

Unemployment: 6.8%. **Median home value:** $141,000. **Median travel time to work:** 19.9 minutes.

LINCOLN COUNTY
225 W Olive St Rm 201   **Ph:** 541-265-4121
Newport, OR 97365   **Fax:** 541-265-4950
www.co.lincoln.or.us

On central western coast of OR; organized Feb 20, 1893 from Benton and Polk counties. **Name Origin:** For Abraham Lincoln (1809-65), sixteenth U.S. president.

Area (sq mi): 1193.79 (land 979.57; water 214.23).

Pop: 44,479 (White 88.3%; Black or African American 0.3%; Hispanic or Latino 4.8%; Asian 0.9%; Other 8.2%). **Foreign born:** 4.2%. **Median age:** 44.1. **State rank:** 17. **Pop change 1990-2000:** +14.4%.

Income: per capita $18,692; median household $32,769. **Pop below poverty level:** 13.9%.

Unemployment: 6.9%. **Median home value:** $148,800. **Median travel time to work:** 20.5 minutes.

LINN COUNTY
300 4th Ave SW   **Ph:** 541-967-3831
Albany, OR 97321   **Fax:** 541-926-5109
www.co.linn.or.us

In northwest OR, northeast of Eugene; original county; organized 1847 (prior to statehood). **Name Origin:** For Lewis Fields Linn (1795-1843), physician and U.S. senator from MO (1833-43); author of the Donation Land Law, which gave free land in the west to settlers.

Area (sq mi): 2310.15 (land 2292.18; water 17.97).

Pop: 103,069 (White 91.2%; Black or African American 0.3%; Hispanic or Latino 4.4%; Asian 0.8%; Other 5.7%). **Foreign born:** 3.5%. **Median age:** 37.4. **State rank:** 8. **Pop change 1990-2000:** +13%.

Income: per capita $17,633; median household $37,518. **Pop below poverty level:** 11.4%.

Unemployment: 8.3%. **Median home value:** $124,100. **Median travel time to work:** 22.2 minutes.

MALHEUR COUNTY
251 B St W   **Ph:** 541-473-5151
Vale, OR 97918   **Fax:** 541-473-5523
www.malheurco.org

On eastern border of OR; organized Feb 17, 1887 from Baker county. **Name Origin:** For the Malheur River, which flows through

All statistics are based on the 2000 Census except the dollar figures given for per capita income, which are based on 1999 estimates.

it; from French 'misfortune', given to the river by trappers who were attacked by Indians and lost all their furs.

Area (sq mi): 9929.99 (land 9887.09; water 42.9).

Pop: 31,615 (White 68.8%; Black or African American 1.2%; Hispanic or Latino 25.6%; Asian 2%; Other 21.1%). **Foreign born:** 8.2%. **Median age:** 34. **State rank:** 20. **Pop change 1990-2000:** +21.4%.

Income: per capita $13,895; median household $30,241. **Pop below poverty level:** 18.6%.

Unemployment: 9%. **Median home value:** $86,900. **Median travel time to work:** 17.7 minutes.

MARION COUNTY
100 High St NE Rm 1331   **Ph:** 503-588-5225
Salem, OR 97301   **Fax:** 503-373-4408
www.co.marion.or.us

In northwest OR, south of Portland; original county; organized as Champoick County Jul 5, 1843 (prior to statehood); name changed 1849. **Name Origin:** For Gen. Francis Marion (c. 1732-95), SC soldier and legislator, known as 'The Swamp Fox' for his tactics during the Revolutionary War.

Area (sq mi): 1194.13 (land 1183.95; water 10.18).

Pop: 284,834 (White 76.5%; Black or African American 0.9%; Hispanic or Latino 17.1%; Asian 1.8%; Other 15.8%). **Foreign born:** 12.6%. **Median age:** 33.7. **State rank:** 5. **Pop change 1990-2000:** +24.7%.

Income: per capita $18,408; median household $40,314. **Pop below poverty level:** 13.5%.

Unemployment: 6.4%. **Median home value:** $132,600. **Median travel time to work:** 23.5 minutes.

MORROW COUNTY
PO Box 338   **Ph:** 541-676-9061
Heppner, OR 97836   **Fax:** 541-676-9876
www.co.morrow.or.us

On central northern border of OR; organized Feb 16, 1885 from Umatilla County. **Name Origin:** For Jackson L. Morrow (1827-99), member of the first state legislature.

Area (sq mi): 2048.53 (land 2032.38; water 16.15).

Pop: 10,995 (White 72%; Black or African American 0.1%; Hispanic or Latino 24.4%; Asian 0.4%; Other 23.1%). **Foreign born:** 14.5%. **Median age:** 33.3. **State rank:** 29. **Pop change 1990-2000:** +44.2%.

Income: per capita $15,802; median household $37,521. **Pop below poverty level:** 14.8%.

Unemployment: 10.8%. **Median home value:** $89,000. **Median travel time to work:** 23 minutes.

MULTNOMAH COUNTY
1021 SW 4th Ave   **Ph:** 503-988-3957
Portland, OR 97204   **Fax:** 503-988-5773
www.co.multnomah.or.us

On central northern border of OR; organized Dec 22, 1854 (prior to statehood) from Clackamas and Washington counties. The smallest county in OR by size and largest by population. **Name Origin:** For

the Multnomah Indian village on Sauvie Island; Lewis and Clark applied the name to all local Indians. From *nemathlonamaq*, probably meaning 'downriver.'

Area (sq mi): 465.65 (land 435.23; water 30.42).

Pop: 660,486 (White 76.5%; Black or African American 5.7%; Hispanic or Latino 7.5%; Asian 5.7%; Other 9.5%). **Foreign born:** 12.7%. **Median age:** 34.9. **State rank:** 1. **Pop change 1990-2000:** +13.1%.

Income: per capita $22,606; median household $41,278. **Pop below poverty level:** 12.7%.

Unemployment: 6.3%. **Median home value:** $157,900. **Median travel time to work:** 23.8 minutes.

POLK COUNTY
850 Main St   **Ph:** 503-623-9217
Dallas, OR 97338   **Fax:** 503-623-0717
www.co.polk.or.us

In northwest OR, west of Salem; original county; organized Dec 22, 1845 (prior to statehood) from the Yamhill district. **Name Origin:** For James Knox Polk (1795-1849), eleventh U.S. president.

Area (sq mi): 744.15 (land 741.03; water 3.12).

Pop: 62,380 (White 85.6%; Black or African American 0.4%; Hispanic or Latino 8.8%; Asian 1.1%; Other 9.2%). **Foreign born:** 6.5%. **Median age:** 36.5. **State rank:** 16. **Pop change 1990-2000:** +25.9%.

Income: per capita $19,282; median household $42,311. **Pop below poverty level:** 11.5%.

Unemployment: 5.7%. **Median home value:** $142,700. **Median travel time to work:** 23.4 minutes.

SHERMAN COUNTY
PO Box 365   **Ph:** 541-565-3606
Moro, OR 97039   **Fax:** 541-565-3312

On central northern border of OR; organized Feb 25, 1889 from Wasco County. **Name Origin:** For Gen. William Tecumseh Sherman (1820-91), officer in the Mexican-American War and the Civil War, remembered for his 'march to the sea' through the South.

Area (sq mi): 831.2 (land 823.21; water 8).

Pop: 1,934 (White 92.1%; Black or African American 0.2%; Hispanic or Latino 4.9%; Asian 0.5%; Other 5.8%). **Foreign born:** 2.5%. **Median age:** 41.8. **State rank:** 34. **Pop change 1990-2000:** +0.8%.

Income: per capita $17,448; median household $35,142. **Pop below poverty level:** 14.6%.

Unemployment: 11%. **Median home value:** $77,400. **Median travel time to work:** 20.6 minutes.

TILLAMOOK COUNTY
201 Laurel Ave   **Ph:** 503-842-3403
Tillamook, OR 97141   **Fax:** 503-842-1384
www.co.tillamook.or.us

On the northwestern coast of OR, west of Portland; organized Dec 15, 1853 (prior to statehood) from Clatsop and Yamhill counties. **Name Origin:** For the Tillamook Indians, from Chinook 'people

Please see sample entry on inside front cover for detailed information about the statistics presented with each county listing.

of Nekelim,' because the tribe lived on the Nehalem and Salmon rivers.

Area (sq mi): 1332.78 (land 1102.15; water 230.63).

Pop: 24,262 (White 91%; Black or African American 0.2%; Hispanic or Latino 5.1%; Asian 0.6%; Other 5.3%). **Foreign born:** 4.2%. **Median age:** 43.5. **State rank:** 22. **Pop change 1990-2000:** +12.5%.

Income: per capita $19,052; median household $34,269. **Pop below poverty level:** 11.4%.

Unemployment: 5.5%. **Median home value:** $143,900. **Median travel time to work:** 20.7 minutes.

UMATILLA COUNTY
216 SE 4th St   **Ph:** 541-278-6236
Pendleton, OR 97801   **Fax:** 541-278-6345
www.co.umatilla.or.us

On northeastern border of OR; organized Sep 27, 1862 from Wasco County. **Name Origin:** For the Umatilla River, which runs through the county; the river is itself named for the Umatilla Indian tribe. The meaning of the name is disputed: possibly 'water rippling over sand.'

Area (sq mi): 3231.25 (land 3215.26; water 15.99).

Pop: 70,548 (White 77.5%; Black or African American 0.8%; Hispanic or Latino 16.1%; Asian 0.8%; Other 16.5%). **Foreign born:** 8.4%. **Median age:** 34.6. **State rank:** 13. **Pop change 1990-2000:** +19.1%.

Income: per capita $16,410; median household $36,249. **Pop below poverty level:** 12.7%.

Unemployment: 7.2%. **Median home value:** $98,100. **Median travel time to work:** 17 minutes.

UNION COUNTY
1106 K Ave   **Ph:** 541-963-1001
La Grande, OR 97850   **Fax:** 541-963-1079
www.union-county.org

In northeastern OR; organized Oct 14, 1864 from Baker County. **Name Origin:** For the town of Union, named in 1862 in support of the Union forces in the Civil War.

Area (sq mi): 2038.55 (land 2036.55; water 2).

Pop: 24,530 (White 93.1%; Black or African American 0.5%; Hispanic or Latino 2.4%; Asian 0.9%; Other 4.3%). **Foreign born:** 2.7%. **Median age:** 37.7. **State rank:** 21. **Pop change 1990-2000:** +3.9%.

Income: per capita $16,907; median household $33,738. **Pop below poverty level:** 13.8%.

Unemployment: 5.8%. **Median home value:** $93,600. **Median travel time to work:** 16.3 minutes.

WALLOWA COUNTY
101 S River St Rm 100   **Ph:** 541-426-4543
Enterprise, OR 97828   **Fax:** 541-426-5901
www.co.wallowa.or.us

On northeastern border of OR; organized Feb 11, 1887 from Union County. **Name Origin:** A Nez Perce word for the 'tripod' used to support netting to catch fish.

Area (sq mi): 3151.69 (land 3145.34; water 6.36).

Pop: 7,226 (White 95.7%; Black or African American 0%; Hispanic or Latino 1.7%; Asian 0.2%; Other 3.2%). **Foreign born:** 0.8%. **Median age:** 44.4. **State rank:** 33. **Pop change 1990-2000:** +4.6%.

Income: per capita $17,276; median household $32,129. **Pop below poverty level:** 14%.

Unemployment: 10.8%. **Median home value:** $111,300. **Median travel time to work:** 17.5 minutes.

WASCO COUNTY
511 Washington St   **Ph:** 541-296-6159
The Dalles, OR 97058   **Fax:** 541-298-3607
www.co.wasco.or.us

On the central northern border of OR; organized Jan 11, 1854 (prior to statehood), from the original Champoeg district; it covered all of Oregon east of the Cascade Range, most of Idaho, and parts of MT and WY. **Name Origin:** For the Wasco or Wascopam Indian tribe of Chinookan linguistic stock; the name means 'cup' or 'bowl.'

Area (sq mi): 2395.32 (land 2381.05; water 14.28).

Pop: 23,791 (White 83.9%; Black or African American 0.3%; Hispanic or Latino 9.3%; Asian 0.8%; Other 12.3%). **Foreign born:** 6.2%. **Median age:** 39.9. **State rank:** 23. **Pop change 1990-2000:** +9.7%.

Income: per capita $17,195; median household $35,959. **Pop below poverty level:** 12.9%.

Unemployment: 10.1%. **Median home value:** $105,500. **Median travel time to work:** 18.6 minutes.

WASHINGTON COUNTY
155 N 1st Ave Rm 130   **Ph:** 503-846-8747
Hillsboro, OR 97124   **Fax:** 503-846-8636
www.co.washington.or.us

In northwest OR, west of Portland; original county; organized as Tuality County Jul 5, 1843 (prior to statehood); name changed Sep 3, 1849. **Name Origin:** For George Washington (1732-99), American patriot and first U.S. president.

Area (sq mi): 726.38 (land 723.75; water 2.63).

Pop: 445,342 (White 77.7%; Black or African American 1.1%; Hispanic or Latino 11.2%; Asian 6.7%; Other 10.1%). **Foreign born:** 14.2%. **Median age:** 33. **State rank:** 2. **Pop change 1990-2000:** +42.9%.

Income: per capita $24,969; median household $52,122. **Pop below poverty level:** 7.4%.

Unemployment: 5.3%. **Median home value:** $184,800. **Median travel time to work:** 23.7 minutes.

WHEELER COUNTY
PO Box 327   **Ph:** 541-763-2400
Fossil, OR 97830   **Fax:** 541-763-2026

In north-central OR; organized Feb 17, 1899 from Crook, Gilliam, and Grant counties. **Name Origin:** For Henry H. Wheeler (1826-1915), who operated the first stage line through the county and later became a prominent rancher in the area.

Area (sq mi): 1715.46 (land 1714.92; water 0.55).

All statistics are based on the 2000 Census except the dollar figures given for per capita income, which are based on 1999 estimates.

Pop: 1,547 (White 92.5%; Black or African American 0.1%; Hispanic or Latino 5.1%; Asian 0.3%; Other 6.3%). **Foreign born:** 2.1%. **Median age:** 48.1. **State rank:** 36. **Pop change 1990-2000:** +10.8%.

Income: per capita $15,884; median household $28,750. **Pop below poverty level:** 15.6%.

Unemployment: 9.3%. **Median home value:** $66,300. **Median travel time to work:** 30.8 minutes.

YAMHILL COUNTY

535 NE 5th St   **Ph:** 503-434-7518
McMinnville, OR 97128   **Fax:** 503-434-7520
www.co.yamhill.or.us

In northwest OR, southwest of Portland; original county; organized 1843 (prior to statehood). **Name Origin:** For the Yamhela or Yamhill Indian tribe; meaning of name is unknown.

Area (sq mi): 718.36 (land 715.56; water 2.79).

Pop: 84,992 (White 84.3%; Black or African American 0.8%; Hispanic or Latino 10.6%; Asian 1.1%; Other 9.1%). **Foreign born:** 7.6%. **Median age:** 34.1. **State rank:** 10. **Pop change 1990-2000:** +29.7%.

Income: per capita $18,951; median household $44,111. **Pop below poverty level:** 9.2%.

Unemployment: 5.9%. **Median home value:** $146,200. **Median travel time to work:** 24.8 minutes.

Please see sample entry on inside front cover for detailed information about the statistics presented with each county listing.

471

PENNSYLVANIA - Counties

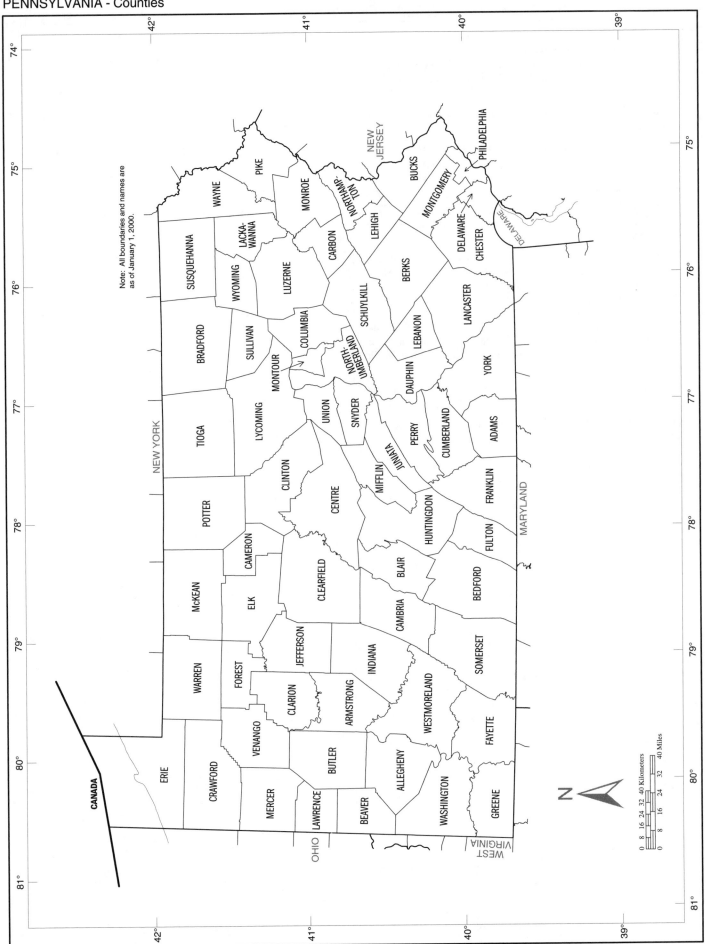

Note: All boundaries and names are
as of January 1, 2000.

NEW YORK

CANADA

OHIO

WEST VIRGINIA

MARYLAND

NEW JERSEY

DELAWARE

ERIE

CRAWFORD

WARREN

McKEAN

POTTER

TIOGA

BRADFORD

SUSQUEHANNA

WAYNE

PIKE

MERCER

VENANGO

FOREST

ELK

CAMERON

CLINTON

LYCOMING

SULLIVAN

WYOMING

LACKA-
WANNA

LUZERNE

MONROE

LAWRENCE

BUTLER

CLARION

JEFFERSON

CLEARFIELD

CENTRE

UNION

SNYDER

MONTOUR

COLUMBIA

NORTH-
UMBERLAND

CARBON

NORTHAMP-
TON

LEHIGH

BEAVER

ALLEGHENY

ARMSTRONG

INDIANA

CAMBRIA

BLAIR

HUNTINGDON

MIFFLIN

JUNIATA

PERRY

DAUPHIN

SCHUYLKILL

LEBANON

BERKS

BUCKS

MONTGOMERY

PHILADELPHIA

WASHINGTON

WESTMORELAND

SOMERSET

BEDFORD

FULTON

FRANKLIN

CUMBERLAND

ADAMS

YORK

LANCASTER

CHESTER

DELAWARE

GREENE

FAYETTE

N

0 8 16 24 32 40 Kilometers
0   8   16   24   32   40 Miles

U.S. Census Bureau, Census 2000

Pennsylvania

PENNSYLVANIA STATE INFORMATION

www.state.pa.us   **Ph:** 717-787-2121

Area (sq mi): 46,055.24 (land 44,816.61; water 1238.63).

Pop: 12,281,054 (White 84.1%; Black or African American 10%; Hispanic or Latino 3.2%; Asian 1.8%; Other 2.8%). **Foreign born:** 4.1%. **Median age:** 38. **Pop change 1990-2000:** +3.4%.

Income: per capita $20,880; median household $40,106. **Pop below poverty level:** 11%.

Unemployment: 6.1%. **Median home value:** $97,000. **Median travel time to work:** 25.2 minutes.

ADAMS COUNTY

111-117 Baltimore St   **Ph:** 717-334-6781
Gettysburg, PA 17325   **Fax:** 717-334-2091

On central southern border of PA, southwest of Harrisburg; organized Jan 22, 1800 from York County. **Name Origin:** For John Adams (1735-1826), second U.S. president.

Area (sq mi): 521.52 (land 520.01; water 1.51).

Pop: 91,292 (White 93.7%; Black or African American 1.2%; Hispanic or Latino 3.6%; Asian 0.5%; Other 2.9%). **Foreign born:** 3.4%. **Median age:** 37. **State rank:** 33. **Pop change 1990-2000:** +16.6%.

Income: per capita $18,577; median household $42,704. **Pop below poverty level:** 7.1%.

Unemployment: 4.1%. **Median home value:** $110,100. **Median travel time to work:** 25.1 minutes.

ALLEGHENY COUNTY

436 Grant St County Courthouse Rm 119   **Ph:** 412-350-5300
Pittsburgh, PA 15219   **Fax:** 412-350-3581
info.co.allegheny.pa.us

In southwestern PA; organized Sep 24, 1788 from Westmoreland and Washington counties. **Name Origin:** For the Allegheny River.

Area (sq mi): 744.71 (land 730.17; water 14.54).

Pop: 1,281,666 (White 83.8%; Black or African American 12.4%; Hispanic or Latino 0.9%; Asian 1.7%; Other 1.5%). **Foreign born:** 3.8%. **Median age:** 39.6. **State rank:** 2. **Pop change 1990-2000:** -4.1%.

Income: per capita $22,491; median household $38,329. **Pop below poverty level:** 11.2%.

Unemployment: 3.8%. **Median home value:** $84,200. **Median travel time to work:** 25.3 minutes.

ARMSTRONG COUNTY

450 E Market St Courthouse Complex   **Ph:** 724-543-2500
Kittanning, PA 16201   **Fax:** 724-548-3285

In central portion of western PA, northeast of Pittsburgh; organized Mar 12, 1800 from Allegheny, Lycoming, and Westmoreland counties. **Name Origin:** For John Armstrong (1758-1843), officer in the Revolutionary War and the War of 1812, U.S. senator from NY (1800-02; 1803-04), and U.S. secretary of war (1813-14).

Area (sq mi): 664.44 (land 653.93; water 10.51).

Pop: 72,392 (White 98%; Black or African American 0.8%; Hispanic or Latino 0.4%; Asian 0.1%; Other 0.7%). **Foreign born:** 0.7%. **Median age:** 40.4. **State rank:** 38. **Pop change 1990-2000:** -1.5%.

Income: per capita $15,709; median household $31,557. **Pop below poverty level:** 11.7%.

Unemployment: 7.3%. **Median home value:** $64,500. **Median travel time to work:** 26.9 minutes.

BEAVER COUNTY

810 3rd St Courthouse   **Ph:** 724-728-5700
Beaver, PA 15009   **Fax:** 724-728-8708
www.co.beaver.pa.us

On central western border of PA, northwest of Pittsburgh; organized Mar 12, 1800 from Allegheny and Washington counties. **Name Origin:** For the Beaver River, which traverses it.

Area (sq mi): 443.9 (land 434.21; water 9.69).

Pop: 181,412 (White 92.1%; Black or African American 6%; Hispanic or Latino 0.7%; Asian 0.3%; Other 1.2%). **Foreign born:** 1.7%. **Median age:** 40.7. **State rank:** 19. **Pop change 1990-2000:** -2.5%.

Income: per capita $18,402; median household $36,995. **Pop below poverty level:** 9.4%.

Unemployment: 4.9%. **Median home value:** $85,000. **Median travel time to work:** 24.5 minutes.

BEDFORD COUNTY

211 S Juliana St   **Ph:** 814-623-4807
Bedford, PA 15522   **Fax:** 814-623-0991

On southern border with MD, southeast of Johnstown; organized May 9, 1771 (prior to statehood) from Cumberland County. **Name Origin:** For Fort Bedford, which became the site of the county seat of Bedford. The fort was named in 1759 to honor England's Duke of Bedford.

Area (sq mi): 1017.4 (land 1014.51; water 2.89).

Please see sample entry on inside front cover for detailed information about the statistics presented with each county listing.

Pop: 49,984 (White 98.2%; Black or African American 0.4%; Hispanic or Latino 0.5%; Asian 0.3%; Other 0.8%). **Foreign born:** 0.6%. **Median age:** 39.5. **State rank:** 43. **Pop change 1990-2000:** +4.3%.

Income: per capita $16,316; median household $32,731. **Pop below poverty level:** 10.3%.

Unemployment: 7.4%. **Median home value:** $80,200. **Median travel time to work:** 27.9 minutes.

BERKS COUNTY
633 Court St 4th Fl   **Ph:** 610-478-6550
Reading, PA 19601   **Fax:** 610-478-6570
www.co.berks.pa.us

In southeastern PA, southwest of Allentown; established Mar 11, 1752 from Chester, Lancaster, and Philadelphia counties. **Name Origin:** The shortened form for Berkshire, England, which also has a Reading as its county seat; site of large land holdings of the Penn family.

Area (sq mi): 865.67 (land 858.88; water 6.79).

Pop: 373,638 (White 84.8%; Black or African American 3.7%; Hispanic or Latino 9.7%; Asian 1%; Other 7.1%). **Foreign born:** 4.3%. **Median age:** 37.4. **State rank:** 9. **Pop change 1990-2000:** +11%.

Income: per capita $21,232; median household $44,714. **Pop below poverty level:** 9.4%.

Unemployment: 4.9%. **Median home value:** $104,900. **Median travel time to work:** 22.3 minutes.

BLAIR COUNTY
423 Allegheny St   **Ph:** 814-693-3000
Hollidaysburg, PA 16648   **Fax:** 814-693-3033

In western PA, east of Johnstown; organized Feb 26, 1846 from Huntingdon and Bedford counties. **Name Origin:** For John Blair, PA legislator and prominent citizen. The only county in PA named for a local citizen.

Area (sq mi): 527.11 (land 525.8; water 1.31).

Pop: 129,144 (White 97.3%; Black or African American 1.2%; Hispanic or Latino 0.5%; Asian 0.4%; Other 0.8%). **Foreign born:** 1%. **Median age:** 39.5. **State rank:** 27. **Pop change 1990-2000:** -1.1%.

Income: per capita $16,743; median household $32,861. **Pop below poverty level:** 12.6%.

Unemployment: 5.9%. **Median home value:** $73,600. **Median travel time to work:** 20.2 minutes.

BRADFORD COUNTY
301 Main St Courthouse   **Ph:** 570-265-1727
Towanda, PA 18848   **Fax:** 570-265-1729
www.bradfordcountypa.org

On northern border of PA, northwest of Scranton; organized as Ontario County Feb 10, 1810 from Luzerne and Lycoming counties. **Name Origin:** For William Bradford (1755-95), associate justice of the PA supreme court (1791) and U.S. attorney general (1794-95). Name changed Mar 24, 1812 from Ontario (named for the lake).

Area (sq mi): 1161.03 (land 1150.67; water 10.37).

Pop: 62,761 (White 97.5%; Black or African American 0.4%; Hispanic or Latino 0.6%; Asian 0.5%; Other 1.2%). **Foreign born:** 1%. **Median age:** 38.9. **State rank:** 40. **Pop change 1990-2000:** +2.9%.

Income: per capita $17,148; median household $35,038. **Pop below poverty level:** 11.8%.

Unemployment: 5.7%. **Median home value:** $73,900. **Median travel time to work:** 22.6 minutes.

BUCKS COUNTY
55 E Court St   **Ph:** 215-348-6000
Doylestown, PA 18901   **Fax:** 215-348-6571
www.buckscounty.org

On southeastern border of PA, north of Philadelphia; original county, organized as Buckingham County Mar 10, 1682. **Name Origin:** Shortened from the original name, Buckingham, for the English county of Buckinghamshire (also called Bucks), home of the Penn family and of many original settlers.

Area (sq mi): 622.11 (land 607.38; water 14.74).

Pop: 597,635 (White 91.1%; Black or African American 3.3%; Hispanic or Latino 2.3%; Asian 2.3%; Other 1.9%). **Foreign born:** 5.9%. **Median age:** 37.7. **State rank:** 4. **Pop change 1990-2000:** +10.4%.

Income: per capita $27,430; median household $59,727. **Pop below poverty level:** 4.5%.

Unemployment: 3.8%. **Median home value:** $163,200. **Median travel time to work:** 28.6 minutes.

BUTLER COUNTY
PO Box 1208   **Ph:** 724-284-5233
Butler, PA 16003   **Fax:** 724-284-5244
www.co.butler.pa.us

In central portion of western PA, north of Pittsburgh; organized Mar 12, 1800 from Allegheny County. **Name Origin:** For Maj. Gen. Richard Butler (1743-91), officer and Indian commissioner after the American Revolution.

Area (sq mi): 794.79 (land 788.53; water 6.26).

Pop: 174,083 (White 97.4%; Black or African American 0.8%; Hispanic or Latino 0.6%; Asian 0.6%; Other 0.8%). **Foreign born:** 1.4%. **Median age:** 37.6. **State rank:** 20. **Pop change 1990-2000:** +14.5%.

Income: per capita $20,794; median household $42,308. **Pop below poverty level:** 9.1%.

Unemployment: 4.3%. **Median home value:** $114,100. **Median travel time to work:** 25.3 minutes.

CAMBRIA COUNTY
200 S Center St   **Ph:** 814-472-6176
Ebensburg, PA 15931   **Fax:** 814-472-6940
www.co.cambria.pa.us

In western PA, west of Altoona; organized Mar 26, 1804 from Somerset, Bedford, and Huntingdon counties. **Name Origin:** For Cambria township in Somerset County. Cambria is an ancient, poetic name for Wales, from Welsh *cymy* or *cumbri* 'brotherhood' or 'fraternity.'

All statistics are based on the 2000 Census except the dollar figures given for per capita income, which are based on 1999 estimates.

Area (sq mi): 693.43 (land 688.02; water 5.41).

Pop: 152,598 (White 95.2%; Black or African American 2.8%; Hispanic or Latino 0.9%; Asian 0.4%; Other 0.9%). **Foreign born:** 1.3%. **Median age:** 41.2. **State rank:** 21. **Pop change 1990-2000:** -6.4%.

Income: per capita $16,058; median household $30,179. **Pop below poverty level:** 12.5%.

Unemployment: 6.8%. **Median home value:** $62,700. **Median travel time to work:** 21.9 minutes.

CAMERON COUNTY

20 E 5th St   **Ph:** 814-486-2315
Emporium, PA 15834   **Fax:** 814-486-3176

In north-west central PA, west of Williamsport; organized Mar 29, 1860 from Clinton, Elk, McKean, and Potter counties. **Name Origin:** For Simon Cameron (1799-1889), U.S. senator from PA (1845-49; 1857-61; 1867-77), U.S. secretary of war (1861-62), and U.S. Minister to Russia (1862).

Area (sq mi): 398.6 (land 397.16; water 1.44).

Pop: 5,974 (White 98.5%; Black or African American 0.4%; Hispanic or Latino 0.6%; Asian 0.1%; Other 0.8%). **Foreign born:** 0.6%. **Median age:** 41.3. **State rank:** 66. **Pop change 1990-2000:** +1%.

Income: per capita $15,968; median household $32,212. **Pop below poverty level:** 9.4%.

Unemployment: 10.1%. **Median home value:** $61,300. **Median travel time to work:** 15.4 minutes.

CARBON COUNTY

PO Box 129   **Ph:** 570-325-3611
Jim Thorpe, PA 18229   **Fax:** 570-325-3622

In eastern PA, south of Scranton; organized Mar 13, 1843 from Northampton and Monroe counties. **Name Origin:** For its rich deposits of anthracite coal.

Area (sq mi): 387.23 (land 381.04; water 6.2).

Pop: 58,802 (White 96.9%; Black or African American 0.6%; Hispanic or Latino 1.5%; Asian 0.3%; Other 1.3%). **Foreign born:** 1.8%. **Median age:** 40.6. **State rank:** 41. **Pop change 1990-2000:** +3.4%.

Income: per capita $17,064; median household $35,113. **Pop below poverty level:** 9.5%.

Unemployment: 6.1%. **Median home value:** $82,100. **Median travel time to work:** 29.2 minutes.

CENTRE COUNTY

420 Holmes St Willowbank Office Bldg   **Ph:** 814-355-6700
Bellefonte, PA 16823   **Fax:** 814-355-6980
www.co.centre.pa.us

In central PA, southwest of Williamsport; organized Feb 13, 1800 from Lycoming, Mifflin, Northumberland, and Huntingdon counties. **Name Origin:** For its location in the geographic center of the state, with the British spelling of the time.

Area (sq mi): 1111.85 (land 1107.53; water 4.32).

Pop: 135,758 (White 90.6%; Black or African American 2.6%; Hispanic or Latino 1.7%; Asian 4%; Other 2%). **Foreign born:** 5.8%. **Median age:** 28.7. **State rank:** 25. **Pop change 1990-2000:** +9.7%.

Income: per capita $18,020; median household $36,165. **Pop below poverty level:** 18.8%.

Unemployment: 2.9%. **Median home value:** $114,900. **Median travel time to work:** 19.6 minutes.

CHESTER COUNTY

2 N High St Suite 512   **Ph:** 610-344-6100
West Chester, PA 19380   **Fax:** 610-344-5995
www.chesco.org

On southeastern border of PA, west of Philadelphia; original county, organized as Upland County Mar 10, 1682; name changed soon after. **Name Origin:** For Chester, Cheshire, England, home of many settlers brought to America by William Penn (1644-1718).

Area (sq mi): 759.81 (land 755.97; water 3.84).

Pop: 433,501 (White 87.2%; Black or African American 6.2%; Hispanic or Latino 3.7%; Asian 2%; Other 2.5%). **Foreign born:** 5.5%. **Median age:** 36.9. **State rank:** 7. **Pop change 1990-2000:** +15.2%.

Income: per capita $31,627; median household $65,295. **Pop below poverty level:** 5.2%.

Unemployment: 3%. **Median home value:** $182,500. **Median travel time to work:** 27.5 minutes.

CLARION COUNTY

421 Main St Courthouse   **Ph:** 814-226-4000
Clarion, PA 16214   **Fax:** 814-226-8069
www.co.clarion.pa.us

In central portion of western PA, northeast of Pittsburgh; organized Mar 11, 1839 from Venango and Armstrong counties. **Name Origin:** For the Clarion River, which flows through it. The rippling waters of the river sounded 'like the notes of a distant clarion' to Daniel Stanard, one of the state surveyors.

Area (sq mi): 608.95 (land 602.44; water 6.51).

Pop: 41,765 (White 97.8%; Black or African American 0.8%; Hispanic or Latino 0.4%; Asian 0.3%; Other 0.7%). **Foreign born:** 1%. **Median age:** 36.3. **State rank:** 53. **Pop change 1990-2000:** +0.2%.

Income: per capita $15,243; median household $30,770. **Pop below poverty level:** 15.4%.

Unemployment: 4.7%. **Median home value:** $68,800. **Median travel time to work:** 22.9 minutes.

CLEARFIELD COUNTY

230 E Market St   **Ph:** 814-765-2641
Clearfield, PA 16830   **Fax:** 814-765-2640
www.clearfieldco.org

In west-central PA, north of Altoona; organized Mar 26, 1804 from Lycoming and Huntingdon counties. Functioned as part of Centre County in early years; first county commissioners elected 1812, courts established 1822. **Name Origin:** For Clearfield Creek, which runs through a part of the county where buffalo had cleared the undergrowth.

Area (sq mi): 1153.8 (land 1147.32; water 6.49).

Please see sample entry on inside front cover for detailed information about the statistics presented with each county listing.

Pop: 83,382 (White 97.1%; Black or African American 1.5%; Hispanic or Latino 0.6%; Asian 0.3%; Other 0.9%). **Foreign born:** 0.7%. **Median age:** 39.3. **State rank:** 36. **Pop change 1990-2000:** +6.8%.

Income: per capita $16,010; median household $31,357. **Pop below poverty level:** 12.5%.

Unemployment: 8.3%. **Median home value:** $62,600. **Median travel time to work:** 24.3 minutes.

CLINTON COUNTY
PO Box 928   **Ph:** 570-893-4000
Lock Haven, PA 17745   **Fax:** 570-893-4041
www.clintoncountypa.com

In north-central PA, west of Williamsport; organized Jun 21, 1839 from Lycoming and Centre counties. **Name Origin:** Most likely for DeWitt Clinton (1769-1828), governor of NY, and supporter of the Erie Canal. The name may have been a substitute to the originally proposed name, Eagle, to thwart political opponents of county formation.

Area (sq mi): 898.09 (land 890.87; water 7.23).

Pop: 37,914 (White 97.9%; Black or African American 0.5%; Hispanic or Latino 0.5%; Asian 0.4%; Other 0.7%). **Foreign born:** 0.9%. **Median age:** 37.8. **State rank:** 57. **Pop change 1990-2000:** +2%.

Income: per capita $15,750; median household $31,064. **Pop below poverty level:** 14.2%.

Unemployment: 6.6%. **Median home value:** $78,000. **Median travel time to work:** 23.5 minutes.

COLUMBIA COUNTY
PO Box 380   **Ph:** 570-389-5600
Bloomsburg, PA 17815   **Fax:** 570-784-0257
www.columbiapa.org

In east-central PA, southwest of Scranton; organized Mar 22, 1813 from Northumberland County. **Name Origin:** Feminine form of Columbus, a poetic and honorific reference to Christopher Columbus (1451-1506) and America.

Area (sq mi): 489.79 (land 485.55; water 4.24).

Pop: 64,151 (White 97.1%; Black or African American 0.8%; Hispanic or Latino 0.9%; Asian 0.5%; Other 1%). **Foreign born:** 1.4%. **Median age:** 37.5. **State rank:** 39. **Pop change 1990-2000:** +1.5%.

Income: per capita $16,973; median household $34,094. **Pop below poverty level:** 13.1%.

Unemployment: 5.5%. **Median home value:** $87,300. **Median travel time to work:** 21.1 minutes.

CRAWFORD COUNTY
903 Diamond Pk   **Ph:** 814-336-1151
Meadville, PA 16335   **Fax:** 814-337-0457
www.co.crawford.pa.us

On northwest border of PA, south of Erie; organized Mar 12, 1800 from Allegheny County. **Name Origin:** For Col. William Crawford (1732-82), surveyor, army officer, and Indian fighter.

Area (sq mi): 1037.74 (land 1012.72; water 25.01).

Pop: 90,366 (White 96.6%; Black or African American 1.6%; Hispanic or Latino 0.6%; Asian 0.3%; Other 1.1%). **Foreign born:** 1.1%. **Median age:** 38.1. **State rank:** 34. **Pop change 1990-2000:** +4.9%.

Income: per capita $16,870; median household $33,560. **Pop below poverty level:** 12.8%.

Unemployment: 7.1%. **Median home value:** $72,800. **Median travel time to work:** 21.5 minutes.

CUMBERLAND COUNTY
1 Courthouse Sq   **Ph:** 717-240-6150
Carlisle, PA 17013   **Fax:** 717-240-6448
www.co.cumberland.pa.us

In south-central PA, west of Harrisburg; organized Jan 27, 1750 from Lancaster County. **Name Origin:** For William Augustus, Duke of Cumberland (1721-65), British general and second son of George II (1683-1760).

Area (sq mi): 551.14 (land 550.17; water 0.98).

Pop: 213,674 (White 93.6%; Black or African American 2.4%; Hispanic or Latino 1.3%; Asian 1.7%; Other 1.5%). **Foreign born:** 3.2%. **Median age:** 38.1. **State rank:** 16. **Pop change 1990-2000:** +9.4%.

Income: per capita $23,610; median household $46,707. **Pop below poverty level:** 6.6%.

Unemployment: 3.1%. **Median home value:** $120,500. **Median travel time to work:** 20.5 minutes.

DAUPHIN COUNTY
2 S 2nd St   **Ph:** 717-255-2810
Harrisburg, PA 17101   **Fax:** 717-257-1604
www.dauphinc.org

In south-central PA, northwest of Lancaster; organized Mar 4, 1785 from Lancaster County. **Name Origin:** To honor France, ally of the American states in the Revolutionary War, by use of the hereditary title of the eldest son of the king of France, dauphin. Louis Joseph (1781-89), son of Louis XVI (1754-93) and Marie Antoinette (1755-93), was *dauphin* at the time the county was established.

Area (sq mi): 557.53 (land 525.29; water 32.24).

Pop: 251,798 (White 75.6%; Black or African American 16.9%; Hispanic or Latino 4.1%; Asian 2%; Other 4.1%). **Foreign born:** 4.1%. **Median age:** 37.9. **State rank:** 15. **Pop change 1990-2000:** +5.9%.

Income: per capita $22,134; median household $41,507. **Pop below poverty level:** 9.7%.

Unemployment: 3.7%. **Median home value:** $99,900. **Median travel time to work:** 21.1 minutes.

DELAWARE COUNTY
201 W Front St Government Center Bldg   **Ph:** 610-891-4000
Media, PA 19063   **Fax:** 610-891-0647
www.co.delaware.pa.us

On southeastern border of PA, west of Philadelphia; organized Sept 6, 1789 from Chester County. **Name Origin:** For the Delaware River, which forms its southeastern border.

All statistics are based on the 2000 Census except the dollar figures given for per capita income, which are based on 1999 estimates.

Area (sq mi): 190.74 (land 184.21; water 6.53).

Pop: 550,864 (White 79.6%; Black or African American 14.5%; Hispanic or Latino 1.5%; Asian 3.3%; Other 1.9%). **Foreign born:** 6.7%. **Median age:** 37.4. **State rank:** 5. **Pop change 1990-2000:** +0.6%.

Income: per capita $25,040; median household $50,092. **Pop below poverty level:** 8%.

Unemployment: 3.9%. **Median home value:** $128,800. **Median travel time to work:** 27.1 minutes.

ELK COUNTY

PO Box 448   **Ph:** 814-776-1161
Ridgway, PA 15853   **Fax:** 814-776-5379
www.co.elk.pa.us

In west-central PA, west of Williamsport; organized Apr 18, 1843 from Jefferson, Clearfield, and McKean counties. **Name Origin:** For the North American elk, once common in the county.

Area (sq mi): 832.23 (land 828.65; water 3.58).

Pop: 35,112 (White 98.7%; Black or African American 0.1%; Hispanic or Latino 0.4%; Asian 0.3%; Other 0.5%). **Foreign born:** 1.1%. **Median age:** 39.4. **State rank:** 59. **Pop change 1990-2000:** +0.7%.

Income: per capita $18,174; median household $37,550. **Pop below poverty level:** 7%.

Unemployment: 9%. **Median home value:** $78,000. **Median travel time to work:** 16.8 minutes.

ERIE COUNTY

140 W 6th St   **Ph:** 814-451-6000
Erie, PA 16501   **Fax:** 814-451-6350
www.eriecountygov.org

At northwestern corner of PA, along southern shore of Lake Erie; organized Mar 12, 1800 from Allegheny County. **Name Origin:** For Lake Erie, which forms its northern border.

Area (sq mi): 1558.4 (land 801.95; water 756.46).

Pop: 280,843 (White 89.8%; Black or African American 6.1%; Hispanic or Latino 2.2%; Asian 0.7%; Other 2.3%). **Foreign born:** 2.7%. **Median age:** 36.2. **State rank:** 13. **Pop change 1990-2000:** +1.9%.

Income: per capita $17,932; median household $36,627. **Pop below poverty level:** 12%.

Unemployment: 5.8%. **Median home value:** $85,300. **Median travel time to work:** 18.5 minutes.

FAYETTE COUNTY

61 E Main St   **Ph:** 724-430-1201
Uniontown, PA 15401   **Fax:** 724-430-1265

On southern border of western PA, southeast of Pittsburgh; organized Sep 26, 1783 from Westmoreland County. **Name Origin:** For the Marquis de Lafayette or La Fayette (1757-1834), French statesman and soldier who fought with the Americans during the Revolutionary War.

Area (sq mi): 798 (land 790.14; water 7.86).

Pop: 148,644 (White 95%; Black or African American 3.5%; Hispanic or Latino 0.4%; Asian 0.2%; Other 0.9%). **Foreign born:** 0.6%. **Median age:** 40.2. **State rank:** 23. **Pop change 1990-2000:** +2.3%.

Income: per capita $15,274; median household $27,451. **Pop below poverty level:** 18%.

Unemployment: 6.9%. **Median home value:** $63,900. **Median travel time to work:** 26.5 minutes.

FOREST COUNTY

526 Elm St Suite 3   **Ph:** 814-755-3537
Tionesta, PA 16353   **Fax:** 814-755-8837

In north-western PA, east of Oil City; organized Apr 11, 1848 from Jefferson County. **Name Origin:** Named by Cyrus Blood (1795-?), pioneer settler, because the county was virgin forestland.

Area (sq mi): 431.4 (land 428.12; water 3.28).

Pop: 4,946 (White 95.4%; Black or African American 2.2%; Hispanic or Latino 1.2%; Asian 0.1%; Other 1.7%). **Foreign born:** 0.6%. **Median age:** 44.2. **State rank:** 67. **Pop change 1990-2000:** +3%.

Income: per capita $14,341; median household $27,581. **Pop below poverty level:** 16.4%.

Unemployment: 15.2%. **Median home value:** $57,300. **Median travel time to work:** 24.4 minutes.

FRANKLIN COUNTY

157 Lincoln Way E   **Ph:** 717-261-3810
Chambersburg, PA 17201   **Fax:** 717-267-3438
www.co.franklin.pa.us

On central southern border of PA, southwest of Harrisburg; organized Sep 9, 1784 from Cumberland County. **Name Origin:** For Benjamin Franklin (1706-90), U.S. patriot, diplomat, and statesman.

Area (sq mi): 772.63 (land 771.92; water 0.71).

Pop: 129,313 (White 94.5%; Black or African American 2.3%; Hispanic or Latino 1.8%; Asian 0.6%; Other 1.7%). **Foreign born:** 2%. **Median age:** 38.3. **State rank:** 26. **Pop change 1990-2000:** +6.8%.

Income: per capita $19,339; median household $40,476. **Pop below poverty level:** 7.6%.

Unemployment: 4.8%. **Median home value:** $97,800. **Median travel time to work:** 23 minutes.

FULTON COUNTY

116 W Market St Suite 203   **Ph:** 717-485-3691
McConnellsburg, PA 17233   **Fax:** 717-485-9411

On central southern border of PA, southeast of Altoona; organized Apr 19, 1851 from Bedford County. **Name Origin:** For Robert Fulton (1765-1815), developer of the *Clermont*, the first commercially successful steamboat.

Area (sq mi): 438.03 (land 437.57; water 0.46).

Pop: 14,261 (White 98%; Black or African American 0.7%; Hispanic or Latino 0.4%; Asian 0.1%; Other 0.9%). **Foreign born:** 0.7%. **Median age:** 38.2. **State rank:** 64. **Pop change 1990-2000:** +3.1%.

Please see sample entry on inside front cover for detailed information about the statistics presented with each county listing.

477

Income: per capita $16,409; median household $34,882. **Pop below poverty level:** 10.8%.

Unemployment: 7.4%. **Median home value:** $83,900. **Median travel time to work:** 31.5 minutes.

GREENE COUNTY

93 E High St   **Ph:** 724-852-5210
Waynesburg, PA 15370   **Fax:** 724-852-5327
www.co.greene.pa.us

At southwestern corner of PA, south of Pittsburgh; organized Feb 9, 1796 from Washington County. **Name Origin:** For Gen. Nathanael Greene (1742-86), hero of the Revolutionary War; quartermaster general (1778-80).

Area (sq mi): 577.95 (land 575.86; water 2.09).

Pop: 40,672 (White 94.3%; Black or African American 3.9%; Hispanic or Latino 0.9%; Asian 0.2%; Other 0.8%). **Foreign born:** 0.7%. **Median age:** 38.2. **State rank:** 56. **Pop change 1990-2000:** +2.8%.

Income: per capita $14,959; median household $30,352. **Pop below poverty level:** 15.9%.

Unemployment: 5.7%. **Median home value:** $56,900. **Median travel time to work:** 28.3 minutes.

HUNTINGDON COUNTY

223 Penn St County Courthouse   **Ph:** 814-643-3091
Huntingdon, PA 16652   **Fax:** 814-643-8152
www.huntingdoncounty.net

In south-central PA, east of Altoona; organized Sep 20, 1787 from Bedford County. **Name Origin:** For the county seat.

Area (sq mi): 889.03 (land 874.05; water 14.98).

Pop: 45,586 (White 92.8%; Black or African American 5.1%; Hispanic or Latino 1.1%; Asian 0.2%; Other 1.3%). **Foreign born:** 0.7%. **Median age:** 37.7. **State rank:** 49. **Pop change 1990-2000:** +3.2%.

Income: per capita $15,379; median household $33,313. **Pop below poverty level:** 11.3%.

Unemployment: 9.3%. **Median home value:** $72,800. **Median travel time to work:** 28.9 minutes.

INDIANA COUNTY

825 Philadelphia St   **Ph:** 724-465-3805
Indiana, PA 15701   **Fax:** 724-465-3953
www.indianacounty.org

In central porton of western PA, northeast of Pittsburgh; organized Mar 30, 1803 from Westmoreland and Lycoming territories. **Name Origin:** For the Indiana Territory, which had been formed as part of the Northwest Territory in 1800.

Area (sq mi): 834.29 (land 829.27; water 5.02).

Pop: 89,605 (White 96.5%; Black or African American 1.6%; Hispanic or Latino 0.5%; Asian 0.7%; Other 0.9%). **Foreign born:** 1.6%. **Median age:** 36.2. **State rank:** 35. **Pop change 1990-2000:** -0.4%.

Income: per capita $15,312; median household $30,233. **Pop below poverty level:** 17.3%.

Unemployment: 6%. **Median home value:** $72,700. **Median travel time to work:** 23.8 minutes.

JEFFERSON COUNTY

155 Main St Jefferson Pl   **Ph:** 814-849-1653
Brookville, PA 15825   **Fax:** 814-849-4084

In central portion of western PA, northeast of Pittsburgh; organized Mar 26, 1804 from Lycoming County. **Name Origin:** For Thomas Jefferson (1743-1826), U.S. patriot and statesman; third U.S. president.

Area (sq mi): 656.87 (land 655.48; water 1.39).

Pop: 45,932 (White 98.7%; Black or African American 0.1%; Hispanic or Latino 0.4%; Asian 0.2%; Other 0.8%). **Foreign born:** 0.6%. **Median age:** 39.8. **State rank:** 48. **Pop change 1990-2000:** -0.3%.

Income: per capita $16,186; median household $31,722. **Pop below poverty level:** 11.8%.

Unemployment: 7.1%. **Median home value:** $59,100. **Median travel time to work:** 22.3 minutes.

JUNIATA COUNTY

PO Box 68   **Ph:** 717-436-7715
Mifflintown, PA 17059   **Fax:** 717-436-7734
www.co.juniata.pa.us

In central PA, northwest of Harrisburg; organized Mar 2, 1831 from Mifflin County. **Name Origin:** For the Juniata River, which flows through it; it is named for an Indian word of uncertain origin.

Area (sq mi): 393.57 (land 391.59; water 1.98).

Pop: 22,821 (White 97.3%; Black or African American 0.4%; Hispanic or Latino 1.6%; Asian 0.2%; Other 1.3%). **Foreign born:** 1%. **Median age:** 37.7. **State rank:** 61. **Pop change 1990-2000:** +10.6%.

Income: per capita $16,142; median household $34,698. **Pop below poverty level:** 9.5%.

Unemployment: 5.2%. **Median home value:** $87,000. **Median travel time to work:** 32.6 minutes.

LACKAWANNA COUNTY

200 N Washington Ave   **Ph:** 570-963-6723
Scranton, PA 18503   **Fax:** 570-963-6387

In northeastern PA, northeast of Wilkes-Barre. Organized Aug 13, 1878 from Luzerne County, the last PA county to be created. **Name Origin:** For the Lackawanna River, which runs through it. From a Delaware Indian word probably meaning 'the stream that forks.'

Area (sq mi): 464.51 (land 458.63; water 5.88).

Pop: 213,295 (White 95.9%; Black or African American 1.3%; Hispanic or Latino 1.4%; Asian 0.8%; Other 1.3%). **Foreign born:** 2.3%. **Median age:** 40.3. **State rank:** 17. **Pop change 1990-2000:** -2.6%.

Income: per capita $18,710; median household $34,438. **Pop below poverty level:** 10.6%.

Unemployment: 5.4%. **Median home value:** $93,400. **Median travel time to work:** 19.8 minutes.

All statistics are based on the 2000 Census except the dollar figures given for per capita income, which are based on 1999 estimates.

LANCASTER COUNTY

50 N Duke St
Lancaster, PA 17602
www.co.lancaster.pa.us

Ph: 717-299-8000
Fax: 717-295-3522

In southeastern PA, southeast of Harrisburg; organized May 10, 1729 from Chester County. **Name Origin:** For Lancaster, Lancashire, England, former home of John Wright, a prime figure in the formation of the county.

Area (sq mi): 983.81 (land 949.06; water 34.75).

Pop: 470,658 (White 89.3%; Black or African American 2.8%; Hispanic or Latino 5.7%; Asian 1.4%; Other 4.3%). **Foreign born:** 3.2%. **Median age:** 36.1. **State rank:** 6. **Pop change 1990-2000:** +11.3%.

Income: per capita $20,398; median household $45,507. **Pop below poverty level:** 7.8%.

Unemployment: 3.2%. **Median home value:** $119,300. **Median travel time to work:** 21.7 minutes.

LAWRENCE COUNTY

County Courthouse 430 Court St
New Castle, PA 16101
www.co.lawrence.pa.us

Ph: 724-658-2541
Fax: 724-652-9646

On central-western border of PA, northwest of Pittsburgh; organized Mar 20, 1849 from Beaver and Mercer counties. **Name Origin:** For the *Lawrence*, the flagship of American commander Oliver Hazard Perry (1785-1819) in the Battle of Lake Erie (1813).

Area (sq mi): 362.76 (land 360.46; water 2.3).

Pop: 94,643 (White 94.6%; Black or African American 3.6%; Hispanic or Latino 0.6%; Asian 0.3%; Other 1.1%). **Foreign born:** 1.3%. **Median age:** 40.5. **State rank:** 31. **Pop change 1990-2000:** -1.7%.

Income: per capita $16,835; median household $33,152. **Pop below poverty level:** 12.1%.

Unemployment: 6.2%. **Median home value:** $72,200. **Median travel time to work:** 21.3 minutes.

LEBANON COUNTY

400 S 8th St
Lebanon, PA 17042

Ph: 717-274-2801
Fax: 717-274-8094

In east-central PA, east of Harrisburg; organized Feb 16, 1815 from Dauphin and Lancaster counties. **Name Origin:** For Lebanon Township, from which the county was formed.

Area (sq mi): 362.6 (land 361.86; water 0.74).

Pop: 120,327 (White 92.3%; Black or African American 1.3%; Hispanic or Latino 5%; Asian 0.9%; Other 3.3%). **Foreign born:** 2.4%. **Median age:** 38.7. **State rank:** 28. **Pop change 1990-2000:** +5.8%.

Income: per capita $19,773; median household $40,838. **Pop below poverty level:** 7.5%.

Unemployment: 3.1%. **Median home value:** $100,700. **Median travel time to work:** 21.8 minutes.

LEHIGH COUNTY

455 W Hamilton St
Allentown, PA 18101
www.pavisnet.com/lehigh

Ph: 610-782-3000
Fax: 610-820-3093

In mideastern PA, northeast of Reading; organized Mar 6, 1812 from Northampton County. **Name Origin:** For the Lehigh River, which forms most of its eastern border. From Algonquian *lechauwekink* 'where there are forks'; shortened by Germans to *Lecha*, then anglicized.

Area (sq mi): 348.34 (land 346.66; water 1.68).

Pop: 312,090 (White 83.2%; Black or African American 3.6%; Hispanic or Latino 10.2%; Asian 2.1%; Other 7.3%). **Foreign born:** 6.2%. **Median age:** 38.3. **State rank:** 12. **Pop change 1990-2000:** +7.2%.

Income: per capita $21,897; median household $43,449. **Pop below poverty level:** 9.3%.

Unemployment: 4.2%. **Median home value:** $113,600. **Median travel time to work:** 22.1 minutes.

LUZERNE COUNTY

200 N River St
Wilkes-Barre, PA 18711
www.luzernecounty.org

Ph: 570-825-1500
Fax: 570-825-9343

In north-central PA, southwest of Scranton; organized Sep 25, 1786 from Northumberland County. **Name Origin:** For Anne Cesar, Chevalier de la Luzerne (1741-91), French diplomat who helped negotiate the termination of the American Revolution.

Area (sq mi): 907.13 (land 890.81; water 16.32).

Pop: 319,250 (White 96%; Black or African American 1.7%; Hispanic or Latino 1.2%; Asian 0.6%; Other 1.1%). **Foreign born:** 1.9%. **Median age:** 40.8. **State rank:** 11. **Pop change 1990-2000:** -2.7%.

Income: per capita $18,228; median household $33,771. **Pop below poverty level:** 11.1%.

Unemployment: 5.5%. **Median home value:** $84,800. **Median travel time to work:** 21.2 minutes.

LYCOMING COUNTY

48 W 3rd St
Williamsport, PA 17701

Ph: 570-327-2256
Fax: 570-327-2505

In north-central PA, west of Wilkes-Barre; organized Apr 13, 1795 from Northumberland County. **Name Origin:** For Lycoming Creek, which runs through it and had for many years been the dividing line between settled and disputed Indian lands. From Delaware Indian word probably meaning 'sandy or gravel-bed creek.'

Area (sq mi): 1243.77 (land 1234.85; water 8.91).

Pop: 120,044 (White 93.6%; Black or African American 4.3%; Hispanic or Latino 0.7%; Asian 0.4%; Other 1.4%). **Foreign born:** 1.2%. **Median age:** 38.4. **State rank:** 30. **Pop change 1990-2000:** +1.1%.

Income: per capita $17,224; median household $34,016. **Pop below poverty level:** 11.5%.

Unemployment: 5.8%. **Median home value:** $86,200. **Median travel time to work:** 19.6 minutes.

Please see sample entry on inside front cover for detailed information about the statistics presented with each county listing.

McKEAN COUNTY

PO Box 1507   **Ph:** 814-887-5571
Smethport, PA 16749   **Fax:** 814-887-2242

On northern border of western PA. Organized Mar 26, 1804 from Lycoming County, but administered through Centre County until 1814, then Potter and Lycoming counties; fully organized in 1826. **Name Origin:** For Thomas McKean (1734-1817), signer of the Declaration of Independence, chief justice of PA (1777-79), and governor (1799-1808).

Area (sq mi): 984.17 (land 981.57; water 2.6).

Pop: 45,936 (White 96%; Black or African American 1.9%; Hispanic or Latino 1.1%; Asian 0.3%; Other 1.3%). **Foreign born:** 1.4%. **Median age:** 38.7. **State rank:** 47. **Pop change 1990-2000:** -2.5%.

Income: per capita $16,777; median household $33,040. **Pop below poverty level:** 13.1%.

Unemployment: 5.9%. **Median home value:** $53,500. **Median travel time to work:** 20.1 minutes.

MERCER COUNTY

Mercer County Courthouse Rm 103   **Ph:** 724-662-3800
Mercer, PA 16137   **Fax:** 724-662-1530
www.merlink.org/mcjac/governmt.htm

On central-western border of PA, north of New Castle; organized Mar 12, 1800 from Allegheny County. **Name Origin:** For Gen. Hugh Mercer (1721-77), Revolutionary War officer and physician.

Area (sq mi): 682.57 (land 671.82; water 10.76).

Pop: 120,293 (White 92.7%; Black or African American 5.3%; Hispanic or Latino 0.7%; Asian 0.4%; Other 1.2%). **Foreign born:** 1.6%. **Median age:** 39.6. **State rank:** 29. **Pop change 1990-2000:** -0.6%.

Income: per capita $17,636; median household $34,666. **Pop below poverty level:** 11.5%.

Unemployment: 5.1%. **Median home value:** $76,000. **Median travel time to work:** 19.6 minutes.

MIFFLIN COUNTY

20 N Wayne St   **Ph:** 717-248-6733
Lewistown, PA 17044   **Fax:** 717-248-3695
www.co.mifflin.pa.us

In central PA, east of Altoona; organized Sep 19, 1789 from Cumberland and Northumberland counties. **Name Origin:** For Gen. Thomas Mifflin (1744-1800), member of the Continental Congress (1774-76; 1782-84), PA legislator, and longest-serving governor of PA (1788-99).

Area (sq mi): 414.6 (land 411.86; water 2.75).

Pop: 46,486 (White 98.2%; Black or African American 0.5%; Hispanic or Latino 0.6%; Asian 0.3%; Other 0.7%). **Foreign born:** 0.8%. **Median age:** 38.8. **State rank:** 45. **Pop change 1990-2000:** +0.6%.

Income: per capita $15,553; median household $32,175. **Pop below poverty level:** 12.5%.

Unemployment: 7%. **Median home value:** $73,300. **Median travel time to work:** 22.1 minutes.

MONROE COUNTY

County Courthouse Sq   **Ph:** 570-420-3400
Stroudsburg, PA 18360   **Fax:** 570-420-3458
www.co.monroe.pa.us

On central eastern border of PA, southeast of Scranton; organized Apr 1, 1836 from Northampton and Pike counties. **Name Origin:** For James Monroe (1758-1831), fifth U.S. president.

Area (sq mi): 617.42 (land 608.5; water 8.92).

Pop: 138,687 (White 84.8%; Black or African American 6%; Hispanic or Latino 6.6%; Asian 1.1%; Other 4.6%). **Foreign born:** 5.8%. **Median age:** 37.2. **State rank:** 24. **Pop change 1990-2000:** +44.9%.

Income: per capita $20,011; median household $46,257. **Pop below poverty level:** 9%.

Unemployment: 5.9%. **Median home value:** $125,200. **Median travel time to work:** 36.7 minutes.

MONTGOMERY COUNTY

Swede & Airy Sts   **Ph:** 610-278-3000
Norristown, PA 19404   **Fax:** 610-278-5188
www.montcopa.org

In southeastern PA, northwest of Philadelphia; organized Sep 10, 1784 from old Philadelphia County. **Name Origin:** For Gen. Richard Montgomery (1736-1775), Revolutionary War officer and hero.

Area (sq mi): 487.45 (land 483.12; water 4.33).

Pop: 750,097 (White 85.3%; Black or African American 7.5%; Hispanic or Latino 2%; Asian 4%; Other 2%). **Foreign born:** 7%. **Median age:** 38.2. **State rank:** 3. **Pop change 1990-2000:** +10.6%.

Income: per capita $30,898; median household $60,829. **Pop below poverty level:** 4.4%.

Unemployment: 3.5%. **Median home value:** $160,700. **Median travel time to work:** 26.5 minutes.

MONTOUR COUNTY

29 Mill St   **Ph:** 570-271-3012
Danville, PA 17821   **Fax:** 570-271-3071

In central PA, southeast of Williamsport; organized May 3, 1850 from Columbia County. **Name Origin:** For Madame Montour (c. 1682-1752), an early PA settler. Of French-Canadian and Indian stock, she was captured and adopted at age ten by an Iroquois tribe. She later used her background as an Indian interpreter and greatly influenced Indian affairs in PA and NY.

Area (sq mi): 132.3 (land 130.75; water 1.55).

Pop: 18,236 (White 96.2%; Black or African American 1%; Hispanic or Latino 0.9%; Asian 1.3%; Other 1.1%). **Foreign born:** 2.2%. **Median age:** 39.8. **State rank:** 62. **Pop change 1990-2000:** +2.8%.

Income: per capita $19,302; median household $38,075. **Pop below poverty level:** 8.7%.

Unemployment: 3.5%. **Median home value:** $93,400. **Median travel time to work:** 19.7 minutes.

All statistics are based on the 2000 Census except the dollar figures given for per capita income, which are based on 1999 estimates.

NORTHAMPTON COUNTY
669 Washington St   **Ph:** 610-559-6700
Easton, PA 18042   **Fax:** 610-559-6702
www.northamptoncounty.org

On central eastern border of PA, east of Allentown; organized Mar 11, 1752 from Bucks County. **Name Origin:** For Northamptonshire, England, home of Thomas Penn's father-in-law, Thomas Fermor, the Earl of Pomfret.

Area (sq mi): 377.36 (land 373.8; water 3.56).

Pop: 267,066 (White 88.2%; Black or African American 2.8%; Hispanic or Latino 6.7%; Asian 1.4%; Other 4.7%). **Foreign born:** 4.6%. **Median age:** 38.5. **State rank:** 14. **Pop change 1990-2000:** +8.1%.

Income: per capita $21,399; median household $45,234. **Pop below poverty level:** 7.9%.

Unemployment: 4.1%. **Median home value:** $120,000. **Median travel time to work:** 24.2 minutes.

NORTHUMBERLAND COUNTY
201 Market St Rt 7   **Ph:** 570-988-4151
Sunbury, PA 17801
www.northumberlandco.org

In central PA, southeast of Williamsport; organized Mar 21, 1772 from Lancaster, Bedford, Berks, Northampton, and Cumberland counties. **Name Origin:** For the county of Northumberland in England.

Area (sq mi): 477.38 (land 459.91; water 17.47).

Pop: 94,556 (White 96.6%; Black or African American 1.5%; Hispanic or Latino 1.1%; Asian 0.2%; Other 1.2%). **Foreign born:** 1.1%. **Median age:** 40.8. **State rank:** 32. **Pop change 1990-2000:** -2.3%.

Income: per capita $16,489; median household $31,314. **Pop below poverty level:** 11.9%.

Unemployment: 5.5%. **Median home value:** $69,300. **Median travel time to work:** 23.4 minutes.

PERRY COUNTY
PO Box 37   **Ph:** 717-582-2131
New Bloomfield, PA 17068   **Fax:** 717-582-5162
www.perryco.org

In south-central PA, northwest of Harrisburg; organized Mar 22, 1820 from Cumberland County. **Name Origin:** For Oliver Hazard Perry (1785-1819), U.S. naval officer during the War of 1812, famous for the message, 'We have met the enemy and they are ours.'

Area (sq mi): 555.77 (land 553.52; water 2.25).

Pop: 43,602 (White 98.1%; Black or African American 0.4%; Hispanic or Latino 0.7%; Asian 0.1%; Other 0.8%). **Foreign born:** 0.9%. **Median age:** 37.5. **State rank:** 51. **Pop change 1990-2000:** +5.9%.

Income: per capita $18,551; median household $41,909. **Pop below poverty level:** 7.7%.

Unemployment: 4.1%. **Median home value:** $96,500. **Median travel time to work:** 34.7 minutes.

PHILADELPHIA COUNTY
City Hall   **Ph:** 215-686-1776
Philadelphia, PA 19107

On southeastern border of PA, southwest of Trenton, NJ; original county, organized Mar 10, 1682. The county is coterminous with the city. **Name Origin:** Named by William Penn (1644-1718) for either Philadelphia, an ancient biblical city of Lydia, in western Asia Minor, seat of one of the seven early Christian churches, or the abstract Greek noun *philadelphia* 'brotherly love.'

Area (sq mi): 142.64 (land 135.09; water 7.55).

Pop: 1,517,550 (White 42.5%; Black or African American 43.2%; Hispanic or Latino 8.5%; Asian 4.5%; Other 7.3%). **Foreign born:** 9%. **Median age:** 34.2. **State rank:** 1. **Pop change 1990-2000:** -4.3%.

Income: per capita $16,509; median household $30,746. **Pop below poverty level:** 22.9%.

Unemployment: 6.4%. **Median home value:** $59,700. **Median travel time to work:** 32 minutes.

PIKE COUNTY
506 Broad St   **Ph:** 570-296-7613
Milford, PA 18337   **Fax:** 570-296-6055
www.pikepa.org

On northeastern border of PA, east of Scranton; organized Mar 26, 1814 from Wayne County. **Name Origin:** For Gen. Zebulon Montgomery Pike (1779-1813), U.S. army officer and discoverer of Pikes Peak, CO.

Area (sq mi): 566.64 (land 546.81; water 19.83).

Pop: 46,302 (White 89.8%; Black or African American 3.3%; Hispanic or Latino 5%; Asian 0.6%; Other 3%). **Foreign born:** 5%. **Median age:** 39.6. **State rank:** 46. **Pop change 1990-2000:** +65.6%.

Income: per capita $20,315; median household $44,608. **Pop below poverty level:** 6.9%.

Unemployment: 4.8%. **Median home value:** $118,300. **Median travel time to work:** 46 minutes.

POTTER COUNTY
1 E 2nd St Rm 22   **Ph:** 814-274-8290
Coudersport, PA 16915   **Fax:** 814-274-8284

On central northern border of PA; organized Mar 26, 1804 from Lycoming County. **Name Origin:** For Gen. James Potter (1729-89), hero of the Revolutionary War.

Area (sq mi): 1081.42 (land 1081.17; water 0.25).

Pop: 18,080 (White 97.7%; Black or African American 0.3%; Hispanic or Latino 0.6%; Asian 0.5%; Other 1.1%). **Foreign born:** 1.1%. **Median age:** 39.1. **State rank:** 63. **Pop change 1990-2000:** +8.2%.

Income: per capita $16,070; median household $32,253. **Pop below poverty level:** 12.7%.

Unemployment: 4.6%. **Median home value:** $68,700. **Median travel time to work:** 23.2 minutes.

Please see sample entry on inside front cover for detailed information about the statistics presented with each county listing.

SCHUYLKILL COUNTY

401 N 2nd St   **Ph:** 570-628-1200
Pottsville, PA 17901   **Fax:** 570-628-1210
www.co.schuylkill.pa.us

In east-central PA, west of Allentown; organized Mar 1, 1811 from Berks and Northampton counties. **Name Origin:** For the Schuylkill River, which traverses it; from Dutch *schuy* 'hidden,' and *kill* 'stream'.

Area (sq mi): 782.61 (land 778.36; water 4.25).

Pop: 150,336 (White 96%; Black or African American 2.1%; Hispanic or Latino 1.1%; Asian 0.4%; Other 0.9%). **Foreign born:** 1%. **Median age:** 40.9. **State rank:** 22. **Pop change 1990-2000:** -1.5%.

Income: per capita $17,230; median household $32,699. **Pop below poverty level:** 9.5%.

Unemployment: 7%. **Median home value:** $63,300. **Median travel time to work:** 24.9 minutes.

SNYDER COUNTY

9 W Market St   **Ph:** 570-837-4207
Middleburg, PA 17842   **Fax:** 570-837-4282

In central PA, south of Williamsport; organized Mar 2, 1855 from Union County. **Name Origin:** For Simon Snyder (1759-1819), member of the PA assembly (1797-1807), speaker of the house (1802-07), and governor (1808-17).

Area (sq mi): 332.16 (land 331.2; water 0.95).

Pop: 37,546 (White 97.4%; Black or African American 0.8%; Hispanic or Latino 1%; Asian 0.4%; Other 0.8%). **Foreign born:** 0.9%. **Median age:** 36.7. **State rank:** 58. **Pop change 1990-2000:** +2.4%.

Income: per capita $16,756; median household $35,981. **Pop below poverty level:** 9.9%.

Unemployment: 3.8%. **Median home value:** $87,900. **Median travel time to work:** 22 minutes.

SOMERSET COUNTY

300 N Center Ave Suite 500   **Ph:** 814-443-1434
Somerset, PA 15501   **Fax:** 814-445-7991
www.co.somerset.pa.us

On the southern border of western PA, south of Johnstown; organized Apr 17, 1795 from Bedford County. **Name Origin:** For Somersetshire, England.

Area (sq mi): 1081.17 (land 1074.66; water 6.51).

Pop: 80,023 (White 97.1%; Black or African American 1.6%; Hispanic or Latino 0.7%; Asian 0.2%; Other 0.8%). **Foreign born:** 0.7%. **Median age:** 40.2. **State rank:** 37. **Pop change 1990-2000:** +2.3%.

Income: per capita $15,178; median household $30,911. **Pop below poverty level:** 11.8%.

Unemployment: 6.4%. **Median home value:** $70,200. **Median travel time to work:** 22.9 minutes.

SULLIVAN COUNTY

PO Box 157 Main & Muncy Sts   **Ph:** 570-946-5201
Laporte, PA 18626   **Fax:** 570-946-4421

In north-central PA, west of Scranton; organized Mar 15, 1847

from Lycoming County. **Name Origin:** For Gen. John Sullivan (1740-95), Revolutionary War officer, member of the Continental Congress (1774-75), and chief executive of NH (1786-88; 1789-90). He led the punitive expedition against the Iroquois Indians (1779) who had caused the Wyoming Massacre.

Area (sq mi): 452.35 (land 449.94; water 2.41).

Pop: 6,556 (White 95.2%; Black or African American 2.2%; Hispanic or Latino 1.1%; Asian 0.2%; Other 2.2%). **Foreign born:** 0.8%. **Median age:** 43. **State rank:** 65. **Pop change 1990-2000:** +7.4%.

Income: per capita $16,438; median household $30,279. **Pop below poverty level:** 14.5%.

Unemployment: 6.2%. **Median home value:** $74,900. **Median travel time to work:** 25.3 minutes.

SUSQUEHANNA COUNTY

PO Box 218   **Ph:** 570-278-4600
Montrose, PA 18801   **Fax:** 570-278-9268
www.susquehanna.pa.us

On northern border of eastern PA, north of Scranton, organized Feb 21, 1810 from Luzerne County. **Name Origin:** For the Susquehanna River, which runs through it.

Area (sq mi): 832.4 (land 822.86; water 9.54).

Pop: 42,238 (White 98.1%; Black or African American 0.3%; Hispanic or Latino 0.7%; Asian 0.2%; Other 0.9%). **Foreign born:** 1.3%. **Median age:** 39.5. **State rank:** 52. **Pop change 1990-2000:** +4.6%.

Income: per capita $16,435; median household $33,622. **Pop below poverty level:** 12.3%.

Unemployment: 6.9%. **Median home value:** $81,800. **Median travel time to work:** 26.2 minutes.

TIOGA COUNTY

118 Main St   **Ph:** 570-723-8191
Wellsboro, PA 16901   **Fax:** 570-723-8206

On central northern border of PA, north of Williamsport; organized Mar 26, 1804 from Lycoming County. **Name Origin:** For the Tioga River, which flows through it; from Iroquoian for 'place between two points' or 'at the forks,' for the Indian town on the Susquehanna River near Athens, PA; the town was called *Diahoga* or *Tioga*.

Area (sq mi): 1137.3 (land 1133.73; water 3.58).

Pop: 41,373 (White 97.8%; Black or African American 0.6%; Hispanic or Latino 0.5%; Asian 0.3%; Other 0.9%). **Foreign born:** 1.1%. **Median age:** 38.5. **State rank:** 55. **Pop change 1990-2000:** +0.6%.

Income: per capita $15,549; median household $32,020. **Pop below poverty level:** 13.5%.

Unemployment: 6.9%. **Median home value:** $72,000. **Median travel time to work:** 23.1 minutes.

UNION COUNTY

103 S 2nd St   **Ph:** 570-524-8600
Lewisburg, PA 17837   **Fax:** 570-524-8635
www.unionco.org

In central PA, south of Williamsport; organized Mar 22, 1813 from

All statistics are based on the 2000 Census except the dollar figures given for per capita income, which are based on 1999 estimates.

Northumberland County. **Name Origin:** As an expression of belief in the federal union of the states.

Area (sq mi): 317.12 (land 316.73; water 0.39).

Pop: 41,624 (White 87.6%; Black or African American 6.9%; Hispanic or Latino 3.9%; Asian 1.1%; Other 2%). **Foreign born:** 3.7%. **Median age:** 35.8. **State rank:** 54. **Pop change 1990-2000:** +15.1%.

Income: per capita $17,918; median household $40,336. **Pop below poverty level:** 8.8%.

Unemployment: 3.5%. **Median home value:** $97,800. **Median travel time to work:** 20 minutes.

VENANGO COUNTY

Courthouse Annex 1174 Elk St   **Ph:** 814-432-9510
Franklin, PA 16323   **Fax:** 814-432-3149
www.co.venango.pa.us

In northwestern PA, southeast of Erie; organized Mar 12, 1800 from Allegheny and Lycoming counties. **Name Origin:** For the Venango River (now called French Creek), which flows through it; from an Indian term of uncertain origin, possibly from *innungah* 'a figure carved on a tree.'

Area (sq mi): 683.02 (land 675.04; water 7.98).

Pop: 57,565 (White 97.3%; Black or African American 1.1%; Hispanic or Latino 0.5%; Asian 0.2%; Other 1.1%). **Foreign born:** 0.6%. **Median age:** 40.2. **State rank:** 42. **Pop change 1990-2000:** -3.1%.

Income: per capita $16,252; median household $32,257. **Pop below poverty level:** 13.4%.

Unemployment: 5.4%. **Median home value:** $55,900. **Median travel time to work:** 21.2 minutes.

WARREN COUNTY

204 4th Ave   **Ph:** 814-728-3400
Warren, PA 16365   **Fax:** 814-728-3479

On northern border of western PA, southeast of Erie; organized Mar 12, 1800 from Allegheny and Lycoming counties. **Name Origin:** For Gen. Joseph Warren (1741-75), Revolutionary War patriot and member of the Continental Congress who dispatched Paul Revere (1735-1818) on his famous ride.

Area (sq mi): 897.81 (land 883.45; water 14.36).

Pop: 43,863 (White 98.4%; Black or African American 0.2%; Hispanic or Latino 0.3%; Asian 0.3%; Other 0.8%). **Foreign born:** 0.9%. **Median age:** 40.5. **State rank:** 50. **Pop change 1990-2000:** -2.6%.

Income: per capita $17,862; median household $36,083. **Pop below poverty level:** 9.9%.

Unemployment: 5.1%. **Median home value:** $64,300. **Median travel time to work:** 19.6 minutes.

WASHINGTON COUNTY

Courthouse Sq 100 W Beau St   **Ph:** 724-228-6700
Washington, PA 15301   **Fax:** 724-228-6965
www.co.washington.pa.us

On western border of PA, southwest of Pittsburgh; organized Mar 28, 1781 from Westmoreland County. **Name Origin:** For George

Washington (1732-99), commander-in-chief of the Revolutionary forces at the time the country was formed; later the first U.S. president.

Area (sq mi): 860.95 (land 857.09; water 3.86).

Pop: 202,897 (White 94.9%; Black or African American 3.3%; Hispanic or Latino 0.6%; Asian 0.4%; Other 1.1%). **Foreign born:** 1.2%. **Median age:** 40.8. **State rank:** 18. **Pop change 1990-2000:** -0.8%.

Income: per capita $19,935; median household $37,607. **Pop below poverty level:** 9.8%.

Unemployment: 5%. **Median home value:** $87,500. **Median travel time to work:** 25.6 minutes.

WAYNE COUNTY

925 Court St   **Ph:** 570-253-5970
Honesdale, PA 18431   **Fax:** 570-253-5432
www.co.wayne.pa.us

At the northeastern corner of PA, east of Scranton; organized Mar 21, 1798 from Northampton County. **Name Origin:** For Gen. Anthony Wayne (1745-1796), PA soldier and statesman, nicknamed 'Mad Anthony' for his daring during the Revolutionary War.

Area (sq mi): 750.54 (land 729.22; water 21.32).

Pop: 47,722 (White 95.7%; Black or African American 1.6%; Hispanic or Latino 1.7%; Asian 0.4%; Other 1.2%). **Foreign born:** 3%. **Median age:** 40.8. **State rank:** 44. **Pop change 1990-2000:** +19.5%.

Income: per capita $16,977; median household $34,082. **Pop below poverty level:** 11.3%.

Unemployment: 5.5%. **Median home value:** $102,100. **Median travel time to work:** 26.3 minutes.

WESTMORELAND COUNTY

2 N Main St Courthouse Sq Suite 101   **Ph:** 724-830-3100
Greensburg, PA 15601   **Fax:** 724-830-3029
www.co.westmoreland.pa.us

In southwestern PA, east of Pittsburgh; organized Feb 26, 1773 (prior to statehood) from Bedford County. **Name Origin:** For the former county of Westmorland in northwest England, with spelling change.

Area (sq mi): 1036.34 (land 1025.48; water 10.86).

Pop: 369,993 (White 96.2%; Black or African American 2%; Hispanic or Latino 0.5%; Asian 0.5%; Other 0.8%). **Foreign born:** 1.4%. **Median age:** 41.3. **State rank:** 10. **Pop change 1990-2000:** -0.1%.

Income: per capita $19,674; median household $37,106. **Pop below poverty level:** 8.6%.

Unemployment: 4.9%. **Median home value:** $90,600. **Median travel time to work:** 25.4 minutes.

WYOMING COUNTY

1 Courthouse Sq   **Ph:** 570-836-3200
Tunkhannock, PA 18657   **Fax:** 570-836-7244
www.wycopa.com

In northeastern PA, west of Scranton; organized Apr 4, 1842 from

Please see sample entry on inside front cover for detailed information about the statistics presented with each county listing.

483

Luzerne County. **Name Origin:** For the Wyoming Valley, the northern extent of which is in the county.

Area (sq mi): 404.79 (land 397.2; water 7.59).

Pop: 28,080 (White 97.8%; Black or African American 0.5%; Hispanic or Latino 0.7%; Asian 0.3%; Other 0.9%). **Foreign born:** 1.2%. **Median age:** 37.8. **State rank:** 60. **Pop change 1990-2000:** +0%.

Income: per capita $17,452; median household $36,365. **Pop below poverty level:** 10.2%.

Unemployment: 4.6%. **Median home value:** $93,900. **Median travel time to work:** 26.2 minutes.

YORK COUNTY

1 W Market Way 4th Fl   **Ph:** 717-771-9612
York, PA 17401   **Fax:** 717-771-9804
www.york-county.org

On southeastern border of PA, south of Harrisburg; organized Aug 19, 1749 from Lancaster County. **Name Origin:** For York and Yorkshire, England, and for James, Duke of York and Albany (1633-1701), later James II, king of England. Name perhaps suggested by its proximity to Lancaster County; the houses of York and Lancaster are linked in English history.

Area (sq mi): 910.25 (land 904.45; water 5.8).

Pop: 381,751 (White 91.5%; Black or African American 3.7%; Hispanic or Latino 3%; Asian 0.9%; Other 2.7%). **Foreign born:** 2.2%. **Median age:** 37.8. **State rank:** 8. **Pop change 1990-2000:** +12.4%.

Income: per capita $21,086; median household $45,268. **Pop below poverty level:** 6.7%.

Unemployment: 4.5%. **Median home value:** $110,500. **Median travel time to work:** 23.9 minutes.

All statistics are based on the 2000 Census except the dollar figures given for per capita income, which are based on 1999 estimates.

RHODE ISLAND - Counties

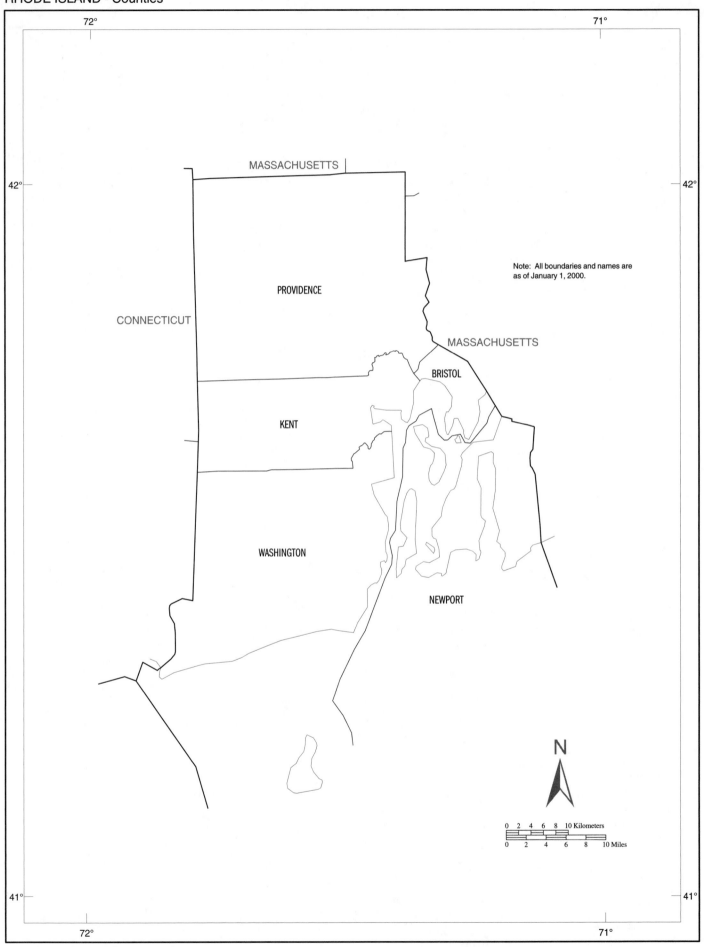

MASSACHUSETTS

72°

71°

42°

42°

Note: All boundaries and names are as of January 1, 2000.

CONNECTICUT

PROVIDENCE

MASSACHUSETTS

BRISTOL

KENT

WASHINGTON

NEWPORT

N

0 2 4 6 8 10 Kilometers
0 2 4 6 8 10 Miles

41°

41°

72°

71°

Rhode Island

RHODE ISLAND STATE INFORMATION

www.ri.gov   **Ph:** 401-222-2000

Area (sq mi): 1545.05 (land 1044.93; water 500.12).

Pop: 1,048,319 (White 81.9%; Black or African American 4.5%; Hispanic or Latino 8.7%; Asian 2.3%; Other 8.3%). **Foreign born:** 11.4%. **Median age:** 36.7. **Pop change 1990-2000:** +4.5%.

Income: per capita $21,688; median household $42,090. **Pop below poverty level:** 11.9%.

Unemployment: 5.1%. **Median home value:** $133,000. **Median travel time to work:** 22.5 minutes.

BRISTOL COUNTY

10 Court St   **Ph:** 401-253-7000
Bristol, RI 02809   **Fax:** 401-253-3080

Largely peninsular area in eastern RI, south of Providence; organized Feb 17, 1747 from Newport County. **Name Origin:** For Bristol, England.

Area (sq mi): 44.71 (land 24.68; water 20.03).

Pop: 50,648 (White 96.1%; Black or African American 0.7%; Hispanic or Latino 1.1%; Asian 1%; Other 1.5%). **Foreign born:** 10%. **Median age:** 39.3. **State rank:** 5. **Pop change 1990-2000:** +3.7%.

Income: per capita $26,503; median household $50,737. **Pop below poverty level:** 6.3%.

Unemployment: 3.4%. **Median home value:** $164,600. **Median travel time to work:** 23.4 minutes.

KENT COUNTY

222 Quaker Ln   **Ph:** 401-822-1311
Warwick, RI 02886

In central RI, south of Cranston; organized Jun 11, 1750 from Washington County. **Name Origin:** For the county in England.

Area (sq mi): 188.1 (land 170.17; water 17.92).

Pop: 167,090 (White 94.6%; Black or African American 0.9%; Hispanic or Latino 1.7%; Asian 1.3%; Other 2.1%). **Foreign born:** 4.9%. **Median age:** 38.9. **State rank:** 2. **Pop change 1990-2000:** +3.7%.

Income: per capita $23,833; median household $47,617. **Pop below poverty level:** 6.6%.

Unemployment: 4.3%. **Median home value:** $118,100. **Median travel time to work:** 22.8 minutes.

NEWPORT COUNTY

45 Washington Sq   **Ph:** 401-841-8330
Newport, RI 028407199   **Fax:** 401-846-1673

In southeastern RI, comprising the islands in Narragansett Bay and mainland along the eastern border of RI, south of Fall River, MA. Original county, organized as Rhode Island County Jun 22, 1703; name changed Jun 16, 1729. **Name Origin:** Descriptive, or possibly recalling Newport, Monmouthshire, England.

Area (sq mi): 313.64 (land 104.05; water 209.59).

Pop: 85,433 (White 90.1%; Black or African American 3.7%; Hispanic or Latino 2.8%; Asian 1.2%; Other 3.6%). **Foreign born:** 4.9%. **Median age:** 38.6. **State rank:** 4. **Pop change 1990-2000:** -2%.

Income: per capita $26,779; median household $50,448. **Pop below poverty level:** 7.1%.

Unemployment: 3.8%. **Median home value:** $164,100. **Median travel time to work:** 21.7 minutes.

PROVIDENCE COUNTY

1 Dorrance Plaza   **Ph:** 401-458-5200
Providence, RI 02903

In northern RI; original county, organized as the County of Providence Plantations Jun 22, 1703; name modified Jun 16, 1729. **Name Origin:** For the city, its county seat.

Area (sq mi): 435.82 (land 413.27; water 22.56).

Pop: 621,602 (White 73.8%; Black or African American 6.5%; Hispanic or Latino 13.4%; Asian 2.9%; Other 12.2%). **Foreign born:** 15.6%. **Median age:** 35.4. **State rank:** 1. **Pop change 1990-2000:** +4.2%.

Income: per capita $19,255; median household $36,950. **Pop below poverty level:** 15.5%.

Unemployment: 5.4%. **Median home value:** $123,900. **Median travel time to work:** 22 minutes.

WASHINGTON COUNTY

4800 Tower Hill Rd   **Ph:** 401-782-4121
Wakefield, RI 02879

In southwestern RI; incorporated as King's County Jun 16, 1729 from Newport County. **Name Origin:** For George Washingtron (1732-99), American patriot and first U.S. president. Name changed from King's County on Oct 29, 1781. Originally called the Narragansett Country; changed to King's Province on Mar 20, 1654.

Area (sq mi): 562.77 (land 332.75; water 230.02).

Please see sample entry on inside front cover for detailed information about the statistics presented with each county listing.

Pop: 123,546 (White 94%; Black or African American 0.9%; Hispanic or Latino 1.4%; Asian 1.5%; Other 2.8%). **Foreign born:** 4.2%. **Median age:** 37.4. **State rank:** 3. **Pop change 1990-2000:** +12.3%.

Income: per capita $25,530; median household $53,103. **Pop below poverty level:** 7.3%.

Unemployment: 3.3%. **Median home value:** $158,600. **Median travel time to work:** 24.7 minutes.

All statistics are based on the 2000 Census except the dollar figures given for per capita income, which are based on 1999 estimates.

SOUTH CAROLINA - Counties

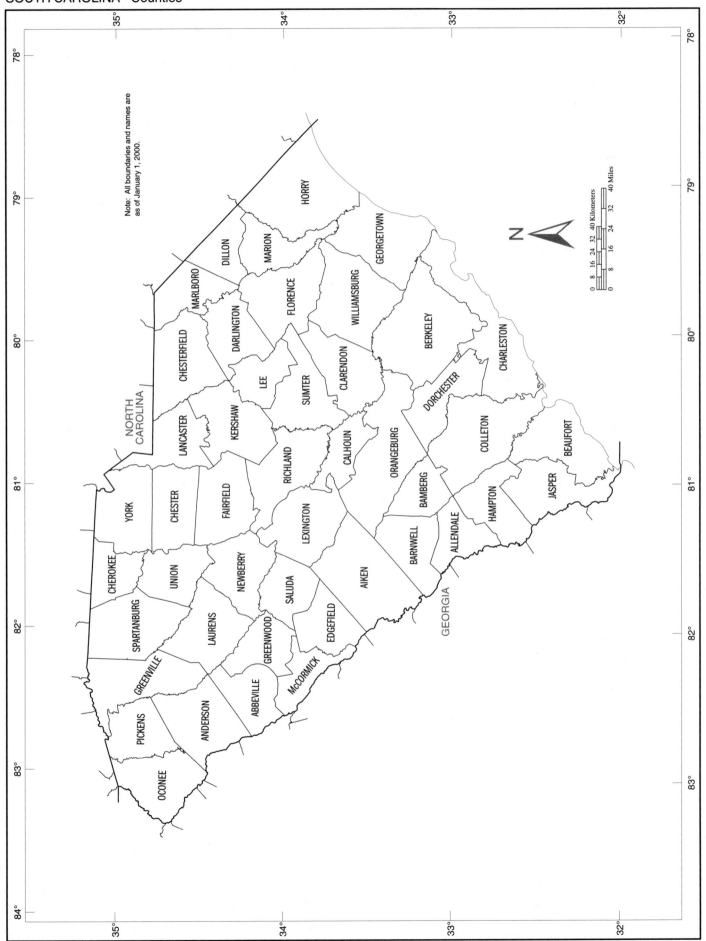

Note: All boundaries and names are as of January 1, 2000.

NORTH CAROLINA

HORRY

DILLON

MARION

GEORGETOWN

MARLBORO

CHESTERFIELD

FLORENCE

WILLIAMSBURG

DARLINGTON

BERKELEY

LEE

CLARENDON

CHARLESTON

SUMTER

DORCHESTER

LANCASTER

KERSHAW

RICHLAND

CALHOUN

ORANGEBURG

COLLETON

BEAUFORT

YORK

CHESTER

FAIRFIELD

LEXINGTON

BAMBERG

HAMPTON

JASPER

CHEROKEE

UNION

NEWBERRY

SALUDA

AIKEN

BARNWELL

ALLENDALE

SPARTANBURG

LAURENS

GREENWOOD

EDGEFIELD

GEORGIA

GREENVILLE

ABBEVILLE

McCORMICK

PICKENS

ANDERSON

OCONEE

N

0 8 16 24 32 40 Kilometers
0 8 16 24 32 40 Miles

U.S. Census Bureau, Census 2000

South Carolina

SOUTH CAROLINA STATE INFORMATION

www.myscgov.com   **Ph:** 803-896-0000

Area (sq mi): 32020.2 (land 30,109.47; water 1910.73).

Pop: 4,012,012 (White 66.1%; Black or African American 29.5%; Hispanic or Latino 2.4%; Asian 0.9%; Other 2.3%). **Foreign born:** 2.9%. **Median age:** 35.4. **Pop change 1990-2000:** +15.1%.

Income: per capita $18,795; median household $37,082. **Pop below poverty level:** 14.1%.

Unemployment: 6.3%. **Median home value:** $94,900. **Median travel time to work:** 24.3 minutes.

ABBEVILLE COUNTY

PO Box 99   **Ph:** 864-459-5074
Abbeville, SC 29620   **Fax:** 864-459-9188

On northwestern coast of SC, south of Greenville; established Mar 12, 1785 from Ninety Six District. (In 1868 all districts were renamed counties.) **Name Origin:** For the city in Somme, France.

Area (sq mi): 511.05 (land 508.03; water 3.02).

Pop: 26,167 (White 68%; Black or African American 30.3%; Hispanic or Latino 0.8%; Asian 0.2%; Other 1.1%). **Foreign born:** 1%. **Median age:** 36.9. **State rank:** 35. **Pop change 1990-2000:** +9.7%.

Income: per capita $15,370; median household $32,635. **Pop below poverty level:** 13.7%.

Unemployment: 8%. **Median home value:** $70,600. **Median travel time to work:** 25.4 minutes.

AIKEN COUNTY

828 Richland Ave W   **Ph:** 803-642-2012
Aiken, SC 29801   **Fax:** 803-642-2124
www.aikencounty.net

On the central western border of SC, east of Augusta, GA; organized Mar 10, 1871 from Edgefield, Barnwell, Lexington, and Orangeburg counties. **Name Origin:** For William Aiken (1806-87), SC governor (1844-46).

Area (sq mi): 1080.46 (land 1072.66; water 7.79).

Pop: 142,552 (White 70.4%; Black or African American 25.6%; Hispanic or Latino 2.1%; Asian 0.6%; Other 2.4%). **Foreign born:** 2.3%. **Median age:** 36.4. **State rank:** 10. **Pop change 1990-2000:** +17.9%.

Income: per capita $18,772; median household $37,889. **Pop below poverty level:** 13.8%.

Unemployment: 5.8%. **Median home value:** $87,600. **Median travel time to work:** 24.8 minutes.

ALLENDALE COUNTY

PO Box 190   **Ph:** 803-584-3438
Allendale, SC 29810   **Fax:** 803-584-7042
www.allendalecounty.com

On southwestern border of SC, south of Augusta, GA; organized Feb 6, 1919 from Barnwell and Hampton counties. **Name Origin:** For the county seat.

Area (sq mi): 412.58 (land 408.2; water 4.38).

Pop: 11,211 (White 27%; Black or African American 71%; Hispanic or Latino 1.6%; Asian 0.1%; Other 1.5%). **Foreign born:** 1.4%. **Median age:** 35.1. **State rank:** 45. **Pop change 1990-2000:** -4.4%.

Income: per capita $11,293; median household $20,898. **Pop below poverty level:** 34.5%.

Unemployment: 4.6%. **Median home value:** $46,900. **Median travel time to work:** 26.7 minutes.

ANDERSON COUNTY

101 S Main St   **Ph:** 864-260-4000
Anderson, SC 29622   **Fax:** 864-260-4106
www.andersoncountysc.org

On the northwestern border of SC, southwest of Greenville; organized Dec 20, 1826 from Old Pendleton District, which was abolished at that time. **Name Origin:** For Gen. Robert Anderson (?-1813), a SC officer in the American Revolution.

Area (sq mi): 757.45 (land 718.02; water 39.43).

Pop: 165,740 (White 80.9%; Black or African American 16.6%; Hispanic or Latino 1.1%; Asian 0.4%; Other 1.4%). **Foreign born:** 1.5%. **Median age:** 37.3. **State rank:** 7. **Pop change 1990-2000:** +14.1%.

Income: per capita $18,365; median household $36,807. **Pop below poverty level:** 12%.

Unemployment: 5.6%. **Median home value:** $88,200. **Median travel time to work:** 23.7 minutes.

BAMBERG COUNTY

PO Box 150   **Ph:** 803-245-3025
Bamberg, SC 29003   **Fax:** 803-245-3088

In south-central SC, south of Columbia; organized Feb 25, 1897 from Barnwell County. **Name Origin:** For the Bamberg family, original settlers of the county seat.

Area (sq mi): 395.47 (land 393.25; water 2.22).

Please see sample entry on inside front cover for detailed information about the statistics presented with each county listing.

Pop: 16,658 (White 36.3%; Black or African American 62.5%; Hispanic or Latino 0.7%; Asian 0.2%; Other 0.8%). **Foreign born:** 0.9%. **Median age:** 35.2. **State rank:** 43. **Pop change 1990-2000:** -1.4%.

Income: per capita $12,584; median household $24,007. **Pop below poverty level:** 27.8%.

Unemployment: 6%. **Median home value:** $61,800. **Median travel time to work:** 26 minutes.

BARNWELL COUNTY

PO Box 723   **Ph:** 803-541-1020
Barnwell, SC 29812   **Fax:** 803-541-1025

On the central western border of SC, south of Augusta, GA; organized as Winston District in 1798 from Orangeburg District. **Name Origin:** For John (1748-99) and Robert (1761-1814) Barnwell, legislators.

Area (sq mi): 557.25 (land 548.41; water 8.84).

Pop: 23,478 (White 54.8%; Black or African American 42.6%; Hispanic or Latino 1.4%; Asian 0.4%; Other 1.8%). **Foreign born:** 0.6%. **Median age:** 35.5. **State rank:** 37. **Pop change 1990-2000:** +15.7%.

Income: per capita $15,870; median household $28,591. **Pop below poverty level:** 20.9%.

Unemployment: 8%. **Median home value:** $66,600. **Median travel time to work:** 27.9 minutes.

BEAUFORT COUNTY

102 Ribaut Rd   **Ph:** 843-470-5218
Beaufort, SC 29902   **Fax:** 843-470-5248
www.co.beaufort.sc.us

On southern border of SC, southwest of Charleston; original county; organized 1768 (prior to statehood). **Name Origin:** For the town.

Area (sq mi): 922.88 (land 586.86; water 336.03).

Pop: 120,937 (White 67.4%; Black or African American 24%; Hispanic or Latino 6.8%; Asian 0.8%; Other 4.6%). **Foreign born:** 6.3%. **Median age:** 35.8. **State rank:** 12. **Pop change 1990-2000:** +39.9%.

Income: per capita $25,377; median household $46,992. **Pop below poverty level:** 10.7%.

Unemployment: 2.6%. **Median home value:** $213,900. **Median travel time to work:** 23.3 minutes.

BERKELEY COUNTY

PO Box 219   **Ph:** 843-719-4403
Moncks Corner, SC 29461   **Fax:** 843-719-4511
www.co.berkeley.sc.us

On southeastern border of SC, north of Charleston; organized Jan 31, 1882 from Charleston County. **Name Origin:** For John Berkeley (1607-78), one of eight original lords proprietor of Carolina, and for his brother Sir William Berkeley (1610-77), governor of VA (1642-49; 1660-77).

Area (sq mi): 1228.07 (land 1097.72; water 130.35).

Pop: 142,651 (White 66.8%; Black or African American 26.6%;

Hispanic or Latino 2.8%; Asian 1.9%; Other 3.5%). **Foreign born:** 3.1%. **Median age:** 32. **State rank:** 9. **Pop change 1990-2000:** +10.8%.

Income: per capita $16,879; median household $39,908. **Pop below poverty level:** 11.8%.

Unemployment: 4%. **Median home value:** $91,300. **Median travel time to work:** 26.5 minutes.

CALHOUN COUNTY

Courthouse Annex Suite 108   **Ph:** 803-874-2435
Saint Matthews, SC 29135   **Fax:** 803-874-1242

In central SC, south of Columbia; organized Feb 14, 1908 from Lexington and Orangeburg counties. **Name Origin:** For John Caldwell Calhoun (1782-1850), U.S. statesman and champion of Southern causes.

Area (sq mi): 392.34 (land 380.22; water 12.11).

Pop: 15,185 (White 49.5%; Black or African American 48.7%; Hispanic or Latino 1.4%; Asian 0.1%; Other 1.1%). **Foreign born:** 1%. **Median age:** 38.9. **State rank:** 44. **Pop change 1990-2000:** +19.1%.

Income: per capita $17,446; median household $32,736. **Pop below poverty level:** 16.2%.

Unemployment: 7.3%. **Median home value:** $72,500. **Median travel time to work:** 29.9 minutes.

CHARLESTON COUNTY

4045 Bridge View   **Ph:** 843-958-4030
Charleston, SC 29405   **Fax:** 843-958-4035
www.charlestoncounty.org

On the southeastern border of SC; original district; organized Mar 12, 1785 (prior to statehood). **Name Origin:** For Charles II (1630-85), king of Great Britian, with whose help the American colonies grew vigorously.

Area (sq mi): 1358.11 (land 918.51; water 439.61).

Pop: 309,969 (White 60.8%; Black or African American 34.5%; Hispanic or Latino 2.4%; Asian 1.1%; Other 2.6%). **Foreign born:** 3.6%. **Median age:** 34.5. **State rank:** 3. **Pop change 1990-2000:** +5.1%.

Income: per capita $21,393; median household $37,810. **Pop below poverty level:** 16.4%.

Unemployment: 3.6%. **Median home value:** $130,200. **Median travel time to work:** 22.6 minutes.

CHEROKEE COUNTY

210 N Limestone St   **Ph:** 864-487-2562
Gaffney, SC 29340   **Fax:** 864-487-2594

On the central northern border of SC, east of Spartanburg; organized Feb 25, 1897 from Union, Spartanburg, and York counties. **Name Origin:** For the Indian tribe of Iroquoian linguistic stock. Name may derive from Creek *tciloki* 'people of a different speech.'

Area (sq mi): 397.28 (land 392.69; water 4.59).

Pop: 52,537 (White 76.2%; Black or African American 20.6%; Hispanic or Latino 2.1%; Asian 0.3%; Other 2.2%). **Foreign born:** 1.3%. **Median age:** 35.3. **State rank:** 24. **Pop change 1990-2000:** +18%.

All statistics are based on the 2000 Census except the dollar figures given for per capita income, which are based on 1999 estimates.

Income: per capita $16,421; median household $33,787. **Pop below poverty level:** 13.9%.

Unemployment: 7.7%. **Median home value:** $74,100. **Median travel time to work:** 23 minutes.

CHESTER COUNTY

PO Box 580   **Ph:** 803-385-2605
Chester, SC 29706   **Fax:** 803-581-7975

In north-central SC, south of Rock Hill; organized Mar 12, 1785 from Camden District. **Name Origin:** For Chester, PA.

Area (sq mi): 586.16 (land 580.52; water 5.64).

Pop: 34,068 (White 59.6%; Black or African American 38.7%; Hispanic or Latino 0.7%; Asian 0.3%; Other 1.1%). **Foreign born:** 0.8%. **Median age:** 36. **State rank:** 30. **Pop change 1990-2000:** +5.9%.

Income: per capita $14,709; median household $32,425. **Pop below poverty level:** 15.3%.

Unemployment: 10.3%. **Median home value:** $62,800. **Median travel time to work:** 27.8 minutes.

CHESTERFIELD COUNTY

PO Box 529   **Ph:** 843-623-2574
Chesterfield, SC 29709   **Fax:** 843-623-6944
www.chesterfield.k12.sc.us

On northeastern border of SC, northwest of Florence; organized 1798 from Cheraws District. **Name Origin:** For Philip Dormer Stanhope (1694-1773), 4th Earl of Chesterfield, English statesman and writer.

Area (sq mi): 805.78 (land 798.6; water 7.18).

Pop: 42,768 (White 63.5%; Black or African American 33.2%; Hispanic or Latino 2.3%; Asian 0.3%; Other 2.1%). **Foreign born:** 1.6%. **Median age:** 35.7. **State rank:** 25. **Pop change 1990-2000:** +10.9%.

Income: per capita $14,233; median household $29,483. **Pop below poverty level:** 20.3%.

Unemployment: 8.8%. **Median home value:** $65,900. **Median travel time to work:** 25.7 minutes.

CLARENDON COUNTY

3 W Key St   **Ph:** 803-435-8424
Manning, SC 29102   **Fax:** 803-435-8258

In central SC, south of Sumter; organized 1855 from Sumter District. **Name Origin:** For Edward Hyde (1661-1724), 3rd Earl of Clarendon, colonial governor of NY and NJ (1702-08).

Area (sq mi): 695.66 (land 607.21; water 88.46).

Pop: 32,502 (White 44.5%; Black or African American 53.1%; Hispanic or Latino 1.7%; Asian 0.3%; Other 1.6%). **Foreign born:** 1.3%. **Median age:** 37. **State rank:** 31. **Pop change 1990-2000:** +14.2%.

Income: per capita $13,998; median household $27,131. **Pop below poverty level:** 23.1%.

Unemployment: 8.9%. **Median home value:** $77,700. **Median travel time to work:** 26.1 minutes.

COLLETON COUNTY

PO Box 157   **Ph:** 843-549-1725
Walterboro, SC 29488   **Fax:** 843-549-7215

In south-central SC, west of Charleston; organized 1798 from part of the Province of Carolina. **Name Origin:** For Sir John Colleton, an original lord proprietor.

Area (sq mi): 1133.21 (land 1056.36; water 76.86).

Pop: 38,264 (White 55.1%; Black or African American 42.2%; Hispanic or Latino 1.4%; Asian 0.3%; Other 2%). **Foreign born:** 1.2%. **Median age:** 36.5. **State rank:** 26. **Pop change 1990-2000:** +11.3%.

Income: per capita $14,831; median household $29,733. **Pop below poverty level:** 21.1%.

Unemployment: 5.1%. **Median home value:** $73,200. **Median travel time to work:** 32.7 minutes.

DARLINGTON COUNTY

PO Box 1177   **Ph:** 843-398-4330
Darlington, SC 29540   **Fax:** 843-393-6871

In northeastern SC, north of Florence; established Mar 12, 1785 from Cheraws District. **Name Origin:** Traditionally for Darlington, Durham, England, but possibly for a Col. Darlington of the Revolutionary War.

Area (sq mi): 566.78 (land 561.14; water 5.63).

Pop: 67,394 (White 56.6%; Black or African American 41.7%; Hispanic or Latino 1%; Asian 0.2%; Other 1.1%). **Foreign born:** 0.9%. **Median age:** 36. **State rank:** 18. **Pop change 1990-2000:** +9%.

Income: per capita $16,283; median household $31,087. **Pop below poverty level:** 20.3%.

Unemployment: 7.4%. **Median home value:** $74,100. **Median travel time to work:** 22.7 minutes.

DILLON COUNTY

PO Box 449   **Ph:** 843-774-1400
Dillon, SC 29536   **Fax:** 843-774-1443

On the northeastern border of PA, northeast of Florence; organized Feb 5, 1910 from Marion County. **Name Origin:** For the county seat.

Area (sq mi): 406.54 (land 404.84; water 1.7).

Pop: 30,722 (White 49.8%; Black or African American 45.3%; Hispanic or Latino 1.8%; Asian 0.3%; Other 3.9%). **Foreign born:** 1%. **Median age:** 34.2. **State rank:** 32. **Pop change 1990-2000:** +5.5%.

Income: per capita $13,272; median household $26,630. **Pop below poverty level:** 24.2%.

Unemployment: 12.5%. **Median home value:** $60,700. **Median travel time to work:** 28.5 minutes.

DORCHESTER COUNTY

101 Ridge St   **Ph:** 843-563-0121
Saint George, SC 29477   **Fax:** 843-563-0178
www.dorchestercounty.net

In south-central SC, northwest of Charleston; organized Feb 25, 1897 from Colleton and Berkeley counties. **Name Origin:** For the town in SC, named for Dorchester, MA, former home of the town founders.

Please see sample entry on inside front cover for detailed information about the statistics presented with each county listing.

Area (sq mi): 576.69 (land 574.73; water 1.96).

Pop: 96,413 (White 70.1%; Black or African American 25.1%; Hispanic or Latino 1.8%; Asian 1.1%; Other 2.8%). **Foreign born:** 2.8%. **Median age:** 34.7. **State rank:** 15. **Pop change 1990-2000:** +16.1%.

Income: per capita $18,840; median household $43,316. **Pop below poverty level:** 9.7%.

Unemployment: 4.1%. **Median home value:** $104,600. **Median travel time to work:** 28 minutes.

EDGEFIELD COUNTY

215 Jeter St   **Ph:** 803-637-4000
Edgefield, SC 29824   **Fax:** 803-637-4056
www.edgefieldcounty.org

On the central western border of SC, north of Augusta, GA; established Mar 12, 1785 from Ninety Six District. **Name Origin:** Said to be so named because the old district of Edgefield was bordered by the Savannah River and by Indian lands, and thus was the edge of SC.

Area (sq mi): 506.54 (land 501.89; water 4.64).

Pop: 24,595 (White 55.5%; Black or African American 41.5%; Hispanic or Latino 2%; Asian 0.2%; Other 1.4%). **Foreign born:** 1.3%. **Median age:** 35.6. **State rank:** 36. **Pop change 1990-2000:** +33.9%.

Income: per capita $15,415; median household $35,146. **Pop below poverty level:** 15.5%.

Unemployment: 4.8%. **Median home value:** $83,400. **Median travel time to work:** 27.1 minutes.

FAIRFIELD COUNTY

PO Drawer 60   **Ph:** 803-635-1415
Winnsboro, SC 29180   **Fax:** 803-635-5969

In north-central SC, north of Columbia; established Mar 12, 1785 from Camden District. **Name Origin:** From Lord Cornwallis' (1738-1805) exclamation when his army first camped there, 'What fair fields!'

Area (sq mi): 709.93 (land 686.59; water 23.34).

Pop: 23,454 (White 39.2%; Black or African American 59.1%; Hispanic or Latino 1.1%; Asian 0.2%; Other 1.2%). **Foreign born:** 0.5%. **Median age:** 36.9. **State rank:** 38. **Pop change 1990-2000:** +5.2%.

Income: per capita $14,911; median household $30,376. **Pop below poverty level:** 19.6%.

Unemployment: 12.6%. **Median home value:** $69,900. **Median travel time to work:** 28.3 minutes.

FLORENCE COUNTY

PO Box E   **Ph:** 843-665-3031
Florence, SC 29501   **Fax:** 843-665-3097
www.florenceco.org/index.htm

In east-central SC, east of Sumter; organized Dec 22, 1888 from Marion, Darlington, Williamsburg, and Clarendon counties. **Name Origin:** For Florence Harllee, daughter of Gen. William Harllee, first president of the Wilmington and Manchester Railroad Co.

Area (sq mi): 803.74 (land 799.84; water 3.9).

Pop: 125,761 (White 58.2%; Black or African American 39.3%; Hispanic or Latino 1.1%; Asian 0.7%; Other 1.3%). **Foreign born:** 1.8%. **Median age:** 35.5. **State rank:** 11. **Pop change 1990-2000:** +10%.

Income: per capita $17,876; median household $35,144. **Pop below poverty level:** 16.4%.

Unemployment: 5.8%. **Median home value:** $85,200. **Median travel time to work:** 24 minutes.

GEORGETOWN COUNTY

PO Drawer 421270   **Ph:** 843-545-3063
Georgetown, SC 29442   **Fax:** 843-545-3292
www.co.georgetown.sc.us

On the central eastern border of SC, northeast of Charleston; original district; organized 1768 (prior to statehood). **Name Origin:** For the county seat.

Area (sq mi): 1035 (land 814.83; water 220.16).

Pop: 55,797 (White 59.2%; Black or African American 38.6%; Hispanic or Latino 1.6%; Asian 0.2%; Other 1.4%). **Foreign born:** 2.2%. **Median age:** 39.1. **State rank:** 22. **Pop change 1990-2000:** +20.5%.

Income: per capita $19,805; median household $35,312. **Pop below poverty level:** 17.1%.

Unemployment: 9.7%. **Median home value:** $114,700. **Median travel time to work:** 26 minutes.

GREENVILLE COUNTY

305 E North St Courthouse Suite 224   **Ph:** 864-467-8551
Greenville, SC 29601   **Fax:** 864-467-8540
www.co.greenville.sc.us

On the northwestern border of SC, west of Spartanburg; organized Mar 22, 1786 from Ninety Six District. **Name Origin:** Either for Gen. Nathanael Greene (1742-86), Revolutionary War hero, or for Isaac Green (1762-1831), pioneer and owner of the mill around which the town of Greenville grew.

Area (sq mi): 794.96 (land 790.08; water 4.88).

Pop: 379,616 (White 75.5%; Black or African American 18.3%; Hispanic or Latino 3.8%; Asian 1.4%; Other 2.7%). **Foreign born:** 4.9%. **Median age:** 35.5. **State rank:** 1. **Pop change 1990-2000:** +18.6%.

Income: per capita $22,081; median household $41,149. **Pop below poverty level:** 10.5%.

Unemployment: 3.2%. **Median home value:** $111,800. **Median travel time to work:** 21.6 minutes.

GREENWOOD COUNTY

600 Monument St Box P-103   **Ph:** 864-942-8500
Greenwood, SC 29646   **Fax:** 864-942-8566
www.co.greenwood.sc.us

In west-central SC, south of Spartanburg; organized June 3, 1897 from Abbeville and Edgefield counties. **Name Origin:** For the county seat.

Area (sq mi): 462.94 (land 455.52; water 7.42).

All statistics are based on the 2000 Census except the dollar figures given for per capita income, which are based on 1999 estimates.

Pop: 66,271 (White 64.1%; Black or African American 31.7%; Hispanic or Latino 2.9%; Asian 0.7%; Other 1.9%). **Foreign born:** 2.8%. **Median age:** 35.2. **State rank:** 19. **Pop change 1990-2000:** +11.3%.

Income: per capita $17,446; median household $34,702. **Pop below poverty level:** 14.2%.

Unemployment: 8.2%. **Median home value:** $81,200. **Median travel time to work:** 20.2 minutes.

HAMPTON COUNTY
201 Jackson Ave W   **Ph:** 803-943-7500
Hampton, SC 29924   **Fax:** 803-943-7502

On the southwestern border of SC, west of Charleston; organized Feb 18, 1875 from Old Beaufort County. **Name Origin:** For Gen. Wade Hampton (1818-1902), SC governor (1876-79), U.S. senator (1858-62; 1878-91), and U.S. railroad commissioner.

Area (sq mi): 562.63 (land 559.78; water 2.85).

Pop: 21,386 (White 41.3%; Black or African American 55.7%; Hispanic or Latino 2.6%; Asian 0.2%; Other 1.2%). **Foreign born:** 0.7%. **Median age:** 34.8. **State rank:** 39. **Pop change 1990-2000:** +17.6%.

Income: per capita $13,129; median household $28,771. **Pop below poverty level:** 21.8%.

Unemployment: 6.8%. **Median home value:** $62,300. **Median travel time to work:** 33.1 minutes.

HORRY COUNTY
PO Box 677   **Ph:** 843-915-5080
Conway, SC 29528   **Fax:** 843-915-6081
www.horrycounty.org

On the central eastern border of SC, southeast of Florence; organized Dec 19, 1801 from All Saints Parish. **Name Origin:** For Gen. Peter Horry (1743-1815), officer in the Revolutionary War and prominent citizen. Referred to by inhabitants as 'The Independent Republic of Horry.'

Area (sq mi): 1254.96 (land 1133.68; water 121.28).

Pop: 196,629 (White 79.9%; Black or African American 15.5%; Hispanic or Latino 2.6%; Asian 0.8%; Other 2.8%). **Foreign born:** 4%. **Median age:** 38.3. **State rank:** 6. **Pop change 1990-2000:** +36.5%.

Income: per capita $19,949; median household $36,470. **Pop below poverty level:** 12%.

Unemployment: 4.7%. **Median home value:** $119,700. **Median travel time to work:** 23.7 minutes.

JASPER COUNTY
PO Box 248   **Ph:** 843-726-7710
Ridgeland, SC 29936   **Fax:** 843-726-7782

On the southwestern border of SC, west of Beaufort; organized Jan 30, 1912 from Beaufort and Hampton counties. **Name Origin:** For Sgt. William Jasper (1750-79), American Revolutionary War soldier from SC.

Area (sq mi): 699.79 (land 656.12; water 43.67).

Pop: 20,678 (White 40.5%; Black or African American 52.7%; Hispanic or Latino 5.8%; Asian 0.4%; Other 4.5%). **Foreign born:** 5.4%. **Median age:** 33.8. **State rank:** 40. **Pop change 1990-2000:** +33.5%.

Income: per capita $14,161; median household $30,727. **Pop below poverty level:** 20.7%.

Unemployment: 3.9%. **Median home value:** $77,600. **Median travel time to work:** 34.2 minutes.

KERSHAW COUNTY
1121 Broad St Rm 202   **Ph:** 803-425-1500
Camden, SC 29020   **Fax:** 803-425-6044

In north-central SC, northeast of Columbia; organized 1798 from old Craven County. **Name Origin:** For Col. Joseph Kershaw, SC army officer during the Revolutionary War and SC legislator.

Area (sq mi): 740.25 (land 726.26; water 14).

Pop: 52,647 (White 70.7%; Black or African American 26.3%; Hispanic or Latino 1.7%; Asian 0.3%; Other 1.7%). **Foreign born:** 1.7%. **Median age:** 37.4. **State rank:** 23. **Pop change 1990-2000:** +20.8%.

Income: per capita $18,360; median household $38,804. **Pop below poverty level:** 12.8%.

Unemployment: 6.4%. **Median home value:** $88,000. **Median travel time to work:** 27.9 minutes.

LANCASTER COUNTY
PO Box 1809   **Ph:** 803-285-1581
Lancaster, SC 29721   **Fax:** 803-416-9388

On the central border of SC, northeast of Columbia; established Mar 12, 1785 from Camden District. **Name Origin:** For Lancaster, PA, home of many early settlers.

Area (sq mi): 555.29 (land 548.99; water 6.3).

Pop: 61,351 (White 70.5%; Black or African American 26.9%; Hispanic or Latino 1.6%; Asian 0.3%; Other 1.8%). **Foreign born:** 1.3%. **Median age:** 35.9. **State rank:** 21. **Pop change 1990-2000:** +12.5%.

Income: per capita $16,276; median household $34,688. **Pop below poverty level:** 12.8%.

Unemployment: 6.1%. **Median home value:** $77,100. **Median travel time to work:** 27 minutes.

LAURENS COUNTY
PO Box 287   **Ph:** 864-984-5214
Laurens, SC 29360   **Fax:** 864-984-3726
www.laurenscountysc.org

In west-central SC, south of Spartanburg; established Mar 12, 1785 from Ninety Six District. **Name Origin:** For Henry Laurens (1724-92), president of the Continental Congress (1777-78).

Area (sq mi): 723.98 (land 715.11; water 8.87).

Pop: 69,567 (White 71%; Black or African American 26.2%; Hispanic or Latino 1.9%; Asian 0.1%; Other 2.2%). **Foreign born:** 1.6%. **Median age:** 36.2. **State rank:** 17. **Pop change 1990-2000:** +19.8%.

Please see sample entry on inside front cover for detailed information about the statistics presented with each county listing.

495

Income: per capita $15,761; median household $33,933. **Pop below poverty level:** 14.3%.

Unemployment: 8.5%. **Median home value:** $74,800. **Median travel time to work:** 23.6 minutes.

LEE COUNTY
PO Box 387   **Ph:** 803-484-5341
Bishopville, SC 29010   **Fax:** 803-484-1632

In north-central SC, north of Sumter; organized Feb 25, 1902 from Darlington, Sumter, and Kershaw counties. **Name Origin:** For Robert E. Lee (1807-70), American general and commander of the Confederate forces during the Civil War.

Area (sq mi): 411.3 (land 410.3; water 1).

Pop: 20,119 (White 34.6%; Black or African American 63.6%; Hispanic or Latino 1.3%; Asian 0.2%; Other 1.2%). **Foreign born:** 2.1%. **Median age:** 35.7. **State rank:** 41. **Pop change 1990-2000:** +9.1%.

Income: per capita $13,896; median household $26,907. **Pop below poverty level:** 21.8%.

Unemployment: 8.2%. **Median home value:** $56,400. **Median travel time to work:** 29.7 minutes.

LEXINGTON COUNTY
139 E Main St Suite 107
County Courthouse   **Ph:** 803-359-8212
Lexington, SC 29072   **Fax:** 803-359-8314
www.co.lexington.sc.us

In west-central SC, west of Columbia; organized Mar 12, 1785 from Orangeburg District. **Name Origin:** For the Battle of Lexington, the first conflict in the Revolutionary War.

Area (sq mi): 757.88 (land 699.25; water 58.63).

Pop: 216,014 (White 83.2%; Black or African American 12.6%; Hispanic or Latino 1.9%; Asian 1%; Other 2.1%). **Foreign born:** 2.9%. **Median age:** 35.7. **State rank:** 5. **Pop change 1990-2000:** +28.9%.

Income: per capita $21,063; median household $44,659. **Pop below poverty level:** 9%.

Unemployment: 2.8%. **Median home value:** $106,300. **Median travel time to work:** 26 minutes.

MARION COUNTY
PO Box 183   **Ph:** 843-423-3904
Marion, SC 29571   **Fax:** 843-423-8306
www.co.marion.sc.us

In east-central SC, east of Florence; organized as Liberty County in 1798; name changed 1800. **Name Origin:** For Gen. Francis Marion (c.1732-95), SC soldier and legislator, known as 'The Swamp Fox' for his tactics during the Revolutionary War.

Area (sq mi): 494.09 (land 489.06; water 5.03).

Pop: 35,466 (White 41.1%; Black or African American 56.3%; Hispanic or Latino 1.8%; Asian 0.3%; Other 1.7%). **Foreign born:** 1.4%. **Median age:** 35.1. **State rank:** 29. **Pop change 1990-2000:** +4.6%.

Income: per capita $13,878; median household $26,526. **Pop below poverty level:** 23.2%.

Unemployment: 17.3%. **Median home value:** $63,500. **Median travel time to work:** 24.7 minutes.

MARLBORO COUNTY
PO Box 419   **Ph:** 843-479-5600
Bennettsville, SC 29512   **Fax:** 843-479-5639

On northeastern border of SC, north of Florence; organized 1798 from Cheraws District. **Name Origin:** For John Churchill (1650-1722), Duke of Marlborough.

Area (sq mi): 485.28 (land 479.71; water 5.57).

Pop: 28,818 (White 44.3%; Black or African American 50.7%; Hispanic or Latino 0.7%; Asian 0.2%; Other 4.5%). **Foreign born:** 0.6%. **Median age:** 35.4. **State rank:** 34. **Pop change 1990-2000:** -1.8%.

Income: per capita $13,385; median household $26,598. **Pop below poverty level:** 21.7%.

Unemployment: 13.4%. **Median home value:** $54,900. **Median travel time to work:** 24 minutes.

McCORMICK COUNTY
133 S Mine St Rm 102   **Ph:** 864-465-2195
McCormick, SC 29835   **Fax:** 864-465-0071

On the central western border of SC, northwest of Augusta, GA; established Feb 19, 1916 from Edgefield, Greenwood, and Abbeville counties. **Name Origin:** For Cyrus Hall McCormick (1809-84), inventor of farm implements and local landowner.

Area (sq mi): 393.85 (land 359.56; water 34.29).

Pop: 9,958 (White 44.4%; Black or African American 53.9%; Hispanic or Latino 0.9%; Asian 0.3%; Other 1.1%). **Foreign born:** 0.6%. **Median age:** 41.1. **State rank:** 46. **Pop change 1990-2000:** +12.3%.

Income: per capita $14,770; median household $31,577. **Pop below poverty level:** 17.9%.

Unemployment: 10.9%. **Median home value:** $70,700. **Median travel time to work:** 33.8 minutes.

NEWBERRY COUNTY
PO Drawer 10   **Ph:** 803-321-2110
Newberry, SC 29108   **Fax:** 803-321-2111

In north-central SC, northwest of Columbia; organized 1789 from Ninety Six District. **Name Origin:** Origin is uncertain, but believed to be for Capt. John Newberry of Gen. Thomas Sumter's (1734-1832) Revolutionary War troops.

Area (sq mi): 647.28 (land 630.77; water 16.51).

Pop: 36,108 (White 61.7%; Black or African American 33.1%; Hispanic or Latino 4.2%; Asian 0.3%; Other 2.6%). **Foreign born:** 3.5%. **Median age:** 37.1. **State rank:** 28. **Pop change 1990-2000:** +8.9%.

Income: per capita $16,045; median household $32,867. **Pop below poverty level:** 17%.

Unemployment: 6.8%. **Median home value:** $78,000. **Median travel time to work:** 25.3 minutes.

All statistics are based on the 2000 Census except the dollar figures given for per capita income, which are based on 1999 estimates.

OCONEE COUNTY

415 S Pine St   **Ph:** 864-638-4242
Walhalla, SC 29691   **Fax:** 864-638-4241
www.oconeesc.com

On the northwestern border of SC, west of Greenville; organized Jan 29, 1868 from Pickens County. **Name Origin:** For an Indian word of uncertain meaning. Possibly refers to the mythical Cherokee snake dragon, or to mean 'water eyes of the hills' or 'beautiful springs.'

Area (sq mi): 673.58 (land 625.41; water 48.17).

Pop: 66,215 (White 88%; Black or African American 8.4%; Hispanic or Latino 2.4%; Asian 0.4%; Other 2.1%). **Foreign born:** 2.4%. **Median age:** 39.5. **State rank:** 20. **Pop change 1990-2000:** +15.2%.

Income: per capita $18,965; median household $36,666. **Pop below poverty level:** 10.8%.

Unemployment: 6.2%. **Median home value:** $97,500. **Median travel time to work:** 23.3 minutes.

ORANGEBURG COUNTY

PO Drawer 9000   **Ph:** 803-533-1000
Orangeburg, SC 29116   **Fax:** 803-533-6104
www.orangeburgcounty.org

In south-central SC, south of Columbia; original district; organized 1768 (prior to statehood). **Name Origin:** For Prince William IV of Orange (1738-1820), who later became King George III of England.

Area (sq mi): 1128.09 (land 1106.16; water 21.93).

Pop: 91,582 (White 36.8%; Black or African American 60.9%; Hispanic or Latino 1%; Asian 0.4%; Other 1.6%). **Foreign born:** 1%. **Median age:** 35.3. **State rank:** 16. **Pop change 1990-2000:** +8%.

Income: per capita $15,057; median household $29,567. **Pop below poverty level:** 21.4%.

Unemployment: 11.1%. **Median home value:** $72,600. **Median travel time to work:** 26.5 minutes.

PICKENS COUNTY

PO Box 215   **Ph:** 864-898-5866
Pickens, SC 29671   **Fax:** 864-898-5863
www.co.pickens.sc.us

On the northeastern border of SC, west of Greenville; organized Dec 20, 1826 from Pendleton District, which was abolished at that time. **Name Origin:** For Gen. Andrew Pickens (1739-1817), Revolutionary War hero and U.S. representative from SC (1793-95).

Area (sq mi): 511.85 (land 496.89; water 14.96).

Pop: 110,757 (White 89.3%; Black or African American 6.8%; Hispanic or Latino 1.7%; Asian 1.2%; Other 1.8%). **Foreign born:** 2.9%. **Median age:** 32.7. **State rank:** 13. **Pop change 1990-2000:** +18%.

Income: per capita $17,434; median household $36,214. **Pop below poverty level:** 13.7%.

Unemployment: 5%. **Median home value:** $96,100. **Median travel time to work:** 24 minutes.

RICHLAND COUNTY

2020 Hampton St   **Ph:** 803-748-4600
Columbia, SC 29204   **Fax:** 803-748-4644
www.co.richland.sc.us

In north-central SC, west of Sumter; established Mar 12, 1785. **Name Origin:** For the fertile farmland along its rivers.

Area (sq mi): 771.72 (land 756.41; water 15.3).

Pop: 320,677 (White 49.2%; Black or African American 45.2%; Hispanic or Latino 2.7%; Asian 1.7%; Other 2.8%). **Foreign born:** 3.9%. **Median age:** 32.6. **State rank:** 2. **Pop change 1990-2000:** +12.2%.

Income: per capita $20,794; median household $39,961. **Pop below poverty level:** 13.7%.

Unemployment: 3.5%. **Median home value:** $98,700. **Median travel time to work:** 21.7 minutes.

SALUDA COUNTY

100 E Church St Suite 6   **Ph:** 864-445-3303
Saluda, SC 29138   **Fax:** 864-445-3772

In west-central SC, west of Columbia; organized 1895 from Edgefield County. **Name Origin:** For the Saluda River, which forms its northern border, itself named perhaps from Cherokee *selu* 'corn,' for the corn-growing area, with ending *tah* 'river': 'corn river.'

Area (sq mi): 461.78 (land 452.48; water 9.3).

Pop: 19,181 (White 62.2%; Black or African American 30%; Hispanic or Latino 7.3%; Asian 0%; Other 4.1%). **Foreign born:** 5.9%. **Median age:** 37. **State rank:** 42. **Pop change 1990-2000:** +17.3%.

Income: per capita $16,328; median household $35,774. **Pop below poverty level:** 15.6%.

Unemployment: 5.3%. **Median home value:** $74,000. **Median travel time to work:** 32.1 minutes.

SPARTANBURG COUNTY

180 Magnolia St   **Ph:** 864-596-2591
Spartanburg, SC 29306   **Fax:** 864-596-2239
www.spartanburgcounty.org

On the central northern border of SC, east of Greenville; established Mar 12, 1785 from Ninety Six District. **Name Origin:** For the Spartan Regiment of SC militia, which distinguished itself in the Revolutionary War.

Area (sq mi): 819.14 (land 810.93; water 8.22).

Pop: 253,791 (White 74%; Black or African American 20.8%; Hispanic or Latino 2.8%; Asian 1.5%; Other 2.6%). **Foreign born:** 3.7%. **Median age:** 36.1. **State rank:** 4. **Pop change 1990-2000:** +11.9%.

Income: per capita $18,738; median household $37,579. **Pop below poverty level:** 12.3%.

Unemployment: 5.2%. **Median home value:** $91,100. **Median travel time to work:** 22.5 minutes.

Please see sample entry on inside front cover for detailed information about the statistics presented with each county listing.

SUMTER COUNTY

141 N Main St   **Ph:** 803-436-2227
Sumter, SC 29150   **Fax:** 803-436-2223
www.sumtercountysc.org

In east-central SC, east of Columbia; organized 1798 from Camden District. **Name Origin:** For Gen. Thomas Sumter (1734-1832), American Revolutionary officer nicknamed the 'Gamecock of the Revolution,' U.S. representative from GA (1789-93; 1797-1801), and U.S. senator (1801-10).

Area (sq mi): 682.03 (land 665.41; water 16.63).

Pop: 104,646 (White 49.4%; Black or African American 46.7%; Hispanic or Latino 1.8%; Asian 0.9%; Other 2.4%). **Foreign born:** 2.1%. **Median age:** 33.4. **State rank:** 14. **Pop change 1990-2000:** +2%.

Income: per capita $15,657; median household $33,278. **Pop below poverty level:** 16.2%.

Unemployment: 7.2%. **Median home value:** $78,700. **Median travel time to work:** 21.5 minutes.

UNION COUNTY

PO Box 703   **Ph:** 864-429-1630
Union, SC 29379   **Fax:** 864-429-1715

In north-central SC, southeast of Spartanburg; organized 1798 from Ninety Six District. **Name Origin:** For the old Union Church, erected in 1765 for use by many different denominations.

Area (sq mi): 515.92 (land 514.12; water 1.8).

Pop: 29,881 (White 67.5%; Black or African American 31%; Hispanic or Latino 0.7%; Asian 0.2%; Other 0.9%). **Foreign born:** 0.6%. **Median age:** 38.6. **State rank:** 33. **Pop change 1990-2000:** -1.5%.

Income: per capita $15,877; median household $31,441. **Pop below poverty level:** 14.3%.

Unemployment: 10.9%. **Median home value:** $61,900. **Median travel time to work:** 27 minutes.

WILLIAMSBURG COUNTY

147 W Main St   **Ph:** 843-355-9321
Kingstree, SC 29556

In east-central SC, north of Charleston; organized 1804 from Georgetown District. **Name Origin:** For William III (1650-1702), king of England with Queen Mary (1689-1702).

Area (sq mi): 936.92 (land 933.9; water 3.02).

Pop: 37,217 (White 32.5%; Black or African American 66.3%; Hispanic or Latino 0.7%; Asian 0.2%; Other 0.9%). **Foreign born:** 0.5%. **Median age:** 35.5. **State rank:** 27. **Pop change 1990-2000:** +1.1%.

Income: per capita $12,794; median household $24,214. **Pop below poverty level:** 27.9%.

Unemployment: 14.6%. **Median home value:** $63,300. **Median travel time to work:** 31.5 minutes.

YORK COUNTY

2 S Congress St   **Ph:** 803-684-8507
York, SC 29745   **Fax:** 803-684-8560
www.yorkcountygov.com

On central northern border of SC, north of Columbia; organized 1798 from Camden District. **Name Origin:** For York, PA, former home of many early settlers. Formerly called *New Acquisition*.

Area (sq mi): 695.72 (land 682.45; water 13.27).

Pop: 164,614 (White 76.4%; Black or African American 19.2%; Hispanic or Latino 2%; Asian 0.9%; Other 2.7%). **Foreign born:** 2.4%. **Median age:** 34.9. **State rank:** 8. **Pop change 1990-2000:** +25.2%.

Income: per capita $20,536; median household $44,539. **Pop below poverty level:** 10%.

Unemployment: 5.1%. **Median home value:** $119,600. **Median travel time to work:** 27.2 minutes.

All statistics are based on the 2000 Census except the dollar figures given for per capita income, which are based on 1999 estimates.

SOUTH DAKOTA - Counties

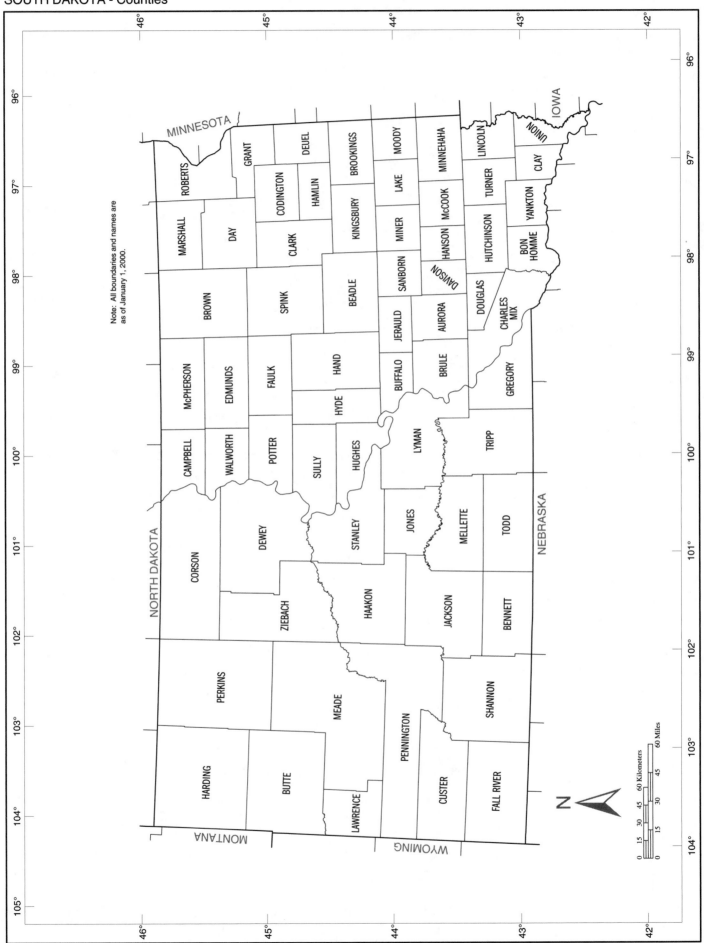

Note: All boundaries and names are as of January 1, 2000.

South Dakota

SOUTH DAKOTA STATE INFORMATION

www.state.sd.us   **Ph:** 605-773-3011

Area (sq mi): 77,116.49 (land 75,884.64; water 1231.85).

Pop: 754,844 (White 88%; Black or African American 0.6%; Hispanic or Latino 1.4%; Asian 0.6%; Other 10.1%). **Foreign born:** 1.8%. **Median age:** 35.6. **Pop change 1990-2000:** +8.5%.

Income: per capita $17,562; median household $35,282. **Pop below poverty level:** 13.2%.

Unemployment: 3.1%. **Median home value:** $79,600. **Median travel time to work:** 16.6 minutes.

AURORA COUNTY

PO Box 366   **Ph:** 605-942-7165
Plankinton, SD 57368   **Fax:** 605-942-7165

In south-central SD, west of Sioux Falls; created Feb 22, 1879 and organized 1882 (prior to statehood) from land that had been parts of Hanson County (what was later Davison, Jerauld and Cragin counties). **Name Origin:** For the Roman goddess of dawn.

Area (sq mi): 712.53 (land 708.18; water 4.35).

Pop: 3,058 (White 95.1%; Black or African American 0.3%; Hispanic or Latino 2.1%; Asian 0.1%; Other 3.9%). **Foreign born:** 1.5%. **Median age:** 40.6. **State rank:** 49. **Pop change 1990-2000:** -2.5%.

Income: per capita $13,887; median household $29,783. **Pop below poverty level:** 11.4%.

Unemployment: 2.4%. **Median home value:** $32,600. **Median travel time to work:** 19.3 minutes.

BEADLE COUNTY

PO Box 1358   **Ph:** 605-353-7165
Huron, SD 57350   **Fax:** 605-353-0118
www.beadlecounty.org

In east-central SD, northwest of Sioux Falls; created Feb 22, 1879 (prior to statehood) from Spink and Clark counties. **Name Origin:** For Gen. William Henry Harrison Beadle (1838-1915), officer in the Civil War, surveyor general of the Dakota Territory (1869-73), and educator.

Area (sq mi): 1264.82 (land 1258.7; water 6.13).

Pop: 17,023 (White 96.4%; Black or African American 0.7%; Hispanic or Latino 0.9%; Asian 0.3%; Other 2%). **Foreign born:** 1.2%. **Median age:** 40.1. **State rank:** 11. **Pop change 1990-2000:** -6.7%.

Income: per capita $17,832; median household $30,510. **Pop below poverty level:** 11.9%.

Unemployment: 3.7%. **Median home value:** $56,000. **Median travel time to work:** 14.6 minutes.

BENNETT COUNTY

202 Main St   **Ph:** 605-685-6969
Martin, SD 57551

On the central southern border of SD, southeast of Rapid City; created Mar 9, 1909 from Indian lands. **Name Origin:** For either John E. Bennett, SD supreme court judge, or jointly for John E. Bennett and Granville G. Bennett, IL legislator and federally appointed judge in Dakota Territory.

Area (sq mi): 1190.59 (land 1185.29; water 5.3).

Pop: 3,574 (White 40.5%; Black or African American 0.3%; Hispanic or Latino 2%; Asian 0.1%; Other 58.8%). **Foreign born:** 0.4%. **Median age:** 29.2. **State rank:** 45. **Pop change 1990-2000:** +11.5%.

Income: per capita $10,106; median household $25,313. **Pop below poverty level:** 39.2%.

Unemployment: 5.9%. **Median home value:** $36,500. **Median travel time to work:** 17.3 minutes.

BON HOMME COUNTY

300 W 18th Ave   **Ph:** 605-589-4215
Tyndall, SD 57066   **Fax:** 605-589-4245

On the southeastern border of SD, west of Sioux Falls; original county; organized Apr 5, 1862 (prior to statehood) from unorganized territory. **Name Origin:** For a village, which was named for a nearby large island in the Missouri River; mentioned in Lewis and Clark's journals. French 'good man,' name used by fourteenth-century French aristocracy for peasants.

Area (sq mi): 581.32 (land 563.34; water 17.98).

Pop: 7,260 (White 95.3%; Black or African American 0.6%; Hispanic or Latino 0.6%; Asian 0.1%; Other 3.8%). **Foreign born:** 0.7%. **Median age:** 40.3. **State rank:** 27. **Pop change 1990-2000:** +2.4%.

Income: per capita $13,892; median household $30,644. **Pop below poverty level:** 12.9%.

Unemployment: 3%. **Median home value:** $46,100. **Median travel time to work:** 18 minutes.

BROOKINGS COUNTY

314 6th Ave   **Ph:** 605-692-6284
Brookings, SD 57006

On the central eastern border of SD, north of Sioux Falls; created

Please see sample entry on inside front cover for detailed information about the statistics presented with each county listing.

501

Apr 5, 1862 (prior to statehood) from unorganized territory. **Name Origin:** For Wilmot W. Brookings (1833-85), prominent legislator and associate justice on the Dakota Territory supreme court (1869-73). He promoted the Southern Dakota Railway, and 'Judge Brookings' was the name of the first locomotive to enter what is now SD.

Area (sq mi): 804.76 (land 794.46; water 10.3).

Pop: 28,220 (White 95.9%; Black or African American 0.3%; Hispanic or Latino 0.9%; Asian 1.3%; Other 1.9%). **Foreign born:** 2.3%. **Median age:** 26.6. **State rank:** 4. **Pop change 1990-2000:** +12%.

Income: per capita $17,586; median household $35,438. **Pop below poverty level:** 14%.

Unemployment: 1.9%. **Median home value:** $88,500. **Median travel time to work:** 14.1 minutes.

BROWN COUNTY
25 Market St   **Ph:** 605-626-7110
Aberdeen, SD 57401
www.brown.sd.us

On the northeastern border of SD; created Feb 22, 1879 (prior to statehood) from Beadle County. **Name Origin:** For Alfred Brown (1836-?), member of the Dakota Territory legislature instrumental in consolidating the then existing counties, which earned him the nickname 'Consolidation Brown.'

Area (sq mi): 1731.21 (land 1713.07; water 18.14).

Pop: 35,460 (White 95.1%; Black or African American 0.3%; Hispanic or Latino 0.7%; Asian 0.4%; Other 3.9%). **Foreign born:** 0.6%. **Median age:** 37.2. **State rank:** 3. **Pop change 1990-2000:** -0.3%.

Income: per capita $18,464; median household $35,017. **Pop below poverty level:** 9.9%.

Unemployment: 2.9%. **Median home value:** $72,700. **Median travel time to work:** 12.6 minutes.

BRULE COUNTY
300 S Courtland St Suite 111   **Ph:** 605-734-4431
Chamberlain, SD 57325

In south-central SD, west of Sioux Falls; created Jan 14, 1875 (prior to statehood) from Buffalo County. **Name Origin:** For the Brule tribe of Sioux Indians. French 'burned,' partial transliteration of *sicangu* 'burned thighs,' a name derisively given to a group of Sioux who tried to raid the Pawnees, who set the plains on fire. Many of the unsuccessful raiders were badly burned but escaped.

Area (sq mi): 846.49 (land 818.96; water 27.54).

Pop: 5,364 (White 89.6%; Black or African American 0.3%; Hispanic or Latino 0.5%; Asian 0.5%; Other 9.4%). **Foreign born:** 0.4%. **Median age:** 36.9. **State rank:** 36. **Pop change 1990-2000:** -2.2%.

Income: per capita $14,874; median household $32,370. **Pop below poverty level:** 14.3%.

Unemployment: 3.3%. **Median home value:** $64,900. **Median travel time to work:** 16.5 minutes.

BUFFALO COUNTY
PO Box 148   **Ph:** 605-293-3234
Gann Valley, SD 57341   **Fax:** 605-293-3240

In south-central SD, southeast of Pierre; organized 1871 (prior to statehood) from territorial country. **Name Origin:** For the once-plentiful herds of buffalo.

Area (sq mi): 487.43 (land 470.59; water 16.83).

Pop: 2,032 (White 16.3%; Black or African American 0.1%; Hispanic or Latino 0.9%; Asian 0%; Other 83.6%). **Foreign born:** 0.4%. **Median age:** 23.4. **State rank:** 61. **Pop change 1990-2000:** +15.5%.

Income: per capita $5,213; median household $12,692. **Pop below poverty level:** 56.9%.

Unemployment: 8.4%. **Median home value:** $26,300. **Median travel time to work:** 16 minutes.

BUTTE COUNTY
PO Box 237   **Ph:** 605-892-2516
Belle Fourche, SD 57717   **Fax:** 605-892-2836

On the central western border of SD; organized Mar 2, 1883 (prior to statehood) from Harding County. **Name Origin:** For nearby buttes (flat-topped mounds or mountains).

Area (sq mi): 2266.36 (land 2248.51; water 17.84).

Pop: 9,094 (White 94.1%; Black or African American 0.1%; Hispanic or Latino 2.9%; Asian 0.2%; Other 4.1%). **Foreign born:** 1.2%. **Median age:** 38. **State rank:** 19. **Pop change 1990-2000:** +14.9%.

Income: per capita $13,997; median household $29,040. **Pop below poverty level:** 12.8%.

Unemployment: 4%. **Median home value:** $60,200. **Median travel time to work:** 18.6 minutes.

CAMPBELL COUNTY
PO Box 146   **Ph:** 605-955-3536
Mound City, SD 57646   **Fax:** 605-955-3308

On the central northern border of SD, northwest of Aberdeen; created Jan 8, 1873 (prior to statehood) from Buffalo County. **Name Origin:** For Norman B. Campbell, Dakota Territory legislator (1872-73).

Area (sq mi): 771.34 (land 735.79; water 35.54).

Pop: 1,782 (White 99.1%; Black or African American 0%; Hispanic or Latino 0.2%; Asian 0.1%; Other 0.6%). **Foreign born:** 0.4%. **Median age:** 41.9. **State rank:** 62. **Pop change 1990-2000:** -9.3%.

Income: per capita $14,117; median household $28,793. **Pop below poverty level:** 14.1%.

Unemployment: 6.8%. **Median home value:** $27,400. **Median travel time to work:** 18.3 minutes.

CHARLES MIX COUNTY
PO Box 490   **Ph:** 605-487-7131
Lake Andes, SD 57356   **Fax:** 605-487-7221

On the southeastern border of SD, southwest of Sioux Falls; original county; created May 8, 1862 (prior to statehood). **Name Origin:**

All statistics are based on the 2000 Census except the dollar figures given for per capita income, which are based on 1999 estimates.

For either Charles E. Mix, a commissioner of Indian affairs, or Charles H. Mix, a scout during the Civil War.

Area (sq mi): 1150.19 (land 1097.57; water 52.61).

Pop: 9,350 (White 69.2%; Black or African American 0.1%; Hispanic or Latino 1.9%; Asian 0.1%; Other 30.2%). **Foreign born:** 0.8%. **Median age:** 35.7. **State rank:** 18. **Pop change 1990-2000:** +2.4%.

Income: per capita $11,502; median household $26,060. **Pop below poverty level:** 26.9%.

Unemployment: 3.3%. **Median home value:** $49,100. **Median travel time to work:** 13.7 minutes.

CLARK COUNTY

200 N Commercial St   **Ph:** 605-532-5921
Clark, SD 57225   **Fax:** 605-532-5931

In east-central SD, southeast of Aberdeen; created Jan 8, 1873 (prior to statehood) from Hanson County. **Name Origin:** For Newton Clark, pioneer schoolteacher and Dakota territorial legislator.

Area (sq mi): 967.79 (land 957.92; water 9.87).

Pop: 4,143 (White 98.5%; Black or African American 0.1%; Hispanic or Latino 0.5%; Asian 0.1%; Other 1.2%). **Foreign born:** 0.8%. **Median age:** 41.6. **State rank:** 42. **Pop change 1990-2000:** -5.9%.

Income: per capita $15,597; median household $30,208. **Pop below poverty level:** 14.8%.

Unemployment: 7.3%. **Median home value:** $36,700. **Median travel time to work:** 18.8 minutes.

CLAY COUNTY

211 W Main St Suite 200   **Ph:** 605-677-7120
Vermillion, SD 57069   **Fax:** 605-677-7104

In southeastern SD, south of Sioux Falls; original county; organized Apr 5, 1862 (prior to statehood) from unorganized territory. **Name Origin:** For Henry Clay (1777-1852), U.S. senator from KY, known as the 'Great Pacificator' for his advocacy of compromise to avert national crises.

Area (sq mi): 416.7 (land 411.6; water 5.1).

Pop: 13,537 (White 92.3%; Black or African American 1%; Hispanic or Latino 0.9%; Asian 2%; Other 4.3%). **Foreign born:** 2.6%. **Median age:** 24.9. **State rank:** 13. **Pop change 1990-2000:** +2.7%.

Income: per capita $14,452; median household $27,535. **Pop below poverty level:** 21.2%.

Unemployment: 1.3%. **Median home value:** $79,500. **Median travel time to work:** 16.3 minutes.

CODINGTON COUNTY

PO Box 1054   **Ph:** 605-882-5095
Watertown, SD 57201   **Fax:** 605-882-5384

In east-central SD, southeast of Aberdeen; organized Aug 7, 1878 (prior to statehood) from Indian lands. **Name Origin:** For the Rev. G.S.S. Codington, clergyman and Dakota Territory legislator.

Area (sq mi): 717.08 (land 687.67; water 29.41).

Pop: 25,897 (White 96.3%; Black or African American 0.1%; Hispanic or Latino 1.1%; Asian 0.3%; Other 2.8%). **Foreign born:** 1.2%. **Median age:** 35.3. **State rank:** 5. **Pop change 1990-2000:** +14.1%.

Income: per capita $18,761; median household $36,257. **Pop below poverty level:** 9%.

Unemployment: 4.6%. **Median home value:** $84,200. **Median travel time to work:** 14.3 minutes.

CORSON COUNTY

PO Box 175   **Ph:** 605-273-4201
McIntosh, SD 57641   **Fax:** 605-273-4597

On the central northern border of SD; organized Mar 2, 1909 from Dewey County. **Name Origin:** For Dighton Corson (1827-1915), WI legislator, a framer of the SD constitution, and SD Supreme Court Justice (1889-1913).

Area (sq mi): 2529.42 (land 2472.93; water 56.48).

Pop: 4,181 (White 37.1%; Black or African American 0.1%; Hispanic or Latino 2.1%; Asian 0%; Other 62.7%). **Foreign born:** 0.3%. **Median age:** 28.3. **State rank:** 41. **Pop change 1990-2000:** -0.3%.

Income: per capita $8,615; median household $20,654. **Pop below poverty level:** 41%.

Unemployment: 8.3%. **Median home value:** $21,600. **Median travel time to work:** 20.9 minutes.

CUSTER COUNTY

420 Mt Rushmore Rd   **Ph:** 605-673-4816
Custer, SD 57730   **Fax:** 605-673-3416

On the southwestern border of SD, south of Rapid City; created Jan 11, 1875 (prior to statehood) from Indian lands. **Name Origin:** For Gen. George Armstrong Custer (1839-76), U.S. soldier and Indian fighter.

Area (sq mi): 1559.14 (land 1557.69; water 1.45).

Pop: 7,275 (White 93.4%; Black or African American 0.3%; Hispanic or Latino 1.5%; Asian 0.2%; Other 5.4%). **Foreign born:** 1.1%. **Median age:** 43.2. **State rank:** 26. **Pop change 1990-2000:** +17.7%.

Income: per capita $17,945; median household $36,303. **Pop below poverty level:** 9.4%.

Unemployment: 3.8%. **Median home value:** $89,100. **Median travel time to work:** 21.9 minutes.

DAVISON COUNTY

200 E 4th Ave   **Ph:** 605-995-8105
Mitchell, SD 57301   **Fax:** 605-995-8112
www.davisoncounty.org

In southeastern SD, west of Sioux Falls; created Jan 8, 1873 (prior to statehood) from Hanson County. **Name Origin:** For Henry C. Davison, prominent merchant and homesteader.

Area (sq mi): 436.78 (land 435.44; water 1.34).

Pop: 18,741 (White 96%; Black or African American 0.3%; Hispanic or Latino 0.7%; Asian 0.4%; Other 3.1%). **Foreign born:** 1%. **Median age:** 36. **State rank:** 10. **Pop change 1990-2000:** +7.1%.

Please see sample entry on inside front cover for detailed information about the statistics presented with each county listing.

503

Income: per capita $17,879; median household $33,476. **Pop below poverty level:** 11.5%.

Unemployment: 2.3%. **Median home value:** $71,600. **Median travel time to work:** 14 minutes.

DAY COUNTY
710 W 1st St   **Ph:** 605-345-3771
Webster, SD 57274

In northeastern SD, east of Aberdeen; created Feb 22, 1879 (prior to statehood) from Clark County. **Name Origin:** For Merritt H. Day (1844-1900), Dakota Territory legislator.

Area (sq mi): 1091.21 (land 1028.57; water 62.63).

Pop: 6,267 (White 91.2%; Black or African American 0.1%; Hispanic or Latino 0.4%; Asian 0.1%; Other 8.5%). **Foreign born:** 0.9%. **Median age:** 42.9. **State rank:** 30. **Pop change 1990-2000:** -10.2%.

Income: per capita $15,856; median household $30,227. **Pop below poverty level:** 14.3%.

Unemployment: 6.5%. **Median home value:** $33,100. **Median travel time to work:** 17.7 minutes.

DEUEL COUNTY
PO Box 308   **Ph:** 605-874-2120
Clear Lake, SD 57226   **Fax:** 605-874-2916

On central eastern border of SD, north of Sioux Falls; created Apr 5, 1862 (prior to statehood) from Brookings County. **Name Origin:** For Jacob S. Deuel (1830-?), sawmill owner and a member of the first Territorial legislature (1862-63).

Area (sq mi): 636.72 (land 623.55; water 13.17).

Pop: 4,498 (White 97.9%; Black or African American 0.1%; Hispanic or Latino 0.8%; Asian 0.2%; Other 1.2%). **Foreign born:** 0.7%. **Median age:** 40.8. **State rank:** 39. **Pop change 1990-2000:** -0.5%.

Income: per capita $15,977; median household $31,788. **Pop below poverty level:** 10.3%.

Unemployment: 5.1%. **Median home value:** $44,400. **Median travel time to work:** 20.5 minutes.

DEWEY COUNTY
PO Box 277   **Ph:** 605-865-3672
Timber Lake, SD 57656   **Fax:** 605-865-3691

In north-central SD, north of Pierre; created as Rusk County in 1883 (prior to statehood); organized 1909 from Indian lands. **Name Origin:** For William Pitt Dewey (?-1900), surveyor general of the Dakota Territory (1873-77).

Area (sq mi): 2445.67 (land 2302.64; water 143.03).

Pop: 5,972 (White 24.1%; Black or African American 0%; Hispanic or Latino 0.9%; Asian 0.1%; Other 75.8%). **Foreign born:** 0.6%. **Median age:** 26.5. **State rank:** 32. **Pop change 1990-2000:** +8.1%.

Income: per capita $9,251; median household $23,272. **Pop below poverty level:** 33.6%.

Unemployment: 16.1%. **Median home value:** $36,000. **Median travel time to work:** 17.2 minutes.

DOUGLAS COUNTY
PO Box 36   **Ph:** 605-724-2585
Armour, SD 57313   **Fax:** 605-724-2508

In south-central SD, southwest of Sioux Falls; created Jan 8, 1873 (prior to statehood) from Charles Mix County. **Name Origin:** For Stephen Arnold Douglas (1813-61), U.S. orator and statesman.

Area (sq mi): 434.13 (land 433.53; water 0.6).

Pop: 3,458 (White 97.9%; Black or African American 0.1%; Hispanic or Latino 0.4%; Asian 0.1%; Other 1.7%). **Foreign born:** 0.4%. **Median age:** 41.8. **State rank:** 46. **Pop change 1990-2000:** -7.7%.

Income: per capita $13,827; median household $28,478. **Pop below poverty level:** 14.6%.

Unemployment: 2.4%. **Median home value:** $34,600. **Median travel time to work:** 14.6 minutes.

EDMUNDS COUNTY
PO Box 384   **Ph:** 605-426-6671
Ipswich, SD 57451   **Fax:** 605-426-6323

In north-central SD, west of Aberdeen; created Jan 8, 1873 (prior to statehood) from Buffalo County. **Name Origin:** For Newton Edmunds (1819-1908), governor of Dakota Territory (1863-66).

Area (sq mi): 1151.16 (land 1145.58; water 5.58).

Pop: 4,367 (White 98.9%; Black or African American 0.1%; Hispanic or Latino 0.5%; Asian 0.1%; Other 0.6%). **Foreign born:** 1%. **Median age:** 41.6. **State rank:** 40. **Pop change 1990-2000:** +0.3%.

Income: per capita $16,149; median household $32,205. **Pop below poverty level:** 13.8%.

Unemployment: 2.2%. **Median home value:** $42,000. **Median travel time to work:** 17.2 minutes.

FALL RIVER COUNTY
906 N River St   **Ph:** 605-745-5132
Hot Springs, SD 57747   **Fax:** 605-745-6835

On the southwestern border of SD, south of Rapid City; organized Mar 6, 1883 (prior to statehood) from Custer County. Seat of government for Shannon County. **Name Origin:** For the Fall River, which flows through the county. Literal translation of the Indian name.

Area (sq mi): 1749.14 (land 1739.86; water 9.28).

Pop: 7,453 (White 89.3%; Black or African American 0.3%; Hispanic or Latino 1.7%; Asian 0.2%; Other 9%). **Foreign born:** 0.6%. **Median age:** 45.5. **State rank:** 25. **Pop change 1990-2000:** +1.4%.

Income: per capita $17,048; median household $29,631. **Pop below poverty level:** 13.6%.

Unemployment: 4.1%. **Median home value:** $54,300. **Median travel time to work:** 19.8 minutes.

FAULK COUNTY
PO Box 309   **Ph:** 605-598-6224
Faulkton, SD 57438

In north-central SD, southwest of Aberdeen; created Jan 8, 1873

All statistics are based on the 2000 Census except the dollar figures given for per capita income, which are based on 1999 estimates.

504

(prior to statehood) from Buffalo County and unorganized territory. **Name Origin:** For Andrew Jackson Faulk (1814-98), a governor of Dakota Territory.

Area (sq mi): 1005.69 (land 1000.14; water 5.55).

Pop: 2,640 (White 99.2%; Black or African American 0.1%; Hispanic or Latino 0.2%; Asian 0%; Other 0.5%). **Foreign born:** 2%. **Median age:** 41.5. **State rank:** 56. **Pop change 1990-2000:** -3.8%.

Income: per capita $14,660; median household $30,237. **Pop below poverty level:** 18.1%.

Unemployment: 2.7%. **Median home value:** $31,600. **Median travel time to work:** 14.8 minutes.

GRANT COUNTY

210 E 5th Ave   **Ph:** 605-432-6711
Milbank, SD 57252   **Fax:** 605-432-9004

On the northeastern border of SD, northeast of Watertown; organized Jun 12, 1878 (prior to statehood) from Codington and Deuel counties. **Name Origin:** For Ulysses Simpson Grant (1822-85), Civil War general and eighteenth U.S. president.

Area (sq mi): 687.91 (land 682.51; water 5.4).

Pop: 7,847 (White 98.5%; Black or African American 0%; Hispanic or Latino 0.5%; Asian 0.2%; Other 1.1%). **Foreign born:** 1.1%. **Median age:** 40.3. **State rank:** 23. **Pop change 1990-2000:** -6.3%.

Income: per capita $16,543; median household $33,088. **Pop below poverty level:** 9.9%.

Unemployment: 4.5%. **Median home value:** $60,400. **Median travel time to work:** 14.3 minutes.

GREGORY COUNTY

PO Box 430   **Ph:** 605-775-2665
Burke, SD 57523

On the central southern border of SD, east of Winner; created May 8, 1862 (prior to statehood) from Yankton County. **Name Origin:** For John Shaw Gregory (1831-?), Indian agent and Dakota territorial legislator (1862-64).

Area (sq mi): 1053.45 (land 1015.93; water 37.51).

Pop: 4,792 (White 92.5%; Black or African American 0%; Hispanic or Latino 0.9%; Asian 0.2%; Other 6.6%). **Foreign born:** 0.7%. **Median age:** 44.3. **State rank:** 37. **Pop change 1990-2000:** -10.6%.

Income: per capita $13,656; median household $22,732. **Pop below poverty level:** 20.1%.

Unemployment: 3.7%. **Median home value:** $32,700. **Median travel time to work:** 13.7 minutes.

HAAKON COUNTY

PO Box 698   **Ph:** 605-859-2800
Philip, SD 57567

In west-central SD, west of Pierre; created Nov, 1914 from Stanley County. **Name Origin:** For Haakon VII (1872-1957), king of Norway; the name was suggested by Hugh J. McMahon, an Irish immigrant who wished to gain the votes of the Norwegian immigrants in favor of the division of Stanley County into two new counties.

Area (sq mi): 1827.22 (land 1812.97; water 14.26).

Pop: 2,196 (White 95.9%; Black or African American 0%; Hispanic or Latino 0.6%; Asian 0.1%; Other 3.5%). **Foreign born:** 1%. **Median age:** 41.3. **State rank:** 59. **Pop change 1990-2000:** -16.3%.

Income: per capita $16,780; median household $29,894. **Pop below poverty level:** 13.9%.

Unemployment: 2.6%. **Median home value:** $46,200. **Median travel time to work:** 14.2 minutes.

HAMLIN COUNTY

PO Box 256   **Ph:** 605-783-3751
Hayti, SD 57241   **Fax:** 605-783-3201

In east-central SD, northwest of Sioux Falls; created Jan 8, 1873 (prior to statehood) from Deuel County. **Name Origin:** For Hannibal Hamlin (1809-91), governor of ME (1857), U.S. senator from ME (1848-67; 1857-61; 1869-81), and vice president (1861-65) under Lincoln.

Area (sq mi): 537.96 (land 506.86; water 31.1).

Pop: 5,540 (White 98%; Black or African American 0.1%; Hispanic or Latino 0.6%; Asian 0.2%; Other 1.2%). **Foreign born:** 0.8%. **Median age:** 38. **State rank:** 35. **Pop change 1990-2000:** +11.4%.

Income: per capita $16,982; median household $33,851. **Pop below poverty level:** 12.1%.

Unemployment: 4.2%. **Median home value:** $49,300. **Median travel time to work:** 22.3 minutes.

HAND COUNTY

415 W 1st Ave   **Ph:** 605-853-3337
Miller, SD 57362   **Fax:** 605-853-3779

In east-central SD, southwest of Aberdeen; created 1873 (prior to statehood) from Buffalo County. **Name Origin:** For George H. Hand (1837-91), secretary of Dakota Territory (1874-83).

Area (sq mi): 1440.21 (land 1436.58; water 3.63).

Pop: 3,741 (White 99.1%; Black or African American 0%; Hispanic or Latino 0.3%; Asian 0.1%; Other 0.5%). **Foreign born:** 1%. **Median age:** 43.6. **State rank:** 44. **Pop change 1990-2000:** -12.4%.

Income: per capita $18,735; median household $32,377. **Pop below poverty level:** 9.2%.

Unemployment: 2.2%. **Median home value:** $45,700. **Median travel time to work:** 16.2 minutes.

HANSON COUNTY

PO Box 127   **Ph:** 605-239-4446
Alexandria, SD 57311   **Fax:** 605-239-9446

In southeastern SD, west of Sioux Falls; organized Jan 13, 1871 (prior to statehood) from Buffalo and Deuel counties. **Name Origin:** For Maj. Joseph R. Hanson (1837-1917), Dakota Territory legislator and Indian affairs official.

Area (sq mi): 435.64 (land 434.76; water 0.87).

Pop: 3,139 (White 99.5%; Black or African American 0%; Hispanic or Latino 0.1%; Asian 0.1%; Other 0.3%). **Foreign born:** 0.5%. **Median age:** 36. **State rank:** 48. **Pop change 1990-2000:** +4.8%.

Income: per capita $14,778; median household $33,049. **Pop below poverty level:** 16.6%.

Please see sample entry on inside front cover for detailed information about the statistics presented with each county listing.

Unemployment: 2.3%. **Median home value:** $45,900. **Median travel time to work:** 23.6 minutes.

HARDING COUNTY

410 Ramsland St PO Box 534 **Ph:** 605-375-3351
Buffalo, SD 57720 **Fax:** 605-375-3432

On the northwest border of SD; organized Feb 26, 1909 from Butte County. **Name Origin:** For J.A. Harding, a Dakota Territory legislator.

Area (sq mi): 2677.58 (land 2670.5; water 7.08).

Pop: 1,353 (White 96.6%; Black or African American 0.3%; Hispanic or Latino 1.6%; Asian 0.6%; Other 1.5%). **Foreign born:** 0.5%. **Median age:** 37.6. **State rank:** 65. **Pop change 1990-2000:** -18.9%.

Income: per capita $12,794; median household $25,000. **Pop below poverty level:** 21.1%.

Unemployment: 3.2%. **Median home value:** $47,100. **Median travel time to work:** 18.3 minutes.

HUGHES COUNTY

PO Box 1238 **Ph:** 605-773-3713
Pierre, SD 57501

In central SD, east of Pierre; organized Nov 26, 1880 (prior to statehood) from Buffalo County. **Name Origin:** For Alexander Hughes, Dakota Territory legislator.

Area (sq mi): 800.29 (land 740.92; water 59.37).

Pop: 16,481 (White 88.4%; Black or African American 0.2%; Hispanic or Latino 1.2%; Asian 0.4%; Other 10.5%). **Foreign born:** 1.3%. **Median age:** 37.5. **State rank:** 12. **Pop change 1990-2000:** +11.2%.

Income: per capita $20,689; median household $42,970. **Pop below poverty level:** 8%.

Unemployment: 2.3%. **Median home value:** $94,400. **Median travel time to work:** 11.3 minutes.

HUTCHINSON COUNTY

140 Euclid St Rm 36 **Ph:** 605-387-4215
Olivet, SD 57052 **Fax:** 605-387-4218

In southeastern SD, southwest of Sioux Falls; created May 8, 1862 (prior to statehood) from unorganized territory. **Name Origin:** For John S. Hutchinson (1821-?), secretary of the Dakota Territory (1861-65), during which time he was frequently acting governor; member of the Hutchinson family singing and bell-ringing group, famous during the mid-1850's.

Area (sq mi): 814.37 (land 812.82; water 1.55).

Pop: 8,075 (White 98.4%; Black or African American 0.1%; Hispanic or Latino 0.5%; Asian 0.1%; Other 1.1%). **Foreign born:** 0.7%. **Median age:** 43.1. **State rank:** 22. **Pop change 1990-2000:** -2.3%.

Income: per capita $15,922; median household $30,026. **Pop below poverty level:** 13%.

Unemployment: 3%. **Median home value:** $42,000. **Median travel time to work:** 17.3 minutes.

HYDE COUNTY

PO Box 306 **Ph:** 605-852-2512
Highmore, SD 57345 **Fax:** 605-852-2767

In central SD, east of Pierre; created Jan 8, 1873 (prior to statehood) from Buffalo County. **Name Origin:** For James Hyde (1842-1902), Civil War prisoner of war at Andersonville and Dakota territorial legislator.

Area (sq mi): 866.59 (land 860.97; water 5.62).

Pop: 1,671 (White 90.9%; Black or African American 0.1%; Hispanic or Latino 0.5%; Asian 0%; Other 8.8%). **Foreign born:** 0.3%. **Median age:** 42.2. **State rank:** 63. **Pop change 1990-2000:** -1.5%.

Income: per capita $16,356; median household $31,103. **Pop below poverty level:** 12.3%.

Unemployment: 2.6%. **Median home value:** $33,800. **Median travel time to work:** 13.6 minutes.

JACKSON COUNTY

PO Box 128 **Ph:** 605-837-2121
Kadoka, SD 57543

In south-central SD, southwest of Pierre; created Nov, 1914 from Stanley County. In 1976 annexed Washabaugh County, which was organized 1883 from Indian lands and continued as an Indian reservation. An original Jackson County, formed in 1883, gradually disappeared as parts of its territory joined other counties. **Name Origin:** For John R. Jackson, Dakota Territory legislator when the original Jackson county was formed in 1883. A claim has been made for Andrew Jackson, but seems to be unjustified.

Area (sq mi): 1871.24 (land 1869.13; water 2.12).

Pop: 2,930 (White 50%; Black or African American 0%; Hispanic or Latino 0.4%; Asian 0%; Other 49.7%). **Foreign born:** 0.9%. **Median age:** 30.6. **State rank:** 50. **Pop change 1990-2000:** +4.2%.

Income: per capita $9,981; median household $23,945. **Pop below poverty level:** 36.5%.

Unemployment: 7%. **Median home value:** $31,500. **Median travel time to work:** 16.9 minutes.

JERAULD COUNTY

PO Box 435 **Ph:** 605-539-1202
Wessington Springs, SD 57382 **Fax:** 605-539-1203

In south-central SD, northwest of Sioux Falls; organized Mar 9, 1883 (prior to statehood) from Aurora County. **Name Origin:** For H.A. Jerauld, Dakota Territory legislator when the county was formed.

Area (sq mi): 532.63 (land 529.91; water 2.72).

Pop: 2,295 (White 98.7%; Black or African American 0%; Hispanic or Latino 0.3%; Asian 0.1%; Other 0.9%). **Foreign born:** 0.3%. **Median age:** 46.3. **State rank:** 58. **Pop change 1990-2000:** -5.4%.

Income: per capita $16,856; median household $30,690. **Pop below poverty level:** 20.6%.

Unemployment: 2.4%. **Median home value:** $39,000. **Median travel time to work:** 18 minutes.

All statistics are based on the 2000 Census except the dollar figures given for per capita income, which are based on 1999 estimates.

JONES COUNTY

PO Box 448   **Ph:** 605-669-2361
Murdo, SD 57559   **Fax:** 605-669-2641

In south-central SD, south of Pierre; organized Jan 16, 1917 from Lyman County. **Name Origin:** For Jones County, IA, former home of some settlers.

Area (sq mi): 971.66 (land 970.52; water 1.14).

Pop: 1,193 (White 95.6%; Black or African American 0%; Hispanic or Latino 0.3%; Asian 0%; Other 4.2%). **Foreign born:** 0%. **Median age:** 41.1. **State rank:** 66. **Pop change 1990-2000:** -9.9%.

Income: per capita $15,896; median household $30,288. **Pop below poverty level:** 15.8%.

Unemployment: 1.5%. **Median home value:** $38,700. **Median travel time to work:** 14.3 minutes.

KINGSBURY COUNTY

PO Box 176   **Ph:** 605-854-3811
De Smet, SD 57231   **Fax:** 605-854-9080

In east-central SD, northwest of Sioux Falls; created Jan 8, 1873 (prior to statehood) from Hanson County. **Name Origin:** For George Washington Kingsbury (1837-1925) and T.A. Kingsbury, brothers prominent in territorial affairs and members of several Territorial legislatures. George was a newspaper publisher and author of *History of Dakota Territory*.

Area (sq mi): 863.67 (land 838.37; water 25.3).

Pop: 5,815 (White 98.1%; Black or African American 0.1%; Hispanic or Latino 0.7%; Asian 0.3%; Other 1.1%). **Foreign born:** 0.6%. **Median age:** 42.7. **State rank:** 34. **Pop change 1990-2000:** -1.9%.

Income: per capita $16,522; median household $31,262. **Pop below poverty level:** 10%.

Unemployment: 3.9%. **Median home value:** $42,900. **Median travel time to work:** 19 minutes.

LAKE COUNTY

200 E Center St   **Ph:** 605-256-5644
Madison, SD 57042   **Fax:** 605-256-5012

In east-central SD, northwest of Sioux Falls; organized Jan 8, 1873 (prior to statehood) from Brookings and Hanson counties. **Name Origin:** For the area's numerous lakes.

Area (sq mi): 575.06 (land 563.23; water 11.83).

Pop: 11,276 (White 97.4%; Black or African American 0.2%; Hispanic or Latino 0.8%; Asian 0.5%; Other 1.5%). **Foreign born:** 0.9%. **Median age:** 36.5. **State rank:** 16. **Pop change 1990-2000:** +6.9%.

Income: per capita $16,446; median household $34,087. **Pop below poverty level:** 9.7%.

Unemployment: 3.3%. **Median home value:** $73,800. **Median travel time to work:** 15.8 minutes.

LAWRENCE COUNTY

PO Box F   **Ph:** 605-578-1941
Deadwood, SD 57732   **Fax:** 605-578-1065
www.lawrence.sd.us

On the central western border of SD, northwest of Rapid City; created Jan 11, 1875 (prior to statehood) from unorganized territory. **Name Origin:** For John Lawrence, Dakota Territory legislator and first treasurer of the county.

Area (sq mi): 800.31 (land 800.04; water 0.28).

Pop: 21,802 (White 94.6%; Black or African American 0.2%; Hispanic or Latino 1.8%; Asian 0.3%; Other 3.7%). **Foreign born:** 1.2%. **Median age:** 37.2. **State rank:** 8. **Pop change 1990-2000:** +5.6%.

Income: per capita $17,195; median household $31,755. **Pop below poverty level:** 14.8%.

Unemployment: 3.1%. **Median home value:** $87,700. **Median travel time to work:** 17.7 minutes.

LINCOLN COUNTY

100 E 5th St   **Ph:** 605-764-2581
Canton, SD 57013   **Fax:** 605-764-5932

On the southeastern border of SD, south of Sioux Falls; created Dec 30, 1867 (prior to statehood) from Minnehaha County. **Name Origin:** For Abraham Lincoln (1809-65), sixteenth U.S. president.

Area (sq mi): 578.59 (land 578.09; water 0.5).

Pop: 24,131 (White 97.3%; Black or African American 0.3%; Hispanic or Latino 0.7%; Asian 0.5%; Other 1.6%). **Foreign born:** 1.1%. **Median age:** 34. **State rank:** 7. **Pop change 1990-2000:** +56.4%.

Income: per capita $22,304; median household $48,338. **Pop below poverty level:** 4.4%.

Unemployment: 1.9%. **Median home value:** $104,100. **Median travel time to work:** 20.7 minutes.

LYMAN COUNTY

PO Box 38   **Ph:** 605-869-2247
Kennebec, SD 57544   **Fax:** 605-869-2203

In south-central SD, southeast of Pierre; created Jan 8, 1873 (prior to statehood) from unorganized territory. **Name Origin:** For W.P. Lyman, member of the Dakota territorial legislature and first settler in Yankton County.

Area (sq mi): 1707.06 (land 1639.96; water 67.1).

Pop: 3,895 (White 64.5%; Black or African American 0.1%; Hispanic or Latino 0.5%; Asian 0.2%; Other 35%). **Foreign born:** 0.6%. **Median age:** 34.5. **State rank:** 43. **Pop change 1990-2000:** +7.1%.

Income: per capita $13,862; median household $28,509. **Pop below poverty level:** 24.3%.

Unemployment: 4.9%. **Median home value:** $44,100. **Median travel time to work:** 19.4 minutes.

Please see sample entry on inside front cover for detailed information about the statistics presented with each county listing.

MARSHALL COUNTY

PO Box 130   **Ph:** 605-448-5213
Britton, SD 57430   **Fax:** 605-448-5213

On the northeastern border of SD, northeast of Aberdeen; organized Mar 10, 1885 (prior to statehood) from Day County. **Name Origin:** For Marshall Vincent of NY, an early homesteader and one of the first Marshall County commissioners.

Area (sq mi): 885.63 (land 837.71; water 47.92).

Pop: 4,576 (White 92.2%; Black or African American 0.1%; Hispanic or Latino 0.8%; Asian 0.1%; Other 7.2%). **Foreign born:** 0.7%. **Median age:** 41.6. **State rank:** 38. **Pop change 1990-2000:** -5.5%.

Income: per capita $15,462; median household $30,567. **Pop below poverty level:** 13.9%.

Unemployment: 7.3%. **Median home value:** $41,300. **Median travel time to work:** 16.8 minutes.

McCOOK COUNTY

PO Box 504   **Ph:** 605-425-2781
Salem, SD 57058   **Fax:** 605-425-3144

In southeastern SD, west of Sioux Falls; created Jan 8, 1873 (prior to statehood) from Hanson County. **Name Origin:** For Edwin S. McCook (1837-73), secretary of the Dakota Territory, killed in a political dispute.

Area (sq mi): 577.16 (land 574.52; water 2.64).

Pop: 5,832 (White 98.3%; Black or African American 0.1%; Hispanic or Latino 0.8%; Asian 0.2%; Other 1%). **Foreign born:** 0.7%. **Median age:** 38.6. **State rank:** 33. **Pop change 1990-2000:** +2.5%.

Income: per capita $16,374; median household $35,396. **Pop below poverty level:** 8.1%.

Unemployment: 3.8%. **Median home value:** $57,400. **Median travel time to work:** 25 minutes.

McPHERSON COUNTY

PO Box 248   **Ph:** 605-439-3361
Leola, SD 57456   **Fax:** 605-439-3394

On the central northern border of SD, northwest of Aberdeen; created Jan 8, 1873 (prior to statehood) from Buffalo County. **Name Origin:** For Gen. James Birdseye McPherson (1828-64), commander of the Union Army of the Tennessee during the Civil War.

Area (sq mi): 1151.85 (land 1136.94; water 14.91).

Pop: 2,904 (White 99.2%; Black or African American 0%; Hispanic or Latino 0.2%; Asian 0.1%; Other 0.5%). **Foreign born:** 0.8%. **Median age:** 47.6. **State rank:** 51. **Pop change 1990-2000:** -10%.

Income: per capita $12,748; median household $22,380. **Pop below poverty level:** 22.6%.

Unemployment: 2.3%. **Median home value:** $20,100. **Median travel time to work:** 16.4 minutes.

MEADE COUNTY

PO Box 939   **Ph:** 605-347-4411
Sturgis, SD 57785   **Fax:** 605-347-3526

In west-central SD, north of Rapid City; created Feb 7, 1889 from Lawrence County. **Name Origin:** For Fort Meade, named for Gen. George Gordon Meade (1815-72), officer in the Mexican-American War and the Civil War, Union commander who defeated Gen. Lee at Gettysburg.

Area (sq mi): 3482.46 (land 3470.63; water 11.82).

Pop: 24,253 (White 91.6%; Black or African American 1.5%; Hispanic or Latino 2.1%; Asian 0.6%; Other 5.2%). **Foreign born:** 1.4%. **Median age:** 33.4. **State rank:** 6. **Pop change 1990-2000:** +10.9%.

Income: per capita $17,680; median household $36,992. **Pop below poverty level:** 9.4%.

Unemployment: 3.2%. **Median home value:** $82,200. **Median travel time to work:** 18 minutes.

MELLETTE COUNTY

PO Box 257   **Ph:** 605-259-3230
White River, SD 57579

In south-central SD, south of Pierre; organized May 25, 1911 from Tripp County. **Name Origin:** For Arthur C. Mellette (1842-96), first governor of SD (1889-93).

Area (sq mi): 1309.75 (land 1306.49; water 3.26).

Pop: 2,083 (White 44.5%; Black or African American 0%; Hispanic or Latino 1.7%; Asian 0.1%; Other 55.1%). **Foreign born:** 0.4%. **Median age:** 32.1. **State rank:** 60. **Pop change 1990-2000:** -2.5%.

Income: per capita $10,362; median household $23,219. **Pop below poverty level:** 35.8%.

Unemployment: 6.5%. **Median home value:** $25,800. **Median travel time to work:** 21.3 minutes.

MINER COUNTY

PO Box 265   **Ph:** 605-772-4612
Howard, SD 57349   **Fax:** 605-772-4412

In east-central SD, northwest of Sioux Falls; created Jan 8, 1873 (prior to statehood) from Hanson County. **Name Origin:** For Capt. Nelson Miner (1827-79) and Ephraim Miner (1833-?), members of the Dakota Territory legislature when the county was formed.

Area (sq mi): 571.99 (land 570.34; water 1.65).

Pop: 2,884 (White 98.2%; Black or African American 0.5%; Hispanic or Latino 0.6%; Asian 0.1%; Other 0.6%). **Foreign born:** 0.4%. **Median age:** 42.5. **State rank:** 52. **Pop change 1990-2000:** -11.9%.

Income: per capita $15,155; median household $29,519. **Pop below poverty level:** 11.8%.

Unemployment: 5.8%. **Median home value:** $26,500. **Median travel time to work:** 17.4 minutes.

MINNEHAHA COUNTY

415 N Dakota Ave   **Ph:** 605-367-4206
Sioux Falls, SD 57104   **Fax:** 605-367-8314
www.minnehahacounty.org

On the southeastern border of SD; original county; organized Apr 5, 1862 (prior to statehood) from Big Sioux, a territorial county. **Name Origin:** Siouan, literally 'waterfall,' popularly 'laughing water.'

All statistics are based on the 2000 Census except the dollar figures given for per capita income, which are based on 1999 estimates.

Area (sq mi): 813.69 (land 809.67; water 4.01).

Pop: 148,281 (White 92.1%; Black or African American 1.5%; Hispanic or Latino 2.1%; Asian 1%; Other 4.5%). **Foreign born:** 4.1%. **Median age:** 33.5. **State rank:** 1. **Pop change 1990-2000:** +19.8%.

Income: per capita $20,713; median household $42,566. **Pop below poverty level:** 7.5%.

Unemployment: 2.3%. **Median home value:** $101,200. **Median travel time to work:** 16.8 minutes.

MOODY COUNTY

101 E Pipestone Ave   **Ph:** 605-997-3181
Flandreau, SD 57028   **Fax:** 605-997-3861

On the central eastern border of SD, north of Sioux Falls; organized Jan 8, 1873 (prior to statehood) from Brookings and Minnehaha counties. **Name Origin:** For Col. Gideon Curtis Moody (1832-1906), officer in the Civil War, Dakota Territory legislator, and one of the first two U.S. senators from SD (1889-91).

Area (sq mi): 521.1 (land 519.67; water 1.43).

Pop: 6,595 (White 84.5%; Black or African American 0.3%; Hispanic or Latino 0.8%; Asian 0.6%; Other 14.3%). **Foreign born:** 1.4%. **Median age:** 37. **State rank:** 28. **Pop change 1990-2000:** +1.4%.

Income: per capita $16,541; median household $35,467. **Pop below poverty level:** 9.6%.

Unemployment: 6.9%. **Median home value:** $58,500. **Median travel time to work:** 21.3 minutes.

PENNINGTON COUNTY

315 Saint Joseph St   **Ph:** 605-394-2171
Rapid City, SD 577012879   **Fax:** 605-394-6833
www.co.pennington.sd.us

On the southwestern border of SD; created Jan 11, 1875 (prior to statehood) from unorganized territory. **Name Origin:** For John L. Pennington, Dakota Territory governor (1874-78).

Area (sq mi): 2784.31 (land 2776.15; water 8.16).

Pop: 88,565 (White 85.6%; Black or African American 0.9%; Hispanic or Latino 2.6%; Asian 0.9%; Other 11.6%). **Foreign born:** 2.1%. **Median age:** 35. **State rank:** 2. **Pop change 1990-2000:** +8.9%.

Income: per capita $18,938; median household $37,485. **Pop below poverty level:** 11.5%.

Unemployment: 3.1%. **Median home value:** $90,900. **Median travel time to work:** 17.3 minutes.

PERKINS COUNTY

PO Box 426   **Ph:** 605-244-5626
Bison, SD 57620   **Fax:** 605-244-7110

On the northwestern border of SD; organized Feb 26, 1909 from Harding and Butte counties. **Name Origin:** For Henry E.Perkins, state senator who helped pass the act that established the county.

Area (sq mi): 2890.71 (land 2871.62; water 19.09).

Pop: 3,363 (White 96.5%; Black or African American 0.1%; Hispanic or Latino 0.7%; Asian 0.2%; Other 2.9%). **Foreign born:**

1.3%. **Median age:** 43.1. **State rank:** 47. **Pop change 1990-2000:** -14.5%.

Income: per capita $15,734; median household $27,750. **Pop below poverty level:** 16.9%.

Unemployment: 2.7%. **Median home value:** $33,200. **Median travel time to work:** 13.6 minutes.

POTTER COUNTY

201 S Exene St   **Ph:** 605-765-9472
Gettysburg, SD 57442

In north-central SD, northeast of Pierre; created as Ashmore County Jan 14, 1875 (prior to statehood) from Buffalo County; name changed 1877. **Name Origin:** For Dr. Joel A. Potter, legislator and steward of the State Hospital for the Insane, Yankton. Originally named for Samuel Ashmore, legislator (1872-73).

Area (sq mi): 898.43 (land 866.49; water 31.94).

Pop: 2,693 (White 98%; Black or African American 0%; Hispanic or Latino 0.2%; Asian 0.2%; Other 1.7%). **Foreign born:** 0.5%. **Median age:** 45.8. **State rank:** 54. **Pop change 1990-2000:** -15.6%.

Income: per capita $17,417; median household $30,086. **Pop below poverty level:** 12.6%.

Unemployment: 3.6%. **Median home value:** $42,800. **Median travel time to work:** 15.8 minutes.

ROBERTS COUNTY

411 2nd Ave E   **Ph:** 605-698-7336
Sisseton, SD 57262   **Fax:** 605-698-4277

On the northeastern border of SD, east of Aberdeen; organized Mar 8, 1883 (prior to statehood) from Grant County. **Name Origin:** Most likely for S.G. Roberts, a publisher and a member of the Dakota territorial legislature when the county was established.

Area (sq mi): 1135.35 (land 1101.28; water 34.08).

Pop: 10,016 (White 68.1%; Black or African American 0.1%; Hispanic or Latino 0.6%; Asian 0.2%; Other 31.4%). **Foreign born:** 0.8%. **Median age:** 37.1. **State rank:** 17. **Pop change 1990-2000:** +1%.

Income: per capita $13,428; median household $28,322. **Pop below poverty level:** 22.1%.

Unemployment: 5.5%. **Median home value:** $43,500. **Median travel time to work:** 16.5 minutes.

SANBORN COUNTY

PO Box 56   **Ph:** 605-796-4515
Woonsocket, SD 57385   **Fax:** 605-796-4515

In south-central SD, northwest of Sioux Falls; organized Mar 9, 1883 (prior to statehood) from Miner County. **Name Origin:** For George W. Sanborn, a Milwaukee Railroad official.

Area (sq mi): 570.21 (land 569.01; water 1.2).

Pop: 2,675 (White 98%; Black or African American 0%; Hispanic or Latino 1%; Asian 0.4%; Other 0.7%). **Foreign born:** 0.6%. **Median age:** 40.8. **State rank:** 55. **Pop change 1990-2000:** -5.6%.

Income: per capita $18,301; median household $33,375. **Pop below poverty level:** 14.9%.

Please see sample entry on inside front cover for detailed information about the statistics presented with each county listing.

Unemployment: 3.4%. **Median home value:** $30,300. **Median travel time to work:** 20.8 minutes.

SHANNON COUNTY

906 N River St   **Ph:** 605-745-5131
Hot Springs, SD 57747   **Fax:** 605-745-5688

On the southwestern border of SD, southeast of Rapid City; created Jan 11, 1875 (prior to statehood) from territorial county. Unorganized; attached to Fall River County for government purposes. County seat is in Fall River County. **Name Origin:** For Peter C. Shannon (1821-?), chief justice of the Dakota Territory Supreme Court (1873-82).

Area (sq mi): 2096.65 (land 2093.88; water 2.77).

Pop: 12,466 (White 4.4%; Black or African American 0.1%; Hispanic or Latino 1.4%; Asian 0%; Other 95.3%). **Foreign born:** 0.6%. **Median age:** 20.6. **State rank:** 15. **Pop change 1990-2000:** +25.9%.

Income: per capita $6,286; median household $20,916. **Pop below poverty level:** 52.3%.

Unemployment: 12.6%. **Median home value:** $25,900. **Median travel time to work:** 17.2 minutes.

SPINK COUNTY

210 E 7th Ave   **Ph:** 605-472-1825
Redfield, SD 57469   **Fax:** 605-472-2410

In east-central SD, south of Aberdeen; created Jan 8, 1873 (prior to statehood) from Hanson and Walworth counties. **Name Origin:** For Solomon Lewis Spink (1831-81), Dakota Territory secretary and territorial delegate to Congress (1869-71).

Area (sq mi): 1510.05 (land 1503.87; water 6.18).

Pop: 7,454 (White 97.3%; Black or African American 0.2%; Hispanic or Latino 0.4%; Asian 0.1%; Other 2.1%). **Foreign born:** 0.6%. **Median age:** 39.9. **State rank:** 24. **Pop change 1990-2000:** -6.6%.

Income: per capita $15,728; median household $31,717. **Pop below poverty level:** 12.8%.

Unemployment: 3.6%. **Median home value:** $34,500. **Median travel time to work:** 15.5 minutes.

STANLEY COUNTY

PO Box 595   **Ph:** 605-223-2673
Fort Pierre, SD 57532   **Fax:** 605-223-3368

In central SD, created Jan 8, 1873 (prior to statehood) from unorganized territory. **Name Origin:** For Gen. David Sloane Stanley (1829-1902), army officer; after retirement, he served as director of the U.S. Soldiers' Home in Washington, D.C.

Area (sq mi): 1516.99 (land 1443.28; water 73.71).

Pop: 2,772 (White 92.9%; Black or African American 0.2%; Hispanic or Latino 0.4%; Asian 0.3%; Other 6.4%). **Foreign born:** 0.7%. **Median age:** 37.6. **State rank:** 53. **Pop change 1990-2000:** +13%.

Income: per capita $20,300; median household $41,170. **Pop below poverty level:** 8.7%.

Unemployment: 2.8%. **Median home value:** $83,900. **Median travel time to work:** 13.4 minutes.

SULLY COUNTY

PO Box 188   **Ph:** 605-258-2535
Onida, SD 57564   **Fax:** 605-258-2270

In central SD, north of Pierre; created Jan 8, 1873 (prior to statehood) from Potter County. **Name Origin:** For Fort Sully, which was named for Gen. Alfred Sully (1821-79), its builder and commander, famous as an Indian fighter and cited several times for bravery during the Civil War.

Area (sq mi): 1070.36 (land 1006.9; water 63.46).

Pop: 1,556 (White 97.4%; Black or African American 0%; Hispanic or Latino 0.8%; Asian 0.1%; Other 2.1%). **Foreign born:** 0.8%. **Median age:** 40. **State rank:** 64. **Pop change 1990-2000:** -2.1%.

Income: per capita $17,407; median household $32,500. **Pop below poverty level:** 12.1%.

Unemployment: 2.4%. **Median home value:** $55,600. **Median travel time to work:** 17.3 minutes.

TODD COUNTY

200 E 3rd St   **Ph:** 605-842-3727
Winner, SD 57580   **Fax:** 605-842-3621

On the central southern border of SD, south of Pierre; created Mar 9, 1909 from Indian lands. Unorganized; attached to Tripp County for governmental purposes. County seat is in Tripp County. **Name Origin:** For Gen. John Blair Smith Todd (1814-72), officer in the Seminole War and the Mexican-American War, U.S. congressional delegate from the Dakota Territory (1862-65), and territorial legislator (1866-67).

Area (sq mi): 1390.9 (land 1388.12; water 2.78).

Pop: 9,050 (White 12.5%; Black or African American 0.1%; Hispanic or Latino 1.5%; Asian 0.1%; Other 87.2%). **Foreign born:** 0.6%. **Median age:** 21.7. **State rank:** 20. **Pop change 1990-2000:** +8.4%.

Income: per capita $7,714; median household $20,035. **Pop below poverty level:** 48.3%.

Unemployment: 8.3%. **Median home value:** $27,500. **Median travel time to work:** 18.6 minutes.

TRIPP COUNTY

200 E 3rd St   **Ph:** 605-842-2266
Winner, SD 57580   **Fax:** 605-842-2267

On the central southern border of SD, southeast of Pierre; created Jan 8, 1873 (prior to statehood) from unorganized territory. Seat of government for Todd County. **Name Origin:** For Bartlett Tripp (1842-1911), promoter of SD's statehood, U.S. minister to Austria-Hungary (1893), chief justice of the Dakota Territory (1886-89), and trustee of Yankton College.

Area (sq mi): 1617.4 (land 1613.52; water 3.88).

Pop: 6,430 (White 87.2%; Black or African American 0%; Hispanic or Latino 0.9%; Asian 0.1%; Other 12.5%). **Foreign born:** 0.4%. **Median age:** 39.5. **State rank:** 29. **Pop change 1990-2000:** -7.1%.

Income: per capita $13,776; median household $28,333. **Pop below poverty level:** 19.9%.

All statistics are based on the 2000 Census except the dollar figures given for per capita income, which are based on 1999 estimates.

Unemployment: 3.1%. **Median home value:** $50,300. **Median travel time to work:** 13.9 minutes.

TURNER COUNTY
PO Box 446   **Ph:** 605-297-3115
Parker, SD 57053   **Fax:** 605-297-3871

In southeastern SD, southwest of Sioux Falls; organized Jan 13, 1871 (prior to statehood) from Lincoln County and part of the now-defunct Jayne County. **Name Origin:** For John W. Turner (1800-83), member of the Dakota Territory legislature (1865-66; 1872) and a superintendent of public instruction.

Area (sq mi): 617.45 (land 616.82; water 0.63).

Pop: 8,849 (White 98.6%; Black or African American 0.1%; Hispanic or Latino 0.4%; Asian 0.2%; Other 0.8%). **Foreign born:** 0.5%. **Median age:** 40.5. **State rank:** 21. **Pop change 1990-2000:** +3.2%.

Income: per capita $17,343; median household $36,059. **Pop below poverty level:** 7.2%.

Unemployment: 3.3%. **Median home value:** $57,600. **Median travel time to work:** 24.4 minutes.

UNION COUNTY
PO Box 757   **Ph:** 605-356-2132
Elk Point, SD 57025   **Fax:** 605-356-3687

In southeastern SD, south of Sioux Falls; organized as Cole County Apr 10, 1862 (prior to statehood) from unorganized territory; name changed 1864. **Name Origin:** For support of the Union in the Civil War. Originally for Austin Cole, member of the first Territorial legislature.

Area (sq mi): 467.08 (land 460.38; water 6.7).

Pop: 12,584 (White 96%; Black or African American 0.3%; Hispanic or Latino 1.3%; Asian 1.3%; Other 1.5%). **Foreign born:** 2.4%. **Median age:** 36.9. **State rank:** 14. **Pop change 1990-2000:** +23.5%.

Income: per capita $24,355; median household $44,790. **Pop below poverty level:** 5.5%.

Unemployment: 4.1%. **Median home value:** $89,600. **Median travel time to work:** 17.9 minutes.

WALWORTH COUNTY
PO Box 199   **Ph:** 605-649-7878
Selby, SD 57472   **Fax:** 605-649-7867

In north-central SD, west of Aberdeen; created Jan 8, 1873 (prior to statehood) from territorial county. **Name Origin:** For Walworth County, WI, former home of early settlers.

Area (sq mi): 744.22 (land 707.81; water 36.41).

Pop: 5,974 (White 86.3%; Black or African American 0%; Hispanic or Latino 0.6%; Asian 0.2%; Other 13.3%). **Foreign born:** 0.7%. **Median age:** 42.8. **State rank:** 31. **Pop change 1990-2000:** -1.9%.

Income: per capita $15,492; median household $27,834. **Pop below poverty level:** 18.2%.

Unemployment: 3.4%. **Median home value:** $40,300. **Median travel time to work:** 12.7 minutes.

YANKTON COUNTY
410 Walnut St   **Ph:** 605-668-3080
Yankton, SD 57078
www.co.yankton.sd.us

On the southeastern border of SD, southwest of Sioux Falls; original county; organized Apr 5, 1862 (prior to statehood) from territorial county. **Name Origin:** For the city of Yankton.

Area (sq mi): 532.62 (land 521.55; water 11.07).

Pop: 21,652 (White 94.1%; Black or African American 1.2%; Hispanic or Latino 1.8%; Asian 0.4%; Other 3.2%). **Foreign born:** 1.5%. **Median age:** 37. **State rank:** 9. **Pop change 1990-2000:** +12.5%.

Income: per capita $17,312; median household $35,374. **Pop below poverty level:** 9.6%.

Unemployment: 3.3%. **Median home value:** $77,900. **Median travel time to work:** 14.4 minutes.

ZIEBACH COUNTY
PO Box 68   **Ph:** 605-365-5157
Dupree, SD 57623   **Fax:** 605-365-5204

In west-central SD, northwest of Pierre; organized Feb 1, 1911 from Pennington County. **Name Origin:** For Frank M. Ziebach (1830-1929), publisher of the *Weekly Dakotian*.

Area (sq mi): 1971.05 (land 1962.33; water 8.72).

Pop: 2,519 (White 26.4%; Black or African American 0%; Hispanic or Latino 1%; Asian 0.1%; Other 73.5%). **Foreign born:** 0.4%. **Median age:** 23.8. **State rank:** 57. **Pop change 1990-2000:** +13.5%.

Income: per capita $7,463; median household $18,063. **Pop below poverty level:** 49.9%.

Unemployment: 14.4%. **Median home value:** $38,300. **Median travel time to work:** 19.7 minutes.

Please see sample entry on inside front cover for detailed information about the statistics presented with each county listing.

TENNESSEE - Counties

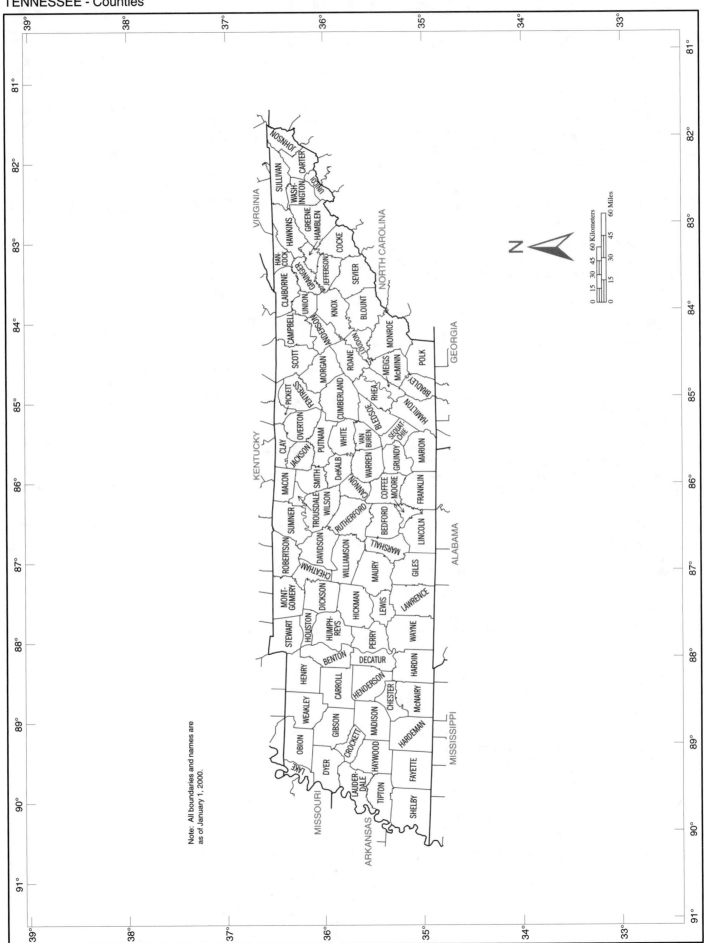

Note: All boundaries and names are
as of January 1, 2000.

Tennessee

TENNESSEE STATE INFORMATION

www.tennessee.gov   **Ph:** 615-741-3011

Area (sq mi): 42,143.27 (land 41,217.12; water 926.15).

Pop: 5,689,283 (White 79.2%; Black or African American 16.4%; Hispanic or Latino 2.2%; Asian 1%; Other 2.4%). **Foreign born:** 2.8%. **Median age:** 35.9. **Pop change 1990-2000:** +16.7%.

Income: per capita $19,393; median household $36,360. **Pop below poverty level:** 13.5%.

Unemployment: 4.6%. **Median home value:** $93,000. **Median travel time to work:** 24.5 minutes.

ANDERSON COUNTY

100 N Main St Rm 111   **Ph:** 865-457-5400
Clinton, TN 37716   **Fax:** 865-259-0116

In northeastern TN, west of Knoxville; organized Nov 6, 1801 from Knox and Grainger counties. **Name Origin:** For Maj. Joseph Anderson (1757-1837), U.S. senator from TN (1797-1815) and first comptroller of the U.S. Treasury (1815-36).

Area (sq mi): 344.82 (land 337.51; water 7.31).

Pop: 71,330 (White 92.7%; Black or African American 3.9%; Hispanic or Latino 1.1%; Asian 0.8%; Other 1.9%). **Foreign born:** 1.9%. **Median age:** 39.9. **State rank:** 15. **Pop change 1990-2000:** +4.5%.

Income: per capita $19,009; median household $35,483. **Pop below poverty level:** 13.1%.

Unemployment: 4%. **Median home value:** $87,500. **Median travel time to work:** 22.9 minutes.

BEDFORD COUNTY

104 Northside Sq   **Ph:** 931-684-1921
Shelbyville, TN 37160   **Fax:** 931-685-9590

In south-central TN, south of Murfreesboro; organized Dec 3, 1807 from Rutherford County and Indian lands. **Name Origin:** For Lt. Col. Thomas Bedford, an army officer.

Area (sq mi): 474.83 (land 473.67; water 1.17).

Pop: 37,586 (White 82.6%; Black or African American 8.5%; Hispanic or Latino 7.5%; Asian 0.5%; Other 4.3%). **Foreign born:** 6.4%. **Median age:** 34.9. **State rank:** 38. **Pop change 1990-2000:** +23.6%.

Income: per capita $16,698; median household $36,729. **Pop below poverty level:** 13.1%.

Unemployment: 5.8%. **Median home value:** $79,000. **Median travel time to work:** 24.1 minutes.

BENTON COUNTY

1 E Court Sq Rm 102   **Ph:** 731-584-6011
Camden, TN 38320   **Fax:** 731-584-4640

In northwestern TN, west of Nashville; organized 1835 from Henry and Humphreys counties. **Name Origin:** For David Benton, an 'old and respectable citizen of said county.'

Area (sq mi): 436.2 (land 394.84; water 41.37).

Pop: 16,537 (White 95.7%; Black or African American 2.1%; Hispanic or Latino 0.9%; Asian 0.2%; Other 1.2%). **Foreign born:** 0.7%. **Median age:** 41.6. **State rank:** 74. **Pop change 1990-2000:** +13.9%.

Income: per capita $14,646; median household $28,679. **Pop below poverty level:** 15.6%.

Unemployment: 7.3%. **Median home value:** $67,000. **Median travel time to work:** 27.1 minutes.

BLEDSOE COUNTY

104 N Frazier St   **Ph:** 423-447-6855
Pikeville, TN 37367   **Fax:** 423-447-7265

In east-central TN, north of Chattanooga; organized Nov 30, 1807 from Roane County and Indian lands. **Name Origin:** For either Anthony Bledsoe (1733-88), member of the VA legislature, active in establishing TN as a state; or for Maj. Abraham Bledsoe, an officer in the Revolutionary War.

Area (sq mi): 406.71 (land 406.32; water 0.4).

Pop: 12,367 (White 93.7%; Black or African American 3.7%; Hispanic or Latino 1.1%; Asian 0.1%; Other 1.7%). **Foreign born:** 0.4%. **Median age:** 37.4. **State rank:** 81. **Pop change 1990-2000:** +27.9%.

Income: per capita $13,889; median household $28,982. **Pop below poverty level:** 18.1%.

Unemployment: 5.1%. **Median home value:** $67,200. **Median travel time to work:** 33 minutes.

BLOUNT COUNTY

341 Court St   **Ph:** 865-273-5700
Maryville, TN 37804   **Fax:** 865-273-5705
www.korrnet.org/blountco

On southeastern border of TN, south of Knoxville; organized Jul 11, 1795 (prior to statehood) from Knox County. **Name Origin:**

Please see sample entry on inside front cover for detailed information about the statistics presented with each county listing.

For William Blount (1749-1800), territorial governor of TN (1790-96) and U.S. senator from TN (1796-97).

Area (sq mi): 566.65 (land 558.56; water 8.08).

Pop: 105,823 (White 94.1%; Black or African American 2.9%; Hispanic or Latino 1.1%; Asian 0.7%; Other 1.6%). **Foreign born:** 1.5%. **Median age:** 38.4. **State rank:** 11. **Pop change 1990-2000:** +23.1%.

Income: per capita $19,416; median household $37,862. **Pop below poverty level:** 9.7%.

Unemployment: 4%. **Median home value:** $103,900. **Median travel time to work:** 24 minutes.

BRADLEY COUNTY
155 Ocoee St   **Ph:** 423-476-0520
Cleveland, TN 37311   **Fax:** 423-478-8845
www.bradleyco.net

On the southwestern border of TN, east of Chattanooga; organized Feb 10, 1836 from Indian lands. **Name Origin:** For Lt. Col. Edward Bradley (?-1829), an officer in the War of 1812 and the Southern Indian wars.

Area (sq mi): 331.5 (land 328.72; water 2.78).

Pop: 87,965 (White 92%; Black or African American 4%; Hispanic or Latino 2.1%; Asian 0.6%; Other 2.5%). **Foreign born:** 2.2%. **Median age:** 35.5. **State rank:** 14. **Pop change 1990-2000:** +19.3%.

Income: per capita $18,108; median household $35,034. **Pop below poverty level:** 12.2%.

Unemployment: 3.8%. **Median home value:** $91,700. **Median travel time to work:** 20.7 minutes.

CAMPBELL COUNTY
PO Box 13   **Ph:** 423-562-4985
Jacksboro, TN 37757   **Fax:** 423-566-3852

On the central northern border of TN, north of Oak Ridge; organized Sep 11, 1806 from Anderson and Claiborne counties. **Name Origin:** For George Washington Campbell (1769-1848), U.S. senator from TN (1811-14; 1815-18), U.S. secretary of the treasury (1814), and ambassador to Russia (1818-20). Others claim Arthur Campbell, a negotiator with the Indians.

Area (sq mi): 498.25 (land 480.07; water 18.19).

Pop: 39,854 (White 97.6%; Black or African American 0.3%; Hispanic or Latino 0.7%; Asian 0.2%; Other 1.4%). **Foreign born:** 0.8%. **Median age:** 38.3. **State rank:** 33. **Pop change 1990-2000:** +13.6%.

Income: per capita $13,301; median household $25,285. **Pop below poverty level:** 22.8%.

Unemployment: 5.8%. **Median home value:** $65,600. **Median travel time to work:** 30.8 minutes.

CANNON COUNTY
County Courthouse Public Sq   **Ph:** 615-563-4278
Woodbury, TN 37190   **Fax:** 615-563-1289

In central TN, southeast of Nashville; organized Jan 31, 1836 from Rutherford, Warren, and Smith counties. **Name Origin:** For Col.

Newton Cannon (1781-1842), U.S. representative from TN (1814-17; 1819-23) and governor (1836-39).

Area (sq mi): 265.71 (land 265.64; water 0.06).

Pop: 12,826 (White 96.1%; Black or African American 1.5%; Hispanic or Latino 1.2%; Asian 0.1%; Other 1.5%). **Foreign born:** 0.8%. **Median age:** 36.8. **State rank:** 79. **Pop change 1990-2000:** +22.5%.

Income: per capita $16,405; median household $32,809. **Pop below poverty level:** 12.8%.

Unemployment: 4.9%. **Median home value:** $79,600. **Median travel time to work:** 32.7 minutes.

CARROLL COUNTY
625 High St Suite 103   **Ph:** 731-986-1961
Huntingdon, TN 38344   **Fax:** 731-986-1978

In western TN, northeast of Jackson; organized Nov 7, 1821 from Western District (Indian lands). **Name Origin:** For Gen. William Carroll (1788-1844), officer in the Battle of New Orleans (1815) and TN governor (1821-27; 1829-35).

Area (sq mi): 599.86 (land 599.02; water 0.84).

Pop: 29,475 (White 87%; Black or African American 10.3%; Hispanic or Latino 1.3%; Asian 0.2%; Other 1.8%). **Foreign born:** 1.1%. **Median age:** 39. **State rank:** 47. **Pop change 1990-2000:** +7.1%.

Income: per capita $16,251; median household $30,463. **Pop below poverty level:** 13.9%.

Unemployment: 9.5%. **Median home value:** $60,900. **Median travel time to work:** 24.1 minutes.

CARTER COUNTY
801 E Elk Ave Courthouse Bldg   **Ph:** 423-542-1814
Elizabethton, TN 37643   **Fax:** 423-542-9279

On the northeastern border of TN, east of Johnson City; organized as Carteret County Apr 9, 1796 from Washington County; name changed later. **Name Origin:** For Col. Landon Carter (1760-1800), officer in the Revolutionary and Indian wars; officeholder in NC, the territories, and in TN, whose statehood he advocated.

Area (sq mi): 347.62 (land 341.05; water 6.57).

Pop: 56,742 (White 96.9%; Black or African American 1%; Hispanic or Latino 0.9%; Asian 0.3%; Other 1.3%). **Foreign born:** 0.8%. **Median age:** 38.5. **State rank:** 21. **Pop change 1990-2000:** +10.2%.

Income: per capita $14,678; median household $27,371. **Pop below poverty level:** 16.9%.

Unemployment: 4.8%. **Median home value:** $77,300. **Median travel time to work:** 24.1 minutes.

CHEATHAM COUNTY
100 Public Sq Suite 105   **Ph:** 615-792-4316
Ashland City, TN 37015   **Fax:** 615-792-2001
www.cheathamcounty.net

In west-central TN, northwest of Nashville; organized Feb 28, 1856 from Dickson, Montgomery, Davidson, and Robertson counties. **Name Origin:** Probably for Edwin S. Cheatham, speaker of the TN senate when county was formed. Others claim Gen. Benjamin F.

All statistics are based on the 2000 Census except the dollar figures given for per capita income, which are based on 1999 estimates.

Cheatham (1820-86), an officer in the Mexican-American War and for the Confederacy; or Nathaniel Cheatham.

Area (sq mi): 307.13 (land 302.66; water 4.47).

Pop: 35,912 (White 96.1%; Black or African American 1.5%; Hispanic or Latino 1.2%; Asian 0.2%; Other 1.5%). **Foreign born:** 1.1%. **Median age:** 35.3. **State rank:** 40. **Pop change 1990-2000:** +32.3%.

Income: per capita $18,882; median household $45,836. **Pop below poverty level:** 7.4%.

Unemployment: 2.8%. **Median home value:** $109,100. **Median travel time to work:** 32.9 minutes.

CHESTER COUNTY
PO Box 205   **Ph:** 731-989-2233
Henderson, TN 38340   **Fax:** 731-989-9602

In southwestern TN, southeast of Jackson; organized Mar 4, 1879 from Hardeman, Madison, McNairy, and Henderson counties. **Name Origin:** For Col. Robert I. Chester (1793-c.1860), officer in the Republic of Texas army and TN state legislator.

Area (sq mi): 288.74 (land 288.52; water 0.22).

Pop: 15,540 (White 87.6%; Black or African American 10%; Hispanic or Latino 1%; Asian 0.2%; Other 1.6%). **Foreign born:** 0.5%. **Median age:** 34.1. **State rank:** 76. **Pop change 1990-2000:** +21.2%.

Income: per capita $15,756; median household $34,349. **Pop below poverty level:** 14.4%.

Unemployment: 4.1%. **Median home value:** $78,900. **Median travel time to work:** 26.1 minutes.

CLAIBORNE COUNTY
1740 Main St   **Ph:** 423-626-3284
Tazewell, TN 37879   **Fax:** 423-626-3604

On central northern border of TN, north of Knoxville; organized Oct 29, 1801 from Grainger and Hawkins counties. **Name Origin:** For William Charles Coles Claiborne (1775-1817), governor of the Mississippi Territory (1801-05), of the Orleans Territory (1804-12), and of LA (1812-16), and U.S. representative from TN (1797-1801).

Area (sq mi): 441.55 (land 434.28; water 7.27).

Pop: 29,862 (White 97.4%; Black or African American 0.8%; Hispanic or Latino 0.6%; Asian 0.3%; Other 1.1%). **Foreign born:** 0.9%. **Median age:** 37.4. **State rank:** 46. **Pop change 1990-2000:** +14.3%.

Income: per capita $13,032; median household $25,782. **Pop below poverty level:** 22.6%.

Unemployment: 5%. **Median home value:** $72,000. **Median travel time to work:** 27.7 minutes.

CLAY COUNTY
PO Box 387   **Ph:** 931-243-2161
Celina, TN 38551   **Fax:** 931-243-2436

On the central northern border of TN, northeast of Nashville; organized Jun 24, 1870 from Jackson and Overton counties. **Name Origin:** For Henry Clay (1777-1852), U.S. senator from KY, known as the 'Great Pacificator' for his advocacy of compromise to avert national crises.

Area (sq mi): 259.25 (land 236.11; water 23.14).

Pop: 7,976 (White 96.1%; Black or African American 1.4%; Hispanic or Latino 1.4%; Asian 0.1%; Other 1.6%). **Foreign born:** 1.1%. **Median age:** 39.9. **State rank:** 88. **Pop change 1990-2000:** +10.2%.

Income: per capita $13,320; median household $23,958. **Pop below poverty level:** 19.1%.

Unemployment: 10%. **Median home value:** $56,400. **Median travel time to work:** 29 minutes.

COCKE COUNTY
360 E Main St Rm 146 Courthouse Annex   **Ph:** 423-623-8791
Newport, TN 37821   **Fax:** 423-623-8792
www.cockecounty.com

On the central eastern border of TN, east of Knoxville; organized Aug 9, 1797 from Jefferson County. **Name Origin:** For William Cocke (1747-1828), explorer with Daniel Boone (c.1734-1820), TN legislator and judge, and U.S. senator (1796-97; 1799-1805).

Area (sq mi): 443.15 (land 434.4; water 8.75).

Pop: 33,565 (White 95.5%; Black or African American 2%; Hispanic or Latino 1.1%; Asian 0.2%; Other 1.7%). **Foreign born:** 0.8%. **Median age:** 38.6. **State rank:** 42. **Pop change 1990-2000:** +15.2%.

Income: per capita $13,881; median household $25,553. **Pop below poverty level:** 22.5%.

Unemployment: 7.4%. **Median home value:** $73,600. **Median travel time to work:** 28.5 minutes.

COFFEE COUNTY
1327 McArthur St   **Ph:** 931-723-5106
Manchester, TN 37355   **Fax:** 931-723-8248

In south-central TN, southeast of Murfreesboro; organized Jan 8, 1836 from Franklin, Warren, and Bedford counties. **Name Origin:** For Gen. John Coffee (1772-1833), officer in the War of 1812 who later oversaw the removal of the Choctaws and Chickasaws to OK Territory.

Area (sq mi): 434.46 (land 428.84; water 5.62).

Pop: 48,014 (White 92.3%; Black or African American 3.6%; Hispanic or Latino 2.2%; Asian 0.7%; Other 2.2%). **Foreign born:** 2.3%. **Median age:** 37.5. **State rank:** 28. **Pop change 1990-2000:** +19%.

Income: per capita $18,137; median household $34,898. **Pop below poverty level:** 14.3%.

Unemployment: 4.4%. **Median home value:** $82,200. **Median travel time to work:** 22.4 minutes.

CROCKETT COUNTY
1 S Bellis St Suite 3   **Ph:** 731-696-5460
Alamo, TN 38001   **Fax:** 731-696-4101

In central-western TN, northwest of Jackson; established Dec 20, 1845 from Dyer, Madison, Gibson, and Haywood counties. **Name Origin:** For David 'Davy' Crockett (1786-1836), soldier, scout, and U.S. representative from TN (1827-31; 1833-35), killed at the Alamo.

Area (sq mi): 265.47 (land 265.27; water 0.21).

Please see sample entry on inside front cover for detailed information about the statistics presented with each county listing.

Pop: 14,532 (White 79.5%; Black or African American 14.4%; Hispanic or Latino 5.5%; Asian 0.1%; Other 3.6%). **Foreign born:** 3.9%. **Median age:** 37.4. **State rank:** 77. **Pop change 1990-2000:** +8.6%.

Income: per capita $14,600; median household $30,015. **Pop below poverty level:** 16.9%.

Unemployment: 5.6%. **Median home value:** $65,200. **Median travel time to work:** 20.9 minutes.

CUMBERLAND COUNTY

2 N Main St Suite 206   **Ph:** 931-484-6442
Crossville, TN 38555   **Fax:** 931-484-6440

In east-central TN, west of Oak Ridge; organized Nov 16, 1855 from Bledsoe, Morgan, Roane, White, Putnam, Rhea, Van Buren, and Fentress counties. **Name Origin:** For William Augustus, Duke of Cumberland (1721-65), British general and second son of George II of England.

Area (sq mi): 684.95 (land 681.61; water 3.34).

Pop: 46,802 (White 97.4%; Black or African American 0.1%; Hispanic or Latino 1.2%; Asian 0.2%; Other 1.6%). **Foreign born:** 1.9%. **Median age:** 42.5. **State rank:** 29. **Pop change 1990-2000:** +34.7%.

Income: per capita $16,808; median household $30,901. **Pop below poverty level:** 14.7%.

Unemployment: 6.4%. **Median home value:** $91,400. **Median travel time to work:** 23 minutes.

DAVIDSON COUNTY

205 Metro Courthouse   **Ph:** 615-862-6770
Nashville, TN 37201   **Fax:** 615-862-6774
www.nashville.gov

In west-central TN, northwest of Murfreesboro; organized Apr 18, 1783 (prior to statehood) from Washington County. **Name Origin:** For Gen. William Lee Davidson (1746-81), officer killed during the Revolutionary War.

Area (sq mi): 526.11 (land 502.26; water 23.85).

Pop: 569,891 (White 65.1%; Black or African American 25.9%; Hispanic or Latino 4.6%; Asian 2.3%; Other 4.8%). **Foreign born:** 6.9%. **Median age:** 34.1. **State rank:** 2. **Pop change 1990-2000:** +11.6%.

Income: per capita $23,069; median household $39,797. **Pop below poverty level:** 13%.

Unemployment: 3.1%. **Median home value:** $115,800. **Median travel time to work:** 23.3 minutes.

DECATUR COUNTY

PO Box 488   **Ph:** 731-852-2131
Decaturville, TN 38329   **Fax:** 731-852-2130

In western TN, southeast of Jackson; organized Nov 1845 from Perry County. **Name Origin:** For Stephen Decatur (1779-1820), U.S. naval officer during the War of 1812 and in actions against the Barbary pirates near Tripoli, who said, '. . . may she always be in the right; but our country, right or wrong.'

Area (sq mi): 344.91 (land 333.9; water 11.01).

Pop: 11,731 (White 93.4%; Black or African American 3.5%; Hispanic or Latino 2%; Asian 0.2%; Other 2.2%). **Foreign born:** 1.7%. **Median age:** 41.2. **State rank:** 82. **Pop change 1990-2000:** +12%.

Income: per capita $17,285; median household $28,741. **Pop below poverty level:** 16%.

Unemployment: 8%. **Median home value:** $58,300. **Median travel time to work:** 25.7 minutes.

DEKALB COUNTY

1 Public Sq Rm 205   **Ph:** 615-597-5177
Smithville, TN 37166   **Fax:** 615-597-1404

In east-central TN, southeast of Nashville; organized 1837 from Cannon, Warren, White, Wilson, and Jackson counties. **Name Origin:** For Johann, Baron de Kalb (1721-80), German-born French soldier who fought with the Americans during the Revolutionary War.

Area (sq mi): 328.98 (land 304.57; water 24.41).

Pop: 17,423 (White 93.8%; Black or African American 1.4%; Hispanic or Latino 3.6%; Asian 0.1%; Other 2.8%). **Foreign born:** 2.7%. **Median age:** 37.7. **State rank:** 71. **Pop change 1990-2000:** +21.3%.

Income: per capita $17,217; median household $30,359. **Pop below poverty level:** 17%.

Unemployment: 5.4%. **Median home value:** $82,600. **Median travel time to work:** 24.3 minutes.

DICKSON COUNTY

PO Box 267   **Ph:** 615-789-4171
Charlotte, TN 37036   **Fax:** 615-789-6075

In west-central TN, west of Nashville; organized Oct 25, 1803 from Montgomery and Robertson counties. **Name Origin:** For William Dickson (1770-1816), physician, TN legislator, and U.S. representative (1801-07).

Area (sq mi): 491.28 (land 489.87; water 1.42).

Pop: 43,156 (White 92.7%; Black or African American 4.6%; Hispanic or Latino 1.1%; Asian 0.3%; Other 1.9%). **Foreign born:** 0.7%. **Median age:** 35.7. **State rank:** 31. **Pop change 1990-2000:** +23.1%.

Income: per capita $18,043; median household $39,056. **Pop below poverty level:** 10.2%.

Unemployment: 4.2%. **Median home value:** $96,200. **Median travel time to work:** 30.5 minutes.

DYER COUNTY

PO Box 1360   **Ph:** 731-286-7814
Dyersburg, TN 38025   **Fax:** 731-288-7719

On northwestern border of TN, northwest of Jackson; organized Oct 16, 1823 from Western District (Indian lands). **Name Origin:** For Robert H. Dyer, a prominent fighter in the Indian wars.

Area (sq mi): 526.48 (land 510.5; water 15.98).

Pop: 37,279 (White 84.8%; Black or African American 12.9%; Hispanic or Latino 1.2%; Asian 0.3%; Other 1.3%). **Foreign born:** 1.3%. **Median age:** 36.5. **State rank:** 39. **Pop change 1990-2000:** +7%.

All statistics are based on the 2000 Census except the dollar figures given for per capita income, which are based on 1999 estimates.

Income: per capita $16,451; median household $32,788. **Pop below poverty level:** 15.9%.

Unemployment: 7.2%. **Median home value:** $74,900. **Median travel time to work:** 19.1 minutes.

FAYETTE COUNTY

PO Box 218   **Ph:** 901-465-5213
Somerville, TN 38068   **Fax:** 901-465-5293

On the southwestern border of TN, east of Memphis; organized Sep 29, 1824 from Shelby and Hardeman counties. **Name Origin:** For the Marquis de Lafayette (1757-1834), French statesman and soldier who fought with the Americans during the Revolutionary War.

Area (sq mi): 706.23 (land 704.5; water 1.73).

Pop: 28,806 (White 62%; Black or African American 35.9%; Hispanic or Latino 1%; Asian 0.2%; Other 1.4%). **Foreign born:** 0.7%. **Median age:** 38.1. **State rank:** 49. **Pop change 1990-2000:** +12.7%.

Income: per capita $17,969; median household $40,279. **Pop below poverty level:** 14.3%.

Unemployment: 5.5%. **Median home value:** $100,100. **Median travel time to work:** 35.4 minutes.

FENTRESS COUNTY

PO Box 823   **Ph:** 931-879-8014
Jamestown, TN 38556   **Fax:** 931-879-8438

In north-central TN, northwest of Oak Ridge; organized Nov 28, 1823 from Overton, White, and Morgan counties. **Name Origin:** For James Fentress, speaker of the TN House of Representatives.

Area (sq mi): 498.97 (land 498.64; water 0.33).

Pop: 16,625 (White 98.8%; Black or African American 0.1%; Hispanic or Latino 0.5%; Asian 0.1%; Other 0.6%). **Foreign born:** 0.4%. **Median age:** 38. **State rank:** 73. **Pop change 1990-2000:** +13.3%.

Income: per capita $12,999; median household $23,238. **Pop below poverty level:** 23.1%.

Unemployment: 11%. **Median home value:** $56,500. **Median travel time to work:** 29.5 minutes.

FRANKLIN COUNTY

1 S Jefferson St   **Ph:** 931-967-2541
Winchester, TN 37398   **Fax:** 931-962-3394

On the central southern border of TN, west of Chattanooga; organized Dec 3, 1807 from Rutherford County and Indian lands. **Name Origin:** For Benjamin Franklin (1706-90), U.S. patriot, diplomat, and statesman.

Area (sq mi): 575.77 (land 554.52; water 21.25).

Pop: 39,270 (White 91.4%; Black or African American 5.5%; Hispanic or Latino 1.6%; Asian 0.4%; Other 1.9%). **Foreign born:** 1.4%. **Median age:** 38.1. **State rank:** 34. **Pop change 1990-2000:** +13.1%.

Income: per capita $17,987; median household $36,044. **Pop below poverty level:** 13.2%.

Unemployment: 3.8%. **Median home value:** $82,600. **Median travel time to work:** 24.1 minutes.

GIBSON COUNTY

1 Court Sq Suite 100   **Ph:** 731-855-7642
Trenton, TN 38382   **Fax:** 731-855-7643

In northwestern TN, north of Jackson; organized Oct 21, 1823 from Western District (Indian lands). **Name Origin:** For Maj. John Gibson, an officer in Gen. Andrew Jackson's (1767-1845) Natchez expedition (1812-13).

Area (sq mi): 603.59 (land 602.67; water 0.92).

Pop: 48,152 (White 78.2%; Black or African American 19.7%; Hispanic or Latino 1.1%; Asian 0.1%; Other 1.5%). **Foreign born:** 0.8%. **Median age:** 38.8. **State rank:** 27. **Pop change 1990-2000:** +4%.

Income: per capita $16,320; median household $31,105. **Pop below poverty level:** 12.8%.

Unemployment: 9.6%. **Median home value:** $66,300. **Median travel time to work:** 22.1 minutes.

GILES COUNTY

1 Public Sq   **Ph:** 931-363-1509
Pulaski, TN 38478   **Fax:** 931-424-4795

On the central southern border of TN, south of Columbia; organized Nov 14, 1809 from Maury County. **Name Origin:** For William Branch Giles (1762-1830), U.S. senator from VA (1804-15) and governor (1827-30).

Area (sq mi): 611.17 (land 610.93; water 0.25).

Pop: 29,447 (White 85.9%; Black or African American 11.8%; Hispanic or Latino 0.9%; Asian 0.3%; Other 1.4%). **Foreign born:** 0.9%. **Median age:** 38. **State rank:** 48. **Pop change 1990-2000:** +14.4%.

Income: per capita $17,543; median household $34,824. **Pop below poverty level:** 11.7%.

Unemployment: 6.1%. **Median home value:** $72,900. **Median travel time to work:** 25.1 minutes.

GRAINGER COUNTY

Hwy 11 W PO Box 126 Courthouse Sq   **Ph:** 865-828-3513
Rutledge, TN 37861   **Fax:** 865-828-4284

In northeastern TN, northeast of Knoxville; organized Apr 22, 1796 from Hawkins County. **Name Origin:** For Mary Grainger Blount, wife of William Blount (1749-1800), governor (1790-95) of the territory south of the Ohio River, present-day TN.

Area (sq mi): 302.44 (land 280.33; water 22.11).

Pop: 20,659 (White 97.7%; Black or African American 0.3%; Hispanic or Latino 1.1%; Asian 0.1%; Other 1.2%). **Foreign born:** 1.1%. **Median age:** 37.7. **State rank:** 61. **Pop change 1990-2000:** +20.8%.

Income: per capita $14,505; median household $27,997. **Pop below poverty level:** 18.7%.

Unemployment: 5.7%. **Median home value:** $74,000. **Median travel time to work:** 29.1 minutes.

Please see sample entry on inside front cover for detailed information about the statistics presented with each county listing.

GREENE COUNTY

204 N Cutler St Suite 200   **Ph:** 423-798-1708
Greeneville, TN 37745   **Fax:** 423-798-1822

On the northeastern border of TN, west of Johnson City; organized Apr 18, 1783 (prior to statehood) from Washington County. **Name Origin:** For Gen. Nathanael Greene (1742-86), hero of the Revolutionary War, quartermaster general (1778-80), and commander of the Army of the South (1780).

Area (sq mi): 624.11 (land 621.69; water 2.42).

Pop: 62,909 (White 95.9%; Black or African American 2.1%; Hispanic or Latino 1%; Asian 0.3%; Other 1.2%). **Foreign born:** 1.3%. **Median age:** 38.9. **State rank:** 18. **Pop change 1990-2000:** +12.6%.

Income: per capita $15,746; median household $30,382. **Pop below poverty level:** 14.5%.

Unemployment: 7.2%. **Median home value:** $80,400. **Median travel time to work:** 22.4 minutes.

GRUNDY COUNTY

PO Box 177   **Ph:** 931-692-3718
Altamont, TN 37301   **Fax:** 931-692-3721

In east-central TN, northeast of Chattanooga; organized Jan 29, 1844 from Franklin and Warren counties. **Name Origin:** For Felix Grundy (1777-1840), U.S. representative from TN (1811-15) who played a leading part in bringing on and sustaining the War of 1812.

Area (sq mi): 361.14 (land 360.56; water 0.58).

Pop: 14,332 (White 97.8%; Black or African American 0.1%; Hispanic or Latino 1%; Asian 0.2%; Other 1.3%). **Foreign born:** 0.7%. **Median age:** 36.6. **State rank:** 78. **Pop change 1990-2000:** +7.3%.

Income: per capita $12,039; median household $22,959. **Pop below poverty level:** 25.8%.

Unemployment: 5.9%. **Median home value:** $52,300. **Median travel time to work:** 32.2 minutes.

HAMBLEN COUNTY

511 W 2nd North St   **Ph:** 423-586-1993
Morristown, TN 37814   **Fax:** 423-318-2508

In northeastern TN, northeast of Knoxville; organized Jun 8, 1870 from Grainger, Hawkins, and Jefferson counties. **Name Origin:** For Hezekiah Hamblen (1775-1854?), member of the Hawkins County court.

Area (sq mi): 175.77 (land 161.03; water 14.74).

Pop: 58,128 (White 88.5%; Black or African American 4.1%; Hispanic or Latino 5.7%; Asian 0.6%; Other 4.6%). **Foreign born:** 5.3%. **Median age:** 37.1. **State rank:** 20. **Pop change 1990-2000:** +15.2%.

Income: per capita $17,743; median household $32,350. **Pop below poverty level:** 14.4%.

Unemployment: 6.2%. **Median home value:** $85,300. **Median travel time to work:** 19.6 minutes.

HAMILTON COUNTY

County Courthouse Rm 201   **Ph:** 423-209-6500
Chattanooga, TN 37402   **Fax:** 423-209-6501
www.hamiltontn.gov

On the southeastern border of TN, west of Cleveland; organized Oct 25, 1819 from Rhea County and Indian lands, and in January 1920 annexed James County, which was organized 1871 from Hamilton and Bradley counties. **Name Origin:** For Alexander Hamilton (1757-1804), first U.S. secretary of the treasury (1789-95).

Area (sq mi): 575.72 (land 542.44; water 33.28).

Pop: 307,896 (White 75.5%; Black or African American 20.1%; Hispanic or Latino 1.8%; Asian 1.3%; Other 2.3%). **Foreign born:** 3%. **Median age:** 37.4. **State rank:** 4. **Pop change 1990-2000:** +7.8%.

Income: per capita $21,593; median household $38,930. **Pop below poverty level:** 12.1%.

Unemployment: 3%. **Median home value:** $94,700. **Median travel time to work:** 22.6 minutes.

HANCOCK COUNTY

PO Box 575   **Ph:** 423-733-2519
Sneedville, TN 37869   **Fax:** 423-733-4509

On the northeastern border of TN, west of Kingsport; organized Jan 7, 1844 from Claiborne and Hawkins counties. **Name Origin:** For John Hancock (1737-93), noted signer of the Declaration of Independence, governor of MA (1780-85; 1787-93), and statesman.

Area (sq mi): 223.5 (land 222.29; water 1.21).

Pop: 6,786 (White 97.6%; Black or African American 0.5%; Hispanic or Latino 0.4%; Asian 0.1%; Other 1.4%). **Foreign born:** 0.3%. **Median age:** 39.2. **State rank:** 92. **Pop change 1990-2000:** +0.7%.

Income: per capita $11,986; median household $19,760. **Pop below poverty level:** 29.4%.

Unemployment: 7.4%. **Median home value:** $53,900. **Median travel time to work:** 32.7 minutes.

HARDEMAN COUNTY

100 N Main St   **Ph:** 731-658-3541
Bolivar, TN 38008   **Fax:** 731-658-3482

On the southwestern border of TN, south of Jackson; organized Oct 16, 1823 from Hardin County and Western District (Indian lands). **Name Origin:** For Col. Thomas Jones Hardeman (1788-1854), TN officer in the War of 1812, later a Texas patriot and legislator.

Area (sq mi): 670.39 (land 667.55; water 2.84).

Pop: 28,105 (White 56.9%; Black or African American 41%; Hispanic or Latino 1%; Asian 0.3%; Other 1.4%). **Foreign born:** 0.7%. **Median age:** 36. **State rank:** 51. **Pop change 1990-2000:** +20.2%.

Income: per capita $13,349; median household $29,111. **Pop below poverty level:** 19.7%.

Unemployment: 8.9%. **Median home value:** $59,900. **Median travel time to work:** 29.4 minutes.

All statistics are based on the 2000 Census except the dollar figures given for per capita income, which are based on 1999 estimates.

HARDIN COUNTY

601 Main St   **Ph:** 731-925-3921
Savannah, TN 38372   **Fax:** 731-926-4313

On the southwestern border of TN, southeast of Jackson; organized Nov 13, 1819 from Western District (Indian lands). **Name Origin:** For Joseph Hardin, a soldier in the Revolutionary War and a TN legislator.

Area (sq mi): 596.31 (land 577.86; water 18.45).

Pop: 25,578 (White 94.2%; Black or African American 3.7%; Hispanic or Latino 1%; Asian 0.2%; Other 1.2%). **Foreign born:** 0.7%. **Median age:** 39.8. **State rank:** 55. **Pop change 1990-2000:** +13%.

Income: per capita $15,598; median household $27,819. **Pop below poverty level:** 18.8%.

Unemployment: 6%. **Median home value:** $69,200. **Median travel time to work:** 24 minutes.

HAWKINS COUNTY

PO Box 790   **Ph:** 423-272-7002
Rogersville, TN 37857   **Fax:** 423-272-5801

On the northeastern border of TN, west of Kingsport; organized Nov 18, 1786 (prior to statehood) from Sullivan County. **Name Origin:** For Benjamin Hawkins (1754-1816), French interpreter for George Washington (1732-99), member of the Continental Congress (1781-84; 1786-87), U.S. senator from NC (1789-95), and Indian agent for all tribes south of the Ohio River.

Area (sq mi): 499.63 (land 486.66; water 12.97).

Pop: 53,563 (White 96.7%; Black or African American 1.5%; Hispanic or Latino 0.8%; Asian 0.2%; Other 1%). **Foreign born:** 0.7%. **Median age:** 37.8. **State rank:** 23. **Pop change 1990-2000:** +20.2%.

Income: per capita $16,073; median household $31,300. **Pop below poverty level:** 15.8%.

Unemployment: 5.6%. **Median home value:** $82,500. **Median travel time to work:** 24.7 minutes.

HAYWOOD COUNTY

1 N Washington St   **Ph:** 731-772-1432
Brownsville, TN 38012   **Fax:** 731-772-3864

In southwestern TN, west of Jackson; organized Nov 3, 1823 from Western District (Indian lands). **Name Origin:** For John Haywood (1753-1826), NC attorney-general (1791-94) and TN supreme court judge (1816-26).

Area (sq mi): 534.15 (land 533.2; water 0.95).

Pop: 19,797 (White 45.9%; Black or African American 51%; Hispanic or Latino 2.6%; Asian 0.1%; Other 2.2%). **Foreign born:** 1.7%. **Median age:** 35.3. **State rank:** 64. **Pop change 1990-2000:** +1.9%.

Income: per capita $14,669; median household $27,671. **Pop below poverty level:** 19.5%.

Unemployment: 9.3%. **Median home value:** $68,400. **Median travel time to work:** 24 minutes.

HENDERSON COUNTY

PO Box 40   **Ph:** 731-968-2856
Lexington, TN 38351   **Fax:** 731-968-6644

In western TN, east of Jackson; organized Nov 7, 1821 from Western District (Indian lands). **Name Origin:** For James Henderson, an officer under the command of Andrew Jackson (1767-1845) in the War of 1812.

Area (sq mi): 525.91 (land 520.02; water 5.89).

Pop: 25,522 (White 89.9%; Black or African American 8%; Hispanic or Latino 1%; Asian 0.1%; Other 1.3%). **Foreign born:** 0.7%. **Median age:** 37.3. **State rank:** 56. **Pop change 1990-2000:** +16.8%.

Income: per capita $17,019; median household $32,057. **Pop below poverty level:** 12.4%.

Unemployment: 6.8%. **Median home value:** $74,000. **Median travel time to work:** 24.6 minutes.

HENRY COUNTY

101 W Washington St Suite 100 PO Box 24 **Ph:** 731-642-2412
Paris, TN 38242   **Fax:** 731-644-0947

On northwestern border of TN, southwest of Clarksville; organized Nov 7, 1821 from Western District (Indian lands). **Name Origin:** For Patrick Henry (1736-99), patriot, governor of VA (1776-79; 1784-86), and statesman, famous for declaring, 'Give me liberty or give me death.'

Area (sq mi): 593.45 (land 561.68; water 31.77).

Pop: 31,115 (White 88.7%; Black or African American 9%; Hispanic or Latino 1%; Asian 0.3%; Other 1.5%). **Foreign born:** 1%. **Median age:** 40.9. **State rank:** 45. **Pop change 1990-2000:** +11.6%.

Income: per capita $15,855; median household $30,169. **Pop below poverty level:** 14.3%.

Unemployment: 6.4%. **Median home value:** $75,800. **Median travel time to work:** 19.9 minutes.

HICKMAN COUNTY

101 S Public Sq   **Ph:** 931-729-2621
Centerville, TN 37033   **Fax:** 931-729-9951

In west-central TN, southwest of Nashville; organized Dec 3, 1807 from Dickson County. **Name Origin:** For Edwin Hickman (?-1791), American explorer killed by Indians.

Area (sq mi): 612.7 (land 612.52; water 0.18).

Pop: 22,295 (White 93.1%; Black or African American 4.5%; Hispanic or Latino 1%; Asian 0.1%; Other 1.7%). **Foreign born:** 0.8%. **Median age:** 36.3. **State rank:** 59. **Pop change 1990-2000:** +33.1%.

Income: per capita $14,446; median household $31,013. **Pop below poverty level:** 14.3%.

Unemployment: 5.6%. **Median home value:** $79,600. **Median travel time to work:** 36.7 minutes.

HOUSTON COUNTY

PO Box 388   **Ph:** 931-289-4165
Erin, TN 37061   **Fax:** 931-289-2603

In west-central TN, southwest of Clarksville; organized Jan 23, 1871 from Dickson, Montgomery, Stewart, and Humphreys counties. **Name Origin:** For Samuel Houston (1793-1863), governor of

Please see sample entry on inside front cover for detailed information about the statistics presented with each county listing.

519

TN (1827-29), president of the Republic of Texas (1836-38; 1841-44), U.S. senator from TX (1846-59), and governor (1859-61).

Area (sq mi): 206.92 (land 200.21; water 6.71).

Pop: 8,088 (White 94.1%; Black or African American 3.3%; Hispanic or Latino 1.2%; Asian 0.1%; Other 2.1%). **Foreign born:** 1.6%. **Median age:** 39.5. **State rank:** 87. **Pop change 1990-2000:** +15.2%.

Income: per capita $15,614; median household $29,968. **Pop below poverty level:** 18.1%.

Unemployment: 10.4%. **Median home value:** $63,300. **Median travel time to work:** 32 minutes.

HUMPHREYS COUNTY

Courthouse Annex Rm 1   **Ph:** 931-296-7795
Waverly, TN 37185   **Fax:** 931-296-5011

In west-central TN, west of Nashville; organized Oct 19, 1809 from Stewart County. **Name Origin:** For Parry Wayne Humphreys (1780-1839), TN superior court judge (1807-13; 1818-36) and U.S. representative (1813-15).

Area (sq mi): 556.72 (land 532.22; water 24.5).

Pop: 17,929 (White 95%; Black or African American 2.9%; Hispanic or Latino 0.8%; Asian 0.3%; Other 1.3%). **Foreign born:** 0.9%. **Median age:** 39. **State rank:** 66. **Pop change 1990-2000:** +13.5%.

Income: per capita $17,757; median household $35,786. **Pop below poverty level:** 10.8%.

Unemployment: 7.5%. **Median home value:** $76,000. **Median travel time to work:** 29.8 minutes.

JACKSON COUNTY

PO Box 617   **Ph:** 931-268-9888
Gainesboro, TN 38562   **Fax:** 931-268-9060

In north-central TN, northeast of Nashville; organized Nov 6, 1801 from Smith County and Indian lands. **Name Origin:** For Andrew Jackson (1767-1845), seventh U.S. president.

Area (sq mi): 319.56 (land 308.88; water 10.67).

Pop: 10,984 (White 98%; Black or African American 0.1%; Hispanic or Latino 0.8%; Asian 0.1%; Other 1.1%). **Foreign born:** 1.6%. **Median age:** 39.8. **State rank:** 86. **Pop change 1990-2000:** +18.1%.

Income: per capita $15,020; median household $26,502. **Pop below poverty level:** 18.1%.

Unemployment: 6.5%. **Median home value:** $68,800. **Median travel time to work:** 29.7 minutes.

JEFFERSON COUNTY

PO Box 710   **Ph:** 865-397-2935
Dandridge, TN 37725   **Fax:** 865-397-3839

In northeastern TN, east of Knoxville; organized Jun 11, 1792 (prior to statehood) from Greene and Hawkins counties. **Name Origin:** For Thomas Jefferson (1743-1826), U.S. patriot and statesman; third U.S. president.

Area (sq mi): 314.33 (land 273.81; water 40.51).

Pop: 44,294 (White 95.1%; Black or African American 2.3%; Hispanic or Latino 1.3%; Asian 0.3%; Other 1.7%). **Foreign born:**

1.5%. **Median age:** 36.5. **State rank:** 30. **Pop change 1990-2000:** +34.2%.

Income: per capita $16,841; median household $32,824. **Pop below poverty level:** 13.4%.

Unemployment: 4.9%. **Median home value:** $88,800. **Median travel time to work:** 26.4 minutes.

JOHNSON COUNTY

222 Main St   **Ph:** 423-727-9633
Mountain City, TN 37683   **Fax:** 423-727-7047

On the northeastern border of TN, east of Kingsport; organized Jan 2, 1836 from Carter County. **Name Origin:** For Cave Johnson (1793-1866), U.S. representative from TN (1829-37; 1839-45) and U.S. postmaster general (1845-49).

Area (sq mi): 302.73 (land 298.47; water 4.26).

Pop: 17,499 (White 95.8%; Black or African American 2.4%; Hispanic or Latino 0.9%; Asian 0.1%; Other 1%). **Foreign born:** 0.6%. **Median age:** 40. **State rank:** 70. **Pop change 1990-2000:** +27.1%.

Income: per capita $13,388; median household $23,067. **Pop below poverty level:** 22.6%.

Unemployment: 8.6%. **Median home value:** $72,200. **Median travel time to work:** 32 minutes.

KNOX COUNTY

City-County Bldg 400 Main St Suite 603   **Ph:** 865-215-2534
Knoxville, TN 37902   **Fax:** 865-521-2038
www.knoxcounty.org

In central eastern TN, east of Oak Ridge; organized Jun 11, 1792 (prior to statehood) from Greene and Hawkins counties. **Name Origin:** For Gen. Henry Knox (1750-1806), Revolutionary War officer and first U.S. secretary of war (1785-95).

Area (sq mi): 525.78 (land 508.46; water 17.32).

Pop: 382,032 (White 87.4%; Black or African American 8.6%; Hispanic or Latino 1.3%; Asian 1.3%; Other 2%). **Foreign born:** 2.5%. **Median age:** 36. **State rank:** 3. **Pop change 1990-2000:** +13.8%.

Income: per capita $21,875; median household $37,454. **Pop below poverty level:** 12.6%.

Unemployment: 2.5%. **Median home value:** $98,500. **Median travel time to work:** 22.2 minutes.

LAKE COUNTY

116 S Court St   **Ph:** 731-253-7582
Tiptonville, TN 38079   **Fax:** 731-253-6815

On the northern border of TN; organized Jun 24, 1870 from Obion County. **Name Origin:** For Reelfoot Lake, on its eastern border. The lake formed in 1811 and 1812, when earthquakes caused the Mississippi River to flow backward.

Area (sq mi): 193.79 (land 163.42; water 30.38).

Pop: 7,954 (White 66.2%; Black or African American 31.2%; Hispanic or Latino 1.4%; Asian 0.1%; Other 2%). **Foreign born:** 0.5%. **Median age:** 35.8. **State rank:** 89. **Pop change 1990-2000:** +11.6%.

Income: per capita $10,794; median household $21,995. **Pop below poverty level:** 23.6%.

All statistics are based on the 2000 Census except the dollar figures given for per capita income, which are based on 1999 estimates.

Unemployment: 5.6%. **Median home value:** $53,000. **Median travel time to work:** 20.4 minutes.

LAUDERDALE COUNTY

100 Court Sq
Ripley, TN 38063

Ph: 731-635-2561
Fax: 731-635-9682

On central western border of TN, northeast of Memphis; organized Nov 24, 1835 from Dyer, Tipton, and Haywood counties. **Name Origin:** For Col. James Lauderdale (?-1814), a soldier killed at the Battle of New Orleans during the War of 1812.

Area (sq mi): 507.14 (land 470.45; water 36.69).

Pop: 27,101 (White 63.4%; Black or African American 34.1%; Hispanic or Latino 1.2%; Asian 0.2%; Other 1.9%). **Foreign born:** 0.7%. **Median age:** 34.9. **State rank:** 53. **Pop change 1990-2000:** +15.4%.

Income: per capita $13,682; median household $29,751. **Pop below poverty level:** 19.2%.

Unemployment: 9.9%. **Median home value:** $59,900. **Median travel time to work:** 23.6 minutes.

LAWRENCE COUNTY

240 W Gaines St
Lawrenceburg, TN 38464
www.co.lawrence.tn.us

Ph: 931-762-7700
Fax: 931-766-2291

On the central southern border of TN, southwest of Nashville; organized Oct 21, 1817 from Hickman and Maury counties. **Name Origin:** For Capt. James Lawrence (1781-1813), U.S. Navy commander in the War of 1812 who said, 'Don't give up the ship!'

Area (sq mi): 617.91 (land 617.17; water 0.74).

Pop: 39,926 (White 96.3%; Black or African American 1.5%; Hispanic or Latino 1%; Asian 0.2%; Other 1.4%). **Foreign born:** 0.9%. **Median age:** 36.2. **State rank:** 32. **Pop change 1990-2000:** +13.1%.

Income: per capita $15,848; median household $30,498. **Pop below poverty level:** 14.6%.

Unemployment: 11%. **Median home value:** $72,400. **Median travel time to work:** 24.2 minutes.

LEWIS COUNTY

110 N Park St Rm 108
Hohenwald, TN 38462

Ph: 931-796-3378
Fax: 931-796-6010

In west-central TN, southwest of Nashville; organized Dec 21, 1843 from Hickman, Maury, Wayne, and Lawrence counties. **Name Origin:** For Meriwether Lewis (1774-1809), co-leader of the Lewis and Clark Expedition (1804-06).

Area (sq mi): 282.48 (land 282.09; water 0.38).

Pop: 11,367 (White 96.2%; Black or African American 1.5%; Hispanic or Latino 1.2%; Asian 0.2%; Other 1.3%). **Foreign born:** 1%. **Median age:** 37.3. **State rank:** 84. **Pop change 1990-2000:** +22.9%.

Income: per capita $14,664; median household $30,444. **Pop below poverty level:** 13.4%.

Unemployment: 9.5%. **Median home value:** $66,700. **Median travel time to work:** 28.5 minutes.

LINCOLN COUNTY

112 Main St S
Fayetteville, TN 37334

Ph: 931-433-2454
Fax: 931-433-9304

On the central southern border of TN, west of Chattanooga; organized Nov 14, 1809 from Bedford County. **Name Origin:** For Gen. Benjamin Lincoln (1733-1810), Revolutionary War officer, U.S. secretary of war (1781-83), and lt. gov. of MA (1788).

Area (sq mi): 570.63 (land 570.23; water 0.39).

Pop: 31,340 (White 89.6%; Black or African American 7.4%; Hispanic or Latino 1%; Asian 0.3%; Other 2%). **Foreign born:** 0.9%. **Median age:** 38.9. **State rank:** 44. **Pop change 1990-2000:** +11.3%.

Income: per capita $18,837; median household $33,434. **Pop below poverty level:** 13.6%.

Unemployment: 4.6%. **Median home value:** $73,900. **Median travel time to work:** 27.9 minutes.

LOUDON COUNTY

101 Mulberry St Suite 200
Loudon, TN 37774

Ph: 865-458-2726
Fax: 865-458-9891

In east-central TN, south of Oak Ridge; organized as Christiana Sumner County Jun 2, 1870 from Blount, Monroe, McMinn, and Roane counties; name changed Jul 7, 1870. **Name Origin:** For John Campbell (1705-82), 4th Earl of Loudoun, commander of British forces during the French and Indian Wars.

Area (sq mi): 247.31 (land 228.88; water 18.43).

Pop: 39,086 (White 95.2%; Black or African American 1.1%; Hispanic or Latino 2.3%; Asian 0.2%; Other 2.7%). **Foreign born:** 1.8%. **Median age:** 41. **State rank:** 35. **Pop change 1990-2000:** +25.1%.

Income: per capita $21,061; median household $40,401. **Pop below poverty level:** 10%.

Unemployment: 3.5%. **Median home value:** $97,300. **Median travel time to work:** 24.8 minutes.

MACON COUNTY

County Courthouse Rm 104
Lafayette, TN 37083

Ph: 615-666-2333
Fax: 615-666-2202

On central northern border of TN, northeast of Nashville; organized 1842 from Smith and Sumner counties. **Name Origin:** For Nathaniel Macon (1757-1837), NC legislator, U.S. representative (1791-1815), U.S. senator (1815-28), and president of the NC constitutional convention (1835).

Area (sq mi): 307.19 (land 307.13; water 0.06).

Pop: 20,386 (White 97%; Black or African American 0.2%; Hispanic or Latino 1.7%; Asian 0.2%; Other 1.7%). **Foreign born:** 1.8%. **Median age:** 35.5. **State rank:** 62. **Pop change 1990-2000:** +28.2%.

Income: per capita $15,286; median household $29,867. **Pop below poverty level:** 15.1%.

Unemployment: 7.2%. **Median home value:** $67,700. **Median travel time to work:** 31.1 minutes.

Please see sample entry on inside front cover for detailed information about the statistics presented with each county listing.

MADISON COUNTY

100 E Main St Rm 105   **Ph:** 731-423-6022
Jackson, TN 38301   **Fax:** 731-424-4903
www.co.madison.tn.us

In western TN, northeast of Memphis; organized Nov 7, 1821 from Western District (Indian lands). **Name Origin:** For James Madison (1751-1836), fourth U.S. president.

Area (sq mi): 558.63 (land 557; water 1.63).

Pop: 91,837 (White 64.4%; Black or African American 32.5%; Hispanic or Latino 1.7%; Asian 0.6%; Other 1.8%). **Foreign born:** 2.3%. **Median age:** 34.7. **State rank:** 12. **Pop change 1990-2000:** +17.8%.

Income: per capita $19,389; median household $36,982. **Pop below poverty level:** 14%.

Unemployment: 4.7%. **Median home value:** $85,100. **Median travel time to work:** 19 minutes.

MARION COUNTY

PO Box 789   **Ph:** 423-942-2515
Jasper, TN 37347   **Fax:** 423-942-0815

On the southeastern border of TN, west of Chattanooga; organized Nov 20, 1817 from Western District (Indian lands). **Name Origin:** For Gen. Francis Marion (c.1732-95), SC soldier and legislator, known as 'The Swamp Fox' for his tactics during the Revolutionary War.

Area (sq mi): 512.32 (land 498.36; water 13.96).

Pop: 27,776 (White 93.9%; Black or African American 4.1%; Hispanic or Latino 0.7%; Asian 0.2%; Other 1.4%). **Foreign born:** 0.5%. **Median age:** 38.2. **State rank:** 52. **Pop change 1990-2000:** +11.7%.

Income: per capita $16,419; median household $31,419. **Pop below poverty level:** 14.1%.

Unemployment: 5.1%. **Median home value:** $76,100. **Median travel time to work:** 29.2 minutes.

MARSHALL COUNTY

1107 Courthouse Annex   **Ph:** 931-359-1072
Lewisburg, TN 37091   **Fax:** 931-359-0559

In south-central TN, south of Nashville; organized Feb 20, 1836 from Giles, Bedford, Lincoln, and Maury counties. **Name Origin:** For John Marshall (1755-1835), American jurist; fourth Chief Justice of the U.S. Supreme Court (1801-35).

Area (sq mi): 376.1 (land 375.36; water 0.75).

Pop: 26,767 (White 88.1%; Black or African American 7.8%; Hispanic or Latino 2.9%; Asian 0.3%; Other 2.5%). **Foreign born:** 1.4%. **Median age:** 36.3. **State rank:** 54. **Pop change 1990-2000:** +24.3%.

Income: per capita $17,749; median household $38,457. **Pop below poverty level:** 10%.

Unemployment: 6.1%. **Median home value:** $83,800. **Median travel time to work:** 25.3 minutes.

MAURY COUNTY

10 Public Sq   **Ph:** 931-381-3690
Columbia, TN 38401   **Fax:** 931-381-1016

In west-central TN, southwest of Nashville; organized Nov 16, 1807 from Williamson County and Indian lands. **Name Origin:** For a prominent local family, whose members included Abram Maury (1801-48), U.S. representative from TN (1835-39).

Area (sq mi): 615.52 (land 612.86; water 2.66).

Pop: 69,498 (White 81%; Black or African American 14.3%; Hispanic or Latino 3.3%; Asian 0.3%; Other 3%). **Foreign born:** 2.1%. **Median age:** 36.3. **State rank:** 17. **Pop change 1990-2000:** +26.8%.

Income: per capita $19,365; median household $41,591. **Pop below poverty level:** 10.9%.

Unemployment: 3.9%. **Median home value:** $96,800. **Median travel time to work:** 26 minutes.

McMINN COUNTY

5 S Hill St Suite A   **Ph:** 423-745-4440
Athens, TN 37303   **Fax:** 423-744-1657
www.mcminnco.org

In southeastern TN, northeast of Chattanooga; organized Nov 13, 1819 from Cherokee Indian lands. **Name Origin:** For Joseph McMinn (1785-1824), governor of TN (1817-21), known as 'the Quaker governor.'

Area (sq mi): 432.22 (land 430.28; water 1.94).

Pop: 49,015 (White 91.9%; Black or African American 4.5%; Hispanic or Latino 1.8%; Asian 0.7%; Other 2.1%). **Foreign born:** 1.3%. **Median age:** 37.9. **State rank:** 26. **Pop change 1990-2000:** +15.6%.

Income: per capita $16,725; median household $31,919. **Pop below poverty level:** 14.5%.

Unemployment: 7.7%. **Median home value:** $80,300. **Median travel time to work:** 23.1 minutes.

McNAIRY COUNTY

County Courthouse Rm 102   **Ph:** 731-645-3511
Selmer, TN 38375   **Fax:** 731-646-1414

On the southwestern border of TN, southeast of Jackson; organized Oct 8, 1823 from Hardin County. **Name Origin:** For John McNairy, a judge in U.S. District Court for TN (1797).

Area (sq mi): 560.84 (land 560.04; water 0.79).

Pop: 24,653 (White 91.6%; Black or African American 6.2%; Hispanic or Latino 0.9%; Asian 0.1%; Other 1.4%). **Foreign born:** 0.9%. **Median age:** 39.1. **State rank:** 57. **Pop change 1990-2000:** +10%.

Income: per capita $16,385; median household $30,154. **Pop below poverty level:** 15.9%.

Unemployment: 6.4%. **Median home value:** $61,400. **Median travel time to work:** 26 minutes.

MEIGS COUNTY

PO Box 218   **Ph:** 423-334-5747
Decatur, TN 37322   **Fax:** 423-334-4819

In southeastern TN, northeast of Chattanooga; organized Jan 20,

All statistics are based on the 2000 Census except the dollar figures given for per capita income, which are based on 1999 estimates.

1836 from Hamilton, McMinn, Rhea, and Roane counties. **Name Origin:** For Return Jonathan Meigs (1764-1824), U.S. senator from OH (1808-1810), OH governor (1810-14), and U.S. postmaster general (1814-23).

Area (sq mi): 216.78 (land 194.86; water 21.92).

Pop: 11,086 (White 97.3%; Black or African American 1.2%; Hispanic or Latino 0.6%; Asian 0.2%; Other 0.9%). **Foreign born:** 0.6%. **Median age:** 36.7. **State rank:** 85. **Pop change 1990-2000:** +38%.

Income: per capita $14,551; median household $29,354. **Pop below poverty level:** 18.3%.

Unemployment: 7.3%. **Median home value:** $87,200. **Median travel time to work:** 33.7 minutes.

MONROE COUNTY

103 College St   **Ph:** 423-442-2220
Madisonville, TN 37354   **Fax:** 423-442-9542
www.monroegovernment.org

On southeastern border of TN, northeast of Chattanooga; organized Nov 13, 1819 from Roane County (Hiwassee Purchase, Indian lands). **Name Origin:** For James Monroe (1758-1831), fifth U.S. president.

Area (sq mi): 652.58 (land 634.91; water 17.67).

Pop: 38,961 (White 94.1%; Black or African American 2.3%; Hispanic or Latino 1.8%; Asian 0.4%; Other 2.6%). **Foreign born:** 1.2%. **Median age:** 36.8. **State rank:** 36. **Pop change 1990-2000:** +27.6%.

Income: per capita $14,951; median household $30,337. **Pop below poverty level:** 15.5%.

Unemployment: 7.2%. **Median home value:** $79,400. **Median travel time to work:** 26 minutes.

MONTGOMERY COUNTY

PO Box 687   **Ph:** 931-648-5711
Clarksville, TN 37041   **Fax:** 931-553-5160

On central northern border of TN, northwest of Nashville; organized Apr 9, 1796 by the division between Montgomery and Robertson counties of Tennessee County, which had been organized in 1788 from Davidson County and was then abolished. **Name Origin:** For John Montgomery (1748-94), explorer of Cumberland County (1771) and Indian fighter.

Area (sq mi): 543.84 (land 539.28; water 4.57).

Pop: 134,768 (White 70.9%; Black or African American 19.2%; Hispanic or Latino 5.2%; Asian 1.8%; Other 5.8%). **Foreign born:** 4.4%. **Median age:** 30. **State rank:** 7. **Pop change 1990-2000:** +34.1%.

Income: per capita $17,265; median household $38,981. **Pop below poverty level:** 10%.

Unemployment: 3.7%. **Median home value:** $85,100. **Median travel time to work:** 25.5 minutes.

MOORE COUNTY

PO Box 206   **Ph:** 931-759-7346
Lynchburg, TN 37352   **Fax:** 931-759-6394

In south-central TN, south of Murfreesboro; organized Dec 14,

1871 from Bedford, Franklin, Lincoln, and Coffee counties. **Name Origin:** For Gen. William Moore, TN officer in the War of 1812 and later a TN legislator.

Area (sq mi): 130.38 (land 129.18; water 1.21).

Pop: 5,740 (White 95.6%; Black or African American 2.7%; Hispanic or Latino 0.8%; Asian 0.1%; Other 1.3%). **Foreign born:** 1%. **Median age:** 39.7. **State rank:** 93. **Pop change 1990-2000:** +21.6%.

Income: per capita $19,040; median household $36,591. **Pop below poverty level:** 9.6%.

Unemployment: 3.2%. **Median home value:** $85,600. **Median travel time to work:** 22.3 minutes.

MORGAN COUNTY

PO Box 301   **Ph:** 423-346-3480
Wartburg, TN 37887   **Fax:** 423-346-4161

In east-central TN, west of Oak Ridge; organized 1817 from Roane County, and in 1903 annexed part of Anderson County. **Name Origin:** For Gen. Daniel Morgan (1736-1802), an officer in the Revolutionary War and U.S. representative from VA (1797-99).

Area (sq mi): 522.4 (land 522.04; water 0.35).

Pop: 19,757 (White 96.2%; Black or African American 2.2%; Hispanic or Latino 0.6%; Asian 0.1%; Other 0.9%). **Foreign born:** 0.4%. **Median age:** 36.5. **State rank:** 65. **Pop change 1990-2000:** +14.2%.

Income: per capita $12,925; median household $27,712. **Pop below poverty level:** 16%.

Unemployment: 6.2%. **Median home value:** $60,200. **Median travel time to work:** 34.8 minutes.

OBION COUNTY

2 Bill Burnett Cir   **Ph:** 731-885-3831
Union City, TN 38261   **Fax:** 731-885-0287

On the northwestern border of TN; organized Oct 24, 1823 from Western District (Indian lands). **Name Origin:** For the Obion River, which runs through it; from an Indian word meaning either 'many forks or branches,' as of a river, or possibly a personal name.

Area (sq mi): 555.35 (land 544.91; water 10.43).

Pop: 32,450 (White 87.3%; Black or African American 9.8%; Hispanic or Latino 1.9%; Asian 0.2%; Other 1.7%). **Foreign born:** 1.3%. **Median age:** 38.7. **State rank:** 43. **Pop change 1990-2000:** +2.3%.

Income: per capita $17,409; median household $32,764. **Pop below poverty level:** 13.3%.

Unemployment: 4.3%. **Median home value:** $67,500. **Median travel time to work:** 18.3 minutes.

OVERTON COUNTY

317 University St Courthouse Annex
Suite 22   **Ph:** 931-823-2631
Livingston, TN 38570   **Fax:** 931-823-7036

In north-central TN, northwest of Oak Ridge; organized Sep 11, 1806 from Jackson County and Indian lands. **Name Origin:** For

---

Please see sample entry on inside front cover for detailed information about the statistics presented with each county listing.

John Overton (1766-1833), founder (with Andrew Jackson, 1767-1845) of Memphis, TN (1819); judge in the TN superior and supreme courts (1804-16).

Area (sq mi): 434.82 (land 433.38; water 1.43).

Pop: 20,118 (White 98.2%; Black or African American 0.3%; Hispanic or Latino 0.7%; Asian 0.1%; Other 1%). **Foreign born:** 0.5%. **Median age:** 38.8. **State rank:** 63. **Pop change 1990-2000:** +14.1%.

Income: per capita $13,910; median household $26,915. **Pop below poverty level:** 16%.

Unemployment: 6.4%. **Median home value:** $71,600. **Median travel time to work:** 26.1 minutes.

PERRY COUNTY

PO Box 16   **Ph:** 931-589-2216
Linden, TN 37096   **Fax:** 931-589-2215

In west-central TN, east of Jackson; established Nov 14, 1821 from Hickman and Humphreys counties. **Name Origin:** For Oliver Hazard Perry (1785-1819), U.S. naval officer during the War of 1812, famous for the message, 'We have met the enemy and they are ours.'

Area (sq mi): 422.9 (land 414.89; water 8).

Pop: 7,631 (White 96.1%; Black or African American 1.7%; Hispanic or Latino 0.8%; Asian 0.1%; Other 1.5%). **Foreign born:** 0.5%. **Median age:** 39.8. **State rank:** 90. **Pop change 1990-2000:** +15.4%.

Income: per capita $16,969; median household $28,061. **Pop below poverty level:** 15.4%.

Unemployment: 7.2%. **Median home value:** $62,600. **Median travel time to work:** 27.9 minutes.

PICKETT COUNTY

PO Box 5   **Ph:** 931-864-3879
Byrdstown, TN 38549   **Fax:** 931-864-7885

In east-central TN, northwest of Oak Ridge; organized Feb 27, 1879 from Fentress and Overton counties. **Name Origin:** For H.L. Pickett, a TN legislator instrumental in forming the county.

Area (sq mi): 174.58 (land 162.92; water 11.66).

Pop: 4,945 (White 98.5%; Black or African American 0.1%; Hispanic or Latino 0.8%; Asian 0%; Other 0.7%). **Foreign born:** 0.3%. **Median age:** 41.6. **State rank:** 95. **Pop change 1990-2000:** +8.7%.

Income: per capita $14,681; median household $24,673. **Pop below poverty level:** 15.6%.

Unemployment: 9.1%. **Median home value:** $66,900. **Median travel time to work:** 25.1 minutes.

POLK COUNTY

PO Box 256   **Ph:** 423-338-4524
Benton, TN 37307   **Fax:** 423-338-8611

On the southeastern border of TN, east of Chattanooga; organized Nov 28, 1839 from Bradley and McMinn counties. **Name Origin:** For James Knox Polk (1795-1849), eleventh U.S. president.

Area (sq mi): 442.35 (land 435.05; water 7.3).

Pop: 16,050 (White 97.8%; Black or African American 0.1%; Hispanic or Latino 0.7%; Asian 0.1%; Other 1.4%). **Foreign born:**

0.8%. **Median age:** 38.6. **State rank:** 75. **Pop change 1990-2000:** +17.6%.

Income: per capita $16,025; median household $29,643. **Pop below poverty level:** 13%.

Unemployment: 5%. **Median home value:** $72,100. **Median travel time to work:** 30.1 minutes.

PUTNAM COUNTY

29 N Washington Ave   **Ph:** 931-526-7106
Cookeville, TN 38501   **Fax:** 931-372-8201

In north-central TN, east of Nashville; organized Feb 2, 1842 from Smith, White, DeKalb, Overton, and Jackson counties. **Name Origin:** For Gen. Israel Putnam (1718-90), Revolutionary War officer and American commander at the Battle of Bunker Hill.

Area (sq mi): 402.56 (land 401.05; water 1.5).

Pop: 62,315 (White 93.2%; Black or African American 1.7%; Hispanic or Latino 3%; Asian 0.9%; Other 2.8%). **Foreign born:** 3.4%. **Median age:** 34.4. **State rank:** 19. **Pop change 1990-2000:** +21.3%.

Income: per capita $16,927; median household $30,914. **Pop below poverty level:** 16.4%.

Unemployment: 4.5%. **Median home value:** $92,600. **Median travel time to work:** 19.6 minutes.

RHEA COUNTY

375 Church St Suite 101   **Ph:** 423-775-7808
Dayton, TN 37321   **Fax:** 423-775-7898

In east-central TN, northeast of Chattanooga; organized Nov 30, 1807 from Roane County. **Name Origin:** For John Rhea (1753-1832), U.S. representative from TN (1803-15; 1817-23).

Area (sq mi): 336.39 (land 315.94; water 20.45).

Pop: 28,400 (White 94.6%; Black or African American 2%; Hispanic or Latino 1.7%; Asian 0.3%; Other 2.3%). **Foreign born:** 1.3%. **Median age:** 37.2. **State rank:** 50. **Pop change 1990-2000:** +16.7%.

Income: per capita $15,672; median household $30,418. **Pop below poverty level:** 14.7%.

Unemployment: 6%. **Median home value:** $76,700. **Median travel time to work:** 24.4 minutes.

ROANE COUNTY

200 E Race St   **Ph:** 865-376-5556
Kingston, TN 37763   **Fax:** 865-717-4121
www.roanealliance.org

In east-central TN, southwest of Oak Ridge; organized Nov 6, 1801 from Knox County and Indian lands. **Name Origin:** For Archibald Roane (1759-1819), governor of TN (1801-03) and judge of the TN supreme court (1815-19).

Area (sq mi): 394.98 (land 360.98; water 34).

Pop: 51,910 (White 94.8%; Black or African American 2.7%; Hispanic or Latino 0.7%; Asian 0.4%; Other 1.6%). **Foreign born:** 1.2%. **Median age:** 40.7. **State rank:** 24. **Pop change 1990-2000:** +9.9%.

Income: per capita $18,456; median household $33,226. **Pop below poverty level:** 13.9%.

All statistics are based on the 2000 Census except the dollar figures given for per capita income, which are based on 1999 estimates.

Unemployment: 4.5%. **Median home value:** $86,500. **Median travel time to work:** 26 minutes.

ROBERTSON COUNTY

511 S Brown St
Springfield, TN 37172

Ph: 615-384-5895
Fax: 615-384-2218

On the central northern border of TN, north of Nashville; organized Apr 9, 1796 by the division between Montgomery and Robertson counties of Tennessee County, which had been organized in 1788 from Davidson County and was then abolished. **Name Origin:** For Gen. James Robertson (1742-1814), office in the Revolutionary War; called 'Father of Tennessee' for his active support of statehood, and founder of present-day Nashville (1780).

Area (sq mi): 476.67 (land 476.47; water 0.2).

Pop: 54,433 (White 87.5%; Black or African American 8.6%; Hispanic or Latino 2.7%; Asian 0.3%; Other 1.9%). **Foreign born:** 2.5%. **Median age:** 35.4. **State rank:** 22. **Pop change 1990-2000:** +31.2%.

Income: per capita $19,054; median household $43,174. **Pop below poverty level:** 9%.

Unemployment: 4.1%. **Median home value:** $107,300. **Median travel time to work:** 29.3 minutes.

RUTHERFORD COUNTY

319 N Maple St
Murfreesboro, TN 37130
www.rc.state.tn.us

Ph: 615-898-7799
Fax: 615-898-7830

In central TN, southeast of Nashville; organized Oct 25, 1803 from Davidson, Williamson, and Wilson counties. **Name Origin:** For Gen. Griffith Rutherford (1731-1800), Revolutionary War hero, NC legislator (1784), and president of the TN legislative council (1796).

Area (sq mi): 623.94 (land 618.91; water 5.03).

Pop: 182,023 (White 84.5%; Black or African American 9.5%; Hispanic or Latino 2.8%; Asian 1.9%; Other 2.8%). **Foreign born:** 3.6%. **Median age:** 31.2. **State rank:** 5. **Pop change 1990-2000:** +53.5%.

Income: per capita $19,938; median household $46,312. **Pop below poverty level:** 9%.

Unemployment: 3.6%. **Median home value:** $113,500. **Median travel time to work:** 26.8 minutes.

SCOTT COUNTY

PO Box 87
Huntsville, TN 37756
www.scottcounty.com/

Ph: 423-663-2588
Fax: 423-663-3969

On the central northern border of TN, northwest of Oak Ridge; established Dec 17, 1839 from Fentriss, Morgan, Anderson, and Campbell counties. **Name Origin:** For Winfield Scott (1786-1866), general in chief of the U.S. Army (1841) and commander of the Union armies at the beginning of the Civil War.

Area (sq mi): 533.22 (land 532.09; water 1.13).

Pop: 21,127 (White 98.1%; Black or African American 0.1%; Hispanic or Latino 0.6%; Asian 0.1%; Other 1.2%). **Foreign born:** 0.4%. **Median age:** 34.7. **State rank:** 60. **Pop change 1990-2000:** +15.1%.

Income: per capita $12,927; median household $24,093. **Pop below poverty level:** 20.2%.

Unemployment: 7.3%. **Median home value:** $60,300. **Median travel time to work:** 27.2 minutes.

SEQUATCHIE COUNTY

PO Box 248
Dunlap, TN 37327

Ph: 423-949-2522
Fax: 423-949-4533

In southeastern TN, northwest of Chattanooga; organized Dec 9, 1857 from Hamilton County (and previously from Bledsoe, Marion, and Grundy counties). **Name Origin:** For the Sequatchie River, which runs through it; name is Cherokee, probably for 'hog river.'

Area (sq mi): 266.02 (land 265.85; water 0.18).

Pop: 11,370 (White 98%; Black or African American 0.2%; Hispanic or Latino 0.8%; Asian 0.1%; Other 1%). **Foreign born:** 1.2%. **Median age:** 36.7. **State rank:** 83. **Pop change 1990-2000:** +28.3%.

Income: per capita $16,468; median household $30,959. **Pop below poverty level:** 16.5%.

Unemployment: 5%. **Median home value:** $80,300. **Median travel time to work:** 27.7 minutes.

SEVIER COUNTY

125 Court Ave Suite 202 E
Sevierville, TN 37862

Ph: 865-453-5502
Fax: 865-453-6830

On the central eastern border of TN, southeast of Knoxville; organized Sep 27, 1794 (prior to statehood) from Jefferson County. **Name Origin:** For John Sevier (1745-1815), only governor of Franklin (original name of the state; 1785-88), then governor of TN (1796-81; 1803-09), and U.S. representative (1811-15).

Area (sq mi): 597.73 (land 592.29; water 5.45).

Pop: 71,170 (White 96.5%; Black or African American 0.6%; Hispanic or Latino 1.2%; Asian 0.6%; Other 1.6%). **Foreign born:** 1.6%. **Median age:** 38.1. **State rank:** 16. **Pop change 1990-2000:** +39.4%.

Income: per capita $18,064; median household $34,719. **Pop below poverty level:** 10.7%.

Unemployment: 5.9%. **Median home value:** $112,500. **Median travel time to work:** 25.3 minutes.

SHELBY COUNTY

160 N Main St Suite 619
Memphis, TN 38103
www.co.shelby.tn.us

Ph: 901-545-4301
Fax: 901-545-4283

On the southwest border of TN; organized Nov 24, 1819 from Hardin County. **Name Origin:** For Gen. Isaac Shelby (1750-1826), officer in the Revolutionary War, NC legislator, and governor of KY (1792-96; 1812-16).

Area (sq mi): 783.63 (land 754.53; water 29.1).

Pop: 897,472 (White 46.2%; Black or African American 48.6%; Hispanic or Latino 2.6%; Asian 1.6%; Other 2.4%). **Foreign born:** 3.8%. **Median age:** 32.9. **State rank:** 1. **Pop change 1990-2000:** +8.6%.

Income: per capita $20,856; median household $39,593. **Pop below poverty level:** 16%.

Please see sample entry on inside front cover for detailed information about the statistics presented with each county listing.

Unemployment: 4.2%. **Median home value:** $92,200. **Median travel time to work:** 23.7 minutes.

SMITH COUNTY

122 Turner High Cir   **Ph:** 615-735-9833
Carthage, TN 37030   **Fax:** 615-735-8252

In north-central TN, northeast of Nashville; organized Oct 26, 1799 from Indian lands. **Name Origin:** For Col. Daniel Smith (1748-1818), officer in the Revolutionary War, member of the first TN Constitutional Convention (1796), and U.S. senator from TN (1798-99; 1805-09).

Area (sq mi): 325.35 (land 314.41; water 10.94).

Pop: 17,712 (White 94.9%; Black or African American 2.5%; Hispanic or Latino 1.1%; Asian 0.2%; Other 1.9%). **Foreign born:** 0.9%. **Median age:** 36.8. **State rank:** 68. **Pop change 1990-2000:** +25.2%.

Income: per capita $17,473; median household $35,625. **Pop below poverty level:** 12.2%.

Unemployment: 4.9%. **Median home value:** $87,100. **Median travel time to work:** 29.9 minutes.

STEWART COUNTY

PO Box 67   **Ph:** 931-232-7616
Dover, TN 37058   **Fax:** 931-232-4934

On the central northern border of TN, west of Clarksville; organized Nov 1, 1803 from Montgomery County. **Name Origin:** For Duncan Stewart, Revolutionary War veteran and early settler.

Area (sq mi): 493.2 (land 458.48; water 34.72).

Pop: 12,370 (White 94.6%; Black or African American 1.3%; Hispanic or Latino 1%; Asian 1.5%; Other 1.9%). **Foreign born:** 1.7%. **Median age:** 38.7. **State rank:** 80. **Pop change 1990-2000:** +30.5%.

Income: per capita $16,302; median household $32,316. **Pop below poverty level:** 12.4%.

Unemployment: 7.2%. **Median home value:** $76,800. **Median travel time to work:** 37.2 minutes.

SULLIVAN COUNTY

3258 Hwy 126   **Ph:** 423-323-6428
Blountville, TN 37617   **Fax:** 423-279-2725
www.sullivancounty.org

On the northeastern border of TN, north of Johnson City; organized Oct 18, 1779 (prior to statehood) from Washington County. **Name Origin:** For Gen. John Sullivan (1740-95), officer in the Revolutionary War, member of the Continental Congress (1774-75; 1780-81), and governor of NH (1786-87; 1789).

Area (sq mi): 429.69 (land 413.02; water 16.67).

Pop: 153,048 (White 96.1%; Black or African American 1.9%; Hispanic or Latino 0.7%; Asian 0.4%; Other 1.1%). **Foreign born:** 1.3%. **Median age:** 40.1. **State rank:** 6. **Pop change 1990-2000:** +6.6%.

Income: per capita $19,202; median household $33,529. **Pop below poverty level:** 12.9%.

Unemployment: 3.9%. **Median home value:** $88,000. **Median travel time to work:** 21.3 minutes.

SUMNER COUNTY

355 N Belvedere Dr   **Ph:** 615-452-4063
Gallatin, TN 37066   **Fax:** 615-452-9371
www.sumnertn.org

On the central northern border of TN, northeast of Nashville; organized Nov 18, 1786 (prior to statehood) from Davidson County (NC), becoming part of the Territory South of the River Ohio (popularly called the Southwest Territory) from its creation in May 1790 until it became the state of TN in 1796. **Name Origin:** For Gen. Jethro Sumner (1733-85), officer in the Revolutionary War who was active in promoting TN statehood.

Area (sq mi): 543.12 (land 529.3; water 13.81).

Pop: 130,449 (White 90.6%; Black or African American 5.8%; Hispanic or Latino 1.8%; Asian 0.7%; Other 2.1%). **Foreign born:** 2.4%. **Median age:** 36.1. **State rank:** 8. **Pop change 1990-2000:** +26.3%.

Income: per capita $21,164; median household $46,030. **Pop below poverty level:** 8.1%.

Unemployment: 4.5%. **Median home value:** $125,800. **Median travel time to work:** 27.2 minutes.

TIPTON COUNTY

PO Box 528   **Ph:** 901-476-0207
Covington, TN 38019   **Fax:** 901-476-0227

On the southwest border of TN, northeast of Memphis; organized Oct 29, 1823 from Western District (Indian lands). **Name Origin:** For Jacob Tipton (?-1791), soldier killed in a battle with Indians.

Area (sq mi): 474.72 (land 459.37; water 15.35).

Pop: 51,271 (White 77.2%; Black or African American 19.9%; Hispanic or Latino 1.2%; Asian 0.4%; Other 1.9%). **Foreign born:** 0.8%. **Median age:** 34.4. **State rank:** 25. **Pop change 1990-2000:** +36.5%.

Income: per capita $17,952; median household $41,856. **Pop below poverty level:** 12.1%.

Unemployment: 5%. **Median home value:** $91,500. **Median travel time to work:** 31.7 minutes.

TROUSDALE COUNTY

200 E Main St Rm 2   **Ph:** 615-374-2906
Hartsville, TN 37074   **Fax:** 615-374-1100

In north-central TN, northeast of Nashville; organized Jan 21, 1870 from Macon, Smith, Wilson, and Sumner counties. **Name Origin:** For Gen. William Trousdale (1790-1872), TN legislator, governor (1849-51), and U.S. minister to Brazil (1852-57).

Area (sq mi): 116.64 (land 114.24; water 2.4).

Pop: 7,259 (White 86.1%; Black or African American 11.4%; Hispanic or Latino 1.5%; Asian 0.1%; Other 1.9%). **Foreign born:** 1.7%. **Median age:** 38.1. **State rank:** 91. **Pop change 1990-2000:** +22.6%.

Income: per capita $15,838; median household $32,212. **Pop below poverty level:** 13.4%.

Unemployment: 10%. **Median home value:** $76,800. **Median travel time to work:** 32.7 minutes.

All statistics are based on the 2000 Census except the dollar figures given for per capita income, which are based on 1999 estimates.

UNICOI COUNTY

PO Box 169   **Ph:** 423-743-9391
Erwin, TN 37650   **Fax:** 423-743-8007

On the northeastern border of TN, south of Johnson City; organized Mar 23, 1875 from Washington and Carter counties. **Name Origin:** For Unicoi Creek, which runs through it, or a variant form of Cherokee *unaka* 'white,' referring to the color of the rocks in the Unaka Mountains.

Area (sq mi): 186.49 (land 186.14; water 0.35).

Pop: 17,667 (White 97.1%; Black or African American 0.1%; Hispanic or Latino 1.9%; Asian 0.1%; Other 1.8%). **Foreign born:** 1.4%. **Median age:** 41.5. **State rank:** 69. **Pop change 1990-2000:** +6.8%.

Income: per capita $15,612; median household $29,863. **Pop below poverty level:** 13.1%.

Unemployment: 5.9%. **Median home value:** $82,400. **Median travel time to work:** 21.2 minutes.

UNION COUNTY

901 Main St Suite 119   **Ph:** 865-992-8043
Maynardville, TN 37807   **Fax:** 865-992-4992
www.unioncountytn.org

In north-central TN, north of Knoxville; organized 1850 from Anderson, Campbell, Grainger, Claiborne, and Knox counties. **Name Origin:** In honor of the strong sentiment of people in the area in favor of the preservation of the Union.

Area (sq mi): 247.13 (land 223.56; water 23.57).

Pop: 17,808 (White 97.9%; Black or African American 0.1%; Hispanic or Latino 0.8%; Asian 0.2%; Other 1.3%). **Foreign born:** 0.3%. **Median age:** 35.8. **State rank:** 67. **Pop change 1990-2000:** +30%.

Income: per capita $13,375; median household $27,335. **Pop below poverty level:** 19.6%.

Unemployment: 3.8%. **Median home value:** $79,000. **Median travel time to work:** 31.5 minutes.

VAN BUREN COUNTY

PO Box 827   **Ph:** 931-946-2121
Spencer, TN 38585   **Fax:** 931-946-7572

In east-central TN, northwest of Chattanooga; organized Jan 3, 1840 from Bledsoe, Warren, and White counties. **Name Origin:** For Martin Van Buren (1782-1862), eighth U.S. president.

Area (sq mi): 274.59 (land 273.46; water 1.14).

Pop: 5,508 (White 98.7%; Black or African American 0.1%; Hispanic or Latino 0.3%; Asian 0.1%; Other 0.8%). **Foreign born:** 0.2%. **Median age:** 38.7. **State rank:** 94. **Pop change 1990-2000:** +13.7%.

Income: per capita $17,497; median household $28,165. **Pop below poverty level:** 15.2%.

Unemployment: 7.6%. **Median home value:** $55,800. **Median travel time to work:** 29.9 minutes.

WARREN COUNTY

201 Locust St Suite 2P   **Ph:** 931-473-2623
McMinnville, TN 37110   **Fax:** 931-473-8622

In east-central TN, northwest of Chattanooga; organized Nov 26, 1807 from White, Jackson, and Smith counties, and Indian lands. **Name Origin:** For Gen. Joseph Warren (1741-75), Revolutionary War patriot and member of the Committee of Safety who dispatched Paul Revere (1735-1818) on his famous ride.

Area (sq mi): 434.08 (land 432.69; water 1.4).

Pop: 38,276 (White 90.6%; Black or African American 3.2%; Hispanic or Latino 4.9%; Asian 0.4%; Other 4.7%). **Foreign born:** 3.7%. **Median age:** 36.6. **State rank:** 37. **Pop change 1990-2000:** +16%.

Income: per capita $15,759; median household $30,920. **Pop below poverty level:** 16.6%.

Unemployment: 7.2%. **Median home value:** $72,800. **Median travel time to work:** 23.4 minutes.

WASHINGTON COUNTY

PO Box 218   **Ph:** 423-753-1621
Jonesborough, TN 37659   **Fax:** 423-753-4716
www.washingtoncountytn.com

In northeastern TN, south of Kingsport; original county; organized Nov 15, 1777 (prior to statehood). **Name Origin:** For George Washington (1732-99), American patriot and first U.S. president.

Area (sq mi): 329.8 (land 326.31; water 3.49).

Pop: 107,198 (White 92.9%; Black or African American 3.8%; Hispanic or Latino 1.4%; Asian 0.7%; Other 1.7%). **Foreign born:** 1.9%. **Median age:** 37.1. **State rank:** 10. **Pop change 1990-2000:** +16.1%.

Income: per capita $19,085; median household $33,116. **Pop below poverty level:** 13.9%.

Unemployment: 4.6%. **Median home value:** $96,700. **Median travel time to work:** 20.6 minutes.

WAYNE COUNTY

PO Box 848   **Ph:** 931-722-3653
Waynesboro, TN 38485   **Fax:** 931-722-5994

On the central southern border of TN, southeast of Jackson; organized Nov 24, 1817 from Hickman and Humphreys counties. **Name Origin:** For Gen. Anthony Wayne (1745-96), PA soldier and statesman, nicknamed 'Mad Anthony' for his daring during the Revolutionary War.

Area (sq mi): 735.59 (land 733.96; water 1.63).

Pop: 16,842 (White 91.3%; Black or African American 6.8%; Hispanic or Latino 0.8%; Asian 0.2%; Other 1%). **Foreign born:** 0.4%. **Median age:** 37.3. **State rank:** 72. **Pop change 1990-2000:** +20.9%.

Income: per capita $14,472; median household $26,576. **Pop below poverty level:** 16.3%.

Unemployment: 9.8%. **Median home value:** $56,600. **Median travel time to work:** 31.3 minutes.

Please see sample entry on inside front cover for detailed information about the statistics presented with each county listing.

WEAKLEY COUNTY

PO Box 587   **Ph:** 731-364-2285
Dresden, TN 38225   **Fax:** 731-364-5236

On northwestern border of TN, north of Jackson; organized Oct 21, 1823 from Western District (Indian lands). **Name Origin:** For Robert Weakley (1764-1845), U.S. representative from TN (1809-11), TN legislator, and member of the TN Constitutional Convention (1834).

Area (sq mi): 581.81 (land 580.19; water 1.62).

Pop: 34,895 (White 89.7%; Black or African American 6.9%; Hispanic or Latino 1.2%; Asian 1.3%; Other 1.4%). **Foreign born:** 2%. **Median age:** 34.8. **State rank:** 41. **Pop change 1990-2000:** +9.1%.

Income: per capita $15,408; median household $30,008. **Pop below poverty level:** 16%.

Unemployment: 5.9%. **Median home value:** $67,900. **Median travel time to work:** 20.2 minutes.

WHITE COUNTY

County Courthouse Rm 205   **Ph:** 931-836-3203
Sparta, TN 38583   **Fax:** 931-836-3204

In east-central TN, west of Oak Ridge; organized Sep 11, 1806 from Jackson and Smith counties. **Name Origin:** For Col. John White (?-1782), an officer in the American Revolution who was an early settler in the area.

Area (sq mi): 379.39 (land 376.58; water 2.8).

Pop: 23,102 (White 96.1%; Black or African American 1.6%; Hispanic or Latino 1%; Asian 0.2%; Other 1.6%). **Foreign born:** 0.8%. **Median age:** 38.8. **State rank:** 58. **Pop change 1990-2000:** +15%.

Income: per capita $14,791; median household $29,383. **Pop below poverty level:** 14.3%.

Unemployment: 5.7%. **Median home value:** $76,300. **Median travel time to work:** 22.4 minutes.

WILLIAMSON COUNTY

PO Box 624   **Ph:** 615-790-5712
Franklin, TN 37065   **Fax:** 615-790-5610
www.williamson-tn.org

In west-central TN, south of Nashville; organized Oct 26, 1799 from Davidson County. **Name Origin:** For Hugh Williamson (1735-1819), member of the Continental Congress (1782-85; 1787; 1788) and U.S. representative from NC (1789-93).

Area (sq mi): 583.62 (land 582.68; water 0.94).

Pop: 126,638 (White 90.2%; Black or African American 5.2%; Hispanic or Latino 2.5%; Asian 1.3%; Other 2%). **Foreign born:** 3.9%. **Median age:** 36.2. **State rank:** 9. **Pop change 1990-2000:** +56.3%.

Income: per capita $32,496; median household $69,104. **Pop below poverty level:** 4.7%.

Unemployment: 2.2%. **Median home value:** $208,400. **Median travel time to work:** 26.3 minutes.

WILSON COUNTY

PO Box 950   **Ph:** 615-444-0314
Lebanon, TN 37088   **Fax:** 615-443-2615
www.wilsoncountytn.com

In north-central TN, east of Nashville; organized Oct 26, 1799 from Sumner County. **Name Origin:** For David Wilson (?-1804), an officer in the Revolutionary War; he later presided over the General Assembly of the Territory South of Ohio River during which the state of TN was organized.

Area (sq mi): 583.2 (land 570.57; water 12.63).

Pop: 88,809 (White 90.8%; Black or African American 6.3%; Hispanic or Latino 1.3%; Asian 0.5%; Other 1.7%). **Foreign born:** 1.4%. **Median age:** 36.3. **State rank:** 13. **Pop change 1990-2000:** +31.2%.

Income: per capita $22,739; median household $50,140. **Pop below poverty level:** 6.7%.

Unemployment: 3.5%. **Median home value:** $136,600. **Median travel time to work:** 29.2 minutes.

All statistics are based on the 2000 Census except the dollar figures given for per capita income, which are based on 1999 estimates.

TEXAS - Counties

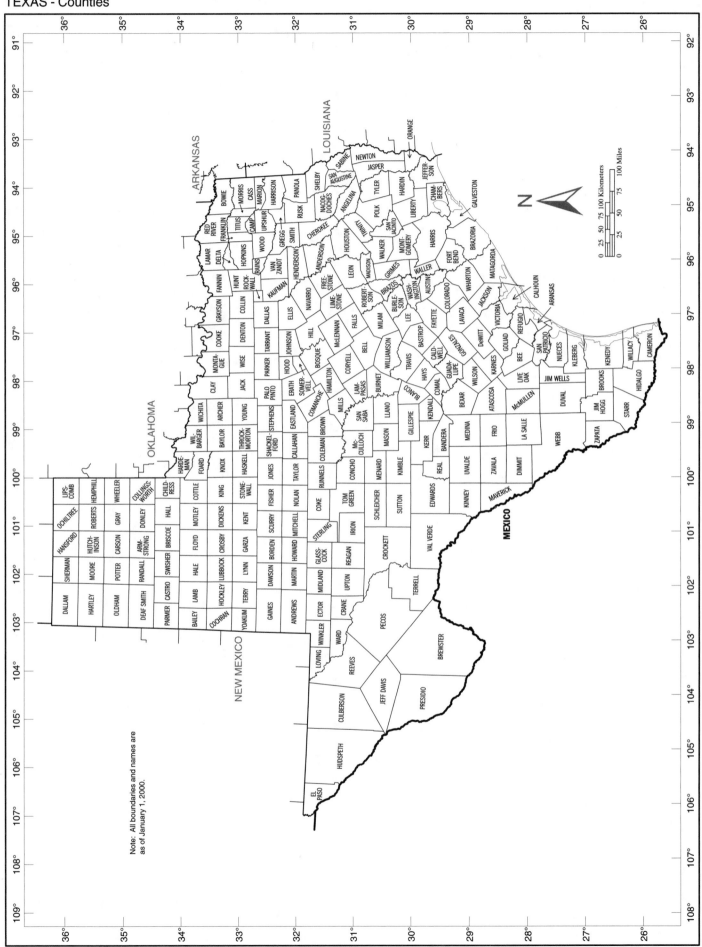

Texas

ANDERSON COUNTY
500 N Church St   **Ph:** 903-723-7432
Palestine, TX 75801
www.co.anderson.tx.us

In east-central TX, southeast of Dallas; organized Mar 24, 1846 from Houston County. **Name Origin:** For Kenneth Lewis Anderson (1805-45), TX legislator and vice president of the Republic of TX (1844).

Area (sq mi): 1077.95 (land 1070.79; water 7.16).

Pop: 55,109 (White 63.1%; Black or African American 23.5%; Hispanic or Latino 12.2%; Asian 0.4%; Other 9.6%). **Foreign born:** 3.2%. **Median age:** 35.8. **State rank:** 53. **Pop change 1990-2000:** +14.8%.

Income: per capita $13,838; median household $31,957. **Pop below poverty level:** 16.5%.

Unemployment: 4%. **Median home value:** $58,900. **Median travel time to work:** 22.8 minutes.

ANDREWS COUNTY
PO Box 727   **Ph:** 915-524-1426
Andrews, TX 79714
www.co.andrews.tx.us

On the southwest border of the TX panhandle, north of Odessa; organized Aug 21, 1876 from Bexar County. **Name Origin:** For Richard 'Big Dick' Andrews (1814-35), the first TX soldier killed in the Texas revolution.

Area (sq mi): 1500.99 (land 1500.64; water 0.36).

Pop: 13,004 (White 56.3%; Black or African American 1.6%; Hispanic or Latino 40%; Asian 0.7%; Other 20.6%). **Foreign born:** 10.6%. **Median age:** 34.1. **State rank:** 151. **Pop change 1990-2000:** -9.3%.

Income: per capita $15,916; median household $34,036. **Pop below poverty level:** 16.4%.

Unemployment: 3.9%. **Median home value:** $42,500. **Median travel time to work:** 20.6 minutes.

ANGELINA COUNTY
PO Box 908   **Ph:** 936-634-8339
Lufkin, TX 75902   **Fax:** 936-634-8460
www.angelinacounty.net

In eastern TX, south of Nacogdoches; organized Apr 22, 1846 from Nacogdoches County. **Name Origin:** For the Angelina River, which forms its eastern border; Spanish diminutive for 'angel.'

Area (sq mi): 864.45 (land 801.56; water 62.89).

Pop: 80,130 (White 69.4%; Black or African American 14.7%; Hispanic or Latino 14.3%; Asian 0.7%; Other 9.5%). **Foreign born:** 6.9%. **Median age:** 34.2. **State rank:** 41. **Pop change 1990-2000:** +14.7%.

Income: per capita $15,876; median household $33,806. **Pop below poverty level:** 15.8%.

Unemployment: 5.8%. **Median home value:** $63,600. **Median travel time to work:** 19.6 minutes.

ARANSAS COUNTY
301 N Live Oak St   **Ph:** 361-790-0122
Rockport, TX 78382   **Fax:** 361-790-0119

On the southeastern coast of TX, northeast of Corpus Christi; organized Sep 18, 1871 from Refugio County. **Name Origin:** For Aransas Bay, on its eastern border; itself named for the Aransas River, which empties into the bay.

Area (sq mi): 527.95 (land 251.86; water 276.09).

Pop: 22,497 (White 73.8%; Black or African American 1.4%; Hispanic or Latino 20.3%; Asian 2.8%; Other 8.3%). **Foreign born:** 5.7%. **Median age:** 42.7. **State rank:** 106. **Pop change 1990-2000:** +25.7%.

Income: per capita $18,560; median household $30,702. **Pop below poverty level:** 19.9%.

Unemployment: 5.8%. **Median home value:** $79,000. **Median travel time to work:** 24 minutes.

ARCHER COUNTY
PO Box 815   **Ph:** 940-574-4615
Archer City, TX 76351

On the central northern border of TX, northwest of Ft. Worth;

Please see sample entry on inside front cover for detailed information about the statistics presented with each county listing.

531

organized Jan 22, 1858 from Fannin County. **Name Origin:** For Dr. Branch Tanner Archer (1790-1856), TX legislator (1836) and secretary of war (1836-42).

Area (sq mi): 925.78 (land 909.7; water 16.09).

Pop: 8,854 (White 93.3%; Black or African American 0.1%; Hispanic or Latino 4.9%; Asian 0.1%; Other 4.2%). **Foreign born:** 2.3%. **Median age:** 38.1. **State rank:** 174. **Pop change 1990-2000:** +11%.

Income: per capita $19,300; median household $38,514. **Pop below poverty level:** 9%.

Unemployment: 2.4%. **Median home value:** $61,200. **Median travel time to work:** 23.6 minutes.

ARMSTRONG COUNTY
PO Box 309 **Ph:** 806-226-2081
Claude, TX 79019 **Fax:** 806-226-5301

In north-central TX panhandle, southeast of Amarillo; organized Aug 21, 1876 from Bexar County. **Name Origin:** For the Armstrong family, early settlers.

Area (sq mi): 913.81 (land 913.63; water 0.18).

Pop: 2,148 (White 93.5%; Black or African American 0.3%; Hispanic or Latino 5.4%; Asian 0%; Other 4.3%). **Foreign born:** 0.9%. **Median age:** 40.7. **State rank:** 237. **Pop change 1990-2000:** +6.3%.

Income: per capita $17,151; median household $38,194. **Pop below poverty level:** 10.6%.

Unemployment: 1.3%. **Median home value:** $60,500. **Median travel time to work:** 24.9 minutes.

ATASCOSA COUNTY
1604 Hwy 97 E Suite 100 **Ph:** 830-767-2511
Jourdanton, TX 78026 **Fax:** 830-769-1021

In south-central TX, south of San Antonio; organized Jan 25, 1856 from Bexar County. **Name Origin:** For the Atascosa River, which runs through it; from Spanish 'wet' or 'swampy.'

Area (sq mi): 1235.61 (land 1232.12; water 3.49).

Pop: 38,628 (White 39.6%; Black or African American 0.6%; Hispanic or Latino 58.6%; Asian 0.3%; Other 25.9%). **Foreign born:** 5.1%. **Median age:** 32.3. **State rank:** 71. **Pop change 1990-2000:** +26.5%.

Income: per capita $14,276; median household $33,081. **Pop below poverty level:** 20.2%.

Unemployment: 4.2%. **Median home value:** $52,900. **Median travel time to work:** 33 minutes.

AUSTIN COUNTY
1 E Main St **Ph:** 979-865-5911
Bellville, TX 77418 **Fax:** 979-865-8786
www.austincounty.com

In eastern TX, west of Houston; original county; organized Mar 17, 1836 (prior to statehood) from Old Mexican Municipality. **Name Origin:** For Stephen Fuller Austin (1793-1836), MO territorial legislator (1814-20), AR jurist (1820), surveyor and explorer of TX (1822), and secretary of state of the Republic of TX (1836).

Area (sq mi): 656.37 (land 652.59; water 3.78).

Pop: 23,590 (White 71.9%; Black or African American 10.6%; Hispanic or Latino 16.1%; Asian 0.3%; Other 8.9%). **Foreign born:** 7.3%. **Median age:** 37.6. **State rank:** 100. **Pop change 1990-2000:** +18.9%.

Income: per capita $18,140; median household $38,615. **Pop below poverty level:** 12.1%.

Unemployment: 2.8%. **Median home value:** $85,000. **Median travel time to work:** 29 minutes.

BAILEY COUNTY
300 S 1st St **Ph:** 806-272-3044
Muleshoe, TX 79347 **Fax:** 806-272-3538

On the central western border of TX panhandle, northwest of Lubbock; organized Aug 21, 1876 from Bexar County. **Name Origin:** For Pvt. Peter James Bailey (1812-36), killed at the Battle of the Alamo.

Area (sq mi): 827.38 (land 826.69; water 0.68).

Pop: 6,594 (White 50.3%; Black or African American 1.3%; Hispanic or Latino 47.3%; Asian 0.1%; Other 32%). **Foreign born:** 13.1%. **Median age:** 34.9. **State rank:** 191. **Pop change 1990-2000:** -6.7%.

Income: per capita $12,979; median household $27,901. **Pop below poverty level:** 16.7%.

Unemployment: 5.1%. **Median home value:** $37,300. **Median travel time to work:** 19.1 minutes.

BANDERA COUNTY
500 Main St PO Box 823 **Ph:** 830-796-3332
Bandera, TX 78003 **Fax:** 830-796-8323

In south-central TX, northwest of San Antonio; organized Jan 26, 1856 from Uvalde County. **Name Origin:** From the Spanish for 'flag'; reason unknown.

Area (sq mi): 797.54 (land 791.73; water 5.81).

Pop: 17,645 (White 84.1%; Black or African American 0.3%; Hispanic or Latino 13.5%; Asian 0.3%; Other 5.5%). **Foreign born:** 3.9%. **Median age:** 41.3. **State rank:** 127. **Pop change 1990-2000:** +67.1%.

Income: per capita $19,635; median household $39,013. **Pop below poverty level:** 10.8%.

Unemployment: 2.7%. **Median home value:** $99,000. **Median travel time to work:** 34.3 minutes.

BASTROP COUNTY
PO Box 770 **Ph:** 512-332-7244
Bastrop, TX 78602 **Fax:** 512-332-7249

In east-central TX, southeast of Austin; organized Mar 17, 1836 (prior to statehood) from Old Mexican Municipality. **Name Origin:** For Felipe Enrique Neri (?-1828), Baron de Bastrop, who established a colony of Germans in TX (1823); first commissioner of Austin's colony (1824).

Area (sq mi): 895.92 (land 888.35; water 7.57).

Pop: 57,733 (White 65.4%; Black or African American 8.8%; Hispanic or Latino 24%; Asian 0.5%; Other 10.6%). **Foreign born:**

All statistics are based on the 2000 Census except the dollar figures given for per capita income, which are based on 1999 estimates.

532

8.1%. **Median age:** 35.4. **State rank:** 52. **Pop change 1990-2000:** +50.9%.

Income: per capita $18,146; median household $43,578. **Pop below poverty level:** 11.6%.

Unemployment: 4%. **Median home value:** $93,400. **Median travel time to work:** 37.1 minutes.

BAYLOR COUNTY
PO Box 689   **Ph:** 940-889-3322
Seymour, TX 76380

In north-central TX, southwest of Wichita Falls; organized Feb 1, 1858 from Fannin County. **Name Origin:** For Henry Weidner Baylor (1818-53), a physician in the Texas Rangers during the Mexican War.

Area (sq mi): 901.01 (land 870.77; water 30.24).

Pop: 4,093 (White 85.8%; Black or African American 3.3%; Hispanic or Latino 9.3%; Asian 0.5%; Other 5.1%). **Foreign born:** 2%. **Median age:** 44.8. **State rank:** 211. **Pop change 1990-2000:** -6.7%.

Income: per capita $16,384; median household $24,627. **Pop below poverty level:** 16.1%.

Unemployment: 4.2%. **Median home value:** $34,200. **Median travel time to work:** 17.9 minutes.

BEE COUNTY
105 W Corpus Christi St Rm 103   **Ph:** 361-362-3245
Beeville, TX 78102   **Fax:** 361-362-3247

In southeastern TX, northwest of Corpus Christi; organized Dec 8, 1857 from Goliad and Refugio counties. **Name Origin:** For Barnard E. Bee (1787-1853), TX soldier, statesman, and Minister from TX to the U.S. (1838-41) who opposed the annexation of TX.

Area (sq mi): 880.31 (land 880.14; water 0.17).

Pop: 32,359 (White 35.1%; Black or African American 9.9%; Hispanic or Latino 53.9%; Asian 0.5%; Other 21.7%). **Foreign born:** 2%. **Median age:** 31.8. **State rank:** 84. **Pop change 1990-2000:** +28.7%.

Income: per capita $10,625; median household $28,392. **Pop below poverty level:** 24%.

Unemployment: 5%. **Median home value:** $47,200. **Median travel time to work:** 24.2 minutes.

BELL COUNTY
550 E 2nd St   **Ph:** 254-933-5160
Belton, TX 76513   **Fax:** 254-933-5176
www.bellcountytx.com

In south-central TX, northeast of Austin; organized Jan 22, 1850 from Bexar County. **Name Origin:** For Peter Hansborough Bell (1812-98), governor of TX (1849-53) and U.S. representative from TX (1853-57).

Area (sq mi): 1087.93 (land 1059.72; water 28.21).

Pop: 237,974 (White 57.3%; Black or African American 20.4%; Hispanic or Latino 16.7%; Asian 2.6%; Other 13.6%). **Foreign born:** 7.3%. **Median age:** 29.2. **State rank:** 19. **Pop change 1990-2000:** +24.5%.

Income: per capita $17,219; median household $36,872. **Pop below poverty level:** 12.1%.

Unemployment: 4.2%. **Median home value:** $78,100. **Median travel time to work:** 21.1 minutes.

BEXAR COUNTY
100 Dolorosa St   **Ph:** 210-335-2011
San Antonio, TX 78205   **Fax:** 210-335-2197
www.co.bexar.tx.us

In south-central TX, southwest of Austin; original county, established Mar 17, 1836 (prior to statehood) from Old Mexican Municipality. **Name Origin:** For the Presidio of San Antonio de Bexas (later known as the Alamo), named for the second son of the Duke of Bexar, of the Spanish royal family. Alternate spelling of *Bejar*.

Area (sq mi): 1256.66 (land 1246.82; water 9.84).

Pop: 1,392,931 (White 35.6%; Black or African American 7.2%; Hispanic or Latino 54.3%; Asian 1.6%; Other 22.3%). **Foreign born:** 10.9%. **Median age:** 32.1. **State rank:** 4. **Pop change 1990-2000:** +17.5%.

Income: per capita $18,363; median household $38,328. **Pop below poverty level:** 15.9%.

Unemployment: 4.1%. **Median home value:** $74,100. **Median travel time to work:** 24 minutes.

BLANCO COUNTY
101 E Pecan Dr Po Box 65   **Ph:** 830-868-7357
Johnson City, TX 78636   **Fax:** 830-868-7788
www.moment.net/~blancoco/

In south-central TX, west of Austin; organized Feb 12, 1858 from Gillespie and Comal counties. **Name Origin:** For the Blanco River, which runs through the south of the county; Spanish 'white'; origin uncertain.

Area (sq mi): 713.41 (land 711.24; water 2.16).

Pop: 8,418 (White 82.1%; Black or African American 0.7%; Hispanic or Latino 15.3%; Asian 0.2%; Other 8.1%). **Foreign born:** 5%. **Median age:** 41.2. **State rank:** 176. **Pop change 1990-2000:** +41%.

Income: per capita $19,721; median household $39,369. **Pop below poverty level:** 11.2%.

Unemployment: 2.7%. **Median home value:** $93,000. **Median travel time to work:** 31.4 minutes.

BORDEN COUNTY
Po Box 156   **Ph:** 806-756-4391
Gail, TX 79738   **Fax:** 806-756-4405

In south-central TX panhandle, southeast of Lubbock; organized Aug 21, 1876 from Bexar County. **Name Origin:** For Gail Borden, Jr. (1801-74), surveyor of Austin's colony (1830), publisher, and inventor of food products, including condensed milk.

Area (sq mi): 906.04 (land 898.8; water 7.24).

Pop: 729 (White 85.6%; Black or African American 0.1%; Hispanic or Latino 11.9%; Asian 0%; Other 9.3%). **Foreign born:** 4.5%. **Median age:** 40.5. **State rank:** 251. **Pop change 1990-2000:** -8.8%.

Please see sample entry on inside front cover for detailed information about the statistics presented with each county listing.

Income: per capita $18,364; median household $29,205. **Pop below poverty level:** 14%.

Unemployment: 2%. **Median home value:** $43,100. **Median travel time to work:** 21.4 minutes.

BOSQUE COUNTY

PO Box 617   **Ph:** 254-435-2201
Meridian, TX 76665   **Fax:** 254-435-2152

In central TX, northwest of Waco; organized Feb 14, 1854 from McLennan County. **Name Origin:** For the N. Bosque River, which runs through it; Spanish 'woods, forest.'

Area (sq mi): 1002.63 (land 989.18; water 13.46).

Pop: 17,204 (White 84.3%; Black or African American 1.9%; Hispanic or Latino 12.2%; Asian 0.1%; Other 7.2%). **Foreign born:** 4.4%. **Median age:** 41.7. **State rank:** 128. **Pop change 1990-2000:** +13.7%.

Income: per capita $17,455; median household $34,181. **Pop below poverty level:** 12.7%.

Unemployment: 4.4%. **Median home value:** $57,900. **Median travel time to work:** 31 minutes.

BOWIE COUNTY

710 James Bowie Dr   **Ph:** 903-628-2571
New Boston, TX 75570   **Fax:** 903-628-6729

On the northeastern border of TX, northwest of Shreveport, LA; organized 1840 (prior to statehood) from Red River County. **Name Origin:** For Col. James A. Bowie (1795-1836), pioneer and officer in the Texas Revolution, killled at the Alamo. The bowie knife is named for him.

Area (sq mi): 922.77 (land 887.87; water 34.9).

Pop: 89,306 (White 70.2%; Black or African American 23.4%; Hispanic or Latino 4.5%; Asian 0.4%; Other 2.8%). **Foreign born:** 1.5%. **Median age:** 36.3. **State rank:** 36. **Pop change 1990-2000:** +9.4%.

Income: per capita $17,357; median household $33,001. **Pop below poverty level:** 17.7%.

Unemployment: 4.6%. **Median home value:** $66,600. **Median travel time to work:** 19.9 minutes.

BRAZORIA COUNTY

111 E Locust St Suite 200   **Ph:** 979-849-5711
Angleton, TX 77515   **Fax:** 979-864-1358
www.brazoria-county.com

On central eastern border of TX, south of Houston; original county; organized Mar 17, 1836 (prior to statehood) from Old Mexican Municipality. **Name Origin:** For the Brazos River, which forms its northern border; a Latinized form of Spanish *brazos* 'arms' or 'forks' as the forks of a river.

Area (sq mi): 1597.44 (land 1386.4; water 211.04).

Pop: 241,767 (White 65.4%; Black or African American 8.5%; Hispanic or Latino 22.8%; Asian 2%; Other 12.3%). **Foreign born:** 8.5%. **Median age:** 34. **State rank:** 18. **Pop change 1990-2000:** +26.1%.

Income: per capita $20,021; median household $48,632. **Pop below poverty level:** 10.2%.

Unemployment: 5.9%. **Median home value:** $88,500. **Median travel time to work:** 28 minutes.

BRAZOS COUNTY

300 E 26th St Suite 120   **Ph:** 979-361-4135
Bryan, TX 77803
www.co.brazos.tx.us

In east-central TX, northwest of Houston; organized Jan 30, 1841 (prior to statehood) from Washington County. **Name Origin:** For the Brazos River, which forms its western border; Spanish 'arms' or 'forks' as forks in a river.

Area (sq mi): 590.29 (land 585.78; water 4.51).

Pop: 152,415 (White 66%; Black or African American 10.7%; Hispanic or Latino 17.9%; Asian 4%; Other 10.9%). **Foreign born:** 10.3%. **Median age:** 23.6. **State rank:** 23. **Pop change 1990-2000:** +25.1%.

Income: per capita $16,212; median household $29,104. **Pop below poverty level:** 26.9%.

Unemployment: 1.6%. **Median home value:** $96,000. **Median travel time to work:** 16.7 minutes.

BREWSTER COUNTY

PO Box 119   **Ph:** 915-837-3366
Alpine, TX 79831   **Fax:** 915-837-6217

On southwestern border of TX, southwest of Odessa; organized Feb 2, 1887 from Presidio County. **Name Origin:** For Henry Percy Brewster (1816-84), TX soldier, secretary to Sam Houston (1836), and attorney general of TX (1847-49).

Area (sq mi): 6192.78 (land 6192.61; water 0.18).

Pop: 8,866 (White 53.1%; Black or African American 1.2%; Hispanic or Latino 43.6%; Asian 0.4%; Other 17.3%). **Foreign born:** 6.9%. **Median age:** 36.2. **State rank:** 173. **Pop change 1990-2000:** +2.1%.

Income: per capita $15,183; median household $27,386. **Pop below poverty level:** 18.2%.

Unemployment: 2.2%. **Median home value:** $67,000. **Median travel time to work:** 12.6 minutes.

BRISCOE COUNTY

PO Box 375   **Ph:** 806-823-2131
Silverton, TX 79257

In the central TX panhandle, southeast of Amarillo; organized Aug 21, 1876 from Bexar County. **Name Origin:** For Capt. Andrew Briscoe (1810-49), Republic of TX officer, signer of the TX Declaration of Independence (1836), and chief justice of Harrisburg, TX (1836-39).

Area (sq mi): 901.59 (land 900.25; water 1.33).

Pop: 1,790 (White 73.7%; Black or African American 2.3%; Hispanic or Latino 22.7%; Asian 0.1%; Other 14.4%). **Foreign born:** 4.9%. **Median age:** 39.9. **State rank:** 240. **Pop change 1990-2000:** -9.2%.

All statistics are based on the 2000 Census except the dollar figures given for per capita income, which are based on 1999 estimates.

Income: per capita $14,218; median household $29,917. **Pop below poverty level:** 16%.

Unemployment: 2.7%. **Median home value:** $30,000. **Median travel time to work:** 18.8 minutes.

BROOKS COUNTY

PO Box 427   **Ph:** 361-325-5604
Falfurrias, TX 78355

In southeastern TX, southwest of Corpus Christi; organized Mar 11, 1911 from Starr and Zapata counties. **Name Origin:** For James Abijah Brooks (1855-1944), TX legislator, ranger (1882-1906), and judge of Brooks County (1911-39).

Area (sq mi): 943.61 (land 943.28; water 0.33).

Pop: 7,976 (White 7.9%; Black or African American 0.2%; Hispanic or Latino 91.6%; Asian 0.1%; Other 24%). **Foreign born:** 6.1%. **Median age:** 34.4. **State rank:** 181. **Pop change 1990-2000:** -2.8%.

Income: per capita $10,234; median household $18,622. **Pop below poverty level:** 40.2%.

Unemployment: 5.7%. **Median home value:** $34,600. **Median travel time to work:** 18.3 minutes.

BROWN COUNTY

200 S Broadway   **Ph:** 915-643-2594
Brownwood, TX 76801

In central TX, southeast of Abilene; organized Aug 27, 1856 from Caldwell County. **Name Origin:** For Henry Stevenson Brown (1793-1834), Republic of TX soldier and delegate to the TX convention (1832-33).

Area (sq mi): 956.94 (land 943.85; water 13.08).

Pop: 37,674 (White 79%; Black or African American 4%; Hispanic or Latino 15.4%; Asian 0.4%; Other 8.3%). **Foreign born:** 3.1%. **Median age:** 37.2. **State rank:** 73. **Pop change 1990-2000:** +9.6%.

Income: per capita $15,624; median household $30,974. **Pop below poverty level:** 17.2%.

Unemployment: 3.7%. **Median home value:** $47,800. **Median travel time to work:** 19.5 minutes.

BURLESON COUNTY

100 W Buck St Suite 203   **Ph:** 979-567-2329
Caldwell, TX 77836   **Fax:** 979-567-2376

In east-central TX, northeast of Austin; organized Mar 24, 1846 from Milam and Washington counties. **Name Origin:** For Gen. Edward Burleston (1798-1852), senator in the first TX congress (1836), vice president of the Republic of TX (1841), and TX legislator.

Area (sq mi): 677.78 (land 665.54; water 12.24).

Pop: 16,470 (White 69%; Black or African American 15.1%; Hispanic or Latino 14.6%; Asian 0.2%; Other 10.7%). **Foreign born:** 3%. **Median age:** 37.9. **State rank:** 131. **Pop change 1990-2000:** +20.9%.

Income: per capita $16,616; median household $33,026. **Pop below poverty level:** 17.2%.

Unemployment: 2.9%. **Median home value:** $55,900. **Median travel time to work:** 28.3 minutes.

BURNET COUNTY

220 S Pierce St   **Ph:** 512-756-5420
Burnet, TX 78611   **Fax:** 512-756-4091

In central TX, northwest of Austin; organized Feb 5, 1852 from Travis County. **Name Origin:** For David Gouverneur Burnet (1778-1870), president of the Republic of TX (1836) and vice president (1838-41).

Area (sq mi): 1020.96 (land 996.04; water 24.93).

Pop: 34,147 (White 82%; Black or African American 1.5%; Hispanic or Latino 14.8%; Asian 0.3%; Other 8.6%). **Foreign born:** 5.4%. **Median age:** 40.2. **State rank:** 79. **Pop change 1990-2000:** +50.6%.

Income: per capita $18,850; median household $37,921. **Pop below poverty level:** 10.9%.

Unemployment: 3.7%. **Median home value:** $93,600. **Median travel time to work:** 28.8 minutes.

CALDWELL COUNTY

PO Box 906   **Ph:** 512-398-1824
Lockhart, TX 78644   **Fax:** 512-398-1816

In east-central TX, south of Austin; organized Mar 6, 1848 from Gonzales County. **Name Origin:** For Matthew 'Old Paint' Caldwell (1798-1842), TX ranger, soldier, and a signer of the TX Declaration of Independence (1836).

Area (sq mi): 547.41 (land 545.73; water 1.69).

Pop: 32,194 (White 49.5%; Black or African American 8.5%; Hispanic or Latino 40.4%; Asian 0.3%; Other 21%). **Foreign born:** 5.1%. **Median age:** 34.4. **State rank:** 86. **Pop change 1990-2000:** +22%.

Income: per capita $15,099; median household $36,573. **Pop below poverty level:** 13.1%.

Unemployment: 4.2%. **Median home value:** $68,000. **Median travel time to work:** 31.4 minutes.

CALHOUN COUNTY

211 S Ann St   **Ph:** 361-553-4411
Port Lavaca, TX 77979   **Fax:** 361-553-4420

On the central eastern coast of TX, northeast of Corpus Christi; organized Apr 4, 1846 from Victoria County. **Name Origin:** For John Caldwell Calhoun (1782-1850), U.S. statesman and champion of Southern causes.

Area (sq mi): 1032.16 (land 512.31; water 519.84).

Pop: 20,647 (White 52.2%; Black or African American 2.6%; Hispanic or Latino 40.9%; Asian 3.3%; Other 16.1%). **Foreign born:** 8.5%. **Median age:** 35.3. **State rank:** 113. **Pop change 1990-2000:** +8.4%.

Income: per capita $17,125; median household $35,849. **Pop below poverty level:** 16.4%.

Unemployment: 7.9%. **Median home value:** $56,400. **Median travel time to work:** 19.6 minutes.

CALLAHAN COUNTY

100 W 4th St   **Ph:** 915-854-1155
Baird, TX 79504   **Fax:** 915-854-1227

In north-central TX, east of Abilene; established Apr 1, 1858 from

Please see sample entry on inside front cover for detailed information about the statistics presented with each county listing.

535

Milam and Travis counties. **Name Origin:** For James Hughes Callahan (1814-1856), soldier and Texas ranger; killed by Indians.

Area (sq mi): 901.26 (land 898.62; water 2.64).

Pop: 12,905 (White 91.6%; Black or African American 0.2%; Hispanic or Latino 6.3%; Asian 0.3%; Other 4.7%). **Foreign born:** 1.4%. **Median age:** 39.8. **State rank:** 153. **Pop change 1990-2000:** +8.8%.

Income: per capita $15,204; median household $32,463. **Pop below poverty level:** 12.2%.

Unemployment: 3.7%. **Median home value:** $49,800. **Median travel time to work:** 24.3 minutes.

CAMERON COUNTY
964 E Harrison St   **Ph:** 956-544-0815
Brownsville, TX 78520   **Fax:** 956-504-0813
www.co.cameron.tx.us

On the southeastern coast of TX, east of McAllen; organized Feb 12, 1848 from Nueces County. **Name Origin:** For Capt. Ewin Cameron (1811-43), a Republic of TX soldier, executed by the Mexicans.

Area (sq mi): 1276.33 (land 905.76; water 370.58).

Pop: 335,227 (White 14.5%; Black or African American 0.5%; Hispanic or Latino 84.3%; Asian 0.5%; Other 18.7%). **Foreign born:** 25.6%. **Median age:** 29. **State rank:** 11. **Pop change 1990-2000:** +28.9%.

Income: per capita $10,960; median household $26,155. **Pop below poverty level:** 33.1%.

Unemployment: 9.2%. **Median home value:** $53,000. **Median travel time to work:** 20.7 minutes.

CAMP COUNTY
126 Church St   **Ph:** 903-856-2731
Pittsburg, TX 75686   **Fax:** 903-856-2309

In northeastern TX, southwest of Texarkana; organized Apr 6, 1874 from Upshur County. **Name Origin:** For Col. John Lafayette Camp (1828-91), officer in the Confederate army, TX legislator (1874), and district judge (1878).

Area (sq mi): 203.2 (land 197.51; water 5.69).

Pop: 11,549 (White 65%; Black or African American 19.2%; Hispanic or Latino 14.8%; Asian 0.2%; Other 11.1%). **Foreign born:** 9.9%. **Median age:** 36.9. **State rank:** 158. **Pop change 1990-2000:** +16.6%.

Income: per capita $16,500; median household $31,164. **Pop below poverty level:** 20.9%.

Unemployment: 5.2%. **Median home value:** $61,000. **Median travel time to work:** 22.1 minutes.

CARSON COUNTY
PO Box 487   **Ph:** 806-537-3873
Panhandle, TX 79068   **Fax:** 806-537-3623

In the north-central TX panhandle, east of Amarillo; organized Aug 21, 1876 from Bexar County. **Name Origin:** For Samuel Price Carson (1798-1838), signer of the TX Declaration of Independence (1836) and secretary of state of the Republic of TX (1836-38).

Area (sq mi): 924.1 (land 923.19; water 0.91).

Pop: 6,516 (White 90.6%; Black or African American 0.6%; Hispanic or Latino 7%; Asian 0.1%; Other 5.4%). **Foreign born:** 2.7%. **Median age:** 38.9. **State rank:** 193. **Pop change 1990-2000:** -0.9%.

Income: per capita $19,368; median household $40,285. **Pop below poverty level:** 7.3%.

Unemployment: 2.8%. **Median home value:** $52,400. **Median travel time to work:** 21.4 minutes.

CASS COUNTY
PO Box 449   **Ph:** 903-756-5071
Linden, TX 75563   **Fax:** 903-756-8057

On northeastern border of TX, south of Texarkana. The area now called Cass Co. has had five names and boundaries: (1) 1924-36, under Mexican rule, part of Paschal Co.; (2) 1836-41 part of Red River Co.; (3) 1841-46 part of Bowie Co.; (4) 1846-60 Cass Co. included Marion Co.; (5) name changed in 1861 to Davis to honor Jeff Davis; name changed back in 1871. **Name Origin:** For Gen. Lewis Cass (1782-1866), OH legislator, military and civil governor of MI Territory (1813-30), U.S. secretary of war (1831-36), and U.S. secretary of state (1857-60).

Area (sq mi): 960.35 (land 937.35; water 22.99).

Pop: 30,438 (White 77.3%; Black or African American 19.5%; Hispanic or Latino 1.7%; Asian 0.1%; Other 2.2%). **Foreign born:** 1.1%. **Median age:** 40. **State rank:** 90. **Pop change 1990-2000:** +1.5%.

Income: per capita $15,777; median household $28,441. **Pop below poverty level:** 17.7%.

Unemployment: 6%. **Median home value:** $53,300. **Median travel time to work:** 27.1 minutes.

CASTRO COUNTY
100 E Bedford St   **Ph:** 806-647-3338
Dimmitt, TX 79027

In the west-central panhandle, southwest of Amarillo; organized Aug 21, 1876 from Wheeler County. **Name Origin:** For Henri Castro (1786-1865), who established a colony in the Republic of TX (1842). Consul general of TX to France (1842).

Area (sq mi): 899.32 (land 898.31; water 1).

Pop: 8,285 (White 45.4%; Black or African American 2.3%; Hispanic or Latino 51.6%; Asian 0%; Other 22.4%). **Foreign born:** 12.1%. **Median age:** 32.3. **State rank:** 178. **Pop change 1990-2000:** -8.7%.

Income: per capita $14,457; median household $30,619. **Pop below poverty level:** 19%.

Unemployment: 4.1%. **Median home value:** $51,000. **Median travel time to work:** 15.5 minutes.

CHAMBERS COUNTY
PO Box 728   **Ph:** 409-267-8309
Anahuac, TX 77514   **Fax:** 409-267-4453
www.co.chambers.tx.us

On the central eastern coast of TX, east of Houston; organized Feb 12, 1858 from Jefferson and Liberty counties. **Name Origin:** For

All statistics are based on the 2000 Census except the dollar figures given for per capita income, which are based on 1999 estimates.

536

Gen. Thomas Jefferson Chambers (1802-65), surveyor general of TX (1829), attorney, and member of secession convention (1861).

Area (sq mi): 871.99 (land 599.31; water 272.68).

Pop: 26,031 (White 77.6%; Black or African American 9.8%; Hispanic or Latino 10.8%; Asian 0.7%; Other 7.7%). **Foreign born:** 5.1%. **Median age:** 35.1. **State rank:** 94. **Pop change 1990-2000:** +29.6%.

Income: per capita $19,863; median household $47,964. **Pop below poverty level:** 11%.

Unemployment: 4.5%. **Median home value:** $85,000. **Median travel time to work:** 25.7 minutes.

CHEROKEE COUNTY

PO Box 420   **Ph:** 903-683-2350
Rusk, TX 75785   **Fax:** 903-683-5931

In northeastern TX, south of Tyler; organized Apr 11, 1846 from Nacogdoches County. **Name Origin:** For the Indian tribe of Iroquoian linguistic stock. Name may derive from Creek *tciloki* 'people of a different speech.'

Area (sq mi): 1061.93 (land 1052.22; water 9.72).

Pop: 46,659 (White 69.3%; Black or African American 16%; Hispanic or Latino 13.2%; Asian 0.4%; Other 9.3%). **Foreign born:** 7.9%. **Median age:** 36. **State rank:** 61. **Pop change 1990-2000:** +13.7%.

Income: per capita $13,980; median household $29,313. **Pop below poverty level:** 17.9%.

Unemployment: 4.3%. **Median home value:** $53,700. **Median travel time to work:** 23.8 minutes.

CHILDRESS COUNTY

Courthouse Box 4   **Ph:** 940-937-6143
Childress, TX 79201   **Fax:** 940-937-3479

On the southeastern border of TX panhandle, northeast of Lubbock; established Aug 21, 1876 from Bexar and Fannin counties. **Name Origin:** For George Campbell Childress (1804-41), one of the drafters of the Texas Declaration of Independence.

Area (sq mi): 713.61 (land 710.34; water 3.27).

Pop: 7,688 (White 64%; Black or African American 14.1%; Hispanic or Latino 20.5%; Asian 0.3%; Other 17.9%). **Foreign born:** 4.7%. **Median age:** 36.6. **State rank:** 184. **Pop change 1990-2000:** +29.1%.

Income: per capita $12,452; median household $27,457. **Pop below poverty level:** 17.6%.

Unemployment: 2.9%. **Median home value:** $44,900. **Median travel time to work:** 10.8 minutes.

CLAY COUNTY

PO Box 548   **Ph:** 940-538-4631
Henrietta, TX 76365
www.co.clay.tx.us

On the central northern border of TX, east of Wichita Falls; organized Dec 24, 1857 from Cooke County. **Name Origin:** For Henry Clay (1777-1852), U.S. senator from KY, known as the 'Great Pacificator' for his advocacy of compromise to avert national crises.

Area (sq mi): 1116.17 (land 1097.82; water 18.36).

Pop: 11,006 (White 93.7%; Black or African American 0.4%; Hispanic or Latino 3.7%; Asian 0.1%; Other 4.1%). **Foreign born:** 1.4%. **Median age:** 40.2. **State rank:** 160. **Pop change 1990-2000:** +9.8%.

Income: per capita $16,361; median household $35,738. **Pop below poverty level:** 10.3%.

Unemployment: 2.4%. **Median home value:** $48,100. **Median travel time to work:** 26.6 minutes.

COCHRAN COUNTY

County Courthouse Rm 102   **Ph:** 806-266-5450
Morton, TX 79346   **Fax:** 806-266-9027

On the central western border of TX panhandle, west of Lubbock; organized Aug 21, 1876 from Bexar County. **Name Origin:** For Robert Cochran (?-1836), a soldier killed at the Alamo.

Area (sq mi): 775.31 (land 775.22; water 0.09).

Pop: 3,730 (White 50%; Black or African American 4.5%; Hispanic or Latino 44.1%; Asian 0.2%; Other 30.7%). **Foreign born:** 9.8%. **Median age:** 35.1. **State rank:** 219. **Pop change 1990-2000:** -14.8%.

Income: per capita $13,125; median household $27,525. **Pop below poverty level:** 27%.

Unemployment: 6.5%. **Median home value:** $25,700. **Median travel time to work:** 18.5 minutes.

COKE COUNTY

PO Box 150   **Ph:** 915-453-2631
Robert Lee, TX 76945   **Fax:** 915-453-2650

In central TX, southwest of Abilene; organized Mar 13, 1889 from Tom Green County. **Name Origin:** For Capt. Richard Coke (1829-97), Confederate Army officer, TX governor (1874-76), and U.S. senator (1876-94).

Area (sq mi): 927.97 (land 898.81; water 29.17).

Pop: 3,864 (White 79.7%; Black or African American 1.9%; Hispanic or Latino 16.9%; Asian 0.1%; Other 9.1%). **Foreign born:** 2.8%. **Median age:** 43.3. **State rank:** 215. **Pop change 1990-2000:** +12.9%.

Income: per capita $16,734; median household $29,085. **Pop below poverty level:** 13%.

Unemployment: 1.9%. **Median home value:** $48,100. **Median travel time to work:** 23.8 minutes.

COLEMAN COUNTY

PO Box 591   **Ph:** 915-625-2889
Coleman, TX 76834

In central TX, southeast of Abilene; organized Feb 1, 1858 from Travis County. **Name Origin:** For Col. Robert M. Coleman (1799-1837), one of the signers of the TX Declaration of Independence.

Area (sq mi): 1281.45 (land 1260.2; water 21.25).

Pop: 9,235 (White 82.3%; Black or African American 2.2%; Hispanic or Latino 14%; Asian 0.2%; Other 9%). **Foreign born:** 3.4%. **Median age:** 43. **State rank:** 169. **Pop change 1990-2000:** -4.9%.

Please see sample entry on inside front cover for detailed information about the statistics presented with each county listing.

Income: per capita $14,911; median household $25,658. **Pop below poverty level:** 19.9%.

Unemployment: 4.8%. **Median home value:** $32,300. **Median travel time to work:** 23.3 minutes.

COLLIN COUNTY

200 S McDonald St Suite 120   **Ph:** 972-548-4134
McKinney, TX 75069   **Fax:** 972-547-5731
www.co.collin.tx.us

In east-central TX, north of Dallas; organized Apr 3, 1846 from Fannin County. **Name Origin:** For Collin McKinney (1766-1861), Republic of TX legislator and a noted signer of the TX Declaration of Independence (1836).

Area (sq mi): 885.85 (land 847.56; water 38.29).

Pop: 491,675 (White 76.1%; Black or African American 4.8%; Hispanic or Latino 10.3%; Asian 6.9%; Other 6.9%). **Foreign born:** 13.3%. **Median age:** 32.9. **State rank:** 8. **Pop change 1990-2000:** +86.2%.

Income: per capita $33,345; median household $70,835. **Pop below poverty level:** 4.9%.

Unemployment: 4.1%. **Median home value:** $155,500. **Median travel time to work:** 28.4 minutes.

COLLINGSWORTH COUNTY

800 West Ave County Courthouse Box 10   **Ph:** 806-447-2408
Wellington, TX 79095   **Fax:** 806-447-5418

On the southeastern border of TX panhandle, southwest of Amarillo; organized Aug 21, 1876 from Bexar and Fannin counties. **Name Origin:** For Maj. James T. Collinsworth (1806-38), aide to Gen. Sam Houston (1793-1863), Republic of TX senator (1836), and first chief justice (1837). Clerical spelling error was allowed to stand.

Area (sq mi): 919.44 (land 918.8; water 0.64).

Pop: 3,206 (White 71.4%; Black or African American 5.3%; Hispanic or Latino 20.4%; Asian 0.2%; Other 14.7%). **Foreign born:** 4.3%. **Median age:** 40.6. **State rank:** 226. **Pop change 1990-2000:** -10.3%.

Income: per capita $15,318; median household $25,438. **Pop below poverty level:** 18.7%.

Unemployment: 1.1%. **Median home value:** $35,400. **Median travel time to work:** 14.8 minutes.

COLORADO COUNTY

PO Box 68   **Ph:** 979-732-2155
Columbus, TX 78934   **Fax:** 979-732-8852

In east-central TX, west of Houston; original county; organized Mar 17, 1836 (prior to statehood) from Old Mexican Municipality. **Name Origin:** For the Colorado River, which flows through it; Spanish 'reddish brown' for the color of its waters from the soil and rocks on its banks.

Area (sq mi): 973.59 (land 962.95; water 10.64).

Pop: 20,390 (White 64.6%; Black or African American 14.8%; Hispanic or Latino 19.7%; Asian 0.2%; Other 12.2%). **Foreign born:**

7.9%. **Median age:** 39.3. **State rank:** 114. **Pop change 1990-2000:** +10.9%.

Income: per capita $16,910; median household $32,425. **Pop below poverty level:** 16.2%.

Unemployment: 3.8%. **Median home value:** $59,200. **Median travel time to work:** 26.2 minutes.

COMAL COUNTY

150 N Seguin St Suite 101   **Ph:** 830-620-5513
New Braunfels, TX 78130   **Fax:** 830-620-3410
www.co.comal.tx.us

In south-central TX, north of San Antonio; organized Mar 24, 1846 from Bexar and Gonzales counties. **Name Origin:** From Spanish 'basin,' descriptive of an area drained by a stream.

Area (sq mi): 574.59 (land 561.45; water 13.15).

Pop: 78,021 (White 74.8%; Black or African American 0.9%; Hispanic or Latino 22.6%; Asian 0.5%; Other 9.5%). **Foreign born:** 4.8%. **Median age:** 39. **State rank:** 42. **Pop change 1990-2000:** +50.5%.

Income: per capita $21,914; median household $46,147. **Pop below poverty level:** 8.6%.

Unemployment: 3.5%. **Median home value:** $117,000. **Median travel time to work:** 28.2 minutes.

COMANCHE COUNTY

County Courthouse 101 W Central Ave   **Ph:** 915-356-2655
Comanche, TX 76442   **Fax:** 915-356-3710

In central TX, southeast of Abilene; organized Jan 25, 1856 from Bosque and Coryell counties. **Name Origin:** For an Indian tribe of Shoshonean linguistic stock; the meaning of the name is unknown.

Area (sq mi): 947.67 (land 937.69; water 9.98).

Pop: 14,026 (White 77.3%; Black or African American 0.4%; Hispanic or Latino 20.9%; Asian 0.1%; Other 12.1%). **Foreign born:** 7.1%. **Median age:** 40.3. **State rank:** 146. **Pop change 1990-2000:** +4.8%.

Income: per capita $14,677; median household $28,422. **Pop below poverty level:** 17.3%.

Unemployment: 2.7%. **Median home value:** $43,600. **Median travel time to work:** 22.2 minutes.

CONCHO COUNTY

PO Box 98   **Ph:** 915-732-4322
Paint Rock, TX 76866   **Fax:** 915-732-2047

In central TX, east of San Angelo; organized Feb 1, 1858 from Bexar County. **Name Origin:** For the Concho River, which runs through it; from the Indian tribal name.

Area (sq mi): 993.69 (land 991.45; water 2.23).

Pop: 3,966 (White 57.1%; Black or African American 1%; Hispanic or Latino 41.3%; Asian 0.1%; Other 10.7%). **Foreign born:** 2.8%. **Median age:** 36. **State rank:** 214. **Pop change 1990-2000:** +30.3%.

Income: per capita $15,727; median household $31,313. **Pop below poverty level:** 11.9%.

All statistics are based on the 2000 Census except the dollar figures given for per capita income, which are based on 1999 estimates.

Unemployment: 1.9%. **Median home value:** $43,600. **Median travel time to work:** 20.6 minutes.

COOKE COUNTY

100 Dixon St   **Ph:** 940-668-5420
Gainesville, TX 76240   **Fax:** 940-668-5440

On the central northern border of TX, north of Fort Worth; organized Mar 20, 1848 from Fannin County. **Name Origin:** For Capt. William G. Cooke (1808-47), officer in the Texas War for Independence and quartermaster general (1839).

Area (sq mi): 898.81 (land 873.64; water 25.17).

Pop: 36,363 (White 84.8%; Black or African American 3.1%; Hispanic or Latino 10%; Asian 0.3%; Other 7.8%). **Foreign born:** 5.5%. **Median age:** 36.7. **State rank:** 76. **Pop change 1990-2000:** +18.1%.

Income: per capita $17,889; median household $37,649. **Pop below poverty level:** 14.1%.

Unemployment: 4.7%. **Median home value:** $73,100. **Median travel time to work:** 25.7 minutes.

CORYELL COUNTY

620 E Main St   **Ph:** 254-865-5016
Gatesville, TX 76528   **Fax:** 254-865-8631

In east-central TX, west of Waco; organized Feb 4, 1854 from Bell and McLennan counties. **Name Origin:** For James Coryell (1801-37), a Texas ranger killed by Indians.

Area (sq mi): 1056.73 (land 1051.76; water 4.97).

Pop: 74,978 (White 60.5%; Black or African American 21.8%; Hispanic or Latino 12.6%; Asian 1.8%; Other 11.2%). **Foreign born:** 5.3%. **Median age:** 27.8. **State rank:** 44. **Pop change 1990-2000:** +16.8%.

Income: per capita $14,410; median household $35,999. **Pop below poverty level:** 9.5%.

Unemployment: 4.9%. **Median home value:** $69,500. **Median travel time to work:** 21 minutes.

COTTLE COUNTY

PO Box 717   **Ph:** 806-492-3823
Paducah, TX 79248   **Fax:** 806-492-3823

In the southeastern TX panhandle, west of Wichita Falls; organized 1892 from Childress County (other sources say organized Aug 21, 1876; first federal census: 1880). **Name Origin:** For Pvt. George Washington Cottle (1798-1836), killed at the Alamo.

Area (sq mi): 901.59 (land 901.18; water 0.42).

Pop: 1,904 (White 70.8%; Black or African American 9.9%; Hispanic or Latino 18.9%; Asian 0%; Other 8.7%). **Foreign born:** 3.6%. **Median age:** 43.9. **State rank:** 238. **Pop change 1990-2000:** -15.3%.

Income: per capita $16,212; median household $25,446. **Pop below poverty level:** 18.4%.

Unemployment: 5%. **Median home value:** $26,900. **Median travel time to work:** 18.8 minutes.

CRANE COUNTY

PO Box 578   **Ph:** 915-558-3581
Crane, TX 79731   **Fax:** 915-558-1185

In west-central TX, south of Odessa; organized 1927 from Ector County (other sources say organized Feb 26, 1887 from Tom Green County; first federal census: 1890). **Name Origin:** For William Carey Crane (1816-85), Baptist minister and president of Baylor University (1863-85).

Area (sq mi): 785.59 (land 785.56; water 0.03).

Pop: 3,996 (White 52.1%; Black or African American 2.9%; Hispanic or Latino 43.9%; Asian 0.4%; Other 23.1%). **Foreign born:** 14.4%. **Median age:** 34.2. **State rank:** 213. **Pop change 1990-2000:** -14.1%.

Income: per capita $15,374; median household $32,194. **Pop below poverty level:** 13.4%.

Unemployment: 6%. **Median home value:** $39,100. **Median travel time to work:** 18 minutes.

CROCKETT COUNTY

PO Box C   **Ph:** 915-392-2022
Ozona, TX 76943   **Fax:** 915-392-3742

In west-central TX, southwest of San Angelo; organized Jan 22, 1875 from Bexar County. **Name Origin:** For David 'Davy' Crockett (1786-1836), frontiersman, U.S. representative from TN (1827-31; 1833-35), fighter for TX independence killed at the Alamo.

Area (sq mi): 2807.43 (land 2807.42; water 0.01).

Pop: 4,099 (White 43.7%; Black or African American 0.7%; Hispanic or Latino 54.7%; Asian 0.3%; Other 22.7%). **Foreign born:** 10.5%. **Median age:** 37.2. **State rank:** 210. **Pop change 1990-2000:** +0.5%.

Income: per capita $14,414; median household $29,355. **Pop below poverty level:** 19.4%.

Unemployment: 2.6%. **Median home value:** $52,400. **Median travel time to work:** 18.4 minutes.

CROSBY COUNTY

201 W Aspen St Suite 102   **Ph:** 806-675-2334
Crosbyton, TX 79322

In the south-central TX panhandle, east of Lubbock; organized Aug 21, 1876 from Baylor County (other sources say organized from Garza County). **Name Origin:** For Stephen F. Crosby (1800-69), chief clerk in TX land office (1853-57; 1859-67).

Area (sq mi): 901.69 (land 899.51; water 2.17).

Pop: 7,072 (White 46.7%; Black or African American 3.9%; Hispanic or Latino 48.9%; Asian 0%; Other 32.3%). **Foreign born:** 3.9%. **Median age:** 34.3. **State rank:** 188. **Pop change 1990-2000:** -3.2%.

Income: per capita $14,445; median household $25,769. **Pop below poverty level:** 28.1%.

Unemployment: 5.7%. **Median home value:** $35,600. **Median travel time to work:** 20.7 minutes.

Please see sample entry on inside front cover for detailed information about the statistics presented with each county listing.

CULBERSON COUNTY
300 La Caverna   **Ph:** 915-283-2058
Van Horn, TX 79855

On the northwestern border of TX, east of El Paso; organized Mar 10, 1911 from El Paso County. **Name Origin:** For Col. David Browning Culberson (1830-1903), Confederate army officer, TX legislator, and U.S. representative (1875-97).

Area (sq mi): 3812.71 (land 3812.46; water 0.25).

Pop: 2,975 (White 24.6%; Black or African American 0.7%; Hispanic or Latino 72.2%; Asian 0.6%; Other 29.8%). **Foreign born:** 15.6%. **Median age:** 32.8. **State rank:** 230. **Pop change 1990-2000:** -12.7%.

Income: per capita $11,493; median household $25,882. **Pop below poverty level:** 25.1%.

Unemployment: 7.6%. **Median home value:** $32,500. **Median travel time to work:** 13.1 minutes.

DALLAM COUNTY
PO Box 1352   **Ph:** 806-244-4751
Dalhart, TX 79022
www.dallam.org/county/

On the northwestern border of TX panhandle, northwest of Amarillo; organized Aug 21, 1876 from Bexar County. **Name Origin:** For James Wilmer Dallam (1818-47), Texas legal writer.

Area (sq mi): 1505.26 (land 1504.69; water 0.56).

Pop: 6,222 (White 68.4%; Black or African American 1.6%; Hispanic or Latino 28.4%; Asian 0.2%; Other 15.5%). **Foreign born:** 7.9%. **Median age:** 31.4. **State rank:** 194. **Pop change 1990-2000:** +13.9%.

Income: per capita $13,653; median household $27,946. **Pop below poverty level:** 14.1%.

Unemployment: 2.2%. **Median home value:** $44,600. **Median travel time to work:** 15.8 minutes.

DALLAS COUNTY
411 Elm St   **Ph:** 214-653-7361
Dallas, TX 75202   **Fax:** 214-653-7057
www.co.dallas.tx.us

In northeastern TX, east of Fort Worth; organized 1846 from Nacogdoches County. **Name Origin:** Traditionally believed to be for George Mifflin Dallas (1792-1864), PA statesman, U.S. vice president (1845-49), and U.S. Minister to Great Britian (1856-61). County historians believe it unlikely that the city founders would honor a vice president when they had several friends so named, especially Joseph Dallas, an old friend from AK.

Area (sq mi): 908.56 (land 879.6; water 28.96).

Pop: 2,218,899 (White 44.3%; Black or African American 20.3%; Hispanic or Latino 29.9%; Asian 4%; Other 17.4%). **Foreign born:** 20.9%. **Median age:** 31.1. **State rank:** 2. **Pop change 1990-2000:** +19.8%.

Income: per capita $22,603; median household $43,324. **Pop below poverty level:** 13.4%.

Unemployment: 5.3%. **Median home value:** $92,700. **Median travel time to work:** 26.9 minutes.

DAWSON COUNTY
PO Box 1268   **Ph:** 806-872-3778
Lamesa, TX 79331   **Fax:** 806-872-2473

In the southwestern TX panhandle, south of Lubbock; organized Feb 1, 1858 from Bexar County. **Name Origin:** For Nicholas Mosby Dawson (1808-42), Republic of TX army officer killed in action.

Area (sq mi): 902.12 (land 902.06; water 0.06).

Pop: 14,985 (White 42.4%; Black or African American 8.7%; Hispanic or Latino 48.2%; Asian 0.2%; Other 18.7%). **Foreign born:** 4.2%. **Median age:** 35.6. **State rank:** 140. **Pop change 1990-2000:** +4.4%.

Income: per capita $15,011; median household $28,211. **Pop below poverty level:** 19.7%.

Unemployment: 4.7%. **Median home value:** $39,300. **Median travel time to work:** 14.3 minutes.

DEAF SMITH COUNTY
235 E 3rd St Rm 203   **Ph:** 806-363-7077
Hereford, TX 79045   **Fax:** 806-363-7023

On the northeastern border of TX panhandle, southwest of Amarillo; organized Aug 21, 1876 from Bexar County. **Name Origin:** For Erastus 'Deaf' Smith (1787-1837), Republic of Texas scout and soldier.

Area (sq mi): 1498.26 (land 1497.34; water 0.92).

Pop: 18,561 (White 40.4%; Black or African American 1.5%; Hispanic or Latino 57.4%; Asian 0.3%; Other 25.9%). **Foreign born:** 11.6%. **Median age:** 30.6. **State rank:** 122. **Pop change 1990-2000:** -3.1%.

Income: per capita $13,119; median household $29,601. **Pop below poverty level:** 20.6%.

Unemployment: 5%. **Median home value:** $46,600. **Median travel time to work:** 19.4 minutes.

DELTA COUNTY
115 E Bonham Ave   **Ph:** 903-395-4118
Cooper, TX 75432   **Fax:** 903-395-4455

In northeastern TX, northeast of Dallas; organized Jul 29, 1870 from Lamar County. **Name Origin:** For its triangular shape, like the Greek letter *delta*.

Area (sq mi): 277.92 (land 277.08; water 0.84).

Pop: 5,327 (White 86.7%; Black or African American 8.3%; Hispanic or Latino 3.1%; Asian 0.1%; Other 3.7%). **Foreign born:** 0.5%. **Median age:** 38.8. **State rank:** 200. **Pop change 1990-2000:** +9.7%.

Income: per capita $15,080; median household $29,094. **Pop below poverty level:** 17.6%.

Unemployment: 4.6%. **Median home value:** $39,400. **Median travel time to work:** 27.7 minutes.

DENTON COUNTY
PO Box 2187   **Ph:** 940-349-2012
Denton, TX 76202   **Fax:** 940-349-2019
www.co.denton.tx.us

In north-central TX, north of Fort Worth; organized Apr 11, 1846

All statistics are based on the 2000 Census except the dollar figures given for per capita income, which are based on 1999 estimates.

from Fannin County. **Name Origin:** For John B. Denton (1806-41), an officer killed by Indians.

Area (sq mi): 957.88 (land 888.54; water 69.34).

Pop: 432,976 (White 76%; Black or African American 5.9%; Hispanic or Latino 12.2%; Asian 4%; Other 8.5%). **Foreign born:** 9.4%. **Median age:** 31. **State rank:** 9. **Pop change 1990-2000:** +58.3%.

Income: per capita $26,895; median household $58,216. **Pop below poverty level:** 6.6%.

Unemployment: 3%. **Median home value:** $133,200. **Median travel time to work:** 28.2 minutes.

DEWITT COUNTY

307 N Gonzales St   **Ph:** 361-275-3724
Cuero, TX 77954   **Fax:** 361-275-8994

In east-central TX, southeast of San Antonio; organized Mar 24, 1846 from Goliad, Gonzales, and Victoria counties. **Name Origin:** For Green C. De Witt (1787-1835), an early colonizer in Mexican Texas.

Area (sq mi): 910.47 (land 909.18; water 1.29).

Pop: 20,013 (White 60.8%; Black or African American 11%; Hispanic or Latino 27.2%; Asian 0.2%; Other 12.3%). **Foreign born:** 2.6%. **Median age:** 40.1. **State rank:** 117. **Pop change 1990-2000:** +6.2%.

Income: per capita $14,780; median household $28,714. **Pop below poverty level:** 19.6%.

Unemployment: 3.6%. **Median home value:** $47,100. **Median travel time to work:** 26.3 minutes.

DICKENS COUNTY

PO Box 120   **Ph:** 806-623-5531
Dickens, TX 79229   **Fax:** 806-623-5319

In the southeastern TX panhandle, east of Lubbock; organized Aug 21, 1876 from Bexar County. **Name Origin:** For J. Dickens (?-1836), killed at the Alamo.

Area (sq mi): 905.21 (land 904.21; water 1).

Pop: 2,762 (White 67.2%; Black or African American 8.2%; Hispanic or Latino 23.9%; Asian 0.1%; Other 14.1%). **Foreign born:** 2%. **Median age:** 39.2. **State rank:** 232. **Pop change 1990-2000:** +7.4%.

Income: per capita $13,156; median household $25,898. **Pop below poverty level:** 17.4%.

Unemployment: 3.1%. **Median home value:** $22,900. **Median travel time to work:** 20.5 minutes.

DIMMIT COUNTY

103 N 5th St   **Ph:** 830-876-2323
Carrizo Springs, TX 78834   **Fax:** 830-876-5036
www.dimmitcountytx.com

On the southwestern border of TX, northwest of Laredo; organized Feb 1, 1858 from Bexar and Maverick counties. **Name Origin:** For Capt. Philip Dimmit (1801-41), Republic of TX officer.

Area (sq mi): 1334.48 (land 1330.91; water 3.57).

Pop: 10,248 (White 13.2%; Black or African American 0.9%; Hispanic or Latino 85%; Asian 0.7%; Other 21.5%). **Foreign born:** 7.6%. **Median age:** 31.6. **State rank:** 164. **Pop change 1990-2000:** -1.8%.

Income: per capita $9,765; median household $21,917. **Pop below poverty level:** 33.2%.

Unemployment: 9.7%. **Median home value:** $29,000. **Median travel time to work:** 21.2 minutes.

DONLEY COUNTY

PO Box U   **Ph:** 806-874-3436
Clarendon, TX 79226   **Fax:** 806-874-5146

In the east-central TX panhandle, southeast of Amarillo; organized Aug 21, 1876 from Jack [sic] County. **Name Origin:** For Stockton P. Donley (1821-71), Confederate army officer and member of the supreme court of TX (1866).

Area (sq mi): 933.05 (land 929.77; water 3.28).

Pop: 3,828 (White 88.1%; Black or African American 3.9%; Hispanic or Latino 6.3%; Asian 0.1%; Other 4.5%). **Foreign born:** 1.6%. **Median age:** 42.8. **State rank:** 216. **Pop change 1990-2000:** +3.6%.

Income: per capita $15,958; median household $29,006. **Pop below poverty level:** 15.9%.

Unemployment: 2.6%. **Median home value:** $46,100. **Median travel time to work:** 23.5 minutes.

DUVAL COUNTY

PO Box 248   **Ph:** 361-279-3322
San Diego, TX 78384   **Fax:** 361-279-3310

In southern TX, west of Corpus Christi; organized Feb 1, 1858 from Live Oak, Starr, and Nueces counties. **Name Origin:** For Capt. Burr H. Duval (1809-36), an officer killed at Goliad during the Texas Revolution.

Area (sq mi): 1795.67 (land 1792.71; water 2.97).

Pop: 13,120 (White 11.1%; Black or African American 0.5%; Hispanic or Latino 88%; Asian 0.1%; Other 19.1%). **Foreign born:** 3.4%. **Median age:** 33.8. **State rank:** 149. **Pop change 1990-2000:** +1.6%.

Income: per capita $11,324; median household $22,416. **Pop below poverty level:** 27.2%.

Unemployment: 7.2%. **Median home value:** $28,600. **Median travel time to work:** 26.5 minutes.

EASTLAND COUNTY

PO Box 110   **Ph:** 254-629-1583
Eastland, TX 76448   **Fax:** 254-629-8125
www.eastlandcountytexas.com

In north-central TX, east of Abilene; organized Feb 1, 1858 from Bosque, Coryell, and Travis counties. **Name Origin:** For William Mosby Eastland (1806-43), Texas Revolutionary officer executed by Mexican Gen. Antonio Lopez de Santa Anna (1794-1876).

Area (sq mi): 931.9 (land 926.01; water 5.89).

Please see sample entry on inside front cover for detailed information about the statistics presented with each county listing.

Pop: 18,297 (White 85.7%; Black or African American 2.2%; Hispanic or Latino 10.8%; Asian 0.2%; Other 6.6%). Foreign born: 4%. Median age: 41.3. State rank: 123. Pop change 1990-2000: -1%.

Income: per capita $14,870; median household $26,832. Pop below poverty level: 16.8%.

Unemployment: 3.6%. Median home value: $33,100. Median travel time to work: 19.7 minutes.

ECTOR COUNTY
PO Box 707
Odessa, TX 79760
www.co.ector.tx.us

Ph: 915-498-4130

In the southwestern TX panhandle, west of Midland; organized Feb 26, 1887 from Tom Green County. Name Origin: For Gen. Matthew Duncan Ector (1822-79), TX legislator and jurist.

Area (sq mi): 901.68 (land 901.06; water 0.62).

Pop: 121,123 (White 51.3%; Black or African American 4.6%; Hispanic or Latino 42.4%; Asian 0.6%; Other 21%). Foreign born: 10.6%. Median age: 32. State rank: 27. Pop change 1990-2000: +1.8%.

Income: per capita $15,031; median household $31,152. Pop below poverty level: 18.7%.

Unemployment: 5.2%. Median home value: $47,700. Median travel time to work: 18.6 minutes.

EDWARDS COUNTY
PO Box 184
Rocksprings, TX 78880

Ph: 830-683-2235
Fax: 830-683-5376

In southwestern TX, northeast of Del Rio; organized Feb 1, 1858 from Bexar County. Name Origin: For Hayden Edwards (1771-1849), founder of a colony at Nacogdoches in Mexican TX (1825).

Area (sq mi): 2119.95 (land 2119.75; water 0.19).

Pop: 2,162 (White 53.7%; Black or African American 0.8%; Hispanic or Latino 45.1%; Asian 0.1%; Other 15.8%). Foreign born: 10.8%. Median age: 39. State rank: 236. Pop change 1990-2000: -4.6%.

Income: per capita $12,691; median household $25,298. Pop below poverty level: 31.6%.

Unemployment: 4.6%. Median home value: $38,200. Median travel time to work: 23.4 minutes.

EL PASO COUNTY
500 E San Antonio Ave
El Paso, TX 79901
www.co.el-paso.tx.us

Ph: 915-546-2000

On the northwestern border of TX, north of Cuidad Juarez, Mexico; organized Jan 3, 1850 from Bexar County. Name Origin: For the city, itself from Spanish for 'the ford,' for a major crossing of the Rio Grande River, or 'the pass' for El Paso del Norte 'the north pass' through either the Sierra Madre or the Franklin mountains: the city lies in a valley between them.

Area (sq mi): 1014.68 (land 1013.11; water 1.57).

Pop: 679,622 (White 17%; Black or African American 3.1%; Hispanic or Latino 78.2%; Asian 1%; Other 22%). Foreign born: 27.4%. Median age: 30. State rank: 6. Pop change 1990-2000: +14.9%.

Income: per capita $13,421; median household $31,051. Pop below poverty level: 23.8%.

Unemployment: 8.2%. Median home value: $69,600. Median travel time to work: 22.7 minutes.

ELLIS COUNTY
1201 N Hwy 77 Suite B
Waxahachie, TX 75165
www.co.ellis.tx.us

Ph: 972-825-5071
Fax: 972-923-5010

In east-central TX, south of Dallas; organized Dec 20, 1849 from Navarro County. Name Origin: Named by Gen. Edward H. Tarrant (1796-1858) for his friend, Richard Ellis (1781-1846), AL jurist and legislator, and member of the Constitutional Congress that declared TX independent from Mexico in 1836.

Area (sq mi): 951.66 (land 939.91; water 11.75).

Pop: 111,360 (White 71.3%; Black or African American 8.6%; Hispanic or Latino 18.4%; Asian 0.4%; Other 10.4%). Foreign born: 7.1%. Median age: 33.2. State rank: 31. Pop change 1990-2000: +30.8%.

Income: per capita $20,212; median household $50,350. Pop below poverty level: 8.6%.

Unemployment: 4.2%. Median home value: $91,400. Median travel time to work: 30.3 minutes.

ERATH COUNTY
100 W Washington St
Stephenville, TX 76401

Ph: 254-965-1482
Fax: 254-965-5732

In north-central TX, southwest of Fort Worth; organized Jan 25, 1856 from Bosque and Coryell counties. Name Origin: For George Bernard Erath (1813-91), Indian fighter, Texas Ranger, and legislator.

Area (sq mi): 1089.8 (land 1086.33; water 3.47).

Pop: 33,001 (White 82.6%; Black or African American 0.8%; Hispanic or Latino 15%; Asian 0.4%; Other 9.1%). Foreign born: 7.3%. Median age: 31.4. State rank: 81. Pop change 1990-2000: +17.9%.

Income: per capita $16,655; median household $30,708. Pop below poverty level: 16%.

Unemployment: 2.3%. Median home value: $67,600. Median travel time to work: 20.1 minutes.

FALLS COUNTY
PO Box 458
Marlin, TX 76661

Ph: 254-883-1408
Fax: 254-883-1406

In east-central TX, southeast of Waco; organized Jan 28, 1850 from Limestone and Milam counties. Name Origin: For the rapids on the Brazos River, which traverses the county.

Area (sq mi): 773.81 (land 769.09; water 4.72).

Pop: 18,576 (White 55.8%; Black or African American 27.5%; Hispanic or Latino 15.8%; Asian 0.1%; Other 10.9%). Foreign born:

All statistics are based on the 2000 Census except the dollar figures given for per capita income, which are based on 1999 estimates.

4.6%. **Median age:** 36.5. **State rank:** 121. **Pop change 1990-2000:** +4.9%.

Income: per capita $14,311; median household $26,589. **Pop below poverty level:** 22.6%.

Unemployment: 3.9%. **Median home value:** $38,800. **Median travel time to work:** 25 minutes.

FANNIN COUNTY

101 Sam Rayburn Dr County
Courthouse Suite 102   **Ph:** 903-583-7486
Bonham, TX 75418   **Fax:** 903-583-7811

On the northeastern border of TX, northeast of Dallas; organized Dec 14, 1837 from Red River County. **Name Origin:** For James Walker Fannin (1809-36), GA soldier killed in action in the TX War of Independence.

Area (sq mi): 899.16 (land 891.45; water 7.71).

Pop: 31,242 (White 84.2%; Black or African American 8%; Hispanic or Latino 5.6%; Asian 0.3%; Other 5.2%). **Foreign born:** 3.1%. **Median age:** 38. **State rank:** 89. **Pop change 1990-2000:** +26%.

Income: per capita $16,066; median household $34,501. **Pop below poverty level:** 13.9%.

Unemployment: 6.4%. **Median home value:** $54,500. **Median travel time to work:** 29.6 minutes.

FAYETTE COUNTY

PO Box 59   **Ph:** 979-968-3251
La Grange, TX 78945   **Fax:** 979-968-8531
www.co.fayette.tx.us

In east-central TX, southeast of Austin; organized Dec 14, 1837 from Bastrop and Colorado counties. **Name Origin:** For the Marquis de Lafayette (1757-1834), French statesman and soldier who fought with the Americans during the Revolutionary War.

Area (sq mi): 959.84 (land 950.03; water 9.81).

Pop: 21,804 (White 79.2%; Black or African American 7%; Hispanic or Latino 12.8%; Asian 0.2%; Other 8.3%). **Foreign born:** 5.6%. **Median age:** 42.6. **State rank:** 109. **Pop change 1990-2000:** +8.5%.

Income: per capita $18,888; median household $34,526. **Pop below poverty level:** 11.4%.

Unemployment: 2.3%. **Median home value:** $71,600. **Median travel time to work:** 23.3 minutes.

FISHER COUNTY

PO Box 368   **Ph:** 915-776-2401
Roby, TX 79543   **Fax:** 915-776-3274

In north-central TX, northwest of Abilene; organized Aug 21, 1876 from Bexar County. **Name Origin:** For Samuel Rhoads Fisher (1794-1839), signer of the TX Declaration of Independence (1836) and secretary of the TX Navy.

Area (sq mi): 901.74 (land 901.16; water 0.58).

Pop: 4,344 (White 74.8%; Black or African American 2.8%; Hispanic or Latino 21.4%; Asian 0.1%; Other 13.4%). **Foreign born:** 2.3%. **Median age:** 42.9. **State rank:** 208. **Pop change 1990-2000:** -10.3%.

Income: per capita $15,120; median household $27,659. **Pop below poverty level:** 17.5%.

Unemployment: 3.2%. **Median home value:** $31,300. **Median travel time to work:** 20.2 minutes.

FLOYD COUNTY

Courthouse Rm 101   **Ph:** 806-983-4900
Floydada, TX 79235   **Fax:** 806-983-4909

In the central TX panhandle, northeast of Lubbock; organized Aug 21, 1876 from Bexar County. **Name Origin:** For Dolfin Ward Floyd (1807-36), killed at the Alamo.

Area (sq mi): 992.51 (land 992.19; water 0.32).

Pop: 7,771 (White 49.9%; Black or African American 3.4%; Hispanic or Latino 45.9%; Asian 0.2%; Other 22.4%). **Foreign born:** 5.9%. **Median age:** 34.8. **State rank:** 183. **Pop change 1990-2000:** -8.5%.

Income: per capita $14,206; median household $26,851. **Pop below poverty level:** 21.5%.

Unemployment: 7.2%. **Median home value:** $37,900. **Median travel time to work:** 16.5 minutes.

FOARD COUNTY

PO Box 539   **Ph:** 940-684-1365
Crowell, TX 79227   **Fax:** 940-684-1947
www.foardcounty.org

In north-central TX, west of Wichita Falls; organized Mar 3, 1891 from Knox and King counties. **Name Origin:** For Maj. Robert J. Foard (1831-98), Confederate army officer and attorney.

Area (sq mi): 707.69 (land 706.68; water 1.01).

Pop: 1,622 (White 78.7%; Black or African American 3.3%; Hispanic or Latino 16.3%; Asian 0.2%; Other 12.3%). **Foreign born:** 1.6%. **Median age:** 41.7. **State rank:** 243. **Pop change 1990-2000:** -9.6%.

Income: per capita $14,799; median household $25,813. **Pop below poverty level:** 14.3%.

Unemployment: 2.8%. **Median home value:** $26,100. **Median travel time to work:** 16.8 minutes.

FORT BEND COUNTY

301 Jackson St Suite 101   **Ph:** 281-341-8685
Richmond, TX 77469   **Fax:** 281-341-8669
www.co.fort-bend.tx.us

In east-central TX, southwest of Houston; organized Dec 29, 1837 from Austin County. **Name Origin:** For the fort built at a bend in the Brazos River, on the western border of the county.

Area (sq mi): 886.05 (land 874.64; water 11.41).

Pop: 354,452 (White 46.2%; Black or African American 19.8%; Hispanic or Latino 21.1%; Asian 11.2%; Other 12%). **Foreign born:** 18.3%. **Median age:** 33.3. **State rank:** 10. **Pop change 1990-2000:** +57.2%.

Income: per capita $24,985; median household $63,831. **Pop below poverty level:** 7.1%.

Unemployment: 3.1%. **Median home value:** $115,100. **Median travel time to work:** 32.3 minutes.

Please see sample entry on inside front cover for detailed information about the statistics presented with each county listing.

FRANKLIN COUNTY

PO Box 68   **Ph:** 903-537-4252
Mount Vernon, TX 75457

In northeastern TX, southwest of Texarkana; organized Mar 6, 1875 from Titus County. **Name Origin:** For Capt. Benjamin Cromwell Franklin (1805-73), an officer in the Republic of Texas army and a jurist.

Area (sq mi): 294.77 (land 285.66; water 9.12).

Pop: 9,458 (White 85.9%; Black or African American 3.9%; Hispanic or Latino 8.9%; Asian 0.2%; Other 6.6%). **Foreign born:** 5.4%. **Median age:** 40.3. **State rank:** 168. **Pop change 1990-2000:** +21.2%.

Income: per capita $17,563; median household $31,955. **Pop below poverty level:** 15.6%.

Unemployment: 2.8%. **Median home value:** $66,100. **Median travel time to work:** 22.8 minutes.

FREESTONE COUNTY

PO Box 1010   **Ph:** 903-389-2635
Fairfield, TX 75840   **Fax:** 903-389-6533

In east-central TX, northeast of Waco; organized Sep 6, 1850 from Limestone County. **Name Origin:** Either for freestone water, which contains little or no dissolved substances, such as calcium, or for any stone that can be cut easily and without splitting.

Area (sq mi): 892.13 (land 877.43; water 14.7).

Pop: 17,867 (White 71.8%; Black or African American 18.9%; Hispanic or Latino 8.2%; Asian 0.3%; Other 5.3%). **Foreign born:** 3.1%. **Median age:** 37.8. **State rank:** 125. **Pop change 1990-2000:** +13%.

Income: per capita $16,338; median household $31,283. **Pop below poverty level:** 14.2%.

Unemployment: 3.6%. **Median home value:** $56,000. **Median travel time to work:** 23.8 minutes.

FRIO COUNTY

500 E San Antonio St Rm 6   **Ph:** 830-334-2214
Pearsall, TX 78061   **Fax:** 830-334-0021

In southern TX, southwest of San Antonio; organized Feb 1, 1858 from Bexar and Uvalde counties. **Name Origin:** For the Frio River, which runs through it; Spanish 'cold.'

Area (sq mi): 1134.28 (land 1133.02; water 1.26).

Pop: 16,252 (White 20.6%; Black or African American 4.9%; Hispanic or Latino 73.8%; Asian 0.4%; Other 22.9%). **Foreign born:** 5.8%. **Median age:** 30.7. **State rank:** 133. **Pop change 1990-2000:** +20.6%.

Income: per capita $16,069; median household $24,504. **Pop below poverty level:** 29%.

Unemployment: 7.1%. **Median home value:** $35,100. **Median travel time to work:** 26.4 minutes.

GAINES COUNTY

101 S Main St Rm 107   **Ph:** 915-758-4003
Seminole, TX 79360   **Fax:** 915-758-4031

On the southwestern border of TX panhandle, north of Odessa; organized Aug 21, 1876 from Bexar County. **Name Origin:** For James Gaines (1776-1850), signer of the TX Declaration of Independence (1836) and TX legislator (1838-42).

Area (sq mi): 1502.84 (land 1502.35; water 0.49).

Pop: 14,467 (White 60.8%; Black or African American 2.3%; Hispanic or Latino 35.8%; Asian 0.2%; Other 17.4%). **Foreign born:** 18.9%. **Median age:** 29.7. **State rank:** 143. **Pop change 1990-2000:** +2.4%.

Income: per capita $13,088; median household $30,432. **Pop below poverty level:** 21.7%.

Unemployment: 4.5%. **Median home value:** $48,000. **Median travel time to work:** 17.4 minutes.

GALVESTON COUNTY

PO Box 2450   **Ph:** 409-766-2200
Galveston, TX 77553
www.co.galveston.tx.us

On the central-eastern coast of TX, south of Houston; organized May 15, 1838 (prior to statehood) from Brazoria County. **Name Origin:** For Bernardo de Galvez (1746-86), Spanish colonial leader active in the Spanish possessions along the Gulf of Mexico. Form of the name is anglicized.

Area (sq mi): 872.93 (land 398.47; water 474.46).

Pop: 250,158 (White 63.1%; Black or African American 15.4%; Hispanic or Latino 18%; Asian 2.1%; Other 9.8%). **Foreign born:** 8.3%. **Median age:** 35.9. **State rank:** 15. **Pop change 1990-2000:** +15.1%.

Income: per capita $21,568; median household $42,419. **Pop below poverty level:** 13.2%.

Unemployment: 6%. **Median home value:** $85,200. **Median travel time to work:** 26 minutes.

GARZA COUNTY

PO Box 366   **Ph:** 806-495-4430
Post, TX 79356   **Fax:** 806-495-4431

In south-central TX panhandle, southeast of Lubbock; organized Aug 21, 1876 from Bexar County. **Name Origin:** For Geronimo Garza, a colonizer who founded San Antonio.

Area (sq mi): 896.19 (land 895.56; water 0.63).

Pop: 4,872 (White 56.7%; Black or African American 4.8%; Hispanic or Latino 37.2%; Asian 0.1%; Other 20.3%). **Foreign born:** 6.3%. **Median age:** 35.1. **State rank:** 204. **Pop change 1990-2000:** -5.3%.

Income: per capita $12,704; median household $27,206. **Pop below poverty level:** 22.3%.

Unemployment: 2.5%. **Median home value:** $38,700. **Median travel time to work:** 16.9 minutes.

GILLESPIE COUNTY

101 W Main St Unit 13   **Ph:** 830-997-6515
Fredericksburg, TX 78624   **Fax:** 830-997-9958

In central TX, west of Austin; established Feb 23, 1848 from Bexar County. **Name Origin:** For Robert Addison Gillespie (?-1846), Texas Ranger killed during the Mexican War.

All statistics are based on the 2000 Census except the dollar figures given for per capita income, which are based on 1999 estimates.

Area (sq mi): 1061.48 (land 1061.06; water 0.42).

Pop: 20,814 (White 82.8%; Black or African American 0.2%; Hispanic or Latino 15.9%; Asian 0.2%; Other 6.8%). **Foreign born:** 7%. **Median age:** 46.3. **State rank:** 111. **Pop change 1990-2000:** +21%.

Income: per capita $20,423; median household $38,109. **Pop below poverty level:** 10.2%.

Unemployment: 1.9%. **Median home value:** $106,400. **Median travel time to work:** 21.8 minutes.

GLASSCOCK COUNTY
117 E Currie St   **Ph:** 915-354-2371
Garden City, TX 79739

In west-central TX, east of Midland; organized Apr 4, 1887 from Tom Green County. **Name Origin:** For George Washington Glasscock (1810-79), a miller at Austin, TX, and TX legislator.

Area (sq mi): 900.93 (land 900.75; water 0.19).

Pop: 1,406 (White 67.9%; Black or African American 0.5%; Hispanic or Latino 29.9%; Asian 0%; Other 21.9%). **Foreign born:** 14.1%. **Median age:** 33.5. **State rank:** 245. **Pop change 1990-2000:** -2.8%.

Income: per capita $18,279; median household $35,655. **Pop below poverty level:** 14.7%.

Unemployment: 3%. **Median home value:** $56,400. **Median travel time to work:** 19.6 minutes.

GOLIAD COUNTY
218 S Commercial St   **Ph:** 361-645-3294
Goliad, TX 77963   **Fax:** 361-645-3858

In southeastern TX, north of Corpus Christi; original county; organized Mar 17, 1836 (prior to statehood) from Old Mexican Municipality. **Name Origin:** Probably originally of biblical origin from *Goliath*; also believed to be an anagram from *Hidalgo* (minus the silent h), referring to Miguel Hidalgo y Costilla (1753-1811), the first promotor of Mexican independence from Spain. Applied to a presidio by the 1829 Congress of Coahuila and Texas.

Area (sq mi): 859.35 (land 853.52; water 5.83).

Pop: 6,928 (White 59.4%; Black or African American 4.8%; Hispanic or Latino 35.2%; Asian 0.2%; Other 12.2%). **Foreign born:** 2.8%. **Median age:** 40.2. **State rank:** 189. **Pop change 1990-2000:** +15.9%.

Income: per capita $17,126; median household $34,201. **Pop below poverty level:** 16.4%.

Unemployment: 3.8%. **Median home value:** $57,400. **Median travel time to work:** 30.9 minutes.

GONZALES COUNTY
1709 Sarah Dewitt Dr   **Ph:** 830-672-2801
Gonzales, TX 78629   **Fax:** 830-672-2636

In east-central TX, east of San Antonio; original county; organized Mar 17, 1836 (prior to statehood) from Old Mexican Municipality. **Name Origin:** For Col. Rafael Gonzales (1789-1857), provisional governor of Coahuila and TX (1824-26).

Area (sq mi): 1069.82 (land 1067.75; water 2.07).

Pop: 18,628 (White 51.2%; Black or African American 8.4%; Hispanic or Latino 39.6%; Asian 0.3%; Other 19.1%). **Foreign born:** 11%. **Median age:** 36.3. **State rank:** 120. **Pop change 1990-2000:** +8.3%.

Income: per capita $14,269; median household $28,368. **Pop below poverty level:** 18.6%.

Unemployment: 3.1%. **Median home value:** $48,500. **Median travel time to work:** 24 minutes.

GRAY COUNTY
PO Box 1902   **Ph:** 806-669-8004
Pampa, TX 79066   **Fax:** 806-669-8054

In northeastern TX panhandle, east of Amarillo; organized Aug 21, 1876 from Bexar County. **Name Origin:** For Capt. Peter W. Gray (1819-74), an officer in the TX army, TX legislator and justice of the TX supreme court (1874).

Area (sq mi): 929.25 (land 928.28; water 0.97).

Pop: 22,744 (White 78.3%; Black or African American 5.8%; Hispanic or Latino 13%; Asian 0.4%; Other 11.5%). **Foreign born:** 4.3%. **Median age:** 38.9. **State rank:** 104. **Pop change 1990-2000:** -5.1%.

Income: per capita $16,702; median household $31,368. **Pop below poverty level:** 13.8%.

Unemployment: 3.5%. **Median home value:** $36,700. **Median travel time to work:** 16.6 minutes.

GRAYSON COUNTY
100 W Houston St   **Ph:** 903-813-4207
Sherman, TX 75090
www.co.grayson.tx.us

On the northeastern border of TX, north of Dallas; organized Mar 17, 1846 from Fannin County. **Name Origin:** For Peter William Grayson (1788-1838), Republic of TX attorney general (1836) who was nominated for presidency of the Republic of Sam Houston (1793-1863), first president of the Republic of TX.

Area (sq mi): 979.19 (land 933.51; water 45.68).

Pop: 110,595 (White 84%; Black or African American 5.9%; Hispanic or Latino 6.8%; Asian 0.6%; Other 6.3%). **Foreign born:** 3.9%. **Median age:** 37.2. **State rank:** 32. **Pop change 1990-2000:** +16.4%.

Income: per capita $18,862; median household $37,178. **Pop below poverty level:** 11.3%.

Unemployment: 5.4%. **Median home value:** $69,100. **Median travel time to work:** 24.9 minutes.

GREGG COUNTY
PO Box 3049   **Ph:** 903-236-8430
Longview, TX 75606   **Fax:** 903-237-2574
www.co.gregg.tx.us

In northeastern TX, northeast of Tyler; organized Apr 12, 1873 from Rusk and Upshur counties. **Name Origin:** For Gen. John Gregg (1828-64), officer in the Confederate Army.

Area (sq mi): 276.37 (land 274.03; water 2.34).

Please see sample entry on inside front cover for detailed information about the statistics presented with each county listing.

545

Pop: 111,379 (White 69%; Black or African American 19.9%; Hispanic or Latino 9.1%; Asian 0.7%; Other 6.6%). **Foreign born:** 5.4%. **Median age:** 35. **State rank:** 30. **Pop change 1990-2000:** +6.1%.

Income: per capita $18,449; median household $35,006. **Pop below poverty level:** 15.1%.

Unemployment: 5.4%. **Median home value:** $76,800. **Median travel time to work:** 19.5 minutes.

GRIMES COUNTY

PO Box 209   **Ph:** 936-873-2662
Anderson, TX 77830   **Fax:** 936-873-2056

In east-central TX, east of Austin; organized Apr 6, 1846 from Montgomery County. **Name Origin:** For Jesse Grimes (1788-1866), signer of the TX Declaration of Independence (1836) and legislator (1836-37; 1841-45).

Area (sq mi): 801.16 (land 793.6; water 7.56).

Pop: 23,552 (White 62.7%; Black or African American 20%; Hispanic or Latino 16.1%; Asian 0.3%; Other 7.8%). **Foreign born:** 5%. **Median age:** 38.1. **State rank:** 101. **Pop change 1990-2000:** +25.1%.

Income: per capita $14,368; median household $32,280. **Pop below poverty level:** 16.6%.

Unemployment: 5.3%. **Median home value:** $56,700. **Median travel time to work:** 32.4 minutes.

GUADALUPE COUNTY

PO Box 990   **Ph:** 830-303-4188
Seguin, TX 78156   **Fax:** 830-401-0300
www.co.guadalupe.tx.us

In south-central TX, east of San Antonio; organized Mar 30, 1846 from Bexar and Gonzales counties. **Name Origin:** For the Guadalupe River, which traverses the county; named for Our Lady of Guadalupe, the patron saint of Mexico.

Area (sq mi): 714.17 (land 711.14; water 3.03).

Pop: 89,023 (White 59.4%; Black or African American 5%; Hispanic or Latino 33.2%; Asian 0.9%; Other 16.5%). **Foreign born:** 6.5%. **Median age:** 34.9. **State rank:** 37. **Pop change 1990-2000:** +37.2%.

Income: per capita $18,430; median household $43,949. **Pop below poverty level:** 9.8%.

Unemployment: 3%. **Median home value:** $91,400. **Median travel time to work:** 24.8 minutes.

HALE COUNTY

500 Broadway St Rm 140   **Ph:** 806-291-5261
Plainview, TX 79072   **Fax:** 806-291-9810

In west-central TX panhandle, north of Lubbock; organized Aug 21, 1876 from Bexar County. **Name Origin:** For Lt. John C. Hale (?-1836), a TX officer killed in the battle of San Jacinto.

Area (sq mi): 1004.77 (land 1004.65; water 0.12).

Pop: 36,602 (White 45.2%; Black or African American 5.8%; Hispanic or Latino 47.9%; Asian 0.3%; Other 27.1%). **Foreign born:** 8.2%. **Median age:** 31.4. **State rank:** 75. **Pop change 1990-2000:** +5.6%.

Income: per capita $13,655; median household $31,280. **Pop below poverty level:** 18%.

Unemployment: 4.8%. **Median home value:** $53,800. **Median travel time to work:** 15.4 minutes.

HALL COUNTY

512 Main St County Courthouse   **Ph:** 806-259-2627
Memphis, TX 79245   **Fax:** 806-259-5078

In east-central TX panhandle, northeast of Lubbock; organized Aug 21, 1876 from Bexar County. **Name Origin:** For Gen. Warren D. C. Hall (1788-1867), TX Republic officer and secretary of war.

Area (sq mi): 904.08 (land 903.09; water 0.99).

Pop: 3,782 (White 63.4%; Black or African American 8.2%; Hispanic or Latino 27.5%; Asian 0.2%; Other 19.6%). **Foreign born:** 9.1%. **Median age:** 40.2. **State rank:** 217. **Pop change 1990-2000:** -3.1%.

Income: per capita $13,210; median household $23,016. **Pop below poverty level:** 26.3%.

Unemployment: 4.2%. **Median home value:** $24,100. **Median travel time to work:** 17 minutes.

HAMILTON COUNTY

County Courthouse   **Ph:** 254-386-3518
Hamilton, TX 76531   **Fax:** 254-386-8727

In central TX, northwest of Waco; created Jan 22, 1858 and organized Jun 2, 1858, being part of the Milam Land District of TX and developed from parts of Bosque, Lampasas, and Comanche counties. **Name Origin:** For Gen. James Hamilton, Jr. (1786-1857), U.S. representative from SC (1822-29), governor (1830-32), and legislator who championed the cause of TX independence and settled there (1855).

Area (sq mi): 836.38 (land 835.71; water 0.67).

Pop: 8,229 (White 91.1%; Black or African American 0.1%; Hispanic or Latino 7.4%; Asian 0.1%; Other 5.8%). **Foreign born:** 3.7%. **Median age:** 43.1. **State rank:** 179. **Pop change 1990-2000:** +6.4%.

Income: per capita $16,800; median household $31,150. **Pop below poverty level:** 14.2%.

Unemployment: 2.4%. **Median home value:** $47,300. **Median travel time to work:** 23.9 minutes.

HANSFORD COUNTY

PO Box 397   **Ph:** 806-659-4110
Spearman, TX 79081   **Fax:** 806-659-4168

In north-central TX panhandle, northeast of Amarillo; organized Aug 21, 1876 from Bexar County. **Name Origin:** For Gen. John M. Hansford (?-1844), TX district court judge (1840-42) and attorney general of TX.

Area (sq mi): 920.4 (land 919.8; water 0.6).

Pop: 5,369 (White 67.1%; Black or African American 0%; Hispanic or Latino 31.5%; Asian 0.2%; Other 19.8%). **Foreign born:** 15.6%. **Median age:** 36.5. **State rank:** 199. **Pop change 1990-2000:** -8.2%.

Income: per capita $17,408; median household $35,438. **Pop below poverty level:** 16.4%.

All statistics are based on the 2000 Census except the dollar figures given for per capita income, which are based on 1999 estimates.

Unemployment: 2.2%. **Median home value:** $49,900. **Median travel time to work:** 15.9 minutes.

HARDEMAN COUNTY

PO Box 30   **Ph:** 940-663-2901
Quanah, TX 79252

On the central northern border of TX, northwest of Wichita Falls; organized Feb 1, 1858 from Fannin County. **Name Origin:** For Lt. Bailey Hardeman (1795-1836), signer of the TX Declaration of Independence (1836) and secretary of the treasury of the TX Republic.

Area (sq mi): 697 (land 695.38; water 1.62).

Pop: 4,724 (White 79%; Black or African American 4.8%; Hispanic or Latino 14.5%; Asian 0.3%; Other 9.5%). **Foreign born:** 2.5%. **Median age:** 41.2. **State rank:** 206. **Pop change 1990-2000:** -10.6%.

Income: per capita $16,824; median household $28,312. **Pop below poverty level:** 17.8%.

Unemployment: 3.5%. **Median home value:** $29,300. **Median travel time to work:** 15.7 minutes.

HARDIN COUNTY

PO Box 38   **Ph:** 409-246-5185
Kountze, TX 77625

In east-central TX, north of Beaumont; organized Jan 22, 1858 from Jefferson and Liberty counties. **Name Origin:** For William Hardin (1801-39), primary judge of Liberty, TX (1834).

Area (sq mi): 897.37 (land 894.33; water 3.04).

Pop: 48,073 (White 89.3%; Black or African American 6.9%; Hispanic or Latino 2.5%; Asian 0.2%; Other 1.9%). **Foreign born:** 1.3%. **Median age:** 36. **State rank:** 58. **Pop change 1990-2000:** +16.3%.

Income: per capita $17,962; median household $37,612. **Pop below poverty level:** 11.2%.

Unemployment: 6.8%. **Median home value:** $75,800. **Median travel time to work:** 29.7 minutes.

HARRIS COUNTY

1001 Preston St 4th Fl   **Ph:** 713-755-5000
Houston, TX 770021899   **Fax:** 713-755-4977
www.co.harris.tx.us

In east-central TX, north of Galveston; organized as Harrrisburg County Mar 17, 1836 (prior to statehood) from Austin and Liberty counties (Old Mexican Municipality); name changed Dec 28, 1839. **Name Origin:** For John Richardson Harris (1790-1829), trading post owner who ran steamboats between Texas and New Orleans.

Area (sq mi): 1777.69 (land 1728.83; water 48.87).

Pop: 3,400,578 (White 42.1%; Black or African American 18.5%; Hispanic or Latino 32.9%; Asian 5.1%; Other 17.7%). **Foreign born:** 22.2%. **Median age:** 31.2. **State rank:** 1. **Pop change 1990-2000:** +20.7%.

Income: per capita $21,435; median household $42,598. **Pop below poverty level:** 15%.

Unemployment: 4.5%. **Median home value:** $87,000. **Median travel time to work:** 28.1 minutes.

HARRISON COUNTY

PO Box 1365   **Ph:** 903-935-4858
Marshall, TX 75671
www.co.harrison.tx.us

On the northeastern border of TX, west of Shreveport, LA; organized Jan 28, 1839 (prior to statehood) from Shelby County. **Name Origin:** For Jonas Harrison (1777-1837), a pioneer lawyer from Shelby County.

Area (sq mi): 915.09 (land 898.71; water 16.38).

Pop: 62,110 (White 69.3%; Black or African American 24%; Hispanic or Latino 5.3%; Asian 0.3%; Other 4.3%). **Foreign born:** 3.3%. **Median age:** 36.1. **State rank:** 49. **Pop change 1990-2000:** +8%.

Income: per capita $16,702; median household $33,520. **Pop below poverty level:** 16.7%.

Unemployment: 5.6%. **Median home value:** $68,400. **Median travel time to work:** 23 minutes.

HARTLEY COUNTY

PO Box Q   **Ph:** 806-235-3582
Channing, TX 79018   **Fax:** 806-235-2316

On the northwestern border of TX panhandle, northwest of Amarillo; organized Aug 21, 1876 from Bexar County. **Name Origin:** For Oliver Cromwell Hartley (1823-59), TX attorney, legislator, and legal scholar.

Area (sq mi): 1463.2 (land 1462.25; water 0.95).

Pop: 5,537 (White 77.1%; Black or African American 8.1%; Hispanic or Latino 13.7%; Asian 0.3%; Other 10.5%). **Foreign born:** 2.6%. **Median age:** 39.6. **State rank:** 198. **Pop change 1990-2000:** +52.4%.

Income: per capita $18,067; median household $46,327. **Pop below poverty level:** 6.6%.

Unemployment: 1.2%. **Median home value:** $94,000. **Median travel time to work:** 13.4 minutes.

HASKELL COUNTY

PO Box 725   **Ph:** 940-864-2451
Haskell, TX 79521   **Fax:** 940-864-6164

In north-central TX, north of Abilene; organized Feb 1, 1858 from Fannin and Milam counties. **Name Origin:** For Charles Ready Haskell (1817-36), Republic of Texas soldier killed in battle.

Area (sq mi): 910.25 (land 902.97; water 7.29).

Pop: 6,093 (White 75.5%; Black or African American 2.8%; Hispanic or Latino 20.5%; Asian 0.1%; Other 14.3%). **Foreign born:** 3.6%. **Median age:** 43.9. **State rank:** 196. **Pop change 1990-2000:** -10.7%.

Income: per capita $14,918; median household $23,690. **Pop below poverty level:** 22.8%.

Unemployment: 2.9%. **Median home value:** $30,600. **Median travel time to work:** 19.4 minutes.

Please see sample entry on inside front cover for detailed information about the statistics presented with each county listing.

HAYS COUNTY

110 E Martin Luther King St   **Ph:** 512-393-7738
San Marcos, TX 78666   **Fax:** 512-393-7735
www.co.hays.tx.us

In south-central TX, southwest of Austin; organized Mar 1, 1848 from Travis County. **Name Origin:** For Capt. John Coffee Hays (1817-83), Texas Ranger, officer in the Mexican War, sheriff of San Francisco County, CA (1849-53), and surveyor general of CA (1859).

Area (sq mi): 679.79 (land 677.87; water 1.92).

Pop: 97,589 (White 64.5%; Black or African American 3.7%; Hispanic or Latino 29.6%; Asian 0.8%; Other 16.7%). **Foreign born:** 5.6%. **Median age:** 28.4. **State rank:** 35. **Pop change 1990-2000:** +48.7%.

Income: per capita $19,931; median household $45,006. **Pop below poverty level:** 14.3%.

Unemployment: 3.3%. **Median home value:** $129,400. **Median travel time to work:** 28 minutes.

HEMPHILL COUNTY

PO Box 867   **Ph:** 806-323-6212
Canadian, TX 79014

On the northeastern border of TX panhandle, northeast of Amarillo; organized Aug 21, 1876 from Bexar County. **Name Origin:** For Gen. John Hemphill (1803-62), chief justice of the TX supreme court (1846-58) and U.S. senator (1859-61).

Area (sq mi): 912.06 (land 909.68; water 2.38).

Pop: 3,351 (White 81.2%; Black or African American 1.6%; Hispanic or Latino 15.6%; Asian 0.3%; Other 10.5%). **Foreign born:** 6.5%. **Median age:** 38.6. **State rank:** 222. **Pop change 1990-2000:** -9.9%.

Income: per capita $16,929; median household $35,456. **Pop below poverty level:** 12.6%.

Unemployment: 1.7%. **Median home value:** $56,800. **Median travel time to work:** 18.1 minutes.

HENDERSON COUNTY

Courthouse Sq Rm 107   **Ph:** 903-675-6140
Athens, TX 75751   **Fax:** 903-675-6105

In northeastern TX, southwest of Tyler; organized Apr 27, 1846 from Houston County. **Name Origin:** For Gen. James Pinckney Henderson (1808-58), TX minister to the U.S. (1844), first governor of the state of TX (1846-47), and U.S. senator (1857-58).

Area (sq mi): 949 (land 874.24; water 74.76).

Pop: 73,277 (White 84.8%; Black or African American 6.6%; Hispanic or Latino 6.9%; Asian 0.3%; Other 4.5%). **Foreign born:** 3.8%. **Median age:** 40.2. **State rank:** 45. **Pop change 1990-2000:** +25.2%.

Income: per capita $17,772; median household $32,533. **Pop below poverty level:** 15.1%.

Unemployment: 3.8%. **Median home value:** $75,300. **Median travel time to work:** 35.4 minutes.

HIDALGO COUNTY

PO Box 58   **Ph:** 956-318-2100
Edinburg, TX 78540   **Fax:** 956-318-2105
www.co.hidalgo.tx.us

On the southern border of TX, west of Harlingen; organized Jan 24, 1852 from Cameron County. **Name Origin:** Either for Guadalupe Hidalgo, D.F., Mexico, or possibly in honor of Miguel Hidalgo y Costilla (1753-1811), Mexican priest and hero of the Mexican war for Independence from Spain. Spanish 'nobleman.'

Area (sq mi): 1582.66 (land 1569.75; water 12.92).

Pop: 569,463 (White 10.4%; Black or African American 0.5%; Hispanic or Latino 88.3%; Asian 0.6%; Other 21.1%). **Foreign born:** 29.5%. **Median age:** 27.2. **State rank:** 7. **Pop change 1990-2000:** +48.5%.

Income: per capita $9,899; median household $24,863. **Pop below poverty level:** 35.9%.

Unemployment: 13.1%. **Median home value:** $52,400. **Median travel time to work:** 20.9 minutes.

HILL COUNTY

PO Box 398   **Ph:** 254-582-4030
Hillsboro, TX 76645   **Fax:** 254-582-4030

In north-central TX, south of Fort Worth; organized Feb 7, 1853 from Navarro County. **Name Origin:** For George Washington Hill (1814-60), secretary of war and navy under Republic of TX presidents Sam Houston (1793-1863) and Anson Jones (1798-1858).

Area (sq mi): 985.65 (land 962.36; water 23.29).

Pop: 32,321 (White 77.6%; Black or African American 7.4%; Hispanic or Latino 13.5%; Asian 0.3%; Other 8.1%). **Foreign born:** 5.9%. **Median age:** 38.3. **State rank:** 85. **Pop change 1990-2000:** +19.1%.

Income: per capita $15,514; median household $31,600. **Pop below poverty level:** 15.7%.

Unemployment: 5.1%. **Median home value:** $54,700. **Median travel time to work:** 29.4 minutes.

HOCKLEY COUNTY

802 Houston St Suite 213   **Ph:** 806-894-4404
Levelland, TX 79336

In southwestern TX panhandle, west of Lubbock; organized 1921 (other sources say organized Aug 21, 1876; first federal census: 1880 with no population). **Name Origin:** For Gen. George Washington Hockley (1802-54), Republic of Texas officer and secretary of war (1838; 1841).

Area (sq mi): 908.55 (land 908.28; water 0.27).

Pop: 22,716 (White 57.9%; Black or African American 3.7%; Hispanic or Latino 37.2%; Asian 0.1%; Other 21.7%). **Foreign born:** 5.2%. **Median age:** 33.3. **State rank:** 105. **Pop change 1990-2000:** -6.1%.

Income: per capita $15,022; median household $31,085. **Pop below poverty level:** 18.9%.

Unemployment: 3.4%. **Median home value:** $50,400. **Median travel time to work:** 22.4 minutes.

All statistics are based on the 2000 Census except the dollar figures given for per capita income, which are based on 1999 estimates.

HOOD COUNTY

PO Box 339   **Ph:** 817-579-3222
Granbury, TX 76048   **Fax:** 817-579-3227
www.co.hood.tx.us

In north-central TX, southwest of Fort Worth; organized Nov 3, 1865 from Johnson County. **Name Origin:** For Gen. John Bell Hood (1831-79), commander of TX troops in the Confederate army and later commander of the Confederate Army of TN.

Area (sq mi): 436.8 (land 421.61; water 15.19).

Pop: 41,100 (White 90.5%; Black or African American 0.3%; Hispanic or Latino 7.2%; Asian 0.3%; Other 4.5%). **Foreign born:** 3.3%. **Median age:** 41.5. **State rank:** 68. **Pop change 1990-2000:** +41.8%.

Income: per capita $22,261; median household $43,668. **Pop below poverty level:** 8.5%.

Unemployment: 4.2%. **Median home value:** $112,100. **Median travel time to work:** 34.1 minutes.

HOPKINS COUNTY

PO Box 288   **Ph:** 903-438-4074
Sulphur Springs, TX 75483   **Fax:** 903-438-4110

In northeastern TX, northeast of Dallas; organized Mar 25, 1846 from Lamar and Nacogdoches counties. **Name Origin:** For the pioneer family headed by Henry Harrison Hopkins and James Elliott Hopkins.

Area (sq mi): 792.74 (land 782.4; water 10.35).

Pop: 31,960 (White 81.2%; Black or African American 8%; Hispanic or Latino 9.3%; Asian 0.2%; Other 6.8%). **Foreign born:** 5.6%. **Median age:** 36.9. **State rank:** 87. **Pop change 1990-2000:** +10.8%.

Income: per capita $17,182; median household $32,136. **Pop below poverty level:** 14.6%.

Unemployment: 4.2%. **Median home value:** $61,000. **Median travel time to work:** 22.6 minutes.

HOUSTON COUNTY

PO Box 370   **Ph:** 936-544-3256
Crockett, TX 75835   **Fax:** 936-544-1954

In east-central TX, west of Lufkin; organized 1837 from Nacogdoches County (prior to statehood). **Name Origin:** For Samuel Houston (1793-1863), governor of TN (1827-29), president of the Republic of Texas (1836-38; 1841-44); U.S. senator from TX (1846-59) and TX governor (1859-61).

Area (sq mi): 1236.83 (land 1230.89; water 5.94).

Pop: 23,185 (White 63.7%; Black or African American 27.9%; Hispanic or Latino 7.5%; Asian 0.2%; Other 3.4%). **Foreign born:** 3%. **Median age:** 40.3. **State rank:** 102. **Pop change 1990-2000:** +8.5%.

Income: per capita $14,525; median household $28,119. **Pop below poverty level:** 21%.

Unemployment: 3.7%. **Median home value:** $49,300. **Median travel time to work:** 23.9 minutes.

HOWARD COUNTY

PO Box 1468   **Ph:** 915-264-2213
Big Spring, TX 79721   **Fax:** 915-264-2215

In south-central TX panhandle, west of Abilene; organized Aug 21, 1876 from Bexar County. **Name Origin:** For Volney Erskine Howard (1809-89), MS legislator, U.S. representative from TX (1849-53), and judge of CA superior court (1878-79).

Area (sq mi): 904.19 (land 902.84; water 1.36).

Pop: 33,627 (White 56.8%; Black or African American 4.1%; Hispanic or Latino 37.5%; Asian 0.6%; Other 15.1%). **Foreign born:** 6%. **Median age:** 36.4. **State rank:** 80. **Pop change 1990-2000:** +4%.

Income: per capita $15,027; median household $30,805. **Pop below poverty level:** 18.6%.

Unemployment: 3.9%. **Median home value:** $39,000. **Median travel time to work:** 17.3 minutes.

HUDSPETH COUNTY

PO Box 58   **Ph:** 915-369-2301
Sierra Blanca, TX 79851   **Fax:** 915-369-2407

In western TX, east of El Paso; organized Feb 16, 1917 from El Paso County. **Name Origin:** For Claude Benton Hudspeth (1877-1941), TX legislator (1902-18) and U.S. representative (1919-31).

Area (sq mi): 4571.93 (land 4571; water 0.93).

Pop: 3,344 (White 23%; Black or African American 0.3%; Hispanic or Latino 75%; Asian 0.2%; Other 12.3%). **Foreign born:** 33.2%. **Median age:** 30.2. **State rank:** 223. **Pop change 1990-2000:** +14.7%.

Income: per capita $9,549; median household $21,045. **Pop below poverty level:** 35.8%.

Unemployment: 4.3%. **Median home value:** $30,500. **Median travel time to work:** 17 minutes.

HUNT COUNTY

PO Box 1316   **Ph:** 903-408-4130
Greenville, TX 75403
www.co.hunt.tx.us

In east-central TX, northeast of Dallas; organized Apr 11, 1846 from Fannin and Nacogdoches counties. **Name Origin:** For Gen. Menucan Hunt (1807-56), Republic of TX officer and statesman.

Area (sq mi): 882.02 (land 841.16; water 40.87).

Pop: 76,596 (White 79.9%; Black or African American 9.5%; Hispanic or Latino 8.3%; Asian 0.5%; Other 6.4%). **Foreign born:** 4.7%. **Median age:** 35.5. **State rank:** 43. **Pop change 1990-2000:** +19%.

Income: per capita $17,554; median household $36,752. **Pop below poverty level:** 12.8%.

Unemployment: 4.9%. **Median home value:** $62,000. **Median travel time to work:** 30.1 minutes.

HUTCHINSON COUNTY

PO Box 1186   **Ph:** 806-878-4002
Stinnett, TX 79083

In north-central TX panhandle, northeast of Amarillo; organized

Please see sample entry on inside front cover for detailed information about the statistics presented with each county listing.

549

Aug 21, 1876 from Bexar County. **Name Origin:** For Anderson Hutchinson (1798-1853), Republic of TX district judge.

Area (sq mi): 894.95 (land 887.37; water 7.58).

Pop: 23,857 (White 80.1%; Black or African American 2.4%; Hispanic or Latino 14.7%; Asian 0.3%; Other 10.3%). **Foreign born:** 5.8%. **Median age:** 37.5. **State rank:** 98. **Pop change 1990-2000:** -7.1%.

Income: per capita $17,317; median household $36,588. **Pop below poverty level:** 11.1%.

Unemployment: 4.2%. **Median home value:** $45,300. **Median travel time to work:** 19.3 minutes.

IRION COUNTY
PO Box 736   **Ph:** 915-835-2421
Mertzon, TX 76941   **Fax:** 915-835-2008

In central TX, west of San Angelo; organized Mar 7, 1889 from Tom Green County. **Name Origin:** For Robert Anderson Irion (1806-61), senator in first TX congress (1836-37) and secretary of state of the Republic (1837-38).

Area (sq mi): 1051.59 (land 1051.48; water 0.11).

Pop: 1,771 (White 74.6%; Black or African American 0.4%; Hispanic or Latino 24.6%; Asian 0%; Other 8.9%). **Foreign born:** 3.5%. **Median age:** 39.9. **State rank:** 241. **Pop change 1990-2000:** +8.7%.

Income: per capita $20,515; median household $37,500. **Pop below poverty level:** 8.4%.

Unemployment: 2.3%. **Median home value:** $60,800. **Median travel time to work:** 25.9 minutes.

JACK COUNTY
100 Main St   **Ph:** 940-567-2111
Jacksboro, TX 76458

In north-central TX, northwest of Fort Worth; organized July 4, 1857 from Cooke County. **Name Origin:** For the Jack brothers, William Houston (1806-44) and Patrick Churchill (1808-44), both TX statesman and legislators.

Area (sq mi): 920.11 (land 916.61; water 3.5).

Pop: 8,763 (White 85.2%; Black or African American 5.5%; Hispanic or Latino 7.9%; Asian 0.3%; Other 5.5%). **Foreign born:** 2.8%. **Median age:** 37. **State rank:** 175. **Pop change 1990-2000:** +25.5%.

Income: per capita $15,210; median household $32,500. **Pop below poverty level:** 12.9%.

Unemployment: 3.2%. **Median home value:** $44,100. **Median travel time to work:** 28.1 minutes.

JACKSON COUNTY
115 W Main St Rm 101   **Ph:** 361-782-3563
Edna, TX 77957

On the central eastern coast of TX, east of Victoria; original county; organized Mar 17, 1836 (prior to statehood) from Old Mexican Municipality. **Name Origin:** For Andrew Jackson (1767-1845), seventh U.S. president.

Area (sq mi): 857.03 (land 829.49; water 27.54).

Pop: 14,391 (White 66.3%; Black or African American 7.6%; Hispanic or Latino 24.7%; Asian 0.4%; Other 15.5%). **Foreign born:** 4.8%. **Median age:** 37.3. **State rank:** 144. **Pop change 1990-2000:** +10.4%.

Income: per capita $16,693; median household $35,254. **Pop below poverty level:** 14.7%.

Unemployment: 3.3%. **Median home value:** $52,700. **Median travel time to work:** 23.6 minutes.

JASPER COUNTY
PO Box 2070   **Ph:** 409-384-2632
Jasper, TX 75951   **Fax:** 409-384-7198

In east-central TX, north of Beaumont; original county; organized Mar 17, 1836 (prior to statehood) from Old Mexican Municipality. **Name Origin:** For Sgt. William Jasper (1750-79), American Revolutionary War soldier from SC.

Area (sq mi): 969.62 (land 937.4; water 32.22).

Pop: 35,604 (White 76.7%; Black or African American 17.8%; Hispanic or Latino 3.9%; Asian 0.3%; Other 3.6%). **Foreign born:** 2.2%. **Median age:** 37.3. **State rank:** 77. **Pop change 1990-2000:** +14.5%.

Income: per capita $15,636; median household $30,902. **Pop below poverty level:** 18.1%.

Unemployment: 11.4%. **Median home value:** $59,900. **Median travel time to work:** 28.1 minutes.

JEFF DAVIS COUNTY
PO Box 398   **Ph:** 915-426-3251
Fort Davis, TX 79734   **Fax:** 915-426-3760

In western TX, southwest of Odessa; organized Mar 15, 1887 from Presidio County. **Name Origin:** For Jefferson Davis (1808-89), president of the Confederate States of America (1862-65).

Area (sq mi): 2264.6 (land 2264.43; water 0.18).

Pop: 2,207 (White 62.3%; Black or African American 0.9%; Hispanic or Latino 35.5%; Asian 0.1%; Other 8.5%). **Foreign born:** 10.9%. **Median age:** 42.5. **State rank:** 234. **Pop change 1990-2000:** +13.4%.

Income: per capita $18,846; median household $32,212. **Pop below poverty level:** 15%.

Unemployment: 1.8%. **Median home value:** $59,800. **Median travel time to work:** 24.1 minutes.

JEFFERSON COUNTY
PO Box 1151   **Ph:** 409-835-8475
Beaumont, TX 77704   **Fax:** 409-839-2394
www.co.jefferson.tx.us

On the northeastern coast of TX, east of Houston; original county; organized Mar 17, 1836 (prior to statehood) from Old Mexican Municipality. **Name Origin:** For Jefferson Beaumont, an early settler.

Area (sq mi): 1111.26 (land 903.55; water 207.71).

Pop: 252,051 (White 51.8%; Black or African American 33.7%;

All statistics are based on the 2000 Census except the dollar figures given for per capita income, which are based on 1999 estimates.

Hispanic or Latino 10.5%; Asian 2.9%; Other 6.1%). **Foreign born:** 6.2%. **Median age:** 35.3. **State rank:** 14. **Pop change 1990-2000:** +5.3%.

Income: per capita $17,571; median household $34,706. **Pop below poverty level:** 17.4%.

Unemployment: 7.9%. **Median home value:** $59,400. **Median travel time to work:** 20.3 minutes.

JIM HOGG COUNTY
PO Box 878   **Ph:** 361-527-4031
Hebbronville, TX 78361   **Fax:** 361-527-5843

In southern TX, southeast of Laredo; organized Mar 31, 1913 from Brooks and Duval counties. **Name Origin:** For James Stephen Hogg (1851-1906), newspaper publisher, attorney general of TX (1886-90), and governor (1891-95).

Area (sq mi): 1136.16 (land 1136.11; water 0.05).

Pop: 5,281 (White 9%; Black or African American 0.5%; Hispanic or Latino 90%; Asian 0.2%; Other 18.9%). **Foreign born:** 5.1%. **Median age:** 33.9. **State rank:** 202. **Pop change 1990-2000:** +3.4%.

Income: per capita $12,185; median household $25,833. **Pop below poverty level:** 25.9%.

Unemployment: 4.5%. **Median home value:** $32,400. **Median travel time to work:** 23.2 minutes.

JIM WELLS COUNTY
PO Box 1459   **Ph:** 361-668-5702
Alice, TX 78333

In southeastern TX, west of Corpus Christi; organized Mar 25, 1911 from Nueces County. **Name Origin:** For James B. Wells, a jurist.

Area (sq mi): 868.22 (land 864.52; water 3.71).

Pop: 39,326 (White 22.9%; Black or African American 0.6%; Hispanic or Latino 75.7%; Asian 0.4%; Other 21%). **Foreign born:** 3.6%. **Median age:** 32.8. **State rank:** 69. **Pop change 1990-2000:** +4.4%.

Income: per capita $12,252; median household $28,843. **Pop below poverty level:** 24.1%.

Unemployment: 5.7%. **Median home value:** $41,300. **Median travel time to work:** 25.1 minutes.

JOHNSON COUNTY
PO Box 662   **Ph:** 817-556-6323
Cleburne, TX 76033   **Fax:** 817-556-6327
www.johnsoncountytx.org

In north-central TX, south of Fort Worth; organized Feb 13, 1854 from McLennan and Navarro counties. **Name Origin:** For Middleton Tate Johnson (1810-66), AL legislator, Texas Ranger, and legislator.

Area (sq mi): 734.46 (land 729.42; water 5.03).

Pop: 126,811 (White 83.2%; Black or African American 2.5%; Hispanic or Latino 12.1%; Asian 0.5%; Other 6.9%). **Foreign born:** 5.2%. **Median age:** 34.3. **State rank:** 25. **Pop change 1990-2000:** +30.5%.

Income: per capita $18,400; median household $44,621. **Pop below poverty level:** 8.8%.

Unemployment: 4.1%. **Median home value:** $81,900. **Median travel time to work:** 31.8 minutes.

JONES COUNTY
PO Box 552   **Ph:** 915-823-3762
Anson, TX 79501   **Fax:** 915-823-4223

In north-central TX, north of Abilene; established Feb 1, 1858 from Bexar and Bosque counties. **Name Origin:** For Anson Jones (1798-1858), secretary of state of the Republic of TX (1841-44) and president of the Republic (1844-46).

Area (sq mi): 937.13 (land 930.99; water 6.14).

Pop: 20,785 (White 66.2%; Black or African American 11.5%; Hispanic or Latino 20.9%; Asian 0.5%; Other 9.3%). **Foreign born:** 1.6%. **Median age:** 36. **State rank:** 112. **Pop change 1990-2000:** +26%.

Income: per capita $13,656; median household $29,572. **Pop below poverty level:** 16.8%.

Unemployment: 2.8%. **Median home value:** $34,600. **Median travel time to work:** 21.3 minutes.

KARNES COUNTY
101 N Panna Maria Ave Suite 9   **Ph:** 830-780-3938
Karnes City, TX 78118   **Fax:** 830-780-4576

In south-central TX, southeast of San Antonio; organized Feb 4, 1854 from Goliad County. **Name Origin:** For Capt. Henry Wax Karnes (1812-40), TX Republic officer and military scout.

Area (sq mi): 753.58 (land 750.32; water 3.27).

Pop: 15,446 (White 40.8%; Black or African American 10.8%; Hispanic or Latino 47.4%; Asian 0.4%; Other 20.3%). **Foreign born:** 3.7%. **Median age:** 34.1. **State rank:** 137. **Pop change 1990-2000:** +24%.

Income: per capita $13,603; median household $26,526. **Pop below poverty level:** 21.9%.

Unemployment: 3.8%. **Median home value:** $41,600. **Median travel time to work:** 27.4 minutes.

KAUFMAN COUNTY
100 W Mulberry St   **Ph:** 972-932-4331
Kaufman, TX 75142   **Fax:** 972-932-8018
www.kaufmancounty.net

In northeastern TX, east of Dallas; organized Feb 26, 1848 from Henderson County. **Name Origin:** For David Spangler Kaufman (1813-51), Republic of TX legislator (1839-45) and U.S. representative (1846-51).

Area (sq mi): 806.81 (land 786.04; water 20.76).

Pop: 71,313 (White 76.3%; Black or African American 10.5%; Hispanic or Latino 11.1%; Asian 0.5%; Other 7.9%). **Foreign born:** 5.7%. **Median age:** 34.9. **State rank:** 46. **Pop change 1990-2000:** +36.6%.

Income: per capita $18,827; median household $44,783. **Pop below poverty level:** 10.5%.

Unemployment: 5.6%. **Median home value:** $85,700. **Median travel time to work:** 35.6 minutes.

Please see sample entry on inside front cover for detailed information about the statistics presented with each county listing.

551

KENDALL COUNTY

201 E San Antonio St   **Ph:** 830-249-9343
Boerne, TX 78006   **Fax:** 830-249-1763

In south-central TX, northwest of San Antonio; organized Jan 10, 1862 from Kerr and Blanco counties. **Name Origin:** For George Wilkins Kendall (1809-67), a founder of the New Orleans *Picayune* and Republic of TX army officer.

Area (sq mi): 663.04 (land 662.44; water 0.6).

Pop: 23,743 (White 80.5%; Black or African American 0.3%; Hispanic or Latino 17.9%; Asian 0.2%; Other 6.5%). **Foreign born:** 5.6%. **Median age:** 39.3. **State rank:** 99. **Pop change 1990-2000:** +62.7%.

Income: per capita $24,619; median household $49,521. **Pop below poverty level:** 10.5%.

Unemployment: 2.3%. **Median home value:** $139,900. **Median travel time to work:** 29 minutes.

KENEDY COUNTY

PO Box 227   **Ph:** 361-294-5220
Sarita, TX 78385   **Fax:** 361-294-5218

On the southeastern coast of TX, south of Corpus Christi; organized as Willacy County 1911 from Hidalgo and Cameron counties; name changed Apr 2, 1921, at which time a new Willacy County was created from Cameron and Hidalgo counties plus a 1.4 mile strip of Old Willacy. **Name Origin:** For Capt. Mifflin Kenedy (1818-95), commercial navigator of the Rio Grande, half-owner of the King ranch (1860-68), and part-owner of the TX narrow gauge railroad (1876-81).

Area (sq mi): 1945.6 (land 1456.77; water 488.83).

Pop: 414 (White 20.3%; Black or African American 0.7%; Hispanic or Latino 79%; Asian 0.5%; Other 34.3%). **Foreign born:** 13.3%. **Median age:** 34.2. **State rank:** 252. **Pop change 1990-2000:** -10%.

Income: per capita $17,959; median household $25,000. **Pop below poverty level:** 15.3%.

Unemployment: 1.8%. **Median home value:** $22,500. **Median travel time to work:** 18.1 minutes.

KENT COUNTY

PO Box 9   **Ph:** 806-237-3881
Jayton, TX 79528   **Fax:** 806-237-2632

In southern TX panhandle, northwest of Abilene; organized Aug 21, 1876 from Bexar County. **Name Origin:** For Andrew Kent (1798-1836), TX soldier killed at the Alamo.

Area (sq mi): 902.91 (land 902.33; water 0.58).

Pop: 859 (White 90.5%; Black or African American 0.2%; Hispanic or Latino 9.1%; Asian 0%; Other 4.2%). **Foreign born:** 1.7%. **Median age:** 47.1. **State rank:** 249. **Pop change 1990-2000:** -15%.

Income: per capita $17,626; median household $30,433. **Pop below poverty level:** 10.4%.

Unemployment: 2%. **Median home value:** $24,200. **Median travel time to work:** 19.7 minutes.

KERR COUNTY

700 Main St Rm 122   **Ph:** 830-792-2255
Kerrville, TX 78028   **Fax:** 830-792-2274
www.kerrcounty.org

In central TX, northwest of San Antonio; organized Jan 26, 1856 from Bexar County. **Name Origin:** For James Kerr (1790-1850), member of the TX constitutional convention (1836) and TX congress.

Area (sq mi): 1107.66 (land 1106.12; water 1.54).

Pop: 43,653 (White 77.4%; Black or African American 1.8%; Hispanic or Latino 19.1%; Asian 0.5%; Other 8.9%). **Foreign born:** 6.6%. **Median age:** 43.8. **State rank:** 64. **Pop change 1990-2000:** +20.2%.

Income: per capita $19,767; median household $34,283. **Pop below poverty level:** 14.5%.

Unemployment: 2.6%. **Median home value:** $96,600. **Median travel time to work:** 18.3 minutes.

KIMBLE COUNTY

501 Main St Courthouse   **Ph:** 915-446-3353
Junction, TX 76849   **Fax:** 915-446-2986

In central TX, southeast of San Angelo; organized Jan 22, 1858 from Bexar County. **Name Origin:** For George C. Kimble (1810-36), a TX officer killed at the Alamo. Name is variously spelled *Kimball* and *Kimbell*.

Area (sq mi): 1250.92 (land 1250.7; water 0.23).

Pop: 4,468 (White 77.9%; Black or African American 0.1%; Hispanic or Latino 20.7%; Asian 0.4%; Other 9.1%). **Foreign born:** 5.5%. **Median age:** 43.1. **State rank:** 207. **Pop change 1990-2000:** +8.4%.

Income: per capita $17,127; median household $29,396. **Pop below poverty level:** 18.8%.

Unemployment: 1.7%. **Median home value:** $50,700. **Median travel time to work:** 21.5 minutes.

KING COUNTY

PO Box 135   **Ph:** 806-596-4412
Guthrie, TX 79236   **Fax:** 806-596-4664

In southeastern TX panhandle, east of Lubbock; established Aug 21, 1876 from Fannin County. **Name Origin:** For William King (1812-26), a soldier killed at the Alamo.

Area (sq mi): 913.33 (land 912.29; water 1.04).

Pop: 356 (White 88.5%; Black or African American 0%; Hispanic or Latino 9.6%; Asian 0%; Other 5.9%). **Foreign born:** 2.2%. **Median age:** 37. **State rank:** 253. **Pop change 1990-2000:** +0.6%.

Income: per capita $12,321; median household $35,625. **Pop below poverty level:** 20.7%.

Unemployment: 3.8%. **Median home value:** $13,800. **Median travel time to work:** 14.4 minutes.

All statistics are based on the 2000 Census except the dollar figures given for per capita income, which are based on 1999 estimates.

KINNEY COUNTY
PO Box 9
Brackettville, TX 78832
Ph: 830-563-2521
Fax: 830-563-2644

On southwestern border of TX, east of Del Rio; organized 1876 from Bexar County. **Name Origin:** For H.L. Kinney, a TX legislator.

Area (sq mi): 1365.31 (land 1363.44; water 1.87).

Pop: 3,379 (White 47%; Black or African American 1.7%; Hispanic or Latino 50.5%; Asian 0.1%; Other 22.3%). **Foreign born:** 11.7%. **Median age:** 43.2. **State rank:** 221. **Pop change 1990-2000:** +8.3%.

Income: per capita $15,350; median household $28,320. **Pop below poverty level:** 24%.

Unemployment: 6.3%. **Median home value:** $45,800. **Median travel time to work:** 22.2 minutes.

KLEBERG COUNTY
PO Box 1327
Kingsville, TX 78364
Ph: 361-595-8548
Fax: 361-595-8546

On the southeastern coast of TX, south of Corpus Christi; organized Feb 27, 1913 from Nueces County. **Name Origin:** For Robert Justice Kleberg (1803-88), German immigrant, Republic of TX soldier, and jurist.

Area (sq mi): 1090.29 (land 870.97; water 219.32).

Pop: 31,549 (White 28.5%; Black or African American 3.7%; Hispanic or Latino 65.4%; Asian 1.5%; Other 22.9%). **Foreign born:** 6.5%. **Median age:** 29.2. **State rank:** 88. **Pop change 1990-2000:** +4.2%.

Income: per capita $13,542; median household $29,313. **Pop below poverty level:** 26.7%.

Unemployment: 4.8%. **Median home value:** $51,800. **Median travel time to work:** 19 minutes.

KNOX COUNTY
PO Box 196
Benjamin, TX 79505
Ph: 940-459-2441
Fax: 940-459-2005

In north-central TX, southwest of Wichita Falls; organized Feb 1, 1858 from Fannin County. **Name Origin:** For Gen. Henry Knox (1750-1806), Revolutionary War officer and first U.S. secretary of war (1785-95).

Area (sq mi): 855.43 (land 849; water 6.43).

Pop: 4,253 (White 66.5%; Black or African American 6.9%; Hispanic or Latino 25.1%; Asian 0.2%; Other 18.6%). **Foreign born:** 6.7%. **Median age:** 40.5. **State rank:** 209. **Pop change 1990-2000:** -12.1%.

Income: per capita $13,443; median household $25,453. **Pop below poverty level:** 22.9%.

Unemployment: 3.3%. **Median home value:** $27,800. **Median travel time to work:** 16.3 minutes.

LA SALLE COUNTY
PO Box 340
Cotulla, TX 78014
Ph: 830-879-3033
Fax: 830-879-2933

In southern TX, northeast of Laredo; organized Feb 1, 1858 from Bexar and Webb counties. **Name Origin:** For Robert Cavelier (1643-87), Sieur de La Salle, French adventurer and explorer who claimed the land west of the Mississippi River for France.

Area (sq mi): 1494.23 (land 1488.85; water 5.38).

Pop: 5,866 (White 19%; Black or African American 3.5%; Hispanic or Latino 77.1%; Asian 0.3%; Other 14.6%). **Foreign born:** 4%. **Median age:** 33. **State rank:** 197. **Pop change 1990-2000:** +11.6%.

Income: per capita $9,692; median household $21,857. **Pop below poverty level:** 29.8%.

Unemployment: 6.2%. **Median home value:** $22,700. **Median travel time to work:** 28.8 minutes.

LAMAR COUNTY
119 N Main St Rm 109
Paris, TX 75460
www.co.lamar.tx.us
Ph: 903-737-2420
Fax: 903-782-1000

On the northeastern border of TX, northwest of Texarkana; organized Dec 17, 1840 from Red River County. **Name Origin:** For Mirabeau Buonaparte Lamar (1798-1859), Republic of TX attorney general, secretary of war, vice president (1836-38), and president (1838-41).

Area (sq mi): 932.47 (land 916.81; water 15.66).

Pop: 48,499 (White 80.7%; Black or African American 13.5%; Hispanic or Latino 3.3%; Asian 0.4%; Other 3.7%). **Foreign born:** 2.1%. **Median age:** 36.9. **State rank:** 56. **Pop change 1990-2000:** +10.4%.

Income: per capita $17,000; median household $31,609. **Pop below poverty level:** 16.4%.

Unemployment: 6.6%. **Median home value:** $57,300. **Median travel time to work:** 20.1 minutes.

LAMB COUNTY
100 6th St Rm 103 Box 3
Littlefield, TX 79339
Ph: 806-385-4222
Fax: 806-385-6485

In west-central TX panhandle, northwest of Lubbock; organized Aug 21, 1876 from Bexar County. **Name Origin:** For Lt. George A. Lamb (?-1836), Republic of TX army officer killed at the Battle of San Jacinto.

Area (sq mi): 1017.73 (land 1016.21; water 1.52).

Pop: 14,709 (White 51.3%; Black or African American 4.3%; Hispanic or Latino 43.5%; Asian 0.1%; Other 19.5%). **Foreign born:** 6.3%. **Median age:** 36.2. **State rank:** 141. **Pop change 1990-2000:** -2.4%.

Income: per capita $15,169; median household $27,898. **Pop below poverty level:** 20.9%.

Unemployment: 6.7%. **Median home value:** $34,300. **Median travel time to work:** 17.9 minutes.

LAMPASAS COUNTY
PO Box 347
Lampasas, TX 76550
Ph: 512-556-8271
Fax: 512-556-8270

In central TX, southwest of Waco; organized Feb 1, 1856 from Bell and Travis counties. **Name Origin:** From a Spanish term meaning 'water lily.'

Please see sample entry on inside front cover for detailed information about the statistics presented with each county listing.

553

Area (sq mi): 713.96 (land 712.04; water 1.92).

Pop: 17,762 (White 79.5%; Black or African American 3.1%; Hispanic or Latino 15.1%; Asian 0.8%; Other 9.4%). **Foreign born:** 6%. **Median age:** 36.9. **State rank:** 126. **Pop change 1990-2000:** +31.4%.

Income: per capita $17,184; median household $36,176. **Pop below poverty level:** 14.1%.

Unemployment: 3.1%. **Median home value:** $72,400. **Median travel time to work:** 25.8 minutes.

LAVACA COUNTY
109 N La Grange St   **Ph:** 361-798-3612
Hallettsville, TX 77964

In southeastern TX, east of San Antonio; organized Apr 6, 1846 from Colorado, Victoria, and Jackson counties. **Name Origin:** For the Lavaca River; Spanish translation of original French *la vache* 'the cow,' for the buffalo in the area, which La Salle thought resembled cows.

Area (sq mi): 970.35 (land 969.9; water 0.45).

Pop: 19,210 (White 81.1%; Black or African American 6.8%; Hispanic or Latino 11.4%; Asian 0.2%; Other 6.1%). **Foreign born:** 2.5%. **Median age:** 41.9. **State rank:** 118. **Pop change 1990-2000:** +2.8%.

Income: per capita $16,398; median household $29,132. **Pop below poverty level:** 13.2%.

Unemployment: 1.6%. **Median home value:** $55,800. **Median travel time to work:** 22 minutes.

LEE COUNTY
PO Box 419   **Ph:** 979-542-3684
Giddings, TX 78942   **Fax:** 979-542-2623

In east-central TX, east of Austin; organized Apr 14, 1874 from Bastrop, Burleson, Washington, and Fayette counties. **Name Origin:** For Robert E. Lee (1807-70), American general and commander in chief of the Confederate forces during the Civil War.

Area (sq mi): 634.03 (land 628.5; water 5.53).

Pop: 15,657 (White 68.5%; Black or African American 12.1%; Hispanic or Latino 18.2%; Asian 0.2%; Other 11.1%). **Foreign born:** 6.1%. **Median age:** 35.6. **State rank:** 136. **Pop change 1990-2000:** +21.8%.

Income: per capita $17,163; median household $36,280. **Pop below poverty level:** 11.9%.

Unemployment: 3.8%. **Median home value:** $75,000. **Median travel time to work:** 30 minutes.

LEON COUNTY
PO Box 98   **Ph:** 903-536-2352
Centerville, TX 75833

In east-central TX, southeast of Waco; organized Mar 17, 1846 from Robertson County. **Name Origin:** For a Martin de Leon, or for Leon Prairie where a 'lion' was killed.

Area (sq mi): 1080.38 (land 1072.04; water 8.34).

Pop: 15,335 (White 80.6%; Black or African American 10.4%; Hispanic or Latino 7.9%; Asian 0.2%; Other 5.9%). **Foreign born:**

4.2%. **Median age:** 42.1. **State rank:** 138. **Pop change 1990-2000:** +21.1%.

Income: per capita $17,599; median household $30,981. **Pop below poverty level:** 15.6%.

Unemployment: 4.7%. **Median home value:** $64,200. **Median travel time to work:** 28 minutes.

LIBERTY COUNTY
1923 Sam Houston St   **Ph:** 936-336-4600
Liberty, TX 77575   **Fax:** 936-336-4640

In east-central TX, northeast of Houston; organized Mar 17, 1836 from Bexar County. **Name Origin:** Honoring TX independence (1836).

Area (sq mi): 1176.22 (land 1159.68; water 16.54).

Pop: 70,154 (White 74.5%; Black or African American 12.8%; Hispanic or Latino 10.9%; Asian 0.3%; Other 7.9%). **Foreign born:** 5.1%. **Median age:** 34. **State rank:** 47. **Pop change 1990-2000:** +33.1%.

Income: per capita $15,539; median household $38,361. **Pop below poverty level:** 14.3%.

Unemployment: 6.4%. **Median home value:** $63,900. **Median travel time to work:** 36.8 minutes.

LIMESTONE COUNTY
PO Box 350   **Ph:** 254-729-5504
Groesbeck, TX 76642   **Fax:** 254-729-2951

In east-central TX, east of Waco; organized Apr 11, 1846 from Robertson County. **Name Origin:** For Lake Limestone.

Area (sq mi): 933.15 (land 908.88; water 24.27).

Pop: 22,051 (White 66.7%; Black or African American 19.1%; Hispanic or Latino 13%; Asian 0.1%; Other 10.1%). **Foreign born:** 5.5%. **Median age:** 37.4. **State rank:** 108. **Pop change 1990-2000:** +5.3%.

Income: per capita $14,352; median household $29,366. **Pop below poverty level:** 17.8%.

Unemployment: 3.5%. **Median home value:** $46,300. **Median travel time to work:** 21.5 minutes.

LIPSCOMB COUNTY
1 Courthouse Sq PO Box 70   **Ph:** 806-862-3091
Lipscomb, TX 79056   **Fax:** 806-862-3004

On the northeastern border of TX panhandle; organized Aug 21, 1876 from Bexar County. **Name Origin:** For Abner S. Lipscomb (1789-1858), AL legislator, secretary of state for the Republic of TX (1839-40), and associate justice of the TX supreme court (1846-58).

Area (sq mi): 932.22 (land 932.11; water 0.11).

Pop: 3,057 (White 76.7%; Black or African American 0.5%; Hispanic or Latino 20.7%; Asian 0.1%; Other 16.6%). **Foreign born:** 11.7%. **Median age:** 39.5. **State rank:** 228. **Pop change 1990-2000:** -2.7%.

Income: per capita $16,328; median household $31,964. **Pop below poverty level:** 16.7%.

All statistics are based on the 2000 Census except the dollar figures given for per capita income, which are based on 1999 estimates.

Unemployment: 2%. **Median home value:** $39,700. **Median travel time to work:** 19.6 minutes.

LIVE OAK COUNTY

PO Box 280   **Ph:** 361-449-2733
George West, TX 78022

In southern TX, northwest of Corpus Christi; organized Feb 2, 1856 from Nueces County. **Name Origin:** For the indigenous live oak trees, *Quercus virginiana* and *Q. chrysolepsis*.

Area (sq mi): 1078.83 (land 1036.3; water 42.53).

Pop: 12,309 (White 58.5%; Black or African American 2.4%; Hispanic or Latino 38%; Asian 0.2%; Other 10%). **Foreign born:** 2.3%. **Median age:** 39.2. **State rank:** 155. **Pop change 1990-2000:** +28.8%.

Income: per capita $15,886; median household $32,057. **Pop below poverty level:** 16.5%.

Unemployment: 2.5%. **Median home value:** $55,200. **Median travel time to work:** 27.2 minutes.

LLANO COUNTY

PO Box 40   **Ph:** 915-247-4455
Llano, TX 78643   **Fax:** 915-247-2406

In central TX, northwest of Austin; organized Feb 1, 1856 from Bexar County. **Name Origin:** For the Llano River, which flows through the county; from its Spanish name, *el rio de los llanos* 'the river of the plains.'

Area (sq mi): 966.18 (land 934.76; water 31.41).

Pop: 17,044 (White 93.1%; Black or African American 0.3%; Hispanic or Latino 5.1%; Asian 0.4%; Other 3%). **Foreign born:** 2%. **Median age:** 53. **State rank:** 129. **Pop change 1990-2000:** +46.5%.

Income: per capita $23,547; median household $34,830. **Pop below poverty level:** 10.3%.

Unemployment: 3.2%. **Median home value:** $102,100. **Median travel time to work:** 27.8 minutes.

LOVING COUNTY

100 Bell St PO Box 194   **Ph:** 915-377-2441
Mentone, TX 79754   **Fax:** 915-377-2701

On the northwestern border of TX, west of Odessa; organized Feb 26, 1887 from Tom Green County. **Name Origin:** For Oliver Loving, pioneer and rancher.

Area (sq mi): 676.85 (land 673.08; water 3.77).

Pop: 67 (White 89.6%; Black or African American 0%; Hispanic or Latino 10.4%; Asian 0%; Other 10.5%). **Foreign born:** 0%. **Median age:** 45.8. **State rank:** 254. **Pop change 1990-2000:** -37.4%.

Income: per capita $24,084; median household $40,000. **Pop below poverty level:** 0%.

Unemployment: 7.9%. **Median travel time to work:** 14.6 minutes.

LUBBOCK COUNTY

904 Broadway St Rm 207   **Ph:** 806-775-1043
Lubbock, TX 79401
www.co.lubbock.tx.us

In south-central TX panhandle, north of Midland; organized 1891

from Baylor County (other sources say organized Aug 21, 1876; first federal census: 1880). **Name Origin:** For Col. Thomas S. Lubbock, signer of the TX Declaration of Independence and an organizer of the Texas Rangers.

Area (sq mi): 900.7 (land 899.49; water 1.2).

Pop: 242,628 (White 62.5%; Black or African American 7.7%; Hispanic or Latino 27.5%; Asian 1.3%; Other 16.7%). **Foreign born:** 3.3%. **Median age:** 30.5. **State rank:** 17. **Pop change 1990-2000:** +9%.

Income: per capita $17,323; median household $32,198. **Pop below poverty level:** 17.8%.

Unemployment: 2.6%. **Median home value:** $69,100. **Median travel time to work:** 17.1 minutes.

LYNN COUNTY

PO Box 937   **Ph:** 806-561-4750
Tahoka, TX 79373   **Fax:** 806-561-4988

In southwestern TX panhandle, south of Lubbock; organized Aug 21, 1876 from Bexar County. **Name Origin:** For W. Linn (?-1836), a soldier killed at the Alamo.

Area (sq mi): 893.46 (land 891.88; water 1.58).

Pop: 6,550 (White 51.6%; Black or African American 2.8%; Hispanic or Latino 44.6%; Asian 0.2%; Other 21.4%). **Foreign born:** 5%. **Median age:** 35.2. **State rank:** 192. **Pop change 1990-2000:** -3.1%.

Income: per capita $14,090; median household $26,694. **Pop below poverty level:** 22.6%.

Unemployment: 5%. **Median home value:** $38,500. **Median travel time to work:** 19.6 minutes.

MADISON COUNTY

101 W Main St Rm 102   **Ph:** 936-348-2638
Madisonville, TX 77864   **Fax:** 936-348-5858

In east-central TX, northeast of Austin; organized 1854 from Montgomery, Walker, Grimes, and Leon counties. **Name Origin:** For James Madison (1751-1836), fourth U.S. president.

Area (sq mi): 472.44 (land 469.65; water 2.8).

Pop: 12,940 (White 60.3%; Black or African American 22.9%; Hispanic or Latino 15.8%; Asian 0.4%; Other 9.9%). **Foreign born:** 4.8%. **Median age:** 33.4. **State rank:** 152. **Pop change 1990-2000:** +18.4%.

Income: per capita $14,056; median household $29,418. **Pop below poverty level:** 15.8%.

Unemployment: 2.7%. **Median home value:** $55,900. **Median travel time to work:** 26 minutes.

MARION COUNTY

PO Box 763   **Ph:** 903-665-3971
Jefferson, TX 75657   **Fax:** 903-665-8732

On the northeastern border of TX, north of Marshall; organized Feb 8, 1860 from Cass and Harrison counties. **Name Origin:** For Gen. Francis Marion (c.1732-95), SC soldier and legislator, known as 'The Swamp Fox' for his tactics during the Revolutionary War.

Please see sample entry on inside front cover for detailed information about the statistics presented with each county listing.

555

Area (sq mi): 420.36 (land 381.21; water 39.15).

Pop: 10,941 (White 71.5%; Black or African American 23.9%; Hispanic or Latino 2.4%; Asian 0.2%; Other 3.1%). **Foreign born:** 0.9%. **Median age:** 43.3. **State rank:** 161. **Pop change 1990-2000:** +9.6%.

Income: per capita $14,535; median household $25,347. **Pop below poverty level:** 22.4%.

Unemployment: 7.9%. **Median home value:** $48,700. **Median travel time to work:** 32.9 minutes.

MARTIN COUNTY
PO Box 906   **Ph:** 915-756-3412
Stanton, TX 79782   **Fax:** 915-607-2212

In southwestern TX panhandle, north of Midland; organized Aug 21, 1876 from Bexar County. **Name Origin:** For Wyly Martin, active in achieving TX statehood.

Area (sq mi): 915.62 (land 914.78; water 0.84).

Pop: 4,746 (White 56.8%; Black or African American 1.6%; Hispanic or Latino 40.6%; Asian 0.2%; Other 19.3%). **Foreign born:** 8.1%. **Median age:** 32.5. **State rank:** 205. **Pop change 1990-2000:** -4.2%.

Income: per capita $15,647; median household $31,836. **Pop below poverty level:** 18.7%.

Unemployment: 4.1%. **Median home value:** $53,800. **Median travel time to work:** 19.3 minutes.

MASON COUNTY
PO Box 702   **Ph:** 915-347-5253
Mason, TX 76856   **Fax:** 915-347-6868

In central TX, northwest of Austin; organized Jan 22, 1858 from Bexar County. **Name Origin:** For Lt. George (G.T.) Mason, army officer who chose locations for forts along the Rio Grande.

Area (sq mi): 932.18 (land 932.07; water 0.11).

Pop: 3,738 (White 77.9%; Black or African American 0.1%; Hispanic or Latino 20.9%; Asian 0.1%; Other 8.2%). **Foreign born:** 4.7%. **Median age:** 46.7. **State rank:** 218. **Pop change 1990-2000:** +9.2%.

Income: per capita $20,931; median household $30,921. **Pop below poverty level:** 13.2%.

Unemployment: 1.6%. **Median home value:** $53,900. **Median travel time to work:** 18.7 minutes.

MATAGORDA COUNTY
1700 7th St Rm 202   **Ph:** 979-244-7680
Bay City, TX 77414   **Fax:** 979-244-7688

On the central east coast of TX, southwest of Houston; original county; organized Mar 17, 1836 (prior to statehood) from Old Mexican Municipality. **Name Origin:** For Matagorda Island; Spanish 'thicket' or 'rough area.'

Area (sq mi): 1612.19 (land 1114.46; water 497.73).

Pop: 37,957 (White 52.4%; Black or African American 12.7%; Hispanic or Latino 31.3%; Asian 2.4%; Other 17.1%). **Foreign born:** 9.9%. **Median age:** 34.8. **State rank:** 72. **Pop change 1990-2000:** +2.8%.

Income: per capita $15,709; median household $32,174. **Pop below poverty level:** 18.5%.

Unemployment: 10.8%. **Median home value:** $61,500. **Median travel time to work:** 23.9 minutes.

MAVERICK COUNTY
PO Box 4050   **Ph:** 830-773-2829
Eagle Pass, TX 78853   **Fax:** 830-752-4479

On the southwestern border of TX, southeast of Del Rio; organized Feb 2, 1856 from Kenedy County. **Name Origin:** For Samuel Augustus Maverick (1803-70), Republic of TX patriot, rancher, and legislator. Many of his cattle went unbranded and were stolen, thus the word 'maverick' to describe a stray animal or a person with no attachment to a place or group.

Area (sq mi): 1291.74 (land 1280.08; water 11.66).

Pop: 47,297 (White 3.4%; Black or African American 0.3%; Hispanic or Latino 95%; Asian 0.4%; Other 28.3%). **Foreign born:** 37.8%. **Median age:** 27.8. **State rank:** 60. **Pop change 1990-2000:** +30%.

Income: per capita $8,758; median household $21,232. **Pop below poverty level:** 34.8%.

Unemployment: 23.3%. **Median home value:** $50,200. **Median travel time to work:** 20.2 minutes.

McCULLOCH COUNTY
County Courthouse Sq   **Ph:** 915-597-0733
Brady, TX 76825   **Fax:** 915-597-1731

In central TX, east of San Angelo; organized Aug 27, 1856 from Bexar County. **Name Origin:** For Gen. Benjamin McCulloch (1811-62), Republic of TX soldier, U.S. marshall (1853), and Confederate army officer.

Area (sq mi): 1073.35 (land 1069.31; water 4.05).

Pop: 8,205 (White 70.6%; Black or African American 1.6%; Hispanic or Latino 27%; Asian 0.2%; Other 13.6%). **Foreign born:** 3.2%. **Median age:** 40.4. **State rank:** 180. **Pop change 1990-2000:** -6.5%.

Income: per capita $14,579; median household $25,705. **Pop below poverty level:** 22.5%.

Unemployment: 5.8%. **Median home value:** $34,000. **Median travel time to work:** 20.3 minutes.

McLENNAN COUNTY
PO Box 1727   **Ph:** 254-757-5078
Waco, TX 76703   **Fax:** 254-757-5146
www.co.mclennan.tx.us

In east-central TX, south of Fort Worth; organized Jan 22, 1850 from Milam, Robertson, and Navarro counties. **Name Origin:** For Neil McLennan (1777-1867), surveyor and pioneer.

Area (sq mi): 1060.23 (land 1041.88; water 18.34).

Pop: 213,517 (White 64.6%; Black or African American 15.2%; Hispanic or Latino 17.9%; Asian 1.1%; Other 11.5%). **Foreign born:** 6.1%. **Median age:** 31.9. **State rank:** 20. **Pop change 1990-2000:** +12.9%.

All statistics are based on the 2000 Census except the dollar figures given for per capita income, which are based on 1999 estimates.

Income: per capita $17,174; median household $33,560. **Pop below poverty level:** 17.6%.

Unemployment: 3.9%. **Median home value:** $67,700. **Median travel time to work:** 20 minutes.

McMULLEN COUNTY

PO Box 235   **Ph:** 361-274-3215
Tilden, TX 78072   **Fax:** 361-274-3858

In south-central TX, south of San Antonio; organized Feb 1, 1858 from Bexar and Live Oak counties. **Name Origin:** For John McMullen, an early settler.

Area (sq mi): 1142.6 (land 1113; water 29.6).

Pop: 851 (White 65.3%; Black or African American 1.2%; Hispanic or Latino 33.1%; Asian 0%; Other 10.4%). **Foreign born:** 4.2%. **Median age:** 43.1. **State rank:** 250. **Pop change 1990-2000:** +4.2%.

Income: per capita $22,258; median household $32,500. **Pop below poverty level:** 20.7%.

Unemployment: 3.1%. **Median home value:** $46,800. **Median travel time to work:** 19.7 minutes.

MEDINA COUNTY

1100 16th St Rm 109   **Ph:** 830-741-6001
Hondo, TX 78861   **Fax:** 830-741-6015

In south-central TX, west of San Antonio; organized Feb 12, 1848 from Bexar County. **Name Origin:** For the Medina River and Lake, in the northern part of the county. Possibly named for a member of Alonzo de Leon's expedition into TX (1689): either Pedro Medina, an engineer, or Nicolas de Medina, a sergeant major.

Area (sq mi): 1334.53 (land 1327.76; water 6.77).

Pop: 39,304 (White 50.7%; Black or African American 2.2%; Hispanic or Latino 45.5%; Asian 0.3%; Other 18.1%). **Foreign born:** 4.1%. **Median age:** 34.4. **State rank:** 70. **Pop change 1990-2000:** +43.9%.

Income: per capita $15,210; median household $36,063. **Pop below poverty level:** 15.4%.

Unemployment: 4.3%. **Median home value:** $68,100. **Median travel time to work:** 30.5 minutes.

MENARD COUNTY

PO Box 1038   **Ph:** 915-396-4682
Menard, TX 76859   **Fax:** 915-396-2047

In central TX, southeast of San Angelo; organized Jan 22, 1858 from Bexar County. **Name Origin:** For Michel Branaman Menard (1803-56), signer of the TX Declaration of Independence (1836), Republic of TX legislator (1840-42), and founder of Galveston.

Area (sq mi): 902.25 (land 901.91; water 0.34).

Pop: 2,360 (White 66.4%; Black or African American 0.5%; Hispanic or Latino 31.7%; Asian 0.3%; Other 11.5%). **Foreign born:** 4.8%. **Median age:** 44.1. **State rank:** 233. **Pop change 1990-2000:** +4.8%.

Income: per capita $15,987; median household $24,762. **Pop below poverty level:** 25.8%.

Unemployment: 4%. **Median home value:** $28,900. **Median travel time to work:** 21.1 minutes.

MIDLAND COUNTY

PO Box 211   **Ph:** 915-688-1070
Midland, TX 79701   **Fax:** 915-688-8973
www.co.midland.tx.us

In west-central TX, east of Odessa; organized Mar 4, 1885 from Tom Green County. **Name Origin:** For its location midpoint on the railway between Fort Worth and El Paso.

Area (sq mi): 901.97 (land 900.25; water 1.72).

Pop: 116,009 (White 62.1%; Black or African American 7%; Hispanic or Latino 29%; Asian 0.9%; Other 14.7%). **Foreign born:** 7.6%. **Median age:** 34.1. **State rank:** 28. **Pop change 1990-2000:** +8.8%.

Income: per capita $20,369; median household $39,082. **Pop below poverty level:** 12.9%.

Unemployment: 3.4%. **Median home value:** $73,400. **Median travel time to work:** 18.5 minutes.

MILAM COUNTY

PO Box 191   **Ph:** 254-697-7045
Cameron, TX 76520   **Fax:** 254-697-7046

In east-central TX, northeast of Austin; original county; organized Mar 17, 1836 (prior to statehood) from Old Mexican Municipality. **Name Origin:** For Benjamin Rush Milam (?-1836), Republic of TX army officer.

Area (sq mi): 1021.67 (land 1016.71; water 4.95).

Pop: 24,238 (White 69.2%; Black or African American 11%; Hispanic or Latino 18.6%; Asian 0.2%; Other 9.8%). **Foreign born:** 5.6%. **Median age:** 38. **State rank:** 97. **Pop change 1990-2000:** +5.6%.

Income: per capita $16,920; median household $33,186. **Pop below poverty level:** 15.9%.

Unemployment: 4.4%. **Median home value:** $49,300. **Median travel time to work:** 27.1 minutes.

MILLS COUNTY

PO Box 646   **Ph:** 915-648-2711
Goldthwaite, TX 76844   **Fax:** 915-648-3251

In central TX, west of Waco; organized Mar 15, 1887 from Brown, Comanche, Lampasas, and Hamilton counties. **Name Origin:** For John T. Mills, Republic of TX district judge.

Area (sq mi): 749.89 (land 748.11; water 1.78).

Pop: 5,151 (White 84.8%; Black or African American 1.3%; Hispanic or Latino 13%; Asian 0.1%; Other 9.4%). **Foreign born:** 4.4%. **Median age:** 44.4. **State rank:** 203. **Pop change 1990-2000:** +13.7%.

Income: per capita $15,915; median household $30,579. **Pop below poverty level:** 18.4%.

Unemployment: 1.4%. **Median home value:** $48,800. **Median travel time to work:** 23.7 minutes.

MITCHELL COUNTY

349 Oak St Rm 103   **Ph:** 915-728-3481
Colorado City, TX 79512   **Fax:** 915-728-5322

In north-central TX, west of Abilene; organized Aug 21, 1876 from

Please see sample entry on inside front cover for detailed information about the statistics presented with each county listing.

557

Bexar County. **Name Origin:** For Asa (1795-1865) and Eli (n.d.) Mitchell, early settlers of Austin's colony.

Area (sq mi): 915.9 (land 910.04; water 5.86).

Pop: 9,698 (White 55.1%; Black or African American 12.8%; Hispanic or Latino 31%; Asian 0.4%; Other 12.3%). **Foreign born:** 2.8%. **Median age:** 38.6. **State rank:** 166. **Pop change 1990-2000:** +21%.

Income: per capita $14,043; median household $25,399. **Pop below poverty level:** 17.7%.

Unemployment: 3.8%. **Median home value:** $31,000. **Median travel time to work:** 18.4 minutes.

MONTAGUE COUNTY
PO Box 77   **Ph:** 940-894-2461
Montague, TX 76251   **Fax:** 940-894-3110

On the central northern border of TX, southeast of Wichita Falls; organized Dec 24, 1857 from Cooke County. **Name Origin:** For Daniel Montague (1798-1876), surveyor and veteran of the Mexican War.

Area (sq mi): 938.44 (land 930.66; water 7.78).

Pop: 19,117 (White 92.7%; Black or African American 0.2%; Hispanic or Latino 5.4%; Asian 0.3%; Other 3.5%). **Foreign born:** 2.4%. **Median age:** 41.3. **State rank:** 119. **Pop change 1990-2000:** +10.7%.

Income: per capita $17,115; median household $31,048. **Pop below poverty level:** 14%.

Unemployment: 4.5%. **Median home value:** $53,200. **Median travel time to work:** 30.2 minutes.

MONTGOMERY COUNTY
PO Box 959   **Ph:** 936-539-7885
Conroe, TX 77305   **Fax:** 936-760-6990
www.co.montgomery.tx.us

In east-central TX, north of Houston; organized Dec 14, 1837 from Washington County. **Name Origin:** For Gen. Richard Montgomery (1736-75), American Revolutionary War officer who captured Montreal, Canada.

Area (sq mi): 1076.81 (land 1044.03; water 32.78).

Pop: 293,768 (White 81.4%; Black or African American 3.5%; Hispanic or Latino 12.6%; Asian 1.1%; Other 7.2%). **Foreign born:** 8.6%. **Median age:** 34.4. **State rank:** 13. **Pop change 1990-2000:** +61.2%.

Income: per capita $24,544; median household $50,864. **Pop below poverty level:** 9.4%.

Unemployment: 3.3%. **Median home value:** $114,800. **Median travel time to work:** 32.9 minutes.

MOORE COUNTY
715 S Dumas Ave Rm 105   **Ph:** 806-935-6164
Dumas, TX 79029   **Fax:** 806-935-9004

In north-central TX panhandle, north of Amarillo; organized Aug 21, 1876 from Bexar County. **Name Origin:** For Edwin Ward Moore (1810-60), a Republic of TX naval officer.

Area (sq mi): 909.61 (land 899.66; water 9.95).

Pop: 20,121 (White 49.9%; Black or African American 0.7%; Hispanic or Latino 47.5%; Asian 0.9%; Other 34.5%). **Foreign born:** 20.9%. **Median age:** 30.4. **State rank:** 115. **Pop change 1990-2000:** +12.6%.

Income: per capita $15,214; median household $34,852. **Pop below poverty level:** 13.5%.

Unemployment: 2.8%. **Median home value:** $60,400. **Median travel time to work:** 17.7 minutes.

MORRIS COUNTY
500 Broadnax St   **Ph:** 903-645-3911
Daingerfield, TX 75638   **Fax:** 903-645-5729

In northeastern TX, north of Tyler; organized Mar 6, 1875 from Titus County. **Name Origin:** For W.W. Morris, thrown off a stagecoach because he was unruly and drunk. He stayed, founded a settlement called Morristown, and became a prominent east TX attorney.

Area (sq mi): 258.64 (land 254.51; water 4.13).

Pop: 13,048 (White 70.6%; Black or African American 24.1%; Hispanic or Latino 3.7%; Asian 0.2%; Other 4%). **Foreign born:** 2%. **Median age:** 40.2. **State rank:** 150. **Pop change 1990-2000:** -1.2%.

Income: per capita $15,612; median household $29,011. **Pop below poverty level:** 18.3%.

Unemployment: 6.8%. **Median home value:** $45,600. **Median travel time to work:** 23.9 minutes.

MOTLEY COUNTY
PO Box 660   **Ph:** 806-347-2621
Matador, TX 79244   **Fax:** 806-347-2220

In east-central TX panhandle, northeast of Lubbock; organized Aug 21, 1876 from Bexar County. **Name Origin:** For Junius William Mottley (1812-36), signer of the TX Declaration of Independence (1836) who was killed at the Battle of San Jacinto. Clerical spelling error was allowed to stand.

Area (sq mi): 989.81 (land 989.38; water 0.43).

Pop: 1,426 (White 82.2%; Black or African American 3.5%; Hispanic or Latino 12.1%; Asian 0.1%; Other 8.9%). **Foreign born:** 3.3%. **Median age:** 44.4. **State rank:** 244. **Pop change 1990-2000:** -6.9%.

Income: per capita $16,584; median household $28,348. **Pop below poverty level:** 19.4%.

Unemployment: 1.7%. **Median home value:** $30,100. **Median travel time to work:** 18.2 minutes.

NACOGDOCHES COUNTY
101 W Main St   **Ph:** 936-560-7733
Nacogdoches, TX 75961   **Fax:** 936-559-5926

In northeastern TX, northwest of Beaumont; original county; organized Mar 17, 1836 (prior to statehood) from Old Mexican Municipality. **Name Origin:** For an Indian tribe of Caddoan linguistic stock, a member of the Hasianai Confederacy.

Area (sq mi): 981.33 (land 946.77; water 34.56).

All statistics are based on the 2000 Census except the dollar figures given for per capita income, which are based on 1999 estimates.

Pop: 59,203 (White 70.3%; Black or African American 16.7%; Hispanic or Latino 11.2%; Asian 0.7%; Other 7.6%). **Foreign born:** 6.2%. **Median age:** 29.7. **State rank:** 51. **Pop change 1990-2000:** +8.1%.

Income: per capita $15,437; median household $28,301. **Pop below poverty level:** 23.3%.

Unemployment: 3.5%. **Median home value:** $73,900. **Median travel time to work:** 19.5 minutes.

NAVARRO COUNTY
PO Box 423   **Ph:** 903-654-3036
Corsicana, TX 75151   **Fax:** 903-654-3097

In east-central TX, south of Dallas; organized Apr 25, 1846 from Robertson County. **Name Origin:** For Juan Jose Antonio Navarro (1795-1870), Republic of TX patriot active in promoting statehood.

Area (sq mi): 1086.17 (land 1007.66; water 78.51).

Pop: 45,124 (White 65.6%; Black or African American 16.8%; Hispanic or Latino 15.8%; Asian 0.5%; Other 11.9%). **Foreign born:** 9.1%. **Median age:** 35.2. **State rank:** 62. **Pop change 1990-2000:** +13%.

Income: per capita $15,266; median household $31,268. **Pop below poverty level:** 18.2%.

Unemployment: 5%. **Median home value:** $56,700. **Median travel time to work:** 26.4 minutes.

NEWTON COUNTY
PO Box 484   **Ph:** 409-379-5341
Newton, TX 75966   **Fax:** 409-379-9049

On the central eastern border of TX, northeast of Beaumont; organized Apr 22, 1846 from Jasper County. **Name Origin:** For Sgt. John Newton (1752-80), a soldier under Gen. Francis Marion (1732?-95) in the Revolutionary War, who saved several colonial patriots from execution by surprising and capturing the British soldiers guarding them.

Area (sq mi): 939.51 (land 932.69; water 6.82).

Pop: 15,072 (White 74%; Black or African American 20.7%; Hispanic or Latino 3.8%; Asian 0.3%; Other 3.2%). **Foreign born:** 0.9%. **Median age:** 36.9. **State rank:** 139. **Pop change 1990-2000:** +11.1%.

Income: per capita $13,381; median household $28,500. **Pop below poverty level:** 19.1%.

Unemployment: 12.6%. **Median home value:** $48,200. **Median travel time to work:** 37.6 minutes.

NOLAN COUNTY
100 E 3rd St Suite 108   **Ph:** 915-235-2462
Sweetwater, TX 79556

In north-central TX, west of Abilene; organized Aug 21, 1876 from Bexar County. **Name Origin:** For Philip Nolan (1771-1801), an American agitator in Spanish-held TX, killed by Spanish soldiers.

Area (sq mi): 913.93 (land 911.98; water 1.94).

Pop: 15,802 (White 66.3%; Black or African American 4.7%; Hispanic or Latino 28%; Asian 0.2%; Other 16.7%). **Foreign born:**

4.2%. **Median age:** 37.4. **State rank:** 135. **Pop change 1990-2000:** -4.8%.

Income: per capita $14,077; median household $26,209. **Pop below poverty level:** 21.7%.

Unemployment: 4.9%. **Median home value:** $35,300. **Median travel time to work:** 16.4 minutes.

NUECES COUNTY
901 Leopard St Suite 201   **Ph:** 361-888-0580
Corpus Christi, TX 78401   **Fax:** 361-888-0329
www.co.nueces.tx.us

On the southeastern coast of TX, north of Brownsville; organized Apr 18, 1846 from San Patricio County. **Name Origin:** For the Nueces River, which forms part of its eastern border; Spanish 'nuts,' for the abundant pecan trees.

Area (sq mi): 1166.42 (land 835.82; water 330.6).

Pop: 313,645 (White 37.7%; Black or African American 4.2%; Hispanic or Latino 55.8%; Asian 1.2%; Other 22.5%). **Foreign born:** 6.5%. **Median age:** 33.3. **State rank:** 12. **Pop change 1990-2000:** +7.7%.

Income: per capita $17,036; median household $35,959. **Pop below poverty level:** 18.2%.

Unemployment: 5.7%. **Median home value:** $70,100. **Median travel time to work:** 20.2 minutes.

OCHILTREE COUNTY
511 S Main St   **Ph:** 806-435-8039
Perryton, TX 79070   **Fax:** 806-435-2081

On the northeastern border of TX panhandle, northeast of Amarillo; organized Aug, 1876 from Bexar County. **Name Origin:** For Col. William Beck Ochiltree (1811-67), Republic of TX secretary of the treasury (1844), TX legislator (1855), delegate to the TX Constitutional Convention (1861), and Confederate officer.

Area (sq mi): 918.07 (land 917.56; water 0.51).

Pop: 9,006 (White 66.3%; Black or African American 0.1%; Hispanic or Latino 31.8%; Asian 0.4%; Other 13.2%). **Foreign born:** 16.1%. **Median age:** 33.7. **State rank:** 171. **Pop change 1990-2000:** -1.3%.

Income: per capita $16,707; median household $38,013. **Pop below poverty level:** 13%.

Unemployment: 2.3%. **Median home value:** $48,800. **Median travel time to work:** 19.2 minutes.

OLDHAM COUNTY
PO Box 360   **Ph:** 806-267-2667
Vega, TX 79092   **Fax:** 806-267-2671

On the northwestern border of TX panhandle, west of Amarillo; organized Aug 21, 1876 from Bexar County. **Name Origin:** For Williamson Simpson Oldham (1813-68), AR legislator, member of the TX secession convention (1861), and TX senator to the Confederate Congress.

Area (sq mi): 1501.42 (land 1500.63; water 0.79).

Please see sample entry on inside front cover for detailed information about the statistics presented with each county listing.

559

Pop: 2,185 (White 84.8%; Black or African American 1.9%; Hispanic or Latino 11%; Asian 0.4%; Other 7.1%). **Foreign born:** 5.4%. **Median age:** 32.9. **State rank:** 235. **Pop change 1990-2000:** -4.1%.

Income: per capita $14,806; median household $33,713. **Pop below poverty level:** 19.8%.

Unemployment: 1.4%. **Median home value:** $50,000. **Median travel time to work:** 20.2 minutes.

ORANGE COUNTY
PO Box 1536   **Ph:** 409-883-7740
Orange, TX 77631   **Fax:** 409-882-0379
www.co.orange.tx.us

On the central eastern border of TX, east of Beaumont; organized Feb 5, 1852 from Jefferson County. **Name Origin:** For the orange groves in the region.

Area (sq mi): 379.54 (land 356.4; water 23.14).

Pop: 84,966 (White 85.9%; Black or African American 8.4%; Hispanic or Latino 3.6%; Asian 0.8%; Other 2.9%). **Foreign born:** 2.1%. **Median age:** 36.1. **State rank:** 39. **Pop change 1990-2000:** +5.5%.

Income: per capita $17,554; median household $37,586. **Pop below poverty level:** 13.8%.

Unemployment: 9.8%. **Median home value:** $66,100. **Median travel time to work:** 22.1 minutes.

PALO PINTO COUNTY
PO Box 219   **Ph:** 940-659-1277
Palo Pinto, TX 76484

In north-central TX, west of Fort Worth; organized Aug 27, 1856 from Navarro County. **Name Origin:** From Spanish for 'painted tree,' but connotation is unclear.

Area (sq mi): 985.5 (land 952.93; water 32.57).

Pop: 27,026 (White 82%; Black or African American 2.3%; Hispanic or Latino 13.6%; Asian 0.5%; Other 9%). **Foreign born:** 4.4%. **Median age:** 38.3. **State rank:** 93. **Pop change 1990-2000:** +7.9%.

Income: per capita $15,454; median household $31,203. **Pop below poverty level:** 15.9%.

Unemployment: 4.4%. **Median home value:** $46,700. **Median travel time to work:** 24.9 minutes.

PANOLA COUNTY
110 Sycamore St Rm 201   **Ph:** 903-693-0302
Carthage, TX 75633   **Fax:** 903-693-2726
www.carthagetexas.com/county.htm

On northeastern border of TX, southwest of Shreveport, LA; organized Mar 30, 1846 from Harrison and Shelby counties. **Name Origin:** For Choctaw word for 'cotton,' but connotation is unclear.

Area (sq mi): 821.34 (land 800.92; water 20.42).

Pop: 22,756 (White 77.5%; Black or African American 17.7%; Hispanic or Latino 3.5%; Asian 0.2%; Other 3.4%). **Foreign born:** 2.9%. **Median age:** 38.8. **State rank:** 103. **Pop change 1990-2000:** +3.3%.

Income: per capita $15,439; median household $31,909. **Pop below poverty level:** 14.1%.

Unemployment: 6.8%. **Median home value:** $60,600. **Median travel time to work:** 25.9 minutes.

PARKER COUNTY
PO Box 819   **Ph:** 817-594-7461
Weatherford, TX 76086   **Fax:** 817-594-9540

In north-central TX, west of Fort Worth; organized Dec 12, 1855 from Bosque and Navarro counties. **Name Origin:** For Isaac Parker (1793-1883), Republic of TX patriot and legislator.

Area (sq mi): 910.09 (land 903.51; water 6.58).

Pop: 88,495 (White 89.2%; Black or African American 1.8%; Hispanic or Latino 7%; Asian 0.3%; Other 5.3%). **Foreign born:** 2.6%. **Median age:** 36.5. **State rank:** 38. **Pop change 1990-2000:** +36.6%.

Income: per capita $20,305; median household $45,497. **Pop below poverty level:** 8.3%.

Unemployment: 3.2%. **Median home value:** $99,400. **Median travel time to work:** 32.8 minutes.

PARMER COUNTY
PO Box 356   **Ph:** 806-481-3691
Farwell, TX 79325

On the central western border of TX panhandle, southwest of Amarillo; organized Aug 21, 1876 from Bexar County. **Name Origin:** For Martin Parmer (1778-1850), Republic of TX legislator, signer of the TX Declaration of Independence (1836), and chief justice of Jasper County (1839-40).

Area (sq mi): 885.17 (land 881.66; water 3.51).

Pop: 10,016 (White 48.7%; Black or African American 1%; Hispanic or Latino 49.2%; Asian 0.3%; Other 32.6%). **Foreign born:** 20.1%. **Median age:** 32.1. **State rank:** 165. **Pop change 1990-2000:** +1.6%.

Income: per capita $14,184; median household $30,813. **Pop below poverty level:** 17%.

Unemployment: 3.1%. **Median home value:** $49,400. **Median travel time to work:** 16.4 minutes.

PECOS COUNTY
103 W Callaghan St   **Ph:** 915-336-7555
Fort Stockton, TX 79735   **Fax:** 915-336-7557
www.co.pecos.tx.us

In west-central TX, south of Odessa; organized May 3, 1871 from Presidio County. **Name Origin:** For the Pecos River, which forms its northeastern border. Believed to be the name of an Indian tribe now lost or unidentified, and to be a Spanish translation of a Keresan word meaning 'watering place.'

Area (sq mi): 4764.73 (land 4763.66; water 1.07).

Pop: 16,809 (White 33.4%; Black or African American 4.4%; Hispanic or Latino 61.1%; Asian 0.5%; Other 19.2%). **Foreign born:** 13.5%. **Median age:** 31.2. **State rank:** 130. **Pop change 1990-2000:** +14.5%.

Income: per capita $12,212; median household $28,033. **Pop below poverty level:** 20.4%.

Unemployment: 5%. **Median home value:** $40,200. **Median travel time to work:** 17.6 minutes.

All statistics are based on the 2000 Census except the dollar figures given for per capita income, which are based on 1999 estimates.

POLK COUNTY

PO Drawer 2119   **Ph:** 936-327-6804
Livingston, TX 77351   **Fax:** 936-327-6874
www.polkcountytexas.com

In eastern TX, northwest of Beaumont; organized Mar 30, 1846 from Liberty County. **Name Origin:** For James Knox Polk (1795-1849), eleventh U.S. president.

Area (sq mi): 1109.81 (land 1057.26; water 52.55).

Pop: 41,133 (White 74.7%; Black or African American 13.2%; Hispanic or Latino 9.4%; Asian 0.4%; Other 6.7%). **Foreign born:** 4.3%. **Median age:** 39.3. **State rank:** 67. **Pop change 1990-2000:** +34%.

Income: per capita $15,834; median household $30,495. **Pop below poverty level:** 17.4%.

Unemployment: 5.1%. **Median home value:** $60,000. **Median travel time to work:** 30.9 minutes.

POTTER COUNTY

PO Box 9638   **Ph:** 806-379-2275
Amarillo, TX 79105   **Fax:** 806-379-2296
www.co.potter.tx.us

In north-central TX panhandle, north of Lubbock; organized Aug 21, 1876 from Bexar County. **Name Origin:** For Robert Potter (1800-42), NC legislator (1826; 1828), U.S. representative from NC (1829-31), Republic of TX official and naval officer.

Area (sq mi): 921.98 (land 909.24; water 12.74).

Pop: 113,546 (White 57.7%; Black or African American 10%; Hispanic or Latino 28.1%; Asian 2.5%; Other 18.9%). **Foreign born:** 9.4%. **Median age:** 32.1. **State rank:** 29. **Pop change 1990-2000:** +16%.

Income: per capita $14,947; median household $29,492. **Pop below poverty level:** 19.2%.

Unemployment: 5.1%. **Median home value:** $54,400. **Median travel time to work:** 17.9 minutes.

PRESIDIO COUNTY

PO Box 789   **Ph:** 915-729-4812
Marfa, TX 79843   **Fax:** 915-729-4313

On the central western border of TX, southeast of El Paso; organized Jan 3, 1850 from Bexar County. **Name Origin:** From Spanish for 'garrisoned fortress.'

Area (sq mi): 3856.26 (land 3855.51; water 0.75).

Pop: 7,304 (White 14.8%; Black or African American 0.3%; Hispanic or Latino 84.4%; Asian 0.1%; Other 14.7%). **Foreign born:** 35.8%. **Median age:** 32.8. **State rank:** 186. **Pop change 1990-2000:** +10%.

Income: per capita $9,558; median household $19,860. **Pop below poverty level:** 36.4%.

Unemployment: 23.5%. **Median home value:** $35,500. **Median travel time to work:** 17.3 minutes.

RAINS COUNTY

PO Box 187   **Ph:** 903-474-9999
Emory, TX 75440   **Fax:** 903-474-9390

In northeastern TX, east of Dallas; organized Jun 9, 1870 from Hopkins, Wood, and Hunt counties. **Name Origin:** For Emory Rains (1800-78), Republic of TX legislator and surveyor.

Area (sq mi): 258.87 (land 232.05; water 26.82).

Pop: 9,139 (White 89.5%; Black or African American 2.9%; Hispanic or Latino 5.5%; Asian 0.3%; Other 4.7%). **Foreign born:** 2.5%. **Median age:** 41. **State rank:** 170. **Pop change 1990-2000:** +36.1%.

Income: per capita $16,442; median household $33,712. **Pop below poverty level:** 14.9%.

Unemployment: 4.4%. **Median home value:** $60,500. **Median travel time to work:** 36.9 minutes.

RANDALL COUNTY

PO Box 660   **Ph:** 806-468-5505
Canyon, TX 79015   **Fax:** 806-468-5509
www.randallcounty.org

In north-central TX panhandle, south of Amarillo; organized Aug 21, 1876 from Bexar County. **Name Origin:** For Gen. Horace Randal (1833-64), Confederate army officer. Misspelling allowed to stand.

Area (sq mi): 922.42 (land 914.43; water 7.99).

Pop: 104,312 (White 85.7%; Black or African American 1.5%; Hispanic or Latino 10.3%; Asian 1%; Other 6.9%). **Foreign born:** 2.6%. **Median age:** 34.9. **State rank:** 33. **Pop change 1990-2000:** +16.3%.

Income: per capita $21,840; median household $42,712. **Pop below poverty level:** 8.1%.

Unemployment: 1.2%. **Median home value:** $93,500. **Median travel time to work:** 18.7 minutes.

REAGAN COUNTY

PO Box 100   **Ph:** 915-884-2442
Big Lake, TX 76932   **Fax:** 915-884-1503

In central TX, west of San Angelo; organized Mar 7, 1903 from Tom Green County. **Name Origin:** For Col. John Henninger Reagan (1818-1905), postmaster general and acting secretary of the treasury of the Confederacy (1861-64), U.S. representative from TX (1875-87), and U.S. senator from TX (1887-91).

Area (sq mi): 1175.98 (land 1175.3; water 0.68).

Pop: 3,326 (White 46.5%; Black or African American 3%; Hispanic or Latino 49.5%; Asian 0.3%; Other 32.1%). **Foreign born:** 16.4%. **Median age:** 32.4. **State rank:** 224. **Pop change 1990-2000:** -26.3%.

Income: per capita $13,174; median household $33,231. **Pop below poverty level:** 11.8%.

Unemployment: 3%. **Median home value:** $50,500. **Median travel time to work:** 18.8 minutes.

REAL COUNTY

PO Box 750   **Ph:** 830-232-5202
Leakey, TX 78873   **Fax:** 830-232-6888

In south-central TX, northwest of San Antonio; organized Apr 3,

Please see sample entry on inside front cover for detailed information about the statistics presented with each county listing.

561

1913 from Bandera and Kerr counties. **Name Origin:** For Julius Real (1860-1944), county jurist and TX legislator (1910-14; 1924-28).

Area (sq mi): 700.04 (land 699.91; water 0.13).

Pop: 3,047 (White 75.7%; Black or African American 0.2%; Hispanic or Latino 22.6%; Asian 0.2%; Other 8.1%). **Foreign born:** 4%. **Median age:** 44.6. **State rank:** 229. **Pop change 1990-2000:** +26.3%.

Income: per capita $14,321; median household $25,118. **Pop below poverty level:** 21.2%.

Unemployment: 3.8%. **Median home value:** $56,700. **Median travel time to work:** 21.8 minutes.

RED RIVER COUNTY

200 N Walnut St   **Ph:** 903-427-2401
Clarksville, TX 75426   **Fax:** 903-427-5510

On the northeastern border of TX, west of Texarkana; original county; organized 1836 (prior to statehood) from Old Mexican Municipality. **Name Origin:** For the Red River, which forms its northern border.

Area (sq mi): 1057.61 (land 1050.18; water 7.43).

Pop: 14,314 (White 75.9%; Black or African American 17.8%; Hispanic or Latino 4.7%; Asian 0.1%; Other 4.1%). **Foreign born:** 2.5%. **Median age:** 40.4. **State rank:** 145. **Pop change 1990-2000:** +0%.

Income: per capita $15,058; median household $27,558. **Pop below poverty level:** 17.3%.

Unemployment: 10.5%. **Median home value:** $34,400. **Median travel time to work:** 27.5 minutes.

REEVES COUNTY

100 E 4th St   **Ph:** 915-445-5467
Pecos, TX 79772   **Fax:** 915-445-3997

In western TX, southwest of Odessa; established Apr 14, 1883 from Pecos County. **Name Origin:** For Col. George R. Reeves (1826-82), TX legislator (1855-61), Confederate army officer, and Speaker of the House (1881-82).

Area (sq mi): 2641.95 (land 2635.88; water 6.07).

Pop: 13,137 (White 23.8%; Black or African American 2.1%; Hispanic or Latino 73.4%; Asian 0.4%; Other 18.2%). **Foreign born:** 14.7%. **Median age:** 32.1. **State rank:** 148. **Pop change 1990-2000:** -17.1%.

Income: per capita $10,811; median household $23,306. **Pop below poverty level:** 28.9%.

Unemployment: 6.8%. **Median home value:** $24,900. **Median travel time to work:** 17.5 minutes.

REFUGIO COUNTY

808 Commerce St   **Ph:** 361-526-2233
Refugio, TX 78377   **Fax:** 361-526-1325

On the southeastern coast of TX, north of Corpus Christi; original county; organized Mar 17, 1836 (prior to statehood) from Old Mexican Municipality. **Name Origin:** For the mission established there, 'Our Lady of Refuge,' honoring the Virgin Mary.

Area (sq mi): 818.64 (land 770.21; water 48.43).

Pop: 7,828 (White 47.3%; Black or African American 6.8%; Hispanic or Latino 44.6%; Asian 0.3%; Other 12.8%). **Foreign born:** 2.6%. **Median age:** 38.6. **State rank:** 182. **Pop change 1990-2000:** -1.9%.

Income: per capita $15,481; median household $29,986. **Pop below poverty level:** 17.8%.

Unemployment: 4.6%. **Median home value:** $42,600. **Median travel time to work:** 22.5 minutes.

ROBERTS COUNTY

PO Box 477   **Ph:** 806-868-2341
Miami, TX 79059   **Fax:** 806-868-3381

In the TX panhandle, northeast of Amarillo; organized Aug 21, 1876 from Bexar County. **Name Origin:** For both Lt. John S. Roberts (1796-1871), a signer of the TX Declaration of Independence, and Oran Milo Roberts, TX governor (1879-83).

Area (sq mi): 924.19 (land 924.09; water 0.1).

Pop: 887 (White 95.8%; Black or African American 0.3%; Hispanic or Latino 3.2%; Asian 0.1%; Other 3.1%). **Foreign born:** 0.5%. **Median age:** 42. **State rank:** 248. **Pop change 1990-2000:** -13.5%.

Income: per capita $20,923; median household $44,792. **Pop below poverty level:** 7.2%.

Unemployment: 1.5%. **Median home value:** $48,800. **Median travel time to work:** 27.2 minutes.

ROBERTSON COUNTY

PO Box 1029   **Ph:** 979-828-4130
Franklin, TX 77856   **Fax:** 979-828-1260

In east-central TX, southeast of Waco; organized Dec 14, 1837 (prior to statehood) from Bexar County. **Name Origin:** For Gen. Sterling Clark Robertson (1785-1842), officer in the Battle of New Orleans (1815), signer of the TX Declaration of Independence (1836), and Republic of TX legislator (1836; 1840).

Area (sq mi): 865.67 (land 854.56; water 11.11).

Pop: 16,000 (White 59.9%; Black or African American 24.2%; Hispanic or Latino 14.7%; Asian 0.2%; Other 9.5%). **Foreign born:** 3.3%. **Median age:** 37.6. **State rank:** 134. **Pop change 1990-2000:** +3.2%.

Income: per capita $14,714; median household $28,886. **Pop below poverty level:** 20.6%.

Unemployment: 5%. **Median home value:** $53,000. **Median travel time to work:** 29.1 minutes.

ROCKWALL COUNTY

1101 Ridge Rd Suite 101   **Ph:** 972-882-0220
Rockwall, TX 75087   **Fax:** 972-882-0229

In northeastern TX, east of Dallas; organized May 1, 1873 from Kaufman County. **Name Origin:** For a subterranean wall or dike that thrusts up in various parts of the county. It is unclear whether the wall is a geological formation or man-made.

Area (sq mi): 148.7 (land 128.79; water 19.91).

Pop: 43,080 (White 83.1%; Black or African American 3.2%; Hispanic or Latino 11.1%; Asian 1.3%; Other 6.3%). **Foreign born:**

All statistics are based on the 2000 Census except the dollar figures given for per capita income, which are based on 1999 estimates.

7.8%. **Median age:** 35.3. **State rank:** 65. **Pop change 1990-2000:** +68.3%.

Income: per capita $28,573; median household $65,164. **Pop below poverty level:** 4.7%.

Unemployment: 3.7%. **Median home value:** $147,100. **Median travel time to work:** 32 minutes.

RUNNELS COUNTY
PO Box 189   **Ph:** 915-365-2720
Ballinger, TX 76821   **Fax:** 915-365-3408

In central TX, northeast of San Angelo; organized Feb 1, 1858 from Coleman County. **Name Origin:** For Hardin Richard Runnels (1820-73), TX legislator (1847-53) and governor (1857-59).

Area (sq mi): 1057.13 (land 1050.73; water 6.4).

Pop: 11,495 (White 67.8%; Black or African American 1.4%; Hispanic or Latino 29.3%; Asian 0.3%; Other 16.8%). **Foreign born:** 4.5%. **Median age:** 39.4. **State rank:** 159. **Pop change 1990-2000:** +1.8%.

Income: per capita $13,577; median household $27,806. **Pop below poverty level:** 19.2%.

Unemployment: 3.8%. **Median home value:** $37,800. **Median travel time to work:** 18.8 minutes.

RUSK COUNTY
115 N Main St Suite 206   **Ph:** 903-657-0330
Henderson, TX 75652

In northeastern TX, east of Tyler; organized Jan 16, 1843 from Nacogdoches County. **Name Origin:** For Gen. Thomas Jefferson Rusk (1803-57), chief justice of the Republic of TX supreme court (1838-42), signer of the TX Declaration of Independence (1836), and U.S. senator (1846-57).

Area (sq mi): 938.62 (land 923.55; water 15.07).

Pop: 47,372 (White 71.2%; Black or African American 19.2%; Hispanic or Latino 8.4%; Asian 0.2%; Other 5.6%). **Foreign born:** 4.4%. **Median age:** 38.1. **State rank:** 59. **Pop change 1990-2000:** +8.3%.

Income: per capita $16,674; median household $32,898. **Pop below poverty level:** 14.6%.

Unemployment: 4.4%. **Median home value:** $60,900. **Median travel time to work:** 23.7 minutes.

SABINE COUNTY
PO Box 580   **Ph:** 409-787-3786
Hemphill, TX 75948   **Fax:** 409-787-2044

On the northeastern border of TX, east of Lufkin; original county; organized Mar 17, 1836 (prior to statehood) from Old Mexican Municipality. **Name Origin:** For the Sabine River, which forms its eastern border. French form of Spanish *sabinas* 'red cedar trees' that grow along the banks.

Area (sq mi): 576.61 (land 490.27; water 86.34).

Pop: 10,469 (White 87.1%; Black or African American 9.9%; Hispanic or Latino 1.8%; Asian 0.1%; Other 2.1%). **Foreign born:** 1.1%. **Median age:** 47. **State rank:** 163. **Pop change 1990-2000:** +9.2%.

Income: per capita $15,821; median household $27,198. **Pop below poverty level:** 15.9%.

Unemployment: 9.9%. **Median home value:** $57,600. **Median travel time to work:** 28.5 minutes.

SAN AUGUSTINE COUNTY
Courthouse Rm 106   **Ph:** 936-275-2452
San Augustine, TX 75972   **Fax:** 936-275-9579

On central east border of TX, north of Beaumont; original county; organized Mar 17, 1836 (prior to statehood) from Old Mexican Municipality. **Name Origin:** For the Presidio de San Augustin de Ahumada (Fort of Saint Augustine of Ahumada), Mission Nuestra Senora de los Dolores de los Ais (Mission of Our Lady of Sorrows of the Ais), which was established on Ayish Bayou by the Marquis de San Miguel de Ahuayo in 1721.

Area (sq mi): 592.21 (land 527.87; water 64.34).

Pop: 8,946 (White 67.8%; Black or African American 27.9%; Hispanic or Latino 3.6%; Asian 0.2%; Other 2.5%). **Foreign born:** 2%. **Median age:** 42.1. **State rank:** 172. **Pop change 1990-2000:** +11.8%.

Income: per capita $15,548; median household $27,025. **Pop below poverty level:** 21.2%.

Unemployment: 5.5%. **Median home value:** $52,000. **Median travel time to work:** 32 minutes.

SAN JACINTO COUNTY
1 State Hwy 150 Rm 2   **Ph:** 936-653-2324
Coldspring, TX 77331   **Fax:** 936-653-8312
www.co.san-jacinto.tx.us

In east-central TX, northwest of Beaumont; organized Aug 13, 1870 from Liberty County. **Name Origin:** For the San Jacinto River, which runs through the county; site of the battle that eventually won Texan independence from Mexico (1836). Spanish 'Saint Hyacinth' for the many water lilies.

Area (sq mi): 627.9 (land 570.65; water 57.25).

Pop: 22,246 (White 80.8%; Black or African American 12.6%; Hispanic or Latino 4.9%; Asian 0.3%; Other 3.5%). **Foreign born:** 2.5%. **Median age:** 40. **State rank:** 107. **Pop change 1990-2000:** +35.9%.

Income: per capita $16,144; median household $32,220. **Pop below poverty level:** 18.8%.

Unemployment: 4%. **Median home value:** $59,400. **Median travel time to work:** 42.2 minutes.

SAN PATRICIO COUNTY
PO Box 578   **Ph:** 361-364-6290
Sinton, TX 78387   **Fax:** 361-364-6112

On the southeastern coast of TX, north of Corpus Christi; original county; organized Mar 17, 1836 (prior to statehood) from Old Mexican Municipality. **Name Origin:** From the Spanish for 'Saint Patrick,' the patron saint of Ireland.

Area (sq mi): 707.06 (land 691.65; water 15.41).

Pop: 67,138 (White 45.8%; Black or African American 2.8%; Hispanic or Latino 49.4%; Asian 0.6%; Other 19.7%). **Foreign born:**

Please see sample entry on inside front cover for detailed information about the statistics presented with each county listing.

563

3.3%. **Median age:** 32. **State rank:** 48. **Pop change 1990-2000:** +14.3%.

Income: per capita $15,425; median household $34,836. **Pop below poverty level:** 18%.

Unemployment: 5.8%. **Median home value:** $66,000. **Median travel time to work:** 23.3 minutes.

SAN SABA COUNTY

500 E Wallace St County Courthouse   **Ph:** 915-372-3614
San Saba, TX 76877

In central TX, southeast of San Angelo; organized Feb 1, 1856 from Bexar County. **Name Origin:** For the San Saba River, which flows through it; Spanish contraction of *San Sabado* 'Holy Saturday,' named for the day before Easter when Spanish explorers discovered it.

Area (sq mi): 1138.25 (land 1134.47; water 3.78).

Pop: 6,186 (White 74.7%; Black or African American 2.7%; Hispanic or Latino 21.5%; Asian 0.1%; Other 12.7%). **Foreign born:** 5.5%. **Median age:** 39.4. **State rank:** 195. **Pop change 1990-2000:** +14.5%.

Income: per capita $15,309; median household $30,104. **Pop below poverty level:** 16.6%.

Unemployment: 2.9%. **Median home value:** $47,000. **Median travel time to work:** 24.8 minutes.

SCHLEICHER COUNTY

PO Drawer 580   **Ph:** 915-853-2833
Eldorado, TX 76936   **Fax:** 915-853-2603

In west-central TX, south of San Angelo; organized Apr 1, 1887 from Crockett County. **Name Origin:** For Capt. Gustave Schleicher (1823-79), TX legislator (1853-54; 1859-61), Confederate army officer, and U.S. representative (1875-79).

Area (sq mi): 1310.65 (land 1310.61; water 0.04).

Pop: 2,935 (White 54.3%; Black or African American 1.5%; Hispanic or Latino 43.5%; Asian 0.2%; Other 21.7%). **Foreign born:** 13.9%. **Median age:** 38.8. **State rank:** 231. **Pop change 1990-2000:** -1.8%.

Income: per capita $15,969; median household $29,746. **Pop below poverty level:** 21.5%.

Unemployment: 2.3%. **Median home value:** $45,700. **Median travel time to work:** 21.6 minutes.

SCURRY COUNTY

1806 25th St Suite 300   **Ph:** 915-573-5332
Snyder, TX 79549   **Fax:** 915-573-7396

In south-central TX panhandle, northwest of Abilene; organized Aug 21, 1876 from Bexar County. **Name Origin:** Either for Gen. William Read Scurry (1821-64), Republic of TX legislator and jurist, publisher of the *Austin State Gazette* and Confederate army officer; or for Gen. Richardson Scurry (1811-62), TX legislator (1842-44) and U.S. representative (1851-53).

Area (sq mi): 907.53 (land 902.5; water 5.03).

Pop: 16,361 (White 65.2%; Black or African American 6.1%; Hispanic or Latino 27.8%; Asian 0.2%; Other 12.4%). **Foreign born:**

3.1%. **Median age:** 37. **State rank:** 132. **Pop change 1990-2000:** -12.2%.

Income: per capita $15,871; median household $31,646. **Pop below poverty level:** 16%.

Unemployment: 5%. **Median home value:** $42,500. **Median travel time to work:** 16 minutes.

SHACKELFORD COUNTY

PO Box 247   **Ph:** 915-762-2232
Albany, TX 76430   **Fax:** 915-762-3966

In north-central TX, northeast of Abilene; organized Feb 1, 1858 from Bosque County. **Name Origin:** For John Shackelford (1790-1857), AL physician and legislator (1822-24) who fought for TX independence then returned to AL to practice medicine.

Area (sq mi): 915.54 (land 913.95; water 1.59).

Pop: 3,302 (White 91.3%; Black or African American 0.5%; Hispanic or Latino 7.6%; Asian 0%; Other 5.2%). **Foreign born:** 2.9%. **Median age:** 40.1. **State rank:** 225. **Pop change 1990-2000:** -0.4%.

Income: per capita $16,341; median household $30,479. **Pop below poverty level:** 13.6%.

Unemployment: 2.2%. **Median home value:** $42,800. **Median travel time to work:** 25.4 minutes.

SHELBY COUNTY

PO Box 1987   **Ph:** 936-598-6361
Center, TX 75935   **Fax:** 936-598-3701

On the northeastern border of TX, northeast of Lufkin; original county; organized Mar 17, 1836 (prior to statehood) from Old Mexican Municipality. **Name Origin:** For Gen. Isaac Shelby (1750-1826), officer in the Revolutionary War, NC legislator, and governor of KY (1792-96; 1812-16).

Area (sq mi): 834.53 (land 794.11; water 40.43).

Pop: 25,224 (White 69.6%; Black or African American 19.4%; Hispanic or Latino 9.9%; Asian 0.2%; Other 7.7%). **Foreign born:** 6.6%. **Median age:** 36.9. **State rank:** 96. **Pop change 1990-2000:** +14.5%.

Income: per capita $15,186; median household $29,112. **Pop below poverty level:** 19.4%.

Unemployment: 6%. **Median home value:** $55,600. **Median travel time to work:** 24.9 minutes.

SHERMAN COUNTY

PO Box 270   **Ph:** 806-396-2371
Stratford, TX 79084   **Fax:** 806-396-5670

In north-central TX panhandle, north of Amarillo; organized Aug 21, 1876 from Bexar County. **Name Origin:** For Gen. Sidney Sherman (1805-73), officer in the Republic of TX army, TX legislator (1842; 1852-53), and organizer of the first railroad in TX.

Area (sq mi): 923.2 (land 923.03; water 0.16).

Pop: 3,186 (White 71%; Black or African American 0.5%; Hispanic or Latino 27.4%; Asian 0%; Other 17%). **Foreign born:** 12.4%. **Median age:** 34.4. **State rank:** 227. **Pop change 1990-2000:** +11.5%.

All statistics are based on the 2000 Census except the dollar figures given for per capita income, which are based on 1999 estimates.

Income: per capita $17,210; median household $33,179. **Pop below poverty level:** 16.1%.

Unemployment: 1.5%. **Median home value:** $48,800. **Median travel time to work:** 19.1 minutes.

SMITH COUNTY
PO Box 1018   **Ph:** 903-535-0630
Tyler, TX 75710   **Fax:** 903-535-0684
www.smith-county.com

In northeastern TX, southeast of Dallas; organized Apr 11, 1846 from Nacogdoches County. **Name Origin:** For Gen. James Smith (1792-1855), officer in the War of 1812 and the war of TX independence; TX legislator (1846-47).

Area (sq mi): 949.45 (land 928.38; water 21.06).

Pop: 174,706 (White 67.9%; Black or African American 19.1%; Hispanic or Latino 11.2%; Asian 0.7%; Other 7.5%). **Foreign born:** 6.6%. **Median age:** 35.5. **State rank:** 22. **Pop change 1990-2000:** +15.5%.

Income: per capita $19,072; median household $37,148. **Pop below poverty level:** 13.8%.

Unemployment: 4.1%. **Median home value:** $82,600. **Median travel time to work:** 22.2 minutes.

SOMERVELL COUNTY
107 NE Vernon St   **Ph:** 254-897-4427
Glen Rose, TX 76043   **Fax:** 254-897-3233

In north-central TX, southwest of Fort Worth; organized Mar 13, 1875 from Hood County. **Name Origin:** For Gen. Alexander Somervell (1796-1854), Republic of TX secretary of war (1836), legislator (1836-38), and collector of customs (1842-45).

Area (sq mi): 191.9 (land 187.17; water 4.73).

Pop: 6,809 (White 84.6%; Black or African American 0.3%; Hispanic or Latino 13.4%; Asian 0.3%; Other 7.3%). **Foreign born:** 5.7%. **Median age:** 36.8. **State rank:** 190. **Pop change 1990-2000:** +27%.

Income: per capita $18,367; median household $39,404. **Pop below poverty level:** 8.6%.

Unemployment: 6.5%. **Median home value:** $91,300. **Median travel time to work:** 27.1 minutes.

STARR COUNTY
County Courthouse Rm 201   **Ph:** 956-487-2954
Rio Grande City, TX 78582   **Fax:** 956-487-6227

On the southwestern border of TX, west of McAllen; organized Feb 10, 1848 from Nueces County. **Name Origin:** For James Harper Starr (1809-90), physician; an official in the Republic of Texas government.

Area (sq mi): 1229.28 (land 1223.02; water 6.26).

Pop: 53,597 (White 2%; Black or African American 0.1%; Hispanic or Latino 97.5%; Asian 0.3%; Other 11.6%). **Foreign born:** 36.9%. **Median age:** 26.1. **State rank:** 54. **Pop change 1990-2000:** +32.3%.

Income: per capita $7,069; median household $16,504. **Pop below poverty level:** 50.9%.

Unemployment: 20%. **Median home value:** $37,800. **Median travel time to work:** 21.4 minutes.

STEPHENS COUNTY
200 W Walker St   **Ph:** 254-559-3700
Breckenridge, TX 76424   **Fax:** 254-559-9645

In north-central TX, northeast of Abilene; established as Buchanan County Jan 22, 1858 from Bosque County; organized Sep 20, 1860. **Name Origin:** For Alexander Hamilton Stephens (1812-83), GA legislator, vice president of the Confederate government (1861), and governor of GA (1882-83).

Area (sq mi): 921.48 (land 894.64; water 26.84).

Pop: 9,674 (White 81.3%; Black or African American 2.9%; Hispanic or Latino 14.7%; Asian 0.3%; Other 9.9%). **Foreign born:** 6.6%. **Median age:** 38.9. **State rank:** 167. **Pop change 1990-2000:** +7.4%.

Income: per capita $15,475; median household $29,583. **Pop below poverty level:** 15.6%.

Unemployment: 3.2%. **Median home value:** $45,800. **Median travel time to work:** 18.7 minutes.

STERLING COUNTY
PO Box 55   **Ph:** 915-378-5191
Sterling City, TX 76951   **Fax:** 915-378-2266

In central TX, northwest of San Angelo; organized Mar 4, 1891 from Tom Green County. **Name Origin:** For W.S. Sterling (?-1881), Indian fighter, rancher, and buffalo hunter.

Area (sq mi): 923.49 (land 923.36; water 0.13).

Pop: 1,393 (White 68.6%; Black or African American 0.1%; Hispanic or Latino 31%; Asian 0%; Other 14.2%). **Foreign born:** 9.2%. **Median age:** 37.9. **State rank:** 246. **Pop change 1990-2000:** -3.1%.

Income: per capita $16,972; median household $35,129. **Pop below poverty level:** 16.8%.

Unemployment: 3.8%. **Median home value:** $53,000. **Median travel time to work:** 24.8 minutes.

STONEWALL COUNTY
PO Drawer P   **Ph:** 940-989-2272
Aspermont, TX 79502   **Fax:** 940-989-2715

In north-central TX, northwest of Abilene; organized Aug 21, 1876 from Fannin County. **Name Origin:** For Gen. Thomas Jonathan 'Stonewall' Jackson (1824-63), Confederate army officer; he earned his nickname from his stand at Bull Run.

Area (sq mi): 920.23 (land 918.67; water 1.56).

Pop: 1,693 (White 83.4%; Black or African American 3%; Hispanic or Latino 11.8%; Asian 0.4%; Other 8.5%). **Foreign born:** 2%. **Median age:** 43.7. **State rank:** 242. **Pop change 1990-2000:** -15.9%.

Income: per capita $16,094; median household $27,935. **Pop below poverty level:** 19.3%.

Unemployment: 4.7%. **Median home value:** $30,100. **Median travel time to work:** 17.8 minutes.

Please see sample entry on inside front cover for detailed information about the statistics presented with each county listing.

565

SUTTON COUNTY

300 E Oak St Suite 3　　　　**Ph:** 915-387-3815
Sonora, TX 76950　　　　　　**Fax:** 915-387-6028

In central TX, south of San Angelo; organized Apr 1, 1887 from Wood County. **Name Origin:** For Lt. Col. John S. Sutton (1821-62), Confederate army officer from TX.

Area (sq mi): 1454.4 (land 1453.76; water 0.63).

Pop: 4,077 (White 47.4%; Black or African American 0.2%; Hispanic or Latino 51.7%; Asian 0.2%; Other 24.3%). **Foreign born:** 13%. **Median age:** 36.5. **State rank:** 212. **Pop change 1990-2000:** -1.4%.

Income: per capita $17,105; median household $34,385. **Pop below poverty level:** 18%.

Unemployment: 2.8%. **Median home value:** $49,900. **Median travel time to work:** 16.2 minutes.

SWISHER COUNTY

County Courthouse 119 S Maxwell St　**Ph:** 806-995-3294
Tulia, TX 79088　　　　　　　　　　**Fax:** 806-995-4121

In central TX panhandle, south of Amarillo; organized Aug 21, 1876 from Bexar County. **Name Origin:** For James Gibson Swisher (1795-1864), Republic of TX soldier and a signer of the TX Declaration of Independence (1836).

Area (sq mi): 900.68 (land 900.43; water 0.25).

Pop: 8,378 (White 57.9%; Black or African American 5.8%; Hispanic or Latino 35.2%; Asian 0.2%; Other 22.2%). **Foreign born:** 4.9%. **Median age:** 34.6. **State rank:** 177. **Pop change 1990-2000:** +3%.

Income: per capita $14,326; median household $29,846. **Pop below poverty level:** 17.4%.

Unemployment: 3.8%. **Median home value:** $38,200. **Median travel time to work:** 17 minutes.

TARRANT COUNTY

100 W Weatherford St　　　　**Ph:** 817-884-1195
Fort Worth, TX 76196　　　　**Fax:** 817-884-3295
www.co.tarrant.tx.us

In north-central TX, west of Dallas; organized Dec 20, 1849 from Navarro County. **Name Origin:** For Gen. Edward H. Tarrant (1796-1858), TX Ranger, legislator, and delegate to the TX Constitutional Convention (1845).

Area (sq mi): 897.48 (land 863.42; water 34.06).

Pop: 1,446,219 (White 61.9%; Black or African American 12.8%; Hispanic or Latino 19.7%; Asian 3.6%; Other 12.4%). **Foreign born:** 12.7%. **Median age:** 32.3. **State rank:** 3. **Pop change 1990-2000:** +23.6%.

Income: per capita $22,548; median household $46,179. **Pop below poverty level:** 10.6%.

Unemployment: 4.2%. **Median home value:** $90,300. **Median travel time to work:** 25.8 minutes.

TAYLOR COUNTY

300 Oak St　　　　　　　　　**Ph:** 915-674-1380
Abilene, TX 79602　　　　　　**Fax:** 915-674-1279

In central TX, northeast of San Angelo; organized Feb 1, 1858 from Bexar County. **Name Origin:** Either for three Taylor brothers who died at the Alamo, or for Edward Taylor, an early settler of Sterling Clark Robertson's colony (1785-1842).

Area (sq mi): 919.25 (land 915.63; water 3.63).

Pop: 126,555 (White 72.7%; Black or African American 6.7%; Hispanic or Latino 17.6%; Asian 1.2%; Other 11.4%). **Foreign born:** 4%. **Median age:** 32.2. **State rank:** 26. **Pop change 1990-2000:** +5.8%.

Income: per capita $17,176; median household $34,035. **Pop below poverty level:** 14.5%.

Unemployment: 3.9%. **Median home value:** $61,700. **Median travel time to work:** 16.4 minutes.

TERRELL COUNTY

PO Box 410　　　　　　　　　**Ph:** 915-345-2391
Sanderson, TX 79848　　　　**Fax:** 915-345-2653

On the southwestern border of TX, northwest of Del Rio; organized Apr 8, 1905 from Pecos County. **Name Origin:** For Gen. Alexander Watkins Terrell (1827-1912), TX judicial district judge (1857-62), legislator (1875-82), and U.S. Minister Plenipotentiary to Turkey (1893-97).

Area (sq mi): 2357.75 (land 2357.72; water 0.03).

Pop: 1,081 (White 48.9%; Black or African American 0%; Hispanic or Latino 48.6%; Asian 0.6%; Other 11%). **Foreign born:** 9.9%. **Median age:** 42. **State rank:** 247. **Pop change 1990-2000:** -23.3%.

Income: per capita $13,721; median household $24,219. **Pop below poverty level:** 25.2%.

Unemployment: 3%. **Median home value:** $26,500. **Median travel time to work:** 17.7 minutes.

TERRY COUNTY

500 W Main St Rm 105　　　　**Ph:** 806-637-8551
Brownfield, TX 79316　　　　**Fax:** 806-637-4874

In southwestern TX panhandle, southwest of Lubbock; organized Aug 21, 1876 from Bexar County. **Name Origin:** For Col. Benjamin Franklin Terry (1821-61), a Confederate army officer.

Area (sq mi): 890.93 (land 889.88; water 1.06).

Pop: 12,761 (White 49.8%; Black or African American 5%; Hispanic or Latino 44.1%; Asian 0.2%; Other 18.2%). **Foreign born:** 7.2%. **Median age:** 35. **State rank:** 154. **Pop change 1990-2000:** -3.5%.

Income: per capita $13,860; median household $28,090. **Pop below poverty level:** 23.3%.

Unemployment: 6%. **Median home value:** $43,800. **Median travel time to work:** 18.2 minutes.

THROCKMORTON COUNTY

PO Box 309　　　　　　　　　**Ph:** 940-849-2501
Throckmorton, TX 76483　　　**Fax:** 940-849-3220

In north-central TX, northeast of Abilene; organized Jan 13, 1858

All statistics are based on the 2000 Census except the dollar figures given for per capita income, which are based on 1999 estimates.

from Bosque County. **Name Origin:** For William Edward Throckmorton (1795-1843), father of Gov. James Webb Throckmorton.

Area (sq mi): 915.47 (land 912.34; water 3.13).

Pop: 1,850 (White 89.5%; Black or African American 0.1%; Hispanic or Latino 9.4%; Asian 0.1%; Other 7.8%). **Foreign born:** 1.6%. **Median age:** 41.8. **State rank:** 239. **Pop change 1990-2000:** -1.6%.

Income: per capita $17,719; median household $28,277. **Pop below poverty level:** 13.5%.

Unemployment: 2.1%. **Median home value:** $34,200. **Median travel time to work:** 19.7 minutes.

TITUS COUNTY
100 W 1st Suite 204   **Ph:** 903-577-6796
Mount Pleasant, TX 75455   **Fax:** 903-572-5078

In northeastern TX, southwest of Texarkana; organized May 11, 1846 from Red River County. **Name Origin:** For Andrew Jackson Titus (1823-55), early settler and TX legislator (1851-52).

Area (sq mi): 425.69 (land 410.54; water 15.15).

Pop: 28,118 (White 59.7%; Black or African American 10.7%; Hispanic or Latino 28.3%; Asian 0.4%; Other 18.7%). **Foreign born:** 17.4%. **Median age:** 31.8. **State rank:** 92. **Pop change 1990-2000:** +17.1%.

Income: per capita $15,501; median household $32,452. **Pop below poverty level:** 18.5%.

Unemployment: 4.1%. **Median home value:** $63,800. **Median travel time to work:** 19.2 minutes.

TOM GREEN COUNTY
124 W Beauregard Ave   **Ph:** 915-659-6553
San Angelo, TX 76903   **Fax:** 915-659-3251
www.co.tom-green.tx.us/county/index.html

In central TX, southwest of Abilene; organized Mar 13, 1874 from Bexar County. **Name Origin:** For Gen. Thomas Green (1814-64), officer in the War for Texas Independence and the Mexican-American War; Confederate Army officer.

Area (sq mi): 1540.54 (land 1522.1; water 18.44).

Pop: 104,010 (White 63%; Black or African American 4.1%; Hispanic or Latino 30.7%; Asian 0.9%; Other 16%). **Foreign born:** 5.9%. **Median age:** 33.8. **State rank:** 34. **Pop change 1990-2000:** +5.6%.

Income: per capita $17,325; median household $33,148. **Pop below poverty level:** 15.2%.

Unemployment: 2.8%. **Median home value:** $63,600. **Median travel time to work:** 17.8 minutes.

TRAVIS COUNTY
PO Box 1748   **Ph:** 512-473-9188
Austin, TX 78767   **Fax:** 512-854-4526
www.co.travis.tx.us

In east-central TX, northeast of San Antonio; organized Jan 25, 1840 (prior to statehood) from Bastrop County. **Name Origin:** For Lt. Col. William Barret Travis (1809-36), an officer in the Republic of TX cavalry, killed at the Alamo.

Area (sq mi): 1022.08 (land 989.3; water 32.77).

Pop: 812,280 (White 56.4%; Black or African American 9.3%; Hispanic or Latino 28.2%; Asian 4.5%; Other 18.2%). **Foreign born:** 15.1%. **Median age:** 30.4. **State rank:** 5. **Pop change 1990-2000:** +40.9%.

Income: per capita $25,883; median household $46,761. **Pop below poverty level:** 12.5%.

Unemployment: 4.1%. **Median home value:** $134,700. **Median travel time to work:** 23.6 minutes.

TRINITY COUNTY
PO Box 456   **Ph:** 936-642-1208
Groveton, TX 75845   **Fax:** 936-642-3004

In east-central TX, southwest of Lufkin; organized Feb 11, 1850 from Houston County. **Name Origin:** For the Trinity River, which forms its southern border; itself probably named for the feast of the Holy Trinity.

Area (sq mi): 714 (land 692.84; water 21.16).

Pop: 13,779 (White 81.9%; Black or African American 11.9%; Hispanic or Latino 4.8%; Asian 0.2%; Other 4.1%). **Foreign born:** 2.7%. **Median age:** 43.3. **State rank:** 147. **Pop change 1990-2000:** +20.4%.

Income: per capita $15,472; median household $27,070. **Pop below poverty level:** 17.6%.

Unemployment: 5%. **Median home value:** $53,400. **Median travel time to work:** 31.1 minutes.

TYLER COUNTY
100 Bluff St Rm 110   **Ph:** 409-283-2281
Woodville, TX 75979   **Fax:** 409-283-6305

In east-central TX, north of Beaumont; organized Apr 3, 1846 from Liberty County. **Name Origin:** For John Tyler (1790-1862), tenth U.S. president.

Area (sq mi): 935.71 (land 922.9; water 12.81).

Pop: 20,871 (White 82.8%; Black or African American 12%; Hispanic or Latino 3.6%; Asian 0.2%; Other 4%). **Foreign born:** 1.2%. **Median age:** 38.9. **State rank:** 110. **Pop change 1990-2000:** +25.4%.

Income: per capita $15,367; median household $29,808. **Pop below poverty level:** 15.8%.

Unemployment: 8.3%. **Median home value:** $50,600. **Median travel time to work:** 34.5 minutes.

UPSHUR COUNTY
PO Box 730   **Ph:** 903-843-4015
Gilmer, TX 75644

In northeastern TX, northeast of Tyler; organized Jul 13, 1846 from Harrison and Nacogdoches counties. **Name Origin:** For Abel Parker Upshur (1791-1844), judge in VA courts (1826-41), U.S. secretary of the navy (1841-43), and U.S. secretary of state (1843-44).

Area (sq mi): 592.67 (land 587.64; water 5.02).

Please see sample entry on inside front cover for detailed information about the statistics presented with each county listing.

Pop: 35,291 (White 84.2%; Black or African American 10.1%; Hispanic or Latino 4%; Asian 0.2%; Other 4%). **Foreign born:** 2%. **Median age:** 37.7. **State rank:** 78. **Pop change 1990-2000:** +12.5%.

Income: per capita $16,358; median household $33,347. **Pop below poverty level:** 14.9%.

Unemployment: 4.9%. **Median home value:** $59,600. **Median travel time to work:** 27.8 minutes.

UPTON COUNTY

PO Box 465   **Ph:** 915-693-2861
Rankin, TX 79778   **Fax:** 915-693-2129

In west-central TX, south of Midland; organized Feb 26, 1887 from Tom Green County. **Name Origin:** For Lt. Col. John Cunningham Upton (1823-62), Confederate army officer.

Area (sq mi): 1241.83 (land 1241.68; water 0.16).

Pop: 3,404 (White 54.5%; Black or African American 1.6%; Hispanic or Latino 42.6%; Asian 0%; Other 20.6%). **Foreign born:** 11.2%. **Median age:** 38.1. **State rank:** 220. **Pop change 1990-2000:** -23.5%.

Income: per capita $14,274; median household $28,977. **Pop below poverty level:** 19.9%.

Unemployment: 4.1%. **Median home value:** $31,100. **Median travel time to work:** 21 minutes.

UVALDE COUNTY

PO Box 284   **Ph:** 830-278-6614
Uvalde, TX 78802   **Fax:** 830-278-8692

In south-central TX, east of Del Rio; organized Feb 8, 1850 from Bexar County. **Name Origin:** For Juan de Ugalde, Mexican army officer, civil and military governor of Coahuila and TX (1777); Indian fighter. The present spelling is a corruption of his name.

Area (sq mi): 1558.6 (land 1556.55; water 2.06).

Pop: 25,926 (White 32.7%; Black or African American 0.4%; Hispanic or Latino 65.9%; Asian 0.4%; Other 23.7%). **Foreign born:** 11.2%. **Median age:** 32.2. **State rank:** 95. **Pop change 1990-2000:** +11.1%.

Income: per capita $12,557; median household $27,164. **Pop below poverty level:** 24.3%.

Unemployment: 7.6%. **Median home value:** $46,000. **Median travel time to work:** 19.8 minutes.

VAL VERDE COUNTY

PO Box 1267   **Ph:** 830-774-7564
Del Rio, TX 78841   **Fax:** 830-774-7608

On the southwestern border of TX, northwest of Laredo; organized Feb 20, 1885 from Kinney and Pecos counties. **Name Origin:** A shortening of the Spanish *valle verde* 'green valley.'

Area (sq mi): 3232.4 (land 3170.38; water 62.02).

Pop: 44,856 (White 21.7%; Black or African American 1.5%; Hispanic or Latino 75.5%; Asian 0.6%; Other 21.6%). **Foreign born:** 23.4%. **Median age:** 30.8. **State rank:** 63. **Pop change 1990-2000:** +15.8%.

Income: per capita $12,096; median household $28,376. **Pop below poverty level:** 26.1%.

Unemployment: 6.2%. **Median home value:** $58,600. **Median travel time to work:** 17.6 minutes.

VAN ZANDT COUNTY

121 E Dallas St Rm 202   **Ph:** 903-567-6503
Canton, TX 75103   **Fax:** 903-567-6722
www.vanzandtcounty.org

In northeastern TX, east of Dallas; organized Mar 20, 1848 from Henderson County. **Name Origin:** For Isaac Van Zandt (1813-47), Republic of TX legislator (1840-42).

Area (sq mi): 859.48 (land 848.64; water 10.84).

Pop: 48,140 (White 88.5%; Black or African American 2.9%; Hispanic or Latino 6.6%; Asian 0.2%; Other 4.9%). **Foreign born:** 3.6%. **Median age:** 39.5. **State rank:** 57. **Pop change 1990-2000:** +26.9%.

Income: per capita $16,930; median household $35,029. **Pop below poverty level:** 13.3%.

Unemployment: 3.7%. **Median home value:** $66,400. **Median travel time to work:** 37.3 minutes.

VICTORIA COUNTY

PO Box 1968   **Ph:** 361-575-1478
Victoria, TX 77902   **Fax:** 361-575-6276

In south-central TX, northeast of Corpus Christi; original county; organized Mar 17, 1836 (prior to statehood) from Old Mexican Municipality. **Name Origin:** For Juan Manuel Felix Fernandez, called Guadelupe Victoria (1789-1843), first president of the Republic of Mexico (1824).

Area (sq mi): 888.73 (land 882.5; water 6.23).

Pop: 84,088 (White 52.9%; Black or African American 6.3%; Hispanic or Latino 39.2%; Asian 0.8%; Other 18.6%). **Foreign born:** 4.3%. **Median age:** 34.2. **State rank:** 40. **Pop change 1990-2000:** +13.1%.

Income: per capita $18,379; median household $38,732. **Pop below poverty level:** 12.9%.

Unemployment: 4%. **Median home value:** $73,300. **Median travel time to work:** 21.4 minutes.

WALKER COUNTY

PO Box 1207   **Ph:** 936-436-4933
Huntsville, TX 77342   **Fax:** 936-436-4930
www.co.walker.tx.us

In east-central TX, northwest of Houston; organized Apr 6, 1846 from Montgomery County. **Name Origin:** Either for Robert James Walker (1801-69), U.S. senator who introduced the resolution to annex TX to the U.S., or for Samuel Hamilton Walker (1809-47), a Mexican War casualty.

Area (sq mi): 801.44 (land 787.45; water 13.99).

Pop: 61,758 (White 60.1%; Black or African American 23.9%; Hispanic or Latino 14.1%; Asian 0.8%; Other 6.3%). **Foreign born:** 4.5%. **Median age:** 31. **State rank:** 50. **Pop change 1990-2000:** +21.3%.

Income: per capita $14,508; median household $31,468. **Pop below poverty level:** 18.4%.

All statistics are based on the 2000 Census except the dollar figures given for per capita income, which are based on 1999 estimates.

Unemployment: 2.7%. **Median home value:** $80,400. **Median travel time to work:** 22.7 minutes.

WALLER COUNTY
836 Austin St　　　　　　　　　　**Ph:** 979-826-3357
Hempstead, TX 77445　　　　　　**Fax:** 979-826-8317

In east-central TX, west of Houston; organized Apr 28, 1873 from Austin County. **Name Origin:** For Edwin Waller (1800-83), signer of the TX declaration of independence (1836) and chief justice of Austin County (1844-56).

Area (sq mi): 518.49 (land 513.63; water 4.87).

Pop: 32,663 (White 49.9%; Black or African American 29.2%; Hispanic or Latino 19.4%; Asian 0.4%; Other 12.6%). **Foreign born:** 9.4%. **Median age:** 30.1. **State rank:** 82. **Pop change 1990-2000:** +39.6%.

Income: per capita $16,338; median household $38,136. **Pop below poverty level:** 16%.

Unemployment: 4.6%. **Median home value:** $84,700. **Median travel time to work:** 32.3 minutes.

WARD COUNTY
County Courthouse 400 S Allen St Suite 101　**Ph:** 915-943-3294
Monahans, TX 79756　　　　　　**Fax:** 915-943-6054

In west-central TX, southwest of Odessa; organized 1891 from Tom Green County (other sources say organized Feb 26, 1887; first federal census: 1890). **Name Origin:** For Thomas William 'Peg Leg' Ward (1807-72), soldier in the TX war of independence, mayor of Austin (1840; 1857; 1865), and U.S. consul to Panama (1840; 1853; 1865).

Area (sq mi): 835.74 (land 835.49; water 0.25).

Pop: 10,909 (White 52.2%; Black or African American 4.6%; Hispanic or Latino 42%; Asian 0.3%; Other 15.3%). **Foreign born:** 6.6%. **Median age:** 36. **State rank:** 162. **Pop change 1990-2000:** -16.8%.

Income: per capita $14,393; median household $29,386. **Pop below poverty level:** 17.9%.

Unemployment: 6.2%. **Median home value:** $34,400. **Median travel time to work:** 19.3 minutes.

WASHINGTON COUNTY
100 E Main St Suite 102　　　　**Ph:** 979-277-6200
Brenham, TX 77833　　　　　　　**Fax:** 979-277-6278

In east-central TX, northwest of Houston; organized Mar 17, 1836 (prior to statehood) from Texas Municipality. **Name Origin:** For George Washington (1732-99), American patriot and first U.S. president.

Area (sq mi): 621.35 (land 609.22; water 12.13).

Pop: 30,373 (White 70.8%; Black or African American 18.7%; Hispanic or Latino 8.7%; Asian 1.2%; Other 5.5%). **Foreign born:** 5.4%. **Median age:** 37.4. **State rank:** 91. **Pop change 1990-2000:** +16.1%.

Income: per capita $17,384; median household $36,760. **Pop below poverty level:** 12.9%.

Unemployment: 2%. **Median home value:** $84,200. **Median travel time to work:** 19.4 minutes.

WEBB COUNTY
1000 Houston County Courthouse　**Ph:** 956-721-2500
Laredo, TX 78040　　　　　　　　**Fax:** 956-726-6906
www.webbcounty.com

On the southwestern border of TX, west of Corpus Christi; organized Jan 28, 1848 from Bexar County. **Name Origin:** For James Webb (1792-1856), Republic of TX Attorney General (1839-41), legislator (1841-44), and judge (1854-56).

Area (sq mi): 3375.53 (land 3356.83; water 18.69).

Pop: 193,117 (White 4.9%; Black or African American 0.4%; Hispanic or Latino 94.3%; Asian 0.4%; Other 17%). **Foreign born:** 29%. **Median age:** 26.5. **State rank:** 21. **Pop change 1990-2000:** +44.9%.

Income: per capita $10,759; median household $28,100. **Pop below poverty level:** 31.2%.

Unemployment: 7.1%. **Median home value:** $74,600. **Median travel time to work:** 21.7 minutes.

WHARTON COUNTY
PO Box 69　　　　　　　　　　　**Ph:** 979-532-2381
Wharton, TX 77488　　　　　　　**Fax:** 979-532-8426

In east-central TX, southwest of Houston; organized Apr 3, 1846 from Colorado and Jackson counties. **Name Origin:** For William Harris Wharton (1802-39), Republic of TX soldier, minister to the U.S. (1836), and legislator (1838).

Area (sq mi): 1094.43 (land 1090.13; water 4.29).

Pop: 41,188 (White 53%; Black or African American 15%; Hispanic or Latino 31.3%; Asian 0.3%; Other 15.7%). **Foreign born:** 6.6%. **Median age:** 35.3. **State rank:** 66. **Pop change 1990-2000:** +3.1%.

Income: per capita $15,388; median household $32,208. **Pop below poverty level:** 16.5%.

Unemployment: 4.8%. **Median home value:** $59,100. **Median travel time to work:** 23.8 minutes.

WHEELER COUNTY
PO Box 465　　　　　　　　　　**Ph:** 806-826-5544
Wheeler, TX 79096　　　　　　　**Fax:** 806-826-3282

On northeastern border of TX panhandle, east of Amarillo; organized Aug 21, 1876 from Bexar County. **Name Origin:** For Royal Tyler Wheeler (1810-64), prominent TX judge.

Area (sq mi): 915.34 (land 914.26; water 1.08).

Pop: 5,284 (White 83%; Black or African American 2.8%; Hispanic or Latino 12.6%; Asian 0.5%; Other 8.8%). **Foreign born:** 5.4%. **Median age:** 42.5. **State rank:** 201. **Pop change 1990-2000:** -10.1%.

Income: per capita $16,083; median household $31,029. **Pop below poverty level:** 13%.

Unemployment: 3%. **Median home value:** $37,000. **Median travel time to work:** 17.9 minutes.

Please see sample entry on inside front cover for detailed information about the statistics presented with each county listing.

WICHITA COUNTY
PO Box 1679   **Ph:** 940-766-8144
Wichita Falls, TX 76307   **Fax:** 940-716-8554
www.co.wichita.tx.us

On the central northern border of TX, northwest of Fort Worth; organized Feb 1, 1858 from Fannin County. **Name Origin:** For the Wichita River, which traverses its northern border; itself named for one of the more important tribes of Caddoan linguistic stock. The name is translated as 'man,' or as taken from Choctaw *owa chito* 'big hunt.'

Area (sq mi): 633.01 (land 627.66; water 5.35).

Pop: 131,664 (White 73.3%; Black or African American 10.2%; Hispanic or Latino 12.2%; Asian 1.8%; Other 9.2%). **Foreign born:** 5.1%. **Median age:** 33.2. **State rank:** 24. **Pop change 1990-2000:** +7.6%.

Income: per capita $16,965; median household $33,780. **Pop below poverty level:** 13.2%.

Unemployment: 3.6%. **Median home value:** $61,500. **Median travel time to work:** 17 minutes.

WILBARGER COUNTY
1700 Wilbarger St County Courthouse
Rm 15   **Ph:** 940-552-5486
Vernon, TX 76384
www.co.wilbarger.tx.us

In north-central TX, west of Wichita Falls; organized Feb 1, 1858 from Bexar County. **Name Origin:** For Josiah Pugh Wilbarger (1801-45), a surveyor, and Mathias Wilbarger, brothers who settled in Austin's colony.

Area (sq mi): 978.1 (land 971.06; water 7.03).

Pop: 14,676 (White 68.7%; Black or African American 8.9%; Hispanic or Latino 20.5%; Asian 0.6%; Other 12.3%). **Foreign born:** 4.2%. **Median age:** 36.3. **State rank:** 142. **Pop change 1990-2000:** -2.9%.

Income: per capita $16,520; median household $29,500. **Pop below poverty level:** 13.1%.

Unemployment: 2.4%. **Median home value:** $46,800. **Median travel time to work:** 12.5 minutes.

WILLACY COUNTY
540 W Hidalgo St 1st Fl   **Ph:** 956-689-2710
Raymondville, TX 78580   **Fax:** 956-689-0937

On the southeastern coast of TX, north of Brownsville; organized 1921 from Cameron and Hidalgo counties plus a 1.4-mile strip of a former Willacy County, which was renamed Kenedy County at the same time that the new county was created. **Name Origin:** For John G. Willacy (1850-1943), TX legislator (1899-1914).

Area (sq mi): 784.23 (land 596.68; water 187.55).

Pop: 20,082 (White 11.7%; Black or African American 2.2%; Hispanic or Latino 85.7%; Asian 0.1%; Other 27.3%). **Foreign born:** 13.3%. **Median age:** 29.8. **State rank:** 116. **Pop change 1990-2000:** +13.4%.

Income: per capita $9,421; median household $22,114. **Pop below poverty level:** 33.2%.

Unemployment: 16.4%. **Median home value:** $34,600. **Median travel time to work:** 22.1 minutes.

WILLIAMSON COUNTY
PO Box 18   **Ph:** 512-930-4300
Georgetown, TX 78627   **Fax:** 512-930-4461
www.co.williamson.tx.us

In central TX, north of Austin; organized Mar 13, 1848 from Milam County. **Name Origin:** For Maj. Robert McAlpin 'Three Legged Willie' Williamson (1806-59), Republic of TX army officer, editor, and legislator.

Area (sq mi): 1134.74 (land 1122.77; water 11.97).

Pop: 249,967 (White 73.5%; Black or African American 5.1%; Hispanic or Latino 17.2%; Asian 2.6%; Other 9.9%). **Foreign born:** 7.4%. **Median age:** 32.3. **State rank:** 16. **Pop change 1990-2000:** +79.1%.

Income: per capita $24,547; median household $60,642. **Pop below poverty level:** 4.8%.

Unemployment: 3.3%. **Median home value:** $125,800. **Median travel time to work:** 28 minutes.

WILSON COUNTY
PO Box 27   **Ph:** 830-393-7308
Floresville, TX 78114   **Fax:** 830-393-7334

In south-central TX, southeast of San Antonio; organized Feb 13, 1860 from Bexar County. **Name Origin:** For James Charles Wilson (1816-61), Republic of TX soldier and legislator (1851-52).

Area (sq mi): 808.57 (land 806.99; water 1.58).

Pop: 32,408 (White 60.9%; Black or African American 1.2%; Hispanic or Latino 36.5%; Asian 0.3%; Other 17.2%). **Foreign born:** 3.3%. **Median age:** 35.9. **State rank:** 83. **Pop change 1990-2000:** +43.1%.

Income: per capita $17,253; median household $40,006. **Pop below poverty level:** 11.3%.

Unemployment: 3.1%. **Median home value:** $85,100. **Median travel time to work:** 35.8 minutes.

WINKLER COUNTY
PO Box 1007   **Ph:** 915-586-3401
Kermit, TX 79745

In western TX, west of Odessa; organized Feb 26, 1887 from Tom Green County. **Name Origin:** For Lt. Col. Clinton McKamy Winkler (1827-82), TX legislator (1848), officer in the Confederate army, and civil appeals court judge (1876-82).

Area (sq mi): 841.24 (land 841.05; water 0.19).

Pop: 7,173 (White 53.3%; Black or African American 1.9%; Hispanic or Latino 44%; Asian 0.2%; Other 23.1%). **Foreign born:** 14.3%. **Median age:** 35.2. **State rank:** 187. **Pop change 1990-2000:** -16.8%.

Income: per capita $13,725; median household $30,591. **Pop below poverty level:** 18.7%.

Unemployment: 5.9%. **Median home value:** $29,600. **Median travel time to work:** 24.5 minutes.

All statistics are based on the 2000 Census except the dollar figures given for per capita income, which are based on 1999 estimates.

WISE COUNTY

PO Box 359   **Ph:** 940-627-3351
Decatur, TX 76234   **Fax:** 940-627-2138

In north-central TX, northwest of Fort Worth; organized Jan 23, 1856 from Cooke County. **Name Origin:** For Maj. Gen. Henry Alexander Wise (1806-76), governor of VA (1856-60), and an officer in the Confederate army.

Area (sq mi): 922.77 (land 904.61; water 18.17).

Pop: 48,793 (White 86.1%; Black or African American 1.2%; Hispanic or Latino 10.8%; Asian 0.2%; Other 7.5%). **Foreign born:** 5.1%. **Median age:** 35.5. **State rank:** 55. **Pop change 1990-2000:** +40.7%.

Income: per capita $17,729; median household $41,933. **Pop below poverty level:** 9.9%.

Unemployment: 3.4%. **Median home value:** $89,100. **Median travel time to work:** 33.3 minutes.

WOOD COUNTY

PO Box 1796   **Ph:** 903-763-2711
Quitman, TX 75783   **Fax:** 903-763-2902

In northeastern TX, east of Dallas; organized Feb 5, 1850 from Van Zandt County. **Name Origin:** For George Tyler Wood (1795-1856), TX legislator (1846) and governor of TX (1847-49).

Area (sq mi): 695.8 (land 650.22; water 45.58).

Pop: 36,752 (White 86.7%; Black or African American 6.1%; Hispanic or Latino 5.7%; Asian 0.2%; Other 4.6%). **Foreign born:** 3.8%. **Median age:** 43. **State rank:** 74. **Pop change 1990-2000:** +25.1%.

Income: per capita $17,702; median household $32,885. **Pop below poverty level:** 14.3%.

Unemployment: 4.9%. **Median home value:** $69,800. **Median travel time to work:** 28.4 minutes.

YOAKUM COUNTY

PO Box 456   **Ph:** 806-456-7491
Plains, TX 79355   **Fax:** 806-456-6175

On southwestern border of TX panhandle, southwest of Lubbock; created Aug 21, 1876 from Bexar County; organized 1907. **Name Origin:** For Col. Henderson King Yoakum (1810-56), army officer in Indian and Mexican wars, and trustee of Austin College (1849-56).

Area (sq mi): 799.76 (land 799.75; water 0.01).

Pop: 7,322 (White 51.8%; Black or African American 1.4%; Hispanic or Latino 45.9%; Asian 0.1%; Other 27.9%). **Foreign born:** 16.6%. **Median age:** 34.1. **State rank:** 185. **Pop change 1990-2000:** -16.7%.

Income: per capita $14,504; median household $32,672. **Pop below poverty level:** 19.6%.

Unemployment: 4.6%. **Median home value:** $40,400. **Median travel time to work:** 15.9 minutes.

YOUNG COUNTY

516 4th St Rm 104   **Ph:** 940-549-8432
Graham, TX 76450   **Fax:** 940-521-0305

In north-central TX, south of Wichita Falls; organized Feb 2, 1856 from Bosque County. **Name Origin:** For William Cocke Young (1812-62), TX sheriff and district attorney, U.S. marshal in IL (1851), and Confederate army officer (1861).

Area (sq mi): 930.84 (land 922.33; water 8.51).

Pop: 17,943 (White 86.5%; Black or African American 1.2%; Hispanic or Latino 10.6%; Asian 0.3%; Other 7.5%). **Foreign born:** 3.7%. **Median age:** 40.7. **State rank:** 124. **Pop change 1990-2000:** -1%.

Income: per capita $16,710; median household $30,499. **Pop below poverty level:** 15.7%.

Unemployment: 4.9%. **Median home value:** $45,200. **Median travel time to work:** 18.1 minutes.

ZAPATA COUNTY

PO Box 789   **Ph:** 956-765-9915
Zapata, TX 78076   **Fax:** 956-765-9933

On the southwestern border of TX, southeast of Laredo; organized Jan 22, 1858 from Starr and Webb counties. **Name Origin:** For Col. Antonio Zapata (?-1840), an officer in the Mexican army and a rancher.

Area (sq mi): 1058.1 (land 996.76; water 61.34).

Pop: 12,182 (White 14.5%; Black or African American 0.4%; Hispanic or Latino 84.8%; Asian 0.2%; Other 15.2%). **Foreign born:** 24.1%. **Median age:** 30.7. **State rank:** 156. **Pop change 1990-2000:** +31.3%.

Income: per capita $10,486; median household $24,635. **Pop below poverty level:** 35.8%.

Unemployment: 6.8%. **Median home value:** $46,500. **Median travel time to work:** 22.6 minutes.

ZAVALA COUNTY

County Courthouse   **Ph:** 830-374-2331
Crystal City, TX 78839   **Fax:** 830-374-5955

In southern TX, southwest of Del Rio; organized Feb 1, 1858 from Uvalde and Maverick counties. **Name Origin:** For Manuel Lorenzo Justiniano de Zavala (1789-1836), a governor of the state of Mexico, vice president of the Repubic of TX, and a signer of the Texas Declaration of Independence (1836).

Area (sq mi): 1301.72 (land 1298.48; water 3.24).

Pop: 11,600 (White 8%; Black or African American 0.5%; Hispanic or Latino 91.2%; Asian 0.1%; Other 34.4%). **Foreign born:** 13.8%. **Median age:** 29. **State rank:** 157. **Pop change 1990-2000:** -4.6%.

Income: per capita $10,034; median household $16,844. **Pop below poverty level:** 41.8%.

Unemployment: 15.8%. **Median home value:** $25,300. **Median travel time to work:** 18.1 minutes.

Please see sample entry on inside front cover for detailed information about the statistics presented with each county listing.

UTAH - Counties

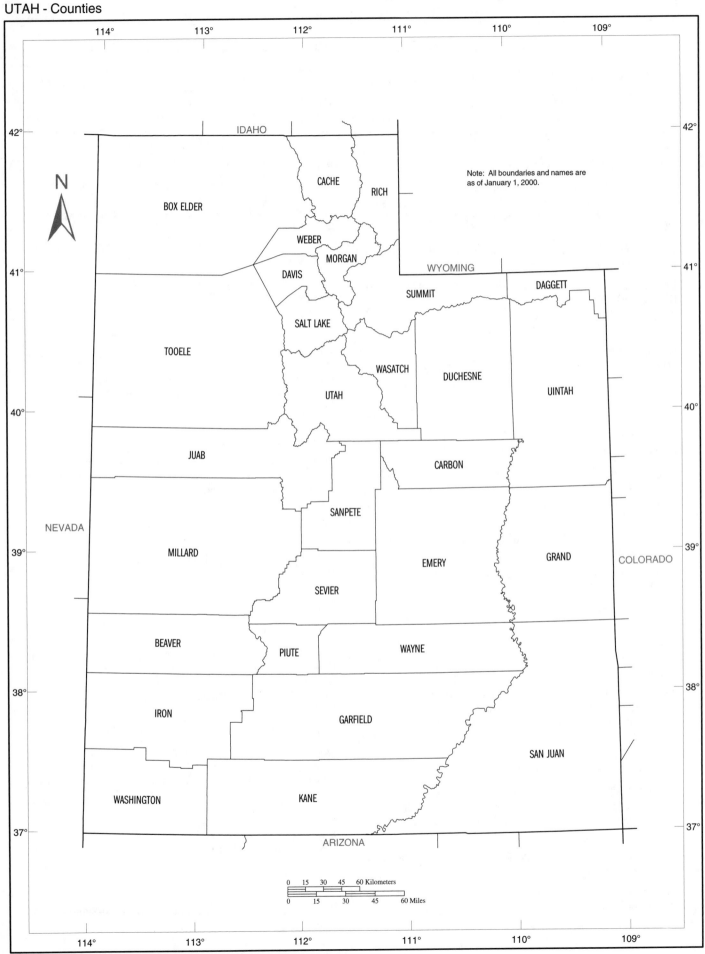

Note: All boundaries and names are as of January 1, 2000.

IDAHO

NEVADA

WYOMING

COLORADO

ARIZONA

BOX ELDER

CACHE

RICH

WEBER

MORGAN

DAVIS

SALT LAKE

SUMMIT

DAGGETT

TOOELE

WASATCH

DUCHESNE

UINTAH

UTAH

JUAB

CARBON

SANPETE

MILLARD

EMERY

GRAND

SEVIER

BEAVER

PIUTE

WAYNE

IRON

GARFIELD

SAN JUAN

WASHINGTON

KANE

N

0 15 30 45 60 Kilometers

0 15 30 45 60 Miles

Utah

UTAH STATE INFORMATION

www.utah.gov **Ph:** 801-538-3000

Area (sq mi): 84,898.83 (land 82,143.65; water 2755.18).

Pop: 2,233,169 (White 85.3%; Black or African American 0.8%; Hispanic or Latino 9%; Asian 1.7%; Other 8.3%). **Foreign born:** 7.1%. **Median age:** 27.1. **Pop change 1990-2000:** +29.6%.

Income: per capita $18,185; median household $45,726. **Pop below poverty level:** 9.4%.

Unemployment: 5.4%. **Median home value:** $146,100. **Median travel time to work:** 21.3 minutes.

BEAVER COUNTY

PO Box 392 **Ph:** 435-438-6463
Beaver, UT 84713 **Fax:** 435-438-6462

On the southwestern border of UT; organized Jan 5, 1856 (prior to statehood) from Iron County. **Name Origin:** For the beaver once plentiful in the area.

Area (sq mi): 2592.28 (land 2589.95; water 2.33).

Pop: 6,005 (White 91.4%; Black or African American 0.3%; Hispanic or Latino 5.5%; Asian 0.6%; Other 5.9%). **Foreign born:** 4.4%. **Median age:** 30.8. **State rank:** 24. **Pop change 1990-2000:** +26%.

Income: per capita $14,957; median household $34,544. **Pop below poverty level:** 8.3%.

Unemployment: 4.2%. **Median home value:** $89,200. **Median travel time to work:** 17.1 minutes.

BOX ELDER COUNTY

01 S Main St **Ph:** 435-734-2031
Brigham City, UT 84302 **Fax:** 435-734-2038

On the northwestern border of UT, west of Ogden; organized Jan 5, 1856 (prior to statehood) from Weber County. **Name Origin:** For the abundant box elder trees in the area. It is more commonly known as the North American maple tree *Acer negundo*.

Area (sq mi): 6729.03 (land 5723.34; water 1005.69).

Pop: 42,745 (White 90.6%; Black or African American 0.2%; Hispanic or Latino 6.5%; Asian 1%; Other 6%). **Foreign born:** 3%. **Median age:** 28. **State rank:** 7. **Pop change 1990-2000:** +17.2%.

Income: per capita $15,625; median household $44,630. **Pop below poverty level:** 7.1%.

Unemployment: 5.6%. **Median home value:** $118,900. **Median travel time to work:** 21.6 minutes.

CACHE COUNTY

170 N Main St **Ph:** 435-716-7150
Logan, UT 84321 **Fax:** 435-752-3597

On the central northern border of UT, northeast of Ogden; organized Jan 5, 1856 (prior to statehood) from unorganized territory. **Name Origin:** For Cache Valley, from the French for 'hiding place,' because early trappers or hunters stored furs and supplies in the valley.

Area (sq mi): 1173.07 (land 1164.52; water 8.55).

Pop: 91,391 (White 89.7%; Black or African American 0.4%; Hispanic or Latino 6.3%; Asian 2%; Other 5.4%). **Foreign born:** 6.7%. **Median age:** 23.9. **State rank:** 5. **Pop change 1990-2000:** +30.2%.

Income: per capita $15,094; median household $39,730. **Pop below poverty level:** 13.5%.

Unemployment: 3.2%. **Median home value:** $131,800. **Median travel time to work:** 16.8 minutes.

CARBON COUNTY

120 E Main St **Ph:** 435-636-3200
Price, UT 84501 **Fax:** 435-636-3210
www.co.carbon.ut.us

In east-central UT, southeast of Provo; organized 1894 (prior to statehood) from Emery County. **Name Origin:** For the abundant coal deposits within its borders.

Area (sq mi): 1484.57 (land 1478.46; water 6.12).

Pop: 20,422 (White 86.5%; Black or African American 0.3%; Hispanic or Latino 10.3%; Asian 0.3%; Other 8.3%). **Foreign born:** 2%. **Median age:** 33.6. **State rank:** 13. **Pop change 1990-2000:** +1%.

Income: per capita $15,325; median household $34,036. **Pop below poverty level:** 13.4%.

Unemployment: 6.3%. **Median home value:** $86,100. **Median travel time to work:** 16.4 minutes.

DAGGETT COUNTY

95 N & 100 W PO Box 219 **Ph:** 435-784-3154
Manila, UT 84046 **Fax:** 435-784-3335

On the northeastern border of UT; organized Jan 7, 1918 from Uintah County. **Name Origin:** For Ellsworth Daggett (1845-1923), mining engineer and first surveyor-general of UT.

Area (sq mi): 723.06 (land 698.36; water 24.71).

Pop: 921 (White 92.6%; Black or African American 0.7%; Hispanic or Latino 5.1%; Asian 0.1%; Other 4.7%). **Foreign born:** 2.7%. **Median age:** 39.2. **State rank:** 29. **Pop change 1990-2000:** +33.5%.

Please see sample entry on inside front cover for detailed information about the statistics presented with each county listing.

Income: per capita $15,511; median household $30,833. **Pop below poverty level:** 5.5%.

Unemployment: 4.6%. **Median home value:** $76,400. **Median travel time to work:** 21.5 minutes.

DAVIS COUNTY

PO Box 618   **Ph:** 801-451-3214
Farmington, UT 84025   **Fax:** 801-451-3421
www.co.davis.ut.us

In north-central UT, north of Salt Lake City; original county; organized Oct 5, 1850 (prior to statehood). **Name Origin:** For Daniel C. Davis (1804-50), commander of 'The Mormon Volunteers.'

Area (sq mi): 633.7 (land 304.48; water 329.22).

Pop: 238,994 (White 89.8%; Black or African American 1.1%; Hispanic or Latino 5.4%; Asian 1.5%; Other 5.2%). **Foreign born:** 3.6%. **Median age:** 26.8. **State rank:** 3. **Pop change 1990-2000:** +27.2%.

Income: per capita $19,506; median household $53,726. **Pop below poverty level:** 5.1%.

Unemployment: 3.8%. **Median home value:** $156,400. **Median travel time to work:** 22.4 minutes.

DUCHESNE COUNTY

PO Box 270   **Ph:** 435-738-1101
Duchesne, UT 84021   **Fax:** 435-738-5522
www.duchesnegov.net

In north-central UT, east of Provo; organized Aug 13, 1914 from Wasatch County. **Name Origin:** For the Duchesne River, which flows through the county. Origin of name unknown. Possibly for Rose Du Chesne (1769-1852), founder of the Society of the Sacred Heart in America; for a fur trapper of that name; or for Fort Duquesne, PA.

Area (sq mi): 3255.97 (land 3238.05; water 17.92).

Pop: 14,371 (White 88.8%; Black or African American 0.1%; Hispanic or Latino 3.5%; Asian 0.2%; Other 9.6%). **Foreign born:** 1.3%. **Median age:** 28.3. **State rank:** 17. **Pop change 1990-2000:** +13.6%.

Income: per capita $12,326; median household $31,298. **Pop below poverty level:** 16.8%.

Unemployment: 6.2%. **Median home value:** $81,800. **Median travel time to work:** 22.4 minutes.

EMERY COUNTY

PO Box 907   **Ph:** 435-381-2139
Castle Dale, UT 84513   **Fax:** 435-381-5183
www.co.emery.ut.us

In east-central UT; organized Feb 12, 1880 (prior to statehood) from Sanpete and Sevier counties. **Name Origin:** For George W. Emery, a territorial governor (1875-80).

Area (sq mi): 4461.54 (land 4451.85; water 9.69).

Pop: 10,860 (White 92.5%; Black or African American 0.2%; Hispanic or Latino 5.2%; Asian 0.3%; Other 3.9%). **Foreign born:**

2.5%. **Median age:** 30.1. **State rank:** 19. **Pop change 1990-2000:** +5.1%.

Income: per capita $14,243; median household $39,850. **Pop below poverty level:** 11.5%.

Unemployment: 9.6%. **Median home value:** $84,200. **Median travel time to work:** 21 minutes.

GARFIELD COUNTY

PO Box 77   **Ph:** 435-676-8826
Panguitch, UT 84759   **Fax:** 435-676-8239

In south-central UT; organized Mar 9, 1882 (prior to statehood) from Iron County. **Name Origin:** For James Abram Garfield (1831-81), twentieth U.S. president.

Area (sq mi): 5208.2 (land 5174.22; water 33.98).

Pop: 4,735 (White 93.8%; Black or African American 0.2%; Hispanic or Latino 2.9%; Asian 0.4%; Other 4.4%). **Foreign born:** 0.8%. **Median age:** 33.8. **State rank:** 25. **Pop change 1990-2000:** +19%.

Income: per capita $13,439; median household $35,180. **Pop below poverty level:** 8.1%.

Unemployment: 9.2%. **Median home value:** $90,500. **Median travel time to work:** 13.9 minutes.

GRAND COUNTY

125 E Center St   **Ph:** 435-259-1321
Moab, UT 84532   **Fax:** 435-259-2959
www.grandcountyutah.net

On the central eastern border of UT; organized Mar 13, 1890 (prior to statehood). **Name Origin:** For the Grand River, which flows through the county; the river was renamed the Colorado in 1921.

Area (sq mi): 3694.08 (land 3681.56; water 12.52).

Pop: 8,485 (White 89.2%; Black or African American 0.2%; Hispanic or Latino 5.6%; Asian 0.2%; Other 6.9%). **Foreign born:** 3%. **Median age:** 36.9. **State rank:** 20. **Pop change 1990-2000:** +28.2%.

Income: per capita $17,356; median household $32,387. **Pop below poverty level:** 14.8%.

Unemployment: 6.7%. **Median home value:** $112,700. **Median travel time to work:** 15 minutes.

IRON COUNTY

PO Box 429   **Ph:** 435-477-3375
Parowan, UT 84761   **Fax:** 435-477-8847
www.ironcounty.net

On the southwestern border of UT; organized as Little Salt Lake County in 1850 (prior to statehood) from unorganized territory; name changed later that year. **Name Origin:** For the county's iron ore deposits and mines.

Area (sq mi): 3301.84 (land 3297.98; water 3.87).

Pop: 33,779 (White 91.3%; Black or African American 0.4%; Hispanic or Latino 4.1%; Asian 0.7%; Other 6%). **Foreign born:** 2.9%. **Median age:** 24.2. **State rank:** 9. **Pop change 1990-2000:** +62.5%.

Income: per capita $13,568; median household $33,114. **Pop below poverty level:** 19.2%.

All statistics are based on the 2000 Census except the dollar figures given for per capita income, which are based on 1999 estimates.

Unemployment: 4.6%. **Median home value:** $112,000. **Median travel time to work:** 15 minutes.

JUAB COUNTY
160 N Main St   **Ph:** 435-623-3410
Nephi, UT 84648   **Fax:** 435-623-5936
www.co.juab.ut.us

On the central western border of UT, southwest of Provo; original county; organized Mar 3, 1852 (prior to statehood). **Name Origin:** From the Juab Valley, named by the local Indians, the Uabs, Yuabs, or Yoabs of the Piute tribe. Meaning is either 'flat, level plain,' or possibly 'thirsty plain.'

Area (sq mi): 3406.28 (land 3391.74; water 14.54).

Pop: 8,238 (White 95.2%; Black or African American 0.1%; Hispanic or Latino 2.6%; Asian 0.3%; Other 2.9%). **Foreign born:** 1.4%. **Median age:** 26.5. **State rank:** 21. **Pop change 1990-2000:** +41.6%.

Income: per capita $12,790; median household $38,139. **Pop below poverty level:** 10.4%.

Unemployment: 5%. **Median home value:** $115,900. **Median travel time to work:** 23.1 minutes.

KANE COUNTY
76 N Main St   **Ph:** 435-644-2458
Kanab, UT 84741   **Fax:** 435-644-2052

On the central southern border of UT; organized Jan 16, 1864 (prior to statehood) from Washington County. **Name Origin:** For Gen. Thomas Leiper Kane (1822-83), Union army officer and friend to the Mormons who acted as an intermediary in the so-called Mormon War of 1858.

Area (sq mi): 4108.42 (land 3991.96; water 116.46).

Pop: 6,046 (White 94.7%; Black or African American 0%; Hispanic or Latino 2.3%; Asian 0.2%; Other 3.7%). **Foreign born:** 2.9%. **Median age:** 39.1. **State rank:** 23. **Pop change 1990-2000:** +17%.

Income: per capita $15,455; median household $34,247. **Pop below poverty level:** 7.9%.

Unemployment: 3.5%. **Median home value:** $103,900. **Median travel time to work:** 18.9 minutes.

MILLARD COUNTY
765 S Hwy 99 Suite 6   **Ph:** 435-743-6223
Fillmore, UT 84631   **Fax:** 435-743-6923

On the central western border of UT, southwest of Provo; organized Oct 4, 1851 (prior to statehood) from Juab County. **Name Origin:** For Millard Fillmore (1800-74), 13th U.S. president, who signed the act creating the Territory of Utah and appointed Brigham Young (1801-77) the first governor.

Area (sq mi): 6828.01 (land 6589.13; water 238.87).

Pop: 12,405 (White 90%; Black or African American 0.1%; Hispanic or Latino 7.2%; Asian 0.5%; Other 5.5%). **Foreign born:** 5.1%. **Median age:** 29.9. **State rank:** 18. **Pop change 1990-2000:** +9.5%.

Income: per capita $13,408; median household $36,178. **Pop below poverty level:** 13.1%.

Unemployment: 4.9%. **Median home value:** $84,700. **Median travel time to work:** 19 minutes.

MORGAN COUNTY
PO Box 886   **Ph:** 801-829-6811
Morgan, UT 84050   **Fax:** 801-829-6176
www.morgan-county.net

In north-central UT, east of Bountiful; organized Jan 17, 1862 (prior to statehood) from Davis and Summit counties. **Name Origin:** For Jedediah Morgan Grant (1816-56), prominent Mormon churchman.

Area (sq mi): 610.79 (land 609.13; water 1.66).

Pop: 7,129 (White 97.3%; Black or African American 0%; Hispanic or Latino 1.4%; Asian 0.2%; Other 1.7%). **Foreign born:** 2.7%. **Median age:** 28.5. **State rank:** 22. **Pop change 1990-2000:** +29%.

Income: per capita $17,684; median household $50,273. **Pop below poverty level:** 5.2%.

Unemployment: 3.6%. **Median home value:** $174,500. **Median travel time to work:** 26.3 minutes.

PIUTE COUNTY
PO Box 99   **Ph:** 435-577-2840
Junction, UT 84740   **Fax:** 435-577-2433

In south-central UT; organized Jan 16, 1865 (prior to statehood) from Beaver County. **Name Origin:** For the sub-tribe of the Ute Indians. The name means 'water Ute.'

Area (sq mi): 765.76 (land 757.81; water 7.95).

Pop: 1,435 (White 93.3%; Black or African American 0.1%; Hispanic or Latino 4.5%; Asian 0.2%; Other 4.1%). **Foreign born:** 2%. **Median age:** 38.9. **State rank:** 28. **Pop change 1990-2000:** +12.4%.

Income: per capita $12,697; median household $29,625. **Pop below poverty level:** 16.2%.

Unemployment: 7.7%. **Median home value:** $80,900. **Median travel time to work:** 26.3 minutes.

RICH COUNTY
20 S Main St   **Ph:** 435-793-2415
Randolph, UT 84064   **Fax:** 435-793-2410

On the northern border of UT, northeast of Ogden; original county. Created as Richland in 1863; organized and name changed Jan 16, 1864 (prior to statehood). **Name Origin:** For Charles Coulson Rich, a Mormon apostle.

Area (sq mi): 1086.29 (land 1028.53; water 57.76).

Pop: 1,961 (White 97.3%; Black or African American 0%; Hispanic or Latino 1.8%; Asian 0.4%; Other 1.5%). **Foreign born:** 1.9%. **Median age:** 34.3. **State rank:** 27. **Pop change 1990-2000:** +13.7%.

Income: per capita $16,267; median household $39,766. **Pop below poverty level:** 10.2%.

Unemployment: 3.9%. **Median home value:** $84,300. **Median travel time to work:** 29 minutes.

Please see sample entry on inside front cover for detailed information about the statistics presented with each county listing.

SALT LAKE COUNTY

2001 S State St Suite S2200   **Ph:** 801-468-3000
Salt Lake City, UT 84190   **Fax:** 801-468-3440
www.co.slc.ut.us

In north-central UT, on the eastern shore of Great Salt Lake; original county. Organized as Great Salt Lake County in 1849 (prior to statehood); name changed Jan 29, 1868. **Name Origin:** For the Great Salt Lake.

Area (sq mi): 807.78 (land 737.38; water 70.4).

Pop: 898,387 (White 80.9%; Black or African American 1.1%; Hispanic or Latino 11.9%; Asian 2.6%; Other 10.1%). **Foreign born:** 10.4%. **Median age:** 28.9. **State rank:** 1. **Pop change 1990-2000:** +23.8%.

Income: per capita $20,190; median household $48,373. **Pop below poverty level:** 8%.

Unemployment: 4.3%. **Median home value:** $157,000. **Median travel time to work:** 22.5 minutes.

SAN JUAN COUNTY

PO Box 338   **Ph:** 435-587-3223
Monticello, UT 84535   **Fax:** 435-587-2425

On the southeastern border of UT; organized Feb 17, 1880 (prior to statehood) from Kane, Iron, Sevier, and Piute counties. **Name Origin:** For the San Juan River, which runs through the county; Spanish 'Saint John.' The origin of th river's name is in dispute.

Area (sq mi): 7933.09 (land 7820.18; water 112.91).

Pop: 14,413 (White 39.6%; Black or African American 0.1%; Hispanic or Latino 3.7%; Asian 0.2%; Other 58.9%). **Foreign born:** 0.9%. **Median age:** 25.5. **State rank:** 16. **Pop change 1990-2000:** +14.2%.

Income: per capita $10,229; median household $28,137. **Pop below poverty level:** 31.4%.

Unemployment: 9.1%. **Median home value:** $68,400. **Median travel time to work:** 21.4 minutes.

SANPETE COUNTY

160 N Main St   **Ph:** 435-835-2131
Manti, UT 84642   **Fax:** 435-835-2135
utahreach.usu.edu/sanpete/govt/index.htm

In central UT, south of Provo; original county; organized 1850 (prior to statehood). **Name Origin:** Corruption of *San Pitch*, name of the Ute Indian chieftain whose people lived in the region.

Area (sq mi): 1602.66 (land 1588.11; water 14.55).

Pop: 22,763 (White 90.5%; Black or African American 0.3%; Hispanic or Latino 6.6%; Asian 0.5%; Other 6.9%). **Foreign born:** 4.8%. **Median age:** 25.3. **State rank:** 12. **Pop change 1990-2000:** +40%.

Income: per capita $12,442; median household $33,042. **Pop below poverty level:** 15.9%.

Unemployment: 5.7%. **Median home value:** $104,800. **Median travel time to work:** 22.4 minutes.

SEVIER COUNTY

250 N Main St   **Ph:** 435-896-9262
Richfield, UT 84701   **Fax:** 435-896-8888
www.sevierutah.net

In south-central UT; organized Jan 16, 1865 (prior to statehood) from Sanpete County. **Name Origin:** For the Sevier River, which runs through the county. Anglicization of Spanish *Rio Severo* 'violent river.'

Area (sq mi): 1918.28 (land 1910.25; water 8.03).

Pop: 18,842 (White 94.2%; Black or African American 0.3%; Hispanic or Latino 2.6%; Asian 0.3%; Other 3.9%). **Foreign born:** 1.3%. **Median age:** 30.3. **State rank:** 14. **Pop change 1990-2000:** +22.1%.

Income: per capita $14,180; median household $35,822. **Pop below poverty level:** 10.8%.

Unemployment: 4.6%. **Median home value:** $95,700. **Median travel time to work:** 17.6 minutes.

SUMMIT COUNTY

PO Box 128   **Ph:** 435-336-3203
Coalville, UT 84017   **Fax:** 435-336-3030
www.co.summit.ut.us

On the central northern border of UT, east of Salt Lake City; organized Jan 13, 1854 (prior to statehood) from Green River Valley. **Name Origin:** For its location on the divide between the Colorado River Valley and the Salt Lake Valley.

Area (sq mi): 1882.05 (land 1871.05; water 11).

Pop: 29,736 (White 89.5%; Black or African American 0.2%; Hispanic or Latino 8.1%; Asian 1%; Other 6.9%). **Foreign born:** 7.7%. **Median age:** 33.3. **State rank:** 10. **Pop change 1990-2000:** +91.6%.

Income: per capita $33,767; median household $64,962. **Pop below poverty level:** 5.4%.

Unemployment: 5.8%. **Median home value:** $296,000. **Median travel time to work:** 24.8 minutes.

TOOELE COUNTY

47 S Main St   **Ph:** 435-843-3140
Tooele, UT 84074   **Fax:** 435-882-7317
www.co.tooele.ut.us

On the northwestern border of UT, west of Salt Lake City; original county. Organized as Tuilla County Jan 31, 1850 (prior to statehood); includes Shambip County, which was abolished in 1862. Spelling was changed Mar 1852. **Name Origin:** Possibly for Tuilla, a Goshute Indian chief, or for the bulrushes (tules) in the swamps, or for Mat Tooele, an Austrian village.

Area (sq mi): 7287.12 (land 6930.35; water 356.76).

Pop: 40,735 (White 84.7%; Black or African American 1.3%; Hispanic or Latino 10.3%; Asian 0.6%; Other 9%). **Foreign born:** 3.7%. **Median age:** 27.1. **State rank:** 8. **Pop change 1990-2000:** +53.1%.

Income: per capita $16,321; median household $45,773. **Pop below poverty level:** 6.7%.

Unemployment: 7.4%. **Median home value:** $127,800. **Median travel time to work:** 32.1 minutes.

All statistics are based on the 2000 Census except the dollar figures given for per capita income, which are based on 1999 estimates.

UINTAH COUNTY

147 E Main St   **Ph:** 435-781-5630
Vernal, UT 84078   **Fax:** 435-781-6701
www.co.uintah.ut.us

On the northeastern border of UT; original county; organized Jan 31, 1850 (prior to statehood). **Name Origin:** For a subtribe of the Utes; named said to mean 'pineland.'

Area (sq mi): 4498.98 (land 4477.07; water 21.91).

Pop: 25,224 (White 85.9%; Black or African American 0.1%; Hispanic or Latino 3.5%; Asian 0.2%; Other 11.9%). **Foreign born:** 1.4%. **Median age:** 29. **State rank:** 11. **Pop change 1990-2000:** +13.6%.

Income: per capita $13,571; median household $34,518. **Pop below poverty level:** 14.5%.

Unemployment: 4.6%. **Median home value:** $84,800. **Median travel time to work:** 19.5 minutes.

UTAH COUNTY

125 N 100 West   **Ph:** 801-429-1000
Provo, UT 84601   **Fax:** 801-429-1033
www.co.utah.ut.us

In north-central UT, south of Salt Lake City; original county; organized Jan 31, 1850 (prior to statehood); includes Cedar County; which was abolished in 1862. **Name Origin:** For the Ute Indians. *Ute* or *Eutaw* is variously defined as 'in the tops of the mountains,' 'high up,' 'the hill dwellers,' 'the land of the sun,' or 'the land of plenty.'

Area (sq mi): 2140.98 (land 1998.33; water 142.64).

Pop: 368,536 (White 89.2%; Black or African American 0.3%; Hispanic or Latino 7%; Asian 1.1%; Other 6.3%). **Foreign born:** 6.3%. **Median age:** 23.3. **State rank:** 2. **Pop change 1990-2000:** +39.8%.

Income: per capita $15,557; median household $45,833. **Pop below poverty level:** 12%.

Unemployment: 3.8%. **Median home value:** $156,400. **Median travel time to work:** 18.8 minutes.

WASATCH COUNTY

25 N Main St   **Ph:** 435-654-3211
Heber City, UT 84032   **Fax:** 435-654-9924
www.co.wasatch.ut.us

In east-central UT, east of Provo; organized Jan 17, 1862 (prior to statehood) from Summit County. **Name Origin:** For the Wasatch Mountains, a Ute word meaning 'mountain pass' or 'low place in a high mountain,' referring to the place where the Weber River cuts through.

Area (sq mi): 1209.17 (land 1177.39; water 31.78).

Pop: 15,215 (White 93.3%; Black or African American 0.2%; Hispanic or Latino 5.1%; Asian 0.3%; Other 3.9%). **Foreign born:** 4.2%. **Median age:** 29.5. **State rank:** 15. **Pop change 1990-2000:** +50.8%.

Income: per capita $19,869; median household $49,612. **Pop below poverty level:** 5.2%.

Unemployment: 5.5%. **Median home value:** $185,300. **Median travel time to work:** 25.3 minutes.

WASHINGTON COUNTY

197 E Tabernacle St   **Ph:** 435-634-5700
Saint George, UT 84770   **Fax:** 435-634-5753
www.washco.state.ut.us

On the southwestern border of UT; organized Mar 2, 1852 (prior to statehood) from unorganized territory. **Name Origin:** For George Washington (1732-1799), American patriot and first U.S. president.

Area (sq mi): 2429.91 (land 2426.62; water 3.28).

Pop: 90,354 (White 91.1%; Black or African American 0.2%; Hispanic or Latino 5.2%; Asian 0.4%; Other 5.7%). **Foreign born:** 4.1%. **Median age:** 31. **State rank:** 6. **Pop change 1990-2000:** +86.1%.

Income: per capita $15,873; median household $37,212. **Pop below poverty level:** 11.2%.

Unemployment: 3.8%. **Median home value:** $139,800. **Median travel time to work:** 17.2 minutes.

WAYNE COUNTY

PO Box 189   **Ph:** 435-836-2731
Loa, UT 84747   **Fax:** 435-836-2479

In south-central UT; organized Mar 10, 1892 (prior to statehood) from Piute County. **Name Origin:** Named by Willis Robinson, a delegate to the state constitutional convention, for his deceased son, Wayne.

Area (sq mi): 2466.47 (land 2460.32; water 6.15).

Pop: 2,509 (White 96%; Black or African American 0.2%; Hispanic or Latino 2%; Asian 0.1%; Other 2.5%). **Foreign born:** 1.7%. **Median age:** 34.1. **State rank:** 26. **Pop change 1990-2000:** +15.3%.

Income: per capita $15,392; median household $32,000. **Pop below poverty level:** 15.4%.

Unemployment: 5.3%. **Median home value:** $97,600. **Median travel time to work:** 19.5 minutes.

WEBER COUNTY

2380 Washington Blvd Suite 350   **Ph:** 801-399-8610
Ogden, UT 84401   **Fax:** 801-399-8314
www.co.weber.ut.us

In north-central UT, north of Salt Lake City; original county; organized Jan 31, 1850 (prior to statehood). **Name Origin:** For the Weber River, which runs through the county. The river is itself named for John H. Weber (?-1859), a Dutch sea captain and trapper who traveled west with Gen. Ashby and was killed near the river, or for another trapper named Weber.

Area (sq mi): 659.46 (land 575.54; water 83.93).

Pop: 196,533 (White 82.8%; Black or African American 1.4%; Hispanic or Latino 12.6%; Asian 1.3%; Other 9.7%). **Foreign born:** 6.4%. **Median age:** 29.3. **State rank:** 4. **Pop change 1990-2000:** +24.1%.

Income: per capita $18,246; median household $44,014. **Pop below poverty level:** 9.3%.

Unemployment: 5%. **Median home value:** $125,600. **Median travel time to work:** 21.6 minutes.

Please see sample entry on inside front cover for detailed information about the statistics presented with each county listing.

VERMONT - Counties

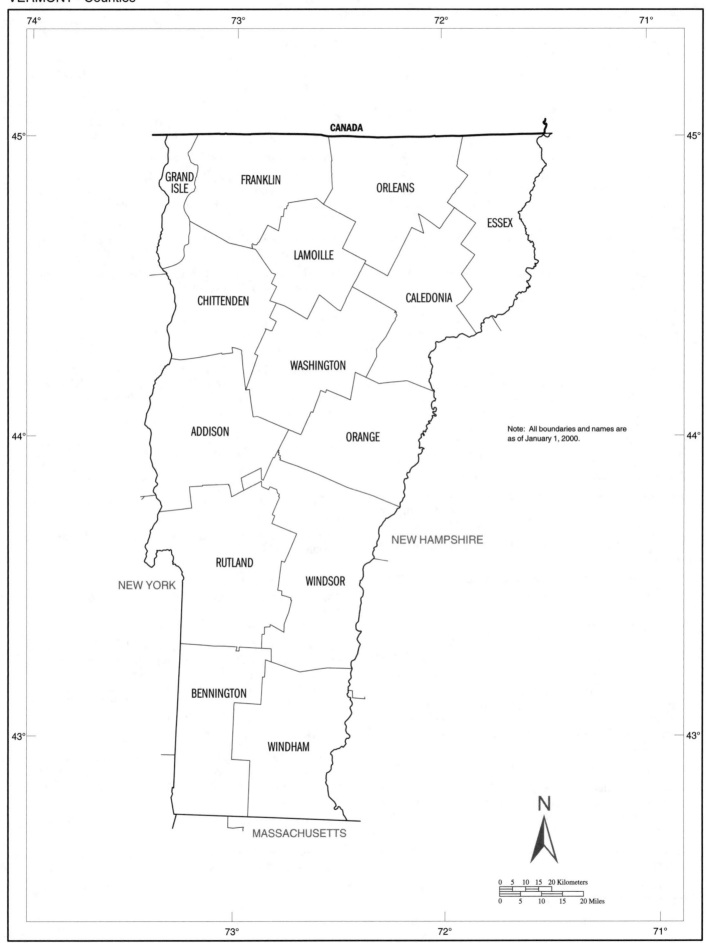

74° 73° 72° 71°

CANADA

45°

GRAND ISLE

FRANKLIN

ORLEANS

ESSEX

LAMOILLE

CHITTENDEN

CALEDONIA

WASHINGTON

ADDISON

ORANGE

Note: All boundaries and names are
as of January 1, 2000.

44°

NEW HAMPSHIRE

RUTLAND

WINDSOR

NEW YORK

BENNINGTON

43°

WINDHAM

MASSACHUSETTS

N

0 5 10 15 20 Kilometers
0 5 10 15 20 Miles

73° 72° 71°

Vermont

VERMONT STATE INFORMATION

www.vermont.gov **Ph:** 802-828-1110

Area (sq mi): 9614.26 (land 9249.56; water 364.7).

Pop: 608,827 (White 96.2%; Black or African American 0.5%; Hispanic or Latino 0.9%; Asian 0.9%; Other 1.8%). **Foreign born:** 3.8%. **Median age:** 37.7. **Pop change 1990-2000:** +8.2%.

Income: per capita $20,625; median household $40,856. **Pop below poverty level:** 9.4%.

Unemployment: 4.1%. **Median home value:** $111,500. **Median travel time to work:** 21.6 minutes.

ADDISON COUNTY

7 Mahady Ct **Ph:** 802-388-7741
Middlebury, VT 05753

On central western border of VT, west of Barre; organized Oct 18, 1785 (prior to statehood) from Rutland County. **Name Origin:** For the town of Addison.

Area (sq mi): 808.3 (land 770.18; water 38.12).

Pop: 35,974 (White 96.2%; Black or African American 0.5%; Hispanic or Latino 1.1%; Asian 0.7%; Other 1.9%). **Foreign born:** 3.5%. **Median age:** 36.1. **State rank:** 8. **Pop change 1990-2000:** +9.2%.

Income: per capita $19,539; median household $43,142. **Pop below poverty level:** 8.6%.

Unemployment: 3.3%. **Median home value:** $111,300. **Median travel time to work:** 23.2 minutes.

BENNINGTON COUNTY

PO Box 4157 **Ph:** 802-447-2700
Bennington, VT 05201 **Fax:** 802-447-2703

On the southwestern border of VT, south of Rutland. Oldest county, organized Feb 11, 1779 (prior to statehood). **Name Origin:** For the town, its county seat.

Area (sq mi): 677.67 (land 676.27; water 1.4).

Pop: 36,994 (White 97.1%; Black or African American 0.4%; Hispanic or Latino 0.9%; Asian 0.6%; Other 1.2%). **Foreign born:** 2.7%. **Median age:** 40.3. **State rank:** 7. **Pop change 1990-2000:** +3.2%.

Income: per capita $21,193; median household $39,926. **Pop below poverty level:** 10%.

Unemployment: 4.6%. **Median home value:** $115,700. **Median travel time to work:** 19.1 minutes.

CALEDONIA COUNTY

1126 Main St **Ph:** 802-748-6600
Saint Johnsbury, VT 05819 **Fax:** 802-748-6603

In northeastern VT, east of Montpelier; organized Nov 5, 1792 from Chittenden and Orange counties. **Name Origin:** For the ancient name of Scotland; name given by the many Scots who had settled in this part of the state.

Area (sq mi): 657.52 (land 650.59; water 6.94).

Pop: 29,702 (White 97%; Black or African American 0.3%; Hispanic or Latino 0.7%; Asian 0.4%; Other 1.8%). **Foreign born:** 2.5%. **Median age:** 38.5. **State rank:** 9. **Pop change 1990-2000:** +6.7%.

Income: per capita $16,976; median household $34,800. **Pop below poverty level:** 12.3%.

Unemployment: 5.2%. **Median home value:** $83,100. **Median travel time to work:** 22.2 minutes.

CHITTENDEN COUNTY

PO Box 187 **Ph:** 802-863-3467
Burlington, VT 05402

In northwestern VT, west of Montpelier, organized Oct 22, 1787 (prior to statehood) from Addison County. **Name Origin:** For Thomas Chittenden (1730-97), first governor of the republic of VT (1778-89; 1790-91), and of the state (1791-97).

Area (sq mi): 619.64 (land 539.04; water 80.6).

Pop: 146,571 (White 94.4%; Black or African American 0.9%; Hispanic or Latino 1.1%; Asian 2%; Other 1.9%). **Foreign born:** 5.9%. **Median age:** 34.2. **State rank:** 1. **Pop change 1990-2000:** +11.2%.

Income: per capita $23,501; median household $47,673. **Pop below poverty level:** 8.8%.

Unemployment: 2.4%. **Median home value:** $139,000. **Median travel time to work:** 19.7 minutes.

ESSEX COUNTY

PO Box 75 **Ph:** 802-676-3910
Guildhall, VT 05905 **Fax:** 802-676-3463

At the northeastern corner of VT; organized Nov 5, 1792 from Chittenden and Orange counties. **Name Origin:** For the county of Essex, England; many early residents had ancestors originally from there.

Area (sq mi): 673.75 (land 665.2; water 8.56).

Pop: 6,459 (White 96.3%; Black or African American 0.2%; Hispanic or Latino 0.5%; Asian 0.3%; Other 2.9%). **Foreign born:** 5.5%. **Median age:** 39. **State rank:** 14. **Pop change 1990-2000:** +0.8%.

Please see sample entry on inside front cover for detailed information about the statistics presented with each county listing.

Income: per capita $14,388; median household $30,490. **Pop below poverty level:** 13.7%.

Unemployment: 6.6%. **Median home value:** $68,700. **Median travel time to work:** 22 minutes.

FRANKLIN COUNTY
PO Box 808   **Ph:** 802-524-3863
Saint Albans, VT 05478

At the northwestern corner of VT, north of Burlington; organized Nov 5, 1792 from Chittenden County. **Name Origin:** For Benjamin Franklin (1706-90), U.S. patriot, diplomat, and statesman.

Area (sq mi): 692.02 (land 637.07; water 54.95).

Pop: 45,417 (White 95.6%; Black or African American 0.3%; Hispanic or Latino 0.6%; Asian 0.3%; Other 3.3%). **Foreign born:** 3.7%. **Median age:** 35.7. **State rank:** 5. **Pop change 1990-2000:** +13.6%.

Income: per capita $17,816; median household $41,659. **Pop below poverty level:** 9%.

Unemployment: 4.2%. **Median home value:** $99,300. **Median travel time to work:** 25.6 minutes.

GRAND ISLE COUNTY
PO Box 7   **Ph:** 802-372-3522
North Hero, VT 05474

Islands and peninsula in Lake Champlain, in northwestern VT; organized Nov 9, 1802 from Franklin and Chittenden counties. **Name Origin:** For the largest of the islands comprising the county. Often referred to as 'The Islands.'

Area (sq mi): 194.67 (land 82.62; water 112.06).

Pop: 6,901 (White 97.1%; Black or African American 0.1%; Hispanic or Latino 0.4%; Asian 0.2%; Other 2.2%). **Foreign born:** 4.2%. **Median age:** 40.1. **State rank:** 13. **Pop change 1990-2000:** +29.8%.

Income: per capita $22,207; median household $43,033. **Pop below poverty level:** 7.6%.

Unemployment: 5.1%. **Median home value:** $127,600. **Median travel time to work:** 33.4 minutes.

LAMOILLE COUNTY
PO Box 490   **Ph:** 802-888-2207
Hyde Park, VT 05655

In north-central VT, north of Montpelier; organized Oct 26, 1835 from Orleans, Franklin, Washington, and Chittenden counties. **Name Origin:** For the Lamoille River, which runs through it; a corruption of French *la mouette* 'the seagull,' the name given to the river by Champlain. The 1744 Charlevois map of discoveries in America showed the river as *La Mouelle* owing to an engraver's neglecting to cross the *tts*; with spelling variations.

Area (sq mi): 463.75 (land 460.97; water 2.78).

Pop: 23,233 (White 96.8%; Black or African American 0.3%; Hispanic or Latino 0.8%; Asian 0.4%; Other 1.9%). **Foreign born:** 3.8%. **Median age:** 36.5. **State rank:** 12. **Pop change 1990-2000:** +17.7%.

Income: per capita $20,972; median household $39,356. **Pop below poverty level:** 9.6%.

Unemployment: 4.9%. **Median home value:** $114,900. **Median travel time to work:** 25.7 minutes.

ORANGE COUNTY
5 Court St   **Ph:** 802-685-4610
Chelsea, VT 05038   **Fax:** 802-685-3246

On the central eastern border of VT, south of Montpelier; organized Feb 22, 1781 (prior to statehood) from the former Cumberland County. **Name Origin:** For William of Orange (1650-1702), later William III, king of England (1689-1702).

Area (sq mi): 691.74 (land 688.56; water 3.18).

Pop: 28,226 (White 97.5%; Black or African American 0.2%; Hispanic or Latino 0.6%; Asian 0.4%; Other 1.4%). **Foreign born:** 1.8%. **Median age:** 38.6. **State rank:** 10. **Pop change 1990-2000:** +7.9%.

Income: per capita $18,784; median household $39,855. **Pop below poverty level:** 9.1%.

Unemployment: 2.7%. **Median home value:** $94,300. **Median travel time to work:** 25.3 minutes.

ORLEANS COUNTY
247 Main St   **Ph:** 802-334-3344
Newport, VT 05855   **Fax:** 802-334-3385

On the central northern border of VT; organized Nov 5, 1792 from Chittenden and Orange counties. **Name Origin:** Probably for Louis Philippe Joseph (1747-93), Duke of Orleans, a friend of Marquis de Lafayette (1757-1834) and supporter of the American Revolution.

Area (sq mi): 721.14 (land 697.7; water 23.44).

Pop: 26,277 (White 96.7%; Black or African American 0.4%; Hispanic or Latino 0.7%; Asian 0.3%; Other 2.2%). **Foreign born:** 5.5%. **Median age:** 39.3. **State rank:** 11. **Pop change 1990-2000:** +9.2%.

Income: per capita $16,518; median household $31,084. **Pop below poverty level:** 14.1%.

Unemployment: 7.1%. **Median home value:** $78,800. **Median travel time to work:** 21.5 minutes.

RUTLAND COUNTY
83 Center St Suite 3   **Ph:** 802-775-4394
Rutland, VT 05701   **Fax:** 802-775-2291

On the central western border of VT, south of Middlebury; organized Feb 22, 1781 (prior to statehood) from Bennington County. **Name Origin:** For the town, its county seat.

Area (sq mi): 944.77 (land 932.53; water 12.24).

Pop: 63,400 (White 97.7%; Black or African American 0.3%; Hispanic or Latino 0.7%; Asian 0.4%; Other 1.1%). **Foreign born:** 2%. **Median age:** 39.5. **State rank:** 2. **Pop change 1990-2000:** +2%.

Income: per capita $18,874; median household $36,743. **Pop below poverty level:** 10.9%.

Unemployment: 4.1%. **Median home value:** $96,000. **Median travel time to work:** 20.6 minutes.

All statistics are based on the 2000 Census except the dollar figures given for per capita income, which are based on 1999 estimates.

WASHINGTON COUNTY

65 State St **Ph:** 802-828-2091
Montpelier, VT 05602

In north-central VT, east of Burlington; organized as Jefferson County Nov 1, 1810 from Addison, Caledonia, Chittenden, and Orange counties. **Name Origin:** For George Washington (1732-99), U.S. patriot and first U.S. president. Originally named Jefferson; changed Nov 8, 1814, by newly elected Federalist majority in VT legislature.

Area (sq mi): 695.43 (land 689.17; water 6.26).

Pop: 58,039 (White 96.1%; Black or African American 0.5%; Hispanic or Latino 1.3%; Asian 0.6%; Other 1.9%). **Foreign born:** 3.6%. **Median age:** 38.5. **State rank:** 3. **Pop change 1990-2000:** +5.7%.

Income: per capita $21,113; median household $40,972. **Pop below poverty level:** 8%.

Unemployment: 3.8%. **Median home value:** $102,500. **Median travel time to work:** 21.8 minutes.

WINDHAM COUNTY

PO Box 207 **Ph:** 802-365-7979
Newfane, VT 05345 **Fax:** 802-365-4360

At the southeastern corner of VT; organized Feb 11, 1781 (prior to statehood) from the former Cumberland County. **Name Origin:** For Windham, CT, former home of early settlers.

Area (sq mi): 798.12 (land 788.72; water 9.4).

Pop: 44,216 (White 96%; Black or African American 0.5%; Hispanic or Latino 1.1%; Asian 0.8%; Other 1.9%). **Foreign born:** 3.1%. **Median age:** 40. **State rank:** 6. **Pop change 1990-2000:** +6.3%.

Income: per capita $20,533; median household $38,204. **Pop below poverty level:** 9.4%.

Unemployment: 3.3%. **Median home value:** $109,500. **Median travel time to work:** 20.5 minutes.

WINDSOR COUNTY

PO Box 458 **Ph:** 802-457-2121
Woodstock, VT 05091 **Fax:** 802-457-3446

On the central eastern border of VT, east of Rutland; organized Feb 22, 1781 (prior to statehood) from the former Cumberland County. **Name Origin:** For the English town of Windsor.

Area (sq mi): 975.74 (land 970.96; water 4.78).

Pop: 57,418 (White 97.1%; Black or African American 0.3%; Hispanic or Latino 0.8%; Asian 0.6%; Other 1.2%). **Foreign born:** 3%. **Median age:** 41.3. **State rank:** 4. **Pop change 1990-2000:** +6.2%.

Income: per capita $22,369; median household $40,688. **Pop below poverty level:** 7.7%.

Unemployment: 2.8%. **Median home value:** $108,500. **Median travel time to work:** 21.3 minutes.

Please see sample entry on inside front cover for detailed information about the statistics presented with each county listing.

581

VIRGINIA - Counties and Independent Cities

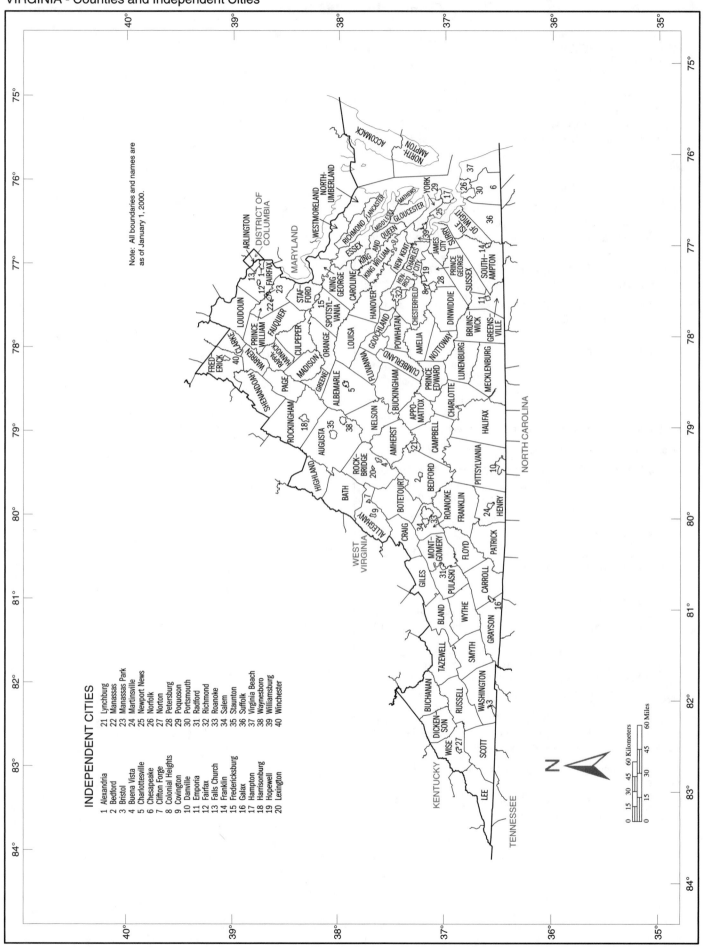

Note: All boundaries and names are
as of January 1, 2000.

INDEPENDENT CITIES

1	Alexandria	21	Lynchburg
2	Bedford	22	Manassas
3	Bristol	23	Manassas Park
4	Buena Vista	24	Martinsville
5	Charlottesville	25	Newport News
6	Chesapeake	26	Norfolk
7	Clifton Forge	27	Norton
8	Colonial Heights	28	Petersburg
9	Covington	29	Poquoson
10	Danville	30	Portsmouth
11	Emporia	31	Radford
12	Fairfax	32	Richmond
13	Falls Church	33	Roanoke
14	Franklin	34	Salem
15	Fredericksburg	35	Staunton
16	Galax	36	Suffolk
17	Hampton	37	Virginia Beach
18	Harrisonburg	38	Waynesboro
19	Hopewell	39	Williamsburg
20	Lexington	40	Winchester

Virginia

VIRGINIA STATE INFORMATION
www.myvirginia.org   **Ph:** 804-786-0000

Area (sq mi): 42774.2 (land 39,594.07; water 3180.13).

Pop: 7,078,515 (White 70.2%; Black or African American 19.6%; Hispanic or Latino 4.7%; Asian 3.7%; Other 4.4%). **Foreign born:** 8.1%. **Median age:** 35.7. **Pop change 1990-2000:** +14.4%.

Income: per capita $23,975; median household $46,677. **Pop below poverty level:** 9.6%.

Unemployment: 4%. **Median home value:** $125,400. **Median travel time to work:** 27 minutes.

ACCOMACK COUNTY
PO Box 388   **Ph:** 757-787-5700
Accomac, VA 23301   **Fax:** 757-787-2468
www.co.accomack.va.us

On the southern Delmarva peninsula, off the east coast of VA; organized 1663 from Northampton County. **Name Origin:** For a subtribe of the Powhatans; name is said to mean 'across the water,' since they lived across Chesapeake Bay from their kinsmen. The county retains the spelling closer to the Indian word *accawmacke*.

Area (sq mi): 1310.05 (land 455.24; water 854.8).

Pop: 38,305 (White 61.9%; Black or African American 31.6%; Hispanic or Latino 5.4%; Asian 0.2%; Other 4.9%). **Foreign born:** 4.2%. **Median age:** 39.4. **State rank:** 41. **Pop change 1990-2000:** +20.8%.

Income: per capita $16,309; median household $30,250. **Pop below poverty level:** 18%.

Unemployment: 4.3%. **Median home value:** $79,300. **Median travel time to work:** 23 minutes.

ALBEMARLE COUNTY
401 McIntire Rd   **Ph:** 434-296-5841
Charlottesville, VA 22902   **Fax:** 434-296-5800
www.co.albemarle.va.us

In central VA, northeast of Lynchburg; organized May 6, 1744 from Goochland County. **Name Origin:** For William Anne Keppel (1702-54), 2nd Earl of Albemarle, absentee governor of the colony of VA (1737-54).

Area (sq mi): 726.18 (land 722.61; water 3.58).

Pop: 79,236 (White 83.6%; Black or African American 9.7%; Hispanic or Latino 2.6%; Asian 2.9%; Other 2.4%). **Foreign born:** 7.3%. **Median age:** 37.4. **State rank:** 21. **Pop change 1990-2000:** +16.5%.

Income: per capita $28,852; median household $50,749. **Pop below poverty level:** 6.7%.

Unemployment: 1.8%. **Median home value:** $161,100. **Median travel time to work:** 22.3 minutes.

ALEXANDRIA (INDEPENDENT CITY)
301 King St Suite 2300   **Ph:** 703-838-4000
Alexandria, VA 22314   **Fax:** 703-838-6433
ci.alexandria.va.us

On the Potomac River, immediately south of Washington, D.C. Established 1749; incorporated as a town in 1779; as a city in 1852. **Name Origin:** For colonial settler John Alexander, who came to the area in 1669. Formerly known as Hunting Creek Warehouse and Belhaven.

Area (sq mi): 15.41 (land 15.18; water 0.23).

Pop: 128,283 (White 53.7%; Black or African American 22.5%; Hispanic or Latino 14.7%; Asian 5.7%; Other 12.1%). **Foreign born:** 25.4%. **Median age:** 34.4. **State rank:** 13. **Pop change 1990-2000:** +15.4%.

Income: per capita $37,645; median household $56,054. **Pop below poverty level:** 8.9%.

Unemployment: 2.8%. **Median home value:** $252,800. **Median travel time to work:** 29.7 minutes.

ALLEGHANY COUNTY
9212 Winterberry Ave Suite C   **Ph:** 540-863-6600
Covington, VA 24426   **Fax:** 540-863-6606

On the central western border of VA, north of Roanoke; organized 1822 from Bath and Botetourt counties, VA, and Monroe County (now WV). **Name Origin:** Probably for the Allegheny River, with a variant spelling.

Area (sq mi): 445.67 (land 444.63; water 1.04).

Pop: 12,926 (White 96.1%; Black or African American 2.5%; Hispanic or Latino 0.4%; Asian 0.2%; Other 0.9%). **Foreign born:** 0.9%. **Median age:** 41.1. **State rank:** 101. **Pop change 1990-2000:** -1.9%.

Income: per capita $19,635; median household $38,545. **Pop below poverty level:** 7.1%.

Unemployment: 3.8%. **Median home value:** $77,500. **Median travel time to work:** 24.6 minutes.

AMELIA COUNTY
PO Box A   **Ph:** 804-561-3039
Amelia Court House, VA 23002   **Fax:** 804-561-6039

In south-central VA, southwest of Richmond; organized Feb 1,

Please see sample entry on inside front cover for detailed information about the statistics presented with each county listing.

583

1734 from Brunswick and Prince George counties. **Name Origin:** For Amelia Sophia (1711-86), second daughter of George II (1683-1760) of England.

Area (sq mi): 358.54 (land 356.8; water 1.74).

Pop: 11,400 (White 70.2%; Black or African American 28.1%; Hispanic or Latino 0.8%; Asian 0.2%; Other 1.2%). **Foreign born:** 0.7%. **Median age:** 38.5. **State rank:** 111. **Pop change 1990-2000:** +29.7%.

Income: per capita $18,858; median household $40,252. **Pop below poverty level:** 8.4%.

Unemployment: 2.8%. **Median home value:** $92,400. **Median travel time to work:** 41.5 minutes.

AMHERST COUNTY

PO Box 390   **Ph:** 434-946-9400
Amherst, VA 24521   **Fax:** 434-946-9370
www.countyofamherst.com

In west-central VA, north of Lynchburg; organized 1761 from Albemarle County. **Name Origin:** For Lord Jeffery Amherst (1717-97), commander of British forces in North America during the French and Indian Wars.

Area (sq mi): 478.78 (land 475.18; water 3.6).

Pop: 31,894 (White 77.3%; Black or African American 19.8%; Hispanic or Latino 1%; Asian 0.4%; Other 2.1%). **Foreign born:** 1.2%. **Median age:** 38. **State rank:** 52. **Pop change 1990-2000:** +11.6%.

Income: per capita $16,952; median household $37,393. **Pop below poverty level:** 10.7%.

Unemployment: 3.8%. **Median home value:** $88,800. **Median travel time to work:** 23.6 minutes.

APPOMATTOX COUNTY

PO Box 672   **Ph:** 434-352-5275
Appomattox, VA 24522   **Fax:** 434-352-2781

In south-central VA, east of Lynchburg; organized 1845 from Buckingham, Campbell, Charlotte, and Prince Edward counties. **Name Origin:** For the Appomattox River, which runs through the county; origin of name is obscure: 'tobacco plant country' and 'curving tidal estuary' have been suggested. Apumetec is mentioned as an Indian queen in John Smith's (c.1580-1631) *The Generall Historie of Virginia, New-England, & the Summer Isles* (1624).

Area (sq mi): 334.73 (land 333.69; water 1.05).

Pop: 13,705 (White 75.7%; Black or African American 22.9%; Hispanic or Latino 0.5%; Asian 0.2%; Other 1%). **Foreign born:** 1.4%. **Median age:** 39.1. **State rank:** 96. **Pop change 1990-2000:** +11.4%.

Income: per capita $18,086; median household $36,507. **Pop below poverty level:** 11.4%.

Unemployment: 6.7%. **Median home value:** $81,600. **Median travel time to work:** 29 minutes.

ARLINGTON COUNTY

2100 Clarendon Blvd Suite 300   **Ph:** 703-228-3130
Arlington, VA 22201   **Fax:** 703-228-7430
www.co.arlington.va.us

On the northeastern border of VA, west of Washington, D.C. Established 1801 as Alexandria County of the Dist. of Columbia; in 1846

county was returned to VA; renamed March 16, 1920. Arlington functions politically as a county in VA. **Name Origin:** For the home of George Washington Parke Custis (1781-1857), grandson of Martha Washington (1732-1802), named for the 1st Earl of Arlington, Henry Bennet (1618-85) who shared Charles II's (1630-85) grant of the colony of VA. It was later the home of Gen. Robert E. Lee (1807-70).

Area (sq mi): 25.96 (land 25.87; water 0.09).

Pop: 189,453 (White 60.4%; Black or African American 9.3%; Hispanic or Latino 18.6%; Asian 8.6%; Other 13%). **Foreign born:** 27.8%. **Median age:** 34. **State rank:** 9. **Pop change 1990-2000:** +10.8%.

Income: per capita $37,706; median household $63,001. **Pop below poverty level:** 7.8%.

Unemployment: 2.3%. **Median home value:** $262,400. **Median travel time to work:** 27.3 minutes.

AUGUSTA COUNTY

PO Box 590   **Ph:** 540-245-5600
Verona, VA 24482   **Fax:** 540-245-5621
www.co.augusta.va.us

On the northwestern border of VA, west of Charlottesville; organized Aug 1, 1738 from Orange County. Part annexed to Waynesboro (independent) city effective July 1, 1994. **Name Origin:** For Princess Augusta of Saxe-Gotha (1719?-72), mother of George III of England.

Area (sq mi): 970.93 (land 970.36; water 0.57).

Pop: 65,615 (White 94.4%; Black or African American 3.6%; Hispanic or Latino 0.9%; Asian 0.3%; Other 1.1%). **Foreign born:** 1.4%. **Median age:** 39. **State rank:** 23. **Pop change 1990-2000:** +20%.

Income: per capita $19,744; median household $43,045. **Pop below poverty level:** 5.8%.

Unemployment: 2.8%. **Median home value:** $110,900. **Median travel time to work:** 23.7 minutes.

BATH COUNTY

PO Box 309   **Ph:** 540-839-7221
Warm Springs, VA 24484   **Fax:** 540-839-7222
www.bathcountyva.org

On the central western border of VA, west of Charlottesville; organized Dec 14, 1790 from Augusta and Botetourt counties, VA, and Greenbrier County (now WV). **Name Origin:** For the city in England, which was also famed for its hot springs.

Area (sq mi): 534.56 (land 531.86; water 2.7).

Pop: 5,048 (White 92%; Black or African American 6.3%; Hispanic or Latino 0.4%; Asian 0.4%; Other 1.1%). **Foreign born:** 4.3%. **Median age:** 41.8. **State rank:** 132. **Pop change 1990-2000:** +5.2%.

Income: per capita $23,092; median household $35,013. **Pop below poverty level:** 7.8%.

Unemployment: 4.6%. **Median home value:** $79,700. **Median travel time to work:** 24.4 minutes.

All statistics are based on the 2000 Census except the dollar figures given for per capita income, which are based on 1999 estimates.

BEDFORD (INDEPENDENT CITY)

215 E Main St   **Ph:** 540-587-6001
Bedford, VA 24523
www.ci.bedford.va.us

In south-central VA, between Roanoke and Lynchburg. Serves as county seat for Bedford County. Annexed part of Bedford County effective July 1, 1993. **Name Origin:** Incorporated as the town of Liberty in 1839; name changed to Bedford City in 1890 for John Russell (1710-71), the fourth Duke of Bedford; shortened to Bedford in 1912. Incorporated as a city in 1969.

Area (sq mi): 6.9 (land 6.89; water 0.01).

Pop: 6,299 (White 74.7%; Black or African American 22.4%; Hispanic or Latino 0.9%; Asian 0.6%; Other 1.7%). **Foreign born:** 1.6%. **Median age:** 40.9. **State rank:** 129. **Pop change 1990-2000:** +3.7%.

Income: per capita $15,423; median household $28,792. **Pop below poverty level:** 19.7%.

Unemployment: 3.5%. **Median home value:** $90,400. **Median travel time to work:** 20 minutes.

BEDFORD COUNTY

122 E Main St Suite 202   **Ph:** 540-586-7601
Bedford, VA 24523   **Fax:** 540-586-0406
www.co.bedford.va.us

In west-central VA, west of Lynchburg; organized 1753 from Albemarle and Lunenburg counties. Part annexed to Bedford (independent) city effective July 1, 1993. **Name Origin:** For John Russell (1710-71), 4th Duke of Bedford, British statesman who negotiated the treaty that ended the French and Indian Wars.

Area (sq mi): 769.25 (land 754.5; water 14.75).

Pop: 60,371 (White 91.7%; Black or African American 6.2%; Hispanic or Latino 0.7%; Asian 0.4%; Other 1.1%). **Foreign born:** 1.8%. **Median age:** 39.7. **State rank:** 27. **Pop change 1990-2000:** +32.2%.

Income: per capita $21,582; median household $43,136. **Pop below poverty level:** 7.1%.

Unemployment: 3.5%. **Median home value:** $127,000. **Median travel time to work:** 27.8 minutes.

BLAND COUNTY

PO Box 295   **Ph:** 276-688-4562
Bland, VA 24315   **Fax:** 276-688-4562

On the southwestern border of VA, west of Roanoke; organized Mar 30, 1861 from Giles, Tazewell, and Wythe counties. **Name Origin:** For Richard Bland (1710-76), member of the VA House of Burgesses (1745-75) and the Continental Congress (1774-75).

Area (sq mi): 358.73 (land 358.67; water 0.06).

Pop: 6,871 (White 94.5%; Black or African American 4.2%; Hispanic or Latino 0.5%; Asian 0.1%; Other 0.9%). **Foreign born:** 0.8%. **Median age:** 40.3. **State rank:** 122. **Pop change 1990-2000:** +5.5%.

Income: per capita $17,744; median household $30,397. **Pop below poverty level:** 12.4%.

Unemployment: 5.9%. **Median home value:** $71,500. **Median travel time to work:** 33.4 minutes.

BOTETOURT COUNTY

1 W Main St Rm 1   **Ph:** 540-473-8220
Fincastle, VA 24090
www.co.botetourt.va.us

In west-central VA, north of Roanoke; organized Nov 7, 1769 from Augusta County. **Name Origin:** For Norborne Berkeley, Baron de Botetourt, the penultimate English governor of VA (1769-70).

Area (sq mi): 545.94 (land 542.66; water 3.28).

Pop: 30,496 (White 94.5%; Black or African American 3.5%; Hispanic or Latino 0.6%; Asian 0.5%; Other 1.1%). **Foreign born:** 0.9%. **Median age:** 40.7. **State rank:** 54. **Pop change 1990-2000:** +22%.

Income: per capita $22,218; median household $48,731. **Pop below poverty level:** 5.2%.

Unemployment: 2.4%. **Median home value:** $130,500. **Median travel time to work:** 26.7 minutes.

BRISTOL (INDEPENDENT CITY)

497 Cumberland St City Hall Rm 210   **Ph:** 276-645-7321
Bristol, VA 24201   **Fax:** 276-645-7345
www.bristolva.org

In southwestern VA on the Tennessee border. **Name Origin:** Established in 1850 as Goodson, for Samuel Goodson, the founder; incorporated as a town in 1856. Incorporated as a city and renamed Bristol in 1890 for the contiguous town in TN of the same name.

Area (sq mi): 13.16 (land 12.9; water 0.27).

Pop: 17,367 (White 91.9%; Black or African American 5.6%; Hispanic or Latino 1%; Asian 0.4%; Other 1.5%). **Foreign born:** 1.4%. **Median age:** 41.3. **State rank:** 82. **Pop change 1990-2000:** -5.7%.

Income: per capita $17,311; median household $27,389. **Pop below poverty level:** 16.2%.

Unemployment: 4%. **Median home value:** $71,400. **Median travel time to work:** 18 minutes.

BRUNSWICK COUNTY

216 N Main St   **Ph:** 434-848-2215
Lawrenceville, VA 23868   **Fax:** 434-848-4307

On the central southern border of VA, southwest of Richmond; organized Nov 2, 1720 from Prince George, Isle of Wight, and Surry counties (prior to statehood). **Name Origin:** For the Royal House of Brunswick, one of the titles of the British royal house of Hanover (the latter was changed to Windsor during World War I to sound less German).

Area (sq mi): 569.37 (land 566.14; water 3.23).

Pop: 18,419 (White 41.4%; Black or African American 56.9%; Hispanic or Latino 1.3%; Asian 0.2%; Other 0.9%). **Foreign born:** 0.7%. **Median age:** 38.1. **State rank:** 79. **Pop change 1990-2000:** +15.2%.

Income: per capita $14,890; median household $31,288. **Pop below poverty level:** 16.5%.

Unemployment: 5.3%. **Median home value:** $73,000. **Median travel time to work:** 30.8 minutes.

Please see sample entry on inside front cover for detailed information about the statistics presented with each county listing.

585

BUCHANAN COUNTY

PO Box 950   **Ph:** 276-935-6500
Grundy, VA 24614   **Fax:** 276-935-4479

On the southwestern border of VA, north of Bristol, TN; organized Feb 13, 1858 from Tazewell and Russell counties. **Name Origin:** For James Buchanan (1791-1868), fifteenth U.S. president.

Area (sq mi): 503.88 (land 503.88; water 0).

Pop: 26,978 (White 96.4%; Black or African American 2.6%; Hispanic or Latino 0.5%; Asian 0.1%; Other 0.5%). **Foreign born:** 0.3%. **Median age:** 38.8. **State rank:** 59. **Pop change 1990-2000:** -13.9%.

Income: per capita $12,788; median household $22,213. **Pop below poverty level:** 23.2%.

Unemployment: 7.7%. **Median home value:** $55,400. **Median travel time to work:** 33.4 minutes.

BUCKINGHAM COUNTY

PO Box 252   **Ph:** 434-969-4242
Buckingham, VA 23921   **Fax:** 434-969-1638

In south-central VA, east of Lynchburg; organized 1761 from Albemarle County. **Name Origin:** Either for the town in Buckinghamshire, England, or the dukedom held by George Villiers and his son, George.

Area (sq mi): 583.56 (land 580.86; water 2.7).

Pop: 15,623 (White 58.8%; Black or African American 39.1%; Hispanic or Latino 0.8%; Asian 0.2%; Other 1.7%). **Foreign born:** 0.8%. **Median age:** 38.2. **State rank:** 91. **Pop change 1990-2000:** +21.4%.

Income: per capita $13,669; median household $29,882. **Pop below poverty level:** 20%.

Unemployment: 2.6%. **Median home value:** $74,900. **Median travel time to work:** 38.8 minutes.

BUENA VISTA (INDEPENDENT CITY)

2039 Sycamore Ave   **Ph:** 540-261-8611
Buena Vista, VA 24416   **Fax:** 540-261-8727
www.buenavistavirginia.org

In south-central VA, north of Lynchburg. Established 1889; incorporated as a town in 1890, and as a city in 1892. **Name Origin:** The town was built on the site of an abandoned iron furnace, dubbed Buena Vista, because it supplied cannonballs used in the Battle of Buena Vista in the Mexican-American War.

Area (sq mi): 6.83 (land 6.83; water 0).

Pop: 6,349 (White 92.8%; Black or African American 4.8%; Hispanic or Latino 1%; Asian 0.4%; Other 1.2%). **Foreign born:** 0.5%. **Median age:** 37.9. **State rank:** 127. **Pop change 1990-2000:** -0.9%.

Income: per capita $16,377; median household $32,410. **Pop below poverty level:** 10.4%.

Unemployment: 3.3%. **Median home value:** $72,900. **Median travel time to work:** 19.6 minutes.

CAMPBELL COUNTY

PO Box 100   **Ph:** 434-332-9599
Rustburg, VA 24588   **Fax:** 434-332-9605
www.co.campbell.va.us

In south-central VA, south of Lynchburg; organized Nov 5, 1781 from Bedford County. **Name Origin:** For Gen. William Campbell (1745-81), officer in the American Revolution.

Area (sq mi): 507.26 (land 504.48; water 2.78).

Pop: 51,078 (White 82.8%; Black or African American 14.7%; Hispanic or Latino 0.8%; Asian 0.6%; Other 1.4%). **Foreign born:** 1.1%. **Median age:** 38.3. **State rank:** 33. **Pop change 1990-2000:** +7.4%.

Income: per capita $18,134; median household $37,280. **Pop below poverty level:** 10.6%.

Unemployment: 5%. **Median home value:** $96,900. **Median travel time to work:** 23.5 minutes.

CAROLINE COUNTY

PO Box 447   **Ph:** 804-633-5380
Bowling Green, VA 22427   **Fax:** 804-633-4970
www.co.caroline.va.us

In east-central VA, north of Richmond; organized Feb 1, 1727 from Essex, King and Queen, and King William counties. **Name Origin:** For Princess Wilhelmina Carolina of Anspach (1683-1737), wife of George II of England.

Area (sq mi): 538.89 (land 532.52; water 6.36).

Pop: 22,121 (White 62%; Black or African American 34.4%; Hispanic or Latino 1.3%; Asian 0.4%; Other 2.7%). **Foreign born:** 1.7%. **Median age:** 37.7. **State rank:** 71. **Pop change 1990-2000:** +15.1%.

Income: per capita $18,342; median household $39,845. **Pop below poverty level:** 9.4%.

Unemployment: 3.1%. **Median home value:** $88,900. **Median travel time to work:** 37.7 minutes.

CARROLL COUNTY

605-1 Pine St   **Ph:** 276-728-3331
Hillsville, VA 24343   **Fax:** 276-728-4938
www.co.carroll.va.us

On the southwestern border of VA, southwest of Roanoke; organized Jan 17, 1842 from Grayson County. **Name Origin:** For Charles Carroll (1737-1832), signer of the Declaration of Independence, U.S. senator from MD (1789-92), and founder of the Baltimore and Ohio Railroad.

Area (sq mi): 477.64 (land 476.34; water 1.3).

Pop: 29,245 (White 97.2%; Black or African American 0.4%; Hispanic or Latino 1.6%; Asian 0.1%; Other 1.4%). **Foreign born:** 0.9%. **Median age:** 40.7. **State rank:** 57. **Pop change 1990-2000:** +10%.

Income: per capita $16,475; median household $30,597. **Pop below poverty level:** 12.5%.

Unemployment: 10.9%. **Median home value:** $68,900. **Median travel time to work:** 26.5 minutes.

All statistics are based on the 2000 Census except the dollar figures given for per capita income, which are based on 1999 estimates.

CHARLES CITY COUNTY

PO Box 128   **Ph:** 804-829-9201
Charles City, VA 23030   **Fax:** 804-829-5819

In east-central VA, west of Williamsburg; original county; organized 1634. Birthplace of two U.S. presidents: William Henry Harrison (1773-1841) and John Tyler (1790-1862). **Name Origin:** For Charles I (1600-49), king of Great Britain.

Area (sq mi): 204.22 (land 182.76; water 21.46).

Pop: 6,926 (White 35.4%; Black or African American 54.9%; Hispanic or Latino 0.6%; Asian 0.1%; Other 9.4%). **Foreign born:** 1.3%. **Median age:** 39.9. **State rank:** 121. **Pop change 1990-2000:** +10.3%.

Income: per capita $19,182; median household $42,745. **Pop below poverty level:** 10.6%.

Unemployment: 6.1%. **Median home value:** $86,700. **Median travel time to work:** 34.6 minutes.

CHARLOTTE COUNTY

PO Box 38   **Ph:** 434-542-5147
Charlotte Court House, VA 23923   **Fax:** 434-542-4336
www.co.charlotte.va.us

In south-central VA, southeast of Lynchburg; organized Mar 1, 1765 from Lunenburg County. **Name Origin:** For Charlotte Sophia, Princess of Mecklenburg-Strelitz (1744-1818) wife of George III (1738-1820) of England.

Area (sq mi): 477.44 (land 474.99; water 2.45).

Pop: 12,472 (White 64.6%; Black or African American 32.9%; Hispanic or Latino 1.7%; Asian 0.2%; Other 1.4%). **Foreign born:** 0.8%. **Median age:** 40. **State rank:** 105. **Pop change 1990-2000:** +6.7%.

Income: per capita $14,717; median household $28,929. **Pop below poverty level:** 18.1%.

Unemployment: 4.2%. **Median home value:** $72,700. **Median travel time to work:** 31.3 minutes.

CHARLOTTESVILLE (INDEPENDENT CITY)

PO Box 911   **Ph:** 434-970-3101
Charlottesville, VA 22902   **Fax:** 434-970-3890
www.charlottesville.org

In central VA, 70 mi. northwest of Richmond. Established 1762; incorporated as a town in 1802; as a city in 1888. Site of University of VA. Serves as county seat for Albemarle County. **Name Origin:** For Princess Charlotte Sophia of Mecklenberg-Stelitz (1744-1818), wife of King George III (1738-1820) of Great Britian.

Area (sq mi): 10.26 (land 10.26; water 0).

Pop: 45,049 (White 68.4%; Black or African American 22.2%; Hispanic or Latino 2.4%; Asian 4.9%; Other 3.2%). **Foreign born:** 6.9%. **Median age:** 25.6. **State rank:** 37. **Pop change 1990-2000:** +11.7%.

Income: per capita $16,973; median household $31,007. **Pop below poverty level:** 25.9%.

Unemployment: 2.6%. **Median home value:** $119,000. **Median travel time to work:** 16.6 minutes.

CHESAPEAKE (INDEPENDENT CITY)

306 Cedar Rd   **Ph:** 757-382-6151
Chesapeake, VA 23322   **Fax:** 757-382-6678
www.chesapeake.va.us

In southeastern VA, southeast of Norfolk. Formed in 1963 by merger of Norfolk County and the former city of South Norfolk, both of which then became extinct. **Name Origin:** For Chesapeake Bay.

Area (sq mi): 350.9 (land 340.72; water 10.18).

Pop: 199,184 (White 65.9%; Black or African American 28.5%; Hispanic or Latino 2%; Asian 1.8%; Other 2.8%). **Foreign born:** 3%. **Median age:** 34.7. **State rank:** 7. **Pop change 1990-2000:** +31.1%.

Income: per capita $20,949; median household $50,743. **Pop below poverty level:** 7.3%.

Unemployment: 2.9%. **Median home value:** $122,300. **Median travel time to work:** 25.1 minutes.

CHESTERFIELD COUNTY

PO Box 40   **Ph:** 804-748-1000
Chesterfield, VA 23832   **Fax:** 804-778-7939
www.co.chesterfield.va.us

In east-central VA, south of Richmond; organized May 1, 1749 from Henrico County. **Name Origin:** For Philip Dormer Stanhope (1694-1773), 4th Earl of Chesterfield, English statesman and writer.

Area (sq mi): 436.99 (land 425.75; water 11.23).

Pop: 259,903 (White 75.4%; Black or African American 17.8%; Hispanic or Latino 2.9%; Asian 2.4%; Other 3%). **Foreign born:** 5.2%. **Median age:** 35.7. **State rank:** 5. **Pop change 1990-2000:** +24.2%.

Income: per capita $25,286; median household $58,537. **Pop below poverty level:** 4.5%.

Unemployment: 2.5%. **Median home value:** $120,500. **Median travel time to work:** 26.1 minutes.

CLARKE COUNTY

102 N Church St   **Ph:** 540-955-5100
Berryville, VA 22611   **Fax:** 540-955-4002
www.co.clarke.va.us

On northern border of VA, northwest of Arlington; organized Mar 8, 1836 from Frederick and Warren counties. **Name Origin:** Alternate spelling for George Rogers Clark (1752-1818), a general in the American Revolution and frontiersman in the Northwest Territory.

Area (sq mi): 178.19 (land 176.62; water 1.57).

Pop: 12,652 (White 90.3%; Black or African American 6.7%; Hispanic or Latino 1.5%; Asian 0.5%; Other 1.7%). **Foreign born:** 2.5%. **Median age:** 40.6. **State rank:** 102. **Pop change 1990-2000:** +4.6%.

Income: per capita $24,844; median household $51,601. **Pop below poverty level:** 6.6%.

Unemployment: 1.8%. **Median home value:** $139,500. **Median travel time to work:** 32.4 minutes.

Please see sample entry on inside front cover for detailed information about the statistics presented with each county listing.

587

COLONIAL HEIGHTS (INDEPENDENT CITY)

PO Box 3401   **Ph:** 804-520-9265
Colonial Heights, VA 23834   **Fax:** 804-520-9207
www.colonial-heights.com

In southeastern VA on the heights overlooking the Appomattox River. Established 1910; incorporated as a town in 1926; as a city in 1948. **Name Origin:** For the Marquis de Lafayette's (1757-1834) artillery, known as the Colonials, which he placed here to shell British positions in Petersburg during the American Revolution.

Area (sq mi): 7.79 (land 7.48; water 0.31).

Pop: 16,897 (White 88.3%; Black or African American 6.3%; Hispanic or Latino 1.6%; Asian 2.7%; Other 1.9%). **Foreign born:** 4.9%. **Median age:** 39.9. **State rank:** 83. **Pop change 1990-2000:** +5.2%.

Income: per capita $23,659; median household $43,224. **Pop below poverty level:** 5.5%.

Unemployment: 3.5%. **Median home value:** $94,800. **Median travel time to work:** 20.7 minutes.

COVINGTON (INDEPENDENT CITY)

333 W Locust St   **Ph:** 540-965-6300
Covington, VA 24426   **Fax:** 540-965-6303
www.covington.va.us

In south-central VA, north of Roanoke. Established 1818; incorporated as a town in 1833, as a city in 1953. Serves as county seat for Alleghany County. **Name Origin:** For Peter Covington, an early settler.

Area (sq mi): 5.67 (land 5.67; water 0).

Pop: 6,303 (White 83.6%; Black or African American 13.1%; Hispanic or Latino 0.6%; Asian 0.7%; Other 2.1%). **Foreign born:** 2.3%. **Median age:** 40.5. **State rank:** 128. **Pop change 1990-2000:** -9.8%.

Income: per capita $16,758; median household $30,325. **Pop below poverty level:** 12.9%.

Unemployment: 5.4%. **Median home value:** $52,500. **Median travel time to work:** 19.2 minutes.

CRAIG COUNTY

PO Box 185   **Ph:** 540-864-6141
New Castle, VA 24127   **Fax:** 540-864-7471
www.co.craig.va.us

On the central western border of VA, west of Roanoke; organized Mar 21, 1851 from Botetourt, Roanoke, Giles, and Monroe counties. **Name Origin:** For Robert Craig (1792-1852), U.S. representative from VA (1829-33; 1835-41).

Area (sq mi): 330.61 (land 330.61; water 0).

Pop: 5,091 (White 98.7%; Black or African American 0.2%; Hispanic or Latino 0.3%; Asian 0.2%; Other 0.7%). **Foreign born:** 0.3%. **Median age:** 39.6. **State rank:** 131. **Pop change 1990-2000:** +16.4%.

Income: per capita $17,322; median household $37,314. **Pop below poverty level:** 10.3%.

Unemployment: 3.3%. **Median home value:** $85,400. **Median travel time to work:** 34.7 minutes.

CULPEPER COUNTY

302 N Main St   **Ph:** 540-727-3427
Culpeper, VA 22701   **Fax:** 540-727-3460
www.co.culpeper.va.us

In north-central VA, northeast of Charlottesville; organized Mar 23, 1748 from Orange County. **Name Origin:** For Sir Thomas Culpeper (1635-89), colonial governor of VA. Also spelled Culpepper or Colepeper.

Area (sq mi): 382.28 (land 381; water 1.27).

Pop: 34,262 (White 77.1%; Black or African American 18.2%; Hispanic or Latino 2.5%; Asian 0.7%; Other 2.8%). **Foreign born:** 3.5%. **Median age:** 36.5. **State rank:** 47. **Pop change 1990-2000:** +23.3%.

Income: per capita $20,162; median household $45,290. **Pop below poverty level:** 9.2%.

Unemployment: 2.1%. **Median home value:** $123,300. **Median travel time to work:** 37.9 minutes.

CUMBERLAND COUNTY

1 Courthouse Cir   **Ph:** 804-492-4280
Cumberland, VA 23040   **Fax:** 804-492-3342

In south-central VA, west of Richmond; organized 1749 from Goochland County. **Name Origin:** For William Augustus, Duke of Cumberland (1721-65), British general and second son of George II (1683-1760) of England.

Area (sq mi): 299.73 (land 298.45; water 1.28).

Pop: 9,017 (White 59.7%; Black or African American 37.4%; Hispanic or Latino 1.7%; Asian 0.4%; Other 1.9%). **Foreign born:** 1.3%. **Median age:** 38.4. **State rank:** 117. **Pop change 1990-2000:** +15.2%.

Income: per capita $15,103; median household $31,816. **Pop below poverty level:** 15.1%.

Unemployment: 2.3%. **Median home value:** $79,300. **Median travel time to work:** 36.9 minutes.

DANVILLE (INDEPENDENT CITY)

PO Box 3300   **Ph:** 434-799-5168
Danville, VA 24543   **Fax:** 434-799-6502
www.ci.danville.va.us

In southern VA on the Dan River, just north of the NC border. Established 1793; incorporated as a town in 1830; as a city in 1890. **Name Origin:** For its location on the Dan River.

Area (sq mi): 43.94 (land 43.06; water 0.88).

Pop: 48,411 (White 53.3%; Black or African American 44.1%; Hispanic or Latino 1.3%; Asian 0.6%; Other 1.5%). **Foreign born:** 1.4%. **Median age:** 40.5. **State rank:** 34. **Pop change 1990-2000:** -8.8%.

Income: per capita $17,151; median household $26,900. **Pop below poverty level:** 20%.

Unemployment: 8.6%. **Median home value:** $71,900. **Median travel time to work:** 18.7 minutes.

All statistics are based on the 2000 Census except the dollar figures given for per capita income, which are based on 1999 estimates.

DICKENSON COUNTY

PO Box 190   **Ph:** 276-926-1616
Clintwood, VA 24228   **Fax:** 276-926-6465
www.dickensonctyva.com

On the southwestern border of VA, north of Bristol, TN; organized Mar 3, 1880 from Buchanan, Russell, and Wise counties. **Name Origin:** For William J. Dickenson (1828-1907), lawyer and legislator.

Area (sq mi): 333.63 (land 331.71; water 1.91).

Pop: 16,395 (White 98.6%; Black or African American 0.4%; Hispanic or Latino 0.4%; Asian 0.1%; Other 0.6%). **Foreign born:** 0.2%. **Median age:** 39.7. **State rank:** 88. **Pop change 1990-2000:** -7%.

Income: per capita $12,822; median household $23,431. **Pop below poverty level:** 21.3%.

Unemployment: 16.9%. **Median home value:** $55,900. **Median travel time to work:** 35.8 minutes.

DINWIDDIE COUNTY

PO Drawer 70   **Ph:** 804-469-4500
Dinwiddie, VA 23841   **Fax:** 804-469-4503

In southeastern VA, south of Richmond; organized Feb 27, 1752 from Prince George County. **Name Origin:** For Robert Dinwiddie (1693-1770), lieutenant governor of VA (1751-58).

Area (sq mi): 506.98 (land 503.67; water 3.31).

Pop: 24,533 (White 64.1%; Black or African American 33.7%; Hispanic or Latino 1%; Asian 0.3%; Other 1.4%). **Foreign born:** 1.4%. **Median age:** 38.5. **State rank:** 63. **Pop change 1990-2000:** +17%.

Income: per capita $19,122; median household $41,582. **Pop below poverty level:** 9.3%.

Unemployment: 2.9%. **Median home value:** $86,900. **Median travel time to work:** 30.8 minutes.

EMPORIA (INDEPENDENT CITY)

PO Box 511   **Ph:** 434-634-3332
Emporia, VA 23847   **Fax:** 434-634-0003
www.ci.emporia.va.us

In southeastern VA, southwest of Norfolk. Incorporated in 1887 from the merger of Hicksford and Belfield. Charter revoked in 1888; reincorporated in 1892; became a city in 1967. Serves as county seat for Greensville County. **Name Origin:** Named in 1887 to indicate that it was to be a center of trade.

Area (sq mi): 6.97 (land 6.89; water 0.07).

Pop: 5,665 (White 41.3%; Black or African American 56.2%; Hispanic or Latino 1.5%; Asian 0.5%; Other 0.9%). **Foreign born:** 3.2%. **Median age:** 38.8. **State rank:** 130. **Pop change 1990-2000:** +6.8%.

Income: per capita $15,377; median household $30,333. **Pop below poverty level:** 16%.

Unemployment: 4.4%. **Median home value:** $68,700. **Median travel time to work:** 19.6 minutes.

ESSEX COUNTY

PO Box 445   **Ph:** 804-443-3541
Tappahannock, VA 22560   **Fax:** 804-445-1216

In east-central VA, on west bank of the Rappahannock River; organized Apr 16, 1692 from Old Rappahannock County, which was organized 1656 from Lancaster County and abolished in 1692. **Name Origin:** For the county of Essex, England.

Area (sq mi): 285.91 (land 257.77; water 28.14).

Pop: 9,989 (White 57.7%; Black or African American 39%; Hispanic or Latino 0.7%; Asian 0.8%; Other 2.2%). **Foreign born:** 1.4%. **Median age:** 40.3. **State rank:** 114. **Pop change 1990-2000:** +15%.

Income: per capita $17,994; median household $37,395. **Pop below poverty level:** 11.2%.

Unemployment: 4.6%. **Median home value:** $98,700. **Median travel time to work:** 33.5 minutes.

FAIRFAX (INDEPENDENT CITY)

10455 Armstrong St   **Ph:** 703-385-7855
Fairfax, VA 22030   **Fax:** 703-385-7811
www.ci.fairfax.va.us

In northeastern VA, west of Washington, D.C. Incorporated as a town in 1874; as a city in 1961. Site of George Mason University. Serves as county seat for Fairfax County. Annexed parts of Fairfax County effective December 31, 1991 and January 1, 1994. **Name Origin:** Established in 1805 as Providence. After the former town of Fairfax (now Culpepper, in Culpepper County), named for Thomas, Lord Fairfax (1692-1780), one of the early great landowners, changed its name in 1859, Providence renamed itself Fairfax.

Area (sq mi): 6.31 (land 6.31; water 0).

Pop: 21,498 (White 66.7%; Black or African American 5.1%; Hispanic or Latino 13.6%; Asian 12.2%; Other 9.9%). **Foreign born:** 25.4%. **Median age:** 37. **State rank:** 72. **Pop change 1990-2000:** +9.6%.

Income: per capita $31,247; median household $67,642. **Pop below poverty level:** 5.7%.

Unemployment: 0.7%. **Median home value:** $192,100. **Median travel time to work:** 30.1 minutes.

FAIRFAX COUNTY

12000 Government Ctr Pkwy   **Ph:** 703-324-2531
Fairfax, VA 22035   **Fax:** 703-324-3956
www.co.fairfax.va.us

On the northeastern border of VA, west of Washington, D.C.; organized May 6, 1742 from Prince William County. Parts annexed to Fairfax (independent) city effective December 31, 1991 and January 1, 1994. **Name Origin:** For Thomas, 6th Baron Fairfax of Cameron (1692-1780), inheritor of the 'Fairfax Proprietary,' vast estates in northern VA; the colonies' only resident peer.

Area (sq mi): 406.61 (land 395.04; water 11.57).

Pop: 969,749 (White 64.4%; Black or African American 8.6%; Hispanic or Latino 11%; Asian 13%; Other 8.6%). **Foreign born:** 24.5%. **Median age:** 35.9. **State rank:** 1. **Pop change 1990-2000:** +18.5%.

Income: per capita $36,888; median household $81,050. **Pop below poverty level:** 4.5%.

Please see sample entry on inside front cover for detailed information about the statistics presented with each county listing.

Unemployment: 2.3%. **Median home value:** $233,300. **Median travel time to work:** 30.7 minutes.

FALLS CHURCH (INDEPENDENT CITY)

300 Park Ave   **Ph:** 703-248-5001
Falls Church, VA 22046   **Fax:** 703-248-5146
www.ci.falls-church.va.us

In northeastern VA, west of Washington, D.C., near the Little Falls of the Potomac River. Established in 1850, incorporated as a town in 1875; as a city in 1948. **Name Origin:** For an Anglican church, so named for its location near the falls, built in the area about 1769.

Area (sq mi): 1.99 (land 1.99; water 0).

Pop: 10,377 (White 79.6%; Black or African American 3.3%; Hispanic or Latino 8.4%; Asian 6.5%; Other 5.2%). **Foreign born:** 16.1%. **Median age:** 39.7. **State rank:** 112. **Pop change 1990-2000:** +8.3%.

Income: per capita $41,051; median household $74,924. **Pop below poverty level:** 4.2%.

Unemployment: 2.6%. **Median home value:** $277,100. **Median travel time to work:** 26.4 minutes.

FAUQUIER COUNTY

40 Culpeper St   **Ph:** 540-347-8680
Warrenton, VA 20186   **Fax:** 540-349-2331
www.fauquiercounty.gov

In north-central VA, west of Alexandria; organized May 1, 1759 from Prince William County. **Name Origin:** For Francis Fauquier (1704-68), lieutenant governor of the colony of VA (1758-68).

Area (sq mi): 651.42 (land 649.7; water 1.72).

Pop: 55,139 (White 87.2%; Black or African American 8.8%; Hispanic or Latino 2%; Asian 0.6%; Other 2.2%). **Foreign born:** 3.6%. **Median age:** 37.8. **State rank:** 31. **Pop change 1990-2000:** +13.1%.

Income: per capita $28,757; median household $61,999. **Pop below poverty level:** 5.4%.

Unemployment: 1.7%. **Median home value:** $162,700. **Median travel time to work:** 36.8 minutes.

FLOYD COUNTY

PO Box 218   **Ph:** 540-745-9300
Floyd, VA 24091   **Fax:** 540-745-9305
www.fin.org

In southwestern VA, southwest of Roanoke; organized Jan 15, 1831 from Montgomery and Franklin counties. **Name Origin:** For Gen. John Floyd (1783-1837), U.S. representative (1817-29) and governor of VA (1830-34).

Area (sq mi): 381.23 (land 381.22; water 0.01).

Pop: 13,874 (White 95.7%; Black or African American 2%; Hispanic or Latino 1.3%; Asian 0.1%; Other 1.2%). **Foreign born:** 1.5%. **Median age:** 40.5. **State rank:** 95. **Pop change 1990-2000:** +15.6%.

Income: per capita $16,345; median household $31,585. **Pop below poverty level:** 11.7%.

Unemployment: 4.5%. **Median home value:** $79,700. **Median travel time to work:** 33.6 minutes.

FLUVANNA COUNTY

PO Box540   **Ph:** 434-591-1910
Palmyra, VA 22963   **Fax:** 434-591-1911
www.co.fluvanna.va.us

In central VA, southeast of Charlottesville; organized May 5, 1777 from Albemarle County. **Name Origin:** For the name by which the upper James River was known until the Civil War; from Latin *fluvius* 'river,' and *anna* for Queen Anne (1665-1714) of England.

Area (sq mi): 290.21 (land 287.37; water 2.84).

Pop: 20,047 (White 78.8%; Black or African American 18.4%; Hispanic or Latino 1.2%; Asian 0.4%; Other 1.7%). **Foreign born:** 2.3%. **Median age:** 38.3. **State rank:** 74. **Pop change 1990-2000:** +61.3%.

Income: per capita $20,338; median household $46,372. **Pop below poverty level:** 5.9%.

Unemployment: 2.1%. **Median home value:** $111,300. **Median travel time to work:** 32.5 minutes.

FRANKLIN (INDEPENDENT CITY)

120 Pretlow St   **Ph:** 757-562-8559
Franklin, VA 23851   **Fax:** 757-562-8561
www.ci.franklin.va.us

In southeastern VA, southwest of Norfolk. Incorporated as a town in 1876; as a city in 1961. Annexed part of Southampton County effective December 31, 1995. **Name Origin:** Origin unclear: possibly for patriot and statesman Benjamin Franklin (1707-90) or for a local storekeeper named Franklin. One story has it that the name originated from the exclamation of a railroad section foreman who, upon driving a spike while working here, said, 'This shall be Franklin!'

Area (sq mi): 8.4 (land 8.35; water 0.05).

Pop: 8,346 (White 45.5%; Black or African American 52.3%; Hispanic or Latino 0.6%; Asian 0.8%; Other 1.1%). **Foreign born:** 0.7%. **Median age:** 39.9. **State rank:** 119. **Pop change 1990-2000:** +6.1%.

Income: per capita $18,573; median household $31,687. **Pop below poverty level:** 19.8%.

Unemployment: 4.5%. **Median home value:** $94,900. **Median travel time to work:** 20.9 minutes.

FRANKLIN COUNTY

40 E Court St   **Ph:** 540-483-3030
Rocky Mount, VA 24151   **Fax:** 540-483-3035
www.franklincountyva.org

In southwestern VA, south of Roanoke; organized Oct 17, 1785 from Bedford, Henry, and Patrick counties. **Name Origin:** For Benjamin Franklin (1706-90), U.S. patriot, diplomat, and statesman.

Area (sq mi): 711.56 (land 692.08; water 19.48).

Pop: 47,286 (White 88.3%; Black or African American 9.3%; Hispanic or Latino 1.2%; Asian 0.4%; Other 1.3%). **Foreign born:** 1.4%. **Median age:** 39.7. **State rank:** 36. **Pop change 1990-2000:** +19.6%.

Income: per capita $19,605; median household $38,056. **Pop below poverty level:** 9.7%.

All statistics are based on the 2000 Census except the dollar figures given for per capita income, which are based on 1999 estimates.

Unemployment: 4.7%. **Median home value:** $105,000. **Median travel time to work:** 29.1 minutes.

FREDERICK COUNTY

107 N Kent St   **Ph:** 540-665-5600
Winchester, VA 22601   **Fax:** 540-667-0370
www.co.frederick.va.us

On the northern border of VA; organized Aug 1, 1738 from Orange County. **Name Origin:** For Frederick Louis (1707-51), Prince of Wales, son of George II (1683-1760) and father of George III (1738-1820) of England.

Area (sq mi): 415.62 (land 414.63; water 1).

Pop: 59,209 (White 94%; Black or African American 2.6%; Hispanic or Latino 1.7%; Asian 0.7%; Other 1.8%). **Foreign born:** 2.4%. **Median age:** 36.7. **State rank:** 28. **Pop change 1990-2000:** +29.5%.

Income: per capita $21,080; median household $46,941. **Pop below poverty level:** 6.4%.

Unemployment: 2.6%. **Median home value:** $118,300. **Median travel time to work:** 27.3 minutes.

FREDERICKSBURG (INDEPENDENT CITY)

PO Box 7447   **Ph:** 540-372-1010
Fredericksburg, VA 22404 **Fax:** 540-372-1201
fredericksburgchamber.org

In northeastern VA on the Rappahannock River, 41 mi. southwest of Alexandria. Founded 1728; incorporated as a town in 1782; as a city in 1879. **Name Origin:** For Frederick Louis (1707-51), Prince of Wales, eldest son of King George II (1683-1760) of Great Britain.

Area (sq mi): 10.52 (land 10.52; water 0).

Pop: 19,279 (White 71.4%; Black or African American 20.4%; Hispanic or Latino 4.9%; Asian 1.5%; Other 4.9%). **Foreign born:** 5.2%. **Median age:** 30.3. **State rank:** 78. **Pop change 1990-2000:** +1.3%.

Income: per capita $21,527; median household $34,585. **Pop below poverty level:** 15.5%.

Unemployment: 4%. **Median home value:** $135,800. **Median travel time to work:** 24.6 minutes.

GALAX (INDEPENDENT CITY)

111 E Grayson St   **Ph:** 276-236-5773
Galax, VA 24333   **Fax:** 276-236-2889

In southern VA, southwest of Roanoke. Incorporated as a town in 1906; as a city in 1954. **Name Origin:** For the mountain evergreen plant, which grows abundantly in the area. Originally called Bonaparte.

Area (sq mi): 8.23 (land 8.23; water 0).

Pop: 6,837 (White 81.2%; Black or African American 6.3%; Hispanic or Latino 11.1%; Asian 0.7%; Other 7%). **Foreign born:** 8.6%. **Median age:** 39.8. **State rank:** 124. **Pop change 1990-2000:** +2.5%.

Income: per capita $17,447; median household $28,236. **Pop below poverty level:** 18.6%.

Unemployment: 8.3%. **Median home value:** $70,300. **Median travel time to work:** 15.7 minutes.

GILES COUNTY

PO Box 502   **Ph:** 540-921-1722
Pearisburg, VA 24134 **Fax:** 540-921-3825
www.gilescounty.org

On the southwestern border of VA, west of Roanoke; organized Jan 16, 1806 from Montgomery and Tazewell counties, VA, and Monroe County (now WV). **Name Origin:** For William Branch Giles (1762-1830), U.S. senator from VA (1804-15) and governor (1827-30).

Area (sq mi): 360.4 (land 357.33; water 3.07).

Pop: 16,657 (White 96.9%; Black or African American 1.6%; Hispanic or Latino 0.6%; Asian 0.2%; Other 0.8%). **Foreign born:** 0.8%. **Median age:** 40.2. **State rank:** 87. **Pop change 1990-2000:** +1.8%.

Income: per capita $18,396; median household $34,927. **Pop below poverty level:** 9.5%.

Unemployment: 6.9%. **Median home value:** $69,200. **Median travel time to work:** 28.2 minutes.

GLOUCESTER COUNTY

PO Box 329   **Ph:** 804-693-4042
Gloucester, VA 23061 **Fax:** 804-693-6004
www.co.gloucester.va.us

On the central eastern border of VA, on east bank of the York River; organized 1651 from York County. **Name Origin:** For Henry, Duke of Gloucester (1639-60), brother of Charles II (1630-85) and James II (1633-1701) of England.

Area (sq mi): 288 (land 216.61; water 71.39).

Pop: 34,780 (White 85.7%; Black or African American 10.3%; Hispanic or Latino 1.6%; Asian 0.7%; Other 2.3%). **Foreign born:** 1.9%. **Median age:** 38. **State rank:** 46. **Pop change 1990-2000:** +15.4%.

Income: per capita $19,990; median household $45,421. **Pop below poverty level:** 7.7%.

Unemployment: 2.4%. **Median home value:** $111,600. **Median travel time to work:** 33.9 minutes.

GOOCHLAND COUNTY

2938 River Rd W   **Ph:** 804-556-5300
Goochland, VA 23063 **Fax:** 804-556-4617
www.co.goochland.va.us

In central VA, northwest of Richmond; organized Feb 1, 1727 from Henrico County. **Name Origin:** For Sir William Gooch (1681-1751), governor of the colony of VA (1727-49).

Area (sq mi): 289.99 (land 284.43; water 5.56).

Pop: 16,863 (White 72.3%; Black or African American 25.6%; Hispanic or Latino 0.9%; Asian 0.5%; Other 1.2%). **Foreign born:** 2%. **Median age:** 40.5. **State rank:** 84. **Pop change 1990-2000:** +19.1%.

Income: per capita $29,105; median household $56,307. **Pop below poverty level:** 6.9%.

Unemployment: 2.2%. **Median home value:** $149,800. **Median travel time to work:** 32.1 minutes.

Please see sample entry on inside front cover for detailed information about the statistics presented with each county listing.

GRAYSON COUNTY

129 Davis St   **Ph:** 276-773-2231
Independence, VA 24348   **Fax:** 276-773-3338
www.ls.net/~grayson/index.html

On the southwestern border of VA, east of Bristol, TN; organized Nov 7, 1792 from Wythe County. **Name Origin:** For Col. William Grayson (1736/40-90), an officer in the Revolutionary War, member of the Continental Congress (1785-87), and U.S. senator from VA (1789-90).

Area (sq mi): 445.9 (land 442.64; water 3.26).

Pop: 17,917 (White 90.9%; Black or African American 6.8%; Hispanic or Latino 1.5%; Asian 0.1%; Other 1.4%). **Foreign born:** 1.2%. **Median age:** 40.5. **State rank:** 80. **Pop change 1990-2000:** +10.1%.

Income: per capita $16,768; median household $28,676. **Pop below poverty level:** 13.6%.

Unemployment: 10.6%. **Median home value:** $65,800. **Median travel time to work:** 29 minutes.

GREENE COUNTY

PO Box 386   **Ph:** 434-985-5208
Stanardsville, VA 22973   **Fax:** 434-985-6723

In north-central VA, north of Charlottesville; organized Jan 24, 1838 from Orange County. **Name Origin:** For Gen. Nathanael Greene (1742-86), hero of the Revolutionary War, quartermaster general (1778-80), and commander of the Army of the South (1780).

Area (sq mi): 156.96 (land 156.58; water 0.39).

Pop: 15,244 (White 90.3%; Black or African American 6.4%; Hispanic or Latino 1.3%; Asian 0.4%; Other 2%). **Foreign born:** 1.6%. **Median age:** 35.5. **State rank:** 93. **Pop change 1990-2000:** +48%.

Income: per capita $19,478; median household $45,931. **Pop below poverty level:** 6.6%.

Unemployment: 2%. **Median home value:** $111,400. **Median travel time to work:** 28.6 minutes.

GREENSVILLE COUNTY

PO Box 631   **Ph:** 434-348-4215
Emporia, VA 23847   **Fax:** 434-348-4020
www.greensvillecountyva.gov

On the southeastern border of VA, south of Richmond; organized Oct 16, 1780 from Brunswick County. **Name Origin:** For either Gen. Nathanael Greene (1742-86) or Sir Richard Grenville (1542-91), leader of the Roanoke settlement.

Area (sq mi): 296.81 (land 295.44; water 1.37).

Pop: 11,560 (White 38.6%; Black or African American 59.7%; Hispanic or Latino 0.9%; Asian 0.4%; Other 0.9%). **Foreign born:** 0.3%. **Median age:** 38.1. **State rank:** 110. **Pop change 1990-2000:** +30.6%.

Income: per capita $14,632; median household $32,002. **Pop below poverty level:** 14.7%.

Unemployment: 3.6%. **Median home value:** $69,000. **Median travel time to work:** 22.4 minutes.

HALIFAX COUNTY

PO Box 699   **Ph:** 434-476-3300
Halifax, VA 24558   **Fax:** 434-476-3384
www.halifax.com/county

On the central southern border of VA, southeast of Lynchburg; organized Feb 27, 1752 from Lunenburg County. Added the former independent city of South Boston effective June 30, 1995. **Name Origin:** For George Montagu Dunk (1716-71), 2nd Earl of Halifax, English statesman and a strong supporter of trade with the American colonies.

Area (sq mi): 829.56 (land 819.3; water 10.27).

Pop: 37,355 (White 59.7%; Black or African American 38%; Hispanic or Latino 1.2%; Asian 0.2%; Other 1.4%). **Foreign born:** 1%. **Median age:** 40.7. **State rank:** 42. **Pop change 1990-2000:** +28.7%.

Income: per capita $16,353; median household $29,929. **Pop below poverty level:** 15.7%.

Unemployment: 9.3%. **Median home value:** $73,300. **Median travel time to work:** 25.1 minutes.

HAMPTON (INDEPENDENT CITY)

22 Lincoln St   **Ph:** 757-727-6000
Hampton, VA 23669
www.hampton.va.us

In southeastern VA, 7 mi. northeast of Newport News. Founded 1680; incorporated as a city in 1952. **Name Origin:** For Hampton Creek, earlier called the Southampton River, itself named for Henry Wriothesley (1573-1624), 3rd Earl of Southampton.

Area (sq mi): 136.23 (land 51.78; water 84.45).

Pop: 146,437 (White 48.5%; Black or African American 44.7%; Hispanic or Latino 2.8%; Asian 1.8%; Other 3.9%). **Foreign born:** 3.9%. **Median age:** 34. **State rank:** 12. **Pop change 1990-2000:** +9.5%.

Income: per capita $19,774; median household $39,532. **Pop below poverty level:** 11.3%.

Unemployment: 3.8%. **Median home value:** $91,100. **Median travel time to work:** 21.8 minutes.

HANOVER COUNTY

PO Box 470   **Ph:** 804-537-6000
Hanover, VA 23069   **Fax:** 804-537-6234
www.co.hanover.va.us

In east-central VA, north of Richmond; organized 1720 from New Kent (prior to statehood). **Name Origin:** For Hanover, the British royal house, which began with George I (1660-1727), the Duke of Hanover. The name was changed to Windsor during World War I to sound less German.

Area (sq mi): 474.08 (land 472.68; water 1.4).

Pop: 86,320 (White 87.8%; Black or African American 9.3%; Hispanic or Latino 1%; Asian 0.8%; Other 1.5%). **Foreign born:** 1.8%. **Median age:** 37.4. **State rank:** 18. **Pop change 1990-2000:** +36.4%.

Income: per capita $25,120; median household $59,223. **Pop below poverty level:** 3.6%.

Unemployment: 2.4%. **Median home value:** $143,300. **Median travel time to work:** 25.4 minutes.

All statistics are based on the 2000 Census except the dollar figures given for per capita income, which are based on 1999 estimates.

HARRISONBURG (INDEPENDENT CITY)

345 S Main St   **Ph:** 540-432-7701
Harrisonburg, VA 22801   **Fax:** 540-432-7778
www.ci.harrisonburg.va.us

In northern VA, 23 mi. northeast of Staunton. Founded in 1780; incorporated as a town in 1849; as a city in 1916. Serves as county seat for Rockingham County. **Name Origin:** For Thomas Harrison, who gave fifty acres for the town site.

Area (sq mi): 17.59 (land 17.56; water 0.03).

Pop: 40,468 (White 80.1%; Black or African American 5.9%; Hispanic or Latino 8.8%; Asian 3.1%; Other 6.1%). **Foreign born:** 9.2%. **Median age:** 22.6. **State rank:** 39. **Pop change 1990-2000:** +31.8%.

Income: per capita $14,898; median household $29,949. **Pop below poverty level:** 30.1%.

Unemployment: 2%. **Median home value:** $122,700. **Median travel time to work:** 14.8 minutes.

HENRICO COUNTY

PO Box 27032   **Ph:** 804-501-4202
Richmond, VA 23273   **Fax:** 804-501-5214
www.co.henrico.va.us

In east-central VA, north of Petersburg; original county; organized 1634. **Name Origin:** For the lost town of Henricus (or Henrico), destroyed by Indians in the Massacre of 1622; itself named for Prince Henry Frederick (1594-1612), son of James I (1566-1625) of England. Originally called *Henricopolis* (the Greek suffix *-polis* 'city of Henry').

Area (sq mi): 244.6 (land 238.06; water 6.54).

Pop: 262,300 (White 67.9%; Black or African American 24.7%; Hispanic or Latino 2.3%; Asian 3.6%; Other 2.8%). **Foreign born:** 6.7%. **Median age:** 36. **State rank:** 4. **Pop change 1990-2000:** +20.4%.

Income: per capita $26,410; median household $49,185. **Pop below poverty level:** 6.2%.

Unemployment: 3.3%. **Median home value:** $121,300. **Median travel time to work:** 21.6 minutes.

HENRY COUNTY

PO Box 7   **Ph:** 276-634-4601
Collinsville, VA 24078   **Fax:** 276-634-4781
henrycounty.neocom.net

On central southern border of VA, south of Roanoke; organized Oct 7, 1776 from Pittsylvania County. **Name Origin:** For Patrick Henry (1736-99), patriot, governor of VA (1776-79; 1784-86), and statesman, famous for proclaiming, 'Give me liberty or give me death.'

Area (sq mi): 384.39 (land 382.35; water 2.04).

Pop: 57,930 (White 72.7%; Black or African American 22.7%; Hispanic or Latino 3.5%; Asian 0.4%; Other 2.5%). **Foreign born:** 2.7%. **Median age:** 39.3. **State rank:** 29. **Pop change 1990-2000:** +1.7%.

Income: per capita $17,110; median household $31,816. **Pop below poverty level:** 11.7%.

Unemployment: 8.6%. **Median home value:** $75,500. **Median travel time to work:** 22.5 minutes.

HIGHLAND COUNTY

PO Box 190   **Ph:** 540-468-2447
Monterey, VA 24465   **Fax:** 540-468-3447
www.highlandcova.org

On the central western border of VA, west of Staunton; organized Mar 19, 1847 from Bath County, VA, and Pendleton County (now WV). **Name Origin:** For its location in the Allegheny Mountains.

Area (sq mi): 415.86 (land 415.86; water 0).

Pop: 2,536 (White 98.9%; Black or African American 0.1%; Hispanic or Latino 0.5%; Asian 0.1%; Other 0.6%). **Foreign born:** 0.4%. **Median age:** 46. **State rank:** 135. **Pop change 1990-2000:** -3.8%.

Income: per capita $15,976; median household $29,732. **Pop below poverty level:** 12.6%.

Unemployment: 2.3%. **Median home value:** $83,700. **Median travel time to work:** 32 minutes.

HOPEWELL (INDEPENDENT CITY)

300 N Main St   **Ph:** 804-541-2243
Hopewell, VA 23860   **Fax:** 804-541-2248
www.ci.hopewell.va.us

In southeastern VA at the confluence of the James and Appomattox rivers, 10 mi. northeast of Petersburg. Incorporated as Hopewell in 1916. **Name Origin:** Established as Charles City Point by Sir Thomas Dale (?-1619) in 1613. Town called City Point until 1913 when Du Pont de Nemours and Co. established a settlement for their workers on Hopewell Farm, itself named by the former owner for the ship on which he arrived in VA.

Area (sq mi): 10.82 (land 10.24; water 0.58).

Pop: 22,354 (White 61.1%; Black or African American 33.5%; Hispanic or Latino 2.9%; Asian 0.8%; Other 3.5%). **Foreign born:** 1.9%. **Median age:** 35. **State rank:** 70. **Pop change 1990-2000:** -3.2%.

Income: per capita $16,338; median household $33,196. **Pop below poverty level:** 14.9%.

Unemployment: 5.4%. **Median home value:** $77,300. **Median travel time to work:** 22.4 minutes.

ISLE OF WIGHT COUNTY

PO Box 80   **Ph:** 757-365-6204
Isle of Wight, VA 23397   **Fax:** 757-357-9171
www.co.isle-of-wight.va.us

In southeastern VA, on the west bank of the James River. Organized 1634 as Warrascoyak County from Upper Norfolk (which was organized 1636 from New Norfolk County and renamed Nansemond County in 1642-43); name changed in 1637. **Name Origin:** For the island off the southern coast of England. Originally named for the local Indians.

Area (sq mi): 362.76 (land 315.87; water 46.89).

Pop: 29,728 (White 70.6%; Black or African American 27.1%; Hispanic or Latino 0.9%; Asian 0.3%; Other 1.5%). **Foreign born:**

Please see sample entry on inside front cover for detailed information about the statistics presented with each county listing.

593

1.1%. **Median age:** 38.9. **State rank:** 56. **Pop change 1990-2000:** +18.7%.

Income: per capita $20,235; median household $45,387. **Pop below poverty level:** 8.3%.

Unemployment: 2.8%. **Median home value:** $129,300. **Median travel time to work:** 29.9 minutes.

JAMES CITY COUNTY
PO Box 8784   **Ph:** 757-253-6728
Williamsburg, VA 23187   **Fax:** 757-253-6833
www.james-city.va.us

In southeastern VA, on the east bank of James River; original county, organized 1634. **Name Origin:** For James I (1566-1625), king of England; also king of Scotland as James VI; son of Mary, Queen of Scots.

Area (sq mi): 179.71 (land 142.92; water 36.79).

Pop: 48,102 (White 81%; Black or African American 14.4%; Hispanic or Latino 1.7%; Asian 1.5%; Other 2.1%). **Foreign born:** 4.1%. **Median age:** 40.8. **State rank:** 35. **Pop change 1990-2000:** +38%.

Income: per capita $29,256; median household $55,594. **Pop below poverty level:** 6.4%.

Unemployment: 2.1%. **Median home value:** $167,300. **Median travel time to work:** 24.6 minutes.

KING GEORGE COUNTY
9483 Kings Hwy Suite 3   **Ph:** 540-775-3322
King George, VA 22485   **Fax:** 540-775-5466

On the northeastern coast of VA, on west bank of the Potomac River; organized Nov 2, 1720 from Richmond and Westmoreland counties. **Name Origin:** For King George I of England (1660-1727).

Area (sq mi): 187.79 (land 180; water 7.79).

Pop: 16,803 (White 76.5%; Black or African American 18.7%; Hispanic or Latino 1.8%; Asian 1%; Other 2.7%). **Foreign born:** 1.3%. **Median age:** 35.1. **State rank:** 85. **Pop change 1990-2000:** +24.2%.

Income: per capita $21,562; median household $49,882. **Pop below poverty level:** 5.6%.

Unemployment: 1.8%. **Median home value:** $123,200. **Median travel time to work:** 31 minutes.

KING & QUEEN COUNTY
PO Box 177   **Ph:** 804-785-5975
King & Queen Court House, VA 23085 **Fax:** 804-785-5999
www.kingandqueenco.net

In east-central VA, northeast of Richmond; organized Apr 16, 1691 from New Kent County. **Name Origin:** For King William (1650-1702) and Queen Mary (1662-94) of England.

Area (sq mi): 326.33 (land 316.26; water 10.06).

Pop: 6,630 (White 60.9%; Black or African American 35.7%; Hispanic or Latino 0.9%; Asian 0.3%; Other 2.9%). **Foreign born:** 0.9%. **Median age:** 40.9. **State rank:** 126. **Pop change 1990-2000:** +5.4%.

Income: per capita $17,236; median household $35,941. **Pop below poverty level:** 10.9%.

Unemployment: 3.9%. **Median home value:** $84,400. **Median travel time to work:** 37.1 minutes.

KING WILLIAM COUNTY
PO Box 215   **Ph:** 804-769-4927
King William, VA 23086   **Fax:** 804-769-4964
www.co.king-william.va.us

In east-central VA, northeast of Richmond; organized Dec 5, 1702 from King and Queen County. **Name Origin:** For William III of England (1650-1702).

Area (sq mi): 285.65 (land 275.43; water 10.22).

Pop: 13,146 (White 73.4%; Black or African American 22.8%; Hispanic or Latino 0.9%; Asian 0.4%; Other 2.9%). **Foreign born:** 1.2%. **Median age:** 37. **State rank:** 98. **Pop change 1990-2000:** +20.5%.

Income: per capita $21,928; median household $49,876. **Pop below poverty level:** 5.5%.

Unemployment: 3.7%. **Median home value:** $100,200. **Median travel time to work:** 34.9 minutes.

LANCASTER COUNTY
PO Box 99   **Ph:** 804-462-5611
Lancaster, VA 22503
www.lancova.com

On the central eastern coast of VA, on east bank of the Rappahannock River; organized 1652 from York and Northumberland counties. **Name Origin:** For the city in England, former home of many early settlers who escaped from Oliver Cromwell's (1599-1658) reign.

Area (sq mi): 231.35 (land 133.14; water 98.2).

Pop: 11,567 (White 69.6%; Black or African American 28.9%; Hispanic or Latino 0.6%; Asian 0.3%; Other 0.8%). **Foreign born:** 1.7%. **Median age:** 49.8. **State rank:** 108. **Pop change 1990-2000:** +6.2%.

Income: per capita $24,663; median household $33,239. **Pop below poverty level:** 12.5%.

Unemployment: 7.8%. **Median home value:** $131,600. **Median travel time to work:** 23.6 minutes.

LEE COUNTY
PO Box 367   **Ph:** 276-346-7714
Jonesville, VA 24263   **Fax:** 276-346-7712

On the southwestern border of VA, west of Kingsport, TN; organized Oct 25, 1792 from Russell County. **Name Origin:** For Henry 'Lighthorse Harry' Lee (1756-1818), VA soldier, statesman, governor (1792-95), and U.S. representative (1799-1801); father of Robert E. Lee (1807-70).

Area (sq mi): 437.32 (land 437.13; water 0.18).

Pop: 23,589 (White 98.1%; Black or African American 0.4%; Hispanic or Latino 0.5%; Asian 0.2%; Other 0.9%). **Foreign born:** 0.5%. **Median age:** 39.7. **State rank:** 65. **Pop change 1990-2000:** -3.7%.

Income: per capita $13,625; median household $22,972. **Pop below poverty level:** 23.9%.

All statistics are based on the 2000 Census except the dollar figures given for per capita income, which are based on 1999 estimates.

Unemployment: 5.5%. **Median home value:** $56,900. **Median travel time to work:** 29.5 minutes.

LEXINGTON (INDEPENDENT CITY)
PO Box 922   **Ph:** 540-463-7133
Lexington, VA 24450   **Fax:** 540-463-5310
www.ci.lexington.va.us

In south-central VA, northeast of Roanoke. Established in 1778; incorporated as a town in 1874; as a city in 1965. Serves as county seat for Rockbridge County. **Name Origin:** Probably for the village in MA where the first battle of the American Revolution was fought.

Area (sq mi): 2.49 (land 2.49; water 0).

Pop: 6,867 (White 85%; Black or African American 10.4%; Hispanic or Latino 1.6%; Asian 1.9%; Other 1.7%). **Foreign born:** 4%. **Median age:** 23.3. **State rank:** 123. **Pop change 1990-2000:** -1.3%.

Income: per capita $16,497; median household $28,982. **Pop below poverty level:** 21.6%.

Unemployment: 1.6%. **Median home value:** $131,900. **Median travel time to work:** 10.5 minutes.

LOUDOUN COUNTY
1 Harrison St SE PO Box 7000   **Ph:** 703-777-0200
Leesburg, VA 20177   **Fax:** 703-777-0325
www.co.loudoun.va.us

On northeastern border of VA, northwest of Washington, D.C.; organized Mar 25, 1757 from Fairfax County. **Name Origin:** For John Campbell (1705-82), 4th Earl of Loudoun, commander in chief of British forces during the French and Indian Wars.

Area (sq mi): 521.1 (land 519.85; water 1.25).

Pop: 169,599 (White 79.6%; Black or African American 6.9%; Hispanic or Latino 5.9%; Asian 5.3%; Other 5%). **Foreign born:** 11.3%. **Median age:** 33.6. **State rank:** 11. **Pop change 1990-2000:** +96.9%.

Income: per capita $33,530; median household $80,648. **Pop below poverty level:** 2.8%.

Unemployment: 2.9%. **Median home value:** $200,500. **Median travel time to work:** 30.8 minutes.

LOUISA COUNTY
1 Woolfolk Ave   **Ph:** 540-967-0401
Louisa, VA 23093   **Fax:** 540-967-3411
www.louisacounty.com

In east-central VA, east of Charlottesville; organized May 6, 1742 from Hanover County. **Name Origin:** For Louisa, queen of Denmark (1724-51), daughter of George II (1683-1760) of England.

Area (sq mi): 510.79 (land 497.14; water 13.65).

Pop: 25,627 (White 76.2%; Black or African American 21.6%; Hispanic or Latino 0.7%; Asian 0.2%; Other 1.6%). **Foreign born:** 1.3%. **Median age:** 38.8. **State rank:** 61. **Pop change 1990-2000:** +26.1%.

Income: per capita $19,479; median household $39,402. **Pop below poverty level:** 10.2%.

Unemployment: 4.5%. **Median home value:** $96,400. **Median travel time to work:** 36 minutes.

LUNENBURG COUNTY
11435 Courthouse Rd   **Ph:** 434-696-2230
Lunenburg, VA 23952   **Fax:** 434-696-3931

In south-central VA, southwest of Richmond; organized 1746 from Brunswick County. **Name Origin:** For King George II (1683-1760) of England who retained the German title, Duke of Brunswick.

Area (sq mi): 432.38 (land 431.7; water 0.68).

Pop: 13,146 (White 58.5%; Black or African American 38.6%; Hispanic or Latino 1.8%; Asian 0.2%; Other 2%). **Foreign born:** 1.2%. **Median age:** 40.5. **State rank:** 99. **Pop change 1990-2000:** +15.1%.

Income: per capita $14,951; median household $27,899. **Pop below poverty level:** 20%.

Unemployment: 6.1%. **Median home value:** $60,200. **Median travel time to work:** 30 minutes.

LYNCHBURG (INDEPENDENT CITY)
PO Box 60   **Ph:** 434-847-1443
Lynchburg, VA 24505
www.ci.lynchburg.va.us

In south-central VA, northeast of Roanoke. Established 1786; incorporated as a town in 1805; as a city in 1852. **Name Origin:** For John Lynch, owner of the original town site.

Area (sq mi): 49.76 (land 49.39; water 0.37).

Pop: 65,269 (White 66%; Black or African American 29.7%; Hispanic or Latino 1.3%; Asian 1.3%; Other 2.4%). **Foreign born:** 3.2%. **Median age:** 35.1. **State rank:** 24. **Pop change 1990-2000:** -1.2%.

Income: per capita $18,263; median household $32,234. **Pop below poverty level:** 15.9%.

Unemployment: 4.5%. **Median home value:** $85,300. **Median travel time to work:** 16.8 minutes.

MADISON COUNTY
PO Box 220   **Ph:** 540-948-6888
Madison, VA 22727   **Fax:** 540-948-3759

In north-central VA, northeast of Charlottesville; organized May 1, 1793 from Culpeper County. **Name Origin:** For James Madison (1751-1836), fourth U.S. president.

Area (sq mi): 321.78 (land 321.42; water 0.36).

Pop: 12,520 (White 86.3%; Black or African American 11.4%; Hispanic or Latino 0.8%; Asian 0.5%; Other 1.3%). **Foreign born:** 2.2%. **Median age:** 40. **State rank:** 103. **Pop change 1990-2000:** +4.8%.

Income: per capita $18,636; median household $39,856. **Pop below poverty level:** 9.6%.

Unemployment: 1.8%. **Median home value:** $100,600. **Median travel time to work:** 30.3 minutes.

MANASSAS (INDEPENDENT CITY)
PO Box 560   **Ph:** 703-257-8200
Manassas, VA 20108   **Fax:** 703-335-0042
www.manassascity.org

In northeastern VA, 25 mi. west of Alexandria. Established 1852;

Please see sample entry on inside front cover for detailed information about the statistics presented with each county listing.

incorporated as a town in 1874; as a city in 1975. Serves as county seat for Prince William County. **Name Origin:** For its location at the Manassas junction of the Manassas Gap Railroad and the Orange and Alexandria Railroad.

Area (sq mi): 9.96 (land 9.93; water 0.02).

Pop: 35,135 (White 66.3%; Black or African American 12.9%; Hispanic or Latino 15.1%; Asian 3.4%; Other 11.7%). **Foreign born:** 14.2%. **Median age:** 31.3. **State rank:** 43. **Pop change 1990-2000:** +25.7%.

Income: per capita $24,453; median household $60,409. **Pop below poverty level:** 6.3%.

Unemployment: 3.3%. **Median home value:** $154,500. **Median travel time to work:** 32.4 minutes.

MANASSAS PARK (INDEPENDENT CITY)

1 Park Center Ct   **Ph:** 703-335-8800
Manassas Park, VA 20111   **Fax:** 703-335-0053
www.ci.manassas-park.va.us

In northeastern VA, west of Alexandria. Established in 1955; incorporated as a town in 1957; as a city in 1975. Annexed part of Prince William County effective December 31, 1990. **Name Origin:** For the nearby city of Manassas.

Area (sq mi): 2.49 (land 2.49; water 0).

Pop: 10,290 (White 67.2%; Black or African American 11.2%; Hispanic or Latino 15%; Asian 4.1%; Other 11.9%). **Foreign born:** 15%. **Median age:** 30.3. **State rank:** 113. **Pop change 1990-2000:** +52.8%.

Income: per capita $21,048; median household $60,794. **Pop below poverty level:** 5.2%.

Unemployment: 1.5%. **Median home value:** $116,000. **Median travel time to work:** 35.6 minutes.

MARTINSVILLE (INDEPENDENT CITY)

PO Box 1112   **Ph:** 276-656-5180
Martinsville, VA 24114   **Fax:** 276-656-5280
www.ci.martinsville.va.us

In southern VA, 32 mi. west of Danville. Founded 1791; incorporated as a town in 1873; as a city in 1928. Serves as county seat for Henry County. **Name Origin:** For Gen. Joseph Martin (1740-1808), pioneer settler and army officer who represented the county in the General Assembly when the town was established.

Area (sq mi): 11.01 (land 10.96; water 0.05).

Pop: 15,416 (White 54.1%; Black or African American 42.5%; Hispanic or Latino 2.3%; Asian 0.5%; Other 1.6%). **Foreign born:** 2.7%. **Median age:** 40.8. **State rank:** 92. **Pop change 1990-2000:** -4.6%.

Income: per capita $17,251; median household $27,441. **Pop below poverty level:** 19.2%.

Unemployment: 11.1%. **Median home value:** $69,100. **Median travel time to work:** 18.1 minutes.

MATHEWS COUNTY

PO Box 463   **Ph:** 804-725-2550
Mathews, VA 23109   **Fax:** 804-725-7456
www.co.mathews.va.us

On the southeastern border of VA, on the western shore of Chesapeake Bay; organized 1791 from Gloucester County. **Name Origin:** For Thomas Mathews, American Revolutionary general and patriot.

Area (sq mi): 251.96 (land 85.68; water 166.28).

Pop: 9,207 (White 86.8%; Black or African American 11.3%; Hispanic or Latino 0.8%; Asian 0.2%; Other 1.2%). **Foreign born:** 2.2%. **Median age:** 46.2. **State rank:** 116. **Pop change 1990-2000:** +10.3%.

Income: per capita $23,610; median household $43,222. **Pop below poverty level:** 6%.

Unemployment: 2.7%. **Median home value:** $118,000. **Median travel time to work:** 45.8 minutes.

MECKLENBURG COUNTY

PO Box 530   **Ph:** 434-738-6191
Boydton, VA 23917   **Fax:** 434-738-6861

On the central southern border of VA, southwest of Richmond; organized Mar 1, 1765 from Lunenburg County. **Name Origin:** For Charlotte Sophia, Princess of Mecklenburg-Strelitz (1744-1818), wife of George III (1738-1820) of England.

Area (sq mi): 679.29 (land 623.93; water 55.36).

Pop: 32,380 (White 58.7%; Black or African American 39.1%; Hispanic or Latino 1.2%; Asian 0.3%; Other 1.4%). **Foreign born:** 1.6%. **Median age:** 40.9. **State rank:** 51. **Pop change 1990-2000:** +10.7%.

Income: per capita $17,171; median household $31,380. **Pop below poverty level:** 15.5%.

Unemployment: 7.2%. **Median home value:** $80,200. **Median travel time to work:** 25.5 minutes.

MIDDLESEX COUNTY

PO Box 158   **Ph:** 804-758-5317
Saluda, VA 23149   **Fax:** 804-758-0792
www.co.middlesex.va.us

On the southeastern border of VA, along the west bank of the Rappahannock River; organized Sep 21, 1674 from Lancaster County. **Name Origin:** For an ancient county in England, most of which became part of Greater London in 1965. The suffix -sex is Old Norman from 'camp' or 'military headquarters.'

Area (sq mi): 210.75 (land 130.3; water 80.46).

Pop: 9,932 (White 78.3%; Black or African American 20.1%; Hispanic or Latino 0.6%; Asian 0.1%; Other 1.3%). **Foreign born:** 2.1%. **Median age:** 46.8. **State rank:** 115. **Pop change 1990-2000:** +14.8%.

Income: per capita $22,708; median household $36,875. **Pop below poverty level:** 13%.

Unemployment: 1.7%. **Median home value:** $124,300. **Median travel time to work:** 35.1 minutes.

All statistics are based on the 2000 Census except the dollar figures given for per capita income, which are based on 1999 estimates.

MONTGOMERY COUNTY

755 Roanoke St   **Ph:** 540-382-6954
Christiansburg, VA 24073   **Fax:** 540-382-6943
www.montva.com

In western VA, west of Roanoke; organized Oct 7, 1776 from Fincastle (organized 1772 from Botetourt County and abolished 1777), Botetourt, and Pulaski counties. **Name Origin:** For Gen. Richard Montgomery (1736-75), American Revolutionary War officer who captured Montreal, Canada.

Area (sq mi): 389.43 (land 388.22; water 1.21).

Pop: 83,629 (White 89.1%; Black or African American 3.7%; Hispanic or Latino 1.6%; Asian 4%; Other 2.3%). **Foreign born:** 5.8%. **Median age:** 25.9. **State rank:** 20. **Pop change 1990-2000:** +13.1%.

Income: per capita $17,077; median household $32,330. **Pop below poverty level:** 23.2%.

Unemployment: 3.1%. **Median home value:** $114,600. **Median travel time to work:** 19.2 minutes.

NELSON COUNTY

PO Box 336   **Ph:** 434-263-7000
Lovingston, VA 22949   **Fax:** 434-263-7004
www.nelsoncounty.com

In west-central VA, southwest of Charlottesville; organized 1808 from Amherst County. **Name Origin:** For Thomas Nelson (1738-89), member of the Continental Congress, signer of the Declaration of Independence, and governor of VA (1781).

Area (sq mi): 474.31 (land 472.35; water 1.95).

Pop: 14,445 (White 81.4%; Black or African American 14.9%; Hispanic or Latino 2.1%; Asian 0.2%; Other 2.2%). **Foreign born:** 1.9%. **Median age:** 42.8. **State rank:** 94. **Pop change 1990-2000:** +13%.

Income: per capita $22,230; median household $36,769. **Pop below poverty level:** 12.1%.

Unemployment: 3.5%. **Median home value:** $95,100. **Median travel time to work:** 33.1 minutes.

NEW KENT COUNTY

PO Box 98   **Ph:** 804-966-9520
New Kent, VA 23124   **Fax:** 804-966-9528
www.newkent.com

In east-central VA, east of Richmond; organized Nov 20, 1654 from York County. **Name Origin:** For Kent, England.

Area (sq mi): 223.48 (land 209.55; water 13.93).

Pop: 13,462 (White 79.7%; Black or African American 16.2%; Hispanic or Latino 1.3%; Asian 0.5%; Other 3%). **Foreign born:** 0.9%. **Median age:** 38.4. **State rank:** 97. **Pop change 1990-2000:** +28.9%.

Income: per capita $22,893; median household $53,595. **Pop below poverty level:** 4.9%.

Unemployment: 3.4%. **Median home value:** $128,100. **Median travel time to work:** 34 minutes.

NEWPORT NEWS (INDEPENDENT CITY)

2400 Washington Ave   **Ph:** 757-926-8411
Newport News, VA 236074300   **Fax:** 757-926-3503
www.newport-news.va.us

In southeastern VA at the mouth of the James River and the entrance to Hampton Roads, 11 mi. northwest of Norfolk. Established in 1880; incorporated as a city in 1896. **Name Origin:** Possibly for Sir Christopher Newport and Sir William Newce, the latter name changed by folk etymology. In 1619 called Newportes Newce.

Area (sq mi): 119.05 (land 68.29; water 50.76).

Pop: 180,150 (White 52%; Black or African American 39.1%; Hispanic or Latino 4.2%; Asian 2.3%; Other 5.1%). **Foreign born:** 4.8%. **Median age:** 32. **State rank:** 10. **Pop change 1990-2000:** +5.9%.

Income: per capita $17,843; median household $36,597. **Pop below poverty level:** 13.8%.

Unemployment: 4.1%. **Median home value:** $96,400. **Median travel time to work:** 23 minutes.

NORFOLK (INDEPENDENT CITY)

1101 City Hall Bldg 810 Union St   **Ph:** 757-664-4242
Norfolk, VA 23510   **Fax:** 757-664-4239
www.city.norfolk.va.us

In southeastern VA on the Elizabeth River just south of Hampton Roads. Established 1682; incorporated as a town in 1736; as a city in 1845. Major port; distribution center for nearby coal-mining regions. Site of Norfolk Naval Base, largest naval installation in the U.S.; headquarters of the Atlantic Command of the North Atlantic Treaty Organization (NATO). Site of Old Dominion University. **Name Origin:** For the county in England, former home of Adam Thoroughgood, an early settler.

Area (sq mi): 96.3 (land 53.73; water 42.58).

Pop: 234,403 (White 47%; Black or African American 44.1%; Hispanic or Latino 3.8%; Asian 2.8%; Other 4.8%). **Foreign born:** 5%. **Median age:** 29.6. **State rank:** 6. **Pop change 1990-2000:** -10.3%.

Income: per capita $17,372; median household $31,815. **Pop below poverty level:** 19.4%.

Unemployment: 5.7%. **Median home value:** $88,400. **Median travel time to work:** 21.7 minutes.

NORTHAMPTON COUNTY

PO Box 36   **Ph:** 757-678-0465
Eastville, VA 23347   **Fax:** 757-678-5410

On the southern border of Delmarva peninsula, bounded on the west by Chesapeake Bay and on the east by the Atlantic Ocean. Original county; organized 1634 as Accawmack County; name changed 1642-43. **Name Origin:** Possibly for Spencer Compton (1601-32), 2nd Earl of Northampton.

Area (sq mi): 795.34 (land 207.37; water 587.97).

Pop: 13,093 (White 52.5%; Black or African American 43%; Hispanic or Latino 3.5%; Asian 0.2%; Other 3.5%). **Foreign born:** 3.4%. **Median age:** 42.4. **State rank:** 100. **Pop change 1990-2000:** +0.2%.

Income: per capita $16,591; median household $28,276. **Pop below poverty level:** 20.5%.

Please see sample entry on inside front cover for detailed information about the statistics presented with each county listing.

597

Unemployment: 4%. **Median home value:** $78,700. **Median travel time to work:** 21.7 minutes.

NORTHUMBERLAND COUNTY

PO Box 217   **Ph:** 804-580-3700
Heathsville, VA 22473
www.co.northumberland.va.us

On central eastern coast of VA, on Chesapeake Bay; organized Oct 12, 1648 from Chicacoun Indian District. **Name Origin:** For the county in England, former home of many early settlers.

Area (sq mi): 285.67 (land 192.3; water 93.36).

Pop: 12,259 (White 71.8%; Black or African American 26.6%; Hispanic or Latino 0.9%; Asian 0.2%; Other 1%). **Foreign born:** 1.6%. **Median age:** 50.1. **State rank:** 106. **Pop change 1990-2000:** +16.5%.

Income: per capita $22,917; median household $38,129. **Pop below poverty level:** 12.3%.

Unemployment: 6.8%. **Median home value:** $129,100. **Median travel time to work:** 28.4 minutes.

NORTON (INDEPENDENT CITY)

PO Box 618   **Ph:** 276-679-1160
Norton, VA 24273   **Fax:** 276-679-3510
www.nortonva.org

In southwestern VA. Incorporated as a town in 1894; as a city in 1954. **Name Origin:** For Eckstein Norton, Louisville and National Railroad president, 1886-91. Originally called Prince's Flats, probably for William Prince, a settler in the area about 1787.

Area (sq mi): 7.53 (land 7.53; water 0).

Pop: 3,904 (White 90.9%; Black or African American 6.1%; Hispanic or Latino 0.9%; Asian 1%; Other 1.3%). **Foreign born:** 1.1%. **Median age:** 39. **State rank:** 134. **Pop change 1990-2000:** -8.1%.

Income: per capita $16,024; median household $22,788. **Pop below poverty level:** 22.8%.

Unemployment: 5.1%. **Median home value:** $62,800. **Median travel time to work:** 18.8 minutes.

NOTTOWAY COUNTY

PO Box 25   **Ph:** 434-645-9043
Nottoway, VA 23955   **Fax:** 434-645-2201

In south-central VA, southwest of Richmond; organized 1789 from Amelia County. **Name Origin:** For the local Indian tribe related to the Iroquois. The name, given to them by their neighbours, means 'rattlesnake' in the sense of 'untrustworthy enemy.' Their own name *Cheroenhaka* is believed to mean 'fork of a stream,' perhaps to signify a favorite campsite.

Area (sq mi): 316.1 (land 314.65; water 1.45).

Pop: 15,725 (White 56.7%; Black or African American 40.6%; Hispanic or Latino 1.6%; Asian 0.4%; Other 1.8%). **Foreign born:** 1.4%. **Median age:** 38.6. **State rank:** 90. **Pop change 1990-2000:** +4.9%.

Income: per capita $15,552; median household $30,866. **Pop below poverty level:** 20.1%.

Unemployment: 3.7%. **Median home value:** $73,200. **Median travel time to work:** 29.1 minutes.

ORANGE COUNTY

PO Box 111   **Ph:** 540-972-1455
Orange, VA 22960   **Fax:** 276-672-1679
www.orangecova.com

In north-central VA, northeast of Charlottesville; organized Feb 1, 1734 from Spotsylvania County. **Name Origin:** For the European ruling family of Orange-Nassau, one of whose princes married Princess Anne, daughter of King George II (1683-1760).

Area (sq mi): 343.41 (land 341.7; water 1.7).

Pop: 25,881 (White 83.6%; Black or African American 13.8%; Hispanic or Latino 1.3%; Asian 0.3%; Other 1.5%). **Foreign born:** 1.9%. **Median age:** 40.4. **State rank:** 60. **Pop change 1990-2000:** +20.8%.

Income: per capita $21,107; median household $42,889. **Pop below poverty level:** 9.2%.

Unemployment: 3%. **Median home value:** $115,000. **Median travel time to work:** 33.1 minutes.

PAGE COUNTY

117 S Court St   **Ph:** 540-743-4142
Luray, VA 22835   **Fax:** 540-743-4533
www.co.page.va.us

In north-central VA, north of Charlottesville; organized Mar 30, 1831 from Rockingham and Shenandoah counties. **Name Origin:** For John Page (1743-1808), U.S. representative from VA (1789-97) and governor (1802-05).

Area (sq mi): 314.09 (land 311.13; water 2.97).

Pop: 23,177 (White 95.7%; Black or African American 2.2%; Hispanic or Latino 1.1%; Asian 0.2%; Other 1.3%). **Foreign born:** 1.5%. **Median age:** 39. **State rank:** 68. **Pop change 1990-2000:** +6.9%.

Income: per capita $16,321; median household $33,359. **Pop below poverty level:** 12.5%.

Unemployment: 3.3%. **Median home value:** $86,300. **Median travel time to work:** 32.5 minutes.

PATRICK COUNTY

PO Box 148   **Ph:** 276-694-7213
Stuart, VA 24171   **Fax:** 276-694-6943
www.co.patrick.va.us

On the southwestern border of VA, southwest of Roanoke; organized Nov 26, 1790 from Henry County. **Name Origin:** For Patrick Henry (1736-99), patriot, governor of VA (1776-79; 1784-86), and statesman, famous for proclaiming, 'Give me liberty or give me death.'

Area (sq mi): 485.87 (land 483.14; water 2.72).

Pop: 19,407 (White 91%; Black or African American 6.2%; Hispanic or Latino 1.9%; Asian 0.2%; Other 1.8%). **Foreign born:** 1.5%. **Median age:** 40.5. **State rank:** 77. **Pop change 1990-2000:** +11.1%.

Income: per capita $15,574; median household $28,705. **Pop below poverty level:** 13.4%.

All statistics are based on the 2000 Census except the dollar figures given for per capita income, which are based on 1999 estimates.

Unemployment: 8.5%. **Median home value:** $75,300. **Median travel time to work:** 27.9 minutes.

PETERSBURG (INDEPENDENT CITY)

City Hall 135 N Union St   **Ph:** 804-733-2301
Petersburg, VA 23803   **Fax:** 804-732-9212
www.petersburg-va.org

In southeastern VA at the head of navigation of the Appomattox River, 23 mi. south of Richmond. **Name Origin:** Named by William Bryd II (1674-1744) for Peter Jones, his companion on expeditions into the VA backcountry. Founded in 1645 as Fort Henry, a trading post; name changed in 1748 when incorporated as a town; incorporated as a city in 1850.

Area (sq mi): 23.19 (land 22.88; water 0.3).

Pop: 33,740 (White 18.2%; Black or African American 79%; Hispanic or Latino 1.4%; Asian 0.7%; Other 1.8%). **Foreign born:** 2.3%. **Median age:** 36.9. **State rank:** 48. **Pop change 1990-2000:** -12.1%.

Income: per capita $15,989; median household $28,851. **Pop below poverty level:** 19.6%.

Unemployment: 6.4%. **Median home value:** $68,600. **Median travel time to work:** 23.3 minutes.

PITTSYLVANIA COUNTY

PO Box 695   **Ph:** 434-432-7879
Chatham, VA 24531   **Fax:** 434-432-7915

On the central southern border of VA, south of Lynchburg; organized Nov 6, 1766 from Halifax County. **Name Origin:** For William Pitt (the Elder; 1708-78), 1st Earl of Chatham, prime minister of England and supporter of the American colonies; with the addition of *-sylvania* 'Pitt's woods.'

Area (sq mi): 978.18 (land 970.76; water 7.42).

Pop: 61,745 (White 74.4%; Black or African American 23.7%; Hispanic or Latino 1.2%; Asian 0.2%; Other 1.1%). **Foreign born:** 1%. **Median age:** 39.6. **State rank:** 26. **Pop change 1990-2000:** +10.9%.

Income: per capita $16,991; median household $35,153. **Pop below poverty level:** 11.8%.

Unemployment: 8.4%. **Median home value:** $80,300. **Median travel time to work:** 25.7 minutes.

POQUOSON (INDEPENDENT CITY)

500 City Hall Ave   **Ph:** 757-868-3000
Poquoson, VA 23662   **Fax:** 757-868-3101
www.ci.poquoson.va.us

In southeastern VA, 9 mi. north of Newport News. Established as a post office between 1885 and 1888; incorporated as a town in 1952; as a city in 1976. **Name Origin:** From an Algonquian term probably meaning 'swamp' or 'overflowed land.'

Area (sq mi): 78.43 (land 15.52; water 62.91).

Pop: 11,566 (White 95.5%; Black or African American 0.7%; Hispanic or Latino 1.1%; Asian 1.6%; Other 1.5%). **Foreign born:** 2.9%. **Median age:** 39.5. **State rank:** 109. **Pop change 1990-2000:** +5.1%.

Income: per capita $25,336; median household $60,920. **Pop below poverty level:** 4.5%.

Unemployment: 2.3%. **Median home value:** $153,400. **Median travel time to work:** 24 minutes.

PORTSMOUTH (INDEPENDENT CITY)

PO Box 820   **Ph:** 757-393-8746
Portsmouth, VA 23705   **Fax:** 757-393-5378
www.portsmouth.va.us

In southeastern VA on the Elizabeth River opposite of Norfolk. Established 1752; incorporated as a town in 1836; as a city in 1858. **Name Origin:** Named by town founder, William Crawford, for the city in England.

Area (sq mi): 46.62 (land 33.16; water 13.46).

Pop: 100,565 (White 45.1%; Black or African American 50.6%; Hispanic or Latino 1.7%; Asian 0.8%; Other 2.8%). **Foreign born:** 1.6%. **Median age:** 34.5. **State rank:** 14. **Pop change 1990-2000:** -3.2%.

Income: per capita $16,507; median household $33,742. **Pop below poverty level:** 16.2%.

Unemployment: 5.4%. **Median home value:** $81,300. **Median travel time to work:** 23.8 minutes.

POWHATAN COUNTY

PO Box 37   **Ph:** 804-598-5660
Powhatan, VA 23139

In east-central VA, west of Richmond; organized May 5, 1777 from Cumberland and Chesterfield counties. **Name Origin:** For chief Powhatan (c.1550-1618), the leader of a confederacy of 32 tribes, whose Indian name was Wahunsonacock; father of Pocahontas (c.1595-1617). Name is believed to mean 'falls in a current of water' or 'at the falls.'

Area (sq mi): 262.4 (land 261.28; water 1.12).

Pop: 22,377 (White 81%; Black or African American 16.9%; Hispanic or Latino 0.8%; Asian 0.2%; Other 1.3%). **Foreign born:** 1.5%. **Median age:** 36.8. **State rank:** 69. **Pop change 1990-2000:** +46%.

Income: per capita $24,104; median household $53,992. **Pop below poverty level:** 5.7%.

Unemployment: 2.1%. **Median home value:** $132,100. **Median travel time to work:** 34.8 minutes.

PRINCE EDWARD COUNTY

PO Box 304   **Ph:** 434-392-5145
Farmville, VA 23901
www.co.prince-edward.va.us

In south-central VA, southeast of Lynchburg; organized 1754 from Amelia County. **Name Origin:** For Prince Edward Augustus (1767-1820), son of George III (1738-1820) of England and father of Queen Victoria (1819-1901).

Area (sq mi): 353.85 (land 352.76; water 1.09).

Pop: 19,720 (White 61.8%; Black or African American 35.8%; Hispanic or Latino 0.9%; Asian 0.5%; Other 1.5%). **Foreign born:** 1.4%. **Median age:** 31.5. **State rank:** 75. **Pop change 1990-2000:** +13.9%.

Income: per capita $14,510; median household $31,301. **Pop below poverty level:** 18.9%.

Please see sample entry on inside front cover for detailed information about the statistics presented with each county listing.

Unemployment: 3.9%. **Median home value:** $93,000. **Median travel time to work:** 25.1 minutes.

PRINCE GEORGE COUNTY

PO Box 68   **Ph:** 804-733-2600
Prince George, VA 23875   **Fax:** 804-733-2602
www.princegeorgeva.org

In southeastern VA, southeast of Richmond; organized 1703 from Charles City County. **Name Origin:** For George of Denmark (1653-1708), husband of Queen Anne (1665-1714) of England.

Area (sq mi): 281.85 (land 265.62; water 16.23).

Pop: 33,047 (White 59.1%; Black or African American 32.5%; Hispanic or Latino 4.9%; Asian 1.7%; Other 4.8%). **Foreign born:** 4.5%. **Median age:** 32.1. **State rank:** 50. **Pop change 1990-2000:** +20.6%.

Income: per capita $20,196; median household $49,877. **Pop below poverty level:** 8%.

Unemployment: 3.4%. **Median home value:** $118,200. **Median travel time to work:** 22 minutes.

PRINCE WILLIAM COUNTY

1 County Complex Ct   **Ph:** 703-792-6600
Prince William, VA 22192   **Fax:** 703-792-7484
www.pwcweb.com

On the northeastern border of VA, southwest of Alexandria; organized 1731 from King George and Stafford counties. Part annexed to Manassas Park (independent) city effective December 31, 1990. **Name Origin:** For Prince William Augustus (1721-65), Duke of Cumberland, son of George II (1683-1760) of England.

Area (sq mi): 348.36 (land 337.78; water 10.58).

Pop: 280,813 (White 64.7%; Black or African American 18.8%; Hispanic or Latino 9.7%; Asian 3.8%; Other 8.4%). **Foreign born:** 11.5%. **Median age:** 31.9. **State rank:** 3. **Pop change 1990-2000:** +30.2%.

Income: per capita $25,641; median household $65,960. **Pop below poverty level:** 4.4%.

Unemployment: 2.4%. **Median home value:** $149,600. **Median travel time to work:** 36.9 minutes.

PULASKI COUNTY

143 3rd St NW Suite 1   **Ph:** 540-980-7705
Pulaski, VA 24301   **Fax:** 540-980-7717
www.pulaskicounty.org

In southwestern VA, southwest of Roanoke; organized Mar 30, 1839 from Montgomery and Wythe counties. **Name Origin:** For Count Casimir Pulaski (1747-79), Polish soldier who fought for America during the Revolutionary War.

Area (sq mi): 329.59 (land 320.57; water 9.03).

Pop: 35,127 (White 92.1%; Black or African American 5.6%; Hispanic or Latino 1%; Asian 0.3%; Other 1.5%). **Foreign born:** 0.6%. **Median age:** 40.3. **State rank:** 44. **Pop change 1990-2000:** +1.8%.

Income: per capita $18,973; median household $33,873. **Pop below poverty level:** 13.1%.

Unemployment: 10.1%. **Median home value:** $80,000. **Median travel time to work:** 21.3 minutes.

RADFORD (INDEPENDENT CITY)

619 2nd St   **Ph:** 540-731-3603
Radford, VA 24141   **Fax:** 540-731-3699
www.radford.va.us

In western VA, 14 mi. northeast of Pulaski. **Name Origin:** Previously called Lovely Mount, English Ferry, Ingle's Ferry, and Central Depot. Established as the town of Central City in 1885; incorporated in 1887. Name changed in 1890 to honor the original landowner, Dr. John Blair Radford; incorporated as a city in 1892.

Area (sq mi): 10.19 (land 9.82; water 0.37).

Pop: 15,859 (White 87.6%; Black or African American 8.1%; Hispanic or Latino 1.2%; Asian 1.4%; Other 2.2%). **Foreign born:** 2.5%. **Median age:** 22.8. **State rank:** 89. **Pop change 1990-2000:** -0.5%.

Income: per capita $14,289; median household $24,654. **Pop below poverty level:** 31.4%.

Unemployment: 4.6%. **Median home value:** $95,100. **Median travel time to work:** 16.1 minutes.

RAPPAHANNOCK COUNTY

PO Box 517   **Ph:** 540-675-3621
Washington, VA 22747

In north-central VA, west of Arlington; organized Feb 8, 1833 from Culpeper County (not to be confused with Old Rappahannock County, with county seat at Lancaster, organized 1656 from Lancaster County and abolished 1692). **Name Origin:** For the Rappahannock River.

Area (sq mi): 266.83 (land 266.57; water 0.26).

Pop: 6,983 (White 91.8%; Black or African American 5.4%; Hispanic or Latino 1.3%; Asian 0.2%; Other 1.7%). **Foreign born:** 3.2%. **Median age:** 42.6. **State rank:** 120. **Pop change 1990-2000:** +5.5%.

Income: per capita $23,863; median household $45,943. **Pop below poverty level:** 7.6%.

Unemployment: 1.6%. **Median home value:** $129,300. **Median travel time to work:** 38.7 minutes.

RICHMOND (INDEPENDENT CITY)

900 E Broad St Rm 201   **Ph:** 804-780-7970
Richmond, VA 232196115   **Fax:** 804-646-7987
www.ci.richmond.va.us

In southeastern VA, northwest of Norfolk. State capital; founded 1742. Major commercial (tobacco products, chemicals, printed material); cultural, educational (Univ. of Richmond and others); and historical center. Capital of the Confederate States of America 1861-65. Established in 1742; incorporated as a town in 1782; as a city in 1842. Serves as county seat for Henrico County. **Name Origin:** Probably for Richmond, Surrey, England.

Area (sq mi): 62.55 (land 60.07; water 2.48).

Pop: 197,790 (White 37.7%; Black or African American 57.2%; Hispanic or Latino 2.6%; Asian 1.2%; Other 3.3%). **Foreign born:**

All statistics are based on the 2000 Census except the dollar figures given for per capita income, which are based on 1999 estimates.

3.9%. **Median age:** 33.9. **State rank:** 8. **Pop change 1990-2000:** -2.6%.

Income: per capita $20,337; median household $31,121. **Pop below poverty level:** 21.4%.

Unemployment: 5%. **Median home value:** $87,300. **Median travel time to work:** 22.1 minutes.

RICHMOND COUNTY

101 Court Cir	**Ph:** 804-333-3781
Warsaw, VA 22572	**Fax:** 804-333-5396
www.co.richmond.va.us	

In east-central VA, on the north bank of the Rappahannock River; organized Apr 16, 1692 from Old Rappahannock County, which was organized 1656 from Lancaster County and abolished in 1692. **Name Origin:** For Richmond, Surrey, England.

Area (sq mi): 216.38 (land 191.46; water 24.92).

Pop: 8,809 (White 63.8%; Black or African American 33.2%; Hispanic or Latino 2.1%; Asian 0.3%; Other 1.8%). **Foreign born:** 1.9%. **Median age:** 40.3. **State rank:** 118. **Pop change 1990-2000:** +21.1%.

Income: per capita $16,675; median household $33,026. **Pop below poverty level:** 15.4%.

Unemployment: 3.5%. **Median home value:** $86,700. **Median travel time to work:** 28.6 minutes.

ROANOKE (INDEPENDENT CITY)

215 Church Ave SW	**Ph:** 540-853-2542
Roanoke, VA 24011	**Fax:** 540-853-1145
www.ci.roanoke.va.us	

In south-central VA, southwest of Lynchburg. Established in 1852 as Big Lick, for the large salt marsh where deer fed; incorporated in 1874. Name changed to Roanoke in 1882, became a city 1884. Convention and railroad center. **Name Origin:** From an Indian name applied to an island, possibly meaning '(place to find) shells that are used for money' or 'place where white shells are found.'

Area (sq mi): 42.91 (land 42.88; water 0.03).

Pop: 94,911 (White 68.8%; Black or African American 26.7%; Hispanic or Latino 1.5%; Asian 1.2%; Other 2.7%). **Foreign born:** 3.1%. **Median age:** 37.6. **State rank:** 15. **Pop change 1990-2000:** -1.5%.

Income: per capita $18,468; median household $30,719. **Pop below poverty level:** 15.9%.

Unemployment: 3.6%. **Median home value:** $80,300. **Median travel time to work:** 19.3 minutes.

ROANOKE COUNTY

5204 Bernard Dr	**Ph:** 540-772-2006
Roanoke, VA 24018	**Fax:** 540-772-2193
www.co.roanoke.va.us	

In west-central VA, west of Lynchburg; organized Mar 30, 1838 from Botetourt and Montgomery counties. **Name Origin:** From an Indian word spelled Roanoak by the first English settlers. Indians applied it to an island, meaning 'place where white shells are found' or perhaps 'shells which are used for money.' Or possibly named for the lost colony of Roanoke.

Area (sq mi): 251.04 (land 250.87; water 0.18).

Pop: 85,778 (White 93%; Black or African American 3.4%; Hispanic or Latino 1%; Asian 1.6%; Other 1.4%). **Foreign born:** 3.1%. **Median age:** 40.9. **State rank:** 19. **Pop change 1990-2000:** +8.1%.

Income: per capita $24,637; median household $47,689. **Pop below poverty level:** 4.5%.

Unemployment: 1.9%. **Median home value:** $118,100. **Median travel time to work:** 20.7 minutes.

ROCKBRIDGE COUNTY

150 S Main St	**Ph:** 540-463-4361
Lexington, VA 24450	**Fax:** 540-463-5981
www.co.rockbridge.va.us	

In west-central VA, northwest of Lynchburg; organized Mar 1, 1778 from Augusta and Botetourt counties. **Name Origin:** For the Natural Bridge or Rock Bridge, the most famous feature in the area.

Area (sq mi): 600.98 (land 599.63; water 1.35).

Pop: 20,808 (White 95%; Black or African American 3%; Hispanic or Latino 0.6%; Asian 0.4%; Other 1.2%). **Foreign born:** 2%. **Median age:** 40.4. **State rank:** 73. **Pop change 1990-2000:** +13.4%.

Income: per capita $18,356; median household $36,035. **Pop below poverty level:** 9.6%.

Unemployment: 2.7%. **Median home value:** $92,400. **Median travel time to work:** 25.1 minutes.

ROCKINGHAM COUNTY

Court Sq	**Ph:** 540-564-3000
Harrisonburg, VA 22801	**Fax:** 540-564-3127
www.co.rockingham.va.us	

On the northwestern border of VA, northwest of Charlottesville; organized Mar 1, 1778 from Augusta County. **Name Origin:** For Charles Watson Wentworth (1730-82), 2nd Marquess of Rockingham, prime minister of England who was largely responsible for the repeal of the Stamp Act.

Area (sq mi): 853.29 (land 851.15; water 2.14).

Pop: 67,725 (White 94.4%; Black or African American 1.4%; Hispanic or Latino 3.3%; Asian 0.3%; Other 1.7%). **Foreign born:** 3.3%. **Median age:** 37.5. **State rank:** 22. **Pop change 1990-2000:** +17.8%.

Income: per capita $18,795; median household $40,748. **Pop below poverty level:** 8.2%.

Unemployment: 1.9%. **Median home value:** $107,700. **Median travel time to work:** 22.8 minutes.

RUSSELL COUNTY

121 E Main St	**Ph:** 276-889-8000
Lebanon, VA 24266	**Fax:** 276-889-8011

In southwestern VA, north of Bristol, TN; organized May 1, 1786 from Washington County. **Name Origin:** For William Russell (1758-1825), VA officer in the Revolutionary War and statesman.

Area (sq mi): 476.77 (land 474.66; water 2.11).

Pop: 30,308 (White 95.6%; Black or African American 3.1%; Hispanic or Latino 0.8%; Asian 0%; Other 0.8%). **Foreign born:** 0.4%. **Median age:** 38.7. **State rank:** 55. **Pop change 1990-2000:** +5.7%.

Please see sample entry on inside front cover for detailed information about the statistics presented with each county listing.

Income: per capita $14,863; median household $26,834. **Pop below poverty level:** 16.3%.

Unemployment: 7.3%. **Median home value:** $69,800. **Median travel time to work:** 31.2 minutes.

SALEM (INDEPENDENT CITY)
PO Box 869   **Ph:** 540-375-3016
Salem, VA 24153   **Fax:** 540-375-4048
www.ci.salem.va.us

In west-central VA, 8 mi. west of Roanoke. Laid out 1802; established in 1806. Incorporated as a town in 1836; as a city in 1968. Serves as county seat for Roanoke County. **Name Origin:** For Salem, NJ, former home of an early settler.

Area (sq mi): 14.59 (land 14.59; water 0).

Pop: 24,747 (White 91.3%; Black or African American 5.9%; Hispanic or Latino 0.8%; Asian 1%; Other 1.2%). **Foreign born:** 2.1%. **Median age:** 39.2. **State rank:** 62. **Pop change 1990-2000:** +4.2%.

Income: per capita $20,091; median household $38,997. **Pop below poverty level:** 6.7%.

Unemployment: 2.4%. **Median home value:** $104,200. **Median travel time to work:** 17 minutes.

SCOTT COUNTY
112 Water St Suite 1   **Ph:** 276-386-6521
Gate City, VA 24251   **Fax:** 276-386-9198
www.scottcountyva.com

In southwest VA, north of Kingsport, TN; organized 1814 from Lee, Russell, and Washington counties. **Name Origin:** For Gen. Winfield Scott (1786-1866), VA officer during the War of 1812 and the Mexican War; general in chief of the U.S. Army (1841-61) and commander of the Union armies at the beginning of the Civil War.

Area (sq mi): 538.63 (land 536.58; water 2.05).

Pop: 23,403 (White 98.2%; Black or African American 0.6%; Hispanic or Latino 0.4%; Asian 0.1%; Other 0.7%). **Foreign born:** 0.3%. **Median age:** 41.4. **State rank:** 67. **Pop change 1990-2000:** +0.9%.

Income: per capita $15,073; median household $27,339. **Pop below poverty level:** 16.8%.

Unemployment: 4.9%. **Median home value:** $69,100. **Median travel time to work:** 30.6 minutes.

SHENANDOAH COUNTY
600 N Main St Suite 102   **Ph:** 540-459-6165
Woodstock, VA 22664   **Fax:** 540-459-6168
www.co.shenandoah.va.us

On the northeastern border of VA, northeast of Harrisonburg; organized as Dunmore County May 15, 1772 from Frederick County; name changed 1778. **Name Origin:** For the Shenandoah River.

Area (sq mi): 512.53 (land 512.2; water 0.32).

Pop: 35,075 (White 94.2%; Black or African American 1.2%; Hispanic or Latino 3.4%; Asian 0.3%; Other 2.9%). **Foreign born:** 3.1%. **Median age:** 40.9. **State rank:** 45. **Pop change 1990-2000:** +10.9%.

Income: per capita $19,755; median household $39,173. **Pop below poverty level:** 8.2%.

Unemployment: 2.1%. **Median home value:** $99,400. **Median travel time to work:** 27.1 minutes.

SMYTH COUNTY
109 W Main St Rm 144   **Ph:** 276-782-4044
Marion, VA 24354   **Fax:** 276-782-4045

In southwestern VA, northeast of Bristol, TN; organized Feb 23, 1832 from Washington and Wythe counties. **Name Origin:** For Gen. Alexander Smyth (1765-1830), U.S. representative from VA (1817-25; 1827-30).

Area (sq mi): 452.31 (land 452.09; water 0.22).

Pop: 33,081 (White 96.4%; Black or African American 1.9%; Hispanic or Latino 0.9%; Asian 0.2%; Other 1.1%). **Foreign born:** 0.5%. **Median age:** 40. **State rank:** 49. **Pop change 1990-2000:** +2.2%.

Income: per capita $16,105; median household $30,083. **Pop below poverty level:** 13.3%.

Unemployment: 8.8%. **Median home value:** $67,900. **Median travel time to work:** 22.5 minutes.

SOUTHAMPTON COUNTY
PO Box 190   **Ph:** 757-653-2200
Courtland, VA 23837

In southeastern VA, west of Norfolk; organized Apr 30, 1749 from Isle of Wight and Nansemond counties. Site of Nat Turner's (1800-31) Rebellion (1831). Part annexed to Franklin (independent) city effective December 31, 1995. **Name Origin:** For Henry Wriothesley (1573-1624), 3rd Earl of Southampton, English statesman and patron of William Shakespeare (1564-1616).

Area (sq mi): 602.35 (land 599.56; water 2.8).

Pop: 17,482 (White 55.8%; Black or African American 42.9%; Hispanic or Latino 0.7%; Asian 0.2%; Other 1%). **Foreign born:** 0.3%. **Median age:** 38.6. **State rank:** 81. **Pop change 1990-2000:** -0.4%.

Income: per capita $16,930; median household $33,995. **Pop below poverty level:** 14.6%.

Unemployment: 2.6%. **Median home value:** $82,500. **Median travel time to work:** 26.6 minutes.

SPOTSYLVANIA COUNTY
PO Box 99   **Ph:** 540-582-7010
Spotsylvania, VA 22553   **Fax:** 540-582-9308
www.spotsylvania.va.us

In east-central VA, north of Richmond; organized 1721 from Essex, King William, and King and Queen counties. **Name Origin:** For Alexander Spotswood (1676-1740), lieutenant governor of the colony of VA (1710-22). Name is a combination of *Spots*wood and *sylvania* 'woodlands,' a play on the surname.

Area (sq mi): 412.27 (land 400.86; water 11.41).

Pop: 90,395 (White 81.4%; Black or African American 12.5%; Hispanic or Latino 2.8%; Asian 1.4%; Other 3.2%). **Foreign born:** 3.2%. **Median age:** 34.3. **State rank:** 17. **Pop change 1990-2000:** +57.5%.

All statistics are based on the 2000 Census except the dollar figures given for per capita income, which are based on 1999 estimates.

Income: per capita $22,536; median household $57,525. **Pop below poverty level:** 4.7%.

Unemployment: 1.7%. **Median home value:** $128,500. **Median travel time to work:** 37.1 minutes.

STAFFORD COUNTY

1300 Court House Rd   **Ph:** 540-658-8605
Stafford, VA 22555   **Fax:** 540-658-7643
www.co.stafford.va.us

On the northeastern coast of VA, on west bank of upper Potomac River; organized 1664 from Westmoreland County. Part of the facility is also in Prince William County. **Name Origin:** For the county of Staffordshire, England.

Area (sq mi): 279.95 (land 270.35; water 9.59).

Pop: 92,446 (White 80.1%; Black or African American 12.1%; Hispanic or Latino 3.6%; Asian 1.6%; Other 4.3%). **Foreign born:** 4%. **Median age:** 33.1. **State rank:** 16. **Pop change 1990-2000:** +51%.

Income: per capita $24,762; median household $66,809. **Pop below poverty level:** 3.5%.

Unemployment: 1.7%. **Median home value:** $156,400. **Median travel time to work:** 37.7 minutes.

STAUNTON (INDEPENDENT CITY)

PO Box 58   **Ph:** 540-332-3800
Staunton, VA 24402   **Fax:** 540-332-3807
www.staunton.va.us

In north-central VA, 35 mi. northwest of Charlottesville. Laid out in 1748; established as a town in 1761. Incorporated as a town in 1801; as a city in 1871. Serves as county seat for Augusta County. **Name Origin:** For Rebecca Staunton, wife of colonial governor William Gooch.

Area (sq mi): 19.71 (land 19.71; water 0).

Pop: 23,853 (White 82.7%; Black or African American 14%; Hispanic or Latino 1.1%; Asian 0.5%; Other 2.3%). **Foreign born:** 2%. **Median age:** 39.8. **State rank:** 64. **Pop change 1990-2000:** -2.5%.

Income: per capita $19,161; median household $32,941. **Pop below poverty level:** 11.7%.

Unemployment: 2.5%. **Median home value:** $87,500. **Median travel time to work:** 19.9 minutes.

SUFFOLK (INDEPENDENT CITY)

PO Box 1858   **Ph:** 757-923-2085
Suffolk, VA 23439   **Fax:** 757-923-2091
www.suffolk.va.us

In southeastern VA on the Nansemond River, 18 mi. southwest of Portsmouth. Established in 1742; incorporated as a town in 1808; as a city in 1910. **Name Origin:** For the county in England.

Area (sq mi): 429.07 (land 400.02; water 29.05).

Pop: 63,677 (White 53.3%; Black or African American 43.5%; Hispanic or Latino 1.3%; Asian 0.8%; Other 1.9%). **Foreign born:** 1.9%. **Median age:** 36. **State rank:** 25. **Pop change 1990-2000:** +22.1%.

Income: per capita $18,836; median household $41,115. **Pop below poverty level:** 13.2%.

Unemployment: 3.5%. **Median home value:** $107,300. **Median travel time to work:** 27.3 minutes.

SURRY COUNTY

PO Box 65   **Ph:** 757-294-5271
Surry, VA 23883   **Fax:** 757-294-5204
www.co.surry.va.us

On southeastern coast of VA, on south bank of the James River; organized 1652 from James City County. **Name Origin:** For Surrey, England; spelling is a clerical error.

Area (sq mi): 310.31 (land 279.09; water 31.22).

Pop: 6,829 (White 46.4%; Black or African American 51.6%; Hispanic or Latino 0.7%; Asian 0.1%; Other 1.3%). **Foreign born:** 0.5%. **Median age:** 39.4. **State rank:** 125. **Pop change 1990-2000:** +11.1%.

Income: per capita $16,682; median household $37,558. **Pop below poverty level:** 10.8%.

Unemployment: 5.4%. **Median home value:** $88,100. **Median travel time to work:** 39 minutes.

SUSSEX COUNTY

PO Box 1337   **Ph:** 434-246-5511
Sussex, VA 23884

In southeastern VA, south of Richmond; organized 1754 from Surry County. **Name Origin:** For the county in England.

Area (sq mi): 492.83 (land 490.73; water 2.1).

Pop: 12,504 (White 36.3%; Black or African American 62.1%; Hispanic or Latino 0.8%; Asian 0.1%; Other 1.3%). **Foreign born:** 1%. **Median age:** 37.6. **State rank:** 104. **Pop change 1990-2000:** +22%.

Income: per capita $14,670; median household $31,007. **Pop below poverty level:** 16.1%.

Unemployment: 4%. **Median home value:** $71,600. **Median travel time to work:** 27.9 minutes.

TAZEWELL COUNTY

PO Box 968   **Ph:** 276-988-1222
Tazewell, VA 24651   **Fax:** 276-988-7501

On the southwestern border of VA, northeast of Bristol, TN; organized 1800 from Russell and Wythe counties. **Name Origin:** For Henry Tazewell (1753-99), VA legislator, chief justice (1785-93), and U.S. senator (1794-99).

Area (sq mi): 519.89 (land 519.74; water 0.15).

Pop: 44,598 (White 95.8%; Black or African American 2.3%; Hispanic or Latino 0.5%; Asian 0.6%; Other 1%). **Foreign born:** 1%. **Median age:** 40.7. **State rank:** 38. **Pop change 1990-2000:** -3%.

Income: per capita $15,282; median household $27,304. **Pop below poverty level:** 15.3%.

Unemployment: 4.4%. **Median home value:** $67,900. **Median travel time to work:** 26.6 minutes.

Please see sample entry on inside front cover for detailed information about the statistics presented with each county listing.

VIRGINIA BEACH (INDEPENDENT CITY)

2401 Courthouse Dr Municipal Ctr Bldg 1   **Ph:** 757-427-4242
Virginia Beach, VA 23456   **Fax:** 757-427-4135
www.virginia-beach.va.us

In southeastern VA on the Atlantic Ocean, 18 mi. east of Norfolk. Incorporated as a town in 1906; as a city in 1952. **Name Origin:** This noted oceanside resort is named for the state.

Area (sq mi): 497.33 (land 248.29; water 249.03).

Pop: 425,257 (White 69.5%; Black or African American 19%; Hispanic or Latino 4.2%; Asian 4.9%; Other 4.7%). **Foreign born:** 6.6%. **Median age:** 32.7. **State rank:** 2. **Pop change 1990-2000:** +8.2%.

Income: per capita $22,365; median household $48,705. **Pop below poverty level:** 6.5%.

Unemployment: 3%. **Median home value:** $123,200. **Median travel time to work:** 23.9 minutes.

WARREN COUNTY

220 N Commerce Ave Suite 100   **Ph:** 540-636-4600
Front Royal, VA 22630   **Fax:** 540-636-6066
www.co.warren.va.us

In north-central VA, west of Arlington; organized Mar 9, 1836 from Frederick and Shenandoah counties. **Name Origin:** For Gen. Joseph Warren (1741-75), Revolutionary War patriot and member of the Committee of Safety who dispatched Paul Revere (1735-1818) on his famous ride.

Area (sq mi): 216.32 (land 213.7; water 2.63).

Pop: 31,584 (White 91.7%; Black or African American 4.8%; Hispanic or Latino 1.6%; Asian 0.4%; Other 2.1%). **Foreign born:** 2.1%. **Median age:** 37.1. **State rank:** 53. **Pop change 1990-2000:** +20.8%.

Income: per capita $19,841; median household $42,422. **Pop below poverty level:** 8.5%.

Unemployment: 2.8%. **Median home value:** $108,800. **Median travel time to work:** 39.1 minutes.

WASHINGTON COUNTY

205 Academy Dr   **Ph:** 276-676-6202
Abingdon, VA 24210   **Fax:** 276-676-6201
www.washcova.com

On the southwestern border of VA, north of Bristol, TN; organized Oct 7, 1776 from Fincastle (organized 1772 from Botetourt County and abolished 1777) and Montgomery counties. **Name Origin:** For George Washington (1732-99), American patriot and first U.S. president.

Area (sq mi): 565.98 (land 562.86; water 3.12).

Pop: 51,103 (White 97%; Black or African American 1.3%; Hispanic or Latino 0.6%; Asian 0.3%; Other 0.8%). **Foreign born:** 0.9%. **Median age:** 40.3. **State rank:** 32. **Pop change 1990-2000:** +11.4%.

Income: per capita $18,350; median household $32,742. **Pop below poverty level:** 10.9%.

Unemployment: 5.9%. **Median home value:** $90,400. **Median travel time to work:** 24.2 minutes.

WAYNESBORO (INDEPENDENT CITY)

PO Box 1028   **Ph:** 540-942-6600
Waynesboro, VA 22980   **Fax:** 540-942-6671
www.waynesborova-online.com

In north-central VA, in the Shenandoah Valley at the foot of the Blue Ridge Mountains, 12 mi. southeast of Staunton. Laid out in 1797; established as a town in 1801. Incorporated as a town in 1834; as a city in 1948. Annexed part of Augusta County effective July 1, 1994. **Name Origin:** For Gen. Anthony Wayne (1745-96), PA soldier and statesman, nicknamed 'Mad Anthony' for his daring during the American Revolution.

Area (sq mi): 15.38 (land 15.36; water 0.02).

Pop: 19,520 (White 84.5%; Black or African American 10%; Hispanic or Latino 3.3%; Asian 0.6%; Other 3%). **Foreign born:** 2.4%. **Median age:** 38.9. **State rank:** 76. **Pop change 1990-2000:** +5.2%.

Income: per capita $17,932; median household $32,686. **Pop below poverty level:** 12.8%.

Unemployment: 4.1%. **Median home value:** $89,300. **Median travel time to work:** 19.3 minutes.

WESTMORELAND COUNTY

PO Box 1000   **Ph:** 804-493-0130
Montross, VA 22520   **Fax:** 804-493-0134
www.westmoreland-county.org

On the central eastern coast of VA, along the west bank of the Potomac River; organized Jul 5, 1653 from Northumberland County. **Name Origin:** For the county in England.

Area (sq mi): 252.64 (land 229.18; water 23.46).

Pop: 16,718 (White 64.1%; Black or African American 30.9%; Hispanic or Latino 3.5%; Asian 0.4%; Other 3.3%). **Foreign born:** 3.1%. **Median age:** 42.8. **State rank:** 86. **Pop change 1990-2000:** +8%.

Income: per capita $19,473; median household $35,797. **Pop below poverty level:** 14.7%.

Unemployment: 5.1%. **Median home value:** $95,300. **Median travel time to work:** 37.1 minutes.

WILLIAMSBURG (INDEPENDENT CITY)

401 Lafayette St   **Ph:** 757-220-6100
Williamsburg, VA 23185   **Fax:** 757-220-6107
www.ci.williamsburg.va.us

In southeastern VA on the peninsula between the James and York rivers, 27 mi. northwest of Newport News. Capital of VA, 1699-1780. Site of College of William and Mary. Serves as county seat for James City County. **Name Origin:** Established in 1633 as Middle Plantation. Renamed in 1699 for William III (1650-1702), king of England; incorporated as a city in 1884.

Area (sq mi): 8.67 (land 8.54; water 0.13).

Pop: 11,998 (White 77.9%; Black or African American 13.3%; Hispanic or Latino 2.5%; Asian 4.6%; Other 2.7%). **Foreign born:** 5.2%. **Median age:** 22.6. **State rank:** 107. **Pop change 1990-2000:** +4.1%.

Income: per capita $18,483; median household $37,093. **Pop below poverty level:** 18.3%.

All statistics are based on the 2000 Census except the dollar figures given for per capita income, which are based on 1999 estimates.

Unemployment: 6%. **Median home value:** $212,000. **Median travel time to work:** 18 minutes.

WINCHESTER (INDEPENDENT CITY)

5 N Kent St   **Ph:** 540-667-5770
Winchester, VA 22601   **Fax:** 540-667-6638
www.ci.winchester.va.us

In northern VA, in the Shenandoah Valley, 70 mi. northwest of Alexandria. Settled 1738; established in 1752. Incorporated as a town in 1779; as a city in 1874. Serves as county seat for Frederick County. **Name Origin:** Named by James Wood, one of the town founders, for Winchester, England, his birthplace. Previously called Opequon, Frederick's Town, and Fredericktown.

Area (sq mi): 9.33 (land 9.33; water 0).

Pop: 23,585 (White 79.4%; Black or African American 10.5%; Hispanic or Latino 6.5%; Asian 1.6%; Other 5.8%). **Foreign born:** 6.8%. **Median age:** 35.2. **State rank:** 66. **Pop change 1990-2000:** +7.5%.

Income: per capita $20,500; median household $34,335. **Pop below poverty level:** 13.2%.

Unemployment: 3%. **Median home value:** $108,900. **Median travel time to work:** 20.1 minutes.

WISE COUNTY

PO Box 570   **Ph:** 276-328-2321
Wise, VA 24293   **Fax:** 276-328-9780
www.wisecounty.org

On the southwestern border of VA, north of Kingsport, TN; organized Feb 16, 1856 from Lee, Russell, and Scott counties. **Name Origin:** For Gen. Henry A. Wise (1806-76), U.S. representative from VA (1833-44), governor (1856-60), and Confederate Army officer.

Area (sq mi): 405.22 (land 404.04; water 1.18).

Pop: 40,123 (White 96.4%; Black or African American 1.8%; Hispanic or Latino 0.7%; Asian 0.3%; Other 1.1%). **Foreign born:** 0.5%. **Median age:** 37.8. **State rank:** 40. **Pop change 1990-2000:** +1.4%.

Income: per capita $14,271; median household $26,149. **Pop below poverty level:** 20%.

Unemployment: 5.6%. **Median home value:** $65,700. **Median travel time to work:** 23.6 minutes.

WYTHE COUNTY

345 S 4th St   **Ph:** 276-223-6020
Wytheville, VA 24382   **Fax:** 276-223-6030
wythe.pcsos.com

In southwestern VA, southwest of Roanoke; organized May 1, 1790 from Montgomery County. **Name Origin:** For George Wythe (1726-1806), VA patriot, first law professor in the U.S., member of the House of Burgesses (1758-68), and signer of the Declaration of Independence.

Area (sq mi): 464.62 (land 463.24; water 1.37).

Pop: 27,599 (White 95.4%; Black or African American 2.9%; Hispanic or Latino 0.6%; Asian 0.4%; Other 1%). **Foreign born:** 0.5%. **Median age:** 39.4. **State rank:** 58. **Pop change 1990-2000:** +8.4%.

Income: per capita $17,639; median household $32,235. **Pop below poverty level:** 11%.

Unemployment: 9.7%. **Median home value:** $77,300. **Median travel time to work:** 24.2 minutes.

YORK COUNTY

300 Ballard St   **Ph:** 757-890-3450
Yorktown, VA 23690   **Fax:** 757-890-3459
www.co.york.va.us

On the southeastern coast of VA, on the west bank of the York River; original county; organized as Charles River Shire 1634; name changed 1642. **Name Origin:** Renamed York for Charles (1600-49), Duke of York, later King Charles I; this to avoid confusion of the original name, Charles River, with Charles City (County).

Area (sq mi): 215.52 (land 105.65; water 109.87).

Pop: 56,297 (White 78.5%; Black or African American 13.4%; Hispanic or Latino 2.7%; Asian 3.2%; Other 3.3%). **Foreign born:** 5.2%. **Median age:** 36.5. **State rank:** 30. **Pop change 1990-2000:** +32.7%.

Income: per capita $24,560; median household $57,956. **Pop below poverty level:** 3.5%.

Unemployment: 2.2%. **Median home value:** $152,700. **Median travel time to work:** 23.7 minutes.

Please see sample entry on inside front cover for detailed information about the statistics presented with each county listing.

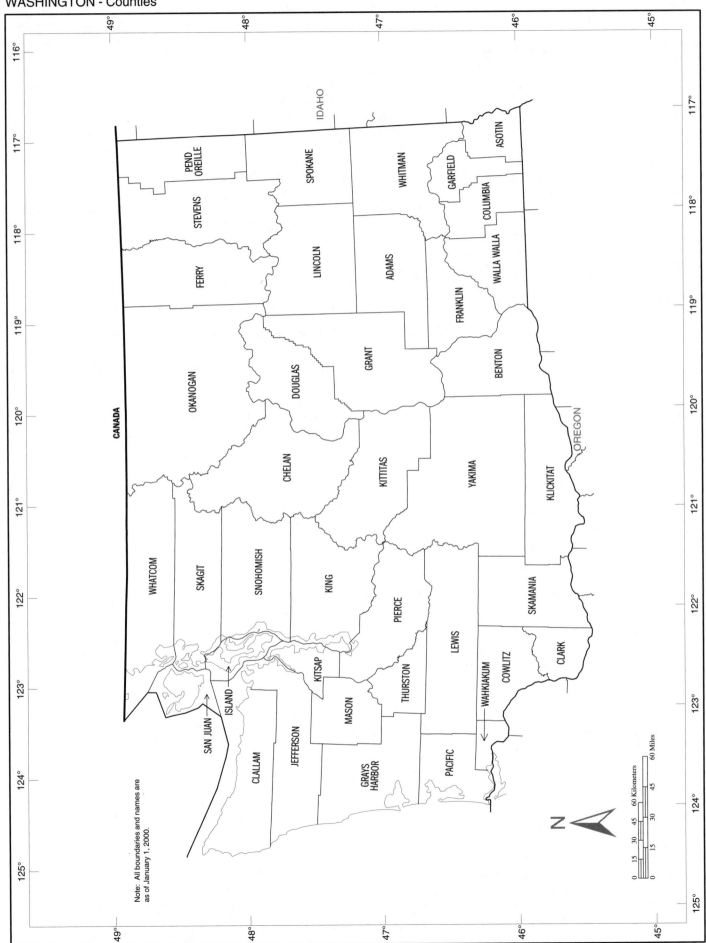

WASHINGTON - Counties

CANADA

IDAHO

OREGON

WHATCOM

SAN JUAN

OKANOGAN

FERRY

STEVENS

PEND OREILLE

SPOKANE

LINCOLN

DOUGLAS

GRANT

ADAMS

WHITMAN

GARFIELD

COLUMBIA

ASOTIN

WALLA WALLA

FRANKLIN

BENTON

CLALLAM

JEFFERSON

SKAGIT

SNOHOMISH

CHELAN

KING

KITTITAS

YAKIMA

KLICKITAT

SKAMANIA

CLARK

COWLITZ

WAHKIAKUM

LEWIS

PIERCE

THURSTON

MASON

KITSAP

ISLAND

GRAYS HARBOR

PACIFIC

Note: All boundaries and names are as of January 1, 2000.

0   15   30   45   60 Kilometers
0   15   30   45   60 Miles

N

Washington

WASHINGTON STATE INFORMATION

access.wa.gov   **Ph:** 360-753-5000

Area (sq mi): 71,299.64 (land 66,544.06; water 4755.58).

Pop: 5,894,121 (White 78.9%; Black or African American 3.2%; Hispanic or Latino 7.5%; Asian 5.5%; Other 9.5%). **Foreign born:** 10.4%. **Median age:** 35.3. **Pop change 1990-2000:** +21.1%.

Income: per capita $22,973; median household $45,776. **Pop below poverty level:** 10.6%.

Unemployment: 6.6%. **Median home value:** $168,300. **Median travel time to work:** 25.5 minutes.

ADAMS COUNTY

PO Box 187   **Ph:** 509-659-3257
Ritzville, WA 99169   **Fax:** 509-659-0118
www.co.adams.wa.us

In southeast WA, southwest of Spokane; organized Nov 28, 1883 (prior to statehood) from Whitman County. **Name Origin:** For John Adams (1735-1826), second U.S. president.

Area (sq mi): 1929.69 (land 1924.96; water 4.73).

Pop: 16,428 (White 50.9%; Black or African American 0.3%; Hispanic or Latino 47.1%; Asian 0.6%; Other 34.1%). **Foreign born:** 22.9%. **Median age:** 29.6. **State rank:** 31. **Pop change 1990-2000:** +20.8%.

Income: per capita $13,534; median household $33,888. **Pop below poverty level:** 18.2%.

Unemployment: 10.8%. **Median home value:** $84,300. **Median travel time to work:** 17.7 minutes.

ASOTIN COUNTY

PO Box 159   **Ph:** 509-243-2081
Asotin, WA 99402   **Fax:** 509-243-4978
www.co.asotin.wa.us

On the southeastern border of WA; organized Oct 27, 1883 (prior to statehood) from Garfield County. **Name Origin:** For Asotin Creek, which runs through the county; Nez Perce word meaning 'eel creek.'

Area (sq mi): 640.69 (land 635.34; water 5.34).

Pop: 20,551 (White 94.5%; Black or African American 0.2%; Hispanic or Latino 2%; Asian 0.5%; Other 3.7%). **Foreign born:** 1.8%. **Median age:** 38.8. **State rank:** 29. **Pop change 1990-2000:** +16.7%.

Income: per capita $17,748; median household $33,524. **Pop below poverty level:** 15.4%.

Unemployment: 4.8%. **Median home value:** $100,500. **Median travel time to work:** 16.8 minutes.

BENTON COUNTY

7320 W Quinault Ave   **Ph:** 509-735-8388
Kennewick, WA 99336   **Fax:** 509-736-3069
www.co.benton.wa.us

On the south-central border of WA; organized Mar 8, 1905 from Yakima and Klickitat counties. **Name Origin:** For Thomas Hart Benton (1782-1858), U.S. journalist and statesman; nicknamed 'Old Bullion' for championing the use of gold and silver currency rather than paper money.

Area (sq mi): 1760.12 (land 1703.09; water 57.03).

Pop: 142,475 (White 81.7%; Black or African American 0.9%; Hispanic or Latino 12.5%; Asian 2.2%; Other 10.6%). **Foreign born:** 8.5%. **Median age:** 34.4. **State rank:** 10. **Pop change 1990-2000:** +26.6%.

Income: per capita $21,301; median household $47,044. **Pop below poverty level:** 10.3%.

Unemployment: 6.5%. **Median home value:** $119,900. **Median travel time to work:** 21.5 minutes.

CHELAN COUNTY

350 Orondo Ave PO Box 3025   **Ph:** 509-667-6380
Wenatchee, WA 98801   **Fax:** 509-667-6611
www.co.chelan.wa.us

In north-central WA, east of Seattle; organized Mar 13, 1899 from Kittitas and Okanogan counties. **Name Origin:** For Chelan Lake; from a Salish Indian tribal name, *tsill-anne*, said to mean 'deep water.'

Area (sq mi): 2993.62 (land 2921.37; water 72.25).

Pop: 66,616 (White 77.4%; Black or African American 0.3%; Hispanic or Latino 19.3%; Asian 0.7%; Other 15.4%). **Foreign born:** 12.9%. **Median age:** 36.3. **State rank:** 17. **Pop change 1990-2000:** +27.5%.

Income: per capita $19,273; median household $37,316. **Pop below poverty level:** 12.4%.

Unemployment: 9.5%. **Median home value:** $148,400. **Median travel time to work:** 17.7 minutes.

CLALLAM COUNTY

223 E 4th St   **Ph:** 360-452-7831
Port Angeles, WA 98361   **Fax:** 360-417-2493
www.clallam.net

On the northwest coast of WA, bordered on the north by the Strait

---

Please see sample entry on inside front cover for detailed information about the statistics presented with each county listing.

of Juan de Fuca; organized as Clalm County Apr 26,1854 (prior to statehood) from Jefferson County; spelling changed soon after. **Name Origin:** For the Indian tribe; name means 'strong people.'

Area (sq mi): 2670.34 (land 1739.45; water 930.89).

Pop: 64,525 (White 87.4%; Black or African American 0.8%; Hispanic or Latino 3.4%; Asian 1.1%; Other 8.9%). **Foreign born:** 4.5%. **Median age:** 43.8. **State rank:** 18. **Pop change 1990-2000:** +14.3%.

Income: per capita $19,517; median household $36,449. **Pop below poverty level:** 12.5%.

Unemployment: 7.8%. **Median home value:** $133,400. **Median travel time to work:** 21.4 minutes.

CLARK COUNTY
1200 Franklin St   **Ph:** 360-397-2000
Vancouver, WA 98660   **Fax:** 360-397-6099
www.co.clark.wa.us

On the southwestern border of WA, north of Portland, OR; original county. Organized as Vancouver County Dec 21, 1845 (prior to statehood); name changed Sep 3, 1849. **Name Origin:** For William Clark (1770-1838), explorer and co-leader of the Lewis and Clark expedition (1804-06).

Area (sq mi): 656.22 (land 628.22; water 27.99).

Pop: 345,238 (White 86.6%; Black or African American 1.7%; Hispanic or Latino 4.7%; Asian 3.2%; Other 6.3%). **Foreign born:** 8.5%. **Median age:** 34.2. **State rank:** 5. **Pop change 1990-2000:** +45%.

Income: per capita $21,448; median household $48,376. **Pop below poverty level:** 9.1%.

Unemployment: 7.1%. **Median home value:** $156,600. **Median travel time to work:** 24.7 minutes.

COLUMBIA COUNTY
341 E Main St   **Ph:** 509-382-4542
Dayton, WA 99328   **Fax:** 509-382-2490
www.columbiaco.com

On the southeastern border of WA; organized Nov 11, 1875 (prior to statehood) from Walla Walla County. **Name Origin:** For the Columbia River.

Area (sq mi): 873.53 (land 868.81; water 4.71).

Pop: 4,064 (White 90.7%; Black or African American 0.2%; Hispanic or Latino 6.3%; Asian 0.4%; Other 5.6%). **Foreign born:** 3.2%. **Median age:** 42.4. **State rank:** 37. **Pop change 1990-2000:** +1%.

Income: per capita $17,374; median household $33,500. **Pop below poverty level:** 12.6%.

Unemployment: 11.4%. **Median home value:** $85,000. **Median travel time to work:** 18.7 minutes.

COWLITZ COUNTY
312 SW 1st Ave   **Ph:** 360-577-3016
Kelso, WA 98626
www.co.cowlitz.wa.us

In southwestern WA, north of Portland, OR; organized Apr 21,

1854 (prior to statehood) from Lewis County. **Name Origin:** For the Cowlitz River, which flows through the county; from an Indian tribal name; meaning uncertain but possibly 'river of shifting sand.'

Area (sq mi): 1166.33 (land 1138.64; water 27.69).

Pop: 92,948 (White 89.9%; Black or African American 0.5%; Hispanic or Latino 4.6%; Asian 1.3%; Other 6.3%). **Foreign born:** 3.7%. **Median age:** 36.9. **State rank:** 12. **Pop change 1990-2000:** +13.2%.

Income: per capita $18,583; median household $39,797. **Pop below poverty level:** 14%.

Unemployment: 11%. **Median home value:** $129,900. **Median travel time to work:** 21.3 minutes.

DOUGLAS COUNTY
PO Box 747   **Ph:** 509-745-8537
Waterville, WA 98858   **Fax:** 509-745-9045
www.douglascountywa.net

In east-central WA, west of Spokane; organized Nov 28, 1883 (prior to statehood) from Lincoln County, just four days after Lincoln Co. was formed. **Name Origin:** For Stephen Arnold Douglas (1813-61), U.S. orator and statesman.

Area (sq mi): 1848.69 (land 1820.53; water 28.17).

Pop: 32,603 (White 77.2%; Black or African American 0.3%; Hispanic or Latino 19.7%; Asian 0.5%; Other 14.5%). **Foreign born:** 13.5%. **Median age:** 35.7. **State rank:** 26. **Pop change 1990-2000:** +24.4%.

Income: per capita $17,148; median household $38,464. **Pop below poverty level:** 14.4%.

Unemployment: 7.6%. **Median home value:** $134,600. **Median travel time to work:** 19.1 minutes.

FERRY COUNTY
290 E Tessie Ave   **Ph:** 509-775-5229
Republic, WA 99166   **Fax:** 509-775-5230

On northeastern border of WA, northwest of Spokane; organized as Eureka County Jan 12, 1899 from Stevens County; name changed Feb 16, 1899. Northern half is part of Colville National Forest; southern half comprises the Colville Indian Reservation. **Name Origin:** For Elisha Peyre Ferry (1825-95), first governor of WA (1889-93).

Area (sq mi): 2257.46 (land 2203.98; water 53.48).

Pop: 7,260 (White 74.9%; Black or African American 0.2%; Hispanic or Latino 2.8%; Asian 0.3%; Other 24.1%). **Foreign born:** 2.5%. **Median age:** 40. **State rank:** 36. **Pop change 1990-2000:** +15.3%.

Income: per capita $15,019; median household $30,388. **Pop below poverty level:** 19%.

Unemployment: 14.5%. **Median home value:** $92,400. **Median travel time to work:** 24 minutes.

FRANKLIN COUNTY
1016 N 4th Ave   **Ph:** 509-545-3535
Pasco, WA 99301   **Fax:** 509-545-3573
www.co.franklin.wa.us

In southeastern WA; organized Nov 28, 1883 (prior to statehood)

All statistics are based on the 2000 Census except the dollar figures given for per capita income, which are based on 1999 estimates.

from Whitman County. **Name Origin:** For Benjamin Franklin (1706-90), U.S. patriot, diplomat, and statesman.

Area (sq mi): 1265.35 (land 1242.4; water 22.95).

Pop: 49,347 (White 47.6%; Black or African American 2.5%; Hispanic or Latino 46.7%; Asian 1.6%; Other 33.9%). **Foreign born:** 25.2%. **Median age:** 28. **State rank:** 21. **Pop change 1990-2000:** +31.7%.

Income: per capita $15,459; median household $38,991. **Pop below poverty level:** 19.2%.

Unemployment: 9.4%. **Median home value:** $102,000. **Median travel time to work:** 20.9 minutes.

GARFIELD COUNTY
PO Box 915   **Ph:** 509-843-3731
Pomeroy, WA 99347   **Fax:** 509-843-1224

In southeastern WA; organized Nov 29, 1881 (prior to statehood) from Columbia County. **Name Origin:** For James Abram Garfiesld (1831-81), twentieth U.S. president.

Area (sq mi): 718.19 (land 710.55; water 7.64).

Pop: 2,397 (White 96.1%; Black or African American 0%; Hispanic or Latino 2%; Asian 0.7%; Other 2.9%). **Foreign born:** 1%. **Median age:** 43. **State rank:** 39. **Pop change 1990-2000:** +6.6%.

Income: per capita $16,992; median household $33,398. **Pop below poverty level:** 14.2%.

Unemployment: 3.7%. **Median home value:** $68,100. **Median travel time to work:** 18.3 minutes.

GRANT COUNTY
35 C St NW   **Ph:** 509-754-2011
Ephrata, WA 98823   **Fax:** 509-754-6098
www.grantcounty-wa.com

In east-central WA; organized Feb 24, 1909 from Douglas County. **Name Origin:** For Ulysses Simpson Grant (1822-85), Civil War general and eighteenth U.S. president.

Area (sq mi): 2791.29 (land 2681.06; water 110.23).

Pop: 74,698 (White 65.4%; Black or African American 1%; Hispanic or Latino 30.1%; Asian 0.9%; Other 21.7%). **Foreign born:** 17.1%. **Median age:** 31.1. **State rank:** 13. **Pop change 1990-2000:** +36.4%.

Income: per capita $15,037; median household $35,276. **Pop below poverty level:** 17.4%.

Unemployment: 10.3%. **Median home value:** $99,500. **Median travel time to work:** 17.7 minutes.

GRAYS HARBOR COUNTY
102 W Broadway St Rm 203   **Ph:** 360-249-3842
Montesano, WA 98563   **Fax:** 360-249-6381
www.graysharbor.com

On the west-central coast of WA, E of Olympia; organized as Chehalis County Apr 14, 1854 (prior to statehood); name changed Mar 15, 1915. **Name Origin:** For Robert Gray (1755-1806), an American who discovered Grays Harbor and named it *Bulfinch* for an owner of his ship. Formerly called *Puerto Grek* by Spanish explorer Martinez y Zayas and *Whidbey* or *Whitbey Harbor* by British explorer David Douglas.

Area (sq mi): 2224.44 (land 1916.89; water 307.55).

Pop: 67,194 (White 86.5%; Black or African American 0.3%; Hispanic or Latino 4.8%; Asian 1.2%; Other 10.2%). **Foreign born:** 4.2%. **Median age:** 38.8. **State rank:** 16. **Pop change 1990-2000:** +4.7%.

Income: per capita $16,799; median household $34,160. **Pop below poverty level:** 16.1%.

Unemployment: 10.6%. **Median home value:** $96,400. **Median travel time to work:** 22.4 minutes.

ISLAND COUNTY
PO Box 5000   **Ph:** 360-679-7354
Coupeville, WA 98239   **Fax:** 360-679-7381
www.islandcounty.net

In northwestern WA, bounded on the north by Deception Pass, on the east by Skagit Bay, on the south by Admiralty Inlet, and on the west by the Strait of Juan de Fuca. Organized Jan 6, 1853 (prior to statehood) from either King County or Thurston County. **Name Origin:** So named because the county is wholly composed of islands.

Area (sq mi): 517.39 (land 208.43; water 308.95).

Pop: 71,558 (White 85.1%; Black or African American 2.4%; Hispanic or Latino 4%; Asian 4.2%; Other 6.2%). **Foreign born:** 6.4%. **Median age:** 37. **State rank:** 14. **Pop change 1990-2000:** +18.9%.

Income: per capita $21,472; median household $45,513. **Pop below poverty level:** 7%.

Unemployment: 4.7%. **Median home value:** $174,800. **Median travel time to work:** 28.8 minutes.

JEFFERSON COUNTY
PO Box 1220   **Ph:** 360-385-9100
Port Townsend, WA 98368   **Fax:** 360-385-9382
www.co.jefferson.wa.us

On the northwestern coast of WA, E of Seattle; original county; organized Dec 23, 1852 (prior to statehood). **Name Origin:** For Thomas Jefferson (1743-1826), U.S. patriot and statesman; third U.S. president.

Area (sq mi): 2183.52 (land 1814.23; water 369.29).

Pop: 25,953 (White 91%; Black or African American 0.4%; Hispanic or Latino 2.1%; Asian 1.2%; Other 6.2%). **Foreign born:** 4%. **Median age:** 47.1. **State rank:** 27. **Pop change 1990-2000:** +28.8%.

Income: per capita $22,211; median household $37,869. **Pop below poverty level:** 11.3%.

Unemployment: 5.8%. **Median home value:** $171,900. **Median travel time to work:** 26 minutes.

KING COUNTY
516 3rd Ave Rm 400   **Ph:** 206-296-4040
Seattle, WA 98104   **Fax:** 206-296-0194
www.metrokc.gov

In west-central WA, bounded on west by Puget Sound; organized Dec 22, 1852 (prior to statehood) from Thurston County. **Name Origin:** For William Rufus King (1786-1853), U.S. senator from AL (1819-44; 1848-52) and vice president for six weeks before his

Please see sample entry on inside front cover for detailed information about the statistics presented with each county listing.

death. In 1986 it was decided the name would honor Martin Luther King, Jr. (1929-68), slain civil rights leader.

Area (sq mi): 2306.53 (land 2126.04; water 180.48).

Pop: 1,737,034 (White 73.4%; Black or African American 5.4%; Hispanic or Latino 5.5%; Asian 10.8%; Other 8.1%). **Foreign born:** 15.4%. **Median age:** 35.7. **State rank:** 1. **Pop change 1990-2000:** +15.2%.

Income: per capita $29,521; median household $53,157. **Pop below poverty level:** 8.4%.

Unemployment: 5.1%. **Median home value:** $236,900. **Median travel time to work:** 26.5 minutes.

KITSAP COUNTY

614 Division St MS 4   **Ph:** 360-337-7146
Port Orchard, WA 98366   **Fax:** 360-337-4632
www.kitsapgov.com

A peninsula in western WA, bounded on east by Puget Sound, west of Seattle. Organized as Slaughter County Jan 16, 1857 (prior to statehood) from Jefferson and King counties; name changed Jul 13, 1857. **Name Origin:** For an Indian chief, whose name means 'brave,' said to have saved area settlers by warning them of a planned massacre. Originally named for Lt. W.A. Slaughter (?-1855).

Area (sq mi): 565.98 (land 395.97; water 170.01).

Pop: 231,969 (White 82.2%; Black or African American 2.9%; Hispanic or Latino 4.1%; Asian 4.4%; Other 8.4%). **Foreign born:** 5.7%. **Median age:** 35.8. **State rank:** 6. **Pop change 1990-2000:** +22.3%.

Income: per capita $22,317; median household $46,840. **Pop below poverty level:** 8.8%.

Unemployment: 6%. **Median home value:** $152,100. **Median travel time to work:** 32.5 minutes.

KITTITAS COUNTY

205 W 5th St Rm 108   **Ph:** 509-962-7508
Ellensburg, WA 98926   **Fax:** 509-962-7679
www.co.kittitas.wa.us

In central WA, southeast of Tacoma; organized Nov 2, 1883 (prior to statehood) from Yakima County. **Name Origin:** Probably from a subtribal name of the Yakima Indians. Meaning uncertain, with 'shoal people' most appropriate, but 'land of bread' has also been suggested, as has 'gray gravel bank,' said to refer to a gravel bank on a river shoal.

Area (sq mi): 2333.11 (land 2297.19; water 35.93).

Pop: 33,362 (White 89.4%; Black or African American 0.7%; Hispanic or Latino 5%; Asian 2.2%; Other 5.3%). **Foreign born:** 5.3%. **Median age:** 31.4. **State rank:** 25. **Pop change 1990-2000:** +24.8%.

Income: per capita $18,928; median household $32,546. **Pop below poverty level:** 19.6%.

Unemployment: 6.5%. **Median home value:** $133,400. **Median travel time to work:** 22 minutes.

KLICKITAT COUNTY

205 S Columbus Ave Rm 204 MS CH3   **Ph:** 509-773-5744
Goldendale, WA 98620   **Fax:** 509-773-4559
www.klickitatcounty.org

On central southern border of WA; original county; organized Dec 20, 1859 (prior to statehood). **Name Origin:** For an Indian nation that lived in the area; name possibly means 'beyond' or 'those who live beyond the mountain,' or even 'thief.'

Area (sq mi): 1904.18 (land 1872.37; water 31.8).

Pop: 19,161 (White 85.2%; Black or African American 0.3%; Hispanic or Latino 7.8%; Asian 0.7%; Other 11.4%). **Foreign born:** 6%. **Median age:** 39.5. **State rank:** 30. **Pop change 1990-2000:** +15.3%.

Income: per capita $16,502; median household $34,267. **Pop below poverty level:** 17%.

Unemployment: 15.1%. **Median home value:** $110,400. **Median travel time to work:** 21.9 minutes.

LEWIS COUNTY

360 NW North St   **Ph:** 360-748-9121
Chehalis, WA 98532   **Fax:** 360-748-1639
www.co.lewis.wa.us

In southwestern WA, south of Tacoma; original county; organized Dec 21, 1845 (prior to statehood). **Name Origin:** For Meriwether Lewis (1774-1809), co-leader of the Lewis and Clark expedition (1804-06).

Area (sq mi): 2436.26 (land 2407.64; water 28.63).

Pop: 68,600 (White 90.6%; Black or African American 0.4%; Hispanic or Latino 5.4%; Asian 0.7%; Other 6%). **Foreign born:** 4.1%. **Median age:** 38.4. **State rank:** 15. **Pop change 1990-2000:** +15.6%.

Income: per capita $17,082; median household $35,511. **Pop below poverty level:** 14%.

Unemployment: 9.4%. **Median home value:** $117,800. **Median travel time to work:** 25.7 minutes.

LINCOLN COUNTY

PO Box 68   **Ph:** 509-725-1401
Davenport, WA 99122   **Fax:** 509-725-1150

In eastern WA, W of Spokane; organized Nov 24, 1883 (prior to statehood) from Spokane County. **Name Origin:** For Abraham Lincoln (1809-65), sixteenth U.S. president.

Area (sq mi): 2339.71 (land 2311.21; water 28.51).

Pop: 10,184 (White 94.6%; Black or African American 0.2%; Hispanic or Latino 1.9%; Asian 0.2%; Other 3.9%). **Foreign born:** 1.2%. **Median age:** 42.8. **State rank:** 34. **Pop change 1990-2000:** +14.9%.

Income: per capita $17,888; median household $35,255. **Pop below poverty level:** 12.6%.

Unemployment: 5.3%. **Median home value:** $83,500. **Median travel time to work:** 22.1 minutes.

All statistics are based on the 2000 Census except the dollar figures given for per capita income, which are based on 1999 estimates.

MASON COUNTY

PO Box 340   **Ph:** 360-427-9670
Shelton, WA 98584   **Fax:** 360-427-8425
www.co.mason.wa.us

In western WA, bordered on east by Puget Sound, west of Tacoma; organized as Sawamish County Mar 13, 1854 from Thurston County; name changed Jan 8, 1864. **Name Origin:** For Charles H. Mason (?-1859), secretary and sometimes acting governor of WA Territory.

Area (sq mi): 1051.03 (land 961.06; water 89.97).

Pop: 49,405 (White 86.3%; Black or African American 1.2%; Hispanic or Latino 4.8%; Asian 1.1%; Other 9.2%). **Foreign born:** 4.4%. **Median age:** 40.3. **State rank:** 20. **Pop change 1990-2000:** +28.9%.

Income: per capita $18,056; median household $39,586. **Pop below poverty level:** 12.2%.

Unemployment: 7.9%. **Median home value:** $132,300. **Median travel time to work:** 30.8 minutes.

OKANOGAN COUNTY

PO Box 72   **Ph:** 509-422-7275
Okanogan, WA 98840   **Fax:** 509-422-7277
www.okanogancounty.org

On the central northern border of WA; organized Feb 2, 1888 (prior to statehood) from Stevens County. **Name Origin:** For the Okanogan River, which traverses the county. From a Salish Indian name possibly meaning 'meeting place [of water]' for the confluence of the Okanogan and Columbia rivers, or 'rendezvous' because they met here for their potlaches.

Area (sq mi): 5315.16 (land 5268.07; water 47.09).

Pop: 39,564 (White 71.7%; Black or African American 0.3%; Hispanic or Latino 14.4%; Asian 0.4%; Other 24%). **Foreign born:** 10.2%. **Median age:** 38.2. **State rank:** 24. **Pop change 1990-2000:** +18.6%.

Income: per capita $14,900; median household $29,726. **Pop below poverty level:** 21.3%.

Unemployment: 10.8%. **Median home value:** $91,400. **Median travel time to work:** 19.6 minutes.

PACIFIC COUNTY

PO Box 67   **Ph:** 360-875-9300
South Bend, WA 98586   **Fax:** 360-875-9321
www.co.pacific.wa.us

On the southwestern coast of WA; original county; organized Feb 4, 1851 (prior to statehood). **Name Origin:** For the Pacific Ocean, which forms the county's western border.

Area (sq mi): 1223.5 (land 932.97; water 290.52).

Pop: 20,984 (White 88%; Black or African American 0.2%; Hispanic or Latino 5%; Asian 2.1%; Other 7.1%). **Foreign born:** 6%. **Median age:** 45.8. **State rank:** 28. **Pop change 1990-2000:** +11.1%.

Income: per capita $17,322; median household $31,209. **Pop below poverty level:** 14.4%.

Unemployment: 9%. **Median home value:** $102,700. **Median travel time to work:** 20.7 minutes.

PEND OREILLE COUNTY

PO Box 5020   **Ph:** 509-447-2435
Newport, WA 99156   **Fax:** 509-447-2734
www.co.pend-oreille.wa.us

On northeastern border of WA; organized Mar 1, 1911 from Stevens County. **Name Origin:** For the Pend Oreille River, which runs through the county, or for the name given to the Kalispel Indians by French-Canadian traders; from the French meaning 'pendant ears' because the Indians wore ear ornaments that probably lengthened their lobes.

Area (sq mi): 1425.32 (land 1400.27; water 25.05).

Pop: 11,732 (White 92.2%; Black or African American 0.1%; Hispanic or Latino 2.1%; Asian 0.6%; Other 5.7%). **Foreign born:** 2%. **Median age:** 41.9. **State rank:** 33. **Pop change 1990-2000:** +31.6%.

Income: per capita $15,731; median household $31,677. **Pop below poverty level:** 18.1%.

Unemployment: 10.1%. **Median home value:** $101,100. **Median travel time to work:** 31.5 minutes.

PIERCE COUNTY

930 Tacoma Ave S Rm 110   **Ph:** 253-798-3495
Tacoma, WA 98402   **Fax:** 253-798-3428
www.co.pierce.wa.us

In west-central WA at the southeastern end of Puget Sound; original county; organized Dec 22, 1852 (prior to statehood). **Name Origin:** For Franklin Pierce (1804-69), fourteenth U.S. president.

Area (sq mi): 1806.5 (land 1678.91; water 127.58).

Pop: 700,820 (White 76%; Black or African American 7%; Hispanic or Latino 5.5%; Asian 5.1%; Other 9.5%). **Foreign born:** 8.1%. **Median age:** 34.1. **State rank:** 2. **Pop change 1990-2000:** +19.6%.

Income: per capita $20,948; median household $45,204. **Pop below poverty level:** 10.5%.

Unemployment: 6.4%. **Median home value:** $149,600. **Median travel time to work:** 28.4 minutes.

SAN JUAN COUNTY

350 Court St Rm 7   **Ph:** 360-378-2163
Friday Harbor, WA 98250   **Fax:** 360-378-3967
www.co.san-juan.wa.us

Islands in northwestern WA, bounded on west and northwest by Haro Strait, on north and northeast by Georgia Strait, and on south by Juan de Fuca Strait. Organized Oct 31, 1873 (prior to statehood) from Whatcom County. **Name Origin:** For Saint John the Baptist, cousin and baptizer of Jesus. Some sources suggest the county may have been named for San Juan Island, for Juan Francisco de Eliza, governor of the Spanish settlement at Nootka Sound in the late 18th century, or for Juan de Fuca, supposedly a Greek navigator in Spanish service.

Area (sq mi): 621.07 (land 174.92; water 446.15).

Pop: 14,077 (White 93.7%; Black or African American 0.3%; Hispanic or Latino 2.4%; Asian 0.9%; Other 3.8%). **Foreign born:** 5.9%. **Median age:** 47.4. **State rank:** 32. **Pop change 1990-2000:** +40.3%.

Income: per capita $30,603; median household $43,491. **Pop below poverty level:** 9.2%.

Please see sample entry on inside front cover for detailed information about the statistics presented with each county listing.

Unemployment: 4%. **Median home value:** $291,800. **Median travel time to work:** 15.8 minutes.

SKAGIT COUNTY
PO Box 837   **Ph:** 360-336-9440
Mount Vernon, WA 98273
www.skagitcounty.net

In northwestern WA, bordered on west by upper Puget Sound, north of Seattle. Organized Nov 28, 1883 (prior to statehood) from Whatcom County. **Name Origin:** For the Indian tribe; meaning of name is unknown.

Area (sq mi): 1920.47 (land 1735.14; water 185.33).

Pop: 102,979 (White 83%; Black or African American 0.4%; Hispanic or Latino 11.2%; Asian 1.5%; Other 11.7%). **Foreign born:** 8.8%. **Median age:** 37.2. **State rank:** 11. **Pop change 1990-2000:** +29.4%.

Income: per capita $21,256; median household $42,381. **Pop below poverty level:** 11.1%.

Unemployment: 7.4%. **Median home value:** $158,100. **Median travel time to work:** 25.1 minutes.

SKAMANIA COUNTY
PO Box 790   **Ph:** 509-427-9430
Stevenson, WA 98648   **Fax:** 509-427-7386

On the southern border of WA, northeast of Portland, OR; organized Mar 9, 1854 (prior to statehood) from Clark County. **Name Origin:** From the Indian name for parts of the Columbia River, which forms the county's southern border. The usual interpretation is 'swift water.'

Area (sq mi): 1683.86 (land 1656.44; water 27.42).

Pop: 9,872 (White 90.4%; Black or African American 0.3%; Hispanic or Latino 4%; Asian 0.5%; Other 7%). **Foreign born:** 3.5%. **Median age:** 38.7. **State rank:** 35. **Pop change 1990-2000:** +19.1%.

Income: per capita $18,002; median household $39,317. **Pop below poverty level:** 13.1%.

Unemployment: 11.1%. **Median home value:** $150,200. **Median travel time to work:** 29.2 minutes.

SNOHOMISH COUNTY
3000 Rockefeller Ave MS 605   **Ph:** 425-388-3466
Everett, WA 98201
www.co.snohomish.wa.us

In northwestern WA, bordered on west by Puget Sound, northeast of Seattle. Organized Jan 14, 1861 (prior to statehood) from Island County. **Name Origin:** For the Snohomish Indians; name is believed to mean 'tidewater people' or 'union.'

Area (sq mi): 2196.41 (land 2089.06; water 107.35).

Pop: 606,024 (White 83.4%; Black or African American 1.7%; Hispanic or Latino 4.7%; Asian 5.8%; Other 7%). **Foreign born:** 9.7%. **Median age:** 34.7. **State rank:** 3. **Pop change 1990-2000:** +30.1%.

Income: per capita $23,417; median household $53,060. **Pop below poverty level:** 6.9%.

Unemployment: 5.4%. **Median home value:** $196,500. **Median travel time to work:** 29.6 minutes.

SPOKANE COUNTY
1116 W Broadway Ave   **Ph:** 509-477-2265
Spokane, WA 99260   **Fax:** 509-477-2274
www.spokanecounty.org

On central eastern border of WA; organized Jan 29, 1864 (prior to statehood) from Stevens County (an earlier Spokane County was merged with Stevens County in 1863). It is the only WA county with township governments in each township. **Name Origin:** For the Spokane Indians, or for the city or river also named for the tribe. The meaning of the name is uncertain; possibly 'sun people' or 'children of the sun', or the name may be from Chief Illum Spokane, whose village was at the base of what became known as Spokane Falls.

Area (sq mi): 1780.72 (land 1763.64; water 17.09).

Pop: 417,939 (White 89.8%; Black or African American 1.6%; Hispanic or Latino 2.8%; Asian 1.9%; Other 5.2%). **Foreign born:** 4.5%. **Median age:** 35.4. **State rank:** 4. **Pop change 1990-2000:** +15.7%.

Income: per capita $19,233; median household $37,308. **Pop below poverty level:** 12.3%.

Unemployment: 6.6%. **Median home value:** $113,200. **Median travel time to work:** 21.2 minutes.

STEVENS COUNTY
215 S Oak St   **Ph:** 509-684-3751
Colville, WA 99114   **Fax:** 509-684-8310
www.co.stevens.wa.us

On the northeastern border of WA, northwest of Spokane; original county. Organized 1854 (prior to statehood). **Name Origin:** For Gen. Isaac Ingalls Stevens (1818-62), an officer in the Mexican-American War and the Civil War; first governor of WA Territory (1853-57).

Area (sq mi): 2540.64 (land 2478.3; water 62.34).

Pop: 40,066 (White 89.1%; Black or African American 0.3%; Hispanic or Latino 1.8%; Asian 0.5%; Other 9.3%). **Foreign born:** 2.4%. **Median age:** 39.2. **State rank:** 23. **Pop change 1990-2000:** +29.5%.

Income: per capita $15,895; median household $34,673. **Pop below poverty level:** 15.9%.

Unemployment: 10.9%. **Median home value:** $112,000. **Median travel time to work:** 27 minutes.

THURSTON COUNTY
2000 Lakeridge Dr SW Bldg 2   **Ph:** 360-786-5430
Olympia, WA 98502   **Fax:** 360-753-4033
www.co.thurston.wa.us

In west-central WA at the southern end of Puget Sound, southwest of Tacoma; organized Jan 12, 1852 (prior to statehood) from Lewis County. **Name Origin:** For Samuel Royal Thurston (1816-54), first delegate to Congress from the Oregon territory (1849-51).

Area (sq mi): 773.64 (land 727.02; water 46.62).

Pop: 207,355 (White 83.4%; Black or African American 2.4%; Hispanic or Latino 4.5%; Asian 4.4%; Other 7.6%). **Foreign born:** 6.1%. **Median age:** 36.5. **State rank:** 8. **Pop change 1990-2000:** +28.6%.

All statistics are based on the 2000 Census except the dollar figures given for per capita income, which are based on 1999 estimates.

Income: per capita $22,415; median household $46,975. **Pop below poverty level:** 8.8%.

Unemployment: 5.7%. **Median home value:** $145,200. **Median travel time to work:** 24.4 minutes.

WAHKIAKUM COUNTY
PO Box 116   **Ph:** 360-795-3558
Cathlamet, WA 98612   **Fax:** 360-795-8813

On the southwestern border of WA at the mouth of the Columbia River; organized Apr 25, 1854 (prior to statehood) from Lewis County. **Name Origin:** For a Chinook tribe and chief, Wakiacum, a name believed to mean 'tall trees' or 'big timber.' The spelling was probably changed to reflect the Indian pronunciation.

Area (sq mi): 286.69 (land 264.24; water 22.45).

Pop: 3,824 (White 92.7%; Black or African American 0.3%; Hispanic or Latino 2.6%; Asian 0.5%; Other 5.8%). **Foreign born:** 1.3%. **Median age:** 44.4. **State rank:** 38. **Pop change 1990-2000:** +14.9%.

Income: per capita $19,063; median household $39,444. **Pop below poverty level:** 8.1%.

Unemployment: 7.3%. **Median home value:** $147,500. **Median travel time to work:** 28.1 minutes.

WALLA WALLA COUNTY
PO Box 1506   **Ph:** 509-527-3200
Walla Walla, WA 99362   **Fax:** 509-527-3235
www.co.walla-walla.wa.us

On the southeastern border of WA; original county; organized Apr 25, 1854 (prior to statehood). **Name Origin:** Apparently for a small tribe, closely related to the Nez Perce, which took its name from the Walla Walla River, 'place of many waters,' referring to the many tributaries, springs, and streams in the area. Lewis and Clark recorded the name as *Wollah Wollah*.

Area (sq mi): 1299.25 (land 1270.51; water 28.74).

Pop: 55,180 (White 78.8%; Black or African American 1.7%; Hispanic or Latino 15.7%; Asian 1.1%; Other 11.8%). **Foreign born:** 9.4%. **Median age:** 34.9. **State rank:** 19. **Pop change 1990-2000:** +13.9%.

Income: per capita $16,509; median household $35,900. **Pop below poverty level:** 15.1%.

Unemployment: 6.5%. **Median home value:** $114,300. **Median travel time to work:** 15.2 minutes.

WHATCOM COUNTY
311 Grand Ave Rm 301   **Ph:** 360-676-6777
Bellingham, WA 98225   **Fax:** 360-676-6693
www.co.whatcom.wa.us

On the northwestern border of WA, bordered on west by Georgia Strait; organized Mar 9, 1854 (prior to statehood) from Island County. **Name Origin:** From the Lummi Indian word *what-coom* or *whuks-qua-koos-ta-qua*, said to mean 'noisy, rumbling water,' referring to Whatcom Falls on Bellingham Bay.

Area (sq mi): 2503.55 (land 2119.53; water 384.02).

Pop: 166,814 (White 86.2%; Black or African American 0.7%; Hispanic or Latino 5.2%; Asian 2.8%; Other 8.1%). **Foreign born:**

9.8%. **Median age:** 34. **State rank:** 9. **Pop change 1990-2000:** +30.5%.

Income: per capita $20,025; median household $40,005. **Pop below poverty level:** 14.2%.

Unemployment: 6.8%. **Median home value:** $155,700. **Median travel time to work:** 20.8 minutes.

WHITMAN COUNTY
PO Box 390   **Ph:** 509-397-4622
Colfax, WA 99111   **Fax:** 509-397-3546
www.co.whitman.wa.us

On the southeastern border of WA, S of Spokane; organized Nov 29, 1871 (prior to statehood) from Stevens County. **Name Origin:** For Dr. Marcus Whitman (1802-47), massacred leader of a missionary colony.

Area (sq mi): 2177.6 (land 2159.37; water 18.23).

Pop: 40,740 (White 86.7%; Black or African American 1.5%; Hispanic or Latino 3%; Asian 5.5%; Other 4.8%). **Foreign born:** 7.7%. **Median age:** 24.7. **State rank:** 22. **Pop change 1990-2000:** +5.1%.

Income: per capita $15,298; median household $28,584. **Pop below poverty level:** 25.6%.

Unemployment: 2.5%. **Median home value:** $119,600. **Median travel time to work:** 15.6 minutes.

YAKIMA COUNTY
128 N 2nd St Rm 323   **Ph:** 509-574-1430
Yakima, WA 98901   **Fax:** 509-574-1473
www.co.yakima.wa.us

In south-central WA; organized Jan 1, 1865 (prior to statehood) from Indian Territory. **Name Origin:** For a tribe of Shahaptian Indians; name is believed to mean either 'runaway,' for a chief's errant daughter, or possibly 'black bear.'

Area (sq mi): 4311.61 (land 4296.23; water 15.38).

Pop: 222,581 (White 56.5%; Black or African American 1%; Hispanic or Latino 35.9%; Asian 1%; Other 32.5%). **Foreign born:** 16.9%. **Median age:** 31.2. **State rank:** 7. **Pop change 1990-2000:** +17.9%.

Income: per capita $15,606; median household $34,828. **Pop below poverty level:** 19.7%.

Unemployment: 11.3%. **Median home value:** $113,800. **Median travel time to work:** 19.4 minutes.

Please see sample entry on inside front cover for detailed information about the statistics presented with each county listing.

WEST VIRGINIA - Counties

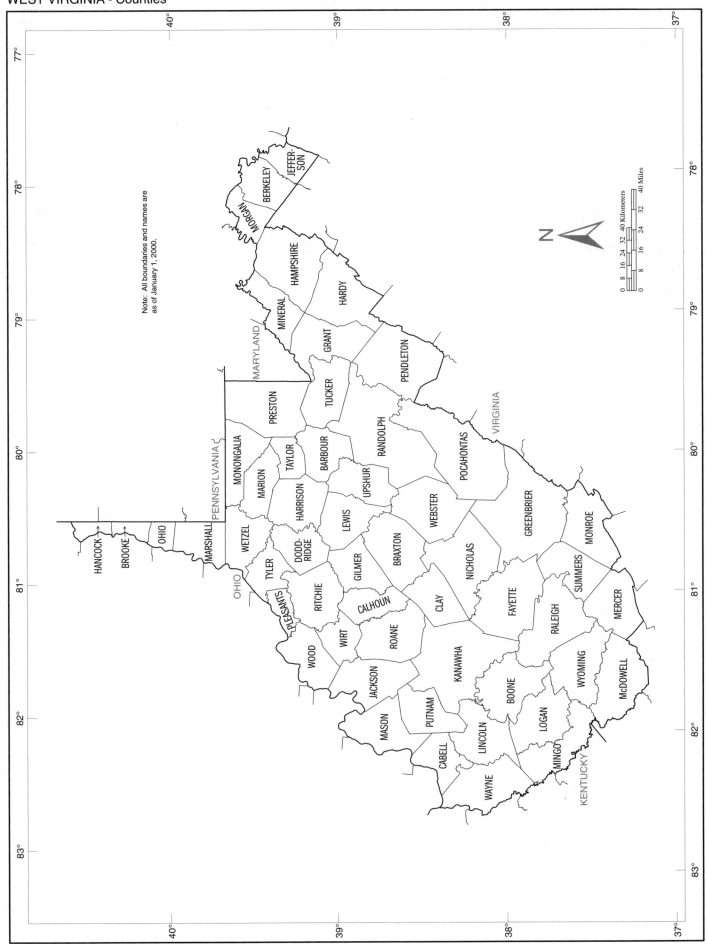

Note: All boundaries and names are as of January 1, 2000.

MARYLAND

PENNSYLVANIA

VIRGINIA

OHIO

KENTUCKY

MORGAN
BERKELEY
JEFFER-SON
HAMPSHIRE
HARDY
MINERAL
GRANT
PENDLETON
PRESTON
TUCKER
RANDOLPH
POCAHONTAS
MONONGALIA
TAYLOR
BARBOUR
MARION
HARRISON
UPSHUR
LEWIS
WEBSTER
GREENBRIER
MONROE
DODD-RIDGE
BRAXTON
NICHOLAS
SUMMERS
TYLER
GILMER
CLAY
FAYETTE
RALEIGH
MERCER
RITCHIE
CALHOUN
PLEASANTS
WIRT
ROANE
KANAWHA
RALEIGH
WYOMING
McDOWELL
WOOD
JACKSON
BOONE
LOGAN
PUTNAM
MASON
LINCOLN
MINGO
CABELL
WAYNE
WETZEL

N

0 8 16 24 32 40 Kilometers
0 8 16 24 32 40 Miles

West Virginia

WEST VIRGINIA STATE INFORMATION

www.state.wv.us   Ph: 304-558-3456

Area (sq mi): 24,229.76 (land 24,077.73; water 152.03).

Pop: 1,808,344 (White 94.6%; Black or African American 3.2%; Hispanic or Latino 0.7%; Asian 0.5%; Other 1.3%). **Foreign born:** 1.1%. **Median age:** 38.9. **Pop change 1990-2000:** +0.8%.

Income: per capita $16,477; median household $29,696. **Pop below poverty level:** 17.9%.

Unemployment: 5.4%. **Median home value:** $72,800. **Median travel time to work:** 26.2 minutes.

BARBOUR COUNTY

8 N Main St   Ph: 304-457-2232
Philippi, WV 26416   Fax: 304-457-2790

In northern WV, southeast of Clarksburg; organized Mar 3, 1843 from Harrison, Lewis, and Randolph counties. **Name Origin:** For Philip Pendleton Barbour (1783-1841), U.S. representative from VA (1814-25; 1827-30) and associate justice of the U.S. Supreme Court (1836-41).

Area (sq mi): 342.75 (land 340.79; water 1.96).

Pop: 15,557 (White 97%; Black or African American 0.5%; Hispanic or Latino 0.5%; Asian 0.3%; Other 1.8%). **Foreign born:** 0.5%. **Median age:** 38.7. **State rank:** 36. **Pop change 1990-2000:** -0.9%.

Income: per capita $12,440; median household $24,729. **Pop below poverty level:** 22.6%.

Unemployment: 7.8%. **Median home value:** $56,100. **Median travel time to work:** 28 minutes.

BERKELEY COUNTY

100 W King St Rm 1   Ph: 304-264-1925
Martinsburg, WV 25401   Fax: 304-267-1794
www.berkeleycountycomm.org

In eastern panhandle of WV, southwest of Hagerstown, MD; organized Feb 10, 1772 (prior to statehood) from Frederick County (in VA). **Name Origin:** For Norborne Berkeley (1718-70), Lord Botetcourt, member of the British Parliament and colonial governor of VA (1768-70) who favored the colonists.

Area (sq mi): 321.58 (land 321.14; water 0.44).

Pop: 75,905 (White 91.9%; Black or African American 4.7%; Hispanic or Latino 1.5%; Asian 0.5%; Other 2.1%). **Foreign born:** 1.7%. **Median age:** 35.8. **State rank:** 6. **Pop change 1990-2000:** +28.1%.

Income: per capita $17,982; median household $38,763. **Pop below poverty level:** 11.5%.

Unemployment: 3.7%. **Median home value:** $99,700. **Median travel time to work:** 28.8 minutes.

BOONE COUNTY

200 State St   Ph: 304-369-3925
Madison, WV 25130   Fax: 304-369-7329

In southwestern WV, south of Charleston; organized Mar 11, 1847 from Kanawha, Cabell, and Logan counties. **Name Origin:** For Daniel Boone (1734?-1820), U.S. frontiersman and KY pioneer, onetime resident of the nearby Kanawha Valley.

Area (sq mi): 503.18 (land 502.98; water 0.2).

Pop: 25,535 (White 98.2%; Black or African American 0.7%; Hispanic or Latino 0.5%; Asian 0.1%; Other 0.7%). **Foreign born:** 0.4%. **Median age:** 38.8. **State rank:** 28. **Pop change 1990-2000:** -1.3%.

Income: per capita $14,453; median household $25,669. **Pop below poverty level:** 22%.

Unemployment: 5.5%. **Median home value:** $63,700. **Median travel time to work:** 33.8 minutes.

BRAXTON COUNTY

PO Box 486   Ph: 304-765-2833
Sutton, WV 26601   Fax: 304-765-2093

In central WV, northeast of Charleston; organized Jan 15, 1836 from Kanawha, Lewis, Nicholas, and Randolph counties. **Name Origin:** For Carter Braxton (1736-97), VA House of Burgesses (1767-71; 1775), a signer of the Declaration of Independence, and a member of the council of state (1786-91; 1794-97).

Area (sq mi): 516.17 (land 513.48; water 2.69).

Pop: 14,702 (White 97.6%; Black or African American 0.7%; Hispanic or Latino 0.4%; Asian 0.1%; Other 1.1%). **Foreign born:** 0.2%. **Median age:** 39.6. **State rank:** 39. **Pop change 1990-2000:** +13.1%.

Income: per capita $13,349; median household $24,412. **Pop below poverty level:** 22%.

Unemployment: 8%. **Median home value:** $59,300. **Median travel time to work:** 36.7 minutes.

BROOKE COUNTY

632 Main St   Ph: 304-737-3661
Wellsburg, WV 26070   Fax: 304-737-3668

In northern panhandle of WV, east of Steubenville, OH; organized

Please see sample entry on inside front cover for detailed information about the statistics presented with each county listing.

615

Nov 30, 1796 from Ohio County. **Name Origin:** For Robert Brooke (1751-99), governor of VA (1794-96) and attorney general (1798).

Area (sq mi): 92.26 (land 88.85; water 3.41).

Pop: 25,447 (White 97.6%; Black or African American 0.8%; Hispanic or Latino 0.4%; Asian 0.3%; Other 0.9%). **Foreign born:** 1.1%. **Median age:** 41.2. **State rank:** 29. **Pop change 1990-2000:** -5.7%.

Income: per capita $17,131; median household $32,981. **Pop below poverty level:** 11.7%.

Unemployment: 4.5%. **Median home value:** $67,000. **Median travel time to work:** 23.9 minutes.

CABELL COUNTY
750 5th Ave Rm 108   **Ph:** 304-526-8625
Huntington, WV 25701   **Fax:** 304-526-8632
www.cabellcounty.org

On western border of WV along the Ohio River, west of Charleston; organized Jan 2, 1809 from Kanawha County. **Name Origin:** For William H. Cabell (1772-1853), governor of VA (1805-08) and judge of various courts (1808; 1811; 1830).

Area (sq mi): 288.02 (land 281.59; water 6.43).

Pop: 96,784 (White 92.9%; Black or African American 4.3%; Hispanic or Latino 0.7%; Asian 0.8%; Other 1.5%). **Foreign born:** 1.3%. **Median age:** 37.5. **State rank:** 2. **Pop change 1990-2000:** +0%.

Income: per capita $17,638; median household $28,479. **Pop below poverty level:** 19.2%.

Unemployment: 4.7%. **Median home value:** $76,200. **Median travel time to work:** 21.7 minutes.

CALHOUN COUNTY
PO Box 230   **Ph:** 304-354-6725
Grantsville, WV 26147   **Fax:** 304-354-6725

In central WV, southeast of Parkersburg; organized Mar 5, 1856 from Gilmer County. **Name Origin:** For John Caldwell Calhoun (1782-1850), U.S. statesman and champion of Southern causes.

Area (sq mi): 280.64 (land 280.62; water 0.02).

Pop: 7,582 (White 98.6%; Black or African American 0.1%; Hispanic or Latino 0.6%; Asian 0.1%; Other 0.8%). **Foreign born:** 0.6%. **Median age:** 41.3. **State rank:** 50. **Pop change 1990-2000:** -3.8%.

Income: per capita $11,491; median household $21,578. **Pop below poverty level:** 25.1%.

Unemployment: 15.4%. **Median home value:** $46,000. **Median travel time to work:** 38 minutes.

CLAY COUNTY
PO Box 190   **Ph:** 304-587-4259
Clay, WV 25043   **Fax:** 304-587-7329

In central WV, east of Charleston; organized Mar 29, 1858 from Braxton and Nicholas counties. **Name Origin:** For Henry Clay (1777-1852), U.S. senator from KY, known as the 'Great Pacificator' for his advocacy of compromise to avert national crises.

Area (sq mi): 343.82 (land 342.4; water 1.42).

Pop: 10,330 (White 97.9%; Black or African American 0.1%; Hispanic or Latino 0.4%; Asian 0%; Other 1.7%). **Foreign born:** 0.1%. **Median age:** 36.8. **State rank:** 45. **Pop change 1990-2000:** +3.5%.

Income: per capita $12,021; median household $22,120. **Pop below poverty level:** 27.5%.

Unemployment: 7.1%. **Median home value:** $55,600. **Median travel time to work:** 45 minutes.

DODDRIDGE COUNTY
118 E Court St Rm 102   **Ph:** 304-873-2631
West Union, WV 26456   **Fax:** 304-873-1840

In northern WV, west of Clarksburg; organized Feb 4, 1845 from Harrison, Tyler, Ritchie, and Lewis counties. **Name Origin:** For Philip Doddridge (1773-1832), VA house of delegates (1815-16; 1822-23; 1828-29) and U.S. representative (1829-32).

Area (sq mi): 320.48 (land 320.43; water 0.05).

Pop: 7,403 (White 98%; Black or African American 0.3%; Hispanic or Latino 0.6%; Asian 0.1%; Other 1.2%). **Foreign born:** 0.6%. **Median age:** 38.7. **State rank:** 52. **Pop change 1990-2000:** +5.8%.

Income: per capita $13,507; median household $26,744. **Pop below poverty level:** 19.8%.

Unemployment: 4.4%. **Median home value:** $57,000. **Median travel time to work:** 38 minutes.

FAYETTE COUNTY
100 Court St   **Ph:** 304-574-4249
Fayetteville, WV 25840   **Fax:** 304-574-4314

In south-central WV, north of Beckley; organized Feb 28, 1831 from Kanawha, Greenbrier, Nicholas, and Logan counties. **Name Origin:** For the Marquis de Lafayette (1757-1834), French statesman and soldier who fought with the Americans during the Revolutionary War.

Area (sq mi): 668.36 (land 663.93; water 4.43).

Pop: 47,579 (White 92.2%; Black or African American 5.6%; Hispanic or Latino 0.7%; Asian 0.3%; Other 1.3%). **Foreign born:** 0.8%. **Median age:** 39.6. **State rank:** 11. **Pop change 1990-2000:** -0.8%.

Income: per capita $13,809; median household $24,788. **Pop below poverty level:** 21.7%.

Unemployment: 6.7%. **Median home value:** $50,800. **Median travel time to work:** 28 minutes.

GILMER COUNTY
10 Howard St   **Ph:** 304-462-7641
Glenville, WV 26351   **Fax:** 304-462-7038

In central WV, southwest of Clarksburg; organized Feb 3, 1845 from Lewis and Kanawha counties. **Name Origin:** For Thomas Walker Gilmer (1802-44), VA legislator, governor (1840-41), U.S. representative (1841-44), and U.S. secretary of the Navy (1844).

Area (sq mi): 340.07 (land 340.05; water 0.02).

Pop: 7,160 (White 96.9%; Black or African American 0.9%; Hispanic or Latino 0.7%; Asian 0.6%; Other 1.2%). **Foreign born:** 1%. **Median age:** 36.8. **State rank:** 54. **Pop change 1990-2000:** -6.6%.

All statistics are based on the 2000 Census except the dollar figures given for per capita income, which are based on 1999 estimates.

Income: per capita $12,498; median household $22,857. **Pop below poverty level:** 25.9%.

Unemployment: 5.1%. **Median home value:** $63,900. **Median travel time to work:** 30.2 minutes.

GRANT COUNTY

5 Highland Ave   **Ph:** 304-257-4422
Petersburg, WV 26847   **Fax:** 304-257-2593

In eastern panhandle of WV, southwest of Cumberland, MD; organized Feb 14, 1866 from Hardy County. **Name Origin:** For Ulysses Simpson Grant (1822-85), Civil War general and eighteenth U.S. president.

Area (sq mi): 480.19 (land 477.21; water 2.99).

Pop: 11,299 (White 97.9%; Black or African American 0.7%; Hispanic or Latino 0.5%; Asian 0.1%; Other 0.9%). **Foreign born:** 0.5%. **Median age:** 39.3. **State rank:** 43. **Pop change 1990-2000:** +8.4%.

Income: per capita $15,696; median household $28,916. **Pop below poverty level:** 16.3%.

Unemployment: 5.1%. **Median home value:** $78,400. **Median travel time to work:** 26.9 minutes.

GREENBRIER COUNTY

PO Box 506   **Ph:** 304-647-6602
Lewisburg, WV 24901

On southeastern border of WV, northeast of Beckley; organized Oct 20, 1778 from Montgomery and Botetcourt counties (in VA). **Name Origin:** For the principal river of the county, whose name refers to the thorny vine *Smilax rotundifolia* found abundantly on its banks.

Area (sq mi): 1024.43 (land 1021.26; water 3.17).

Pop: 34,453 (White 94.7%; Black or African American 3%; Hispanic or Latino 0.7%; Asian 0.2%; Other 1.5%). **Foreign born:** 0.6%. **Median age:** 41.6. **State rank:** 17. **Pop change 1990-2000:** -0.7%.

Income: per capita $16,247; median household $26,927. **Pop below poverty level:** 18.2%.

Unemployment: 6.2%. **Median home value:** $71,300. **Median travel time to work:** 24.3 minutes.

HAMPSHIRE COUNTY

PO Box 806   **Ph:** 304-822-5112
Romney, WV 26757   **Fax:** 304-822-4039
www.co.hampshire.wv.us

In eastern panhandle of WV, southeast of Cumberland, MD. Oldest county of what is now WV; organized Feb 27, 1754 from Frederick and Augusta counties (in VA). **Name Origin:** For the county in England.

Area (sq mi): 644.62 (land 641.72; water 2.9).

Pop: 20,203 (White 97.7%; Black or African American 0.8%; Hispanic or Latino 0.6%; Asian 0.2%; Other 0.9%). **Foreign born:** 0.6%. **Median age:** 38.5. **State rank:** 32. **Pop change 1990-2000:** +22.5%.

Income: per capita $14,851; median household $31,666. **Pop below poverty level:** 16.3%.

Unemployment: 4.5%. **Median home value:** $78,300. **Median travel time to work:** 39.7 minutes.

HANCOCK COUNTY

PO Box 367   **Ph:** 304-564-3311
New Cumberland, WV 26047   **Fax:** 304-564-5941

In northern panhandle of WV, northeast of Steubenville, OH; organized Jan 15, 1848 from Brooke County. **Name Origin:** For John Hancock (1737-93), noted signer of the Declaration of Independence, governor of MA (1780-85; 1787-93), and statesman.

Area (sq mi): 88.35 (land 82.82; water 5.53).

Pop: 32,667 (White 95.8%; Black or African American 2.3%; Hispanic or Latino 0.7%; Asian 0.3%; Other 0.9%). **Foreign born:** 1.8%. **Median age:** 41.7. **State rank:** 18. **Pop change 1990-2000:** -7.3%.

Income: per capita $17,724; median household $33,759. **Pop below poverty level:** 11.1%.

Unemployment: 3.7%. **Median home value:** $70,500. **Median travel time to work:** 21.6 minutes.

HARDY COUNTY

204 Washington St Rm 111   **Ph:** 304-538-2929
Moorefield, WV 26836   **Fax:** 304-538-6832

In eastern panhandle of WV, south of Cumberland, MD; organized Oct 17, 1786 from Hampshire County. **Name Origin:** For Samuel Hardy (1758-85), member of VA house of delegates (1780) and a member of the Continental Congress (1783-85).

Area (sq mi): 584.48 (land 583.39; water 1.09).

Pop: 12,669 (White 96.5%; Black or African American 1.9%; Hispanic or Latino 0.7%; Asian 0.1%; Other 1.1%). **Foreign born:** 0.5%. **Median age:** 38.9. **State rank:** 42. **Pop change 1990-2000:** +15.4%.

Income: per capita $15,859; median household $31,846. **Pop below poverty level:** 13.1%.

Unemployment: 2.7%. **Median home value:** $74,700. **Median travel time to work:** 26 minutes.

HARRISON COUNTY

301 W Main St County Courthouse   **Ph:** 304-624-8611
Clarksburg, WV 26301   **Fax:** 304-624-8575
www.harrisoncountywv.com

In northern WV, southwest of Fairmont; organized May 3, 1784 from Monongalia, Randolph, and Ohio counties. **Name Origin:** For Benjamin Harrison (1726-91), a signer of the Declaration of Independence, governor of VA (1782-84), and father of President William Harrison (1773-1841).

Area (sq mi): 416.6 (land 416.04; water 0.56).

Pop: 68,652 (White 95.8%; Black or African American 1.6%; Hispanic or Latino 1%; Asian 0.6%; Other 1.2%). **Foreign born:** 1.4%. **Median age:** 39.2. **State rank:** 7. **Pop change 1990-2000:** -1%.

Income: per capita $16,810; median household $30,562. **Pop below poverty level:** 17.2%.

Unemployment: 5%. **Median home value:** $67,600. **Median travel time to work:** 22.2 minutes.

Please see sample entry on inside front cover for detailed information about the statistics presented with each county listing.

JACKSON COUNTY

PO Box 800   **Ph:** 304-372-2011
Ripley, WV 25271   **Fax:** 304-372-1107

On western border of WV along the Ohio River, south of Parkersburg; organized May 1, 1831 from Kanawha, Mason, and Wood counties. **Name Origin:** For Andrew Jackson (1767-1845), seventh U.S. president.

Area (sq mi): 471.59 (land 465.79; water 5.8).

Pop: 28,000 (White 98.6%; Black or African American 0.1%; Hispanic or Latino 0.3%; Asian 0.2%; Other 0.9%). **Foreign born:** 0.5%. **Median age:** 38.8. **State rank:** 22. **Pop change 1990-2000:** +7.9%.

Income: per capita $16,205; median household $32,434. **Pop below poverty level:** 15.2%.

Unemployment: 6%. **Median home value:** $78,500. **Median travel time to work:** 27.1 minutes.

JEFFERSON COUNTY

PO Box 208   **Ph:** 304-728-3215
Charles Town, WV 25414   **Fax:** 304-728-1957
170.215.149.18/

In eastern panhandle of WV, south of Hagerstown, MD; organized Jan 8, 1801 from Berkeley County. **Name Origin:** For Thomas Jefferson (1743-1826), U.S. patriot and statesman; third U.S. president.

Area (sq mi): 211.57 (land 209.53; water 2.03).

Pop: 42,190 (White 90%; Black or African American 6.1%; Hispanic or Latino 1.7%; Asian 0.6%; Other 2.3%). **Foreign born:** 2.1%. **Median age:** 36.8. **State rank:** 14. **Pop change 1990-2000:** +17.4%.

Income: per capita $20,441; median household $44,374. **Pop below poverty level:** 10.3%.

Unemployment: 2.5%. **Median home value:** $116,700. **Median travel time to work:** 36.8 minutes.

KANAWHA COUNTY

409 Virginia St E   **Ph:** 304-357-0130
Charleston, WV 25301   **Fax:** 304-357-0585
www.kanawha.us/home.htm

In west-central WV, east of Huntington; organized Nov 14, 1788 from Greenbrier County (WV) and Montgomery County (in VA). **Name Origin:** For the Kanawha River, which traverses it; named for an Indian tribe, possibly the Conoy of Algonquian linguistic stock. The name has been said to mean 'hurricane.'

Area (sq mi): 910.99 (land 903.1; water 7.89).

Pop: 200,073 (White 90.1%; Black or African American 7%; Hispanic or Latino 0.6%; Asian 0.8%; Other 1.7%). **Foreign born:** 1.4%. **Median age:** 40.2. **State rank:** 1. **Pop change 1990-2000:** -3.6%.

Income: per capita $20,354; median household $33,766. **Pop below poverty level:** 14.4%.

Unemployment: 4%. **Median home value:** $80,700. **Median travel time to work:** 21.9 minutes.

LEWIS COUNTY

110 Center Ave   **Ph:** 304-269-8215
Weston, WV 26452   **Fax:** 304-269-8202

In north-central WV, south of Clarksburg; organized Dec 18, 1816 from Harrison and Randolph counties. **Name Origin:** For Charles Lewis (?-1774), a soldier killed during the Revolutionary War.

Area (sq mi): 389.75 (land 382.14; water 7.61).

Pop: 16,919 (White 98.1%; Black or African American 0.1%; Hispanic or Latino 0.5%; Asian 0.3%; Other 1%). **Foreign born:** 0.5%. **Median age:** 40.1. **State rank:** 34. **Pop change 1990-2000:** -1.8%.

Income: per capita $13,933; median household $27,066. **Pop below poverty level:** 19.9%.

Unemployment: 5.9%. **Median home value:** $63,400. **Median travel time to work:** 25.7 minutes.

LINCOLN COUNTY

PO Box 497   **Ph:** 304-824-7990
Hamlin, WV 25523   **Fax:** 304-824-2444
www.co.lincoln.wv.us

In southwestern WV, southwest of Charleston; organized Feb 23, 1867 from Boone, Cabell, and Kanawha counties. **Name Origin:** For Abraham Lincoln (1809-65), sixteenth U.S. president.

Area (sq mi): 438.59 (land 437.43; water 1.16).

Pop: 22,108 (White 98.5%; Black or African American 0.1%; Hispanic or Latino 0.5%; Asian 0.1%; Other 0.9%). **Foreign born:** 0%. **Median age:** 37.4. **State rank:** 31. **Pop change 1990-2000:** +3.4%.

Income: per capita $13,073; median household $22,662. **Pop below poverty level:** 27.9%.

Unemployment: 8.5%. **Median home value:** $60,000. **Median travel time to work:** 39.2 minutes.

LOGAN COUNTY

300 Stratton St Rm 101   **Ph:** 304-792-8600
Logan, WV 25601   **Fax:** 304-792-8621

In southwestern WV, west of Beckley; organized Jan 12, 1824 from Cabell and Kanawha counties (WV), and Giles and Tazewell counties (in VA). **Name Origin:** For John Logan (1725-80), a Mingo Indian chief originally named *Tah-gah-jute*, who was educated by James Logan of PA.

Area (sq mi): 455.61 (land 454.21; water 1.4).

Pop: 37,710 (White 95.9%; Black or African American 2.6%; Hispanic or Latino 0.5%; Asian 0.3%; Other 0.8%). **Foreign born:** 0.5%. **Median age:** 39.3. **State rank:** 15. **Pop change 1990-2000:** -12.4%.

Income: per capita $14,102; median household $24,603. **Pop below poverty level:** 24.1%.

Unemployment: 5.5%. **Median home value:** $62,500. **Median travel time to work:** 30.2 minutes.

MARION COUNTY

PO Box 1267   **Ph:** 304-367-5440
Fairmont, WV 26555   **Fax:** 304-367-5448
www.marioncountywv.com

In northern WV, southwest of Morgantown; organized Jan 14, 1842

All statistics are based on the 2000 Census except the dollar figures given for per capita income, which are based on 1999 estimates.

from Harrison and Monongalia counties. **Name Origin:** For Gen. Francis Marion (c.1732-95), SC soldier and legislator, known as 'The Swamp Fox' for his tactics during the Revolutionary War.

Area (sq mi): 311.49 (land 309.69; water 1.8).

Pop: 56,598 (White 94.5%; Black or African American 3.2%; Hispanic or Latino 0.7%; Asian 0.4%; Other 1.2%). **Foreign born:** 1%. **Median age:** 39.9. **State rank:** 9. **Pop change 1990-2000:** -1.1%.

Income: per capita $16,246; median household $28,626. **Pop below poverty level:** 16.3%.

Unemployment: 5.4%. **Median home value:** $63,600. **Median travel time to work:** 23.9 minutes.

MARSHALL COUNTY

PO Box 459   **Ph:** 304-845-1220
Moundsville, WV 26041   **Fax:** 304-845-5891

In northern panhandle of WV, southeast of Wheeling; organized Mar 12, 1835 from Ohio County. **Name Origin:** For John Marshall (1755-1835), American jurist and fourth Chief Justice of the U.S. Supreme Court (1801-35).

Area (sq mi): 312.18 (land 306.99; water 5.19).

Pop: 35,519 (White 97.9%; Black or African American 0.4%; Hispanic or Latino 0.6%; Asian 0.3%; Other 0.9%). **Foreign born:** 0.7%. **Median age:** 40.4. **State rank:** 16. **Pop change 1990-2000:** -4.9%.

Income: per capita $16,472; median household $30,989. **Pop below poverty level:** 16.6%.

Unemployment: 6.2%. **Median home value:** $62,600. **Median travel time to work:** 26.4 minutes.

MASON COUNTY

200 6th St   **Ph:** 304-675-1110
Point Pleasant, WV 25550   **Fax:** 304-675-4982

On western border of WV along the Ohio River, northeast of Huntington; organized Jan 2, 1804 from Kanawha County. **Name Origin:** For George Mason (1725-92), VA statesman and author of the VA Declaration of Rights, a model for the American Bill of Rights.

Area (sq mi): 444.8 (land 431.85; water 12.95).

Pop: 25,957 (White 98%; Black or African American 0.5%; Hispanic or Latino 0.5%; Asian 0.3%; Other 0.9%). **Foreign born:** 0.5%. **Median age:** 39.7. **State rank:** 26. **Pop change 1990-2000:** +3.1%.

Income: per capita $14,804; median household $27,134. **Pop below poverty level:** 19.9%.

Unemployment: 10.8%. **Median home value:** $65,100. **Median travel time to work:** 28.5 minutes.

McDOWELL COUNTY

90 Wyoming St Suite 109   **Ph:** 304-436-8544
Welch, WV 24801   **Fax:** 304-436-8576

On southern border of WV, southwest of Beckley; organized Feb 20, 1858 from Tazewell County (in VA). **Name Origin:** For James McDowell (1796-1851), member of the VA house of delegates (1830-35; 1838), governor (1842-46), and U.S. representative (1846-51).

Area (sq mi): 534.9 (land 534.72; water 0.18).

Pop: 27,329 (White 86.7%; Black or African American 11.9%; Hispanic or Latino 0.5%; Asian 0.1%; Other 1%). **Foreign born:** 0.5%. **Median age:** 40.5. **State rank:** 23. **Pop change 1990-2000:** -22.4%.

Income: per capita $10,174; median household $16,931. **Pop below poverty level:** 37.7%.

Unemployment: 6.9%. **Median home value:** $22,600. **Median travel time to work:** 32.6 minutes.

MERCER COUNTY

1501 Main St   **Ph:** 304-487-8311
Princeton, WV 24740   **Fax:** 304-487-8351

On southern border of WV, southeast of Beckley; organized Mar 17, 1837 from Giles and Tazewell counties (in VA). **Name Origin:** For Gen. Hugh Mercer (1721-77), Revolutionary War officer and physician.

Area (sq mi): 420.69 (land 420.43; water 0.26).

Pop: 62,980 (White 92.2%; Black or African American 5.8%; Hispanic or Latino 0.5%; Asian 0.5%; Other 1.1%). **Foreign born:** 0.8%. **Median age:** 40.2. **State rank:** 8. **Pop change 1990-2000:** -3.1%.

Income: per capita $15,564; median household $26,628. **Pop below poverty level:** 19.7%.

Unemployment: 4.5%. **Median home value:** $63,900. **Median travel time to work:** 24.9 minutes.

MINERAL COUNTY

150 Armstrong St   **Ph:** 304-788-3924
Keyser, WV 26726   **Fax:** 304-788-4109
www.mineralcountywv.com

In eastern panhandle of WV, southwest of Cumberland, MD; organized Feb 1, 1866 from Hampshire County. **Name Origin:** For its mineral resources, particularly coal.

Area (sq mi): 329.13 (land 327.73; water 1.4).

Pop: 27,078 (White 95.7%; Black or African American 2.5%; Hispanic or Latino 0.6%; Asian 0.2%; Other 1.1%). **Foreign born:** 0.6%. **Median age:** 39.1. **State rank:** 24. **Pop change 1990-2000:** +1.4%.

Income: per capita $15,384; median household $31,149. **Pop below poverty level:** 14.7%.

Unemployment: 6.2%. **Median home value:** $73,500. **Median travel time to work:** 29.2 minutes.

MINGO COUNTY

PO Box 1197   **Ph:** 304-235-0381
Williamson, WV 25661   **Fax:** 304-235-0365

On southwestern border of WV, southeast of Huntington; organized Jan 30, 1895 from Logan County. **Name Origin:** For the Indian tribe of Iroquoian linguistic stock. The name derives from Algonquian *Mingwe*, probably 'stealthy, treacherous.'

Area (sq mi): 423.64 (land 422.61; water 1.03).

Pop: 28,253 (White 96%; Black or African American 2.3%; Hispanic or Latino 0.5%; Asian 0.2%; Other 1%). **Foreign born:** 0.3%. **Median age:** 37.2. **State rank:** 21. **Pop change 1990-2000:** -16.3%.

Please see sample entry on inside front cover for detailed information about the statistics presented with each county listing.

Income: per capita $12,445; median household $21,347. **Pop below poverty level:** 29.7%.

Unemployment: 6.9%. **Median home value:** $61,100. **Median travel time to work:** 29.6 minutes.

MONONGALIA COUNTY
243 High St Rm 123
Morgantown, WV 26505
www.co.monongalia.wv.us

Ph: 304-291-7230
Fax: 304-291-7233

On northern border with PA, north of Fairmont; organized Oct 7, 1776 from District of West Augusta. **Name Origin:** Variant spelling for the Monongahela River, which traverses the county.

Area (sq mi): 365.89 (land 361.16; water 4.73).

Pop: 81,866 (White 91.6%; Black or African American 3.4%; Hispanic or Latino 1%; Asian 2.5%; Other 1.9%). **Foreign born:** 3.8%. **Median age:** 30.4. **State rank:** 4. **Pop change 1990-2000:** +8.4%.

Income: per capita $17,106; median household $28,625. **Pop below poverty level:** 22.8%.

Unemployment: 2.2%. **Median home value:** $95,500. **Median travel time to work:** 20.6 minutes.

MONROE COUNTY
PO Box 350
Union, WV 24983

Ph: 304-772-3096
Fax: 304-772-4191

On southeastern border of WV, southeast of Beckley; organized Jan 14, 1779 from Greenbrier County (WV) and Botetourt County (in VA). **Name Origin:** For James Monroe (1758-1831), fifth U.S. president.

Area (sq mi): 473.66 (land 473.37; water 0.3).

Pop: 14,583 (White 92.2%; Black or African American 6%; Hispanic or Latino 0.5%; Asian 0.2%; Other 1.1%). **Foreign born:** 0.5%. **Median age:** 39.7. **State rank:** 40. **Pop change 1990-2000:** +17.5%.

Income: per capita $17,435; median household $27,575. **Pop below poverty level:** 16.2%.

Unemployment: 4%. **Median home value:** $64,700. **Median travel time to work:** 35 minutes.

MORGAN COUNTY
77 Fairfax St Suite 1A
Berkeley Springs, WV 25411

Ph: 304-258-8547
Fax: 304-258-8545

In eastern panhandle of WV, west of Hagerstown, MD; organized Feb 9, 1820 from Berkeley and Hampshire counties. **Name Origin:** For Gen. Daniel Morgan (1736-1802), an officer in the Revolutionary War and U.S. representative from VA (1797-99).

Area (sq mi): 229.67 (land 228.98; water 0.68).

Pop: 14,943 (White 97.7%; Black or African American 0.6%; Hispanic or Latino 0.8%; Asian 0.1%; Other 1%). **Foreign born:** 1.4%. **Median age:** 40.7. **State rank:** 38. **Pop change 1990-2000:** +23.2%.

Income: per capita $18,109; median household $35,016. **Pop below poverty level:** 10.4%.

Unemployment: 3.5%. **Median home value:** $89,200. **Median travel time to work:** 36.3 minutes.

NICHOLAS COUNTY
700 Main St
Summersville, WV 26651

Ph: 304-872-7829
Fax: 304-872-9600

In central WV, east of Charleston; organized Jan 30, 1818 from Greenbrier, Kanawha, and Randolph counties. **Name Origin:** For Wilson Cary Nicholas (1761-1820), U.S. senator from VA (1799-1804), U.S. representative (1807-09), and governor (1814-16).

Area (sq mi): 654.4 (land 648.63; water 5.77).

Pop: 26,562 (White 98.5%; Black or African American 0.1%; Hispanic or Latino 0.5%; Asian 0.2%; Other 0.8%). **Foreign born:** 0.6%. **Median age:** 39.4. **State rank:** 25. **Pop change 1990-2000:** -0.8%.

Income: per capita $15,207; median household $26,974. **Pop below poverty level:** 19.2%.

Unemployment: 6%. **Median home value:** $60,100. **Median travel time to work:** 28.9 minutes.

OHIO COUNTY
1500 Chapline St Rm 205
Wheeling, WV 26003

Ph: 304-234-3656
Fax: 304-234-3829

In northern panhandle of WV, southeast of Steubenville, OH; organized Oct 7, 1776 from Augusta County. **Name Origin:** For the Ohio River, which forms its western border.

Area (sq mi): 108.86 (land 106.18; water 2.68).

Pop: 47,427 (White 94.1%; Black or African American 3.6%; Hispanic or Latino 0.5%; Asian 0.8%; Other 1.1%). **Foreign born:** 1.3%. **Median age:** 40.6. **State rank:** 12. **Pop change 1990-2000:** -6.8%.

Income: per capita $17,734; median household $30,836. **Pop below poverty level:** 15.8%.

Unemployment: 3.5%. **Median home value:** $71,400. **Median travel time to work:** 19.5 minutes.

PENDLETON COUNTY
PO Box 1167
Franklin, WV 26807

Ph: 304-358-2505
Fax: 304-358-2473

In eastern panhandle of WV; organized Dec 4, 1788 from Hardy County (WV) and Augusta and Rockingham counties (in VA). **Name Origin:** For Edmund Pendleton (1721-1803), VA House of Burgesses (1752-54), VA House of Delegates (1776-77), and presiding judge of VA court of appeals (1779).

Area (sq mi): 698.15 (land 697.87; water 0.28).

Pop: 8,196 (White 95.8%; Black or African American 2.1%; Hispanic or Latino 0.9%; Asian 0.2%; Other 1.4%). **Foreign born:** 0.7%. **Median age:** 41.1. **State rank:** 49. **Pop change 1990-2000:** +1.8%.

Income: per capita $15,805; median household $30,429. **Pop below poverty level:** 11.4%.

Unemployment: 3.1%. **Median home value:** $76,600. **Median travel time to work:** 35.4 minutes.

All statistics are based on the 2000 Census except the dollar figures given for per capita income, which are based on 1999 estimates.

PLEASANTS COUNTY

301 Court Ln Rm 101   **Ph:** 304-684-7542
Saint Marys, WV 26170   **Fax:** 304-684-7569

On northwestern border of WV, northeast of Parkersburg; organized Mar 29, 1851 from Ritchie, Tyler, and Wood counties. **Name Origin:** For James Pleasants, Jr. (1769-1836), U.S. representative from VA (1811-19), U.S. senator (1819-22), and governor (1822-25).

Area (sq mi): 134.59 (land 130.73; water 3.86).

Pop: 7,514 (White 98%; Black or African American 0.5%; Hispanic or Latino 0.4%; Asian 0.2%; Other 1.1%). **Foreign born:** 0.5%. **Median age:** 38.9. **State rank:** 51. **Pop change 1990-2000:** -0.4%.

Income: per capita $16,920; median household $32,736. **Pop below poverty level:** 13.7%.

Unemployment: 6.8%. **Median home value:** $75,300. **Median travel time to work:** 24.4 minutes.

POCAHONTAS COUNTY

900C 10th Ave   **Ph:** 304-799-4549
Marlinton, WV 24954   **Fax:** 304-799-6947

On central eastern border of WV; organized Dec 21, 1821 from Pendleton, Randolph, and Greenbrier counties (WV) and Bath County (in VA). **Name Origin:** For Indian princess Pocahontas (1595?-1617), daughter of Chief Powhatan (1550?-1618), whom she convinced to spare the life of VA colonist John Smith (c.1580-1631).

Area (sq mi): 941.85 (land 940.29; water 1.56).

Pop: 9,131 (White 98%; Black or African American 0.8%; Hispanic or Latino 0.4%; Asian 0.1%; Other 0.8%). **Foreign born:** 0.6%. **Median age:** 41.9. **State rank:** 48. **Pop change 1990-2000:** +1.4%.

Income: per capita $14,384; median household $26,401. **Pop below poverty level:** 17.1%.

Unemployment: 7.3%. **Median home value:** $64,000. **Median travel time to work:** 31.3 minutes.

PRESTON COUNTY

101 W Main St Rm 201   **Ph:** 304-329-0070
Kingwood, WV 26537   **Fax:** 304-329-0198

On northern border of WV, east of Morgantown; organized Jan 19, 1818 from Monongalia and Ranolph counties. **Name Origin:** For James Patton Preston (1774-1843), VA legislator, officer in the War of 1812, and governor of VA (1816-19).

Area (sq mi): 651.39 (land 648.32; water 3.06).

Pop: 29,334 (White 98.3%; Black or African American 0.3%; Hispanic or Latino 0.6%; Asian 0.1%; Other 0.6%). **Foreign born:** 0.6%. **Median age:** 39.1. **State rank:** 19. **Pop change 1990-2000:** +1%.

Income: per capita $13,596; median household $27,927. **Pop below poverty level:** 18.3%.

Unemployment: 4.6%. **Median home value:** $63,100. **Median travel time to work:** 30.2 minutes.

PUTNAM COUNTY

3389 Winfield Rd   **Ph:** 304-586-0202
Winfield, WV 25213   **Fax:** 304-586-0280

In western WV, northwest of Charleston; organized Mar 11, 1848 from Kanawha, Mason, and Cabell counties. **Name Origin:** For Gen. Israel Putnam (1718-90), Revolutionary War officer and American commander at the Battle of Bunker Hill.

Area (sq mi): 350.4 (land 346.23; water 4.17).

Pop: 51,589 (White 97.6%; Black or African American 0.6%; Hispanic or Latino 0.5%; Asian 0.6%; Other 0.9%). **Foreign born:** 1%. **Median age:** 37.7. **State rank:** 10. **Pop change 1990-2000:** +20.4%.

Income: per capita $20,471; median household $41,892. **Pop below poverty level:** 9.3%.

Unemployment: 3.7%. **Median home value:** $102,900. **Median travel time to work:** 27.1 minutes.

RALEIGH COUNTY

215 Main St   **Ph:** 304-255-9126
Beckley, WV 25801   **Fax:** 304-255-9166

In south-central WV, southeast of Charleston; organized Jan 23, 1850 from Fayette County. **Name Origin:** For Sir Walter Raleigh (1522?-1618), British naval commander and first lord proprietor of the colony of VA (1584-1603).

Area (sq mi): 609.34 (land 606.93; water 2.41).

Pop: 79,220 (White 88.9%; Black or African American 8.5%; Hispanic or Latino 0.9%; Asian 0.7%; Other 1.1%). **Foreign born:** 1.2%. **Median age:** 39.5. **State rank:** 5. **Pop change 1990-2000:** +3.1%.

Income: per capita $16,233; median household $28,181. **Pop below poverty level:** 18.5%.

Unemployment: 4.2%. **Median home value:** $69,800. **Median travel time to work:** 26.3 minutes.

RANDOLPH COUNTY

PO Box 368   **Ph:** 304-636-0543
Elkins, WV 26241

In east-central WV; organized May 5, 1787 from Harrison County. **Name Origin:** For Edmund Jennings Randolph (1753-1813), governor of VA (1786-88), first U.S. attorney general (1789), and U.S. secretary of state (1794-95).

Area (sq mi): 1039.92 (land 1039.72; water 0.2).

Pop: 28,262 (White 97.2%; Black or African American 1.1%; Hispanic or Latino 0.7%; Asian 0.4%; Other 0.9%). **Foreign born:** 0.7%. **Median age:** 38.8. **State rank:** 20. **Pop change 1990-2000:** +1.7%.

Income: per capita $14,918; median household $27,299. **Pop below poverty level:** 18%.

Unemployment: 5.9%. **Median home value:** $71,800. **Median travel time to work:** 22.5 minutes.

RITCHIE COUNTY

115 E Main St Rm 201   **Ph:** 304-643-2164
Harrisville, WV 26362   **Fax:** 304-643-2906

In north-central WV, east of Parkersburg; organized Feb 18, 1843 from Harrison, Lewis, and Wood counties. **Name Origin:** For Thomas Ritchie (1778-1854), newspaper owner and editor of the Richmond *Enquirer* (1804-45) and manager of the Washington, DC *Union* (1845-51).

Please see sample entry on inside front cover for detailed information about the statistics presented with each county listing.

Area (sq mi): 453.58 (land 453.51; water 0.07).

Pop: 10,343 (White 98.3%; Black or African American 0.1%; Hispanic or Latino 0.5%; Asian 0.1%; Other 1.1%). **Foreign born:** 0.3%. **Median age:** 39.9. **State rank:** 44. **Pop change 1990-2000:** +1.1%.

Income: per capita $15,175; median household $27,332. **Pop below poverty level:** 19.1%.

Unemployment: 8.1%. **Median home value:** $51,100. **Median travel time to work:** 32.9 minutes.

ROANE COUNTY

PO Box 69   **Ph:** 304-927-2860
Spencer, WV 25276   **Fax:** 304-927-2489

In west-central WV, northeast of Charleston; organized Mar 11, 1856 from Kanawha, Jackson, and Gilmer counties. **Name Origin:** For Spencer Roane (1762-1822), justice of the VA supreme court of appeals and son-in-law of Patrick Henry (1736-99).

Area (sq mi): 483.75 (land 483.57; water 0.18).

Pop: 15,446 (White 98%; Black or African American 0.2%; Hispanic or Latino 0.7%; Asian 0.2%; Other 1%). **Foreign born:** 0.6%. **Median age:** 39.5. **State rank:** 37. **Pop change 1990-2000:** +2.2%.

Income: per capita $13,195; median household $24,511. **Pop below poverty level:** 22.6%.

Unemployment: 13.4%. **Median home value:** $56,600. **Median travel time to work:** 34.8 minutes.

SUMMERS COUNTY

PO Box 97   **Ph:** 304-466-7104
Hinton, WV 25951   **Fax:** 304-466-7146

In southern WV, east of Beckley; organized Feb 27, 1871 from Greenbrier, Monroe, and Mercer counties. **Name Origin:** For George William Summers (1804-68), U.S. representative from VA (1831-45) and judge of VA's eighteenth judicial circuit (1852-58).

Area (sq mi): 367.72 (land 361.17; water 6.54).

Pop: 12,999 (White 96.1%; Black or African American 2.2%; Hispanic or Latino 0.5%; Asian 0.1%; Other 1.2%). **Foreign born:** 0.4%. **Median age:** 43.4. **State rank:** 41. **Pop change 1990-2000:** -8.5%.

Income: per capita $12,419; median household $21,147. **Pop below poverty level:** 24.4%.

Unemployment: 6.4%. **Median home value:** $56,100. **Median travel time to work:** 33.3 minutes.

TAYLOR COUNTY

214 W Main St   **Ph:** 304-265-1401
Grafton, WV 26354   **Fax:** 304-265-3016

In northern WV, south of Fairmont; organized Jan 19, 1844 from Harrison, Barbour, and Marion counties. **Name Origin:** For Col. John Taylor (1754-1824), officer in the Revolutionary War and U.S. senator from VA (1792-94; 1803; 1822-24).

Area (sq mi): 175.69 (land 172.78; water 2.91).

Pop: 16,089 (White 97.7%; Black or African American 0.8%; Hispanic or Latino 0.6%; Asian 0.2%; Other 0.9%). **Foreign born:**

0.6%. **Median age:** 39.1. **State rank:** 35. **Pop change 1990-2000:** +6.2%.

Income: per capita $13,681; median household $27,124. **Pop below poverty level:** 20.3%.

Unemployment: 5.5%. **Median home value:** $61,900. **Median travel time to work:** 25.2 minutes.

TUCKER COUNTY

215 1st St Suite 3   **Ph:** 304-478-2414
Parsons, WV 26287   **Fax:** 304-478-2606

In eastern WV, southeast of Clarksburg; organized Mar 7, 1856 from Randolph County. **Name Origin:** For Capt. Henry Saint George Tucker (1780-1848), cavalry officer in the War of 1812, U.S. representative from VA (1815-19), and president of the VA court of appeals (1831-41).

Area (sq mi): 421.11 (land 418.87; water 2.24).

Pop: 7,321 (White 98.7%; Black or African American 0.1%; Hispanic or Latino 0.2%; Asian 0%; Other 1.1%). **Foreign born:** 0.2%. **Median age:** 42. **State rank:** 53. **Pop change 1990-2000:** -5.3%.

Income: per capita $16,349; median household $26,250. **Pop below poverty level:** 18.1%.

Unemployment: 5.6%. **Median home value:** $61,100. **Median travel time to work:** 30.1 minutes.

TYLER COUNTY

PO Box 66   **Ph:** 304-758-2102
Middlebourne, WV 26149   **Fax:** 304-758-2126

On northwestern border of WV along the Ohio River, west of Fairmont; organized Dec 6, 1814 from Ohio County. **Name Origin:** For John Tyler (1747-1813), judge in the VA general court (1789-1808), governor (1808-11), and father of U.S. President John Tyler (1790-1862).

Area (sq mi): 260.69 (land 257.56; water 3.14).

Pop: 9,592 (White 99%; Black or African American 0%; Hispanic or Latino 0.4%; Asian 0.1%; Other 0.5%). **Foreign born:** 0.3%. **Median age:** 40.8. **State rank:** 47. **Pop change 1990-2000:** -2.1%.

Income: per capita $15,216; median household $29,290. **Pop below poverty level:** 16.6%.

Unemployment: 5.3%. **Median home value:** $61,500. **Median travel time to work:** 30.5 minutes.

UPSHUR COUNTY

40 W Main St Rm 101   **Ph:** 304-472-1068
Buckhannon, WV 26201   **Fax:** 304-472-1029

In central WV, south of Clarksburg; organized Mar 26, 1851 from Randolph, Barbour, and Lewis counties. **Name Origin:** For Abel Parker Upshur (1791-1844), judge in VA courts (1826-41), U.S. secretary of the Navy (1841-43), and U.S. secretary of state (1843-44).

Area (sq mi): 354.86 (land 354.76; water 0.1).

Pop: 23,404 (White 97.7%; Black or African American 0.6%; Hispanic or Latino 0.6%; Asian 0.3%; Other 0.9%). **Foreign born:** 0.4%. **Median age:** 37.4. **State rank:** 30. **Pop change 1990-2000:** +2.3%.

All statistics are based on the 2000 Census except the dollar figures given for per capita income, which are based on 1999 estimates.

COLUMBIA COUNTY

PO Box 177　　　　　　　　　　**Ph:** 608-742-9654
Portage, WI 53901　　　　　　　**Fax:** 608-742-9602
www.co.columbia.wi.us

In south-central WI, northwest of Milwaukee; organized Feb 3, 1846 (prior to statehood) from Portage, Brown, and Crawford counties. **Name Origin:** Feminine form of Columbus, a poetic and honorific reference to Christopher Columbus (1451-1506) and America.

Area (sq mi): 795.7 (land 773.79; water 21.91).

Pop: 52,468 (White 96.2%; Black or African American 0.9%; Hispanic or Latino 1.6%; Asian 0.3%; Other 1.6%). **Foreign born:** 1.3%. **Median age:** 38. **State rank:** 26. **Pop change 1990-2000:** +16.4%.

Income: per capita $21,014; median household $45,064. **Pop below poverty level:** 5.2%.

Unemployment: 5%. **Median home value:** $115,000. **Median travel time to work:** 24.7 minutes.

CRAWFORD COUNTY

220 N Beaumont Rd　　　　　　　**Ph:** 608-326-0200
Prairie du Chien, WI 53821　　　**Fax:** 608-326-0213

On southwestern border of WI; organized Oct 26, 1818 (prior to statehood) from a territorial county. **Name Origin:** For Fort Crawford, or possibly for Willliam Harris Crawford (1772-1834), U.S. senator from GA (1807-13), U.S. secretary of war (1815-16), and U.S. secretary of the treasury (1816-25).

Area (sq mi): 599.22 (land 572.69; water 26.53).

Pop: 17,243 (White 96.8%; Black or African American 1.4%; Hispanic or Latino 0.7%; Asian 0.3%; Other 1.1%). **Foreign born:** 0.7%. **Median age:** 38.9. **State rank:** 57. **Pop change 1990-2000:** +8.2%.

Income: per capita $16,833; median household $34,135. **Pop below poverty level:** 10.2%.

Unemployment: 5.1%. **Median home value:** $75,100. **Median travel time to work:** 21.8 minutes.

DANE COUNTY

210 ML King Jr Blvd Rm 112　　**Ph:** 608-266-4121
Madison, WI 53703
www.co.dane.wi.us

In south-central WI, west of Milwaukee; organized Dec 7, 1836 (prior to statehood) from Iowa County. **Name Origin:** For Nathan Dane (1725-1835), U.S. representative from MA (1782-85) who proposed the Ordinance of 1787 establishing the Northwest Territory.

Area (sq mi): 1238.32 (land 1201.89; water 36.42).

Pop: 426,526 (White 87.4%; Black or African American 4%; Hispanic or Latino 3.4%; Asian 3.5%; Other 3.5%). **Foreign born:** 6.3%. **Median age:** 33.2. **State rank:** 2. **Pop change 1990-2000:** +16.2%.

Income: per capita $24,985; median household $49,223. **Pop below poverty level:** 9.4%.

Unemployment: 2%. **Median home value:** $146,900. **Median travel time to work:** 19.9 minutes.

DODGE COUNTY

127 E Oak St　　　　　　　　　**Ph:** 920-386-3602
Juneau, WI 53039　　　　　　　**Fax:** 920-386-3928
www.co.dodge.wi.us

In southeastern WI, west of Milwaukee; organized Dec 7, 1836 (prior to statehood) from territorial county. **Name Origin:** For Gen. Henry Dodge (1782-1867), an officer in the War of 1812 and Black Hawk War, first governor of WI Territory (1836-41;1845-48), and U.S. senator from WI (1848-57).

Area (sq mi): 906.99 (land 882.28; water 24.71).

Pop: 85,897 (White 93.8%; Black or African American 2.5%; Hispanic or Latino 2.5%; Asian 0.3%; Other 1.9%). **Foreign born:** 1.6%. **Median age:** 37. **State rank:** 17. **Pop change 1990-2000:** +12.2%.

Income: per capita $19,574; median household $45,190. **Pop below poverty level:** 5.3%.

Unemployment: 5.3%. **Median home value:** $105,800. **Median travel time to work:** 20.8 minutes.

DOOR COUNTY

PO Box 670　　　　　　　　　　**Ph:** 920-746-2200
Sturgeon Bay, WI 54235　　　　**Fax:** 920-746-2330
www.co.door.wi.us

On the peninsula in northeast WI, bordered on west by Green Bay and on east by Lake Michigan; organized Feb 11,1851 from Brown County. **Name Origin:** Origin uncertain. A legendary incident involving Indians is said to be the reason the strait between Washington Island and the peninsula is named in French *La Porte des Morts,* 'Door of the Dead.' Or possibly 'the door' refers to the entrance to Green Bay. The county later took the name from the strait.

Area (sq mi): 2369.83 (land 482.72; water 1887.11).

Pop: 27,961 (White 97.4%; Black or African American 0.2%; Hispanic or Latino 1%; Asian 0.3%; Other 1.7%). **Foreign born:** 1.5%. **Median age:** 42.9. **State rank:** 44. **Pop change 1990-2000:** +8.8%.

Income: per capita $21,356; median household $38,813. **Pop below poverty level:** 6.4%.

Unemployment: 5.2%. **Median home value:** $120,800. **Median travel time to work:** 17.8 minutes.

DOUGLAS COUNTY

1313 Belknap St　　　　　　　　**Ph:** 715-395-1341
Superior, WI 54880　　　　　　　**Fax:** 715-395-1421
www.co.douglas.wi.us

On northwestern border of WI, at southwestern end of Lake Superior; organized Feb 9, 1854 from unorganized territory. **Name Origin:** For Stephen Arnold Douglas (1813-61), U.S. orator and statesman.

Area (sq mi): 1479.91 (land 1309.13; water 170.78).

Pop: 43,287 (White 94.9%; Black or African American 0.6%; Hispanic or Latino 0.7%; Asian 0.6%; Other 3.4%). **Foreign born:** 1.6%. **Median age:** 37.7. **State rank:** 31. **Pop change 1990-2000:** +3.7%.

Income: per capita $17,638; median household $35,226. **Pop below poverty level:** 11%.

Please see sample entry on inside front cover for detailed information about the statistics presented with each county listing.

Unemployment: 5.1%. **Median home value:** $69,900. **Median travel time to work:** 20.9 minutes.

DUNN COUNTY

800 Wilson Ave   **Ph:** 715-232-1677
Menomonie, WI 54751   **Fax:** 715-232-2534
www.co.dunn.wi.us

In west-central WI, east of Saint Paul, MN; organized Feb 3, 1854 from Chippewa County **Name Origin:** For Charles Dunn, a legislator and first chief justice of WI Territory.

Area (sq mi): 863.91 (land 852.03; water 11.89).

Pop: 39,858 (White 95.6%; Black or African American 0.3%; Hispanic or Latino 0.8%; Asian 2.1%; Other 1.5%). **Foreign born:** 2.1%. **Median age:** 30.6. **State rank:** 36. **Pop change 1990-2000:** +11%.

Income: per capita $17,520; median household $38,753. **Pop below poverty level:** 12.9%.

Unemployment: 4.1%. **Median home value:** $92,900. **Median travel time to work:** 21.8 minutes.

EAU CLAIRE COUNTY

721 Oxford Ave   **Ph:** 715-839-4803
Eau Claire, WI 54703   **Fax:** 715-839-4854
www.co.eau-claire.wi.us

In west-central WI, east of Saint Paul, MN; organized Oct 6, 1856 from Clark County. **Name Origin:** For Eau Clair River, which runs through it; French transliteration of an Indian word meaning 'clear water.'

Area (sq mi): 645.28 (land 637.64; water 7.64).

Pop: 93,142 (White 94.4%; Black or African American 0.5%; Hispanic or Latino 0.9%; Asian 2.5%; Other 1.9%). **Foreign born:** 2.2%. **Median age:** 32.4. **State rank:** 16. **Pop change 1990-2000:** +9.3%.

Income: per capita $19,250; median household $39,219. **Pop below poverty level:** 10.9%.

Unemployment: 4.1%. **Median home value:** $96,300. **Median travel time to work:** 17.3 minutes.

FLORENCE COUNTY

PO Box 410   **Ph:** 715-528-3201
Florence, WI 54121   **Fax:** 715-528-4762
www.florencewisconsin.com

On northeastern border of WI; organized Mar 18, 1882 from Marinette and Oconto counties. **Name Origin:** For Florence Terry Hulst, wife of an early developer and mine owner, Dr. N. P. Hulst.

Area (sq mi): 497.46 (land 488.03; water 9.43).

Pop: 5,088 (White 97.9%; Black or African American 0.2%; Hispanic or Latino 0.5%; Asian 0.3%; Other 1.3%). **Foreign born:** 0.6%. **Median age:** 41.9. **State rank:** 71. **Pop change 1990-2000:** +10.8%.

Income: per capita $18,328; median household $34,750. **Pop below poverty level:** 9.1%.

Unemployment: 6.7%. **Median home value:** $82,200. **Median travel time to work:** 20.3 minutes.

FOND DU LAC COUNTY

PO Box 1557   **Ph:** 920-929-3000
Fond du Lac, WI 54936   **Fax:** 920-929-3293
www.co.fond-du-lac.wi.us

In east-central WI; organized Dec 7, 1836 (prior to statehood) from a territorial county. **Name Origin:** For its location at the southern end of Lake Winnebago; French 'end of the lake,' transliterated from *Wanikamiu*, name of an Indian village, with the similar meaning 'farthest point of the lake.'

Area (sq mi): 765.8 (land 722.91; water 42.89).

Pop: 97,296 (White 95.1%; Black or African American 0.9%; Hispanic or Latino 2%; Asian 0.9%; Other 2%). **Foreign born:** 2%. **Median age:** 36.9. **State rank:** 14. **Pop change 1990-2000:** +8%.

Income: per capita $20,022; median household $45,578. **Pop below poverty level:** 5.8%.

Unemployment: 4.3%. **Median home value:** $101,000. **Median travel time to work:** 18.7 minutes.

FOREST COUNTY

200 E Madison St   **Ph:** 715-478-2422
Crandon, WI 54520   **Fax:** 715-478-5175
www.forestcountywi.com

On northeastern border of WI; organized Apr 11, 1885 from Langlade and Oconto counties. **Name Origin:** Descriptively named for the forests in the area.

Area (sq mi): 1046.4 (land 1014.05; water 32.34).

Pop: 10,024 (White 85.5%; Black or African American 1.2%; Hispanic or Latino 1.1%; Asian 0.2%; Other 12.7%). **Foreign born:** 1.1%. **Median age:** 39.9. **State rank:** 68. **Pop change 1990-2000:** +14.2%.

Income: per capita $16,451; median household $32,023. **Pop below poverty level:** 13.1%.

Unemployment: 6.5%. **Median home value:** $77,400. **Median travel time to work:** 23 minutes.

GRANT COUNTY

111 S Jefferson St   **Ph:** 608-723-2675
Lancaster, WI 53813   **Fax:** 608-723-4048
grantcounty.org/govt/index.html

On southwestern border of WI; organized Dec 8, 1836 (prior to statehood) from Iowa County. **Name Origin:** For the Grant River, which runs through it; itself named for a trapper and Indian trader who lived on the banks.

Area (sq mi): 1183.31 (land 1147.85; water 35.46).

Pop: 49,597 (White 97.9%; Black or African American 0.5%; Hispanic or Latino 0.6%; Asian 0.5%; Other 0.7%). **Foreign born:** 1%. **Median age:** 35.9. **State rank:** 28. **Pop change 1990-2000:** +0.7%.

Income: per capita $16,764; median household $36,268. **Pop below poverty level:** 11.2%.

Unemployment: 5.3%. **Median home value:** $78,000. **Median travel time to work:** 20.4 minutes.

All statistics are based on the 2000 Census except the dollar figures given for per capita income, which are based on 1999 estimates.

GREEN COUNTY

1016 16th Ave
Monroe, WI 53566
www.co.green.wi.us

Ph: 608-328-9430
Fax: 608-328-2835

On central southern border of WI, south of Madison; organized Dec 8, 1836 (prior to statehood) from Iowa County. **Name Origin:** For Gen. Nathanael Greene (1742-86), Revolutionary War officer and quartermaster general (1778-80). The missing *e* not explained.

Area (sq mi): 584.56 (land 583.99; water 0.58).

Pop: 33,647 (White 97.7%; Black or African American 0.3%; Hispanic or Latino 1%; Asian 0.3%; Other 1.4%). **Foreign born:** 1.3%. **Median age:** 37.9. **State rank:** 40. **Pop change 1990-2000:** +10.9%.

Income: per capita $20,795; median household $43,228. **Pop below poverty level:** 5.1%.

Unemployment: 4.8%. **Median home value:** $97,700. **Median travel time to work:** 22.3 minutes.

GREEN LAKE COUNTY

PO Box 3188
Green Lake, WI 54941
www.co.green-lake.wi.us

Ph: 920-294-4005
Fax: 920-294-4009

In east-central WI, west of Lake Winnebago; organized Mar 5, 1858 from Marquette District. **Name Origin:** For the large lake in the middle of the county, named for the color of the water.

Area (sq mi): 380.44 (land 354.28; water 26.15).

Pop: 19,105 (White 96.7%; Black or African American 0.2%; Hispanic or Latino 2.1%; Asian 0.3%; Other 1.7%). **Foreign born:** 1.8%. **Median age:** 40.9. **State rank:** 53. **Pop change 1990-2000:** +2.4%.

Income: per capita $19,024; median household $39,462. **Pop below poverty level:** 7%.

Unemployment: 5.6%. **Median home value:** $90,100. **Median travel time to work:** 22.4 minutes.

IOWA COUNTY

222 N Iowa St Suite 102
Dodgeville, WI 53533
www.iowacounty.org

Ph: 608-935-5445
Fax: 608-935-3024

In southwestern WI, west of Madison; organized Oct 9, 1829 (prior to statehood) from a territorial county. **Name Origin:** For either the Iowa River, or the Iowa Indians. Name is a French version of the Dakota name for the tribe, variously *Ayuhwa, Ouaouia, Aiouez,* and *Ioways* 'the sleepy ones.'

Area (sq mi): 768.08 (land 762.67; water 5.41).

Pop: 22,780 (White 98.5%; Black or African American 0.2%; Hispanic or Latino 0.3%; Asian 0.3%; Other 0.8%). **Foreign born:** 0.6%. **Median age:** 37.1. **State rank:** 48. **Pop change 1990-2000:** +13.1%.

Income: per capita $19,497; median household $42,518. **Pop below poverty level:** 7.3%.

Unemployment: 3.7%. **Median home value:** $91,800. **Median travel time to work:** 24.7 minutes.

IRON COUNTY

300 Taconite St
Hurley, WI 54534
Ph: 715-561-3375
Fax: 715-561-2928

On central northern border of WI; organized Mar 1, 1893 from Ashland and Oneida counties. **Name Origin:** For the huge deposits of iron ore found in the Mesabi Range.

Area (sq mi): 919.24 (land 757.23; water 162.01).

Pop: 6,861 (White 97.9%; Black or African American 0.1%; Hispanic or Latino 0.7%; Asian 0.1%; Other 1.5%). **Foreign born:** 1.8%. **Median age:** 45. **State rank:** 70. **Pop change 1990-2000:** +11.5%.

Income: per capita $17,371; median household $29,580. **Pop below poverty level:** 11.1%.

Unemployment: 6.9%. **Median home value:** $58,900. **Median travel time to work:** 19.8 minutes.

JACKSON COUNTY

307 Main St
Black River Falls, WI 54615
www.co.jackson.wi.us
Ph: 715-284-0208
Fax: 715-284-0270

In west-central WI, northwest of Madison; organized Feb 11, 1853 from Crawford County. **Name Origin:** For Andrew Jackson (1767-1845), seventh U.S. president.

Area (sq mi): 1000.11 (land 987.32; water 12.79).

Pop: 19,100 (White 89%; Black or African American 2.3%; Hispanic or Latino 1.9%; Asian 0.2%; Other 8%). **Foreign born:** 1.9%. **Median age:** 37.6. **State rank:** 54. **Pop change 1990-2000:** +15.1%.

Income: per capita $17,604; median household $37,015. **Pop below poverty level:** 9.6%.

Unemployment: 5.2%. **Median home value:** $76,800. **Median travel time to work:** 21.2 minutes.

JEFFERSON COUNTY

320 S Main St Rm 109
Jefferson, WI 53549
www.co.jefferson.wi.us
Ph: 920-674-7140
Fax: 920-674-7368

In southeastern WI, east of Milwaukee; organized Dec 7, 1836 from Dodge and Waukesha counties. **Name Origin:** For Thomas Jefferson (1743-1826), U.S. patriot and statesman; third U.S. president. Others claim it was named for Jefferson County, NY, former home of some prominent early settlers.

Area (sq mi): 582.75 (land 557.01; water 25.73).

Pop: 74,021 (White 94.3%; Black or African American 0.3%; Hispanic or Latino 4.1%; Asian 0.4%; Other 2.8%). **Foreign born:** 2.8%. **Median age:** 36.6. **State rank:** 21. **Pop change 1990-2000:** +9.2%.

Income: per capita $21,236; median household $46,901. **Pop below poverty level:** 5.7%.

Unemployment: 3.9%. **Median home value:** $123,800. **Median travel time to work:** 21 minutes.

Please see sample entry on inside front cover for detailed information about the statistics presented with each county listing.

JUNEAU COUNTY

220 E State St   **Ph:** 608-847-9300
Mauston, WI 53948   **Fax:** 608-847-9402
www.juneaucounty.com

In south-central WI, northwest of Madison; organized Oct 13, 1856 from Adams County. **Name Origin:** For Solomon Juneau (1793-1856), early French trader, the first postmaster and first mayor of Milwaukee, called 'the father of the city.'

Area (sq mi): 804.13 (land 767.61; water 36.53).

Pop: 24,316 (White 95.9%; Black or African American 0.3%; Hispanic or Latino 1.4%; Asian 0.4%; Other 2.6%). **Foreign born:** 1.5%. **Median age:** 39.4. **State rank:** 46. **Pop change 1990-2000:** +12.3%.

Income: per capita $17,892; median household $35,335. **Pop below poverty level:** 10.1%.

Unemployment: 9.1%. **Median home value:** $71,200. **Median travel time to work:** 22.1 minutes.

KENOSHA COUNTY

1010 56th St   **Ph:** 262-653-2552
Kenosha, WI 53140   **Fax:** 262-653-2564
www.co.kenosha.wi.us

On southeastern border of WI; organized Jan 30, 1850 from Racine County. **Name Origin:** For the name of Potawatomi (Algonquian) Indian villages, meaning 'pike' or 'pickerel,' for the abundance of this fish in the local creeks.

Area (sq mi): 754.31 (land 272.83; water 481.48).

Pop: 149,577 (White 85.1%; Black or African American 5.1%; Hispanic or Latino 7.2%; Asian 0.9%; Other 5.6%). **Foreign born:** 4.8%. **Median age:** 34.8. **State rank:** 9. **Pop change 1990-2000:** +16.7%.

Income: per capita $21,207; median household $46,970. **Pop below poverty level:** 7.5%.

Unemployment: 4.9%. **Median home value:** $120,900. **Median travel time to work:** 25.3 minutes.

KEWAUNEE COUNTY

613 Dodge St   **Ph:** 920-388-7144
Kewaunee, WI 54216   **Fax:** 920-388-3199
www.kewauneeco.org

On the peninsula in eastern WI, bordered on west by Green Bay and on east by Lake Michigan; organized Apr 16, 1852 from Manitowoc County. **Name Origin:** A Potawatomi word whose meaning is unclear; possibly 'to cross a point,' referring to the river between Green Bay and Lake Michigan or 'prairie hen' or 'wild duck.'

Area (sq mi): 1084.52 (land 342.64; water 741.89).

Pop: 20,187 (White 98.2%; Black or African American 0.2%; Hispanic or Latino 0.8%; Asian 0.1%; Other 1.2%). **Foreign born:** 0.9%. **Median age:** 37.5. **State rank:** 51. **Pop change 1990-2000:** +6.9%.

Income: per capita $18,456; median household $43,824. **Pop below poverty level:** 5.8%.

Unemployment: 4.2%. **Median home value:** $92,100. **Median travel time to work:** 22.5 minutes.

LA CROSSE COUNTY

400 N 4th St Rm 102   **Ph:** 608-785-9581
La Crosse, WI 54601   **Fax:** 608-789-4821
www.co.la-crosse.wi.us

On southwestern border of WI, northwest of Madison; organized Mar 1, 1851 from unorganized territory. **Name Origin:** For the village of the same name, from the French name for an Indian game *baggataway*, from a resemblance they saw to their tennis game, played with a racquet that resembled a bishop's crozier or cross.

Area (sq mi): 479.92 (land 452.74; water 27.18).

Pop: 107,120 (White 93.7%; Black or African American 0.9%; Hispanic or Latino 0.9%; Asian 3.2%; Other 1.7%). **Foreign born:** 2.5%. **Median age:** 33.5. **State rank:** 13. **Pop change 1990-2000:** +9.4%.

Income: per capita $19,800; median household $39,472. **Pop below poverty level:** 10.7%.

Unemployment: 3.7%. **Median home value:** $96,900. **Median travel time to work:** 17.3 minutes.

LAFAYETTE COUNTY

PO Box 40   **Ph:** 608-776-4850
Darlington, WI 53530   **Fax:** 608-776-8893
wicip.uwplatt.edu/lafayette

On southwestern border of WI, southwest of Madison; organized Jan 31, 1846 (prior to statehood) from Iowa County. **Name Origin:** For the Marquis de Lafayette (1757-1834), French statesman and soldier who fought with the Americans during the Revolutionary War.

Area (sq mi): 634.56 (land 633.57; water 1).

Pop: 16,137 (White 98.7%; Black or African American 0.1%; Hispanic or Latino 0.6%; Asian 0.2%; Other 0.6%). **Foreign born:** 0.8%. **Median age:** 38.1. **State rank:** 60. **Pop change 1990-2000:** +0.4%.

Income: per capita $16,811; median household $37,220. **Pop below poverty level:** 9.1%.

Unemployment: 5.2%. **Median home value:** $74,600. **Median travel time to work:** 23.9 minutes.

LANGLADE COUNTY

800 Clermont St   **Ph:** 715-627-6200
Antigo, WI 54409   **Fax:** 715-627-6303
www.langlade-county.com

In northeastern WI, northeast of Wausau; organized Feb 27, 1879 as New County from Oconto County; name changed Feb 19, 1880. **Name Origin:** For Charles Michael de Langlade (1729-1800), an Indian leader who fought with the French against the British in the French and Indian War and with the British against the Americans during the Revolutionary War; he established the first permanent settlement at Green Bay (1764). Some claim for his father, Augustin de Langlade (1695-1771), a French settler who married an Indian woman.

Area (sq mi): 887.88 (land 872.67; water 15.2).

Pop: 20,740 (White 97.4%; Black or African American 0.1%; Hispanic or Latino 0.8%; Asian 0.3%; Other 1.6%). **Foreign born:** 1%. **Median age:** 40.5. **State rank:** 50. **Pop change 1990-2000:** +6.3%.

All statistics are based on the 2000 Census except the dollar figures given for per capita income, which are based on 1999 estimates.

Income: per capita $16,960; median household $33,168. **Pop below poverty level:** 10.1%.

Unemployment: 7.8%. **Median home value:** $68,600. **Median travel time to work:** 20.3 minutes.

LINCOLN COUNTY

1110 E Main St   **Ph:** 715-536-0312
Merrill, WI 54452   **Fax:** 715-536-6528
www.co.lincoln.wi.us

In northeastern WI, north of Wausau; organized Mar 4, 1874 from Marathon County. **Name Origin:** For Abraham Lincoln (1809-65), sixteenth U.S. president.

Area (sq mi): 907.05 (land 883.3; water 23.75).

Pop: 29,641 (White 97.4%; Black or African American 0.4%; Hispanic or Latino 0.8%; Asian 0.4%; Other 1.4%). **Foreign born:** 1.6%. **Median age:** 38.9. **State rank:** 42. **Pop change 1990-2000:** +9.8%.

Income: per capita $17,940; median household $39,120. **Pop below poverty level:** 6.9%.

Unemployment: 5.8%. **Median home value:** $86,500. **Median travel time to work:** 19.2 minutes.

MANITOWOC COUNTY

PO Box 2000   **Ph:** 920-683-4030
Manitowoc, WI 54221   **Fax:** 920-683-2733
www.co.manitowoc.wi.us

On central eastern coast of WI, south of Green Bay; organized Dec 7, 1836 (prior to statehood) from a territorial county. **Name Origin:** From an Indian name probably meaning 'land of the spirit,' possibly with a connotation of evil.

Area (sq mi): 1493.87 (land 591.53; water 902.34).

Pop: 82,887 (White 95%; Black or African American 0.3%; Hispanic or Latino 1.6%; Asian 2%; Other 1.8%). **Foreign born:** 2.3%. **Median age:** 38.3. **State rank:** 18. **Pop change 1990-2000:** +3.1%.

Income: per capita $20,285; median household $43,286. **Pop below poverty level:** 6.1%.

Unemployment: 5.7%. **Median home value:** $90,900. **Median travel time to work:** 18.2 minutes.

MARATHON COUNTY

500 Forest St   **Ph:** 715-261-1500
Wausau, WI 54403   **Fax:** 715-261-1515
www.co.marathon.wi.us

In central WI, east of Eau Claire; organized Feb 9, 1850 from Portage County. **Name Origin:** For the site of the famous battle in Greece (490 B.C.).

Area (sq mi): 1576.14 (land 1544.96; water 31.18).

Pop: 125,834 (White 93.4%; Black or African American 0.3%; Hispanic or Latino 0.8%; Asian 4.5%; Other 1.3%). **Foreign born:** 3.5%. **Median age:** 36.3. **State rank:** 10. **Pop change 1990-2000:** +9%.

Income: per capita $20,703; median household $45,165. **Pop below poverty level:** 6.6%.

Unemployment: 4.1%. **Median home value:** $95,800. **Median travel time to work:** 18.4 minutes.

MARINETTE COUNTY

1926 Hall Ave   **Ph:** 715-732-7406
Marinette, WI 54143   **Fax:** 715-732-7532
www.marinettecounty.com

On northeastern border of WI, north of Green Bay; organized Feb 27, 1879 from Oconto County. **Name Origin:** For Marguerite Chevallier (1784-1865), a successful female fur trader, also known as *Marinette*, a combined form of Marie Antoinette (1755-93), then Queen of France.

Area (sq mi): 1550.07 (land 1401.76; water 148.32).

Pop: 43,384 (White 97.6%; Black or African American 0.2%; Hispanic or Latino 0.7%; Asian 0.3%; Other 1.4%). **Foreign born:** 1.2%. **Median age:** 40.5. **State rank:** 30. **Pop change 1990-2000:** +7%.

Income: per capita $17,492; median household $35,256. **Pop below poverty level:** 8.3%.

Unemployment: 6.7%. **Median home value:** $69,800. **Median travel time to work:** 20.1 minutes.

MARQUETTE COUNTY

PO Box 187   **Ph:** 608-297-9136
Montello, WI 53949   **Fax:** 608-297-9188
www.co.marquette.wi.us

In south- central WI, west of Lake Winnebago; established Dec 7, 1836 (prior to statehood) from Marquette District. **Name Origin:** For Jacques Marquette (1637-75), French missonary known as Pere Marquette; explorer with Louis Jolliet (1645-1700) of the Wisconsin and Mississippi Rivers.

Area (sq mi): 464.42 (land 455.49; water 8.94).

Pop: 15,832 (White 92%; Black or African American 3.4%; Hispanic or Latino 2.7%; Asian 0.3%; Other 2.6%). **Foreign born:** 1.5%. **Median age:** 40.9. **State rank:** 62. **Pop change 1990-2000:** +28.5%.

Income: per capita $16,924; median household $35,746. **Pop below poverty level:** 7.7%.

Unemployment: 7.3%. **Median home value:** $87,000. **Median travel time to work:** 25.9 minutes.

MENOMINEE COUNTY

PO Box 279   **Ph:** 715-799-3311
Keshena, WI 54135   **Fax:** 715-799-1322

In east-central WI, northwest of Lake Winnebago; organized May 1, 1961 from Shawano and Oconto counties. **Name Origin:** For the Menominee Indians, a tribe of Algonquian linguistic stock, who lived in the lake region where wild rice grows. The name probably means 'wild rice people.'

Area (sq mi): 364.99 (land 357.96; water 7.03).

Pop: 4,562 (White 11.5%; Black or African American 0.1%; Hispanic or Latino 2.7%; Asian 0%; Other 88.3%). **Foreign born:** 2.7%. **Median age:** 27.7. **State rank:** 72. **Pop change 1990-2000:** +17.3%.

Income: per capita $10,625; median household $29,440. **Pop below poverty level:** 28.8%.

Please see sample entry on inside front cover for detailed information about the statistics presented with each county listing.

Unemployment: 11.6%. **Median home value:** $72,700. **Median travel time to work:** 18.4 minutes.

MILWAUKEE COUNTY
901 N 9th St   **Ph:** 414-278-4067
Milwaukee, WI 53233
www.co.milwaukee.wi.us

On southeastern coast of WI; organized Aug 25, 1835 (prior to statehood). **Name Origin:** An Algonquian word of uncertain meaning; possibly 'rich beautiful land' or 'gathering place by the river.' The area had long been a council ground for different tribes.

Area (sq mi): 1189.7 (land 241.56; water 948.14).

Pop: 940,164 (White 62.1%; Black or African American 24.6%; Hispanic or Latino 8.8%; Asian 2.6%; Other 7.1%). **Foreign born:** 6.8%. **Median age:** 33.7. **State rank:** 1. **Pop change 1990-2000:** -2%.

Income: per capita $19,939; median household $38,100. **Pop below poverty level:** 15.3%.

Unemployment: 5.6%. **Median home value:** $103,200. **Median travel time to work:** 21.9 minutes.

MONROE COUNTY
202 S 'K' St   **Ph:** 608-269-8705
Sparta, WI 54656   **Fax:** 608-269-8747
www.co.monroe.wi.us

In southwestern WI, east of La Crosse; organized Mar 21, 1854 from unorganized territory. **Name Origin:** For James Monroe (1758-1831), fifth U.S. president.

Area (sq mi): 908.29 (land 900.77; water 7.52).

Pop: 40,899 (White 95.7%; Black or African American 0.5%; Hispanic or Latino 1.8%; Asian 0.5%; Other 2.4%). **Foreign born:** 1.8%. **Median age:** 36.8. **State rank:** 33. **Pop change 1990-2000:** +11.6%.

Income: per capita $17,056; median household $37,170. **Pop below poverty level:** 12%.

Unemployment: 5.4%. **Median home value:** $77,500. **Median travel time to work:** 19 minutes.

OCONTO COUNTY
301 Washington St   **Ph:** 920-834-6800
Oconto, WI 54153   **Fax:** 920-834-6867
www.co.oconto.wi.us

On northeastern coast of WI, bordered on east by Green Bay; organized Feb 6, 1851 from unorganized territory. **Name Origin:** For the Oconto River, which flows through it; from a Menominee word of unclear meaning, possibly 'place of the pike fish' or 'red river.'

Area (sq mi): 1149.04 (land 997.97; water 151.07).

Pop: 35,634 (White 97.4%; Black or African American 0.1%; Hispanic or Latino 0.7%; Asian 0.2%; Other 1.9%). **Foreign born:** 0.7%. **Median age:** 38.8. **State rank:** 39. **Pop change 1990-2000:** +17.9%.

Income: per capita $19,016; median household $41,201. **Pop below poverty level:** 7.1%.

Unemployment: 6.8%. **Median home value:** $89,900. **Median travel time to work:** 25.8 minutes.

ONEIDA COUNTY
PO Box 400   **Ph:** 715-369-6144
Rhinelander, WI 54501   **Fax:** 715-369-6230
www.co.oneida.wi.us

In north-central WI; organized Apr 11, 1885 from Lincoln County. **Name Origin:** For the Oneida Indians, one of the Five Nations of the Iroquois. The name is thought to mean 'stone people,' perhaps in praise of their bravery.

Area (sq mi): 1235.88 (land 1124.5; water 111.38).

Pop: 36,776 (White 97.3%; Black or African American 0.3%; Hispanic or Latino 0.7%; Asian 0.3%; Other 1.7%). **Foreign born:** 1%. **Median age:** 42.4. **State rank:** 38. **Pop change 1990-2000:** +16.1%.

Income: per capita $19,746; median household $37,619. **Pop below poverty level:** 7.4%.

Unemployment: 5.4%. **Median home value:** $106,200. **Median travel time to work:** 17.8 minutes.

OUTAGAMIE COUNTY
410 S Walnut St   **Ph:** 920-832-5077
Appleton, WI 54911   **Fax:** 920-832-2200
www.co.outagamie.wi.us

In east-central WI, west of Green Bay; organized Feb 17, 1851 from Brown County. **Name Origin:** Ojibway *O-dug-am-eeg* 'dwellers on the other side,' in reference to the Fox Indians.

Area (sq mi): 644.4 (land 640.34; water 4.06).

Pop: 160,971 (White 93%; Black or African American 0.5%; Hispanic or Latino 2%; Asian 2.2%; Other 3.3%). **Foreign born:** 3.1%. **Median age:** 34.4. **State rank:** 6. **Pop change 1990-2000:** +14.6%.

Income: per capita $21,943; median household $49,613. **Pop below poverty level:** 4.7%.

Unemployment: 3.7%. **Median home value:** $106,000. **Median travel time to work:** 18.1 minutes.

OZAUKEE COUNTY
PO Box 994   **Ph:** 262-284-8110
Port Washington, WI 53074   **Fax:** 262-284-8100
www.co.ozaukee.wi.us

On southestern coast of WI, north of Milwaukee, organized Mar 7, 1853 from Milwaukee County. **Name Origin:** Said to be the true name of the main Sauk Indian tribe; meaning is either 'people at the mouth of the river' (the Ojibway name for the tribe), or 'yellow earth,' from their tradition that the first Sauk male sprang from yellow earth.

Area (sq mi): 1116.2 (land 231.95; water 884.26).

Pop: 82,317 (White 95.8%; Black or African American 0.9%; Hispanic or Latino 1.3%; Asian 1.1%; Other 1.2%). **Foreign born:** 3.3%. **Median age:** 38.9. **State rank:** 19. **Pop change 1990-2000:** +13%.

Income: per capita $31,947; median household $62,745. **Pop below poverty level:** 2.6%.

All statistics are based on the 2000 Census except the dollar figures given for per capita income, which are based on 1999 estimates.

Unemployment: 3%. **Median home value:** $177,300. **Median travel time to work:** 22.1 minutes.

PEPIN COUNTY
740 7th Ave W   **Ph:** 715-672-8857
Durand, WI 54736
www.co.pepin.wi.us

On central western border of WI, southeast of Saint Paul, MN; organized Feb 25, 1858 from Chippewa County. **Name Origin:** For Pepin Lake, a widening of the Mississippi River. Named before 1700 by French explorers either for a member of the Duluth expedition, or for the French king, Pepin le Bref (715-768), the father of Charlemagne (742-814).

Area (sq mi): 248.68 (land 232.28; water 16.4).

Pop: 7,213 (White 98.7%; Black or African American 0.1%; Hispanic or Latino 0.3%; Asian 0.2%; Other 0.8%). **Foreign born:** 0.6%. **Median age:** 38.7. **State rank:** 69. **Pop change 1990-2000:** +1.5%.

Income: per capita $18,288; median household $37,609. **Pop below poverty level:** 9.1%.

Unemployment: 5.9%. **Median home value:** $79,200. **Median travel time to work:** 25.7 minutes.

PIERCE COUNTY
PO Box 267   **Ph:** 715-273-3531
Ellsworth, WI 54011   **Fax:** 715-273-6155
www.co.pierce.wi.us

On central western border of WI, east of Saint Paul, MN; organized Mar 14, 1853 from Saint Croix County. **Name Origin:** For Franklin Pierce (1804-69), fourteenth U.S. president.

Area (sq mi): 591.59 (land 576.49; water 15.1).

Pop: 36,804 (White 97.5%; Black or African American 0.2%; Hispanic or Latino 0.8%; Asian 0.4%; Other 1.3%). **Foreign born:** 1%. **Median age:** 32.1. **State rank:** 37. **Pop change 1990-2000:** +12.3%.

Income: per capita $20,172; median household $49,551. **Pop below poverty level:** 7.7%.

Unemployment: 4%. **Median home value:** $123,100. **Median travel time to work:** 25.1 minutes.

POLK COUNTY
100 Polk County Plaza Suite 110   **Ph:** 715-485-9271
Balsam Lake, WI 54810   **Fax:** 715-485-9104
www.co.polk.wi.us

On central western border of WI, northeast of Saint Paul, MN; organized Mar 14, 1853 from Saint Croix County. **Name Origin:** For James Knox Polk (1795-1849), eleventh U.S. president.

Area (sq mi): 956.28 (land 917.27; water 39.01).

Pop: 41,319 (White 97.1%; Black or African American 0.2%; Hispanic or Latino 0.8%; Asian 0.3%; Other 2%). **Foreign born:** 1%. **Median age:** 38.7. **State rank:** 32. **Pop change 1990-2000:** +18.8%.

Income: per capita $19,129; median household $41,183. **Pop below poverty level:** 7.1%.

Unemployment: 6%. **Median home value:** $100,200. **Median travel time to work:** 28.7 minutes.

PORTAGE COUNTY
1516 Church St   **Ph:** 715-346-1351
Stevens Point, WI 54481   **Fax:** 715-346-1486
www.co.portage.wi.us

In east-central WI, northwest of Lake Winnebago; organized Dec 7, 1836 (prior to statehood) from territorial county in the area now occupied by much of Columbia County, expanded northward in 1841 (into territory from Crawford County); Columbia County detached in 1846. **Name Origin:** For the portage of canoes or other craft between the Fox and Wisconsin rivers.

Area (sq mi): 822.76 (land 806.31; water 16.45).

Pop: 67,182 (White 94.9%; Black or African American 0.3%; Hispanic or Latino 1.4%; Asian 2.2%; Other 1.7%). **Foreign born:** 2.2%. **Median age:** 33. **State rank:** 22. **Pop change 1990-2000:** +9.4%.

Income: per capita $19,854; median household $43,487. **Pop below poverty level:** 9.5%.

Unemployment: 4.5%. **Median home value:** $98,300. **Median travel time to work:** 18.3 minutes.

PRICE COUNTY
126 Cherry St   **Ph:** 715-339-3325
Phillips, WI 54555   **Fax:** 715-339-3089
www.co.price.wi.us

In north-central WI, northwest of Wausau; organized Feb 26, 1879 from Chippewa and Lincoln counties. **Name Origin:** For William Thompson Price (1824-86), WI jurist, legislator, and U.S. representative (1883-86).

Area (sq mi): 1278.43 (land 1252.56; water 25.87).

Pop: 15,822 (White 97.7%; Black or African American 0.1%; Hispanic or Latino 0.7%; Asian 0.3%; Other 1.3%). **Foreign born:** 0.6%. **Median age:** 41.7. **State rank:** 63. **Pop change 1990-2000:** +1.4%.

Income: per capita $17,837; median household $35,249. **Pop below poverty level:** 8.9%.

Unemployment: 7%. **Median home value:** $70,100. **Median travel time to work:** 18.9 minutes.

RACINE COUNTY
730 Wisconsin Ave   **Ph:** 262-636-3121
Racine, WI 53403   **Fax:** 262-636-3491
www.co.racine.wi.us

On southeastern coast of WI, south of Milwaukee; organized Dec 7, 1836 (prior to statehood) from territorial county. **Name Origin:** French 'root,' referring to the county's principal town, located on the Root River, which had so many roots growing out of its banks that navigation was difficult.

Area (sq mi): 791.9 (land 333.1; water 458.81).

Pop: 188,831 (White 79.6%; Black or African American 10.5%; Hispanic or Latino 7.9%; Asian 0.7%; Other 5.8%). **Foreign born:** 4.1%. **Median age:** 36.1. **State rank:** 5. **Pop change 1990-2000:** +7.9%.

Income: per capita $21,772; median household $48,059. **Pop below poverty level:** 8.4%.

Please see sample entry on inside front cover for detailed information about the statistics presented with each county listing.

Unemployment: 6.7%. **Median home value:** $111,000. **Median travel time to work:** 22 minutes.

RICHLAND COUNTY

181 W Seminary St   **Ph:** 608-647-2197
Richland Center, WI 53581   **Fax:** 608-647-6134
www.co.richland.wi.us

In southwestern WI, northwest of Madison; organized Feb 18, 1842 (prior to statehood) from Crawford, Sauk, and Iowa counties. **Name Origin:** For the fertile soil, and possibly because an early settler came from Richland Co., IA.

Area (sq mi): 589.38 (land 586.2; water 3.18).

Pop: 17,924 (White 97.9%; Black or African American 0.2%; Hispanic or Latino 0.9%; Asian 0.2%; Other 1.3%). **Foreign born:** 1%. **Median age:** 39.2. **State rank:** 56. **Pop change 1990-2000:** +2.3%.

Income: per capita $17,042; median household $33,998. **Pop below poverty level:** 10.1%.

Unemployment: 4.8%. **Median home value:** $75,200. **Median travel time to work:** 24.1 minutes.

ROCK COUNTY

51 S Main St   **Ph:** 608-757-5660
Janesville, WI 53545   **Fax:** 608-757-5662
www.co.rock.wi.us

On central southern border of WI, southeast of Madison; organized Dec 7, 1836 (prior to statehood) from a territorial county. **Name Origin:** For the Rock River, which flows through it.

Area (sq mi): 726.2 (land 720.47; water 5.73).

Pop: 152,307 (White 89.2%; Black or African American 4.6%; Hispanic or Latino 3.9%; Asian 0.8%; Other 3.6%). **Foreign born:** 3.3%. **Median age:** 35.9. **State rank:** 8. **Pop change 1990-2000:** +9.2%.

Income: per capita $20,895; median household $45,517. **Pop below poverty level:** 7.3%.

Unemployment: 6.4%. **Median home value:** $98,200. **Median travel time to work:** 20.3 minutes.

RUSK COUNTY

311 Miner Ave E   **Ph:** 715-532-2100
Ladysmith, WI 54848   **Fax:** 715-532-2237
www.ruskcounty.org

In northwestern WI, northeast of Saint Paul, MN; organized May 15, 1901 as Gates County from Chippewa County; name changed Jun 19, 1905. **Name Origin:** For Col. Jeremiah McLain Rusk (1830-93), an officer in the Civil War, statesman, governor of WI (1882-89), and U.S. secretary of agriculture (1889-93).

Area (sq mi): 930.89 (land 913.13; water 17.77).

Pop: 15,347 (White 97.4%; Black or African American 0.5%; Hispanic or Latino 0.8%; Asian 0.3%; Other 1.6%). **Foreign born:** 1.7%. **Median age:** 40. **State rank:** 65. **Pop change 1990-2000:** +1.8%.

Income: per capita $15,563; median household $31,344. **Pop below poverty level:** 11.8%.

Unemployment: 7.3%. **Median home value:** $63,200. **Median travel time to work:** 21.6 minutes.

SAINT CROIX COUNTY

1101 Carmichael Rd   **Ph:** 715-386-4600
Hudson, WI 54016   **Fax:** 715-381-4396
www.co.saint-croix.wi.us

On central western border of WI, east of Saint Paul, MN; organized Jan 9, 1840 (prior to statehood) from a territorial county. **Name Origin:** For the river, which flows through it; French 'holy cross,' probably for an early French explorer of that name who drowned in it.

Area (sq mi): 735.81 (land 721.82; water 13.98).

Pop: 63,155 (White 97.4%; Black or African American 0.3%; Hispanic or Latino 0.8%; Asian 0.6%; Other 1.3%). **Foreign born:** 1.1%. **Median age:** 35. **State rank:** 23. **Pop change 1990-2000:** +25.7%.

Income: per capita $23,937; median household $54,930. **Pop below poverty level:** 4%.

Unemployment: 4.5%. **Median home value:** $139,500. **Median travel time to work:** 26.1 minutes.

SAUK COUNTY

505 Broadway   **Ph:** 608-355-3288
Baraboo, WI 53913   **Fax:** 608-355-3292
www.co.sauk.wi.us

In south-central WI, northwest of Madison; organized Jan 11, 1840 (prior to statehood) from a territorial county. **Name Origin:** Shortened form of Saukie, a local Indian tribe; French form is *Sac*. Meaning of the name is unclear: possibly 'something sprouting up' or 'yellow earth' from which their tradition says their first male sprang.

Area (sq mi): 848.43 (land 837.63; water 10.8).

Pop: 55,225 (White 96.4%; Black or African American 0.3%; Hispanic or Latino 1.7%; Asian 0.3%; Other 2.1%). **Foreign born:** 1.9%. **Median age:** 37.3. **State rank:** 24. **Pop change 1990-2000:** +17.6%.

Income: per capita $19,695; median household $41,941. **Pop below poverty level:** 7.2%.

Unemployment: 3.6%. **Median home value:** $107,500. **Median travel time to work:** 20.3 minutes.

SAWYER COUNTY

PO Box 836   **Ph:** 715-634-4866
Hayward, WI 54843   **Fax:** 715-634-3666
www.sawyercountygov.org

In northwestern WI, north of Eau Claire; organized Mar 10, 1883 from Ashland and Chippewa counties. **Name Origin:** For Philetus Sawyer (1816-1900), U.S. representative from WI (1865-75) and U.S. senator (1881-93).

Area (sq mi): 1350.32 (land 1256.42; water 93.9).

Pop: 16,196 (White 81.4%; Black or African American 0.3%; Hispanic or Latino 0.9%; Asian 0.3%; Other 17.6%). **Foreign born:** 1.6%. **Median age:** 42.1. **State rank:** 59. **Pop change 1990-2000:** +14.2%.

All statistics are based on the 2000 Census except the dollar figures given for per capita income, which are based on 1999 estimates.

Income: per capita $17,634; median household $32,287. **Pop below poverty level:** 12.7%.

Unemployment: 5.7%. **Median home value:** $94,300. **Median travel time to work:** 18.4 minutes.

SHAWANO COUNTY
311 N Main St   **Ph:** 715-526-9150
Shawano, WI 54166   **Fax:** 715-524-5157
www.co.shawano.wi.us

In east-central WI, northwest of Green Bay; organized Feb 16, 1853 from Oconto County. **Name Origin:** For Shawano Lake, a Menominee word probably meaning 'to the south.'

Area (sq mi): 909.33 (land 892.51; water 16.82).

Pop: 40,664 (White 91.2%; Black or African American 0.2%; Hispanic or Latino 1%; Asian 0.3%; Other 7.8%). **Foreign born:** 1%. **Median age:** 38.5. **State rank:** 34. **Pop change 1990-2000:** +9.4%.

Income: per capita $17,991; median household $38,069. **Pop below poverty level:** 7.9%.

Unemployment: 5.4%. **Median home value:** $84,000. **Median travel time to work:** 22.8 minutes.

SHEBOYGAN COUNTY
508 New York Ave   **Ph:** 920-459-3003
Sheboygan, WI 53081   **Fax:** 920-459-0304
www.co.sheboygan.wi.us

On central eastern coast of WI, southeast of Lake Winnebago; organized Dec 7, 1836 (prior to statehood) from a territorial county. **Name Origin:** For the Sheboygan River, from an Algonquian word whose meaning is unclear: possibly either 'reed like,' 'something that pierces,' or 'thundering under the ground.'

Area (sq mi): 1270.97 (land 513.63; water 757.34).

Pop: 112,646 (White 91.1%; Black or African American 1.1%; Hispanic or Latino 3.4%; Asian 3.3%; Other 3%). **Foreign born:** 4.3%. **Median age:** 36.8. **State rank:** 12. **Pop change 1990-2000:** +8.4%.

Income: per capita $21,509; median household $46,237. **Pop below poverty level:** 5.2%.

Unemployment: 3.8%. **Median home value:** $106,800. **Median travel time to work:** 16.9 minutes.

TAYLOR COUNTY
224 S 2nd St   **Ph:** 715-748-1460
Medford, WI 54451   **Fax:** 715-748-1415
www.co.taylor.wi.us

In north-central WI, northwest of Wausau; organized Mar 4, 1875 from Clark and Lincoln counties. **Name Origin:** For William Robert Taylor (1820-1909), governor of WI (1874-76), known as the 'farmer governor.'

Area (sq mi): 984.49 (land 974.86; water 9.63).

Pop: 19,680 (White 98.3%; Black or African American 0.1%; Hispanic or Latino 0.6%; Asian 0.2%; Other 1%). **Foreign born:** 0.9%. **Median age:** 37.4. **State rank:** 52. **Pop change 1990-2000:** +4.1%.

Income: per capita $17,570; median household $38,502. **Pop below poverty level:** 9.8%.

Unemployment: 5.8%. **Median home value:** $75,600. **Median travel time to work:** 18.5 minutes.

TREMPEALEAU COUNTY
36245 Main St   **Ph:** 715-538-2311
Whitehall, WI 54773   **Fax:** 715-538-4210
www.tremplocounty.com

On central western border of WI, southeast of Saint Paul, MN; organized Jan 27, 1854 from Chippewa County. **Name Origin:** For the town at the foot of a high elevation surrounded by water; French transliteration *la montagne qui termpe a l'eau* of an Indian word probably meaning 'mountain drenched with water.' The Trempealeau River forms the lower western border of the county.

Area (sq mi): 741.98 (land 734.08; water 7.9).

Pop: 27,010 (White 98.3%; Black or African American 0.1%; Hispanic or Latino 0.9%; Asian 0.1%; Other 1%). **Foreign born:** 0.8%. **Median age:** 38.3. **State rank:** 45. **Pop change 1990-2000:** +6.9%.

Income: per capita $17,681; median household $37,889. **Pop below poverty level:** 8.3%.

Unemployment: 5.8%. **Median home value:** $77,000. **Median travel time to work:** 21.9 minutes.

VERNON COUNTY
411 Courthouse Sq   **Ph:** 608-637-5380
Viroqua, WI 54665

On southwestern border of WI, southwest of Madison; organized as Bad Axe County Mar 1, 1851 from Richland and Crawford counties; name changed Mar 22, 1862. **Name Origin:** For either Mount Vernon, first U.S. President George Washington's (1732-99) home overlooking the Potomac River in VA, or for George Vernon Weeks, a friend of the county judge. Originally for the Bad Ax River, which traverses it.

Area (sq mi): 816.41 (land 794.87; water 21.54).

Pop: 28,056 (White 98.4%; Black or African American 0.1%; Hispanic or Latino 0.7%; Asian 0.2%; Other 0.9%). **Foreign born:** 0.8%. **Median age:** 39.1. **State rank:** 43. **Pop change 1990-2000:** +9.5%.

Income: per capita $15,859; median household $33,178. **Pop below poverty level:** 14.2%.

Unemployment: 5%. **Median home value:** $73,400. **Median travel time to work:** 23.7 minutes.

VILAS COUNTY
330 Court St   **Ph:** 715-479-3600
Eagle River, WI 54521   **Fax:** 715-479-3605
www.co.vilas.wi.us

On central northern border of WI; organized Apr 12, 1893 from Oneida County. **Name Origin:** For Col. William Freeman Vilas (1840-1908), officer in the Civil War, U.S. postmaster general (1885-88), U.S. secretary of the interior (1888-89), and U.S. senator from WI (1891-97).

Area (sq mi): 1017.85 (land 873.72; water 144.13).

Pop: 21,033 (White 89.2%; Black or African American 0.2%; Hispanic or Latino 0.9%; Asian 0.2%; Other 10%). **Foreign born:**

Please see sample entry on inside front cover for detailed information about the statistics presented with each county listing.

635

2.4%. **Median age:** 45.8. **State rank:** 49. **Pop change 1990-2000:** +18.8%.

Income: per capita $18,361; median household $33,759. **Pop below poverty level:** 8%.

Unemployment: 5.2%. **Median home value:** $120,200. **Median travel time to work:** 17.9 minutes.

WALWORTH COUNTY

PO Box 1001
Elkhorn, WI 53121
www.co.walworth.wi.us

Ph: 262-741-4241
Fax: 262-741-4287

On southeastern border of WI, southwest of Milwaukee; organized Dec 7, 1836 (prior to statehood) from a territorial county. **Name Origin:** For Col. Reuben Hyde Walworth (1788-1867), officer in the War of 1812, jurist, and U.S. representative from NY (1821-23); unconfirmed nominee to the U.S. Supreme Court (1844).

Area (sq mi): 576.5 (land 555.31; water 21.19).

Pop: 93,759 (White 91.1%; Black or African American 0.8%; Hispanic or Latino 6.5%; Asian 0.7%; Other 3.9%). **Foreign born:** 5.4%. **Median age:** 35.1. **State rank:** 15. **Pop change 1990-2000:** +25%.

Income: per capita $21,229; median household $46,274. **Pop below poverty level:** 8.4%.

Unemployment: 3.7%. **Median home value:** $128,400. **Median travel time to work:** 24 minutes.

WASHBURN COUNTY

PO Box 639
Shell Lake, WI 54871
www.co.washburn.wi.us

Ph: 715-468-4600
Fax: 715-468-4725

In northwestern WI; organized Mar 27, 1883 from Burnett County. **Name Origin:** For Cadwallader Colden Washburn (1818-82), U.S. representative (1855-61; 1867-71) and governor of WI (1872-74).

Area (sq mi): 853.06 (land 809.68; water 43.37).

Pop: 16,036 (White 96.7%; Black or African American 0.2%; Hispanic or Latino 0.9%; Asian 0.2%; Other 2.3%). **Foreign born:** 1%. **Median age:** 42.1. **State rank:** 61. **Pop change 1990-2000:** +16.4%.

Income: per capita $17,341; median household $33,716. **Pop below poverty level:** 9.9%.

Unemployment: 6.3%. **Median home value:** $85,700. **Median travel time to work:** 22.4 minutes.

WASHINGTON COUNTY

432 E Washington St PO Box 1986
West Bend, WI 53095
www.co.washington.wi.us

Ph: 262-335-4305
Fax: 262-306-2208

In southeastern WI, northwest of Milwaukee; organized Dec 7, 1836 (prior to statehood) from a territorial county. **Name Origin:** For George Washington (1732-99), American patriot and first U.S. president.

Area (sq mi): 435.89 (land 430.82; water 5.07).

Pop: 117,493 (White 96.9%; Black or African American 0.4%; Hispanic or Latino 1.3%; Asian 0.6%; Other 1.4%). **Foreign born:**

1.9%. **Median age:** 36.6. **State rank:** 11. **Pop change 1990-2000:** +23.3%.

Income: per capita $24,319; median household $57,033. **Pop below poverty level:** 3.6%.

Unemployment: 3.8%. **Median home value:** $155,000. **Median travel time to work:** 23.2 minutes.

WAUKESHA COUNTY

1320 Pewaukee Rd Rm 120
Waukesha, WI 53188
www.waukeshacounty.gov

Ph: 262-548-7010

In southeastern WI, west of Milwaukee; organized Jan 31, 1846 (prior to statehood) from Milwaukee County. **Name Origin:** For the Fox River and the Fox Indian tribe, from Potawatomi *wakusheg* 'foxes.'

Area (sq mi): 580.48 (land 555.58; water 24.91).

Pop: 360,767 (White 94.2%; Black or African American 0.7%; Hispanic or Latino 2.6%; Asian 1.5%; Other 2%). **Foreign born:** 3.6%. **Median age:** 38.1. **State rank:** 3. **Pop change 1990-2000:** +18.4%.

Income: per capita $29,164; median household $62,839. **Pop below poverty level:** 2.7%.

Unemployment: 3.3%. **Median home value:** $170,400. **Median travel time to work:** 22.2 minutes.

WAUPACA COUNTY

811 Harding St
Waupaca, WI 54981
www.co.waupaca.wi.us

Ph: 715-258-6200
Fax: 715-258-6212

In east-central WI, west of Green Bay; organized Feb 17, 1851 from Winnebago and Brown counties. **Name Origin:** From an Indian name of various interpretations; the most probable is 'place of clear water.'

Area (sq mi): 765.33 (land 751.09; water 14.24).

Pop: 51,731 (White 97.2%; Black or African American 0.2%; Hispanic or Latino 1.4%; Asian 0.3%; Other 1.6%). **Foreign born:** 1%. **Median age:** 38.5. **State rank:** 27. **Pop change 1990-2000:** +12.2%.

Income: per capita $18,664; median household $40,910. **Pop below poverty level:** 6.8%.

Unemployment: 5%. **Median home value:** $89,300. **Median travel time to work:** 21 minutes.

WAUSHARA COUNTY

PO Box 507
Wautoma, WI 54982
www.1waushara.com

Ph: 920-787-0441
Fax: 920-787-0481

In east-central WI, west of Lake Winnebago; organized Feb 15, 1851 from Marquette County. **Name Origin:** From an Indian word possibly meaning 'good land river' or for a Winnebago word meaning 'foxes.' Corruption of the name of a Winnebago chief, an ancient Winnebago village, and the Indian name for Fox Lake.

Area (sq mi): 637.39 (land 626.03; water 11.36).

Pop: 23,154 (White 94.8%; Black or African American 0.3%; Hispanic or Latino 3.7%; Asian 0.3%; Other 2.6%). **Foreign born:** 2%. **Median age:** 42.1. **State rank:** 47. **Pop change 1990-2000:** +19.4%.

All statistics are based on the 2000 Census except the dollar figures given for per capita income, which are based on 1999 estimates.

Income: per capita $18,144; median household $37,000. **Pop below poverty level:** 9.1%.

Unemployment: 5.8%. **Median home value:** $85,100. **Median travel time to work:** 27.1 minutes.

WINNEBAGO COUNTY

PO Box 2808
Oshkosh, WI 54903
www.co.winnebago.wi.us

Ph: 920-236-4800
Fax: 920-303-3025

In east-central WI, west of Lake Winnebago; organized Jan 6, 1840 (prior to statehood) from Brown County. **Name Origin:** For the Winnebago Indians, a tribe of Siouan linguistic stock; their name believed to mean 'fish eaters.'

Area (sq mi): 578.7 (land 438.58; water 140.12).

Pop: 156,763 (White 93.9%; Black or African American 1.1%; Hispanic or Latino 2%; Asian 1.8%; Other 2.1%). **Foreign born:** 2.8%. **Median age:** 35.4. **State rank:** 7. **Pop change 1990-2000:** +11.7%.

Income: per capita $21,706; median household $44,445. **Pop below poverty level:** 6.7%.

Unemployment: 3.5%. **Median home value:** $97,700. **Median travel time to work:** 17.8 minutes.

WOOD COUNTY

PO Box 8095
Wisconsin Rapids, WI 54495
www.co.wood.wi.us

Ph: 715-421-8460
Fax: 715-421-8808

In central WI, southwest of Wausau; organized Mar 29, 1856 from Portage County. **Name Origin:** For Joseph Wood, legislator, county judge, and mayor of Grand Rapids.

Area (sq mi): 809.46 (land 792.78; water 16.68).

Pop: 75,555 (White 95.9%; Black or African American 0.3%; Hispanic or Latino 0.9%; Asian 1.6%; Other 1.7%). **Foreign born:** 2.1%. **Median age:** 38. **State rank:** 20. **Pop change 1990-2000:** +2.6%.

Income: per capita $20,203; median household $41,595. **Pop below poverty level:** 6.5%.

Unemployment: 5.3%. **Median home value:** $81,400. **Median travel time to work:** 17.4 minutes.

Please see sample entry on inside front cover for detailed information about the statistics presented with each county listing.

637

WYOMING - Counties

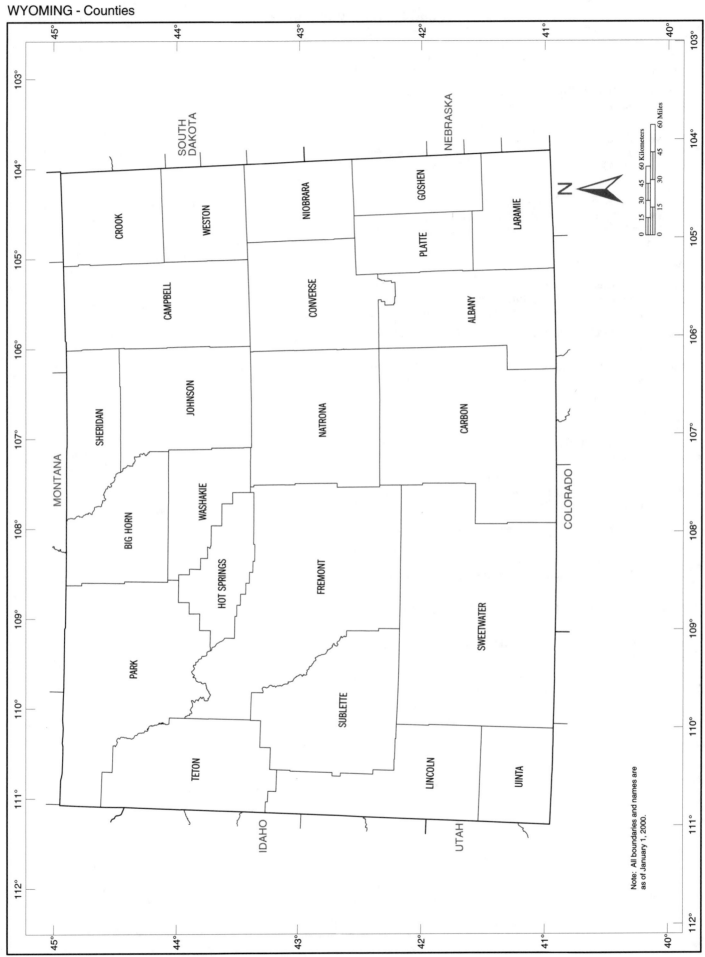

SOUTH DAKOTA

NEBRASKA

CROOK

WESTON

NIOBRARA

GOSHEN

LARAMIE

PLATTE

CAMPBELL

CONVERSE

ALBANY

MONTANA

JOHNSON

SHERIDAN

NATRONA

CARBON

WASHAKIE

BIG HORN

HOT SPRINGS

FREMONT

COLORADO

PARK

SWEETWATER

SUBLETTE

TETON

LINCOLN

UINTA

IDAHO

UTAH

N

0 15 30 45 60 Kilometers
0 15 30 45 60 Miles

Note: All boundaries and names are
as of January 1, 2000.

Wyoming

WYOMING STATE INFORMATION

www.state.wy.us   **Ph:** 307-777-7220

Area (sq mi): 97,813.56 (land 97100.4; water 713.16).

Pop: 493,782 (White 88.9%; Black or African American 0.8%; Hispanic or Latino 6.4%; Asian 0.6%; Other 6.7%). **Foreign born:** 2.3%. **Median age:** 36.2. **Pop change 1990-2000:** +8.9%.

Income: per capita $19,134; median household $37,892. **Pop below poverty level:** 11.4%.

Unemployment: 4%. **Median home value:** $96,600. **Median travel time to work:** 17.8 minutes.

ALBANY COUNTY

525 Grand Ave County Courthouse Rm 202   **Ph:** 307-721-2541
Laramie, WY 82070   **Fax:** 307-721-2544

On the southeastern border of WY, west of Cheyenne; organized Dec 16, 1868 (prior to statehood) from Laramie County. **Name Origin:** For Albany, NY, former home of Charles D. Bradley, a member of the legislature.

Area (sq mi): 4308.79 (land 4272.75; water 36.04).

Pop: 32,014 (White 87.5%; Black or African American 1.1%; Hispanic or Latino 7.5%; Asian 1.7%; Other 5.9%). **Foreign born:** 3.8%. **Median age:** 26.7. **State rank:** 6. **Pop change 1990-2000:** +4%.

Income: per capita $16,706; median household $28,790. **Pop below poverty level:** 21%.

Unemployment: 2%. **Median home value:** $118,600. **Median travel time to work:** 13.6 minutes.

BIG HORN COUNTY

420 W 'C' St   **Ph:** 307-568-2357
Basin, WY 82410   **Fax:** 307-568-9375

On the central northern border of WY; organized 1896 from Fremont and Johnson counties. **Name Origin:** For the Big Horn River, which traverses the county, and the Big Horn Mountains, which form its eastern border; both are named for the bighorn sheep in the area.

Area (sq mi): 3158.96 (land 3136.99; water 21.97).

Pop: 11,461 (White 91.9%; Black or African American 0.1%; Hispanic or Latino 6.2%; Asian 0.2%; Other 5.8%). **Foreign born:** 2.2%. **Median age:** 38.7. **State rank:** 15. **Pop change 1990-2000:** +8.9%.

Income: per capita $15,086; median household $32,682. **Pop below poverty level:** 14.1%.

Unemployment: 5%. **Median home value:** $71,800. **Median travel time to work:** 15.7 minutes.

CAMPBELL COUNTY

PO Box 3010   **Ph:** 307-682-7285
Gillette, WY 82717   **Fax:** 307-687-6455
ccg.co.campbell.wy.us

On northeastern border of WY; organized Feb 13, 1911 from Crook and Weston counties. **Name Origin:** Probably for Gen. John Allen Campbell (1835-80), Civil War officer and first territorial governor of WY (1869-75); or possibly for Robert Campbell, member of an expedition into the Missouri River area in 1822.

Area (sq mi): 4801.56 (land 4796.76; water 4.8).

Pop: 33,698 (White 94.1%; Black or African American 0.2%; Hispanic or Latino 3.5%; Asian 0.3%; Other 3.4%). **Foreign born:** 1.7%. **Median age:** 32.2. **State rank:** 5. **Pop change 1990-2000:** +14.7%.

Income: per capita $20,063; median household $49,536. **Pop below poverty level:** 7.6%.

Unemployment: 2.9%. **Median home value:** $102,900. **Median travel time to work:** 20.1 minutes.

CARBON COUNTY

PO Box 6   **Ph:** 307-328-2668
Rawlins, WY 82301   **Fax:** 307-328-2669

On the central southern border of WY; organized Dec 16, 1868 (prior to statehood) from Laramie County. **Name Origin:** For vast coal deposits within its boundaries.

Area (sq mi): 7964.03 (land 7896.14; water 67.89).

Pop: 15,639 (White 82.4%; Black or African American 0.7%; Hispanic or Latino 13.8%; Asian 0.7%; Other 8.7%). **Foreign born:** 2.9%. **Median age:** 38.9. **State rank:** 11. **Pop change 1990-2000:** -6.1%.

Income: per capita $18,375; median household $36,060. **Pop below poverty level:** 12.9%.

Unemployment: 4.4%. **Median home value:** $76,500. **Median travel time to work:** 13.7 minutes.

CONVERSE COUNTY

107 N 5th St Suite 114   **Ph:** 307-358-2244
Douglas, WY 82633   **Fax:** 307-358-4065
www.conversecounty.org

In east-central WY, east of Casper; organized Mar 9, 1888 (prior to statehood) from Albany County. **Name Origin:** For Amasa Converse

Please see sample entry on inside front cover for detailed information about the statistics presented with each county listing.

639

(1842-85), WY Territory official and Cheyenne businessman who established the Converse Cattle Company.

Area (sq mi): 4265.1 (land 4254.72; water 10.38).

Pop: 12,052 (White 91.9%; Black or African American 0.1%; Hispanic or Latino 5.5%; Asian 0.3%; Other 4.9%). **Foreign born:** 1.9%. **Median age:** 37.5. **State rank:** 14. **Pop change 1990-2000:** +8.3%.

Income: per capita $18,744; median household $39,603. **Pop below poverty level:** 11.6%.

Unemployment: 4.2%. **Median home value:** $84,900. **Median travel time to work:** 25.9 minutes.

CROOK COUNTY
309 Cleveland St   **Ph:** 307-283-1323
Sundance, WY 82729   **Fax:** 307-283-3038

On the northeastern border of WY, northeast of Gillette; created Dec 8, 1875 (prior to statehood). **Name Origin:** For Gen. George H. Crook (1829-90), officer in the Oregon Territory and Indian fighter; called 'Gray Fox' by the Shoshones.

Area (sq mi): 2870.52 (land 2858.59; water 11.93).

Pop: 5,887 (White 97.3%; Black or African American 0.1%; Hispanic or Latino 0.9%; Asian 0.1%; Other 2%). **Foreign born:** 0.9%. **Median age:** 40.2. **State rank:** 21. **Pop change 1990-2000:** +11.2%.

Income: per capita $17,379; median household $35,601. **Pop below poverty level:** 9.1%.

Unemployment: 3.8%. **Median home value:** $85,400. **Median travel time to work:** 22.4 minutes.

FREMONT COUNTY
450 N 2nd St Rm 220   **Ph:** 307-332-2405
Lander, WY 82520   **Fax:** 307-332-1132
www.fremontcounty.org

In west-central WY, west of Casper; organized Mar 5, 1884 (prior to statehood) from Sweetwater County. **Name Origin:** For John Charles Fremont (1813-90), soldier and explorer who led five expeditions to the West, U.S. senator from CA (1850-51), and governor of the AZ Territory (1878-81).

Area (sq mi): 9265.8 (land 9182.27; water 83.53).

Pop: 35,804 (White 74.6%; Black or African American 0.1%; Hispanic or Latino 4.4%; Asian 0.3%; Other 23.1%). **Foreign born:** 0.8%. **Median age:** 37.7. **State rank:** 4. **Pop change 1990-2000:** +6.4%.

Income: per capita $16,519; median household $32,503. **Pop below poverty level:** 17.6%.

Unemployment: 6.4%. **Median home value:** $89,300. **Median travel time to work:** 17.1 minutes.

GOSHEN COUNTY
2125 E 'A' St PO Box 160   **Ph:** 307-532-4051
Torrington, WY 82240   **Fax:** 307-532-7375

On the southeastern border of WY, northeast of Cheyenne; created Feb 9, 1911 from Platte and Laramie counties. **Name Origin:** For Goshen Hole Valley, which was probably named for the Biblical

Egyptian home of the Israelites before the Exodus; generally interpreted as 'land of abundance or plenty.'

Area (sq mi): 2232.16 (land 2225.32; water 6.84).

Pop: 12,538 (White 89.1%; Black or African American 0.2%; Hispanic or Latino 8.8%; Asian 0.2%; Other 5.8%). **Foreign born:** 1.9%. **Median age:** 40. **State rank:** 13. **Pop change 1990-2000:** +1.3%.

Income: per capita $15,965; median household $32,228. **Pop below poverty level:** 13.9%.

Unemployment: 3.6%. **Median home value:** $77,000. **Median travel time to work:** 18.7 minutes.

HOT SPRINGS COUNTY
415 Arapahoe St   **Ph:** 307-864-3515
Thermopolis, WY 82443   **Fax:** 307-864-3333
www.hscounty.com

In west-central WY; created Feb 9, 1911 from Fremont, Johnson, and Big Horn counties. **Name Origin:** For the hot springs located in the county seat.

Area (sq mi): 2006.21 (land 2003.89; water 2.32).

Pop: 4,882 (White 94.5%; Black or African American 0.3%; Hispanic or Latino 2.4%; Asian 0.2%; Other 3.4%). **Foreign born:** 1.3%. **Median age:** 44.2. **State rank:** 22. **Pop change 1990-2000:** +1.5%.

Income: per capita $16,858; median household $29,888. **Pop below poverty level:** 10.6%.

Unemployment: 4.3%. **Median home value:** $80,400. **Median travel time to work:** 14.6 minutes.

JOHNSON COUNTY
76 N Main St   **Ph:** 307-684-7272
Buffalo, WY 82834   **Fax:** 307-684-2708
www.johnsoncountywyoming.org

In north-central WY, north of Casper; created as Pease County Dec 8, 1875 (prior to statehood) from Pease County; name changed Dec 13, 1879. **Name Origin:** For E.P. Johnson, a Cheyenne lawyer. Originally named for Dr. E. L. Pease.

Area (sq mi): 4174.71 (land 4166.28; water 8.42).

Pop: 7,075 (White 95.7%; Black or African American 0.1%; Hispanic or Latino 2.1%; Asian 0.1%; Other 2.8%). **Foreign born:** 0.8%. **Median age:** 43. **State rank:** 18. **Pop change 1990-2000:** +15.1%.

Income: per capita $19,030; median household $34,012. **Pop below poverty level:** 10.1%.

Unemployment: 3.1%. **Median home value:** $115,500. **Median travel time to work:** 19.6 minutes.

LARAMIE COUNTY
309 W 20th St   **Ph:** 307-633-4264
Cheyenne, WY 82001   **Fax:** 307-633-4240
webgate.co.laramie.wy.us

On the southeastern border of WY; first county in WY; created Jan 9, 1867 (prior to statehood). **Name Origin:** For Jacques LaRamie (?-c.1818), a respected French-Canadian trapper killed by Indians

All statistics are based on the 2000 Census except the dollar figures given for per capita income, which are based on 1999 estimates.

near the river, which was later named for him. Also spelled *LaRamie* or *LaRamee*.

Area (sq mi): 2687.63 (land 2686.05; water 1.58).

Pop: 81,607 (White 83.2%; Black or African American 2.6%; Hispanic or Latino 10.9%; Asian 1%; Other 7.5%). **Foreign born:** 2.9%. **Median age:** 35.3. **State rank:** 1. **Pop change 1990-2000:** +11.6%.

Income: per capita $19,634; median household $39,607. **Pop below poverty level:** 9.1%.

Unemployment: 3.5%. **Median home value:** $106,400. **Median travel time to work:** 16.3 minutes.

LINCOLN COUNTY

PO Box 670   **Ph:** 307-877-9056
Kemmerer, WY 83101   **Fax:** 307-877-3101
www.co.lincoln.wy.us

On the southwestern border of WY; created Feb 20, 1911 from Uinta County. **Name Origin:** For Abraham Lincoln (1809-65), sixteenth U.S. president.

Area (sq mi): 4089.01 (land 4069.09; water 19.92).

Pop: 14,573 (White 96.1%; Black or African American 0.1%; Hispanic or Latino 2.2%; Asian 0.2%; Other 2.6%). **Foreign born:** 1.4%. **Median age:** 36.8. **State rank:** 12. **Pop change 1990-2000:** +15.4%.

Income: per capita $17,533; median household $40,794. **Pop below poverty level:** 9%.

Unemployment: 5.4%. **Median home value:** $95,300. **Median travel time to work:** 25.1 minutes.

NATRONA COUNTY

PO Box 863   **Ph:** 307-235-9210
Casper, WY 82602   **Fax:** 307-235-9367
www.natrona.net

In east-central WY; created Mar 9, 1888 (prior to statehood) from Carbon County. **Name Origin:** For the mineral natron, or trona, a sodium carbonate, found in the area.

Area (sq mi): 5375.72 (land 5339.88; water 35.83).

Pop: 66,533 (White 91.7%; Black or African American 0.8%; Hispanic or Latino 4.9%; Asian 0.4%; Other 4.6%). **Foreign born:** 1.8%. **Median age:** 36.4. **State rank:** 2. **Pop change 1990-2000:** +8.7%.

Income: per capita $18,913; median household $36,619. **Pop below poverty level:** 11.8%.

Unemployment: 4.1%. **Median home value:** $84,600. **Median travel time to work:** 16.7 minutes.

NIOBRARA COUNTY

PO Box 420   **Ph:** 307-334-2211
Lusk, WY 82225   **Fax:** 307-334-3013

On the central eastern border of WY, east of Casper, created Feb 14, 1911 from Converse County. **Name Origin:** For the Niobrara River, which flows through the county, or for the Niobrara Indian tribe; from an Omaha-Poca Indian word *ni obthantha ko* 'spreading water river.'

Area (sq mi): 2627.9 (land 2625.81; water 2.09).

Pop: 2,407 (White 97.1%; Black or African American 0.1%; Hispanic or Latino 1.5%; Asian 0.1%; Other 1.7%). **Foreign born:** 0.7%. **Median age:** 42.8. **State rank:** 23. **Pop change 1990-2000:** -3.7%.

Income: per capita $15,757; median household $29,701. **Pop below poverty level:** 13.4%.

Unemployment: 3.3%. **Median home value:** $60,300. **Median travel time to work:** 14.8 minutes.

PARK COUNTY

1002 Sheridan Ave   **Ph:** 307-754-8600
Cody, WY 82414   **Fax:** 307-527-8626
www.wtp.net/parkco

On the northwestern border of WY; organized Feb 15, 1909 from Sweetwater, Fremont, and Big Horn counties. **Name Origin:** For Yellowstone National Park, which forms the northwestern part of the county.

Area (sq mi): 6968.51 (land 6942.39; water 26.11).

Pop: 25,786 (White 94.5%; Black or African American 0.1%; Hispanic or Latino 3.7%; Asian 0.4%; Other 3.1%). **Foreign born:** 1.8%. **Median age:** 39.8. **State rank:** 8. **Pop change 1990-2000:** +11.3%.

Income: per capita $18,020; median household $35,829. **Pop below poverty level:** 12.7%.

Unemployment: 4.4%. **Median home value:** $107,300. **Median travel time to work:** 17.6 minutes.

PLATTE COUNTY

PO Box 728   **Ph:** 307-322-3555
Wheatland, WY 82201   **Fax:** 307-322-2245

In southeastern WY, north of Cheyenne; created Feb 9, 1911 from Laramie County. **Name Origin:** For the North Platte River, which flows through the county; French 'flat' or 'still.'

Area (sq mi): 2110.9 (land 2084.93; water 25.97).

Pop: 8,807 (White 92.9%; Black or African American 0.2%; Hispanic or Latino 5.3%; Asian 0.2%; Other 3.5%). **Foreign born:** 1.5%. **Median age:** 41.2. **State rank:** 16. **Pop change 1990-2000:** +8.1%.

Income: per capita $17,530; median household $33,866. **Pop below poverty level:** 11.7%.

Unemployment: 3.9%. **Median home value:** $84,100. **Median travel time to work:** 14.5 minutes.

SHERIDAN COUNTY

224 S Main St Suite B-2   **Ph:** 307-674-6822
Sheridan, WY 82801   **Fax:** 307-674-2529
www.sheridancounty.com

On the central northern border of WY; created Mar 9, 1888 from Johnson County. **Name Origin:** For the county's major town and county seat, itself named for Gen. Philip Henry Sheridan (1831-88), Union officer during the Civil War and commander in chief of the U.S. army (1883-88).

Area (sq mi): 2527.07 (land 2523.32; water 3.75).

Please see sample entry on inside front cover for detailed information about the statistics presented with each county listing.

Pop: 26,560 (White 94.6%; Black or African American 0.2%; Hispanic or Latino 2.4%; Asian 0.4%; Other 3.5%). **Foreign born:** 1.6%. **Median age:** 40.6. **State rank:** 7. **Pop change 1990-2000:** +12.7%.

Income: per capita $19,407; median household $34,538. **Pop below poverty level:** 10.7%.

Unemployment: 4%. **Median home value:** $102,100. **Median travel time to work:** 17.8 minutes.

SUBLETTE COUNTY

PO Box 250   **Ph:** 307-367-4372
Pinedale, WY 82941   **Fax:** 307-367-6396

In west-central WY; organized Feb 15, 1921 from Fremont County. **Name Origin:** For William Lewis Sublette (1799-1845), fur trader and explorer of the Rocky Mountain region.

Area (sq mi): 4935.66 (land 4882.57; water 53.08).

Pop: 5,920 (White 96.4%; Black or African American 0.2%; Hispanic or Latino 1.9%; Asian 0.2%; Other 2.1%). **Foreign born:** 1.6%. **Median age:** 39.8. **State rank:** 20. **Pop change 1990-2000:** +22.2%.

Income: per capita $20,056; median household $39,044. **Pop below poverty level:** 9.7%.

Unemployment: 2.1%. **Median home value:** $112,000. **Median travel time to work:** 20.2 minutes.

SWEETWATER COUNTY

PO Box 730   **Ph:** 307-872-6400
Green River, WY 82935   **Fax:** 307-872-6337
www.co.sweet.wy.us

On the southern border of WY; largest county in WY. Created as Carter County Dec 27, 1867 (prior to statehood) from Laramie County; name changed Dec 13, 1869. **Name Origin:** For the Sweetwater River, which flows through Fremont County, at that time still a part of Sweetwater County. Originally named for Judge W.A. Carter.

Area (sq mi): 10,491.17 (land 10425.3; water 65.87).

Pop: 37,613 (White 86.9%; Black or African American 0.7%; Hispanic or Latino 9.4%; Asian 0.6%; Other 7%). **Foreign born:** 2.7%. **Median age:** 34.2. **State rank:** 3. **Pop change 1990-2000:** -3.1%.

Income: per capita $19,575; median household $46,537. **Pop below poverty level:** 7.8%.

Unemployment: 4.6%. **Median home value:** $104,200. **Median travel time to work:** 21.1 minutes.

TETON COUNTY

PO Box 1727   **Ph:** 307-733-4430
Jackson, WY 83001   **Fax:** 307-739-8681
www.tetonwyo.org

On the northwestern border of WY; created Feb 15, 1921 from Lincoln County. **Name Origin:** For the Teton Mountains.

Area (sq mi): 4221.8 (land 4007.76; water 214.04).

Pop: 18,251 (White 91.3%; Black or African American 0.1%; Hispanic or Latino 6.5%; Asian 0.5%; Other 5.6%). **Foreign born:**
5.9%. **Median age:** 35. **State rank:** 10. **Pop change 1990-2000:** +63.4%.

Income: per capita $38,260; median household $54,614. **Pop below poverty level:** 6%.

Unemployment: 2.2%. **Median home value:** $365,400. **Median travel time to work:** 17.1 minutes.

UINTA COUNTY

PO Box 810   **Ph:** 307-783-0306
Evanston, WY 82931   **Fax:** 307-783-0511
www.uintacounty.com

On the southwestern border of WY; original county, organized Dec 1, 1869 (prior to statehood); smallest county in WY. **Name Origin:** For the Uintah Mountains or the Uinta Indian tribe.

Area (sq mi): 2087.56 (land 2081.66; water 5.9).

Pop: 19,742 (White 92.2%; Black or African American 0.1%; Hispanic or Latino 5.3%; Asian 0.3%; Other 5.4%). **Foreign born:** 2.5%. **Median age:** 31.4. **State rank:** 9. **Pop change 1990-2000:** +5.5%.

Income: per capita $16,994; median household $44,544. **Pop below poverty level:** 9.9%.

Unemployment: 5%. **Median home value:** $89,400. **Median travel time to work:** 20.9 minutes.

WASHAKIE COUNTY

PO Box 260   **Ph:** 307-347-3131
Worland, WY 82401   **Fax:** 307-347-9366
www.washakiecounty.net

In north-central WY; created Feb 9, 1911 from Big Horn and Johnson counties. **Name Origin:** For Washakie (1804-1900), the Shoshone Indian chief and ally of the whites; meaning of name is uncertain but possibly 'rattler,' for the one he made and used to lead his men to battle.

Area (sq mi): 2242.75 (land 2240.06; water 2.69).

Pop: 8,289 (White 86.2%; Black or African American 0.1%; Hispanic or Latino 11.5%; Asian 0.7%; Other 9%). **Foreign born:** 2.4%. **Median age:** 39.4. **State rank:** 17. **Pop change 1990-2000:** -1.2%.

Income: per capita $17,780; median household $34,943. **Pop below poverty level:** 14.1%.

Unemployment: 4.5%. **Median home value:** $83,600. **Median travel time to work:** 12.5 minutes.

WESTON COUNTY

1 W Main St   **Ph:** 307-746-4744
Newcastle, WY 82701   **Fax:** 307-746-9505

On the northeastern border of WY; organized Mar 12, 1890 from Crook County. **Name Origin:** For John B. Weston, geologist and surveyor who located large anthracite deposits that eventually brought the railroad to WY.

Area (sq mi): 2400.07 (land 2397.86; water 2.21).

Pop: 6,644 (White 94.8%; Black or African American 0.1%; Hispanic or Latino 2.1%; Asian 0.2%; Other 3.7%). **Foreign born:** 0.8%. **Median age:** 40.7. **State rank:** 19. **Pop change 1990-2000:** +1.9%.

All statistics are based on the 2000 Census except the dollar figures given for per capita income, which are based on 1999 estimates.

Income: per capita $17,366; median household $32,348. **Pop below poverty level:** 9.9%.

Unemployment: 4.3%. **Median home value:** $66,700. **Median travel time to work:** 21.7 minutes.

Please see sample entry on inside front cover for detailed information about the statistics presented with each county listing.

643

Counties Index

Counties Index

Counties USA